1688

THE LEWIS WALPOLE SERIES IN EIGHTEENTH-CENTURY CULTURE AND HISTORY

The Lewis Walpole Series, published by Yale University Press with the aid of the Annie Burr Lewis Fund, is dedicated to the culture and history of the long eighteenth century (from the Glorious Revolution to the accession of Queen Victoria). It welcomes work in a variety of fields, including literature and history, the visual arts, political philosophy, music, legal history, and the history of science. In addition to original scholarly work, the series publishes new editions and translations of writing from the period, as well as reprints of major books that are currently unavailable. Though the majority of books in the series will probably concentrate on Great Britain and the Continent, the range of our geographical interests is as wide as Horace Walpole's.

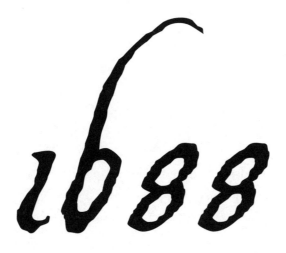

THE FIRST MODERN REVOLUTION

STEVE PINCUS

YALE UNIVERSITY PRESS   NEW HAVEN & LONDON

Published with the assistance of the Frederick W. Hilles Publication Fund of Yale University;
the Kingsley Trust Association Publication Fund established by the Scroll and Key Society of Yale College;
and the Annie Burr Lewis Fund.

Designed by James J. Johnson and set in Adobe Garamond type by Duke & Company,
Devon, Pennsylvania.
Printed in the United States of America.

The Library of Congress has catalogued the hardcover edition as follows:
Pincus, Steven C. A.
1688 : the first modern revolution / Steve Pincus.
p.   cm. — (The Lewis Walpole series in eighteenth-century culture and history)
Includes bibliographical references and index.
ISBN 978-0-300-11547-5
1. Great Britain—History—Revolution of 1688. 2. Great Britain—History—Revolution of 1688—
Historiography. 3. Great Britain—History—Revolution of 1688—Social aspects. I. Title.
DA452.P53 2009
941.06′7—dc22
2009004607

ISBN 978-0-300-17143-3 (pbk.)

A catalogue record for this book is available from the British Library.

10   9   8   7   6   5   4   3   2

Contents

PART IV. REVOLUTIONARY TRANSFORMATION

PART V. CONCLUSION

Illustrations

Acknowledgments

Like the Revolution of 1688–89 itself, this book has been long in the making. Over the decade that I worked on this book I have amassed a number of debts, most of which can never be repaid.

I began the project with modest aims. I hoped to write an interpretative essay suggesting that the international dimension of the Revolution of 1688–89 was underappreciated. A number of conversations I had when a postdoctoral fellow in Harvard's Society of Fellows convinced me there was something more to be done. Bernard Bailyn was one of the first to encourage me to think bigger. Wallace MacCaffrey, my dissertation supervisor, was as always unflaggingly supportive and helpful. Blair Worden not only urged me on but asked some tough questions along the way. After a lunch at Churchill College, Mark Goldie suggested that I look further into the commercial and mercantile contexts of the 1680s. When Tim Harris and I learned that we were writing parallel books, we had numerous discussions to make sure that we would not duplicate our efforts.

Many of the ideas developed in this book bear the mark of my time at the University of Chicago. My colleagues there, not only in the history department, but in sociology, political science, and English, all asked good questions and helped think of new paths by which I could find answers. Wilder House, the Chicago Humanities Center and the Early Modern Workshop, offered stimulating cross-disciplinary environments in which to discuss, argue about, and test ideas. Some friends and colleagues were subjected to an unusually large number of coffees with me in the Classics Café and elsewhere. They deserve special thanks. Bill Novak always had an open door and an encouraging word. Andy Abbot had excellent advice and was willing to offer an informed and critical ear. Richard Strier, despite wishing fervently that I worked on the late Elizabethan or Jacobean periods, asked important questions and offered provocative suggestions. Claudio Lomnitz was a willing tennis partner and an excellent reader of my work. Lynn Sanders not only playfully discussed ideas and concepts but bravely killed arachnids at key moments. Cornell Fleischer, Jules Kirshner, and Tamar Herzog helped create a vibrant early modernist community.

In my last few years at Chicago, the Nicholson Center for British Studies created a new context to think about my project. Janel Mueller played an instrumental role not only in creating the center but as a friend and colleague as well. Discussions on the Board with Dipesh Chakrabarty, Jacob Levy, Josh Scodel, Andy Abbot, Janel, and others could not but suggest new kinds of questions. Eva Wilhelm was not only a terrific administrator but an intellectual force and a dear friend as well.

Since coming to Yale I have benefited from discussions with and suggestions from a wide variety of colleagues, including Keith Wrightson, Stuart Schwartz, Julia Adams, Phil Gorski, David Underdown, Francesca Trivellato, David Quint, Annabel Patterson, Karuna Mantena, Jim Whitman, and Bryan Garsten. The participants in the Transitions to Modernity, British Historical Studies, and Comparative Sociology colloquia all provided me with friendly and critical audiences.

This project is a necessarily transatlantic one. Many scholars and friends in the United Kingdom and on the Continent have provided support, the occasional bed, and the more frequent patient ear during the long gestation of this project. Adam and Carolyn Fox have often housed me and provided me with much-needed good food and great cheer. Adam has more often than he would care to remember discussed English political history with me and raised important questions. Mark Knights has shared ideas and his passion for a similar terrain. Blair Worden has always been willing to lend a critical eye and suggest useful resources. Jean-Fredric Schaub invited me to spend time at the EHESS and provided an opportunity to present my ideas before a French audience.

I owe a great debt to my students, graduate and undergraduate, at both Chicago and Yale. Not only have I subjected them to my crazy ideas—to which they have had the good taste to listen patiently with only a few smirks and incredulous tosses of the head—but, more important, they helped to shape them in seminars, over innumerable coffees, and across the occasional lunch or dinner table. Several worked with me as research assistants: Abby Swingen (now of Auburn University), Ryan Frace (now of Wellesley College), Brent Sirota (now of North Carolina State University), Gerry Siarny, and Alice Wolfram. Others have read chapters, discussed themes, and provided invaluable insights, including Amanda Behm, Lisa Diller, Chris Dudley, Amy Dunagin, Justin DuRivage, Arvind Elangovan, Jessica Hanser, Elizabeth Herman, Sarah Kinkel, Fredrik Jonsson, Megan Lindsay, Leslie Theibert, James Vaughn, and Heather Welland. I could not have brought the manuscript to a conclusion without the incredible help of Alice Wolfram. Alice read every chapter several times, helped chase down images, and patiently waited as I missed every one of my self-imposed deadlines.

Many, many friends and scholars have read and commented on sections of the manuscript. In particular, Peter Lake, Jim Livesey, Frank Trentmann, Alan Houston, Don Herzog, and Adam Fox have provided reliable sounding boards throughout the project. Meg Jacobs has had many useful suggestions and was always willing at a moment's notice to look at particularly turgid bits of my prose. In the later stages of the project Chris Rogers, my editor at Yale University Press, provided critical nudges that I very much hope have made this a better and more readable book.

My greatest debt, of course, is owed to my long-suffering family. Sam has lived with this book as long as he has lived with me. I only wish this book had developed as much as he grown as a physical being, as a student, and above all as a person. Andy has only the vaguest notions that this book was being written. Nevertheless his 5:00 a.m. wakeup calls have provided great inspiration. For David, "going to the office" is the moral equivalent of "going to the playground," only that Daddy gets to stay in his office longer than anyone will allow Day-Day to stay at the playground. But Day-Day is right to think that writing this book has been a whole lot of fun. Above all I want to thank my wife, Sue, who has been an academic model, a stern critic, and a loving companion. Without her support, encouragement, criticism, and compassion this book would never have been written. Without her this book (probably) and my life (certainly) would be less rich.

PART I

Introductory

HISTORIC COUNTIES of ENGLAND

SCOTLAND

IRELAND

NORTHUMBERLAND

CUMBERLAND

DURHAM

WESTMORELAND

YORK SHIRE

LANCASTER

ANGLESEY

CARNARVAN SHIRE

DENBIGH SHIRE

FLINT SHIRE

CHESTER

DARBY SHIRE

NOTTINGHAM SHIRE

LINCOLN SHIRE

MERIONETH

MONTGOMERY SHIRE

SHROP SHIRE

STAFFORD SHIRE

LEICESTER SHIRE

RUTLAND

NORFOLK

CARDIGAN SHIRE

RADNOR SHIRE

WORCESTER SHIRE

WARWICK SHIRE

NORTHAMPTON SHIRE

HUNTINGDON SHIRE

CAMBRIDGE SHIRE

SUFFOLK

HEREFORD SHIRE

BEDFORD SHIRE

CARMARTHEN SHIRE

BRECKNOCK SHIRE

PEMBROKE SHIRE

MONMOUTH SHIRE

GLOUCESTER SHIRE

OXFORD SHIRE

BUCKINGHAM SHIRE

HERTFORD SHIRE

ESSEX

GLAMORGAN

BERK SHIRE

MIDDLESEX

WILT SHIRE

SURREY

KENT

SOMERSET

HAMP SHIRE

SUSSEX

DEVON

DORSET

ISLE OF WIGHT

CORNWALL

After
"The South Part of Great Britain
called *England and Wales"*
by
HERMAN MOLL
1710

Introduction

England's Glorious Revolution of 1688–89 holds a special place in our understanding of the modern world and the revolutions that had a hand in shaping it. For the better part of three centuries scholars and public intellectuals identified England's Revolution of 1688–89 as a defining moment in England's exceptional history. Political philosophers have associated it with the origins of liberalism. Sociologists have contrasted it with the French, Russian, and Chinese revolutions. Historians have pointed to the Revolution as confirming the unusual nature of the English state. Scholars of literature and culture highlight the Revolution of 1688–89 as an important moment in defining English common sense and moderation. All of these interpretations derive their power from a deeply held and widely repeated narrative of England's Revolution of 1688–89. Unfortunately, that narrative is wrong. Replacing that historical narrative with a new one will necessarily force us to revise many of the basic historical, political, moral, and sociological categories we use to make sense of the modern world. This book aims to explain both the ways in which this traditional view is mistaken and why that view has been so widely accepted for such a long time. The old narrative emphasized the Revolution of 1688–89 as a great moment in which the English *defended* their unique way of life. The argument I advance in this book is that the English revolutionaries *created* a new kind of modern state. It was that new state that has proved so influential in shaping the modern world.

Men and women all over the English-speaking world once knew what happened in England's Revolution of 1688–89. In 1685, the Catholic King James II inherited the crown of England. In 1689 the English people agreed to replace him with the Protestants King William III and Queen Mary II. In the intervening years, James II gradually and myopically alienated the moderate and sensible English people. He did this in a series of well-known missteps. In late 1685 he overreacted to the romantic but hopeless rebellion of his nephew, the Protestant Duke of Monmouth, by judicially murdering hundreds of humble inhabitants of the English West Country in the Bloody Assizes. Determined to improve the social and political status of his Catholic coreligionists, James then ran roughshod over English law. He insisted on his right to defy parliamentary statute and awarded Roman Catholics military and naval commissions. In 1687 he used his newly formed and illegal ecclesiastical commission to force England's Protestant universities to accept Roman Catholic fellows. When the fellows of Magdalen College Oxford resisted their king's demands, he had the dons stripped of their fellowships, turning the institution into a Catholic seminary.

According to this once well-known narrative, after James II had failed to persuade the House of Commons or the House of Lords to repeal England's laws against Roman Catholicism, he decided to emasculate Parliament. He first asserted his right to nullify the Test Acts and Penal Laws. These parliamentary statutes—requiring, in the case of the Test Acts, that all political or military officeholders take the sacrament according to the rites of the Church of England and, in the case of the Penal Laws, punishing those who officiated at or attended non–Church of England services—had successfully insulated the English from Continental Catholic practices. Then James determined to have his royal fiat ratified by a Parliament packed with men whom he knew would do his bidding. When, in June 1688, seven bishops of the Church of England defied James II by refusing to have his Declaration of Indulgence, emasculating the Penal Laws and Test Acts, read from England's pulpits on the grounds of its illegality, James had the seven prelates dragged into court for a show trial. That even a carefully picked English jury acquitted the bishops demonstrated the extent to which the English were willing to go in support of their king. Soon after the trial, the English invited the Dutchman William III, Prince of Orange, to England to vindicate their religious and political liberty.

The English people enthusiastically welcomed William on his arrival in the west of England in 1688. James's army quickly melted away after a series of spectacular defections, including that of the future Duke of Marlborough. James himself, preceded by his wife and newborn son, fled to France. The English people, in what was thought to have been a remarkable moment of political unanimity, agreed to replace James with William and Mary in February 1689. The English justified the crowning of the new monarchs with the publication of the Declaration of Right, detailing the ways that James II had violated English law, thereby insisting on the limited power of English kings. In the traditional account of the Glorious Revolution, the English people, led by their natural leaders in the two Houses of Parliament, changed the English polity in the slightest of ways in 1688–89. They slightly altered the succession, they made it illegal for a Catholic ever to inherit the throne, and they passed the Toleration Act, allowing Protestant Dissenters to worship freely. There were, to be sure, some significant unintended consequences of this bloodless revolution. But these outcomes were to be understood less as a direct consequence of these events than as the natural outgrowth of the English national character—a character that the Catholicizing Stuart monarchs had done much to pervert.

This was the story that every English schoolchild, and many North American ones, used to know. This was the story that the great Victorian historian Thomas Babington Macaulay laid out in his magisterial *History of England,* first published in the middle of the nineteenth century. That *History* was an immediate and runaway best seller and has deservedly been deeply influential ever since. Macaulay told his story in beautiful and accessible prose. He based his account on exhaustive research. Any scholar with an interest in the late seventeenth century should begin his or her research by examining Macaulay's notes, now preserved in the British Library. Very few subsequent scholars of the events Macaulay described have achieved his level of archival mastery. And in many ways, subsequent scholars have quibbled with the details of Macaulay's story while accepting his general thesis.

Macaulay's thesis became *the* classic statement of the Whig interpretation of the Revolution of 1688–89. It had a number of distinctive facets. First, the revolution was unrevolutionary. Unlike other subsequent revolutions, England's revolution was bloodless, consensual, aristocratic, and above all sensible. The English had no desire to transform their polity, their society, or their culture. Instead they worried that James II had intended to do just that. Second, the revolution was Protestant. James II had tried to reinstitute Catholicism in England. The revolution insured that England would remain a Protestant polity. Third, the revolution demonstrated the fundamentally exceptional nature of English national character. Continental Europeans vacillated between the wild extremes of republican and popular government on the one hand and tyrannical royal absolutism on the other. The English, by contrast, were committed to limited monarchy, allowing just the right amount of tempered popular liberty. Just as the English church was a sensible middle way between the extremes of Roman Catholicism and radical Protestant sectarianism, so the English polity, by maintaining its ancient constitution, was sensible and moderate. In this context the English remained committed to their hierarchical social structure precisely because it did not impose unbridgeable gaps between the aristocracy and the people. Fourth, there could have been no social grievances undergirding the Revolution of 1688–89 because English society had changed little in the period before James II's flight. It was only after English property rights were secured by the revolution, only after absolutism was no longer possible in England, that the English economy could truly flourish.

This book challenges every element of this established account. It is my claim that England's Revolution of 1688–89 was the first modern revolution. I came to this conclusion after more than a decade of research in archives across the United Kingdom, North America, and Europe. Macaulay built his story on a mountain of evidence; but much new material has become available in the intervening century and a half, and new bibliographic techniques have made it easier to locate materials. Macaulay assumed he knew what a Catholic king must have wanted to achieve; but I decided to try to uncover the aims, ideals, and contexts in which James II and his Catholic advisers operated. Macaulay assumed that European affairs were of little interest to the English people; I chose, by contrast, to take seriously the mass of ephemeral publications discussing Continental power politics. Macaulay assumed that conflicts over economic policy would become central political questions only in his own day; I chose, instead, to investigate the links between the aspirations and activities of England's merchant communities and late-seventeenth-century politics. I have benefited immensely from the research of twentieth-century scholars into England's social and economic history. All told this new historical evidence, it seems to me, makes it possible to tell a radically different story about the Revolution of 1688–89. In this story the English experience is not exceptional but in fact typical (if precocious) of states experiencing modern revolutions. The Revolution of 1688–89 is important not because it reaffirmed the exceptional English national character but because it was a landmark moment in the emergence of the modern state.

England in the later seventeenth century was rapidly becoming a modern society. Its economy was booming. Its towns were growing and becoming more comfortable. Its trade was expanding. These developments made it possible for English statesmen to conceive of a more active role for the English government. But social and economic change did not make the Revolution of 1688–89 inevitable. James II, deeply influenced by the particular brand of Catholicism he practiced and by the successful political model of his cousin, Louis XIV of France, sought to develop a modern absolutist state. James and his supporters created a centralizing bureaucratic state, a professional standing army, and a world-class navy. At the same time, James fashioned a modern Catholic polity. James, like his cousin Louis XIV, wanted Catholic subjects but not a papal overlord. Instead James insisted on absolute sovereignty within his own dominion while at the same time seeking to Catholicize his Protestant country. James successfully promoted the spread of Catholic apologetic literature, the proliferation of Catholic schools and colleges, and the opening of Catholic churches. No one living through the 1680s in England could have failed to appreciate the new prominence of Catholicism in English everyday life. James and his advisers appreciated that his modern state needed an expanding set of resources to support his more interventionist state. They quickly concluded that a centralized overseas territorial empire, with bases in India, North America, and the West Indies were essential props. James marshaled newly available resources, and devised plans for a vastly increased empire, to create a modern Catholic state.

James's opponents were, by and large, revolutionaries, not reactionaries. They appreciated that only a modernized English state could compete in contemporary Europe. Unlike James, however, the revolutionaries looked to the Dutch Republic rather than to the French monarchy for political inspiration. They, too, wanted a state that could support a powerful army and a first-class navy. They, too, imagined that such a state would have to be centralized and interventionist. But unlike James and his advisers, the revolutionaries imagined that England would be most powerful if it encouraged political participation rather than absolutism, if it were religiously tolerant rather than Catholicizing, and if it were devoted to promoting English manufactures rather than maintaining a landed empire. The revolutionaries understood full well that these political preferences put them at ideological loggerheads with Louis XIV's modern Catholic monarchy. The revolutionaries were therefore fully committed to fighting an all-out war against France, not only to protect the British Isles against a potential French-backed Jacobite restoration, but also to ensure that there would be European markets available to English manufactures and that European liberty would be preserved against French-style absolutism.

James II and his opponents did not only advocate radically different modernizing programs, they also were able to deploy a modern arsenal of political tools. James had succeeded in raising, maintaining, and deploying an efficient and disciplined army. He was in the process of molding most corporations throughout England and Wales into loyal instruments of local politics. James used the press and various political institutions to spread his regime's values and silence alternative viewpoints. James's regime may look brief and fragile in retrospect, but from the perspective of the later seventeenth century he had created a powerful edifice. It was precisely because James had been able to create such a powerful state that many of James's opponents realized that it could only be resisted with violence and that only a revolutionary transformation could prevent a future English monarch from re-creating his modern absolutist state. Those who overthrew James II in 1688 and shaped the new regime in the following decade were necessarily revolutionaries.

Though we have come to view the Glorious Revolution as bloodless, aristocratic, and consensual, the actual event was none of these things. The Revolution of 1688–89 was, of course, less bloody than the violent revolutions of the twentieth century, but the English endured a scale of violence against property and persons similar to that of the French Revolution at the end of the eighteenth century.[1] English men and women throughout the country threatened one another, destroyed each other's property, and killed and maimed one another throughout the revolutionary period. English men and women, from London to Newcastle, from Plymouth to Norwich, experienced violence or threats of violence, or lived in terrifying fear of violence. This was not a tame event. Nor was it a staid negotiation conducted by elites. Men and women of all social categories took to the streets, marched in arms on England's byways and highways, and donated huge amounts of money—some in very small quantities—to support the revolutionary cause. When the members of the House of Lords tried calmly to settle the succession issue after James II had fled the country, an angry crowd numbering in the tens of thousands cut short the nobles' deliberations and forced their hands. Given the power, efficiency, and ideological cohesion of James II's new regime, it was not surprising that many supported their king with great enthusiasm even in 1688 and beyond. Since many of the revolutionaries sought to replace James II's French-style modernization program with one based on a Dutch model, it was also predictable that many others would support the undoing of James II's new state edifice while doing everything they could to prevent the creation a Williamite alternative. The English throughout the 1680s, 1690s, and thereafter were politically and ideologically divided. There was no moment of English cohesion against an un-English king. There was no period in the late seventeenth century in which the sensible people of England collaborated to rid themselves against an irrational monarch. The Revolution of 1688–89 was, like all other revolutions, violent, popular, and divisive.

My central argument in this book, then, is that the English in the later seventeenth century forged the first modern revolution. This revolution had long-term causes and long-term consequences. The English could not have transformed their state and society in the ways that they did in the 1680s and 1690s had the events of the previous century—especially those of the crisis of the 1640s and 1650s—not unleashed a series of ideological debates that informed and transformed conceptions of state, religion, and society. English politicians, whether supporters of James II or of William and Mary, could not have transformed England's state institutions had the English economy not diverged from the late-seventeenth-century European pattern of recession and retrenchment. Because there were long-term causes of the Glorious Revolution, the consequences of that revolution were not necessarily unintended. The creation of the Bank of England, war against France, and religious toleration were all explicit goals of many of the revolutionaries. Precisely because the debates over these issues had long pedigrees, it would be wrong to understand 1688 or 1689 as a fundamental break in English history. The debates over these issues continued, albeit modified and reshaped by new institutional realities. Early Modern England did not come to an end in 1688, nor did Modern England begin then. It would, however, be fair to say that the character of English state and society relations was fundamentally transformed.

The revolutionaries created a new kind of English state after 1689. They rejected the modern, bureaucratic absolutist state model developed by Louis XIV in France. But they did not reject the state. Instead the revolutionaries created a state that was intrusive in different ways. Their state sought to transform England from an agrarian into a manufacturing society, oversaw the massive military buildup that was necessary to fight a war against the greatest military power that Europe had ever seen, and sought to promote a religiously tolerant society. John Locke, often described as one of the earliest and most influential liberal thinkers, was one of these revolutionaries. If the Glorious Revolution was a critical moment in the development of modern liberalism, that liberalism was not antagonistic to the state. The liberalism spawned in 1688–89 was revolutionary and interventionist rather than moderate and antistatist.

The Glorious Revolution, in my view, was not the triumph of a group of modernizers over defenders of traditional society. Instead the revolution pitted two groups of modernizers against each other. Both sides tried, against long odds, to appeal for the hearts and minds of the reactionaries. This, I believe, was a pattern typical of all modern revolutions. Revolutionary situations, in the vast majority of cases, have been created when the regime in power decides, for whatever reason, that it needs to modernize. In so doing the regime extends the tendrils of the state deeper and more extensively into society than they had ever gone before, necessarily generating resentment. At the same time, by announcing a break with the past, the regime has lowered the bar for opposition movements. Potential revolutionaries no longer need to persuade their fellow subjects to break with traditional and trusted ways of life. They merely need to persuade them that they have a superior model for change. The regime in power can no longer rely on the habitual loyalty of elites. The revolutionaries of late-seventeenth-century England set the model for this now typical political pattern.

What do I mean by modern, modernizers, and modernization? The terms have become flashpoints in contemporary public discussion. Many scholars, scholars for whom I have the utmost respect, would prefer that we do away with them or at least severely limit their use.[2] These scholars, and many others, dislike the family of terms around "modernity" for two reasons. First, it is said that the term *modern* or *modernity* is never specified. It is a term that means everything and nothing. Second, it is claimed that modernization stories are always reading history backward from the perspective of contemporary advanced democracies. All modernization stories are measured against the outcome of modern capitalist (read non–state interventionist) democracy. These are serious concerns. When, throughout this book, I use the terms *modernization, modernity,* or *modern* I mean them in very specific ways. I do not conceive of modernity as a coherent and integrated whole. Nor do I think modernization implies one narrow and particular path. Instead, it makes sense to discuss an epochal break in the construction of the state, and perhaps only the state, in later seventeenth-century Europe as a whole, and in England in particular. Although changes in the state, I believe, had profound consequences for foreign policy, the nature of imperial aspirations, English economy, and English society, I am not asserting that modernization determined these outcomes. In fact, it is my central claim that different conceptions of the modern state made possible different political and social consequences. Above all, I am not saying that state modernization necessarily implied a complete and total break with the past in intellectual, religious, or social life.

What, then, do I mean by the emergence of a modern state? I mean two interrelated sets of changes. I mean, first, a set of sociostructural innovations in statecraft. State modernizers usually try to centralize and bureaucratize political authority. They attempt to transform and professionalize the military. They use the tools of the state to accelerate economic growth and shape the contours of society. They undertake to gather directly detailed information about and occasionally suppress social and political activities taking place in a wide range of geographical locales and social levels within the polity. Second, a modern state implies an ideological break with the past. State modernizers insist on their own novelty, on a sense that they are undertaking a project that is utterly new. James II frequently mentioned that he was basing his state on a "New Magna Carta." One of those active on the other side in 1688, John Evelyn, hoped that the consequence of the revolution would be to make a new state, to "produce a kind of new creation amongst us."[3] But state modernization does not just imply a one-time break. Instead, a modern state is one that imagines itself to be always changing and adjusting. Both James II and his revolutionary opponents understood themselves to be laying new foundations, not creating novel but unchanging edifices.[4]

In this book, then, I retell the story of the Glorious Revolution, but I retell it in significantly new ways. Instead of a story of triumphant English exceptionalism emphasizing the far-seeing actions of a few men, I tell a story about a wide range of actors reacting not only to developments in English high politics and in the English church but to changes in society, in the economy, and on the broader European scene. To get that story right, to understand why so many people took the drastic and dangerous step of revolutionary action, we must take seriously the ways in which James II and his advisers transformed English politics and society. Whereas Macaulay's magisterial account focuses on English events, reactions of the Protestant community, and elite actors, my story adds to that mix a European context, the Catholic ideological perspective of James II and his entourage, popular politics, and issues of political economy. These additional elements make it possible to see that the Revolution of 1688–89 had long-term causes and long-term consequences for England and the wider world. It was, in fact, the first modern revolution.

This book operates at three levels: narrative, historiographical, and conceptual. The three are closely interlinked throughout. But readers with particular interests might find different entry points to the book more to their tastes. Those who are mostly interested in the narrative history of the Revolution of 1688–89 may wish to begin with chapter 3. Readers whose primary interest is in how my story relates to other accounts of the revolution but are less interested in broader theoretical implications may wish to start with chapter 1 and then skip the second chapter. And those who are primarily interested in revolutions as a general subject of inquiry may find starting with chapter 2 most to their tastes.

CHAPTER ONE

The Unmaking of a Revolution

O n 30 November 1789, just after the outbreak of the French Revolution, one Monsieur Navier stood up to address the Patriotic Society of Dijon, the chief city of Burgundy. "Why should we be ashamed, Gentlemen," he asked his auditors, "to acknowledge that the Revolution which is now establishing itself in our country, is owing to the example given by England a century ago? It was from that day we became acquainted with the political constitution of that island, and the prosperity with which it was accompanied; it was from that day our hatred of despotism derived its energy. In securing their own happiness, Englishmen have prepared the way for that of the universe. Whilst on all sides tyrants were attempting to extinguish the sacred flame of liberty, our neighbors with intrepid watchfulness and care cherished it in their bosoms. We have caught some of these salutary sparks; and this fire enflaming every mind, is extending itself all over Europe, for ever to reduce to ashes those shackles with which despotism has oppressed mankind."[1]

That late-eighteenth-century revolutionaries turned to the Revolution of 1688–89 for inspiration is hardly surprising. The Revolution of 1688–89 was a radically transformative event. The English revolutionaries reoriented their country's foreign policy—from virulent hostility against the Dutch Republic before the revolution to war against France immediately after it. The revolutionaries completely transformed the direction of English economic policy. The postrevolutionary regime created England's first national bank,

---

(above) *Centenary of the Revolution, 1788.* Struck in 1788, in commemoration
of the centennial of the Revolution of 1688–89, this medal emphasizes
the revolution's pivotal role in guaranteeing the liberty of British subjects.

the Bank of England, to signal its newfound enthusiasm for manufacturing. England's new governors also transformed the religious character of the nation. The prerevolutionary Church of England had been intolerant, insisting that Englishness and communion in the Church of England were one and the same thing. The postrevolutionary church leaders demanded a broader church, and one that was willing to tolerate religious practice outside that church. The revolution, and the Toleration Act of 1689, separated church from nation. All three of these transformations were intimately tied to a new vision of the English polity. The revolutionaries had rejected a French-inflected modernity in favor of a Dutch-inspired modern state.

Throughout the eighteenth century many Britons proclaimed that their revolution represented a fundamental break with the British and European past. They saw the revolution as inaugurating a new age of liberty. "The Revolution forms a new epoch in the constitution," David Hume proclaimed in his widely celebrated *History*. From that period, the great Scottish philosopher asserted, the English enjoyed "the most entire system of liberty that ever was known amongst mankind." "From the era of the revolution," agreed Hume's fellow Scottish light John Millar, "we may trace . . . a new order of things." This was not merely a Scottish view. "Since the Revolution in eighty-eight," declared the former ambassador Robert Molesworth in 1711, "we stand upon another and better bottom." In the middle of the century the most flamboyant of English politicians, John Wilkes, maintained that "the Revolution is the great era of English liberty." "From this most auspicious period," Wilkes explained, "freedom has made a regular uninterrupted abode in our happy island." The great Whig politician Charles James Fox dated "the brightest era of freedom known to the annals of our country" to the Revolution of 1688–89. "The Revolution is looked upon by all sides as a new era," agreed the Tory leader Viscount Bolingbroke, whose principles, however, were rather different from Fox's, "from thence we must date both king and people."[2]

Not only did many eighteenth-century Britons believe that the Revolution of 1688–89 marked a fundamental turning point in their history, they also saw the revolution as setting an example for the rest of the world. At the beginning of the century Molesworth thought "no man can be a sincere lover of liberty," none could be a sincere exponent of revolution principles, who was not "for increasing and communicating that blessing to all people." By the second half of the century many thought the principles of the revolution had indeed been communicated far and wide. The English, thought John Wilkes, had since the revolution become "the patrons of universal liberty, the scourge of tyrants, the refuge of the oppressed." The Glorious Revolution, chimed in the Presbyterian minister and translator extraordinaire Henry Hunter in 1788, ushered in a new "era" not only for the British Isles "but to Europe; nay to mankind during the period of a hundred years." The benefits of the revolution, agreed Andrew Kippis, "have not been confined to our country alone, but have extended to Europe in general." The great defender of liberty Richard Price was clearly not alone in believing that in 1688 an "era of light and liberty was introduced among us, by which we have been made an example to other kingdoms, and become the instructors of the world."[3]

Because the Revolution of 1688–89 marked a fundamental break in the history of the British state, because the revolution was thought to be the harbinger of an era of liberty not only in Britain but all of Europe, the anniversary of the revolution was widely celebrated throughout the British Isles. "The Revolution in 1688 in every view of it was an event of such distinguished and indeed unspeakable importance," noted the Revolution Society in 1789, that it was widely commemorated. Both the established church and other "religious societies" had annual celebrations of the revolution. "Social meetings and festivals" also feted the occasion yearly. "Various institutions" devoted exclusively to the memory of 1688 "have subsisted in different parts of the kingdom and in different quarters of the metropolis." Though the minute books of the Revolution Society have survived only from 1788, its members were certain that it had been "established soon after the Revolution and that it has annually met without interruption from that time to the present." The Bristol Baptist minister and friend of the American Revolution Caleb Evans proclaimed that "even Popish priests avow and openly justify the principles of the Revolution." The Revolution of 1688–89, though interpreted by different groups in different ways, was understood by Britons of every social class and every geographical locale as *the* decisive event in British history. "Not to be acquainted with the great event which distinguishes this illustrious day of the revolving year," said Henry Hunter of the official revolution anniversary of 4 November, "is, in a citizen of Great Britain, a proof of the most shameful ignorance, or the most criminal coldness and indifference."[4]

Popular familiarity with the Revolution of 1688–89 had diminished dramatically by the time of its tercentenary. By the 1980s, concluded Barry Price, the author of a government report on the tercentenary, the revolution was "a relatively unknown period in our history which nowadays seldom gets a place in our school history syllabus." Price recalled of his own school days that "1688 was a black hole in our history syllabus." The former headmaster of Westminster School, John Rae, doubted "whether one school leaver in a thousand could give an account of 1688, let alone say why it was a turning point in our history." No wonder the leader of the House of Lords, Viscount Whitelaw, could assert confidently that there was no "general wish" for a lavish celebration of the Revolution of 1688–89. The Glorious Revolution, opined Patricia Morrison in the *Daily Telegraph,* had "little box office appeal." The Victoria and Albert Museum was so "unenthusiastic" about plans for an exhibit commemorating the event that it "foundered." In the end, the Tercentenary of the Revolution of 1688–89 was "passing largely unnoticed."[5]

Why has the Revolution of 1688–89 receded from the popular imagination? Why has an event that was once almost universally understood to be the touchstone of British identity become an obscure occurrence familiar only to learned antiquarians? The answer, most commentators would agree, is that the events of 1688–89 are no longer thought to have been transformative. "British history," observes the political scientist Charles Tilly, "now provides a much-thumbed manual for the avoidance of revolution." The image of English stability, inevitably contrasted with French volatility, has now been long in the making. "The English have for the last century and more been insistent that their revolution [of 1688–89] was unique—so unique as to have been practically no revolution at all," notes the scholar of comparative revolutions Crane Brinton.[6]

How did the Revolution of 1688–89 come to be a nonevent? While many have assumed that the disappearance of the Glorious Revolution has gone hand in hand with the demise of a naive, progressive Whig history, this is not the case. The hegemonic "neo-conservative interpretation" of the revolution is in fact nothing new. As outside observers like Tilly and Brinton are well aware, British historians have long insisted on the unrevolutionary nature of 1688–89. In fact, this became the establishment Whig interpretation of the revolution by the 1720s, and the virtually universal view by the turn of the nineteenth century. Britain's sensible revolution was increasingly contrasted with the revolutionary excesses first of Europeans and then of non-Europeans. The Revolution of 1688–89 that had once been a model for revolutionaries instead became a symbol of British exceptionalism. England's radical revolution had been transformed into a uniquely unrevolutionary revolution. It had become an exercise in restoration rather than in innovation. England in the seventeenth century, and Britain in the nineteenth and twentieth centuries, offered a stark and ostensibly successful historical contrast to the Continental pattern of development. This process of unmaking the revolution, I suggest, had less to do with historical scholarship than with political positioning and historiographical fashion.[7]

Eighteenth-century Britons were obsessed with the Glorious Revolution. The revolution was not only commemorated and remembered, it anchored discussions of contemporary politics, society, and culture. "Throughout the eighteenth century," writes the historian Harry Dickinson, "no major debate involving any discussion of fundamental political principles took place without the events of 1688–89 being used as a source of inspiration or guidance."[8]

Political developments ensured that partisan interpretations of the revolution took some time to congeal. In the immediate aftermath of James II's flight in 1688, especially in the early 1690s, many radicals were temporarily disappointed by the new regime's limited achievements. In their view the revolution had been incomplete and was thus liable to subversion from within as well as invasion from abroad.[9] Whig radicals feared that because William and Mary had wanted to consolidate their power by working with the Tories the opportunity for fundamental reform had been lost.

By the middle of the 1690s, Whigs began to speak with a united voice about the revolution. Clearly, by the first decade of the eighteenth century they had united behind a radical interpretation of the revolution. That interpretation was given a full airing in the Whig regime's politically disastrous, but ideologically revealing, show trial of the conservative cleric Henry Sacheverell in 1710. Sacheverell had long been a fierce critic of the Whigs and the postrevolutionary regime, but he attracted the interest of the government with his inflammatory sermon *The Perils of False Brethren,* delivered in front of the lord mayor of London at St. Paul's Cathedral on 5 November 1709. In that sermon Sacheverell argued forcefully that political resistance to James II in 1688 had been illegitimate. Whigs everywhere were outraged.[10]

In 1710 the parliamentary managers of Sacheverell's very public trial carefully outlined what was then the mainstream interpretation of the Revolution of 1688–89. Against Sacheverell's assertions, the Whig politicians argued, in short, that in 1688–89 the English people rose up all across the land to overthrow a despotic king and that they were justified in doing so. The revolutionaries, they asserted, had not only dethroned a tyrant, they had engineered a fundamental transformation of the English state.

The revolution, the Whig managers and their allies insisted in front of the House of Lords, acting in their capacity as judges, established the principle of popular sovereignty. In 1688, the Whigs unanimously claimed, the people had legitimately resisted a tyrannical king. "The glorious enterprise for delivering this kingdom from popery and arbitrary power," the parliamentary managers maintained in the articles they presented against Sacheverell, was brought about by "diverse subjects of this realm, well affected to their country." "That there was a resistance, is most plain," explained Sir John Holland, highlighting the fact that the English people took "up arms in Yorkshire, Nottinghamshire, Cheshire, and almost all the counties of England." "It cannot be necessary to prove resistance in the Revolution," asserted the future prime minister Robert Walpole, who was then very much a defender of a radical interpretation of the revolution. "I should as well expect that your Lordships would desire me for form's sake, to prove the sun shines at noonday," he added sarcastically. "Self-defense and resistance" is lawful in cases of "extreme necessity," chimed in Gilbert Burnet, bishop of Salisbury, and "this was the case at the Revolution." "We owe the late Revolution" to "the people of all ranks and conditions, from the highest and holiest order, to the meanest and most secular employment," added the London cleric and Whig polemicist Benjamin Hoadly in what was then an uncontroversial statement of the Whig position. For Hoadly, as for the Whig establishment in 1710, there was a close "connection between the present settlement, and that resistance which brought it about."[11]

The ideological stakes in the Whig case were spelled out most clearly by another of the parliamentary managers of the case against Sacheverell, Nicholas Lechmere. Lechmere was both a prominent lawyer and closely associated with powerful Whig politicians. In 1688, Lechmere informed the House of Lords, in making his case against Sacheverell, "the subjects had not only a power and right in themselves to make that resistance, but lay under an indispensable obligation to do it." This was because there was "an original contract between the crown and the people." When "the executive part endeavors the subversion and total destruction of the government," which Lechmere asserted had clearly happened by 1688, "the original contract is thereby broke." This contract stipulated not only a right in the people but a duty as well. "The nature of such an original contract of government proves," Lechmere explained, "that there is not only a power in the people, who have inherited its freedom, to assert their own title to it, but they are bound in duty to transmit the same constitution to their posterity also."[12]

While the setting and context of Sacheverell's trial necessarily focused the attention of the Whig managers on questions of resistance and popular sovereignty, some Whigs did make clear as well the religious and political economic consequences of the revolution. "The toleration of Protestant Dissenters," asserted Lechmere, was "one of the earliest and happiest effects of the late Revolution." Not only did the Whigs believe there had been a transformation of religious affairs, they also believed that the events of 1688–89 had ushered in a radical transformation of social policy. Robert Molesworth, who had been a strong supporter of the Whig ministry in the first decade of the century, clearly enunciated this position. Because defenders of the revolution believed, along with John Locke, that labor rather than land was the basis of all wealth, Molesworth argued that a government according to the revolution's principles would have a wide-ranging social agenda. "The supporting of public credit, promoting of all public buildings and highways, the making of all rivers navigable that are capable of it, employing the poor, suppressing idlers, restraining monopolies upon trade, maintaining the liberty of the press, the just paying and encouraging of all in the public service," all this and more, Molesworth argued was the consequence of the revolution.[13]

In 1710 the Whigs asserted with one voice that the revolution was fundamentally transformative. The Whig parliamentary managers and their allies saw the revolution as ushering in a new age of civil and religious liberty buttressed by a new social agenda. This liberty, they warned, was threatened not only by the combined forces of the French and the Jacobites but also by High Churchmen and Tories like Henry Sacheverell.

The Sacheverell trial and the ensuing Tory electoral triumph not only put an end to the Whig ministry, it also eventually severed the close connection between the Whig establishment and the radical interpretation of the revolution. When Robert Walpole, one of the most eloquent defenders of the radical reading of the revolution, came to power as England's chief minister in 1720, he brought with him a change of heart. Walpole and his political allies now claimed that the revolution had instantiated parliamentary rather than popular sovereignty and that it had established a constitution rather than a blueprint for further reform. Walpole, in short, insisted that the revolution was necessary and brief. The era of revolutionary transformation had come to an end. Because Walpole himself held onto the reins of government for two decades and his political heirs quickly returned to power after his fall, those who remained committed to a radical interpretation of the revolution were forced into opposition. The Whig party split between those who understood the revolution to have been a brief and necessary adjustment in England's constitutional arrangements—the establishment Whigs—and the Opposition Whigs, who insisted that the events of 1688–89 had initiated a period of revolutionary transformation in politics, religion, and society.[14]

From the early 1720s Walpole as chief minister modified many of the policies associated with the revolution. He maintained peace with France, he sought no further relief for religious Dissenters, and he reversed the progressive taxation schemes implemented after the revolution. As a result, defenders of the Walpolian Whig establishment emphasized a narrow and conservative account of the revolution. "The principle, the great, the only end of the Revolution," argued one typical pro-Walpole pamphleteer, "was then to settle the government upon its ancient and proper basis, which the measures of a mad bigot had almost destroyed." There was, this pamphleteer insisted, no evidence to suggest that the revolutionaries had any intention of increasing the power of the people or indeed of altering the government in any way. James had been the innovator; the revolutionaries were conservative and virtuous defenders of the ancient constitution. Not only did the establishment Whigs now distance themselves from the potentially reformist implication of the revolution, but they insisted that the revolution had nothing to do with popular sovereignty. Those "who say our government is founded upon resistance," wrote Walpole's henchman John Hervey, "are as great enemies to this constitution, at least to the peace of it, as those who would advise the Crown, instead of maintaining its legal prerogative, to be watching every favorable opportunity to increase it." While Walpole and his supporters still ascribed the revolution an important role, it was in the re-establishment of liberty rather than in the initiation of an age of progressive improvement. The revolution did not initiate a process of reform; it ended forever attempts to establish absolutism in Britain. Walpolians emphasized the tyrannical activities of James II, rather than the creative potential of the revolutionaries.[15]

From the 1720s, then, it was the Opposition Whigs who argued that the revolution had dramatically and fundamentally altered not only British politics but British society and culture as well. It was the Opposition Whigs who continued to argue that the revolution marked the beginning of a new era in British and ultimately world history. The Opposition Whigs claimed that the revolution was in fact based on popular resistance, that it changed the moral foundation of government, that it inaugurated a new era that celebrated the principle of religious liberty, that it radically altered the direction of English (then British) foreign policy, and that it transformed the socioeconomic basis of the polity.

In pamphlets, treatises, formal histories, and popular toasts, Opposition Whigs from the 1720s to the 1790s insisted that widespread popular resistance had occurred in 1688. They thus maintained that the revolution established popular, not parliamentary, sovereignty. Violence, observed Walpole's great enemy William Pulteney, "hath often proved salutiferous, and preserved the liberty of popular states." "When King Charles's deluded brother attempted to enslave the nation," reasoned the great legal theorist Sir William Blackstone, "he found it was beyond his power: the people both could, and did, resist him; and, in consequence of such resistance, obliged him to quit his enterprise and his throne together." The revolution, agreed the author of the Opposition pamphlet the *Livery-Man* in 1740, "was brought about not by the Parliament, by the freeholders, or by any particular body of men, but by the people of Great Britain; and what they then did is the foundation of our present constitution." By the "people," this author made clear, he meant "the son of the peasant as well as of the peer." Henry Hunter was merely repeating a well-worn Opposition Whig credo when he preached in November 1788 that "the insulted genius of an injured people at length awoke to just vengeance" in November 1688.[16]

For Opposition Whigs, the popular resistance of the revolutionaries in 1688–89 was lawful because they believed deeply in the principle of popular sovereignty. William Pulteney referred his readers to John Locke's *Two Treatises* and its endorsement of popular resistance as "the true principles of liberty; the principles of the Revolution." Half a century later, the Bristol Baptist and Whig Caleb Evans argued that the revolution marked the triumph of "the immortal Locke, the assertor of liberty" over the defender of patriarchal kingship Robert Filmer. "There is no man scarcely to be met with," claimed Evans, "who is not familiar with [Locke's] writings on the interesting subject of government by which the very soul of despotism in Great Britain has received its death wound." It was therefore very much consonant with the historical views of the Opposition Whigs that the Revolution Society declared that the first principle "confirmed by the Revolution" was that "all civil and political authority derived from the people."[17]

Opposition Whigs placed far less emphasis on the restoration of the ancient constitution than they did on the transformation of the moral and practical basis of politics brought about by the revolution. Andrew Kippis was not alone in arguing that the revolution not only halted James II's infringements on the privileges granted by the ancient constitution but "brought new ones of the utmost value. It conferred additional rights on the subject; fixed additional limitations on the crown; and provided additional security for the continuation of our felicity." In particular, Opposition Whigs maintained that, at the revolution, "a decisive blow was struck at the doctrine of non-resistance, and passive obedience." Radicals and Opposition Whigs also emphasized that changes in "the direction of the national revenue" at the revolution created "a necessity of convening the Parliament annually." Opposition Whigs and radicals placed less emphasis on formal institutions than on a change of political culture. While "a notion of general liberty had strongly pervaded and animated the whole constitution" before 1688, argued Sir William Blackstone, it was only at the revolution that "particular liberty, the natural equality, and personal independence of individuals" were widely "applauded." John Wilkes adopted Blackstone's definition when he insisted that "liberty was the direct avowed principle of the English at the Revolution." It was from the period of "The Revolution," that Henry Hunter thought, "the country, possessed of spirit, wisdom, virtue, and power to assert their rights, to form and establish a system of government favorable to general liberty and happiness, began to enjoy the sweets of them." As early as 1712, the Tory political journalist Delarivier Manley had observed correctly that the Whigs did not understand the revolution to be merely "a re-establishment" but as initiating a "Great Change" so that "changing of law, liberty, and religion came to be the only true Revolution principles."[18]

Opposition Whigs, like the parliamentary managers of 1710, emphasized that the revolution inaugurated an era of religious liberty. "Scarce can a period be assigned, in all ancient and modern history," bragged the Presbyterian minister and fierce anti-Walpolian Robert Wallace, "of such a long continuance as the period of 66 years since the Revolution, in which any people have enjoyed such solid and substantial blessings," chief among which were "an entire freedom from all kinds of persecutions; [and] a perfect liberty of worshipping God according to our consciences." After the revolution, argued the author of *The Advantages of the Revolution,* "our minds are now happily freed from the ignominious bondage of ecclesiastical and state slavery, the flaming brands of bigotry being well nigh extinguished." "Soon after the Revolution," agreed John Wilkes, "the English in a good degree, adopted the Dutch system of government, as to a general toleration of religious parties." Many Dissenters and Opposition Whigs believed that the principles of religious liberty set forth at the revolution needed further statutory expansion and elaboration. The Revolution was a beginning not an end. But, they insisted, the revolution had marked a fundamental turning point. The Dissenter Andrew Kippis admitted that the religious liberty established at the revolution was "far short" of the "enlarged and philosophical principles" of the late eighteenth century. "Nevertheless," he explained to his auditors, "when we consider the temper of the preceding age, it was a glorious advantage gained in favor of the interests of truth and conscience, and the natural rights of mankind." It was on the basis of similar reasoning that the Revolution Society insisted that the "Glorious Revolution of 1688" gave birth to "the civil and religious liberties of the people of this country."[19]

Opposition Whigs frequently noted that the revolutionaries of 1688–89 transformed English foreign policy. In the 1720s and 1730s Sir Robert Walpole's opponents emphasized that his pacific foreign policy represented a betrayal of revolution principles. In 1742 one Opposition Whig asked the now-deposed Walpole, "How do you think will the aggrandizing the House of Bourbon, at the expense of that of Austria, square with Revolution principles?" Political engagement with Europe, specifically opposition to French imperial designs, continued to be a central theme throughout the century. Blackstone recalled that the revolutionaries of 1688–89 "introduced a new system of foreign politics." "From this period of the Revolution," John Wilkes commented approvingly, "England has continued regularly and steadily to oppose the ambitious views of France." The exceptions, according to Wilkes, were "two short, critical and convulsive intervals"—the aftermath of the Tory peace of 1713 and Walpole's ministry—during which "the national interest" was sacrificed to the "views of a few particulars."[20]

Finally, radicals and Opposition Whigs emphasized that the revolution transformed the political economy of Britain. "Great changes in the state of society," argued the Scottish philosopher and supporter of the Opposition Whig Charles James Fox, John Millar, "may be dated from the revolution." In particular, in the late seventeenth century, "the feudal institutions natural to a rude nation, were, in a great measure, abolished and forgotten." "The full establishment of a regular and free constitution," establishing "the secure possession and enjoyment of property," was, in Millar's view, "obtained by the memorable Revolution in 1688," ensuring that "commerce and manufactures assumed a new aspect." "The feudal constitution was far from being favorable to commerce," noted the commercial historian and friend of Freemasonry Adam Anderson in the 1760s. So "the establishment of this free constitution" in 1689, he concluded, "did most certainly contribute greatly in its consequences (as it was natural to suppose and expect) to the increase and advancement of our own commerce."[21]

The Opposition Whigs did not believe that the revolutionaries of 1688–89 had single-handedly demolished the feudal system; rather, they believed that a variety of developments had begun to alter dramatically English state and society. These were the necessary preconditions of revolution. The revolution dealt the deathblow to the feudal system. David Hume, for example, emphasized that "the commerce and riches of England did never during any period increase so fast as from the restoration to the revolution." Anderson highlighted the role that the "discovery of the East-Indies, and of Brazil by the Portuguese; and of the West-Indies" had in transforming the European commercial world. Blackstone pointed to the development of the post office, the proliferation of hackney coaches, the "discovery of the Indies," and the advancement of learning as paving the way for the great climacteric of 1688. "The great revolutions that had happened in manners and in property," he noted, "had paved the way, by imperceptible yet sure degrees, for as great a revolution in government." Yet, Blackstone was careful to note, "while that revolution was effecting, the crown became more arbitrary than ever, by the progress of these very means which afterwards reduced its power."[22]

The revolution, according to the Opposition Whigs, had remarkably beneficial effects on British manufacturing and commerce. This was in large part because of the activities of the postrevolutionary state. In the 1730s especially Opposition Whigs emphasized that the revolutionaries had adopted Lockean economic principles. They developed their economic policies on the assumption "that the lands of Great Britain are only made valuable by the number of people employed in foreign and domestic trade, and in the woolen and other manufactures of this kingdom." The implication, based on "the authority of Mr. Locke," was a policy of progressive taxation. After the revolution, the regime, on Lockean principles, recommended "a Land Tax in preference to any duties on commodities, whether imported or our own production." Others emphasized the postrevolutionary regime's assault on "exclusive trading companies." Still others pointed to the rage for social legislation, "salutary laws for the welfare of the public," that became possible only after the revolution.[23]

The Opposition Whigs emphasized the tremendous political economic consequences of the revolution. John Millar marveled at "the rapid improvements of arts and manufactures, and the correspondent extension of commerce, which followed the clear and accurate limitation of the prerogative." These in turn "produced a degree of wealth and affluence, which diffused a feeling of independence and a high spirit of liberty through the great body of the people." "Another undeniable instance of the advantage which has accrued to this nation by the Revolution," argued a polemicist at midcentury, "is the vast increase and flourishing condition of our manufactures." "The good effects" of the Revolution of 1688–89, agreed Adam Anderson, "have in nothing been more conspicuous than in the great increase in commerce, shipping, manufactures, and colonies, as well as of riches and people, since that happy period." At no other period in British history have "agriculture, manufactures and commerce" "been enjoyed in any such degree," gushed Andrew Kippis, "as since the Revolution."[24]

Opposition Whigs, then, developed an interpretation of the revolution that differed dramatically from that offered by the establishment or Walpolian Whigs. Where the establishment Whigs, in what would become known as *the* Whig interpretation of the Glorious Revolution, understood the event to have been restorative and brief, the Opposition Whigs understood the revolution to be transformative and chronologically open-ended. The establishment Whigs argued that the revolution ended in 1689 or 1690; the Opposition Whigs insisted that the revolution's principles should continue to drive a reformist agenda. In short, by the 1720s the establishment Whigs were emphasizing the immediate tyrannical *causes* of the events of 1688–89, whereas the Opposition Whigs were highlighting *long-term* structural causes and the revolutionary *consequences* of 1688–89.

The centenary celebrations of 1788 proved to be the high-water mark of discussion about the Glorious Revolution. Not only were the celebrations of the revolution ubiquitous in 1788, but they were wide-ranging and multivalent. Clerics, journalists, pamphleteers, and poets all expressed their interpretations of the great event. No one in England, Scotland, or Ireland, indeed few in Britain's colonies, could have been unaware of the centenary of 1688. However, Continental developments soon halted these discussions and debates. The establishment Whig interpretation of the revolution quickly achieved hegemonic status.

In November 1789, just months after the outbreak of the French Revolution, the most celebrated English Dissenting cleric of the eighteenth century and a prominent supporter of the American Revolution, Richard Price, delivered a sermon at the meetinghouse in the Old Jewry just outside London's Guildhall, a sermon that indirectly ended the historiographical controversy about the Glorious Revolution. His sermon, which instantly became a best seller in Britain and on the Continent, developed what had already become the Opposition Whig interpretation of revolution principles. "By a bloodless victory, the fetters which despotism had long been preparing for us were broken," Price recalled, "the rights of the people were asserted, a tyrant expelled, and a Sovereign of our own choice appointed in

This banner, created for local celebrations of the centennial of the
Glorious Revolution, depicts the alehouse near Chesterfield, Derbyshire,
where the Earls of Devonshire and Danby met in November 1688
to plot an uprising against James II.

his room. Security was given to our property, and our consciences were emancipated. The
bounds of free enquiry were enlarged; the volume in which are the words of eternal life,
was laid more open to our examination; and the era of light and liberty was introduced
among us, by which we have been made an example to other kingdoms, and became the
instructors of the world. Had it not been for this deliverance, the probability is, that, instead
of being thus distinguished, we should now have been a base people, groaning under the
infamy and misery of popery and slavery." The Revolution of 1688–89 had been an act of
popular resistance, allowing the British people to "frame a government for ourselves."[25]

      Price's optimistic, reformist, and radical commentary on the meaning of the Revo-
lution of 1688–89 elicited a number of critical responses. But there was no more famous,
more widely read, or more politically influential response to Richard Price's *Discourse on the
Love of Our Country* than the interpretation of the revolution offered by Edmund Burke.
In the context of the disturbing developments across the Channel, Burke felt himself im-
pelled to write his *Reflections on the Revolution in France* to dispel the dangerous principles
espoused and embraced by Dr. Price. Burke duly recorded "the dislike I feel to revolutions,
the signals which have so often been given from pulpits"—reminding his readers that Price
had celebrated the principles of 1688–89 from the pulpit of the Dissenting meetinghouse in

the Old Jewry. Burke, like his antagonist Price, found much to celebrate in 1688–89. But, unlike Price, Burke argued that there had been no innovation, no revolution, but merely a sensible and backward-looking restoration of the old order. The Revolution of 1688–89 was motivated by not a single new idea. James II had been the radical revolutionary; the English people had merely restored normalcy in 1688–89. "The Revolution was made to preserve our ancient indisputable laws and liberties, and that ancient constitution of government which is our only security for law and liberty," Burke explained. "The very idea of the fabrication of a new government is enough to fill us with disgust and horror. We wished at the period of the Revolution, and do now wish, to derive all we possess as an inheritance from our forefathers. Upon that body and stock of inheritance we have taken care not to inoculate any cyon alien to the nature of the original plant. All the reformations we have hitherto made, have preceded upon the principle of reference to antiquity; and I hope, nay I am persuaded, that all those which possibly may be made hereafter, will be carefully formed upon analogical precedent, authority and example." Although Burke could imagine future tinkering with the British constitution, unlike Price he believed that further reformation would never be needed. Burke claimed that the people of England "look on the frame of their commonwealth, *such as it stands,* to be of inestimable value."[26]

Burke's rhetorically brilliant exposition of the establishment Whig position attracted a last gasp of Opposition Whig scorn. The lifelong radical John Horne Tooke, for example, denounced Burke's *Reflections* as "a libel on the constitution." But with the French Declaration of War against Great Britain in February 1793, it had become unpatriotic to imagine that Britain had provided the model for French political developments. Britons now castigated revolutionary radicalism and denounced the inevitable excesses brought about by popular political insurrections. The Revolution Society's 1789 and 1790 calls for unity with the French people discredited their interpretation of the Revolution of 1688.[27]

Radicals were not completely silenced in the 1790s, but they did abandon the notion that Britain had spawned a new universal age of liberty in 1688. Radical disquiet about the revolution had begun much earlier. After the accession of George III, many began to feel that revolution principles had been abandoned. John Wilkes noted with dismay in 1762 that "almost every friend of liberty and of revolution principles has retired, or been dismissed." The radical pamphleteer and journeyman printer Joseph Towers lamented the recent "extraordinary change in political affairs" by which those who adhered to "the old Whig principles" were "stigmatized as factious, seditious, disaffected, and even rebellious." Wilkes and Richard Price claimed that this development proved that the revolution was imperfect. Blackstone pointed out that while "the nominal" power of the crown had been weakened at the revolution, the "real power" remained. "The stern commands of prerogative have yielded to the milder voice of influence," he explained.[28]

In the context of George III's turn to new advisers with Tory and neo-Tory ideological leanings, the outbreak of the American Revolution, and the creation of a new, more authoritarian empire in India, some radicals came to see the Revolution of 1688–89 as a disaster rather than as merely imperfect. The revolution, some thought, had not created an age of liberty but rather an age of oligarchy. Instead of "admitting the plebeians into the full possession of liberty, according to their natural right," complained the political reformer John Cartwright, those who brought about the revolution "strove all they could to establish an aristocratical tyranny upon the ruins of the royal one, and they succeeded but too well." Catherine Macaulay similarly, if more bitterly, argued that the Revolution of 1688–89 established "an unexampled mode of tyranny" and occasioned "an universal depravity of manners." The reason was that at the revolution "under the specious appearance of democratical privilege, the people are really and truly enslaved to a small part of the community."[29]

The end of the American war and the passage of economic reform no doubt dulled the discontent among the radicals, making possible the enthusiastic celebrations in 1788. British opposition to the French Revolution, however, encouraged those who continued to defend the French cause to abandon the Revolution of 1688–89. Thomas Paine set the tone of future radical interpretations of 1688. He responded to Burke's assault on the Opposition Whig interpretation not with a spirited defense but with a tactical surrender. "The Revolution of 1688," he said in *The Rights of Man,* "may have been exalted beyond its value." It was now "eclipsed by the enlarging orb of reason, and the luminous revolutions of America and France." This was because, in Paine's view, the Revolution of 1688–89 was a mere courtier revolution in which "the nation" was left to choose between "the two evils, James and William." There was no possibility of radical reform. From the 1790s onward, radicals abandoned the Revolution of 1688–89. They ceased, in the words of one historian, "to examine the events of 1688–89 for what they were, rather than for what they wished them to be."[30]

From the time of the French Revolution, the Revolution of 1688–89 was celebrated less as a turning point in British history than as an event that distinguished Britain from the Continent and the rest of the world. After the French Revolution, establishment Whig history became *the* Whig historical narrative. Thomas Babington Macaulay's magisterial Whig *History of England,* published in 1849, was implicitly a study in comparative history. Macaulay set out to distinguish Britain from a Europe convulsed with revolution. Macaulay shared with Burke and the establishment Whigs the conviction that 1688–89 was a fundamentally conservative event. The "calamities" of Continental revolutions were averted in England because the revolution in England "was a revolution strictly defensive, and had prescription and legitimacy on its side." Neither in act nor idea was there anything innovative in the English Revolution of 1688–89. "Not a single flower of the crown was touched," Macaulay famously observed, "not a single new right was given to the people. The whole English law, substantive and adjective, was, in the judgment of all the greatest lawyers . . . exactly the same after the Revolution as before it." Nor did the actors behave as if they were doing something new. "As our revolution was a vindication of ancient rights, so it was conducted with strict attention to ancient formalities. In almost every word and act may be discerned a profound reverence for the past," Macaulay wrote, very much echoing Burke. "Both the English parties agreed in treating with solemn respect the ancient constitutional traditions of the state. The only question was in what sense those traditions were to be understood." Macaulay also shared Burke's contempt for modern revolutions, claiming that "it is because we had a preserving revolution in the seventeenth century that we have not had a destroying revolution in the nineteenth." Indeed Macaulay, in what would become a mantra for future commentators, believed that the events in England in 1688–89 were conceptually distinct from modern revolutions. "To us who have lived in the year 1848," Macaulay argued, "it may seem almost an abuse of terms to call a proceeding, conducted with so much deliberation, with so much sobriety, and with such minute attention to prescriptive etiquette, by the terrible name of revolution."[31]

Macaulay's great-nephew George Macaulay Trevelyan reached similar conclusions in his establishment Whig history of the Revolution of 1688–89. While Macaulay wrote in the shadow of Jacobins and their atrocities, Trevelyan picked up his pen in the late 1930s filled with hatred for fascists whom he compared to the French Jacobins. Like Macaulay, Trevelyan insisted that in 1688–89 "there are no new ideas." Like Macaulay, Trevelyan saw the revolution as "a victory of moderation." Nor did Trevelyan see the actions of those who expelled James II as particularly revolutionary. "The merit of the Revolution," he insisted, "lay not in the shouting and the tumult, but in the still small voice of prudence and wisdom that prevailed through all the din." Unsurprisingly, like both Burke and Macaulay, Trevelyan thought "the spirit of this strange Revolution was the opposite of revolutionary."[32]

The works of Burke, Macaulay, and Trevelyan reasserted the establishment Whig interpretation of the revolution. For these three—all of whom wrote hoping Britain would not replicate the violent and extremist revolutions that were consuming the Continent in their own ages—the great virtue of the events of 1688–89 was precisely that they prevented a real revolution from happening in Britain. Their interpretations became hegemonic not because they had uncovered new, irrefutable historical evidence but because in the face of contemporary political events their interpretative opponents had abandoned the field. For all of the archival industriousness of Macaulay, for all of the rhetorical brilliance of Burke and Trevelyan, they assumed that their burden was to account for the resistance against James II's tyranny, rather than to explain and detail the revolutionary consequences of 1688–89. Burke, Macaulay, and Trevelyan did not so much refute the arguments of the Opposition Whigs as assume that in the contemporary political climate their claims were irrelevant.

Late-twentieth-century accounts of the Revolution of 1688–89 elaborated and reinforced the establishment Whig interpretation. Again and again scholars have narrowed their focus to the reign of James II and its immediate aftermath. Again and again scholars have discussed the revolution narrowly in terms of issues of domestic high politics and anti-Catholicism. Unsurprisingly, then, recent scholars have concluded, along with the establishment Whigs, that the revolution was restorative rather than innovative. The revolution, unlike more modern revolutions, did not mark a decisive turning point.[33]

Scholars across the ideological and methodological spectrum have chimed in with a single voice. The Revolution of 1688, they all claim, was an act of recovery and conservation rather than one of innovation. The purpose of the Revolution of 1688–89, argues J. R. Jones, "was restorative and conservationist." The revolutionaries in England, he affirms, "did not aim, like the dominant revolutionaries in France a century later, at transforming government, the law, society, and changing the status of all individuals who composed the nation." In an essay explicitly defending Trevelyan's account, John Morrill proclaims that "the Sensible Revolution of 1688–89 was a conservative revolution." The Revolution of 1688–89 "was a 'glorious revolution'—in the seventeenth century sense of that word," concurs Jonathan Scott, "because at last it restored, and secured, after a century of troubles, what remained salvageable of the Elizabethan church and state." Hugh Trevor-Roper notes that since the revolution "was essentially defensive, the product of determined resistance to innovation, it too was necessarily conservative."[34]

The events of 1688–89, in these accounts, were in no sense akin to modern revolutions. The Glorious Revolution was not a social revolution in terms of either its participants or its consequences. Dale Hoak has dismissed the Revolution of 1688–89 as "a dynastic putsch." Because "the revolution was a successful coup d'état," argues David Hosford, "what happened in England during this period was not a revolution, except in the narrowest sense of the word." There could be no popular radicalism in 1688–89, argues John Pocock, because "the peers were in charge." "The Glorious Revolution was astonishingly conservative in its ruling illusions," comments Mark Goldie, "in the welter of vindicatory words, talk of popular revolution was marginal."[35]

Since those who took part in the events of 1688–89 came from the narrow political elite and had no revolutionary program and no social agenda, they were necessarily not modern revolutionaries. "The 'glorious revolution' of 1688," notes John Western, "was so called precisely because so much of it was not in the modern sense revolutionary." Robert Beddard has insisted on "the particularly unmodern character of the Revolution of 1688." William Speck makes clear that the Revolution of 1688–89 was no social revolution.[36]

By the late twentieth century, the scholarly debate over the Revolution of 1688–89 was narrow indeed. To most observers there appeared to be no debate at all. "It was generally accepted," notes Howard Nenner, that "what had transpired in 1688–89 was essentially conservative." Harry Dickinson remarks that "the latest works on the Glorious Revolution agree that it was a conservative settlement." "Most scholars have reached a consensus," chimes in Kathleen Wilson, "that the Revolution was largely an episode in patrician politics, unrelentingly 'conservationist' in ideological, political and social effect." The establishment Whig understanding of the Revolution of 1688–89 has achieved hegemonic status.[37]

The Tercentenary of the Revolution of 1688–89 fell flat because there was little left to celebrate. Two centuries of historical scholarship had reduced what had once been seen as a fundamental shift in the history of humanity to an aristocratic parlor game. English or British identity had not been reshaped; it had been reaffirmed. The British constitution had not been remade; its ancient constitution had been recovered. Above all, scholars have claimed with a united voice, the lives of most Britons were remarkably little affected. The Revolution of 1688–89, if it did anything at all, changed high politics.

In public and in private, historians and politicians of all ideological stripes agreed that not much had happened. The Catholic conservative Auberon Waugh dismissed the revolution as "the last successful invasion and conquest of England by a foreign power." The long-serving Labour MP Tony Benn, who shared few political principles with Waugh, told the House of Commons that "what happened in 1688 was not a glorious revolution. It was a plot by some people." "Of course the glorious revolution did nothing to change the social order," agreed the Conservative MP Sir Bernard Braine, "it did nothing immediate for the lot of the common man."[38]

There may have been political changes as a result of the events of 1688–89, all could agree, but they did not constitute a revolution. When asked whether the events that began in November 1688 should be considered a revolution, Charles Wilson, the head of the historians' committee involved in the tercentenary celebrations, replied that "if by revolution you mean an upheaval comparable to the French Revolution, the Russian Revolution, even the American Revolution . . . certainly not. The magnates who invited William to England had no intention to change the political or social order." Noel Annan thought it was fair to conclude that, whatever their value, the events of 1688–89 were "not a real revolution." "It was certainly a revolution," insisted Sir Bernard Braine in the face of Labour attacks, "but more in the sense of the turning a wheel back to normality." In 1988 politicians of the left and right could agree that there had been no revolution in 1688–89. Lord Hailsham was left the unenviable task of opening the Banqueting House exhibit marking the tercentenary. He told the assembled audience that the Revolution of 1688–89 should be celebrated for what it was not and what it may have prevented. "Our own Glorious Revolution," he explained, "coming when it did, spared us any convulsions comparable to the French Revolution of 1789 or even the Russian Revolution of 1917 or the fall of the Weimar Republic in 1933." The significance of the Revolution of 1688–89, argued Prime Minister Margaret Thatcher, was that it showed the irrelevance of popular radicalism. "Political change should be sought and achieved through Parliament," she claimed, "it was this which saved us from the violent revolutions which shook our continental neighbors."[39] Given this remarkable consensus, given the hegemonic exposition of the establishment Whig interpretation of revolution principles, it is hardly surprising that the tercentenary events were sedate and dull affairs. Popular celebrations would have been antithetical to the spirit of the revolution.

The Revolution of 1688–89 has receded from the popular imagination because it has ceased to be an interesting event. Scholars, politicians, and journalists have come to agree that the revolution merely restored the English ancient constitution. It affirmed, rather than created, British exceptionalism. It was at best a heroic moment for a few British aristocrats standing up for their honor against an innovative and tyrannical monarch. The people were hardly involved. The revolution set no new precedent for future political action—it merely reasserted parliamentary sovereignty. The revolution set no model that was followed by others. If anything should be celebrated, it is the recurrent moderation of the British. We have all become establishment Whigs.[40]

This was not, however, always the only available interpretation of the Revolution of 1688–89. Throughout the eighteenth century some Britons, some Europeans, and some North Americans understood the revolution to be a politically, morally, and socially transformative event. That this view, contested as it was throughout the eighteenth century, has disappeared owes little to historical research. Scholars have investigated the nature of James's rule, not the content and origins of the revolutionary consequences of 1688–89. This oversight derives from Britons' vision of themselves, since the 1790s, as the opponents of revolutionary change on the Continent and as the targets of anticolonial revolutions elsewhere. The political climate, rather than scholarly research, has narrowed the kinds of questions that have been asked about the Revolution of 1688–89. It is now time to find answers to the questions that the Opposition Whigs raised in the eighteenth century.

This book is an attempt to do just that. Inspired by the insights of the eighteenth-century debate about the revolution, this book differs from most scholarly work on the Glorious Revolution in two fundamental ways. First, rather than assuming that the Glorious Revolution was a high political event that took place between 1688 and 1690 and had origins that must be found in the reign of James II, I expand the lens of investigation. I ask whether there were long-term causes of the revolution—whether socioeconomic, political, religious, or broadly ideological. And I ask whether there were longer-term consequences of the revolution that might be missed by curtailing the investigation with the Battle of the Boyne (1690) or the Treaty of Limerick (1691), the events that may be said to have ended the military conflict in the British Isles between King James and King William. Second, I have insisted on placing developments in England within broader European and extra-European contexts. Rather than assuming that English men and women thought in exclusively insular terms, I have explored economic, religious, and political interactions with Europe and the wider world. I have, for example, tried to interpret James II's Catholicism in terms of European Catholic debates and tried to understand how the English thought about Europe and the possibilities of extra-European empire. It is because I have adopted a radically different method from most scholars that I have come up with very different conclusions about the causes, nature, and consequences of the Revolution of 1688–89.

Instead of asking why James II was overthrown in 1688–89—the unacknowledged question for most scholars—I ask why English state and society was transformed in the 1680s and 1690s. In Part II of this book, then, I part ways with the establishment Whig interpretation of the Glorious Revolution by insisting that English economic life, and England's place in the European economy, was changing dramatically in the second half of the century. James II, I suggest, tried to harness these energies to create one version of a modern English state. James II's efforts, modeled as they were on a French version of a modern Catholic state, did inspire widespread and passionate opposition. In Part III, I show that the revolutionary energies unleashed from 1687 onward did not give rise to the moderate and sensible revolution celebrated in establishment Whig historiography and modern scholarship. Far from being aristocratic, peaceful, and consensual, I show that the Revolution of 1688–89, like most modern revolutions, was popular, violent, and extremely divisive. Part IV traces the long-term causes and consequences of the revolution in three vital areas: the revolution in political economy, the revolution in the Church, and the revolution in foreign policy. In Part V, I highlight the radically transformative effect of the Revolution in two very different ways. In chapter 14, I use the Assassination Plot of 1696 to show how dramatically the revolution had transformed the contours of political discussion in late-seventeenth-century England. In the conclusion I ask: When was the English Revolution? Here I make it clear that although the Revolution of 1688–89, and its radical consequences, would have been impossible had there not been a civil war and an interregnum in midcentury, the midcentury upheaval did not make 1688–89 and its aftermath inevitable. French-style absolutism was a real possibility in later seventeenth-century England. Only a radical revolution prevented England from following a very different developmental path.

Before turning to my account of later seventeenth-century England, however, it is important to establish my understanding of revolution. So, chapter 2 sets out a theory of revolution that draws heavily on the extensive literature on revolutions in the social sciences and the humanities. Based on that literature I advance a new agenda for studying revolutions in a comparative framework. Although I hope the theory and agenda will stimulate further research in areas far beyond English history, this chapter makes clear why I think the Revolution of 1688–89 must be considered the first modern revolution.

CHAPTER TWO

Rethinking Revolutions

There is no part of history better received than the account of great changes and revolutions of states and governments," wrote the Anglican cleric and future revolutionary Gilbert Burnet in the middle of the seventeenth century. This was so, he claimed, because "the variety of unlooked for accidents and events, both entertains the reader and improves him." Another early commentator on revolutions emphasized that revolutions were not only entertaining but difficult to interpret. "When great revolutions are successful their causes cease to exist," explained Alexis de Tocqueville. "The very fact of their success has made them incomprehensible." Little has changed in the century and a half separating us from Tocqueville. Revolutions continue to fascinate and to baffle. In the late 1970s Theda Skocpol observed that "during the last two decades theories of revolution have sprung up thick and fast in American social science."[1] The pace of scholarship on the subject of revolution has only accelerated since Skocpol wrote those words.

Revolutions continue to fascinate and amaze because each new revolution seems to raise doubts about the previous generation of sophisticated theorizing. Unfortunately, each new revolution has encouraged scholars to develop ever-more elaborate explanations, with new variables and new sets of possible outcomes. Each new account of revolutions is more complex than the last. Along with new causes have come new distinctions in the

---

(above) *Centenary of the Revolution*, 1788. Struck in 1788, in commemoration of the Revolution of 1688–89, this medal depicts the British lion, with symbols of Catholic domination underfoot. See Laurence Brown, *A Catalogue of British Historical Medals, 1760–1960*, Vol. 1: *The Accession of George III to the Death of William IV* (London: Seaby, 1980), 68.

typology of revolutions. We now hear of political revolutions, social revolutions, great revolutions, lesser revolutions, Third World revolutions, and twentieth-century revolutions. This chapter offers a more parsimonious explanation for the causes of revolutions *tout court* and suggests some new directions in explaining their outcomes. The general model developed here makes clear why the Revolution of 1688–89 in England should be understood to be the first modern revolution.

Revolutions are relatively rare and distinctive events. They fundamentally transform states and societies. "A revolution," suggests the political scientist Samuel Huntington, "is a rapid, fundamental, and violent domestic change in the dominant values and myths of a society, in its political institutions, social structure, leadership, and government activity and policies." Revolutions are thus distinguishable from violent leadership changes in which social and political structures remain as they were. They are also separable from wars of independence in which the former colony's social and political structures remain but the locus of sovereignty is shifted. Useful as Huntington's definition is, it needs to be qualified and amplified. The rapidity of revolutions must be measured in years, not in months. "Revolutions," one recent commentator has pointed out, "are best conceptualized not as events, but as processes that typically span many years or even decades." Revolutions, too, possess a common ideological element: a self-conscious commitment to epochal change. Revolutionary actors insist that their achievements, or their aspirations, represent a fundamental temporal break from the past. "True revolution," notes the political theorist Isaac Kramnick, "seeks a new beginning." So for Richard Price, the American Revolution "opens a new prospect in human affairs, and begins a new era in the history of mankind." Almost a century earlier the Swiss observer of English society Guy Miege had described England's Glorious Revolution as spawning "a new face of things."[2] It was this same conception of a temporal break that prompted the French Jacobins to construct a new calendar in 1793.

Revolutions thus constitute a structural and ideological break from the previous regime. They entail changes to both the political and socioeconomic structures of a polity. They involve an often violent popular movement to overturn the previous regime. Revolutions change the political leadership and the policy orientations of the state. And revolutionary regimes bring with them a new conception of time, a notion that they are beginning a new epoch in the history of the state and its society.

Class conflict, then, is incidental to revolutions. Despite the central role that class struggle plays in some influential accounts of revolutions and the role that class divisions clearly have played in some revolutions, to insist that class struggle is constitutive of revolution is to narrow unnecessarily the field of analysis. The French Revolution of the late eighteenth century, once the classic case of class-based social revolution, is no longer universally thought to have had the class basis that Georges Lefebvre and Albert Soboul among others assumed.[3] Some twentieth-century revolutions, such as the Iranian Revolution, would also appear to be excluded from a definition of revolution that places class struggle at its center. Class conflict may have determined the shape of some revolutionary movements, may have been the outcome of revolutionary transformations, and may have informed the political goals of the revolutionaries and their opponents in some cases. But not all revolutions have been about class conflict. Such a narrow definition of revolution would seem to have little social scientific value. Revolutions must involve popular movements; those popular movements need not be class based.

Nor is it useful to distinguish between social and political revolutions. Events that "transform state structures but not social structures" are civil wars, rebellions, or coups d'état; they are not revolutions. Revolutions must involve both a transformation of the socioeconomic orientation and of the political structures. That transformation must take place through a popular movement, and the transformation must involve a self-consciousness that a new era has begun. The distinction usually drawn in the literature between social and political revolutions, it seems to me, is normative as much as it is analytical.[4] Scholars draw a bold line between social and political revolutions because they admire some revolutionary outcomes and disdain others. Analytical language has been used to disguise political preferences.

Why, then, do revolutions happen? Social scientists and historians have not been at a loss for explanations. As books and articles have proliferated, so have the stories scholars have told about the causes of revolutions. Despite the richness of the literature, it is possible to discern two types of explanations that now dominate the discussion, both associated with prominent social scientists. The first explanation of revolution is that the old regime is overturned by modernizers. The second analysis specifies that the old regime is done in by a new social group, a class that seizes power and overturns the structures of the state and society. For all of their differences, both explanations of revolution are modernization stories.

"Revolution," Huntington declares, "is characteristic of modernization. It is one way of modernizing a traditional society." In particular Huntington argues that revolution "is most likely to occur in societies which have experienced some social and economic development and where the processes of political modernization and political development have lagged behind the processes of social and economic change." Although Huntington distinguishes between a Western and an Eastern pattern of revolution, in both cases, as Charles Tilly perceptively points out, "the immediate cause of revolution is supposed to be the discrepancy between the performance of the regime and the demands being made upon it. . . . Which in turn occurs as a more or less direct effect of rapid social and economic change."[5]

The class struggle explanation for revolution differs from the classic modernization story in two fundamental ways. Whereas the classic modernization story focuses on a generalized transition from a traditional to a modern society, the class struggle model highlights the transition from one mode of economic production to another. "The conception of social revolution used here," Theda Skocpol emphasizes, "draws heavily upon Marxist emphases on social structural change and class conflict." And whereas the classic modernization story focuses exclusively on internal domestic transitions, Skocpol, in particular, highlights the international context. "Modern social revolutions have happened only in countries situated in disadvantaged positions within international arenas," she points out. "The realities of military backwardness or political dependency have crucially affected the occurrence and course of social revolutions." This situation of comparative backwardness is itself inextricably tied to modes of production. "All modern social revolutions," says Skocpol, "must be seen as closely related in their causes and accomplishments to the internationally uneven spread of capitalist economic development and nation-state formation on a world scale." It is in this sense that Skocpol argues that "revolutionary crises developed when the old-regime states became unable to meet the challenges of evolving international situations."[6] For defenders of the class struggle paradigm, revolutions happen when members of a particular class overturn the old regime because the old sociopolitical structure had made the state uncompetitive on the world stage.

Despite these important interpretive, analytical, and (one suspects) normative differences, these two dominant explanations for revolution share a great deal. Both are fundamentally stories about modernization. Both emphasize that revolutions occur in societies in which social and economic modernization has made the state appear to be outmoded, to be an ancien régime. Despite the differences in approach, Skocpol shares with Huntington the notion that "epochal modernizing dynamics in part cause and shape revolutionary transformations."[7]

In contrast to both the classical modernizing and class struggle perspectives, I suggest that revolutions occur only when states have embarked on ambitious state modernization programs. Revolutions do not pit modernizers against defenders of an old regime. Instead revolutions happen when the political nation is convinced of the need for political modernization but there are profound disagreements on the proper course of state innovation. For all the emphasis that the approaches of Huntington and Skocpol place on "political and institutional factors," I suggest, they have missed this crucial point.[8] State modernization, as political aim and as political process, is a necessary *prerequisite* for revolution. The extent and nature of modernizing social movements may encourage state modernization. These social movements may help to shape the nature of the revolutionary process. But social movements do not spark revolution unless state modernization is already under way.

Before I lay out the case that state modernization is a necessary prerequisite to revolution, it is important that I acknowledge one powerful analysis of revolutions that does not stress modernization. Jack Goldstone, in his widely discussed *Revolution and Rebellion in the Early Modern World,* has advanced an altogether different thesis. "Revolutions," Goldstone insists, "are not provoked by a battle between the past and the future, or between good and evil; they are instead provoked by imbalances between human institutions and the environment." The key factor in promoting state breakdown, according to Goldstone, has nothing to do with social or economic modernization. "The motivation for change," Goldstone insists, "[comes] from ecological shifts in the relation of the population size to agricultural output, which produce[s] diverse conflicts between elites and states, among elite factions, and between popular groups and authorities."[9] In Goldstone's breathtaking analysis, which traverses the early modern world from Europe to East Asia, traditional Malthusian crises, not modernizing economies, promote state breakdown and revolution.

The demographic explanation for revolutions and state breakdown relies on an important empirical claim. Goldstone suggests that there was "state breakdown not merely in Europe but on a world wide scale, clustered in two marked 'waves,' the first culminating in the mid-seventeenth century, the second in the mid-nineteenth, and separated by roughly a century, from 1660 to 1760, of stability." The periods of instability were periods of demographic growth; the period of stability was one of population stagnation. "If population decline restores a traditional balance of people and resources," Goldstone explains, "traditional institutions may be revived."[10]

Though innovative and interpretatively exciting, Goldstone's analysis fails to make sense of the early modern world that is his focus. Monumental state breakdowns and revolutions occurred during his "century of stability" of 1660–1760. Goldstone dismisses England's Glorious Revolution of the later seventeenth century as "not really a revolution." This view contrasts with that of classic commentators and the interpretation developed here. Karl Marx thought the Glorious Revolution marked "the first decisive victory of the bourgeoisie over the feudal aristocracy." The great jurist Sir William Blackstone agreed that it was the Glorious Revolution, "the happy revolution," that marked the decline of feudalism in England and the full establishment of England's "civil and political liberties."[11] The Glorious Revolution, I will show, was a popular and violent event in which both the nature of English governance and the socioeconomic orientation of the regime were radically transformed. Not only did the new regime alter its foreign, imperial, economic, and religious policies, but subsequent commentators—whether supportive or critical of the revolution—almost universally described the revolution as a new beginning in English history.

England was not the only European state to undergo a state breakdown, a state transformation, or a revolution in the century of so-called stability. The United Provinces of the Netherlands were convulsed by violent and spectacular state upheavals. In the face of military reverses at the hands of the French in the summer of 1672, a wave of popular protests and riots swept across the wealthiest state in Europe. The rioters eventually forced the great republican leader John De Witt to resign from office in early August. Then, on 20 August, De Witt and his brother Cornelius were ripped limb from limb on the streets of The Hague. The result was to make William of Orange stadholder in July 1672, "transforming the structure of power." Popular political violence had changed the Netherlands from a republican into a quasi-monarchical regime.[12]

Scandinavia, too, suffered state breakdowns between 1660 and 1760. Between 1660 and 1683, Frederik III and Christian V transformed Denmark from an elective monarchy into one of the most absolute states in Europe. Frederik III, in the wake of Denmark's disastrous military defeat by the Swedes in 1657–60, "staged a coup" to ensure that the monarchy would become hereditary in 1660. In the following decades "the old oligarchical social order" was replaced "by a meritocracy in which the talented could reach the top irrespective of their social origins." The Danish Law of 1683 created "order and transparency in every aspect of life." The Danish political and social order had been permanently transformed.[13] Despite its victory over Denmark, the Swedish state was also dramatically transformed after 1680. In the Swedish case, in fact, it was not so much defeat and comparative backwardness but anxiety that Sweden did not have the resources to maintain its hard-won status as a great power that provoked the transformation from an elective to an absolute monarchy. In 1680 Charles XI formally achieved the status of absolute monarch. In the words of one scholar, Charles XI "effected a revolution in the power of the monarchy." The Swedish diets lost the power to limit his authority. He was then able to restructure radically the Swedish army, the Swedish navy, and Swedish finances. Significantly, the transformation of the Swedish state, which some interpreted as a royal coup, involved a massive transfer of resources from "private hands to the public domain." In essence, the Swedish nobility was emasculated.[14] Swedish state and society had been transformed.

Northern Europe was not the only region that underwent state breakdown in the so-called era of stability. The Spanish state was spectacularly transformed in a pan-European war, the War of the Spanish Succession. Europeans from London to Vienna and beyond were convulsed by the downfall of the Spanish Habsburg monarchy in the early eighteenth century. Spain devolved into civil war. The Bourbon monarchy that emerged from the war altered the nature of the Spanish state. The new state generated a new "bureaucratic elite" and "a shift in power towards the central government." After 1714 the new Spanish royal line engaged in further state reforms.[15]

The demographic explanation for revolution and state breakdown asserts that states are at risk of upheaval only during periods when population growth outstrips economic resources. During periods of population stability, there should be state stability. Yet the period of population stability, 1660–1760, was an era of frequent and dramatic state breakdown and revolution throughout Europe. We must therefore look elsewhere for the causes of revolution.

The key factor in explaining revolutions was neither population pressure nor socio-economic modernization. In some cases both factors may have played a role, but the key factor was state modernization. In all revolutions the old regime had ceased to exist before the revolution. Revolutions, then, do not pit modernizing elements against defenders of the traditional order. Instead revolutions occur only after the regime in power has set itself on a modernizing course. State modernization itself cannot occur without prior socio-economic modernization. But that socioeconomic modernization is a necessary though not a sufficient cause of state modernization.[16] It is for that reason that revolutions are the often-violent working out of competing state modernization programs.

Scholars have long perceived empirical problems with both the classic and class struggle versions of the modernization story. Charles Tilly, for one, has pointed out that the historical record suggests "no direct relationship [between] the pace of structural change" and revolution. Indeed, Tilly notes the evidence suggests a negative relationship: "rapid change, diminution of political conflict." "Large-scale structural changes" indirectly affect "the probabilities of revolution," Tilly concludes, but "there is no reliable and regular sense in which modernization breeds revolution."[17] Social and economic transformation—that is, social modernization—may lead to political changes but not to state breakdown. Rather, state modernization makes a regime ripe for revolution.

By state modernization I mean a self-conscious effort by the regime to transform itself in fundamental ways. State modernization will usually include an effort to centralize and bureaucratize political authority, an initiative to transform the military using the most up-to-date techniques, a program to accelerate economic growth and shape the contours of society using the tools of the state, and the deployment of techniques allowing the state to gather information about and potentially suppress social and political activities taking place in a wide range of social levels and geographical locales within the polity. State modernizers almost always deploy the same rhetoric of creating new beginnings that we normally associate with revolutionaries. They insist that they are initiating a fundamental break with past modes of governance.

Louis XVI's France, Tocqueville long ago suggested, was a classic case in which attempts to modernize the state made the regime ripe for revolution. "Experience teaches us," writes Tocqueville, that "the most perilous moment for a bad government is one when it seeks to mend its ways." Tocqueville was generalizing from his knowledge of the French case. There, in the decades before the revolution, "modern institutions" had emerged "within the shattered framework of the feudal system." So extensive were the programs of state modernization that "the whole nation seemed to be in the throes of a rebirth." Far from being a reactionary, Louis XVI was a determined reformer. "During his entire reign Louis XIV was always talking about reform," notes Tocqueville, "and there were few institutions whose destruction he did not contemplate." In the later eighteenth century the French state was becoming increasingly centralized, "more systematic in its methods and more efficient." In 1787 Louis XVI initiated a "wholesale remodeling of the entire administration." The following year, 1788, the king "issued an edict overhauling the entire judicial system." In response to France's demoralizing and devastating defeat in the Seven Years' War (1757–63), "the government had become more energetic [and] had launched into a host of activities to which until then it had not given a thought." The point is neither that Louis XVI's regime anticipated all the changes later brought about by the revolutionaries nor that Louis XVI was a misunderstood radical but that Louis XVI was a modernizer.[18] His activities shifted the terrain of political discussion and activity. The French Revolution was the violent working out of competing modernization programs.

The French Revolution was not the first example of this phenomenon. A century earlier, England had been convulsed with a similar revolutionary pattern. James II and the English political nation were also concerned that recent military setbacks, this time against the Dutch, had rendered the kingdom a second-rate power. James II also benefited from an expansion of English foreign trade that enabled him to modernize and expand the English army, to massively increase the state bureaucracy, and to impose central control on local government. James also developed a wide-ranging and efficient surveillance system, deploying numerous informers in England's coffeehouses, taverns, and churches. He used the newly created post office to open letters and thereby keep tabs on the political pulse. He also used extensive political surveys to assess political sentiment and to ease the removal of political dissidents and replace them with loyalists. The revolutionaries who overthrew James implemented an alternative modernization program. The postrevolutionary regime was also determined to modernize, centralize, and augment the state. But that regime did so with a very different economic strategy—one committed to developing England's manufacturing sector rather than seeking to expand the agrarian sector through territorial acquisition—a different foreign policy, and a profound commitment to religious toleration.[19]

Twentieth-century revolutions followed the same pattern as those of the seventeenth and eighteenth centuries. State modernization was a necessary prerequisite to revolution. The Mexican Revolution was preceded by a period of extensive state modernization. Mexico's president Porfirio Díaz had initiated a series of reforms that the historian Friedrich Katz has christened the "Porfirian road to modernization." Díaz modernized the Mexican army along Prussian lines, making it into a career open to talents. Díaz's finance minister, José Limantour, "balanced the budget, reformed the treasury, abolished internal tariffs and overhauled the country's banking institutions." As a result, the size of the state bureaucracy "greatly increased." Díaz also used his power to bring Mexico's opposition press "under control." Díaz's achievement was to create a "national ruling class" that ran "a strong, centralized regime."[20]

The Russian and Turkish Revolutions of the early twentieth century both followed attempts to modernize the state, though in both cases the modernization was in part forced on the old regime. In Russia, the czars had already taken steps toward emancipating the serfs in the nineteenth century. By the early twentieth century, state reforms "had managed to turn the state administration into a uniform and modern institution."[21] Russia's defeat in the Russo-Japanese War and the subsequent 1905 Revolution quickened the pace of state modernization. Czar Nicholas created the Duma, a national elected parliament, and legalized political parties and trade unions. He had at his command the largest standing army in Europe. And before the Revolution that began in October 1917 Nicholas had initiated "a major program of social reform."[22]

Sultan Abdulhamid II similarly embarked on a series of state reforms before the Turkish Revolution of 1908. Aware that European powers were anxiously awaiting the opportunity to carve up the once formidable Ottoman Empire, the sultan reluctantly but actively pursued modernization. He greatly expanded the state school system and the railway network. He initiated a wide-ranging program to modernize the Turkish army along German lines. Before the revolution of 1908, then, the sultan "had managed to create major modernized sectors within the Ottoman military and bureaucracy, sectors that began to operate on the basis of legal/rational rules of conduct."[23]

State modernization was also a precursor to the Chinese Revolution. In this case, China's defeat at the hands of the Japanese (1895), followed by the Boxer Rebellion (1899–1901), had encouraged a series of rapid and far-reaching reforms. Large sections of the military were reformed in the Western tradition. In 1905 the classical Confucian examination system was abandoned, making possible wide-ranging educational reforms. According to the historian of China Jonathan Spence, "government control of the economy was also strengthened, as more state-directed but merchant-run companies were founded and the railway network was gradually extended." In September 1906, the government proclaimed that a constitution and further administrative reforms were being prepared. In early-twentieth-century China all parties "were advocates of political modernization." The conflict that would soon rise to the level of revolution "concerned the form of modern government China should have and the method by which modern government should be introduced."[24]

The Iranian Revolution of 1979, so problematic for scholars who understand revolutions to be about the triumph of modernization or the ultimate victory of the peasant class, was yet another example of an ambitious state modernizer paving the road to revolution. Shah Mohammad Reza Pahlavi was the architect of a thoroughgoing modernization program. His army of more than four hundred thousand men was supplied with modern weapons, advisers, and technologies. His vast "bureaucracy managed such diverse functions and enterprises as the oil industry, the steel industry, ports, railroads, and even atomic energy." The shah, of course, had also fine-tuned a secret police force that was widely feared and despised. According to one commentator, the Iranian Revolution was "a political struggle set in motion by the centralization and modernization of the state." The revolutionaries were not reactionaries. They had different visions for a modern Iran. This reflected the broad base of the opposition to the shah, including, in addition to the clergy, "the bazaar merchants, the tribes, the intellectuals, the technocrats, the students, the industrial workers, the usually timid civil servants, and in the end even a segment of the armed forces." Even the ultimately triumphant Islamists could be said to have had a vision of a modern Islamic republic.[25]

The Cuban Revolution of 1959 would at first glance appear to pose the greatest interpretative problems. Most commentators suggest that Fulgencio Batista's vulnerability stemmed in large part from his desire to deprofessionalize the army. Yet even Batista was an aggressive, if quirky, state modernizer. Batista's recipe for political survival included promoting rapid economic growth, which he fostered in part "by the state's development banks." He had, in the view of another commentator, "embarked on an industrialization program." Batista, who had emerged as Cuba's leading political figure in 1933, had developed an immense state bureaucracy in which one in nine Cubans was a state employee. Of course, one element of Batista's modernizing state—as in all the other examples of state modernization—was an arm of political repression. As many as twenty thousand Cubans may have been killed by the state between 1952 and 1959.[26] Fidel Castro rose to power offering an alternative vision of Cuban modernization.

Why should state modernization be a necessary step on the road to revolution? The answer is both sociostructural, the social effects of the extension of the bureaucratic state, and ideological. State modernization necessarily brings a huge swath of people into contact with the state. Modernizing states tend to create vast new centralized bureaucracies. Tax collectors, local governors, postmasters, and secret police descend into the localities as never before. This new contact with the state in everyday life encourages those for whom national politics was previously distant and largely unimportant to care deeply about the state's ideological and political direction. By creating a demand for information and a means of supplying it, modernizing states create newly politicized peoples. Modernizing state institutions also employ large new sectors of the population.[27] Modernizing armies and bureaucracies not only make large groups state employees but educate these new employees in new methods and new worldviews, and, in many cases, teach them to embrace a national rather than regional or local identity. It is for this reason that many revolutions involve radical cadres from within the modernizing institutions, such as the Young Turks in early-twentieth-century Turkey, or the army deserters led by the future Duke of Marlborough in late-seventeenth-century England. Modernizing states create new publics that suddenly care about national politics.

By announcing a break with the past, modernizing states create an ideological opening. In order to explain and justify state expansion, state transformation, and the necessary intrusions in everyday life, modernizing states have to proclaim and explain their new direction. In so doing, they are compelled to concede the need for radical change. Would-be revolutionaries are no longer obliged to explain to a potentially skeptical or conservative populace why change is necessary. Revolutionaries have the far less imposing task of explaining why the state's chosen modernization path is doomed to failure or deleterious. Modernizing states necessarily stir up wide-ranging debates about the means

and ends of modernization. Modernizing states create the ideological space for a modernizing opposition.

Modernization of the old regime is not one step in an ineluctable progression to revolution. States have not necessarily modernized in response to revolutionary pressures. The Russian Romanovs and the Chinese Qing may have modernized their states in unsuccessful attempts to thwart revolution. But in other cases the regime was responding to other pressures. James II modernized the English state apparatus at the apex of his domestic popularity. The great state reforms proposed by Louis XVI were a response not only to domestic discontent but to a perceived competitive disadvantage in the face of British power. The ambitious programs of state development embarked upon by Díaz in Mexico and Pahlavi in Iran were not counterrevolutionary programs. In both cases the agendas appear to have more to do with international status than with silencing a well-defined revolutionary opposition. Statesmen rarely developed modernization programs to stave off revolution. However, statesmen who chose to initiate ambitious and transformative modernization programs did, in some instances, unintentionally spawn revolutionary opposition.

What are the differences between my account and previous ones? Most theorists of revolution have emphasized the creation of social movements with the potential to overthrow the old regime. I argue by contrast that the origins of revolution are to be found in the state modernization that begins within the old regime, a modernizing program that makes the old regime into a modern state. This account contrasts with that of Huntington, who claims that "revolutions are unlikely in political systems which have the capacity to expand their power and to broaden participation within the system." It is precisely the state's capacity to broaden contact that creates new politicized groups. Although I share with Skocpol the view that international developments may place extreme pressure on old regimes, I don't agree with her suggestion that "the repressive state organizations of the pre-Revolutionary regime have to be weakened before mass revolutionary action can succeed." In the English, Cuban, or Iranian cases, the repressive elements of the state were strengthening rather than weakening at the moment of the revolution. In fact, the expanding power of the state often creates a desperation to act before resistance becomes futile. I disagree, in turn, with Jeff Goodwin that revolutionary movements develop on the periphery of states that are "organizationally incoherent and militarily weak especially in outlying areas of society."[28] It is precisely the modernizing state's actions to extend its authority more deeply into society that politicize and mobilize people on the periphery. State modernization, not state breakdown—increasing state strength, not impending state weakness—is a presage to revolution.

Of course, not all state modernization programs have given rise to popular revolutions. The ambitious and extensive reformulations of the state in Sweden and Denmark created more stable rather than more volatile regimes. Louis XIV pursued a remarkable program of state modernization that centralized his power, limited the possibility for judicial opposition, created a variety of new state industries, and modernized both the army and the navy. The outcome was not revolution but a golden age of French government.[29] Similarly, the Meiji Restoration in Japan (1868) "established a system of universal education, formed a modern army and navy, and recruited an efficient administrative bureaucracy both nationally and locally."[30] In this case, too, the new state was not overturned by a revolutionary movement but rather created an effective military machine.

Why, then, have some state modernizations led directly to revolution while others have produced a stable and efficient state? In answering this question I am on shaky ground. Because most scholars have focused on the social prerequisites for revolution rather than on state modernization, there is a paucity of scholarship on which to draw. The work of historians, because not usually comparative, is largely unhelpful in this regard.

The best explanation for why some modernizing regimes suffer revolution and others enjoy stability and political success is offered by Carles Boix. "Given some uncertainty about the technology of repression in the hands of the wealthy," Boix posits, "revolutions and some forms of armed conflict should erupt with some positive probability."[31] This suggests that revolutions are more likely in situations in which the modernizing regime is not clearly perceived to have a monopoly of the forces of violence. This may happen when the modernization program has been so rapid as to create the perception of administrative weakness, as in the case of late-eighteenth-century France or late-seventeenth-century England. Or it may happen when the regime has proven unable to repress fledgling opposition movements, as in Cuba and China. When the modernizing state quickly demonstrates its control of resources and disarms the opposition, as in seventeenth-century Denmark and Sweden or late-nineteenth-century Japan, revolutions do not occur.

Ideology must play a role as well. Opposition groups can be silenced either by physical repression or by high levels of ideological consensus. Louis XIV was almost certainly aided in his massive modernization project by his successful self-representation as the leader who would allow France to achieve universal dominion.[32] In general, when regimes can marshal patriotic rhetoric so as to depict successfully their political opponents as enemies of the nation, they are much more likely to avoid revolution. Naturally, should the patriotic language be cause or consequence of international conflict, military victory becomes essential to remaining in power. Would the Russian Revolution have happened if the czar's armies had been victorious in World War I?

Why did some revolutions generate relatively open regimes whereas others produced more repressive, closed societies? Why did some revolutions, like the Glorious Revolution and the American Revolution, create more competitive political cultures whereas the Russian and Chinese Revolutions created less pluralistic regimes?

This, of course, is a modification of the classic question posed by Barrington Moore in *Social Origins of Dictatorship and Democracy*. Why, Moore asks, did some states become democracies, other states fascist, still others communist? His answer is rich in historical detail and analytical subtlety. But it can be neatly summarized. Moore suggests that in England, France, and the United States, "capitalism and democracy" were achieved "after a series of revolutions." These revolutions, Moore concludes, were "bourgeois revolutions." This is because "a vigorous and independent class of town dwellers has been an indispensable element in the growth of parliamentary democracy." "No bourgeois, no democracy," Moore crisply puts it. In Germany and Japan, by contrast, Moore sees the development of capitalism without democracy. Economic modernization happens in those countries without "a strong revolutionary surge," culminating ultimately in "fascism." In these cases, in contrast to England, France, and the United States, modernization was brought about by a strong "landed upper class." Although Moore refers to this model as "revolution from above," he makes it clear that these are revolutions without revolutionary activity. Modernization happened without "popular revolutionary upheaval." The cases Moore describes in this category are what I have called state modernization projects that are not followed by revolution. Finally, communist revolutions, those that occurred in China and Russia, were revolutions that had "their main but not exclusive origins among the peasants."[33]

For all of Moore's historical sophistication and analytical acumen, his account is ultimately not persuasive. Both the French Revolution and the English Civil War were followed by periods that could hardly be called democratic. Napoleon certainly celebrated the image of the Frenchman, and he did codify French law, but Napoleon's pursuit of the old French goal of universal dominion was not based on the political support of a democratic regime. The English Civil War, which was quickly followed by the execution of Charles I in 1649, did not lead—as I argue in the next section—seamlessly to parliamentary democracy. Charles II and especially James II (1685–88) created a strong absolutist state that had to be overthrown by a violent popular revolution in 1688. Had Napoleon not been defeated, had James II crushed the revolutionaries in 1688, the path to parliamentary democracy would have been far less smooth in both countries. A strong bourgeoisie does not ineluctably produce parliamentary democracy. Nor does state transformation from above necessarily lead to fascism. Both Denmark and Sweden experienced state modernization led by an absolutist king. Yet both countries are more closely associated with social democracy than with fascism. There are basic truths in Moore's analysis, but the argument depends heavily on feats of historical gymnastics.[34]

An alternative answer to the question why some revolutions result in more democratic regimes while others spawn more authoritarian ones has been advanced by Hannah Arendt. For Arendt, the reason why the French Revolution ultimately followed "a disastrous course" whereas the American Revolution created a democratic society had everything to do with the aims of the revolutionaries.[35] From "the later stages of the French Revolution up to the revolutions of our own time," laments Arendt, "it appeared to revolutionary men more important to change the fabric of society . . . than to change the structure of the political realm." Revolutions focused on social rather than political questions inevitably produced authoritarian regimes. This was because, as in the French Revolution, the revolutionary energy was diverted away from attention to freedom. "The direction of the French Revolution was deflected almost from its beginning from this course of foundation [of freedom] through the immediacy of suffering," Arendt posits. "It was determined by the exigencies of liberation not from tyranny but from necessity." This logic, according to Arendt, "helped in the unleashing of a stream of boundless violence.[36]

Arendt's explanation for the varying political outcomes of revolution is even more pessimistic than Moore's. Like Moore, Arendt relates her outcomes to "historical stages." Whereas Moore suggests that the democratic and fascist stages have passed, Arendt posits that ever since the French Revolution, revolutionaries have sought to remedy social rather than political problems. Nevertheless, there are significant historical problems with Arendt's analysis. Social issues *were* part and parcel of England's Glorious Revolution, the revolution that paved the way for parliamentary democracy. That social issues played a prominent role in England's later seventeenth-century revolution is hardly surprising since it was John Locke (1632–1704) who, in Arendt's view, invented the central idea of social revolutionaries: the notion that "labour and toil" were not the activities "to which poverty condemned those who were without property" but "were, on the contrary, the source of all wealth." Locke's notion that labor created property made property potentially infinite; therefore it would be humanly possible to eliminate poverty. It was precisely this ideology that motivated many of the revolutionaries of 1688–89 to transform England from an agrarian to a manufacturing society, from a society bounded by limited raw materials to a society fueled by the limitless possibilities of human creation. Even more damaging for Arendt's argument is the fact that her quintessential political revolution, the American Revolution, had a social dimension. Tim Breen's recent work has placed the "consumer boycott" at the center of his account of the American Revolution. "The American Revolution was," Breen argues, "the first large-scale political movement to organize itself around the relation of ordinary people to manufactured consumer goods."[37] Colonial subjects in North America were turned into revolutionaries when British taxes deprived them of the consumer goods that had made them feel civilized. Social questions were at the heart of the concerns of America's revolutionaries.

Why then have some revolutions created democratic states while others have given birth to authoritarian societies? The answer has a great deal to do with economic structures of the societies in which the revolutions have taken place. The French Revolution, like all other revolutions, as Tocqueville noted, "created an atmosphere of missionary fervor and, indeed, assumed all the aspects of religious revival."[38] Revolutionaries are certain of their own position. They voluntarily brook no compromises. Faced with political resistance, revolutionaries left to their own devices are willing to force people to be free. However, when the revolutionary states depend on foreign trade for their economic survival, they in turn depend on merchant communities. Merchant communities demand free flows of information to conduct their trade and are thus hostile to authoritarian regimes that monopolize information. It was the economic and political clout of the foreign trading communities, I suspect, that prevented England after 1688 and the United States in the early national period from adopting one-party rule. In both cases the resources of the merchant communities were vital to national defense. In relatively economically self-sufficient states—France under Napoleon, China, and the Soviet Union—relatively authoritarian regimes with a single dominant party triumphed. Iran has been able to remain a closed society because of the state's control of the vast oil revenues. Cuba, though not economically self-sufficient, is a special case. In its formative years the Castro regime was able to depend on a single trading partner, the Soviet Union.

In a sense, I am offering a refinement of Barrington Moore's thesis. It is not so much that the lack of a bourgeoisie means no democracy. Iran had a robust bourgeoisie, Cuba a significant one. Rather, unless the survival of the state depends on the economic activities of the bourgeoisie—especially those involved in foreign trade—there will be no democracy. Because revolutionary states have a tendency toward missionary zeal, they find it difficult to accommodate ideological opposition. Democracy persists only when the state has insufficient resources to survive without negotiating with the bourgeoisie and international economic interests. It is not the size or quality of the bourgeoisie that matters. It is their economic power. Scholars interested in explaining the political outcomes of revolutions should focus less on the class composition of the revolutionary society and more on the financial structure of the state within that society.

The methodological and interpretative stakes in the analysis I have been tracing are profound. If state modernization is a prerequisite for revolution, then scholars have been asking the wrong questions. Instead of offering a bewildering set of causal factors that trigger revolutions or, as in the older literature, a broad menu of preconditions and precipitants, scholars should separate the study of revolutions into three questions.[39] First, why have states modernized? Here, it seems to me, the kind of analysis of the international context proposed by Skocpol is most useful. Second, why have some modernizing states and not others undergone revolutions? The answer to this question is still not well understood. Third, why have revolutions that have pitted competing models of the modern state against one another had different political outcomes? Again, the answers are not well known to this important question. The smorgasbord of causal factors offered by students of revolution fails to distinguish among these questions. I suspect that the answer to the first question has very much to do with the international political context, the second has much to do with the ideological and economic resources of the state, and the third is best answered by understanding the degree to which the country in question can achieve economic self-sufficiency.

Whatever the answers to these questions, the prevailing models for explaining revolutions have wrongly assumed that revolutions occur when an old regime is incapable of adjusting to changed circumstances. Instead, revolutions happen only when the old regime commits itself to state modernization. "One of the most evident uniformities we can record," offers Crane Brinton almost as an afterthought in his preliminary discussion, "is the effort made in each of our societies to reform the machinery of government." Similarly, in her analysis of the Russian Revolution, Sheila Fitzpatrick concludes that "there was progress" in the political realm before 1917. "But," she suggests, that very progress "contributed a great deal to the society's instability and likelihood of political upheaval: the more rapidly a society changes (whether that change is perceived as progressive or regressive) the less stable it is likely to be."[40] These historical insights should inform the way we think about revolutions. Revolutions are not struggles to overturn traditional states. They occur only after regimes have determined, for whatever reasons, to initiate ambitious modernization programs. Revolutions, then, pit different groups of modernizers against one another.

The rest of this book is devoted to charting the development of two competing modernizing programs in later seventeenth-century England. In 1688–89 these two modernizing programs came into direct conflict, but their proponents had been honing their arguments for much longer. And although 1688–89 was a turning point, the full implications of the triumph of one modernizing program over the other would not be clear until well into the 1690s. Both the Jacobite and Williamite modernizing programs, it is clear, were made possible by England's remarkable social and economic divergence from the Continent in the later seventeenth century. Both were made urgent because of the implications of the great ideological, geopolitical, and military confrontation between France and the United Provinces of the Netherlands in the later seventeenth century.

PART II

Prerevolutionary England

CHAPTER THREE

Going Dutch
English Society in 1685

Later seventeenth-century English men and women were fascinated by their country. Travel narratives, topographical descriptions, and urban histories flooded the book market. Time and again contemporaries noted that the great works of the previous age—William Camden's *Britannia* (1586), John Stowe's *Survey of London* (1598), Sir Thomas Smith's *De Republica Anglorum* (1565)— were hopelessly outdated. Though some complained that their Elizabethan forebears had relied on hearsay rather than "experience," most felt that the country had changed so dramatically that new description was imperative. The future bishop of London, Edmund Gibson, undertook in the years immediately after James II's fall from power the most ambitious and comprehensive project, the updating of Camden's *Britannia*. The project was sufficiently promising that the London printer Awnsham Churchill was able to advance Gibson more than two thousand pounds to undertake it. Gibson lined up a variety of noted antiquaries, virtuosos, and local experts to "compare Camden's account with the present condition and furnish us with some short description of it." Gibson's revised *Britannia*

(above) *British Colonization,* by John Roettier, 1670. By the late seventeenth century, the English empire included growing colonies in North America and the Caribbean and trading settlements on the Indonesian archipelago, in Africa, and in India. Trading networks linked England with West Africa, the Americas, and Asia, and overseas trade was becoming ever more important. Descriptions of this and all subsequent medals in this book rely on Edward Hawkins, *Medallic Illustrations of the History of Great Britain and Ireland to the Death of George II,* 2 vols. (Trustees of the British Museum, 1885; reprint ed., London: Spink and Son, 1969).

was elegant, impressive, and popular. It gave the impression that England had changed rapidly and profoundly since Camden's day. In "the space of sixty or eighty years," Gibson concluded, there had been "a strange alteration in the face of things." Gibson noted that "the growth of trade, the increase of buildings, the number of inhabitants, do all make the appearance very different."[1]

This perception that England was a rapidly changing society stands in uneasy tension with most scholarly accounts of the Glorious Revolution. Thomas Babington Macaulay nearly two centuries later offered a detailed and memorable account of later seventeenth-century English society, in the conviction that the absence of the social context "would render the subsequent narrative unintelligible or uninstructive." Macaulay compared England in the later 1600s to England in his own day and found it severely wanting. Were one transported back to 1685, Macaulay thought, "we should see straggling huts built with wood and covered with thatch where we now see manufacturing towns and sea-ports renowned to the farthest ends of the world." "A large part of the country beyond Trent," Macaulay insisted, was "in a state of barbarism." Communications by land and sea were horrid for both passengers and goods. London, though more sophisticated by far than the rest of the country, was "squalid." The country gentleman, to say nothing of his social inferiors, was marked by "his ignorance and uncouthness" as well as his insularity. "It was very seldom that the country gentleman caught glimpses of the great world," wrote Macaulay, "and what he saw of it tended rather to confuse than to enlighten his understanding."[2] Later seventeenth-century England was more barbaric than civilized, more backward than modern. England could not, in Macaulay's view, have a modern revolution in 1688 because it was not a modern but a traditional society.

More recent historians of the Glorious Revolution have done little to modify this impression of the society they are describing. Scholars have taken one of two tacks in dealing with English society. The first is to decide that English political history could be described without reference to the society in which it occurred. Despite the increased interest in popular politics evinced by many of these historians, the social and economic organization of the lives of the people have not figured in their accounts.[3] A second tack is to affirm Macaulay's classic Whig view of English society. Jonathan Clark has suggested "that England from Restoration to Reform possessed an economy not driven by manufacturing industry and that its diverse social order was contained within a patrician hegemony." Jonathan Scott has insisted that "the events, structures, and issues in the reign of Charles II . . . are almost xerox copies of events, structures, and issues of the early Stuart period."[4] Rapid and profound social change figures in neither account.

Historians of the Glorious Revolution should take the contemporary perceptions of rapid and significant social and economic change before the Revolution of 1688–89 more seriously. Economic development was a cause, not an unintended consequence, of the Revolution. England in the later 1600s was quickly becoming more urban, more economically diverse, and more committed to manufacturing. All of these developments were supported by an increasingly sophisticated economic infrastructure. This rapid economic growth was remarkable in that it diverged sharply from major trends on the Continent. The source of England's dynamism was the indirect effects of its colonial trade with the East and West Indies and with North America. The English had met the standards that economic historians have set for a modern economy. England had developed a variety of markets for land, labor, and capital. England had become a net exporter of agricultural goods, making it capable of supporting "a far-reaching division of labor." The political nation had taken to heart the notion that economic productivity was essential to the kingdom's welfare. And unlike most other European countries, England had achieved "a level of technology and organization capable of sustained development." In short, English society by the later seventeenth century had come to look increasingly like that of its neighbors across the North Sea. If, as the most recent scholarship suggests, the Dutch United Provinces had become "the first modern economy" in the 1600s, the English were quickly learning from Dutch success.[5]

Unlike current scholars of British social and economic history, commentators in later seventeenth-century England were obsessed with comparative economic development. They tried to account for Venetian economic decline, the surprising prominence of Genoa, and the trading success of imperial free cities. The Tory-leaning economic writer John Houghton promised that his economic periodical would provide "as good an account as may be had of the trade, strength and policy of other nations."[6]

Late-seventeenth-century commentators disagreed, and disagreed sharply, about the causes and consequences of the economic developments they observed. But there was little debate about two salient developments in contemporary Europe. Spain, recently perhaps the greatest power in Europe, was in serious economic decline. Spain was now a country with little or no domestic manufactures, clinging desperately to its dispersed overseas empire. Its sole aim, thought one adviser to James II, was "how to stave off some approaching ruin." Spanish decline was invariably contrasted with the remarkable economic efflorescence of the Northern Netherlands. Although there was little agreement about the causes of the Dutch economic miracle, commentators were certain that it had nothing to do with agriculture. The United Provinces of the Netherlands "affords neither grain, wine, oil, timber, metal, stone, wool, hemp, pitch, nor, almost any other commodity of use; and yet we find, there is hardly a nation in the world which enjoys all these things in greater affluence."[7] The trick, English commentators agreed, was to make their economy more Dutch than Spanish.

In fact, the society James II inherited in 1685 was going Dutch. Travelers noted the sheer agrarian beauty of Kent, the exclusive focus on agriculture in Northamptonshire, and the pastoral character of Dorset, but above all they commented on the extent and variety of English manufactures. "In most parts of England," commented the well-traveled

Andrew Yarranton, "there are fixed manufactures already that do in great measure set the poor at work."[8]

Although England in the sixteenth century had been almost entirely an agricultural society, it had ceased to be so by the later 1600s. Fen drainage and enclosures were controversial topics in the seventeenth century as they are now, but their effect on the employment profile of England's rural population was clear. Whereas over 80 percent of the population was employed primarily in agriculture in the early sixteenth century, less than 60 percent was so employed in the later seventeenth century. The number of rural laborers dependent on the market doubled between the second quarter of the sixteenth century and the last quarter of the seventeenth century. By the later 1600s, then, the percentage of England's population primarily involved in agriculture had reached the levels achieved by the precocious Dutch Republic at midcentury, clearly differentiating itself from the rest of Europe. To place this in an even broader perspective, the percentage of English men and women primarily employed in agriculture in later seventeenth-century England was about the same as in the United States on the eve of the American Civil War.[9]

Compared to the rest of Europe, England had been economically backward in the early 1500s. This was true whether one measured the value of manufacturing output or the percentage of the population so employed. This was no longer the case by the later 1600s. By 1700 the manufacturing and commercial sectors were responsible for fully one-third of English national product. Again, this placed England on a par with the United Provinces and well ahead of every other kingdom and state in Europe. Although the economic statistics do not exist to describe the development with precision, the evidence suggests that England's transformation was not gradual. "The later decades of the seventeenth century," notes the economic historian D. C. Coleman, "were marked by brisk industrial advance" and by "an abnormally rapid progress of internal change."[10]

The growth of manufacturing and the decline in the relative importance of agrarian employment dramatically altered the economic geography of England. New towns emerged devoted to particular industries; old towns declined. Regions increasingly developed economic specializations while at the same time these regions diversified their manufactures within a particular sector. In the later 1600s observers were increasingly aware of the pronounced differences between agricultural and manufacturing regions.[11]

Cloth was England's leading manufacture in the late seventeenth century, as it had been in the sixteenth century. "English wool is famous all over the world, both for its fineness and goodness," noted the Lausanne native Guy Miege, "the English being now the best cloth-makers in the world." This observation, however, conceals the rapid and significant transformation of English clothing manufactures. Even though English wool retained its high reputation both domestically and internationally, the English were no longer finishing their own raw wool exclusively. By 1700 fully one-quarter of English raw wool was imported from Ireland, Spain, and elsewhere. English textile manufacturing was now more significant than English raw wool production. English cloth manufactur-

These playing cards, from an
early-eighteenth-century deck,
reflect contemporary awareness
that England had become
a manufacturing nation. They
depict three of England's
buoyant industries: coal mining,
sugar refining, and shipbuilding.

ing exports, even though they no longer dominated overall English production, almost doubled between 1650 and 1700.[12]

The English not only greatly increased their exportation of finished cloth but began to exploit new markets. Whereas in the sixteenth and early seventeenth centuries the English exported mostly heavy woolen broadcloths to northern Europe, by the later seventeenth century they were selling the lighter new draperies to southern Europe, the eastern Mediterranean, and beyond. The Mediterranean merchant John Joliffe told the House of Commons in 1670 that "our woolen trade begins to thrive." So important had English cloth exports to Spain and Portugal become that some advised the English to increase their consumption of Iberian wine so as not to jeopardize the trade. In the grand duchy of Tuscany, despite laws prohibiting the sale of English cloths, "all the nobility and gentry, even in [Florence] wear little or nothing else but English cloth." Not only were the new cloths lighter but they were produced and sold for lower prices. Between the late sixteenth and the late seventeenth centuries the price of English fabrics dropped by over 50 percent.[13] The English now produced textiles for mass consumption.

The advent of the new draperies and the relative decline of markets for English heavy woolens dramatically altered England's manufacturing landscape during the seventeenth century. After 1614 English exports of heavy cloths began an inexorable if uneven decline. Towns and regions that had depended on this old manufacture experienced noticeable downturns. Coventry's clothiers complained in the 1680s that "for some years past" they had "labored under the manifest decay of their trade to their very great impoverishment and the utter ruin of some hundred families that depended thereon." Salisbury apparently suffered a similar fate. Needham, like so many cloth-making towns and villages in Suffolk, was trading "less than formerly." Reading experienced the same decline as the Weald of Kent, in which the old broadcloth manufacture was "in a great measure laid aside."[14]

By contrast, new areas emerged as centers of production of the new draperies. Serges and kerseys were made in the West Country, making Taunton into a "neat and populous town" and transforming Tiverton in Devon into a manufacturing center. The grand duke of Tuscany observed over thirty thousand people making "different sorts of light cloth" in Devonshire in the 1660s. Exeter grew from a town of eight thousand in the late sixteenth century to about thirteen thousand in the late seventeenth century because it was "much inhabited and resorted unto by merchants and tradesmen" buying and selling serges and kerseys at home and abroad. Norwich surged from a population of twenty thousand in the 1620s to thirty thousand by 1700 because of its commitment to Norwich stuffs, another form of new drapery. Bays and says, again lighter woolen hybrid fabrics typical of the new draperies, were manufactured in Essex. There, despite the devastation of Colchester during the Civil War, fifty to sixty thousand families were employed in the "woolen manufactory." Ralph Thoresby marveled at "the increase of the clothing trade" in the West Riding of Yorkshire, which was "inconsiderable" in the middle of the sixteenth century, "but now the very life of these parts."[15]

Macaulay's barbaric north benefited significantly from the new draperies. Manchester, "justly noted for the manufactures there made called from the place Manchester wares," was "much" larger than it had been in Camden's day. These Manchester wares or Manchester cottons were being manufactured in and around Manchester from the late seventeenth century. Bolton had become sometime in the early 1600s "a place for great trade for fustians"—a wool-linen-cotton blend—"which anciently were credible wearing in England for persons of primest quality" but were now inexpensive enough for much broader consumption. Even the most barbarous counties of all, Cumberland and Westmoreland, experienced a manufacturing boom. Kendal and its surrounding district was one among many places that diversified its manufacturing portfolio in the late seventeenth century. Not only were Kendal's cottons "famous all England over," but its inhabitants were now manufacturing "druggets, serges, hats, and worsted stockings." Kendal, whose "people seem to be shaped out for trade," earned Sir Daniel Fleming's praise as "a place for excellent manufactures, and for civility, ingenuity and industry." Even the garrison town of Carlisle had become "a place of good trade, chiefly for fustians."[16]

The development of the new draperies was not autochthonous. There was no gradual evolution of the domestic English manufacturing industry. Instead immigrants, especially immigrants from the Netherlands, played a crucial role in developing the new lighter clothing. "The Dutch chiefly manage" the Essex new drapery trade, discovered Narcissus Luttrell in the late 1670s. Thomas Baskerville declared that Maidstone's thread manufacturers learned their trade from Flemish-speaking immigrants. Norwich's booming trade, declared Guy Miege, "is beholding to the Dutch that came to inhabit here." The new wave of late-seventeenth-century Huguenot immigrants taught the English more new manufacturing skills, as the French envoy Bonrepaus was only too painfully aware.[17]

England's cloth manufacturing had been transformed and its exports had doubled by the later 1600s. And yet cloth suffered a relative decline in importance during the seventeenth century. This was because the English developed—in some cases rapidly—new manufactures. Regional specialties familiar to students of the nineteenth century had emerged by 1685.

Extractive industries—the mining of coal, lead, iron, and tin—were certainly not new in the later seventeenth century. However, collectively the developments in these industries from the mid-1500s through the late 1600s deeply altered England's commercial profile.

In the middle of the seventeenth century William Grey of Newcastle estimated "that there was more coals vented in one year, than was in seven-years forty years by-past." Recent scholarship has confirmed and quantified the impression of this seventeenth-century topographer. The most comprehensive analysis of coal production finds that between the 1560s and 1700 coal production increased twelvefold. Production in the northeast alone more than doubled between the early 1600s and 1685. The figure is impressive, given that demand might have been met by producers outside the northeast, where coal pits were proliferating. Coal production grew dramatically in Derbyshire, Cumberland and Westmoreland, the Mendip Hills, South Wales, and Kingswood Chase. But the greatest center of coal production was undoubtedly the northeast, where "many thousand people" were said to be employed in mining, conveying, and shipping. The northeastern coal mines, thought Guy Miege, who may well have been involved in the coal trade, "supply with coals, not only this country (where that fuel is always bought at very easy rates) but a good part of England besides." Areas beyond Durham and Northumberland benefited from the boom in coal shipments. Ipswich, quickly losing its trade in old broadcloths, for example, maintained a high level of prosperity by shipping "Newcastle coals."[18]

Contemporaries were well aware that coal consumption set England apart from the Continent. John Evelyn complained that in London there was "such a cloud of sea-coal, as if there be a resemblance of Hell upon Earth." Continental commentators were just as conscious of the effects of coal pollution but were more appreciative of the economic benefits. One of the marquis de Seignelay's industrial spies marveled at the colliers docked at Bristol, noting that "everyone used coal and it is extremely widely consumed." Henri Misson pointed out that new chimney technology had somewhat contained the "horribly thick" coal smoke, which was a good thing, since coal was now "the common fuel" in England. The "cheapness" of coal, maintained in part by government regulation, made a huge difference for the lower orders, thought Guy Miege. "Whatever the Parisians say to the praise of their wood-fires," Miege pointed out, "I dare say the common sort of people there would be glad, could they compass it, to change in Winter-time fuel with the Londoners."[19]

Although coal kept many people throughout England warm, in the later seventeenth century it also came to play a commercial role. The development of metal manufacturing in and around Birmingham "was bound to the development of the coal-field at every point." So significant was coal in later seventeenth-century manufacturing that the modern historian of the coal industry has emphasized the "sweeping changes [that] occurred in the pattern of industrial coal consumption."[20]

Lead mining was also a booming industry in seventeenth-century England. Since lead was heavily used in domestic building and for military and naval uses, one might expect some modest development. In fact, English lead output more than doubled in the 1600s, with "much of the growth" in the 1660s and 1670s. New demand sparked "rapid change" in the industry, leading to the "growing domination of large-scale capitalism." Contemporaries were well aware of the growing importance of lead and lead mining. The Mendip Hills were "famous for the lead-mines," many of whose miners were slain in the Duke of Monmouth's ill-fated 1685 rebellion. The north also had its share of mines. The best lead mines "not in England only but Europe for quality and quantity" were in Derbyshire's Peak District. There mining had "in a great measure" stripped the hills of their woods and made Wirksworth "rich . . . and well inhabited."[21]

Cornish tin mining was a much older industry. But while the output from the mines was largely stagnant from 1500 to 1660, between the 1660s and 1680s it more than doubled. This is why Narcissus Luttrell could observe that Cornish tin was sold "to all parts of the world." Tin, like lead, was increasingly mined by wage laborers working for large owners like Sir William Stroude, who escorted Cosimo de' Medici through his tin works. It was perhaps the increasingly capitalistic nature of the enterprise that allowed miners in some works to "dig up as much tin as would yield a thousand pounds in one day from some time together."[22]

Iron manufacturing also grew significantly in the 1600s. Both iron mining and iron smelting increased. Travelers commented on the impressive ironworks in Sherwood Forest, Herefordshire, and Pontypool and on iron mining in Cumberland. Sussex, an iron center in decline, still had ironworks in "several places." The most vibrant iron-producing region appears to have been the Forest of Dean in Gloucestershire. There "no less than sixty thousand persons" worked in the mines and furnaces. In the 1680s two experts concluded that England had at least eight hundred iron furnaces. Many commented on the deleterious effects of the booming iron trade on the English countryside. Guy Miege and Thomas Newsham blamed the deforestation of Gloucestershire and Warwickshire on the iron industry. "It were well if there were no iron works in England; and it was better when no iron was made in England," complained many in the later seventeenth century, because "the iron-works destroy all the woods."[23]

Despite the proliferation of English ironworks in the 1600s, England became, in this period, a net importer of iron. By the 1680s the English imported almost half of their bar iron. Domestic production could simply not satisfy the voracious appetite of the burgeoning English metalware trades. Sheffield, always a center of metal production, transformed itself in the later seventeenth century into a diverse and vibrant industrial center. The Company of Cutlers in Hallamshire claimed that "there are above one thousand cutlers, scissors-smiths, [and] shear-smiths" in and around Sheffield in 1680. Sheffield and the Hallamshire area also became the home of button makers, file makers, and a steel industry in the late seventeenth century. In 1672 there were about six hundred smithies in and around Sheffield. Sheffield was already responsible for England's reputation for producing "the best knives" in the world. A wide variety of metalworking trades also developed "in the years following the Civil War" in the West Midlands. "At Stourbridge, Dudley, Wolverhampton, Sedgeley, Walsall, Birmingham and thereabouts," iron was "wrought and manufactured into all small commodities, and diffused all England over, and when manufactured sent into most parts of the world." By the later seventeenth century, the trades that were to make mid-Victorian Birmingham famous had already established themselves. Andrew Yarranton, himself a former ironmaster, thought that Midland iron manufacturers employed well over one hundred thousand people by 1677. Between 1600 and 1700 the Midlands metalware trades had been transformed. Whereas in 1600 Midland smiths had barely penetrated the London market, by the Restoration they had gained control of royal naval contracts, and their commercial products were sold worldwide.[24]

Over the seventeenth century the English also established a variety of new manufactures. Between 1600 and the 1670s England had gone from being a glass-importing to a glass-producing nation. England's remarkable development in this industry, much like the development of the new draperies, depended on skills learned from foreign handicraftsmen, in this case Venetian and Huguenot refugees. By the later seventeenth century more than sixty houses turned out glass in England—almost three times as many as there had been in the 1630s—with great concentrations in and around London, Stourbridge, Newcastle, and Gloucester. In Herefordshire bottle makers developed a symbiotic relationship with cider makers in the later seventeenth century, producing enough red-streak cider "to furnish London and other parts of England." Although the glass industry had not reached the same scale as the Midland iron manufactures, it did employ "several thousand poor people" and had developed its own lobbying cartel by the 1690s. The results were startling. The Venetian envoy in London thought that the English would soon bring the famous Venetian glass trade to "utter ruin." "There is so great an improvement of the art or mystery of making glass within this our kingdom," agreed the workmen glassmakers, that virtually all imports had ceased. John Houghton thought that English glass had become "the best in the world." No wonder, then, that in the later seventeenth century "hardly any people [were] without" English glasswares.[25]

English ceramics developed later than glasswares. John Dwight of Christ Church, Oxford, was one of many in the late 1600s who devised ways of imitating imported pottery from China, Germany, and the Netherlands. Staffordshire quickly became the center of this new industry, which like glass depended heavily on cheap coal for firing. Between the 1660s and 1700 there was an "especially rapid" explosion of commercial pottery making in Staffordshire: the number of potteries doubled, and the size of each individual outfit increased. By one report, "upwards of 3000 families depend[ed] wholly upon the manufacturing of stone and earthenwares" by the 1690s. The potters thought that they could "with ease" soon supply the needs "of the whole nation."[26]

Sugar refining and processing exploded in England in the later seventeenth century as well, growing alongside the development of England's West Indian colonies. In the 1650s "there were but four or five refining houses in England," but that number had reached fifty by the 1690s. Sugar imports doubled between 1660 and 1700, suggesting that an increasing percentage of sugar coming from the West Indies was unrefined. The majority of sugar refiners were in London and Bristol, where much of the West Indian sugar entered England, but sugar bakers also set up shop in Newcastle, York, Chester, Liverpool, Worcester, Plymouth, and Exeter. By the late seventeenth century the refiners claimed, probably with exaggeration, that they employed "some thousands of subjects." It is important to note that England's "sugar revolution," like so much of England's commercial development, was not a native growth but relied on Dutch expertise brought from Brazil to the English islanders of the Caribbean.[27]

It was in the later 1600s that the English developed a great shipbuilding industry. While contemporaries remarked on the large amount of commercial shipbuilding in London and Bristol, English naval production underwent the most dramatic transformation. When he heard that Edmund Gibson was planning to revise Camden's *Britannia*, Samuel Pepys insisted that he undertake "an historical account" of England's naval development, which had "been very considerable" since Camden's day. The statistics Pepys ultimately provided were startling. Pepys calculated that the Royal Navy had five times as many ships, almost six times the tonnage, and six times the crew as it had in Camden's time. The median peacetime expenditure on the navy was more than twenty times what it had been in Camden's day. Not surprisingly, then, it was in the later seventeenth century that England's naval dockyards "underwent their most rapid expansion." Portsmouth, Pepys noted, "is very much altered since Mr. Camden's time, and even since the Restoration of Charles II." It had replaced its "much decayed" neighbor Southampton as one of the "principal chambers of the kingdom, for the laying up of its Royal Navy." Its dry and wet docks, storehouses, and rope yards made it ideal "for the building, repairing, rigging, arming, victualling, and complete fitting to sea [of] ships of the highest rates." Deptford was an older center of naval shipbuilding, but its shipyard was "more than double what it was" at Charles II's accession. Chatham and Sheerness also developed notably in the later seventeenth century. Robert Plot bragged that the "station of the Navy-Royal" was "far advanced by the Kings, Charles and James 2." The late Stuart kings had added new docks, storehouses, launches, mast houses, and boathouses "exceeding what had ever been before known in the navy of England." Woolwich and the rapidly developing dockyards at Plymouth also became large naval-building centers in the later 1600s. Harwich, a modest market town in Camden's day, had become in the later seventeenth century a major royal naval base, ideal for "ready cleaning and refitting of ships of war." Charles II built the King's Yard at Harwich, which became a center for shipbuilding as well. The prodigious growth of naval shipbuilding in England captured the attention of foreign visitors, one of whom pronounced, a fortnight after James II's coronation, that the English naval frigates "instill fear and terror all over Europe."[28]

England had become a nation of manufactures between the 1580s and 1680s. Early modern English social historians have been riveted by the years before 1640. Yet it is clear that English manufacturing grew fairly spectacularly after the outbreak of the Civil War. Wool remained the most important manufacture, but its relative importance declined. Coal mining, metalworking, and shipbuilding all came to play a significant economic role in the century separating Camden's *Britannia* from the accession of James II. Although much of the manufacturing took place in the countryside, it would be wrong to describe this development as exclusively rural. Metalworking was based in Sheffield, Birmingham, and other towns in the Midlands. Shipbuilding was centered in London, Portsmouth, and Harwich. Sugar was refined in Bristol, Newcastle, and London. In fact, late-seventeenth-century London "was the greatest manufacturing city in Europe and was at its all-time peak as an industrial centre relative to the rest of the country."[29] England in 1685 was not an agrarian capitalist society; it was a capitalist society.

Not only did England become a more commercial society in the 1600s, it became a more urban society. The percentage of English men and women living in urban environments rose dramatically. Whereas between 10 and 12 percent of English people lived in towns in the early sixteenth century, the most recent estimates suggests that as many as 40 percent lived in urban areas by 1700. This was slightly below the 45 percent urbanization rate achieved in 1675 by the United Provinces, the most urban state in Europe outside Venice. The United States did not achieve England's rate of 40 percent in 1700 until 1870. Significantly, it was in the late seventeenth century that England's urban development surged ahead of its Continental neighbors. Whereas most European countries experienced urban stagnation or deurbanization from the later seventeenth century, England's towns enjoyed sustained growth.[30] England was urbanizing more rapidly than any place in Europe.

Much of this urbanization was the result of the remarkable growth of the capital. London was a modest city in 1550—its population of seventy-five thousand placed it alongside such cities as Lyon, Milan, and Palermo. It was much smaller than Lisbon, Antwerp, Paris, Venice, and Naples. By 1700 all that had changed. French visitors, not usually noted for their modesty when it came to assessing their native land, were "amazed with the vastness of this city," noting that "one may safely venture to affirm that London, including Westminster, is the biggest city in Europe." Contemporary scholarship has confirmed their assessment. London had a population of around 575,000 people, sixty-five thousand more than Paris. It was more than twice the size of Amsterdam, Lisbon, or Naples and about five times the size of Vienna and Madrid.[31]

Not only was London a larger city than most of its Continental rivals, it was also a different kind of city. Only Amsterdam shared London's remarkably bourgeois character. London, as both native and visitor noted, lacked the great noble palaces with their enclosed courtyards scattered throughout Paris. Instead London had merchants' houses, shops, and taverns. Late-seventeenth-century London was a shopper's paradise. "For conveniencies and delight, here all is at hand," marveled the well-traveled Guy Miege, "and scarce anything wanting that money can purchase." "I believe no body is ignorant that London has as rich and extensive a commerce as any city in the world," gushed the Huguenot exile Henri Misson. "The river that runs by London bears a great floating city, and its streets are a perpetual fair." Few would have disagreed with William Petty's claim "that London is the best housed, best peopled and wealthiest city of the known world."[32]

Although London grew and grew tremendously, it was not alone responsible for England's increasing urbanization. Outside London, two sorts of towns grew substantially: new manufacturing centers, and ports oriented toward overseas, and increasingly, Atlantic trade.

Birmingham, Manchester, Leeds, Halifax, and Sheffield all developed into major urban centers by 1700. Birmingham, which one historian has described as being "no more than a group of villagers" in the sixteenth century, had a population of at least eight thousand in 1700. The statistics are not solid, but it is clear that most of Birmingham's rapid growth occurred after 1660. "The ancient and modern state of Birmingham, must divide

Top: The Thames by Westminster Stairs, by Claude de Jongh, 1631 or 1637. *Bottom: The Thames from the Terrace of Somerset House, Looking toward St. Paul's,* by Canaletto, c. 1750. These two paintings depict the transformation of London from a medieval to a recognizably modern city. London was already expanding rapidly in the early seventeenth century, and its growing population had spread well east and west of the medieval City walls. By the early eighteenth century, the medieval city of half-timbered houses along narrow alleyways had given way to a city built in brick along widened streets. London's population had surpassed half a million by 1700, making the metropolis not only the capital of a growing empire but also the largest city in Europe, larger than both Paris and Amsterdam.

at the restoration of Charles the Second," wrote the eighteenth-century local historian William Hutton, "at this period the curious arts began to take root, and were cultivated by the hand of genius." Manchester had a similar meteoric rise in the seventeenth century. It, too, had a population well under five thousand in 1600, but had an estimated population of between eight and nine thousand in 1700. Manchester was already famous "for excelling all the towns lying round about it" and "for the vast quantity of wares and commodities made there." So significant was its "growth" that, "of an inland town[,] it has the best trade of any one in the north of England." Though Sheffield was not as large as Birmingham or Manchester, its growth was even more remarkable. Between 1672 and 1736 Sheffield experienced a thirty-five-fold increase in population, a growth that mirrored its growing prominence as a manufacturing center. The inhabitants of Halifax, "noted for their industry in making of cloth and other manufactures," increased substantially between the mid-sixteenth and the late seventeenth century. Population estimates vary, but no one doubted "the vast growth and increase of this town." Halifax's West Riding neighbor Leeds also rose to prominence in the seventeenth century. By 1700 it had grown from humble, though ancient, beginnings to have a population of between seven and eight thousand. Guy Miege remarked that in the recent past Leeds had grown to be "so considerable, that it is counted one of the best towns in Yorkshire." John Conyers similarly expressed surprise that Leeds, hitherto a relatively unimportant place, was both "a town of good trade" and "a thriving town."[33]

Two older manufacturing towns developed rapidly in the 1600s. Coal was responsible for turning Newcastle from "a poor hamlet" into a town "considerable for its numerous, trading, wealthy inhabitants." Newcastle's population grew by over 50 percent from 1600 to 1700, from about ten thousand to about sixteen thousand people. Newcastle had become "the wealthiest" and "the most trading place in the whole Northern tract." Newcastle's "wealth and commerce are wonderfully increased since Camden's time," concurred the northern antiquary and future bishop of Carlisle William Nicolson. While praising its growing importance as the great emporium of the north, Nicolson knew that Newcastle achieved prominence because its "coal trade is incredible." The rise of the new draperies was responsible for Norwich's growth in the seventeenth century. And grow it did. The Dutch visitor and painter William Schellinks was right to observe of Norwich in 1662 that it was "a famous, old town." It was already England's second city in the early sixteenth century. But the population of Norwich "multiplied in the course of the seventeenth century some two-and-a-half times," growing to thirty thousand by 1700. Much of this growth happened after 1650. When Thomas Baskerville visited Norwich after the Restoration, he praised it as "a great city and full of people."[34] New manufactures were the keys to prosperity for new and ancient towns alike.

Ports had always been important for England. Yet between 1600 and 1700 ports grew in importance and shifted in focus. London and the southeast remained important, but new ports emerged, shifting England's orientation toward the Atlantic and colonial trades. Liverpool in 1660 "was an insignificant seaport," but by 1700 it had "emerged as one of England's leading ports." By 1700 Liverpool's population ranged somewhere between five and seven thousand. Already it was a town whose fortunes were intimately tied to "the trade to the West Indies." So significant was this trade, and the trade with Ireland, that Liverpool's customs income had increased between eightfold and tenfold "within these 28 years last past." Contemporaries celebrated Liverpool's new and "fair building," including the new townhouse with a merchant exchange down below. The growth of Whitehaven in the later seventeenth century was even more spectacular. Between 1667 and 1685 Whitehaven tripled in size under the guidance of Sir John Lowther of White-haven, reaching a population of three thousand by 1700. The virtual creation of a new and thriving town did not escape contemporary notice. All remarked that Whitehaven was "absolutely the most thriving town in these parts" and praised its "much improved" buildings. Whitehaven's growth depended on the exploitation of local coal deposits and overseas trade. Coal was shipped from Whitehaven in large quantities to Dublin. Pitch, tar, and cordage were imported from Denmark and Norway, and increasingly "tobacco and sugar [came] from [the] West Indies." So important had the West Indian trade become by the later seventeenth century that Sir John Lowther himself kept a record of "goods vendable at Jamaica from Whitehaven."[35]

The southwest as well as the northwest benefited from the new orientation toward the Atlantic. Plymouth had grown from "a poor village, inhabited by fishermen," into a major port in the late sixteenth century. The town grew only modestly after 1600, reaching a population of nine thousand by 1700. The relatively stagnant population, however, masks a reorientation of Plymouth's trade. Despite Charles II's anxiety to "overawe the town," which had been so "prone to sedition" during his father's reign, Plymouth remained "a very populous, rich and thriving place." This was because Plymouth had diversified its mercantile portfolio. It continued to trade with France and Spain but added a vibrant commerce with the Canary Islands, Barbados, and North America. Falmouth in Cornwall was incorporated only in 1660. The town was still relatively small in 1700, but it became a major trading center in a few years. When he visited Falmouth in 1677, Narcissus Luttrell met people "that remember the time when there was not above two or three houses in the whole town; but now it is very large, having several fair houses and inns for entertainment." Falmouth became "the most frequented place in these parts for mariners" because it exported Cornish tin to Spain and Portugal and served as a haven for returning Newfoundland fishermen. The older port of Exeter also prospered in the seventeenth century. It had already been a big place in the early sixteenth century, and although it had remained relatively stagnant with a population of around eight thousand throughout the sixteenth century, it almost doubled again in size over the seventeenth century. The Earl of Bath was probably right to claim that Exeter "is a city so considerable in wealth and trade, that it is deservedly accounted one of the greatest after London." Exeter's sustained growth in the 1600s owed in part to the development of the new draperies in the West Country and in part to its growing involvement in the Atlantic trade with New England, Newfoundland, and the West Indies.[36]

Bristol's growth pattern was very similar to Exeter's. Bristol's population almost doubled between 1600 and 1700, to twenty-one thousand. Its prosperity in the later seventeenth century led one visitor to declare it "a second London." Bristol, thought Narcissus Luttrell, was "a place of great trade and merchandize and a man may have anything here." Bristol was more heavily dependent than Exeter on Atlantic imports for its economic surge in the later seventeenth century. Bristol's shipping devoted to the West Indian trade, largely sugar, almost tripled between 1670 and 1700 at the same time that it doubled its ships committed to the Chesapeake tobacco trade. In 1670 Sir John Knight claimed that trade with North America and the West Indies "employs half the ships of Bristol." The French commercial spy M. Robert thought that in 1685 the "greatest commerce" of Bristol's merchants was with the West Indies and North America, from whence they imported "tobacco, indigo, cotton, and sugar which they refine in this same town." When Roger North visited Bristol in 1680, he found it "remarkable" that "all men that are dealers, even in shop trades, launch into adventures by sea, chiefly to the West India plantations and Spain."[37]

East coast ports grew as well, but not as consistently. Sunderland, like Newcastle dependent on the coal trade, developed into a significant town of five to seven thousand inhabitants in the seventeenth century. Among the East Coast ports Great Yarmouth expanded most rapidly, doubling in size from five to ten thousand between 1600 and 1700. Yarmouth certainly benefited from exporting Norwich worsted cloth, but contemporaries tended to believe that its "chief trade" was smoked herring.[38]

Three North American ports had also grown into substantial towns by the later seventeenth century. Philadelphia, on the Delaware River, was founded only in the 1680s. But within "ten year's time there was above one thousand houses built and inhabited." By 1700 it had a population of five thousand. The development of Boston and New York was less dramatic. But they, too, had populations of at least five thousand by century's end.[39]

Growing prosperity necessarily meant more disposable income. The result was the proliferation in later seventeenth-century England of "leisure towns." This period saw the transformation of medicinal watering places into tourist towns. Bath, a medicinal center from Roman times, shed its cloth-making pretensions in the late seventeenth century and diversified its entertainment portfolio. When William Schellinks visited Bath in 1662, the town was a place where "people are sent by their doctors to bathe." By the 1670s and 1680s it had already become much more of a resort. From May through August, "not only . . . the nobility and gentry, but . . . the commonalty too, from all parts of the nation" flocked to Somerset. "Thousands go thither," observed Henri Misson, not so much for the medicinal virtues of the hot baths "but only to divert themselves with good company." The opportunities for such diversion were proliferating. When Narcissus Luttrell visited in the late 1670s he found tourists going to plays, dancing at balls, competing on the bowling green, and "walking in the meads." Bath, like today's fashionable resorts, was not inexpensive.

Bath was "very well served with provisions," warned Luttrell, "but it is extraordinary dear living here, the people being mighty exacting."[40]

After 1660 Tunbridge Wells began to rival Bath. Robert Plot, predictably, highlighted the medicinal aspects of the "famous chalybiat springs." But most came to Tunbridge for its variety of entertainment. So popular had the resort become that James Fraser complained in the summer of 1687 that London "is become so empty by reason of the resort to Tunbridge." By the 1680s Tunbridge Wells had developed a series of walks, along which visitors passed houses and booths to fully enjoy the waters. More important, it had become "an emporium of all diversions," transforming itself in John Evelyn's opinion from a place of "natural philosophic solitude" into a "mart of vanity." The villages round about had developed a range of accommodation for the nobility, gentry, and citizenry who came to partake of the waters. Good vintners, high-quality butchers, fresh fruit, and good poultry were readily available. Tourists were well fed, and they were entertained. The "pipe office," a sort of smoking club, was by 1680 well established. The most fashionable preachers of the day could be heard at Tunbridge parish church in the summer. For those drawn more to mammon than to God, the Royal Oak Lottery opened at ten each morning for gambling. Each evening in season, the various villages hosted music and dancing. Auctions offered opportunities for those interested in different kinds of risks. Perhaps the most popular diversion at Tunbridge Wells was conversation. James II's mistress Catharine Sedley warned Justice George Jeffreys that any restriction on free speech, any refusal to "suffer persons to vent their own fancies, and to use freedom in conversation and discourse," would "destroy Tunbridge Wells."[41]

Less fashionable but still very popular spas developed throughout the country. Epsom Wells, which John Aubrey recalled was discovered in the late 1630s, developed a variety of facilities. By the 1680s one wag exclaimed that "every Mother's son" could be found at Epsom in the summer. Buxton in Derbyshire, Harrogate in Yorkshire, Astrop Wells in Northamptomshire, Bourne in Lincolnshire, Lanercost in Cumberland, and Barnet in Hertfordshire all emerged as regional or national resorts in the later seventeenth century. Even Islington developed as a spa. By the 1680s it was known as "the New Tunbridge Wells" with more than a thousand visitors every day in the season partaking of the waters as well as the gaming, walking, and dancing.[42]

Spas did not capture the entire tourist market. Charles II's love of horse races stimulated the development of Newmarket as a tourist destination. After the Restoration, Newmarket's buildings were "beginning to improve in appearance, and to increase in numbers." There was no local manufacture, and "the townsmen live chiefly upon passengers." Burford in Oxfordshire and Lichfield in Staffordshire had also become centers for regular horse races by the later seventeenth century. The years after 1680 have been described as a "boom" period for the development of regular horse racing meetings. Although seaside resorts were largely a later development, Saltfleet in Lincolnshire was already "much frequented by the gentry in the summer season" during the Restoration.[43]

Not only did England become more urban, not only did tourist destinations emerge, but the quality of everyday life in England's towns and cities significantly improved in the later seventeenth century. Houses, both urban and rural, became much more comfortable. John Houghton thought that houses were "built like palaces over what they were in the last age." Improved building materials were partly responsible. "Glass windows were very rare, only used in churches and the best rooms of gentleman's houses," averred John Aubrey, "even in my remembrance, before the Civil Wars, copyholders and ordinary people had none." "Now," Aubrey concluded, even "the poorest people that are upon alms have it." After 1650 brick became the most fashionable building material, stimulating a variety of local brick-making industries. The result was more substantial and permanent domiciles for all but the poorest of people. Whereas it was once thought that England was substantially rebuilt in the decades preceding the Civil War, recent scholarship has taught us that "the period from 1660–1739 was far more important, with every decade producing more dated houses than even the peak decade of the pre–civil war period." The transformation was evident by the last decades of the century. "When I compare the modern English way of building with the old way," testified Guy Miege, "I cannot but wonder at the genius of old times." Older houses were so cramped and dark "that one would think the men of former ages were afraid of light and good air." By contrast, "the genius of our time" was for "lightsome staircases, fine sash-windows, and lofty ceilings."[44]

Anecdotal evidence confirms the impression that Macaulay's thatched villages were disappearing rapidly long before the mid-nineteenth century. Before the Great Fire of 1666 John Evelyn thought London "deformed" and thoroughly lacking in "modern architecture." After the fire London rose from its ashes, but differently. The French visitor M. de Sainte-Marie who came to view James II's coronation was astounded by the transformation since his previous visit. "I am enthralled," he exclaimed. "I find a different city newly built of brick in place of the one of wood, and badly built, that I left in 1660." Glass was used liberally now, and rooms were larger and better ventilated. Londoners constructed about ten thousand new buildings between 1656 and 1677, convincing one Italian visitor that they had constructed a "more modern" city.[45]

The capital may have taken the lead, but it was not alone in replacing timber-framed houses with more spacious stone and brick dwellings. Northampton, which also was devastated by fire in the late seventeenth century, rebuilt all its houses "either of brick or stone." In the 1670s Ralph Thoresby rebuilt his house in Leeds with brick, "which were scarce known in the beginning of my grandfather's time." Sheffield soon followed suit. Derby and Newcastle each had a number of new brick buildings in the later seventeenth century. Yarmouth had "many very handsome new brick houses" in 1679. Preston in Lancashire, too, was largely a town of brick in the 1680s. Nearby, Manchester's tradesmen were also building in brick. Launceston in Cornwall was newly built in stone, while Norwich banned thatched roofs in the later seventeenth century.[46]

More and more towns and cities paved their streets in the later seventeenth century.

There was a remarkable transformation of the urban landscape in late-seventeenth-century England when streets were paved, cleaned, and lit and public and private buildings were reconstructed, often in a grandiose neoclassical style, in brick and stone.

John Evelyn and Sir John Denham were involved in the post-1660 paving of London's streets. Within thirty years "the principal streets" were all "paved a good convenient breadth on each side with smooth hewn stone, for the benefit of foot-passengers." Dorking in Surrey had paved streets in 1649. By the 1670s Preston was "evenly" paved, as was Barnstaple. Shrewsbury began paving its streets in the 1670s. Morpeth and Wakefield in Northumberland were "paved high in the middle with the kernells on each side, after the manner of the new paving of streets in London." The streets of Bridlington in Yorkshire, "which before [were] troublesome to pass for dirt," were paved in the later seventeenth century. Plymouth, too, had paved streets, though Luttrell thought them "very slippery."[47]

Streetlighting, in all likelihood like the new draperies a Dutch import, came to English towns in the 1680s. Edmund Heming began in the early 1680s, deploying convex gas lamps on the streets of London. The new lamps, a rarity outside Amsterdam, were so effective that they "seem to be but one great solar light." London soon required that the new lights be placed outside all public buildings. Canterbury and York deployed the new streetlamps during the reign of James II, while Exeter and Norwich developed them soon thereafter.[48] The effect, no doubt, was to make towns safer and to encourage a variety of evening cultural activities.

Late-seventeenth-century towns had a variety of cultural amenities. Libraries are usually thought to have emerged in the eighteenth century. But there were already libraries available for public use in the seventeenth century. Leeds had a new library in the later seventeenth century, as did Stainbrough in Yorkshire. Ipswich, Manchester, Colchester, Norwich, Bristol, Gloucester, Leicester, and Durham all had publicly accessible collections. Peterborough's cathedral library was expanded in the 1670s. Before the erection of Tenison's London library, inhabitants of the capital could consult books at Lambeth palace or public records in the Tower of London. Public walks and pleasure gardens began to be features of English towns in the late seventeenth century. The new Spring Gardens at Vauxhall gave people venues to smoke, stroll, and watch occasional performances. Promenades, walks, or pleasure gardens were also constructed at Bath, Tunbridge Wells, Preston, and Shrewsbury.[49]

The growth of new manufacturing towns, port towns, leisure towns, and above all London had a dramatic effect on the nature of English society. The new urban amenities, combined with the old attraction of the alehouses and taverns, created a large cultural pull. In the previous age "the gentry and nobility of England lived altogether in the country," but now they spent more time in towns and cities, and "their way of living is quite differing from that used heretofore."[50] Although the transformation was no doubt exaggerated by the defenders of rural culture, there was no doubting the overall trend. In the later seventeenth century, the English increasingly took their cultural cues from urban and commercial society.

The rapid development and improvement of England's infrastructure in the later seventeenth century did a great deal to support the growth of urban society and urban culture. English communications by both land and sea, which Macaulay claims were virtually nonexistent, improved dramatically in this period. These developments supported an ever-expanding network of inns and accommodation. Perhaps more important, the emergence of a national and accessible postal system in the later 1600s made it easier for merchants to conduct business, for communication networks to fan out across wider areas, and for political gossips to spread the news ever more rapidly. Merchants and consumers alike benefited greatly from the development of two typically modern conveniences, insurance and deposit banking. All of these developments facilitated the gradual transformation of the English from a nation of consumers dependent exclusively on the rhythms of market fairs into a nation of shoppers.

Although many English rivers were navigable in the early seventeenth century, many more were by 1700. English engineers, financiers, and projectors almost doubled the number of navigable river miles between 1660 and 1700. The Thames and the Avon in Warwickshire were improved in the 1630s, the Wey in Surrey in the 1650s, the Avon in Wiltshire and the Stour in Worcestershire after 1660, and the River Wye in the West Midlands in the 1690s. The Severn, long navigable, experienced a massive increase in river traffic in the latter half of the century. The number of commercial voyages passing through

Gloucester annually, for example, more than doubled between 1637 and 1700. Barges on the Severn delivered ever-increasing quantities of coal to Shrewsbury, Gloucester, and Bristol and brought "merchantable goods up stream again." Maidenhead in Berkshire was one of those towns that in the later seventeenth century could send two passenger barges per week up the Thames to London. Regular barges carried lead from Derbyshire, tin from Cornwall, and coal from Newcastle to London.[51]

Foreign visitors were invariably impressed by the variety, efficiency, and speed of the various forms of water transport available in and around London in the later seventeenth century. The Thames was "all covered" with "small boats," remarked one French visitor in 1685. There was "a perpetual motion of wherries and small boats" agreed Guy Miege, perhaps as many as two thousand in number, supported by more than three thousand watermen. Unlike in France, Henri Misson implied, there were no financial "disputes" because the carriage rates were "fixed by authority."[52]

English coastal shipping, taking advantage of England's long coastline, also grew remarkably after the Restoration. Between 1660 and the early eighteenth century there was a growth of over 27 percent in the number of ships plying the English coasts. Between 1628 and 1683 the number of ships traveling from London to other English ports increased threefold. By the time of James's accession, for example, it was possible to take regularly scheduled wherries from Ipswich to Harwich, from Norwich to Yarmouth, and from London to Gravesend. William Schellinks found it easy to hire "a post boat" to carry his injured friend Thierry from London to Dover.[53]

Ground transportation improved just as dramatically. Even though the cost of transport by land was still substantially higher than that by sea, Sir John Lowther ranked "commodious carriage by land" as the highest priority in his "rules for increase of trade." His fellow members of the House of Commons acted on his desires. In 1663 Parliament passed the first turnpike act that effectively shifted the burden of road improvements from local parishes to those who used the roads. This first act created just one turnpike on the New Great North Road in Hertfordshire, Huntingdonshire, and Cambridgeshire, and there would not be another turnpike act until a flurry in the 1690s and first decade of the eighteenth century. In passing that first act, however, English politicians recognized the rapidly expanding demand for road transport.[54]

By the end of the century improved roads, coupled with increased demand, had created a boom in ground transport. One modern expert claims that "the later seventeenth century appears as a crucial phase in the development of the road carrying industry." There was, for example, 127 percent more land carriage out of London by 1715 than there had been in 1637. Although contemporaries noted that were some bad roads in Somerset and Cornwall, and that, unlike in France, not all roads were paved, the general quality of English roads in the later seventeenth century was remarkably high. Guy Miege opined that "the English nation is the best provided of any for land travel," claiming that "no city in Europe" had better communications than London. Regular carriers took goods from

Kendal and Whitehaven in less than two weeks when they took the direct road. In fact, the north of England, which had no regular carrying service to London before the English Civil War, had six weekly services by the early eighteenth century. Wagons and carriers regularly plied the roads from Ipswich, Norwich, and Yarmouth to London. Roads in and out of Newcastle were "as much frequented" as "almost any other in the kingdom." Even the "totally decayed" town of Bodmin in Cornwall had roads that supported regular carriers to Truro and Exeter.[55]

The English began to use stagecoaches in the 1630s. By the later seventeenth century, the English could take stagecoaches throughout the width and breadth of the country. York, Chester, and Exeter had regular stagecoaches to London, as did Gloucester, Hereford, Reading, Harwich, Portsmouth, Southampton, Winchester, Bristol, Bath, Salisbury, Reading, Canterbury, and many places besides. Several stagecoaches, "especially in Summer time," served Tunbridge Wells. "Flying coaches" made the trip between London and Cambridge or Oxford in less than a day. By the 1680s there were stagecoaches "to almost every town within twenty or twenty-five miles of London." Local stages connected small towns to larger ones, like the service that connected Bridport in Dorset to Exeter. Stagecoaches were so popular that John Aubrey complained that the gentry were forgetting how to ride hunting horses. Others moaned that stagecoaches had decreased the demand for saddle horses in general by three quarters. "England excels all other nations" in having stagecoaches, thought Guy Miege. This new form of transport, he marveled, was cheap, comfortable, and fast, and it could take the interested traveler "to most noted places in England."[56]

Within London itself hackney coaches had become widely available to transport passengers from one end of the city to the other. One finds hackney coaches "in all quarters of this city," wrote one French visitor to London at the time of James II's coronation, "in all parts of the street, always ready to depart, and always with the same great speed." These urban coaches were already established in London by 1660, long before they appeared in Paris. By the 1660s, all agree that there were at least eight hundred hackney coaches plying their trade on London's streets, catering to all social classes. Sir Richard Temple was only one of the earliest to complain that the proliferation of hackney coach drivers made it impossible to cross the street in London and Westminster "without great obstruction and hazard."[57]

The English state in the later seventeenth century used the newly improved and expanded road system to develop a national post office. Successive postmasters general in the later seventeenth century, beginning with John Thurloe in 1657, transformed the postal service from one that carried royal messages and the letters of a select elite into a national service that circulated the correspondence of thousands of English men and women. Charles I had established a letter office in 1635, but by 1639 that office employed just forty-eight people and took in £1,536 in revenue. By contrast, in 1686 the post office employed well over four hundred people—including clerks of the road, sorters, window men, letter receivers, letter bringers, porters, and letter carriers—and took in close to £100,000. By

1696 the post office employed almost seven hundred workers. "The number of letters missive in England were not at all considerable in our ancestors' days," noted one observer in the 1680s, but the volume of correspondence had become "so prodigiously great" in part because even "the meanest people have generally learnt to write."[58]

After the Restoration the English postmasters general, Roger Whitley in particular, aggressively sought to expand the English mail service. Whitley wrote constantly to local postmasters or would-be postmasters seeking to open new offices and new routes. New postmasters were promised that they would be "free from all public offices, [and] quartering soldiers" and would receive copies of the *London Gazette* "free of charge" in order to help "in their common trade of selling drink." By the 1680s the postmasters had established six postal roads, running as far as Plymouth in the west and Edinburgh in the north, and 182 deputy postmasters. There was, wrote Guy Miege, "no considerable market town but has an easy and certain conveyance for letters." Philip Frowde, Whitley's successor as postmaster general, developed a strategy to ensure that all towns and villages within sixty miles of London had daily mail service "to accommodate merchants." Whitley also sought to entice letter writers to use the newly expanded post office. He promised to provide an inexpensive service, insisting on the "necessity of containing the rates as they are." Whitley also worked to provide a speedy and reliable standard of delivery. He told his postmasters that the "late carrying in of mail is not to be longer endured." The mail, he advised, needed to travel at least five miles per hour and 120 miles per day. Because of Whitley's vigilance, letters traveled from London to Edinburgh in five days and from London to Plymouth in three. By 1690 Sir Willoughby Aston remarked that only a heavy snowfall could prevent the timely delivery of the post to him in Warrington, Cheshire. By the 1670s Whitley was surely right to assert that "the commerce of the nation is maintained by the ministration of this office." Since that commerce was increasingly foreign as well as domestic, it was hardly surprising that the post office delivered huge quantities of overseas mail. Whitley claimed that on a single day in 1673 his office handled more than four thousand letters that arrived in Plymouth from overseas. In 1686 the post office delivered more than sixty thousand letters "brought from New England, Jamaica, Barbados, Lisbon, Cadiz and other foreign parts."[59]

Not surprisingly, as the post office became increasingly important not only for the nation's commerce but for the circulation of political news and the dissemination of political propaganda, the postmasters became political appointees. One Mr. Castleton, for example, lost his job as postmaster in 1689 in part because he "was a great frequenter of clubs . . . that were commonly called Tory clubs." William and Mary chose as their first governor of the post office the long-time radical operative and former employee of Thurloe in the Protectorate postal service John Wildman, who lost his position when the Marquess of Carmarthen, a Tory, consolidated his hold on power.[60] The transformation of England's economy and the creation of new infrastructure vastly expanded the range and social depth of politics.

The new London Penny Post soon became even faster, more efficient, cheaper, and briefly more heavily politicized than the national post office. In 1680 two Whigs, William Dockwra and Robert Murray, set up an office in London that promised "cheap and frequent" conveyance of letters in and around London. The office was an immediate success. Letters were collected every two hours at more than four hundred offices in the city and once a day in over 148 towns and villages within ten miles of London. Dockwra himself bragged that the Penny Post soon "set on foot thousands of things that never would have been done" without it. The Duke of York, the future James II, was convinced that some of these things were Whig political projects. So in 1682 James secured a King's Bench decision stripping Dockwra of the Penny Post. Nevertheless, the Penny Post survived under the control of the central post office. By 1688 the Penny Post was delivering more than seven hundred thousand letters a year. The Frenchman Henri Misson was so impressed that he thought it "a wonder" that no other city in Europe had set up such a system. John Evelyn later lobbied for a medal commemorating Dockwra, "who has brought to perfection the now so useful, cheap, certain and expeditious intercourse of letters by the Penny Post."[61]

Londoners launched another innovative project in the 1680s: fire insurance. Although a system of fire insurance had been established in Hamburg in the 1590s, London was certainly a European leader in this field. Perhaps energized by the economic disaster resulting from the Great Fire of 1666, a number of Londoners began floating proposals for a fire insurance office in the 1670s. Fire insurance, like the Penny Post, generated a good deal of controversy that may have been partly political. The Tory Nicholas Barbon opened his Fire Office in 1680. The following year the Whig-dominated London Common Council inaugurated its own scheme. Although that insurance company failed, William Hale and Henry Spelman established the Friendly Society in 1683 to compete with Barbon. All told, the competing companies insured more than seven thousand houses and helped create fire departments to protect their investments.[62]

Londoners provided deposit-banking facilities for the first time in the second half of the seventeenth century. Before the middle of the century there were no English banks, but by the 1690s there were well over forty in London alone. The old Cavalier William Blundell offered a plea for improved credit facilities in 1659, but by 1683 he thought things were extremely "convenient to borrowers and lenders." The Tory Sir Edward Seymour complained in 1670 that the proliferation of bankers had encouraged the English to "carry all their money to London." London was in fact quickly becoming a "a new kind of hub for international finance." Not only did London bankers like Edward Backwell operate at the center of a web of financiers across Europe, but other London bankers provided financial services to clients throughout England. From the 1680s Francis Child, based in Fleet Street, provided services to more than eight hundred customers. Beginning in the 1670s Richard Hoare, in Cheapside, began building a national network of customers that by 1700 included clients in Shropshire, Lancashire, Leicestershire, Pembrokeshire, Somerset, Yorkshire, Lincolnshire, and Northumberland as well as all across the Home Counties.[63]

Amicable Society Instituted, 1696. The Amicable Society was one of several fire insurance schemes established in the late seventeenth century.

Better roads, easier water transport, an extensive post office, insurance, and improved financial services not only made trade easier for wholesalers but transformed the nature of retail in later seventeenth-century England. England was quickly becoming a nation of shoppers and shopkeepers. Whereas retailing had been castigated as a moral hazard in the late sixteenth and early seventeenth centuries, shops and shopkeepers were accepted as a necessary part of the domestic economy by the later 1600s. Not surprisingly, this shift in perception was accompanied by a proliferation of shops and shopkeepers across the country. John Houghton's contemporary estimate that "we have six times the traders, and most of their shops and warehouses better furnished than in the last age," has been confirmed by more recent research. Many more market towns and villages had shops than before the English Civil War, and those shops were better stocked with a wider variety of goods. In contrast to what was "wont to be formerly," reported one pamphleteer, "now in every country village, where is (it may be) not above ten houses, there is a shop-keeper . . . and many of those are not such as deal only in pins or such small wares, but such that deal in as many substantial commodities as any that do that live in cities and market towns." At the turn of the century one economic writer guessed that there were eight thousand shops in London and more than 1.2 million across England. These numbers were staggering by European standards. One observer thought that "there are ten thousand retailing shop-keepers more in London than are in Amsterdam," the most commercial city in Europe. "The number of shops both in the City and suburbs" is "so great, and indeed so far beyond that of any foreign city," wrote another, "that it is to strangers a just matter of amazement."[64]

All across England, though perhaps faster in some regions than in others, the open market was losing the retail trade to fixed shops. Naturally, London led the way. Visitors to London invariably lavished praise on the New Exchange, with over two hundred shops in which "well-dressed women" sold "the richest sort of commodities." But perhaps more impressive for those who got to know the city was the fact that "every lane, turning, street and corner" was "full of shops of all kinds of ware." By the later seventeenth century much smaller towns offered the same range of emporiums to eager shoppers. Nottingham was a "town full of shops." The streets of Ipswich in Suffolk, long a trading center, were also "full of shops." Nearby Bury St. Edmunds was "full of rich shops and tradesmen" when Thomas Baskerville visited in the later seventeenth century. Taunton, the West Country clothing center, had "long, wide streets full of shops." Gloucester was "a fairly large town" with "some fine streets and shops." Chester's major streets had "galleries (or rows as they call them) with shops on one side through which galleries one may walk free from wet in the greatest storms." The cathedral towns of Canterbury and Winchester were "full of handsome shops." The market village of Billericay in Essex, which sent five men to New England on the *Mayflower,* had "a wide street with fine houses and shops." Narcissus Luttrell discovered that in the tin-mining town of Truro in Cornwall, "a man may have almost anything" in the 1670s.[65]

The English developed a remarkable array of new, and recognizably modern, institutions in the later seventeenth century. Stagecoaches, turnpike trusts, the Penny Post, fire insurance, deposit banking, an increasingly robust retail sector all helped support England's increasingly commercial society. These new institutions and this vastly expanded infrastructure helped soften the shock of England's transition from agrarian to urban culture. It was much easier to leave the countryside to work in the city, or to migrate between country house and town house, if goods, people, and ideas could travel more easily between the two. As these social and cultural connections deepened, it became increasingly possible for the English to have truly national political discussions. Interests, anxieties, and aspirations were communicated far more quickly in the later seventeenth century than they had been in earlier periods. And, just as important, these ideas could now be communicated to an English people who shared an increasingly large number of social and cultural reference points.

The emergence of the coffeehouse in later seventeenth-century England, perhaps more than any other institution, both transformed and marked the transformation of English national culture. Coffee and coffeehouses took England by storm in the later 1600s. Although coffee was available as an exotic novelty good in the early seventeenth century, the first coffeehouses opened in England in the 1650s. By the 1670s coffee was so widespread that one contemporary could remark with only slight exaggeration that "coffee has so generally prevailed that bread itself though commonly with us voted the staff of life is scarce of so universal use." Coffee, John Evelyn noted in the late 1650s, had "universally besotted the nation."[66]

London became the epicenter of English coffeehouse culture. Already in November 1659 the Londoner Thomas Rugg noted that there was "at this time a Turkish drink to be sold almost in every street, called coffee." Londoners such as the natural philosopher Robert Hooke and the civil servant par excellence Samuel Pepys worked, debated, and relaxed in dozens of different coffeehouses in the 1660s, 1670s, 1680s, and 1690s. In the early eighteenth century Dudley Ryder of Hackney regularly visited a dozen coffeehouses in and around London, where he discussed politics, gossiped about the law, and refined his conversation. When the Swiss traveler Antoine Muralt visited London in the early eighteenth century he reported on the "prodigious number of coffee-houses in London." One surveyor of the London scene estimated that in the first decade of the eighteenth century there were "near 3000" coffeehouses in London and Westminster.[67]

Coffeehouses were not merely metropolitan phenomena in England. One pamphleteer noted correctly that there were coffeehouses "in both universities and most cities and eminent towns throughout the nation." England's first coffeehouse opened in Oxford in the 1650s, and several others soon followed in that university town. Roger North complained that there was already a coffeehouse in Cambridge in the 1660s. By the early eighteenth century things had gotten worse, for there were "diverse" coffee establishments "where hours are spent in talking; and less profitable reading of newspapers." Soon most of the manufacturing towns of England had their own coffeehouses. Thomas Baskerville found a coffeehouse in the cloth-making town of Gloucester in the 1670s. Exeter, Coventry, and Kendal in Westmorland—all cloth manufacturing towns in the seventeenth century— had coffeehouses by the 1680s and 1690s. Sheffield, already famous for its ironwares, and Newcastle, renowned for coal, had their coffeehouses in the later seventeenth century. English ports also hosted coffeehouses. Bristol, the center of trade with the West Indies, had "three or four coffee houses in the 1670s." Plymouth and Dorchester had their own establishments in the later seventeenth century as well. The fishing town of Great Yarmouth had a coffeehouse by the late 1660s. Not to be outdone, old county towns such as Penrith in Westmorland, Preston in Lancashire, Chester, Stamford, Buckingham, Nottingham, and York soon had their own coffeehouses. By the time of the Glorious Revolution even Boston in New England had a coffeehouse.[68] English coffeehouses were neither the preserve of Londoners in the later seventeenth century nor limited geographically to the centers of elite, gentlemanly, or scientific culture.

Coffeehouses spread more slowly on the Continent. The observation of the cosmopolitan Guy Miege that coffeehouses were "more common [in England] than anywhere else" is borne out by recent research. In the Holy Roman Empire coffee "was a relatively expensive and exotic drink up to the 1720s." Vienna, normally thought of as the center of coffeehouse culture, did not have its own coffeehouse until 1683. The trading town of Hamburg, unsurprisingly, had one earlier, in 1671. Amsterdam had a vibrant coffeehouse

Figures in a Tavern or Coffeehouse, attributed to Joseph Highmore, 1720s.
English coffeehouses were sparsely decorated, aspiring to little of the aristocratic elegance
of the French cafés. English coffeehouse owners created a climate for free and open
conversation rather than intimate exchange. Their clientele was overwhelmingly drawn
not from the gentry and aristocracy but from the urban middle classes.

scene by the late seventeenth century. But even there its thirty-two coffeehouses were an
order of magnitude smaller than the hundreds or even thousands in London. The first
café opened in Paris in the 1670s, but the real boom period of the French coffee-drinking
establishments was in the eighteenth century.[69]

Not only were there more, many more, coffeehouses in England than in Continental cities, English coffeehouses were physically quite different. The archetypal French
café, the Café Procope, was opened by the Sicilian Francesco Procopio Coltelli in the
rue des Fosses-Saint-Germain in 1686. The Café Procope was from the first an elegant
establishment, with little marble tables, crystal chandeliers, and mirrors throughout. It
was, in the words of one historian, a "luxurious place." Coltelli's success soon encouraged
competitors. By 1690 "the entire heart of elegant Paris—from the Bussy crossroads to the
Saint Germain Fair and on to the Seine River" had taken to the coffeehouse. The Parisian
café had taken on the elegance and luxury of the aristocratic town home. In London, by
contrast, the center of coffeehouse life was the "heart of London's mercantile sector." They
were anything but genteel. One Francophone visitor complained that English coffeehouses "are loathsome, full of smoke like a guard-room, and as much crowded." Ned
Ward, an admittedly hostile witness, compared the clientele of the coffeehouse as "a parcel of muddling muck-worms [who] were as busy as so many rats in an old cheese-loft;
some going, some coming, some scribbling, some talking, some drinking, others jangling
and the whole room stinking of tobacco like a Dutch barge." The small, elegant marble
tables in Paris were replaced with long, communal wooden ones in London. The typical
coffeehouse, recalled one commentator, had "three or four tables set forth, on which are

placed small wax-lights, pipes, and diurnalls." The French visitor M. de Sainte Marie, no doubt familiar with the urbane elegance of the French cafés, compared the long wooden tables in English coffeehouses to those in monastic refectories.[70] Where the Parisian cafés were organized to invite intimate and private dialogues, the London coffeehouses were ideal for group discussions.

The physical environment of the English coffeehouse catered perfectly to its clientele. Coffeehouses from the first sold their wares cheaply. A cup of coffee could be had anywhere in England for a penny. An evening at the coffeehouse was relatively cheap, whereas "a tavern reckoning soon breeds a purse—consumption." Opponents and proponents of the new social venues agreed that coffeehouses were thus able to host socially diverse clientele. In a coffeehouse, noted Samuel Butler, "people of all qualities and conditions meet." The coffee man, Butler averred, "admits of no distinction of persons, but gentleman, mechanic, Lord, and scoundrel mix, and are all of a piece, as if they were resolv'd into their first principles." In a coffeehouse there was no regard "to degrees or order," asserted one pamphleteer, there "you may see a silly fop, and a worshipful justice, a griping rook, and a grave citizen, and an errant pickpocket, a Reverend Nonconformist, and a canting mountebank." The "ugly Turkish enchantress," complained one scribbler, "attracts both rich and poor." Another more neutrally observed that "persons of all qualities from all parts resorted to" coffeehouses. Foreign observers agreed. In English coffeehouses "a boatman and a Lord smoke at the same table," remarked one French visitor. In general the early-eighteenth-century Swiss visitor Antoine Muralt thought the English were devoid of the pronounced social distinctions so prevalent on the Continent. Coffeehouses in particular "are the constant rendezvous for men of business as well as the idle people, so that a man is sooner asked about his coffee-house than his lodging."[71]

The earliest English coffeehouses were associated with trade. Not only did coffee beans have to be imported from the Middle East, but the coffeehouse itself had Levantine origins. Coffeehouses had existed in Damascus, Cairo, Aleppo, and Baghdad since at least the sixteenth century. In the 1560s there were thought to be over six hundred coffeehouses in Istanbul. It was, of course, merchants trading with the Ottoman Empire who first came into contact with this novel institution. Unsurprisingly, then, John Houghton recorded that the first coffeehouse in London—in St. Michael Cornhill—was introduced by two English merchants, Rastall and Edwards, who had come to learn the Ottoman custom of drinking coffee in Smyrna and Livorno. A Jewish man name Jacob, almost certainly of Levantine descent, had opened the first English coffeehouse in Oxford two years earlier. In the early 1660s George Davenport reported to the future archbishop of Canterbury William Sancroft that two baptized Jews were about to open new coffeehouses in London. One can only assume that the first French coffee store, opened in 1671 in the Mediterranean port town of Marseille rather than in Paris, had a similar origin.[72]

The English coffeehouse quickly emerged as a place to conduct business. London's Jamaica Coffee House provided a comfortable venue for West Indian merchants to catch up on the latest news and to make deals for sugar, indigo, and slaves. The governing court of the Moscovy Company met at Jonathan's Coffeehouse. Londoners could "every noon and night on working-days, go to Garroway's Coffee-House, and see what prices the actions bear on most companies trading in joint-stocks." In the 1690s John Houghton's *Collection for the Improvement of Husbandry and Trade,* which included a range of commodity prices as well as political and commercial news, could "be found in all the coffee houses and read for free." In the 1670s Andrew Yarranton lectured "in public coffee-houses" about the need for a public bank and the shortcomings of goldsmith-bankers. In the early 1680s London's short-lived Bank of Credit invited potential clients to visit any of eight coffeehouses to enter their subscriptions. By the later seventeenth century projectors were typically depicted peddling their schemes in one coffeehouse or another. One government memorandum of the 1680s warned that it was the country's newfound addiction to "trade" that "causes that eternal noise and wild manner of talk in City coffee houses." "No bargain can be drove, or business concluded between man and man," observed one pamphleteer, "but it must be transacted at some public house" and more often than not in a "coffee-house." In that sense the Huguenot exile Henri Misson was absolutely correct to suggest that coffeehouses were "extremely convenient" locales to "meet your friends for the transaction of business, and all for a penny."[73]

Merchants, shopkeepers, and businessmen in the seventeenth century needed to have the most up-to-date information not only on commodity prices but also on world events that might affect those prices. Predictably, then, coffeehouses quickly emerged as centers of news and information. As soon as one entered a coffeehouse one heard "that threadbare question, 'What news have you Master?'" or "Gentlemen, here's fresh news from all parts." The Florentine Lorenzo Magalotti discovered that in coffeehouses "there are diverse bodies or groups of journalists where one hears what is or is believed to be new, be it true or false." Two decades later Henri Misson, reflecting on England's vibrant coffeehouse culture, reported that "England is a country abounding in printed papers, which they call pamphlets, wherein every author makes bold to talk freely upon affairs of state, and to publish all manner of news." In coffeehouses, agreed Antoine Muralt in the early eighteenth century, the English "smoke, game, and read the *Gazettes,* and sometimes make them too. Here they treat of matters of state, the interests of princes, and the honour of husbands, &c." The English did not disagree with this assessment of their new cultural attachment. "There's nothing done in all the world, / From monarch to the mouse," rhymed one minor poet of the 1670s, "But every day or night 'tis hurl'd, / Into the Coffee-House." "Every coffee-house now seems, as it were, a Cabal of State," observed another pamphleteer.[74]

Although coffeehouses no doubt purveyed a good deal of local gossip, they were also the locales par excellence where city dwellers could go and learn about recent developments overseas. Thomas Sheridan found that in coffeehouses one could "hear the state-affairs of all nations adjusted." The Frenchman M. de Sainte-Marie marveled that in

England's coffeehouses one could find "all the gazettes printed in England, France, and Holland, [as well as] handwritten newsletters." It was in coffeehouses that "doubting politicians" discussed the illness of Louis XIV and speculated on its significance for English affairs. A decade later James Brydges took a coach to Tom's Coffeehouse to hear the latest developments in the Nine Years' War (1689–97).[75]

Seventeenth-century politicos quickly discovered the dynamic political potential of the coffeehouses. The nascent Whig party used coffeehouses from the first to publicize their ideas. The poet and propagandist Andrew Marvell used the coffeehouse as a stage from which to offer his gloss on each day's *London Gazette*. It was hardly a surprise, then, when his most influential political pamphlet, *An Account of the Growth of Popery and Arbitrary Government*, was thought by Roger North to be "calculated proper for use in clubs and coffeehouses." The Whig leader and John Locke's patron, the Earl of Shaftesbury, aired "all his thoughts and designs in John's coffeehouse." By the time of the Exclusion Crisis (1679–81) the list of Whig coffeehouses included Fair's, the Rainbow, Procter's, Man's, Garraway's, Ford's, Jonathan's, and Combe's. It was not only Whigs who used the medium of the coffeehouse. During the Second Anglo-Dutch War (1665–67) the government sought to circulate stories of Dutch atrocities "at the coffeehouses," where it was hoped they would "spread like a leprosy." During the Exclusion Crisis the Countess of Powis, an intimate friend of the future king James II, "sent a very great number of pamphlets" defending the government's position into "little petty coffee-houses about the town." Will's Coffeehouse in Covent Garden developed a reputation as a center of Tory political activity. No wonder any aspiring politician sent agents to coffeehouses to collect political gossip.[76]

Some coffeehouses also became centers of learned culture. John Dryden, Samuel Butler, and "all the wits of the town" frequented Will's Coffeehouse as early as the 1660s. When Ned Ward visited Will's in the 1690s, he still found the wits "communicating to one another the newest labors of their brains." Playwrights offered readings of scenes from their plays in coffeehouses. Critics, too, used the coffeehouses to advertise their views on the latest literary productions. The virtuosi of the Royal Society were great frequenters of coffeehouses, having established a regular "coffee club" early in the 1660s. By the later 1670s a group of merchants established a religious evening lecture series "in a large room belonging to a coffee-house in Exchange-Alley." It was perhaps this development that led the playwright Aphra Behn to scoff that coffeehouses now hosted disputes about "those things which ought to be the greatest mysteries in religion." James Brydges sought out and found companions eager to discuss books, rare manuscripts, and paintings in London's coffeehouses. John Houghton was surely right to proclaim that "coffee houses make all sorts of people sociable; they improve arts, and merchandize, and all other knowledge."[77]

It was only in this last sense—as the home of polite culture—that English and Continental coffeehouses were comparable. The French café was always and exclusively a "literary café." French cafés did not bustle with merchants and tradesmen making business deals. While frequenters of English coffeehouses could peruse competing financial

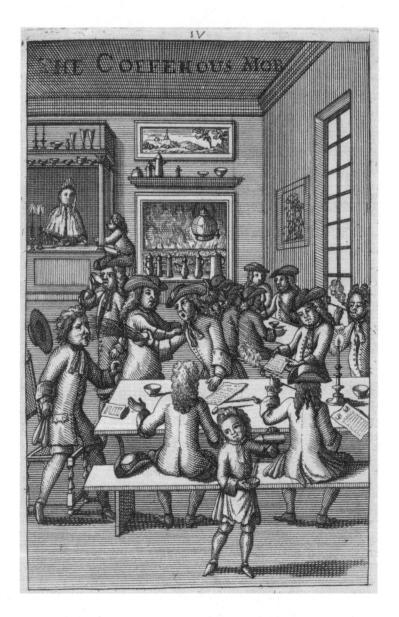

The Coffeehouse Mob, from Edward Ward, *Vulgus Britannicus; or, The British Hubridas,* 1710. English coffeehouses were hubs for political discussion and argument and for the dissemination of news and gossip among the urban commercial classes.

publications from the early 1680s, there was no continuous French-language commodity price lists to be had anywhere in France until the third quarter of the eighteenth century. Whereas foreign visitors to England marveled at "the license assumed by this nation to scrutinize events," in Paris "there is very little noise . . . of public cries of things to be sold, or any disturbance from pamphlets and hawkers." There was comparatively little interest in news. Dr. Martin Lister was amazed that in Paris "the *Gazette* comes out but once a week, and but few people buy them." When the marquis de Seignelay expressed concern about political gossip in Parisian coffeehouses in the 1680s, he ascribed the dangerous speech to "foreigners." The difference was not one of taste. The French, Martin Lister thought, now drank coffee, tea, and chocolate "daily," but unlike the English, most did so "in private houses." This impression was confirmed by the journalists Joseph Addison and Richard Steele in the early eighteenth century. "As for politicians," they told the readers of the *Tatler,* the French "do not abound with that species of men as much as we." The French, they thought, specialized in the literary memoir, while the English were famous "for extemporary dissertations in coffeehouses." The *Tatler* writers made their point chillingly clear in a later comparison. While passing Will's Coffeehouse, now a notorious Tory and Jacobite stronghold, they overheard "a very loud voice swearing, with some expressions towards treason, that the subject in France was as free as in England. His distemper would not let him reflect, that his own discourse was an argument of the contrary."[78] Only in England did a political and economically vibrant coffeehouse culture emerge.

English coffeehouses were novel institutions in the later seventeenth century. Within a few decades every English village or market town with any pretensions had its own coffeehouse. Although each coffeehouse must have had its own particular charm, by and large English coffeehouses all shared the same cultural characteristics. They were venues where locals could come to exchange news, read the most recent newspapers and pamphlets, and conduct business. The coffeehouse was an institution ideally suited to a society experiencing rapid urbanization and commercialization. It fostered a modern politics in which the increasingly ambitious activities of the state were subject to the scrutiny of an expanding political nation.

Why did England change so quickly in the seventeenth century? What sparked the development of English manufactures? Why did manufacturing and port towns develop so rapidly? Why did England's road improve, its shops proliferate? Why did England develop a post office, insurance agencies, new economic instruments? Why did the intellectual and cultural horizons of English men and women of even relatively modest means expand during this period?

These questions can best be answered by placing England in a comparative European context. The social change and economic growth that England experienced in the sixteenth and early seventeenth centuries mirrored developments in the rest of Europe.

Economic historians agree that in the long sixteenth century "the volume of trade expanded everywhere," that in Western Europe "the trend in absolute and relative prices and in population growth was everywhere the same." It was only in the middle of the seventeenth century that the Dutch first and then the English diverged from the general European pattern. For most of Europe the seventeenth century was an age of crisis. In the Netherlands it was a golden age. In England, especially in the later seventeenth century, the economy expanded greatly even though population stagnated. The Venetian resident Alberti reported in the 1670s "that the City of London has never had so much trade as now." "We have increased more in trade" since 1665, noted John Houghton in his new economically oriented periodical, "than it is possible any nation has done in like space." This impression of substantial late-seventeenth-century English economic growth was confirmed by more statistically minded contemporaries as well as later scholars.[79] The relevant question, then, is not why did the English economy expand, but why did the English economy expand while the rest of Europe (besides the Netherlands) was in relative or absolute decline?

Much recent work in social and economic history of the British Isles has failed to grapple with this question because it has become insular in two senses. First, as Jacob Price has suggested, "economic historians of Britain have shown a diminishing interest in placing the evolution of the nation's economy in a world context." Second, the role of England's foreign trade has been downplayed. "The bulk of incomes from employment," asserts John Chartres, "were dependent upon home trades and services." "The greater part of G.N.P.," he concludes, was "generated internally, and the great bulk of domestic products was destined for the home market." In particular, "the impact of the colonial re-export trades before 1690 has been overstated." More ships carried goods destined for the internal market, so, naturally, that market must have been more important to England's economy. The driving force in England's economic history as in its political history, contend most scholars, was national and exceptional rather than external and international.[80]

Recent work in comparative economic development has demonstrated conclusively the implausibility of this internalist story. Using indexes of production and demographic change, scholars have now shown that "almost all the differential growth of Western Europe during the sixteenth, seventeenth, eighteenth and early nineteenth centuries is almost entirely accounted for by the growth of nations with access to the Atlantic ocean," those people most "directly involved in trade and colonialism in the New World and Asia." In other words, the key factor in explaining differences in economic development, the key factor in accounting for English and Dutch prosperity in the face of crisis elsewhere in Europe, is the growth of long-distance trade and the development of overseas colonies. In fact, these scholars have shown that before the opening up of Atlantic trade routes, the regions that would later benefit performed much like neighboring non-Atlantic regions. Internalist stories of social change and economic development in the late sixteenth and early seventeenth centuries are not wrong. England did develop in the period that has been the focus of so much

Panoramic View of the City of London and Stepney, by William Morgan, 1682. The growth of domestic and overseas trade fueled the growth of East London, in particular, and East London suburbs like Stepney were consequently transformed into busy and teeming districts populated overwhelmingly by those in the maritime trades.

attention from social and economic historians. Its development in this period was, however, much like the development experienced in most areas of Europe. In fact, the dynamism that the comparative approach assigns to long-distance trade explains the oddity that French Atlantic areas were uniquely economically vibrant in the French "age of difficulties."[81]

Foreign trade, and especially long-distance foreign trade, did provide England with an economic jolt. English merchant shipping more than doubled its tonnage between 1640 and 1686. Much of this growth was in foreign trade. Imports grew sixfold and exports 650 percent between 1660 and 1700. By 1700 trade with the North American and West Indian plantations on one hand and India on the other represented 30 percent of English imports and 15 percent of English exports. These figures had been negligible at the beginning of the century. Indeed, the export figures would be much higher if one included the massive reexport trade of colonial and East Indian products to Europe. This change in scale of English foreign trade was accompanied by a qualitative shift. Whereas 80–90 percent of English exports were woolen cloths in 1640, by 1700 textiles accounted for less than 50 percent of exports. Foreign trade, and especially overseas trade, created what one economic historian has called "a new context," another "a revolution in trade."[82]

Contemporaries were well aware of the transformative impact of overseas trade on England. One widely circulated merchant's handbook reminded its readers that England's customs revenues had increased more than tenfold since the reign of Henry VIII. Gregory King attributed England's economic boom in the later seventeenth century "chiefly to an increase in foreign trade." In particular, contemporaries pointed to the importance of the new extra-European trades. "Whatever mistaken notions unthinking men have to the contrary," affirmed one late-seventeenth-century pamphleteer, "it may be truly affirmed that it is the planters and settlers of our American plantations, to whom England owes its greatest riches and prosperity." When William Blathwayt surveyed England's overseas endeavors in 1685, he concluded that "those plantations which heretofore were looked upon as desperate adventures are now become necessary and important members of the main body." Two years later Richard Blome affirmed that James II's dominions in the New World were just as important for national prosperity as the king of Spain's possessions there. Sir Robert Southwell reminded the Earl of Nottingham that North America and the West Indies furnished "a full third part of the whole trade and navigation of England." Almost all who cared to comment were convinced that England's prosperity depended on commerce with the East and West Indies. "It is foreign trade that is the main sheet-anchor of us islanders," commented one commercial expert. "No man ever doubted but that foreign trade and commerce is the great concern and interest of every nation," averred another. This was particularly true of England. "The wealth, strength and glory of the King and Kingdom of England depends much (under God) upon the Navigation and foreign trade."[83]

Imported colonial goods had a noticeable effect on English consumption in the later seventeenth century. Tobacco imports grew dramatically from 1615 to 1700. Between 1615 and 1700 English imports rose from fifty thousand pounds per year to thirteen million pounds per year, a twenty-six-fold increase. In addition England in 1700 reexported another twenty-five million pounds per year to the Continent. By the later seventeenth century consumption of tobacco in England was "universal." "The common people love tobacco," agreed Sir George Downing. "Most part of the corporations of England do subsist by this trade of tobacco, what in tap-houses, and strong-water shops," one MP told the House of Commons in 1670. When William Schellinks visited Penzance in 1662 he found that "everyone, men and women, young and old," were "puffing tobacco, which is here so common that the young children get it in the morning instead of breakfast, and almost prefer it to bread." By 1670, it has recently been shown, English men and women consumed one pound of tobacco per person yearly.[84]

Coffee and tea consumption also increased substantially in the seventeenth century. Both hot beverages were extremely exotic in the early seventeenth century, but with the proliferation of coffeehouses after 1650, they became extremely popular drinks. "The use of coffee and tea" had become "so prevalent," thought one observer with some exaggeration, that they "take off people considerably from drinking of strong liquors." English coffee imports from the Middle East and the East Indies more than doubled between 1664 and 1685. Although it is difficult to calculate precisely, it appears that about 3 percent of the English population was consuming one cup of coffee per day by the end of the century. No good price series exists for coffee or tea, but anecdotal evidence from a range of sources suggest that the price of coffee was plummeting in the later seventeenth century, making the drink more accessible to those of modest means.[85] Coffee lacked the mass market

The Island of Barbados, by Isaac Sailmaker, c. 1694. By the middle of the
seventeenth century, Barbados had become the site of large-scale sugar cultivation,
which transformed English consumption patterns and revolutionized English trade.

that tobacco did in the late seventeenth century, but it was nevertheless very popular for
a relatively new nonessential food.

Sugar, too, changed in the late seventeenth century from an occasional luxury
gift to an indispensable part of the English diet. Sugar was soon added to a variety of
fruits to create "many brave and exhilarating drinks," to "the noble nut called the cocoa,"
which without sugar "would be but of little use," to say nothing of the transformations
wrought by the variety of England's confectioners. By 1700 sugar was said to have "spread
its generous and sweet influences through the whole nation." Thomas Tryon's impressions,
though colorful, were not without foundation. Sugar imports more than doubled between
the 1660s and 1690s while prices simultaneously plummeted. Isaac Sailmaker's detailed
painting captured the new economic vibrancy of one of England's sugar islands in the
later seventeenth century. Barbados alone, the island depicted by Sailmaker, more than
tripled the quantity of sugar it sent to England between 1650 and 1700. Enough sugar was
imported by the end of the century for the entire English population to consume about
4 pounds each per year.[86]

Overseas trade was not a one-way affair. The West Indies and North America,
much more than the East Indies, developed an appetite for English manufactures. Sir
George Downing proclaimed as early as 1670 that the "plantations do not only bring home
and send abroad too, but vend your manufactures." Coal, cloth, stockings, gloves, glass,
coaches, shoes, and hats were all sent regularly to the West Indies and North America.
The prominent Quaker metalware manufacturer Thomas Fell was selling his products in
Jamaica in the late seventeenth century. Suffolk cheese, "disesteemed in England," was

deemed appropriate for the long voyages to the New World. "Most certain it is," one polemicist confidently and correctly asserted, "that our American plantations take off more
of the manufactures of England than any other trade abroad whatsoever." In fact, exports
of English manufactures beyond Europe more than tripled between the 1660s and the
1690s. The colonies in the New World had by the later seventeenth century created "the
true new market for English manufactures."[87]

Although trade beyond Europe still accounted for only about 20 percent of English
trade by 1700, its effects were much broader than that figure suggests. Contemporaries were
well aware, as have been economic historians, that overseas trade's largest impact was not
direct but was felt in its "innumerable multiplier, feedback, and spin-off effects." Sir John
Lowther of Whitehaven chose to emphasize that "foreign trade has collateral advantages."
It was these indirect effects which allowed Thomas Tomkins to claim that "there is scarce
any man so mean, but that he doth in one degree or other receive some benefit by our
commerce with other nations."[88]

It is possible to identify some but not all of these indirect multiplier effects of foreign trade. The new popularity of coffee, tea, sugar, and tobacco—all perishable goods—
created a need for local shops able to dispense these products in small quantities relatively
frequently. Contemporaries often noted that after 1640 the English began eating lighter
evening meals. English men and women tended in the later seventeenth century to supplement a light meal with a sweet, a hot caffeine beverage, or a smoke. Together the change
in taste and consumptive practices, both owing to "the creative effects of overseas trade,"
helps to explain the proliferation of shops in towns and small villages in the later seventeenth century. Shops such as that of Benjamin Paramore in Sheffield, which stocked
cinnamon from the East Indies, tobacco, sugar and molasses from the West Indies, and
North American sarsaparilla, became ever more common in the late seventeenth century.
Of course, the new hot beverages could not be consumed at home or in coffeehouses in
the pewter tankards used for beer and ale. The demand for earthenware utensils for these
new hot drinks may well have stimulated the rapid development of the potteries.[89]

Overseas trade was also "the hot-house of the British economy" in other ways. The
risk associated with overseas trade probably encouraged the creation of large firms to share
the financial risk. More sophisticated financial instruments allowed for multilateral systems
of payments based on signatures rather than face-to-face communications.[90] The arrival of
cargoes on large ships encouraged the expansion of warehouses in which to store the goods.
Denizens of England's growing port towns were thus stimulated to build new wharves,
warehouses, docks, and distribution facilities. And of course, overseas trade necessitated
the building of larger ships than were normal in the coastal or even European trades.

Overseas trade became increasingly important in the seventeenth century in political as well as economic terms. European markets, especially those markets influenced
directly or indirectly by French policies, were increasingly closed to the English. The late-
seventeenth-century protectionism became increasingly sophisticated and widespread.

Jean-Baptiste Colbert, Louis XIV's minister of finance in the later seventeenth century, may not have succeeded completely in stimulating French industry or in eliminating internal French tolls and trade barriers, but he did erect steep barriers to English and Dutch imports. From the late 1660s the English were increasingly aware that French tolls were eliminating markets for English manufactures. Even after Colbert's death the French were using "all the art that can be found out . . . to obstruct and ruin the woolen manufactures of England." Merchants in London and Exeter, as well as elsewhere, were well aware that French policies had "ruined" their profitable Continental trade in the new draperies.[91] Increasing French power and increasing French diplomatic pressure would undoubtedly have gradually shut the English out of Continental markets.

English overseas trade with the colonies, itself protected by economic legislation, gave manufacturers a guaranteed market for their products. Colonial consumption of English manufactures was small but growing rapidly in the late seventeenth century. The growing demand from the colonies meant that England did not have to reorient away from manufacturing. Inability to adjust to a protectionist world ultimately cut short the Dutch economic miracle. Despite Dutch initial success in combating French protectionist measures, the Dutch economy "was bound to decay as soon as protectionist policies were adopted more widely." Dutch colonies, like those of Spain and Portugal and unlike their English counterparts, were comparatively self-sufficient economically. There was no safe outlet for Dutch manufactures. So the English uniquely benefited from the late-seventeenth-century rage of tariffs and countertariffs. Because of its linking of England with growing demand from the colonies, the Atlantic trade provided a comparative advantage over trade with the East—a trade that provided rich spices and valuable cloths but very limited demand for English and European products. The development of the West Indian and North American colonies, one scholar has correctly noted, provided "an exclusive market for English industrial output precisely when intra-European trade was depressed and competition intensifying."[92] Foreign trade, and in particular colonial trade, provided the jolt that allowed the English economy to grow during a European economic crisis. Atlantic trade provides the only plausible explanation for England's divergence from the European pattern.

Rapid economic development in later seventeenth-century England necessarily changed the political environment. England was a very different place than it had been a century earlier. It housed new industries, boasted new towns, engaged with new trading partners, developed a new infrastructure, and created new social institutions. All of this created new political opportunities, new resources for the state, and new political bureaucracies to manage new resources. Social and economic changes informed a new kind of politics. Macaulay and the historians who have almost all followed in his wake wrongly assumed that because English economic transformation was a consequence of the Revolution of 1688–89 there was no need to investigate the relationship between socioeconomic and political history. These two realms of scholarly inquiry could be safely segregated. This assumption can no longer be sustained.

The separation of social and economic from political history appears, at first glance, to be warranted by the historical record. The percentage of MPs involved in trade remained steady at about 10 percent from the age of Elizabeth through the end of the seventeenth century. James II's Parliament of 1685 was indisputably "a landed Parliament," one in which most MPs seemed to be bent on policies that "favour their lands." Samuel Pepys and John Houghton both complained that the gentry, when it came to trade, "are more ruled by vulgar error, and false maxims, than the dictates of their own reason."[93]

This apparent continuity, the apparent continued lack of interest of the political nation in trade, was in fact exaggerated. In the early 1680s John Houghton published an entire periodical devoted to issues of commerce and industry because "trade is a subject that hath not only taken up the thoughts and time of private men, but also of late years especially hath been one of the main concerns of the greatest princes." An increasing number of those holding landed estates were taking an interest in commerce. The Duke of Buckingham, for example, was deeply involved in London glass manufacturing. The Earl of Thanet set up a textile manufacture in Appleby. Sir John Lowther was personally responsible for creating the thriving port of Whitehaven and was a great supporter of state support for new manufactures. Sir Daniel Fleming developed lead and copper mines on his properties in Lancashire and Westmorland. The Earl of Rochester, normally seen exclusively as a committed defender of the Church of England, was "very well informed about the details of commerce and made that his principal study." Of course, the greatest landed gentlemen of all, Charles II and James II, set a new example of commercial commitment. Charles II famously took "peculiar pleasure in experiments relating to navigation" and set up a school for boys designed to promote "the security and advancement of our trade." "The great and almost only pleasure of mind he seemed addicted to was shipping and sea affairs," commented one intimate of Charles II soon after the monarch's death. James II, thought the French special envoy Bonrepaus, was particularly interested in financial and commercial affairs. The Marquis of Ailesbury, who perhaps knew James II better still, thought he had trade "much at heart." In the 1660s and early 1670s James had been responsible for reviving the Royal African Company, investing huge amounts of time and money in the venture. On his accession James created a commerce committee within the Privy Council and initiated discussions on a number of commercial projects.[94]

Trade was increasingly a topic of interest for the political nation. Charles II created a series of parliamentary and extraparliamentary committees and boards to gather "matters of fact" and develop proposals regarding trade. The Royal Society created a Georgic Committee to discuss agrarian issues and their relationship to trade. Contemporaries were convinced that trade was penetrating the culture in all sorts of ways. Ralph Thoresby thought that the new importance of trade required the penning of biographies "that are applicable to the trading part of the nation of persons involved in business." "Though here-tofore it was esteemed a disparagement to be a merchant or to marry with the daughter of such," wrote Sir Daniel Fleming of Lancashire, "yet now the inhabitants here have grown wiser and several gentlemen of very great quality are become merchant-adventurers." Sir Francis Brewster commented how much better his contemporaries understood issues of commerce than "our forefathers." Recently, agreed John Cary, many MPs "began to be much in love with trade, and have often lamented the dark notion that house had of it." The Venetian envoy, no stranger to commercial culture, described the House of Commons in the 1670s as filled with "persons skilled in economics and acquainted with the readiest ways of obtaining ready money from the public."[95]

Contemporaries were keenly aware that English political culture was diverging significantly from those of its Continental counterparts. The Newcastle lead merchant Ambrose Barnes, who had himself spent significant time on the Continent, observed that in both Denmark and Sweden "trade is below a gentleman." Most, however, contrasted the English with the French. The French visitor M. de Sainte-Marie marveled at the extent to which merchandizing had penetrated English culture. England, unlike France, was a place in which "King, Lords, gentlemen, and the bourgeoisie live all together." "In France indeed," commented Guy Miege, who hailed from Lausanne, "where if a gentleman-born betakes himself to trade forfeits his gentility, the gentry stand so much upon their honor, that it is very rare to see a French gentleman turn to merchandizing."[96]

Later seventeenth-century English men and women were relentless commentators on recent changes in the sociology of power. This perception crossed party lines. The Tory John Houghton knew that "many of our poor cottagers' children [have] turned merchants and substantial traders." "As England is one of the most trading countries in Europe," agreed the Whig Guy Miege, "so the greatest body of its commonalty, is that of traders, or men that live by buying and selling." Most thought that as England became a nation of tradesmen and shopkeepers, the locus of political power had shifted. John Aubrey was convinced that "the balance of the government [is] quite altered, and put into the hands of the common people." Dr. Charles Aldworth, a fellow of the ill-fated Magdalen College, confided to his commonplace book that recently "the commons" had "got the riches of the nation in their hands by trade" and had thus become "a match both for Kings and Lords." James II's friend and loyal supporter Sir Edward Hales knew that as a result of "the great increase in trade since Henry VIIIth's time," the English people had achieved "an equality of riches" and therefore power. Sir Henry Capel argued in Parliament that political trust was placed where "there is most property," and to him it was clear that "the property of England was in the Commons." Significantly, this was the conclusion of a memorandum circulated widely in James II's court in 1685. "Trade and negotiation has infected the whole kingdom, and no man disdains to marry or mix with it," the author of the memorandum contended, "by this means the very genius of the people is altered, and it will in the end be the interest of the crown to proportion its maxims of power suitable to this new nature come among us." A variety of arithmetical calculations proved unequivocally that "trade is much the over-balance of the wealth of the nation, and consequently must influence the power for good or ill."[97]

Again and again, the English described themselves as a trading nation in the later seventeenth century. "Trade is the true and intrinsic interest of Britain without which it cannot subsist," wrote one popular pamphleteer. "England is properly a nation of trade, and extremely well situated for commerce," agreed another. "The whole project of the nation," opined the economic writer Carew Reynell, was "trade." "It is a mistake," warned Sir John Cotton, "to think that trade doth not concern our being but our well being." "Trade is the true and intrinsic interest of England," averred Slingsby Bethel in an unusually uncontroversial statement. This was because "from trade there doth not only arise riches to the subjects, rendering a nation considerable, but also increase of revenue, and therein power and strength to the sovereign." On this point, if on few others, Bethel agreed with the Tory civil lawyer Charles Molloy. In England, Molloy contended, "navigation and commerce were never . . . in greater esteem than now."[98]

In 1685 England was a radically different place than it had been in 1600. It was more urban, more mercantile, more industrial, and more prosperous. Communications were dramatically better by both sea and land. England had developed much more of a national market, with regional specialization. Insurance made trade less risky. The post office made it easier to carry out. The coffeehouse provided a new venue in which to conduct business. More important, perhaps, England had diverged from the general European economic pattern. Although its population was not growing in the later seventeenth century, its economy was dynamic while the rest of Europe largely lay stagnant. "For merchandizing and navigation," observed one commentator correctly, "no people can compare with [the English] but the Hollanders."[99] England had indeed followed the Dutch economic path to modernity. And like the Dutch, foreign trade had provided the stimulus to English economic modernization.

The English were well aware that the transformation of their society and economy required a new politics. Both James II and his critics were fascinated with trade. They were convinced that England's political future lay as a commercial society. Thomas Babington Macaulay knew that it was impossible to describe England's politics without first coming to grips with its social situation. Because Macaulay thought that seventeenth-century English society shared few characteristics with the England of his own day, he concluded that English politics at the accession of James II was anything but modern. In this assessment Macaulay was fundamentally mistaken. By most measures the England that James II came to rule in February 1685 was a modernizing commercial society. The English in the later seventeenth century were a people concerned with issues of commercial policy and foreign affairs as much as they were with religious and legal or constitutional controversies. Only by first understanding that fact, only by broadening our conception of the political, can we hope to understand the revolution that occurred in 1688.

CHAPTER FOUR

English Politics at the Accession of James II

Despite premature reports of his recovery from a severe stroke, on the morning of 6 February 1685 King Charles II "gave up the ghost." All England was soon consumed by uncontrollable grief. The Duke of Newcastle was "so very ill with grief" that he "could scarce stir out of [his] chamber." The news "drew tears" from Colley Cibber, who would in 1688 take up arms against James II. "What is all this world! What is all the glory of it," exclaimed the virtuoso John Evelyn on hearing of the king's death, "I cannot speak without disorder." "Now the whole nation is in a general sadness for the death of our beloved King Charles," the London merchant Henry Hunter told one of his trading partners. The Londoner's perception of national sentiment was not far off the mark. John Curtois, a Lincolnshire cleric, recalled that as the news of Charles II's death spread across the country, "we looked as half dead our selves and stood staring upon one another as men at our wits' end: every eye was ready to drop a tear and every heart to breathe a sigh, I think I may truly say, never was King of England so generally and so heartily lamented."[1]

Undoubtedly the lamentation for the death of Charles II stemmed from a variety of causes. Charles II's convivial and informal manner appealed to many. His recent determined support of the Church of England and the rights of his brother the Duke of York gained the sympathy of others. But perhaps more than anything else, Charles's twenty-

---

(above) *James, Duke of Monmouth, and Archibald, Earl of Argyle; Beheaded,* by R. Arondeaux, 1685. The king's forces put down the Duke of Monmouth's Rebellion in July 1685. The leaders of the rebellion were executed later that month. This medal, cast in commemoration of the executions, warns that "ill-advised ambition fails."

five-year reign symbolized political and social stability after the tumultuous 1640s and 1650s. Charles's younger brother, James, by contrast, was a controversial figure. After his reconciliation with the Roman Catholic Church, James had become the focus of intense political scrutiny. His well-known absolutist temperament frightened many. The Whig political party had coalesced in the later 1670s in a failed campaign to exclude James from the throne. While Whig hopes of a parliamentary act altering the succession were dashed by the deft political activities of their Tory rivals, and their political prestige was shattered by a failed plot to murder Charles II and James at Rye House in the spring of 1683, no one could be certain how the English people would receive James II. The Earl of Burlington was typical in recommending to Lord Fairfax's "particular care the preventing of all disorders or disturbances that may happen by any false reports or seditious practices on this occasion."[2] The tears that flowed as the news of the king's death spread were as much tears of anxiety as tears of mourning.

Nevertheless, the moment of anxiety proved fleeting. The vast majority of the political nation welcomed the accession of James II in February 1685. That summer, few people joined the armed rebellion in the west of England led by the charismatic and Protestant James, Duke of Monmouth, natural son of Charles II. Why did so many in England welcome James enthusiastically in 1685? Why was James able to defeat his nephew's rebellion so quickly?

The answer can tell us a great deal about the nature of English political culture in the later seventeenth century and ultimately about the causes of the Revolution of 1688–89. These questions provide an opportunity to scrutinize assumptions about late-seventeenth-century English political culture that lie at the heart of the establishment Whig interpretation of the revolution as a fundamentally conservative event.

Many scholars now insist that the English people replaced the Catholic James II with the Protestants William and Mary for overwhelmingly religious reasons, implying that James's religion doomed his reign from the start. According to William Speck, author of a scholarly monograph produced at the three-hundredth anniversary of the revolution, "it was not [James II's] absolutism . . . so much as his Catholicism which alienated his subjects." "Religion," Speck concludes, "was thus at the heart of the Revolution." "England's domestic troubles centered on a religious polarity which divided the whole of Europe in the early modern period: between the forces of the reformation and the counter-reformation," argues Jonathan Scott. "All of the major crises of the century—the three crises of popery and arbitrary government of 1637–42, 1678–83 and 1687–9, were fundamentally about religion. It was concern about religion, not about politics or economics, which drove seventeenth-century English people to compromise their political allegiances and mire themselves in one another's blood." Writing as an expert of eighteenth-century political culture, Jonathan Clark reaches the same conclusion. "Through all the vicissitudes of English politics from the 1530s to the 1830s and beyond, the most consistent theme both of popular sentiment and of ideological exegesis was anti-Catholicism," Clark argues. "Popular political vocabulary was largely expressed in a dichotomy of papist and anti-papist. The apotheosis of this tradition in England was the Glorious Revolution."[3]

Instead of positing that the English people *as a whole* were always united against Catholic James, a second group of scholars insists on the central role played by a small group of Whig opponents of James II. These historians highlight what they have called a heroic and ultimately triumphant "radical" tradition. What defined this radicalism, in their view, was not so much an innovative ideological agenda—the Whig opponents were not modern revolutionaries—but a willingness to use force to promote their religious agenda. Melinda Zook defines radicals as those who were willing "to use and justify violence to obtain their ends." That end "between 1679 and 1685" was "to bar Catholic James from the throne." While Zook defines the domain of radicalism as the political, she makes it clear that "to the English mind, Catholicism and absolutism were indistinguishable." For Richard Greaves, "no issue aroused more concern in British politics in the period 1673–88 than James' Catholicism." "Religious issues," Greaves concludes, "were fundamental to the radical cause."[4] The Whigs, in this view, were committed to radical practices in defense of a conservative ideological agenda.

Where the first group of scholars emphasizes English political consensus, this second interpretative tradition emphasizes the partisan triumph of the Whigs in 1688. The Revolution of 1688–89 was a Whig victory because the Whigs were the only group in England willing and able to act in defense of their principles. Melinda Zook suggests that "the Exclusion Crisis, the Rye House Plot [of 1683], and the Revolution of 1688—episodes that historians have often examined separately—were" for the Whigs "all part of one long struggle over which many of their brethren lost their lives." Immediately on the death of Charles II, in Zook's view, the committed Whigs "turned their attention and hopes to Charles's bastard son, the Duke of Monmouth." The failure of the 1685 rebellion was prologue to the Whig triumph of 1688. Richard Greaves, author of an exhaustive trilogy examining the radical underground from the Restoration of 1660 to the Revolution of 1688–89, reaches similar conclusions. "The revolution of 1688–89," Greaves maintains, "fulfilled many of the radicals' hopes, and in that sense Monmouth, Argyle, and their associates prepared the way for William even as the core of their program became that of the political nation."[5] This second group argues that a small group of Whigs, a group that failed to exclude James from the throne 1679–81 and then failed to overthrow him in 1685, finally succeeded in ousting James in 1688 because, unlike their similarly religiously motivated fellow English men and women, they were willing to resort to violence to achieve their goals. The Whigs made the Revolution of 1688–89 not because they had radical political objectives but because they were willing to use radical political means to achieve conservative aims.

The subtle differences between these two interpretative traditions should not blind us to their shared assessment of the nature of English political culture. Both groups argue that opposition to James was largely religious in nature. Both groups deny that the revolutionaries had any transformative political or social agenda. Both schools, then, depict 1688–89 as a conservative revolution, a revolution in defense of Protestantism against a Catholic king. English men and women ultimately ceased to support their king because of his commitment to the Roman Catholic Church. The English in 1688–89 struggled against Catholicism just as their forefathers had fought against Philip II's Catholic Armada in 1588, just as they had abhorred the Gunpowder Plot of 1605, just as they had risen up against the Catholicizing policies of Charles I, just as they had attempted to prevent James from being made heir to the throne in 1678–81. The Revolution, in this view, was based on no new principles. In fact, the events of 1688–89 were a return to Protestant normality after the aberration of a Catholic monarch.

Close examination of the early months of James II's reign, however, reveals that this interpretation of English political culture is flawed. Far from demonstrating a prevailing atmosphere of religious paranoia, the initial response of English men and women to the accession of James II, the parliamentary elections of 1685, and the Duke of Monmouth's failed rebellion in the summer of 1685 reveals the depth of support for the Catholic monarch at his accession. While no doubt some of James II's support did reflect the "zenith" of Tory "enthusiasm" in the wake of the botched Whig attempt to assassinate Charles II and his brother James at Rye House in 1683, as Thomas Babington Macaulay claimed, most of it stemmed from a sophisticated assessment that the English had more to lose from a regime led by Protestant religious enthusiasts than they did from a Catholic prince who promised to protect the religion and liberties of the English. Not only Tory high fliers but also moderates and Whig politicos supported James II in 1685. Few English political radicals supported the Duke of Monmouth's religious uprising. Just as the English were radically transforming their social and economic environment in the later seventeenth century, so were they shifting their political attitudes. Religion remained an important element of English political life, but it had ceased to dominate it. The English, by 1685, had begun to move beyond identity politics.[6]

The English people welcomed James II to the throne with open arms and enthusiastic toasts, not with anti-Catholic paranoia. "The ark of God was not shaken as many feared it would have been at the death of our late gracious sovereign Lord, Charles the second," recalled the dean of Ripon Thomas Cartwright the following year, "but continued steady without the least commotion. No cry in our cities, no complaining in our streets, no tears but those of love and loyalty." The young Presbyterian Edmund Calamy agreed that "the acclamations" at James II's accession "were very general." "Over all England his Majesty is with so great and general applause proclaimed king," enthused the Earl of Burlington. "His Majesty begins his reign with auspicious acclamations from all parts," chimed in Sir Robert Southwell, who would be far less enthusiastic about James in 1688. "Every man believes he will take to heart the glory of his nation: that he will chastise the late insolency of vice, and by his own example bring morality into reputation; that he will be at the head of all his affairs and retrench in a high degree every superfluous expense; that he will be very soft and sociable towards those who show obedience and formidable to those who do not. In these points all seem to concur."[7]

Reports from all over England and Wales confirmed these impressions of widespread support for the new Catholic king. In London the proclamation was greeted with "great acclamations of joy." In York the news elicited "loud and repeated acclamations of the citizens" who spent "the rest of the day and part of the night . . . in ringing of bells, bonfires and all other expressions of a general satisfaction." Sir Robert Southwell reported that "at Bristol and all these parts," parts which would soon be scarred by the Duke of Monmouth's rebellion and its aftermath, "his Majesty hath been proclaimed with the solemnity and joy that could be wished for." Even at Lyme Regis, where the Duke of Monmouth would land in June 1685 to begin his rebellion against James, there were "repeated acclamations of joy." "Great numbers" demonstrated their joy at Durham, while in Newcastle there was "gladness in every man's countenance." "General acclamations of the people," "ringing of bells," and "bonfires" marked the proclamation of James II in Reading, Colchester, and Winchester. Sir John Lowther, who would later become William III's secretary of state, proclaimed the new king enthusiastically at Appleby in Westmorland. "No county in England could proclaim [James II] with more acclamations or joy or express more entire resolutions to serve him with their lives and fortunes," bragged the sheriff of Northumberland. The Midlands were no less enthusiastic, no more fearful, at James II's accession. There were great celebrations at Boston in Lincolnshire, while at Stamford there was "a general satisfaction." Loughborough, thought Sir Henry Beaumont, "exceeded all others in their zeal of proclaiming the King." "What unanimous and cheerful acclamations, and bravery of resolution" to serve the new king did Benjamin Canfield perceive at Leicester.[8]

England's two universities, both of which ultimately proved troublesome to James II, fell over themselves with demonstrations of loyalty in February 1685. In Oxford riotous celebrations greeted James II's proclamation as king. Beer was provided in the town hall "to be drunk by all comers." The "conduits" were well supplied "with claret." There were "bonfires in all college quadrangles, or before their gates, where the respective societies drunk a health, kneeling, to King James II, his queen, princess of Orange, and princess of Denmark; and left the rest of the ceremony to be carried on by the juniors with wine and beer, and letting off guns and cracks." At Cambridge there was "public feasting with ringing of bells all day. The whole concluded at night with bonfires in the several colleges, and all other testimonies of zealous affection and loyalty to His Sacred Majesty." Both universities presented James II with splendid books of poetry predicting great achievements during his reign. The Oxford book included verses from Christopher Wase, who would enthusiastically support William III, Richard Wright of Magdalen College, who would support the college in its celebrated struggle against James, and Philip Bertie, who would take up arms in support of the Prince of Orange in November 1688.

The Cambridge volume included works by the future Whig poet and diplomat Matthew Prior, the long-serving Williamite diplomat George Stepney, and Charles Montague, who would play an instrumental role in the establishment of the Bank of England.[9]

While there can be no doubt that most people in England, Wales, and the colonies welcomed the accession of the Catholic king James II, he certainly did not enjoy universal support. After all, three successive houses of commons harbored majorities in support of excluding James from the throne. The West Country Quaker John Whiting recalled that in February 1685 "many were under dreadful apprehensions of what would follow." "The gloomy prospect of popery" overwhelmed the west Yorkshire occasional conformist Ralph Thoresby, who was celebrating his nuptials when James II came to the throne. Edmund Calamy, who was in London at the time of Charles II's death, thought there were many "that had very terrifying apprehensions of what was to be expected" from a Catholic king. In Lancaster, William Stout was sure that "the sober, conscientious and observant people of all Protestant professions" shared his apprehensions about the Catholic James II. Once James began to attend Mass publicly at Whitehall, concerns about Catholicism were voiced by "the great Tories as well as the Whigs" in the country's "coffeehouses." Nevertheless these concerns about the king's Catholicism were relatively rare and were perhaps magnified in hindsight. Sir John Lowther, hardly one of the king's great supporters, acknowledged that though those who "were zealous in their religion" and "timorous in their natures" harbored some fears resulting from the new king's religious beliefs, "yet a far greater number had then no such apprehensions."[10]

Those who were apprehensive were largely reassured by the king's actions on taking the throne. As soon as Charles II died, the new king "went immediately to the Council, and before entering into any business" delivered a passionate and politically brilliant speech. "I have been reported to be a man of arbitrary power," James II admitted, "but I shall make it my endeavor to preserve this government both in church and state as it is now by law established. I know the principles of the Church of England are for monarchy, and the members of it have showed themselves good and loyal subjects, therefore I shall always take care to defend and support it. I know too that the laws of England are sufficient to make the king as great a monarch as I can wish, and as I shall never depart from the just rights and prerogatives of the crown, so I shall never invade any man's property."[11] James could have made no more reassuring statement. Indeed, that he delivered this speech extemporaneously as he rushed from his dead brother's side made it all the more poignant and powerful.

James II's declaration to his Privy Council, which was immediately printed in the official newspaper and read aloud in each town and village, had an immediate and decisive effect on English public opinion. Public confidence in the capital was almost instantaneously restored. "This gracious speech," the Whitehall press censor James Fraser informed Sir Robert Southwell, "has already healed in a great measure the wounds the late king's death made in the minds of many people, who are overjoyed to have their fears removed upon so sudden a change." The Earl of Burlington thought that the declaration "has given an universal satisfaction to everybody that has heard it." "His Majesty's expressions of a very great care and tenderness for his people had that good influence that the suspicions of the most timorous did immediately vanish," recalled the rector of St. Andrew Undershaft Robert Grave. James II "has given such assurances of the security of our religion and properties," reported the London-based West Indies merchant Christopher Jeaffreson, "that all fears and jealousies being removed, we hope for a happy and flourishing government." One London pundit was even confident that the king's declaration in council would turn "Whigs and Trimmers" into "loyalists."[12]

Political observers around the country were relieved to report similar transformations as the news of James II's declaration was announced in each town and village. From Warminster in Wiltshire Sir Henry Coker reported the king's "royal and gracious words to the Lords of his Council to maintain the laws and religion established did with excessive joy enliven all spirits to cry out God save King James the second." After reading James II's declaration aloud and posting it in market places throughout Warwickshire, Sir Andrew Hacket found that "it begat great satisfaction among the people and prevailed much upon their affections towards his Majesty." At York and throughout Yorkshire the king's "declaration to maintain the liberties, properties and religion of his subjects as now by law established" "made no small impressions upon the people of all sorts for it was presently in every man's mouth and that seconded with such universal loud acclamations as we conceive has not been exceeded at any time or upon any occasion." Indeed, Sir William Trumbull learned that "all peoples' hearts were transported with joy, thinking themselves secure enough upon his Royal word." The poet John Baber correctly captured the popular mood created by James II's well-publicized speech when he rhymed that "all his Declaration did behold, / And wished it writ in characters of gold."[13]

English men and women throughout the country soon expressed in writing their excitement at their new king's declaration to protect the religion and liberties established by law. "Innumerable addresses" of thanks arrived "from all the quarters of these his kingdoms," "from all counties, corporations and societies throughout the king's dominions." Not only did these addresses express how willing thousands of English were to overlook the king's Catholicism and accept him as their lawful and legitimate monarch, the addresses also emphasized the role which the king's word in council had played in assuaging their fears. While a few, a very few, of the addresses insisted like that of Oxford University that "no consideration whatsoever shall be able to shake that steadfast loyalty and allegiance" which is owed to a king, the overwhelming majority did not.[14] The addresses reveal an English people who were able to overcome traditional anti-Catholic prejudices, as well as a people very much committed to their liberties and religion established by law. Neither rabid anti-Catholicism nor enthusiastic absolutism defined English political culture at the accession of James II.

Greater London, which had so recently been the scene of extreme Whig exclusionist sentiment, produced an impressive series of addresses always emphasizing the importance of the new king's declaration. The bishop and clergy of London, who would be so influential in turning public opinion against James II in coming years, thanked their new king "for making our duty so easy and pleasant by your gracious assurance to defend our religion established by law, which is dearer to us than our lives." The free shipwrights of London expressed their "infinite satisfaction" for their king's promise to protect the "government both of church and state as now established by law." For the inhabitants of Westminster, James II's declaration merely expressed "what no honest man ever doubted."[15]

Boroughs and corporations throughout the country soon followed the London addresses with statements of their own, remarks that invariably emphasized the importance of James II's promises to protect the laws and Church of England. The Corporation of Canterbury thanked James for his "royal word," which they were certain would convince his "enemies of their folly and injury" as well as adding "a further happiness to all those that have been admirers of your great worth." The "gracious declaration" has given "new life to us," averred the city of Chichester in Sussex. "Though your Majesty through a succession of several ages has an undoubted right to the imperial crown of this realm," announced the members of the borough of Warwick, "yet has your Majesty by your late gracious declaration crowned yourself anew in the hearts of your loyal subjects." Places diverse as Portsmouth, Hereford, Westbury in Wiltshire, and Brackley in Northamptonshire all expressed similar sentiments. The town of Nottingham, which would be the location of one of the best-publicized and best-attended risings in support of the Prince of Orange in November 1688, also addressed James II to thank him for his "late gracious declaration."[16]

The counties were just as enthusiastic in their support for the king and his declaration to protect the laws and church. The perception that the inhabitants of Devon could trust the declaration of a king "whose word has ever been dearer to him than his life" was all the more poignant in that the address was delivered by the Whig Sir John Rolle. After the king's declaration to protect "our lives, liberties, and religion," the people of Hertfordshire could have "no other just fears but what arise from our infinite value of your Majesty's person." James II's declaration was something on which the inhabitants of Berkshire were able to "build [their] confidence as on a rock." The declaration set the "hearts" of the inhabitants of Sussex "at perfect rest," while the grand jury of Essex thought it would "certainly oblige the worst of men to repent their former mistakes, and make them double their diligence in performing their duty hereafter."[17]

The Welsh welcomed James II's promise to protect the laws and church with similar enthusiasm. The gentry of Carnarvon informed James that they "have already shared in the happy effects which your late Declaration wrought in the hearts of your subjects." The inhabitants of Anglesey enthused that the king's "resolution to maintain the present government by law established in both church and state . . . renders us the happiest subjects in the world." "The happy fruits of this invaluable blessing which we do find in your Majesty's most gracious declaration, must needs have filled the hearts of all your people with joy and ravishment," announced the people of Carmarthen, "but amongst all your subjects you have not any in whom the effects of so much grace and goodness can have made their impressions deeper . . . than they have done with us."[18]

Although James II's Catholicism at his accession raised some concerns, they were initially limited among the English population. Most in England, including many who had misgivings about a Catholic king, were largely reassured by James's promise to govern within the legal framework of church and state. Moreover, a careful reading of the veritable plethora of addresses that poured in from around the country soon after James became king reveals that James was so enthusiastically feted precisely because the English thought he would govern as an English monarch constrained by the law. The experience of the previous century and a half had apparently diminished the religious prejudices of the English people while at the same enhancing their commitment to their laws in church and state. By the accession of James II identity politics played only a limited role in shaping English political culture. James II, then, was welcomed enthusiastically in 1685 because most people thought the risks engendered by excluding the rightful heir from the throne far outweighed the dangers of allowing him to rule.

James II not only promised to defend the English church and state established by law at his accession, he also immediately issued writs for Parliament to meet in April. This announcement reinforced his commitment to rule by law. It also created an opportunity to test public opinion. If anti-Catholic sentiment was dominant in English political culture, surely it would be revealed in the election campaigns taking place throughout England and Wales.

Before Charles II was buried the new king and his advisers began preparing for the parliamentary elections. The Earl of Sunderland quickly pressured all the king's supporters to exercise their influence in the localities. He urged each one "to use his best interest to choose such men who will act for the support and honor of the crown and the peace, quiet and welfare of the public." This meant supporting candidates who "would rather heal than make breaches betwixt the king and his people, which cannot be expected from such who have openly declared against the succession of the crown in the right line, or not heartily declared in defense of it."[19] James II very much wanted a Parliament devoid of the Whigs who had tried to exclude him from the throne.

The Crown's plea for organizational support was met with great enthusiasm. The Earl of Plymouth lobbied the Hull electors "to oppose the election of any person that was for the bill of Exclusion." The Duke of Newcastle, who had been so depressed at the news of Charles II's death that he would not leave his house, promised to "take all the care I can in this county that good men may be chosen to serve in the next Parliament." Heneage Finch, Earl of Winchilsea, whom James later dismissed as lord lieutenant of Kent, insisted that he would do "what I can that good members be chosen for the approaching Parliament." The

Earl of Derby, who threw in his lot with the revolutionaries in 1688, announced he would crisscross the country, attending "as many of the elections as possible I may, and take all due care that none be chosen but persons of approved loyalty." A variety of noblemen and gentlemen from all over the country expressed similar sentiments.[20] "I am doing what I can" in Hampshire and Cornwall "to have loyal and fit persons chosen to serve in Parliament," reported Charles Pawlet, Marquis of Winchester, whose son would later join the Prince of Orange in the Netherlands. Clerics were equally active in the court campaign. "I have toiled myself extremely ever since I came into the country in making interest for Parliament men," the bishop of Chichester, John Lake—who would later become famous as one of the Seven Bishops tried by James II for defying his commands—testified to his metropolitan, William Sancroft.[21]

Despite the organizational muscle of the government, a number of former Whigs did test the electoral waters. "My Lord Brandon uses great endeavors to be chosen at Lancaster, where the commonalty are very factious," one Whitehall gossip informed Sir Richard Bulstrode. George Jeffreys, never known for his moderation, feared that Sir Roger Hill, "a horrid Whig," was campaigning heavily in Buckinghamshire. At Harwich "the Dissenting party" were observed making "a great interest." The mayor of Chichester worried that the local "factious spirits" might "set up for electing their old seditious members." Similarly Thomas Penn, mayor of Bridgwater, was terrified that "the grand fanatics" were making "great preparations for a party."[22]

While this Whig agitation might be interpreted as evidence of deep anti-Catholic prejudice, the rhetoric of the Whigs who did stand was devoid of inflammatory religious language. "The Exclusion men are very busy everywhere pretending they are ashamed of their transactions in the late Parliaments and therefore desire to be in this that they may testify their repentance to the King and the world," observed Sir Charles Holt from Warwickshire. The Whig Sir Edward Abney, who had the support of "a bad party" and was "not recommended by any loyal person," vehemently denied to the Earl of Huntingdon that he had "any disloyal or fanatical principles." Similarly, Sir Richard Newdigate, who had served in the Oxford Parliament of 1681 as a Whig, assured the Earl of Sunderland that he had "been zealous to persuade the people to own their allegiance to our present king (whom I pray God to preserve)," even going so far as to turn out a tenant who had expressed pro-Monmouth sentiments.[23] Clearly, those Whigs who stood for Parliament in 1685 did not do so on anti-Catholic platforms.

As it turned out, the elections overwhelmingly returned Tories and long-term supporters of the new king. In Bedfordshire the Whig Russell interest was decisively defeated, showing, according to the Tory Lord Bruce, that "the eyes of the nation" were "well opened." "The best of gentlemen of the county (besides other freeholders)" in Derbyshire "heartily agreed" to return the Tories Sir Robert Coke and Sir Gilbert Clarke. The Whigs found "few for them" in Essex as well. "The whole county opposes [the Whig] Sir Scroope Howe," John Mellington informed the Marquis of Halifax. On the day of the election one group led by Lord Lexington carried a long pole into Newark market "at the end of which was a black box and great piece of parchment like a banner upon which was written in a large character: no black box, no bill of exclusion, no association." The Leicestershire election proved "fatal to the fanatics and their favorites," who experienced an "entire defeat." "The fanatics and Trimmers" were routed in Cornwall, bragged the Earl of Bath, returning instead a slate of MPs "entirely devoted to his Majesty's service." In London the radical Whig slate of 1681 was replaced by "Sir John Moore, Sir William Pritchard, Sir Samuel Dashwood and Sir Peter Rich, all gentlemen who have eminently shown their loyalty in the late times of trial."[24]

Contemporaries were convinced that the election of 1685 represented an over-whelming victory for the Tories, James II, and his government. James II's new lord treasurer the Earl of Rochester bragged to the Prince of Orange that "the elections for Parliament men are generally so good that there is all reason in the world to believe it will be a very happy meeting between the King and them, which is the best thing that can happen to both." Sir Richard Bulstrode heard that "loyal good men" were "everywhere chosen." "We do not hear of three ill men that are chosen," Edward Dering crowed to Sir John Percival. The important East India and Africa merchant and committed Tory Sir Benjamin Bathurst thought "almost all the members chosen are very loyal and good men." "The inward as well as outward joy" of the English people at James II's accession, the Earl of Ailesbury recalled, was confirmed by the "great and wise choice the kingdom made at the elections for Parliament that commenced in April 1685."[25]

Although it is true that Charles II's campaign to tamper with borough charters guaranteed that many boroughs would return candidates favorable to the government, there is strong evidence that public opinion in the political nation was firmly behind the new king. An analysis of the county elections, where Charles and James were powerless to alter the voting qualifications, reveals a remarkable electoral shift.[26] The potential electorate in the English counties was about 140,000 voters. In the last election of Charles II's reign, the election to the Oxford Parliament of 1681, the counties returned sixty-five Whigs, thirteen Tories, and two moderates. By 1685, despite the moderation of Whig rhetoric across the country, public sentiment had shifted dramatically. In this election the English counties returned seven Whigs, seventy Tories, two moderates, and one MP for whom there is insufficient evidence to classify. These returns make it hard to believe that concern about the new king's Catholicism determined English voting behavior. They make it hard to believe that anti-Catholicism still dominated English political culture.

While these returns do suggest a radical shift in public attitudes toward James, the king's new support remained limited and conditional. Close examination of the sur-viving evidence suggests that the English were persuaded that James II could be trusted to protect the constitution in church and state. The English political nation did not shift from enthusiastic Whiggery to rabid Toryism. Instead the political hotbed of the Exclu-sion Crisis and its aftermath made the English political nation wary of the destabilizing implications of the Whigs. In 1685 the English felt that supporting a constitutionalist James II afforded the best chance of political stability.[27]

There was good reason to believe that the electorate's rejection of extreme exclusionists did not mean an endorsement of royal absolutism. Many of the Tories returned from the counties were men of moderate views, men like Richard Southby of Berkshire, John Egerton of Buckinghamshire, Edward Montagu of Northamptonshire, Sir William Clifton of Nottinghamshire, or Alan Bellingham of Westmorland. Precious few of the Tories elected would prove future Jacobites. It was a telling mark of the attitudes of the MPs that James II received his most enthusiastic reception among them when he repeated his promise "to support the government in church and state as by law established." It was equally significant that John Evelyn, long a supporter of the Stuart monarchy and currently employed by James II, condemned the tenor of Roger L'Estrange's *Observator,* "which rather kept up animosities than appeased them, especially now that nobody gave the least occasion." Sir John Reresby appreciated the nuanced political situation that so many historians have missed. The Parliament, he noted, "consisted of a great many loyal gentlemen, and the generality, however, good patriots and Protestants."[28]

The surviving pamphlets written in anticipation of the Parliament of 1685 also reveal a remarkable degree of political moderation. Though the pamphleteers made their opposition to Whiggery manifest, they also emphasized their devotion to the English constitution in tones redolent of the Marquis of Halifax's classic affirmation of moderate principles *The Character of a Trimmer.* "Let other nations call themselves free, let potent princes assume what titles they please, there is none can boast of more liberty than the Englishman enjoys," boasted Robert Grove in his *Seasonable Advice to the Citizens, Burgesses, and Free-Holders of England,* "there is no monarch more absolute and really great than a king of Great Britain enthroned in the hearts and affections of his people." Grove made the limits of this absolutism clear to his readers. He lamented that "the Parliamentary way of consulting for the public good" was disappearing across Europe but celebrated the fact that "the freedom and dignity of those noble assemblies has been no where so entirely preserved as it is" in England. Freedom of speech and security of property, Grove thought, were paradigmatic English liberties. "Where every man is concerned, every man may be allowed to speak his own judgment, and to differ from whom he pleases, provided he do it with modesty and due respect," Grove insisted, "and to be menaced and frighted out of this innocent freedom, is of all slaveries the most intolerable." England was a place where industry was duly encouraged because there everyone is "assured that whatever he gains is his own property, and that not one farthing shall be demanded of him, without the consent of prudent and worthy persons, freely chosen and entrusted by the body of the nation." Grove acknowledged that some still harbored fears that James II would alter the constitution. But these fears were rendered unreasonable by the king's declaration in council, for James "was never known to fail of his word." "Liberty and property are words that chime well enough," Grove remarked, but he felt sure that the "experience" of the English would convince them that they were in no danger. He offered a simple test to the English to prove his point, a test that he was sure the regime would pass in 1685: "Has he ever been illegally imprisoned? Has any part of his goods been violently wrested from him? Has his house been rifled? Have his barns been robbed? Have his cattle been driven off his grounds? Has he suffered anything under color of authority that could not be justified by the known laws?"[29]

Other writers, though less forceful in their insistence on political moderation, made their opposition to absolutism quite apparent. The author of *The Mischief of Cabals* balanced his caustic distaste for Whig extremism with fulsome praise of the English constitution. After drawing attention to James's declaration in council, which should satisfy "the most scrupulous amongst us," this polemicist insisted that he could imagine no greater constitutional protections for English liberties since "the laws formerly made are as full and as binding, as any can be framed anew." Nor did it make any sense, from this author's perspective, for James II to want to arrogate more power to himself. "It is not to be imagined by rational men," opined the author of *The Mischief of Cabals,* "that any King of England will ever be so far overseen, as to hazard the loss of all the hearts of his people, the only support and security of Princes, to make himself somewhat more absolute, while he may even by the laws of the land, be as great a monarch as any good Christian can wish; and the frequent meetings and counsels of King and Parliament are the only means to make both Prince and people happy." Similarly, Dr. Edward Chamberlaine, in a pamphlet "making some seasonable application and proposals to the approaching Parliament," praised the efficacy of England's balanced constitution. England was, for Chamberlaine, a mixed government in which the king and subject both had significant duties and rights.[30] Clearly in the spring of 1685 anti-Whig sentiment in the nation outside Whitehall was also largely constitutionalist in sentiment.

When Parliament met in April, the members of the lower house made the limits of their royalism quite clear. The court quickly signaled a wide-ranging legislative program, which just as quickly met with resistance. The court hoped for "the repeal of the law of Habeas Corpus," which Sir John Reresby found "the great men opposed in their private discourse." Similarly, rumors circulated that the king was contemplating an act for liberty of conscience, which "if it were general, some seemed willing to grant, but resolved at the same time not in any alteration to give a capacity to the papists to come into any place or employment in the government." Interestingly, a range of MPs, including the Tories Sir Edward Seymour and the moderate Sir John Lowther of Whitehaven, complained that the government "had by their new charters altered the old way and chosen representatives themselves." Apparently many MPs felt committed simultaneously to doing their "duty to the crown but yet with a good conscience to my religion and country."[31]

Despite the moderate Toryism of the parliamentary contingent of 1685, there could be no doubting the remarkable transformation that had taken place in England. After years of concern about a "Popish Plot," the English were willing to accept and even celebrate a Catholic king. Contemporaries were well aware of this sea change in English public opinion. Sir John Reresby thought it "strange" that "so strong a party as has not long before appeared in Parliament to exclude the Duke of York from the crown of his ancestors should submit to his coming to it with so great deference and submission." Not five years earlier James "was writ against by every scribbler; vilified and abused and scandalized; talked against by most wise men who seemed very loyal," marveled the Oxford antiquary Anthony Wood, and yet "he was now proclaimed generally throughout with great applause and settled in his throne without a bloody nose. Such is the world's career." For Wood the botched Whig attempt to assassinate the king and Duke of York at Rye House in 1683 explained this change. "If the execrable design against the King be fully discovered and broken," the bishop of Oxford John Fell predicted as soon as he heard of the Rye House Plot, it would produce a profound "turn of men's minds."[32] Whig extremism combined with the apparent moderation of James on his accession, then, combined to convince most in England that the greater threat to political and social stability came from the Crown's enemies, not its supporters. There was not so much a swing to extreme Toryism as there was a revulsion against unconstitutional Whiggery. By April 1685, it was clear, the vast majority of English men and women were willing to accept a Catholic king as long as he was willing to rule within the parameters established by the English constitution in church and state.

On 11 June 1685, after a few months' planning, James, Duke of Monmouth, bastard son of Charles II, arrived at Lyme Regis in Dorset and raised the standard of rebellion against James II. Monmouth brought with him a handful of men—including the radical pamphleteer Robert Ferguson, the Scots political writer Andrew Fletcher of Saltoun, and the Rye House plotter Ford, Lord Grey—and a large supply of arms. Within days people from all over the West Country flocked to his banner. A little over a week later, on 20 June, Monmouth had himself declared king. While James II was quick to respond to the threat, it soon became clear that the local militias were insufficiently reliable to risk battle. The regular troops under the Earl of Feversham reached battle strength only in early July. They finally fought the Duke of Monmouth's army, achieving a spectacular victory at Sedgemoor, on 6 July. Monmouth's troops were broken and utterly defeated. The royalist forces captured huge numbers, and many more fled the field of battle, including Monmouth himself. Two days later Monmouth and Lord Grey were captured hiding in a cornfield. After pleading pathetically for his life, Monmouth was executed in the Tower of London on 15 July 1685. While many mourned the death of King Monmouth and others persisted in the belief that he had miraculously survived, most in England staged wild celebrations at the news of Monmouth's defeat and capture. Monmouth's defeat, rhymed one poet, "does our bliss complete, / A kingdom happy made, and monarch great."[33]

James, Duke of Monmouth and Buccleuch, by William Baillie, c. 1774. Monmouth was long seen as a charismatic and Protestant alternative to the Catholic James II.

Monmouth's Rebellion raises a number of important questions about James II's reign and the Revolution of 1688–89. Why was Monmouth resoundingly defeated in the west of England in 1685 when William III would succeed in overthrowing James II by landing in the west three years later? Why was Monmouth able to elicit some popular support for revolt in a country that had just signaled its enthusiasm for the new regime in its elections to Parliament and in hundreds of loyal addresses? Does the rebellion demonstrate the persistence of Whig radicalism, as some scholars have suggested? What does the rebellion tell us about the religiosity of English political culture in 1685?

The Duke of Monmouth raised the standard of rebellion ostensibly in defense of Whig principles. However, historians who have paid attention only to the intellectual content of Monmouth's published statements while ignoring the extent of their distribution have been misled. The Duke of Monmouth's *Declaration* poorly describes the ideology of his rebellion. Monmouth raised his standard in defense of Protestantism against a Catholic king. The vast majority of his supporters fought a religious rebellion. They risked

The Duke of Monmouth did attract
a group of religiously motivated
supporters in the West Country, but
his troops were routed by James II's
forces at Sedgemoor just weeks after
the rebellion began.

their lives not for revolutionary principles but to crown a Protestant king James in place of a Catholic one.

"Immediately upon his landing" at Lyme Regis on 11 June 1685, the Duke of Monmouth "gave forth his declaration." Supporters of the regime quickly denounced and belittled the document. The Earl of Rochester called the *Declaration* "the most villainous and abominable in its language that was ever put forth." The Earl of Ailesbury, who was extremely fond of Monmouth personally, thought the *Declaration* could only be the work of "a madman."[34] Following in this tradition of interpretation, the Whig historian Thomas Babington Macaulay later dismissed the *Declaration* as "a libel of the lowest class, both in sentiment and language."[35]

These dismissive assessments of Monmouth's *Declaration* are far too critical. The *Declaration* was a powerful and sophisticated statement of radical political aspirations. It was "the glory of England above most other nations," claimed the authors of the *Declaration,* that the power of the king had always "stood so limited and restrained by the fundamental terms of the constitution." Unfortunately, "all the boundaries of government have of late been broken and nothing left unattempted for turning our limited monarchy into an absolute tyranny."[36]

The specific criticisms that the *Declaration* leveled at the government were remarkably similar to those enunciated in the Prince of Orange's *Declaration* issued three years later. "In defiance of all the laws and statutes of the realm," Monmouth's *Declaration* complained, James II "hath called in multitudes of priests and Jesuits," allowing them to practice their religion publicly. The regime had blocked the streams of justice by "advancing those to the bench who were the scandal of the bar." James had threatened property by collecting taxes without parliamentary consent. By "packing" Parliament, by preventing free and fair elections, James and his brother had transformed that institution "which ought to be the people's fence against tyranny and the conservators of their liberties" into "the means of subverting all our laws and of establishing his arbitrariness and confirming our thralldom." The *Declaration* also complained of the new king's illegal "standing military force."[37]

Monmouth's *Declaration* called for religious toleration but condemned religious war. "Our religion," the *Declaration* did insist, was "the most valuable blessing we lay claim unto." Monmouth was "resolved to spend our blood for preserving it to ourselves and posterity." But this meant defending the religion established by law, not imposing it on others. The *Declaration* did not envision an apocalyptic struggle against Catholics, a religious war such as that called for by early Reformation enthusiasts. "We do declare," the document stated clearly and boldly, "we will not make war upon or destroy any for their religion how false and erroneous soever." Catholics were specifically comprehended among those protected. "The very Papists," the document insisted, "provided they withdraw from the tents of our enemies and be not found guilty of conspiring our destruction, or abettors of them that seek it, have nothing to fear from us, except what may hinder their altering our laws and endangering our persons, in the profession of the reformed doctrine, and exercise of our Christian worship."[38]

Although historians have assumed that the *Declaration* set the ideological agenda of Monmouth's rebellion, this claim appears unwarranted. Monmouth himself insisted that Robert "Ferguson drew [up the *Declaration*] and made me sign it before ever I read it." Whatever the truth of this assertion, there can be no doubt that Monmouth soon rejected one of the *Declaration*'s central claims. On 20 June in Taunton he had himself proclaimed king despite the *Declaration*'s promise that Parliament would decide who would be king.[39]

Not only did Monmouth himself appear uncommitted to the *Declaration*, but he and his supporters were remarkably unsuccessful in distributing the document in England. Although the *Declaration* was immediately translated into Dutch and enjoyed a wide circulation in the Netherlands and northern Germany, it was never well known in England. Unlike William's *Declaration*, which had a massive circulation before the Prince of Orange arrived in November 1688, few copies were available in England, so few that Macaulay later marveled at their rarity. Indeed, the *Declaration* probably received its widest and most detailed reading when it was presented in the House of Lords to be condemned on 15 June. If the *Declaration* had not been read there, thought Lord Delamere, who was suspected of complicity in the rebellion, "it had been a secret to them, as well as to the world that there was such a thing; for as that was the first time that it was heard of, so not any more of those prints came publicly abroad, and not one man of a million that either saw or heard the contents of that print." This was no doubt in part because Monmouth's printer, William Disney, was arrested and executed by James II and his government.[40]

More decisively, Monmouth and his followers placed a low priority on the *Declaration*. Not only did Robert Ferguson, the probable author, advise Monmouth to take the crown contrary to the *Declaration,* but Lord Grey failed even to mention the document in his excruciatingly detailed account of the rebellion. The result was that sophisticated and radical though the *Declaration* certainly was, it failed to set the ideological agenda for the rebellion. James II was right to claim that "this bitter and false invective made [very] little impression upon the sober part of the nation." If the double agent Edmund Everard was right that "the press has formerly and is of late made the chief tool of sedition both in church and state," Monmouth and his followers singularly failed in their deployment of that powerful weapon.[41]

Unsurprisingly the rebels made little or no reference to the *Declaration* during the rebellion itself or in their retrospective accounts of the parts they played in it. Most understood the rebellion either as a war of religion—the one explanation for their activities that the *Declaration* specifically denied—or as a struggle to place the legitimate king of England on the throne. The rebels, in other words, saw themselves engaged in a conservative rather than a radical activity.

From the outset many of Monmouth's supporters claimed they were fighting a great religious war. Monmouth's supporters recruited in Rotterdam by claiming they were there "to engage in this Holy War." An eyewitness to the disembarkation of Monmouth and his men at Lyme Regis on 11 June recorded that "he saw the enemy coming in a full body half way down the street and observed many townsmen and others rejoicing and joining with the enemy crying out A Monmouth, A Monmouth, the Protestant religion." One of the soldiers accompanying Monmouth on that day bragged that "we come to fight the papists." When the twenty-six maidens of Taunton presented Monmouth with a Bible, he kissed the book and proclaimed that "he came to defend the truths contained in it, or to seal them with his blood." The rebels' "banners were painted with Bibles," recalled Sir Hugh Cholmondley, and they claimed they came to "fight against a papist king and the whore of Babylon." Andrew Paschall discovered that when Monmouth's troops left Glastonbury, they were "declaring with great assurance, taken from the sudden growth in their bulk, that God was with them." Given these sentiments it is hardly surprising that when Monmouth's men reached Wells they "rifled" the cathedral. Those few rebels who

The godly maids of Taunton were
among the many who saw the Duke of
Monmouth's rebellion as a religious
uprising—part of a great Protestant
struggle against the Catholic James II.

succeeded in escaping to the Netherlands after their defeat were known to say that "the Duke of Monmouth was a martyr for his religion."[42]

Contemporary supporters of James II also thought that the rebellion was a religious war. "That which was the ground (or at least, the pretence) for the late rebellion," opined the Duke of Somerset's chaplain Edward Pelling in Westminster Abbey, "was this unreasonable jealousy which some weak men have entertained that the ark of God, which hath been (blessed be God) fixed in this kingdom hath been so glorious since the Reformation, is now in a tottering, in a falling condition, so that nothing but strong and armed hands can support it." "Look now into the very late rebellion, and then tell me what you think of it, whether it was not purely and solely fanatical?" asked the Earl of Ailesbury's chaplain and future nonjuror Shadrach Cooke. The Cornish cleric Charles Hutton reviled "the impudence" of the rebels "to appeal for heaven for the justice of their arms, and to challenge God to decide for them in the day of battle." John Churchill's troops were told before they marched to face Monmouth's forces that they were fighting men who had "drawn the sword of rebellion" upon the pretence of "fears and jealousies of popery, and a reformation in matters of religion, and to fight for the Protestant religion."

"In vain you your rebellion would excuse, / By saying 'tis for pure religion's sake," chided one contemporary poet.[43]

Most important, many of the rebels themselves claimed that they joined Monmouth for narrowly religious reasons. "I die a martyr for the Protestant religion, and merely for doing my duty in opposing of that flood of popery, which seemed to be just overwhelming the Church and interest of Christ in these nations," the condemned rebel William Jenkyn wrote to his mother just before his execution. When asked to account for his joining in the rebellion Roger Satchel replied that "he always hated the name of a Papist, and as it fell out did foresee Popery advancing." The constable of Crookhouse, John Madden, claimed that he joined Monmouth when he was convinced he was fighting "for the maintenance of the Protestant religion." William and Benjamin Hewling joined Monmouth's men, their uncle William Kiffin recalled, because they and their friends "were under great dissatisfaction seeing popery encouraged and religion and liberty like to be invaded." On hearing the news of Monmouth's landing, "the hearts of the people of God gladdened," wrote the author of the *Axminster Ecclesiastica,* the collective memoirs of the gathered church at Axminster. This community of Dissenters, a community that sent several men to fight and die with Monmouth, hoped "that this man might be a deliverer for this nation, and the interest of Christ in it, who had been even harassed out with trouble and persecution, and even broken with the weight of oppression under which they had long groaned. Now also they hoped that the day was come in which the good old cause of God and religion that had lain as dead and buried for a long time would revive again: and now was the sounding of trumpets and alarm for wars heard." "My whole design in taking up arms under the Duke of Monmouth was to fight for the Protestant religion, which my own conscience dictated me to, and which the said Duke declared for," Joseph Speed of Culleton explained to "some rude soldiers" while on the scaffold. Major Abraham Holmes, a former Cromwellian officer and Rye House plotter, adventured his life because he "believed the Protestant religion was bleeding, and in a step towards extirpation." At Sherborn the convicted rebel John Sprague explained that "he believed no Christian ought to resist a lawful power; but the case being between Popery and Protestantism altered the matter; and the latter being in danger, he believed it was lawful for him to do what he did." "O God confound our cruel foes, / Let Babylon come down," wrote Joseph Tyler a little before his execution. "Let England's king be one of them / shall raze her to the ground."[44]

While many emphasized that they supported Monmouth because they could not stomach a Catholic king, others highlighted their belief that Monmouth was in fact the rightful king of England. These two positions were not at all incompatible. Indeed, those whose anti-Catholicism was particularly strong were more likely to believe that Monmouth's mother, Lucy Walters, had been legally married to Charles II. Significantly, unlike the ideological position staked out in Monmouth's *Declaration,* both sets of beliefs were fundamentally conservative. They offered no radical criticism of the existing constitution in church and state. James II, in the eyes of Monmouth's supporters, was a usurper.

The claim that Monmouth was a legitimate son of Charles II was not new in 1685. The story had circulated widely during the Exclusion Crisis. Less than a week after Charles II's death, two soldiers proclaimed in the Black Boy tavern at Tower Ditch that "the Duke of Monmouth is right Prince of Wales and shall sway." The Presbyterian minister John Hickes made it clear on the scaffold that he shared the political principles if not the religious convictions of his Anglican brother George. "I did approve of the ancient and present form of civil government, English monarchy I am fully satisfied with," Hickes insisted. He also argued "that it is not warrantable for any subject to take up arms against, and resist their lawful sovereign and rightful princes." Hickes joined Monmouth because he was "convinced by several things that I have read and heard . . . that the late Duke of Monmouth was the legitimate son of his father Charles the Second." The Baptist Benjamin Keach, writing of John Hickes's commitment to nonresistance, thought "the rest in general [of the rebels] were of that mind." The Lyme Regis seaman Henry Boddy announced that had he believed James II "had been my lawful prince," he never would have taken up arms. The Anabaptist Samson Lark of Honiton refused under intense pressure to "own the Duke of Monmouth was a rebel." The Church of England minister Christopher Heyricke of Market Harborough was convinced that the rebellion "in the West of England was for monarchy." The Londoner Sir John Fryer, whose sympathies were clearly with the rebels, later recalled that the struggle was over who had the "right to the crown." Dissenters in many parts of the country defended Monmouth's legitimacy. Nathaniel Gauden in Essex, for example, warned Sir John Bramston that "care" was necessary in administering the oaths of allegiance and supremacy, "for the fanatics will take it with applying it to Monmouth and so have an equivocation whilst they take that oath." Similarly in Stockport in Lancashire "one Robert Gibson and Abigail his wife did much justify the Rebellion of the late Duke of Monmouth and said they did not know but that he was the king."[45]

Not only did those who fought for Monmouth do so for conservative reasons, many of England's most prominent radicals—most of whom were to support William of Orange enthusiastically in 1688–89—would have nothing to do with the duke and his rebels. Remarkably, even the English exile community in the Netherlands, men and women who had fled their native country for largely political reasons, was not unanimous in its support of the Duke of Monmouth. The exiles based in Utrecht separated themselves from the supporters of Monmouth in both geographical and ideological terms. Sir Thomas Papillon, the former East India merchant and Whig sheriff of London, refused even to lend money at interest to Monmouth and his cause. The former Whig mayor of London Sir Patience Ward refused to budge from Utrecht. James II's spies in the area reported that he was "never involved with the rebels" and that he and Papillon publicly accused Monmouth and his friends of "building castles in the air." John Starkey, the radical printer and friend of John Locke, was known by the English ambassador to be "a great rogue," but none of the government's spies were able to turn up any evidence "to put him in with" the rebels.[46] Indeed, during the rebellion the English diplomat Bevil Skelton reported that the "whole party" at Utrecht "have expressed great dislike that Monmouth hath caused himself to be proclaimed King by his rout of rebels."[47]

The great Whig polemicist and political agitator John Locke had nothing to do with Monmouth's rebellion. There can be no doubt that Locke knew and socialized with many of Monmouth's supporters. However, the evidence suggests that he, like Papillon, knew what the rebels were up to and disapproved. Just before Monmouth's departure one of Skelton's well-informed spies reported that Locke was thinking of fleeing to the East, insisting that "whenever these sorts of people begin speaking of affairs in England in his presence he would leave them dissatisfied." There seems no reason to distrust the account of Locke's close friend and biographer Jean Le Clerc, writing when it would have been no shame to admit Locke's role in the rebellion had he had one. "I believe one may rest satisfied," Le Clerc concluded, that Locke "had no correspondence with the Duke of Monmouth, of whom he had not such high thoughts as to expect anything from his undertaking."[48]

Other prominent radicals also kept their distance from Monmouth and his conservative cause. Sir Robert Peyton, the London Whig who was heard in the coffee houses of Amsterdam lecturing that "monarchs sought [only for] themselves and commonwealths the good of the people," refused to support Monmouth, accusing those who did of being "cowardly and prating fools." The former Whig sheriff of London Slingsby Bethel protested his "innocence" of involvement, pointing out that he was "not accused by any of the affidavits or informations" of any complicity in Monmouth's rebellion. The Commonwealthman and future Williamite postmaster John Wildman did all he could to temper the enthusiasm of the rebels and did little to raise support in London. He sent a message to Monmouth that he was "very much disturbed that the Duke should continue so resolved [on the invasion], contrary to the opinion of all his friends on this side." The plan, he predicted would receive no popular or financial support, "for it looked like a heedless thing and doubted it would prove so." Wildman himself, Nathaniel Wade later testified, gave Monmouth "no money for which he hath heard Monmouth curse him." The radical Taunton MP and postrevolutionary secretary of state John Trenchard "went out of England four days before" Monmouth landed England, so "mean" were his thoughts of the duke and his cause. Other West Country Whig radicals like Sir Walter Young and Sir Francis Rolle failed to support Monmouth, which made the duke "grow very melancholy." Sir John Thompson, the son of the radical merchant Maurice Thompson and "one of the earliest subscribers to invite the Prince of Orange over in the year 1688," was one of those who spoke in favor of the Duke of Monmouth's prosecution by bill of attainder in the House of Commons in June 1685. Gilbert Burnet, who would play such a prominent role as propagandist extraordinaire in 1688, "went to Paris, where he lived in great retirement, in order to avoid being involved in any of the conspiracies which the Duke of Monmouth's friends were then forming in his favor." The great Commonwealthman Edmund Ludlow, who returned to England temporarily after nearly three decades in exile in 1689, was "no ways disposed" to support Monmouth in 1685. Another prominent Whig radical, though one who would play a rather more prominent role in English politics after 1689, Richard Hampden, "would not speak with" Robert Cragg when he sought to deliver a message from Monmouth.[49]

Political radicalism and political radicals had little to do with Monmouth's rebellion. When Monmouth "took the title of king by the advice of Ferguson" at Taunton, few expressed dismay. Nathaniel Wade, who was one of the tiny group who were "for a Commonwealth" in Monmouth's camp, later lamented that "that party is much the least in the nation," much the smallest group of Monmouth's supporters. Lady Rachel Russell, whose husband had been executed for his insistence on the right to rebel against tyrannical rulers in 1683, knew quite well that Monmouth's "wild attempt" had little to do with the cause for which Lord William Russell had died. Monmouth's, she insisted, was "a new project not depending on, or being linked in the least to any former design."[50] Monmouth's rebellion was not a design engineered by political radicals. Had the rebels succeeded, they would have crowned a new king; they would not have spawned a revolution.

Despite James II's later convictions, there is strong evidence that the Prince of Orange himself strongly opposed Monmouth's invasion and rebellion. Although there had been tension between James and William almost from the moment that William had married the Duke of York's eldest daughter in 1677, that tension quickly evaporated in early 1685. James, suspicious that William's deep anti-French feelings would lead the prince to sympathize with his English political opponents, demanded "that the Prince should absolutely abandon the Duke of Monmouth and command all that depend or favor him out of the" United Provinces. To the king's surprise, William "absolutely resigned himself and them to his Majesty's pleasure." Outwardly at least there was "a wonderful reconciliation" between the Prince of Orange and the new king of England. While James remained "jealous" of the prince, there can be no doubt of William's abhorrence of Monmouth's rebellion. "I never saw the Prince of Orange so much concerned as he is for the disorder that is now in England," Bevil Skelton reported to Lord Middleton. "Monmouth's *Declaration* hath galled him to the quick, his Highness exclaiming against him as the most perfidious perjured man upon earth." Not surprisingly given his outrage, William sent his close friend Hans Willem Bentinck to England to "offer his Highness's service against the Duke of Monmouth and to let his Majesty know that there were regiments, I forgot how many, and ships ready to convey them over at an hour's warning should his Majesty desire it."[51] There can be no doubting that William had no desire to see James overthrown in 1685.

Monmouth's was not a radical rebellion. Although the political manifesto drawn up by Robert Ferguson did outline a radical agenda, that document never outlined the ideological contours of the rebellion. Monmouth and the other leaders, including Ferguson himself, were never fully committed to the *Declaration*. Perhaps as a result, the *Declaration* was never widely circulated within England. Nor did the *Declaration* strike a chord with the men who risked their lives and fortunes to support the popular duke. Instead of fighting for elective monarchy and popular sovereignty, they saw their cause as hereditary legitimacy and anti-Catholicism. In the rebels' view Monmouth stood for tradition and James for dangerous innovation.

Although Monmouth's rebellion was clearly conservative in nature, it nonetheless has retained a certain romantic appeal not unlike that of the Jacobite risings in the eighteenth century. And yet, despite the fears of contemporary supporters of the regime and the retrospective drunken boasts of the defeated rebels, the rebellion never had much chance of success. Unlike in 1688, when Englishmen of all social ranks joined William in droves and staged their own risings throughout the country, there was no support from any but religious extremists in the spring of 1685. The maverick politician Sir Richard Temple recalled that "the downright fanatical-independent ran into Monmouth upon his invasion, but very few of any note." "Monmouth's followers are a mere rout of people," noted Sir Robert Southwell, "no gentleman has gone into him." The West Country cleric Andrew Paschall later recalled the fury and rage exhibited by Monmouth and his council as it became clear that few of the Nonconformist clergy and none of the "greater men" were willing to support their cause.[52] Clearly they had made a calculation that whatever their fears, James II's promise to protect the laws in church and state offered the potential of social and political stability. Their experience of James II's regime in the first few months had been anything but tyrannical. Monmouth offered only the prospect of devastating civil war.

It is true, of course, that Monmouth did attract the support of thousands of more humble men in the West Country, men who believed that he was the legitimate king of England and that James II would soon return England to the fold of the Roman Catholic Church. But one should not overestimate the quantity or quality of that support. The most painstaking analyst of Monmouth and his supporters has concluded that Monmouth's "was not a very big army." Contemporary estimates of Monmouth's strength were wildly exaggerated. Monmouth probably had only about three thousand men at his disposal. Those who did come in to Monmouth were not crack troops but were "undisciplined and without arms." Those who had access to the widest range of information, those able to sift through and analyze the wild rumors circulating in the West Country, never seemed to have doubted the ultimate outcome. The regime was well prepared for "this mad attempt of these infatuated rebels," William Lloyd, bishop of St. Asaph, noted perhaps a bit cavalierly, "so that probably the work will be done before I shall have written this letter." "No man doubts but this insurrection will come to a very short and fatal issue to the undertakers of it," wrote Sir Robert Southwell on hearing the news of Monmouth's landing and raising troops. The lord treasurer Rochester, who had every reason to be alarmist had it been warranted, wrote to the Prince of Orange that "I think there is little fear to be had, but that the late Duke of Monmouth will pass his time as he deserves." Indeed Sir William Trumbull,

These playing cards depict the raucous celebrations that followed the defeat of Monmouth's rebellion and the fate of the unfortunate rebels. The support James gained by defeating the rebels paved the way for his modernization programs.

who served James successively as ambassador to France and the Ottoman Empire, argued in Parliament in 1685 against the creation of a large standing army on the grounds that James and his forces were able to defeat the rebels so easily.[53]

Whereas in 1688 William of Orange gained men, money, and momentum with each step he took toward an encounter with James II, the closer Monmouth and his men came to an engagement, the more likely his men were to flee. By 23 June, not two weeks after Monmouth had landed, the Duchess of Beaufort told her husband, "the rebels begin to desert their mock king." After James II issued a proclamation offering a pardon to those who deserted within four days, "a great many of the rebels" deserted. The Earl of Clarendon confirmed to the Earl of Abingdon that by early July, the rebels' "numbers decrease daily." Included in those numbers were John Speke, whose propagandistic efforts would do so much to help William's cause in 1688, and many of the members of the Axminster congregation who sought "by any means to return to their own habitations."[54]

It is of course impossible to know what would have happened had Monmouth won at Sedgemoor. However, all the evidence suggests that Monmouth's defeat was no historical accident. The conservatism of his cause meant that few political radicals—those who were active in the Exclusion Crisis and would be active again in the heady days of 1688–89—were willing to risk their all in his cause. Most in England must have reasoned that James had offered assurances not to alter the constitution in church and state, and had in fact called a Parliament. He had done nothing, or at least nothing that Charles II hadn't been doing for several years, to justify commencing an unpredictable civil war. And Monmouth did not provide a palatable alternative. No one was sure, in the words of John Wildman, "what he intended to set up or declare."[55] The only consistent themes widely espoused were Monmouth's desire to be king and the detestation that many of the rebels felt for Catholicism and a Catholic king. In 1685, it was clear, a rebellion based almost exclusively on anti-Catholicism had little chance of success. The political nation, though still a deeply religious one, was not willing to reject a monarch exclusively for his religious beliefs.

The defeat of Monmouth and his rebels in early July 1685 left James II in an extremely enviable position. Not only had he been welcomed to the Crown with unexpected and unprecedented enthusiasm, not only had he and his supporters enjoyed an overwhelming endorsement from the electorate that spring, but he had resoundingly defeated a rebellion led by his most popular personal foe.

English men and women from a wide range of political persuasions were optimistic about the new king. "The general opinion" held James II "to be a Prince steady above all others to his word," wrote Sir John Lowther, which "made him at that time the most popular Prince that had been known in England of a long time." The Earl of Burlington soon concluded that his new king was "the most indefatigable Prince in his business that ever wore the crown." Sir Richard Bulstrode learned that "all men admire and esteem [James II], the foreign ministers [are] highly satisfied in him, and he is certainly like to be the most glorious prince that ever sat upon the throne." "As the King is known to be steady in his resolutions in those things he knows to be for the good of his people and government," wrote the East India and Africa merchant Sir Benjamin Bathurst just before Monmouth's arrival in England, "so his people seem to be entirely satisfied and ready in their obedience to his law and will."[56]

After James had defeated Monmouth's rebellion, the king's subjects elevated their praise to even higher levels. The political economist William Petty now thought that James would "do such things for the common good that no king since the Conquest besides his present Majesty can so easily effect." "Never King more directly pursued the true interest of England," enthused the former Whig Sir Edmund Warcup, "and if God bless him with a long life, he will make this a more glorious nation than ever we have been." Clearly it was not only sycophantic poets who believed that with James II's accession, "the Golden Age begins anew."[57]

Far from exhibiting a deep anti-Catholic prejudice against their new king, then, the English welcomed James II with great expectations. Although a few were clearly willing to join in a religious rebellion against their monarch, the evidence suggests just how limited the appeal of an eschatological struggle was in 1685. Most people, and certainly almost everyone who had anything to lose, were willing to think and hope for the best from their new king. James II's promise to his Privy Council immediately after his brother's death had convinced a great many that the fears of arbitrary government and Catholic tyranny expressed during the Exclusion Crisis were greatly exaggerated. One should not, however, read the loyal addresses and the parliamentary elections of 1685 as evidence of popular support for absolutism. While a few certainly felt that Whig activity in the Exclusion Crisis and the machinations of the Rye House plotters in 1683 meant that the power of the king could never be too great, they were clearly a small minority. Most people in England wanted a king who would make England great and who would do so by maintaining the constitution in church and state. By the summer of 1685, the vast majority of English men and women thought that James II would do just that.

CHAPTER FIVE

The Ideology of Catholic Modernity

James II had an immense amount of political capital in the summer of 1685. He had ascended the throne peacefully, held a remarkably successful first session of Parliament, and easily brushed back a religious rebellion in England (and in Scotland as well). Those rebellions, though never posing significant military threats, had done everything to confirm that James's political opponents were fanatics, willing to destroy civil society to advance their extremist religious agendas. If the political nation had seemed supportive of James in the spring of 1685, there could be little doubt that after the summer James could count on political adulation. James appeared the perfect king for the moment. He had extensive political and military experience and, unlike his brother, did not waver in the face of adversity. Yet by the winter of 1688–89 James had apparently squandered all of this political capital. Many rose in arms against him, many more arrived in the battleships of his nephew William, Prince of Orange, and precious few were willing to defend their legitimate king, who less than four years before had been the object of popular adoration. Why did James II lose the support of his people?

Contemporaries were well aware of the interpretative problems they faced in explaining the collapse of James II's regime. In December 1688, one Londoner noted that "a history of the mobile," by which he meant the English people, "is a problem no author I meet with has encountered" successfully. The polymath John Evelyn, a historian of some note, doubted "whether in any age or place of this habitable world there is to be found

(above) *James II and Queen Mary; Accession and Coronation,* by George Bower, 1685. This medal, struck early in James's reign, compared the new king to the sun. Contemporaries would have noted the iconographic similarity with Louis XIV's self-depictions.

more convincing instances of the mutability and uncertainty of human affairs than in this little fragment of it." James II's demise, he acknowledged, presented real challenges of interpretation. "To assign the causes of these effects I undertake not," Evelyn modestly proclaimed. The explanation would fill "a volume," requiring the expertise not only of "statesmen, but of divines, historians, physicians, and natural philosophers too."[1]

Two basic lines of interpretation have emerged, one associated with the great Whig historians of the nineteenth and twentieth centuries, the other associated with a more recent school of revisionist historians. Both schools base their interpretations on wide reading in the sources, and both seek to explain not the revolution—since both schools insist that that event was largely conservative and restorative—but, narrowly, King James's fall from power.

Thomas Babington Macaulay, in his classic account, emphasizes James's misguided policies. Everything, Macaulay maintains, was "subordinate to one great design on which the king's whole soul was bent": the restoration of Roman Catholicism in the British Isles. To achieve this goal, James adopted policies that, in Macaulay's eyes, could be described only as a "tyranny, which approached to insanity," or as at best "stupid and perverse." Macaulay's great-nephew George Macaulay Trevelyan observes more neutrally that James "found it necessary to become an absolute monarch like the other princes in Europe." In Macaulay's view, James had precious few intellectual resources with which to pursue these policies. James relied on the advice of "a few Roman Catholic adventurers, of broken fortune and tainted reputation, backed by France and the Jesuits." These were "a small knot of Roman Catholics whose hearts had been ulcerated by old injuries, whose heads had been turned by recent elevation" and "having little to lose, were not troubled by thoughts of the day of reckoning." The old English Catholic families were no help. They held "a hereditary faith, sincerely, but with little enthusiasm," differing from their neighbors only "by being somewhat more simple and clownish than they." Nor could James rely on sophisticated Catholic apologetic to help in his enterprise. The Roman Catholics were able to produce "nothing of the smallest value," nothing that contemporary Protestants would have perceived as being more than "of the third rate."[2]

The results of such a misguided, reactionary, and unsophisticated policy were predictable: the entire nation turned against their king. James was forced to abandon his natural allies the Tories and the Church of England and, through the Declarations of Indulgence (1687, 1688), make a desperate bid for the support of the religious Dissenters and Whigs. Offered liberty of conscience in return for their support, "the Dissenters wavered" at first. Many eagerly embraced the freedom to worship in public after years of brutal repression. But in the end "the great body of Protestant Nonconformists" turned against James. They abandoned James gradually over the course of 1687 and 1688, with some who had initially supported the king's offer of liberty concluding that "their spiritual privileges had been abridged rather than extended by the indulgence." Experience of James II's rule led them to conclude that freedom of worship under James required "sacrificing religious

liberty." The Tories, long the supporters of a strong monarchy and defenders of the notion that kings could not be resisted, also slowly turned against James. In 1686 and 1687,
Macaulay writes, the Tories and "the church had not yet been provoked and insulted into
forgetfulness" of the doctrine of passive obedience; that time would soon come. The experience of James II's rule turned the Tories and churchmen against their monarch in 1687 and
1688. Despite their rhetoric, Macaulay points out, "the great body of Tories . . . heartily
abhorred despotism. The English government was, in their view, a limited monarchy." By
the summer of 1688, then, James's policies had alienated the entire political nation. "The
name of Whig and Tory were for a moment forgotten," Macaulay recalls. "Episcopalians,
Presbyterians, Independents, Baptists, forgot their long feud, and remembered only their
common Protestantism and their common danger." While "the fanatical and ignorant"
people had long despised James because of their "prejudice" against Roman Catholicism,
by 1688 they were joined by "the most judicious and tolerant statesmen" who had "by a
very different road" come "to the same conclusions."[3]

    James, in Macaulay's view, was not doomed to failure by virtue of his religious
beliefs. A Roman Catholic king could well have succeeded in ruling late-seventeenth-
century England. Had James "carefully abstained from violating the civil or ecclesiastical
constitution of the realm," Macaulay suggests, he would have "quieted the public apprehensions." Had James pursued "a moderate and constitutional policy, it is probable that the
great revolution which in a short time changed the whole state of European affairs would
never have taken place."[4] Macaulay's case, then, emphasizes English exceptionalism. James
failed because he pursued misguided, unrealistic, and irrational policies that had no hope
of acceptance by the people of England.

    Revisionist scholars, who self-consciously distance themselves from Whig histo-
riography, argue that James was not a religious zealot pursuing irrational policies but a
political moderate committed to the principle of religious toleration and uninterested in
claiming new or unprecedented powers. In their view, James had modest and pragmatic
objectives. Devout Catholic though he was, Robert Beddard writes, James "meant only
to ensure [Catholicism's] survival by putting his co-religionists on an equal footing with
members of the Church of England." James, writes his modern biographer John Miller,
merely wanted to allow Catholics "to worship freely and to hold public office." James had a
deep and lasting commitment to liberty of conscience, never dreaming "that the Catholics
could ever be more than a minority in England." James's modest aims for his coreligionists
were complemented by his moderate state-building agenda. He was no absolutist. James,
Miller insists, had no desire "to overthrow the laws and constitution and establish an
absolutism like that of Louis XIV."[5]

    Given James II's commitment to toleration, in the view of the revisionists, it was
hardly surprising that he received the political support of the Whigs and religious Dissenters. The revisionists, sharing the views of seventeenth- and eighteenth-century Tories,
portray the Whigs as a party united around the single issue of religious toleration and

relatively unconcerned about other political or economic issues. James II was not a Catholic king as much as he was a king committed to the principle of religious liberty. "Whig support for James," notes Mark Goldie, "went far beyond an eccentric handful." In particular the circle around John Locke, the thinker most closely associated with the Whig party, "reached a cautious accommodation with James's regime." Locke's friend James Tyrell was apparently typical of the Whigs in being "prepared to allow his objections to the King's suspension of law to be overruled by the desirability of toleration."[6]

In the revisionist account, then, it was the Tories and the members of the Church of England who turned against James in 1687 and 1688, and they did so for exclusively religious reasons. The Tories abhorred James's commitment to religious toleration. James "provoked widespread opposition from his Protestant subjects, and particularly from Tory-Anglican interests," notes Tim Harris. It was the Tories, argues Mark Goldie in the most thoroughgoing explication of the revisionist case, who "had risen in order to restrain James's popery and whiggery," who had risen "as much in horror at the spectre of upstart Baptist colonels and canting quaker merchants stalking Whitehall and guildhall, as out of repugnance for Popery and jesuitry." The Tories and the churchmen, to be sure, had not embraced theories of political resistance—they retained their commitment to passive obedience. "Anglican political theology" provided "a legitimating ideology for resistance to the crown," not by advocating overt political resistance, but by emphasizing "the duty of spiritual pastors to school their prince in true religion." These men were motivated to act "chiefly" because of their "abhorrence" of James II's policy of toleration. "It was not the absolutism of James that provoked Tory anger," Goldie states, "but the uses to which it was put." The opponents of James were defending "the law of God rather than the law of the land."[7] James failed, in the revisionist rendering, not because he managed to provoke a fundamentally liberal English political nation, but because in pursuing liberal policies James angered a narrow and bigoted political elite.

James II, in the Whig interpretation, pursued irrational Catholic policies that united the English political elite against him. In the revisionist account James II pursued moderate and tolerationist policies that provoked an intolerant and prejudiced Church of England. In my view James pursued an aggressive and very modern ideological agenda—modern not because it was particularly tolerant but because it adopted the most up-to-date notions of state building. James's political program provoked a variety of responses, many of which were themselves revolutionary. Neither the Whig nor revisionist accounts, I believe, do justice to James's ideological agenda. Neither view places James's aspirations in the sophisticated European intellectual terrain in which they developed. James was not merely a Roman Catholic. He was a Roman Catholic deeply convinced by the modern views and concerns developed at the court of Louis XIV. Louis XIV's Gallicanism, fiercely defended by the Jesuits, and bitterly criticized by Innocent XI and the rest of Catholic Europe, exalted the power of the prince and insisted on eliminating religious pluralism. James did not seek to become like other Continental monarchs, he actively sought to model his kingship on the successful and thoroughly innovative strategies specific to Louis XIV. James sought simultaneously to Catholicize the country and modernize his government. It was these practices rather than prejudice against James's religion that provoked resistance. Although the revisionists are not wrong to assert that some Anglicans opposed James on purely religious grounds and that many of those felt James could be stopped by civil disobedience, this was a small part of the story. Some Tories came to believe that James's policies merited resistance. Some more Whiggishly inclined members of the Church of England came to believe that James had subverted the constitution and should be resisted. Indeed, while many Whigs eagerly embraced James's Declaration of Indulgence in 1687, the vast majority had come to prioritize civil over religious liberty by the middle of 1688. In fact, many Roman Catholics—those whose beliefs accorded more with Innocent XI than with Louis XIV—turned against James. Nevertheless, James's policies were neither foolish nor unrealistic. It was for that reason that some Englishmen felt it necessary to draw up plans for revolutionary transformation. James II's modernizing policies demanded a modernizing response.

Historians have misunderstood James II's ideological agenda because they have insisted on studying him in a narrowly British context, whereas he and his contemporaries understood their world in European terms. James II was a Gallican Roman Catholic of the late seventeenth century. His conversion was deeply felt and well informed. But European Catholicism in the late seventeenth century was not unitary. Deep theological and political questions exercised the Church. James, when he rejoined the Church, necessarily took a position in these quarrels. It is only by taking the nature of James's Catholic commitments seriously that it becomes possible to understand his practices as king.

Europeans were keenly aware by the later 1680s that there was no love lost between His Most Christian Majesty Louis XIV and Pope Innocent XI. "That which makes most noise now is the dispute between France and the Court of Rome," observed the English envoy and playwright George Etherege of the European political scene. By late 1687 tensions between the courts of Versailles and Rome had escalated out of control. The pope refused to receive the new French ambassador, the marquis de Lavardin. In January 1688, the English ambassador in Paris Bevil Skelton heard that "two couriers come from Rome" were reporting that "the Pope has excommunicated Monsieur de Lavardin." Louis XIV was predictably outraged. He publicly declared he would take measures that "perhaps would not be very agreeable to the Pope." Rumors spread that those measures included a French invasion of papal territories and that the French king intended "to throw off the Pope's authority." For his part Innocent XI let it be known that he "firmly expects the worst his M[ost] C[hristian] M[ajesty] can do to him and that he will meet all the force he sends against him with a crucifix." Although no French troops arrived to sack Rome and Louis XIV never repudiated the pope's authority, relations between Paris and Rome remained icy. "We must expect another Pope before we see an end to this matter," observed George Etherege correctly.[8]

Tensions between the papacy and the French King did not subside over the course of the fateful year of 1688. Louis infuriated the pope by forcing the election of his candidate, William von Furstenberg, as bishop-elector of Cologne. Innocent XI claimed that the appointment was "an intrusion, a usurpation, and simioniacal." By August 1688 European observers agreed that the struggle over Cologne created "all the likelihood of a war in those parts." Louis XIV further enraged the pope by invading the papal city of Avignon in September. The papal court "is now in the height of resentment for Avignon, and the Bishop taken away prisoner," reported the English envoy at Rome John Lytcott, "so that the Pope cannot but be exasperated more and more, and if he is not able to resist with temporal arms 'tis apprehended he will employ the spiritual." The pope and his propagandists denounced Louis XIV to all who would listen. Innocent himself called the French king "the common enemy of West-Europe." His propagandists accused Louis of seeking to be "the Universal Monarch of Europe." No wonder then that the Dutch diplomat Everard van der Weede, Heer van Dijkveldt, kept a portrait of Innnocent XI in his chamber, dubbing him the "Protestant Pope."[9]

Not only did Innocent XI fear and loathe Louis XIV, he also detested the increasingly Francophile Society of Jesus. Both the Scottish Catholic William Leslie and the Scottish Protestant Gilbert Burnet concluded that in Rome the Jesuits "are looked upon as rather adversaries than friends to this court." In particular the pope feared that the Jesuits "stir up the Princes against this court, and especially France in their present conjunctures that Rome may have its mortification."[10]

At the heart of the tension between Louis XIV and Innocent XI was a conflict over sovereign authority. Their struggle began with a dispute over the right of the *regalia,* the right to enjoy the revenues of vacant bishoprics and to appoint clerics to fill the benefices dependent on those sees. By insisting on his rights to the *regalia,* Louis XIV was said by the defenders of the papacy "to have snatched out of [the pope's] hands the Patrimony of the Church." In 1682 the bishop of Meaux, Jacques-Benigne Bossuet and the archbishop of Paris, François de Harlay de Champvallon, played a pivotal role in drafting the Gallican *Declaration of the Clergy of France,* defending Louis XIV's position and denying both the pope's temporal power and his infallibility. In 1687 Louis XIV also sought to limit the pope's authority in his own dominions. Louis XIV's ambassador refused to relinquish the so-called diplomatic franchises that in effect extended diplomatic immunity to the entire quarter that housed the French embassy. Louis XIV was preventing the pope from asserting sovereignty within his own city.[11]

Innocent XI also disapproved of the violent measures Louis XIV adopted to reconcile the Huguenots to Roman Catholicism. Despite attempts by the French court, with the apparent complicity of the pope's secretary Cardinal Cybo, to keep Innocent XI ignorant of the forced conversion of the Huguenots the pope eventually learned of the extent of the *dragonnades.* He responded by elevating one of the most vocal French opponents of the dragonnades, Bishop Le Camus of Grenoble, to the dignity of cardinal in 1686. The author of the Francophobe pamphlet *The Spirit of France* was right to suggest that Innocent XI thought the conversion of the Huguenots "should have been carried on by reasonings, and good examples, and not by force and violence."[12]

Contemporaries in Britain were well aware that these Franco-papal tensions and the pope's antipathy for the Jesuits had potentially significant consequences in the British Isles. "Our gazettes and newsletters have been of late so filled with the contests between the Pope and the French King, that it has been no small part of the conversations of the town," reported Gilbert Burnet in 1682. In fact, Burnet's own tract provided a detailed account for English audiences of the Jesuit reversal on the issue of sovereignty and Pope Innocent XI's detestation of the Society of Jesus. By James II's reign, then, English audiences were well versed in these ideological disputes. "We are as impatient to hear how the great affair betwixt the Pope and the French monarch is to be determined as you can possibly imagine us to be," wrote James Fraser from London to Sir Robert Southwell. James II's courtiers were not the only ones who anxiously followed the steadily deteriorating relations between the French monarch and the pope. "I am heartily sorry for the too too great appearance of an ugly breach" between the pope and Louis XIV, wrote the Scottish Catholic Alexander Dunbar from Edinburgh. This was because the breach was doing much "hurt of the Church of God . . . whereof we begin to find in this island the sad effects, which I am afraid are just beginning." "The Pope is well known to be of the anti-Jesuitical faction, and to be implacably maligned by them, and consequently in the opposite policies to the French King, who is now the Patron General to the Jesuits as formerly the King of Spain was," the Presbyterian Roger Morrice of London noted in his entering book.[13]

Political and ideological tensions between the king of France and the pope provided the context in which James II and his court discussed Catholics and Catholicism in the later seventeenth century. As Louis XIV and Innocent XI took increasingly entrenched and belligerent positions, contemporaries were well aware that they fundamentally disagreed about royal sovereignty and the proper way of dealing with religious minorities. Both of these issues, of course, were also central concerns in the British Isles.

James II left little doubt about his ideological sympathies in the struggle between Innocent XI and Louis XIV. He increasingly surrounded himself with Jesuit and Francophilic advisers while keeping the papal nuncio and Francophobic advisers at arm's length.

James was deeply influenced by French Catholicism. He had made his abjuration in 1669 to a French-based Jesuit, Father Edward Simeon. Throughout his life James expressed "great affection" for the Jesuits. One eighteenth-century Catholic historian, very much alive to the ideological differences within European Catholicism, described James as "unfortunately bigoted to the Jesuits." A modern scholar has suggested that the Jesuits were the "guiding spirit in James's conversion and devotional life." He maintained a warm and intimate correspondence with Louis XIV's Jesuit confessor, Père de La Chaise. In the 1680s James developed a serious interest in the writings of Bossuet, a charismatic preacher and perhaps the most influential Gallican theologian of his generation. The conclusion was inescapable to interested contemporaries. "The Jesuitical party has a very great interest at court, and are very many and have the king's ear even entirely," observed Roger Morrice, "and the King of France stands by them to the utmost of his power and influence."[14]

From the moment of his abjuration, James never wavered in his commitments. To his old friend and committed Anglican the Earl of Dartmouth he professed his hope that "God would give me his grace to suffer death for the true Catholic religion." No matter what the political advantage, even if it might prevent the attempts of his political enemies to exclude him from the throne, James insisted that he would never "dissemble" nor "alter my mind in point of religion, from what it is now." That religion had from the first a French orientation. When James first told his brother Charles II in early 1669 that he had rejoined the Catholic Church, the brothers discussed "the ways and methods fit to be taken for advancing the Catholic religion in his dominions," concluding "that there was no better way for doing this great work, than to do it in conjunction with France." Though this early project of Catholicizing England never came to fruition, James retained his affinity for French-style Catholicism. As king he never missed an opportunity to praise "the greatness of spirit, the virtue and the piety" of Louis XIV. It was hardly surprising, then, that the Spanish ambassador Don Pedro de Ronquillo told his confidants that Louis XIV and James II were "in complete agreement" and were "equally opposed to the pretensions of the Pope." James was well known for his "firmness in any resolution he had once taken."[15]

Soon after his accession to the throne, James's political alliances fell into line with his devotional sympathies. Within weeks of Charles II's death, James created a separate Roman Catholic Cabinet Council that included his old friends Richard Talbot (the future Earl of Tyrconnell) and Henry Jermyn, Lord Dover. This group was at first supplemented by a second Cabinet Council that included James II's brother-in-law, the influential Earl of Rochester. James, however, placed increasing pressure on Rochester to convert to Catholicism. Rochester's refusal and his subsequent dismissal by James transformed the Catholic Cabinet into England's real governing body. This modern, svelte, and ideologically coherent group replaced the traditional and cumbersome Privy Council, the traditional royal advisory group, as the font of political power. It was in this cabinet that "principle affairs" were discussed and resolutions adopted. The religiously pluralist Privy Council had become honorific, merely ratifying the decisions of the exclusively Catholic Cabinet Council. The Privy Council, noted James's trusted Catholic military man Sir Edward Hales, existed "rather for name than business," existing merely "to declare the king's resolutions" after they had been debated and discussed in the modern "Cabinet."[16]

It was soon clear, however, that "the Catholics were not in complete agreement among themselves." The French ambassador Paul Barillon characterized the split as between "the more talented" party that had the king's ear on one hand and "the rich and established Catholics" on the other. In all of his dispatches, Barillon made clear that the Jesuits were in league with those offering "the wisest" counsel. The well-informed Roger Morrice knew that there was a struggle at court between "the Jesuitical interest under the King of France here," including the new arrivals Father Warner and Father Morgan, and the "Pope's interest" or "anti-Jesuitical party." By 1687, Morrice learned, the Jesuits supported by Père de La Chaise and Louis XIV, had "quite borne down and broken the strength of the Pope and Italian interest with us." The Augustinian abbot of Ratisbon, Placidus Fleming, who had spent a good deal of time at James II's court, concluded that the Jesuits "are there omnipotent and carry all before them like a torrent, without keeping any measures with the clergy or with us." The eighteenth-century Catholic historian Charles Dodd, who had access to a range of Catholic manuscripts that are no longer extant, agreed that "affairs were managed entirely by a cabinet council" that consisted of recent converts "and hot-headed Catholics."[17]

By 1687 all commentators agreed that James II took his advice exclusively from the French party among the Catholics. William Leslie complained bitterly from Rome that James II had a "blind preoccupied passion to only give ear to Jesuits and not hear others." Ambassador Barillon reported triumphantly to his master that "the Catholic Cabal," by which he meant the pro-French faction, "has entirely prevailed, and all the credit and all the authority is in their hands or those who openly favor them." In Germany James II was universally thought to be a "bon françois." "All, even the very best Protestants at Whitehall," Roger Morrice confided despairingly to his journal, "make their court entirely to Father Peters, Warner, Morgan, White, or some other Jesuit for no other person have any interest at all." The Dutch ambassador Arnoud Van Citters agreed that the Jesuits "daily increase in credit at the court." Though it is true, as some scholars have noted, that the Jesuits did not have an absolute monopoly of influence, all of James's advice tended in the same direction. "The Jesuits and all the regulars, even the Benedictines though professed enemies to the Jesuits, are in the French interest," observed the Scots spy James Johnston.[18]

James II surrounded himself with advisers who, invariably, had close ties to the French court and French Catholicism. One of the most prominent, and most controversial, advisers of James II was Father Edward Petre, a Jesuit. Petre came from an old English Catholic aristocratic family but had lived in France for many years before James II's accession. His sympathy for France and French Catholicism was never in doubt. Both Ambassador Barillon and Special Envoy Usson de Bonrepaus were convinced of Petre's "veneration" of Louis XIV. Those in the papal party, by contrast, complained that Petre was "too attached to the interests" of Louis XIV. When Father Petre was admitted to James's Privy Council in November 1687, Roger Morrice saw it as a signal to the pope "that he is governed by the Jesuits and not by his faction, and to let the King of France know as

*The Scientifik Three Horned Doctor, Father Peters, a Great Labourer, in Works of Darkness /
Het Stookhuys van Pater Peters, en der Jesuiten in Engeland,* 1689. This print,
published in London, satirizes Father Petre, the French-educated Jesuit who was
widely seen by contemporaries as one of the most influential of James's advisers.

much, who will be greatly satisfied therewith." Nor was there much doubt of the extent of
Petre's influence over James. Both the Protestant Earl of Ailesbury and the author of the
Jesuit provincial letters agreed that Father Petre had the new king's ear from the outset of
his reign. Petre soon replaced the apparently apolitical Father Mansuet as James's confessor
and was rewarded with elegant chambers at Whitehall. As a result, James II's courtiers
"thought no one had a greater part of the King's confidence." Surely James's repeated
appeals to the pope to confer a cardinal's cap on Father Petre confirm the Jesuit's special
relationship with his king.[19]

   Robert Spencer, Earl of Sunderland, was along with Father Petre one of "the two
principal ministers" during James II's reign. All commentators agreed that from the moment of James's accession to the throne Sunderland enjoyed the king's complete confidence.
Though Sunderland remained nominally a Protestant until June 1688, both Catholics and
Protestants knew that it was merely a matter of time before he made his religious preferences public. Sunderland, thought the son of the archbishop of York, Gilbert Dolben, "gets
nearer the king's heart than any of his fellow councilors, as being of all the most advanced
on the way to popery." Although we know little of Sunderland's private devotional proclivities, his political leanings had a decidedly French orientation. Sunderland was "an

intimate friend" of Ambassador Barillon. Both the Spanish ambassador and Roger Mor-rice described Sunderland as "the head" of the French faction at court. Sunderland was so closely tied to the Gallican group that he thought nothing of accepting a substantial bribe from Barillon to further French interests in early 1688.[20]

In 1687 and 1688 Sir Nicholas Butler joined Father Petre and the Earl of Sunderland in James II's Cabinet Council. Roger Morrice thought Butler "was as much in favor" with James II "as any one subject whatsoever, and to be privy to all counsels and to have a great influence on them." Butler's background remains murky, but it is clear that, as commis-sioner of the customs and of the treasury, he had long been a "secret councilor" to both James and his brother, Charles II. Previously a Presbyterian and a member of an Anabaptist conventicle, Butler converted to Catholicism in April 1687. Although little is known of his Catholic commitments, the facts that he was "closely allied with Lord Sunderland and Father Petre" and was well liked by Barillon hint at his Francophilia.[21]

James relied almost as heavily on the Scottish Drummond brothers as he did on Petre and Sunderland. James Drummond, Earl of Perth, was James's lord chancellor in Scotland and was widely known to be the king's chief minister north of the Tweed. His brother John, Earl of Melfort, served James II as secretary for Scottish affairs and as an increasingly influential adviser. Melfort, most commentators agree, was a man of remark-able talent. Roger Morrice thought him "a man of great abilities and policies and craft, and . . . a principal man in laying down and promoting the late methods both in Scotland and England for the setting up of the dispensing power and all things depending thereupon." William Fuller, who as a servant of the Marquis of Powis, had a chance to observe many of James II's most private debates, agreed that Melfort was "a man of most penetrating wisdom, sober, honest and zealous for his royal master's service." He added that "no noble person at court had more frequently the King and Queen's ear than my Lord Melfort had." Both Drummond brothers converted to Catholicism under James II, and both owed their conversion in part to Bishop Bossuet. "The excellent book of the Bishop of Meaux, explicat-ing the doctrine of the church," Perth wrote to Anne Huntly of his conversion, "was such a great help to me, that I should kiss the feet of this honorable bishop everyday." "One would have to close one's eyes to the light to avoid the truth," Perth wrote to Bossuet himself, "so clearly is it exposed by your excellent pen." Perth's admiration for Bossuet resulted in a lifelong correspondence between the two men. Melfort, who converted several months after his brother, also maintained close contacts with France. He conducted a regular and secret correspondence with the marquis de Seignelay, one of Louis XIV's secretaries of state. Melfort also worked closely with Père de La Chaise. James II's employment of the Drummond brothers reflected both his ability to rely on clever and competent administra-tors and his ideological attachment to French Catholicism.[22]

Not only did James choose advisers with a French Catholic orientation, but he made sure that his sons shared his Gallican orientation. James's illegitimate son James Fitzjames, Duke of Berwick, recalled that "as soon as I was seven years old [I] was sent into France, to be educated there in the Catholic, apostolic and Romish religion." In 1684 he returned to France "and by the advice of Father Peters" was placed at the Jesuit school at La Flèche. James immediately appointed his own French Jesuit chaplain, Louis Sabran, to secretly baptize and serve as chaplain to his legitimate child and heir, James Francis Edward.[23]

James did all he could to make French Catholic writings generally available. He recommended Bossuet's writings against the Huguenots to all who would listen at Whitehall. The king's printer, the recent Catholic convert Henry Hills, printed a variety of translations of French works, including those of Bossuet. Barillon thought Hills's English edition of Bossuet's *Exposition of the Doctrine of the Catholic Church* was having "a very good effect." Special Envoy Bonrepaus, apparently on orders from the marquis de Seignelay, also had a number of controversial Gallican works translated into English. For this task, Bonrepaus turned to an eager and expert translator at St. James's Palace, Henry Joseph Johnston, one of the sixteen Benedictine monks installed by James at St. James's. Professed as a monk in Lorraine in 1675, Johnston had acquired a familiarity with French Catholic apologetics. After his own conversion in 1685, Perth employed Johnston to translate and defend the writings of his favorite Catholic expositor, Bossuet. Francis Turner, bishop of Ely, observed correctly that "the arguments lately used in France" to "bring in shoals of proselytes" to the Catholic Church were being deployed in England. Bossuet, "the famous founder of this new set of expositors" of the Catholic faith, all agreed, provided the model and much of the content of Catholic publication in the 1680s.[24] The preparation and production of Catholic apologetic in England during the reign of James II had a clear French bias.

Just as the French Catholic group was winning the battle for control of James's agenda at home, so by the autumn of 1686 they had achieved hegemony over James's foreign service. James set the tone in September 1685 when he appointed Roger Palmer, Earl of Castlemaine, as his ambassador to Rome. Castlemaine had long been "a noble and cordial friend" of the Jesuits. Barillon thought that in Rome the general of the Jesuits "guided his conduct." Contemporaries were well aware that such a man was hardly calculated to curry favor with Innocent XI. His instructions from James insisted on the same rights of royal appointment that had provoked Innocent's anger against Louis XIV. Castlemaine's own views of European politics could not have been closer to those of the French king and further from the pope's. In Rome he told Cardinal Cybo that Innocent's differences with Louis XIV were "frivolous" and that the Catholic world should unite in war against the United Provinces, which were nothing but "a haven for rebels, pirates, and heretics."[25]

James's decision to appoint Ignatius White, Marquis d'Albeville, to replace Bevil Skelton as ambassador to the United Provinces was another great victory for the French faction. D'Albeville was not only an old and trusted servant of the Stuart cause but also a trusted agent of Ambassador Barillon. D'Albeville accepted money from France just before his departure for the Netherlands, making "all possible engagements" with Barillon. The

In 1685 James appointed the Earl of
Castlemaine, widely seen as sympathetic
to the Jesuits, his ambassador to Rome.
Given the open hostility between
the pope and the Jesuits, contemporaries
understood this move as an open
declaration of the king's French
sympathies.

Spanish ambassador Ronquillo had good reason to be "furious" with D'Albeville's appointment, knowing full well that he "was in the interests of France." Once in the United Provinces, D'Albeville met "nightly" with the French ambassador D'Avaux, coordinating their efforts. They clearly shared the same opinion of the United Provinces. D'Albeville thought that James II always "needed a pretext in hand to declare war against Holland, when the occasion presented itself." D'Albeville did both James II and the French a good turn when he secured the "reentrance into the bosom of the Catholic Church" of James's envoy in Hamburg Peter Wyche. It was no surprise, given the ideological orientation of James's increasingly Catholic diplomatic corps, that Wyche attended services at the French resident's chapel in Hamburg.[26]

The appointment of Bevil Skelton to replace Sir William Trumbull as ambassador to France was only an apparent contradiction of James's new policy to employ exclusively Catholics in foreign affairs. Skelton's pathological hatred of the Dutch was legendary, making him an enemy of the papal nuncio and the "country" Catholic group. Almost as important, he conducted himself as a Catholic in France. Abbot Placidus Fleming assured Charles Whyteford, the assistant principal of the Scots College in Paris, that "you will certainly find him your very good friend" even though he was unable to verify rumors that Skelton "had made public profession of the Catholic faith."[27]

James II surrounded himself not only with Catholic advisers but with advisers who had a particular orientation in European Catholic debates. Just as the increasingly hostile conflict between Louis XIV and Innocent XI forced European Catholics to take sides, so James II was compelled to choose between the pope and the French king. Although James did consult a wide variety of British and European Catholics, those Catholics were invariably on the French side of this epic dispute. No wonder Louis XIV insisted that "though there is no treaty" linking himself to James, "nevertheless the ties of agreement since his coming to the throne, have formed a more strict one than if stipulated by a formal treaty."[28]

Was James II's association with French Catholicism merely a personal affinity? Was there ideological content of the French-style Catholicism practiced at James II's court? Was the Catholicism espoused by James and his Gallicanized followers indeed uncontroversial, as historians have claimed?

Powerful evidence indicates that James and his court were taken as much with the ideological implications of French Catholicism as with its devotional precepts. Bossuet, who was so deeply influential at James II's court, was well known not only for his defense of Catholicism against its Protestant detractors but also for his enthusiastic support of royal absolutism. Bossuet's role in the absolutist Gallican *Declaration of the Clergy* of 1682 and his celebration of the effects of the revocation of the tolerationist Edict of Nantes were well known in Whitehall. Cardinal Richelieu's equally absolutist *Testament politique* was known to be "the most admired book that our great men here have seen of a long time." Another popular author at James II's court was the former Jesuit Louis Maimbourg, who was, according to the poet laureate and historiographer royal John Dryden, himself a Catholic convert, "forced to quit his order" because he "supported the temporal power of sovereigns" against "the usurpations and encroachments of the papacy." Two of Maimbourg's tracts were translated and published in England in the 1680s. In both works he more than lived up to Dryden's billing. He enthusiastically condemned the resistance theorists Robert Bellarmine and Francisco Suarez because "they most dangerously follow the conduct of heretics" in allowing resistance to kings. "Neither Popes nor Councils can ever depose kings," according to Maimbourg, because "Jesus Christ and the apostles" were the "first that have taught us that the Church and the Popes have nothing at all to do with temporal affairs." The sincere loyalty of the primitive Christians to the Roman emperors proved unequivocally, reasoned Maimbourg, that it was "the express command of God made to us in Scriptures of obeying our Princes, whoever they be."[29]

The English publications of Catholics favored by James II enunciated the same absolutist ideology advanced in the Gallican tradition. In pamphlet after pamphlet and sermon after sermon, James's Catholic supporters exalted the power of kings. The Benedictine James Maurice Corker, who lived in St. James's Palace during the later 1680s, denied that "Catholics (as Catholics) believe that the Pope hath any direct, or indirect authority over the temporal power and jurisdiction of Princes." The Roman Catholic recorder of Gloucester Charles Trinder agreed that in England there was "a monarchy, wherein the King has all the power." John Wilson, whose work was published by the Catholic royal printer Henry Hills, insisted that "the Kings of England are absolute monarchs." The Catholic author of the tract *Lex Coronae* explained that the king "holds his crown immediately from God to whom only he is accountable for his failures in the government and not to the people." In fact two tracts published by the new English Roman Catholic presses explicitly endorsed the notions of the "royal prerogative" advanced by the Gallican church.[30]

A slew of Catholic publications explained that the Jesuits had turned away from their old king-killing doctrines and were now the greatest defenders of royal authority. The author of one Catholic tract reminded his English audience that the Jesuit order publicly burned Juan de Mariana's famous tract *De Rege* "for handling problematically" the question of "killing kings." Now, the author assured his readers, the Jesuits "in all the Catholic territories where they are seated, do generally renounce that doctrine so fatal to civil authority." The Jesuit author of a 1680s commonplace book copied out a tract that insisted that "the Pope has no power or authority direct or indirect," even in the case of "apostasy, heresy, schism or any other pretext, for any matter or cause whatsoever, to depose his Sacred Majesty." No one spoke more clearly than the French-educated Jesuit and royal chaplain Edward Scarisbrick. The absolute authority of princes, he preached "is spoken to all kings, to all sovereign powers, under what form soever; and so it is to all people, in all places, at all times, and for ever; without any sort of condition, limitation, or restriction, in respect of customs, degrees, or any political sanction, or provisions."[31]

James's Catholic supporters insisted that there were no circumstances under which the king might be resisted actively or passively. John Dryden insisted that "the people are not judges of good or ill administration in their King; for 'tis inconsistent with the nature of sovereignty that they should be so." The king, in Dryden's view, "is only punishable by the king of kings." "A sovereign power, or absolute monarch," agreed John Wilson, "if he offend against these [positive] laws, is unaccountable to them, as having no superior in his dominions but God." "Is his government heavy upon us by oppression, by injustice, by all sorts of vexations?" asked Scarisbrick. "The good and the bad prince are creatures both of the same power, stamped with the same impress, and as inviolably sacred the one as the other."[32]

Contemporaries were aware that Gallicanism under Louis XIV was friendlier to the king's powers than previous theories of absolutism. This was also the case in the Catholicism of James II's court. First, James's Catholic apologists insisted on an active as well as a passive obedience to the king. Philip Michael Ellis, a Benedictine inhabitant of St. James's, preached before the king and queen that one who "behaves himself merely passive to the community" was "a monstrous member of the common-wealth, and is obliged to restitution, that is to rectify, and atone for his former coldness and indifference." Scarisbrick agreed that when it came to loyalty "sins of omission are sins of commission." "The want of love and affection is a grand failure of duty," he thundered from the pulpit, "neuters are lost to the end and service of government; and men grow cold by example." The newly created English Catholic bishops made this obligation explicit in 1688. "You lie under not only [the obligation] of a passive obedience to His Majesty's orders relating to the government," the bishops informed English Catholics in their first pastoral letter, "but also of an active and cheerful concurrence with him therein."[33]

Second, James II's French-influenced court Catholics denied that subjects had the right to question (or petition against) the king's policies. "We conjure you all to abstain from speaking or acting anything that may seem to have the least indecent reflection upon the government," wrote the Catholic bishops in their pastoral letter. The people had no right to question or query. "Their duty is," continued the bishops, "not to approach [the] persons [of kings] but with respect, nor discourse of their Councils but with submission." Scarisbrick was no less cautious. "Wherever you find private meddlers in politics, commenting upon the king's prerogatives, or haranguing to the people upon the subject of mal-administration; know it to be a seditious post and practice, that they have taken up for the undermining of the crown." "To deface the character of your temporal or spiritual superiors," agreed Philip Ellis, "is so much worse than prophaning churches and robbing altars."[34]

Gallican Catholicism clearly went much further in exalting royal authority than most High Churchmen were willing to go. Even in the wake of the Rye House Plot and Monmouth's rebellion, Anglican defenders of the royal prerogative asked only for a passive obedience to kings. The High Churchman John Kettlewell warned that when a prince "happen[s] to be misled of religion," his subjects "must not embrace his errors, nor conform to his opinion and practice in religion if they happen to be different from what the Scripture teaches." In that case the subjects must avail themselves of "their legal privileges in their own defence," and failing that, "they may have recourse to prayers and tears, or any other peaceable arts to still a Prince's rage." Even the dean of Bristol, Richard Thompson, preaching in the midst of the Monmouth rebellion, allowed that if the king's commands "are sinful," Christians "may suspend their active obedience." There were certainly a few in the Church of England, such as Thomas Cartwright, bishop of Chester, and Samuel Parker, bishop of Oxford—and perhaps others as well—who "urged that the Church of England taught an unconditional and unlimited obedience." But this was clearly new doctrine, "never believed in former ages," and advocated by few in England alongside the "French divines."[35]

James II's Catholic advisers did not merely discuss the theoretical possibilities of royal power. They sought to put those powers into practice. Both the Scottish Proclamation and English Declarations of Indulgence, establishing liberty of conscience by royal fiat in each kingdom in 1687, drew heavily on language developed in the Gallican Catholic tradition. Contemporaries were keenly aware that the Scottish Declaration's insistence that "all our subjects are to obey without reserve" was an ideological innovation. Gilbert Burnet quickly identified the provenance of the new language. "All princes, even the most violent pretenders to absolute power, till Lewis the Great's time, have thought it enough to oblige their subjects to submit to their power, and to bear whatsoever they thought good to impose upon them," Burnet observed, "but till the days of the late dragoons, it was never so much as pretended, that subjects were bound to obey their Prince without reserve."[36] The Gallican insistence on active rather than merely passive obedience provided the ideological backdrop for the Scottish Proclamation.

James's attitude toward Parliament in both England and Scotland was deeply influenced by his Gallican connections. "The Catholic Lords have forcefully represented the inconveniences of calling a Parliament," Barillon informed his master in September 1686. "They made it clear that no good could be hoped for as long as the court was divided." Similarly, the Drummond brothers thought the best hope for "placing the Catholics in security" in Scotland lay with avoiding Parliament and acting on the king's prerogative. The strategies pursued in the two kingdoms developed from the same ideological roots. It was hardly surprising that in England the recent Catholic convert Sir Nicholas Butler sought to remake the English corporations by deploying commissioners "with a power not unlike that of the Intendants of provinces in France." One of James's most intimate advisers clearly hoped to go much further in exalting royal authority. Sir Edward Hales, who was one of the lords of the Admiralty, deputy governor of the Cinque Ports, lieutenant of the Tower of London, and a recent Catholic convert left a detailed plan for augmenting royal power. Hales advised James to "abolish" parliaments because "these popular assemblies are inconsistent with monarchy as well as justice." He wanted to replace the English county militia with "dragoons." Hales also hoped to massively increase the intelligence powers of the state. "Lord Lieutenants should have some in every suspected family to send him notice of what passes," and each lord lieutenant should keep a file on "every man of any figure in his county, of what estate, what parts, what interest, what relations, what he is fit for." The ideal, Hales made clear, was "to reduce the government of our counties nearer to that of the provinces of France and consequently strangely increase the king's power."[37]

English court Catholicism, then, bore a remarkable resemblance to French Catholicism. Just at the moment that papal propagandists were calling for limitations on the powers of kings, the Catholic sermons and pamphlets promoted by James II and his courtiers emphasized the unquestionable absolute authority of their king. The court Catholics of James II's reign were not shy about exalting royal absolutism or about parading their close ideological associations with the court of Louis XIV. James and his courtiers were not political moderates as revisionist scholars have claimed. They had great plans to transform the English polity following the model of the modern French state. James did a great deal to put his Gallican ideology into practice. But even that achievement paled in comparison to what some of his intimate advisers intended.

French Catholicism also influenced the attitudes that James and his courtiers had toward religious toleration. Gallicans were not only absolutist, they also believed that force was sometimes necessary to break the will of obstinate schismatics and heretics. Because James and his closest advisers embraced the full force of Gallican beliefs, revisionist scholars are wrong to describe them as religious moderates willing to tolerate a religiously pluralist society. James, it is true, publicly and frequently, asserted his belief that "none has or ought to have any power over conscience but God." He reportedly told the Scottish Quaker Robert Barclay on the eve of William's arrival in England in 1688 that he would make any concession to appease his people "except to part with liberty of conscience, which he never would, while he lived." James told William Penn, "It was always my principle that conscience ought not to be forced and it was always my judgment men ought to have the liberty of their conscience."[38] It is also true that many Protestant Dissenters published sophisticated defenses of toleration timed to coincide with James's policy pronouncements. However, James's commitment to French-style Catholicism placed limits on his commitment to toleration.

French Catholic writings were not tolerationist. They drew on the full arsenal of Augustinian arguments for intolerance, arguing that Protestantism was both heresy and schism, emphasizing according to one recent scholar "the notion of 'conversion' through compulsion." Bossuet, who was so influential in court Catholic circles, hoped to hear soon that no former Huguenot "absents himself" from Catholic services. Louis Maimbourg praised Louis XIV for "the reduction of the remnant of our Protestants." John Evelyn, who held office under James II, was "showed" the speech of the bishop of Valence "celebrating the French King (as if he were a God) for his persecuting the poor Protestants." Of course, neither Bossuet nor Maimbourg acknowledged that force had been used in the miraculous conversion. Their denial of the existence of the dragonnades did not imply any condemnation of conversion by force. Force, they were suggesting, was a last resort that fortunately was unnecessary in this case. The language with which the French Catholics discussed the Huguenots left little doubt of the limits of their tolerance. Bossuet referred to the Protestant Reformation as a "deplorable apostasy which hath torn from the church whole nations, and which seems to prepare for the kingdom of Antichrist." The French Jesuit Dominique Bouhours was no less concerned about the implications of Protestantism. The Protestants, Bouhours recalled, "having shaken off the yoke of ecclesiastical obedience, and of allegiance to their sovereigns . . . abandoned themselves to all those disorders, which men are capable of, when they are governed by the spirit of lying." This was inevitable because "the manners of men generally grow corrupt by the same degrees that they loose their faith; so were these new heresies followed by a general licentiousness."[39] Given these dire consequences of toleration, those steeped in Gallican teaching could hardly be expected to yearn for long-term indulgence to religious minorities.

Catholic literary production promoted by James and his court was no friendlier to religious toleration. The Catholic convert and master of Sidney Sussex College, Cambridge, Joshua Basset, in a text published by the royal printer Henry Hills, sneered that in tolerant Holland he "saw such a medley of faiths, that it looked to me as Babel might have done, when God confounded their language." The English Jesuit William Darrel described the Protestant Reformation as a "disease." This was, in part, because for these English Catholics as for French Catholics, Protestantism and political rebellion were ineluctably yoked. John Dryden observed that "both the French and English Presbyterians were fundamentally and practically rebels." "This so great decay from the ancient vigor of our government, and the many difficulties in which it is of late so deeply involved, have arisen principally, if not purely, from the course of religion," posited the Catholic recorder of Gloucester Charles Trinder. Since he dated the decay from Henry VIII's succumbing to his "unbridled appetite," Trinder left his auditors and readers in little doubt that the religious troubles began with the Reformation. Surely such a dangerous religion could not be tolerated. John Betham, who was both a doctor of the Sorbonne and a future preceptor of the Prince of Wales, predicted that God would not tolerate those who refused to accept the blessings of the one true faith. "God will not have patience to expect their natural death," he warned, "but will hurry them away without the least warning."[40] These were hardly the utterances of a tolerationist lot.

The actions and statements of Catholics close to James were no friendlier to toleration. James's ambassador to the papacy, the Earl of Castlemaine, publicly displayed at Rome "his Majesty's picture with John Calvin under his feet." James's lord chancellor of Scotland, the Earl of Perth, hoped fervently that there would be no spread of Protestant conventicles in Scotland since "they are destructive to all government." The French-based commissary general of the Irish Capuchins, Lawrence Dowdall, described the newborn Prince of Wales as "the Messiah of Great Britain, whose cradle is the tomb of heresy and schism." Sir Edward Hales, though he made no specific comment about toleration among the general population, left no doubt that the state could not be religiously pluralist. The Cabinet Council, which Hales thought was the only proper forum for policy making, "must be all of a piece, uniting in the king's interest and loving one another like brothers, therefore they must all be Catholics." Similarly "the great offices should be all in Catholic hands for these are the only sorts of men the king may rely upon in all seasons." Hales's son, also Edward, described the mission of University College, Oxford, now with a Catholic master and two Jesuit chaplains, as being "to begin the restitution of the religion," which would put an end to the "deplorable breach" with the one true Church. These sentiments give a certain plausibility to Gilbert Burnet's claim to have seen in Rome a series of letters from English Catholics asserting they had "no doubt left of their succeeding in the reduction of England" to the Roman Catholic faith.[41]

There is good reason to suppose that James shared these views. Though James had long professed his sympathy for liberty of conscience, it is clear that for James, liberty of conscience was a means to an end, not a deeply felt principle. James believed deeply that with proper religious teaching his subjects would convert to Catholicism. Over and over again he informed the French ambassador Barillon that "he would do all he could to advance the Catholic religion," that "his principal goal was the establishment of the Catholic religion," and that "the end of all his designs was uniquely the establishment of the Catholic religion in England." Fortunately, James claimed, the Protestants had left him with ecclesiastical powers—powers not far distant from those being claimed by Louis XIV in his struggle against Innocent XI—"greater than those enjoyed by Catholic Kings in other countries." James apparently was quite taken with the arguments advanced in one French treatise based on Augustine's epistles on the Donatist question in which he justified imperial power to impose religious uniformity. One Jesuit reported that James told him privately "that he would convert England or would die a martyr." No wonder one well-informed French observer thought James was merely following "the example of what he had seen done in France, which served him as a model."[42]

James's response to Louis XIV's Revocation of the Edict of Nantes was hardly what one would expect from someone committed to the principle of liberty of conscience. Far from expressing outrage at the French king's reversal of a century-old policy of religious indulgence, Barillon reported that James "could not have been more overjoyed" at seeing what Louis XIV had done "to destroy heresy in his kingdom." He told the Spanish ambassador Ronquillo that the revocation "is very laudable, and that since [Louis XIV's] predecessors could" offer Protestants liberties "against the laws with much more reason could he now revoke them." James celebrated each report of the mass conversions of French Huguenots. The French governor James chose for his natural sons made no secret of his belief that "the French King had done well to oblige all his subjects to be of one religion, that [the Huguenots] were of anti-monarchical principles . . . and they were to expect no protection in England." Following Bossuet's lead, James chose to deny the extent of violence perpetrated by Louis XIV's dragoons. He had Jean Claude's gory *Account of the Persecutions and Oppressions of the Protestants of France* publicly burned as an infamous libel. More than once James told the French ambassador that Louis XIV's successes increased his own "zeal and ardor" for the "advancement of the Catholic religion in England."[43]

James's statements about religious minorities were not those of a committed tolerationist. When James spoke of Ireland, he made clear that he hoped not only to allow the Catholic majority "the free exercise of their religion" but also to award them "all the offices of war, justice and police." Nor did the king sound like a religious pluralist when he came to speak of his northern kingdom. James spoke disparagingly of Scottish "phanaticks" who visited conventicles. He had a "strong desire that only Catholics should have the right to practice their religion" in Scotland, only reluctantly conceding the political folly of such a policy. James spoke so passionately about the Catholicization of Scotland that the Catholic priest Louis Innes exclaimed, "I never in my life heard so many zealous expressions for the conversion of our poor country as from his Majesty at that time." When the English envoy in Lisbon complained that the English merchants were not allowed "the benefit of the free exercise of their religion," the Portuguese secretary of state replied that he knew James "would be no way displeased with their proceeding in this affair." To the French ambassador James "often had the occasion" to "speak against the Calvinists whom he groups along with the Presbyterians and other Nonconformists," proclaiming that they "all had republican principles and were extremely opposed to monarchy."[44]

James himself expressed views of Protestantism reminiscent of the opinions of the Gallicans. In a volume of James's writings published posthumously by his Jesuit confessor Francis Sanders, the king explained that the Protestant Reformation owed its origins and success to the worst of motives. "Pride was the occasion that Luther and Calvin revolted from the Church their Mother," he wrote. "In the lay people it was avarice that engaged them to follow these false guides, and to embrace their doctrine, to enrich themselves with the spoils of so many churches, which they robbed and whose possessions they took away by force," James lamented. The consequences of such a pernicious social movement were entirely predictable to James. "Since what they call reformation has been introduced among us," James wrote of the advent of Protestantism in England, "all the world knows the disorders it has caused there, and how our isle has been troubled by a variety of sects in the Church, and several rebellions in the state." Although James stopped short of calling for the eradication of British Protestantism, he made his predilections clear. "When we begin ill," he cautioned, referring to confessional allegiance, "and take not the right way, we ought not to wonder if we always go more and more astray."[45]

James was not the defender of religious pluralism imagined by revisionist historians. James and his Gallican supporters clearly did not shy away from anti-Protestant polemic. Instead they adopted the Gallican theology and adapted the political ideology of Maimbourg and Bossuet. Despite James's public defense of liberty of conscience before his Protestant political allies, he had no trouble giving voice to the opposite ideology among his coreligionists. The statements of James's inner circle and those Catholics whom he promoted bore no resemblance to the tolerant effusions of the Quaker William Penn or the Dissenting newspaperman Henry Care or even the West Country natural philosopher Richard Burthogge. James understood that he could gain a strategic advantage by professing support for religious toleration. But among his most trusted friends and most intimate confidants he made clear his real feelings. James's court was not suffused with an aura of religious tolerance. James, the evidence suggests, wanted to establish a Catholic church reminiscent of the Gallican church of Louis XIV.

French Catholic thinking did not, however, achieve hegemonic status during the reign of James II. Many Catholics opposed James's policies. Far from being led by cautious men, temperamentally unwilling to risk unsettling their provincial tranquility, the opposition took their cue from the Italian papal nuncio and the Spanish ambassador. Both James and his Catholic opponents had cosmopolitan ideological positions. Catholic opposition to James was part and parcel of the papal struggle against the policies and practices of Louis XIV. Sharp ideological divisions split both the English and European Catholic communities, making nonsense of descriptions of later-seventeenth-century politics and the Glorious Revolution as a straightforwardly confessional struggle.

Innocent XI was a fierce critic of James and his policies. The Earl of Ailesbury recalled that "Innocent the eleventh disapproved all that was done here." This was because Innocent knew that James sided with the Gallican faction. James Wellwood recalled that Innocent XI "was not over-fond" of James because he had "an aversion in his nature to a faction he knew King James was embarked in." Both the Frenchman Eustache Le Noble and the king's friend Ailesbury agreed that "the little indulgence which his Holiness had for King James proceeded from his intimate union with the King of France."[46]

The pope treated the ambassador from the first openly Catholic monarch of England for more than a century with the utmost contempt. By all accounts the Earl of Castlemaine had to wait out innumerable delays to receive a papal audience, and when he was at last admitted, "the Pope was seasonably attacked with a fit of coughing, which broke off the ambassador's discourse." The pope's affect gave a good indication of his policy predilections. Barillon soon reported to his master that "people are very dissatisfied here with the harshness with which the Pope has refused everything that the earl of Castlemaine has asked of him on behalf of His British Majesty." In particular Innocent XI refused first to make Father Petre a bishop and then a cardinal, despite repeated personal pleas from James. Observers were unanimous in their belief that Innocent would never willingly prefer a Jesuit or a member of the French faction. By contrast, Innocent was known to have had "frequent private audiences" in 1687 with Henry Sidney, known to be a "creature of the Prince of Orange."[47]

The papal nuncio in London soon began criticizing James's policies and his Gallican proclivities. Just as the papal envoy (he formally became nuncio in 1687) Ferdinando d'Adda was arriving in London in November 1685, Barillon warned that "ministers of the Pope and people entirely attached to the court of Rome are not well disposed to France." There was no love lost between d'Adda on one hand and Father Petre and the Jesuits on the other. Petre told James II that "Daada was a Whig." It was equally clear that d'Adda's distaste for Petre was ideological more than personal. The Scottish Catholic Richard Hay lamented that d'Adda often publicly "did no other thing but cry out against the French as heretics." In general d'Adda found much to fault in James's catholicizing policies. He discussed James's actions with Ailesbury, with whom he was quite friendly, "in a lamenting tone." James Wellwood also reported that the papal nuncio "had too much good sense to approve of all the measures that were taken [by James]." Barillon also noted d'Adda's resistance to a variety of James's policy initiatives.[48] In particular d'Adda was extremely critical of the controversial proceedings against Magdalen College in 1687 and James's use of the dispensing power.[49]

The papal nuncio's ideological proclivities were shared by the ambassador of His Most Catholic Majesty the king of Spain. Ronquillo and d'Adda worked together against the dominant French Catholic faction at court. At his first audience with the new king, Ronquillo warned James against taking advice from "the several priests about him." Already by the end of 1685 Ronquillo publicly deplored the English king's treatment of Parliament. He went so far as to proclaim that "the safety of the monarchy depended on Parliament"—a statement as radically opposed to the Gallican pronouncements on sovereignty as possible. Ronquillo complained to all who were willing to listen "that the King of England was entirely devoted to the King of France, and had made a private league or contract with him, for the destruction of Germany, Flanders and Holland." It was hardly surprising, then, that the Spanish ambassador was providing copies of William's *Declaration of Reasons* to "whosoever desired them" in late 1688.[50]

The papal nuncio and Spanish ambassador had a good deal of support from segments of the English Catholic community. Many English Catholics had long been averse to the Jesuits and the regular clergy more generally. Recent scholarship has shown that there was a lively and profound debate within the English Catholic community from the early seventeenth century between the advocates of a revived Catholic episcopate and the defenders of treating England "as a missionary territory, more like the New World than a European Christian state." The seculars, the opponents of the Jesuits, argued that "a Catholic episcopate in England would help to curb political extremism in England." These issues, it is now known, "lost none of their vigour and intensity after 1660." There was, then, a long tradition of sophisticated, cosmopolitan, anti-Jesuit, and antiregular sentiment within the English Catholic community. These divisions, no doubt, became increasingly intense when the French province of the Jesuits aligned themselves with the absolutist principles espoused by the Gallicans. During the Exclusion Crisis many English Catholics "began to calumniate the Jesuits, whom they would have exterminated forthwith by fire and sword." Father Hamerton recalled that "most Catholics" at that time castigated Jesuit "principles as pernicious to government, and leading to sedition." Little had changed by James's reign. The Presbyterian Roger Morrice knew that "most of our English papists do secretly like and favour the anti-Jesuitical faction." In the newly consecrated Catholic chapel in Holyroodhouse, a priest delivered a sermon whose "whole discourse ran against the Jesuits." After the revolution the Earl of Tyrconnel, himself no critic of the Jesuits, admitted that even among Catholics "this age will not bear being too fond of Jesuits."[51]

The deep-rooted antipathy of many British Catholics to Jesuits provided fertile ground for the development of ideological opposition to the French-style Catholicism promoted by James II's court. "All those displeased with the good intelligence with France think that the King is moving too quickly with respect to Catholicism," reported Barillon. A Jesuit intelligencer concurred, noting that "several Catholic Lords represented to the King that His Majesty was moving too quickly and too zealously for the reestablishment of his faith." "Most moderate Catholics have always, and hitherto without effect, endeavored to bring His Majesty to other maxims," noted the Dutch ambassador Van Citters. The Protestant commentators Daniel Defoe and James Wellwood both noted that James was supported by a minority of Catholics, a minority Wellwood identified as "chiefly the bigots of some religious orders and the new converts." "The Papists who have estates begin to have qualms," noted the Marquis of Halifax, who was always well informed about political maneuvers, "and would be willing to stop a career which maybe so dangerous to them in the conclusion." Many Catholics followed Innocent XI in their abhorrence of the appointment of Father Petre to the Privy Council. Roger Morrice observed along with many others that Petre "meets with far greater opposition, not only from the aversion of the English nation, but from Count Daada and all the anti-Jesuitical papists than could be foreseen."[52]

Many individual Catholics were willing to make known their opposition to James's Gallican-inflected policies. The Catholic gentleman Sir William Goring of Sussex "reproached his friends of the same religion for their folly and vanity, adding, 'you will ruin us all by it.'" Both Lord Baltimore and the Duke of Gordon let it be known that they were "of the anti-Jesuitical and anti-French faction and for the Pope's faction, and have had ill treatments therefore for some years past." This may well explain why James II had Sir Robert Sawyer call into question the charter to Maryland granted "to the Lord Baltimore's ancestors." Both the Marquis of Powis and the Earl of Middleton had little influence at court before the Revolution because they opposed the policies of the Gallican group. Powis's opposition was so well known that when a virulently anti-Catholic mob came before his London house in Lincoln's Inn Fields in 1688, the mob spared it because some cried out, "Let it alone, the Lord Powis was against the Bishops going to the Tower." The vicar apostolic John Leyburn, who had close ties to the most powerful group of pre–Civil War Catholic secular priests and later served as head of the anti-Jesuit English college at Douai, was denounced as a cowardly moderate by the Jesuits. Cardinal Philip Howard, Leyburn's former employer, also opposed "the violent courses" being taken in England, advising instead "slow, calm and moderate courses." This perhaps explains why he was so detested by the Jesuits, who "rule the roost" at James II's court.[53]

Just as the French-tinged Catholics surrounding James enunciated a clear ideological position, so the Catholics who were closer to the pope and the Habsburgs developed an alternative set of aspirations. By 1685 it was clear that those Catholics "who are closest to the court of Rome" were advising that should the king "join with the interests opposed to France, he would have the hearts of the people and great support from Parliament." These Catholics wanted "an accommodation with the Prince of Orange and Parliament," and thought of themselves as "good Englishmen" who opposed giving the king "too much absolute authority" at the expense of the "privileges and liberties" of the nation. James's November 1685 speech to Parliament in which he announced his intention to keep Roman Catholic officers illegally in the army elicited a wave of criticism from this group of Catholics. Lord Bellasis asked the Earl of Ailesbury, "Who could be the framer of this speech? I date my ruin and that of all my persuasion from this day." Still more Catholics, such as the wealthy Marquis of Powis, opposed the appointment of the Francophilic Earl of Tyrconnel as lord lieutenant of Ireland. Catholic opposition to James's plans to repeal the Test Acts and pack Parliament was more widely known. John Leyburn was among those who was extremely pessimistic about James's chances for success. While many Catholics agreed to serve their king as lord lieutenants and justices of the peace, many more did not. After perusing a variety of private manuscript collections, the Catholic historian Charles Dodd reported, "I don't find that all the Catholics were unanimous with relation to the Test."[54]

From the perspective of Catholics opposed to France and critical of the Jesuits, James II's policies were both politically unwise and ideologically offensive. These Catholics, whose views were in line with the sentiments of the Italian papal nuncio and the Spanish ambassador, detested the French-style absolutist policies advocated by James and his French-influenced advisers. Father Conne lamented in London in November 1688 that "all the mischief come upon us by [our] own faults," meaning the advice of James's chosen Catholic advisers. Abbot Placidus Fleming attributed "all the misfortunes of the late king to the ill counsel he took from the Jesuits" and in particular Father Petre, whom he deemed "one of the chief causes of all this trouble."[55] Scholars have long known that Protestants friendly to James had blamed his demise on French and Jesuit counsels. The same points were made by well-connected Roman Catholics. By the late 1680s, it is clear, a significant segment of the Roman Catholic community in England (and Britain more generally) shared Innocent XI's concerns about royal absolutism and conversion by force.

James II was ideologically committed to avant-garde French Catholicism. James had a long association with Jesuit and Gallican Catholicism, an association that he maintained and nurtured until his death. In addition to a devotional style, Gallican Catholicism involved a commitment to a heightened royal absolutism and to an Augustinian opposition to religious pluralism. These twin commitments defined the ideological program of James II's court. Although historians have tended to underestimate the influence of Gallican Catholicism because of their narrowly British interpretative focus, it would be wrong to see James's religious style as a foreign imposition. The broad European struggle between Louis XIV and Innocent XI, between Gallican and Roman Catholicism, mapped nicely onto the older struggle in England between regular and secular priests. Both sides, then, were drawing simultaneously on sophisticated cosmopolitan arguments and on deep local support within the Catholic community. The bitter ideological divisions within the Catholic community both within England and on the Continent make nonsense of understanding James II's reign as part of the great struggle between the Protestant and Catholic Reformations. The fact that the tolerationist Anglican Gilbert Burnet, so deeply despised by Anglican High Churchmen, could commiserate in Rome with Cardinal Philip Howard highlights the transformation of religious alignments since the early seventeenth century.

CHAPTER SIX

The Practice of Catholic Modernity

J ames II not only embraced French-style Catholicism as a devotional and ideological orientation, he actively sought to put his deeply held ideas to work. From
the moment of his accession to the throne, he did everything he could to create
a modern, rational, centralized Catholic state. Though not all of James's new
subjects perceived their king's intentions immediately, most soon understood the
enormity of James's project. They did so because James and his new state apparatus, with remarkable rapidity, transformed the daily lives of English men and women
of all social classes across the width and breadth of England.

The coherence and sophistication of James II's modern style of governance, however, has frequently been obscured by historians insistent on writing the history of James's
reign in periods defined by his choice of Protestant allies. In this reading James's reign
is divided between an early Tory phase and a later Whig phase. In the first phase James
depended on those, largely members of the Church of England, who defended his cause
during the attempt to exclude him from the throne (1679–81). The leaders of James's Tory
advisers were said to be his two brothers-in-law, the Earls of Rochester and Clarendon.
The Whig phase, which began with the fall of Rochester, was a time when James turned to
his former political enemies, many of whom were critics of the Church of England. Some

---

(above) *The Religious State of England,* attributed to Jan Smeltzing, 1688. The dog depicted
in this medal represents James II wearing a rosary and eating his coronation oath.
The medal, cast in Holland, records James's efforts to overturn the Test and Penal Acts,
which imposed penalties on both Catholics and Nonconformists. James II's enemies
highlighted his desire to rule in arbitrary manner with little regard for English law.

suggest that in this second phase James was able to enunciate his lifelong commitment to liberty of conscience. For others this phase was marked by incoherence. "It is difficult to say," comments J. P. Kenyon, whether Sunderland or James "possessed" a policy at all during these years.[1]

In fact, James pursued a coherent, consistent, and sophisticated political ideology—one bearing a striking resemblance to that of his neighbor Louis XIV—that he did much to put into practice during the entirety of his reign. James consistently pursued the twin goals of augmenting his own royal authority and of Catholicizing England.

James, who had spent much of his early adulthood in the French and then the Spanish army, had long believed that England needed to acquire a more efficient and powerful army. From his exile in Scotland during the Exclusion Crisis, he urged his old friend the Earl of Dartmouth that the garrisons at Chester and Berwick should not be neglected but be improved. Chester could be used "to keep that country in awe," while Berwick was "a great bridle to the south parts of this kingdom [Scotland] which are much poisoned by phanaticks; and in case of anything to do in England it could be of great consequence to have arms there to put into the hands of the loyal party that are very numerous in the four northern shires."[2] James, it is clear, saw the army as simultaneously an instrument of foreign and domestic policy.

Soon after his accession to the throne in 1685, James began to implement his long-held desire of creating a military force that would rival Continental armies. James put his deeply held beliefs in the authority of kings into political practice. The failed rebellion of his nephew the Duke of Monmouth, James openly declared, "had rendered an essential service" by demonstrating "that no reliance" could be placed on the traditional militia. The rebels "had thereby given reasons for levying and maintaining troops." The implications of Monmouth's rebellion were immediately clear to contemporaries. "We have now got a standing army, a thing the nation hath long been jealous of," wrote Humphrey Prideaux from Oxford in July 1685. Many MPs complained vociferously in the parliamentary session that autumn that England now had an army which threatened "to give up all our liberties at once."[3]

James II transformed the English military and in so doing radically altered the balance between state and society in late-seventeenth-century England. James, in the words of one historian, "created a 'modern' army." The extent of James II's military reforms makes it clear that James's political ambitions went much further than merely allowing his coreligionists to worship freely. The army that James inherited from his brother in February 1685 was "pathetically small," numbering under nine thousand troops. By November 1688 James had more than quadrupled his army in England, having about forty thousand troops at his disposal. Even though expenditures on the army had been steadily increasing in the last years of Charles II's reign, James more than tripled even those expanded average yearly outlays.[4]

The dramatic growth in the size of the army does not capture the impact of James II's standing army on English society. James transformed England's twenty-seven garrisons from dilapidated and almost abandoned stations into military strongholds. Chester in the west, Carlisle in the northwest, Berwick in the northeast, and Yarmouth in the east joined Hull, Portsmouth, and London in having prominent and powerful garrisons.[5]

England's garrisons were not large enough to house James II's standing army, so the new king requisitioned houses, inns, taverns, and coffeehouses for its use. The Petition of Right of 1628 technically prevented James from quartering troops on the civilian population. Even so, many people were compelled to quarter troops. The Leeds Dissenter Ralph Thoresby recalled that "one of the first hardships put upon us" in James II's reign was "quartering soldiers in gentlemen's houses and private families," noting with regret that "I had two for my share." The Preston Anglican Lawrence Rawsthorne similarly noted that he "had two officers quartered with me." In Carlisle landlords asserted that "they are undone by quartering of soldiers." The inhabitants of both Aylesbury in Buckinghamshire and Chester "grumbled" when the Irish Catholic military man John Eames quartered his soldiers on them.[6]

James hit on a far more extensive and legal solution to quartering his troops. Late in the summer of 1685 James decided that all inns, taverns, alehouses, and coffeehouses—all public houses that needed to purchase licenses to carry on their trades—were to be given a choice "either to receive soldiers or to lose their licenses." James's bureaucrats fanned out across the country to survey the available beds in every corner of the kingdom. The resulting document, produced in 1686, was remarkable both for its detail and for its reach. The surveyors calculated that there were just under forty-three thousand beds available in public houses scattered across 284 towns and villages. Some places, such as Bristol, Newcastle, Salisbury, and Oxford, could accommodate more than five hundred soldiers each in their public houses. Other smaller towns, like Tadcaster in Yorkshire, Trowbridge in Wilsthire, Dorking in Surrey, Tamworth in Staffordshire, or Penryn in Cornwall, could provide beds for a little more than fifty men. This was not merely a bureaucratic exercise. Troops were quartered "in public houses" in Hull, "which the town looks on as a grievance." Marmaduke Ayscough, a coffeehouse owner and barber surgeon in York, complained when he had four soldiers quartered on him, making it impossible for him to support his wife and six small children. People raised concerns about the soldiers' free quartering from "Salisbury and other places in the West" to Lancashire and Cheshire. In London, wrote one pamphleteer, "the king doth exceed the bounds of his prerogative to quarter soldiers." In fact, during the winter 1686–87, James's standing army was housed in more than a hundred towns and villages all over England.[7] In the reign of James II, the army was ubiquitous.

Not only was James II's army larger and more widely dispersed than any previous English military force, it was also more professional. James made every effort to distinguish and insulate his army from civil society. In June 1686 James decided, contrary to earlier pronouncements, that "the soldiery should be placed under martial law"—that is, that "no soldier henceforward will ever be tried by the common or statute law." James's army was no longer governed by the same rules as the rest of English society.[8]

Just as James II took devotional inspiration from French Catholicism, so he turned to France when he chose to modernize the English military. James made every effort to instill a new discipline, a new spirit, and a new efficiency in his army. To do this, James consciously imitated the most modern army in Europe, that built up in France by Louis XIV and his minister of war the marquis de Louvois. James told the French ambassador Barillon that he had learned "all he knew in the armies" of Louis XIV. The result was that he was convinced that only French military methods were good "to shape the troops and the officers" in the English army. Unsurprisingly, in early January 1686 James's secretary-at-war William Blathwayt wrote urgently to Sir William Trumbull in Paris to "make a collection of all the French military edicts, ordinances, and regulations" because these would provide the basis of instruction of the English troops gathering at Hounslow Heath the following summer. Blathwayt made clear that the French model would be followed "in these parts where the art of war has been so little practiced." Blathwayt's wishes were soon put into effect. Richard Legh of Lyme in Lancashire learned that his son "has now begun to learn the exercise of his arms according to the new mode, as is used now in the guards and abroad in the French army." Blathwayt himself reminded Sir John Reresby to drill his troops according to order "which differs from the former practice in England but is agreeable to the Rules abroad."[9]

James made the entire nation take notice of his new modern army. Each summer James organized a spectacular review of his forces at Hounslow Heath. "The entire court and almost the entire city of London" ventured out to take in the martial display. They were treated not only to precise drilling but also to reenactments of the army's great victory over Monmouth's rebel forces. The Scot William Hay was probably typical of those witnessing these displays in opining that James's new army "are the finest troops and the best mounted of any in Europe." The point, both James's supporters and critics knew well, was "to over-awe the nation." No wonder the author of one mock Catholic litany prayed that "we humbly beseech the Lord / That we may govern by the sword."[10]

Not only was the new army a novel and intrusive force in English society, it was an extremely disruptive one as well. The army may have been well drilled for battlefield operations, but it was not well disciplined when it came to interactions with civilians. Almost from the moment of the army's creation in 1685, people all over the country complained of extensive abuse from the soldiery. The West Country, where the Duke of Monmouth had raised his standard of rebellion, was the first area ravaged by the soldiers. The inhabitants were anxious to be rid of the royal army almost as soon as it arrived, explained Henry Sheres, because "we have been hitherto much their greater enemies than the rebels." The defeat and trial of the rebels did not put an end to bitter relations between the soldiers and the inhabitants of Somerset, Wiltshire, Devon, and Cornwall. Over the next three years,

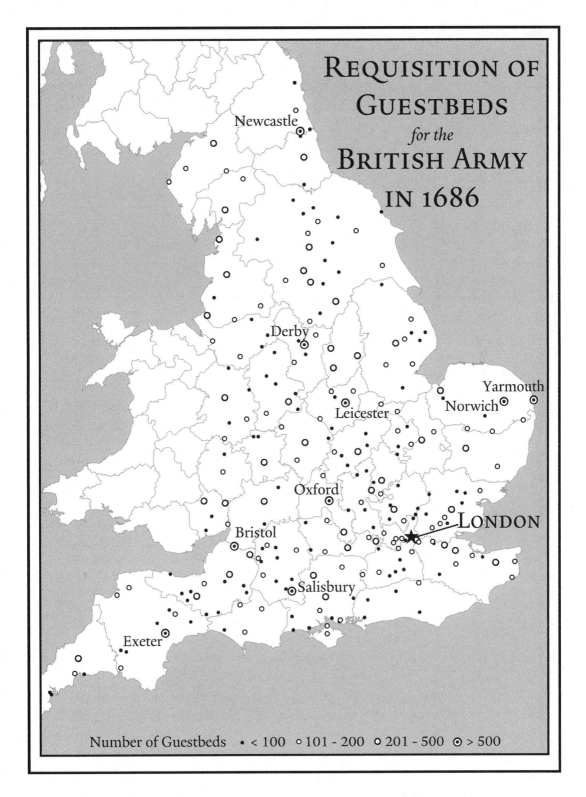

REQUISITION OF GUESTBEDS *for the* BRITISH ARMY IN 1686

Number of Guestbeds • < 100 ○ 101 - 200 ○ 201 - 500 ◉ > 500

In an effort to disperse his new professional army as widely as possible,
James surveyed the available beds in England. He demanded that innkeepers
house his soldiers or lose their license to operate. The result was an unprecedented
level of military presence throughout the width and breadth of England.

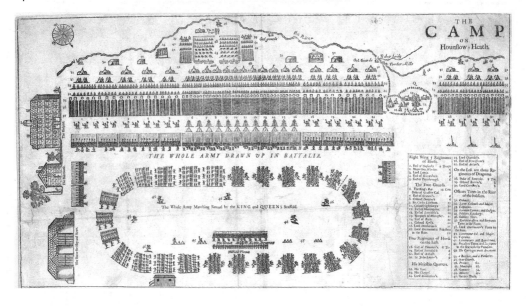

The Camp on Hounslow-Heath, 1686. Each summer James put his modernized army on display on Hounslow Heath, near London, with the intention of inspiring awe among his subjects.

the experience of the West Country was repeated over and over again all over England. Wherever soldiers were stationed, they came into conflict with civilians. Townsmen and women complained of atrocities in Carlisle near the Scottish border, in Hull in the northeast, in Wigan in Lancashire, in Leicester in the Midlands, in Chester, in Norwich, in York, and in London. In London and Norwich women were raped and killed. In York the cooper of one Edward Thompson was "run up the nostril with a sword." George Mawson, the former chamberlain of Hull, was "dragged from his own house . . . by a file of soldiers" and "fettered in an unmerciful manner" for so long that "blood gushed out both from his mouth and ears" until he "died in a miserable manner."[11]

Although James professed his commitment to liberty of conscience and promised to relieve Dissenters from the rigors of the laws against religious dissent, the message did not apparently get to his new standing army. From the West Country to the suburbs of London, soldiers disrupted Dissenting religious gatherings and made Dissenters fearful of traveling in public. The Presbyterian Daniel Defoe was speaking for thousands when he bitterly recalled "the unspeakable oppressions of the soldiery, by virtue of whose quartering at pleasure, neither men's families or persons were secure from the greatest violence."[12]

James, contrary to the impression fostered by most studies of his reign, was not focused narrowly on developments within the British Isles. He wanted a modern military machine that would make him a force to be reckoned with on the European and world stage. His standing army was much larger than necessary to maintain the peace within England. Similarly, James, who had long served as lord high admiral of England, was committed to creating a modern naval establishment.

James informed both houses of Parliament in May 1685 that the navy "was the strength and glory of the nation" and that he was determined "to carry the reputation of it yet higher in the world than ever yet it was in the time of his ancestors." In this, too, James sought to follow the model established by Louis XIV. Although we think of the French navy as second-rate, recalling its defeats at the hands of the British navy in the Seven Years' War and the Napoleonic wars, in the second half of the seventeenth century the French navy was thought to be the most modern and most powerful in Europe. Jean-Baptiste Colbert and his successors transformed France "into a great naval power," concludes one scholar. Colbert did this not just by building up the French fleet but by improving and augmenting the dockyards, increasing administrative efficiency, and retiring obsolete vessels in favor of "the most modern type" of warships. In frequent conversations with Barillon and with the French naval expert Usson de Bonrepaus, James expressed his admiration for the French navy and his desire "to imitate it." He told Bonrepaus in no uncertain terms that the French navy "was the best in Europe," emphasizing its discipline, "the good construction of its ships," and "the experience of its officers."[13]

Contemporaries agreed that the navy James inherited from his brother was in terrible condition. In 1684 Samuel Pepys, who served as secretary of the Admiralty in the last year of Charles II's and the entirety of James's reign, complained of "slackness" in the dockyards, "lewdness of discipline," and the "poverty of the captains." Years later Pepys recalled that in 1685 the best ships in the fleet were "with difficulty kept above water." Little had improved the following year when French spies reported that the English navy "was in great disorder and a very miserable state." It was at this point that James, at Pepys's request, undertook an "extraordinary application" to put the navy into a "condition of force and discipline." James, influenced by what had been done in France, created a special commission that unified the Admiralty and Navy Board, seeking to make the navy more rational, efficient, and modern.[14]

The reforms of 1686 followed the French model. Although James II spent a smaller proportion of his overall budget on the navy than had his brother, this was only because the size of James's state was so much larger. James spent one-third as much again per year on the navy as Charles II had done. The focus, however, was not on increasing the size of the fleet but on modernizing existing ships and on improving naval infrastructure. The new special commission improved the pay of naval officers, put the naval artillery in good condition, augmented the naval stores, and made an array of repairs and improvements to the fleet. The commission made significant improvements in the naval dockyards, accounting for some portion of the dramatic growth in those state industries in the second half of the seventeenth century.[15]

Contemporaries were quick to appreciate the dramatic improvement in the quality of James's navy. By November 1686 one newsletter writer predicted that the "navy will be suddenly in a better condition than it hath been in many years." Bonrepaus, never lavish in his praise, thought in 1687 that the English fleet was "in a very different condition from what it had been the previous year." James II had the confidence to brag to his French guests that his ships were now in a better condition than theirs. Pepys himself was later able to defend the proposition that during James's reign, he had helped raise "the navy of England from the lowest state of impotence, to the most advanced step towards a lasting and solid prosperity . . . the nation had ever seen it at."[16]

Not only did James modernize his military in emulation of Louis XIV, but he sought to use the tools of the state to limit public discussion and public debate. He sought, like Louis XIV, to dictate the terms of public opinion. James and his supporters felt, as had their predecessors, that public political discussion was both improper and of little value. Sermons, plays, and poems all advised people to avoid political discussion. Preaching at Westminster Abbey, Edward Pelling reminded his auditors that the primitive Christians provided a good model for political as well as religious behavior. These men and women, he pointed out, "were very diligent and honest in their several callings; they minded their own business, not meddling with matters that were out of their sphere, especially with the business of their governors." Sir George Pudsey, who would serve in James II's only Parliament and who remained a passionate supporter of the king throughout his reign, insisted that "shops were made for trade and commerce, and not for stating the question about politics, and the *arcana* of government." "Honest fellow live content, / Kindly take what God hath sent, / Think what way to pay the rent, / And strive to fly no higher," rhymed one popular balladeer, because "He's a fool (at any rate), / Medl'th with affairs of state." The epilogue to a 1685 stage play advised that all "who leave their awls, their needles, hammers, shears / To meddle with, and prate of state affairs" should be sent summarily to the madhouse.[17]

While James and his apologists may have only amplified views expressed by kings and their defenders in the last century, James had new resources and techniques with which to limit popular political discussion. James used a wide variety of government-paid spies to keep him abreast of political opposition. Politicians had used informants time out of mind, but they become an integral part of the English state only in the later seventeenth century. Between the 1650s and 1670s the yearly sums devoted to gathering domestic intelligence tripled. James almost certainly expanded those activities even farther. Barillon thought James relied heavily on his spy networks "among the factious." One of those confirmed that "men cannot be too cautious what company they keep nor what they say." "Hell scarce has more intelligence and spies, than this suspicious court in every corner," commented one fictional character about James II's regime.[18]

The new Post Office, long controlled by James, became an intrusive and effective means of surveillance. Postal spying was all the more effective and obtrusive because of the remarkable growth and development of the postal service in the later seventeenth century. All sorts of communication—business, personal, and political—was conducted through the mail. While Oliver Cromwell's secretary John Thurloe had used the still limited post office of the 1650s as a means of political surveillance, that practice had all but stopped by the 1670s. Sir Roger Whitley, who served as deputy postmaster from 1672 to 1677, insisted that "opening the mails is a thing not sufferable." Only when James consolidated his control over the post office and the new London Penny Post in the early 1680s, did political surveillance become the norm. In 1683 Charles II's Privy Council reaffirmed James's monopoly of the post and prohibited the use of alternate means of delivering mail. In 1685 the new king insisted on his monopoly rights, making it clear that he would prosecute unauthorized letter carriers.[19]

James and his postmasters throughout the country were remarkably effective in stifling the exchange of information through the post. The evidence from the London Penny Post suggests that James could depend on politically reliable postmasters to sift through the mails. Letter writers complained that the mail was opened at Preston, Oxford, Grantham, Gloucester, Dublin, and Aberdeen. No one's letters were safe. Lady Sunderland complained that "all letters are opened," as did the official Whitehall intelligencer Owen Wynne. Overseas letters were especially liable to search and seizure. "Letters to me have been frequently opened," lamented the Earl of Winchelsea, "which makes me write less frequently to my friends." In particular, friends stopped writing to friends about news. Overseas merchants, prominent clerics, Dissenters, and country gentlemen all concluded that it was "imprudent as well as dangerous to write any news." When the Marquis of Halifax received a letter from Sir William Trumbull in Paris, presumably filled with news, he promised to "burn [it] after reading." The son of the archbishop of York, Gilbert Dolben, reported that a private letter containing news "must now serve to light my pipe, for I dare not trust it by the post."[20]

James's government, again very much like Louis XIV's regime in France, was just as active in suppressing commercially produced, and ideologically unreliable, newsletters. These newsletters that the mayor of Newcastle was sure "poisons so many of his Majesty's liege people, and alienates their affections" were officially prohibited in early 1686. Judges on their circuits throughout the country reminded potential readers in the country that "all newsletters" were illegal. The result was that even Catholic supporters of the Crown were "discharged from speaking or writing any" news. James's regime particularly targeted coffeehouses, notorious as resorts for avid consumers of news. In early 1686 the mayor of London ordered the Common Council to examine every coffeehouse owner in the city as to whether "they take in any such newspapers or letters," warning them "for the time to come" they must "altogether forbear to receive or expose any manner of newsletters or papers." That summer at least one coffee man was accused "of receiving and spreading of seditious and factious letters in his coffee house." Presumably by quartering the new standing army in coffeehouses, inns, and taverns throughout the country, James was able to restrict the public dissemination of newsletters. However, newsletters had clearly reappeared in the autumn of 1688 as rumors spread of an impending descent from the Netherlands, forcing Lord Chancellor Jeffreys to warn coffeehouse owners in and around London that they would forfeit their licenses if they were found displaying newsletters.[21]

Whatever James's commitment to religious liberty, the English king was not friendly to those who took the liberty to criticize his regime in print. The Stationers Company raided booksellers in pursuit of unlicensed books. Illegal printing presses were seized. James even instructed the new governor of the Dominion of New England to ensure that "no person keep any printing press for printing." The regime actively prevented the sale and resale of Whig pamphlets. James and his supporters were especially vigilant to prevent a pamphlet debate over foreign affairs. Anti-French tracts were stopped in the press, and Dutch publications were routinely seized. The government seized "whole impressions" of Gilbert Burnet's ideologically charged account of his travels through Catholic Europe. In 1687 and 1688 James and his regulators of the press made every effort to silence the most eloquent critics of his policy of toleration by royal fiat. Authors were hounded. Printers were bullied. And booksellers' stocks were seized.[22]

James was no friendlier to popular political gatherings than he was to highbrow printed polemic. Bonfire celebrations were prohibited on Guy Fawkes Day and on Queen Elizabeth's birthday in order to disappoint "the evil designs of persons disaffected to the government who commonly make use of such occasions to turn those meetings into riots and tumults." James's government insisted on strictly licensing the peddlers and chapmen that roamed the country because so many of them were no more than "rebels" that "carry abroad and disperse without inspection schismatical and scandalous books and libels." James's handpicked lord mayor of London even went so far as to prohibit ballad singing in the streets of London because these songs might cause "great scandal to the government."[23]

James had made it clear from the outset that his government was determined to do more than merely make pronouncements: it was prepared to enforce its will ruthlessly. In his notebook the London Whig and future director of the Bank of England Brook Bridges documented the sense of political foreboding. From 1684, when James was by all accounts his brother's chief minister, through late 1685 Bridges duly recorded trial after trial of Englishmen for saying or writing things critical of James and his government. In February 1684 the radical Church of England divine Samuel Johnson was fined "upon an indictment of sedition" for the publication in 1682 of *Julian the Apostate,* a thinly veiled political diatribe against James, Duke of York. Two years later, while still in jail for his inability to pay the fine for his previous infraction, Johnson was again tried and convicted "for making and publishing two scandalous libels." Three days after Johnson's first conviction, Bridges recorded the guilty verdict against Sir Samuel Barnardiston "for writing libelous and scandalous letters reflecting upon the government." In May Bridges learned of the conviction of the Whig John Dutton Colt on a charge brought by James himself. Dutton Colt's crime was to have declared publicly, "I will be hanged at my own door before such a damned popish rascal as the Duke of York shall ever inherit the crown of England." James's accession simply accelerated the drum roll of prosecutions. In May Titus Oates, the star witness whose account of the Popish Plot led to calls to exclude James from the throne in the late 1670s and early 1680s, was found guilty of perjury and sentenced to be whipped through the streets of London five days a year for the remainder of his life. The sober and scholarly Presbyterian minister Richard Baxter was, Bridges knew, fined "for publishing a seditious comment on the New Testament." At his trial Lord Chief Justice Jeffreys shouted at Baxter, "Hadst thou been whipped out of the writing trade forty years ago, it had been happy." Unsurprisingly given Jeffreys's sentiments, the government continued to harass Baxter even after this conviction. In June 1685 another Popish Plot witness, Thomas Dangerfield, was sentenced "for publishing of libels" against James when Duke of York. His brutal sentence of public whipping proved fatal when the rabid loyalist Robert Frances of Gray's Inn "thrust the end of his cane" into Dangerfield's eye. Three days before Dangerfield's murder, Bridges recorded the conviction and execution of the longtime Whig activist William Disney for "printing a traitorous paper called the Duke of Monmouth's Declaration."[24] Just before the notebook peters out, Bridges noted the conviction of the former Whig sheriff Henry Cornish for his supposed role in the Rye House Plot to assassinate Charles II and James in 1683.

Although Brook Bridges apparently stopped noting prosecution for dangerous speech and libelous writings in 1685, it is clear that the government did not let up. Quarter sessions rolls throughout the country are filled with charges against humble men and women for publicly criticizing the regime. In Norwich, as in many other places, those "that were drunk or mad with loyalty" had "watched" those "who did either speak or insinuate that we were in danger of popery." William Penn sought and received permission from James "to bring an action" against a minister of the Church of England for calling him a Jesuit. Two of James's most loyal supporters, the Duke of Beaufort and the Earl of Peterborough, brought actions of *scandalum magnatum* against men who criticized their political behavior. In 1686 Dr. Edes of Chichester was tried and convicted for "commending in discourse" at a dinner party Philip Hunton's antiabsolutist *Treatise of Monarchie* of 1643.[25]

It was soon clear that James II had effectively implemented a very modern surveillance state. "In former time / Free conversation was no crime," rhymed one wag in 1686, "But now the place / has chang'd its face." James had "taken such care of the presses," wrote one pamphleteer days after William's arrival in 1688, "that never a malcontent in England durst whisper." John Cotton thought he lived in such "dangerous times" that it was unsafe to maintain a private library. John Lauder was so fearful that he felt obliged "to hide" his manuscript of historical observations in 1686 "and intermit my Historick Remarks till the Revolution in the end of 1688." The virtuoso Richard Bentley even advised his friend John Evelyn not to enter into a list of subscribers for a scholarly book "for fear of a *scandalum magnatum*." Samuel Masters, the preacher at Bridewell Hospital and a great supporter of the revolution, recalled that under James II the English lived in "a slavish fear" and, he thought, had "almost lost" the "liberty of thinking freely."[26]

Just as James was devoted to a French style of Catholicism, just as he built up a standing army inspired by French military methods, just as he chose to follow Colbert and Seignelay in his reforms of the navy, so he tried to shape the judiciary in the style of Louis XIV. Louis, one scholar has noted, tried "to create a solid core of loyal, capable judges at each court." James similarly applied ideological tests to judicial appointees in a modern way. In the reign of Charles II judges began to be appointed to serve at the king's pleasure rather than contingent on their good behavior. This innovation meant that both Charles and James felt emboldened to remove those judges from the common law courts whose opinions clashed with their royal masters' views. Charles removed twelve judges for political reasons in a quarter of a century of effective rule. James greatly accelerated that trend. He dismissed twelve judges from his already ideologically purified bench in less than four years.[27]

James was determined to appoint and retain judges who shared his exalted view of royal authority, who shared the view of royal authority promulgated by Louis XIV's Gallican supporters. The refusal of the majority of MPs in the House of Commons to countenance James's employment of Catholics in the army—the Test Act of 1673 made it illegal for the Crown to employ Catholics in any office—encouraged James to insist on his authority above Parliament. At the end of the Parliamentary session James pardoned the seventy-four newly commissioned Catholic officers, thus putting them beyond the sanctions of the Test Act. The "heart burning" of some people over the issue, convinced James that he needed to clarify his powers. James immediately set about canvassing legal opinions. By late November the king was convinced that he had the right to dispense with the laws against Catholics for the future and that "the judges would declare that by the laws of England the king's prerogative gave him the right to dispense with the penalties of the laws and to suspend their execution." He secured written opinions of his extensive powers to dispense. James dismissed four of the twelve common law judges—William Montagu, Sir Job Charlton, Sir Thomas Jones, and Sir Creswell Levinz—for refusing to accept that English kings had the right to dispense with parliamentary laws and claiming that such a right would "overturn the English constitution." Subsequently James dismissed three more judges, Sir Edward Herbert, Sir Francis Wythens, and Richard Holloway, for their refusal to accept the extension of martial law in peacetime. James II had certainly made it clear, as Paul Barillon observed, that he would only employ "people entirely attached to his interests and who placed no limits on his authority."[28]

Unsurprisingly, James was able to secure a judicial opinion that established virtually unlimited royal authority. In April 1686 the coachman Arthur Godden brought an action against his employer, Sir Edward Hales, for having accepted a commission as colonel in the army despite his professed Catholicism. In a widely publicized and eagerly followed case, eleven of the twelve judges ruled for the defendant Hales, on the grounds that he had a valid dispensation from the king. To most observers it was clear that the case was to ascertain "which be like to get and continue uppermost, the prerogative or the hitherto pretended liberties of the subject." Lord Chief Justice Herbert left his auditors and readers in no doubt about his opinion. "This is a case of great consequence," he admitted, "but of as little difficulty as ever any case that raised so great an expectation." Herbert ruled in favor of Hales, and the king, on the grounds that "the laws of England are the King's laws," "that it is an inseparable prerogative in the King, to dispense with penal laws upon necessity and urgent occasions," and "that the King is sole judge in that necessity." The ruling, achieved through purging the judicial bench, was of momentous significance. In the view of the French ambassador, no critic of royal power, "the prerogative attributed to the King of England has overturned the laws entirely," has put James "in a position to do many things that he could not otherwise have done without Parliament."[29]

James also followed Louis XIV in his intense desire to reform all levels of government, both in the center and in the peripheries. Both Louis and James sought to assert central control over local governance. A main feature of Louis XIV's modern governance was his control over the localities. He restricted judicial authority of the local *parlements*. He manipulated and intimidated the French provincial estates. The municipalities, according to one authority, "suffered most from the extension of royal power."[30] James, it is clear, followed a similar agenda.

James's decision to remake English government completely began with his disappointments in late 1685. Frustration with high politics at the center of government ultimately led James to the most modern and thoroughgoing set of political maneuvers that England had ever experienced. When Parliament failed to approve of James's desire to employ Roman Catholics in the army, James felt it was time to reevaluate his political circle. The king rejected the notion that he should seek advice from a broad spectrum of political opinion. He insisted that all of Charles II's problems had arisen from "divided councils." Instead, James told the French ambassador, he would retain at court and in his councils only "those who were entirely attached to his interests." The king took swift action. He dismissed the Marquis of Halifax, who was serving as lord president of the Privy Council, for his opposition to removing the Test Acts and his concerns about a standing army. In December James dismissed Henry Compton, bishop of London, both from his position of dean of the chapels royal and from the Privy Council for his "speaking more forcefully than anyone against the Catholic officers" in the House of Lords. The following year the Duke of Queensberry was dismissed from the Scottish Privy Council and from the Scottish Treasury for his Hollandophilia and for his "bad conduct" in opposing James's religious policies. When the archbishop of Canterbury, William Sancroft, was dismissed from the Privy Council in the autumn of 1686, Barillon commented simply, "The King of England has taken the resolution not to suffer anyone in the principal offices who are not entirely in his interests."[31]

It was soon clear that James wanted ideological purity not only in the great offices but in every office. James had, after all, already transformed the Privy Council into a cipher. Dismissing political moderates from this toothless body had only symbolic significance. More significantly, James began a campaign of individually "closeting" or meeting with recalcitrant MPs in order to change their points of view on key issues. James did not believe that his subjects should be free to choose to support his program of religious liberty.

The refusal of both houses of Parliament to support James in his desire to employ Catholic officers in the army not only led him to remodel the judiciary, it also provoked him to reshape Parliament. Rumors began to fly in late 1685 that James was determined to seek a statutory toleration for Catholics and Protestant Nonconformists and that he saw no way to achieve that end with the current Parliament. In order to alter the political balance in Parliament James conducted a thorough campaign of private meetings with members of both houses. In particular James targeted those who held state offices or positions in the royal household. Each man was asked individually whether he would consent to the repeal of penal laws and the revocation of the Test Acts. "Those that will not give a promise," the Westmorland Tory Sir Christopher Musgrave, who was himself closeted, explained, "but reserve themselves to the debate, it is interpreted a denial, and lose their employments." The results were dramatic. Many prominent politicians and military men, including the earl of Rochester, lost their places.[32]

Both James's supporters and his critics were aware of the novelty of the king's methods. James's predecessors had met with a few individuals in preparation for a parliamentary session. James's innovation was in the thoroughness and efficiency of his approach. Paul Barillon, not usually sensitive to such sentiments, informed Louis XIV that James's closeting campaign seemed to "many people" to be "an innovation that threatened their liberties and their privileges."[33]

Despite the king's best efforts, it had become clear by the spring of 1687 that his closeting campaign could not deliver the desired results. Although James remained optimistic—some said blindly optimistic—throughout the campaign, even he was forced to admit to the Earl of Perth that "some I depended on as to the repealing of the Tests and Penal Laws, have not answered my expectations." James finally and definitively abandoned his closeting campaign when Arthur Hebert, the rear admiral of the fleet and a man known more for his flamboyant escapades with women than for his deeply felt beliefs, refused to agree to repeal the penal laws and tests because it was "contrary to his judgment, conscience and profession." Herbert's actions apparently convinced James that even those "who should be most attached to his interests and his person" were capable and willing to disappoint him. James needed new allies.[34]

The failure of the closeting campaign led James to pursue two complementary strategies. James decided to offer liberty of conscience by royal fiat and to reform comprehensively the infrastructure of English government. James was adamant that all of his servants—whether the national political elite or local customs officers—share fully his political aspirations. James's decision to pursue the twin goals of indulgence for tender consciences—Protestant Dissenters and Roman Catholics—by royal declaration, and remodeling local and national and political life did not represent a change of course. Instead it represented a change of strategy. James remained ideologically committed to promoting

French-style government and a Gallican-tinged Catholicism. But he chose to do so now in alliance with a different set of Protestants—England's Dissenters rather than the Church of England. James, commented Barillon knowingly, had achieved "un coup d'authorité" by establishing liberty of conscience through his royal prerogative.[35]

James sought a far greater accretion of royal power by his comprehensive plan to reform local government—a plan he pursued in part to pack a parliament that would agree to repeal the Penal Laws against religious nonconformity and the Test Acts preventing dissenters from accepting office or sitting in Parliament. In order to achieve his ambitious and very modern goals, James conducted a remarkable political survey. The lords lieutenant of all the counties in England and Wales were told to ask all deputy lieutenants, justices of the peace, and members of all the corporations within their jurisdiction three questions:

1. If in case he shall be chosen Knight of the Shire, or Burgess of a town, when the king shall think fit to call a Parliament, whether he will be for taking off the Penal Laws and the Tests.
2. Whether he will assist and contribute to the elections of such members as shall be for taking off of the Penal Laws and Tests.
3. Whether he will support the King's Declaration for Liberty of Conscience, by living friendly with those of all persuasions, as subjects of the same prince, and good Christians ought to do.

The work of the lords lieutenant was supplemented by a series of local agents, all reporting to a central committee meeting in London. Although many of the regulators in the localities were Presbyterians, Quakers, and Baptists, the central committee was made up overwhelmingly of Gallican Catholics. That committee was organized by the Catholic lawyer Robert Brent and included the Catholic noblemen Powis and Castlemaine, the recent convert Sir Nicholas Butler, Father Edward Petre, the crypto-Catholic Sunderland, and Lord Chancellor Jeffreys as the lone Protestant.[36]

On 2 July 1687 James decided to dissolve his first parliament and "to attempt everything" to secure a parliament willing to repeal the Penal Laws and Test Acts. Throughout 1687 and 1688 the country was abuzz with the activities of the regulators. They fanned out across the country, made contacts with local informants, interviewed thousands of officeholders and potential officeholders, and gathered relevant local political gossip. They, along with the lords lieutenant, kept records of the results of their inquiries. The returns from the lords lieutenant began to filter back to London in October. By December the national committee was sitting "daily about regulating corporations." They continued to work diligently through the new year and into the following spring. Although opinions were and remain mixed as to whether James would have succeeded in procuring parliamentary majorities for repeal of the Penal Laws and Test Acts, no one doubted that the regulators had "as full an account of the persons and things for each corporation and place as hath

By 1687 James had embarked on
an ambitious effort to create an
ideologically sympathetic Parliament
by intervening in local government,
discovering and purging those who
would resist his program of
Catholic modernization.

hitherto been collected." The whole enterprise was remarkably careful, bureaucratic, and modern.[37]

Soon town corporations, commissions of the peace, and county lieutenants were being purged all over the country. The central committee began replacing High Churchmen and Tories with Dissenters, Catholics, and Whigs. The scale of the purges was unprecedented. The commissioners dismissed 2,199 corporation members in 103 towns, almost five times as many as had lost their places in the great corporate purge at the Restoration of the monarchy in 1662–63. This meant that in 1687–88, almost three quarters of corporate members lost their places. A separate committee headed by the Catholics Sir Nicholas Butler, Robert Brent, and John Trinder purged the London guilds. That committee did its work in two waves, the first of which, noted the Presbyterian Roger Morrice, eliminated "the drunken rotten Tories," the second, the "malicious cankered Tories." Most of the new names added to the livery lists were clearly "Dissenters or Roman Catholics." Again the extent of the transformation was astounding. More than three thousand wardens, masters, assistants, and liverymen were displaced. This was "a great alteration" indeed. The numbers were more modest among the lords lieutenant, but the results equally dramatic. Between September 1687 and March 1688 twenty-one counties changed hands in what one scholar has called "by far the most radical purge the lieutenancy had ever experienced." The three questions led to the dismissal of more than half of the deputy lieutenants as well. The carnage among the justices of the peace was no less dramatic. In a sample of nine counties, one scholar has shown, more than three quarters of the justices lost their places between 1685 and 1688. This meant that almost four hundred men lost their posts in those counties alone.[38]

Contemporaries had no trouble placing James's massive interventions into local government in their proper ideological context. William of Orange's confidant the Sieur de Dijkveld predicted that the campaign to pack Parliament would either fail miserably or create a government modeled on France. James, recalled John Milton's nephew John Phillips, had through his massive purges made "way for the introduction of a French Parliament."[39]

Not only were James's actions modeled on those of France, they were also remarkably modern. James's political interventions did not require complex negotiations with local governors. James and his committee of regulators clearly had the upper hand. They relied, in the words of one scholar, on "visiting professional bureaucrat[s]." Neither in London nor in the country at large did James depend on "the old style of mixed unity." "This," comments another student of James's activities, "was a new way of thinking." James was not a reactionary seeking to restore a world of "parliamentary selection" in which the great and the good in local communities gathered to agree upon members of Parliament rather than pursue divisive contests. James wanted to create reliable parliamentary constituencies from above. He cared more about ideological purity than local influence. In so doing he was identifiably modern. This is because local adversarial politics is not, as one historian has asserted, "fundamental to modern participation in politics." Adversarial politics is but one form that modern electoral politics might take. Modern politics just as frequently involves electoral manipulation from above.[40] In that sense, James's electoral strategy was both French and very modern.

James sought ideological purity even in branches of the government that had no direct effects on parliamentary returns. James's regulators reformed the nonparliamentary corporations of Basingstoke, Doncaster, Kingston upon Thames, and Macclesfield. James was committed to maintaining an ideologically committed army. In 1686 he dismissed a large group of "subaltern officers whom he did not think entirely attached to him." In 1687 and 1688 James had his officer corps respond to the same three questions posed by the lord lieutenants in the counties. He even attempted to have one officer who answered unsatisfactorily court-martialed. Others were merely dismissed. In early 1688 rumors spread that "all officers" in the navy who were not in favor of repealing the Test Acts and Penal Laws would be discharged. The drive for ideological purity in the navy so permeates the Admiralty papers for James's reign that one scholar commented, "It was necessary for even a chaplain to be politically sound." The Dutch ambassador heard in the spring of 1688 that any purveyors of drink—wine, beer, ale, or coffee—who required a license to ply their trade would need to reply positively to the three questions to remain in business. "All the officers of the customs and excise" were surveyed in early 1688 as to where they stood on the three questions, with the clear implication that their jobs depended on the answers.[41]

James vastly augmented the English state in the later 1680s. A recent macroanalysis of the development of the English fiscal state from 1485 to 1815 demonstrates that it was in the 1680s that English taxes began "their steep and almost continuous ascent." Although most scholars still highlight the period after 1688 as that of the rapid growth of the English state, the evidence suggests that the break with the previous tradition of state building actually took place in the reign of James II. James's massive state-building project was very expensive. James's revenue, remarked Ambassador Barillon, was much greater than that of Charles II, and so he was able to maintain his much larger army and the other "dependencies of the government." In fact, James's annual revenue was almost five hundred thousand pounds annually, or a third again larger than the last, most comfortable years of his brother's reign. How did James manage significantly to increase his revenues, facilitating the remarkable growth in the state? The answer was not that Parliament had augmented his regular income. Instead James's revenue increased because of the growth in customs revenues, in the excise tax, and in the hearth tax. The growth in hearth tax revenue was attributable to increased efficiency brought about by James's administrative centralization. The large growth in excise and customs had everything to do with the boom in overseas trade—the new duties on wine, tobacco, sugar, and vinegar alone produced an increase in James's revenue of more than three hundred thousand pounds. In other words, James was able to disrupt domestic economic production, which surely must have been the effect of the massive purges of the country's corporations and London's livery companies, because he had plumped for a political economy that emphasized the importance of colonial trade. England's rapid social and economic development in the later seventeenth century made James II's modernizing state possible. James, Bonrepaus understood, had "augmented his revenues by commerce."[42]

James sought to extend royal authority into the localities, into the lives of English men and women, as had never been achieved before. In purging the corporations, in vetting the London liveries, in surveying the lords lieutenant and JPs, James was not merely packing a parliament that he hoped would repeal the Penal Laws and Test Acts, he was establishing his power to pack future parliaments in order to pursue whatever policies he wished. James was establishing that authority in England was no longer a negotiation between the people and the king, between the localities and the center. Power descended from the king in both theory and practice.

Contemporaries were well aware that James was ruling in a new way, a new way heavily modeled on the methods and practices of Louis XIV. Both James's enemies and his friends marveled at the rapid increase in royal power. James II's "power swelled so

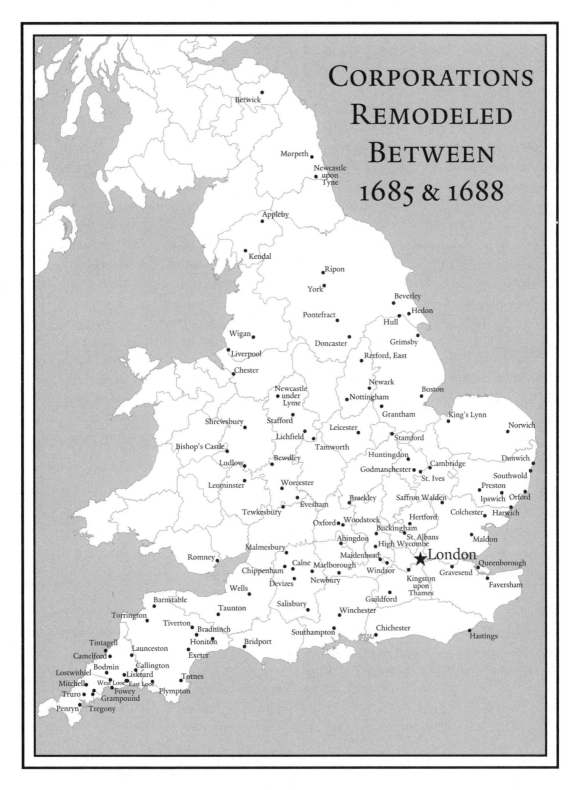

Corporations Remodeled Between 1685 & 1688

Berwick

Morpeth
Newcastle upon Tyne

Appleby

Kendal

Ripon
York
Beverley
Hedon
Pontefract
Hull
Wigan
Doncaster
Grimsby
Liverpool
Retford, East
Chester
Newark
Newcastle under Lyme
Nottingham
Boston
Grantham
King's Lynn
Shrewsbury
Stafford
Leicester
Norwich
Lichfield
Stamford
Bishop's Castle
Tamworth
Dunwich
Ludlow
Huntingdon
Southwold
Bewdley
Godmanchester
Cambridge
Preston
Leominster
St. Ives
Orford
Worcester
Ipswich
Brackley
Saffron Walden
Colchester
Harwich
Tewkesbury
Evesham
Oxford
Woodstock
Hertford
Buckingham
Abingdon
St. Albans
Maldon
Malmesbury
High Wycombe
Romney
Maidenhead
★ London
Calne
Marlborough
Queenborough
Chippenham
Windsor
Gravesend
Devizes
Newbury
Kingston upon Thames
Faversham
Wells
Guildford
Barnstable
Taunton
Salisbury
Winchester
Torrington
Tiverton
Bradninch
Southampton
Chichester
Tintagell
Honiton
Bridport
Hastings
Camelford
Launceston
Exeter
Lostwithiel
Bodmin
Callington
Mitchell
Liskeard
Totnes
Truro
West Looe
East Looe
Penryn
Fowey
Plympton
Grampound
Tregony

James extensively remodeled local government in an attempt to centralize his authority.
No region in England and Wales remained untouched.

fast," recalled the Whig critic Lord Delamere, "that he quickly makes all people to feel the intolerable burden of an unbounded prerogative." Barillon agreed that "the royal authority increases everyday by means of the firm conduct of the King of England." James, all concurred, took his measures from Louis XIV. "The French precedent was too exactly followed," lamented one pamphleteer in 1688. "Our King in imitation of his brother of France," wrote another pamphleteer drawing a similar parallel, "strives to bring all the offices and magistracy of the kingdom, that were legally of the people's choice, to be solely and immediately depending on his absolute will for their being." John Evelyn, who knew James well, recalled that that "unhappy" Prince had attempted to "make himself absolute in imitation of the French." This was not only the opinion of hostile witnesses. Usson de Bonrepaus reported on frequent conversations with James in which the English king praised "all the great actions" of Louis XIV, "his firmness, his conduct in the execution of his projects, and the marvelous order he had achieved in his realm." James had told many people that "he had rather reign one month as the King of France, than twenty years as his brother the King of England had."[43]

James's policies were not insane, stupid, or perverse. Nor did James pursue policies typical of later seventeenth-century monarchs. Instead he carefully, methodically, and above all bureaucratically promoted a series of centralizing policies that were both modern and proven to be successful. James followed a blueprint that had been perfected by Louis XIV in France. James was not merely seeking equal standing for his coreligionists. His total reshaping of English government at every level was much more ambitious than that. James was creating a centralized modern state system not dissimilar from those that political scientists have associated with electoral authoritarianism.

James, following the example of Louis XIV, rapidly built up a modern army and a modern navy, made all branches of government subservient to royal authority, and extended the power of central government deep into the localities. Neither James's political ambitions nor his political achievements were modest. But, some scholars argue, James did all this in the service of modest ideological objectives. James merely wished to place his coreligionists on an equal footing. To achieve that end in a deeply prejudiced society was no mean task. James needed to acquire the means to enforce liberty of conscience. Liberty of conscience, in other words, demanded the creation of a massive state. Does the evidence support the claim that James merely sought civil equality for Roman Catholics?

From the first James made it clear that his would be an openly Catholic court. A Catholic oratory, complete with a French Capuchin preacher, was quickly established at Whitehall, where Mass was heard publicly every morning. Roman Catholics were welcomed in Whitehall. So quick and dramatic was the transformation of the religious culture at the center of power that John Evelyn scribbled disgustedly in his diary that "the Romanists [were] swarming at court with greater confidence than had ever been seen in

England since the Reformation." Within a year the French ambassador Barillon informed his royal master that the public celebration of the Mass at Whitehall convinced many courtiers that their prejudices against the Catholic faith were misguided.[44]

Though the public reintroduction of the Catholic liturgy at the royal palace shocked some and educated others, it was not until two years after James acceded to the throne that most in England began to experience a transformation in their daily lives. Not until 1686 were most people in England exposed to Roman Catholic religious practice. But the transformation was dramatic if slow in coming. Before 1685, English men and women all over the country, no doubt, were well aware that a minority of their neighbors did not attend the parish church. But Catholic recusancy was necessarily quiet and circumspect. Catholic chaplains hid in priest holes. Catholic priests were never seen wearing their robes in the streets. There were no Catholic colleges, no publicly advertised Catholic churches. From 1686 to 1688, for the first time in more than a century, England was infused with Catholic chapels, Catholic books, Catholic sermons, Catholic schools, Catholic monks, and ambitious Catholic building programs.

James took the lead in promoting his faith in England. Immediately after his accession he released all Roman Catholics imprisoned for recusancy or for their parts in the Popish Plot. Soon the royal chapels at St. James's Palace, Somerset House, and the chapels of foreign ministers in the capital were opened for Londoners to worship. In 1686, at James's behest, a sumptuous Catholic chapel was opened in Lyme Street to accommodate Catholic merchants. James was also able to celebrate several spectacular and prominent conversions. The Earls of Peterborough and Salisbury; Thomas Chudleigh, a former envoy to the United Provinces; John Dryden the poet laureate; Dr. Robert Sibbald, a leading Scottish natural philosopher; Charles Trinder, the recorder of Gloucester; and Edward Sclater, minister of Putney all made very public conversions. James and his Gallican Catholic friends expected these were just the beginning. James as well as many others felt certain that given the freedom to choose, many would inevitably return to the faith of their forefathers.[45]

That there was a trickle rather than a flood of reconciliations with Rome convinced many contemporary Protestants, and many subsequent observers, that James was delusional in his hopes to convert England. The court's attempts to promote conversions, recalled Gilbert Burnet, "failed in most instances." "The papists are very busy to make proselytes," sneered John Lake, bishop of Chichester, "but God be blessed it is with little success."[46]

These pessimistic assessments of the efficacy of the Catholic missionary efforts in James II's reign should not, however, be taken at face value. They were, by and large, the views of Anglicans anxious to demonstrate that despite the support of the monarchy, Catholic apologetic was being defeated by the success of the Anglican counterattack. More significantly, these pessimistic assessments reflected an elitist view of conversion. It was true, as these commentators maintained, that James was not able to achieve a second or third round of spectacular reconciliations among the elite. However, these accounts reveal little about the effect and extent of the Catholic effort beyond the court and outside of the aristocracy.

Catholic sources and sources not focused so heavily on the court tell a very different story. The vicar apostolic, after touring England in 1687, came to believe that the "laity in general will not be backward in their cooperation to so pious and necessary a work."[47] John Leyburn's quiet confidence was based not on his belief in the inherent superiority of Catholic apologetic but in the knowledge of the extent and sophistication of the Catholic missionary effort.

Soon after James's accession Catholic priests began pouring into the British Isles from the Continent. The number of Jesuit priests active in England tripled between 1681 and 1685. James himself ordered home "instantly and without delay" all Scottish priests in order to aid in the missionary effort. Given the bishop of London's complaints about the widespread efforts of Catholic priests among English Dissenters, one can suppose that James made a similar request to English Catholics abroad as well.[48]

When the General Assembly of the secular English clergy resolved unanimously in 1687 "to set up chapels for the increase and propagation of the faith," they were recognizing a movement that was already well under way. Encouraged by the newly invigorated priests, many Catholic laymen "were very free of their money in erecting little chapels in several parts of the kingdom." In Worcester, for example, a Catholic chapel was already open in late 1686. The following summer "great numbers" attended services there, forcing the anti-Catholic dean of Worcester George Hickes to concede that the Catholics "are very zealous and busy to save the souls of the heretics." The Jesuits established a chapel at Norwich in which Father Charles Gage "effected wonderful conversions by his sermons." In York the Council Chamber was converted to a Catholic chapel, while the manor that was once St. Mary's Abbey was transformed into a Benedictine monastery. In Fishwick, just outside Preston in Lancashire, a barn was converted into a Catholic chapel, while a purpose-built chapel was erected in Bristol. The transformation of England's architectural landscape was manifest to all. "Throughout the entire kingdom," noted one Jesuit, "sacred edifices were seen to rise in most of the principal cities."[49]

The Catholic community did not merely provide the superstructure for religious worship, it also made sure that the intellectual and spiritual lives of Catholics received ample nourishment. Catholic devotional works, Catholic catechisms, Catholic apologetic, Catholic histories, and Catholic Bibles all spewed forth from the newly created Catholic printing presses in London and Oxford. James encouraged the dissemination and consumption of these works. In one month alone the court distributed gratis more than a hundred thousand books. Catholic schools opened all over the country. With the public support of James II, the Jesuits opened a school in the Savoy in London in May 1687. That school was so popular that the Jesuits continually added masters to accommodate the throngs wishing to enroll. The new Jesuit academy in the Savoy was joined by a school for girls in St. Martin's Lane and John Goad's private school in Piccadilly. Catholic schools and colleges

These playing cards depict the influx of Jesuit priests—part of the energetic
missionary effort that took place under James's watch—and the revival of
Catholic forms of worship, nurtured by the new Jesuit schools and chapels
established with the king's encouragement. Townspeople and villagers throughout
England quickly became aware of a pervasive new Catholic presence.

were not merely metropolitan phenomena. Mary of Modena helped finance the opening
of a Jesuit college in Wigan in Lancashire. Other Jesuit schools and colleges opened in
Lincoln, Pontefract, Gateshead, Bury St. Edmonds, and Wolverhampton. The English
secular clergy probably opened schools and colleges as well. There were certainly plans to
create an academy in Staffordshire. The Protestant Whig polemicist James Wellwood was
not exaggerating when he claimed that "Jesuit schools and seminaries [were] erected in
the most considerable towns."[50]

Catholic books, Catholic chapels, and Catholic schools provided the infrastructure
for an extensive missionary effort throughout England. It was no doubt with this effort
in mind that the political arithmetician William Petty assured his king that the English
Catholic population could be quickly and significantly augmented. Although Catholics
represented a tiny percentage of the English population at James's accession—Petty's
calculations seem to be based on the Compton Census (1676) estimate that there were
fewer than fourteen thousand Catholics—Petty was sure this could be quickly remedied.
Petty told James that with "the present liberty in England" the number of Catholics "may
within one year be 100 times their present number and proportion." Petty may have been

optimistic, but he was not outlandish in his estimates. The Jesuit Father John Penketh alone converted about five hundred to the Catholic faith between 1685 and 1688. John Leyburn, the vicar apostolic, in a tour of the north of England personally admitted to the sacrament almost twenty-one thousand people, or 150 percent of the number of Catholics thought to be in England in 1676. These figures lend plausibility to John Paul Jameson's assertion in 1685 that "there is so many becoming Catholic at London that there cannot be found priests to receive them." Small wonder that the English Jesuits reported before James II's demise that "the abundant fruit of their labors greatly increased the expectation of restoring in time the ancient religion to England."[51]

James was not misguided in thinking that, at the very least, England could become a much more heavily Roman Catholic country. Nevertheless, revisionists might claim that as extensive as the missionary effort was, as public as was the royal support it received, this was still a campaign of persuasion not of compulsion. James, revisionists might argue, was committed to liberty of conscience in part because he believed that given a free market of ideas, he was confident that the English people would choose to return to their ancient faith. However, the evidence suggests that James was not supportive of a free and open discussion of religion. His notion of liberty of conscience was quite limited indeed.

James never offered his subjects a free and open terrain on which to discuss and debate their religious beliefs. The king, it is true, twice issued Declarations of Indulgence, in 1687 and 1688, proclaiming his commitment to allowing his subjects "the free exercise of their religion for the time to come." In many ways the declarations were extremely wide-ranging, making it clear that English men and women would no longer be penalized in any way for failure to attend the Church of England. However, James was also careful to place severe limits on the kinds of expression allowable in religious assemblies. "Nothing," the authors of the Declaration insisted, could "be preached or taught" in any religious assembly "which may any ways tend to alienate the hearts of our people from Us or Our government."[52] This limitation was interpreted quite broadly by James and his Gallican supporters.

From the moment he became king, James II made it clear that criticism of his religion would be interpreted as criticism of his regime. In September 1685 the Earl of Sunderland warned the archbishop of Canterbury that sermons criticizing the king's religion were "meant against him personally" and in such cases "the minister ought to be punished." Gilbert Burnet learned that there had been much talk at court of proposing legislation in which "everything said to the dishonour of the king's religion" would have been comprehended as treason. In the spring of 1686 James infuriated many Protestants when he promised to punish severely preachers if they treated matters that would "excite the spirits" of Protestants against Catholics.[53]

James insisted that the Declaration of Indulgence was not meant to allow freedom of anti-Catholic polemic. Two pamphleteers closely associated with the court published widely read treatises on the limits of allowable religious speech. John Gother, a famous

Roman Catholic controversialist, wrote a tract published by the royal printer Henry Hills in which he offered *Good Advice to the Pulpits*. Although Gother began with a plea for civility, asking that preachers "forbear all scurrility, prophaneness, irreverent expressions, and comical declamations" when referring to other religions, it soon became clear that his concerns had a far more specific ideological thrust. Anyone who "inveighs" against the religion of the sovereign, Gother insisted, "does not look like the part of a good subject." Excoriating Catholicism "reflects upon the government of the sovereign," making James II's subjects unlikely to give the "hearty service" to their prince required by law. To underscore his point, Gother peppered his pamphlet with references to sermons that should be disallowed. Gother singled out exactly those Low Churchmen who were most critical of royal absolutism, exactly those men who would become Whig bishops in the 1690s: Thomas Tenison, Edward Fowler, Gilbert Burnet, John Tillotson, and Edward Stillingfleet. Gother's arguments and subtle hints were made explicit by the Anglican bishop of Chester, Thomas Cartwright. "If you teach the rabble to scorn the religion of the Supreme Magistrate," he warned, "they will not continue long to reverence his person or authority." Given that the king was a practicing Roman Catholic, Cartwright lectured, it was "impudent" for any member of the Church of England to preach that "St. Peter was never at Rome, or that the Pope is Antichrist; or that no man in his right wit can turn Papist." "Railing therefore against Popery," Cartwright concluded, was only to heap contempt on the king himself, "on whom all ill language against his religion does ultimately redound."[54]

Contemporaries were aware that the Declaration of Indulgence was not an invitation for frank and open discussion of religious and civil questions. Indeed, James's subjects knew well that the king's liberty of conscience was meant to mark an end of political discussion as well as an end of religious persecution. When the Presbyterian Vincent Alsop welcomed James's Declaration of Indulgence in 1687, he did so with the promise that he and his fellows "pretend not to any refined intellectuals, nor presume to philosophize upon the mysteries of government, neither to pry into the mysteries of state." James responded to Alsop by insisting that "there be no reflection on the ancient government of this nation or disloyal expressions in your assemblies." Poem after poem celebrating the declaration reiterated the same theme. "But count it a blessing sent down from above, / To end our debates and unite us in love," rhymed one popular ballad. Cartwright was typically blunt. Dissenters who misused James's gracious grant of liberty of conscience "for a cloak of maliciousness" deserved "the rod."[55]

James did not merely want to restrict hate speech in the pulpit. James wanted to put an end to religious controversy. Protestants of all denominations were supposed to refrain from discussing and elucidating their differences with Roman Catholicism. This severely circumscribed allowable topics for Protestant ministers. The clergy of the Church of England and Dissenting preachers were limited, in the view of James and his supporters, to teaching their auditors to live well. "As long as the pulpits employ themselves in correcting the vices of their congregations, in teaching them to lead good lives, not to use frauds, nor cheat, nor lie, nor swear, nor blaspheme, to avoid all excesses," John Gother explained, "I applaud them." Going beyond that was exceeding what was allowable. "Practical preachers will do the church more service than polemical," agreed Cartwright, by which he meant those who taught their auditors "to become better livers and better subjects." James did not create a space for open and free discussion of differing religious positions. Instead James created a situation in which Gallican Catholics were freed to publish and preach polemical expositions of their faith while Protestants were allowed to preach good morals. Protestants, James Wellwood recalled, were forbidden "to defend their religion in the pulpit, when it was at the same time attacked by Romish priests with all the vigor they were capable of, both in their sermons and their books."[56]

As always, James made sure that his ideological commitments were put into practice. Protestants quickly learned that they would have little freedom of religious expression during his reign. Although scholars have correctly emphasized the cruel and vindictive roles that informers played among Dissenters in the early 1680s, it would be a mistake to think that James halted those practices. James and his government were just as reliant on religious spies. James maintained a wide array of "emissaries" among the factious, reported Barillon, and these made "a great impression upon his spirit." James widened the scope of the activities of informers. "Such fellows were posted in all churches," remembered James's friend the Earl of Ailesbury. A range of Anglican clerics confirmed that the Catholics "have their spies in our churches." There is every reason to believe one report that claimed that a group of Catholic clergy in England and Wales had determined "that in every parish one or two persons shall be appointed to attend the Protestant meetings to see or hear what may fall amiss from them and to inform their superiors of what they shall find worth observation."[57]

In the summer of 1686 James created a new institution, the Commission for Ecclesiastical Causes, that had as its prime purpose "the prevention of indiscreet preaching" because James's "exhortations" had "proved ineffectual." This official account of the commission's genesis accords exactly with other evidence. Over the course of 1686 James had become increasingly irritated with the extent of anti-Catholic preaching in his kingdoms. When he heard about an anti-Catholic tumult in Edinburgh in late January 1686, James immediately wrote to the Earl of Perth that he hoped "to make good use of this disorder and have told some of the Bishops here they may now see the effects of indiscretion in the pulpits." Unfortunately, James was unable to impress upon the English bishops the urgency of the situation. By the early summer, Paul Barillon was relaying to Louis XIV reports on James's quickly escalating frustration with the extent and intensity of anti-Catholic sermons. By early July the king had had enough and resolved to create the commission based on one established by Henry VIII in order to punish "preachers who abuse their station and who preach too violently against Roman Catholicism." James's goal, Barillon made clear, was "to bridle the zealous Protestants and to support those who favor the Catholic religion."[58]

A new Comishond Cort for to inquier into the Ecclesiasticall Afairs.

James's ecclesiastical commission,
which energetically investigated
and punished anti-Catholic speech,
was widely seen as an innovative
and dangerous tool for suppressing
religious and political dissent.

The ecclesiastical commission made its ideological commitments clear at its first meeting. It was then that the commissioners cited Henry Compton, bishop of London, to appear before them. The commissioners ultimately suspended Compton from his duties as bishop for his refusal to punish Dr. John Sharp for preaching a fiery anti-Catholic sermon. Compton had long infuriated James. Initially James had hoped that he could work through the bishop of London to silence anti-Catholic preaching in the city. But the king soon discovered that that hope was badly misguided. By early March 1685 James was blaming Compton for the openness with which London preachers delivered "sermons against that which they call Popery." Compton responded by declaming against Catholic officers in the autumn parliamentary session. In April 1686 James sensed Compton's hand in the violent opposition of many Londoners to the opening of the elector palatine's Catholic chapel in the City. There was thus very good reason for Compton to be "fearful," as he was said to be, when the ecclesiastical commission was created. The prominence of Compton and the urgency with which the commission attacked him convinced many James intended to silence Protestant defenses of their religion in the face of the onslaught of Catholic apologetic. The archbishop of Canterbury declared at court that the ecclesiastical commission was "established solely to destroy the Protestant religion." Gilbert Burnet later commented that the intent of the commission was "to proceed very severely" against some so that "they might intimidate the rest."[59]

The Commission for Ecclesiastical Causes continued to pursue anti-Catholic speech long after it had suspended the bishop of London. The future first lord of the Treasury Charles Montagu reported that one Cambridge master of arts "was made recant some reflections on the papists which had made a great noise here." In January 1687 the commission suspended Dr. Beversham in Norfolk for "having used some unhandsome expressions concerning the king in his pulpit." Thomas Cartwright, who was himself a member of the commission, noted in his diary the admonishment of one Merrels for "reflecting as impudently as he did upon the king's religion." One Southall of Pedmore near Stourbridge was suspended in April, while the commission cited the bishop of Worcester for refusing to admit two Catholic priests into Church of England benefices. The rabid High Churchman Anthony Wood later recalled that the ecclesiastical commissioners "punished those ministers that acted and preached against" Catholicism. The Whig military man Captain Robert Parker agreed that "before this court the Bishops and clergy were summoned to answer for every thing they said against Popery, either in their pulpits or elsewhere."[60]

Royal admonishment and the ecclesiastical commission were not the only means James deployed to curtail Protestant responses to the onslaught of Catholic apologetic. James's soldiers were known to take it upon themselves to silence preachers who were too enthusiastic in their criticisms of Catholicism. In Stretton-on-Fosse in Warwickshire a group of soldiers warned one minister that "he should be called to an account" for his "sermon against Popery." One pamphleteer commented that experiences in both England and France should incline one to doubt whether "dragoons mind charters or arguments," whether the troops would protect freedom of religion when the government was so manifestly bent on re-Catholicization.[61]

The quality and quantity of the pamphlet debates over theology and toleration itself in the latter years of James II's reign has blinded scholars to the extent that James and his government were willing to go to stifle such discussion. James was eager to promote Catholic apologetic and promote tracts advocating repeal of the Penal Laws and Test Acts, but he did all he could to silence contrary views. In March 1686, for example, the lord mayor of London, no doubt with instructions from Whitehall, tried to suppress a broadside responding to Charles II's reasons for his deathbed conversion. In September 1686 the Stationers Company seized all of the copies they could find of *Episcopalia,* a book of letters written by the suspended bishop of London in which he outlined important differences between the Church of England and the Church of Rome. Days later the printer and bookbinder were arrested. As Edward Stillingfleet was contemplating answering a pamphlet written by Samuel Parker defending the Church of Rome against the charge of idolatry, James let it be known that he "would resent it in the highest manner." So, when William Wake, a future archbishop of Canterbury, took it upon himself to reply to Parker, he went to elaborate lengths to prevent anyone from knowing his authorship. In fact, James wanted to make it as difficult as possible for casual readers to consume the vast outpouring of Protestant literature. According to Wake, he forbade "any account to be given in the term catalogues of the books printed against Popery."[62]

Although James made every effort to expose his subjects to the most recent and fashionable French Catholic apologetic, he did not want that apologetic to initiate a free and open discussion of comparative religions. At the same time that Catholic presses were licensed, that Catholic chapels opened to the public, and that Catholic missionary priests were readmitted to England, James and his government made every effort to suppress the Protestant polemical response. Any criticism of Catholicism, whether by Dissenters or Anglicans, was interpreted as a potentially treasonable affront against the king. For James liberty of conscience clearly meant freedom of expression for Catholics and severely circumscribed freedom to worship for everyone else. Although James was able to garner the support of sophisticated and precocious defenders of unlimited toleration, such as William Penn, Henry Care, and Richard Burthogge, he did not share their views. James was clearly not committed to religious toleration.

Not only did James seek to give Catholic polemicists every possible advantage in their ideological battle against their Protestant opponents, but he sought to give Catholic Englishmen every possible advantage in the competition for place and office in late-seventeenth-century England. James did not merely use his prerogative to render inoperative the laws barring Catholics from office; he also did all he could to secure as many offices and places as possible for his coreligionists.

James's push for his coreligionists began with those closest to him. He not only created a Catholic Cabinet Council upon which he relied exclusively for political advice but also began to create an increasingly Roman Catholic household and circle of intimates. James distanced himself from his lifelong friends the Earls of Feversham and Dartmouth on the grounds that both were Protestants and that Dartmouth especially was "always opposed to everything that might benefit the Catholic religion." The increasing openness with which James proclaimed that "it was impossible to be a loyal subject and declare that the religion he professed was idolatrous" created an uncomfortable situation for many Protestants. The king's "zeal for the Catholic faith" made many officeholders both at court and elsewhere conclude "that in the end they must either declare themselves to be Catholics or resign their places." The general sense within the royal household was that James was determined to employ only servants who would "declare themselves Catholics or engage openly to do whatever was in their power in Parliament to promote the Catholic religion." Unsurprisingly sixteen former members of the royal household petitioned for financial relief in 1689 because under James they had been "put out of their respective places (and Papists admitted into several of them) without any manner of allowance or consideration." James did not reserve any special favors even for his most intimate acquaintances. He placed significant pressure on both of his daughters, Anne and Mary, to convert to Roman Catholicism. It was with good reason that one commentator friendly to James concluded that the English king "thought nobody entirely in his interest, except they were of his religion also."[63]

Throughout his reign James favored the employment of Roman Catholics in one arena after another. In the army, in many ways the quintessential institution of the Gallican-style modern state, James made every effort to augment the percentage of Catholic officers and troops. The *Arthur Godden v. Sir Edward Hales* show trial, which confirmed the king's prerogative to dispense with the Test Acts and Penal Laws when he saw fit, was but a necessary first step toward a much larger program of Catholicization. James made certain that the summer training grounds of his modern army at Hounslow Heath would be equipped with a splendid central Catholic chapel and many smaller ones. Each of the garrisons scattered throughout the country also provided a prominent place for Catholic worship. James made significant headway in Catholicizing the officer corps. By October 1688 about 11 percent of the officer corps was Roman Catholic, about ten times their proportion in the population at large and one and a half times that of the gentry and aristocracy. Although these numbers may not seem astounding, they were limited by James's desire for a professional army. There were simply not that many Catholics with the requisite military experience. James, however, made clear the disproportionate trust that he placed in his coreligionists. "All considerable places of trust everywhere" were to be placed in the hands of Roman Catholics, wrote one Whitehall insider. The important garrisons of Hull, Berwick, and Portsmouth as well as the Tower of London were all given to Roman Catholics to command. Sir Martin Beekman was dismissed from his post despite James's "great kindness" for him, because, as Father Petre explained, the king "was resolved that the Engineer general should be a Roman Catholic."[64]

The rank and file of the army in England was more heavily Roman Catholic. According to one reasonably reliable estimate there were between five and six thousand Catholic soldiers in England in October 1688, many of whom had clearly arrived from Ireland. These figures suggest that Catholics made up between 12 and 15 percent of James II's army, a figure much higher than the slightly greater than 1 percent of Catholics in the overall population. Catholics were therefore significantly overrepresented in James II's army. James, it appears, was not unsympathetic to the views of Sir Edward Hales, the Catholic commander of the Tower of London, who advised that without a Catholic army "all our labour is vain and frivolous."[65]

Many believed that James sought to Catholicize the government. The former Tory lord mayor of London Sir John Moore warned after a private meeting with James that "there was an intention to bring in Popery." "Popery is rolled up hill with great force and many machines," commented one of Sir William Trumbull's friends. These sentiments cannot be dismissed merely as the comments of the politically paranoid or the politically disappointed. By 1688 thirteen, or more than a third, of the lords lieutenant of England were Roman Catholics. This was a remarkable number given that before James's accession Catholics had been barred from holding such an august office. James told Barillon that he was "resolved to make the justices of the peace in the counties Catholic." Research has shown that James was as good as his word. In 1687 and 1688 James pursued a thoroughgoing policy of purging justices of the peace who were unsympathetic to his Catholicizing policies while at the same time infusing the commissions of the peace with Roman Catholics. About 64 percent of the new JPs named in 1687 and 1688 were Catholics, bringing the overall percentage up to almost 25.[66]

James's Catholicizing policies extended much lower down the ladder of government appointment. In late 1686 the new heavily Catholic Treasury commission, with the efficient Roman Catholic lawyer Sir Robert Brent as secretary, began a systematic purge of local customs officers and watermen. Although the extent of the purge cannot be shown with statistical precision, the dozens of Catholics who lost their jobs in 1689 suggests that there had been a significant effort. James also sought to Catholicize the Inns of Court, the pinnacles of the English legal profession, while at the same time some effort was made to appoint Roman Catholic grand juries.[67]

James's effort to Catholicize every level of government was impressive for its thoroughness and efficiency. It was, however, limited by the availability of qualified Catholics. After a century and a half of proscription, there were simply not many Catholics who had been able to qualify themselves for public office. This James sought to remedy by Catholicizing the ancient universities.

James began his assault on the twin pillars of English learning in early 1687. In January the king insisted that Sidney Sussex College, Cambridge, appoint as master the recent Catholic convert Joshua Basset. The appointment of a known intolerant Catholic was said to "alarm much the university." In July the ecclesiastical commission sent the Sidney Sussex fellows an instrument revising their statutes, "dashing out all that was against popery, and giving the Master the power to admit fellows without the consent of the rest of the society." Sidney Sussex had become England in miniature, with an absolute intolerant Catholic master. Even though Basset had appointed only one other Catholic fellow by October 1688, it was clear which direction the confessional winds were blowing. The college had ceased to be "a nursery to the Church of England," the Protestant fellows complained to archbishop Sancroft. "Mass and the other Popish service have been publicly celebrated within our College."[68]

In April 1687 the ecclesiastical commission intervened in the confessional politics of Cambridge University. In early May the commissioners deprived the vice-chancellor of the university, Dr. John Peachell, of his office and suspended him from exercising the mastership of Magdalene College for refusing to confer the degree of master of arts on the Benedictine monk Alban Francis. While the deprivation of the vice-chancellor sent a strong signal that James would brook no opposition to his will, those close to the court knew that the commission's decision had much wider significance. "The ruling made a big splash," Barillon informed Louis XIV, because it established "the royal prerogative for placing Catholics in all religious offices."[69]

James also made substantial headway in Catholicizing Oxford. The English political world was abuzz in early 1686 when the well-known and widely respected master of University College, Obadiah Walker, converted to Catholicism. Although those who knew him well thought that Walker had long held a deep sympathy for the Roman Catholic Church, others were taken aback. John Evelyn, for example, lamented that he had recommended Walker, "an hypocritical concealed papist," as a potential tutor for his sons. That Walker was allowed to keep his prominent place at Oxford, have Mass publicly said at his college, and have a printing press at Oxford pour forth Catholic apologetic convinced Evelyn that "all engines" were "now at work to bring in popery amain."[70]

Walker's University College was not the only Roman Catholic stronghold at Oxford. In October 1686 James appointed John Massey as the new dean of Christ Church. Within months Massey converted to Catholicism, established a Catholic oratory, and appointed a Jesuit chaplain. Massey's appointment, Burnet noted, "was set up for a maxim to encourage all converts." Both Walker and Massey were soon appointed justices of the peace, allowing them to punish those guilty of anti-Catholic behavior. Although the master of University and the dean of Christ Church were the most prominent and powerful Catholics in Oxford, they were not alone. Nathaniel Boyse and Thomas Deane, both fellows of University, were also prominent Catholic converts. Stephen Hunt of Trinity College, Robert Charnock of Magdalen, Matthew Tindall of All Souls, and George Clarke of Balliol all converted. John Barnard, a fellow of Brasenose, was known to speak openly "in behalf of Popery" in Oxford's coffeehouses. The Jesuit Father Thomas Fairfax, also known as Dr. Beckett, was appointed professor of philosophy at Oxford and was popular for his expertise in Oriental languages.[71]

Although rumors spread across the country "as if Oxford converts came in by whole shoals, and all the university were just ready" to declare themselves Roman Catholics, it was immediately clear that Catholicism would face stiff resistance in the university. Walker "was abused to his face when met with in the public streets and lanes, and had songs made of him." Instead of attending the lessons taught by the new converts, Usson de Bonrepaus learned, the scholars hurled "terms of ridicule" at them. Few came to hear Mass at University College. So vitriolic was the opposition that Obadiah Walker had to walk the streets of Oxford with a bodyguard from the moment he announced his reconciliation with the Roman Church.[72] Nevertheless, public ridicule could not halt the slow but steady advance Catholicism was making at Oxford.

It was in this context of slow but significant Catholicization in Oxford that James turned his attention to Magdalen College. In March 1687 Henry Clerke, the college's elderly president, died at Gawthorp Hall in Lancashire, setting off a round of speculation as to who would succeed him. James wanted the new president to be someone "favourable to his religion." The master of University College recommended to James that he appoint the new convert Anthony Farmer as president. Farmer's only recommendation turned out to be his recent conversion. His morals were none of the best. He was said to have "kissed a woman and tongued her," "put his hands under a fair lady's coats," and when pressed to explain his conversion, he replied that it was "only for preferment." In these circumstances the fellows of Magdalen rejected James's mandamus and elected one of their own, John Hough, as president. This action provoked a citation from the ecclesiastical commission. Over the summer the commissioners heard witnesses against Farmer and dropped his candidacy. In August James issued a new mandamus naming Samuel Parker, bishop of Oxford, as president. The fellows replied that they already had a president and that Parker did not meet the statutory requirement of being a fellow of Magdalen or New College.[73] James reacted by appointing Bishop Thomas Cartwright of Chester to lead a visitation of the college.

By this point the case had become a national cause célèbre. "All eyes and ears are bent that way," wrote Owen Wynne of Magdalen College in October 1687. Each stage of the proceedings was detailed in newsletters, transcribed in widely circulated separates, and eagerly gossiped upon by English men and women all over the country.[74] The interest in the case was twofold: it was both a test of the king's ability to override the law and a measure of the limits that might be placed on James's policy of Catholicization. In the end James proved that there were no theoretical limits on his authority. The college fellows were unable to assert their property right in their fellowships against the king's will. And the fellows were unable to prevent another college from becoming a center of Catholic education.

James made it clear to anyone who would listen that the fellows of Magdalen College were questioning his sovereign authority. The Frenchmen Barillon and Bonrepaus recalled that faced with the recalcitrant fellows in Oxford, James "worked himself into an extraordinary fury and transported with anger he told them he knew well how to make them obey." "I have been affronted and abused more than ever King was," he stormed in an interview with the king's council Dr. Charles Hedges, "and I would have my honor vindicated." This was exactly the tone taken by the bishop of Chester in his speech to the fellows during his visitation. "You have dealt with His Sacred Majesty as if he reigned only by courtesy and you were resolved to have a king under you, but none over you," Cartwright told the fellows. He made it clear "that the heinousness of their crime was next to rebellion." The fellows, led by John Hough, stood their ground and soon accepted their inevitable doom. The visitation commissioners ordered Hough to cease acting as president, installing Samuel Parker as his replacement. By mid-November twenty-five of Magdalen's fellows had resigned.[75]

The Magdalen College case demonstrates the limits of James II's commitment to liberty of conscience. The fellows of Magdalen College explicitly defended their refusal to appoint a president of the king's choosing on the grounds that they could not do so "without violence to their consciences." Thomas Cartwright had replied that "conscience being always a pretext for rebellion, they ought to sacrifice their conscience."[76] The fellows defended their rights to adhere to their statutes and their principles as a private society. Their position was analogous to that of a church insisting on its right to appoint its own officers and discipline its members. James, following the precepts of French Augustinian apologetic, insisted on his authority to enforce what was true and right in his eyes. The principle of liberty of conscience counted for little when it conflicted with James's authority and his plans for Catholicization.

Magdalen soon became, as its fellows had feared, "a Catholic seminary." When Samuel Parker died in March 1688, the Sorbonne-educated Catholic Bonaventure Giffard was named as the new president. Magdalen College's chapel was quickly transformed, with mass being performed daily. By August 1688 all but two of the fellows of the College were Roman Catholics.[77]

The spectacular case of Magdalen College needs to be understood not as an isolated incident of Anglican suffering, but as part and parcel of James's catholicizing program. This was certainly how contemporaries understood the affair. "The Papists have already got Christ Church and University, the present struggle is for Magdalen," wrote John Hough, "and in a small time they threaten they will have the rest." This was not mere paranoia on the part of a defeated man. In November 1687 the ecclesiastical commission commenced a thorough examination of all the college statutes at Oxford and Cambridge. That they did so immediately after resolving the Magdalen College case suggests that they had plans for further Catholicization. No wonder "all the heads and fellows of Houses" at both Oxford and Cambridge were said to "tremble."[78] James was moving inexorably toward turning Cambridge and Oxford into Catholic centers of learning.

James pursued a wide-ranging strategy of Catholicizing England. He was not merely content to ease Catholic disabilities and wait in confidence that given a level playing field the truth of Catholic arguments would triumph. James was determined to do as much as he could to place Gallican-infused Catholics at the center of political power and to give Catholics as much authority at all levels of government as possible. James was following the blueprint established by Louis XIV.

Why, then, did James welcome Huguenots fleeing persecution in France? Why did he appear to offer refuge to those Protestants resisting Louis XIV's Revocation of the Edict of Nantes? Thousands of Huguenots arrived in England during the reign of James II; the pace of new arrivals appeared to quicken in 1687 and 1688. By 1687 there were at least seven active Huguenot congregations in London alone.[79] Surely, one might claim, the English king must have supported such a massive emigration.

In fact, James did as much as was politically possible to discourage the French refugees. On at least two separate occasions James explained to the French ambassador Barillon that there was necessarily a distinction between his private sentiments toward the persecuted French Protestants and what he was able to state publicly. The Huguenots, he said, "were badly disposed" toward the English king and "their stay in his kingdom dis-

Qualis Vir Talis Oratio, by Romeyn de Hooghe, 1688. This print depicts James II at the end of his reign, dressed as a Jesuit and regurgitating reptiles that spew forth, in Dutch, the tenets of James's Catholic absolutism: "No Free Parliament," "Jesuit Colleges," "French Alliance."

pleased him," but "he did not wish to speak publicly on this subject." Privately James and his closest advisers consistently denounced the Huguenots. James regarded the Huguenots as "his enemies" and wished they were gone from his kingdom. James's wife shared his views. Mary of Modena openly told the French agent Bonrepaus that "she regarded all Protestants as republicans, and particularly those who fled from France." James's Catholic Cabinet Council thought the Huguenots "dangerous to the government." Lord Chancellor Jeffreys, the one Protestant who retained James's favor throughout his reign, was a well-known critic of the Huguenots, denouncing them as for "the most part holding principles opposed . . . to the government."[80]

James and his government took actions against the Huguenots consonant with these privately expressed sentiments. James suppressed the public discussion of the French persecution of the Huguenots. The *London Gazette,* noted John Evelyn, "never all this time, spake one syllable of this wonderful proceeding in France." This omission, the French agent Bonrepaus knew well, was by direct "order of the King of England." The following year James insisted that Jean Claude's *Account of the Persecutions and Oppressions of the French Protestants* be burned by the common hangman, an act that seemed to many to be to indicate approval "of all that has been done in France against the Protestants."[81]

James and his court not only tried to limit discussion of the persecution, they also took actions to make the Huguenot refugees feel unwelcome. James sought to suppress the Huguenot churches in London on the grounds "that they are all Presbyterians and in correspondence with the Dutch to the prejudice of himself and government." James had refused "a great number" of requests to naturalize individual Huguenots. Although the king could not prevent the circulation of charity briefs on behalf of the refugees, he restricted the distribution of sums to those who would conform to the Church of England. Those who did donate to the Huguenot relief fund earned their sovereign's ire. James did nothing to prevent Usson de Bonrepaus from locating and rounding up Huguenot families and returning them to France. Far from demonstrating his commitment to religious toleration, James's actions toward the Huguenot refugees show the limits of his commitment to liberty of conscience.[82]

James II, the evidence suggests, was committed to a thoroughgoing project of Catholic modernization. He went a long way toward transforming the English state into a centralized, efficient, and bureaucratic machine. James made certain that both the English army and navy had the most modern equipment and learned the most up-to-date techniques. And like many modernizing regimes, James extended the tendrils of the state much wider and deeper into society than any of his predecessors. Like Louis XIV across the Channel, James's modernization program had a religious dimension. He shared the disdain of French Catholics for Protestantism. Although it was politically impossible for James, in an overwhelmingly Protestant country, to suppress the established religion, James did everything he could to promote re-Catholicization. He relied increasingly heavily on Gallican Catholic advisers, military men, and naval officers. He promoted Catholic schools, helped disseminate Catholic apologetic, and did everything he could to shackle the Protestant response. James not only adopted a Gallican religious outlook, he did everything he could to create a French-style regime and to re-Catholicize England along Gallican lines.

CHAPTER SEVEN

Resistance to Catholic Modernization

J ames II's extensive and ambitious program of Catholic modernization was bound
to provoke a response. No ruler could embark on a program designed to radically
transform the English polity and expect complete quiescence. Nevertheless, James
certainly did not expect to provoke a revolution. James was an experienced and
accomplished statesman by the time he ascended the throne in 1685. Why did the
English people so unexpectedly and so decisively turn against him?

Historians have not been at a loss for explanations. Scholars in the Whig tradition
maintain that James's irrational and un-English policies united the country against him.
England's natural leaders put aside their party differences and determined to undermine
their king's innovative policies. James was therefore bound to fail.

Revisionist scholars, by contrast, argue that it was, above all, James's alienation
of the intolerant Anglican establishment that caused him to lose his throne. This understanding has led some revisionists to dub the developments in the second half of 1688
an "Anglican Revolution," by which they have meant a revolt led narrowly by intolerant
churchmen for exclusively confessional reasons. These scholars argue that James's aims were
in fact modest and plausible, and that his tolerationist measures were eagerly endorsed
by most Whigs, including John Locke's circle of West Country Whig friends. They have
followed James II himself and some contemporary Tories in arguing that James lost the

(above) *Invitation to William and Mary of Orange,* 1688. This medal,
struck in commemoration of the English invitation to William III, is inscribed
"For the liberty and faith of our ancestors," and depicts, on the reverse,
a figure of Religion with one of her hands upon the cap of liberty.

support of the Anglican churchmen by promoting religious toleration. "It was liberty of conscience," James II told his Irish parliament in 1689, that provoked his enemies "to set themselves up against me," fearing that once such liberty was established by law, the English people "would have been too happy, and I . . . too great." The Tories, James implied, were religious bigots who could not and would not allow others who believed and worshipped other than themselves to be tolerated. The Tories and the Church of England men, in the view of the revisionists and their early modern forbears, undid James not in defense of law and the English polity but in the narrow defense of their church. The Tories, recalled the great eighteenth-century Tory leader and polemicist Viscount Bolingbroke, "had taken the lead in the revolution." It was the Tories, agreed the late-seventeenth-century statesman Sir Joseph Williamson, who could not bear the thought "of living under a Popish king. None did their duties with more courage than that body of men."[1] Revisionist scholars have followed early modern Tories in insisting that the English in the later seventeenth century were driven by identity politics. Revisionist scholars have taken this party political interpretation of the revolution for an account of the revolution itself.

In fact, James's modernizing strategy was more coherent than Whig historiography has allowed, and this chapter will demonstrate that the opposition to that strategy was more politically widespread than revisionists have posited. English men and women of all political stripes appreciated, or came to appreciate, that James II had an ambitious plan to remake the English state. That plan, they quickly learned, involved sacrificing English civil liberties to create a more powerful state. Many Tories, as the revisionists have said, did turn against James, but they did so because they thought that both his plans to modernize the state and to Catholicize the country violated English law. Though many no doubt were concerned about the religious implications of James's policies, most Tories made their stand on more secular grounds. Many Whigs were deeply appreciative that James ultimately ended the vicious wave of religious persecution that had begun in the early 1680s, but—contrary to the claims of revisionist scholars—few were willing to embrace James's policies. Indeed, many Whigs, including the friends of John Locke, thought that civil liberty was a necessary *prerequisite* to real religious liberty. In 1687 and 1688 the vast majority of Whigs and Dissenters throughout the country made it clear that they were unwilling to work with James II. In 1688 the Whigs, like many Tories, were working to overthrow their king. When the Seven Anglican Bishops were tried for seditious libel in presenting their petition against James's toleration by royal fiat in June 1688, Whigs and Tories, Anglicans and Dissenters interpreted the event as a great threat to English liberties. The wild celebrations that followed the bishops' acquittal indicated the extent of popular discontent with James's Catholic modernization project. They did not initiate an Anglican revolution. In fact when James II, having learned that an Anglo-Dutch fleet was preparing to sail for England, pledged to dismantle his modernizing state, the vast majority of English people rejected his gambit as insufficient. Few believed that a conservative "Anglican Revolution," a restoration of the hegemony of the Church of England and the mere dismantling of James II's bureaucratic regime, could guarantee English religious and civil liberties. England's traditional political arrangements were insufficient to contain the ambitions of a modernizing monarch. This was why many English people hoped for revolutionary change.

James II's remarkable program of state modernization, a program that reached extensively across the country and deeply into English society, provoked widespread resentment. Although revisionist historians have recently emphasized the reorientation of James II's policies in 1686 and 1687, James's ostensible turn away from support of the intolerant Church of England to his adoption of a policy of religious indulgence, most in England perceived a coherent and consistent project of state centralization and modernization. James and his inner circle turned to new political allies in 1686 and 1687 but never hesitated in their efforts to transform the English state. When the king's subjects came to understand his absolutist designs, many of them reacted with fury.

James's massive military modernization program and his efforts to secure a state monopoly on the use of violence provoked and was no doubt intended to provoke a good deal of comment from his subjects. When, in the wake of the Duke of Monmouth's rebellion of June and July 1685, James made it clear that he not only would employ Catholic officers but also intended to maintain a standing army, he provoked intense and unanticipated hostility in both houses of Parliament. In the Commons both issues stimulated impassioned speeches from members across the ideological spectrum. The lifelong Tory Sir Thomas Clarges "set out the great consequence of melting the militia and establishing a standing force," adding that James's decision to employ Roman Catholic officers was "illegal." The political maverick Sir Thomas Meres, a number of army officers, and servants of the royal household soon joined Clarges in opposing a standing army. Sir John Thompson was probably typical of the Whigs in being "very violent" against "keeping a standing army." In the Lords the Whigs Viscount Mordaunt, Charles Paulet, Earl of Winchester, William Cavendish, Earl of Devonshire, and the moderate George Savile, Marquis of Halifax, were all conspicuous in their opposition both to the employment of Catholic officers and to the creation of a standing army. Both houses made their opposition to James's plans to create a modern army clear. "No man would have given a supply for the maintenance of a standing force," reported Gilbert Dolben.[2]

The issue of the Catholic officers provoked more debate but was clearly unpopular. Those opposed to employing Catholic officers were not motivated by anti-Catholic bigotry. "They were not concerned at heart with thirty or forty Catholic officers in the army," explained the French ambassador Paul Barillon—who was always alive to English prejudices—"but that their establishment in the army was directly contrary to the laws." The issue, Barillon made clear to his king, was that if James could ignore the laws against employing Catholics in military and civil office, then he could "alter the laws as he pleased." "The consequence of this," many in Parliament were certain, was "a complete transformation of the government which could be soon followed by an entire change of the religion." It was this principled opposition to his innovations in the military that convinced James to prorogue and ultimately to dissolve his parliament.[3]

Many beyond Parliament detested James II's massive and modern military force. As soon as James deployed his new military force across the nation, the English people came to resent the new intrusion. In town after town where troops were quartered, where troops were garrisoned, or where troops merely marched through, the inhabitants bitterly complained. Quartering troops was expensive. The young men that made up the new army were often unruly. And for many, the existence of the army signaled a new political order. Troops were soon quartered at Ailesbury in Buckinghamshire "to the great grief of very many." In Leeds and in Carlisle locals moaned that "they are undone by the quartering of soldiers." In Hull it was clear that the citizens "hate soldiers," while in York the people complained about the imposition of martial law. Opposition to martial law was one of the reasons that the inhabitants of the island of Guernsey disputed the power of James's new military men "inch by inch." The citizens of both Bristol and Chester deeply resented their garrisons. Salisbury was only one of many places in the West Country brutalized by the army in which there were loud complaints against "free quartering" of troops. In the capital the spectacular encampment at Hounslow Heath "infuriated the people of London," in part no doubt because "they were a company of troublesome rogues and rascals." But the fury was also in part a reflection, as the French ambassador understood too well, of Londoners' deep appreciation that their new army was transforming the political tenor of their country.[4]

Popular antipathy to the new military regime soon became violent. There were street battles between soldiers and citizens in the capital, in Tory Oxford, and in Whiggish Yarmouth. Tensions between soldiers and citizens ran particularly high in York. In 1686 more than five hundred apprentices and "lusty young fellows," armed with "great clubs under their coats," attacked the local garrison in "a most terrible manner," shouting, "Let's knock the black guards' brains out." In early 1688 military men appear to have initiated a battle against a taunting crowd, beating them "with their swords, their muskets being loaded with ball." So frequent was the "quarreling of the military men" that Thomas Comber, the Tory precentor of York, felt it necessary to preach sermons against their violent behavior.[5]

Many English people loathed and feared James II's modern army. Within months the new standing army had become a national grievance. The political moderate John Evelyn recorded "the great complaints" registered "throughout the kingdom" against the army, noting that the camp on Hounslow Heath in particular created "many jealousies and discourse [of] what the meaning of this encampment of an army should be." The young Yorkshireman Abraham de la Pryme recorded that "everyone says that a standing army will be England's ruin." "A standing army, in time of peace," argued the Whig Gilbert Burnet in a widely read pamphlet, could not but be "looked upon by this nation as an attempt upon the whole property of the nation in gross."[6] The French ambassador Barillon thought in 1687 that the army was the greatest single grievance in the nation. "Those who are attached to the laws and to the established government in England," he informed Louis XIV, "are more shocked and more alarmed to see a standing army than everything that has been done in favor of the Roman Catholics."[7]

The army was not the only unpopular element of James II's Catholic modernization program. From the moment of James's accession the French ambassador anticipated that there would be opposition to the king's plans to augment, regularize, and modernize his revenue. When James announced his intentions of collecting the excise taxes and customs revenue before receiving parliamentary consent, one commentator warned that this demonstrated that the new king would ignore his promise "to defend every man's property." As James took steps to regularize collection of the hearth and excise taxes, as he took measures to ensure the ideological purity of the customs officers, popular unease continued to grow. James's chosen agents of modernization, Sir Nicholas Butler, Sir John Buckworth, and Sir Dudley North were men who "the City do exceedingly dislike." In fact, James's modernized revenue was so unpopular that it was the target of an extensive parliamentary inquiry in 1689.[8]

James's use of the courts to emasculate his enemies and authorize his innovations also provoked hostile comment. When James had the Whig peer Henry Booth, Lord Delamere, tried for high treason before a special court made up of a carefully selected group of Tory lords, he received surprisingly little public support. Despite Delamere's well-known Whig political commitments, the fact that James sought to destroy him on the basis of flimsy evidence earned Delamere a unanimous acquittal. It was perhaps not surprising that the Dissenter Henry Newcome looked on Delamere's acquittal as an "unexpected mercy." Less predictable, and therefore much more troubling for James II and his regime, was the response of others less sympathetic to Delamere's politics. The courtier William Haward reported of Delamere that he "behaved himself very knowingly and prudently to the admiration of his friends and displeasure of his enemies." When his acquittal was announced, "the bells in several places rung that evening for joy of so just a sentence." The lifelong Tory and one of James's most loyal supporters in his hour of need Henry Cavendish, Duke of Newcastle, confided to fellow Tory Sir John Reresby, "I am very glad," when he heard the results of Delamere's trial.[9]

There was similar dismay several months later when the Court of King's Bench affirmed the king's right to dispense with the Test Act in the case of *Arthur Godden v. Sir Edward Hales.* Even though no one "openly contested the decision," Ambassador Barillon was hardly alone in thinking that "many were deeply opposed to the decision." Barillon and the Whig exile Gilbert Burnet, who agreed on little else, both thought the King's Bench decision threatened to "dissolve all our laws" by making them all dependent "on the royal will."[10]

By 1688 it was clear that a good number of English people had lost confidence in the English judicial system. They had come to believe that James, instead of impartially enforcing the rule of law, was using the judicial system as a political tool. James's lord chancellor and chief legal adviser George Jeffreys had long been hated by Whigs for presiding over the trials of the Rye House plotters and for overseeing the bloody assizes in the aftermath of Monmouth's rebellion. But his vigorous support of James II's Catholic modernization program made him "universally hated." One Buckinghamshire man captured a widespread sentiment when he declared that the Protestant Jeffreys "is for Popery." Perhaps more telling was the shifting popular attitude toward the flamboyant rogue Titus Oates. Oates's fabrications had touched off the Popish Plot scare in 1678, which in turn led to the Whig attempts to exclude James from the throne. Convicted of perjury in May 1685, Oates was sentenced to life imprisonment and ordered to stand in the pillory five times a year for the remainder of his life. When he first appeared in the pillory in 1685 he was "pelted with eggs" while the crowd screamed "cut off his ears" and "hanging is too good for him." Though Oates had remained a hero among committed Whigs even in 1685—John, Lord Lovelace, had embraced him on the way to the pillory—by 1687 and 1688 he had become the symbol of the injustice of James's regime. When he appeared in the pillory in August 1687, "the mob was not at all uncivil to him." The following August Oates stood in the pillory at Westminster, Charing Cross, and Temple Bar "without any of the least injury offered him." Many in England had apparently come to agree with the Guernsey man Eliazar Saumaree, who declared that "the king was a rogue, and did not stand to the law as he promised to do."[11]

James II's ambitious plan to modernize and centralize the English state by remodeling England's corporations also met with widespread resistance. Throughout the country a number of people from both political parties actively resisted their king's demands. Knowing as the French ambassador Barillon did that James aimed through the reform of the corporations to make all England more "dependent" on him, many sought to thwart the king. The Whig Lord Lovelace was apparently unusual only in his brashness when he responded to a warrant from two newly empowered Catholic magistrates that they had no legal authority, as Catholics they "were disabled by law to act," and that therefore he would "wipe his breech" with the offending warrant. In both Chester and Cambridge townsmen withstood substantial pressure from the Crown and rejected the court's candidate for mayor. Many religious Dissenters who were intruded into the corporations by the king's regulators refused to serve. Urban leaders, both Whig and Tory, made it known that they would "not only not elect" those who had declared their support of James's policies but would embrace "such as they positively know and have before declared never" to support them. Evidence from all over England suggests that a wide variety of corporations resisted James's maneuvers at every stage. One scholar has suggested that "by early September 1688, corporate governance nationwide was rumbling along awkwardly; in many places, especially those sent new charters, it ceased altogether."[12]

Even more pronounced than active resistance was the level of voluble complaint.

By calling together the county and urban elite to query their political intensions, James II and his advisers had succeeded in creating numerous local arenas for political debate. And unlike the political chatter heard in local coffeehouses, taverns, and marketplaces, these gatherings included by definition all of those who mattered politically. These sorts of gatherings in England, Barillon knew well, were sites in which people "assembled together, concert and form political alliances which they would not otherwise make." Both Whigs and Tories agreed that James's attempt to modernize and centralize the English polity, by extending the tendrils of the state ever deeper into the localities, had called into being a new political consciousness. "The examination of the minds of the nobility and gentry has made such an union," observed the Tory Earl of Danby, that James II's advisers "begin to despair of supplanting it by violent means, and it is certain they can do it no other way." The remarkable "engine" of James II's state "seemeth to move fast," agreed the moderate Marquis of Halifax, but the net result of all the querying and purging was that "men are more united" in opposing the king's wishes. "The method of questions has angered and united the nation," opined the radical Whig James Johnston in November 1687. The following month he elaborated that "the sending down of Lord Lieutenants to know the opinions of the gentry has not only healed our sores by uniting people, but been the happiest occasion to show the people that they are united again."[13]

It was this pronounced opposition in the localities, in terms of both political resistance and aroused public opinion, that convinced many that James II's plan to create a compliant parliament would fail. In letter after letter both the French ambassador Barillon and the French special envoy Bonrepaus—two men who were hoping against hope that James would succeed in his endeavors—reported on the difficulties James's regulators were encountering in the localities. Bonrepaus was appalled at the tiny numbers of supporters James had in the counties: in one county there were six, in another three, and in "some others there were none." "All of the signs are that the Parliament will not do what His Majesty wants," agreed Barillon. After sifting through the available evidence from the regulators the imperial envoy Philippe Hoffmann wrote that there was "neither hope nor appearance that things were happening in the fashion that the court had imagined." "The nobility and the people are deeply opposed" to the English king's designs, reported the Polish ambassador in the Netherlands Antoine Moreau in December 1687. In the spring of 1688 he announced that "the King of England is farther than ever from achieving his design" of a compliant parliament.[14]

International observers doubted the viability of a packed Parliament for two good reasons. First, those who promised to do the king's bidding would likely not do so in the face of a manifestly hostile public. The Whitehall insider Robert Yard believed that because "there is a strange humor among the people in the country," it was likely that "many who were before for repealing the penal laws and tests, are now of a quite contrary opinion." "They who have promised such high things" to James, thought the Tory Earl of Huntingdon's skeptical Derbyshire informant, "are neither able to perform it, and I am well assured some of them never designed it farther than to please for the present." The well-connected Whig Roger Morrice thought if the court believed a packed Parliament would do their bidding, "it is certain they are misinformed." "It is a question after all, whether the Parliament which K[ing] James was laboring to model would have answered his expectation had they come to sit," thought the Whig James Wellwood, "for men's eyes were opened more and more every day; and the noble principles of English liberty began to kindle themselves afresh in the nation, notwithstanding all the endeavors had been used of a long time to extinguish them." Both French and Dutch diplomatic channels agreed that despite all of James's purges, despite the extent of his propaganda campaign, despite everything, it seemed that with respect to a compliant Parliament, "the King of England had achieved nothing."[15]

Second, it was not even certain that the king's chosen candidates would secure their elections. Just as the candidates themselves were likely to have been influenced by public opinion, so the electors in the counties and boroughs, even though handpicked, were liable to be swayed. One of William of Orange's informants said that he expected "great disturbance" and "shows of violence" on the hustings because the elections "will be contested." "I hear all the good men in every county will stand to be members," wrote Cary, Lady Gardiner, from London in the summer of 1688, and she had good reason to believe that despite a variety of court "tricks," many of these "good men" would be elected. The Leicestershire court supporter Theophilus Brookes confirmed that his county was "full of fears and projects prepared to make a great opposition in choosing a parliament." "Both the people of the city and country" in and around Canterbury were "resolved to oppose" the chosen court candidates, according to Colonel John Hales, who thought that there would be "but very few" who would toe the royal line. The story was similar in Oxford, where it was "presumed" that two opponents of the king would be elected.[16]

It was precisely because James and his advisors could not be certain that they would get a compliant parliament that so many well-informed observers of every political persuasion doubted that a parliament would be seated in the autumn of 1688. "Many great wagers" were laid in the summer of 1688 against the meeting of Parliament, noted the political insider James Fraser, who himself doubted Parliament would sit in November. The Marquis of Halifax remained an "unbeliever" with respect to the eventual meeting of Parliament in 1688. "I can hardly yet believe we will have any parliament," chimed in the well-informed Derbyshire Tory Sir William Boothby.[17]

James II's ambitious state modernization project had provoked widespread and bipartisan opposition throughout England. This was not, as Whig historians have suggested, because James II's plans were myopic or unrealistic. Rather English men and women opposed James and his supporters because they realized just how serious and plausible James II's state-building strategy was. James's radical actions had provoked, and must have been expected to provoke, outrage among many.

The Election in the Guildhall, 1687, by Egbert van Heemskerk. This painting illustrates one example among many of local men resisting James's attempts to reform local government.

James II did eventually decide that he could not achieve his aims by working with the traditional allies of the Stuart monarchs, the Tory party, and the Church of England. But James's decision to embrace Whigs and Dissenters was not reciprocated. Instead a broad and uneasy coalition of Whigs and Tories resisted every move initiated by James II and his inner circle. James did not provoke a conservative Anglican reaction—what revisionist scholars have dubbed an "Anglican Revolution"—so much as create a revolutionary situation. Both Anglicans and Dissenters appreciated that James's modernizing regime threatened the liberties of all English men and women.

James II's modernization project was not purely secular. He hoped to use his newly created Commission for Ecclesiastical Causes to emasculate the Church of England. James reversed the monopoly on publicly sanctioned religious argument Protestants had enjoyed since the reign of Queen Elizabeth by employing his royal printer, Henry Hills, to publish

French Catholic apologetic. But he and his advisers sought much more than to create an environment for the free discussion of religious ideas. They sought to silence anti-Catholic preaching and publication. They hoped to create an environment in which Catholic schools would dominate the educational landscape. James created a Cabinet Council in which only the views of Francophilic Catholics, crypto-Catholics, and Catholic sympathizers would be heard. Each move that James and his advisers made in their project of Catholic modernization made their intentions increasingly clear, provoking ever greater levels of protest and outrage. Despite his best efforts to highlight divisions among his English opponents, James's positive actions, his willingness to deploy the weapons of a modernizing state, compelled his opponents to eschew identity politics.

From the outset James II's ecclesiastical commission stimulated much interest and speculation throughout England. By the summer of 1686 the document establishing James II's new court could be found in "all the coffeehouses" for a penny. The result, noted the courtier Owen Wynne, was that "all give freely their conjectures and reflections upon it." One such speculator was John Evelyn, who noted darkly that its powers were "greater" than the disbanded midcentury Court of High Commission and that its "main drift was to suppress zealous preachers." Another was Cary Gardiner, who overheard a lawyer say, "There was a great power given them, the greatest as words could make it."[18]

Such a controversial court was bound to provoke interest as soon as it took on a high profile case. That happened in August when the ecclesiastical commissioners heard the case against the bishop of London, Henry Compton, for refusing to suspend John Sharp for his virulently anti-Catholic sermon. Almost instantly news of the case spread throughout England. Compton's case was discussed in newspapers, newsletters, private correspondence, and coffeehouse gossip. It was "the great discourse of the town," wrote the West Indian merchant Christopher Jeaffreson. The case was "the talk all over England." Sir Ralph Verney gossiped about the case in Buckinghamshire. Sir Richard Newdigate, like so many others, kept a manuscript transcription of the case among his papers in Warwickshire. When Compton was suspended, Barillon heard through his extensive network of contacts that "it made a good deal of noise not only in London but in the counties as well." As far away as Aleppo, the young Dr. John Guise learned of the bishop of London's suspension and worried about what "will follow."[19]

Unsurprisingly, the suspension of Compton, a prominent Anglican bishop, disciple of the High Churchman John Fell, and member of an impeccably royalist and Tory family, infuriated a wide range of Anglicans. During the commission's proceedings, the Tory Sir Thomas Clarges could not restrain himself from shouting his support for the bishop of London with "a loud voice," insisting to all that "my Lord speaks nothing but reason." The devout Anglican Sir Robert Southwell wrote from his house outside of Bristol that "my heart aches for the good Bishop of London." When Compton was suspended by the court, John Evelyn was surely not exaggerating when he said the verdict was "universally resented" among his coreligionists. One later pamphleteer captured the gist of Anglican clerical sentiment when he declared that the ecclesiastical commission's verdict "turned our clergy into their right wits, and filled our pulpits with the same complaints, which before only filled lay-men's mouths."[20]

It would be wrong, however, to claim that only High Church Anglicans and Tories were infuriated by Compton's suspension. Whatever Compton's earlier attitudes toward Protestant Dissenters might have been, he was suspended in 1686 defending the right of Protestant clergymen to respond aggressively to the new barrage of French Catholic apologetic. As a consequence Dissenters felt his cause to be their own. Much to his dismay, the Frenchman Barillon was soon forced to admit that "the Huguenot refugees and the Presbyterians, who resemble them, are extremely disconcerted to see the most violent enemy of Catholics brought to court and placed in peril." Indeed, the London Presbyterian Roger Morrice observed that "all the Dissenters fall in with" the bishop of London. "It was never known of late years," he opined, "that so universal an interest of churchmen, Trimmers, and Dissenters did follow any one cause." This was because they understood well that they were "all struck at" by the ecclesiastical commission. The available evidence suggests that Morrice was almost certainly correct. The Westmorland Whig Sir John Lowther was only more vocal than most when he announced while leaving the ecclesiastical commission itself, "I will not be afraid, nor ashamed, to vindicate my Lord Bishop's cause before the commissioners themselves."[21]

The following year the Commission for Ecclesiastical Causes again made manifest the extent of James II's Catholic modernization program. When the commission sought to compel the recalcitrant fellows of Magdalen College to accept the king's choice of president, many saw their actions as an important step in a Catholic program to seize control of England's educational institutions. The creation of prominent and successful Catholic schools throughout the country had been threatening enough, but this new step suggested that James was willing to go so far as arbitrarily to seize property, in the form of college fellowships, to advance the cause of his coreligionists.

With so much at stake, the case quickly became "the whole concern of the university," "the common talk of the town," and the discourse of the whole "nation." Once again the new activism of the state forced people throughout the country to react to its newfound power. Once again the Catholicizing implications of James II's political actions provoked a response that cut across confessional lines. The Magdalen College case, remarked Barillon with not a little contempt, provoked the English throughout the country to insist on "their privileges and their liberty." The case, recalled one pamphleteer, "kindled such a fire of hatred in the people, as never could be put out." Since the Magdalen fellows were not only deprived of their fellowships but also made "incapable of a livelihood," agreed another later commentator, the actions of the ecclesiastical commission "made every Englishman a party complainant."[22]

Churchmen were infuriated with their king. Both the Anglican lord chief justice Edward Herbert and the bishop of Rochester, Thomas Sprat, heretofore loyal servants

James's attempt to appoint a Catholic
president of Magdalen College,
Oxford, and in particular, his
subsequent expulsion of the fellows,
seemed to many contemporaries an
unprecedented encroachment on the
liberty and property of his subjects.

of the king, dissented from the general opinion of the ecclesiastical commission. When
Thomas Ken, bishop of Bath and Wells and a High Churchman, heard of the decision, he
asked his friend William Wake for reasons to believe in "the illegality of the commission."
Other High Churchmen and Tories anxiously invited the dismissed Magdalen fellows into
their households and offered them substantial financial assistance. James told the West
Country Tory Sir Edward Seymour that if these rumors of assistance from churchmen
proved true, "he would look on it as a combination against him." The Magdalen College
case "did so inflame the Church party and the clergy," Gilbert Burnet learned while at
William's court in the Netherlands, "that they sent over very pressing messages upon it
to the Prince of Orange desiring that he would interpose, and espouse the concerns of
the Church." If James II refused, the churchmen made clear, they hoped William would
"break" with James II and declare war.[23]

Although Magdalen was an Anglican establishment in the heart of Tory Oxford,
Whigs, Dissenters, and even Catholics who were not of the French party were irate at

James's actions against the president and fellows. They, too, understood the case as part of James II's program of Catholic modernization. "The business of Magdalen College," James Johnston informed William and his circle in December 1687, "has lost [James II and his supporters] a great many of the Dissenters." "The ejection of the President and fellows of Magdalen College," coming so soon after "the illegal proceedings against the Bishop of London," opined Charles Caesar, "opened the eyes of all sorts, and quickly taught the Dissenters what they were to expect . . . when such open invasions were made on that Church that was firmly established by law." "The master and fellows of Magdalen College are a sufficient proof" of James II's plan to modernize the state to the cost of all English men and women, insisted the Presbyterian Daniel Defoe, since the fellows "were deprived of their freeholds by a most arbitrary sentence of a court." The consequence, Defoe noted, was that "all our freeholds and estates shake by this sentence."[24]

Whigs and Catholics opposed to the French and Jesuit party also condemned the injustice of the proceedings against Magdalen College. The recent action against Magdalen, argued the radical Whig cleric Samuel Johnson, "shakes all the property in England." "You all remember Magdalen College," the West Country Whig Sir Richard Cocks urged his auditors in the 1690s. "That was enough to justify us and to show the world that force and nothing but force could persuade the late king to restore us our laws, liberties, churches, properties, charters, and colleges." This view was shared by one of England's most prominent anti-Jesuit and anti-French Catholics, Bishop John Leyburn. Leyburn, who had opposed using Magdalen College chapel for Roman Catholic services after the eviction of the fellows, declared that the ecclesiastical commission's actions in the Magdalen College case "had been a spoliation, and that the possession in which the Roman Catholics now found themselves was one of violence and was illegal."[25]

Six months later James II again enraged a wide variety of English men and women by prosecuting seven English bishops for seditious libel. Once again James and his advisers chose to silence their political opponents on a religious issue—this time whether Anglican clerics should be compelled to read James's second Declaration of Indulgence aloud from the pulpit. Once again James and his advisers demonstrated that whatever their commitment to liberty of conscience, that liberty did not an imply a liberty to disagree, much less to criticize. Once again James's decision to mobilize the ever-growing resources and powers of his modernizing state provoked an angry and widespread response.

After issuing his second Declaration of Indulgence, promising liberty of conscience, in April 1688, James II decided in council on 4 May to compel all Church of England clergymen to read the Declaration of Indulgence aloud in their parishes. Surprisingly, this move infuriated not only Anglican clerics but many Whigs and Dissenters. James II's decision to compel the clergy to give voice to his policies sparked a wildfire of comment and outrage all across the country. Many Anglican clerics supported broader religious toleration, though some did not. Yet very few felt that tolerance by royal fiat was either legal or desirable. Many must have shared the sentiments of the Buckinghamshire

The June 1688 trial of the Seven Bishops, shown here, infuriated
a wide range of English men and women. Dissenters and Anglicans
alike celebrated their acquittal. A few Anglicans interpreted
the bishops' acquittal as a providential vindication of their church.
The vast majority in England regarded the event as an indication
that popular action might possibly frustrate James II's
Catholic modernization strategy.

cleric William Butterfield, who confided to Sir Ralph Verney that the clergy "could not
be instrumental in promoting a thing which we do not approve." As a result a number of
meetings took place among the London clergy on 7, 8, and 9 May to determine a course
of action. There it was resolved to take the pulse of the London clergy and to meet again
with a number of England's bishops. Eventually, in a meeting held at the archbishop of

Canterbury's residence in Lambeth, the clerics decided that they would oppose reading the declaration in their churches later that month and that seven of the eight bishops present would petition the king. The news of these meetings quickly spread within London's Presbyterian community, and Richard Baxter "commended the Church of England for what they have done."[26]

The petition submitted "in the most submissive and respectful manner" to James II by William Sancroft, archbishop of Canterbury; William Lloyd, bishop of St. Asaph; Francis Turner, bishop of Ely; John Lake, bishop of Chichester; Thomas Ken, bishop of Bath and Wells; Thomas White, bishop of Peterborough; and Jonathan Trelawney, bishop of Bristol emphasized political rather than theological objections to James II's actions. Their refusal to read the king's declaration, the bishops maintained in their petition, did not arise from "any want of due tenderness to dissenters." Instead they objected to the declaration because it was "founded upon such a dispensing power as hath been often declared illegal in Parliaments."[27]

The Seven Bishops' petition, secretly printed, became an immediate sensation and "the soul subject of discourse among all sorts of people." When Sir Robert Southwell received a copy at his home in the West Country, he could no more "forbear sending it" along to his friend Viscount Weymouth than he could become "weary with reading it." From Carlisle Thomas Smith reported that "all wise and good men applaud[ed] what" the bishops had done. James II reacted rather differently. "What! The Church of England against my dispensing power! The Church of England! They that always preached it!" exclaimed the king. "This," James said "was a sounding of Sheba's trumpet, and that the seditious preachings of the puritans in the year [16]40 was not of so ill consequence as this." James immediately announced that "he knew well how to make them obey."[28]

If the Seven Bishops' petition was a trumpet of rebellion, it was a trumpet heard far and wide. The Anglican clergy in London and in the rest of the kingdom overwhelmingly refused to read the king's declaration. A small handful of clerics read the declaration in London, and in one parish where it was read, "the people generally went out of the Church." The Anglican clergy's near unanimity in the face of royal pressure emboldened Londoners. "From this day," William Westby confided to his diary, "people discourse with great freedom against the suspending power and that with great plainness." "The country," all reports agreed, soon "followed the example of the city." The majority of clergy refused to read the king's declaration in county after county. Even in those few dioceses in which the local bishop had refused to support the petitioning bishops, "the inferior clergy following the example of those of London have refused to read" the Declaration of Indulgence.[29]

Faced with such manifest and national resistance to his policy of Catholic modernization, James deployed another tool of the state to silence the opposition. He sued the bishops for seditious libel. This decision, and the subsequent trial, highlighted for everyone the issues at stake. Both William Sancroft and William Lloyd had intended to deliver speeches at their trial to clarify their positions. Sancroft claimed to have discovered that

About 200 Ministers Suspended in y Country of Duram for not reading the Kings Declaration

Even as late as the summer of 1688, James II still had a formidable state apparatus at his disposal, and he put it to use in a campaign to suspend those clergymen who refused to read his second Declaration of Indulgence.

the king's declaration "seemed to alter the whole frame of government and introduce a new constitution." In "ecclesiastical affairs," he was certain the king's intention was that "all the laws" passed "in opposition to the groundless and unjust usurpations of the Pope and Church of Rome" would be "suspended and in effect abolished." "The consequence of [this case]," William Lloyd intended to say in open court, "extends to the Protestant religion and all the laws of England. The happiness of this and future ages depends upon it."[30] Perhaps the two bishops did not deliver their orations because they did not have to. The arguments they intended to advance were already ubiquitous.

English people everywhere had been debating the same issues that Sancroft and Lloyd had intended to raise at their trial for well over a year. "The whole kingdom was filled with pamphlets which daily appeared concerning the dispensing power and taking off the tests and other penal laws," recalled one Catholic historian. There was "a war of words," thought the French ambassador; an extensive "debate," agreed the king's propagandist Henry Care. Some individual contributions to this pamphlet war scored remarkable popular successes. Samuel Parker, the bishop of Oxford and one of James II's staunchest supporters, found that his detailed polemic, *Reasons for Abrogating the Test,* sold more than two thousand copies in two days in December 1687. But some of the works of the king's opponents were even more popular. "At least twenty thousand copies" of the Marquis of Halifax's *Letter to a Dissenter* were distributed to every "corner of the land" in late 1687. Some, like the Roman Catholic Henry Neville Payne, thought it the most "disloyal and dangerous" paper ever published. Others claimed that Halifax had written "one of the most admired pieces for style, close reasoning and expression that has appeared abroad of a long time." James Johnston subsequently claimed that the pamphlet did the Orangist cause "more service" than anything else. Gilbert Burnet also wrote a number of popular tracts criticizing James II's Declarations of Indulgence.[31]

Two other pamphlets published just months before the bishops' trial also created quite a stir. In January 1688 Gaspar Fagel, the grand pensionary of Holland, published his *Letter* objecting strenuously to James II's plans to repeal the Penal Laws and Test Acts. Perhaps because it was known that Fagel accurately represented the views of the Prince and Princess of Orange, "thousands of copies" of the tract were eagerly bought up "across the entire kingdom." The tract gave "great offence at court" in large part because, in the opinion of the Scottish Catholic Louis Innes, it did "much mischief." Within days a sequel, *Reflexions on Monsieur Fagel's Letter,* surpassed the commercial and polemical success of Fagel's *Letter.* That pamphlet, circulated "both in town and country for nothing," provoked the Earl of Sunderland to search high and low for its author and its printer. By the time James II decided to prosecute the Seven Bishops for seditious libel, few in England could have been unaware of the issues involved. In both London and the country there were a "variety of pamphlets on all sides." "The general discourse this year," noted William Westby, speaking for the country as a whole, "was about the King's power in dispensing with the laws."[32]

Not only were the English people saturated with pamphlets about the king's right to dispense with laws by fiat, many had, by all appearances, begun to side with the king's opponents. In 1687 and 1688 an increasing number of people in England insisted that James II's actions were not only illegal but tantamount to declaring that there was no law in England other than the king's word. Anyone who spoke up in favor of the Declaration of Indulgence, argued the Marquis of Halifax, looked "like counsel retained by the prerogative against your old friend Magna Carta." "If the King could grant an indulgence against acts of Parliament," asserted some English exiles in the Netherlands, "then welcome arbitrary government and popery." Gilbert Burnet decided to "serve in the Revolution" in spring 1688. This was because, he recalled later, James II's Second Declaration of Indulgence in which "many laws were dispensed with at pleasure," combined with the king's insistence on employing those "who were under legal disabilities" in local and national political offices, convinced him that "there was a total subversion of our constitution; which from being a legal one was made precarious, subject to mere will and pleasure." Another Anglican agreed that reading James II's Second Declaration of Indulgence aloud to the congregation "is to teach the dispensing power, which alters what has been formerly thought the whole constitution of this church and state." During the Seven Bishops' trial itself, the council for the defendants "said often bluntly that the dispensing power was a change of the government." One observer interpreted the thousands who gathered at Charing Cross, Whitehall, and in front of Lambeth Palace as celebrating the defeat of "the too earnest assertors of the Dispensing Power" and the victory of England's "unvariable laws."[33]

Not only did the bishops give voice to widely repeated fears that James II was assuming unprecedented political power and subverting England's constitution, they did so on the national stage. Everyone in England was obsessed with the Seven Bishops and their trial in late May and June 1688. Great throngs of people lined the route when the bishops were sent to the Tower. Many of the nobility, gentry, and "vast multitudes" of more humble folk visited the bishops in the Tower. All of them, it appeared, were convinced that the bishops were suffering "in defense of religion, liberty, and property." Mary Woodforde in Binstead on the Isle of Wight, Sir Ralph Verney in Middle Claydon in Buckinghamshire, and Sir William Boothby in Ashbourne in Derbyshire prayed for the bishops' deliverance. "Men, women, and children" all over the country eagerly gossiped about the bishops and their trial. News, reliable and unreliable, was widely distributed in printed newspapers, manuscript newsletters, private correspondence, and coffeehouse chatter. John Locke's friend Anna Grigg thought that "many hundred thousands" were "perpetually" thinking or talking about the bishops' case. England's most prominent nobles and gentlemen came from all across the country to attend the bishops' trial. But it was not just those present who hung on every word uttered in the courtroom. When the bishops were bailed on 18 June, for example, bonfires were lit in towns and villages throughout the land. When supporters of James II attempted to quell the celebration in the Midland cathedral city of Lichfield, "there happened a very great riot."[34]

The enthusiasm was even greater and more universal the moment the Court of King's Bench announced the bishops' acquittal on 29 June 1688. When the verdict was revealed in the courtroom itself, "there was a most wonderful shout, that would one would have thought the hall had cracked," enthused the Earl of Clarendon, an eyewitness. As soon as the spectators left the courthouse, the news "was taken up by the watermen, and in a moment, like a train of gunpowder set on fire, went up and down the river and along the streets." "The generality" of the people, from noblemen to the "giddy rabble," soon joined in two wild and raucous days of celebration in the streets of London. Some lit bonfires, others rang bells, and almost everyone, it seemed, shouted nonstop. Crowds mercilessly attacked friends of James II who refused to contribute to the celebrations. When the newly converted Roman Catholic James, Earl of Salisbury, tried to put out a bonfire in front of his house, "the rabble" opened fire and "killed the beadle of the parish who came on purpose to quench the bonfire."[35]

The celebrations spread with the news of the acquittal across the nation. In Buckingham "there were a great many bonfires." In Bristol there were "such doings as never were before in the tokens of joy." "A great part of the night was spent in rejoicing" in

Peterborough, recalled the future bishop Simon Patrick. People, "rich and poor," military and civilian, Church of England and Nonconformist, celebrated "throughout the kingdom."[36]

Commentators across the political spectrum later claimed that after the Seven Bishops' case the entire political nation turned against James II and his regime. As soon as the "seven trumpets of rebellion" were freed from the Tower of London, recalled the Jacobite John Stevens bitterly, they spread seditious sentiments among "not only their own insignificant flock, commonly distinguished by the name of Church of England men, but [to] all the other herds of wild animals that ranged the vast forest of the English heresy and schism." The consequence, Stevens felt sure, was that the country "was now grown drunk with rebellion." "The late business concerning the bishops hath had such a great effect that it is hardly to be imagined," agreed the moderate Marquis of Halifax; it "hath brought all the Protestants and bound them up into a knot that cannot easily be untied." The June 1688 trial, chimed in the Whig James Wellwood, "awakened the people of England to shake off their chains."[37]

The English people were furious with their king in the summer of 1688. The Seven Bishops' trial convinced many that James II was determined to destroy religious and political liberty in England. The trial was not, as the revisionist scholars have claimed, a triumph of Anglicanism. It did not initiate a conservative "Anglican Revolution." No doubt many High Churchmen did celebrate the bishops' acquittal as a partisan triumph. No doubt the popularity of the theologically inflected medals and prints celebrating the bishops as "seven pillars" of wisdom reflected the views of many of those who purchased them. But Dissenters as well as High Churchmen were overjoyed with the verdict. Since the bishops had framed their case as a defense of the law against royal prerogative, as liberty against arbitrary government, most of England's Dissenters saw the bishops' battle as their own. One Quaker from Wells offered to stand bail for Thomas Ken, bishop of Bath and Wells. A wide range of other Whigs including the Earl of Bedford, the Earl of Shrewbury, the Earl of Manchester, the Earl of Carlisle, the Earl of Clare, the Earl of Radnor, Viscount Newport, Lord Paget, and Lord Grey of Warke actually stood bail for the bishops. The great Presbyterian leader Richard Baxter praised "the zeal of the Bishops" in "high terms" before his congregation. Dissenters enthusiastically celebrated the bishops' acquittal. "Clergy and laity, as well Dissenters as Church of England," were "unanimous in their expressions of joy at the Bishops' deliverance," observed eyewitnesses in London. The Lancashire Dissenting minister Henry Newcome probably expressed the sentiments of many others when he declared that he "was not sorry" to hear the bishops were acquitted.[38]

At every step in which James II and his advisers sought to consolidate power and advance their program of Catholic state modernization they were met with increasing resistance. But while many of James II's opponents may have been motivated by profound and long-held anti-Catholic prejudices, most of them publicly justified their actions in secular and legal terms. "Here's no talk of religion," Sir Roger L'Estrange correctly noted.[39]

James, they said over and over again, in ever shriller tones, was destroying the English constitution in church and state. It was precisely because James II's opponents deployed the language of liberty rather than that of salvation, highlighted the threat to England's legal establishment rather than to the true church, that it makes little sense to discuss their triumphs as an Anglican revolution. Both Anglicans and Dissenters excoriated the ecclesiastical commission, condemned the proceedings against Magdalen College, and cherished the acquittal of the Seven Bishops. They wanted an English revolution, not a narrowly Anglican one.

James II's Catholic modernization strategy provoked widespread resistance. Many throughout England chose to voice their opposition. Those revisionist scholars who claim that James's opponents were motivated primarily by religious bigotry, however, have not focused exclusively on James's enemies. Instead they have argued that those most sympathetic to religious toleration were the king's most enthusiastic supporters. James II, these scholars claim, promoted religious pluralism, and the majority of England's Whig and Dissenting community understood that point quite well.

Did Whigs and religious Dissenters support James II? Had James II, in the eyes of those who had tried to exclude him from power in the late 1670s and early 1680s, become a Whig king?

Dissenters certainly had good reason to embrace James II. When he began making overtures to them in late 1685 and 1686, and ultimately issued his first Declaration of Indulgence in 1687, he ended one of the most vicious periods of religious persecution in English history. Ever since the failed Whig attempt to exclude James from the throne in 1681, Tories had initiated "great severities against Dissenters." They were "run down universally," their meetings "were weekly (not weakly) disturbed." "What Protestant age or Church can parallel such barbarities and cruel persecution?" asked the Quaker leader George Whitehead. The leaders of the gathered church at Axminster in the West Country expressed similar sentiments. "The rage of adversaries increasing more and more," they noted in 1683, so "the hearts of professing people [are] ready to faint." In 1685 alone, state authorities had more than fourteen hundred Quakers imprisoned. The government had unleashed a thick web of informers who terrorized Dissenting congregations across the country. After Monmouth's failed rebellion in the summer of 1685, the state persecution of Dissenters reached new levels of cruelty. The Low Churchman Gilbert Burnet was not alone in claiming that James II's regime "seemed to delight in blood."[40]

When James II halted the persecutions and reached out to the Dissenters, many thought the transformation could only have been the result of divine intervention. The Yorkshire Presbyterian Oliver Heywood was surely not alone in exclaiming, "What hath God wrought!" "I should have been tempted to think the Dissenters such stupid creatures, as wanted even the sense of feeling," wrote one pamphleteer, had they not been grateful to

James II for relieving them "from burdens, as innumerable, as unsupportable." Catholic and High Church observers all commented on the enthusiasm with which Dissenters embraced James II and his new policy. "Our liberty of conscience has charmed all the old fanatics," asserted one Anglican observer. "The whole body of Nonconformists" now enthusiastically supported James II, wrote the Catholic Marquis d'Albeville. Another Roman Catholic noted that "the fanatics are now become the King's loyal subjects."[41]

Immediately after James issued the Declaration of Indulgence in April 1687, Whigs and Nonconformists *did* appear to support his regime. Prominent Dissenters like the Quakers William Penn and Robert Barclay, the Presbyterians Vincent Alsop and Sir James Stewart, and the Independent Stephen Lobb soon frequented the inner circles of power and took up their formidable pens in defense of their king's policies.[42]

Unsurprisingly, more than eighty addresses of thanks for the Declaration of Indulgence poured in from Dissenting congregations. Prominent Whig polemicists soon began writing on behalf of James and his policies. Henry Care, whose bitter and popular attacks on James and the Tories in the early 1680s ensured that he was "identified in the public mind with Dissenters and Whigs," wrote a number of pamphlets defending James's policies and published the government-supported weekly newspaper *Publick Occurrences*. When Care died in August 1688, Elkanah Settle, another veteran Whig polemicist, took over *Publick Occurrences*. James Vernon, who not only had sat as a Whig MP in 1679 but had also served as the duke of Monmouth's private secretary until his execution, wrote the other prominent government newspaper, the *London Gazette*. Richard Burthogge, "who always kept pace with the fanatics," wrote the theoretically sophisticated *Prudential Reasons for Repealing the Penal Laws* (1687) and was rewarded by being made a justice of the peace in Devon. Many proscribed Whigs, including George Speke, John Trenchard, John Hampden, John Dutton Colt, and Samuel Barnardiston, accepted royal pardons. Other Whigs were more active still. Several accepted high office. The Whig lawyer Sir William Williams accepted the office of solicitor-general in December 1687. Silius Titus, "one of the most violent" Whigs, attended court frequently beginning in September 1687. In July 1688 Titus joined the Whig Christopher Vane, son of the regicide Sir Henry Vane Jr., on James II's Privy Council.[43]

James II clearly did turn to Whigs and Dissenters for political support. The vast majority of Dissenters were thrilled that years of violent persecution and imprisonment had ended. A few prominent Dissenters and Whigs certainly worked closely with James II and his regime. But did the majority of Dissenters and Whigs come to believe that James was in fact a Whig king? Did they provide James II with a solid political base of support?

The evidence, though complex, suggests that many Dissenters and Whigs had misgivings about James II's Declaration of Indulgence from the beginning. Though they welcomed their newfound religious liberty, they wondered what had provoked James's concession. Then, with each step that James took to promote his Catholic modernization program, with each step that James took to consolidate and centralize his political authority, Dissenters began to distance themselves from the regime. Over the course of 1687 and 1688 more and more Dissenters made it clear that they felt religious liberty was meaningless without civil liberty.

From the outset many Dissenters were uncertain how to respond to James II's Declaration of Indulgence. As gossip circulated in the Dissenting community that James intended to issue his Declaration of Indulgence, many began to make clear their misgivings. Some, it is true, were "much joyed at it," reported the Whitehall insider Owen Wynne, "but others seem less transported than they were in 1672 and do not seem to have yet resolved whether to accept or refuse the benefit of it." In the immediate aftermath of the declaration, many Dissenters remained perplexed. There was a deep "division among the Presbyterians." Both the French and Spanish ambassadors, who agreed on little else, thought that among the Presbyterians, "the most considerable and those who guided the others were in league with the Church of England" against James II. Barillon even claimed that almost "all the sects" believed that James's declaration was "a means to establish the Catholic religion and destroy all the others."[44]

Dissenters were no more enthusiastic supporters of James's new policies in the counties than they were in the metropolis. "The only Dissenters that seem pleased with their toleration are the Quakers and Independents, the numbers of either not considerable," Sir John Reresby reported from York. The Dissenters had deep-seated "fears" about the intensions of James II and his regime, thought Samuel Sanders of Normanton in West Yorkshire. "For all their hypocritical addresses," wrote one Hereford Anglican of the Dissenters, it was certain that "whenever there is an opportunity offered," these same people would "act according to their avowed king-killing principles." Jonathan Trelawney, bishop of Bristol, was more sympathetic to the Dissenters. "Those of the better rank even among the Presbyterians," he averred, were furious that their names had been affixed to addresses against their consent and refused to contribute to the construction of new meetinghouses. "The most considerable Dissenters in this city," observed John Lake, bishop of Chichester, chose to attend Anglican services rather than build new places for their own worship after James issued his declaration. "If the King expects the Presbyterians here" to assist him, "he will find himself much mistaken," wrote the Duke of Hamilton from Scotland, where ambivalence was similar to that in England.[45]

Many Dissenters, especially prominent Presbyterians, immediately expressed concern about James II's larger political project. The Presbyterians and Independents "were enemies to the high prerogative that the King was assuming," recalled Gilbert Burnet, so while they were "generally of a mind as to the accepting of the King's favor," they would not "concur in taking off the Tests." "The greatest part of the Dissenters," averred the Presbyterian polemicist Daniel Defoe, were "so sensible of the mischief" planned by James II "that though they had smarted somewhat hardly under the lash of the penal laws but a little while before, yet they would rather venture the continuance of them, than run the hazard of ruining the substance and being of the Protestant religion amongst us." James II's

Declaration of Indulgence, because it granted liberty of conscience by "prerogative," did not "come forth in the way we could have wished for," agreed the Quaker John Whiting. Although James II did all he could to advertise the large number of addresses thanking him for his Declaration of Indulgence, many prominent leaders of Dissenting opinion, such as Richard Baxter, John Howe, and William Bates, made their opposition to addressing public. And as the Presbyterian Roger Morrice made clear, "most of those that did address owned not the dispensing power."[46]

Though grateful for their religious liberty, many Dissenters made it clear that they were uneasy with James II's plan to repeal both the Test Acts, which made conformity to the Church of England a prerequisite for holding government office, and the Penal Laws, which punished those who failed to attend Anglican services. "People generally agree," wrote one well-informed observer, "that to take away the all the Penal Laws by the lump, is cutting up the Reformation by the roots, and leaving the old Popish ones only in force." Instead of James II's program of Catholic modernization, which involved unmaking the legislation that had made England Protestant, the Dissenters advocated "making a new law to exempt men's persons and estates from punishment in matters of mere religion and conscience." Although scholars have been at pains to highlight those who agreed to work with James II throughout the country, an impressionistic analysis of the returns from the national surveys circulated by James and his bureaucrats suggests that the overwhelming majority of Dissenters and Whigs refused to do so. In Lancashire, at least, this was the perception of well-informed Anglicans as well. "The Presbyterians" and "the Quakers southward of Lancaster," thought Sir Daniel Fleming of Rydal, all answered the first two of James's three questions negatively.[47]

Over the course of 1687 and 1688 Dissenters and Whigs increasingly voiced their opposition to James II's Catholic modernization project. Whereas some Dissenters and some Whigs had greeted the end of persecution in 1686 and the Declaration of Indulgence in 1687 with stunned relief, within a few months most had turned against James II and his regime. Whigs and Dissenters were coming to realize—perhaps influenced by the pervasiveness of James II's modern army, the determination of the ecclesiastical commission to silence religious debate, and the willingness of James II to override English law at Magdalen College—that at best James II meant to offer a circumscribed religious liberty in exchange for relinquishing civil liberty. "The Presbyterians and Independents are coming off from the fondness they had at first for the toleration," reported one of William of Orange's English informants. Many, it turns out, had told James's commissioners that they were "for taking off the Tests" while promising "their voices to men who have told them they will never consent to it." Nathaniel Johnston, who was very closely connected to James's inner circle and was himself employed by James as a propagandist, was concerned in January 1688 that "the Dissenters may cool" toward the king's projects. "The wiser sort of Dissenters" had always been wary of James II's plans, recalled Daniel Defoe in 1689, but "the generality of them in a short time" came to share their concerns. James II's "plot," agreed the Baptist William Kiffin, "took with several Dissenters—but indeed they were but few." "It were great injustice," agreed the Low Churchman Gilbert Burnet, to judge all Dissenters by "the impudent strains of an Alsop or a Care." Two men hostile to Dissenters and Whigs had the same opinion. "Our Dissenters were not so easily wheedled into a forgetfulness of what they had so lately suffered," maintained Edmund Bohun, who had been a hammer of Dissenters during his time as a Suffolk justice of the peace, so when given the "opportunity, they gave . . . bold hints of their resolution to defeat the expectations" of James and his Catholic advisers. The Dissenters who had appeared "to have so great a zeal for His Majesty," agreed the Exeter prebend Thomas Long, who was a prolific critic of Dissenters in print, "were most forward to unite against him."[48]

By the spring of 1688 no one was in any doubt that the main body of the Dissenters had turned against James II. The Dissenters, wrote the Dutch envoy Van Citters, who had strong ties to the Dissenting community, "openly" declared "that they seeing what is intended" by their king, "will rather as before remain under the persecution of the Penal Laws in the hopes and expectation of receiving at the proper period some alleviation, than by separating from the English church . . . go surely one after the other to the ground."[49]

James II and his advisers themselves appreciated that Dissenters and Whigs were turning against them. "The kindness we had for the Dissenters is much cooled," reported James Fraser in February. Since James II and his fellow Catholic modernizers did not find "their expectations answered by the Dissenters," the Marquis of Halifax informed William in April, "they have thoughts of returning to their old friends the high churchmen." By May James Johnston learned that "the court is turning out everywhere the Presbyterians and Independents that were lately put in the corporations."[50]

This general evidence that Dissenters and Whigs did not embrace James II's regime is confirmed by an examination of particular cases. With some remarkable and well-publicized exceptions, Dissenters did not believe that James II offered them their only and best hope of religious liberty. With remarkable courage, these deeply devout men—though one suspects there were just as many important women who shared their views—rejected the terms on which they were offered an end to religious persecution.

Presbyterian leaders were especially prominent in their opposition to James and his policies. Richard Baxter had made it clear even before James issued his declaration that he had no intention of addressing the king in thanks. John Howe, who counted among his friends the prominent Low Churchmen and future bishops Gilbert Burnet, Richard Kidder, and Edward Fowler, was persuaded by William of Orange himself not to address James. Howe not only followed the prince's instructions, believing that if James achieved his designs it would have "fatal consequences," but he also used "his utmost influence in order to the restraining of others." The Lincolnshire Presbyterian John Rastrick "refused" to sign an address of thanks to James II in 1687, hinting darkly that "the meaning and design of it was pretty well understood." George Trosse of Exeter began frequenting "the prelatical assemblies with great frequency" when he learned of James II's Declaration of Indulgence. He based his decision on two considerations. He thought the declaration "against law," and he suspected that "the design of the King was to withdraw the people from the public, and so to weaken the party of the Church of England, whom if he had once brought into contempt, the Dissenters would have been easily crushed." Not surprisingly, Trosse was much happier with the Toleration Act of 1689, which provided statutory authority for religious freedom. These sentiments were similar to those of the Derbyshire minister William Bagshawe, known as the Apostle of the Peak, who "was far from owning the dispensing power on which King James's indulgence was founded, and could not but discern his design in it." A sermon delivered before the students at Richard Frankland's Dissenting academy at Attercliffe near Sheffield warned against "grounding thy expectations upon absolute power."[51]

In his long and detailed Entering Book Roger Morrice described his distaste for and opposition to James II's religious policies. In May 1688 he copied out an Anglican paper denouncing the Declaration of Indulgence for asserting "a transcendancy of prerogative above law" as a prelude to leading his own campaign to prevent Dissenting ministers from reading the declaration to their congregations. Even Thomas Rosewell of Rotherhithe on the South Bank of the Thames, who did publicly thank James II for his Declaration of Indulgence, had no great fondness for James or his politics. "No man rejoiced in [the Glorious Revolution] more than he," recalled his son and biographer. "Some few" Presbyterian ministers "who had personal and particular favors shown them, might be drawn into the snare," wrote Edmund Calamy, who was very close to a number of the leading clerics of the time; however, "they were but very few . . . the far greater number stood it out" and opposed the king's policies.[52]

Independents (or Congregationalists) also greeted James's policies with distrust. "Not one member" of the gathered church in Axminster in Devon consented to sign an address of thanks to James II. The chronicler of that congregation recorded that "it was too evident unto such as were men of understanding, as had any right discerning of the times, that a popish design was still carrying on amain under all the fair and plausible carriages of authority." The independent master of the Free School in Exeter, Zachary Mayne, no doubt took full advantage of James II's Indulgence but was still "well pleased with the great revolution" that began in 1688. "Though no one in Lancashire has suffered more by the Penal Laws in matters of religion than myself," wrote the Independent minister Thomas Jollie, still he thought the king's new policies "hath done harm." He believed deeply in "free liberty for all persuasions" but bristled at any thought of removing the Test Acts.[53]

Even the groups that contemporaries most closely associated with James II's policies in 1687 and 1688, the Baptists and the Quakers, did not prove to be reliable political allies. Not only did the venerable London Baptist leader William Kiffin refuse to act as London alderman, he also did everything he "could to prevent those Dissenters of my acquaintance" from serving the regime. Kiffin was one of more than twenty leading

Baptists who refused to work with James and his regime. "Some few persons (from their own sentiments)" did agitate "for the taking off the Penal Laws and Tests," but, wrote one Baptist in early 1689, no Baptist congregation did so. In fact, some Baptist congregations "have not only reproved those among them that were so engaged, but in a regular way have further proceeded against them."[54]

The Quakers, too, cooled in their support for James after some initial enthusiasm for indulgence. William Penn himself apparently came to believe it best to "have the Penal Laws taken off and the Test let alone." Of course, such a plan would have made it impossible for James to pursue his Catholic modernization strategy, perhaps explaining why Penn and Father Petre had become bitter political enemies by June 1688. Meanwhile Penn, to the extent that he did back James II's policies, had lost the support of many Quakers. "His own people" began to "see now only the French interest supports the liberty," one of William's informants wrote of Penn, "for toleration they perceive they must give up property." Penn, agreed the French special envoy Bonrepaus, was "strongly denounced among his own party." The Carlisle Quaker Thomas Story was one who excoriated those "who approached daily nearer and nearer towards the Papists" because he and the "steady part" retained their "dreadful apprehensions."[55]

Prominent Whig politicians and polemicists similarly opposed James II and his Catholic modernization program. Despite James II's best efforts, both the king's closest advisers and foreign observers thought his chief opponents in 1687 and 1688 were Whigs. When William's agent Everard van Weede van Dijkveldt came to England to organize support for his master in 1687, many observers noted his close contacts with Whig leaders. In the summer and autumn of 1687, long after James II had issued his Declaration of Indulgence, "secret cabals" of Whigs continued to organize opposition to royal policies. Unsurprisingly, most contemporaries were far less optimistic than some scholars about James's chances of garnering parliamentary support from the Whigs. The Marquis of Halifax doubted that a Whig parliament would "comply with whatever shall be expected" by the court. "It may reasonably be expected that such Dissenters as shall be chosen [to sit in Parliament] will not in our present circumstances concur to the repeal," agreed the Tory Earl of Nottingham. The Presbyterian minister Roger Morrice, who was as well informed about Whig sentiment as anyone, thought that at most they "will take off the Penal Laws only against mere matters of religion, but that reacheth not the King's point." Experienced political observers came to the same conclusion. "The court begins to be mighty weary of their new friends for they do not find them so cheerful in concurring with their designs," wrote the Whitehall insider James Fraser. James II had no reason "to be satisfied with the face of his affairs," wrote one Orangist after observing Whig attitudes during James II's progress of 1687. The Polish ambassador Antoine Moreau thought it very much an open question whether those James was counting on would actually support him. "None of the principal opponents of the court are willing to change their conduct or their sentiments," concluded the Frenchman Barillon in December 1687.[56]

Most prominent Whigs were inveterate enemies of James II and his policies. While James and his ministers "complemented and caressed" the Earl of Shrewsbury, he remained adamant in his opposition. Shrewsbury traveled back and forth to The Hague to consult with William, he organized a covert political cabal at his house in London, and was thought by many to be "zealous" in deploying his considerable talents in opposition to James. The Earl of Devonshire made no secret of his contempt for James II's policies, assuring William in May 1687 that there were "thousands here" who shared his sentiments. Thomas Wharton, the author of the revolutionary song "Lilibulero," though "despised" by James II, was known to be "very averse to the King of England." Another aristocratic Whig, the Earl of Stamford, was regarded as "one of the leading opponents of James II because of his spirit and talents."[57]

Several past and future Whig members of Parliament were just as adamant in their opposition to James II's Catholic modernization program. Tom Foley of Worcestershire, though approached several times by James's electoral agents, responded that the king's three questions were not "fit to be put, neither shall he give any answer" to them. Another Warwickshire man, Thomas Mariet, who was more closely associated with Baptists and Quakers than the Presbyterian-leaning Foley, advised William Penn at the height of James's attempts to pack Parliament, that there was "no way to heal" the nation but by "a parliament freely and legally chosen." The Cornwall Whig Hugh Boscawen responded to James II's approach to the Whigs by dismissing any Dissenting ministers who hinted at collaboration with the king. It surely must have come as no surprise when he took up arms against his king in Truro in 1688. "Nothing was more known throughout the court than that the King numbered" the flamboyant playwright and Whig politician Sir Robert Howard among his most bitter enemies because "he could not be brought to sacrifice the religion and laws of his country to the arbitrary lust of a priest-ridden tyrant." In Surrey the experienced exclusionist George Evelyn, brother of the diarist, promised to stand for the county in 1688 in order "to preserve our religion and properties now they are in so great danger." The great natural philosopher Isaac Newton, who would sit in the Commons as a Whig in 1689, wrote in 1687 that to support James's Indulgence was "to throw up all the laws for liberty and property." In early January 1688 radical Whigs on both sides of the North Sea made their opposition to James explicit. Despite being begged by the court to engage on their behalf, both Richard Hampden and his son John declared their opposition to the abrogation of the Penal Laws and Test Acts. The younger Hampden, Harry Neville, "and all the old republicans" declared their support for William against James because he would "restore English honor by treating France as his ancestors did Spain, revive European liberty and tolerate different opinions in matters of religion." A few weeks later in Amsterdam a "cabal" was held at John Wildman's lodgings. Attendees included the Whigs Robert Ferguson, John Starkey, who had just assisted in the publication of Gaspar Fagel's *Letter,* and the former Monmouth rebel John Manley.[58]

Whig booksellers and printers like John Starkey and Awnsham Churchill were joined by Whig polemicists. The "passionately Whig" almanac writer John Partridge never wavered in his criticism of James II and his regime. His *Annus Mirabilis* of 1688 cheerfully predicted and encouraged the downfall of James II. In 1688 John Milton's nephew John Phillips resumed his prolific polemical career by publishing a nimble attack on James II's deployment of the prerogative and then by translating the *Monthly Account,* which warned the English of the dire international consequences of James's politics. Daniel Defoe, who was just beginning his long career as an effective political writer, also made clear that Whig principles necessitated opposition to James. He belittled those who claimed that "it hat always been His Majesty's persuasion that conscience ought not to be forced," pointing out that "we know whose hand was most concerned in making and executing Penal Laws in the last reign." James, Defoe pointed out, was a "Roman Catholic prince whose conscience was directed by a Jesuit" whose actions in England would surely be similar to "the mild and gentle usage of the French Protestants by a King whose conscience is directed by a tender-hearted Jesuit."[59]

Although historians have frequently highlighted those Whigs and Dissenters who agreed to work with James and his regime, they have paid less attention to those who either refused to serve, or who served with great reservations. One of the first Whigs approached by James was the Duke of Buckingham. Despite personal pleas from his old comrade William Penn, Buckingham refused to serve with the disingenuous claim that he was "now an errant country gentleman." In 1688 James did manage to employ a number of former radicals in his Privy Council. But one of them, Silius Titus, had already made clear his suspicions about the king's policies. Titus informed James Johnston that while he had given "ear to their proposals," he concluded that James II and his French Catholic advisers aimed "to bring in their religion right or wrong, and to model this army for the taking of it; and if that is not sufficient to take assistance from France." Others, including Colonel Richard Norton, Sir Thomas Lee, Sir Charles Wolseley, and perhaps Lord Wharton, all refused to serve on James's Privy Council.[60]

John Locke's circle of friends reacted to James's policies like many other Whigs. Initially some of them were enthusiastic. In Otterton, Devon, Isabella Duke enthused to Locke in the wake of James's declaration that "'tis the merriest time in England that ever I remember." Inviting Locke to return from his Dutch exile to England, James Tyrell claimed that he "would find a strange alteration in men's humors"; now only "the High Church men" were "highly displeased" with the direction of politics. But like many Dissenters and Whigs, Locke's circle quickly tempered their enthusiasm. Or rather, their doubts about James quickly outpaced their hopes for his commitment to religious liberty. Locke himself rebuffed offers of a pardon from James. Only when James had been overthrown did Locke's friend Philip van Limborch think it possible for the Whig polemicist "to return thither without apprehension." Locke's friends came to share the same sentiments. In the same letter that Tyrell invited Locke back to England he enthused about Gilbert Burnet's *Letters,* a tract that made clear the dangers from French-style Catholicism and was therefore "forbid to be brought in" to England. In the autumn of 1687 the Magdalen College case filled Tyrell with "fear." When James's regulators asked Tyrell himself the three questions in Buckinghamshire in February, he refused the first two. Not surprisingly, he was "turned out" of his place as justice of the peace within a fortnight. Tyrell's Whig cousins Sir Peter and Sir Thomas fared better but made it clear that they like "a great many honest gentlemen" would "not act." Locke's close friend Edward Clarke of Taunton, who shared his interest in wool manufacture, was a longtime Whig politician. Clarke counted the Earl of Shaftesbury and John Trenchard as friends and had been arrested in the wake of Monmouth's rebellion. Clarke kept in close contact with Locke and was visiting him in the Netherlands in the summer of 1688, just as William was preparing his Anglo-Dutch force to invade England. Like Locke himself, Clarke was an enthusiastic supporter of the new regime after 1688 and did all he could to make life difficult for Jacobites. Locke's "noble friend" Thomas Herbert, Earl of Pembroke, "refused to propose the choosing of such members as will take off the Penal Laws and Test" when approached by the Wiltshire regulators. Locke's friend Dr. David Thomas, who also visited Locke in the Netherlands in 1688, refused to serve as alderman of Salisbury. The Dorset Whig John Freke, though identified as a "moderate" supporter of the regime by the regulators, could not have been more explicit in his distaste for James's Catholic modernization program. He discussed going into exile in February 1687, he categorically rejected the three questions, and he refused the enticements of his cousin William Penn. Another of Locke's friends, Sir Walter Yonge, failed to act when named to James II's Commission of Enquiry in Devon. The man who kept John Locke's goods while in exile, Dr. Charles Goodall, thought the events of November and December 1688 might well "deliver our miserable and distressed kingdoms from popery and slavery."[61] Some of Locke's Whig friends, like so many other Dissenters and Whigs, initially welcomed the end of persecution promised by James II but quickly came to dread the loss of civil and eventually religious liberty that his policies would surely bring.

Whigs and Dissenters reacted to James's enticements similarly at the local level. London proved to be the most spectacular case. When James and his regulators sought to replace London's largely Anglican political leadership with Whigs and Dissenters, they met with active and passive resistance. The court removed the Whig recorder Sir John Holt "because he would not give his hand to the taking away the Test." In late November James invited the former Whig recorder Sir George Treby to assume his old duties. Treby refused, taking the opportunity to lecture James in a private audience that his policies had alarmed the people "with the apprehension of the loss of their religion" and "also of their estates and lands, and of their lives." Whigs were no more anxious to serve as sheriff. Although James and his regulators did ultimately appoint a Whig lord mayor and a number of Independent, Presbyterian, and Baptist aldermen, these hardly proved to be a compliant bunch. The Baptist lord mayor, Sir John Shorter, refused to avail himself of James's Declaration of Indulgence, insisting that he was "required by law to take the Oath of Allegiance and Supremacy" according to the rites of the Church England. Not only did his insistence on "going to the Sacrament and taking the Test" infuriate James and his supporters, but it set the standard for the vast majority of the Dissenting London aldermen. Many Dissenters did all they could to avoid serving. The Quaker William Mead, who was to be George Fox's literary executor, refused office, saying, "he will be tool and property for nobody." Others, like the Presbyterian Humphrey Edwin and the Baptist William Kiffin, delayed taking the aldermanic oaths for "above six weeks" before succumbing. To make their opposition to James and his policies manifest, the new Whiggish aldermen quickly voted to celebrate the traditionally anti-Catholic day of 5 November. Court attempts to regulate the London livery companies were no more successful. Dissenters were just as ambivalent about serving in purged guilds as they were about serving James as aldermen of the City. The evidence suggests that in London "by the spring of 1688 James's campaign to win the political support of the Nonconformists had run out of steam."[62]

James, it is clear, did attempt to persuade Whigs and Dissenters to support his regime. For the king this move represented not so much a shift in his political goals as a shift in political strategy. Throughout his reign James remained committed to pursuing a policy of Catholic modernization. What is remarkable is that even after years in the political wilderness and decades of intermittent and increasingly severe persecution, many Whigs and Dissenters did not rush to embrace their liberator. Though some did certainly accept office, though a few did deploy their considerable literary and political talents on behalf of their king, most Whigs and Dissenters did not.

Whigs and Dissenters largely concluded that James was offering religious liberty in exchange for surrendering civil liberty. The Whigs were not so enthusiastic about James's declaration, thought the Tory Sir John Dugdale, because they had "liberty only to play with their consciences; a very airy good little pleasing to them." Dissenters could not be satisfied with mere religious liberty, the vice-principal of Magdalen College Charles Aldworth implied, because they "are for a government so circumstantiated and limited as may only give liberty and power of doing good . . . the end of government being for the good of the community." Whigs and Dissenters were explicit on this point. When rallying his friends and tenants to take up arms against James II on Boden Downs in November 1688 Lord Delamere warned that "if the King prevails, farewell liberty of conscience." This promised liberty was necessarily insecure, he later explained, because it was not based on civil liberty. "It will not be denied but that liberty is a great security to the free exercise of religion," Lord Delamere argued, recalling the English situation before the Revolution, "but if our civil rights are assaulted, I do not see by what means religion can rescue them out of violent hands; because there are many instances where religion has been used as a stalking horse to introduce slavery." John Howe claimed in 1687 that the Presbyterians "generally" believed that "the suffering they had met with, had been on the account of their firm adherence to the civil interest of the nation, in opposition to Tory schemes, rather than on the account of their religious principles," implying that there was no reason to abandon those principles. "Their professed principles," agreed Roger Morrice, "ever inclined" the

Dissenters "tenaciously to adhere to the maintaining and asserting religion, liberty, and property." The Whig Gilbert Burnet told the Prince of Orange in 1686 that "I was such a friend to liberty, that I could not be satisfied with the point of religion alone, unless it was accompanied with the securities of law."[63]

Whigs argued in pamphlet after pamphlet in late 1687 and throughout 1688 that they were both Protestants and Englishmen, that they wanted both religious and civil liberty. They refused to be seduced by religious identity politics. "The sum of my opinion is this," maintained the Dissenter in Thomas Brown's popular 1688 dialogue *Heraclitus Ridens Redivivus,* "that I consider myself an Englishman as well as a Protestant, and whatever I conceive may directly or by consequence prejudice my religion or civil rights, I think myself obliged not to consent to it, as I am to answer to God and my country." Many were provoked by suggestions by William Penn and James himself that liberty of conscience would be the new Magna Carta. The English must "watchfully attend to any encroachment of our civil rights whatever is pretended," warned the author of a 1687 treatise on the Magna Carta. The Dissenters "can not but discern that a new Magna Charta for liberty of conscience will be of no validity to them, for a new Declaration may dispense with it at pleasure," chimed in another. Once the English surrender "our laws" to gain liberty of conscience, predicted yet another scribbler, then James and his supporters would "soon take away . . . our beloved liberties." An England governed by William would be preferable to one governed by James, insisted the author of the runaway best seller *Reflexions on Monsieur Fagel's Letter,* because the Prince of Orange knew it was his "interest to settle matters at home, which only can be done by a legal toleration or comprehension in matters of religion; and by restoring the civil liberties of the nation, so much invaded of late."[64]

Not only must James be understood as a promoter of Catholic modernization rather than a precocious defender of religious liberty, but James's political actions gradually convinced those who benefited the most from his Declarations of Indulgence that this was the case. Although a few Dissenters and Whigs remained convinced that religious liberty was a prior good to civil liberty, the experience of living under James II's government gradually persuaded the majority of them to think otherwise. Most Whigs and Dissenters moved beyond a narrow politics of religious identity in 1687 and 1688. They did not believe that religion was unimportant—far from it—rather, Whigs and Dissenters developed the claim that religious liberty was impossible without the protection of the law. Civil liberty, they thought, must be guaranteed before religious liberty could be enjoyed.

Dissenters and Anglicans, Whigs and moderate Tories increasingly despised James II's Catholic modernization program. A wide range of English men and women across the country and of various social strata turned against James II and his government. James had enraged a far wider group than just the High Churchmen. Are Whig historians, then, right to believe that James's actions, while more sophisticated than they have allowed, united the Protestant English against their king? Are the Whig historians correct to assume that by June 1688 a conservative and Protestant revolution had become inevitable? There are two powerful reasons for doubting this argument. First, James's critics did not express their opposition in confessional terms; they did not describe their actions as a renewal of the struggle between the forces of the Protestant and Catholic Reformations. Second, the events culminating in the trial of the Seven Bishops in June 1688 by no means made James II's downfall inevitable.

Even though many Protestants—both Dissenters and Anglicans—genuinely feared that James II's policies aimed to restore Catholic hegemony in England, they chose to cast their struggle in the language of English liberty rather than in terms of the defense of the true religion. Many no doubt feared and loathed Roman Catholicism. Many certainly held onto to age-old anti-Catholic prejudices. But most criticized the new standing army, the growth and centralization of the state, the intrusive ecclesiastical commission, and James's Declaration of Indulgence as invasions of property and violations of the English constitution. Whigs and Tories, Dissenters and Anglicans expressed most of their discontent in legal rather than confessional terms. When they did criticize Catholics, they did so in specific ways: they made clear that they blamed their troubles not on all Catholics but on Jesuits and French-style Catholics. The English were well aware that it was Jesuits and French-trained Catholic apologists, rather than all Catholics, who defended the absolute power of princes and insisted that force might sometimes be necessary to convert heretics.

Because James's opponents defended English liberty rather than the true religion, they made it possible for Catholic critics of the regime to join them. This they did in large numbers. Even at court there was a "very considerable" party opposed to James's proceedings, including John, Lord Belasyse, of Worlaby; Robert Brudenell, 2nd Earl of Cardigan; the papal nuncio; and Bishop John Leyburn. Belasyse later claimed that "he had been very averse (though a Papist) to the measures used in that reign for promoting that religion, as the putting of papists into office in counties and corporations, the high commission court, the laying aside Protestants for taking away the Test and the Penal Laws." Outside the court, Catholic discontent was more widespread. Many "who were Roman Catholics themselves," recalled one pamphleteer, "abhorred so much the government by priests, that they were eventually disgusted at it and left the court." The "moderate" Catholic party, those who thought James "was too much a creature of the Jesuits," only wanted freedom to practice their religion, fearing that the king's "virulent courses" may cost them their "estates and fortunes." The English Catholics, thought the Dutchman Van Citters, were "more inclined for moderation." Many English Catholics "refused to be sheriffs or deputy lieutenants," reported James Johnston, and those who did agree to serve made it clear that they would have no part in "false returns" so as to create a more pliable House of Commons. The fear of absolutism so dominated "the spirit of the nation," reported the French special envoy Bonrepaus, that the Catholics themselves "opposed the repeal of Test Acts."[65]

Many Catholic priests followed Bishop Leyburn in welcoming their newfound ability to teach and catechize while at the same abhorring James II's French-influenced politics. "Many of the principal Catholics," including Cardinal Howard and his relatives, were surprised and furious when Father Petre was made a member of the king's Privy Council. By making his Jesuit confessor a member of the Privy Council, they reasoned, James had made it all too plausible for people to claim that he aimed "to establish arbitrary power." The well-connected abbot of Ratisbon Placidus Fleming was not alone in worrying that the "proceedings" of the Francophile Drummond brothers in James II's court would "ruin the affairs of religion in our country." "Two great anti-Jesuit" Catholic polemicists, John Sergeant and Peter Walsh, would have nothing to do with James II and his court, presumably because they objected to James's political strategies.[66]

It was because many English (and Scottish) Catholics had such misgivings about James's French-style modern Catholicism, because they embraced notions of English civil liberty, that so many of them worked for and ultimately benefited from James's overthrow. When Dijkveld visited England in 1687, in part to shore up the opposition to James's regime, he not only made contacts with Whigs and some alienated Anglicans but approached a number of Catholics. To their horror the French diplomatic team of Barillon and Bonrepaus soon discovered that many "considerable Catholics" were working with William's agent. By the summer of 1687 they were certain that several had taken "secret measures" with the Prince of Orange. At a time when tensions between Pope Innocent XI and King Louis XIV were so high that the pope contemplated excommunicating His Most Christian Majesty, it is perhaps not surprising that many English Catholics were willing to flirt with treason to prevent a French Catholic takeover of their country. In the aftermath of the revolution, many English Catholics surely felt they had been right to oppose their Catholic monarch. "The Roman Catholics" were never "more at ease and less disturbed in all my observations than here at present," wrote John Evelyn to Lady Tuke, a Catholic, in 1693. English Catholics served in William's armies and welcomed his government not only because the postrevolutionary regime was often reticent to enforce the Penal Laws against them but also, presumably, because the new regime had no interest in promoting French-style religiosity. This was why some Catholics signed the Association of 1696 denouncing the Jacobite Assassination Plot of 1696 as violating "the laws of nature and nations."[67]

Not only are Whig historians wrong to assume that James inspired a narrowly confessional opposition, an opposition that enunciated its grievances in exclusively religious terms, but they are also wrong to assume that the demise of James's regime was inevitable by the summer of 1688. James and his advisers may have acted with uncertainty and some hesitancy in the aftermath of the Seven Bishops' trial, but they did not cease to act. James was surely stunned by the reaction to the bishops' trial, but he and his advisers knew full well that they still had a formidable state apparatus at their disposal. Almost immediately the Commission for Ecclesiastic Causes began gathering names of those clergy who refused to read the king's Second Declaration of Indulgence. By August they had begun to take action. The bishops of Chester and Durham suspended large numbers of

Anglican clerics in their dioceses. Some justices of the peace and army officers took it upon themselves to punish those who had celebrated the bishops' acquittal. When the judges fanned out across the country for their summer circuits, they showed no signs of tactical retreat. According to the archbishop of Canterbury William Sancroft, the bishops were "condemned" by James II's judges "as seditious libelers in their circuits all over England." In Leicester and Northampton Sir Robert Heath said that "the Bishops were guilty of a factious and seditious libel, but were so crafty as to take care there should be no evidence against them." Another baron of the exchequer, Sir John Rotherham, called the bishops "blockheads" at the assizes in Berkshire and agitated "for taking off the Test and Penal laws." In Gloucestershire the Roman Catholic JP William Rogers told the Quarter Sessions that the "factious Bishops" were "cleared by a packed jury." Not a few individuals were "called to account in the circuits for speaking irreverently of His Majesty's Declaration for Liberty of Conscience."[68]

In the summer of 1688 many well-informed observers called for immediate action against James II. Their point was not that James's regime was about to crumble but rather that if his opponents did not act with alacrity, James's position would be impregnable. John Hampden and Sir Thomas Lee agreed that "the King in two years' time would have done his business," so "this Summer" was the time to act. Their fellow Whig the Earl of Devonshire agreed that James's position was only getting stronger and that the friends of the Prince of Orange were "like to suffer." There was no "other means but force" to deal with James II, wrote the Cheshire Whig Lord Delamere justifying his resort to arms in 1688; the alternative was to "pretend to bind the Leviathan with words." "I had rather lose my life in the field than live under an arbitrary power, and see our laws and religion changed," wrote the Earl of Danby to a fellow Tory in September 1688, and that was "now visibly the King's intention."[69]

James's opponents understood what many of the king's supporters had long maintained. It would be best for James if he could procure a compliant Parliament, but James did not need to pack Parliament to succeed. The Marquis of Powis suggested that James could use "money and an army" to achieve a compliant Parliament should persuasion and electoral manipulation fail. "'Tis not improbable" that James would use "French force" to get a Parliament to his liking should the regulators fail, opined one of William's informers. Others close to James thought the king was prepared to dispense with Parliament altogether. "Should it prove impossible to procure a favorable Parliament," thought the French ambassador Barillon, "His Britannic Majesty could still achieve many things on his own authority." Father Petre "and his cabal" were willing in April 1688 to give the regulating plan one last try, but should it fail, they were convinced the king's aims could be achieved by "extreme and violent methods." The Presbyterian Roger Morrice heard rumors in August 1688 that "His Majesty is very indifferent whether this Parliament comply or no," because if they failed him he was happy to "proceed to govern without a Parliament, by such force as he has at home or can have from abroad."[70]

The acquittal of the Seven Bishops in June 1688 was neither an Anglican triumph nor the moment when English Protestants combined to force the Catholic James off the throne. Instead contemporaries understood the trial of the Seven Bishops as one of many steps taken by James in his Catholic modernization program. Since James's program simultaneously sought to promote the king's religion and the king's power, it offended those of his coreligionists who did not share his Sorbonniste view of royal authority. James's opponents were united by their antipathy to royal absolutism. It was this widespread opposition that made James and his regime vulnerable in 1688. James's power, like that of all modernizing regimes, was at its most fragile exactly during its transformative phase. Both the Whig Sir Thomas Lee and the Tory Earl of Danby understood this point all too well. But revolution was not inevitable. James did not depend on public support. Rather, the king placed his faith in the institutions of his modernizing state. And James, in all likelihood, would have survived had his domestic opponents not been able to seize on an international crisis in the autumn of 1688.

James was in the process of modernizing the English state in 1688. That he had been able to achieve as much as he had without a compliant Parliament and despite widespread popular disaffection demonstrated that the rules of government had changed. English rulers in the later seventeenth century no longer relied on negotiation and cooperation with local authorities as much as their predecessors had done. James had new wealth, new technologies of governance, and a new foreign model, Louis XIV, on which to draw. James was able, using the resources, institutions, and traditions he had inherited, to mold a modern state. It was precisely because of James's achievement that many in England realized it would not be enough merely to unmake the modernizing Jacobite state. England, they realized, needed a new governmental form. The Whigs had no ready-made plan in 1688, but there were not a few who understood the necessity of devising one.

It was because James had been able to do so much to modernize and transform the English state that very few were satisfied when he abruptly changed course in late September 1688. Claiming disingenuously that "none of this is done" in response to the "emergency" created by news that William was about to set sail with a massive fleet filled with Dutch and English men, funded by the Dutch States General and the English discontented, James quickly moved to dismantle much of the state apparatus he had created. He restored the Bishop of London, the Magdalen College fellows, eliminated the Ecclesiastical Commission, and restored corporation charters throughout the country. He had decided, wrote the Dutch ambassador Van Citters, "that the Dissenters are too powerless or too unwilling to procure him a favorable Parliament." According to Roger Morrice, James had decided to return to the Tories.[71]

While James's about-face sparked brief celebrations, he convinced almost no one. Almost everyone realized that James was taking temporary and desperate action to forestall

From *Engelants Schouwtoneel* (*The English drama*), by Romeyn de Hooghe, 1692. This print depicts James II in late 1688, finally persuaded to retreat from his absolutist posture and summon a free Parliament. This tactical surrender was part of James's unsuccessful last-ditch strategy to regain Tory support by rolling back his modernization program.

revolution. There was nothing that would prevent him from quickly resurrecting the state apparatus as soon as the crisis had passed. James had appeared to reverse course "without giving any satisfaction to the people," noted John Evelyn in his diary. Even though he had done almost everything demanded by the Tories, Evelyn later observed, the people "seem to long for and desire the landing of that Prince [of Orange], whom they looked on as their deliverer from Popish tyranny." The Dutch ambassador heard people say "that as soon as the storm has passed, the King may retract in everything." "Almost everyone in England" had concluded, agreed the Frenchman Barillon, that James "placed his trust in none of the English nation."[72] James had bowed to the forces of reaction, and it pleased almost no one.

Most people in England realized that merely forcing James to unmake his state was not enough to protect religious and civil liberty. It was therefore not surprising that many in England began sketching blueprints for a new English polity. A few of these have survived. Had James been willing to negotiate, he would have been required to accept a "reformation of the state in civil matters." The former servant of both Charles II and

James II, John Evelyn, provided just such a blueprint for revolutionary transformation in November 1688. Evelyn hoped to prevent forever the kind of state James had constructed. He demanded free elections, parliamentary reform, parliamentary control of the army and navy, and the elimination of the dispensing power. But Evelyn did not merely want to destroy James II's state; he wanted to erect a modern edifice in its place. He hoped for an Anglo-Dutch union to fight France, a new land tax, a state-supported civil service, and a new committee to promote public projects. Evelyn proposed that the Anglican Church be retained, but with toleration for "sober Dissenters" and Roman Catholics. He also called for a wide-ranging plan for the reformation of English manners, including the extension of social benefits to the poor and the erection of a public library in each county.[73]

Others drew up plans that were less comprehensive. The Cheshire Whig nobleman Lord Delamere, who expected to lose his life when he took up arms against James, drew up several memoranda that, taken together formed a call to revolution. Delamere was committed to the transformation of the state, but in 1688 he was less specific about the nature of his imagined new government. Above all, he reminded his children in September 1688, "God almighty did on purpose permit the Jewish constitution to be changed," showing that "if any people found theirs to be out of order, the blame rested at their doors if it was not reformed." Delamere was no defender of the ancient constitution. He also hoped for a new state in which the clergy were prevented from discussing politics, "for none are blinder guides than they, and no one thing has done more mischief in this nation than their politics." Delamere had long been committed to religious toleration; in 1688, however, he did not specify its nature. He demanded free and regular Parliaments, "for the government cannot long continue well when Parliaments are neglected." Government, he insisted, was instituted for "the good" of the people, and any king who "forsakes the guidance of the law" should not be obeyed. Only when Delamere became dissatisfied with Tory government under William and Mary did he think it necessary to specify what he meant by the "good" of the people.[74]

The Presbyterian John Humfrey was more detailed and explicit in his vision for a postrevolutionary state. The English, Humfrey thought, had a unique and unprecedented opportunity. "The state we are in," he observed, was "a state that puts the supreme power in the hands of the people, to place it as they will: and therefore to bound and limit it as they see fit, for the public utility; and if they do it not now, the ages to come will have occasion to blame them forever." Like most Whigs and Dissenters Humfrey had come to prioritize civil over religious liberty. "The delivery of the people from slavery," had to be the primary object, "which can never be done effectually and radically but upon this advantage." "The settling our religion," by contrast, was "a work of great length" and was "the business more properly of a Parliament." Humfrey believed that the only way to prevent future kings from reviving James II's political program was to lodge power over the military and judiciary in the hands of the legislature. In addition, Humfrey advocated replacing the current regressive taxation scheme with a new system of progressive taxation. He wanted "a register of estates" preparatory to a land tax on the wealthiest Englishmen, coupled with the elimination of "the Chimney Money," which was not only intrusive but taxed the manufacturing sector most heavily. He wanted a more efficient state, with "a provision against buying and selling offices" and "a regulation of Westminster Hall." Finally, Humfrey hoped for "freedom from persecution (by a bill for Comprehension and Indulgence) in the business of religion."[75] Much of Humfrey's revolutionary program soon became that of the nation at large.

James II was committed to a program of Catholic modernization. He appreciated that Europe was rapidly changing. To become a major player on the European scene, England needed to develop a large and powerful state. James perceived that England was well positioned to take advantage of new economic opportunities. In particular, James thought—as will be detailed in chapter 11—that England could displace the United Provinces of the Netherlands as Europe's primary imperial power in the East and West Indies. James and his state could tap resources from these new and expanding possessions to create a governmental edifice on a par with that of Louis XIV. James thought that England's best chance for imperial greatness was to create a modern absolute government. His preference for absolutism was deeply informed by his French Catholic belief system. Not only had he been reconciled to the Catholic Church by French-educated Jesuits, but he had adopted their vision of the modern Catholic state. He believed deeply, along with Louis XIV, both that Catholic theology demanded the absolute sovereignty of princes and that force was sometimes necessary to break the will of heretics and bring them to the true faith. James II was committed both to absolute monarchy and the reestablishment of Catholicism in England.

James did a great deal to achieve his vision of a modern Catholic monarchy. He was not the bumbling, bigoted, and hopelessly unrealistic king described in Whig historiography. He did much to centralize political power in England. He reformed countless corporations, he established nationwide ideological tests for political office, he transformed and modernized the English bureaucracy both in the metropolis and in the counties, he created a modern standing army and a more modern navy, and he did a great deal to centralize and rationalize imperial governance.

Like most modernizers, however, James II provoked and energized widespread opposition. Whigs and Tories, Anglicans, Dissenters, and many Catholics resented the new intrusive and aggressive state apparatus. The majority of English men and women almost certainly objected to James II's measures. They rioted against them. They applauded James II's political reverses. They refused to support his chosen candidates for local and national office. In the final analysis, however, they would have been unable to unmake James II's modern state. James II's political opponents, as many as they were, were not strong enough to combat the modern military and modern bureaucracy that their king was creating. Conservative reaction was impossible. Revolution had become the only option.

James II was undone because his actions had broad international implications. He was deposed neither by an indigenous consensus nor by a foreign invasion. James II was overthrown by a combination of English popular uprisings and an Anglo-Dutch military force because many in England as well as many in Europe came to share an alternative vision for the modern state.

PART III

Revolution

CHAPTER EIGHT

Popular Revolution

The English "have been always inclined to rebellion and intestine commotions," observed the German natural law thinker and comparative historian Samuel Pufendorf. Robert Ferguson, who had a great deal of personal experience in the matter, noted that "in all our histories of Great Britain, we meet with nothing more frequent than mobs and insurrections." The enthusiastic supporter of the Revolution of 1688–89 James Wellwood agreed that "scarce any kingdom we know upon earth has suffered so many and various convulsions" as England. The English are "a nation prone to rebellion," lamented one committed Jacobite. Since so many in Britain and Europe were convinced of English political volatility, it was inevitable that some would speculate on the broader consequences of the Revolution of 1688–89. The Scottish Episcopalian Robert Kirk expressed what would soon become a common sentiment. "England," he wrote, "is like to be a precedent to all states and armies hereafter, for defeating their prince in a time of need, if he rule not by laws."[1]

This Early Modern image of England could not be farther from our contemporary understanding of the Revolution of 1688–89 as an unrevolutionary revolution. The Revolution of 1688–89, it is claimed, failed three standards met by proper revolutions. First, the Revolution of 1688–89 was not a popular revolution. Social scientists agree that "top-down social transformations do not qualify as revolutions." For more than two centuries scholars have followed establishment Whigs in insisting on English popular political passivity. It

(above) *Landing of William of Orange at Torbay,* by Jan Luder, 1688. William III landed in England in November 1688 and was welcomed by large crowds of English men and women. This medal shows his troops disembarking at Torbay, Devon.

"seems to be certain," asserts Thomas Doubleday in 1847, "that the revolution in this period was not brought about by any effort on the part of the English people." This assessment has only been reinforced by more recent scholarship. "In 1688 the Glorious Revolution was popular in that all save Catholics applauded it, but not in the sense that the masses played any part in planning it or executing it," concludes Robin Clifton. "To the political nation indeed 1688 was glorious precisely because it was so far from being a popular rebellion." Both John Western and Jonathan Scott have insisted on the "relative passivity of the English" people in 1688–89. "The events of 1688 were no revolution," agrees Stephen Saunders Webb. "They were not even a revolt, whether by peers, parliament or people."[2]

Many scholars have concluded that the Revolution of 1688–89 was an aristocratic coup d'état. For G. M. Trevelyan "the Revolution was indeed a demonstration of the power of the landowning classes," it took place firmly under "aristocratic and squirearchical leadership." Christopher Hill concurs with Trevelyan in this, if in little else. "The Revolution" of 1688, he writes, "demonstrated the ultimate solidarity of the propertied class." "The revolution did not in any significant sense represent a popular rising against James," concludes David Hosford, reviewing the evidence he gathered from northern England. "It was an upper class movement initiated and dominated by members of the nobility and scions of aristocratic houses." The provincial risings in 1688, agrees J. R. Jones, "were a conclusive demonstration of the social cohesion and (admittedly temporary) political unity of the landowning classes, who had an obvious interest in preserving order."[3]

For other scholars the Revolution of 1688–89 was fundamentally a foreign invasion. Jonathan Israel has pointed out that William of Orange invaded England with an army of at least twenty-one thousand men. The northern risings, according to Israel, had little effect. "Most of England's nobility and gentry evinced so healthy a respect for James's standing army, and the practical side of his authority," Israel suggests, "that they preferred to sit on the fence, declining to commit themselves. . . . Consequently, the Revolution in the north and midlands was merely a by-product." The collapse of James's regime had nothing to do with indigenous resistance. "The plain fact was that it was the Prince of Orange acting in collusion with a tiny group of lords . . . who made the king leave," Israel contends. The invasion thesis has now all but become orthodoxy. "The armies, not the people, would decide the issue" in 1688, chimes in Craig Rose in one standard narrative history.[4]

Second, the Revolution of 1688–89 is said to have been bloodless, falling short of the standard of great revolutions in yet another way. "Political change through violent means is the single defining characteristic of revolution most often cited in the literature" on revolution, notes Isaac Kramnick. Accounts of the Revolution of 1688–89 almost invariably highlight its bloodless character in contrast to the French or Russian Revolutions. "This revolution, of all revolutions the least violent," Thomas Babington Macaulay bragged of the Revolution of 1688–89, "has been, of all revolutions, the most beneficent." "It is England's true glory," remarks G. M. Trevelyan with an implicit nod to the French Revolution, "that the cataclysm of James's overthrow was not accompanied by the shedding of English blood either on the field or on the scaffold." Jonathan Scott also celebrates the bloodlessness of 1688–89 in contrast this time to the English upheavals of midcentury. "Within five months events had traversed the entire passage from successful invasion (as in 1640) to restoration (1660)," Scott points out, "missing out most of the bloodshed and revolution between." Tim Harris, looking narrowly at London crowd activity in 1688, concludes "that the violence was often constrained."[5]

Third, whereas modern revolutions are extremely divisive, the Revolution of 1688–89 is said to have occurred by consensus. According to Macaulay, both Whigs and Tories agreed to establish a moderate solution to England's political crisis. During England's Revolution, in contrast to Continental events, "extreme opinions were generally held in abhorrence." "In our Revolution," Trevelyan concurs drawing an implicit contrast with the continent, "the two great parties in Church and State united to save the laws of the land from destruction by James." The Revolution of 1688–89 was therefore necessarily "a victory of moderation, a victory not of Whig or Tory passions." More recent scholars have come to similar conclusions. The "belief that the king had to be constrained provided a sufficient binding force to hold the movement together until after the final outcome had been decided," Hosford observes. John Western contrasts the divisions in Scotland in 1688 with the "consensus" in England. For John Morrill "the Sensible Revolution of 1688–89 was a conservative Revolution" precisely because "it did not create damaging new rifts in the English nation."[6]

Against these traditional views, I suggest that the Revolution of 1688–89 does indeed meet the theoretical standard of revolution. Scholars have significantly underestimated the extent of English popular involvement in the Revolution. Thousands took up arms in support of William. There were popular risings throughout England—as well as in Scotland and parts of Ireland. Many Englishmen went into exile to join William's invasion force. Still others contributed financially to the overthrow of James's regime. Although many aristocrats did play a significant role in these activities, the masses who took arms should not be understood as taking part in a baronial revolt. Crowd activity in 1688–89 was remarkably similar to that in other revolutions. "Revolutions," Crane Brinton has reminded us, "are not begun by the poor and downtrodden." In France, George Rudé has pointed out, the *sans-culottes* "were not at variance with, or isolated from, those of other social groups." In fact, they were able "to assimilate and to identify themselves with the new political ideas promoted by the liberal aristocracy and the bourgeoisie." In neither the French nor the English case should this coordination render popular political activity irrelevant. In England as in France a century later popular elements worked in coordination with the higher orders. In part because of the extensive popular activity in 1688–89, the revolution was far from bloodless. There was extensive mob violence throughout England in late 1688, violence that terrified local populations and resulted in extensive damage to property and individuals, violence that was on the same scale as the violence in France subsequent to July 1789.[7] It is true that the expected civil war never occurred in England because of the rapid collapse of James's army. Instead James chose to conduct his war in Scotland and Ireland, conflicts that need to be seen as part of the bloody Nine Years' War against France.

Last, the ostensible consensus of 1688–89 was, under closer examination, a mirage. Not only was there extensive, and deeply felt, Jacobite sentiment from the start but ideological divisions were always evident among James's opponents. The revolution settlement was not a consensual compromise but the result of profound disagreements and subject to party political interpretation. The settlement settled nothing. James's departure only reframed debates that persisted well into the eighteenth century and beyond.

The Revolution of 1688–89 was neither a coup d'état nor a foreign invasion but a popular revolution. Just as in the French and Russian Revolutions, there was extensive and violent crowd activity. And just as in other modern revolutions, the revolutionary events resulted not in consensus and compromise but in deep ideological cleavages.

In early June 1688 James appeared both secure on the throne and successful in his attempt to modernize the British state. He had successfully remodeled borough corporations and county magistracies throughout England and Wales. He and his regulators had ostensibly made it certain that all future Parliaments would compliantly do the king's bidding. He had transformed England's two ancient universities so that they would now train Catholic priests as well as Anglican clergymen. He had talented and loyal men running the governments of both Ireland and Scotland. James had also done a great deal to create a modern and efficient standing army. In tandem with his efficient secretary of the navy, Samuel Pepys, James had gone a long way to creating a world-class navy. Besides all of that, James was on very friendly terms with the most powerful monarch in Europe, Louis XIV.

Yet in a little over half a year, the English people chased their king and his family from England. The contrast between the events of 1688 and Monmouth's failed invasion of 1685 was stunning. In 1685 James crushed the uprising led by the popular and charismatic Duke of Monmouth. In 1688 it was James and his army that were routed. The difference was not that William of Orange arrived with a more powerful army but that in 1688 William's Anglo-Dutch army was supported by mass popular uprisings throughout England.

When news began to pour in from James's various diplomats and international informants in August 1688 that his son-in-law, William of Orange, was planning a bold invasion, James II appeared prepared. Throughout England observers commented on the "great preparations." John Verney marveled that James's government "work hard as well Sunday as workdays to get out a fleet, and the dragoons are going to the sea coasts, as well as other regiments." Sir John Lowther recalled that "nothing was left undone that might put the king in a posture to defend himself."[8]

By the time that William landed at Torbay in November 1688, James had a for-midable fighting machine at his disposal. Levies had augmented the standing regiments. Crack troops had arrived from Scotland and Ireland. Reliable contemporaries reported that "the garrisons are everywhere well provided, and the King has now 40,000 men in England standing forces, including those that are come from Scotland and Ireland." "I grow stronger every day at land by the Scots and Irish coming near the town, and the forwardness of some of the regiments of horse and foot," wrote a confident James II to his friend and naval commander the Earl of Dartmouth. "In a very few days time, I shall be much stronger than I am." When James set up camp at Salisbury he could rely on about thirty thousand trained soldiers, in addition to those in training and manning the gar-risons.[9] This was a substantially larger army than even the most generous estimates of the forces at William's disposal.

The news from the navy was also promising. "The maritime preparations advance successfully," reported Robert Yard from the secretary's office. "Now we begin to look in earnest," Dartmouth informed the king, "and though our men are not so good as they will be, yet they are generally for their number as good as any I saw at the first fitting out of ships." James himself felt reassured "that all the fleet are in so good heart."[10]

There was good reason to believe that despite rumors of discontent, the people of the three kingdoms would enthusiastically support their king in the face of a foreign invasion. "I doubt not," confided Robert Yard to the Marquis d'Albeville, that the people will "on this occasion give fresh proofs of their fidelity to the king and their readiness to serve him against all foreign as well as home enemies." "The English are more resolute than ever to fight for their king," reported another, "when these three nations are united, what can the king fear?" "Those who so faithfully adhered to the crown in the suppression of the Monmouth Rebellion still hold their true principles of duty and loyalty and will exert themselves again with as much vigor against any foreign invader be the pretences never so plausible," reasoned one newsletter writer with a telling comparison. The Earl of Sunderland's account—even if he was playing the double agent—chimed in with others. "All the Dissenters are satisfied, and the Church of England's principles will keep them loyal, though they may be indiscreet," he asserted. "In short I believe there never was in England less thoughts of rebellion."[11]

Most supporters of James II were confident that the Dutch invasion of 1688 would prove to be yet another in a long line of failed attacks against the Stuart monarchy. "I question not," wrote Thomas Bligh from London in September, that if the Dutch do come, "His Majesty and his loyal people here will be able to beat them out, to their eter-nal shame." The English were so strong, agreed Nathaniel Molyneux, "that we are able almost to blow them home again." Elizabeth Herbert told her son that the Dutch were coming "but to be beaten." Sir Ralph Verney, who was no friend of James II's regime, informed Lady Bridgeman that "the confused noise of the Dutch has never been able to break my sleep, nor I believe would not if they actually landed since the King has forces sufficient to repel them." From Salisbury plain in November Thomas Brathwait wrote to his countryman Sir Daniel Fleming that he would soon be sending him "an account of a second Monmouth's success."[12]

Yet James II fared very differently in 1688 than he had in 1685. Even though the king was far better prepared to face an armed enemy in 1688 than he had been in 1685, the outcome was a complete disaster for James. Within a month of William's landing, James's standing army had dissolved. His fleet never fired a salvo against the Dutch navy. By the end of December James himself had fled the country. In February 1689 William and Mary were crowned king and queen. What had happened? Why had James's ostensibly powerful regime been toppled so quickly?

The answer to the puzzle is that James had lost the support of a large proportion of his subjects. Many opposed his modernizing and centralizing state. Some were concerned with his sympathy for and promotion of French-style Catholicism. A very few detested his promotion of liberty of conscience. Others were concerned about his use of royal fiat to promote his policy of liberty of conscience. Still others were concerned about James's failure to align his kingdoms firmly and publicly against French expansionism.

By the middle of 1688 it was clear to a variety of observers that England was seething with discontent. Already that spring one observer was predicting that James's policies were merely "cobwebs . . . that have more art than strength" that will soon "come to be thrown out." The bishop of Carlisle thought that that garrison town had "grown extreme sullen and unmanageable." The Jacobite soldier John Stevens later recalled that in Wales in the summer of 1688, "I could not but easily discern, how prone all were to mutter about breach of laws, and invading of religion, and it was plainly to be discerned, that many who said Well Well thought very evil." "It were almost incredible to tell you," recounted the enthusiastic Williamite and northerner Colley Cibber, "at the latter-end of King James's time (though the rod of arbitrary power was always shaking over us) with what freedom and contempt the common people in the open streets talked of his wild measures to make a whole Protestant nation Papists; and yet, in the height of our secure and wanton defiance of him, we of the vulgar had no farther notion of any remedy for this evil than a satisfied presumption that our numbers were too great to be mastered by his mere will and pleasure." The normally cautious John Evelyn thought in August that "the whole nation [is] disaffected and in apprehensions." "The whole nation is alienated from the government in their inclination," agreed the radical Richard Hampden.[13]

The imminence of William's arrival in the autumn failed to turn popular opinion toward James. In London "most men either carried a tacit treason in their faces, or palliated in their words." The Earl of Bath found Exeter to be "miserably divided and distracted." From the northwest Sir Christopher Musgrave reported on "great distractions." "The commotions of the kingdom are very great," wrote the experienced political observer Sir Charles Cotterell. Another observer could not but lament that "England [is] extraordinary disunited." One Catholic purveyor of news castigated the ingratitude "of the rabble and people of this kingdom" who were "publishing and venting many villainous scandals." The Marquis d'Albeville could not believe the "enthusiasm or rather madness" of an "English nation" that "refuses liberty of conscience, the only thing that can increase their wealth and tranquility, [and] runs headlong into civil wars, and after such a manner as must entail them upon themselves and posterity."[14]

Most commentators thought that England had "grown ripe for a revolution." One observer recalled that "there was a wonderful consternation among some people." "Most people wished for any means to be relieved," wrote the archbishop of Canterbury William Sancroft in January 1689. "Many encouraged a foreign force to invade England."[15]

English encouragement played a decisive role in framing William of Orange's bold invasion of England in November 1688. William and his advisers did a nearly miraculous job in convincing the often-divided Dutch United Provinces to support his militarily daring adventure in the autumn of 1688. One experienced European diplomat commented that "he had never seen the Dutch so resolute in supporting, rather than fearing, a war." Alexander Dunbar, who was a hostile Catholic observer, marveled at "the greatest sea preparations that has been heard of out of memory." But it is important to remember that William's endeavor was never imagined as a Dutch invasion. William would not have sailed to England without assurances of substantial indigenous support. William would not have and could not have raised an army of twenty thousand without British aid.[16]

William was interested in accurately assessing English sentiment, not in creating false hopes on which to base a doomed invasion. In 1687 and 1688 William sent two of his trusted servants, the Heer van Dijkveldt and Count Zuylestein, to sound out political opinion in the British Isles. William himself, it is true, insisted on a formal invitation "by some men of the best interest, and the most valued in the nation" as a necessary prerequisite to his taking up arms. But William's focus on formal guarantees and aristocratic acquiescence should not blind us to the depth of popular sentiment against James II and his regime. Count Zuylestein reported that "the whole nation was in a high fermentation." English contemporaries echoed the extent of popular disaffection. James Wellwood insisted that it was "the people of England" who were forced "upon an inevitable necessity of calling in the Prince of Orange to retrieve the expiring liberties of their country." "What did we discourse of everywhere to one another, as the sole foundations of our hopes of freedom and relief," Daniel Defoe asked rhetorically, referring to the Prince of Orange. "It's no ways to be doubted but [William III] has been encouraged and invited by the leading persons of the hierarchical party in the church and state in the army and in the fleet," exclaimed the Presbyterian Roger Morrice, "they that always condemned that principle of taking up arms in defense of their religion or civil rights, now think it both lawful, highly laudable and absolutely necessary." Dissenters, including Roger Morrice himself, were no less forward in venting their frustrations with the regime. The treasonous roll of those pledged to support William in 1688 kept by the Earl of Shrewsbury, the archbishop of Canterbury "and some other eminent persons" only captured a tiny fraction of popular support.[17]

The Invitation of the Seven of June 1688—the authors of which were themselves a diverse set of gentlemen and aristocrats—did more than assure William that "much the greatest part of the nobility and gentry are as much dissatisfied" as the signatories and that "the most considerable of them would venture themselves with your Highness at your first landing." They also thought it vital to report on the state of public opinion more generally. They knew that much more than the support of a few aristocrats was needed to overturn James's powerful regime. "The people," they wrote, "are so generally dissatisfied with the present conduct of the government in relation to their religion, liberties, and properties (all which have been greatly invaded) and they are in such expectation of their prospects being daily worse, that your Highness may be assured there are nineteen parts of twenty of the people throughout the kingdom, who are desirous of a change, and who we believe would willingly contribute to it if they had such a protection to countenance their rising, as could secure them from being destroyed before they could get to be in a posture to defend themselves."[18]

These were not the views of overly optimistic revolutionaries. Diplomats throughout Europe came to similar conclusions about the state of English public opinion. The Austrians were sure, reported the Earl of Carlingford, that William has "already a great faction in England formed and ready to receive him, that the inclinations of two parts in three are already with him." In the Spanish Netherlands Sir Richard Bulstrode heard talk of "a great revolt in England as soon as the States fleet should appear on our coasts." The diplomatic contacts of the Hamburg-based Peter Wyche revealed that the Prince of Orange's party in England "have promised home and are engaged too far to be able to retreat." George Etherege heard in Ratisbon, but very much doubted, "that great revolutions will be in our country and that no less than a civil war is upon the point of breaking out." In Paris it was said "very openly that the Prince of Orange has many friends in England who can do him service and will declare for him, if ever he appear amongst them." The Dutch, the Marquis d'Albeville knew, were literally betting on British popular support. They so counted on "great assistance in England and Scotland" that "they can not see one another in the streets, but they cry out embracing one another." "It is known to all the world that the English nation has long since murmured," announced the States General of the United Provinces based on their extensive diplomatic networks, "nothing but a general disorder and confusion could be expected in that kingdom."[19]

Contemporary observers within England sensed immense goodwill for William and little support for James's government in the autumn of 1688. "After it was known that the Prince's forces were shipped and all things ready," noted Sir Robert Southwell, "the people here generally longed for their coming." One "witty gent" observed "that the people were divided, the one half hoped the Prince would come, and the other half feared he would not come." When Samuel Clarke surveyed his countrymen on the prospect of the arrival of the Dutch, he found "but few melancholy faces." "People yet speak of it smilingly," William Westby wrote of the impending arrival of the Dutch fleet. In Yorkshire Sir John Reresby noted that "neither the gentry nor common people seemed much afraid."

Sum of ye Nobillety of England are sending their memorialls of their Distreses to ye Prince of Oring

The Invitation to William of Orange of June 1688 assured
the Dutch stadholder that the vast majority of English men
and women would rally to his support against James II.

"Many would be glad to hear of the landing," agreed the Dutch ambassador Van Citters, "the conversation on this subject being general among all classes of society, excepting the Roman Catholics and courtiers."[20]

The English did more than passively wish the Dutch well. The English people actively subverted James II's regime before November 1688 and put their lives on the line to support William's enterprise. William's arrival should be seen less as a Dutch invasion than as a joint Anglo-Dutch venture against James II's regime. The sequence of events that began in the autumn of 1688 need to be understood not as the fourth Anglo-Dutch war of the seventeenth century but as a central event in England's revolutionary century.

English governance was in a state of crisis in the summer and autumn of 1688—a crisis that was only made acute by the prospect of an Anglo-Dutch invasion. By the middle of August Roger Morrice observed that "public affairs seem now to be in a tottering posture, there seems to be no party engaged to the Crown." When James, in a panic, reversed his course, restored the corporation charters, abolished the ecclesiastical commission, abandoned his projects for reforming the universities, and appeared to appeal once again for the support of the Tories, he was still unable to place the government on a firmer footing.[21]

County militias and urban trained bands refused to act on behalf of their king throughout the crisis of 1688–89. When the Duke of Newcastle convened the nobility of the three ridings of Yorkshire to ask for their support against the impending arrival of William and his men, they instead "drank among themselves, first confusion to the Catholics, the welfare of the protestant religion and those who hold with it, and lastly a good easterly wind." Many if not most refused to serve in the militia with those who were not qualified to do so by law. Lord Fairfax was not the only one in Yorkshire who lamented that "we are in a very distracted condition here; not being in any sort of posture to defend or offend an enemy ourselves." "Several other counties followed the example of Yorkshire and refused to act in the lieutenancy in conjunction with the Roman Catholics," remembered Sir John Lowther. In Staffordshire there was "no militia at all." In Lancashire, while some agreed to serve, many refused, saying "it was against law and they could not do it in conscience being no one can bear office without taking the oaths." In Leicestershire the muster "ended in nothing" because there, as in Derbyshire, "the gentlemen of the country who had the greatest interest being removed out of the several commissions [of the peace] were so exasperated in this time of difficulty and danger that those who would not act against the king, sat still and would not appear for him." In Cheshire, where the Earl of Derby accepted the position of lord lieutenant only after consulting the Prince of Orange, the militia was unable to raise the necessary money to muster. Things were no better in the west. In Somerset "at present there is no deputy lieutenant nor militia officer in this county," lamented the Earl of Bristol. When the Duke of Beaufort arrived in Bristol in November 1688, he "found the militia of that city so backwards to oppose the Prince, that he has left it and gone home to his own house at Badminton." From the Isle of Wight Sir Robert Holmes reported that "part of the militia is grown mutinous already and refuses to follow their commanders' orders." The pattern was similar nearer London. Sir Ralph Verney was not unusual in advising his grandson to avoid service in the Buckinghamshire militia. From Kent Lord Teynham reported on "the great difficulty I find will be to find out such as will take commissions."[22]

Not only were the English in the countryside reluctant to serve their king, but there are signs that English urban dwellers were equally backward. England's metropolis had ground to an administrative standstill. When James restored London's charter in October 1688, he was not able to regain the goodwill of Londoners. When Lord Chancellor George Jeffreys came to the city to restore the charter "the people made no huzzahs at the sight of the seal, but several people when they saw it looked at the coach and said, there was the fellow that took away the charter, they could expect no good from him." The "old honest aldermen" who were asked to govern the city were "unwilling to enter into employment." The newly appointed lord mayor Sir William Prichard refused to act on the grounds that he was not properly elected. Many prominent Londoners, both Whigs and Tories, similarly refused the office. Jeffreys bemoaned the fact that "the City remains now without any seeming magistracy, which is not fit long to remain in this posture." Sir John Chapman who was meant to assume the mayoralty in November "made difficulties to the King"—presaging greater acts of resistance after William's arrival.[23]

The situation was little better in Exeter. There the purges in the corporation had created such great "animosities" that even after the restoration of the city charter, "few gentlemen come near the City; the most considerable merchants are leaving it; the trade decays, distractions increase." Evidence from elsewhere in the country suggests that James II's last-ditch attempt to cultivate the Crown's traditional supporters simply created political confusion.[24]

James II and his government were sufficiently unpopular in the autumn of 1688 that despite the manifest national danger, the regime had trouble attracting seamen and soldiers. "Drums are beating up about Wapping for seamen but few come in" reported John Verney. Thames watermen were being impressed to serve on the fleet, "for few volunteers come in." The problem was apparently national. "Hardly any one will voluntarily enter into the King's service," noted the Dutch ambassador Van Citters, "particularly as it might turn to a war with Holland." By early October "most of the seafaring men and a great number of watermen" had fled inland to avoid the government's increasingly desperate press gangs. There was no great influx of men into the army either. Although James's army did swell in size, it grew through compulsion rather than an outpouring of loyalist sentiment. Anthony Heyford thought that Norfolk was "the worst county in England for recruiting our troops." His assessment probably reflected his despair rather than a genuine comparative assessment. Other localities shared the experience of Exeter where agitators were "persuading people not to list themselves in His Majesty's Service.[25]

The English were far from pulling together in the face of a foreign invasion in the autumn of 1688. Coal prices skyrocketed because of fears that coastal shipping would be curtailed. There was a general run on the banks. Money became scarce. Most agreed that there had "been a general stop to all matters of trade." The prominent London bankers Kent and Duncombe significantly refused to lend James II money in his hour of need. In the face of this manifest unpopularity it was hardly surprising that Whitehall was full of "confusion and distraction." Roger Morrice thought with good reason in early October that "the government seems now to be like a vessel tossed up and down the sea, and ready to sink."[26]

The extent of popular disaffection and institutional breakdown in England in the autumn of 1688 should caution against an interpretation of the Revolution of 1688–89 as the result primarily of a Dutch invasion. The active role that the English, Scots, and Irish played in assisting William's enterprise further weakens the case for the Williamite thesis. The Dutch in general, and William in particular, were remarkably successful in raising money and assembling a formidable fighting force in the 1688, but they did this in concert with a substantial proportion of the English population.

A wide variety of English men and women contributed financially to William's enterprise. "A great deal of money comes daily out of England" to support the Dutch enterprise, reported the Marquis d'Albeville to Lord Middleton in the late summer of 1688. Daniel Petit's information was more precise. He learned that "near £200,000 sterling had been remitted hither from London within a month or six week's time"—an astounding figure when the gross estimated yearly revenue collected by James and his government was less than two million pounds for 1687–8. One Dane remarked after being taken to see William's war chest that he saw "such prodigious heaps of English gold as by his computation less must be left in the kingdom." Another government informant heard that the Dutch had "millions of Spanish coin that was brought over from England."[27]

Unfortunately, we have no complete list of the British contributors to William's effort. Nevertheless, there is strong evidence that John Churchill, the Earl of Shrewsbury, and the Earl of Danby mortgaged parts of their estates to transfer thousands of pounds to William's cause through the Bank of Amsterdam. Sir Hugh Owen sent "eight chests of silver" from Wales to Rotterdam to support William and his Anglo-Dutch force. One suspects that a great many more made more modest financial contributions.[28]

As soon as William arrived in England, hundreds donated money to his cause. The West Country Whig Hugh Speke claimed to have donated "above a thousand pounds." Sir John Morgan, who later became governor of Chester castle, reminded the Earl of Shrewsbury that he, too, had "laid out in the late revolution a considerable sum maintaining out of my own pocket the greatest part of those men we had then in arms." The Earl of Rutland contributed a thousand pounds. The Earl of Devonshire collected over fourteen thousand pounds at Nottingham, Leicester, and Coventry. The Earl of Bristol, apparently with some success, asked the inhabitants of Dorset to support "his Highness" and the "glorious undertaking." The Dutch ambassador Van Citters learned in Reading that "some private individuals in this town and most of the nobility of Wiltshire have from pure inclination given several sums of money and offered more for the support" of William and his army.[29]

The account book fragments that survive from the popular uprisings in November and December 1688 reveal the extent and depth of popular financial support for the uprising against James. Whereas some substantial gentlemen, such as Sir William Boothby and Justice Candall of Leicester, donated in excess of a hundred pounds each, most contributed much smaller amounts. One Henry Candish of Loughbridge donated thirty pounds, while Sir Thomas Gragely of Nottingham gave fifteen. More common still were anonymous and smaller donations. "A little leather bag" from Derby contained just over nine pounds, almost a hundred pounds came "in one bag" from Nottingham, and "two other boys brought from Melborn" £120. John Wright gathered almost a thousand pounds from seven individuals. If anything, the Scottish Episcopalian Robert Kirk's later estimate that the English paid eighty thousand pounds in November and December 1688 seems a bit conservative.[30]

The money continued to pour into William's coffers after James had fled the country, but before William was crowned king. In January 1689 the Common Council of the London agreed to subscribe a loan to the prince to support the interim government. Londoners were soon falling over themselves to contribute. People were "thronging in to make subscriptions none of which are to be under fifty pounds; Guildhall hath not hands enough to receive the sums of money that flows in." Within two days the City had collected more than £150,000 and it was thought that ultimately "the subscriptions will be three times as much." Naturally there were some very large loans—the great Whig merchants Sir Patience Ward, Sir Robert Clayton, Sir William Ashurst, and John Joliffe subscribed a thousand pounds each—but most subscribed fifty or one hundred pounds. In all more than thirteen hundred male and female inhabitants of London contributed to the loan. The Royal African Company gave William an outright gift of one thousand pounds.[31]

Not only was William's expedition partly underwritten with British silver, but it included many British bodies. Many prominent men joined William in the Netherlands and came over with his fleet. The Earl of Shrewsbury was instrumental in planning "the extraordinary undertaking." The committed Whigs Lord Mordaunt, the Earl of Macclesfield, Sir Rowland Wynne, Sir John Guise, Sir Robert Peyton, Sir John Hotham, John Wildman, and Robert Ferguson had long been in the United Provinces waiting for their opportunity to return in triumph. In 1688 many sons of prominent noblemen joined William, including the sons of the Earl of Winchester, the Earl of Lindsey, the Earl of Danby, and the Marquis of Halifax. Many prominent Scots also joined William's forces, including the Earls of Sutherland, Fforfar, and Leven, as well as Lords Cardross, Lorne, Elphinstone, and Melville and a wide range of lairds. Two prominent English naval officers also joined William. Edward Russell, a nephew of the Earl of Bedford and one of the signatories of the invitation, rejoined William in the autumn. Arthur Herbert, an experienced naval officer who had long ties to James II, arrived in the Netherlands in July 1688. No greater evidence of the Anglo-Dutch nature of William's enterprise can be adduced than that Herbert served as the admiral in charge of William's fleet and Russell served as secretary for the expedition.[32]

Those who joined William in the Netherlands came from more diverse social backgrounds than the usual lists of noblemen and gentry would suggest. English and Scots came over in huge numbers to serve in the Anglo-Dutch force. The Polish ambassador told his king that the English were arriving "en foule" to embark on the newly readied ships. The Marquis d'Albeville, hardly a friendly witness, admitted that "a man cannot step one step at The Hague, and at Rotterdam but he will meet with English in gangs." Even though many British volunteers were turned away, Daniel Petit knew well that the fleet then preparing in the Dutch harbors had "many English among them." Among those embarking were almost four thousand men who were part of the regular Scots and English regiments stationed in the Low Countries. Since these men had refused to heed James's request for them to return to England in January 1688, they were almost certainly deeply committed to the overthrow of James's regime. D'Albeville, with more than a grain of truth, referred to these men as "Cromwellians." They were men who "prefer this service before their king's, and boldly disobey his proclamation" and were "resolved for any kind of rebellion." These men were augmented by almost five thousand British volunteers. The number of Britons in arms in the Netherlands in November 1688 was about half the size of Cromwell's New Model Army. Not only did the English (and presumably Scots) make significant financial contributions to William's enterprise, but almost half of his "invasion" force was in fact British.[33]

James had done a great deal to make sure that the army and navy that would fight the Dutch were professional outfits largely insulated from public opinion. But in 1688 he had not had enough time to create truly independent fighting forces. As a result, some elements of both the army and navy turned against James in the autumn of 1688. Nevertheless, it would be wrong to overemphasize the significance of army defections and naval disaffection. Neither would have doomed James had there not been mass popular uprisings across the length and breadth of England. Popular disaffection rather than military revolt destroyed James II's modernizing regime.

While many people throughout England feared and loathed James II's standing army, there was some discontent within the army itself. Rumors circulated throughout the summer that "the army is most wonderful out of sorts." The seven who invited William in June were perhaps overly optimistic when they predicted that the army would be "so divided among themselves" that there was the "greatest probability imaginable of great numbers of deserters which would come from them should there be such an occasion." But their exaggeration was almost certainly based on a kernel of fact. Both the Duke of Grafton and Ambrose Norton later recalled that James's decision to take a census of Catholic army officers in the summer of 1688 raised latent fears of purges to a level of extreme agitation. These fears accelerated when a number of officers and men in the Duke of Berwick's regiment were cashiered for refusing to serve with Irish Catholics. The "murmurings" after that affair, recalled Sir John Lowther, had become "universal." There were, thought Francis Gwyn, "great jealousies and suspicions" among the soldiers and officers at Warminster in November 1688 that should James "overcome" William, he would "destroy the Protestant religion and especially the Church of England."[34]

It was in this context of military discontent that a two-pronged conspiracy developed among the army officers. William and his supporters in the Netherlands held "frequent and secret conversations" with a group of "chief officers in the army." These were the Anglican veterans of the Caroline occupation of Tangier John Churchill (the future Duke of Marlborough), Charles Trelawney, and Percy Kirke. A second and very much distinct group gathered in the Treason Club at the Rose Tavern in Covent Garden. This group, led by the Whig Richard Savage, Viscount Colchester, also included Colonel Charles Godfrey, Thomas Wharton, "and many others of their party." Whereas experience in Tangier had defined the first group, experience in the Dutch military characterized this Whiggish "association." These two groups, and perhaps others, played on and amplified fears that James had concluded an anti-Protestant alliance with Louis XIV. Many in the army had come to believe that James "had overturned the constitution." Orangist propaganda must also have circulated among James's Scottish troops. On their march from Scotland in November the soldiers "drank the Prince of Orange's health in several places." It was no doubt based on the knowledge of these conspiracies, his expectation that "the king's army for the most part will come over to him," that William turned away many volunteers at Exeter.[35]

The army desertion in November and December 1688 was, however, not nearly as great as William had hoped. In November Lord Cornbury and Viscount Colchester revolted to the Prince of Orange with many of their men. They were soon joined in their treason by Lord Churchill, the Duke of Grafton, the Duke of Ormond, and Prince George of Denmark. Sir Henry Shere was not the only one who exclaimed against the "knaves" who chose to desert the king "in his distress." Military historians, and some contemporary military men, saw this defection as the central event of the revolution. However, the military significance of the defections was not in fact so great. There can be no question that James took the defections in the army very hard. "Never any prince took more care of his sea and land men than I have done and been so very ill repaid by them," he wrote to Dartmouth. But he knew well that the actual numbers of those who defected was quite small. "It is hard to say which was most surprising to see so general defection in the officers from a Prince that paid them well and cherished them so much, or so much loyalty among the common soldiers when almost all their officers gave them so ill an example," James later wondered. Both the loyal Sir John Reresby and James's hostile critic Lord Delamere thought that fewer than two thousand men had revolted to William.[36] Even with the defections James had a sizeable military advantage over the force William brought from the Netherlands. James, unlike many historians, was well aware that William was not his sole enemy. He was facing, as two London merchants acutely observed, "a universal defection throughout the nation of nobility, gentry and commonalty."[37]

The situation in James's navy was similar to that in the army. James had upset many seamen when he rationalized the collection of his customs revenue. This "rigid exaction" that went "much beyond what had been used in former times" did "no small disservice" to James in the crucial months of 1688. Many naval men were upset with James's prosecution of the Seven Bishops. When the recent Catholic convert and longtime naval officer Sir Roger Strickland asked each individual naval captain to subscribe an address to James in abhorrence of the bishops, he found little support, and one captain "swore bloodily at him and threatened to beat him." Strickland's own dramatic rise to the post

The ould Oxford Regiment of
Horse with 2 more, first left
the King and went to the
Prince.

Desertions in the army weakened
James's resolve, though the
revolution could not have succeeded
without support from the broader
populace as well.

of rear admiral was part of a larger attempt by James to introduce a significant Roman
Catholic element into the naval officer corps. As in the army, this move provoked great
fears among the seamen. James appears to have barely headed off a naval mutiny in July
by agreeing to allow Protestant chaplains on ships with Roman Catholic captains. The
general mood on the fleet was not happy. Sir Roger Strickland had provoked "a general
dislike" among the seamen, and discontent was thought to be simmering just below the
surface. The claim made to William that "there is not one in ten" seamen who would serve
James II in a naval conflict was certainly an exaggeration, but it did capture something
of the mood on the fleet.[38]

Every effort was made by James's opponents to augment the discontent on the
fleet. The Duke of Grafton, after a lightning visit to Holland in October 1688, "made it
his business to wheedle abundance of officers and seamen." James II later claimed that
Grafton's endeavors "to corrupt the commanders" had succeeded, and "two thirds of them
had engaged their words to join the Prince of Orange." Grafton was not acting alone.
Matthew Aylmer and George Byng had met with several army conspirators in London and
promised to persuade key officers of the fleet. Pamphlets and newsletters were circulating

widely among the fleet and "at Wapping and other seafaring places." Both William himself and Arthur Herbert had pamphlets printed and circulated among naval men warning of the impending "ruin" of the "laws and liberties of England" and the "Protestant religion" should James not be defeated. Admiral Herbert, who sent personal copies of his letter to his friends among the fleet, made it clear that this was to be no foreign invasion. He appealed to the fleet "as a true Englishman" who was concerned that James's continued rule would only "enslave you deeper."[39]

Nevertheless, the English fleet never had a chance to play a decisive role in November 1688. The weather prevented the English fleet from sailing out to meet the Anglo-Dutch force en route from the Netherlands in late October and early November. On 5 November, when action was meteorologically possible, the naval Council of War "unanimously declared" that the opposing "fleet was much superior to ours" and it "was not advisable to attack or give them battle." This decision—apparently based on an overestimate of William's naval strength—was clearly not the result of conspiracy. The Catholic Sir Roger Strickland, the man in the navy most unequivocally loyal to James, "earnestly pressed" the Earl of Dartmouth not to risk an attack on the Dutch.[40]

Neither the conspiracy in the army nor the navy proved decisive in the autumn of 1688. At most two thousand soldiers defected to William, a fraction of James's force. Disaffection at sea may well have been more widespread—James had been unable to insulate the navy from civilian opinion—but the navy never had any opportunity to take political action. However, both conspiracies revealed the extent of popular discontent with James II's government. These two sectors in which James had the most reason to be able to count on complete and unquestioning loyalty gave him good cause for suspicion. The conspiracies in the fleet and in the army, it turns out, were but small parts of the larger story of popular insurrections against James.

Those who took up arms against James in England, Scotland, Ireland, and the colonies dwarfed in number those who joined William in the Netherlands or acted on his behalf within James's army and navy. Many in England had long known of the Anglo-Dutch expedition planned for the autumn of 1688. Not only were there the select few who had invited William and the much larger number who had contributed financially to the expedition, but by the summer of 1688 the scheme was an open secret. Roger Morrice learned that "the Northern nobility and gentry were very many of them privy to the Prince's arrival." So widespread was the anticipation of the arrival of the Anglo-Dutch force that Captain Humphrey Okeover had heard one prediction in late August "that at their landing the whole kingdom will be in a flame and an uproar."[41]

Many contemporaries believed that only James's standing army was preventing the uproar from commencing. Despite profound popular discontent, argued the Whig Lord Delamere, "the nation had been rid so long, that little of the old English spirit was left." The Tory Earl of Dartmouth also thought "there are many will be cautious enough, let their wishes be what they will." Both John Whittle and Sir Robert Southwell sensed great fear in the West Country "that there might be such hanging as had been in those parts after the defeat of the late Duke of Monmouth." The conclusion was inescapable for some contemporaries. "It is evident that the people were suppressed by the fears of a strong standing army," asserted the author of *A Political Conference,* "for before the Prince of Orange came near them, they rose in all corners of the kingdom, and would certainly have done so when the king declared his dispensing power of making all the laws of the land precarious and invalid, if they might securely have done the same."[42]

Rise, the English people certainly did. Plans for an insurrection in Yorkshire and Derbyshire were far advanced in the autumn of 1688. The Earl of Middleton learned that "great numbers of horses have been of late bought up" preparatory to a rebellion in Yorkshire. Sir Henry Belasyse, a long-term officer in the English brigade stationed in the United Provinces, "lurked long" in Yorkshire on behalf of the Prince of Orange, learned Sir John Reresby. The Earl of Danby, James II later claimed, "had taken pains to go about the country to prepare and solicit the gentry in favor of this invasion." The Earls of Devonshire and Danby met at both Whittington in Derbyshire and Sir Henry Goodricke's house in Yorkshire to coordinate their activities.[43]

These preparations gave rise to rebellion in Yorkshire before news had arrived of any of the army defections. On 22 November a range of gentlemen gathered in York's common hall on the pretext of petitioning for a free Parliament. When a rumor of a rising of Catholics against the county gentry spread through the hall, the men, acting on a prearranged sign, ran to get their horses. The county militia had "come to town without orders" to join in the rising. This was not a narrowly aristocratic and gentry affair. One contemporary described the scene as having been promoted by "a diabolical rabble." Another noted that at least three thousand armed men took control of York that day. Within two days the governor of the garrison, Sir John Reresby, had been seized, the citizens had joined in a petition for a free Parliament, and a Catholic chapel in the city was "demolished." "The whole city almost . . . either for fear or inclination declared for them," lamented the deposed governor Reresby. The rebel forces "increase[d] daily at York," allowing them to seize nearby Scarborough Castle. This was not merely an urban movement, as one observer noted, "the whole county being in arms."[44]

A few days earlier, on 17 November, Lord Delamere—well aware that he was risking his life and fortune—had placed himself at the head of a thousand horse at Boden Downs in Cheshire after having set forth to them "the great danger our lives, religion and liberties were in at this present juncture" and declaring that "he would venture his life for the Prince of Orange." These were joined by "great numbers of the populacy on foot . . . and more would resort unto them, but they restrain them, notwithstanding there has been several thousands together." From Boden Downs Delamere marched to the manufacturing town of Manchester. There "though danger stood on every side/ And Molyneux advanc'd his pride/ they vow'd to venture all with Delamere." Though Delamere accepted the support of at least 280 "gentlemen and tradesmen of very great fortunes" he again felt compelled to turn away "abundance" of the "ordinary sort" because the "Prince of Orange had foot enough, it was horse he wanted." It was apparently at this point that Captain Thomas Bellingham was ordered, perhaps by Viscount Molyneux, to raise the Lancashire militia and oppose Delamere. Instead it was soon reported that "Mr. Bellingham is gone over to the Prince of Orange." Within a week Delamere had by some accounts two thousand and by others four thousand horse at his disposal. Their numbers increased as they marched through Staffordshire and Warwickshire, stopping outside of Birmingham at Edgbaston Hall to seize "a great quantity of arms." Delamere, it was said, also had a significant following in Derbyshire. His "prudence, courage and forwardness in this design together with his exemplary carriage gained him such a great interest about Derbyshire" that he could have had raised "as many [forces] as he pleases." Meanwhile, in his home county of Cheshire, Lord Molyneux threatened to burn Delamere's house, "but the county rose up to the number of 4 or 5000 men with such arms as they had to defend the house."[45]

From his base in Derbyshire the Earl of Devonshire had no trouble mobilizing an armed force to oppose James II and support a free Parliament. He arrived in Derby on 21 November with five hundred men who declared "that they would, to their utmost, defend the protestant religion, the laws of the kingdom, and the rights and liberties of the subject." Though Derby itself proved cautious, more Derbyshire men poured in to augment Devonshire's force that day, including a group of Derbyshire dissenters led by Philip Prince. When this group reached Nottingham they were met by large numbers of men from elsewhere in the Midlands. One group came from Northamptonshire, having risen in arms on 10 November—long before they could have heard any substantial news from the Prince of Orange in the West. They were joined by James's daughter, Princess Anne, the bishop of London, and the Earl of Dorset.[46]

Although historians have followed contemporaries in emphasizing the participation of the aristocracy and gentry in the gathering at Nottingham, it was clear that those involved came from across the social spectrum. The stonemason Caius Gabriel Cibber, who had at the time been hard at work transforming Chatsworth House "from a Gothic to a Grecian magnificence" was among those in arms at Nottingham to secure "the redress of our violated laws and liberties." He was soon joined by his eldest son, Colley, who described himself as "one among those desperate thousands, who, after a patience sorely tried, took arms under the banner of necessity, the natural parent of all human laws and government." Among those thousands was "a collector of hearth money of Nottingham" who "had joined himself to the soldiery there carrying with him his books and the money he had collected upon them." Another Nottinghamshire collector of the hearth tax, John Borradale, "was the first man that listed himself" under the command of the radical Whig Scroope Howe "and brought in several other persons to whom he furnished horses and accoutrements." This huge crowd of revolutionaries, despite the presence of aristocrats, was hardly orderly and peaceful. They were known to have "seized some priests and many that belonged to the excise."[47]

Once in Nottingham, Devonshire was joined not only by Princess Anne, the Earl of Northampton, and his brother Henry Compton, bishop of London, but thousands more volunteers. Both Compton and Devonshire were ecstatic at the popular support they received. "We are here a considerable body of men, and there are daily coming in from all parts," reported Compton. Devonshire calculated that he had at his disposal more than a thousand horse and that he could muster "great numbers of foot if we had arms." By the time Devonshire marched out of Nottingham the number of horse had swelled to several thousand.[48] By all appearances Devonshire could have had as many foot soldiers—men drawn from the lower orders—as he wished, but he was limited by the amount of arms available. The evidence strongly suggests that the gathering of thousands at Nottingham was no staid concourse of aristocrats but a meeting of revolutionaries from a wide range of social strata.

In the face of the enigmatic activity of the Earl of Derby, common folk struck the decisive blows against James II's regime in Lancashire and Cheshire. Derby's activities were so circumspect that one resident of Lancaster, in reference to an earlier Earl of Derby's failure to act in the battle that determined Richard III's fate in 1485, predicted "he would be as cunning as his predecessor in Crookback Richard's time." In fact, Derby claimed he had already taken action against James II. On 24 November he conspired with the governor of Chester Castle, Sir Peter Shakerley, to raise the militia. When the Roman Catholic regiment under the command of Colonel Gage arrived in the city a few days later, they were "not received into any quarters." The citizens of Chester, encouraged by the military governor, had in fact risen up against James's standing army. The result of "the accident at Chester between the citizens and Colonel Gage's men" was that the loyalist troops marched north into Lancashire. The Earl of Derby was convinced that Gage and his men had designs on his life—they had certainly threatened "to fire some houses in the country"—and fled to Wigan. There he met with an outpouring of support, not only from his friends, but "from the whole town," amounting to three thousand men "who did secure all the highways and footways about the town." In both Wigan and Chester, Derby played a role in opposing James's standing army, but in each case it was the citizens who actually rose up in arms against the regime. In fact, in Chester less than two weeks later, "the inhabitants and some country troops disarmed Colonel Gage's regiment and two troops of Irish dragoons which were there in garrison, and thrust them out of the city, after which they read the Prince's Declaration and resolved that they would live and die by the same."[49]

In town after town, in county after county, the English people rose up against James II's regime. Not much more than a week after William had arrived in England, James's trusted servant the Duke of Beaufort informed him "that he could not answer for the city of Bristol, if he had not sufficient troops to keep the people in obedience, as most of them seemed desirous to embrace the party of his Highness." Less than two weeks later the citizens of Bristol circulated a petition for a free Parliament "signifying that the people are generally bent that way." It was hardly surprising, then, that the Earl of Shrewsbury was able to take the city with only five hundred soldiers and one hundred horse confident of the citizens' "fidelity." Shrewsbury was preaching to the converted when he promised to defend "the Protestant religion, their liberties and properties." Sir Edward Harley and Thomas Foley led a revolutionary party that took control of Worcester with widespread support throughout the county. In Hereford a group of four hundred gentlemen from Wales declaring for the Prince of Orange were soon joined by a local "rabble" that "defaced the mass house and much to our regret spoiled and stole a great deal of [goods]" and seized Ludlow Castle.[50]

There was extensive popular revolutionary activity in Wales itself. The Earl of Middleton learned correctly that "Sir Rowland Gwynne is gone or going into [Wales] to endeavor to make disturbance." Gwynne's task was apparently not difficult. The Jacobite loyalist John Stevens "found the generality of the people" in Wales "open hearted" and "not at all averse to the Prince of Orange or his designs." By mid-November up and down the principality people were "preparing horse and arms under pretence of a militia for an insurrection." Lord Herbert of Cherbury and Sir John Price rose in arms and were "soon reinforced from all parts of the country, fathers sending their sons, and masters their servants with their best horses and arms, giving out for fear of any misfortune that they ran away from them." Sir Willoughby Aston was being too socially exclusive when he noted on 21 November that "the gentry in Wales [are] in arms."[51]

Popular activity in Norfolk was little different from the West Country or Wales. The Duke of Norfolk, despite his family's long and deep associations with Catholicism, was "not satisfied with the court." Although Norfolk had assured the Earl of Sunderland that he and the county were "truly loyal to the king and will show it upon this present or any other occasion as far as any county in England," both the duke himself and popular opinion in East Anglia inclined in another direction. By the middle of November the future nonjuring bishop of Norwich William Lloyd was reporting that in Norfolk the demand for a free Parliament had become "*vox populi* and they begin to say there is little hope for safety without a Parliament." It was to this popular voice that the Duke of Norfolk responded announcing to enthusiastic crowds first in Norwich and then in King's Lynn that he would "ever stand by you to defend the laws, liberties and Protestant religion and . . . procure a settlement both in church and state in concurrence with the Lords and gentlemen in the North and pursuant to the Declaration of the Prince of Orange."[52]

Popular support was overwhelmingly for William when he landed in the West Country in November 1688. When he arrived at Torbay on 5 November, "the people in great numbers from the shore welcomed his Highness with loud acclamations of joy." Not content to sit idly by, the local populace provided William and his forces with "provisions in great plenty" as they disembarked. As the army marched toward Exeter, "sundry companies of young men met them, with each a club in his hand; and as they approached near, they gave sundry shouts and huzzahs, saying God bless the Prince of Orange and grant him victory over his enemies." When William marched into Exeter with "kettle-drums beating and trumpets sounding joyfully," he received a similar greeting. The citizens exploded

Het lande van Syn Hoogh in Engelant (The arrival of His Highness in England),
by Bastiaen Stoopendaal, 1689. William arrived in England with the support of
a massive Anglo-Dutch invasion force.

"with loud huzzahs, ringing of bells, bonfires and such loud acclamations of joy as the convenience of the place and their abilities could afford." One eyewitness recalled that "the
windows of every house were extremely crowded and beautified." So numerous were the
crowds, observed another, that it "was impossible to ride a horse in the streets."[53]

Popular support for William in Exeter extended far beyond polite applause and good
wishes. "As soon as the Prince came to Exeter," noted Sir Robert Southwell, "the common people came in great numbers offering themselves to be listed as soldiers." "The common people,"
lamented the loyal Earl of Huntingdon just two days after William's arrival, "runs into" join
the Anglo-Dutch army. "Men came in to the city from all parts to list themselves," remembered another eyewitness, "insomuch that many captains picked and chose their soldiers."[54]

There could be no question that the lower orders led the charge to join William
and the Anglo-Dutch force. William himself bemoaned the fact that despite "the great
acclamation of the people" at Exeter, "no gentlemen, clergy or the mayor the city" had
joined him. "When the Prince of Orange landed at Torbay none of the gentry came to
him but most of them fled from their houses," concurred Sir Robert Southwell. Even the
triumphant Gilbert Burnet had to admit, along with every other eyewitness, that "the
gentry of the country were a little backward at first."[55]

Only on 10 November, almost a full week after William and his force had landed at Torbay, did the gentry begin to come into Exeter. The Whig Thomas Wharton was the first to arrive, with twenty of his friends, "where he found few so forward as himself." After Wharton came a flood of gentry and aristocratic support. By the time William left Exeter, reported Sir Robert Southwell, "almost all the gentry of Devonshire and some few of Cornwall and diverse of Dorset and Somerset came in to him." Those who joined William in those early days included the moderate Sir William Portman of Taunton, the Whig Narcissus Luttrell, the Tory Edward Seymour, and the future Jacobite Sir Copplestone Bampfield. The clergy in the West Country soon followed, as Gilbert Burnet reported to Edward Herbert, and began "promoting a petition for a free Parliament which is understood by all to be a declaring for us." By the end of November the Anglo-Dutch army had so many volunteers that William "refuse[d] to take any more." The East India Company captured the social balance if not the chronology of the support for William in the West when its directors told the general and council in Bombay that "very many of the English nobility and gentry flock into him with multitudes of the common people."[56]

James, by contrast, received almost no support whether from the people, the gentry, or the aristocracy. The Earl of Middleton complained from Salisbury that "none of the gentry of this or the adjacent counties come near to the court, and the commons are spies to the enemy." "Very few of the gentlemen of the country come to" support James, agreed the Earl of Nottingham, "for indeed most of them are gone to the Prince of Orange." There were a few "sectaries" who hurried to aid the king who had worked so hard to indulge their consciences, but Roger Morrice was sure that there were in fact "not many" collaborators of that persuasion. When James returned to London from Salisbury, he was "attended with few nobility, the greatest part being gone over to the Prince of Orange."[57]

The response in the West could not have been more different than when the Duke of Monmouth had arrived in the summer of 1685. Whereas in 1685 Monmouth and his small group of followers received some popular support, that support came exclusively from those who wanted to replace Catholic king James with Protestant king Monmouth.[58] Monmouth's immediate entourage included some radical Whig veterans of the Exclusion campaigns, but most of his support came from confessional opponents of James II. The popular, and ultimately gentry, support that William received in the first few weeks after his landing dwarfed the numbers who came out in arms for Monmouth in 1685.

John Trenchard was perhaps typical of political radicals who had avoided involvement with Monmouth in 1685 but enthusiastically embraced the Revolution of 1688–89. Trenchard had fled from the West Country to the Netherlands before Monmouth arrived in 1685. In the spring of 1688 he held high-level meetings with William at Loo. In July 1688 Trenchard returned to England, accepted a pardon, and kissed the king's hand. But like so many who accepted pardons from James in 1687–88, Trenchard was no supporter of the regime. By the beginning of December 1688 William had appointed Trenchard, along with fellow committed radicals William Harbord and John Row, overseers of revenue collection in the West—hardly a job he would have assigned to one whose commitment he could not trust. No wonder Sir William Portman praised Trenchard for "his early and hearty promoting the Prince of Orange's service."[59]

As the Anglo-Dutch army marched toward London, there was ever-increasing popular support for the uprising. "All the corporations of the West engage themselves" to the prince's cause, announced one pamphlet in early December, "and declare for a free Parliament and the Protestant religion." When the Anglo-Dutch army entered Salisbury, recently vacated by James and his standing army, "never were windows more crowded with faces of both sexes than here; never were bells ringing more melodiously than now at Sarum; never were people shouting and echoing forth huzzahs more in the air than now."[60]

A group of soldiers and horse, from a wide array of social backgrounds, under the command of Lord Lovelace joined the main Anglo-Dutch force. Lovelace, who was one of the signers of the June invitation, was well known to have been conspiring with William. He crossed the North Sea frequently as he plotted "to raise men underhand, and to cause others to raise men." Lovelace did raise a troop at Cirencester but was quickly captured and sent to Gloucester Gaol. An Orangist crowd freed him, allowing him to raise a new force that marched to Oxford. There the familiar pattern was repeated. Lovelace arrived in Oxford with about two hundred horse and was greeted enthusiastically "by the townsmen on foot, who unanimously rose in his behalf, but coldly seconded by the passive obedience men," who included the mayor. According to Sir Ralph Verney, it was "the mobile" that compelled the town's support of Lovelace. The extent of popular support in Oxford, for what one participant called a "rebellion," can be gauged by the fact that Lovelace's force soon swelled from two hundred to more than two thousand.[61]

As the Anglo-Dutch force made its way toward London, the revolutionaries, with broad popular support at every stage, took garrison after garrison. On 26 November, after having promised William his support a week earlier, the Earl of Bath had the Earl of Huntingdon seized and read the Prince of Orange's *Declaration* to the officers and soldiers stationed at Plymouth. They, in turn, "unanimously declared their readiness to concur" in the "generous great design of defending the Protestant religion, our laws and liberties and ancient constitutions of England." Huntingdon, whose regiment had almost entirely joined the Orangist cause, could only lament that "the king is betrayed, his counsels are betrayed, and I am betrayed."[62]

In Hull, on 3 December, Lieutenant Colonel Sir John Hanmer and Captain Lionel Copley, acting "with the help of the townsmen, all of the same inclination," seized the governor of the garrison Lord Langdale and a few of his loyal Catholic officers. When Langdale pleaded his right to command based on the dispensing power, Captain William Carvell replied that he "had no right according to the laws of the country." The next day all the shops of Hull were "shut up, and all the bells in the town set a ringing, the Prince of Orange's colours put upon the high church and other places." For over a century the popular revolution in Hull was celebrated as "town-taking day."[63]

This late-seventeenth-century print depicts William's progress toward London. From the upper left, William arrives at Exmouth Bay, enters Exeter, is greeted by the Duke of Grafton, and is welcomed to Salisbury. William and his troops were hailed by cheering crowds, many of whom volunteered to serve in his army or offered financial support.

Less than a week later Dover Castle and town declared for the Prince of Orange. In this case, the military stronghold fell to an exclusively civilian crowd. The castle, Samuel Pepys informed the Earl of Dartmouth, was taken on behalf of the Prince of Orange "by some of the rabble of that town, not headed by any officer that I can hear of civil or military." In Berwick, by contrast, the officers of the garrison decided to declare for "a free Parliament and to assist the Prince of Orange." In the Scilly Isles the governor, Sir Francis Godolphin, was seized by his lieutenant working in conjunction with "the inhabitants." They then immediately "declared for the Prince of Orange and read his *Declaration*."[64]

The pattern of popular uprisings was similar in James's other kingdoms and territories. In Scotland, wrote William Carstares, just as in England, James's wooing of the Dissenters proved a mixed blessing. "The body of the nobility, gentry and commons of the South and West parts is zealous for the interest of the Protestant successors," he learned, and this zeal was promoted by "the Nonconform ministers." Carstares added that many who had recently returned from the Netherlands "had done considerable service." His information proved remarkably reliable. When James decided in October to march his Scottish forces south for support against the imminent arrival of the Anglo-Dutch force, the Scottish state was left severely weakened. "The Presbyterian and discontented party" soon flocked to Edinburgh, where "they took off their mask, and formed several clubs, where they deliberated upon what was to be done as freely as if allowed by authority." Popular uprisings quickly broke out in much of Scotland. In the southwest Daniel Ker of Kersland emerged from his hiding place in the mountains, joined with "some hundreds of the Whigs," and "over-ran the whole kingdom"—including a bold attack on Traquair House in the Borders—seized "the revenues of the Crown in several places, and expelled the Episcopal clergy from their churches." In Edinburgh student-led pope-burning processions soon widened into "a kind of carnival liberty" in which the citizens indulged "their two passions of joy and revenge in the general confusion, which is the rabble's holiday." In Glasgow William was proclaimed "Protestant Protector" by the citizens. The citizens of Dumfries "have taken and imprisoned the Provost with some other Papists and priests, and guard their town with six companies–a-night." James, thought Sir John Clerk of Penicuik, had provoked a "popular rebellion." "Nor was it to be admired," commented another Scot after observing the remarkable similarities between crowd activities in London and Edinburgh, "that the desire of such a change should reach so far as Scotland, where the causes were the same, and the cries of oppression were no less loud than in England."[65]

There were popular insurrections in Ireland as well. In December 1688 "the inhabitants of Londonderry shut up their gates against the earl of Tyrconnel and the Irish forces, and together with the several counties in Ulster and Connaught, declared for his Highness the then Prince of Orange." There were plans for similar risings in Dublin and Limerick. In February 1689 the inhabitants of Bandon in Cork "turned out some royal dragoons and then shut their gates."[66] That Viscount Mountcashel was able speedily to reduce Bandon, and that Tyrconnel was able to regain political and military control over all of Ireland, should not blind us to the revolutionary fervor among many in Ireland. It suggests that the very different revolutionary experiences in England, Scotland, and Ireland had much to do with where James chose to fight and with local demographics. All three kingdoms experienced popular revolutionary fervor.

There was also popular revolutionary sentiment in North America. In Boston in April 1689 more than five thousand men took to the streets, "seizing and carrying to prison" their political enemies, and threw "down all manner of government there, and set up for themselves." The rhetoric of the Bostonians and their supporters was familiar. They complained of the unjust deprivation of their charter and the subsequent "exercise of an illegal and arbitrary power over them" by Sir Edmund Andros. Contemporaries noted the parallels with developments in Britain. The New Englanders' "seizing and securing the governor," wrote two Bostonians, "was no more than was done in England at Hull, Dover, Plymouth, &c." In New York the revolutionaries took longer to achieve their objectives. In mid-May Lieutenant Governor Francis Nicholson warned that some "ill affected and restless spirits amongst us, use all imaginable means to stir up the inhabitants of this city to sedition and rebellion." In Queen's County, Westchester County, and Suffolk County on Long Island, "all magistrates and military officers were put out by the people and others chosen by them." The revolutionaries in New York, too, complained of the "arbitrary powers" of the governor, including "that of levying money without calling an assembly, whereby we reckoned that our lives, as well as estates were subject to the arbitrary will of a Governor, contrary to the known laws of England." By mid-June Nicholson had fled, and the New Yorkers had "set up their former government like those in New England." In Maryland, the radical John Coode led a rebellion that resulted ultimately in the deposition of the governor, Lord Baltimore. Among other things, the revolutionaries complained of "the absolute authority exercised over us, and of the greatest part of the inhabitants, in the seizure of their persons, forfeiture and loss of their goods, chattels, freeholds, and inheritances."[67]

Popular uprisings, then, spread throughout England, Wales, Scotland, Ireland, and North America with bewildering rapidity in the autumn of 1688 and winter of 1689. In some cases, townspeople rose up against their governors; in others, aristocrats and gentry coordinated with their tenants and local yeomen to defy loyalist elements. An outpouring of popular support transformed William's Anglo-Dutch expeditionary force into a massive army. While revolutionary activity took different shapes in the various regions, a development in December 1688 served to unify national support for what had clearly become a revolution: the "the Irish Fright."

The Irish Fright of December 1688 bore a striking resemblance to the French Great Fear of 1789 that followed the fall of the Bastille. Just as in France a century later, rumors of massacres by royal forces that spread along byways and highways and through the post provoked local men and women throughout the country to arm themselves. In both cases concerns about the awesome and arbitrary power of the agents of the collapsing regime coupled with the realization that there was no central authority guiding the activities of those agents to produce an extremely volatile situation. The historian of the Great Fear noted perceptively that the situation in France in the summer of 1780 was "exactly the same" as that in England in December 1688.[68]

Just as in France, the Irish Fright of December was preceded by widespread concern. Fears that James's army would attempt to maintain control by force escalated as it became known that James had summoned troops from Scotland and Ireland to reinforce his position. That Irish troops committed well-publicized atrocities at Portsmouth ratcheted up the tension still further. In September and October 1688 the stationing of Irish troops at the royal garrison in Portsmouth provoked a number of English officers to resign their posts, followed by "great complaints of the rude Irish who have caused many families to leave that place." Conflicts between the Irish soldiers and the locals culminated in the death of forty when some Irish troops fired "bullets into the church during service." In late November the widely distributed *Third Declaration* of the Prince of Orange, which was actually written without any authority by Hugh Speke, warned that "great numbers of armed papists have of late resorted to London and Westminster" with the intention of making some "desperate attempt" to burn the cities or subject their inhabitants to "a sudden massacre." Fears of a massacre by Irish, Scottish, or French troops were voiced in London, Stoke-on-Trent, Carlisle, Manchester, Wigan, and Killaloe in Ireland. In general, wrote Sir Charles Cotterell in late October, the Irish in particular have provoked "great jealousy and discontent." These fears were stoked when in the wake of James II's first attempt to flee overseas, the Earl of Feversham, commander of the royal army, disbanded his troops without disarming them.[69]

Just at this moment someone or perhaps some group began circulating a rumor that a marauding group of Irish soldiers, numbering around eight thousand, was on the march with the intention of "cutting the English Protestants' throats." Far from being an example of premodern paranoia, the sophisticated methods used to spread the rumor are more reminiscent of modern smear campaigns. Hugh Speke, who claimed credit for spreading the rumors throughout England and Scotland, openly bragged that he made use of his vast knowledge of "the coaches, wagons, and carriers by which goods, parcels, and letters might be conveyed, and of the times and days of their several setting out to and fro London." Marshal Schomberg, who also did much to spread the rumor spent six thousand pounds to have the post office circulate anonymous letters detailing the threat.[70]

The effect of the rumor was dramatic and national. Early in the morning of 13 December "a universal terrible alarm was taken all over London and Westminster with a fear and confident persuasion that they should have their throats cut by the French and by the Papists." The whole city was soon aglow with candles lit in each and every window. By one count more than a hundred thousand men "were upon their weapons" that night to protect their fellow citizens. From London the fear of a massacre spread rapidly along the country's vastly expanded road system and through the improved post office. By the next day the alarm had put the country people into "a consternation" in Herefordshire and Derbyshire. From his home in Ashbourne, Derbyshire, Sir William Boothby appears to have played a remarkable role in spreading the news that there was "a part of the Irish army coming into these parts and destroying all before them." On 15 December people were arming themselves in Oxford, Chester, Lancaster, Wigan, and Warrington. Fears spread throughout Yorkshire and north to Berwick and, ultimately, to lowland Scotland. The exact content of the rumor varied from locality to locality—in some areas the marauding forces numbered eight thousand, in others as many as twenty thousand; in some areas the marauders were Irish, in others French; in still others they were identified merely as Catholics. This unstable identity permitted Theophilus Brookes, a Roman Catholic, to quell fears in Derbyshire. Despite the different meaning ascribed to the rumor, the response everywhere was similar. Englishmen everywhere took to their arms. Sir Christopher Musgrave's report that three thousand were in arms in Carlisle and above four hundred were armed in Cockermouth was typical of the country at large.[71]

The "Irish Fright" of 1689 was the product of a sophisticated and decidedly
modern propaganda campaign, reminiscent in many of its particulars
to the French "Great Fear" of 1689.

Although the fears quickly subsided, the extent and consequence of the Irish Fright
cannot be doubted. "Invisible fears possessed most parts of the kingdom," recalled Roger
Morrice; the rumor "circulated so generally throughout the kingdom that it's vain to name
particular counties but in none was it greater than in Buckinghamshire, Northamptonshire,
Leicestershire, and especially Staffordshire, Derbyshire, and Nottinghamshire." Hugh
Speke was, for once, probably not exaggerating when he claimed that the mass mobilization as a result of the Irish Fright persuaded many Jacobites that there could be no chance
of an English-based counterrevolution.[72]

On 18 December William marched into London confident of widespread popular
support. He was not disappointed. His route was lined "for some miles" with enthusiastic
supporters, many of whom had "oranges on swords, pikes, &c." In London "a vast number
of people of all sorts and ranks" cheered on the revolutionary hero. One woman outside
Ludgate "gave diverse baskets full of oranges to the Prince's officers and soldiers as they
marched by to testify her affection towards them." Roger Morrice also witnessed "diverse
ordinary women in Fleet Street" congratulating William's soldiers as they passed, crying,
"Welcome, welcome, God bless you, you came to redeem our religion, laws liberties, and
lives." The "joy and concourse of people" was "free and unconstrained," remarked one

Receptie van S.K.H. den H. Prince van Orange ap zyn intrede tot London (*The reception of the Prince of Orange on his entrance to London*), by Romeyn de Hooghe, 1689. When William reached London, thousands of English men and women from all social ranks welcomed him enthusiastically. These crowds would play a decisive role in making sure that William and Mary were crowned king and queen of England.

contemporary. Another compared it to the enthusiasm "at the restoration in all things except for debaucheries." "The bells and bonfires proclaim as much joy as these [people] are capable of who have seen so many changes and revolutions, without being able to divine how all this will conclude at last," noted John Evelyn cautiously. "The ringing of bells, the blazing of bonfires, and all the public demonstrations of joy imaginable," thought another eyewitness, indicated popular "satisfaction at so great a revolution." Another marveled at "the repeated huzzahs and loud acclamations of the inhabitants who showed no other concern for the Revolution but what might express their satisfaction and approbation."[73]

Contemporaries were convinced they were witnessing a popular or national revolution. There were risings "in all counties," lamented the Countess of Huntingdon in early December. In Paris Joseph Hill heard that "some whole counties, Cheshire, Derbyshire, Yorkshire, and Lancashire [were] all up in arms." The Dissenter Henry Newcome spoke

Enthusiastic crowds awaited William at his arrival in London in December 1688.
Men, women, and children throughout England began singing the Whig Tom Wharton's
song "Lilibulero." The song's lyrics emphasized that James, influenced by the French,
would do away with all legal protections in England, and called for revolutionary change.

of "a general revolt," while others referred to "great revolutions" and the ubiquity of "the
cloud of rebellion." The Levant Company informed Sir William Trumbull that "the whole
nation" had turned against James II. Colley Cibber, who joined the rising at Nottingham,
observed both the extent and broad social range of the revolutionaries in his march south.
"Through every town we passed the people came out, in some sort of order, with such rural
and rusty weapons as they had, to meet us, in acclamation of welcome and good wishes,"
he remembered fondly. The Jacobite John Stevens was less wistful in his recollection that
"the spirit of witchcraft or rebellion (which the Scripture tells us are alike) had well possessed itself, and as it were fixed its abode in the hearts of most of His majesty's dissembling
enthusiastic subjects." James himself testified to the universality and social inclusiveness
of the revolution. "The contagion was spread so universally," he bitterly recorded, "that
all parts of England furnished the same news of risings and defections, the only strife was
who would be forwardest in abandoning the king."[74]

The evidence overwhelmingly suggests that the events of 1688–89 were not the
result of a Dutch invasion. William's force included large numbers of British exiles and
was financed in part by significant quantities of British money. Though there can be no
doubt that William's arrival with a substantial force gave courage to many to rise up in

rebellion, contemporaries were not persuaded that the Anglo-Dutch force alone would have put an end to James's rule. Indeed, one commentator in early 1689 insisted that to call the revolution "an invasion" was "a piece of lunacy."[75]

Contemporaries of all political stripes maintained that James's overthrow was the work of the people. The maverick Tory Sir Richard Temple claimed that William's arrival was the desire of "universally all the people (except popish recusants)." The Jacobite John Stevens thought there was "universal consent" to the rebellion. The Mediterranean merchants Thomas and Robert Ball reported that James had been "quite deserted by all men." Even those "trained up in a course of passive obedience, did generally revolt and rise up," noted several. "Those who have appeared for the Prince of Orange are by far the majority of the whole kingdom," observed another scribbler. "Almost all people in the nation of all ranks and conditions" were opposed James and his policies, reported Philip Warre from Whitehall. "The weight of the people cannot be withstood," admitted James's friend the Earl of Huntingdon. "This is," opined the *Dilucidator,* "one of the greatest events of our age, wherein the English nation have newly manifested the power it has ever retained to itself, of looking to the conservation of its government in extraordinary and pressing cases." "This revolution might perhaps seem surprising to strangers," noted one contemporary newsletter writer, "but to those who know what has been agitated here for several years without any regard for the law, promises, nobility, clergy, gentry and others are not stunned, knowing well that such universal discontent could have had no other outcome as soon as an opportunity presented itself." So powerful was popular outrage at the government of James II, so profound was the desire for revolutionary change, that one experienced international observer thought a popular uprising would have occurred absent the Prince of Orange. "All the great men, the peers, the cities, the provinces" agreed with William's complaints against James's government, observed the Huguenot exile Pierre Jurieu. But, he said pointedly, "if this Prince had refused to have afforded succor to the nation, she would have done the very same without him, that she does under his banners; and from thence there would have unavoidably followed the ruin of the monarchy."[76]

Although historians have been virtually unanimous in denying that the Revolution of 1688–89 was a popular revolution—asserting either that it was an aristocratic putsch or that it was a Dutch invasion—two well-placed contemporaries from opposing political camps saw things differently. Lord Delamere believed deeply that those who "moved forward to join the Prince's army"—meaning all who rose up against the government—forced James to flee the country. These Britons, Delamere said, "were resolved not to look back, but would either conquer or die." It was these Britons who "did not mince the matter, but spoke plain English to King James, and of our condition, and thereby animated the country as they marched, and made all sure behind them, so that the further they marched the greater service they did; for 500 men thus moving would in a short time occasion 40,000 to rise in arms." In a short time it was clear that they would either reduce "King James to measures, or drive him out of the kingdom." It was this rising, Delamere was sure, "that so astonished King James, and put him to his wit's end." Significantly, James himself agreed. In his memoirs James commented that in the critical days after his retreat from Salisbury he heard "nothing but insurrections, desertions, and treasons." He told his friend the Earl of Feversham that he did not expect him to "expose" himself "by resisting a foreign army and a poisoned nation." By mid-December "the general defection of the nobility, gentry, and clergy, and others in the army . . . gave little reason to trust those who remained; so that no other Council could reasonably be embraced, but to quit the kingdom with as much secrecy as possibly he could."[77]

CHAPTER NINE

Violent Revolution

In early December 1688 the London Presbyterian Roger Morrice found it almost unbelievable "that the decision of this adorable transaction," by which he meant the Revolution of 1688–89, "will be without the effusion of blood."[1] Apparently Morrice's testimony provides contemporary support for the bloodlessness and orderliness of the Revolution of 1688–89. But only apparently. Morrice, and most in England and elsewhere, had every reason to believe that William's arrival would unleash a civil war not unlike the one that had ripped apart German lands from 1618 to 1648 or that had devastated England in the middle of the seventeenth century. An all-out civil war on the scale of the Thirty Years' War never happened. But the events of 1688 and beyond were far from peaceable. Although historians have long emphasized that events in Scotland and Ireland were hardly bloodless, they have underplayed how much violence pervaded everyday life in England itself. In 1688 and after, England as well as Scotland and Ireland—and then much of Europe—were plagued by battles, rioting, and property destruction that were eerily similar to the events following the fall of the Bastille in the next century.

There were no great set-piece battles in England in 1688–89. There was, however, a good deal of violence involving James's army and what remained of his militia. "The first bloodshed" in the revolution occurred at Cirencester in the west when the county militia intercepted Lord Lovelace. A sharp battle followed in which Lovelace and his seventy

(above) *Roman Catholic Chapels Destroyed*, 1689. In November and December 1688 crowds in London unleashed their fury on the visible symbols of James's faith and absolutist government. Here they pull down the Portuguese Chapel on Duke's Street, London, and burn Catholic artifacts.

More Williamite and royalist troops were killed in the December 1688
skirmish at Reading than in the 1791 "massacre of the Champs de Mars"
—one of the bloodiest events of the French Revolution.

followers were overwhelmed after having killed the militia captain and his son. Less than
two weeks later a revolutionary crowd freed Lovelace from Gloucester Gaol, insisting that
the sheriff of Gloucestershire had no legal standing. Another short but bloody skirmish
took place at Wincanton in the West Country between Williamite and royal troops. In
early December a more extended battle took place near Reading. There about two hundred
Williamite dragoons along with fifty horse encountered some of James's Irish dragoons.
The royalist forces were defeated and then attacked by "the people" of Reading on their
retreat. Although contemporaries referred to the event as a "slight skirmish," more than
sixty troops were killed in the encounter, far outnumbering the number of Parisians killed
in the famous "massacre of the Champ de Mars" in July 1791.[2]

Crowd violence against James's standing army was much more common than
pitched battles in late 1688. In early November "some of the inhabitants of Sherburne"
in Dorset attacked and seriously wounded a group of soldiers under the command of
Captain Counteney. In late November a group of James's newly raised soldiers under the
command of Captain Jones were told that Uxbridge, where they were quartered, "was
a Whiggish town so they might use their discretion." The townsmen soon rose up and
"soundly" mauled the soldiers. "'Tis said above fifty (some say a hundred) on both sides are
killed," reported one Londoner. The fracas ended with "abundance of broken pates" and

the revolutionary townsmen in complete control. At Bury St. Edmunds in Suffolk, "the mobile disarmed some new raised forces and diverse were killed"—a scenario repeated in "diverse other parts" of England. A similar scene was narrowly avoided in Brentford, just outside of London. In that case "the country people came down in great numbers to be revenged on the Irish regiment," but Sir John Edgworth was able to convince the unruly crowd that they were Irish Protestants bitterly opposed to James and his regime. The crowd and soldiers then joined together in crying, "The Prince of Orange forever."[3]

Military-civilian relations had been tense in garrison towns throughout James II's reign. So it was hardly surprising when violence erupted in town after town late 1688. Popular uprisings in York, Hull, and Carlisle achieved quick victories. Chester was seething with discontent. The seventeen companies of foot and two troops of dragoons quartered were so frequently reviled and attacked by the townsmen that many of the military men "wish themselves at home." Portsmouth was even more of a flashpoint. In early December rumors were already circulating that the townsmen had allied themselves with the "English" soldiers and "killed and disarmed all the Irish and declared for the Prince." Perhaps because this rumor was based on a grain of truth, the deputy governor of Portsmouth, Sir Edward Scott, threatened the inhabitants "with plunder and massacre in case of the approach of any of the Prince of Orange's forces," going so far as to cane the mayor. Predictably, given the climate of late 1688, the response was swift and violent. The townsmen, in alliance with a group of seamen, "beat out the soldiers and shut the gates."[4]

James's soldiers were not the only servants of the state who were the targets of violent attacks in late 1688. James's newly modernized and efficient revenue collection and agencies were the focus of much popular ire. People "everywhere" were taking "all the money the king's collectors have in their hands," Philip Warre complained from Whitehall. John Stevens, who had worked for James's government in Wales, knew well "that the rebels seized the king's money wherever they found it." These were not merely generalized complaints of demoralized Jacobites. The commissioners of the revenue received detailed reports "from most parts of England that the officers of the excise are disturbed in their business by the rabble." "Several persons," they told the lords of the treasury, "intermeddle in receiving the duty of excise and hearth money, some force what is collected from the officers, others collect it by officers appointed by themselves."[5]

Not only was there extensive violence against the symbols and officers of the Jacobite state in late 1688, but anti-Catholic violence was also ubiquitous. The Revolution of 1688–89 was certainly not bloodless in Catholic historiography and popular memory. However, one should not assume that this rash of anti-Catholicism provides unequivocal evidence of premodern crowd behavior, not only because violent paranoia has been characteristic of crowd behavior in many modern revolutions, but also because in targeting Catholics they were very often attacking the most visible symbols and the most vocal proponents of James II's absolutist state. James had, after all, relied heavily on his coreligionists to construct his modernizing absolutist state. He had placed Gallican Catholics in offices after purging corporations, he had inserted a wide range of Catholics in the various branches of revenue collection, and he had recruited many Catholics to serve in his newly expanded army and navy. In addition James had relied heavily on Gallican-inflected Catholic polemic to justify his political practices. There was good reason for antiabsolutists as well as anti-Catholics to attack Jesuit schools, Catholic army officers, and recently converted customs men. No doubt many attacks on Catholic persons, institutions, and symptoms, especially many attacks carried out by Tory crowds, were manifestations of religious bigotry. But the evidence does not suggest, nor can it demonstrate, that religious bigotry was the exclusive motivation for anti-Catholic behavior in either England or Scotland. Above all, what is unequivocal was that English Catholics did not experience a bloodless revolution in 1688–89.

No region of England escaped anti-Catholic violence in 1688–89. There was "scarce a county" in England in 1688, wrote one eighteenth-century Catholic historian, "where the mob did not leave the marks of their indignation." "The popular fury was now uncontrolled, and broke loose against all Catholics and sacred edifices, some of which were stripped and plundered, some virtually destroyed, and some actually leveled to the ground," agreed the authors of the Jesuit Annual Letter for 1688. Sir Richard Bulstrode learned from Catholic exiles in Brussels that most Catholic houses in the country were "pulled down," that many practicing Catholics were killed, and that "such insolencies [were] committed that it would make one's heart bleed to hear them."[6]

Anti-Catholic violence broke out in London before William's Anglo-Dutch fleet landed at Torbay in early November. James, perhaps sensing the pent-up hostility to his Catholicizing policies, had the Catholic chapels in Lyme Street and Bucklersbury closed in early October. On the Lord Mayor's Day, 29 October 1688, London erupted in violence. By all accounts the crowd that had gathered to celebrate the swearing in of the new lord mayor traveled the three blocks from the Guildhall to the Jesuit college and chapel at Bucklersbury. They had targeted the London headquarters of the group most closely associated with absolutist rhetoric and most adamant about re-Catholicizing England. There the "rioters," "great rabble" or "mobile," broke into the chapel, "took out many of their vests, copes, ornaments and trinkets some say to the value of £400 and burnt them." The priests, who had apparently not heeded James's order, "were disturbed when celebrating at the altar." Soon the congregants themselves were "pelted" with stones. By the end of the evening the chapel and college had been burned to the ground.[7]

A week after William's landing, mobs once again took to the streets in London. A crowd of more than a thousand broke the windows and threatened far worse to the house of the king's Catholic printer, Henry Hills, in Blackfriars. "The prentices do daily commit disorders in great numbers," reported the Earl of Nottingham. In fact, large crowds attacked the new Benedictine abbey in St. James's Palace—the workshop that had translated so much French Catholic apologetic for English consumption—and unleashed "their fury" against the new chapel recently built by the Catholic Lord Berkeley. Eventually the king's

Anti-Catholic violence broke out in the capital in the autumn and winter of 1688.
These playing cards depict the burning of two Catholic chapels in London:
Lyme Street in late October and Lincoln's Inn Fields in December.

horse guards dispersed the crowds, but not before killing several people. James's order to suppress all Catholic chapels in London other than those belonging to the royal family and foreign dignitaries appeased the crowds for the moment.[8]

James's first flight from London, on the morning of 11 December 1688, unleashed another round of mob violence unlike anything that had gone before. That evening a group of more than twenty thousand gathered in Lincoln's Inn Fields, first destroying the large new Roman Catholic chapel near the arch. The crowd then turned its fury on Wild House, the home of the Spanish ambassador, also in Lincoln's Inn Fields. Although the ambassador was well known to have been a fierce critic of James and was long rumored to have been a supporter of William's plans, he was also known to have stored the valuables of many of the prominent Catholics who had supported James's regime. It was perhaps because of this, or because he notoriously failed to pay his debts to London's tradesmen, that "the rabble" "tore and plundered all." "They ransacked, destroyed and burnt all the ornamental and inside part of the chapel," they "plundered the ambassador's house of plate, jewels, money, rich goods &c." Worst of all, in the eyes of the antiquary John Aubrey, they "burned manuscripts and antiquities invaluable, such as are not left in the world." By one account the damage done to the library alone was valued at over fifteen thousand pounds. The entire loot seized by the mob was worth a remarkable fifty thousand pounds.[9]

"The multitude" then "proceeded from place to place, pulling down and burning Popish chapels and mass houses, carrying the images and crosses in triumph." One group, "a great many thousands" by one account, demolished the Catholic church at St. John's near Smithfield. Another assembled in front of Henry Hills's press in Blackfriars to complete the destruction begun the previous month. "The mobile" destroyed six printing presses and burned cartload after cartload of books. James's own servants at Whitehall "plundered his chapel and clapped their hands and hissed out all the Catholic domestics." Another crowd gathered at Hammersmith to destroy the Roman Catholic school there. Only at the house of the Florence resident in Haymarket did the mob encounter resistance. There the Middlesex militia under the command of a cheesemonger called Captain Douglas was ordered to open fire on the crowd. As in so many revolutionary situations, however, the militia turned on their commander and shot him instead. The crowd then proceeded to pull down the Catholic chapel and burn the resident's possessions.[10]

London, on the night of 11 December, was alight with revolutionary flames. "The rabble has illuminated several places in this city in an extraordinary manner," reported one observer. The postmaster Philip Frowde marveled that "the sky [was] so very red, that I can see it out of the rooms here at the post office." On that night, thought Edmund Bohun, "the rabble of London" were in "such a ferment as has scarce been seen." After that night's "pulling-down, burning and destroying" of Catholic edifices and symbols, wrote another, "the London rabble" had "hardly left one stone upon another."[11]

It would be wrong to think that anti-Catholic violence in 1688 was a largely metropolitan affair. "The common people entered and destroyed the places lately set up for the public worship [of Catholicism] in most of the cities and biggest towns," learned Edmund Poley, the English consul in Hamburg. This report both rhetorically and factually understated the extent of popular violence in the English countryside. The mood in Kent was not dissimilar from London. "The people of Kent," recalled Sir Robert Southwell, "were up in the roads leading to Dover and in boats near the Thames mouth" to prevent Catholic priests from escaping. Unsurprisingly, the crowds in Kent were not content merely to prevent the escape of Catholic priests. In Canterbury "an armed mob of at least three hundred men" ransacked an inn where Jesuit priests were rumored to be staying. When it was confirmed that the priests were in fact there, "several thousands" assembled to ensure that the Jesuits were captured. An angry mob boarded James II's vessel at Feversham, preventing the king in his first attempt to escape to France. While James, once shed of his disguise, was treated well by the crowd, his absolutist confidant Sir Edward Hales was not. "The rabble," it was reported, as soon as they heard that Hales had been seized, "assaulted his house at a place called St. Stephens, which they very much defaced, entirely destroying his library and what else was valuable." In Northamptonshire a large group of "the vulgar" marched on the Earl of Peterborough's house, destroyed his chapel and much of his furniture, and then tied his steward to a stake before he revealed where his master had hid a cache of arms. In Hampshire "a numerous mob riotously attacked" Burton Castle and seized Father Anthony Selosse, a Jesuit who served as chaplain there. A crowd of seamen burned "all the Popish trinkets" in the chapel of Judge Christopher Milton, the younger brother of the poet John Milton, at Rushmere St. Andrew, near Ipswich.[12]

Both of England's university towns suffered through waves of anti-Catholic violence. As soon as news reached Oxford that William had landed, "the insults of the rabble" forced the famous University College don, and Catholic convert, Obadiah Walker to flee. The situation quickly deteriorated even after the arrival of Lord Lovelace's liberating force. The Jesuit Thomas Beckett of Magdalen "was flung down in the kennel, trampled upon, and had been killed, had not one, upon the noise, come up with a candle." Soon all members of the Society of Jesus, who just months before had congratulated themselves on having support in three prominent colleges, were forced to flee for their lives. In Cambridge "the mobile" similarly attacked a variety of the Catholic fellows, dragging many new converts "through the dirt" and publicly burning the scarlet gown of the former Catholic lord mayor. It was a Cambridge mob that ventured out to James II's privy councillor Lord Dover's house at Cheveley Park near Newmarket, destroying the Catholic chapel and refraining from doing the same to the house only when offered a substantial bribe.[13]

All across the country the English people attacked the persons and property of Catholic supporters of James's modernizing regime and did all they could to demolish the nearly ubiquitous new Catholic edifices. The "mobile" in Gloucester "pulled down the Mass-house, burnt the pulpit, and all the trinkets and materials, demolished some Papists' houses," and then some of them marched out of town to destroy the chapel of a Gloucestershire Catholic gentleman. James's ambassador to Rome, the Earl of Castlemaine, had hoped to escape the wrath of the London crowds by retiring to Montgomeryshire, but there he "fell into the hands of the rabble" and was imprisoned at Oswestry for more than seven weeks. Within days of William's landing, a great "abundance" of people "burnt the new Mass House at Birmingham and secured the Papists." In Stafford, already the heart of the developing ceramic industry, the Jesuit father Philip Philmott was "seized by the mob" and imprisoned. Then "an immense mob, numbering full five thousand," returned to the jail three times demanding summary justice on the unfortunate priest. The Jesuit school and chapel in Lincoln were similarly destroyed by "the rabble." The same thing happened in Pontefract in Yorkshire, where the local Jesuit priest Father Hamerton was apparently lucky to escape with his life. Even those Catholics and priests who were imprisoned could not feel safe. On Christmas in York a crowd gathered to see the burning of an effigy of Father Edward Petre, when some one "cried out that nothing was wanting but some live Jesuits to burn upon it," at which point several attempts were made to take the jail and all the Jesuit priests incarcerated there. At Durham in early December "a numerous and violent mob rushed into the chapel with such a fury that in a few moments everything was destroyed from top to bottom." Not content to destroy the center of Catholic worship, "the mob turned off to the houses of the Catholics, where they rioted with almost equal violence." The Jesuit father Clement Smith luckily escaped a crowd of nearly three hundred who attacked his house in Furness, Lancashire. The new Jesuit church and school in Wigan were not so lucky. These elaborate buildings were "destroyed to the foundations" by "a furious and excited mob."[14]

Mobs all over England and Scotland violently destroyed Catholic chapels, ransacked Catholic property, and threatened many Catholic individuals associated with James II's modernizing regime. Edmund Bohun listed off the litany of destruction in early 1689: "The Popish chapels at York, Bristol, Gloucester, Worcester, Shrewsbury, Stafford, Wolverhampton, [Birmingham], Cambridge and St. Edmund's Bury were about this time demolished."[15] By placing the list in the passive voice, Bohun obscured the active violence perpetrated by thousands of English and Scots throughout both kingdoms. These were not the acts exclusively of the poor and ill informed. College students at Edinburgh, Aberdeen, Oxford, and Cambridge were hardly members of the lower orders of society. The contemporary use of "mob" and "vulgar" reflects more on the acts committed than on the social status of those committing them.

One should not read the anti-Catholic violence in late 1688 and early 1689 as a simple manifestation of religious prejudice. No doubt religious bigotry did motivate some in the crowds. However, that much of the violence was directed at Jesuit institutions and at individuals closely associated with James II's regime in England suggests a more political interpretation of the violence. This interpretation is enhanced by the plethora of violence directed against Protestant props of James's state apparatus. Violence against James II's regime cut across confessional lines.

Political violence was the rule rather than the exception in England in 1688. In his underappreciated *History of All the Mobs, Tumults, and Insurrections in Great Britain*, Robert Ferguson, who had himself been involved in a number of rebellious acts from the 1660s through the early eighteenth century, recalled that "upon the news that the Prince of Orange was landed, a strange disorder spread itself in an instant all over the kingdom. The rabble got up in great bodies in several counties." These were not peaceful demonstrations. "It would be endless to enumerate the many outrages that happened before the nation could come to any tolerable state of settlement," Ferguson informed his readers. Though Ferguson was keenly sensitive to the power of political violence, his assessment was not an unusual one. Mary Woodforde confided to her diary that "ever since" William landed, "we have the sounds of wars and desolation in our land." The Countess of Huntingdon warned her Protestant husband that "the mobile is so unruly in all places that it is extremely dangerous to all that has had malicious lies made of them." Less than three weeks after William's landing, Lord Delamere lamented "the effusion of blood" and the "civil wars" that were already taking place. The French ambassador Paul Barillon, who clearly feared for his safety, lamented the "civil war" that had erupted in England.[16]

In the middle of December London erupted in a wave of revolutionary violence. Although the city had been seething with unrest before that time, most of the violence before James's departure had been of an anti-Catholic nature. This led contemporaries, and more recent commentators, to "rejoice" that "bloody and outrageous sacrifices are not made considering" the numbers that had taken to the streets. Their glee was relatively short-lived. Two days after Tory Philip Musgrave marveled at London's quiescence, he complained bitterly that "the insolencies committed by the rabble have been insupportable." London's crowds made their political agenda more legible after James's departure from the capital. Huge numbers "marched down the Strand with Oranges upon their sticks," clearly enunciating their political preference. Soldiers stood by as citizens tore Whitehall apart, exclaiming "against [the king's] wicked, pernicious, and Jesuitical council." Sir Edmund King complained to his fellow high churchman Viscount Hatton that "the mobile have been extremely insolent and ungovernable and yet are not suppressed." The Presbyterian Roger Morrice also lamented the "many tumultuous insolencies" committed by the mob, highlighting their "invasion upon liberty and property."[17]

Although the crowds did not cease their assault on Catholic places of worship, the most vitriolic anger in December 1688 was directed to the secular and mostly Protestant instruments of Jacobite absolutism. Lord Chancellor George Jeffreys, the man responsible for the Bloody Assizes in the West Country and one known to be part of James II's inner circle, was seized in seaman's clothing in Hope and Anchor Alley in Wapping. A huge and angry crowd escorted Jeffreys to the lord mayor in Cheapside, calling him "the great rogue of all," "a perverter of the laws and a betrayer of the liberties of the people." So furious was the mob, so obvious their desire to "dissect" him and "have him out of the coach," that the lord chancellor told one bystander that "he knew he was a dead man and cared not though [the] rabble would pull him in pieces that minute." On the same day "the rabble plundered" the house of James II's privy councillor, corporation regulator, and chief revenue collector Sir Nicholas Butler. A few days later Sir Roger L'Estrange, one of the chief ideological defenders of Stuart absolutism, was seized and committed to Newgate because "his writings" threatened "against the government." London had become a revolutionary city. Its citizens had given up on traditional means of securing political redress. Instead they had taken to the streets and subjected the capital to "violent concussions."[18]

Political violence was endemic not just in London but throughout England during the revolutionary period. In Gloucestershire, for example, there were rumors that some supporters of the Prince of Orange would burn down Badminton, the sumptuous home of James II's loyal and Protestant supporter the Duke of Beaufort. Sometime thereafter a "tumultuous rabble" destroyed much of the Forest of Dean and "the enclosures about the land of the Duke of Beaufort." These activities may well have been related to those of the crowd of citizens in Gloucester itself who forced the resignation of Mayor Anselm Fowler and his replacement by a Williamite in late November. Farther west, in Wales, John Stevens reported that "all the country round was in open rebellion" in December, "having taken arms, plundered several houses." In Exeter in Devon, the "mobile" were so "incensed" against the loyal lord mayor that they would have ripped him limb from limb—"dewitted" him ran one press report—had he not been first imprisoned. In Cheshire there were a

The Lord Chancellor Taken Disguis'd in Wapping, 1688. London crowds attacked not only symbols of James's Catholic faith in 1688 but also those responsible for creating his centralized and bureaucratic state. In December they unleashed their anger on Lord Chancellor George Jeffreys, a Protestant and the man responsible both for increasing the power of the Tory East India Company and for many of the executions after Monmouth's rebellion.

series of violent assaults on the supporters of James II's regime. In late November Roger
Whitley witnessed a confrontation between Colonel Gage's regiment and the "city officers"
in which "high words passed," leading many citizens to "fall to their arms." The city streets
were soon "full of the rabble and very great disorder." James's decision to disband his army
in early December did not diminish the popular hostility. William Fleming reported in
mid-December that Chester "boys," as soon as "they met any of the officers in the streets
after they were disbanded went into their pockets and took what as they had." In nearby
Nantwich "the rabble" seized Dr. Arden, the Protestant dean of Chester Cathedral and a
devoted follower of the absolutist bishop of Chester, Thomas Cartwright. He was placed
on a "wooden engine," paraded through the town, and threatened with a severe "penalty"
before he was rescued by some "moderate persons."[19]

Violence was no less frequent in areas farther from William's landing point in the
west. In Cambridge "many scholars" had taken up arms, acts that Vice-Chancellor John
Covel thought were "very dangerous to the whole university, as well as destructive to all
good manners." Student activity was certainly dangerous to the absolutist bishop of St.
David's, Dr. Thomas Watson, who was seized by "the Cambridge mob." At Bury St. Edmund's in Suffolk "the poor mobile that had nothing to hazard or lose" took to the streets,
attacking the houses of Roman Catholic and Protestant aldermen while "imposing on some
taxes." Hatred of the Jacobite state rather than confessional bigotry appeared to motivate
this crowd. "The mobile" in Norfolk acted equally indiscriminately in confessional terms,
"having committed many notorious riots and robberies." In York in late November the
"volunteers" "did not touch any property but the king's and the papists"—though included
in the king's property was that of the Protestant governor Sir John Reresby.[20]

Violence did not end with the calling of the Convention Parliament or the crowning of William and Mary. A series of struggles took place within England, in Scotland,
Ireland, and Wales, in North America and the West Indies, and above all on the Continent.
The period 1689–97 is best understood as an era of revolutionary warfare. The notion that
the revolution ended with the coronation of William and Mary is untenable. From 1689
the British Isles were ripped apart by what one historian has rightly called "two years of
bitter civil war." These were followed by a fierce struggle on the Continent to establish the
revolutionary regime and its principles against French-style absolutism, a struggle that was
punctuated at home with a series of more or less serious violent attempts to overthrow
the regime.[21] England's late-seventeenth-century revolutionary regime, like most modern
revolutionary regimes, was established only after a long period of social, political and
military conflict.

In England political developments in Westminster did little to quell violent sentiments or violent actions. A culture of violence was ensured as early as January 1689 when
William ordered James's standing army disbanded and reordered. "The changing of officers
and the ordering of them for Holland and Ireland," Lord Yester explained to his father,
the Earl of Tweeddale, has occasioned "several disorders and almost mutinies among the

soldiers so that many desert and it is feared more will." Unlike the violence perpetrated by James's standing army in the localities, the postrevolutionary violence had everything to do with irregular payment and victualing caused by the rapid change of regime. The indiscipline of Colonel Henry Wharton's regiment quartered at Doncaster was entirely typical. In town after town they took whatever they pleased to eat or drink and often "wandered six or seven miles from their quarters and spoiled and pillaged all they could."[22]

People throughout the country seized on opportunities presented by the change of regime to vent their political frustrations at their old political opponents. In February the Earl of Arran, who had been an officer in James's army and was steadfast in his support of his old master, was attacked in London "in his chair" by six men who "ran the chair through and scarred his throat." After Arran escaped, he reported that his assailants were "English, and he heard them call him a 'Papist dog' though he is none of that religion." "The multitude assaulted a minister's house" in Canterbury in June, "broke the windows and took away what things of value they could find" because they suspected him of Jacobite sentiments. "The rabble of the town" of Chester attacked two dozen disbanded soldiers and threatened to stone them to death before they were able to escape. So bad were things in Lancashire and Staffordshire that Lord Massarene, an Irish Protestant, claimed that he saw no "face of government but frequent disorders up and down the country." The London Presbyterian Roger Morrice confirmed that he knew of frequent actions by the "mobile in Lancashire and Staffordshire" against local Catholics.[23]

A large crowd in Newcastle-upon-Tyne took part in a typical act of revolutionary violence. On 11 May Captain Killegrew climbed on a stage before "a great multitude of people together," pointed to the statue of James II standing nearby, and shouted that "our laws, liberties and properties were taken away and all by that picture." Soon "a man in a red coat" marched up to the statue, "put a rope about the neck of the picture and it was pulled down." The crowd then pulled the statue of James off horseback and were seen "beating of it with stones and breaking it." The "rabble" then made it clear that they did not think the revolution was over; James II's statue was not merely a historical oddity. The crowd left the Sandhill and "broke several of the disaffected people's windows in this town."[24] The crowd in Newcastle was well aware that the revolution had not ended, that the struggle against the ideological orientation of the Jacobites was not concluded once constitutional arrangements had been settled.

Although much of the violence in 1689 was directed against the symbols and supporters of James's regime, it would be wrong to think that English opinion was univocal. In his lengthy visit to London, the Episcopalian minister of Aberfoyle in the Trossachs observed and remarked on the acute ideological tensions in the capital. In particular he witnessed a near brawl between "Williamites in the pit" and Jacobite noblemen above at a performance of Sir Robert Howard's *The Committee*. In Lancaster there was open conflict between supporters of King James and King William when "the governing part of our town" had a violent "contest" with the "mobile," who were supported by Colonel

In a typical revolutionary act, a Newcastle crowd tore down this
statue of James II in May 1689, responding to the cry that "our laws,
liberties and properties were taken away and all by that picture."

Kirkby. Already in early 1689 there was talk that some Jacobites were seeking revenge for
revolutionary violence perpetrated against them. William Harbord reported to the House
of Commons that he had heard about a Catholic in Norwich setting fire to a house in
March. A month earlier William Banks learned that in Lancashire "the papists in our
country are inquiring who those were that pulled down or defaced their chapels" with an
eye to taking revenge.[25]

   After James's flight in late December, the prospect of a traditional military encounter in England itself receded. However, the military phase of the Revolution had
not ended. James and his ally Louis XIV chose to fight their battles on different terrain.

The military struggle in Scotland, Ireland, and on the Continent, taken together, was simultaneously about whether the revolutionary regime would survive and whether that regime would be able to extend its vision of European liberty to the Continent. These were England's revolutionary wars.

The extent of violence against the agents and symbols of Jacobite government in Scotland masked the depth of political division and the continued existence of armed support for James II. The Williamite regime established itself in Scotland only after years of armed struggle. Catholic networks confidently reported that "the Highlands and the North are in arms for their true king." Charles Whyteford added, "It's very probable the whole country will declare for the King whenever they hear he is landed in Ireland." William himself confided to the Marquis of Halifax in late December 1688 that "Scotland by their divisions would give him more trouble than anything." Others, accurately reflecting popular sentiment that was being expressed in the elections being held across Scotland, thought that the Scottish "nobility are divided, some for King William and Queen Mary and some for King James. But the commonalty are generally resolved to follow the example of England." In the event, the elections held for the Scottish convention of estates provided a great boost for the Williamite case. Rupert Browne's assessment from Whitehall that "the elections are very good for King William's interest" proved remarkably accurate. In an unusually large turnout in the Scottish burghs and counties, the Scots returned a convention full of men hostile to James's regime and sympathetic with the revolution. On 4 April, less than a month after the men had gathered, the convention overwhelmingly declared that James had forfeited the Crown. The Earl of Shrewsbury and William himself had good reason to be "satisfied with the zeal many of the Lords and gentlemen assembled in Edinburgh have showed for the preservation of their religion and liberties."[26]

By gaining control of the convention in Scotland, the Williamites had won an important battle but not the war. Unlike in England, where military confrontation preceded the meeting of the convention, in Scotland it was Jacobite political defeat that created the conditions for military action. As soon as it was clear that Williamites, under the presidency of the Duke of Hamilton, had won the day in Edinburgh, many Jacobite lords, including the brilliant and charismatic Protestant Viscount Dundee, left the city. Meanwhile, Edinburgh itself was still bitterly divided between Jacobites and Williamites. The Jacobite Duke of Gordon held Edinburgh Castle for his king, occasionally raining small shot on the town. One attack "killed one woman, two men, two horses, and a dog." In Edinburgh itself, "several disaffected persons gathered together" on 29 May to drink the health of King James, the Duke of Gordon, and Viscount Dundee, prompting a street battle between two competing crowds.[27]

The Jacobite leader Dundee's activities were more threatening still to Williamite Scotland. Dundee was known by both Jacobites and Williamites to be travelling "up and down the northern parts," where he was, in the words of one Catholic Jacobite, "confirming all true Scots in their allegiance to their lawful Prince." Dundee, an Episcopalian, was able to gain the support of a number of Catholic highland clans. By May Dundee was able to muster raid after raid on territories held by the Williamites. An exasperated Duke of Hamilton informed the Earl of Melville in early July that "we shall never be in quiet" until Dundee and his Glen Cameron allies were "reduced and a garrison put in Inverlochy." The newly restored Earl of Argyll complained that the "trimming" of the Highland leaders made it impossible to predict the political future. As a result Major General Mackay, himself a Presbyterian Highlander, was sent north with four thousand troops to force a battle with Dundee and his two thousand men, who were based at Blair Atholl.[28]

For both sides the anticipation before what would become known as the Battle of Killiecrankie was great. Not only were the numbers mustered comparatively large but the stakes were greater still. Both Jacobites and Williamites had reason to believe that control of Scotland would be determined on the battlefield. Although Dundee's forces were certainly outnumbered, there were not a few who thought the question of who "will have the best of it, is yet uncertain." In the event, on 27 July Dundee was able to trap MacKay's forces in the narrow pass at Killiecrankie, between Pitlochry and Blair Castle. His Highlanders achieved a great victory, but at a great cost. By some estimates, over a quarter of Mackay's troops were killed and another five hundred taken prisoner. The Jacobite army lost one third of its force. The greatest loss for the Jacobites was their commander, Dundee, who was mortally wounded. The Williamite Duke of Hamilton was able to claim that "our advantage is more than our loss." This perception of the Williamites was confirmed the next month when the advancing Jacobite forces were thoroughly defeated by a Presbyterian force at the small Episcopal burgh of Dunkeld.[29]

In the event the Battle of Killiecrankie and its aftermath at Dunkeld marked the beginning rather than the end of armed conflict in Scotland. Some had reasoned, along with the London merchants Francis Barrington and Benjamin Steele, that with Viscount Dundee "being killed in a late battle" and the Highlanders having "received so many routs," things in Scotland were "in a fair way of settlement." This was not to be. It was soon clear to a variety of commentators that the struggle to establish the new regime was far from over in Scotland. James Hay remarked to the Earl of Tweeddale that far from marking "the ruin of the Dundee party," the Jacobites had "grown more numerous" since the Battle of Killiecrankie. Robert Kirk of Aberfoyle thought that had James followed up Killiecrankie with a landing, he could have taken control of Edinburgh and played "a far better game" than he did in Ireland. In fact, in December James ordered General Thomas Buchan to the Highlands, where he was assured there "a great many friends" who could be influenced to "rise for the king." By early 1690 most keen observers were of the opinion that though "things are at present quiet in Scotland," it was "certain there is a great ferment and discontent there."[30] The violent struggle to establish the revolution in Scotland, as in England, had not ended at Killiecrankie. It had entered a new phase.

James was never able to fulfill his many promises to lead the Jacobite cause in Scotland, but he did take control of Ireland in person. It was in Ireland, rather than in

Scotland or England, that James and his supporters sought to fight to recover his kingdoms. By making this choice, James ensured that Ireland would host a violent confrontation between Williamites and Jacobites.

As soon as news reached Ireland that King James's position in England was collapsing, James's lord deputy of Ireland, the Earl of Tyrconnel, began making preparations to defend Ireland for his king. Even before replacing the Earl of Clarendon in January 1687, Tyrconnel had done a great deal to modernize and Catholicize the army in Ireland. After a brief flirtation with William, which may well have been a clever delaying tactic, Tyrconnel stepped up the recruitment of his army. By late December 1688 he was said to have twenty thousand men in arms. By the middle of January estimates ran as high as thirty thousand. In January and February, one Jacobite recalled, "the nobility and gentry from all parts of the realm [did] fly up to Dublin." More humble Irishmen were just as enthusiastic. One Jacobite claimed that "in the space of two months above fifty thousand enlisted themselves for the war." The English government estimated that after the troops were regularized, Tyrconnel had more than forty-five thousand men in arms.[31]

The lord deputy's military preparations quickly received a double boost. First, Louis XIV decided to make a considerable contribution to the war effort in Ireland. In February it was known in London that Louis intended to "speedily send" Tyrconnel "a supply of men and ammunition." The following month English "coffee house talk" reported quite accurately that "the French have put out to sea twenty-five sail of ships with tenders for Ireland, men, money and ammunition." Louis XIV was clearly "using all his arts and skill" to promote "the rebellion in Ireland."[32] The French king understood that the conflict in Ireland was much more than a British problem: at stake was the future of the revolution in the British Isles and the balance in the struggle for European mastery.

Second, James—after prodding from Louis XIV himself—left France to lead the Irish cause in person. He arrived at Kinsale in the middle of March 1689, accompanied by the French ambassador Jean-Antoine de Mesmes, comte d'Avaux, several French military officers, his two natural sons, James and Henry, the Duke of Powis, the Earl of Melfort, the bishop of Chester, and a number of Scottish, English, and Irish loyalists. From Kinsale James and his entourage traveled to Cork, where he was received "with great joy and acclamations of the magistrates," who escorted him into town "with a great number of young females dancing in white." From Cork, James proceeded to Dublin in a great triumphal procession. "The way," recalled one Jacobite, "was like a great fair, such crowds poured forth from their habitations to wait on his Majesty, so that he could not but take comfort amidst his misfortunes at the sight of such excessive fidelity and tenderness for his person in his Catholic people of Ireland."[33]

Contemporaries disagreed about the quality of James's massive new Franco-Irish army, but there could be no doubting its initial achievements. By the end of spring all of Ireland—with the exception of Londonderry and Enniskillen—was in Jacobite hands. As early as January 1689 the Protestant archbishop of Armagh, Michael Boyle, worried that

Ireland would "in a short time . . . be reduced to the very last extremeties." One Scottish Jacobite bragged from Dublin to the Earl of Perth about "how entirely the King is master here." The normally pessimistic English Jacobite John Stevens wrote in May that "almost all the kingdom [was] settled under His Majesty's obedience," adding that "nothing was thought of could obstruct the speedy conquest" of the remaining two Protestant garrisons. From the perspective of the Protestant Irish refugee Lord Massarene, Ireland was "forcibly torn and ravished by an alienation to the French crown."[34]

Williamites in England were well aware of the desperate situation in Ireland. In December 1688 a group of Irish gentlemen presented William with an address that urged him to take action in Ireland. Many in England shared their concern. Sir William Boothby, whose support for the revolution was at best lukewarm, averred that he was "in great trouble for the poor Protestants in Ireland, if some speedy help be not sent they will be destroyed." "I wish," chimed in the more enthusiastic Williamite Cary Gardiner, "that timely helps might be sent to Ireland for by delays many perish." In early January William responded to these concerns by asking the city of London for a loan "for the affairs of Ireland." Two months later his secretary of state, the Earl of Shrewsbury, insisted that "his Majesty's greatest concern hath been for Ireland." Nevertheless, financial shortfalls and fears about the loyalty of the troops repeatedly delayed the dispatch of relief from England. As a result, the reports from Londonderry were increasingly desperate. In April 1689 the Jacobite army besieged the city with at least ten thousand men. "Though Londonderry be not yet delivered up," lamented Roger Morrice in a statement typical of English sentiment in the spring of 1689, "it must necessarily be so when King James commands it, for it cannot entertain any hopes of relief." The situation inside the besieged town was truly horrific. "This garrison hath lived upon cats, dogs and horse flesh this three days," reported its governors, George Walker and John Mitchelburne, in July; "above 5000 of our men are dead already for want of meat and those that survive are so weak that they can scarce creep to the walls, where many of them die every night at their post."[35]

That the English Parliament and William himself laid such stress on the relief of Ireland had little to do with narrowly British sensibilities. Ireland, they knew, was a vital battleground in England's revolutionary wars and the great European struggle against Louis XIV. "'Tis more than an Irish war," John Hampden Jr. informed the House of Commons, "I think 'tis a French war. The French King has carried King James into Ireland; and there is no way possible to bear that great force, but by securing Ireland." The Irish refugee Lord Massarene celebrated the Commons' vote to give "vigorous assistance" as a "full one for reducing Ireland and opposing the French king." Into 1690 contemporaries continued to view the battle in Ireland as part of the larger European conflict and the struggle to settle the revolutionary regime in England. "The allies and the French will stand at a gaze and look one upon the other to see what is acted and done in Ireland," reported Paul Rycault from Hamburg, "as the successes are there, the measures will be taken in all the world." "Our all depends" on "a successful campaign in Ireland," affirmed Alexander

Stanhope. Even William King, the dean of St. Patrick's Dublin, understood the conflict in European rather than narrowly British terms. The "design" of the Jacobites, he preached, was to "enslave all Europe under the tyranny of the French king." Many Jacobites shared this European vision. John Stevens noted that many of those in arms in Ireland fancied their chances against the revolutionaries because they placed a great faith in "the power of France." Another supporter of James reckoned that William knew he "could not be any great helper unto the allies till he had put an end to the war of Ireland, which the Irish Catholics undertook against his usurpation."[36]

It was with this conviction, then—that the fate of the revolution and of all Europe lay in the balance—that Parliament sent Major General Percy Kirke to relieve Londonderry. After six weeks, on 28 July, Kirke finally broke the blockade by sending ships to destroy the boom obstructing Lough Foyle into Londonderry. Within days the Jacobite army had abandoned their positions surrounding the city. "It's with all joy imaginable," wrote Captain George Rooke to the Duke of Hamilton, "that I tell you the siege of Londonderry is raised." In Preston, as in many places throughout England, the news was greeted enthusiastically "by bells ringing, bonfires." The celebrations were so fervent, the excitement so tremendous, because the relief of Londonderry was understood to be so central to the revolutionary cause. It was Londonderry's stubborn resistance, recalled Captain Robert Parker, that "prevented [James] from passing over into Scotland, as he intended with a body of between seven and eight thousand foot, whom he brought with him from France." Had James's army been able to join up with Viscount Dundee's Highlanders, the balance would certainly have tipped against the revolutionaries. "Had King James on his landing in Ireland, found no opposition in it, but been entirely at liberty to join his forces with that party that appeared for him in our neighboring kingdom," insisted William King, "everyone is sensible how fatal the event might have proved, not only to England, but also to the liberty of all Europe."[37]

Soon after the relief of Londonderry, the long-awaited Williamite force under the command of Marshal Schomberg arrived in Ireland near Carrickfergus. The force under his command may have been as large as twenty-six thousand men. Their first action was to take Carrickfergus, allowing fifteen hundred to march out of the town. However, "the Scotch Protestants of the country" badly abused the newly surrendered townspeople, "stripped them and killed many of them." Despite predictions that Schomberg's arrival would encourage James to "make as much haste out of that kingdom as he did out of" England, the Williamite army achieved little over the next several months. In fact, by the time Schomberg retired into winter quarters in Ulster, his troops were dying at an alarming rate: by some estimates, almost half of his expeditionary force had died.[38]

The Jacobites remained confident of victory in the winter of 1689–90. Jacobite news networks in England boldly circulated tales of Schomberg's imminent demise. From Dublin Father Maxwell asserted that "the people's minds are so turned towards their duty" that Jacobite victory was inevitable. Since James's army in Ireland now had "thirty-five thousand men armed and already in good discipline," Lord Waldegrave did not "doubt but that kingdom is in a good condition to defend it, if against a considerable force."[39]

Parliament, England's Continental allies, and William himself felt the urgency of the situation in Ireland. "All our discourse now is of the King's going for Ireland," reported one London newsletter in January 1690, "and the preparations thereto are very great." In order to best carry "on the war against the common enemy," Lord Dursley wrote from The Hague, "nothing was more necessary than quick dispatch," and "for that reason . . . his Majesty did intend to expose his own person at the head of his army in Ireland." In June William set sail for Ulster with fifteen thousand reinforcements. The composition of William's force made clear the European nature of the struggle in Ireland. Along with more than seven thousand English troops, William sailed with more than ten thousand Dutch, seven thousand Danish, and thirty-five hundred Scottish troops. A number of Germans and French Huguenots were included in the army as well. All told, William had at his command an army of more than thirty-five thousand in Ulster in the summer of 1690.[40]

In June 1690, then, two large and newly reinforced armies faced each other in Ireland. In retrospect it is clear that the Williamite army was both much larger and better trained. But for contemporaries, the outcome was not inevitable. "All will depend on your Majesty's successes" in Ireland, the Marquis of Carmarthen wrote to William. "I fear," wrote Queen Mary, who was governing England in William's absence, "besides the disheartening of many people, the loss of a battle would be such an encouragement to disaffected ones that might put things here in disorder." Rather than emphasizing the probability of Jacobite uprisings in England, the English ambassador to the Holy Roman Emperor chose to emphasize the positive. "God send us good news from Ireland," William, Lord Paget, wrote from Vienna. "If all go well there, when our Glorious master returns triumphant from thence, everything will go well and merrily on."[41]

In the event, things did go well for the Williamites. On 30 June 1690 the Williamite and Jacobite armies faced one another across the River Boyne not far from Drogheda. The battle took place the next day, with the Williamites winning a decisive if not overwhelming victory. In all about a thousand Jacobites and five hundred on the Williamite side, including Marshal Schomberg, were killed. James and the Jacobite army withdrew, but in great disorder. John Stevens poignantly recalled "the horror of a routed army, just before so vigorous and desirous of battle and broke without scarce a stroke from the enemy. . . . Scarce a regiment was left but what was reduced to a very inconsiderable number by this, if possible, more than panic fear." James quickly fled to France. Meanwhile, the Williamite army followed up its victory by sweeping to take Dublin. In the autumn John Churchill, Earl of Marlborough, landed in Munster and swiftly captured Cork and Kinsale. Although Limerick held out for more than a year, William felt confident enough of the situation in Ireland to return to England, leaving the army under the command of General Godard van Reede Ginkel.[42] William had won the only battle in which the two claimants to the British throne faced off against each other.

The thousands of deaths on the battlefield at the Boyne and later at Aughrim in 1691, at the sieges of Londonderry and at Limerick, only scratched the surface of the extraordinary violence in Ireland during the revolutionary years. Protestant fears of persecution that had begun when the Earl of Tyrconnel became lord deputy accelerated during the revolution. Rumors circulated that Tyrconnel had threatened to "turn his army loose to do what they please" if any Williamite army landed in Ireland. Robert Parker recalled that many thought the massacre at midcentury, "the fatal scene of Forty-One, might be repeated." Hundreds, perhaps thousands, of Protestants fled their homes and took sail for England. As soon as Tyrconnel felt confident in his military and administrative position, he took measures to disarm the country's Protestants and seize their horses. In Dublin, Tyrconnel's men were quartered on Protestants, where they were said to "daily commit so great outrages, that they force them to abandon their habitations, and to sit up all night long, for fear of being murdered in their beds." Irish Protestant information networks no doubt exaggerated the atrocities committed. But the extent of the devastation was real. "The rapines, assaults, robberies and outrages of the papists committed daily upon the Protestants increase," lamented Lord Massarene, almost certainly referring in part to the devastation wrought by the marauding bands. "The condition of the Protestants," wrote the natural philosopher Thomas Aske, was "very lamentable, they being generally throughout the kingdom imprisoned." Protestants in Dublin enjoyed more freedom. But in June 1690, according to William King, "at least 3000" were incarcerated, many ironically in Protestant Trinity College, which had been seized and converted into a garrison and prison.[43] In 1689–90 Ireland was a dangerous place for anyone who could be suspected of Williamite sympathies.

The war fought on Irish soil in 1689–91 wreaked havoc on the local economy and landscape. Ulster was devastated. "The Irish have harassed and burnt much of the North of Ireland," reported the Earl of Melville. Melville's interim report was given much more specificity after the siege. "I found the land almost desolate, country houses and dwellings burnt," William King noted when he took up his position as bishop of Derry. "On an inquiry being made I ascertained there were in the diocese of Derry, before the troubles, about 250,000 head of cattle, there were left, after the siege was raised, about 300; out of 460,000 horses 2 horses remained, lame and wounded, with 7 sheep, and 2 pigs, but no fowl, whence the miserable state of the province was sufficiently manifest." Williamite activities were no less destructive. Drogheda, "since this rebellion . . . is totally ruined," observed the Jacobite John Stevens, "its trade lost, most of the inhabitants fled, and the buildings ready to fall to the ground." James's decision to coin brass money to keep his regime financially afloat made the cost of everyday provisions beyond the means of most inhabitants of Ireland. The Williamite embargo deprived Dublin in particular of fuel, driving many soldiers to do much "mischief by night" including cutting down trees and destroying hedges. The net effect was desolation. Ireland "is so harassed by two armies of different complexions," wrote one Englishman sympathetically, "that no less than an age of peace can recover it."[44]

Despite the war's disastrous effects on Ireland, the Williamite victory at the Boyne and the revolutionaries' ultimate triumph at Aughrim were decisive moments in the establishment of the revolutionary regime in England and ultimately for the hopes of the confederate cause in Europe. When the news of the victory at the Boyne reached London, the city erupted in "great demonstrations of joy." One political insider wrote, "Our fears with relation to Ireland are wholly vanished." In Derbyshire the Earl of Chesterfield claimed that the news "revived the drooping spirits." The Independent congregation at Axminster in Somerset was no doubt typical of many Dissenting congregations in their "great gladness" of the Williamite victory "over that malignant generation of men."[45]

The response was similar among England's allies on the Continent. "'Tis impossible to express the great joy the late success brought to these parts and consequently to all the allies," wrote William Dutton Colt from Hanover. In The Hague people were "filled" with joy. In Amsterdam the price of stock in the East India Company—always a great measure of the Dutch public mood—rose "50% upon the news of our happy success in Ireland."[46]

This euphoria was based, no doubt, on an overestimation of the ease with which William's armies would complete the conquest of Ireland. But Williamite glee was exactly matched by Jacobite gloom. "King James diverts himself with hunting and good meat and drink" in France, wrote one Jacobite sympathizer, since after his ignominious return from Ireland "he sees nothing will do" to restore his throne but a French invasion. The news from the Boyne "having quite undone me . . . I have been sick ever since," wrote the Earl of Melfort to Mary of Modena, "nor do I think my heart will ever come to its place again." The survival of the Jacobite army over the winter of 1690–91 did not cheer up Jacobite politicos in France. Sir Edward Hales wrote to Tyrconnel that "our only hopes" were for an invasion of England. "The King," concurred Melfort, "cannot be restored except by force"—by which he made clear he meant a French invading force—"so long at least as the Prince of Orange lives."[47]

At the same time that the Williamites decisively defeated the Jacobite army on land in Ireland, a French invasion of England by sea was, however, a real possibility. Only because William and his allies understood better than most historians that the Revolution of 1688–89 was of European rather than narrowly British significance were they able to prevent the expected French assault. Only a brilliant diplomatic maneuver prevented a successful French invasion in the summer of 1690.

After a huge naval buildup, the French fleet soundly defeated a joint Anglo-Dutch naval force off Beachy Head just a few days before the Battle of the Boyne. The victory gave the French naval supremacy, making it possible for them to invade England and Scotland with their massive army. "The news of this action struck England into a terror," rightly observed one Jacobite. Queen Mary agreed after the news of Beachy Head reached her that "things have but a melancholy prospect." "My trouble at our unfortunate sea fight . . . was so great," wrote the radical ambassador to Denmark Robert Molesworth, "that

I had not the courage either to go to court or to set pen to paper." Logic and a wealth of reports convinced the Marquis of Carmarthen, lord president of the Privy Council, that the French intended a landing "with a strong force and that very speedily." Similar rumors about French preparations for an invasion of England circulated in European merchant circles that summer as well. Jacobites, too, expected a French invasion. Knowing that "England was left almost naked of soldiers," wrote one Jacobite, Louis XIV "immediately took up a resolution to transport a moderate army, in the absence of the Prince, into England, which would soon, with the assistance of the loyal party, reduce that kingdom to its obedience."[48]

People all over England girded themselves for a French invasion. In the West Country there were "frequent tidings and great fears" that summer that the nation was "in danger to be invaded by the French." The mood in London was somber "for fear of the French's landing." Elizabeth Oxenden recalled that in Hampshire "an invasion by the French . . . was expected after they beat our fleet last year." English fears appeared well grounded when soon after Beachy Head "a body of Frenchmen landed in the west of England and burned some places on the coast." The French also landed some men in Northumberland "and plundered Lord Waddrington's house (a Papist) burnt his outhouses and two or three thatched houses in the village." These preliminary raids convinced the government to place the country on high alert. Carmarthen told William that "the militias of all England are ordered to be in arms." "The whole nation almost is united against" the French, wrote one Londoner. This was no exaggeration. An astounding ninety-two thousand English militiamen were raised to fight off the French invasion in the summer of 1690.[49]

Yet there was no French invasion. By the middle of August Carmarthen felt safe enough to have the militias "dismissed."[50] What had happened? Why did the French not invade? The answer to this question reveals the danger of attempting to understand the revolution in narrowly British terms.

For William, Louis XIV, and most in the British Isles, the Revolution of 1688–89 was part of a European struggle. While William was fighting in Ireland, and the French and Anglo-Dutch fleets were facing each other off Beachy Head, the confederate allies conducted a successful diplomatic campaign on the Continent. In late May diplomatic channels were abuzz with the news that the Duke of Savoy was about to join the confederacy. Nothing, wrote one European observer, could be "more useful and more advantageous" for the cause of "humbling France." "I could never begin in a more favorable conjuncture nor with more favorable news," gushed Lord Dursley to the Marquis of Carmarthen, "than the hearty declaration of the Duke of Savoy for the common cause. . . . A better way of humbling the pride of France could never have prevented itself." The reason for all the excitement was not far to seek. The Duke of Savoy's support made it possible for the allies to attack France directly. When William, Lord Paget, learned of the news in Vienna, he emphasized the obvious point that "a door is now opened into France." When the Duke of

From *Engelants Schouwtoneel* (*The English drama*), by Romeyn de Hooghe,
1692. This depiction of James fleeing England belies descriptions of
the Revolution of 1688–89 as "bloodless" or "sensible."

Savoy ordered his army to march toward France, Louis XIV was forced to send "a counter-
mand to the army he had destined for England . . . to face about and march straight to
Savoy against the said confederate army." "Thus," one Irish Jacobite lamented, "the best
occasion that ever France could have" of restoring James II to his throne was lost.[51]

The Revolution of 1688–89 was neither bloodless nor quick. Revolutionary violence, and the potential for further violence, continued in England long after William and
Mary were crowned in 1689. The struggle to establish the revolutionary regime in England,
though, was fought out in Scotland, Ireland, and on the Continent. Only after James had
fled Ireland and the Duke of Savoy had prevented Franco-Jacobite invasion in 1690 was
it clear that the new regime could be overthrown by French force alone. Sir Charles Cotterell expressed sentiments typical of those sympathetic to the regime. Our affairs "never
seemed to me so hopeful as at present," he wrote to Sir William Trumbull after the final
defeat of the Jacobite army in Ireland in 1691, "for Ireland being now totally reduced and
all quiet both here and in Scotland, the King is peaceful master of the three kingdoms."
Nevertheless, these British achievements were not sufficient to establish the revolutionary
regime. To ensure long-term stability, the English needed to "bring Monsieur to reason."

Not until after the creation of the Bank of England in 1694 was the future Duke of Chandos, James Brydges, able to convince his Jacobite-leaning father that the new regime was firmly in place. It was at that moment, he argued, "the opinion of most persons here as well as strangers abroad, that the present government is so firm, and if not well settled nevertheless settled so well for King William's advantage, that there is no likelihood of its ever changing in favor of King James."[52] Not until 1694 would this well-connected lifelong politician admit that no domestic rising could quickly overturn the revolutionary regime. Lord Chandos understood better than most subsequent historians just how fragile the new regime was in the 1690s. The English revolution would be insecure until the English state could parry any thrust from the powerful French monarchy.

The Williamite regime was insecure because like most modern postrevolutionary regimes it came to power on the strength of popular uprisings and extensive violence. As in most revolutions, the number of people killed was much smaller than the amount of property damaged and destruction done to the structures of power. Most people in England and Scotland were well aware that any calm was extremely fragile. From 1688 to 1691 angry crowds, disbanded and disgruntled soldiers, and Jacobite plots were ubiquitous. The culture of violence was pervasive. In both Scotland and England James was overthrown with widespread popular violence. In both cases crowds attacked both Catholic and High Church supporters of James II's regime. In Ireland the story was very different. There the overwhelming majority of the population supported James's loyal lord deputy, Tyrconnel. However, even there the revolution began with violent popular uprisings that were largely beaten back. In all three kingdoms, however, the violence was organized around the establishment of a revolutionary regime. In none of the kingdoms was there a bloodless or peaceful revolution. Throughout the British Isles the violent establishment of the revolution was part of a broader struggle over European liberty.

CHAPTER TEN

Divisive Revolution

The Revolution of 1688–89 was neither aristocratic nor bloodless. Nor was it consensual. This claim runs counter to one of the central tenets of the Whig interpretation of the Revolution of 1688–89. The proponents of this view have always maintained that James II's reign spawned an unusual period of political consensus in England. For Macaulay and his fellow Whig interpreters of the Revolution, the English displayed their exceptional national character in 1688 by putting aside party divisions to dismiss James II with a united voice. The events of 1688–89 were neither a Whig nor a Tory triumph; they were an English triumph.

Revisionists, by contrast, have argued that Tories played the leading role in 1688–89: they led the charge against James II's tolerationist policies in defense of an exclusive church. Many Whigs, the revisionists imply, had a great deal invested in James's regime. Although Tories may not have anticipated or desired William's arrival and his decision to seize the Crown, they quickly adjusted.

The evidence runs counter to both interpretations. Whereas James II's enemies had every incentive to maintain a united front in the face of a modern standing army and a modern state apparatus, the revolutionaries could not silence or even hide their profound ideological disagreements. Party political differences—above all between Whigs and Tories—reemerged before James II had fled the country. Both Whigs and Tories wanted

---

(above) *Throne of England Declared Vacant*, by Jan Smeltzing, 1689. James II, portrayed as a bear, is driven from England by bees flying from three hives, representing the three kingdoms of England, Scotland, and Ireland. The inscription on the front of the medal reads: "Thus the British vindicate their liberty and religion from the spoilers. 1688."

to dismantle James II's Catholic modernizing regime; they disagreed profoundly about what they hoped would replace it. The Tories hoped the revolution would merely undo James II's Catholic modernization program and return to the heady days of Tory political hegemony that characterized the final years of Charles II's reign. They accepted that regime change would have to be defended by force, but they had no desire to transform European politics. The cost of defeating James and his political allies, they thought, might require great exertion in the short term but no fundamental rearrangement of English society. The Whigs, by contrast, wanted the revolution to radically remake English politics and society. They wanted to initiate their own modernization agenda. The substantial minority that remained loyal to James did so in part because they remained committed to his French style of modern government. The events of 1688–89 did not usher in an age of political stability, much less one of placidity. The rage of party dominated the English political scene from late 1688. Party differences rather than political consensus characterized England's Revolution of 1688–89.

Many contemporaries did marvel at the apparent unanimity of the English in 1688–89. James was so unpopular, noted Lady Sunderland, that England stands "all as one man" against him. "England is now all of one mind," lamented the Jacobite loyalist Countess of Huntingdon in December 1688. The Whiggish rector of Almer in Dorset John Ollyffe praised the "union of all parties" that had appeared in 1688. In 1688, agreed the Whig Colley Cibber, England was "of one mind, Whigs, Tories, Princes, prelates, nobles, clergy, common people, and a standing army were unanimous." One postrevolutionary play even suggested that the events of 1688 had finally reconciled the "old Cavalier" with the former Roundheads.[1] Nevertheless, unity remained an ideal never quite realized. Many in England could agree in their opposition to James—though even on that issue there was hardly unanimity—but they differed deeply about what should follow the dismantling of his version of a modern English polity.

William did all he could to promote English unity. He worked hard to curb the enthusiasms of his more committed Whig followers. He tempered the language and the content of his official manifesto, the *Declaration of Reasons,* so that it was moderate in both tone and content. William's *Declaration* focused narrowly on the misdeeds of James II's reign rather than offering the broader critique of the post-Restoration monarchy desired by the Whigs. The emphasis in the document was on those issues that appealed across the ideological spectrum. William made heroic efforts to have the *Declaration* define the events of 1688–89. The *Declaration* went through twenty-one editions in 1688. Printing houses in Amsterdam, Rotterdam, and The Hague each printed twenty thousand copies of the manifesto for distribution in England. Supporters of William such as Sir Rowland Gwynne were each given three thousand copies for distribution among their "friends." Although some of the copies were seized, many more made their way into "the hands of the generality of the nation." William's supporters used the new Penny Post to distribute the *Declaration* in London. By the middle of November copies were to be found from Cornwall to Yorkshire and everywhere in between. In town after town the revolutionaries frequently read out William's *Declaration*. As the prince marched from Torbay, crowds celebrated his arrival with demands to hear the *Declaration* in Newton Abbot and then at Exeter Cathedral. When the Earl of Bath surrendered Plymouth to William, he "caused the Prince of Orange's *Declaration* to be read in his presence." When the revolutionaries took control of York, they, too, "read the Prince of Orange's *Declaration*." The same pattern was followed clear across England. In Falmouth, in Chester, in Maidstone in Kent, in Leeds, and in Preston in Lancashire the revolutionaries proudly read out the moderate manifesto.[2]

Nevertheless, even though many were extremely grateful to William and shared many of the sentiments expressed in his *Declaration,* the English did not put aside their long-held party differences to tamely follow the Dutch stadholder. There were many popular uprisings throughout the country in the autumn of 1688, not a single Dutch invasion. In many cases the speeches, declarations, and manifestos of the revolutionaries gave a party spin on William's more politically anodyne manifesto.

The groups associated with Lord Delamere and the Earl of Devonshire, who had led popular uprisings in the Midlands, were overwhelmingly Whiggish and Dissenting. They maintained that sovereignty lay with the people, insisted religious and civil liberty could be guaranteed only through revolutionary change, and implied that the English needed to radically transform their social and institutional arrangements. James himself recalled that Delamere's "interest lay most among the Presbyterians." Delamere's troops displayed their Whig sympathies by spending "their diverting hours" in shooting effigies of "the Bishop of Chester and the Bishop of St. David's," the two most absolutist Anglican bishops, as well as that of the French-style Catholic Father Petre. When Delamere first gathered his forces at Boden Downs, he told them that if they did not prevail, "farewell liberty of conscience." Delamere, his cousin the Earl of Ailesbury recalled, was "a person of implacable spirit against the King and the Crown." This must have been the impression of those thousands gathered to hear Delamere at Boden Downs, where he insisted that "our deliverance must be by force," and at Derby, where he denounced James II and extolled "the rights and liberties of the subject." It was characteristic of Delamere that on his arrival in London, he declared to anyone who would listen, "that if the King was King, he and his were rebels." The implication was clear and clearly anathema to Tories. The revolutionaries had already deposed James II, and now all power had devolved to "the body of the people." It was no doubt because he found Delamere's Whiggery so distasteful that the Tory 9th Earl of Derby refused to join Delamere's rebellion. Devonshire's politics were little different. At Nottingham he and his men issued and disseminated a *Declaration* stating that James "was always accounted a tyrant, that made his will the law; and to resist such a one, we justly esteem no rebellion, but a necessary defense." No wonder "only one major Tory joined Devonshire."[3]

The uprisings in the northeast of England tended, on the whole, to be Tory and High Church affairs; both the leaders and participants were Anglicans who hated James's Catholicism but were uninterested in broader social or political change. The men who took York, Hull, and most of Yorkshire were overwhelmingly Tories. One historian has called the events in Yorkshire "a Tory rebellion." Unlike the risings in the northwest, for example, these men emphasized their support "for the Church of England and the downfall of Popery." Danby himself repeatedly said that he was "the last man in the kingdom" who would resort to use force against his lawful sovereign. But there were no other hopes of "saving the Protestant religion," since "if the King beat the Prince, popery will return upon us." Sir Richard Temple remembered that in Yorkshire it was "the Church Party" and "only" the Church Party that had "made a stand." By the time this group arrived in Nottingham, it could positively be affirmed that they made up "a differing party." Indeed, many among Danby's men, like the Earl of Chesterfield, "had a natural aversion to the taking arms against my king, which the law justly terms designing the king's death."[4] One cannot imagine a political theory more distant from that espoused by Lord Delamere and his supporters.

So ideologically divided was the opposition to James that in Westmorland and Cumberland opposing Whig and Tory groups competed with each other even before James II's garrison at Carlisle had relinquished control of the region. Attempts by Sir Daniel Fleming to get the Whig Sir John Lowther and the Tory Sir Christopher Musgrave to work together came to nothing. Musgrave and his Tory ally Sir George Fletcher refused to sign the Whig petition calling for "a free parliament." Opposing Whig and Tory bands marched on the military garrison at Carlisle, competing to accept the commander's surrender and take over the city. In the end, the Tories gained control of the garrison. But bitter feelings remained. One of Musgrave's henchmen, Basil Fielding, on entering Carlisle said of Lowther, "God damn him for a Whig." Lowther, who never missed an opportunity to dispute any position taken by Musgrave in the parliamentary debates of the 1690s, recorded in his memoirs bitterly that Musgrave and the Tories had "complied with those times" in the reign of James II.[5]

In the immediate aftermath of James's flight, Whigs and Tories each claimed that they and they alone had been responsible for the revolution. Neither side claimed that the revolution was a moment of ideological consensus. In a debate in the House of Commons in December 1689, the Tory Sir Thomas Clarges announced that he was "sure the King came in by the Church of England, their peers, sermons, and sufferings." Clarges was merely enunciating what had already become Tory orthodoxy. "The Whigs were entirely closed with King James and did not in the least contribute to this change," remarked the former political maverick turned orthodox Tory Sir Richard Temple. The Whigs had an entirely different memory of the events of 1688 and 1689. The Whig Sir John Guise, who had himself been in arms in 1688 and had taken Bristol "with 600 horse," immediately responded that Clarges had clearly not been "upon the spot when the change was" because he knew that "the Church of England ran away from us, and the Dissenters stayed." One Whig pamphleteer agreed, aptly summarizing the Whig case by stating that "the present happy change is owing to Whiggism." Those Tories who did support the movement to rid the nation of James II did so for "private ends" whereas the Whigs acted "for a public good."[6]

Both versions of events were at best partial truths. Both Whigs and Tories had taken up arms in 1688. What is important is that even before any decision had been taken on the settlement of the kingdom party battle lines had been drawn. Tories and Whigs had not acted in a consensual manner. They had never buried party differences. Instead, both groups had decided, for very different reasons, that James II's modern polity needed to be overthrown.

In this context, it is hardly surprising that the English did not celebrate James's flight to the Continent with united cheers. Instead, the overwhelming majority of those who cared to comment described a bitterly divided polity. James II's flight in December 1688 did nothing to remedy these divisions. A deeply divided nation now faced the daunting task of reaching a settlement.

The elections to the Convention Parliament, convened in late January 1689 to bring the nation to that settlement, were anything but consensual. England's counties and boroughs could not put party strife behind them. The elections were, according to a wide range of contemporaries, "very free, all soldiers having been removed from the places where they were made." Yet free elections did not imply calm, peaceful, or consensual elections. All across the country, seats were bitterly contested among "such as had been Tories, Whigs and Trimmers," noted Sir Robert Southwell in his manuscript account of the revolution. Another observer commented that in the elections to the convention, "the Church party was almost as much opposed as the Jacobites." One very conservative modern estimate suggests that there were at least eighty contested elections in 1689, an unusually high if not unprecedented number.[7]

Evidence from the localities confirms this general assessment. In Derby, for example, Sir William Boothby roused the "honest free men of our Church"—the Church of England—to turn out in hordes to oppose the candidacy of the radical Dissenter William Sacheverell. The Whig Sir William Cowper prepared a paper for the election in Hertford in which he poured venom both on Tory "arbitrary magistrates" and "electors" who had kept him from Parliament in 1685 but also on the "Popish regulators" who had aimed to pack Parliament for James II. The party animosities between the Whig Sir John Lowther of Lowther and the Tory Sir Christopher Musgrave colored the campaigning season in Cumberland and Westmoreland. Lowther balanced his failure to take Carlisle for the Whigs by forcing Sir Christopher Musgrave to abandon attempts to sit for the county of Westmoreland. "Sir John Lowther is so violent against my father," complained Philip

Musgrave to the Earl of Dartmouth, "that he is making interest to oppose him and his friends in all places where he or any of them think to stand." In this Lowther failed; as Sir Christopher was elected for Carlisle and Philip for Appleby. Taunton in Somerset had long been known for violent party animosities. On election day the supporters of the Whig candidates, John Trenchard and Edward Clarke, gathered at the Angel Inn in Taunton, where they were soon accosted by a Tory crowd that included many soldiers. Some escaped "over a wall," but others, when they tried to vote, were "knocked down and grievously wounded." According to Trenchard and Clarke, at least thirteen men suffered serious injury. In the event the Tories Sir William Portman and John Sanford were returned as they had been in 1685. The Whig petition no doubt exaggerated the extent of Tory violence, but there was no denying the intensity of party animosity. In London, by contrast, where four Whigs were returned for Parliament, Tories were bitterly denounced. Sir Peter Daniel was decried as "the most active and crafty Tory in all the City." The powerful Tory and former lord mayor Sir John Moore was "hissed at." In general the Tories were accused of being "the chief agents in betraying the City and the nation." These party divisions were ultimately well represented in the Convention Parliament. Far from producing a consensual body, the elections produced a House of Commons neatly poised between Whig and Tory—the Whigs probably had a majority of fewer than twenty in a House made up of more than five hundred members.[8]

The Convention Parliament's meeting did little to dampen ideological contestation. One London newsletter commented that "all the discourse in town is about settling the government"—with every group offering its own solution. All were talking "in coffee houses and better places of fine things for you to do," observed the Whig John Maynard. English men and women throughout the kingdom were discussing a bewildering array of options. Some, mostly High Church Tories, thought it illegal to alter the succession and therefore wanted James to remain king with limitations placed on his authority. A sizable and articulate group argued for a commonwealth. Others argued that the Princess of Orange should be made queen, with William acting as regent. Still others insisted that William and Mary should jointly be made king and queen. These were heady and unpredictable times. John Locke relished the "opportunity" the convention provided "to find remedies and set up a constitution that may be lasting for the security of civil rights and the liberty and property of all the subjects of the nation." "The public affairs of this unsettled kingdom seem now to be brought to a crisis," preached William Stainforth in York Minster in late January. "How things will go and what will be the issue and event of them, God only knows."[9]

The Convention Parliament itself was bitterly divided. Throughout London and Westminster there was "much caballing about affairs." A group of Dissenting ministers met to discuss "what was fit to be offered about church matters for themselves and those of their persuasion," while other Whigs offered proposals on constitutional issues. The Tories, including Sir Robert Sawyer, Heneage Finch, Sir Thomas Clarges, Sir Christopher

Musgrave, Sir Joseph Tredenham, "and a great many more," had probably been meeting at the Devil Tavern long before the Presbyterian Roger Morrice heard of them in mid-March. It was hardly surprising, then, that the debates of the convention quickly divided on party lines. On 28 January 1689 the parties settled into a heated debate about the state of the nation. In the end, perhaps influenced by the "common talk" in favor of settling the Crown on William and Mary, the House of Commons adopted a resolution declaring "the throne vacant" because James had "endeavoured to subvert the constitution of this kingdom, by breaking the original contract between King and People; and, by the advice of Jesuits and other wicked persons" he had "violated the fundamental laws" and "having withdrawn himself out of the kingdom; has abdicated the government." Although many Tories in the Commons argued vehemently in favor of a regency and against the throne being vacant, they were probably appeased by the very ambiguity of the resolution. The Tories desperately wanted to deny the legitimacy of popular political resistance. The throne was certainly vacant, but it was left unclear whether James had been deposed or had simply fled. Tories could continue to maintain that there had been no political resistance in 1688, that the constitutional crisis was caused by James II's voluntary and unfortunate abandonment of the nation. Since it was unclear whether James's demise should be treated like a royal death or as the result of resistance to the monarchy, it was also unclear whether the throne should be filled by the ordinary rules of hereditary succession or whether the Convention Parliament was empowered to select a new ruler. Even so, many Tories were unhappy. Only a handful voted against the resolution, but the well-connected Scottish Episcopalian minister Robert Kirk later claimed that "160 were against advancing King William and Queen Mary."[10]

The Tories made their stand in the House of Lords. Lord Yester predicted correctly as soon as the Convention assembled that "there are not a few and those considerable men especially among the peers and clergy" who would oppose any move to replace James with William and Mary. Instead of declaring the throne vacant, a number of lords, led by the Tory Earl of Nottingham, proposed that England be governed by a regency during James's lifetime. The proposal was defeated, "but only by three votes." Over the next two days the lords proceeded with "great heats" to pass motions rejecting the Commons' use of the term "abdicated" and refusing to admit that the throne was "vacant." Although the divisions did not strictly follow party lines—the Marquis of Halifax, who was at the time a moderate Tory, had been convinced that James could no longer be king—the basic pattern was clear. "The Whigs were the most zealous for the abdication and giving the crown to King William and those that argued for it did own that the Whigs were in the right whilst others were in the wrong during the two late reigns," recalled Lord Delamere. "On the other side," pulling "as hard as they could the other way," he noted, were "the Tories and High Church party."[11]

The Convention Parliament was at an impasse. Whigs and Tories could not agree about the most basic issues preliminary to a settlement. A conference between the leaders of the Commons and Lords was leading nowhere. It was at this moment that those in and around London acted in a manner typical of all modern revolutions: they used the pressure of mass politics. A petition was hastily drawn up demanding that William and Mary be declared king and queen. Although it is difficult to specify who was behind the petition, it was clearly a Whig document. Sir John Reresby heard that it was "the Lords that were for confirming the crown immediately upon the Prince" who "sent some instruments to stir up the mobile, who came in a tumultuous manner with a petition." Roger Morrice, who had rather better sources in London's Whig community, claimed that the Whig merchant, Francophobe, and violent critic of Josiah Child's East India Company, James Houblon, promoted the petition "as the only way to prevent a war." The only known manuscript copy of the petition survives in the papers of the Whig William Cowper. The petition received mass support. When the petitions were "delivered by ten of the mobile," they claimed that for "every one of the ten was deputed to this by 5000 of the like." Even if this figure of fifty thousand was an exaggeration—others reported that only fifteen thousand signatures had been gathered—the Whig petition of February 1689 was clearly on the same scale of the monster petition in favor of Exclusion presented in January 1680 and included at least as many signatures as the Root and Branch petition of December 1640. In fact, the petition probably rivaled in scope the petitioning campaigns of the later eighteenth century. Unsurprisingly the radical Whig Anthony Rowe presented "the petition from great numbers of persons" to the House of Commons, while the Whig Lord Lovelace presented the petition in the House of Lords.[12]

Even though neither the House of Commons nor the House of Lords agreed to read the Whig petition, the petition had a decided effect. The petition, it turns out, was a piece a paper backed by thousands of angry English men and women. Many were in great fear that "the City apprentices were coming down to Westminster in a violent rage against all who voted against the Prince of Orange's interest." "There are some sort of people that begin to threaten the bishops," William Banks warned his fellow Tory Roger Kenyon. "The Lords were threatened yesterday by the mob," complained the Tory Sir Edward Seymour, "and they are not yet dispersed." "Diverse persons, not being members of the House," were said to have been "in the speaker's chamber and gallery." Members of the House of Lords were "hindered" from attending the house by "hackney-coaches, carts, and drays." The Earl of Clarendon complained that the "rabble" had come "in great numbers this morning to Westminster, conducted or invited thither by Lord Lovelace or William Killegrew." The Presbyterian Henry Newcome must not have been the only one in England who thought that "things at present look like a tendency to confusion."[13]

In less than a week, on 6 February, the House of Lords agreed that James II had abdicated and that the throne was vacant. They then agreed to have William and Mary declared king and queen of England. There can be no doubt that William's last-ditch lobbying campaign had some effect. However, it is hard to imagine that the angry crowds demonstrating in Westminster, claiming to have the support of thousands more, did not powerfully persuade the lords. In a revolutionary crisis that had already had its fair share of political violence, the threat posed by the Whig crowds must have been intimidating indeed. The story printed years later, that Lord Lovelace threatened the recalcitrant Tory lords that "if they did not agree within two or three days, and crown the Prince of Orange, he would bring fifty thousand men to the House that shall make them do it," is certainly plausible. Some contemporaries thought that Whig popular political activity tipped the balance. On 2 February Roger Morrice had predicted that the Tories would not "be able to carry it," because "many Lords, Commons and many gentlemen of great interest, and the universality of the middle gentlemen and of the best freeholders who are the strength of the kingdom" were "all in a brave fermentation." Though no friend of "popular petitioning," he thought it much "more warrantable" in circumstances like the present when "war may be prevented."[14]

The news of the Whig victory was welcomed enthusiastically by much of England's population. For those still gathered "about the Parliament House," this was "a very joyful vote." That night there were "several bonfires and great ringing of bells for so great a mercy as such a happy concurrence between the Lords and Commons." The following week there were official celebrations all across the country. Although most of the extant accounts are too general to describe the political character of these events, there is some evidence that Whigs were especially pleased. One group of Londoners, at "no small cost and charge," constructed and then burned an effigy of the Whig bogeyman Lord Chancellor George Jeffreys. In Newcastle "a spirit of crossness" overcame most in the town, but "all the Dissenters in that town unanimously" celebrated "with great joy and solemnity."[15]

Party strife did not end after Whig politicians and Whig crowds had replaced James II with William and Mary. Many Tories accommodated themselves to the new regime, but many others did not. Almost forty members of the House of Lords formally protested against declaring the Crown vacant.[16] More important, James's strategic decision to abandon England in late 1688 was not because he lacked supporters. In fact, James's program of Catholic modernity generated deep passions. There were, we should not forget, passionate supporters as well as passionate opponents.

Three groups in particular remained loyal and active in James's cause. First, servants of James II's modernizing state remained committed to his regime. In particular, soldiers in James II's standing army proved remarkably loyal to their old master. These men, drilled in loyalty for several years, had a host of grievances against the new regime ranging from irregular pay to threats of deployment in Ireland or on the Continent. Second, many Church of England ministers, men who had spent their lives teaching their parishioners the value of loyalty and passive obedience, could not accept the new regime. Third, the religious groups who thought they had benefited most from James's government—French-style Roman Catholics and the Quakers most loyal to William Penn—actively supported a Jacobite restoration.

From the moment that James fled England there was good reason to suspect that his soldiers would remain loyal. They had, after all, been treated extremely well by James, who had transformed England's army from a ragtag group of soldiers into one of the best-trained and disciplined armies in Europe. By late January 1689 Roger Morrice was already concerned that "a great part" of James II's army was predisposed "to a defection." The Jacobite Charles Whyteford knew that there were "great grudgings in England, especially among the soldiers." Anthony Cary, Lord Falkland, reported to the House of Commons that "the old army is discontented." Many leaders of James's army, including the Earl of Arran, Theophilus Oglethorpe, and Sir John Fenwick, were prominent in Jacobite activities. Soldiers who had served in the garrison of Carlisle met frequently to discuss plans for opposing the regime. The former members of the Earl of Dunbarton's regiment stationed at Ipswich did rebel and proclaim James, "declaring they had no other king." When the Duke of Grafton's regiment was ordered to the Continent, many officers resigned their commissions and "many of the soldiers deserted."[17]

Reports came in from all over the country of army opposition to the new regime. The "insolent" soldiers in Cirencester "proclaim King James" and "drank King William's and Queen Mary's damnation." Hugh Boscawen reported that the disbanded soldiers in Cornwall "are as bad as the rest." While many locals were celebrating "the happy change" of government, "the soldiers killed a man." In Buckingham the troops were said to have "forced the Mayor to drink the late King James's health." In the west of England disbanded soldiers "often rifle the post." John Wildman was furious that soldiers "at Newbury, Abingdon and other places . . . would not suffer the crier or bell-man to say, 'God Bless King William and Queen Mary.'" The recently disbanded Captain Motley was heard to say at a London coffeehouse that "in three weeks time King James would be possessed of Whitehall; and that King William would abdicate in three months."[18]

Soldiers were not the only loyal servants of James II. Two of James's lords lieutenant, the Dukes of Beaufort and Newcastle, were involved in Jacobite conspiracies. Peter Shakerley, the former governor of Chester, was arrested in May 1689 at "a Papist's house" in possession of a stash of James II's declarations. The former governor of Upnor Castle in Kent, one Captain Minors, was overheard drinking "King James's health" and "damnation to King William and Queen Mary." The former governor of the freemen of Dorchester, Edward Lester, accused William of breaking "faith with the nation," asserting that "the times were like those of '41 and '42." The magistrates of Exeter, presumably the Church of England men restored to authority by James II in October 1688, similarly displayed "much disaffection to the King." The attitudes of lower-level bureaucrats are harder to trace. But there is good reason to suspect that the actions of the hearth money collectors were not atypical. "Many of the collectors," the postrevolutionary commissioners of the revenue reported in November 1689, "run away with great sums of money and with the books of collection."[19]

Many High Church clergymen remained loyal to James, or at least extremely critical of the new regime. Though Oxford remained the home of High Churchmanship and Nonjurors, Cambridge college fellows were little more enthusiastic about the new regime. The fellows of St. John's College refused to join the official prayers for William and Mary. These were undoubtedly the "ringleaders," but most of the college masters and the vast majority of the fellows of the various colleges failed to attend the official ceremony proclaiming William and Mary. Although most of the fellows eventually took the official oaths to the government, William Whiston later recalled that they took "them with a doubtful conscience and against its dictate." The rector of Stalbridge in the vale of Blackmore in Dorset, the home of the natural philosopher Robert Boyle, eventually fled, but not before he had uttered "scurrilous abuses against the Prince of Orange." The curate of Sutton Coldfield in Warwickshire refused to pray for William and Mary. "In and about York" many ministers similarly refused to pray for the new monarchs. The Duke of Bolton complained that the clergy at Winchester Cathedral in Hampshire "did not pray for King William and Queen Mary." The parson in Stamford, Lincolnshire, worked with the mayor to encourage the militia "to load with ball" to break up celebrations for the newly proclaimed William and Mary while he himself "drank a health to the old gentleman [James II]." In 1690 a parson was convicted at the Northampton assizes for "saying that King William and Queen Mary were not lawfully King and Queen" and for praying for James II. When William called for a fast in support of the war effort in 1690, the minister of the church of St. Mary of Charity in Faversham, Kent, compared his actions to those of "that rogue Oliver [Cromwell]." The Jacobite clergy that gathered at Sam's coffeehouse in London were a "numerous gang" who croaked "like frogs in March against the government." Though the number of clergymen who refused to take the oaths to the new regime was relatively small—they numbered about four hundred as against about two thousand who refused to conform to the restored Church of England in 1660–63[20]—their influence should not be underestimated. This was in part because many, like the Cambridge college fellows, took the oaths grudgingly and in part because they "draw after 'em some numbers of the gentry and commonalty of the nation."[21]

Catholics—one suspects those practicing a French-style Catholicism—and some Quakers formed a third group of Jacobites. Even if the Gallican bent of James II's Catholicism had alienated many of England's Catholics, James's policy of Catholic modernization had reconciled many others to the Catholic Church and his Catholicizing policies made it possible for many crypto-Catholics to espouse their beliefs openly. So it was hardly surprising that, when James returned to the capital from his first attempted flight in December 1688, London's Catholics "were very high and made bonfires." Popular anti-Catholic violence, James's final departure, and the crowning of William and Mary did not eliminate Jacobite activity in London. The sheer size and diversity of London no doubt made it easy for Catholic Jacobites to survive. Despite various crackdowns, there were constant reports of Catholics "acting in London for the interest of King James." Late in 1689 some London Catholics were heard to predict that "before Michaelmas they shall yet see a great change to King James's advantage."[22]

Catholic Jacobite activity was not exclusive to London. The Harleys complained of the "insolence of the Papists" in Herefordshire and of their "confident expectation of their king's return in spring [1690]." In Cheshire there were similar reports of "frequent and great meetings of Roman Catholics," some of whom were also certain that "King James would speedily be among them" and could count on significant support in their county. Lancashire, which had a significant Roman Catholic population and had been a center of Jesuit activity in James II's reign, was from the first a center of Catholic Jacobitism. Reports poured in from both Whig and Tory informants of frequent meetings and rumors of uprisings long before the discovery of the Lancashire Plot of 1694. Sir Jonathan Jennings informed the House of Commons that in Ripon, Yorkshire, "the Papists are very high, ride in numbers, and have cabals." A Jacobite postmaster was known to have distributed large quantities of James's *Declaration* to Catholics throughout that county. Catholic Jacobites were active in Northumberland as well.[23]

Some Quakers, such as the leader William Penn, were also involved in Jacobite activity. Despite his denials, the evidence suggests that immediately after James's fall from power, William Penn remained loyal and active in the cause of his old master. Some of Penn's coreligionists shared his sentiments. Robert Harley complained that "the Quakers are very nought and stick not publicly to declare they are for King James and have constant instructions by letters." The Jacobite Earl of Melfort bragged to Cardinal Howard of the assistance that the Jacobite cause in Ireland had received from Quaker middlemen.[24]

Jacobites were remarkably successful in disseminating their bitter criticisms of the postrevolutionary regime. Surviving commonplace books from the 1690s are filled with Jacobite poems and doggerel verse. Within days of William and Mary having been declared king and queen, one "scurrilous paper was set over Whitehall gates" that proclaimed "this house is to let and within may be seen / A crooked nose K—— and a fat a——d Q——." Less witty, but perhaps more politically significant, were the extensive Jacobite pamphleteering efforts. "There are papers cast about to fright people with the change of government," complained John Wildman in March 1689. "Go where you will," agreed Wildman's fellow Whig John Birch, "you see rebellious pamphlets." The following year Edward Harley bemoaned "the malicious reports which the enemies of religion and common liberty everywhere spread." These were not exaggerated fears. Jacobites scattered their pamphlets everywhere. Some were undoubtedly printed in France and smuggled into England, while most were probably printed domestically. Jacobites successfully distributed their tracts in London, Cambridge, Buckinghamshire, Yorkshire, Lancashire, and Scotland in 1689. In June 1689 James II's *Declaration,* appealing to the English people, was successfully distributed in London and as far afield as Cornwall and Lancashire.[25]

The existence of Jacobite social networks and the ready availability of Jacobite propaganda naturally resulted in a good deal of Jacobite activity. Jacobite sentiments could be heard everywhere as soon as James fled England in 1688. Jacobites took "great liberty in coffee houses and churches," observed John Howe. Robert Harley noted that they were "very free in their discourse." The lawyer John Bayley, for example, was heard to say at the Rose and Crown in Chippenham, Wiltshire, that "he owned no king but King James." Thomas Thompson, a soldier, proclaimed at the White Hart Tavern in Rochester that "he hoped to see the heart of the Prince of Orange upon the highest spike" on London Bridge. In London the prominent Tory merchant Thomas Paige exclaimed, "God Damn him he would murder King William and Queen Mary." Another Jacobite "cut the crown and scepter" off the painting of William in London's Guildhall. Other Jacobites rang London church bells on 10 June 1689, the first birthday of James II's son James Francis Edward. Many expressed their Jacobite sentiments by drinking health to King James and "confusion to their present Majesties."[26]

There is good reason to believe that Jacobites were involved in more than symbolic gestures against the postrevolutionary regime. From 1689 through the 1690s there were constant rumors of Jacobite plots. Newsletters and newspapers reported frequently on arrests of Jacobites. In many cases these were undoubtedly sham plots, political fabrications, or merely the creative exaggerations of those with genuine Jacobite sympathies. Nevertheless, some Jacobites clearly were willing to take violent action against the new regime. In early March 1689 the government saw fit to arrest some who were gathering in London and conspiring "against the government, for the interest of King James." In the late spring evidence came in from Cheshire, Hampshire, Lancashire, Nottinghamshire, and Northumberland of clandestine Jacobite military preparations. In July the government issued warnings that they had evidence of a substantial London-based conspiracy. Then in early September the government seized over two dozen Jacobite conspirators who were hatching a plot that involved assassinating William and fomenting rebellion throughout the country. The following summer there were "great discoveries" of another Jacobite effort, that some thought explained the ignominious English naval defeat at Beachy Head. This was followed by the more serious Ailesbury Plot of 1691–92, organized from the Continent by the Earl of Melfort. Although the authenticity of each individual assertion of Jacobite plotting may be questioned—and no doubt a good deal of paranoia and political calculation was involved—contemporaries did not doubt the reality and seriousness of the Jacobite threat. The Tory Sir Henry Goodrick believed that there was a "general conspiracy." On this, if on little else, the Whig Lord Delamere agreed. He warned that while William was away fighting in Ireland there might well be military uprisings on behalf of James in England because there were "too many who openly discover their inclinations for him."[27]

How significant was the Jacobite party in England? The evidence is complex and contradictory. In 1689 and 1690 many enthusiastic Jacobites and paranoid Williamites thought that James's restoration was imminent. "The usurper's power" will "by all appearances shortly be overthrown and our gracious sovereign restored," wrote David Nairne from Dublin in the spring of 1689. At the court of St. Germain, Jacobites confidently said in April 1689 that "before three months are at an end, the King will be an absolute monarch of his kingdoms." By the end of the year the Earl of Tyrconnel assured James's Mary that "the people of England were never in such a disposition to throw off the usurper and receive their own King as at this time." In the spring and summer of 1690, the Earl of Melfort told a number of his correspondents that "this summer shall give us the happiness of seeing the King again in his throne, all things seem to work for it." Some supporters of the regime in 1689 and 1690 also sensed a significant threat from domestic Jacobite activity. John Birch was one of the first to admit that "the country is in many ways disaffected to the government." Edward Harley was another who lamented "the visible growth of King James's party" in early 1690.[28]

These assessments of the strength of popular Jacobitism must be balanced with the equally numerous claims that Jacobitism was weak and growing weaker. There were some Jacobite pessimists. Almost as soon as he heard that James had been deposed, Walter Lorenzo Leslie wrote from Rome that "we despair anything from England without a conquest." The once optimistic Tyrconnel thought in the spring of 1690 that if James II did not become "master of England" by the end of the year, "I fear his friends there will despair of it and consequently secure themselves." Some supporters of the revolution also felt Jacobitism was a spent force. Lord Brandon, despite his own success in rounding up Lancashire Jacobites, thought his "country was unanimously for the King's service." The Tory Edmund Bohun claimed that the number of committed Jacobites "is not great." Robert Kirk, the Episcopalian minister from Aberfoyle, found "that in England and Scotland, few ministers and people" still supported James in October 1689.[29] By 1691, one observer with Tory sympathies claimed that the Tory government had "taken away all occasions of discontents except to Lord Feversham, Sir John Fenwick, and about twenty more who dare still own their old master."[30]

The balance of contemporary evidence makes it difficult to come to firm conclusions about the strength of domestic Jacobite sentiment. However, it is likely that Jacobitism was not negligible. James's Catholic modernizing policies had clearly alienated a large portion of the political nation. Most Whigs and most Tories had wanted to put an end to James's pro-French and pro-Catholic policies in 1688. There had been widespread popular rebellion. But unpopular as James undoubtedly was, he almost certainly had a significant minority who supported his policies till the end. James, the evidence suggests, had a hard core of support in the military, in the government bureaucracy, and among his fellow French-style Catholics.[31] From the moment William and Mary took power, each political action was carefully scrutinized by the political nation. The more the new regime began to pursue its own very different program of political modernization—when it pursued a policy of Continental commitment in the war against Louis XIV, when it sought to promote a radical new political economic vision, when it sought to transform the Church of England—it created a broader scope for Jacobite opposition. Faced with the choice of two competing modernizing programs, the conservatives—that is the mainstream Tories—were faced with an uncomfortable choice. At moments in which the new regime seemed to be more radical than that of James II, many were willing to flirt with

Jacobitism. When William and Mary turned to Tory ministers and pursued more cautious policies, the Jacobites received comparatively less popular support.

Until the Assassination Plot of 1696 and the widespread popular revulsion to Jacobitism that it caused, moments when the revolutionary regime appeared most radical were moments when contemporaries noticed the increase of popular Jacobitism. "The breaking of the succession and the making of the Convention a Parliament is not agreeable to the judgment of many of the Bishops, nobility or gentry of the nation," noted Rupert Browne in March 1689. "There has been a great reformation everywhere," agreed another Tory sympathizer at the height of Whig parliamentary success in 1689, "and some very honest folks turned out for not seeming enough pleased with the change." It was this, he thought, which "makes many discontented and still keeps up hopes in King James's party."[32] It was hardly surprising, then, that with Tory political triumphs and as William turned away from the Whigs, many—and especially many Tories—could be confident that Jacobitism was a diminishing force. When the revolution appeared less revolutionary, Jacobite discontent was less prominent.

Despite the ebbs and flows of Jacobite sentiment, and notwithstanding the contradictory evidence, it is clear that the Revolution did not produce the political consensus assumed in the Whig historiography. A significant minority in England remained committed to James II—and many of those no doubt remained committed because they shared in the ideology of Franco-Catholic modernization. Others supported counterrevolution when the Williamite regime appeared to pursue policies even more radical than James had done. The events of 1688–89 may have made it risky to voice Jacobite sentiments, but those events did not produce a consensus in favor of revolution.

Not only was there no consensus in favor of regime change, party strife continued unabated after William and Mary had been crowned. Whigs continued to push for a series of radical transformations, while Tories tended to argue that replacing James with William and Mary was the only change necessary. Whigs, in short, understood the deposition of James II as the first necessary step toward revolutionary transformation, whereas the Tories imagined that James's abdication was an unfortunate, albeit necessary adjustment. For Tories the revolution ended with the change of regime.

Even before Parliament had agreed that the throne was vacant and that William and Mary should fill it, Whigs and Tories had begun a new party debate over what was to become the *Declaration of Rights,* a document that enumerated in detail the wrongs committed by James II's government and specified the English rights that no monarch could transcend. The *Declaration,* scholarship has now shown, was a compromise, but it was not a bipartisan affair. Its "principle supporters" were "radical Whigs"—including John Hampden, Henry Pollexfen, John Somers, Sir George Treby, Thomas Wharton, and Sir William Williams—who were willing to temper their demands to placate Tories in the House of Lords. There was tactical compromise, not ideological consensus. In the end several of the thirteen clauses in the *Declaration* did specify new limitations on royal authority—for example, prohibitions on having a standing army in peacetime, the requirement that there would be frequent Parliaments, and the stipulation that excessive bail could not be required of a defendant. While much of what was stated had long been assumed by Whigs to be part of their ancient constitution, it was only in 1689 that they had the power and the opportunity to offer the claims as explicit limitations. It was in this sense that the Whigs succeeded in achieving Sir William Williams's aim of settling "your safety for the future." It was in this sense that some described William and Mary having accepted the Crown "with many limitations." It was for this reason that William needed to be assured that the articles "contained nothing in them but the known laws."[33]

The passage of the *Declaration of Rights* presaged the fierce partisan struggles that characterized the balance of the Convention Parliament and the tenor of the Parliaments of the 1690s. By March 1689 it was already clear that there were deep party differences over the direction of England's policy, the nature of taxation, and the orientation of England's political economy. It was also in March that bitter partisan debates began over the future direction of the Church of England. Although almost everyone was in favor of an act of toleration for those Protestants who could not accommodate themselves to any version of the Church of England, there were sharp partisan divisions over both a comprehension bill to broaden the Church of England and a proposal to eliminate the requirement—known as the Test Act—that all prospective officeholders receive the sacrament in the Church of England. By early April it was clear that a settlement more to the liking of the Tories than the Whigs was inevitable. No change was made in the sacramental test, and there was "but a very slender prospect of a comprehension." In the event, the plan of comprehension was removed from Parliament and turned over to the convocation of the clergy, where it ultimately died. Although the Tories did not achieve all they had hoped for—the Tory Earl of Nottingham had proposed and supported a narrow comprehension bill—it was clear that "Toryism is now in the ascendant." The passage of the Toleration Act without revision of the Test Act or the addition of a comprehension bill, though welcomed by many Dissenters as a vast improvement on the previous regime, was a partisan political victory for the Tories.[34]

Disagreements between Whig and Tory supporters of the regime change of 1689 were not limited to Westminster. When the Convention Parliament passed an act in April 1689 requiring that all civil and ecclesiastical officeholders take an oath of allegiance to King William and Queen Mary, it set off a remarkable national pamphlet debate that lasted for the better part of six years. The question was not only whether one should take the oaths to the new regime but on what terms. Had James been deposed by the people? Had he broken the original contract? Or had James merely run away creating a vacancy that needed to be filled so that England could be governed? One historian has counted almost two hundred pamphlets published during this period that engaged in this debate.

The number of readers was probably between forty thousand and a hundred thousand. In Oxford the debate over the oaths had been "the general discourse." The Derbyshire Tory Sir William Boothby had "a great curiosity" to collect "all the stitched pamphlets" available on the subject. William Wake, who would take the oaths to the new regime, devoted "the greatest part of [his] vacant hours" to reading "the greatest part" of the works available to him. Unsurprisingly, given the breadth of interest and the extent of publication, there was no consensus. Just under half of the pamphlets were Whiggish, while the others were divided fairly evenly between Tory supporters of the revolution and Jacobite opponents. There was no general agreement that resistance had taken place. Nor was there general agreement that James had broken an original contract. The public debate over the nature of the revolution was just as deeply contested along party lines as the decision whether to declare the throne vacant had been.[35]

Political partisanship continued unabated in 1688 and after. But the nature of party differences did shift after James II was overthrown. The events of 1688–89 shifted the political center of gravity. Few Tories after 1688, for example, opposed giving civil relief, as opposed to civil rights, to Protestant Dissenters. This marked a dramatic change from Tory attitudes immediately after Monmouth's rebellion in 1685. English men and women were willing to extend the boundaries of legal subjecthood if not yet legal citizenship.

The allegiance controversy, though bitterly divisive, also revealed two subtle yet significant shifts in the nature of English political debate. First, polemicists, whether Tory or Whig, were much more anxious than hitherto to frame the debate in particularist or national as opposed to universalist or confessional terms. The basis for political action was firmly grounded on English law or English political tradition rather than on the universal and timeless truths to be found in the Bible. The Bible, lamented the Scottish Episcopalian Robert Kirk, had become just another resource in political debate. It was, he said, "as if all subjects were indifferent to talk of, and religion were no more sacred than merchandise, and everything might be alike safely used which furthered the present purpose and design." Over and over again polemicists during the allegiance controversy insisted on the national, as opposed to universal, basis of politics. "Particular forms (I say) are not determined by God or nature, as government in general is," argued the author of *A Brief Vindication*. "It is left to every nation and country to choose that form of government which they shall like best." "The Supreme Governor of the world hath not seen fit to prescribe one form of government to be everywhere observed," wrote Samuel Masters in one of the most oft-cited pamphlets of the revolutionary era, "he hath permitted to every nation a liberty of framing to themselves such a constitution as may be most useful and agreeable; and as it is inconceivable that all nations should conspire in the platform of governments; so it is most unreasonable to seek in Judea, Italy, or France, for the measures or properties of the English government, which was made, and is therefore to be found only at home."[36]

Throughout the revolution clerics and laymen, Anglicans and Dissenters, insisted on the national diversity of forms of government. Richard Claridge, the rector of Peopleton in Worcestershire, announced, "Almighty God has no where determined in his word a model for our civil government, but has left us, as all other nations, to such a form as shall be agreed upon by the people." "The ordinance of government is from God and nature," insisted the High Church cleric Thomas Long, "but the species of it, whether by one or more, is from man." Richard Booker, the Tory rector of Icklingham All-Saints in Suffolk, laid it "down for a foundation not to be overthrown" that "god hath left all nations and people, to be ruled by that government and those laws, which are most suitable to the constitution and temperament of the people." Those with more radical pedigrees and reputations made similar statements about the national basis of political power. "As far as I can discover," concluded Daniel Defoe, "the power that our Savior found Kings invested with, was what the people first consented to, and afterwards by laws obliged themselves to: but there can be no universal rule, because that the laws vary according to the differing constitution of government that is in several nations." The Whig divine Daniel Whitby thought that because God had given only a "general appointment or ordinance, that all nations shall have some government placed over them," no one could claim to rule by divine right. "Although some governments seem to be built upon firmer and more unalterable foundations than others, yet there is none but ought to adapt itself to the circumstances and disposition of the people governed," insisted John Wildman in January 1689, "and as these do daily change, so ought the government to shift and tack with them, that it may the better hit with the necessities and changing circumstances of those for whom it was first instituted."[37]

Second, Whigs engaged in the allegiance controversy felt free to enunciate positions that had been illegal before the revolution. In most cases Whigs were not developing new ideas, although there were some subtle innovations, so much as resuscitating notions that had become so unfashionable as to have become almost extinct. Over and over again polemicists denounced claims that subjects must passively obey rulers even when they violated the law of the land. "The doctrine of passive obedience and non-resistance, which a sort of men did of late, when they thought the world would never change, cry up as a divine truth," observed one contemporary, "is by means of the happy Revolution in these nations, exploded, and the assertions of it become ridiculous." The Earl of Bridgewater noted simply, "The clergy fall from their doctrine of passive obedience." Many Whigs now argued that the people had a right, in some cases a duty, to resist unlawful governors. When Robert Harley heard the charge at the Herefordshire sessions "that Kings are made by the people," he remarked, "The charge would have been high treason eighteen months since." "How things change!" exclaimed the Dissenter Henry Newcome. "The opinions condemned" in the Oxford University decree of 1683 were "those very principles acted upon in this revolution." When the Tory lawyer Whitelocke Bulstrode heard a sermon in his parish church praising the resistance that had occurred the previous autumn, he could not but "observe how various this doctrine is from our former preachments about ten or twelve years ago, wherein the King's power was taught as irresistible, that the king was only accountable to God, and that the people had no other weapon as Christians but prayers and tears." John Locke published his *Two Treatises of Government* anonymously, thought his friend and biographer Jean Leclerc, because "the principles which he there establishes" were "contrary to those which were generally taught in England before the Revolution." "Many courtiers, divines, and writers flattered King James with passive obedience, non-resistance, absolute power without reserve, dispensing with execution of laws" and other claims "to all their ruins," summarized the visiting Scottish minister Robert Kirk, "but now they hold that the subjects have got a share of the government in taking cognizance of maladministration of both the monarch and ministers of state."[38]

The parliamentary decision to crown William and Mary king and queen did not end partisan debate in England. Whigs and Tories, in Parliament and throughout the country, continued to argue and argue passionately about the nature of the English monarchy, the extent of the Church of England, and the basis on which the Revolution had occurred. In many ways these arguments built on disagreements established in the early 1680s. Nevertheless, it was clear that the revolution had spawned important changes in party polemic and English political culture. On constitutional and religious matters the political center of gravity had shifted.

The achievements of February, March, and April 1689—the accession of William and Mary, the declaration of war against France, and the repeal of the regressive hearth tax—represented the high point of Whig political achievement immediately after James's flight. From the late spring of 1689 through the parliamentary elections of the following year and well into 1693, the Tories enjoyed a series of political and ideological triumphs. These triumphs, in turn, infuriated the Whigs. Far from agreeing with the Tories on the aims and principles of the revolution, a wide variety of Whigs believed that in giving political power to the Tories, William and Mary had put the revolution at risk.

By the end of March 1689 a number of observers were convinced that the Tories were gaining the upper hand in Parliament. The moderate Scottish Episcopalian Lord Yester noted that their successful obstruction of the revisions to the Test Act and the broader plans for religious comprehension demonstrated "how strong the church party is" and testified "to their animosity against the Dissenters." "The Church of England has a majority in both houses," agreed an English observer. "The Tories in Parliament are still rampant," chimed in Sir Edward Harley on the first of April. The London Non-conformist Roger Morrice was convinced that the Tories, successfully organizing in the Devil Tavern, were well on their way to their goal of reducing "all things in church and state to the condition they were in in the year 1662 (and ever since)." Morrice feared that Tory obstructionism in 1689 allowed them to restore Anglican royalist dominance of the

1660s and the period of Tory political hegemony from 1681 to 1686. "The Church party in the Parliament is become so zealous that they retard and render all resolutions in vain," lamented the Scottish Whig Sir John Dalrymple in May. The Tories may not have been able to achieve all they wanted in the remaining months of the Convention Parliament, but they did obstruct further revolutionary change by the Whigs.[39]

By the summer of 1689, William began to put his trust in Tory ministers. He became convinced that the Whigs were unable or unwilling to do his business. Instead of settling the country, he found the Whigs too intent on righting old wrongs. They were, he thought, wasting valuable time pursuing reforms in church and state rather than supporting the war effort. Convinced that the country needed administrative experience rather than political flamboyance, William increasingly turned from his Whig ministers and placed renewed trust in the experienced Tory secretary of state the Earl of Nottingham and the Tory lord president of the Privy Council the newly created Marquis of Carmarthen (the former Earl of Danby).[40]

By the end of January 1690 William had decided that he could no longer work with the Convention Parliament, which he prorogued and then dissolved. There was little doubt that William hoped that the new elections would produce a Tory majority. Gilbert Burnet recalled that after "a great struggle all England over," the Tories proved "by much the superior party in the new Parliament." In fact, although the Tories did gain a majority, it was an extremely slender one. Nevertheless, with the king's support, the Tories were clearly the dominant force. The Tory Sir John Trevor was named speaker of the House of Commons "by many hundreds of votes, by which all do judge the general intent and strain of the parliament." Carmarthen was soon seen as "the most active man" both in the House of Lords and in the Privy Council. In the Commons the Tory Sir Thomas Clarges "and that side are like to carry all before them." The future Whig architect of the Bank of England, Charles Montagu, calculated that "the Tories have a majority by fifty at least, and carried whatever they had a mind to." In the ensuing months, the Tories only further consolidated their hold on power.[41] After the summer of 1689 the political nation remained deeply divided, but now the political initiative both in the House of Commons and in William's inner circle lay with the Tories.

These developments infuriated the Whigs. It was not just Whig radicals, not just those who may have preferred a commonwealth rather than a monarchy in 1689, who were concerned that the revolution had been for naught. The Whigs were convinced, with some justice, that they had gotten rid of James and replaced him with William and Mary. Although the Tories appeared lukewarm to the new regime, noted the London Whig Roger Morrice in early March, "all the Whigs and all the fanatics do most sincerely, universally, and absolutely adhere to King William." It was therefore galling for the Whig Edward Harley to observe "the preferment of some men to places of trust that were the promoters of tyranny and the disregard of those that always opposed it." Morrice was convinced that the navy was in "Tory's hands," that the army was "under the command of Tories," that "the list of Deputy Lieutenants" was "generally Tories," and that "the civil power" was "in the hands of the Tories." "Why then we are little better than slaves," rhymed one Whig poet in 1689, "we have changed our K—— but kept all his knaves."[42]

In late May 1689 London Whigs sought to take action against the Tory drift of politics. Convinced that "the ecclesiastical power, the civil power, and the military power" was in the hands of the regime's enemies—that is, in Tory control—city Whigs circulated a petition complaining that they "as yet have not found their grievances redressed nor any of those persons brought to justice who were the instruments of introducing that tyrannical government under which we groan." In three days they were able to collect "some thousands" of signatures. In the event the petition was never presented. A second Whig petition was prepared later that month demanding repeal of the Test for civil employment.[43]

Not only London Whigs were disenchanted. Whig politicians, from radical to moderate, became increasingly concerned with the Tory drift in 1689 and 1690. The Whig John Skeffington, 2nd Viscount Massereene, complained in late 1689 that "things are not right." After the 1690 election, which Whigs were convinced was tainted by "false returns," complaints became shriller. One friend of the old Whig John Swynfen commented after the election that "our public concerns look very dismally." The committed West Country Whig Mary Clarke wrote sarcastically to her husband in April 1690 that "the men do so little good" that after William's departure to fight in Ireland, Queen Mary "will certainly have a parliament of women and see if they will agree any better." "The Whigs are turned against Carmarthen," James Johnston correctly noted of his party's attitude to the Tory lord president of the Privy Council. John Hampden found it "most melancholy and discouraging" that William and his advisers had not only embraced the Tories but had begun to voice their opinions of "secure the Church; no Bishop, no King." In December 1689 the Earl of Shrewsbury had warned William "that your Majesty and the government are much more safe depending upon the Whigs" because many of the Tories "would bring in King James, and the very best of them, I doubt, have a regency still in their heads." The Tory party had "so unreasonable a veneration for monarchy, as not altogether to approve the foundation yours is built upon." When William refused to heed his advice, Shrewsbury felt he had little choice. He had become so adamant in his belief that Tory principles, and the actions of the Tory ministers Carmarthen and Nottingham, were inconsistent with the revolution, that he resigned from his office of secretary of state.[44]

The ensuing years in the political wilderness merely deepened Whig displeasure. Even the moderate Whig Sir John Lowther briefly retired to Lowther "in some discontent." Captain Harry Mordant spoke for most Whigs when he complained in 1692 that "most of the people that King James left behind him, are continued in places of trust and profit." "But now we come to count our gains / We find we did but shift our chains," rhymed the Whig physician John Lower. "The whole world are at this time mournfully reflecting upon the miserable state we are fallen into from that happy and glorious prospect of things we had in 1688 and 1689," wrote another discontented Whig in the 1690s. "The causes of the unhappy change of affairs," this author concluded, was "from entrusting those with the government of all, who were the creatures and tools of the two last reigns." The Whig historian John Oldmixon later recalled that "the rise" of all William's political problems was his placing faith in "a party in England at the Revolution, that had nothing in their mouths but clemency and moderation, that were for forgetting who were the instruments in the invasions made upon the charters of England, of the dispensing power, of the murder of the best patriots, and all the tyrannical practices of he former reigns."[45]

William's turn to the Tories disappointed the vast majority of mainstream Whigs. For these men and women the revolution was about much more than merely changing kings. They had hoped for a brave new beginning. They had hoped that the injustices not just of James II's reign but of the entirety of Stuart policy since the Restoration would be reversed. So bitter and general was Whig discontent that two prominent Whig nobles, men known to be at the ideological center rather than the extremist fringes of their party, wrote letters of bitter political disappointment in the early 1690s.

Lord Delamere, who had been elevated to Earl of Warrington in 1690, could not conceal his displeasure with the turn of events by 1690.[46] Some time before his death in early 1694 he penned an essay denouncing William's turn to Toryism. The Convention Parliament, he thought, had been "upon the right scent." They had sought to punish evil councillors, were enthusiastic supporters of the war with France, and were doing "what then was necessary to support that power which they had set up." Yet, that promising Parliament "was sent away before it had finished its work." The reason, Warrington was certain, was "a pretence to have a Parliament of another complexion." That aim was achieved through extensive "foul play," so extensive that "scarcely one half of the House of Commons that were returned had a right to sit." "There is not anything in the last age that has been so remarkable," scoffed Warrington, as William's "treatment of the Whigs and particularly those that are eminent or had suffered under either of the last reigns." Convinced "that those who gave him the crown acted by Whiggish principles," Warrington was aghast that William "does now so much endeavor to depress the reputation of all men that are of that principle and to baffle the doctrine that kings hold their crowns upon condition." "The Whigs and those that suffered from that principle under the two late reigns," he remarked bitterly, "have nothing to boast of from the Revolution, but that they were so much the poorer for the expense they were at in contributing to it." In making this claim, Warrington did a great deal to clarify his understanding of mainstream Whig principles. England's problems, he wrote, had begun long before James II came to the throne. For that reason he and the Whigs demanded radical change, for "if the root be not cut up it will in time bring forth the like fruit again." The claim that he and his fellow Whigs were "for a Commonwealth" was at best "far-fetched." So was the argument that the events of 1688 were a mere anti-Catholic rebellion. "Had King James been content with the exercise of his religion for himself and those of his opinion, so as to have left others secure in the enjoyment of theirs and of their liberties," he insisted, "few would have grudged at it." The problem was that James was not interested in liberty of conscience. For Warrington it was clear that "arbitrary power would be set up by the self-same means whereby popery would be established, or rather that we must first be bereaved of our civil rights before that popery can prevail in England." That was why for Warrington, as well as for most mainstream Whigs, civil liberty had come to be more highly valued than religious liberty.[47]

Warrington's sentiments were almost identical to those of Thomas Wharton, who would become one of the most prominent Whigs serving the king. When William arrived in England in November 1688, Wharton told the king, "your friends adored you, and your enemies melted before you." A year later, however, William had squandered this political capital. "You have lost the hearts of a great part of your people," "many thousands talk against you in all public places," and "the spirit that is risen up against you is spread over England as well as about the town," warned Wharton. Why had this happened? Wharton and most Whigs were certain of the answer. William, "who came in upon one principle," had chosen to "employ men who had professed another." In the "treasury, admiralty, customs, navy and excise, you will find in every place some whom all England are amazed to see employed and trusted by you." In short, William had come to rely on the old servants of Charles II and James II, "the Tories and high churchmen," instead of the "honest old Whig interest." It was for this reason that "those, who twelve months since would have poured out their hearts' blood to have served you, have sacrificed their fortunes and all the hopes of their families for your sake, do now grudge every penny that is given for the necessary defense of your government and repent their too forward zeal for a man who despises his best and only true friends, and mistakes the right way to advance both his own and his people's glory."[48]

From middle of 1689 until late in 1693 Tories dominated the postrevolutionary political agenda. Tories held critical offices not only at the highest levels but throughout the ever-growing government bureaucracy. As in all modern revolutions, so in England after 1688, the ousting of the old modernizing regime was not immediately followed by political or ideological consensus. As in all modern revolutions, there was a political ebb and flow between those who simply wanted to dismantle the modernizing program of the ousted leader and those who wanted to implement an alternative modernization agenda. Because of this political give and take, because the Tories had the upper hand from 1689–93, it would be a mistake to measure the Revolution by the achievements of 1689–91 or even 1689–94. The full implications of England's revolution would begin to be realized only when most in England were convinced that it was politically and ideologically impossible merely to undo what James had achieved.

Few contemporaries were under the illusion that the Revolution of 1688–89 had been the result of, or had spawned, political consensus in England. The country was overrun with political discussion from the moment of James's departure. "The late public revolutions in these parts have so busied and indeed engrossed men's thoughts, discourses, and pens, that very little has of late appeared from the press besides pamphlets and other tracts about political affairs," wrote the great natural philosopher Robert Boyle. These effusions were not all making the same point. Everyone was impressed with the depth of England's divisions. Though there had been a "general desire" for "deliverance" in 1688, wrote Sir Charles Cotterell to Sir William Trumbull in early 1689, immediately "men began to differ in their opinions concerning the ways of settlement." "We are now a divided people," agreed Sir William Williams. "All here is full of brigues, jealousies and murmurs of all sorts," observed the Scot Lord Yester. "Discontents seem every day to increase," noted the Nonjuror Charles Trumbull. So violent were the political passions, wrote one of Sir Ralph Verney's friends, that some members of Parliament almost "fought in the Parliament house." Nothing that happened in the ensuing years dampened these divisions. Jacobites, Whigs, and Tories were all vying for power. "In all companies, they talk of our divisions," remarked William Sacheverell in early 1690. William's victory at the Boyne in 1690 did not end these disputes. "To my thinking," wrote Queen Mary to her husband at the end of July 1690, political divisions "increase here daily."[49]

Most contemporaries were well aware that the political passions manifested themselves in deep party divisions. "The Whig and Tory parties at home," recalled Robert Parker, "were driving the nation into confusion." "I'm sorry to see so great a violence of spirit as is in both parties," agreed one of Abigail Harley's friends. Lord Dursley could not but lament the "silly names which we give one another in England of Whigs and Tories." That "there are factions, and factions are the gangrenes of state," gave the Jacobite Earl of Melfort hope that "England must be strongly dismembered before it get rid of them." Although the parties may have looked like religious groupings in the immediate aftermath of James's fall, most observers understood that the issues were much broader than narrowly confessional politics. It was because foreign policy had become such a central issue that one of Sir William Trumbull's informants thought that "the names of Whig and Tory will at last change into English and Dutch."[50]

Whatever their origins and their nature, most observers were convinced of the grim reality of Whig-Tory ideological and political animosity. "We are unhappy to continue in parties, without being upon one bottom," regretted Paul Foley. "That there are parties is well known," stated one pamphleteer matter-of-factly. "The Whigs and Tories" appealed to their various publics in order to "form their parties," observed the Dutch resident L'Hermitage. John Howe was more evenhanded than most when he opined that "the opposition of the two violent parties is equally honest, and equally well intentioned to the government."[51]

These party divisions were not restricted to Parliament or to a narrow band of the political elite. "Almost in every parish there are persons of different persuasions," wrote the High Churchman Thomas Long, referring to the variety of political attitudes in the wake of James's departure. The Whig Sir John Guise thought it likely that in "every county, and every borough in England," political differences had provoked "hard words and sharp censures." The Marquis of Carmarthen could not but conclude that "faction is very natural to us." The Tory Dorset MP William Ettrick was not alone in asserting that "without doors, we are divided into parties." That "the whole country is divided into Whig and Tory" was the opinion of the vast majority of contemporary observers.[52]

What, then, divided Whig and Tory? Many scholars have assumed that the political parties in the age of William and Mary were narrowly concerned with issues of the previous age, with the problems of religious Dissent and the extent of royal power. These issues did play an important role. However, the postrevolutionary party divisions had a broader foundation. Looking back on the divisions of the 1690s, Viscount Bolingbroke noted that in addition to the differences about "our constitution in church and state," Whigs and Tories differed about "the affairs of the continent" and the direction of political economy. The Tories insisted that the point of the revolution was merely to unmake James II's modern polity. That is why the Tory directors of the Royal African Company described in February 1689 "the sudden revolution in our government, which now God be praised is in a great measure resettled." Once James had been replaced, and his restoration made nearly impossible, the revolution was over in the Tory view. For a Whig, like the Earl of Warrington, however, displacing James was "the *first step* towards repairing our breaches." The Whigs wanted their own modernization program. They wanted "a new heaven and a new earth, even so clean of a reformation of the state, that nothing of the old rust should have remained."[53] It was the fact that the Whigs ultimately were able to promote such a modernization scheme, to bring about such a "reformation of state," that explains why Bolingbroke described the party divisions of the 1690s in much broader terms.

Scholars have rarely included the Revolution of 1688–89 in their lists of great modern revolutions. They have failed to do so because the Revolution of 1688–89 simply did not appear similar to the dramatic developments in France, Russia, or China. The English revolution was unrevolutionary because it was aristocratic, bloodless, and consensual. This description of the Revolution of 1688–89, it turns out, is an artifact of historical narration more than of historical investigation. In the nineteenth and twentieth centuries Britons of both the left and the right insisted that English history bore little resemblance to Continental patterns. Most Britons had an investment in some version of British exceptionalism. This ideological consensus has made it difficult to recover the social history of English politics in the late seventeenth century. The archival record, however, tells a far different story. The historical evidence suggests that, in fact, the Revolution of 1688–89 was every bit as popular, violent, and divisive as most modern revolutions.

PART IV

Revolutionary Transformation

CHAPTER ELEVEN

Revolution in Foreign Policy

The English in the later seventeenth century were obsessed with European affairs. The vast majority desperately wanted their kings to put a halt to the overweening power of France. "England has these thirty and odd years past always groaned after a war with France," noted one pamphleteer, "and the friendship between our two last kings and Lewis the fourteenth was none of the least grievances of these reigns." "At last," agreed another after James II had been overthrown and war against France declared, "the people, the Lords, the Protestant clergy opened their eyes and thought of delivering themselves, and with them all Europe, from those shackles which were forging for them."[1]

That English concerns about European affairs, that English foreign policy, was central to the revolutionaries' agenda in 1688 sits uneasily with most accounts of the Glorious Revolution. Scholars do not quibble with Craig Rose's claim that there was "a radical reorientation in England's foreign policy" after 1688.[2] Nevertheless they deny that the English intended to foment this radical reorientation. There was, scholars say, a remarkable change in orientation at the level of high politics, but there were no long-term causes of that change, nor was there a transformation in the contours of policy making. In essence, the revolution in foreign policy involved an English monarch adopting for the first time since

---

(above) *Louis XIV and William III Contrasted,* by F. D. Winter, 1691. The wars of the 1690s pitted the English and the Dutch against France in a contest over the future of Europe and its empires. This medal, cast in the early stages of the Nine Years' War, contrasts Louis XIV, the "decrepit oppressor," with William III, "the flourishing liberator." Notions of European liberty were central to the Whig defense of the war effort.

the Restoration of 1660 a consistent anti-French orientation. If there was anything modern about this transformation, it lay in its unintended consequences, not in its causes.

There have been two discernable approaches to England's entry into the Nine Years' War against France (1689–97). Both approaches essentially describe the making of English policy both before and after the Revolution of 1688–89 in premodern terms. The first approach describes the revolution in foreign policy in terms of the concerns of the two different monarchs. In this view, foreign policy remained both the constitutional preserve and the exclusive concern of the monarch. The English political nation, if it existed at all, had no sustained or sophisticated interest in foreign affairs. The English, we are told by this first group of historians, were far more interested in local affairs than in European developments. Members of Parliament might be "men of considerable local standing and influence," but they had "often limited their mental and political horizons." By 1685, it is claimed, "politics in a popular sense no longer existed." Consequently, when the Dutch stadholder William III looked to England for support in his European crusade against Louis XIV, he received little sympathy. The English, apparently, were unimpressed by Louis XIV's numerous and spectacular victories. Popular opinion remained "woefully uninformed." Even those who invited William to intervene in English politics looked "at matters from a strictly insular point of view," Jonathan Israel asserts, hoping that the Dutch stadholder would tilt the domestic political situation in their favor but knowing little and caring less about the European situation.[3]

Most scholars who take this view have followed Thomas Babington Macaulay in arguing that James II pursued no constructive or consistent foreign policy. After the Duke of Monmouth's rebellion in 1685, Macaulay maintains, James II had had "visions of dominion and glory," seeing himself as "the umpire of Europe, the champion of many states oppressed by one too powerful monarchy." But as soon as it became clear that Parliament would not meekly acquiesce to his domestic goals, James II relinquished "all thought of arbitrating between contending nations," sinking "into a potentate of the third or fourth class." James had no ideological sympathy with Louis XIV, and his "pro-French inclinations have been exaggerated," agree most modern scholars. Poverty and domestic affairs kept James preoccupied so that, in the view of many, "Charles II and James II turned away from Europe."[4]

When William of Orange came to the throne, in this view, he simply imposed his Francophobic policies on an indifferent English nation. William brought his European war against Louis XIV into England. William III, Jeremy Black argues in the spirit of Macaulay, "was able to impose his views" because the English "political nation felt obliged to follow William" as the inevitable cost of Dutch intervention in English domestic politics. It was "William's actions in 1689" that "marked a sharp reversal in the then prevailing tendencies of British foreign policy," notes Gibbs. It was William, argues Jonathan Israel, who "brought England and (separately) Scotland into the war against France."[5] In the view of these scholars, the war against France may have generated public debates, but English public opinion did not agitate for the war or for a revolution that would make the war possible.

A second group of scholars, the revisionists, have argued that foreign policy was transformed in 1688–89 and that this transformation may have had long-term causes. Those causes, however, were confessional, not modern. William III's polemicists, Tony Claydon insists, understood the revolution "as part of an international protestant crusade." Protestant beliefs need to be "returned to the centre stage" in our understanding of the revolution because there can be no doubting "the persisting influence of the *early* Protestant worldview." Restoration English men and women were fighting the same fight that their Elizabethan forebears had fought, the same fight that the Huguenots had fought unsuccessfully in France. Louis XIV had merely replaced Philip II as the bugbear of the international protestant cause. Religious war against Spain had precipitated the political crises of the Elizabethan era, the crisis of the early Stuart regime was a direct result of the confessional strife known as the Thirty Years' War, and it was to be the need for a holy war against Louis XIV that would precipitate the final Stuart struggle over popery and arbitrary government in 1688–89. Craig Rose, who has read widely in the postrevolution literature, concurs that "for many" the Nine Years' War was about "religion."[6]

Against these views, I maintain that there was a lively and vital debate among a wide range of English men and women of a variety of social classes about England's proper role in European politics. The English were far from insular or indifferent about foreign affairs. The content of the debate reflected a sophisticated and well-informed understanding of the subtleties of European politics and culture. Although some of the terms in which the debate was conducted, universal monarchy or just war, for example, were old, the uses and meanings they were assigned were decidedly novel. Far from being neutral or otherwise preoccupied, Charles II and especially James II had an ideologically specific understanding of European politics—an understanding that the Dutch Republic represented the greatest threat to monarchy, stability, commerce, and European peace. By contrast, many, if not most, in the political nation had come to believe that absolutist and imperialist France represented the greatest threat to European peace. These men and women became revolutionaries, in part, to reverse England's political position on the European scene. James II, his supporters, and his opponents pursued a modern foreign policy in that they analyzed the world in terms of shifting national and group interests, not in terms of stable confessional identities. Whig historians are wrong to assume that William imposed his European agenda on the English. Instead, the English invited William to England because they knew he would support their image of the national interest.

Revisionist scholars are wrong, I suggest, to assume that the revolutionary majority agreed about the nature of the war with France. Whigs overwhelmingly felt that France needed to be fought, and fought on the Continent, until the liberties of Europe could be secured. They were fighting against hegemonic absolutism. Tories, by contrast, thought that the aims of the war should be simply to guarantee the Williamite revolution in the British Isles. Tories wanted to limit French imperialism to the Continent, leaving England in control of the seas. The Tories advocated a blue-water policy. Although French propaganda sought to portray the struggle as a confessional one, most in England—and especially those most closely associated with the regime—insisted that this was not a war of religion but a new kind of war—a war to protect liberties, whether English or European, against imperialism.[7]

The English in the later seventeenth century had unprecedented access to information about foreign affairs. In the 1640s and 1650s English men and women had developed an interest in both foreign and domestic news. The development of new institutions like the vastly expanded post office, the increasingly ubiquitous coffeehouses, and the ever proliferating committee rooms of trading companies provided the English with access to information, news, and gossip from overseas like never before. Quickly growing merchant fleets brought a wealth of information, books, and foreign goods into the booming old port towns and into the quays and docks of new ones. From there the expanding networks of stagecoaches, carts, and wagons could bring information ever more quickly into the interior on the newly expanding road networks. By the later seventeenth century the English had access to a sophisticated range of material discussing European politics, culture, and geography.

The middling and upper classes throughout England made it a point to provide their children a solid grounding in European learning. By the 1670s Sir Daniel Fleming could record that that the Lancashire gentry "are most of them good scholars and many of them have been beyond sea." "Almost all" of the Englishmen Lorenzo Magalotti encountered in the 1660s "speak French and Italian and readily apply themselves to learn the latter language from the good-will which they entertain towards our nation." The young Ralph Thoresby was sent by his Leeds cloth merchant father to the Netherlands "in order to my learning Dutch." No wonder a group of booksellers thought that "foreign books" were "much desired" by a wide range of people in England.[8]

A much broader range of people sought information about foreign affairs. The young Thomas Isham of Lamport in Northamptonshire eagerly gathered news about European politics in the 1670s. Ambrose Barnes, a Newcastle merchant, noted that "the desolations of Bohemia and in the valleys of Piedmont lay very near his heart." Sir John Lowther kept a large collection of books about European affairs at his home in the northwest of England. John Verney quickly relayed the latest news from Dutch newspapers to his father in Buckinghamshire. Lady Damaris Masham kept up with the latest French newspapers, while Sir Walter Yonge had the monthly *Mercure Politique et Historique* sent to his West Country home. In Yorkshire Sir John Reresby derived great "joy" from the king of Poland's military victory against the Turks in 1683. James Brydges "talked of the peace and the succession of Spain" with his friends in a Westminster chocolate house. A decade earlier the Earl of Burlington was eagerly relaying gossip of the Spanish succession into the countryside. John, Lord Ashburnham, grew quite cross with his newsman when he failed to deliver to his Sussex home the Amiens and Paris gazettes for several weeks running. In the later 1670s one of Sir Joseph Williamson's country correspondents exclaimed, "What a din there is now amongst many in these (and some other parts)" for news of "the grand actions now on foot in the world of Europe."[9]

English men and women did not have to rely on private letters or their own copies of books and journals to collect the most up-to-date information on European affairs. Local coffeehouses were virtual clearinghouses of information about the Continent. Foreign as well as domestic news was both readily available and eagerly sought after. People were always discoursing of "the sacking of towns, the cutting in pieces of gallant troops, the approaching catastrophes of nations, the misfortunes of eminent statesmen, the fantastic crises under which puissant monarchies groan." "No secrets are the court for peace, or the camp for war," rhymed one coffeehouse denizen, "but straight they're here disclosed and known; / men in this age are so wise grown." Cardplayers in coffeehouses and taverns could even gamble while reading political commentaries on European affairs on their aces and knaves. Indeed, so adept had the coffeehouses become at collecting news about European affairs that one official newsletter writer had to admit in 1677 that the caffeine consumers had information to which he was not yet privy.[10]

By the later seventeenth century, most observers agreed, the English were extremely well informed about foreign affairs. In contrast to the Irish, the English, noted William King, the dean of St. Patrick's Dublin, "had the advantage of enquiry and correspondence" and hence were no "strangers to the full extent" of the designs of foreign princes. There were many in England, agreed the French ambassador Paul Barillon, "who were extremely capable of discerning the true interests of the powers of Europe." "The wisdom of the nation," chimed in George Philips, was not "ignorant of all matters foreign or domestic, that concern the honor, safety and advantage of it."[11]

What news about foreign affairs did patrons of coffeehouses and country taverns, readers of newspapers and highbrow pamphlets, frequenters of the London exchange and country markets collect so eagerly? How did they understand the developments about which they so viciously gossiped? Instead of reacting with a visceral xenophobic reaction to all things foreign, Restoration English men and women placed the news they received within sophisticated ideological frameworks. They were eager to gather information about European power politics because they understood it and thought that it vitally affected their lives.

England, most members of the political nation knew, had spent the better part of the past century trying to prevent the Spanish kings from achieving their long-sought-after goal of universal monarchy, or world dominion. In the later seventeenth century, however,

The Coffee-house Politicians, 1733. Coffeehouses made
newspapers, newsletters, and mercantile correspondence,
all of which were packed full of foreign news,
available to their patrons and were important sites
for the public discussion of foreign policy.

Spanish power was clearly on the wane. Although English commentators fiercely debated
the origin of Spain's decline, the reality was undeniable. "The Spanish Monarchy, and
the House of Austria, (whose great accessions of territory gave rise to those observations
on which the policy of the last age was founded)," noted the author of *Europae Modernae
Speculum* uncontroversially, "are concluded to be consumptive and to stand merely on
the defensive part."[12] The problem now was to identify and prevent the next aspirant.
English men and women identified two possible candidates: the Dutch Republic and the

kingdom of France. In the 1660s and early 1670s the English engaged in hot debates over which country was more dangerous. But by the later 1670s, most, though certainly not all, agreed that Louis XIV was well on his way to making his new palace at Versailles the seat of universal dominion.

The most enthusiastic supporters of the restored monarchy, the Anglican royalists and future Tories, quickly became convinced that the Dutch Republic sought universal dominion through commercial hegemony. The repeated Spanish bankruptcies during the Dutch Revolt, and the obvious financial exhaustion of both the Spanish and Austrian branches of the Habsburg family in the latter stages of the Thirty Years' War, convinced many observers that stable financial resources rather than crack troops were the keys to military success. "Trade and commerce are now become the only object and care of all Princes and Potentates," claimed the Tory jurist and favorite of James II Charles Molloy, for in so doing the "opulency and greatness of such a kingdom or state" could be guaranteed. The English in the later seventeenth century felt certain that the most lucrative commercial endeavors were the new long-distance maritime trades. Control of the sea thus became the key to the universal monarchy. After all, Columbus's discovery of the New World and the resultant Spanish claims to the monopoly of the South American silver mines had led the Habsburgs to think "of no less than an Universal Monarchy." By the 1670s it was "a maxim as true as common, that he who is the master of the sea, carries the keys of the world in his hand." "That people that can get the trade of the world," agreed an economic observer during the reign of James II, "may quietly, without pursuing the toils of the Caesars and Alexanders, be, (in effect) Lords of their neighbours, and give laws to the world."[13] Clearly, control of the sea was widely felt to be the first step toward the universal monarchy.

The Dutch Republic, an apparently modest collection of loosely allied provinces in Europe, had built up a vast and powerful overseas empire by the mid-seventeenth century, thanks to its naval strength. "The Netherlanders," one pamphleteer pointed out during the Second Anglo-Dutch War (1665–67), "from the beginning of their trade in the Indies, not contented with the ordinary course of a fair and free commerce, invaded diverse islands, took some forts, built others, and labored nothing more than the conquest of countries and the acquiring of new dominion." "Scarce any subject occurs more frequent[ly] in the discourses of ingenious men," William Aglionby reported, "than that of the marvelous progress of this little state which in the space of about one hundred years . . . hath grown to a height, not only infinitely transcending all the ancient Republics of Greece, but not much inferior in some respects even to the greatest monarchies of these latter ages."[14]

For many Tories the Dutch Republic was not only a commercial rival but also a model for political iniquity. The Dutch Revolt against their Spanish sovereign had set a terrible precedent. Elizabeth had been well aware, argued Charles Molloy, that though an independent Dutch Republic would "fortify the Queen's outworks; yet it could not but as much dismantle the Royal Fort of Monarchy, by teaching subjects the way to depose their Princes, and be no losers by the bargain." Tory poets drew the obvious conclusions. The

Dutch, often referred to as "frogs" in the argot of the seventeenth century, were "vermin antimonarchical"; their republic was an "academy of revolting," actively "planting sedition in the nation"; their political leader of the 1660s and 1670s, John De Witt, was none other than the biblical "Achitophel."[15]

Anglican royalists and Tories were convinced that once the Dutch had control of the seas, they would have all but established the universal monarchy. "You think the Narrow Seas for us too much," complained one poet during the Second Anglo-Dutch War, "yet the whole globe too little for the Dutch." It had become a commonplace that the Dutch "thought to grasp a pow'r great as old Rome, / Striving to carry all commerce away, / And make the universe their only prey." When a Dutchman in a tavern asked why the English insisted on calling his compatriots "butterboxes," he was reputedly told it was because "you are so apt to spread everywhere, and for your sauciness must be melted down." Although "no nation can be rich that abounds not in some part of his dominions in shipping, or who neglects trade," the moderate Anglican royalist Sir Philip Warwick insisted, "yet it is no policy to think to engross it, or be monarchs of it, as Holland hath for a time affected, and pursued that Sea-Monarchy as eagerly as Charles the Fifth or Francis the First did the Land Monarchy."[16]

For Anglican royalists and Tories—whether at the Council table, in trade company committee rooms, or in country taverns—the Dutch needed to be fought not just because they were England's greatest economic rivals, but because they threatened to subvert all that Restoration England stood for. Their republicanism was a cancer that ate away at monarchy. Their religious pluralism threatened to replace religion with atheism and grasping ambition. The Dutch, who no longer benefited from the civilizing effects of monarchy and true religion, had become economic Machiavellians. For most Tories the Dutch were both the most plausible aspirants to universal dominion and posed the greatest threat to the English way of life.

Against the Anglican Royalist and Tory claim that the religiously pluralist and antiabsolutist Dutch were seeking universal dominion, Whigs and proto-Whigs maintained that the absolutist and intolerant Gallican French king Louis XIV was attempting to establish a new universal monarchy.

Far from accepting the Tory claim that the Dutch Republic was a political cancer, the future Whigs praised the Dutch as defenders of liberty and industrious self-improvers. The Dutch, argued the author of *The Present Interest of England Stated,* were the "principle instruments in preventing the House of Austria in their grand design for the Universal Monarchy." The extraordinary wealth of the Dutch was "alone the effects of industry and ingenuity." All of the Dutch "advantages in point of trade which we term wrongs," testified Robert MacWard, "do proceed directly on their part from their sobriety and industry, and on England's part from our idleness and luxury."[17]

The three Anglo-Dutch wars (1652–54, 1665–67, and 1672–74) were not merely pieces of good fortune for the French, they were part of their grand strategy to gain control of the seas. The author of *The French Intrigues Discovered* aptly summarized the Whig and proto-Whig conviction that the French had fomented all three wars, "dreading nothing more than a durable and firm friendship between the two nations; blowing up the feuds on both sides, pretending to take part with each, that they might with less opposition invade their neighbors, and increase their naval strength, but not really purposing it with either, having the same design of weakening both parties, for your weakness is his strength." The French were well aware that they wanted "nothing to facilitate their universal design more than an interest in the Northern Seas." Consequently, Louis XIV and his great minister Jean-Baptiste Colbert devised a comprehensive economic system. In order to make his subjects "sole merchants of all trades," Louis XIV placed "all manner of discouragements upon all foreign factories and merchants by difficulty in their dispatches, delays in point of justice, subjecting them to foreign duties and seizures, not suffering them to be factors in the French or any other nation but their own, and in case of death to have their estates seized as aliens." The net effect of these measures was predictably devastating for English merchants. England, which continued to import French luxury items without the large protectionist imposts that Louis XIV placed on English goods, began to run up a huge trade deficit. The result was "that in few years (if some timely expedient be not applied) all the money of this nation will be drawn into France." The conclusion was inescapable: "The French doth deal far more unkindly with us than the Dutch."[18]

At the same time that he was discouraging foreign commercial activity, Louis XIV did everything in his power to advance French mercantile prowess. He encouraged the French nobility to engage in the Indies trades. More important, Louis deployed his vast treasures to build up a huge merchant marine and a vast navy. "If some timely power be not applied from this naval power of France," fumed one pamphleteer, "the destruction of Europe may take its date before we be much older." "France has been dangerous enough to the rest of Europe, whilst they were in a manner without shipping," the author of the *Discourses upon the Modern Affairs of Europe* wrote with trepidation; now nothing seemed to prevent them from driving "on that huge design of ambition for the Universal Monarchy which has so long swelled their hearts." No one could now doubt that they were "setting up an Universal Monarchy of commerce."[19]

Whigs proclaimed with a united voice that universal monarchy was in fact the sole aim and purpose of French policy. They, like many all over Europe, were aware of "the great design of France, who seemeth no less now to endeavor and affect the same design of an Universal Monarchy and direction of affairs as Spain was once doing." "It is agreed at all hands," insisted the London Whig Slingsby Bethel in pamphlet after pamphlet, "that the French set up for an Universal Monarchy." It "is the utmost excess of madness" not to oppose the growing power of France, exclaimed the future Whig martyr Algernon Sidney. For "though France may have many hard steps before it can arrive at such a monarchy as can deserve the name of universal; yet that King doth at present enjoy many advantages that may reasonably give him higher expectations that way than any other Prince in

Europe. And having a mind equal to his fortune, he is not like to omit any opportunity." The French "are of an aspiring genius," observed the former French ambassador and future Whig Denzil Holles, "which is so much the more dangerous to Europe, as the object they have fixed upon is great, and that is no less than to erect an Universal Monarchy in Europe." Louis XIV, Andrew Marvell declared, was the "master of absolute dominion, the presumptive monarch of all Christendom."[20]

From a Whig point of view, then, there could be no doubting that France was seeking a universal monarchy. Not only were French armies pillaging Europe, but Colbert's economic policies were making Louis XIV into the richest prince in Christendom. Protectionism had transformed France from a maritime midget into a true Leviathan on the seas. This was made possible because France, unlike the previous aspirant to universal dominion, had succeeded in dividing the two great maritime powers and in setting them at each other's throats. France was able to do this, the Whigs claimed, by bewitching England with the twin sins of popery and arbitrary government. Instead of assuming its proper role of maintaining the balance of Europe, England had become little better than a client state of France.

In the wake of the Restoration, while memories of the anarchy and confusion of the later 1650s were still fresh in the minds of most English men and women, the Anglican royalist and Tory case against the United Provinces seemed particularly strong. A broad range of moderate opinion, including many who had opposed the king in the 1640s or who had accommodated themselves to the Protectorate, remained convinced that the threats from the radical sects and from the republicans demanded a foreign policy directed against their European allies, the Dutch. Louis XIV's invasion of the United Provinces in the Dutch Year of Wonders of 1672, however, changed their thinking. The image of the Dutch forced to flood their own country in a desperate attempt to prevent French armies from overrunning the republic made claims that the Dutch were seeking universal monarchy seem incredible to many. More important, the demise of the Dutch republican regime—the grand pensionary of Holland John De Witt and his brother Cornelius "were torn in pieces by the rude rabble of The Hague, their privities cut off, their bodies dragged through the streets and hanged at the gallows"—and William III's consequent assumption of the offices of captain general and stadholder alleviated the concerns of many political moderates.[21]

The Dutch political revolution of 1672 was greeted with unbridled enthusiasm from the broad middle segment of the English political nation. For these men and women, many of whom would become moderate Tories, Louis XIV had become the greatest possible threat to England. Their opposition to France was, unlike their more radical compatriots, less ideological and more geopolitical. France was dangerous not because it was absolutist and intolerant but because it was imperialist and militarily aggressive. France, for these men and women, represented a real and present danger to the British Isles. The

United Provinces, by contrast, had ceased to be an ideological threat. The Dutch Republic no longer seemed likely to advocate aggressive radical expansionism. "The plotters have been punished sufficiently, though in a tumultuary way, but whose irregularity has been recompensed with the public good," Stephen Temple reported to his uncle Sir Richard from the United Provinces; "great and rational hopes are builded here upon a league with the House of Austria, and some Princes of Germany, who fear the French King's design towards the Universal Monarchy of Christendom." After the Third Anglo-Dutch War, most moderates joined the proto-Whigs in believing that the most serious aspirant to the universal monarchy was Louis XIV rather than the Orangist-led Dutch Republic.[22]

French economic policies, French military victories, and manifest French perfidy convinced Whigs, moderates, and moderate Tories that England needed to join the European struggle against the intended French universal monarchy. Throughout the 1670s anti-French sentiment was building in a powerful crescendo of vituperation. William Garroway informed the House of Commons that "our fears of ruin from the French are in everybody's mouth." "There are ninety in a hundred against France, all England over," chimed in the Whig Colonel Birch. The London weavers were said to be "in a mutiny against the French." Indeed, it was well known that the fateful last session of the Cavalier Parliament in 1677 was called principally "to alarm the French." "There is no discourse here but of war" against the French, the Earl of Huntingdon reported from London in the winter of 1678. The Earl of Danby, who was in a position to know, wrote to the Earl of Essex that "truly things appear to me more like a war with France than otherwise." Nor were the English unaware of the costs involved in fighting the world's greatest power. "They of the country seem not to be afraid of war, nor what is the necessary concomitant of it, taxes," Thomas Thynne informed Halifax, "so universal is their dread of the growth of France." Indeed, so certain was one English army officer that there would be war with France that he prepared and published an inspirational speech for his troops. In this context, it does not seem that Marchamont Nedham was exaggerating by much when he claimed "that if it were put to the vote of the people, whether a war or no war with France, I believe not one in a thousand, but would be for a war."[23]

Charles II, however, never intended to go to war against his cousin and friend Louis XIV. The king, Danby understood well, "had no mind to fall out with France." It was a measure of his political deftness that he managed to avoid war while simultaneously doing damage to his political opponents. Charles argued, and argued effectively, that the Exclusion Crisis of 1679–81, the political crisis that centered on fears of political absolutism, made it impossible for him to start a war against Europe's greatest power. Whig factiousness promoted national disunity, and a nation at odds with itself was in no condition to begin a war against so great a power as France.[24]

Charles II's polemical strategy proved a brilliant success. The bitter divisions resulting from the fierce debate over excluding James, Duke of York, from the throne really did seem to threaten a new civil war. In this context, Tories—even Tories who were predisposed to believe that the threat from France was very real and had to be stopped—insisted that English unanimity was a prerequisite to intervention in European affairs. Charles II, then, was able to avoid war against Louis XIV by insisting that he very much wanted to join in the fight but was prevented by Whig political intransigency.

James II came to the throne in 1685 in this ideological setting. For well over two decades English men and women had been engaged in a lively debate about England's proper place in European affairs. The English were far from being an isolationist or xenophobic people. They were extremely interested in and well informed about developments on the Continent. For the English of all social levels in the later seventeenth century, foreign affairs were not peripheral concerns. The English were not content to leave decisions about foreign policy to the king and a narrow band of specialist politicians. This was because England's relations with Europe mattered to the people's everyday lives. The English knew that the price of the cloths they made had a great deal to do with European and colonial markets. They knew that the types of luxury goods available in their local markets—from silks to spices, from wines to papers—were determined by the vagaries of European politics. They also knew that the culture in which they partook—from the types of dances they performed to the books they read—were all part of a broader European discussion. More important, perhaps, the English knew that there was a great ongoing struggle for political hegemony in Continental Europe. It was a struggle in which most moderate Tories and almost all Whigs felt the English should be playing a greater role. The English in the 1680s, like many prerevolutionary publics described in the social scientific literature on revolutions, were terribly concerned that they were becoming a second-rate power.

Most in England desperately hoped that the new king—a king who had, after all, a long history of military accomplishments—would lead the united nation into war against France. Poems, broadsides, coins, and pamphlets issued in the early months of the new king's reign trumpeted James's military reputation. Sir John Lowther was one among many who recalled that "reports of a misunderstanding betwixt the French King and" James II were "industriously spread abroad to amuse the ignorant" in order to "put men in hopes of what they had long wished," a war "to reduce France," which had "now become the terror of Christendom." Contemporaries, even well-connected contemporaries, avidly circulated rumors that the new king was "setting up against the French interest which if true, we may hope to see this as glorious and redoubtable a nation as ever it was in ages before." The London Presbyterian Roger Morrice correctly noted in 1685 that "the grand enquiry is whether we enter into a close correspondency with France or Holland."[25]

Despite avid political gossip and popular hopes, there was never much doubt in which European direction James would turn. James had been trained in a French army, he had been reconciled to the church by a French Jesuit, he had married Louis XIV's choice of bride, he was active in mercantile concerns that were in regular competition with the

Wie Boren Zynen Staet (The lessons of state), by Romeyn de Hooghe, 1688.
This print draws critical attention to the close relations between James and Louis XIV.
The English king and the French king appear together in the foreground, while
William's landing at Torbay is depicted in the background. James's ties to Louis XIV
were the cause of much consternation in England and across Europe during the 1680s.

Dutch, and he was a great and outspoken admirer of the modern absolutist state created
by Louis XIV. That contemporaries and many subsequent historians were in doubt about
James's foreign policy orientation demonstrates the king's sensitivity to English popular
Francophobia. James knew all too well that his admiration for French politics and culture
did not sit well with many of his subjects.[26]

James had long been one of the most powerful advocates of a close alliance between
England and France. He had advised his brother, Charles II, in 1681 "that an alliance
with France was the only means to support the king and preserve the monarchy and even
the Church of England itself, by according a supply without a Parliament, which aimed
manifestly at the ruin of them all." "Matters were come to such a head," James had advised,

"that the monarchy must be either more absolute or quite abolished," and he was certain that "France would be sorry to see England a commonwealth, that Spain desired it, and Holland would not be displeased at it." James, however, was an extremely sophisticated politician. He knew that he could leave no paper trail of his ties of affection and interest to France and Louis XIV. This was why he conducted important affairs personally in London. Sir William Trumbull, who had been appointed James's ambassador in Paris, recalled that "all matters of moment were to be transacted by Barillon, the French ambassador here [in London]." Paul Barillon had been the French ambassador in England since 1677, and by the time of James's accession to the throne he knew well the range of English politicians. Since he also enjoyed the patronage of the marquis de Louvois, Louis XIV's powerful minister of war, it was hardly surprising that "Barillon knew all [James II's] secrets and executed his pleasure, and the king no doubt communicated to Barillon all that he knew."[27]

From the moment of his accession James II affirmed his close ties to France and Louis XIV. French Catholic news networks immediately reported that James, unlike his likely successors, would never go to war with France. James affirmed this heartfelt commitment in his darkest hour, promising Barillon in December 1688 that "he would never consent to enter a war against [Louis XIV]." Over and over again James repeated that his ties to France were both those of affection and those of interest. From the moment of his accession James was at pains to emphasize that his ties to Louis XIV came from "his heart." He told Barillon that "the King his brother had almost been ruined when he allowed himself to be detached from his alliance" with Louis XIV. Barillon was convinced after innumerable lengthy conversations—conversations that were the envy of every other foreign minister at James's court—that James wanted "sincerely to attach himself to the interests of [Louis XIV] for his entire life." Louis XIV's special envoy Usson de Bonrepaus, who also had unusual access to James, reported that the English king "regarded Louis XIV as his oldest ally and the most solid that he had." James's most powerful minister, the Earl of Sunderland, assured both Barillon and Bonrepaus that the king of England was determined to maintain "a strict alliance" with Louis XIV. These ties of affection no doubt led James II to celebrate publicly Louis XIV's recovery from a serious illness in April 1686 and to have Louis XIV named godfather of the Prince of Wales in 1688.[28]

James was a modern prince for whom ties of affection meant a great deal but ultimately far less than pursuing what he perceived to be England's national interest. James, the French knew, was tied to them most closely because of his political interests. When James discussed his connection to Louis XIV he frequently emphasized his "inviolable attachment to the interests" of the French king. Barillon was convinced that "the projects and the designs of the King of England necessarily engage him to remain in a great alliance with" Louis XIV. In particular, James's tense relations with Rome as he was attempting to Catholicize England pushed him toward closer ties with France. Just as important, James did not share the concerns of many of his subjects, and many Continental observers, about the balance of power. James told Bonrepaus that "he would not risk the establishment of the [Catholic] religion in order to pursue the vain honor of maintaining the balance equal among European powers." "Those men sincerely attached to the King of England," Barillon reported, "considered this idea of a balance of affairs in Europe as something chimerical." Given these views, given that James II was not at all concerned about the growing power of France, the French had little to fear from James's growing authority within England.[29]

Instead of balancing the growing power of France, James imagined that he and Louis XIV could divide the world up between themselves. The exact nature of James II's plans is difficult to discover because so few papers have survived. However, James had "private and ample conferences" with the political arithmetician William Petty in 1686 and 1687 to sketch out possible arrangements. Petty began his various papers with the assumption that there was an alliance involving France, Denmark, and England. France, Petty assumed, would by means of this alliance soon conquer both the United Provinces and the Spanish Netherlands, as well as half of Germany and Italy, all of which would be "no destruction to England." This was because England, in return for French dominance in Europe and in the Mediterranean, would be granted hegemony in the East Indies, the West Indies, and "the carriage of Norway timber and boards." In Petty's vision, a vision that James II and his closest advisers almost certainly shared, England would be in no danger of truckling under to France. This was because "the King of England's territories being islands, fitted with ships, seamen and trade doth (at least as to defense) balance the French advantages."[30] James did not imagine that he would be dependent on France, but rather that Louis would gain hegemony on land while he would become the supreme power at sea. James, in short, had a very modern imperial vision.

James was not merely telling Louis XIV's representatives what they wanted to hear or drawing up utopian imperial visions. Instead, all of his actions reinforced his words. Just as James shaped his circle of advisers so as to best advance his French-style domestic priorities, so he promoted those who were the most enthusiastic supporters of a French alliance. The Marquis of Halifax, who was lord president of the Privy Council at James's accession, and the Earl of Dartmouth, one of James's oldest friends, both lost favor because of their known opposition to France.[31] The Earl of Sunderland, by contrast, who had a "profound knowledge of the intentions and designs of his king," was insistent that "the interest of the Catholic religion would be the foundation of a more strict alliance [with France] in the near future." Father Petre, who had increasing influence at James II's court, was explicit and insistent that "the interests of the King his master, and of those of the Catholic religion demanded a strict alliance and a perfect intelligence with" Louis XIV.[32]

If Louis XIV and James II were always careful to protect their interests in their mutual dealings, there is ample evidence that they invariably treated each other as friends and allies rather than as potential enemies. During James II's reign the French and the English entered negotiations assuming that they had a shared ideological outlook and overlapping interests.

As soon as his brother died, James entered high-level negotiations with the French for a new subsidy. James immediately sent his former master of the wardrobe, John Churchill, to Paris to negotiate. Churchill, who had been James's loyal adviser when in exile, "was already in on the secret of the intimate alliance" between James and Louis. As it turned out, the subsidy was settled in London. James was, according to Barillon, indescribably overjoyed at Louis XIV's generous grant of half a million pounds.[33]

In James's first year in power he made several gestures of friendship toward the French king. In June 1685 he issued an order in his Privy Council to "obliterate" the inscription on the monument blaming the French for setting the Fire of London of 1666. James, "having great occasion for the friendship of the French King," ensured that Parliament repealed the prohibition on the importation of French goods. The result, according to one eighteenth-century estimate, was "an inundation of French commodities, to the value of above four millions sterling, within the compass of less than three years time." Finally, James refused to intervene on behalf of his son-in-law, William of Orange, who was seeking compensation for the damage done by French troops to his ancestral principality of Orange. That James failed to "intercede for Orange," argued James's envoy in Copenhagen, Gabriel de Sylvius, showed that "there was too good a correspondence betwixt [James II] and the French King."[34]

At the same time, James did all he could to quell lingering Anglo-French tension in North America. French encroachments threatened both New England and the profitable Tory-run fur-trading Hudson's Bay Company. Despite the growing tension, the immense profits at stake, and his hopes that he would gain sole control of North America and the West Indies, James made it clear to the French negotiators that he desired an amicable settlement. He needed to "please" England's mercantile companies and merchants by "discussing all of their complaints in general" before concluding a treaty of neutrality. James made it clear that he placed a greater value on his relationship with Louis XIV than the potential lost customs revenue from the New World trade. The treaty was largely concluded in the spring and published in November. It was so favorable to France that rumors quickly circulated that a secret alliance had also been signed. The Hudson's Bay Company later proclaimed that the treaty did nothing to stop the Company of New France's plans to "extirpate" them. James's capitulation, they thought, had everything to do with his "greatly favoring the Jesuits who have the sole benefit of this trade and the interest of the Canada Company." In the eighteenth century Adam Anderson declared that in this treaty "the French King imposed on his dupe, King James." Barillon was not incorrect to tell Louis XIV that the treaty would be "entirely" to his liking.[35]

The Treaty of Neutrality of 1686 did not put an end to disputes in North America or to James's support of the interests of the French king. News soon reached Europe that the French had taken a further three English forts, worth one hundred thousand pounds, at the base of Hudson's Bay. James was concerned about a significant decline in his customs revenue. Investors were furious about their plummeting stocks. The English, reported Bonrepaus and Barillon, were extremely "heated over the loss of the three forts." Leading the charge for compensation and restitution was John, Lord Churchill, James's former confidant and current director of the Hudson's Bay Company. Yet James and his government ultimately allowed the three forts to remain in French possession. James made it clear that this was because he saw France as a vital ally. His initial proposal to the French negotiating team in June 1687 was that he would "declare war against the Hollanders" if the French promised to compromise on Hudson's Bay. In late 1687 Sunderland told a delegation from the Hudson's Bay Company, led by Churchill himself, that James "would not go to war with France over an affair of so little importance," an affair that paled in significance compared to the Dutch seizure of Bantam.[36] James was not a man to sacrifice English interests easily. But, at the end of the day, he was more willing to let English trading interests slip in the face of claims made by a political and ideological ally than against those advanced by a bitter opponent.

James and Louis XIV continued to negotiate and ultimately agree on areas of mutual interest throughout the last two years of James's reign. In October 1687 James, the Earl of Tyrconnel, and the Earl of Sunderland suggested that Louis XIV support and finance a regiment of English Catholics on French soil, claiming that the establishment of such a regiment "would be of great advantage for the Catholic religion." Though Louis was unwilling to accept this proposal, he did agree to pay for the maintenance and upkeep of two regiments of a thousand men apiece in England—enabling James to contemplate recalling the British regiments stationed in the United Provinces. In addition to this subvention, the French king promised James that "whenever he needed help," he could be certain that a sufficient number of French troops would be made available "to oppress his enemies and to make his subjects obey." In the event, Louis XIV proved to be almost as good as his word. In the desperate days of November and December 1688 Louis XIV did promise and deliver aid. Affairs on the Continent prevented him from sending troops, but he dispatched fifty thousand écus in gold, though the funds apparently never made it into James's coffers.[37]

James had good reason both to maintain a close alliance with Louis XIV and to keep it secret. He knew that his interests, his vision for England's future, depended on good relations with and support from Louis XIV. He was also well aware that such an arrangement would infuriate moderate Tories and Whigs. James's alignment with France was certainly not the invention of Whig politicians or of subsequent overly credulous historians. The entire European diplomatic community suspected the existence of such an alliance. They were simply unaware of its extent.

Informed observers of the European diplomatic scene, no matter what their ideological orientation, were certain that there were intimate ties between James II and Louis XIV. Just after James II's accession, Scottish Jesuits in Rome had already learned of Louis XIV's stipend to James II and proclaimed confidently that "there is a great correspondence between the King of France and our king." Walking with Sir William Trumbull in the Tuileries in 1686, Monsieur Vaudeuil, the governor of James's natural sons by Arabella Churchill, confided "that there was a secret treaty and league between our King" and Louis XIV. The papal nuncio at Louis XIV's court was also convinced that there was an offensive and defensive alliance between France and England by early 1686. Political gossips throughout the German lands asserted that "His Majesty is of intelligence with the French King for [the] extirpation [of Protestants]." In the United Provinces rumors circulated both in official circles and on the streets of Amsterdam of a dangerous connection between the kings of France and England. "We are assured," wrote one well-connected purveyor of diplomatic news from The Hague, "that the alliance between the Kings of France and England is established in order to make war against this state." James II for his part, the story went, could never "govern as he wished" as long as his subjects "had recourse" to the assistance of the Dutch.[38]

Many diplomats with more direct connections to the English court were certain of an Anglo-French alliance. The Spanish ambassador in England, Don Pedro de Ronquillo, had concluded that "even if there was not a Secret Treaty and formal alliance, the interests and designs of [Louis XIV] and those of the King of England were so conformable that it produced the same effects as if there was an express union." "France continues to enjoy its great and long-standing influence at this court," wrote the imperial ambassador Philippe Hoffmann from London in early 1688. The London resident of the Grand Duke of Tuscany, Francesco Terriesi, also commented on the "great friendship between His Majesty [James II] and France." In Istanbul, the French ambassador asserted confidently that "now an alliance was concluded" between Louis XIV and James II. It was perhaps this declaration that definitively convinced Sir William Trumbull, who was then posted in Istanbul, "of the friendship between the two Kings, cemented by the designs of promoting of Popery." So, when the French ambassador in the United Provinces, Jean-Antoine de Mesmes, comte d'Avaux, announced the existence of an Anglo-French alliance, it surprised almost no one in Europe.[39]

Despite growing English Francophobia, then, James II maintained a close personal and political attachment to Louis XIV. James believed, and believed deeply, that he and Louis XIV had overlapping geopolitical and ideological interests. Knowing full well that his subjects feared and loathed the French king, James did everything he could to avoid leaving a paper trail. Nevertheless his actions, his conversations, and those of the French King convinced almost everyone in Europe—both Catholics and Protestants— of the reality of the Anglo-French connection. James, it should be emphasized, did not see the French alliance in traditional terms of Catholic universalism. He did believe that the alliance would promote the cause of the true faith. But James also believed that the Anglo-French connection would allow England to develop a formidable seagoing empire. This, James was convinced, was very much in the national interest.

James not only sought alliance with France but pursued an aggressive policy toward the United Provinces. He did not seek to maintain neutrality in European politics. Nor did James hope to maintain the balance of power. James had an activist and belligerent foreign policy. Like so many of his contemporaries, James understood European politics in terms of a great struggle between two competing models of the modern state. Most in England believed that Louis XIV had perfected an absolutist and intolerant state that focused on territorial empire. The United Provinces, by contrast, had come for many to represent a modern popular or mixed state committed to religious toleration and commercial expansion. James was unusual in the 1680s not for his characterization of the European struggle but for his conclusion that English interests lay in supporting France and in eviscerating the Dutch Republic. James, in short, concluded that his brother's Anglo-Dutch wars were fought on the right principles.

The English monarch had made clear his detestation of the Dutch long before he acceded to the throne in 1685. He had been active both as lord admiral and as one of his brother's trusted advisers during the Anglo-Dutch War of 1665–67. James's reconciliation to the Catholic Church in 1669 occurred at a time when plans were afoot "to join with France in making war upon Holland." While it is true that James was no enthusiastic supporter of the Third Anglo-Dutch War, his opposition was to the timing not to the cause. He "feared," James confided to his old friend the Earl of Dartmouth, a war "would run [Charles II] in debt, and consequently put him into power of the Parliament." By the early 1680s, James made clear that he could not trust his son-in-law, William, because he was "so led away with the flatteries of [the Whig] party." Not surprisingly, once the Exclusion Crisis was over and Charles II again felt safe to have his younger brother by his side, Anglo-Dutch tensions increased noticeably. In the weeks before Charles's death both he and James affirmed that their "true interest" was to oppose William of Orange and the Dutch, judging that reconciliation with William "had no utility" and "could only do injury to their affairs."[40]

Why did James so thoroughly detest the Dutch and his son-in-law, William of Orange? Why did he reverse the political and ideological calculus of so many of his subjects? The answer is that James had embraced the view of the Dutch polity so widely shared by the vast majority of Anglican royalists before the political revolution of 1672 and still held by Tory highfliers. James believed that the Dutch Republic was far from being an unthreatening neighbor. For James, and his inner circle of advisers, the Dutch represented the greatest threat to England's future.

James believed deeply that the Dutch Republic was a dangerous source of political instability. By late September 1685 James had made public and "frequent" statements that the Dutch were "enemies in general to all royalty, and in particular to that of England." This was a natural position for the Dutch to take, reasoned James, because "all the world knew" that Dutch Republic was itself founded in rebellion against their legitimate sovereign Philip II of Spain. The political culture of the Northern Netherlands was so dangerous and so contagious that James believed that anyone who "spent a long time in Holland" became a rebel.[41]

James's conviction that the Netherlands was the ideological spawning ground for rebellion was only reinforced by revelations that many of his political opponents had been welcomed in the Dutch Republic. James, his advisers, and his diplomats complained obsessively that the Dutch embraced his most rebellious subjects. He told the Dutch ambassador in London that "all the English merchants residing" in Amsterdam "were evil disposed toward His Majesty and the Royal Family, that they were all republicans." James's ambassador to the United Provinces, Bevil Skelton, complained to anyone who would listen both on the Continent and in England that the Dutch offered "security" to "our English rebels" that had become their "darling villains." One of Skelton's many agents in the Netherlands, Edmund Everard, reported that Amsterdam was "the sanctuary of all the King's enemies, and the shameless forge of all rebellious and licentious contrivances." Skelton's successor at The Hague, the Marquis d'Albeville, found every reason to concur in his assessment of Dutch attitudes to the English malcontents. D'Albeville complained to James that the provincial "states offer open retreat and protection to your rebellious subjects and to traitors." In fact, he noted, "the worst intentioned of your subjects who live in these territories are much better treated . . . than those who are known to be loyal to Your Majesty."[42]

James and his advisers were not imagining things. There really was a large and ever growing English (and Scottish) exile community in the Netherlands. The radicals John Wildman and Robert Ferguson, the booksellers John Starkey and Awnsham Churchill, and the almanac writer John Partridge were among the large numbers who spent time in Amsterdam in the later 1680s. There were "many outlaws" in Rotterdam, including the Whig philosopher John Locke, where one government agent reported that "a man that's not known to be a Whig" could not be "secure for his life." The Hague attracted those exiles that could rely on the protection of William and Mary. Living in Utrecht was a large group who both hated James II and "expressed great dislike that Monmouth hath caused himself to be proclaimed King by his rout of rebels." Among the 150 or so Scottish and English families living at Utrecht were the wealthy merchant Sir Thomas Papillon, the former London sheriff Slingsby Bethel, and the former Whig lord mayor of London and vitriolic Francophobe Sir Patience Ward. In addition to these more middling communities, there were communities of English cloth weavers in the Low Countries. The exiles developed significant factories in Leeuwarden in Friesland, in Groningen, and across the border in Luneburg near Hamburg. James II's government learned that, as in England, "several English take liberty to vilify his Majesty in public coffee houses and reflect on the government." The exiles haunted Nesbit's and Colbert's coffeehouse in Rotterdam, the coffeehouse in Delft, and the Croom Elbow coffeehouse in Amsterdam. Since Peter Kidd, who ran the notoriously Whiggish Amsterdam coffeehouse in London, settled in Utrecht, he was soon likely plying his old trade there as well.[43]

Not only did Dutch provincial governments welcome English and Scottish rebels, but Dutch printing presses spewed out venomous attacks on James II's government.
Amsterdam soon became "the scene of all seditious and treasonable pamphletting against
England." Samuel Johnson's inflammatory antiabsolutist tract *Of Magistracy* was almost
certainly printed there and smuggled into England. As the ideological temperature rose in
England in 1687 and 1688, so did the number of politically significant pamphlets published
in the Netherlands. James was infuriated by the flurry of pamphlets written by Gilbert
Burnet, who not only enjoyed the protection of William of Orange but also had his works
printed in the Netherlands and smuggled into England. Burnet's works may have been the
most prominent, but they were hardly the sum total of works critical of James II pouring
forth from Dutch presses. There were "several seditious pamphlets and libels," including
such as John "Milton himself would not have owned," which were "printed in Holland
and privately conveyed over hither by ill people." Included among these Dutch prints were
"reproachful pictures that some time since, and of late they have drawn of us." "The Hollanders at this time," wrote the Londoner William Westby in the summer of 1688, "take care
to heighten and aggravate all things by their pamphlets which are privately brought over
and sold at great prices which hint irreverent reflections on the government and endeavor
to spirit away the affections of the people and debauch their love to their prince." Whether
or not the Dutch print campaign did "debauch" the English—and there is good reason to
believe that the pamphlets were widely read and discussed—there can be no doubt that
James II was deeply irritated. These "sour pills" from the Netherlands, Barillon informed
his king, could soon lead James II to go "a long way" to put an end to them.[44]

James was also convinced that Dutch political meddling, in particular political
meddling by William and his circle, was fostering political instability in England. James II
agreed with the French ambassador Barillon that the Prince of Orange's "intentions" were
completely opposed to his own and that William hoped to "instigate troubles" in England.
By the spring of 1688 James was certain that William's design had "always" been "to excite
troubles when he could in England." A variety of James's advisers, including Barillon, Bevil
Skelton, and the Earl of Grannard, repeatedly warned the English king that William represented an ever-present danger to his throne. One court memorandum, almost certainly
circulated among the Catholic inner circle, warned that the tensions between James and the
Prince and Princess of Orange represented the greatest "danger to His Majesty's safety or
repose whilst he lives." This tension, the author of the memorandum claimed, would "render all His Majesty's endeavors for a Catholic and national interest feeble and ineffectual
to his perpetual disturbance and the diminution of his glory." Sure enough, James soon
declared that it was Dutch meddling that made his first Parliament intractable, foiled his
closeting strategy, and threatened his plans to pack a new Parliament. It was also clear to
James that the Dutch ambassador Van Citters as well as the Prince and Princess of Orange
were doing all they could to thwart the king's plans to repeal the Test and Corporation
Acts, which prevented him from employing Roman Catholics and Protestant Dissenters.

In this context of ineluctable political and ideological confrontation, one can only suppose that James gave some credence to rumors that the Dutch were behind plans to assassinate him 1686 and to kidnap the Prince of Wales in 1688.[45]

James was not only concerned about the political implications of the Dutch ideological orientation but also saw the Dutch as England's great political economic competitor. Unconcerned about French territorial acquisitions, James was deeply disturbed by Dutch economic imperialism. He shared the view of those who claimed that the Dutch were seeking a universal monarchy of trade, or a sea-based empire. James had always been active in London's trading circles, and he was long convinced by the arguments advanced by his friends in the East India and Royal African Companies that the Dutch sought to drive the English from the seas by fair means or foul. In 1681 James told his friend Dartmouth that the Dutch "will do anything to engross the trade" of the world. In 1687 he confided to Bonrepaus that he feared the Dutch "were putting themselves into a position to become masters of all the commerce" of the East Indies. Sunderland, who played a dominant role in James's inner circle until November 1688, also thought that the Dutch "will make themselves masters of all trade and that soon they will absolutely control the entire pepper trade." One memorandum that circulated at court in 1685 asserted that the Dutch were "a people whose counsel being composed of traders, lay as long schemes for engrossing the sole negotiation of any foreign commerce, as ambitious monarchs do for enlarging dominions." The Dutch, the author of this memorandum warned, were about to achieve "the dominion of both the Indies." In the summer of 1687, it was common gossip at court that the Hollanders "omit no measures and no longer deny that they desire to expel the English completely from the commerce of the Indies." James and his advisers were convinced that England needed to act quickly and decisively. The goal of English policy, William Petty asserted in two papers drawn up at James's behest, was "to take away the trade of Holland &c. and bring it into England." Petty devised strategies, including "giving liberty of religion," whereby "the principal point of engrossing trade"—that is, the seizing "the trade of freight, fishing, and East India Commodities from the Hollanders"—could be achieved.[46]

Last, James detested the foreign policy pursued by the Dutch States General and their captain general William of Orange. From the moment of his accession James and his advisers were convinced that the English "parliament, the Prince of Orange and the house of Austria" had "inseparable interests." James thought all three were determined to limit his power at home, disrupt English trade, and contain French power. The Dutch pursued these aims in order to maintain what was, in James's view, a chimerical European balance of power. He was certain that William, in particular, was doing everything he could "to trouble the repose of Europe." The Dutch and their agents, many believed at Whitehall, were fomenting "a war in the North" between the Scandinavian princes, agitating for peace between the Ottoman sultan and the Holy Roman Emperor Leopold I so that he could go to war against France, and enticing the elector of Brandenburg into a Francophobic entente. James, it must be admitted, frequently expressed his worries in confessional terms. William, he said, "was working arduously" in the hopes of "starting a war of religion." But James did not mean "war of religion" in any traditional sense. He did not think that William was espousing an early Protestant worldview. James knew well, and frequently told the French ambassador, that this "Protestant League" included "the House of Austria and its adherents."[47] In essence, James feared an alliance of all those who were opposed to the Gallican version of Catholicism, a league that included a number of the most important Roman Catholic princes.

Clearly James had little interest in maintaining the European balance of power. He simply did not perceive French activities in Europe to be a threat to English national interests. The Dutch Republic and its political leader, William of Orange, by contrast, did represent a terrifying danger to James II. The Dutch polity, in James's view, was based on a set of heinous principles. The Dutch believed in popular government at home, commercial imperialism on the seas, and a balance of power in Europe. The consequence of these beliefs, James and his advisers were certain, was that the Dutch would do everything in their power to destabilize England, would seek to drive the English from the Indies East and West, and would convulse all Europe in a pointless conflagration. For all of these reasons, James felt, the Dutch—not the French—needed to be stopped.

James's ideological antipathy for the Dutch did not automatically translate into an aggressively Hollandophobic foreign policy. There was certainly a great deal of difference—even in the seventeenth century—between a cold war of ideological antagonism and a hot war of military confrontation. James had, after all, always detested the Dutch polity. Yet he had been skeptical about the Third Anglo-Dutch War precisely because he felt the English treasury could not yet support the all-out confrontation that such a war demanded.[48] Nevertheless, James did come to desire, and desire passionately, a war against the Dutch by the end of 1687. Although the scholarly consensus is that James was either too obsessed with his domestic agenda to pay attention to foreign affairs or that his sole extra-British aim was to maintain the balance of power in Europe, this overlooks James's strong pro-French orientation. Scholars have mistaken James's understanding of the financial limitations of his regime immediately after Monmouth's rebellion for his ideological and political commitments. In fact, James always knew he would go to war against the Dutch. The only question was *when* he would deem it necessary to do so. By late 1687, James had decided he could wait no longer. He made his desires to go to war so clear that William and the Dutch had to react. James's political actions, not the birth of his son, provoked military action in 1688. This was because English revolutionaries, Dutch politicians, and most of the rest of Europe understood that what was at stake was not the narrow question of succession to the English throne but the broader one of the political, economic, and ideological orientation of northern Europe.

There is indeed a good deal of evidence to suggest that in the first two years of his reign, James thought that maintaining the peace in Europe was very much in his interest. In 1685 Barillon reported to Louis XIV that James believed "a foreign war would create great obstacles for achieving all of his designs for English domestic affairs." But this was not because James prioritized domestic affairs or because James wished to remain neutral in European affairs. James believed both that he could not yet afford an Anglo-Dutch war without throwing himself on the mercy of Parliament and that such a conflict would make it all too easy for the Dutch to foment insurrection at home.[49] James accepted that conflict with the United Provinces was inevitable. He simply wanted to wait until he was wealthy enough and strong enough to strike.

The evidence overwhelmingly suggests that James's political calculus slowly altered after each new Dutch affront, each new strand of evidence pointing to the nefarious effects of Dutch political meddling, each new development that suggested that no domestic agenda could be accomplished without altering the international situation.[50]

In the summer of 1686, despite England's financial limitations, James and his inner circle of advisers discussed seriously the possibility of initiating a new Anglo-Dutch war. In early August both the Spanish ambassador Ronquillo and the Dutch ambassador Van Citters heard from "diverse persons, and among others by Catholics of note" that there were serious plans afoot "to declare war" along with France "against the Dutch." James's inner circle of Catholic advisers, and one must suppose that these were largely the French Catholic party, were doing everything in their power to convince James "that the Netherlands [are] the source and nursery of all the obstacles which encounter him in point of religion, ought first of all to be exterminated." "One of the most creditable ministers" warned the Dutch ambassador that James was prepared "to apply all possible means" to compel the Dutch to expel the British exiles and to restore all territories seized from the English East India Company. It was just at this period that the Cabinet Council discussed a proposal calling for "a war for the purpose of exterminating the Netherlands." The authors of this memorandum, which subsequently was widely circulated in European diplomatic circles and perhaps shared with Pope Innocent XI, argued that "the injuries and injustices committed by the Dutch" were "insupportable." The Dutch, it was claimed, "fomented the last rebellion, and give every asylum to His Majesty's rebels." "We shall never see the last of their factions," the authors insisted, "until that Republic is destroyed." The time to act was now. "There never was such an opportunity to destroy them as the present, when all the forces that could assist them"—that is, the forces of the Holy Roman Emperor and his allies—"are employed against the Turks."[51]

James's Cabinet Council not only talked tough, they took provocative actions. James had Samuel Pepys step up naval preparations "for what design is not yet fully known." By the middle of July 1686 more than five thousand men were working feverishly in the naval dockyards. That summer, the Algerine corsairs who were at war with the Dutch "were shamefully encouraged" by James II and given free use of English ports and allowed to sell their Dutch prizes in England. To make sure that no one missed the point of these actions, James heaped honor upon honor on the most vitriolic of Hollandophobic polemicists, Charles Molloy. In April Molloy was knighted, and in September he became recorder of London.[52]

The chattering classes in both England and the Netherlands began to discuss seriously the possibility of war. As early as January 1686 Robert Harley had heard "some whispering of a war against the D[utch]." In the following months those whispers gradually built into a roar. In June one well-connected court watcher noted that "a war with the Dutch is confidently reported." By August both Sir Robert Holmes and the Duke of Grafton were scrambling to secure the most desirable commissions for the eventual fighting. Across the North Sea the Dutch were already beginning to be "alarmed" about James II's "intentions" in early January. In the spring, these alarms quickly translated into naval preparations as the Dutch anticipated an attack from either the French or the English or both. It was these potent rumors "prevalent in Holland and elsewhere" that ultimately compelled the Dutch ambassador Van Citters to confront James about his intentions.[53]

James decided not to declare war against the Dutch in the summer of 1686. James and his inner circle of advisers apparently concluded that England was "not ready" at the time.[54] Not only was the English fleet not yet at full strength, but James must have feared the concessions that a skeptical Parliament would have demanded. Having decided that he could not secure a loyal Parliament through closeting, James probably hoped that his plans to remodel the corporations would secure a more supportive set of MPs in the future. He knew well, however, that such a Parliament could not be called immediately. The Dutch Republic must be destroyed, James almost certainly reasoned, but not this year.

Not until late 1687 did James determine to take decisive action against the Dutch Republic. He now decided to recall from the United Provinces the six British regiments in the service of the Dutch States General. Although later historians have downplayed the significance of James's decision, contemporaries were not similarly misled. They all knew that James's actions signaled a willingness to go to war with the Dutch. The Dutchman Van Citters reacted to the news of the recall by exclaiming that "this was a certain mark of war against the States General." The following week Van Citters told his "most intimate" friends that "there was a formed project to make war against the States General" by James II and Louis XIV. The Spanish ambassador Ronquillo reasoned that "at the least" this action indicated a "strict alliance between [the King of France] and the King of England." When he asked the Earl of Sunderland whether the English would "make war on the States General," he was told that James II "was in a condition to go to war." Many of the "principal Catholics" at James's court "regarded this recalling of the troops as a rupture with the States General and principally with the Prince of Orange." This was why moderate Catholics, like the Marquis of Powis and the Earl of Arundel, and the increasingly Francophobic John Churchill, so adamantly opposed the move. It was also why the French-inclined Catholics like Father Petre so enthusiastically supported James's decision.[55]

Why had James, who was reticent about going to war with Dutch as recently as the summer of 1686, decided to risk provoking a conflict? The answer is that James became convinced that the Dutch provided an insuperable barrier to achieving both his foreign and his domestic agendas. Whereas in the middle of 1686 it appeared as if an Anglo-Dutch war would make it more difficult for James to secure his international and domestic position, by late 1687 James felt that the Dutch needed to be destroyed for him to achieve anything. In the view of James and his inner circle of advisers, Dutch political meddling had proven sufficiently successful that the cost of not going to war was greater than the not insignificant costs of an all-out naval conflict.

The decision against an immediate war in the summer of 1686 had done little to diminish Anglo-Dutch tensions. By November 1686 there was another rash of rumors, fueled in part by the public knowledge of James II's naval buildup. "Most talk of a probability of a war with Holland the next year," remarked one gossip. Another reported that "there is a great rumor, and has been a considerable time, of a war with Holland the next spring." In the Netherlands, too, there was much talk of war. "The people are much concerned," noted Daniel Petit in Amsterdam. "How great an apprehension people are in here of a war with England," exclaimed James Kennedy from Delft.[56]

This renewed wave of rumors was sparked by new concerns about Dutch imperialism in the East Indies. In 1682 Cornelis Speelman, the governor-general of the Dutch East Indies, had overrun the sultanate of Bantam and destroyed the English factory there. Since Bantam had played a significant role in the English spice trade with Java and Sumatra, and since James was a great friend of the English East India Company, this development had long been considered "very important." In fact, the Dutch refusal to pay £1.3 million in reparations for Bantam was a significant source of tension in the early months of 1686. Two developments in the autumn of 1686 sparked renewed fears of Anglo-Dutch hostilities. "Fresh complaints" were brought to the English court of successful Dutch efforts to drive the English completely out of what is now Indonesia. James responded by ordering his new Catholic envoy to the United Provinces, the Marquis d'Albeville to increase the pressure on the Dutch by not only demanding satisfaction but "the restitution" of Bantam. "The Hollander does not give that satisfaction as was expected and demanded," commented the London merchant Christopher Jeaffreson, "the consequences of which may be expected." As fresh reports seeped into England in 1687 of new Dutch encroachments, James maintained a moderate demeanor, but he was known to be "furious." The Earl of Sunderland lectured the French ambassador Barillon in June 1687 that if England and France did nothing to put a stop "to the insolence of the Dutch in the Indies" their commercial hegemony would render them sufficiently powerful "to make war or to block all of the projects of the" kings of England and France.[57] James and his government were coming to realize that short of war they were impotent to stop Dutch hegemony in the East Indies.

Not only did James come to believe that the Dutch represented an insuperable roadblock to the achievement of his imperial and commercial goals, but he decided that Dutch political meddling threatened the very existence of his regime. In 1686 and 1687

Dutch actions had helped to foil James's attempt to cajole recalcitrant MPs into supporting him through closeting, Dutch-produced propaganda had turned many of James's people against his Declaration of Indulgence, and Dutch lobbying had done a great deal to make the remodeling of England's corporations more difficult. By late 1687 James had had enough. He told everyone that he detested the Dutch. Before the Roman Catholics at court and again before his Cabinet Council James recounted "with a great deal of force" the history of Anglo-Dutch relations since his accession. He highlighted Dutch connivance at Monmouth's enterprise, "the Bantam affair and the other things that had happened in the East Indies," the stream of demeaning Dutch propaganda, and the protection "that the States had given to rebels and particularly to [Gilbert] Burnet." James did not, as he had done before, keep his anger in check. The imperial ambassador Philippe Hoffmann soon heard the same litany of Dutch abuses, adding that what "was particularly disagreeable to the King" was the fact that the Prince of Orange, the States General, even the Dutch burgers themselves "meddled in an insufferable fashion in English politics and above all in religious affairs." James's fulminations reached the ears of the Rotterdam Quaker Benjamin Furley. "The King of England publicly declared that the Dutch had broke treaty with him in protecting his declared rebels," he informed his good friend John Locke. The Polish ambassador at The Hague Antoine Moreau was really summarizing James's actions since January 1688 when he declared that the English king "had not ceased threatening this State . . . since his accession to the throne."[58]

So, while some contemporaries thought the decision to recall the regiments in Dutch service had been an impulsive response to the publication of the Dutch grand pensionary Gaspar Fagel's notorious *Letter* criticizing James's desire to repeal the Test and Corporation Acts, James's decision was more considered and more wide-ranging. James's profound ideological antipathy to the Dutch Republic grew exponentially with each new provocation. As early as the summer of 1686, the Dutch ambassador Van Citters noted that even though "the king is not in a condition to enter in a foreign war" this year, the feverish English naval buildup at immense cost "causes many penetrating persons to be apprehensive that the intentions against Spring may prove quite different." The following year, Bonrepaus and Barillon—who had been the most adamant in their insistence that England was unprepared for war in 1686—changed their assessments dramatically. In June 1687 Barillon rushed into Bonrepaus's quarters at midnight to announce that James's fury against the Prince of Orange was such that "it was impossible there would not be an open rupture with the Dutch." Although Bonrepaus remained more skeptical that James was willing immediately to start a war in Europe, both Barillon and Bonrepaus agreed that James "was so furious with the Prince of Orange and so dissatisfied with what was happening daily in the Indies" that war might well begin between the two companies in the East, with James willingly supporting the English East India Company's claims. Within weeks of these discussions, James initiated serious discussions with Barillon about uniting "the Catholic powers" against the international efforts of the Prince of Orange. When

Louis XIV promised to bankroll the repatriated regiments from the Netherlands, James's uneasiness must have been overcome.[59]

War had become inevitable from the moment that James decided to recall the British regiments from the Netherlands. James's actions set in motion a spiral of escalating tension that neither side could or wanted to reverse. Initially the Dutch refused to return the regiments to James, claiming that "men are born free and that they had the right to choose which country they wished to inhabit." In the end only about a third of the soldiers returned. Each side lodged ever more strident complaints against their opponent's propaganda machines. The English ambassador in the Netherlands accused the Prince of Orange of inciting "disorders in England." The Dutch, in turn, complained bitterly of the officially sanctioned squib *Parliamentum Pacificum,* which rehearsed all of the arguments for eviscerating the Dutch Republic.[60]

Soon the pamphlet wars turned into a dangerous arms race. James, encouraged at every step by Louis XIV, accelerated his naval preparations in February 1688. The Dutch responded in kind, provoking James to remark to Van Citters that "it was apparent their intention was to make war." The French court soon caught wind of rumors of a massive mobilization in the Netherlands to defend itself against "the war threatened by the English for the restitution of Bantam." It was probably on the basis of this knowledge that Barillon warned the Earl of Sunderland to be prepared to deal with the possibility of a Dutch invasion. James and his inner circle of advisers needed little convincing. They were certain that the States General and the Prince of Orange were merely seeking a pretext for war. Rumors began again to circulate abut a joint Anglo-French assault on the Dutch. Perhaps more significantly, the Earl of Sunderland no longer denied English interest in such a conflict. He told Barillon that if Louis XIV saw fit to go to war against the Dutch, then James II "would take the necessary measures to execute this important project." In fact, Sunderland added, if the Dutch could be painted as the aggressors, then "all England" would surely support "the crown in a just war."[61]

James II and his inner circle, it is clear, did not seek merely to maintain the balance of power in Europe. Nor were they so obsessed with their domestic agenda that they neglected European affairs. Instead James and his closest confidants harbored a deep and unswerving ideological hatred for the Dutch Republic. Initially they had hoped to modernize the English state, regularize the English empire, and establish the Catholic religion before commencing the inevitable confrontation with the Dutch Republic. However, James, Sunderland, Father Petre, and others became convinced that the Dutch were a fundamental impediment to their achieving their domestic and imperial agenda. They concluded that the Dutch must be destroyed. Rapidly accelerating Anglo-Dutch tensions made conflict inevitable by late 1687. The Anglo-Dutch force that set sail for England in the autumn of 1688 had long been anticipated. Indeed, the belligerent actions of William III and the British exiles in coordination with the Dutch States General need to be understood as a preemptive first strike against an equally bellicose English polity. The Dutch thought the success of the enterprise, wrote Antoine Moreau from The Hague in October 1688, was the only way to "preserve their religion, their liberty, and was the only means to restore their commerce."[62] James had succeeded in provoking the Dutch Republic.

James and his advisers were unable to convince the majority of English men and women to share their assessment of the international situation. Just as James and his inner circle became increasingly convinced of the perniciousness of the States General and William of Orange, most English people became increasingly convinced that Louis XIV's France represented the greatest ideological and geopolitical threat that England had ever faced. In fact, most English people came to understand their own problems in remarkably modern and nationalist terms, even if this nationalism—as I will show later on—never implied ideological consensus about the aims and directions of English foreign policy.[63]

Many in England loathed and feared Louis XIV because of his perceived universalism, because of his aspirations to be universal monarch. In the later seventeenth century, the English unlike their forebears, had no intention of replacing a Catholic universal monarch with a Protestant one. Instead they condemned aspirations to universal dominion as archaic, in a world now organized along national lines.

Despite Crown attempts to limit the extent and ferocity of anti-French propaganda, England was saturated with Francophobic sentiment by the time of the revolution. "Everybody takes the freedom of censuring all the actions of the King France," wrote one London observer. The Manchester area Dissenting minister Henry Newcome could hardly contain his contempt for "the tyrant of France." "It is agreed at all hands," asserted another commentator, "that the French set up for an Universal Commerce as well as for an Universal Monarchy." "No man in his wits will deny that the French King has been these many years past, and is like to continue" the greatest threat to England, advised one conservative Anglican scribbler in 1685, because Louis XIV was committed to "his long hatch'd designs of an universal monarchy." The Buckinghamshire gentleman Edmund Verney thought that Louis XIV "never will have done demanding, claiming and destroying, and taking forcibly, until the devil hath him." In October 1688 one journalist proclaimed that Louis XIV was determined to make "a war with all Europe." Barillon, surely one who was quite sensitive to popular opinion on this issue, thought that "most" in England, those who were "the good English and the Protestant zealots," thought it was England's "true interest to oppose the grandeur" of Louis XIV. This was why "the generality of people," those the French ambassador labeled "the factious and the discontented," were always "desirous of war with France."[64]

The English were well aware that Louis XIV posed a threat to the national integrity not only of themselves but of all Europe. Louis XIV, one polemicist averred, is "the old enemy of the English nation, one who desires nothing more than to destroy and ruin the people; to change and subvert their laws and religion." Louis XIV, explained the author of *True Interest of Christian Princes,* made a habit of "ill treating the sovereign states and princes" of Europe. The English in the 1680s anxiously commented on every French assault on national sovereignty throughout Europe. The French, complained Gabriel de Sylvius, were trying "to put all Germany into intestine broils." Louis XIV shamelessly meddled in the selection of the elector of Cologne and, what was worse, invited the Ottoman Turks to invade the Holy Roman Empire with the ultimate aim of gaining "either the title of Emperor or so much of the Empire himself as he thought fit." Others worried that French agents were hard at work encouraging subjects of the various Spanish territories "to change their master." The West Country gentleman William Lawrence summed up English sentiment when he explained that "the French King thinks that for men to obey other Princes is to taste of the forbidden fruit, and therefore with his flaming sword he drives whole nations from the paradise of peace and plenty; it equally kills and burns, no reason can stop his rage, nor can any force as yet repulse his ambition. Attila who was only styled the *flagellum dei,* was not a greater tyrant, he only whipped the nations and away, but this insatiable monarch designs a perpetual bondage."[65] Lawrence captured perfectly the national basis of English opposition to French universalism in 1688–89. Louis XIV was dangerous not only because of his tyrannical governmental style but also and centrally because he refused to recognize the legitimacy of separate national governments and identities.

Many English men and women necessarily came to interpret, with some justice, their king's domestic political activities in the context of the growing greatness of Louis XIV and James II's remarkable inaction in the face of this threat to universal dominion. The English in the late seventeenth century understood their political situation not in splendid isolation but in the context of French activities in Europe and beyond.

James II, most English men and women came to believe, sought to replace the English national political culture with that of France. Many in England understood James II's Catholic modernization program as an attempt to replace an English with a French government. James II was following his French cousin's "perfect pattern . . . of governing all by one sovereign will," warned one poet in the summer of 1688. Another was sure that England's "oppressors" were "fleshed with the barbarous precedent in France." "The French King's example and assistance inspired" James II "with mighty courage," wrote the Tory Whitelock Bulstrode in June 1688. The author of *The Justification of the Whole Proceedings* thought James II had erected "an insupportable tyranny, just modeling after the French fashion." "King James had in a great measure enslaved these nations," James Wellwood later recalled, and "in conjunction with Lewis the 14th," he planned "to teach us a French kind of subjection."[66]

The English sense that their political culture was being Frenchified was both well developed and quite sophisticated. Since the early 1680s many English wits had complained that "French councilors and whores, French education / Have changed our natures, and enslaved our nation." James II so promoted French fashion, French travels, and French education, thought one poet, he "with ill breeding corrupted the nation." At court, of course, the French presence was manifest in Francophilic privy councillors and Jesuit advisers. It was for this reason that the English blamed all their nation's "misfortunes these many years unto French councils." James's advisers, scowled Daniel Defoe, "were politicians by the book, and never consulted the genius and humor of that people they had to do with. It may be they are thought very wise men and great politicians in other countries, but they can never in England expect anything but the reputation of the most impudent and unpolitic of men."[67]

The policies pursued by James and his Frenchified counselors were naturally French policies. James II's standing army—whose central base camp at Hounslow Heath was explicitly modeled on Louis XIV's military installations—was thought to turn "the civil government into a military; and that is not the government of England." English law was turned into a French mockery. In subverting "the civil government and established laws," one angry English controversialist proclaimed, "the French precedent was too exactly followed," so much so that "it may well be said, that the methods here observed were the same with those which had been taken in France." Another fulminated that "in all his undertakings," James II "went quite counter to the fundamental institution of an English monarch: instead of maintaining our laws, he usurped a power to suspend and null them: instead of preserving the true course of judicature, he appointed such as were enemies of the constitution to be judges and jurors."[68]

James II's attempts to overturn the Test Act and Penal Laws by declaration and to pack Parliament to have them statutorily reversed were widely interpreted in a French context. It was "the doings in France" that taught the English to beware "what feeble things edicts, coronation-oaths, laws and promises repeated over and over again prove to be." By first closeting privy councillors and MPs, and then by submitting the entire country to his notorious three questions regarding the Test Act and Penal Laws, James II had threatened "the freedom and being of our Parliaments, just as the French King first invaded the supreme legal authority of France, which was vested in the Assembly of Estates." "The King, by this dispensing power," thundered Sir George Treby in the Convention Parliament of 1689, "might have packed members of Parliament, like the Parliament of Paris, which is in the nature of registers, only to record the King's will and pleasure by his dragoons." James II, recalled one historian soon after the revolution, "resolves the utter subversion of English Parliaments" in order "to make way for the introduction of a French Parliament, that should at once have surrendered all the ancient liberty of this kingdom, and the whole power of government into his hands."[69]

Over the course of James II's reign, the English people came to believe that their king's love for things French perfectly accorded with his style of government. French government, they knew, brought with it nothing but misery. "In the realm of France (where the people are governed by regal power alone)," warned the Tory Jacob Bury in 1685, the people "do live in great misery and thralldom; for there the Prince's pleasure standeth in force of a law, so that by reason thereof, their kings at their pleasure change laws, make new laws, execute Parliaments, burden their subjects with charges." "When I have named France," preached the Whig Gilbert Burnet several years later, "I have said all that is necessary to give you a complete idea of the blackest tyranny over men's consciences, persons and estates, that can possibly be imagined."[70] English nationalist ire was raised because in the eyes of many, James II had come to mimic this tyranny.

Most English people in the later 1680s knew they must choose between two distinct national political cultures. Popular political activity throughout England left little doubt of the drift of public opinion on the question. In June 1687, for example, the leader of one set of West Country rioters, William Hurford of Burnham-on-Sea, announced his ephemeral triumph with the claim that "now Holland . . . had conquered France." In December 1688 the English coastal towns were repeatedly filled with rumors of French landings in support of James II. When a French merchantman was cast ashore at Weymouth by foul weather, "the people imagining that French soldiers were coming to land they run to the sea shore and without further inquiry killed most of them."[71]

At the same time that English popular political Francophobia was at its highest pitch, the English people had come to believe that their government was in strict alliance with the national enemy. In August 1688 the Anglican divine Dr. William Denton was "certain the King expects a squadron of French ships to be at his command." Roger Morrice heard a rumor that "the French would send forces over hither to awe the Parliament, to do whatever they are directed both for the altering of the constitution here and for the precluding of the Prince and Princess of Orange from the crown." Almost as soon as d'Avaux, the French ambassador in the United Provinces, revealed the existence of an Anglo-French alliance, it was eagerly believed by England's "coffee drinkers." "Everybody speaks of a holy league" between James II and Louis XIV, averred the Londoner William Westby in late September.[72]

The English knew in late 1688 that they had to act immediately if they wished to maintain their national integrity. Sir Richard Cocks later summarized the choice facing the English nation in the 1680s in the starkest terms. "That government that is settled upon the biased designing will and pleasure of one frail man is that despotical tyrannical government the thinking Englishman abhors," Cocks lectured in 1694. "It is French government where the will of the prince is the law, reason and religion of the people. Such is the admirable virtue and excellency of our laws and statutes that they not only make us live honestly and justly one with another but they secure us and save us from the ambitious designs and ill disposition of the great one." It was, recalled the Episcopalian cleric Robert Kirk, James II's "intimacy with the French King and learning his methods" that "cooled the hearts of many who wished well to King James." It was precisely because much more than "a very small but far-sighted minority" in England perceived a connection between James's Francophilia and his style of government that Admiral Herbert could confidently appeal for support from "all true Englishmen" on William of Orange's arrival at Torbay.[73]

Nationalist revolutionaries deposed James II in late 1688 in part because the English people—ranging from radical Whigs to moderate Tories—desperately desired to replace a French with an English political culture. In the 1690s and thereafter they would disagree and disagree bitterly over the content of that English political culture. But in 1688–89 the English across a broad political spectrum agreed that a central aspect of the English national interest was to go to war with France.

English men and women had been active participants in a long national debate about the proper orientation of English foreign policy. That debate—much like the debate about the Cold War in the second half of the twentieth century—informed discussions of almost every aspect of political and social life. By late 1688 it was clear that the majority of the political nation favored opposing the growing power of France by force of arms. It was hardly surprising, then, that for most of the revolutionaries the deposition of James II necessarily implied the rejection of his Francophilic foreign policy. William did not have to impose his foreign policy on an unwilling nation.[74] Instead, the English political nation had chosen to support the Prince of Orange in 1688 and 1689 precisely because he was likely to lead the country into the long-desired war against Louis XIV.

Even before William and his entourage had reached London in December 1688, English men and women throughout the nation were convinced that they would finally go to war against France, that they would finally engage in the struggle against the aspiring universal monarch Louis XIV. The news of the revolution "will be most of all menacing in France," thought Sir Robert Southwell, "all our thunderbolts will light there besides what may fall from the rest of Europe. They have great desolations and inhumanities to account for and it looks as if Heaven were now disposed to send an avenger." "This sudden revolution of affairs," the Levant Company informed Sir William Trumbull, "may occasion a speedy breech with France." War with France was clearly the desire of the political nation. The Dutch ambassador Van Citters learned that "the City in the next Parliament will very strongly insist upon a war with France." Sir Edmund Warcup, no Whig, hoped "the Parliament will assist gloriously in carrying on the Protestant interest, and reducing France; which too much threatens the quiet of Christendom, and is too big for all its neighbors." The directors of the East India Company reported in early December 1688 that "war against France" was "the most general inclination of the English Protestants of all qualities and degrees."[75]

The squabbles over the constitutional settlement did nothing to lessen the popular enthusiasm for war in the new year. John Locke thought that no one in England "can sleep" until "they see the nation settled in a regular way of acting and putting itself in a posture of defense and support of the common interest of Europe." The old Whig exclusionist Henry Powle was quick to remind his countrymen "of the growth of France, and the aspiring hopes of their turbulent monarch." The English, he thought, should prepare not only to defend themselves against such a powerful foe but also to fight on the Continent so "that our former conquests in France may be remembered, and the provinces formally belonging to the crown of England recovered." The Livorno-based merchants Thomas and Robert Balle expressed their fervent hopes that the members of the Convention Parliament would "unite for the common safety under that eminent danger at hand and join in a war against France." One Parliament-watcher commented in early February 1689 that "our old-fashioned heroes . . . talk big how they will thump the French." Francophobic effusions streamed forth from the newly unregulated English presses. Louis XIV will soon discover, announced the author of one cheap print, "that his Bordeaux claret has not quite damped the English spirits, but there are a generation of men alive who dare make him a bold visit."[76]

A remarkably high proportion of the ballads and doggerel verses—genres targeting less learned and less literate audiences—that appeared in the immediate aftermath of the revolution called for war against France. One versifier called on "English arms by mighty Nassau led" to "break the long leagues with Mahommet and Hell; / And the world's ravager, Europe's monster quell." "Nip France's pride, pull Hell's great Lewis down" advised another poet. Yet another rhymer promised, "If it should be our happy chance, / With Monsieur to engage O, / with forces thither we'll advance, / And shake the very crown of France." "Let Gallia then beware the mortal blow," warned a classically minded contemporary. "Our brave Prince and we, will unite and agree / For to drive Lewis King out of France," predicted the rhyming shoemaker Richard Rigby. The author of the *Civil Orange* promised that "Great Britain and Holland's each flourishing fleet, / As soon as they're fitted and perfect complete, / Will challenge our foes to fight on the main / Shou'd France have the mighty Armado of Spain." "Our British lions" now led by William of Orange, predicted the Whig politician Sir William Cowper in verse, "once more shall stalk through France with furious state." Henry Pollexfen captured this popular spirit when in calling for war against France he asked to "let the world see we are returned to our senses, and that we are truly English."[77]

English men and women in late 1688 and early 1689 were determined to put a halt to Louis XIV's universalist designs. Revolutionaries across a wide spectrum of political commitments demanded war against France with a united voice. Those who had taken up arms to defend the Church and those who wanted full civil rights for Dissenters, those who merely wanted to change kings and those who wanted to radically restrict the power of the executive—in short, almost everyone who wanted a change of regime also wanted to fight the growing power of France. William did not have to impose his Francophobic views on an unwilling nation. The English in 1688–89 were just as anxious to join battle with Louis XIV as the Prince of Orange.

The Revolution of 1688–89 was a successful act by the English political nation to replace a government that they increasingly perceived to be ruling in the French style with an English government. It was a Protestant revolution in the sense that the English national religion was explicitly defended and celebrated as one of the elements—arguably one of the most important elements—of English national identity threatened by James. It was not, however, a war of religion, a war in defense of universal religious truth. War against the aspiring French universal monarch was one of the central goals of the English revolutionary nationalists, so it was in proclaiming and defending that war that the nationalists were able to give their ideology more precise definition. The English—including William's own propagandists—understood the war against France as a war to protect national integrities against an aspiring universal monarch, not as a war of religion. Indeed, English polemicists constantly pointed out that it was only Louis XIV's propagandists who were raising the crusading banner in a desperate, but mendacious, attempt to garner allies. The argument for confessional war, however effective it might have been in the sixteenth and early seventeenth centuries, was no longer persuasive. Europe was no longer divided into two neatly divided confessional camps of Catholics and Protestants. Catholics were bitterly divided between supporters of the pope and defenders of Gallican Catholicism. Northern European Protestants were themselves increasingly divided into Lutheran and Calvinist camps.[78] Opponents of French Catholic universalism in the later seventeenth century, then, turned not to an alternative universalism but to a universal defense of particularism. Religion did not cease to be important; it ceased to be all-important in the making of foreign policy. For most Europeans, and especially for England, the war pitted the entire community of European nations against the supreme violator of national identity, Louis XIV.

It was in this nationalist context, then, that William and Mary, as king and queen of England, heeded their subjects' call for war against Louis XIV. The war the revolutionaries asked the English nation to fight was not, as some recent historians have claimed, a war of religion. Instead William, his regime's defenders, and the revolutionaries more broadly were careful to describe the war as an international struggle against Louis XIV, a tyrant and aspiring universal monarch who was equally threatening to Catholic and Protestant. For the new English regime, the war against France was a war that pitted a multiconfessional alliance of European nations against a tyrant who threatened the existence of each and every one of them.

William, the Dutch States General, and the prince's inner circle of advisers were careful never to depict the revolution in confessional terms. The invasion fleet itself sailed under St. George's cross, the arms of England, the arms of William of Orange, and the nonconfessional motto "Pro Libertate et Libero Parlamento"—for liberty and a free Parliament. Even before his departure William had suppressed a Dutch pamphlet printed in Rotterdam declaring his actions to have been undertaken "under pretext of religion." William told anyone who cared to listen that he was determined to improve the conditions of English Catholics. The States General for their part instructed their representatives in Catholic courts and told the Catholic diplomats in The Hague that "their intention and that of the Prince was not to persecute anyone for their religion"; instead of "a religious alliance they wanted the opposite."[79]

Hardly a week after the coronation, a committee of the House of Commons led by the Whigs John Somers and John Hampden drafted an address to their new monarchs calling for war against France. "We have examined the mischiefs brought upon Christendom in late years by the French King," they reported, "who, without any respect to justice, has by fraud and force endeavored to subject it to an arbitrary and universal monarchy." Far from rejecting arguments "about the strategic and commercial dangers of allowing France to dominate Europe," the Commons committee emphasized just those claims. Louis XIV, the committee claimed, had pursued a variety of means to devastate and weaken Europe in general and England in particular. "The whole series of the French King's actions for many years past has been so ordered, as if it were his intention not only to render his own people extremely miserable," they contended, "but likewise to hold all the neighboring powers in perpetual alarm and expense for the maintaining of armies and fleets, that they may be in a posture to defend themselves against the invader of their common safety and liberties." Louis XIV "has constantly had recourse to the vilest and meanest acts, for the ruin of those whom he had taken upon him to subdue to his will and power." It was by these "practices against England" that Louis XIV was able under Charles II and James II to "undermine the government and true interest of this flourishing kingdom." In addition, the committee reported, Louis XIV deployed "another art" in order "to weaken England and subject it to his aspiring designs": that was "never to admit an equal balance of trade, nor consent to any just treaty or settlement of commerce, by which he promoted our ruin at our own charge." Far from being motivated by religious zeal, far from doing all this from his "zeal for the Catholic religion," Louis XIV used this language only as "a cloak for his unmeasurable ambition." Thinking men and women were not duped, the committee averred, "for at the same time when the persecution grew hottest against the Protestants of France, letters were intercepted (and published) from [Louis XIV] to [the Protestant] Count Teckeley, to give him the greatest encouragement, and promise him the utmost assistance in the war, which in conjunction with the Turk he then managed against the first and greatest of all the Roman Catholic Princes." The addressers concluded with a plea for war so that "a stop may be put to that growing greatness of the French King, which threatens all Christendom with no less than absolute slavery." This war could only serve to protect the "justice and liberty" of "all Europe in general, and this nation in particular."[80]

A month later William enthusiastically accepted the Commons' call to arms and declared war against France. The *Declaration* made it clear that William did not intend to fight a war of religion. The document opened by recounting Louis XIV's crimes against the Holy Roman Emperor, who was William's ally. These perfidious actions of Louis XIV made it clear that he was no religious crusader but the "disturber of the peace, and the common enemy of the Christian world." Louis XIV had long been devastating the property of English men and women in Hudson's Bay, New York, and the Caribbean Islands.

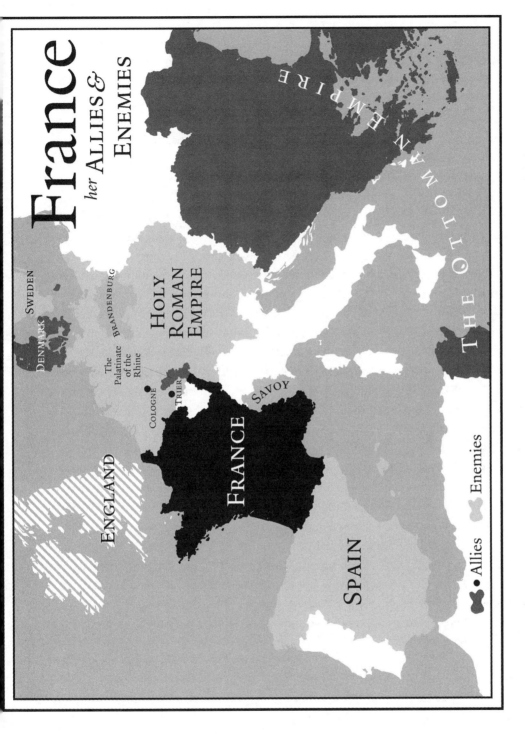

European politics in the late seventeenth century no longer hinged on confessional divisions. Among France's enemies were the Catholic king of Spain and the Holy Roman Emperor.

These acts, coupled with Louis XIV's protectionist measures, William and Mary declared, "are sufficient evidences of his designs to destroy the trade, and consequently to ruin the navigation upon which the wealth and safety of this nation very much depends." When the new monarchs did come to discuss Louis XIV's attacks on Protestants, they made no mention of his religious zeal, of his desire to re-Catholicize Europe, or even of his persecution of Huguenots in France; they merely complained that Louis's attacks on "our English Protestant subjects in France" was "contrary to the law of nations, and express treaties." Louis XIV had violated the rights of English men and women. William and Mary raised a wildly popular nationalist sword, not a religious crusading one.[81]

The instructions and official correspondence of William's diplomatic corps made it clear that the postrevolutionary English state was fighting a nationalist war against French universalist pretensions, not a war of religion. Diplomats sent to Protestant states were told nothing of a great confessional struggle. When William and Mary sent Thomas, Earl of Pembroke, to the States General in May 1689, he was told to work "for the common good of Christendom as well as the particular advantage of our dominion." The new regime's envoy to Denmark, Robert Molesworth, was instructed to emphasize that "we are now engaged in one common interest for our mutual assistance and defense as well as for the common good of Christendom." Charles Berkeley, Viscount Dursley, who replaced Pembroke at The Hague, was told to "concur in all such measures as may best tend to promote the good of Christendom," including "entering into the alliance concluded between the Emperor" and the Dutch. Unsurprisingly William, Lord Paget's instructions as envoy to the Catholic imperial court also emphasized that the war against France was not a war of religion. He was ordered to "press" the emperor to send a mission to the Catholic Swiss cantons "to enter into the common measures with us and our allies for the public good against the encroachments and exorbitant designs of France." Over and over again the English diplomatic corps reminded one another that despite French and Jacobite propaganda, the Nine Years' War was not a confessional struggle. When negotiating with the Duke of Savoy, Viscount Dursley warned, "we must have a care of giving jealousy to our Popish allies," being certain not to "appear any ways over partial to our religion." Paul Rycaut wrote from Hamburg of his feeling that not just Protestants but "all the Christian world is now united" against France, "the common enemy." "That this is not a war of religion is plain by the French encouraging the Turks as they do," insisted the English envoy Sir William Dutton Colt.[82]

The official fast sermons—the genre in which the English were most likely to highlight the religious aspects of the war against France—delivered on 5 June 1689 reinforced the nationalist and antiuniversalist nature of the war. Before the House of Commons Thomas Tenison emphasized that the English were going to war against Louis XIV, "who is reputed, even by the head of the Roman Church" to be "the common enemy of West-Europe." "We are at war with one," Tenison preached, emphasizing the well-known ecumenical nature of the struggle, "who (how unlike soever he is to be governor of the world) hath set himself in the seat of God, by making his personal glory his ultimate end." For Tenison, the war against France was evidence that the postrevolutionary regime was set upon "repairing the breaches" of the previous era. Rather than pursuing policies based on self-interest or the interest of a faction, the new regime was "pursuing the true end of government, the good of the whole body; of raising the figure of the nation, and making us that which we are capable of being, by our natural genius, and by the advantages of our situation, a great and flourishing people." That same day, William Wake, one of the new monarchs' chaplains, rehearsed many of the same themes before the Commons. Wake called on the English to become "the scourge and terror of the universal enemy of truth, peace, religion, nature; in short, of all the common laws and rights of God and of all mankind." This war against France, he made clear, was neither a religious crusade nor a war of secular aggrandizement. It was a war to be fought "not of your nation only, but of all the nations round about us." Nor were the fortunes "of your own country and religion only" at stake. "This is the fatal crisis," Wake warned, "that must secure or ruin both them and us forever."[83]

Prominent clergymen, especially Low Churchmen, continued to promote this multiconfessional and antiuniversalist interpretation throughout the war. The French "design was universal, and aimed at the enslaving all the Kingdoms and States of Europe: no distinction of Protestant or Papist," preached the dean of St. Patrick's and future archbishop of Dublin William King in November 1690. The fact that the pope, the Holy Roman Emperor, and the king of Spain were engaged with William in an alliance against France rendered it "ridiculous to pretend a Holy War." The first postrevolutionary archbishop of Canterbury, John Tillotson, argued in a sermon delivered before William and Mary at Whitehall that the war did involve "the necessary defense" of Protestantism against Louis XIV's antiheretical crusade. But, he made clear, the Nine Years' War was not an old-fashioned confessional struggle. The war, he repeatedly emphasized, was fought "in the public cause of the rights and liberties of almost all Europe"; it was fought in "the vindication of the common liberties of mankind, against tyranny and oppression." By the middle years of the war, the multiconfessional and nationalist understanding of the war had become commonplace among the clerics most closely associated with the regime and the war. So John Petter was merely reinforcing what the English army already knew quite well when he preached before a regiment of horse fighting in Flanders that Louis XIV was "the common enemy of Christendom." In Alsace, in Catalonia, and elsewhere Louis XIV had treated Roman Catholics so badly that "all of them exclaim against his arbitrary and unjust ways of proceeding." This was why "it concerns both Papist and Protestant to adventure their distinct power and interest in one common bottom and resolution to oppose him, and to hinder the obstinate pursuit of his project of universal monarchy."[84]

The extraordinarily vibrant discussion of the war against France—which took place in provincial parish churches, in coffeehouses, in newsletters, in periodicals, and in hundreds of pamphlets—largely emphasized the novel nature of the war against France.

Whereas earlier struggles against aspiring universal monarchs had sought to replace a false aspirant with the true inheritor of the Roman imperium, this struggle denied the propriety of universal dominion. This was not a war of religion, a war to replace a Catholic universal monarch with a Protestant one, but a war to protect the national integrity of each and every European state. Even though the English repeatedly emphasized that Protestantism was an essential part of their national identity threatened by France, they also made clear that France threatened all national identities. Precisely because this was no war of religion, no anti-Catholic crusade, the Williamite regime made every effort to translate and publish imperial, papal, and occasionally Spanish Francophobic propaganda as well as material produced by Protestant polemicists. In contrast to James II's appeasement of Louis XIV abroad, while imitating him at home, the postrevolutionary regime—its defenders tried to make clear—would pursue English nationalist policies both at home and abroad.

While French propagandists feverishly scribbled tracts, treatises, and sermons proclaiming that Louis XIV was fighting a war of religion against the Protestant William III, only English Jacobites and some English Tories echoed their views. By the end of December 1688 Louis XIV, James II, and their Jesuit allies were proclaiming the beginning of a religious crusade in all the courts of Europe. Catholic European states quickly signaled their disagreement with the French interpretation of international politics. Don Manuel Coloma, the Spanish envoy to the States General, prayed ostentatiously in his chapel in November 1688 for the "happy success of the enterprise of the Prince of Orange." The Catholic elector of Bavaria, Maximilian II Emanuel, was one of the first to send an envoy to England "to compliment the Prince upon his success." The Holy Roman Emperor was also not backward in wishing William "success in his expedition in England."[85]

Almost as quickly, controversialists from both Catholic and Protestant Europe—whose works were widely disseminated in England, often at the government's behest—insisted on the perfidious and mendacious nature of the French king's claims to be fighting a war of religion. "In good truth," explained one Spanish polemicist, "it is apparent that the Most Christian King [of France] derides religion and Christianity; and laughs at all Europe beside." "This ought not to be concealed," wrote the Holy Roman Emperor himself in a published letter, "that the greatest injuries which have been done to our religion have flowed from no other than the French themselves." "It is a matter of astonishment," scowled another pamphleteer, "that the French who have been the authors of so much mischief, and damage to the Catholic Princes, and to the Catholic religion, should go about to persuade the world, that the present revolution in England is a war on the score of religion." "It is not religion that pushes the French King" but fear that the tide had turned against him, insisted the English author of *The Means to Free Europe*. If the grand monarch ever got the upper hand, "after he had pulled down William III [and] overcome the Protestant Princes, he would do the like to all the Roman Catholics, one after another, and thus become Master of Europe."[86]

The profound antipathy between Louis XIV and the leaders of European Catholicism made a mockery of his claim to be leading a pan-Catholic struggle against Protestantism. It was clear to most English in the 1680s and 1690s that Innocent XI neither supported Gallican-style Catholicism nor understood politics in confessional terms. Innocent XI, the English nation came to understand, restricted his universalism to the spiritual sphere. Sir Robert Southwell heard that "the Emperor and some other Popish Princes and even the Pope himself" were well informed of William's intended invasion, and far from joining in a confessional alliance against the revolution, they "wished well to it," hoping it would lead England "to join with the confederates against France." The pope and England's new governors made common cause in insisting that the European war now on foot was no war of religion. One papal polemic, republished in England, denounced Louis XIV as "the Christian Turk, and as great an enemy to Europe as the Mahometan one." The Jacobite diplomat John Lytcott confessed from Rome that the pope had no intention of aiding James II against William, because "provided France may be suppressed," the pope was "willing to sacrifice all other considerations and interests." Papal support for the war against France and Innocent's refusal "to send anything to King James" was well advertised in London. Roger Morrice heard in London that the pope was proclaiming throughout Italy that "the French King makes not . . . war upon the account of religion, but only to tyrannize over his neighbors and to increase his own dominions."[87]

The English were equally well informed about their alliance with the Holy Roman Emperor and that Catholic monarch's insistence that the war against France was no war of religion. France, they knew, had done everything possible to alienate the emperor. While insisting on the extirpation of heresy at home, Louis XIV had covertly aided a Protestant rebellion in Hungary. He had encouraged the Ottomans to refuse a negotiated peace with the Austrian Habsburgs, prompting Sir John Lowther to comment that "religion" is "insignificant" in cases "where interest comes in competition." On the eve of the revolution even James II's man in Vienna, Thomas Lane, had to admit that the imperialists "wished well to the Protestant party, which they imagined was a hearty enemy to France." So little did the court in Vienna think that they still lived in an age of religious wars that "none was so popular [t]here as the Prince of Orange." Edmund Bohun thought that the emperor's support of William against the Catholic James II made perfect sense. James, the Habsburgs knew, had "embraced a design" that "would raise France to such an height of power as could never be retrieved." "The Emperor of Germany is as religious and as zealous a Prince for the Roman Catholic religion as ever sprung out of that family," Bohun continued, "but he has no mind, after all, to lose his life, his empire, and his liberty; he had rather there should be some heretics in Germany, than to suffer the French King to send his apostolic dragoons to convert them, and drive him into exile."[88]

For most English the struggle against France—the struggle that did so much to define the thinking of the revolutionaries in 1688–89—was a struggle to protect European and English national liberties against an aspiring universal monarch, not a war of religion. The Anglo-Dutch alliance made possible by the revolution allowed both nations to be "the

This controversial painting, *Innocent XI Blessing William III,* c. 1690s,
attributed to Pieter van der Muelen, is thought to depict the pope posthumously
celebrating William III's key victory over the Jacobite and French forces.

restorers of Europe to her liberties." The Revolution of 1688–89, and the international alliance against France made possible by it, proclaimed another commentator, made it certain
that "the project of France concerning the Universal Monarchy of Christendom will fall to
the ground." The revolution placed William III in the position, a position that his ancestors
had traditionally filled, "to rescue Europe from its oppressors, and to resettle governments
upon the primitive and immortal foundation of liberty and property."[89]

Most people in England were well aware that the alliance against Louis XIV was
multiconfessional; most knew they were not engaged in a war of religion. "It is certain
that the diversity of religion has always been as a large and vast abyss betwixt the Catholic
and the Protestant Princes," conceded one pamphleteer, "but the cruelty and perfidiousness of the French has filled up that abyss, and leveled the way between them, and all
difficulties are at present laid aside." "Who will be so silly as to fall into that trap" of
thinking the current conflict a war of religion, asked one journalist incredulously. "Can it
be well imagined that this war should be a war of religion, and that these three Potentates
[the pope, the emperor, and the king of Spain] should, with the Protestant Princes, have
conspired the ruin of the Church of Rome?" "This war," explained Sir Richard Cox to a

grand jury, "is for the defense of the laws, liberties, customs, and religion as well papist and protestant from the barbarous and avaricious tyranny and invasion of the French King. The Emperor, the King of Spain, the confederate Princes, the supporters of the Roman See help us and assist."[90]

Contemporaries understood perfectly well that nationality was determined by a variety of issues and interests. Religion was but one of them. "The four main interests of a nation are religion, reputation, peace and trade," theorized one revolutionary writer. While everything that Louis XIV did threatened the reputation, peace, and trade of England, there were no signs that faith played any consistent role in the French king's agenda. The nature of Louis XIV's ambition, coupled with the multiconfessional nature of the alliance against him, convinced this author that "the question now on foot is a communion of state, not of faith."[91]

There was, of course, a league of Protestant princes. But these allies were interested in preventing, not promoting, a war of religion. "Nor does it appear that the Protestant states, the English and Hollanders, either have or can have any prospect of conquest, nor any other interest than that of the public safety and the preservation of the liberty of Europe," wrote one pragmatic commentator. The memorial issued by the elector of Brandenburg "tends to prove," concurred another, "that the Union of Protestant Princes has in no wise for its scope a war of religion, as France would fain persuade the world, but that it only exerts the interests which they have in common with other Catholic Princes." The Protestant princes "rest satisfied with maintaining themselves in the possession of their rights, and their religion," the *Dilucidator* asserted. "Neither their genius nor their interests, prompt them to think of invading or oppressing the Catholic States; that on the contrary, in the war now depending, they support the common cause of the Emperor and the Pope, by maintaining the election and confirmation of the Prince of Bavaria, and in opposing the invasions of France, which cannot in this occasion cover itself with the pretense of religion, while that it is at daggers' drawn with the Holy See."[92]

Many English commentators argued that religious diversity was inevitable and that therefore international relations should be, and indeed were, organized around principles of interest. Alliance against France should be entered into "without having respect for the diversity of religions of which they make profession; neither ought any differences therein to stand in competition with their interest," posited one thinker, "since there have been and always will be diverse opinions amongst Christians concerning matters of religion, as there have also been heretofore amongst the Jews, whatsoever care may be taken to oblige all men to hold one and the same faith." "The difference of [religious] sentiments ought never to prevail against the common notions which the whole world is agreed upon," advised one Dutch writer serialized in England, "nor serve by consequence for cause, or pretext, for violating the natural or civil rights." The Whig Roger Morrice was convinced by his observations of contemporary politics that "those who have very opposite church interests, may come to a hearty conjunction as to the promoting of their civil interests." "His late

Majesty seems to have been the only Prince in Christendom who made it his great, and almost only design to advance the interests of the Church of Rome, without, and against his own temporal interest," the Tory Edmund Bohun came to understand. "The rest of the Princes and their council look in the first place to their own concerns at home and abroad, and make the affairs of religion subservient to their other designs."[93]

Europeans had not lost their profound religious beliefs in the seventeenth century, but most had ceased to call for wars of religion. The zeal of the early Reformation and Counter-Reformation had not been lost, but it had been tempered. The experience of almost two centuries of unending bloody and devastating religious wars made most Europeans more skeptical in analyzing crusading calls. They struggled to find a basis of political relationships that would avoid ineluctable and insoluble conflicts. Nationalism offered just such a solution. Goaded into action by Louis XIV's universalist political and cultural aspirations, many Europeans called for multiconfessional alliances based on mutual national interest to oppose the French European menace. Many in the English political nation, which had long hoped to enter the fray against France, embraced the revolution and the opportunity that it gave them. They did so because they understood their revolution and its consequences in nationalist terms.

England's later seventeenth-century revolution was a nationalist revolution. Europeans did not have to wait for the Industrial Revolution or events in France in the late eighteenth century to witness a mass political movement in defense of a bounded community sharing a public culture. The commercial nature of English society meant that information and ideas spread remarkably rapidly throughout the community, allowing English men and women from Preston to Dorchester, from Dartmouth to Newcastle, from London to Carlisle, to imagine themselves as sharing in common national characteristics.

It was precisely these cultural, political, and economic national characteristics that Gilbert Burnet, the postrevolutionary bishop of Salisbury, outlined in his *Exhortation to Peace and Union*, which was both preached and printed in November 1689. "We are Englishmen," he informed both his audience and his readership, "all of the same nation under the same laws, and the same protection." "Our climate it is true, is none of the best; we have but a faint sun, and the product of our soil cannot be compared with that of more Southern regions," he admitted, "but our ports and rivers give us such advantages, that we send out both colonies and manufactures all the world over, and fetch home rich returns; so that we have both security and wealth beyond any of our neighbors." What distinguished the English, Burnet was saying, was their industry, not their agriculture. They were a manufacturing nation. They were also a nation with a peculiarly felicitous form of government. "Oh! the difference between us and some happier climates where men's estates and liberties, and often their lives are at the mercy of mere humor and passion," Burnet gushed. There the people's "ruined houses, their ragged clothes, their hungry looks, and their half-naked children, give evident proofs of the tyranny of their governments that can render the people extremely miserable, in spite of all that abundance which nature has set before them, while millions of people are pining away in want and beggary, that so a few may surfeit themselves with all the excess of fullness and vice." It is for this reason that Burnet was sure the English "have the greatest blessing that can be found in government in as high degrees as wise men can desire." The English were intensely aware that they were a constructed nation—Burnet said they were really united only at "the beginning of this century"—and consequently emphasized their shared public culture rather than any racial traits. As a result, anyone could become English. "Whatever they are before," Carew Reynell testified, "when once they come here to be under our laws, customs and government, they are soon one with us."[94]

These shared national characteristics—cultural, economic, and political—had been profoundly threatened by the growing power of Louis XIV and by James II's adoption of French political style. It was not hatred of France but love of their own nation that so agitated English men and women. "I must tell you," exclaimed Sir Richard Cox, "it is not the eating of our beef or the consuming the English corn and taking, I mean, breathing an English air from one's infancy that makes a man an Englishman: it is the mind and principles and actions pursuant to such principles. My birth is where my Mother pleases, it is mere accidental but my settling my affection to this or that place or country is my own choice and judgment. I take him for an Englishman that is for securing our properties and maintaining the liberties of Europe against the French King . . . I take him for a Frenchman, a Papist, a foreigner or anything that being born here and enjoying the freedom of an Englishman can ever entertain thoughts of changing this present government or making any interest for the French King or our late tyrant." The Marquis of Halifax's Trimmer—easily one of the most influential political characters of the 1680s—"is far from idolatry in other things, in one thing only he cometh somewhat near it; his country is in some degree his idol: he doth not worship the sun, because it is not peculiar to us, it rambleth about the world and is less kind to us than it is to other countries; but the earth of England, though perhaps inferior to that of many places abroad, to him there is divinity in it, and he had rather die than see a spire of English grass trampled upon by a foreign trespasser." Halifax was certain that such was the cultural attachment of the English to their nation that "before the French blood can be let into our bodies, every drop of our own must be drawn out of them."[95]

This deep nationalist sensibility that was so profoundly challenged by the policies and actions of James II led the English to insist that ultimate political authority lay in the nation—though they disagreed whether the nation meant Parliament or the people more broadly defined. They claimed that their allegiance was to English liberty, English religion, and English law rather than to a particular king. And the English of all social classes took political action based on those beliefs. Those who were Whiggish in their outlook claimed a right to resist James II in defense of their nation. Unlike earlier Protestants who had resisted their governments, the English in 1688 did not claim to resist James because he was an ungodly king but because he was an un-English king. Others who were

Tory in political persuasion argued that James II had unkinged himself, had abdicated, by governing in a French rather than an English fashion. The Convention of 1689 merely registered that abdication. Both groups of men and women justified their actions with appeals to the nation.

It was precisely because the English recognized and valued national diversity in early modern Europe that they could insist that the desired war against France—a desire that was as much cause as consequence of the revolution—was not a religious war. The English supported the Holy Roman Emperor, the king of Spain, and the pope himself because they knew they were engaged in a desperate struggle to protect national integrities, including their own, against the aspiring universal monarch Louis XIV. Since different nations had different religious cultures, no nation had the right to impose its beliefs on others. Government propaganda and national sentiment were in full agreement: the age of religious wars was over. It was the interest of all European nations, whatever their confessional practices, to unite against France.

To say that there was a nationalist revolution in foreign policy, to say that there was a widespread popular desire for war against France long before William called for such a war, is not to say that there was a foreign policy consensus at the revolution. Whigs and moderate Tories, even some very conservative Tories, could agree that James II's foreign policy was disastrous while also disagreeing and disagreeing violently as to the contours and shape of James's error. Almost from the moment that James departed England in 1688, it became clear that Whigs and Tories had radically different preferences for the direction of postrevolutionary foreign policy. The Whigs were convinced that Louis XIV was a great and powerful enemy who could be stopped only by reversing his Continental expansion. For the Whigs Louis XIV and the spread of absolutism needed to be halted and turned back on the Continent. The Whigs were determined to protect European as well as English liberty. The Whigs, in short, were committed to understanding England as a European power. Tories agreed that Louis XIV needed to be fought. But in their view the primary goal was to contain Louis XIV's power within Continental Europe. England's future, they argued, lay in protecting the British Isles and expanding overseas. They therefore defended a blue-water policy devoted to containing the French and dominating the seas. The Tories, like many subsequent historians, saw the revolution in narrowly British terms. The goal of Williamite foreign policy must be, they thought, to protect the revolution in the British Isles and in England's overseas possessions. After 1690 and 1691 the Tories came to argue that English interests were best served by ending England's European commitments.[96]

For Williamite Tories the war was always about defending the regime change in the British Isles. The struggle on the Continent was a peripheral concern. So, for Tories like Colonel John Granville, it was clear that "of your enemies, your chiefest, [is] King James." Not surprisingly, given this assessment, Tories were always far more interested in the course of the struggle in Scotland and Ireland than in the European and extra-European war with Louis XIV. The reliable Tory Sir Thomas Clarges was typical in claiming that "if the King be not master of Ireland this Summer, we shall not hope to keep England long." This set of priorities explained why the Tories "could not bear" the long, detailed, and very Whiggish *Address* calling for war against France in April 1689. It was the Tories in the House of Commons, a group that the Dissenter and Whig Roger Morrice mischievously called "the French interest," that "set all their interest at work in the House of Commons to set aside that long address, and they did set it aside." In fact, the Tories in the house succeeded in having the printer of the *Address* questioned before the Commons. By midsummer it was clear to some Whigs that the opposition to the Grand Alliance stemmed from fears that the Continental war would "destroy the Tory interest in England." Several years later Daniel Defoe offered a polemical edge to what had become a clear point of party contention. The opponents of the Continental war that now "set up for patriots," Defoe charged, were "those very men who in former reigns, had sacrificed our religion and civil rights."[97]

Tories quickly seized on the immense cost of the war, the massive interruption in English trade, and the failings of England's European allies to make their case for a blue-water, as opposed to a Continental, war strategy. The Nine Years' War was in fact larger than any previous English military commitment. The army ballooned to almost double what it had been under James II, and the naval forces were much more numerous as well. In all, England had on average more than 115,000 men in arms during the Nine Years' War. The average military expenditure was almost £5.5 million, or about 74 percent of the annual state budget. The average annual tax revenue during the war was about twice what it had been before 1689. Numbers such as these made Tories and their political allies quick to insist that the country simply could not afford a massive Continental war. "If you make not an end of the war this year," insisted prominent Tory Sir John Trevor in November 1689, "I know not how we can supply another." "I do believe that we cannot supply the war above a year longer," chimed in the ancient and quirky William Garraway, who had again fallen in line with the Tories. The diehard Tory Sir Edward Seymour told the House of Commons that it was "mistaken" to believe that "England was in a condition to carry on the war for themselves and the confederates."[98]

One did not have to be a Tory to believe that the immense tax burden generated by the war was causing severe economic dislocation. On this point the West Country Whig Mary Clarke, who found "everyone complaining of scarcity of money," was of one mind with the Oxfordshire Tory Sir Edmund Warcup. "Our taxes are so great," he lamented, "that we want money for all other things." This growing sense of economic exhaustion soon augmented the Tory ranks. Old Tories like Sir Christopher Musgrave and Sir Thomas Clarges became more strident in their warnings about "the poverty of the nation," the taxes that were "so great that we can hardly live under them." True-blue Tories were soon joined by former Whigs whose assessment of the war and political economy caused them to abandon their party. The former Whig Paul Foley exclaimed that "never so much was paid to the navy and army" in November 1691. He advised the house that he could "not see any necessity for so many men." Sir John Thompson, the son of the midcentury radical Maurice Thompson, also began to drift toward the Tories because of concerns about the war's financial imperatives. "The poverty of the nation cannot come up to the greatness and firmness of our king's spirit," he explained almost apologetically.[99]

Tories also complained that the commitment to Continental war had deleterious effects on English foreign trade. Instead of protecting English merchant fleets, the government had committed its resources to raising Continental armies and preparing for set-piece naval battles. The results, they claimed, were disastrous. "The loss of trade and treasure by neglect of guarding the sea" contributed greatly, in the view of Sir Edward Seymour, to the "ill condition" of the nation. Seymour's fellow Tory Clarges chimed in that the "ill success of the government" in protecting trade was of dire consequences: "if trade be lost, land will fall." The Tories may have been quick to blame the decline of overseas trade on the government's war strategy, but they were not imagining things. Because of the war "no one" knows "how to steer or govern himself in any one maritime concern," observed the Whiggishly inclined Mediterranean merchants Barrington and Steele. "These times of war have cut off all intercourse by sea," agreed one of Sir William Trumbull's English informants. The French decision to attack English merchant shipping had dramatic effects. In 1690 it was said that more than a thousand English ships had been taken. By 1693 that number had grown to more than fifteen hundred, with the consequence that "many merchants, grocers, drapers, salesmen, mercers, milliners" were suffering and "many thousands have quite broke." One Levant merchant heard that already by the end of 1689 the English had lost "one quarter of our navigation." These estimates have been confirmed by recent scholarship that shows a 25 percent decline from prewar levels in England's trade with southern Europe, a 60 percent drop in reexports to northwestern Europe, and a massive decline in the trade with West Indies and North America.[100]

Tories increasingly complained of the conduct of England's allies in the Grand Alliance. In essence, Tories argued that England was footing the bill for Europe's war against Louis XIV. Many English people of all political stripes were in constant fear that one ally or another would succumb to French diplomatic seduction and sign a separate peace. Many also whined that the allies were not doing their part financially and militarily. But it was the Tories and their allies in Parliament who developed these concerns into a full-scale critique of Continental commitment. "Though we came into the war last yet we shall pay for all," fulminated Sir Thomas Clarges. "Our coming into the war was of more advantage to the confederates than it was to us," he explained. "The only way for you to oppose France is to strengthen yourself by sea." Clarges's increasingly reliable ally and passionate defender of the Tory Old East India Company Theodore Bathurst demanded pointedly that "we may know what sums of money have been sent to the Duke of Savoy, to the Dutch, and to the beggarly princes of Germany." Paul Foley asserted in the Commons that if the allies "had been unanimous to attack" Louis XIV "we might have brought him to our terms." The Tory secretary of state the Earl of Nottingham was more circumspect in his criticisms, but his correspondence makes clear his belief that had the allies only done their part, it would have led inexorably to "the establishment of a just and honorable peace." In this context, it is clear that Nottingham's advocacy of a descent on France in 1692 needs to be understood not as a commitment to European engagement but an attempt to use sea power to secure a quick peace and extricate England from European affairs. When the project of the descent failed to develop, in part because the Tories were unwilling to support a full-scale invasion, Tory leaders like the Earl of Rochester and Sir Edward Seymour recommended replacing commitments to support the allies in Flanders with increased support for the English navy.[101]

Tory assaults on the conduct of the allies not only presaged eighteenth-century Tory rhetoric, they also connected with prerevolution anti-Dutch arguments and with Jacobite accounts of the revolution itself. The Jacobites had been the first to understand the events of 1688–89 as a Dutch invasion conducted to further Dutch, not English interests. In making this claim they had drawn on the entire panoply of anti-Dutch arguments from the 1660s and 1670s. The Dutch, Jacobites argued, were interested only in seizing England's trade and impoverishing the country by making it pay for Dutch wars. The Tory Sir Edward Seymour quickly enunciated these same concerns in 1689. It was impossible, he said, "for Holland and England to be heartily united, they both courting the same mistress, trade." By 1690 Tory supporters of the revolution enunciated the same arguments in condemning the war effort. "The Hollanders adoring only profit, Mammon and trade (say some)," heard Robert Kirk in London's coffeehouses, taverns, and newly fashionable down-market eateries, "they will treat for their advantage with France or any common enemy and leave England in the lurch to defend itself or sink." The Tory opponents of the Continental war effort, agreed Daniel Defoe, argued that the Dutch were "more dangerous" than the French or the Turks because "of the strength of their shipping, and their rivalship with us in trade."[102]

For Tories, the remedy was increasingly clear: England should sever its Continental commitments and adopt a blue-water policy. Such a strategy, the Tories argued, would be much less expensive, would allow England to protect its trade, and would obviate the necessity of relying on untrustworthy and perfidious allies. Sir Thomas Clarges had long insisted that "the strength of England consists in our navy." In the 1690s he continued to defend a blue-water strategy in the war against France. By sending "all our force into Flanders," where Louis XIV was "irresistible," the only outcome would be to "ruin England." "The most natural way" for England to fight the war, Clarges suggested, was "by sea." The English should become "masters of America" rather than dominant in Europe. "As we are an island," he pointed out, "if the French have all the seventeen provinces [of the Dutch Republic and the Spanish Netherlands], and we are superior at sea, we may still be safe." England's "security," agreed Sir Edward Seymour, was "to be found only in the fleet." The new Tory ally Robert Harley agreed "that the sea must be our first care, or else we are all prisoners to our island." Sir Richard Temple, who was a committed Tory after 1689, believed passionately that "it imports this monarchy to have a vigorous militia at sea both for defense, offense and commerce." A land army, he thought, was unnecessary for England. Instead of alliances and conquests on the Continent, Temple argued, "the enlargement of trade and Dominion of the Sea ought to be the proper object of our Empire." Tory advocates of a blue-water strategy had coalesced around the notion "that England is not much concerned in the general fate of Europe," "that the sea which divides us from the rest of the world is our safeguard against all dangers from abroad," and "that when we engage in any foreign war, it is not so much for our preservation, as to make a show of our power."[103]

The Whigs, by contrast, advocated a foreign policy of Continental commitment. Whigs believed passionately that their revolution was not merely a British solution to a British problem. Instead they understood the revolution as part of a greater struggle to protect the liberty of Europe against French universalist aspirations and French-style absolutism. Whig Continental commitment was as much ideological opposition to the spread of absolutism as it was geopolitical opposition to French imperialism. So, whereas the Tories argued that James was England's chief enemy, Whigs like Thomas Papillon and John Maynard insisted that Louis XIV was the "great enemy" and that "King James is but his tool." Whereas Tories did everything in their power to tone down Francophobic rhetoric in early 1689, it was the Whigs John Somers and John Hampden who were most active in drafting the *Address* and the Declaration of War against France. Whigs almost invariably described the revolution and the war against France that followed it in European terms. "What were become of the liberty of Europe" had the Revolution not happened, asked the lifelong Whig Robert Molesworth rhetorically. The answer he knew was that "the Emperor and all the allies . . . must have set down quietly and submitted to the French yoke." It was because he focused on European liberty, rather than narrowly British concerns, that Molesworth "wished that thorn [of Ireland] were once out of our foot" so that the English could throw all of their energy behind "the common cause" in Europe. Sir John Lowther, who had come of political age as a supporter of the Earl of Shaftesbury and the Whigs during the Exclusion Crisis and had taken up arms against James II in 1688, was clear that he supported the war effort because it was "not only the concern of this nation but of all Europe." Sir William Dutton Colt, one of three active Whig brothers, made clear that he thought his role as envoy extraordinary from England to various German states was to make it possible for the Grand Alliance to "free Europe." The Gloucestershire Whig Sir Richard Cocks was a great supporter of the war "to preserve the liberties and properties of Europe against the monstrous, avaricious and barbarous tyranny of the French King." "The common liberty of Europe" rather than "the increase of dominions" was England's war aim, argued the West Country merchant and son and namesake of the Dorset Whig lawyer William Lawrence. William and the English, rhymed the flamboyant Whig Sir Charles Sedley, "ne're will consent to a treaty, / Till each neighboring crown / Have what's justly his own." When answering the question "why the English hate the French," it was hardly surprising that the Whiggish authors of the *Athenian Mercury* opined that "they don't care to be slaves themselves, nor to see any of their neighbors so, unless they have a mind to continue in their bondage."[104]

The Whigs were in no position to deny that the war was both costly and that it interrupted trade. But they maintained that the war was necessary whatever the cost. Sir John Lowther could not but admit the "extraordinary charge" of the war, but he pointed out that this was because England had never before gone to war "with so potent a prince as the French King." "I have always been of opinion that the French king is the most likely to trouble England," the ancient Whig William Sacheverell testified truthfully, "and I doubt not but gentlemen will give a million in trade" to support the war effort. The Gloucestershire Whig and former political exile Sir John Guise responded to Tory complaints about the cost of the war by insisting in November 1691 that "when I voted for the war against France, I was in earnest, and I have not abated since the war." "The taxes indeed fall heavy upon everybody," wrote Anne Pye, whose husband, Sir Robert Pye, had taken up arms in the parliamentary cause and again in the revolutionary cause in 1688, "but considering the slavery we are freed from, I wonder people complain." "We must do anything rather than be slaves to the French," argued succinctly the Whiggish absentee Barbados planter Edward Littleton.[105]

Whereas Tories advocated turning away from Europe—focusing exclusively on British and Atlantic concerns—Whigs warned that giving free rein to France on the Continent would have dire consequences for England. Again and again Whig polemicists outlined the domino effect that would be set off by the advance of French power. Each state or principality that fell under French sway would make the next target that much more vulnerable to French coercion or rough persuasion. The Spanish Netherlands, where much of the fighting in the Nine Years' War took place, was increasingly seen as the crux of the issue. Were France to gain control of this region, argued one pamphleteer, "she would have gained a considerable number of new soldiers, having more ports, more men of war, she would absolutely depose of the commerce of the world; and that her riches multiplying with her subjects, would open her way to an universal monarchy." In other words, "if the Low Countries are delivered up to the French, they will be in a position to give England the law." Should the Spanish Netherlands yield to French power, Daniel Defoe argued, then Holland "must necessarily truckle," since "they are like nine-pins, the throwing down one carries the rest." And "if France had no enemy but England," Defoe warned, "what could England hope for, but to be a field of blood." Were the English to abandon their Continental commitments, argued the Whig Sir George Treby in the House of Commons, "then you cannot possibly be defended with a standing army and a standing fleet too."[106]

Instead of a blue-water policy, Whigs advocated firm commitments to Continental alliances and a full-scale invasion of France. "Since France is in the bottom of all slavery," argued the radical Whig John Wildman, England had "need of all the confederates against King James and France." Sir John Lowther was a consistent advocate of "assisting your confederates against the common enemy, the French." Instead of allowing Louis XIV to break the Grand Alliance with bribes and peace offerings, Lowther thought England should "attack him vigorously, and that in his own country with a force sufficient." "The next Summer for France, / We will boldly advance," predicted the Whig Sir Charles Sedley in 1690. "We may justly dread the consequences of it, if by sea and land we do not oppose them with more vigor than ever," warned one Whiggish wartime critic of a blue-water strategy. More positively, another Whig suggested that England's aims should not be merely "to maintain the empire of the sea" but to have sufficient strength on the Continent "to decide the success of wars, and the conditions of treaties for the future."[107]

Immediately after the revolution William and his inner circle gave full support to the Whig position of Continental commitment. William's first diplomatic appointments were almost all committed to a Whiggish foreign policy. The new regime quickly "turned out all foreign ministers that served the last reign" and made it clear that the revolutionaries would be "backward to employ any that had commission from King James." The absolutists, Catholics, and crypto-Catholics that made up James II's diplomatic corps were replaced by committed Whigs. John Locke and John Hampden were offered diplomatic posts in 1689. Though they declined, both exerted influence over some aspects of the diplomatic corps. The first postrevolutionary ambassador to the United Provinces, Thomas Herbert, 7th Earl of Pembroke, had traveled abroad with Locke and had "weekly conferences" with him after the revolution. Pembroke's successor at The Hague was Viscount Dursley, whom Locke also counted as a "friend and former pupil." Dursley, who also had a close friendship with the Whig Earl of Shrewsbury, helped imbue his son and heir James with "staunch Whig" principles. It was on John Hampden's "recommendation" that the Whig Thomas Coxe was sent as envoy to the Swiss cantons. Coxe had been an exile in Utrecht during the reign of James II and was a friend of both the midcentury radical Edmund Ludlow and the radical Whig James Vernon. Gilbert Burnet's cousin James Johnston, who had provided William with vital intelligence in 1687 and 1688, was appointed England's envoy extraordinary to the elector of Brandenburg. There, Johnston proved a staunch defender of the Whig principle that England must remained committed to the "confederacy" because in the case of France "the public quiet can be no longer secured by the faith of treaties"; indeed, "a firm peace is only to be obtained by a thorough war." Sir William Dutton Colt, who was sent envoy extraordinary to various German states, including Hanover, in 1689, came from a radical Whig Herefordshire family. William's first envoy in Vienna was the radical Whig William, Lord Paget, who had shuttled back and forth to the United Provinces during the reign of James II and been quick to join the revolutionaries in 1688. Robert Molesworth, who would come to define radical Whiggery and had taken up arms in support of William in 1688, was made the new regime's first envoy to Denmark. One of the few holdovers from James II's diplomatic corps was Sir William Trumbull, whose pathological Francophobia had earned his recall from Paris and deployment in the harmless post of ambassador to the Ottoman Empire before the revolution. Afterward, it was thought, he would do his utmost to sever the close ties between France and the Ottomans and further the cause of the Continental war.[108] With few exceptions, the overall character of the postrevolutionary diplomatic corps was extremely Whiggish.

Given this ideological outlook, England's diplomats understandably grew concerned as the direction of policy making in England took a decidedly Tory turn from 1690 to 1693. It looked initially to many Whigs as if the high Tory blue-water views of Sir Edward Seymour and Sir Thomas Clarges carried little weight with the Commons or the ministry. But those in the diplomatic corps were not long deceived. From their various posts in Europe, they complained vociferously that English lack of commitment to the Continental cause was costing them dearly. In letter after letter the Whig and Whig-inclined diplomats reported that the English were being outmaneuvered and outspent by the French, who were unambiguously committed to winning the war on the Continent. French endeavors were seducing German princelings one at a time with caresses of various sorts. Louis XIV's agents "court and flatter" the Swiss cantons while "we neglect and say nothing them," complained Thomas Coxe. "The consequences," he lamented, are "easily guessed at." Only a dedication to military victory against France and a commitment to buying "off the ministers which is the best purchase that can be made" would have any effect in Sweden, predicted William Duncombe and Viscount Dursley. England's failure on both counts meant that almost "all the ministers of Sweden were sold to France." Despite the high priority the Whiggish diplomats placed on convincing the Ottomans to come to terms with the Holy Roman Emperor, in Istanbul, too, it soon became clear that French commitments, French promises, and French bluster was keeping the sultan in the war. In the Dutch Republic the marquis de Louvois was able briefly to control the news being distributed to the country's many gazetteers, while other forces were at work—albeit unsuccessfully—to persuade "underhand for a separate peace." The French apparently used similar tactics to much greater effect in North Africa.[109]

While the postrevolutionary Whig diplomats were never slow to denounce the unsavory tactics of their enemies, they were equally quick to contrast French commitment and French resources with English ambivalence and English parsimony. Viscount Dursley was one of the first to sound the alarm. He was thoroughly "convinced that we can not be strong enough to resist France alone." In order to "keep our allies steady" in the face of frequent French temptations "with money to buy them off from us," the English, especially in the House of Commons, needed to signal their complete devotion to the common cause. They needed to demonstrate their Continental commitment. This commitment, Dursley hinted to an unsympathetic Carmarthen, was not consistent with support for a blue-water strategy. Perhaps, Dursley suggested, "I may not be unserviceable to His Majesty by making appear especially to members of Parliament" how "absolutely necessary" it was to support the common cause. "France," Robert Molesworth complained, "does his business much more vigorously and effectually than we." Molesworth's growing frustration with the foreign policy ineptitude of England's increasingly Tory-leaning ministers was of a piece with the feelings of his fellow Whig diplomats. After England's naval defeat at Beachy Head in June 1690, Molesworth warned that "if some people's heads do not fly now, no foreign prince or state will believe there is a King or Queen in England." The problem, Molesworth and his diplomatic friends knew, was that they had "little encouragement" from the blue-water advocates then at the helm in England. English inaction, English indifference, and English failure to demonstrate a commitment to the war on the Continent were all having a deleterious effect on the Grand Alliance. "We have made a fine shift with labor and great pain to lose all our friends on this and your side the world," Molesworth wrote to the sympathetic Sir William Dutton Colt. The weakening of confederate resolve, Molesworth insisted, was not the result of "ill fortune" but of English—and implicitly Tory—inaction. After the fall of Mons in the Spanish Netherlands to the French in the spring of 1691, Molesworth shared with modern scholars the belief that English indecisiveness had been at least partly to blame. England needed to commit itself fully to the war on the Continent, the Whig diplomats all believed. "'Tis more than time something were done to show we can be brisk and that the English courage is not quite enervated," Molesworth exclaimed.[110]

Whig frustration with Tory blue-water foreign policy provides the context for the publication of Molesworth's spectacularly successful *Account of Denmark*. After taking up arms on the side of the revolutionaries in 1688, Molesworth had been posted to Denmark at the moment of the revolution. He had witnessed firsthand that Protestant monarchy's slow drift from active membership in the Grand Alliance into the French sphere of influence. He had come to understand through the cut and thrust of diplomatic correspondence that William's turn toward Tory ministers after 1689 increasingly implied, despite William's own wishes, a withdrawal from European commitment. After his return to England in 1692 Molesworth distilled his arguments for Continental commitment and his understanding of the trends of modern European politics. In late 1693—perhaps at the moment that the Earl of Nottingham fell from power—he sensed that it was time to shift the tone of the public debate. Molesworth elegantly, trenchantly, and dramatically expressed the concerns of the Whig diplomatic corps, Whig politicians, and Whig sympathizers that the Tory foreign policy of 1690–93 would have disastrous results. He made a passionate plea for a return to full-scale Continental commitment.

The *Account of Denmark* was a runaway best-seller from the moment it appeared in late 1693. According to Molesworth's publisher, the very Whiggish Timothy Goodwin, the tract went through "three large editions" in "less than three months." The book sold at the astonishing rate of almost a thousand copies per week in late 1693, with more than six thousand copies having been sold in the first three months. Anthony Wood was being cautious when he stated that the book "hath made a great noise in London." By 1700 at least thirteen editions of Molesworth's *Account* had been published in French, Dutch, and German, as well as English. The pamphlet also spawned a variety of virulent attacks in English, Dutch, French, and German—some of them sponsored by the Danish government. Not surprisingly, the Danish envoy in London, Mogens Skeel, quickly protested against the "extreme malignity and bad faith" of the book. Molesworth's *Account* was soon the talk of diplomats all over Europe.[111]

That the *Account* attracted so much international attention makes it unlikely that it was a work designed for British audiences about narrowly British issues. Nevertheless, that is how Molesworth's *Account* has long been understood in an Anglo-American historical tradition that has insisted on English insularity. According to the historian Caroline Robbins in her influential classic *The Eighteenth-Century Commonwealthman*, Molesworth's book "was at least as much an attack on the short-comings of the English as those of the Danish government." As such Molesworth was part of a group of "Real Whigs" who "worked for a federal system in the British Isles, an amendment of Parliament, a diminution of ministerial prerogative, an increased toleration, and some modification of mercantilist regulation." Neither they nor their agenda, unfortunately, ever "received support or encouragement from Whigs in office." Molesworth was, in this view, a radical opposition figure. The diplomatic historian D. B. Horn agrees that Molesworth's "attention was more directed to the British Isles than to Denmark." "The somewhat tactless diplomat wanted," according to Knud Jespersen, "to impress upon his compatriots the terrible misfortunes resulting from free people giving up their right to self-determination and entrusting an absolutist regime with all political power."[112]

In fact, Molesworth's dynamic and influential tract attracted so much interest both in England and on the Continent because it was part of a desperate attempt by Whigs to regain the initiative in English foreign policy. Molesworth insisted on the continuing ideological importance of the Grand Alliance in the great struggle for European liberty. Molesworth, in other words, was denouncing Tory blue-water foreign policy and demanding, as he later recalled, a return to a foreign policy based on "Whiggish principles." He was reaffirming mainstream Whig principles, shared by those who would be returning to power in 1694. He was not, he insisted, attacking the Whigs or William III. How some had come to believe that he had done so, Molesworth scoffed, "I cannot possibly imagine."[113]

Molesworth published his *Account of Denmark* to revive English enthusiasm for the Continental struggle in defense of European liberty. "Through the encouragement and design of our late rulers," he reminded his readers, England had for "too long" failed to oppose "our formidable neighbor and enemy," the king of France. Since the revolution, however, "we make a greater figure in the world than formerly." This was, he explained, advancing the central tenet of Whig foreign policy, because "we have more foreign alliances," and instead of promoting traditional confessional politics, the English "are become the head of more than a Protestant league." The English now had "a right to intermeddle in the affairs of Europe beyond what we ever pretended to in any of the preceding reigns."[114] Molesworth was calling on his fellow patriots to act on that right.

The kingdom of Denmark provided a case study in the pernicious effects of French political ideology. Before 1660 the Danes had shared in the benefits of the Gothic constitution that had once prevailed "in most, if not all parts of Europe." It was to the Goths, according to Molesworth, that Europe owed "the original of Parliaments," with "frequent meetings" in which "all matter relating to good government were transacted," the right to elect their kings, and the right to depose "cruel, vicious, tyrannical, covetous, or wasteful" rulers. Then, "at one instant the whole face of affairs was changed" in Denmark, and the kings became "absolute and arbitrary" with "not the least remnant of liberty remaining to the subject." Denmark's turn to absolutism was not unique. "The King of Denmark," like many monarchs in Europe, explained Molesworth, had become "a pupil" of Louis XIV. Following what "is practiced in France," the Danish kings assumed the power of disposing all estates at the owners' death. To augment their armies, Danish kings, always imitating "the French king's practice," sought "to make the gentry poor and render traffic unprofitable or dishonorable." Once in the army, "the gentlemen and officers go very fine in their dress after the French mode." The outward consequence of this new French-style absolutism was that the Danes "affect French modes, French servants, and French officers in the army."[115]

Along with French-style absolutism came a French political alliance. "The King of Denmark," lamented Molesworth, "loves the alliance of France, and keeps a stricter correspondence with that crown than with any other." The French ambassador in Copenhagen, he recalled, "was favored by the King of Denmark and his whole court." In his diplomatic correspondence Molesworth had complained that the Danes were "French in their hearts" and that they did "heartily wish" for a Jacobite restoration.[116]

The implications of this analysis for England were profound. Danish friendship for France was not just an elective affinity, it was the structural consequence of absolutist policies. The turn to absolutism in Denmark, as was the case everywhere else, necessitated "frequent and arbitrary taxes" to support the enlarged military machine. This in turn impoverished the country. "The value of estates in most parts of the kingdom is fallen three fourths." More generally, the policies of the Danish kings had caused "poverty in the gentry, which necessarily causes extremity of misery in the peasants," which, Molesworth pointed out, was "the constant effects of arbitrary rule in this and all other countries where it has prevailed." This grinding poverty, the inevitable result of absolutist politics, necessarily created instability in international politics. Those states "that consider soldiers as the only riches, never cease enlarging their number, till they are necessitated for their subsistence, either to come to blows with their neighbors, or to create animosities between others" that would necessitate employing their forces as mercenaries. Absolutism bred endless arms races. No leader dared risk disarmament for fear that his neighbors were only waiting "for an opportunity to fall upon him that is worst provided to make resistance." This, Molesworth concluded, was "none of the least calamities which the French tyranny has forced upon the world."[117] His analysis generated a clear imperative for English foreign policy. The only way to stop the spread of economic depredation and unending warfare was to block the spread of French absolutism. This implied, at a minimum, constant vigilance and involvement in Europe or, most likely, a full-scale invasion of France.

Molesworth's analysis made it clear that the age of confessional warfare had ended.

The threat to the welfare of Europe was absolutism, not Roman Catholicism. Denmark, Molesworth, reminded his readers, was a Protestant country. "Whoever takes the pains to visit the Protestant countries abroad," he observed, "will be convinced that it is not Popery as such, but the doctrine of blind obedience in what religion soever it be found, that is the destruction of the liberty, and consequently of the happiness of any nation." The spread of "slavery" in "most of the Protestant as well as Popish countries," Molesworth argued, was because "the spirits of the people" had been weakened by clergy who preached "that subjects should obey without reserve." This pernicious doctrine was the inevitable consequence of having priests "who depend upon the prince" for their livelihood. The problem was not priests, but priests who depended on the absolutist state. The danger came not from the spread of the Catholic or Lutheran reformation but from the growing power of absolutist states. "I wish every Englishman would read the *Account of Denmark*," wrote the Lancashire Whig William Phillips to the Somerset Whig Edward Clarke, for then "they'll find a slave is the same thing be he a Papist or a Protestant."[118]

Molesworth's was not a lone voice crying out in the wilderness. Molesworth was not expressing the views of a disenchanted commonwealth opposition. His *Account* was merely the most sophisticated voice in a chorus of Whig complaints about the Tory direction of English foreign policy. Indeed, the *Account* was published just as the House of Commons was engaged in a vitriolic party debate on English foreign policy. Many of the arguments Molesworth developed in his analysis of Denmark were found in the works of others advocating a policy of Continental commitment.

In 1693 and 1694 Whigs were complaining with one voice of the spread of absolutism on the Continent. Samuel Johnson described the similar absolutist policies being pursued in Sweden, Denmark, Hungary, and France. "We see what Spanish Parliaments, what French Parliaments are come to," warned John Smith, who would soon serve the Whig Junto in the treasury. "Sweden," he continued, "since then, and Denmark by trusting their power with their kings, upon their most urgent occasions, are now slaves for their pains." The Whig lord chief baron of the exchequer Sir Robert Atkyns pointed that Louis XIV "doth endeavor to make all other princes seek to be absolute and arbitrary, too, in their dominions."[119]

Molesworth was not the only Whig to point out that modern absolutism could be found in Protestant as well as Catholic countries. In 1692 William Duncombe, the English envoy to Sweden, presented his own account in parallel with Molesworth's. He, too, lamented the decline of the Gothic constitution in a northern kingdom. Charles XI "has enlarged his own authority and the forces of his kingdom beyond any of his predecessors." These ends were achieved by "the ruin of the nobility and gentry of Sweden, together with the loss of that liberty formerly enjoyed by the subject and the share they had in the administration of the government." As in Denmark, France, and elsewhere, the effect of all this was "a general poverty and as general a discontent and an earnest longing to be delivered." Though Sweden had originally taken the lead in the war against France, since then it had "obstinately adhered to its own neutrality, and with great care prevented all endeavors used to engage it in the common cause." This was hardly surprising, since along with French absolutism came French political influence. Indeed, it was "not easy to find one man in Sweden" trained in the arts of diplomacy and affairs of state "who is not already in the French interest." Although Duncombe's report was not printed in the 1680s, the assessment of his secretary and successor, John Robinson, was. Robinson's *Account,* published by Molesworth's printer, Timothy Goodwin, also highlighted the transformation of the Swedish government in 1680 that "lay the foundations of as absolute a sovereignty, as any Prince in Europe possesses." Robinson, like Molesworth, emphasized the role of the Lutheran clergy—which he elsewhere castigated for their intolerance—in persuading the Swedish people among whom "the priests have a very great and uncontrollable interest" to accept the new absolutist regime.[120]

Molesworth was also not the only Whig to argue that absolutism demanded militarization and unending warfare. Whigs pointed out that the inevitable consequence of absolutism was the impoverishment of the people. In France, for example, the people "were so miserably harassed, ransacked, and oppressed" that it would "require a pen of iron dipped in blood to describe it." "No absolute monarch," agreed the Low Church bishop William Lloyd, "likes that his subjects should grow rich by trade." This poverty created a double imperative for warfare. First, impoverished absolutist states needed to gain wealth to feed their insatiable war machines. "The care that is taken to form it to slavery" required that the absolutist state engage in "frequent wars abroad." Second, the widespread misery of absolutist subjects, particularly in France, required the destruction of other polities so "that the slaves of France might not understand that there was a milder government in the world than the tyranny of their master."[121]

It was this sort of analysis that convinced so many Whigs in 1693 and 1694 to argue vociferously against Tory blue-water policy. There were, admitted one Whig pamphleteer, "many" who maintained that "we being an island should mind nothing but our fleet." Such a view was, however, myopic. If "we neglect our confederates and suffer them to be ruined, we must be ruined ourselves." France would gradually conquer each confederate, "and then, whoever is King of England, we shall be in the French King's power." Again and again Whigs reaffirmed their Continental commitment in the debates of 1693 and 1694. Again and again they argued, as Molesworth had, for continued support of the allies against French encroachments. Oliver Cromwell, Charles II, and James II had "neglected Europe" to their cost, warned the Whig Sir John Darrell. "Either we must be at the charge to pull down this vigorous monarch or not," he blustered. If England abandoned the confederates, the Whig Sir Thomas Littleton predicted, "the French King will be quickly full of money, and over-run us all." "If Holland be destroyed, it is our turn next," chimed in Sir Charles Sedley. "We cannot be safe without an army; neither safe at home nor considerable abroad." Richard Savage, Lord Colchester, was succinct and predictably Whiggish: "If you do not increase your forces, the honor of England will be lost."[122]

Most Tories responded to the renewed challenge from the Whigs in general, and from Molesworth in particular, by reasserting their advocacy of a blue-water strategy, but those polemicists who engaged with Molesworth directly tried to marginalize his arguments by accusing him of republican extremism. They claimed that instead of describing disturbing developments on the contemporary European political landscape, Molesworth was merely rehearsing well-worn classical tropes. The arguments of the tract, asserted William King, who would soon associate closely with the Tory circles surrounding Princess Anne, "savor very much of a commonwealth."[123] Faced with a wildly successful pamphlet, Tories responded by denouncing their opponent as an extremist. It is a measure of their polemical success that scholars have persistently misread Molesworth's *Account* as the contribution of an eloquent but politically marginal defender of classical values rather than as a mainstream Whig intervention in the party controversy over modern English foreign policy of the 1690s.

From the moment that James departed England, the English with an almost-united voice called for war against France. The majority of English men and women believed that James II had not followed the national interest in pursuing alliance with France and war with the Dutch. Few called for a renewal of sixteenth- and early-seventeenth-century confessional strife. However, it would be a mistake to assume that though there was widespread enthusiasm for war, there was a popular consensus. Instead, from 1689 there were two distinct visions of the proper nature of English foreign policy. Both sides deployed passionate nationalist arguments. Tories argued that it was in the national interest to pursue a blue-water foreign policy. Louis XIV needed to be fought only so long as he posed a real and immediate threat to the British Isles and could plausibly undo the events of 1688–89. England had no interest in financing a Continental war against France that would merely benefit the weak and unreliable confederates. For the advocates of blue-water policy, England's future lay in an overseas empire, not in European engagement. Whigs, by contrast, argued that England needed to be strong both at sea and on land. The French threat was ideological as well as geopolitical. England could be safe only when European liberty was secure. As long as states continued to be seduced or compelled to adopt the absolutist political model, Europe and England would be dragged into a hopeless spiral of massive military expenditures and unending warfare. It was not enough to defend the British Isles; England needed to humble France and thereby halt the spread of absolutism.

The revolutionaries of 1688–89 radically transformed the shape and direction of English foreign policy. The revolutionaries of 1688–89 aimed to transform the orientation of England's foreign policy. This was not an unintended consequence but a central aim of the revolutionaries. The English people demanded war with France in 1689. This was not a policy imposed on them by William of Orange. This was because from the middle of the seventeenth century English men and women throughout the country had been engaged in a lively and exciting debate about England's proper role in European affairs. While many committed Anglicans and Tories had argued passionately that the Dutch were England's natural enemies because of their pernicious republicanism and their unbridled materialism, Louis XIV's political and military achievements in the 1660s, 1670s, and 1680s convinced most people in England that France represented a greater threat. France was far more likely to gain a universal monarchy based on Continental hegemony than the Dutch were to gain universal dominion through commercial monopoly. From the late 1670s most English men and women from all ranks of society anxiously looked forward to a war against France that would, at the least, make England the arbiter of the European balance of power.

James II, however, understood England's interest and European politics differently from the majority of his subjects. He believed that England's future lay as an imperial power that would control the seas. James wanted to make England into a modern commercial empire. France, which in James's view was fundamentally a land power, posed a far smaller threat than the Dutch, who already controlled vast areas in the East and West Indies. And of course, James shared with Louis XIV a commitment to Gallican-style Catholicism. It was for this reason that James cast in his lot with Louis XIV and was inching increasingly toward war with the United Provinces. James was not blindly following his religious passions and sacrificing his country's secular interests. He was pursuing a sophisticated and plausible strategy to make England into a modern power of the first class.

James's foreign policy infuriated large segments of the political nation. It was because they believed that James was "wholly devoted" to his alliance with France, explained one pamphleteer, that "the English have found themselves constrained to prevent their following into the same predicament their neighbors were in." The revolutionaries freed themselves to "deliver all Europe also from the slavery in which it was going to fall." Fears of a French alliance, wrote the Tory-leaning Anglican William Sherlock, "did as much as anything to alienate the minds of his late Majesty's subjects and gave as great a blow to his affairs as the Dutch army." There would have been no revolution, asserted another, if James II "had only constrained the French King to disband his armies, or to employ them in delivering the Turks out of Europe." In an account directed at the former king himself, another writer told James that, having "allied yourself with the French nation, our old and inveterate enemies . . . you have forsaken and abandoned the ancient interest of England," so "we have also abandoned and left you." One newsletter writer insisted that James "has lost all" by "following [Louis XIV's] measures and espousing his interest." The Whig James Wellwood thought that had James sought to provide for "the common safety of Europe," he "would have preserved the crown upon his head." Sir William Trumbull later recalled that he had warned James that his friendship with France would lead to "his certain ruin." "If your Majesty had put a stop by your force and authority" to the rapid augmentation of French power, wrote the Holy Roman Emperor Leopold I, then "by this means you should have in great measure quieted the minds of your people." This was the view of the

French as well. Usson de Bonrepaus was certain that the English "would give James all the money that he wished without restrictions, if he would only declare war against France." As James's regime was collapsing around him in late October 1688, he confided to Paul Barillon that he would never abandon France, even though "he knew well it would be his ruin and his destruction."[124]

The revolutionaries of 1688–89 were not narrowly concerned about "the succession," about the constitution, or about advancing an early Protestant worldview.[125] Instead, the revolutionaries had much more sweeping, more general, and more modern aims. Like more recent revolutionaries, those who overthrew James II in 1688–89 were desperately concerned with their nation's diminishing world standing. They were furious that James appeared to be appeasing the aspiring world hegemon Louis XIV. One of their chief aims was to reverse the foreign policy of Charles II and James II and instead align with the Dutch against the growing French power. They were certain that in doing so they were pursuing England's national interest. They believed that they were deposing a king who was pursuing a foreign rather than a national interest.

Nevertheless, even those who knew that James had sacrificed the nation to France, disagreed and disagreed fundamentally about the proper way of combating France. Nationalism did not necessitate consensus. Patriots could, and did, disagree. Tories shared with James the conviction that England's future was as an Atlantic, not Continental power. War was necessary to emancipate the British Isles from French influence. But there was no need to intervene in Continental affairs. Tories were committed to a blue-water policy. Whigs, by contrast, were convinced that the only way to halt French universalism was to reverse the slide of European states toward absolutism. Whigs believed that the revolution was the first step toward regaining European liberty. As a result, they argued, France needed to be fought both on land and on the seas.

Whigs and Tories alike knew and knew well that James II's commitment to re-Catholicize England had thrown him into the arms of Louis XIV. James's belief in a French-style Catholicism and his admiration for Louis XIV's Catholic absolute monarchy made the two kings natural allies. In that sense religion did play a vital role in the revolution in foreign policy. However, all but a tiny minority of English men and women were opposed to initiating a new war of religion. They had learned in the last age that wars of religion were devastating and ultimately unwinnable. They were also keenly aware that Europe was no longer divided into two neat confessional camps. The pope and the king of France were bitter enemies. Lutherans and Calvinists despised one another in northern Europe. The alternative to a Catholic foreign policy, they knew, was not a Protestant foreign policy. Instead, the English entered into, and were happy to enter into, a multiconfessional alliance against the imperialism of Louis XIV. Both Whigs and Tories understood their foreign policy commitments in modern, national terms.

CHAPTER TWELVE

Revolution in Political Economy

W hat greater demonstration can the world require concerning the excellence of our national government, or the particular power and freedom of this city, than the Bank of England," gushed one later seventeenth-century Englishman. This new institution, this bedrock of the so-called Financial Revolution, was so much to be lauded because it, "like the Temple of Saturn among the Romans, is esteemed so sacred a repository, that even foreigners think their treasure more safely lodged there than with themselves at home; and this not only done by the subjects of absolute princes, where there can be no room for any public credit, but likewise by the inhabitants of those Commonwealths where alone such banks were hitherto reputed secure." For the Whig John Toland the creation of the bank marked England's emergence as a modern economic powerhouse. This emergence, Toland implied, was possible only after the English had radically transformed their polity and adjusted their attitudes toward their own economy. The Bank of England was a consequence of a prior revolution in political economy, a transformation that Toland hinted was central to the agenda of the revolutionaries of 1688–89.[1]

Toland's celebration of the bank, suggesting that such an institution was possible and desirable only after the events of 1688–89 had altered England's political arrangements, raises a number of questions about the relation between political economy and the Revolution of 1688–89. Was there a revolution in political economy in 1688–89? If so,

(above) *Louis XIV: Indian Trade Molested,* by Thomas Bernard, 1695. Debates about trade and empire were central to English politics in the late seventeenth century. This medal depicts French privateering in the Indian trade during the Nine Years' War.

what had been the contours of the debate before the accession of William and Mary in 1689? What was the ideological, as opposed to the narrowly political, background to the establishment of the Bank of England? What was the relation between party politics and the Financial Revolution?

Most humanists, following the influential account of the relation between political economy and the Glorious Revolution developed by John Pocock, argue that the vast majority in England lacked the conceptual tools to argue for political economic innovation. For Pocock, commercial society, "the assertion of the commercial order," was not "a crucial issue in English ideological debate" at the time of the Glorious Revolution. Indeed, the truly revolutionary consequences of 1688–89—the reorganization of "military, financial, and political structures in order to achieve effective participation in continental and imperial warfare"—were "not fully foreseen or desired by those who invited" William to England. It was because William imposed these changes from outside that he is to be seen as "a revolutionary actor in the history of the British monarchy." The Financial Revolution, then, was the result of foreign imposition rather than domestic ideological debate. It was at best an unintended, at worst an undesired, consequence of the events of 1688–89. The English, it turns out, deployed well-worn ideological tools to criticize this foreign imposition. In this interpretation of the relation between political economy and the Revolution of 1688–89, the English turned almost unanimously against the new capitalist institutions of the 1690s. Indeed, in Pocock's view, whatever the differences between the defenders of the Financial Revolution and their critics, "all Augustan analysts of political economy accept the interdependence of land, trade and credit"; both Whigs and Tories "share not only the same reading of the economic facts, but the same underlying value system, in which the only material foundation for civic virtue and moral personality is taken to be independence and real property." All groups in the English political nation shared the same economic assumptions. All held what would later be called mercantilist assumptions. In other words, they all believed that property was necessarily finite and defined by landed property. Trade was merely the exchange of the products of the land. In such a world, landed property was necessarily the basis for political power.[2]

Those few historians—and they are very few—who have ventured into the terrain of political economic thought of the 1690s have largely agreed that instead of a revolutionary demand for modern financial institutions, there was an ideological consensus against their creation in the period. "In the main," notes P. G. M. Dickson in his account of the institutional transformations of the 1690s, "public reactions to the Financial Revolution were as hostile as they were later to be to the Industrial Revolution." John Brewer has similarly argued that a revolution in political economy was no part of the agenda of the English revolutionaries of 1688–89. Almost no one "envisaged the transformation that the wars would wreak upon the nation's institutions." There was no ideological drive by the English to create the Bank of England; rather, it "was established"—passive voice— "after a bitter political battle, in 1694." Given this profound consensus, there could be no ideological explanations for the Financial Revolution. A radical reorientation of England's political economy could be no part of the revolutionaries' agenda in 1688–89.[3]

In the social sciences, by contrast, many have followed Douglass North and Barry Weingast in arguing that a very modern capitalist consensus emerged in England in the wake of the Glorious Revolution. In contradistinction to the anticapitalist consensus posited by humanists, Weingast and North posit that the Revolution of 1688–89 created a new ideological climate favorable to capitalism and hostile to state intervention in the economy. In 1688–89, they claim, a coalition of interests came together to solve England's "financial problems" and provide "appropriate constraints on the crown." The revolution, elaborates Weingast, ended many of the old arguments dividing Whigs and Tories and "created a consensus about many disputed issues," a consensus that was "codified through various constitutional changes." The revolution, in essence, established "an elite pact." In particular, North and Weingast suggest, the pact ushered in three institutional changes: parliamentary supremacy, Parliament's "central role in financial matters," and the curtailing and subordination of the Crown's prerogative powers. All of these changes were durable because the revolution had "established a credible threat to the crown regarding future irresponsible behavior." So whereas in Pocock's view the Revolution of 1688–89 had given the state newfound power to create capitalist institutions against which English thinkers reacted, in the view of North and Weingast the revolution had effectively created political institutions "that limit economic intervention and allow private rights and markets to prevail in large segments of the economy." The new institutions acted to limit mercurial governmental interventions in the economy and "significantly raised the predictability of government." In so doing the revolution had created the conditions by which eighteenth-century Britain "was on the verge of the Industrial Revolution" while its main Continental rival, France, teetered "on the verge of bankruptcy." North and Weingast have effectively mapped Whig political history onto an account of economic transformation.[4]

Against these views—the first that the Revolution of 1688–89 created an intellectual consensus against capitalism; the second that the revolution was brought about by a political consensus in favor of unbridled accumulation—I suggest that there was a revolution in political economy in 1688–89. But, I insist, the radical transformation was the consequence of a widespread and heavily politicized argument between two rival modern economic programs. There was no consensus for or against capitalism. Although the English agreed that theirs was a trading society, they disagreed vociferously over whether England should commit itself to a policy of territorial acquisition or to becoming a manufacturing society. This debate, which became increasingly associated with the Tory and Whig parties in the late 1670s and 1680s, began long before the revolution and continued long after it. The creation of the Bank of England and the institutions of the Financial Revolution were neither imposed by external Dutch forces nor resulted from a pact among the English political elite. Instead, the Bank of England was a Whig creation against Tory resistance. Humanists have missed the theoretical richness and subtlety of this debate over political economy because they have chosen to focus on "imaginative literature" and on "the ground of intellectual history" rather than on the economic practices and programs of merchants and politicians.[5] Social scientists have not seen the deep ideological divisions that made political consensus impossible in the 1690s because they have chosen to analyze measurable economic behavior rather than the mass of ephemeral writings on political economy or on the evidence of party political activity. By focusing attention on commercial debates and political actions both before and after 1688–89, I will show how central political economic issues were to the causes and consequences of the revolution. The events of 1688–89 produced neither ideological nor political consensus. Instead, there was a fierce debate between a land-based Tory political economy and labor-centered Whig one. Just as both Tories and Whigs were committed to war against France, so both sides desperately wanted the state to intervene in the economy. Neither Tory nor Whig campaigned for state noninterference. Instead, both Tories and Whigs wanted the postrevolutionary state to deploy its resources in support of their economic program.

Since at least the 1650s, English radicals had embraced the possibilities of commercial society. Marchamont Nedham, Slingsby Bethel, Henry Robinson, and Benjamin Worsley among others were all men deeply invested in the radical politics of the Commonwealth and critical in a variety of ways of the Protectorate. All of them defended two propositions. First, they argued that property was primarily a human creation, not a natural endowment. Second, they claimed that a national bank would play a vital and constructive role in promoting national prosperity and in providing a bulwark to national security.[6] Although the bank they hoped for was not established in the 1650s, the economic ideas of these writers were remembered and deeply influential after the Restoration. Many of these same writers, joined by a variety of younger pamphleteers, politicians, and merchants, reiterated their ideas and proposals throughout the 1660s, 1670s, and 1680s.

One of the most eloquent and well-developed defenses of commercial political economy was offered in 1685 by Carew Reynell. Although Reynell did not explicitly announce his party preferences, his pronouncements were decidedly Whiggish. He was clearly no friend of absolutism. "And if his Majesty desires to advance his empire," Reynell advised, "it is but granting more privileges to trade, and security to men's persons and properties from arbitrary power and control than his fellow princes; and he shall not fail to draw to him all the hands, hearts and purses of the neighbouring nations." Reynell's political beliefs were determined by his economic convictions. And the touchstone of his economic thought was that "England is properly a nation of trade."[7]

Reynell believed along with almost everyone in the later seventeenth century that "trade and populousness of a nation are the strength of it." However, the basis of that strength, of trade and populousness, according to Reynell, was labor rather than land, manufacturing rather than raw materials. "It is the manufacturers of a commodity that is in general sale, that employs people and produces the great profit," he explained, "although the original materials are not in the country, as silks for example, the making of which employs abundance of people, and with them brings in other things by exportation." "It is manufactures must do the work," he enthused, "which will not only increase people, but also trade and advance it. It saves likewise money in our purses by lessening importation, and brings money in by exportation." Manufacturing set in motion a process that rendered property infinite; trade was not a zero-sum game. "Where abundance of manufacturing people are, they consume and sweep away all country commodities, and the wares of ordinary retail trades, with all sorts of victuals, wearing apparel, and other necessaries, and employ abundance of handicraftsmen, in wooden and iron work for tools, and instruments that belong to their trades, and so maintain and increase abundance of husbandmen, retailers and artificers of all sorts," Reynell detailed, "and they again increasing, take up more manufactures, and so they thrive one by another, ad infinitum." "Though we are a nation already pretty substantial," Reynell concluded, "yet it is easy for us to be ten times richer."[8]

While Reynell was confident that a massive increase in English wealth and consequently English power was attainable, he did not think it would happen of its own accord. He deemed it essential that "the confusion of trade [be] taken away" and that "the mysteries of exchange were more publicly known." He hoped thereby to generate a "public spirit" that "gave countenance to brave actions and industrious men, and minded the business of trade and populacy, as much as we do pleasures and luxury." More important even than a more commercially informed public, however, was a more commercially inclined state. The government action that he called for was not only an elimination of detrimental laws and customs but also the positive creation of state agencies to advance trade. Reynell hoped that "such laws might be made and contrived for the encouragement of trade and manufactures," of which "the chief things that promote trade and make it flourish are that it be free, naturalization, populacy, [religious] comprehension, freedom from arrests, certainty of property and freedom from arbitrary power, small customs, all conveniency and advantages for trading people: loans of interest, public places of charity for all wanting and distressed people, and also employments ready for all persons that want it." Though he was a friend to manufactures and to banks, Reynell was no capitalist critic of government intervention in the economy. He wanted the national state to work for the economic betterment of the people. "The happiness and welfare of all people arises by having or acquiring, through some industry or other, such conveniency of livelihood, as may not only keep them from want and poverty, but render them pleasant and sociable to one another," Reynell elaborated. "This holds both in private persons and families, and also in bodies politic: that they may best be able to grow and flourish, at least bear up against the malignity of enemies and adverse fortune."[9]

Indeed, Reynell was careful to distinguish in his treatise between trades that promoted the public good and those that did not. Significantly, in the ideological context of the 1680s, he singled out the East India trade as particularly deleterious because "to the East Indies we carry nothing but ready money, and bring in again nothing worth anything but spices."[10] For Reynell the goal of trade was to bring in raw materials not readily available at home to be manufactured. Since the East India trade did none of that, but only brought in goods for reexport, it potentially benefited the private merchant but not on balance the nation.

Reynell's voice may have been an unusually eloquent one, but his views were similar to those of a number of other later seventeenth-century commentators. Many others were committed to the notion that labor, not natural endowment, created property, that manufactures, not land, was the key to wealth and power. Richard Blome, an expert on the West Indies, endorsed the view "which is agreed on all hands," that it is the "labour" of the lower orders "that improves countries, and to encourage them is to promote the real benefit of the public." The violent Francophobe William Carter observed that "where a nation is not rich in mines of gold and silver, it is not capable of being enriched any other way, than by its manufacture." This premise led Carter to conclude that it was the government's interest to promote manufactures. "If it be from our manufactures alone that the riches of this nation comes, and if it be from our manufacture chiefly that our shipping is employed, and our mariners bred, if it be from our trading alone, and from the riches which our trading brings in, that his Majesty's customs are raised, and that our fleets have been hitherto built and maintained, and the dominion of the seas hath been preserved," Carter reasoned, "then it is and must be from our manufacture only that our bullion hath been brought in, and that the rents of our nobility and gentry doth depend and are sustained. And therefore it must be granted me, that there is no higher interest in the nation." John Locke, who was one of the earliest supporters of and investors in the Bank of England, was sure that "if we rightly estimate things as they come to our use, and cast up the several expenses about them, what in them is purely owing to nature, and what to labour, we shall find that in most of them 99/100 are wholly to be put on the account of labour." No wonder he was convinced that for states "the honest industry of mankind" and "numbers of men are to be preferred to largeness of dominions."[11]

The notion of a public bank had equally wide support in the 1670s and 1680s. An English national bank was already the subject of hot dispute "in public coffeehouses" in the late 1670s. "If it shall please God once to raise a Bank in London of six hundred thousand pounds fund and anchorage," thought Andrew Yarranton, who sensibly looked to the future Whig Earl of Anglesey for support. "Out of such a bank will sprout out many lumber houses and smaller banks to quicken trade. . . . I could write a whole volume of the advantage it would be to our English trades, the growth and manufactures of our kingdom." "All people are satisfied a bank is very advantageous to a nation, especially to a trading people," agreed Mark Lewis in 1678. In 1683, recalled the political economic writer Adam Anderson, "Dr. Hugh Chamberlain, a physician, and one Robert Murray, both great projectors, made a mighty stir with their scheme for a bank for circulating bills of credit on merchandize to be pawned therein, and for lending money to the industrious poor on pawns at six percent interest—but it came to nothing." The Whig Sir John Lowther described a public national bank in his "rules for increase of trade."[12]

At the accession of James II, then, many Whigs believed that wealth and political power was determined not by land but by labor. They insisted that wealth was potentially infinite, limited not by the size of the kingdom's possessions but only by the industriousness of the population. Since the key to promoting manufactures, the efficient deployment of labor in creating wealth, was the circulation of money to the productive parts of the economy, many continued to advocate the notion of a public national bank first espoused by the radicals of the 1650s. While these later seventeenth-century merchants, politicians, and thinkers were passionate advocates of commercial society, they were not possessive individualists but promoters of the good of the national community. They believed simultaneously in capitalism and in the necessity of state intervention to promote the right kind of economic growth.

James II, however, embraced a Tory rather than a Whig political economy. Just as he never embarked on Sir John Lowther's desired war against France, so James never took up Lowther's understanding of political economy. The king chose Sir Josiah Child rather than John Locke or Carew Reynell as his economic adviser. He chose to understand property exclusively as land and finite rather than as mobile and infinite. Instead of supporting the creation of a national bank, James II supported the exclusive monopoly privileges of the English East India Company and the Royal African Company.

In the last few years of Charles II's reign, when political economic debates were becoming closely associated with the emerging Whig and Tory Parties, the Tory Sir Josiah Child, long one of the most important merchants in the kingdom, successfully took control of the East India Company. In 1682 "on a sudden," Child "forsook all his old friends that first introduced him, with great difficulty into the [governing] Committee [of the East India Company], and afterwards raised him to the honour of Governor, throwing them totally out of the management"—Whig friends like Sir Samuel Barnardiston, Thomas Papillon, and Major Robert Thompson—"betaking himself to new counselors that were very ignorant in this trade." These new counselors, it turns out, were a motley collection of Catholic and Tory courtiers. "Child manages totally by the interest of his son-in-law Lord Worcester and his Father Duke of Beaufort who he has brought deep into stock together with several others of Grandees by their means and some of the judges," angrily and accurately wrote the disgruntled Whiggish East India merchant Nathaniel Cholmley, "so that now [Child] has the sole power by the disposal of their voices that no part is able to withstand him on the other side." "Sir Josiah Child and a few of his adherents," wrote another commentator, "do tumble the members in and out of the committee, according as they serve their own turns." Besides James II's loyal followers Worcester and Beaufort, these adherents appear to have been the lifelong rabid Tory Sir Benjamin Bathurst, the Tory Sir Joseph Herne, and Sir John Moore, who was voted after the revolution "to be a principal actor in the late illegal and arbitrary proceedings for the subversion of the government of the City of London."[13]

Unsurprisingly, given the nature of the coup that he had engineered, Josiah Child and the East India Company soon became favorites at James II's court. Scholars have shown that the East India Company "became closely tied to James II's monarchy" and that "Child and the East India Company's directorate . . . wedded themselves to the Tory position of support for the crown." James himself owned at least ten thousand pounds' worth of stock in the company. This association, of course, had its ideological repercussions. Child, according to his enemies, was "supported by an interest purchased at court at a dear rate, espoused for the sake of prerogative which the Company desire to have thought concerned in their charter." "The great ministers and chief men at court fell in with Sir Josiah," recalled another commentator, "not doubting but to have found a sufficient fund for carrying on any public design either of war or otherwise." Child and his cronies were "cultivated, cherished and influenced by the hand of tyranny and arbitrary power." Naturally, then, the East India Company "was of the first that made addresses to the late king, with a promise of slavish compliance to that illegal arbitrary demand of continuing the customs then expired, to the encouraging and setting up of popery and tyranny, and was a leading card to the rest of the lesser companies and particular merchants to a tame submission to that badge of slavery, raising money by proclamation, and of this action they publicly and highly boasted, valuing themselves mightily thereon." Not only did Child's company endorse James II's claim to tax without consent of Parliament, but it arrogated to itself "an unbounded despotic power . . . an unhoopable power over goods, liberties and properties of English men at pleasure." Small wonder that the East India Company continued to funnel large sums of money to James II and his court after the revolution.[14]

Josiah Child, then, seized almost total control of the East India Company with the aid and support of James II and his courtiers. Just as Child and the East India Company provided unwavering financial support of the king, so James II appears to have embraced Child's economic policies and aspirations.[15] What, then, was Child's—and by extension James II's regime's—understanding of political economy? Child, unlike Sir John Lowther or Carew Reynell, was convinced that "trading merchants, while they are in the busy and eager prosecution of their particular trades, although they be very wise and good men, are not always the best judges of trade, as it relates to the profit or power of the kingdom."[16] Kings should listen to the advice not of mere traders but of men who had—like Child himself—settled down to the life of country gentlemen. Child believed that those who owned landed property had the best political judgment.

Child was committed to the notion that property was natural, not created by human endeavor, and hence necessarily finite. Possession of land was therefore the basis of political power. While at first humans lived off the uncultivated products of the land,

Child recounted in a story echoed almost verbatim by Lord Chief Justice George Jeffreys, "but when the inhabitants of the earth began to increase and multiply; those who had first gained the possession thereof, and assumed to themselves a distinct propriety and right therein, had excluded the succeeding race of men, from all other livelihood and subsistence, but what was subordinate to, and dependent on such proprietors, who having power and means to support them, did thereby claim a right of dominion over them." Since dominion was based in land, Child was certain that commerce was merely the exchange of the growth of that land. "The principal advantage and foundation of trade in England is raised from the wealth which is gained out of the produce of the earth," Child contended. Where Reynell had seen a series of knock-on effects from manufactures leading to a possibility of unlimited economic growth, Child saw a finite economy totally "derived out of this principal stock of good husbandry." Agriculture and the fisheries, a kind of farming of the sea, were the fundamentals of trade, which in turn consisted merely of merchants buying "commodities purely to sell again, or exchange the commodities of one nation, for those of another, for no other end but that of their own private benefit or profit." Since no wealth was created by human labor, international trade was necessarily a zero-sum game: "whatever weakens" Italy, France, or Holland "enriches and strengthens England."[17]

Child's basic premise that property can be understood only in terms of land and that therefore trade was necessarily a vicious international competition for limited resources led him to enunciate criticisms of capitalist, commercial, and urban society long associated both with classical republicanism and Tory political culture. He was convinced that "luxury and prodigality are as well prejudicial to kingdoms as to private families." Because land and not exchange or manufactures was the real basis of England's wealth and power, Child urged "the gentry of England" to leave London and its "wicked course of life" and return "to their own countries" to "betake themselves to a way of husbandry." Child's East India Company warned that those employed in manufacturing should be limited because they were "so apt and ready for disorders." Finally, Child thought that the government "for promoting the credit, and securing those privileges which the land is justly entitled to" should replace "public taxes that are laid on the land" with an "excise" or tax on consumer goods, thereby "easing those few that are the proprietors of land, to lay it on those many that raise their estates out of the produce of the land."[18]

Child's understanding of political economy, an understanding certainly shared by James II and his court, had significant implications for the organization of the East India trade in particular and for English foreign and imperial policy in general. The notions that trade was finite and international competition necessarily fierce led Child and his fellow exponents of Tory political economy to insist that foreign trade be conducted in monopolistic fashion. Competition among English merchants could only be disastrous for England. "Our affairs in India had been in a wonderful prosperous condition in every place but for the interlopers who unite interests with the Dutch," Child complained to Secretary Middleton. "In those interloping times," Child later recalled, referring to the period before the establishment of the East India Company's monopoly, the English in India were "divided and contending among themselves, like Guelphs and Ghibelines, under the distinction of the Old and New Company; which latter appellation the interlopers assumed to themselves, and under that name made contracts of commerce and alliance with Princes and Governors in India, without any authority from their sovereign, which our law accounts a crime of a high nature, and which is in itself by the experience and confession of all men, of most destructive consequence to any kingdom or Commonwealth trading to the East Indies."[19]

James's preference for Child's political economy was hardly surprising. As director and the largest shareholder of the Royal African Company, James himself had provided a model for the East India Company. From the first the Royal African Company, founded in 1672 with the strong personal support of James (then Duke of York), had extremely close ties to the Crown. Very quickly the company developed a partisan profile. Critics of the court and future Whigs, such as John Locke and the Earl of Shaftesbury, sold their stock in the company in the late 1670s. By the 1680s the company had an overwhelmingly Tory profile. When James had the chance to fill aldermanic vacancies after London's charter was vacated in the late 1680s, almost half of the king's nominees were shareholders in the Royal African Company.[20]

The Royal African Company, so closely tied to James, espoused a political economic vision identical to that of the East India Company. Company arguments invariably began with the assumption that "the increase and wealth of all states, is evermore made upon the foreigner." Trade, James and his fellow company members were convinced, was a viciously competitive zero-sum game. Because it was a form of organized international competition, the notion that trade in Africa could be conducted without a mercantile monopoly was "short and erroneous." The experience of African trade before the establishment of the African Company's predecessor in 1662 was an unmitigated disaster. The company claimed that merchants, unprotected by a joint-stock company, lost thousands of pounds. This was because trade in Africa as in the East Indies could never be a purely commercial endeavor. "By long experience it is evident," insisted one company spokesman, that "this trade cannot be carried on but by a constant maintaining of forts upon the place, and ships of war to protect the ships of trade, and this occasioned by the natural perfidiousness of the natives, who being a barbarous and heathen people, cannot be obliged by treaties without being awed by a continuous and permanent force, and partly because the Dutch, Danes, French, and other nations, that likewise trade in the same country, are ever more vigilant for their own profit, frequently instigating the natives against us, as well as by their own force, to extirpate and destroy the English commerce there."[21] In the vicious world of international trade England could compete only if its joint-stock companies were awarded sovereign powers to enforce their monopolies and protect their exclusive trading privileges by whatever means necessary.

In fact, before 1685 the law was not so clearly on the side of the joint-stock com-

panies against the interlopers. It was in January 1685 that the matter of "the East India
Company's charter and the power of the King to grant such charters and prohibit his other
subjects" was decided in King's Bench in the case of the *East India Company v. Thomas
Sandys*. The East India Company had sought a ruling against the interloper Thomas
Sandys for trading without a license. In so doing, the company and its lawyers laid out
the ideological suppositions of land-based political economy. Sir John Holt and Daniel
Finch—the future Earl of Nottingham—argued that exclusive joint-stock companies were
justifiable despite prohibitions on monopolies for three reasons. First, since "the main end
of government" was "the preservation of Christianity," the kings of England had a special
interest in regulating commerce with infidels, such as the inhabitants of the East Indies.
The religious practices of merchants in exclusive trading companies with royal charters
were more easily supervised. Second, they argued that "'tis necessary for the king to have a
power to restrain a foreign trade, because a foreign trade, as the case may be, may be very
inconvenient and mischievous." It was therefore necessarily within the royal prerogative
to create limited trading companies that existed at the king's pleasure. Third, as Finch
argued, the vicious zero-sum nature of international trade in the Indies created "an absolute
necessity of a company to manage this trade."[22]

Against this position the defendants outlined a different understanding of political economy. First, both lawyers for the defendant, the prominent Whigs Sir Henry
Pollexfen and Sir George Treby, denied that the propagation of religion was the primary
end of government. "I must take leave to say," fulminated Treby, "that this notion of
Christians not to have commerce with infidels is a conceit absurd, monkish, fantastical,
and fanatical. 'Tis akin to *dominium fundatur in gratia*"—it was the same as asserting
that political dominion was founded in grace. Pollexfen more moderately warned "that
religion too often has been made a cloak and veil for other ends and purposes. It should
not be so, and I hope will not be so used in this case." Second, where the plaintiffs claimed
that property was based in land and that international trade was necessarily a zero-sum
game, the defendants' lawyers defined property quite differently. Property, the defendants
claimed, was the creation of human labor and consequently potentially limitless. "There
is a natural necessity that every man that will live must eat and thence a necessity and
obligation to labor," Treby argued, "and there is a property in this means of livelihood as
well as in life." "I do not know a greater property than freedom of trade and labor," he
elaborated, "the King cannot take away goods that a man has got by his trade, much less
can he take away his whole trade; if the profit which a man gets by his trade be his own,
the liberty whereby he acquires it is his own. Otherwise the whole property of traders were
precarious." Third, the defendants offered a more restrictive understanding of the prerogative. "The prerogative is great," they allowed, "but it has this general and just limitation,
that nothing is to be done thereby that is mischievous or injurious to the subject." If kings
were allowed to restrict trade by prerogative, "they might by the means of that have made
an undeniable title to such a revenue [based on taxing trade] without the consent of their

Lords and Commons."[23] In other words, were kings allowed to restrict trade by prerogative they could do away with Parliaments.

After much consideration the justices in King's Bench sided with the plaintiffs on every issue in dispute. Both Justices Walcott and Holloway insisted that it was essential to the king's being "to protect us in our religion," that the king "is the Defender of the Faith." The justices also endorsed the plaintiffs' understanding of property. "As to manu-factures," the creation of goods by human labor, argued Chief Justice Jeffreys in his most expansive opinion, "the public weal is little concerned therein." Land, not manufactures or exchange, was what mattered for Jeffreys. "The King is the only person truly concerned in this question" of the East India Company, Jeffreys reasoned, "for this island supported its inhabitants in many ages without any foreign trade at all, having in it all things neces-sary for the life of man." Property and livelihood depended on land. Trade was clearly a luxury not a necessity, and therefore it was well within the king's prerogative to regulate all foreign trade as he saw fit. Justice Holloway asserted that the king "hath the sole right and power of trade." Justice Witkins concluded that the king had the right "to control all trade in general." Significantly, Jeffreys spelled out the necessary imperial corollary of this reasoning. Because they could regulate trade, "His Majesty and his predecessors have always disposed of the several plantations abroad that have been discovered or gained by any of their subjects, and may do for the future, in case any other be discovered or acquired."[24]

Figured in this way, then, it is hardly surprising that the justices were unanimous in declaring *East India Company v. Sandys* to be of monumental importance for the royal prerogative. Jeffreys declared the case to be "of so great concern and consequence as perhaps there was none ever so great (I am sure none greater) in Westminster Hall wherein the prerogative of the King was more concerned on the one hand, and the liberty and prop-erty of the subject on the other."[25] Jeffreys went so far as to suggest that the emergence of the East India interlopers and the rise of radical rebellious principles exactly coincided in England. Similarly, Jeffreys proclaimed, lawyers had "of late years" been making a habit of "lessening the power of the king, and advancing, I had almost said the prerogative of the people," "making the power of the king thought so inconsiderable, as though he were a mere duke of Venice, being absolutely dependent on the Parliament." All of this, he insisted, must end. By defining property as a natural creation, measured only in land, Jeffreys was able to show that English kings had the power to regulate all trade. Where the defendants' lawyers worried that this would make Parliament irrelevant, Jeffreys reveled in the possibility. "God be praised," he exclaimed, "it is the king's power to call and dissolve Parliaments, when and how he pleases; and he is the only judge of these *ardua regni,* that he should think fit to consult with the Parliament about."[26]

The Court of King's Bench had determined that granting exclusive trading charters was the king's "undoubted prerogative." In other words, the court ruled that property was indeed finite, that all property was potentially the king's, and that the king could grant a monopoly with unlimited powers to conduct overseas trade. This ruling allowed the East

India and Royal African Companies immediately to indict the interlopers in their specific trades. It was also the legal basis on which James II based his ambitious imperial project, creating the Dominions of New England, the West Indies, and India.[27]

The King's Bench decision in *East India Company v. Sandys* paved the way for the development of territorial empire in India in the reign of James II. Not only did Child's—and by extension the East India Company's—ideological commitment to an agrarian political economy demand exclusive trading privileges, but it demanded that the company have property on which to base their trade in India. The East India Company was convinced, as they hoped were "all English men that have any love for their native country, since this matter has now been beat so thin in debates as well before his Majesty as almost in all other public places," that "the English must learn to raise revenues to support their power and increase their strength in India, or give up the whole trade of India to the Dutch in a short time." To achieve these ends James II granted to the company "all the powers we can possibly desire and all that the Dutch have or can pretend unto." This allowed the company to transform itself from "a parcel of mere trading merchants or peddlers" into a "formidable martial government in India." The company promptly sent Sir John Child as governor in India, with "entire and absolute command" over the entire English nation in India. His brief was to establish "an English political government in India" complete with "coercive laws and a strict execution of those laws." No person was allowed to dispute the governor's "authority in any kind," since "unity in our councils and entire obedience to superiors can only settle the English affairs in India upon a firm foundation of policy, power and justice."[28] The company mapped a land-centered notion of political economy onto James II's notions of unrestricted sovereignty.

These were not the flights of fancy of an overly ambitious merchant and his faction in London merely dreaming of empires in the East. A fledgling Indian empire quickly took shape. James II incorporated Bombay, making it, as one newsletter writer put it, "the English metropolis in India" complete with mayor, recorder, sheriffs, aldermen, and courts of law and admiralty. Indeed, Child boasted, Bombay was improved by the company from a town of four thousand families to a city of "fifty thousand families, all subject to the company's laws." Similarly, Madras had become "one of the finest and largest cities in those parts of the world, and secured by a good garrison, and containing at least one hundred thousand families of all nations, which inhabit within that city and the territory about it, all subject to such laws for life and goods, as the Company by virtue of their charter think fit to impose upon them." With a population of about a hundred thousand, Madras was the second largest English city during the reign of James II.[29]

Given the commitment of Child, and by extension both the East India Company and James II's court, to land-based zero-sum political economy, and given the company's newfound commitment to territorial empire in the East Indies, it is not surprising that England and the East India Company pursued a belligerent policy toward their imperial competitors—the Dutch and the Mogul Empire. Child, like James and his closest advisers,

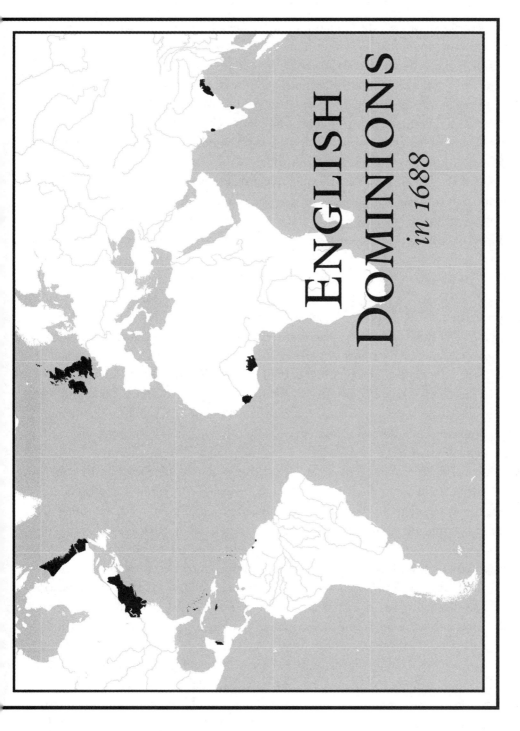

ENGLISH DOMINIONS *in 1688*

By 1688 Britain had possessions in North America, the Caribbean, Canada, West Africa, and India. The future of the empire was a central issue in debates about foreign policy and political economy in the later seventeenth century.

had long been obsessed with the United Provinces, alternating between pleas for emulation and vitriolic condemnation. Child frequently called on his compatriots to imitate
their neighbors across the North Sea and set up an empire in the East Indies, while at the
same time blaming the Dutch for the decline of all fifteen areas of English exchange that
he chose to analyze. After they took the English trading post of Bantam on the island of
Java in 1682, Child became ever more convinced that England's economic rivals were on
the brink of monopolizing the entire East India trade. Should the Dutch achieve this goal,
Child was sure, it would "render them irresistible." "The consequences of the designed
sole empire of the Dutch in India are so fatal to this kingdom," Child implored Lord
Middleton, "that this national gangrene needs speedier and stronger remedies than can be
applied by any private merchants." Child and the East India Company steadily increased
the shrillness of their calls for national support once James II ascended the throne. Child
and his friends repeatedly advanced the same arguments about the dangers of Dutch
commercial hegemony in discussions at court, in conversations with foreign ministers, in
printed pamphlets, and in letters to their factors in the Indies. They warned the president
and council at Fort St. George in Madras to be prepared to do military battle with "the
Dutch tyranny in India." The following year they informed their new general in Bombay, Sir John Child, that the stakes of a war in India would be of much more than local
import. "If the present misunderstandings between the two nations should ferment to an
open war," the London-based committee wrote of the English and Dutch, "it would be
thought by the vulgar but a war for pepper which they think to be a slight thing, because
each family spends but a little of it. But at the bottom it will prove a war for the British
as well as Indian Seas."[30]

Just as English public opinion outside the court was whipping itself into a frenzy
of Francophobic excitement, the East India Company along with James II and his court
were demanding a war against the Dutch—a war justified because commerce was integral
to power and commerce depended on imperial landed possessions. In this ideological vision, trade was a zero-sum game, and England's competitors for trade were the Dutch, not
the French. Indeed, Child had long advocated making common cause with the French
in the East Indies against the Dutch—a call for coordination of efforts to which James II
responded positively. By 1687 it was known, and indeed advertised, that James II had offered his "royal assistance" in raising "some thousands of men" to advance the company's
cause in India.[31]

The East India Company did begin a war in India. But it proved to be a war
against the Mogul Empire rather than one against the Dutch. Sir Josiah Child, according to his critics, by means of "great annual presents . . . could command both at court
and in Westminster-Hall what he pleased." And what he pleased was "a great fleet" full
of "soldiers and all other warlike preparations." Child, the East India Company, and England declared war against the Mogul emperor "by his Majesty's commission under the
great seal of England." Despite every effort by the company and the court to publicize

English successes, it was soon known on the Exchange and throughout England that the war was going badly. "Sir Josiah Child is preparing a relation of his late successes against the great Mogul," one London newsletter writer sneered in the summer of 1688, "yet 'tis thought his rhetoric will scarce longer gain belief since our actions [stock prices] fall to the lowest ebb." The Moguls soundly defeated the English, threatening the very existence of the English empire in India. "Most men conclude that the East India trade is all lost" as a result of this ignominious war, wrote another.[32]

James II had made political and ideological common cause with Josiah Child and his restructured East India Company. In tandem they were committed to a vision of wealth as a zero-sum game, a territorial imperial policy, and an anti-Dutch foreign policy. Together they had achieved legal confirmation of the royal right to create exclusive trading monopolies. All of this clearly angered large segments of the English mercantile community. Not only did Child alienate his former allies in the East India Company like Thomas Papillon and Sir Samuel Barnardiston, his complicity with James II's regime managed to upset a wide variety of merchants. The exclusive nature of trading rights that he secured and James II insisted on deprived merchants all over the kingdom, and the entire Jewish community, of access to trade. No wonder the Whig merchant community so spectacularly turned against the regime. No wonder there was a "great grumbling in the City against a certain great East India merchant whose first name rhymes with Goliah."[33] No wonder Whig merchants poured money into William of Orange's coffers in 1688. No wonder merchants, especially Whig merchants, were so quick to support the new regime with their purses in the heady days of 1689.

James II, then, did embrace a commercial policy—the policy espoused by Sir Josiah Child, the East India Company, and the Royal African Company. James II had a coherent and modern imperial policy. He was "a mature imperialist."[34] But James II's commercial and imperial policies were at odds with the newly consolidated Whig commercial tradition—the tradition that property was created by human endeavor and that banks could do much to increase the nation's wealth. The implications of James's policy, alliance with France and war with the Mogul Empire and the United Provinces accorded nicely with the king's own foreign policy predilections but put him at loggerheads with large swaths of the political nation. James II thus alienated not only the East India Company's traditional enemies but also those powerful Whig merchants who rejected Child's commercial and imperial vision. The result was that large segments of England's merchant community actively supported William's plan for invasion and provided a key financial prop to the regime in the critical early months. Questions of political economy had played a crucial role in bringing about the Revolution of 1688–89. "Economic arguments" did not have to wait until "after the Glorious Revolution," as the humanists have maintained, to "become political and constitutional argument."[35] Arguments about political economy played a pivotal role in generating the ideological energy that gave rise to the Revolution of 1688–89; interest in political economy was not an unintended consequence of those events.

The revolutionaries of 1688–89 not only dislodged James II and his political regime, they also ended the Tory stranglehold on economic ideology. A cacophony of different voices soon began to be heard. The ideology of the radicals of the 1650s, an ideology that had gained a following among those more politically moderate than the brave Commonwealth critics of Oliver Cromwell, quickly reemerged. "Notwithstanding the great influence that trade now hath in the support and welfare of states and kingdoms," observed Nicholas Barbon, the Tory son of the 1650s radical Praisegod Barbon, "yet there is nothing . . . that men differ more in their sentiments than about the true causes that raise and promote trade."[36]

The newly invigorated debate over political economy, though initiated by an English people very much alive to the power of liberty, did not rely on the classics or their Renaissance and republican popularizers. The ancients were simply no longer relevant in the realm of commerce. "Livy and those ancient writers, whose elevated genius set them upon the inquiries into the causes of the rise and fall of governments, have been very exact in describing the several forms of military discipline, but take no notice of trade," observed Barbon, "and Machiavel, a modern writer, and the best, though he lived in a government, where the family of Medicis had advanced themselves to the sovereignty by their riches acquired by merchandizing, doth not mention trade, as any way interested in the affairs of state." The military revolution of the sixteenth and early seventeenth centuries, however, had necessarily changed the relation between trade and politics. "Until trade became necessary to provide weapons of war," Barbon correctly perceived, "it was always thought prejudicial to the growth of empire, as too much softening the people by ease and luxury, which made their bodies unfit to endure the labour and hardships of war." One Whig polemicist noted similarly that "trade was in all ages till within little more than a hundred years past counted a contemptible thing, as it is still by some mighty and famous kingdoms, and is indeed but a modern system of politics, little descanted on by the great writers and professors of that science." This was because "since the discovery of the East and West Indies, and increase in navigation thereon, the state of Europe in general, and every nation in it in particular, is much altered, more especially in the course of war." "Now," this polemicist observed, "we see all corners of Europe crowded with listed, disciplined and standing armies in pay, which as it cannot be done without huge funds of money, and the ancient demesnes of the Prince not sufficing, taxes are everywhere increased on the subject." "Home manufactures and foreign trade" were essential to raise the newly required revenue. Times had changed. So, argued another commentator, "whatever low conceits Aristotle or some other pedants may have had of merchandize in old times," they were irrelevant given the "dignity" to which trade "has long since arrived to."[37] Neither the classics nor the ancient constitution provided the wisdom necessary to deal with modern problems of political economy.

James II's government had embraced the Tory notion of a land-based, zero-sum understanding of wealth. After the king's departure the Whig claim that wealth was potentially infinite and created by human labor was everywhere to be found. Many claimed that manufactures rather than land was the key to England's future strength and prosperity. "It is manifest by experience," claimed William James, echoing the views expressed by Carew Reynell half a decade previously, "that where a manufacture and much people are settled in any part of the nation, there the lands are not only occupied, but yield the greatest rents, and the fruits thereof the greatest price." It is "manufactories," insisted Daniel Defoe, that "is the treasure of this nation, and keeps our exports to a balance with our imports; otherwise this kingdom would have been as poor as Spain, and as effeminate as Italy." James Whiston, who had long been known for his publication of mercantile price lists, thought that "industrious inhabitants," not land, were the "original riches, as well as strength of the nation." The "labors" of the people were capable of infinitely improving nature's blessings, thought the author of *England's Glory,* so that human endeavor indeed "is the real riches and strength of the nation; and the more the merrier, like bees in a hive, and better cheer too." Sir Francis Brewster was certain that those nations that combine natural resources "are more to be feared, than those that abound with the blessings of nature, but want that of industry." It was because "the numbers of people are the original of the strength of any nation," argued the Whig Roger Coke, that land-poor and population rich Holland was "much more rich than Spain." A king "is nothing if he have no subjects," preached the Low Churchman and future bishop Simon Patrick, "but the more numerous they are, the greater is his force and his splendor at home, and his fame and reputation abroad; which very much depends on the populousness of his country." The Whig friend of Locke and plantation trader John Cary knew it to be "the great interest of England to advance its manufactures." Through manufactures "we not only employ our poor, and so take off that burden which must otherwise lie heavy on our lands, but also grow rich in our commerce with foreign nations, to whom we thereby sell our product at greater prices than it would otherwise yield, and return them their own materials when wrought up here, and increased in their value by the labor of our people."[38]

Given the new mood in political economic discourse, given the violent distaste much of the merchant community displayed toward James II's policies, it is hardly surprising that many of the implications of land-based zero-sum economic reasoning came in for criticism.

The House of Commons quickly reversed the orientation of England's tax policies. Soon after the Restoration of Charles II, Parliament had, with more than a little pressure from the king and his court, granted the Crown in perpetuity revenue from the new Hearth Tax. Under the provisions of this new tax, the Crown would receive one shilling for each hearth. Because fires were essential for so many stages in early modern manufacturing, it was inevitable that the Hearth Tax would breed resentment. Almost immediately the new tax provoked complaints, evasion, and riots. Although much of the resentment against the Hearth Tax was part of a general resentment against taxpaying and intrusion by inspectors, the pattern of complaint reveals particular concern from the manufacturing sector. "The smiths in and about Birmingham" captured the government's attention for their resistance to the Hearth Tax in 1672. The future Whig Sir John Lowther was sympathetic to the anguished cries "of the poorer inhabitants," who particularly objected to the levying the tax on "smiths' hearths and private ovens." A central aim of the Hallamshire Cutlers' Company throughout the 1670s and 1680s was to secure repeal of the Hearth Tax, which heavily assessed the burgeoning cutlery trade in and around Sheffield. During James II's reign, Hearth Tax disturbances were closely associated with manufacturing districts. In 1687 there were Hearth Tax riots in tin-making areas of Cornwall and pottery-making regions of Staffordshire. Predictably, in the cloth-making town of Leeds, and elsewhere in Yorkshire, William's arrival was quickly followed by Hearth Tax riots with a strongly Orangist tinge. Immediately after William and Mary were declared England's new sovereigns, a bill was passed in the Commons repealing the antimanufacturing Hearth Tax. Whigs like Colonel John Birch celebrated the repeal for removing "a badge of slavery." One noted during the debate that nothing was "more unequal" than this tax because urban "corporations must needs pay a hundred times as much for their candle rents as we pay for our land." By contrast, the Marquis of Halifax, who had Tory inclinations on political economic issues, feared that removal of the Hearth Tax was a radical "design."[39]

The new regime, intent on fighting a war against Europe's greatest power, France, could not forego revenue. The House of Commons soon provided William and Mary with a new source of income. In December 1689, the Commons passed a new land tax that had more in common with taxation practices in the 1650s than with any since the Restoration. Lifelong Whigs such as John Hampden and John Swynfen enthusiastically supported this resurrection of progressive taxation. The reemergence of a tax on landed wealth provoked bitter criticism from the Tory defenders of the land-based, zero-sum political economy. One pamphleteer complained that the gentry would soon bear "the whole burden" for the war against France. "I would not have us follow the example of Holland," this author darkly warned. Sir Richard Temple, who had developed business contacts with both the East India and Royal African Companies in the 1670s and 1680s, was another bitter and eloquent opponent of land taxes. He highlighted the Civil War origins of the tax and complained that it "lies so heavy upon the nobility and gentry above all others, to the weakening and diminishing their estates, who are the chief supporters of the monarchy." By contrast, the "rich usurer or tradesman" and "the considerable free-holder" got off lightly and would inevitably form "the proper basis of a democracy or commonwealth." No wonder, Temple felt that the land tax was upheld by the "zealous endeavors" of members of Parliament from the manufacturing parts of the country. In speech after speech in the years after the Revolution, Tory MPs stood to denounce the land tax. The revolutionary regime's land tax quickly became the bogeyman of the Tories.[40]

Tax policy, the English knew, had become a central issue of party political contestation. "All nations have from time to time declined or flourished, in proportion to their due or undue methods of contribution," explained one commentator. So important had taxation become in modern politics that to it "may be fairly imputed most of the famous revolts of provinces, enthrallments of free countries, violent changes of government." In particular, the postrevolutionary tax policies produced "a great noise," reported one Jacobite, making the new king "very popular" among some while generating "innumerable enemies" in other quarters. Whig sponsorship of the revolutionary transformation in England's tax policy almost immediately became an election issue. In Cheshire the Whig Sir Robert Cotton came under attack from the Tory Lord Cholmondley for having supported the new land tax, "which is not for the interest of these Northern parts." The Whig Roger Kirkby was similarly able to defeat Tory opposition in Lancaster based on his own support of the land tax.[41]

The reorientation of English tax policy—from favoring land to favoring manufacturing—presaged a new attitude toward the Royal African and East India Companies. "Several owners of the interloping vessels and goods condemned in Guinea" now had the confidence to bring "actions at law" against the Royal African Company and its monopoly. In 1689, in the case of *Nightingale v. Bridges,* Chief Justice John Holt reversed *East India Company v. Sandys.* Jeffreys's famous ruling which provided the legal basis for Tory political economy was now "legally disclaimed." The antimonopolist lawyer Sir Bartholomew Shower argued successfully for the plaintiff that property was not limited to land but also included "goods as well as other franchises and liberties which the subject hath." Shower maintained that property was potentially mobile, implicitly created by human labor, and consequently necessary to the common welfare. As a result "the altering of a property of a subject's goods required Parliamentary assistance," "and that is the fittest way for ordering that fundamental property which the subject hath in his goods, because each subject's vote is included in whatsoever is there done: an act of Parliament hath the consent of many men, both past, present and to come." The king had no right to create an exclusive trading monopoly—such as the East India Company and the Royal Africa Company—because the property so involved was not his to manage. "The Kings of England have always claimed a monarchy royal not a monarchy seigniorial," Shower adverted. By this he meant that English common law "gives a true property in contradistinction to the superintendant power, and for this purpose it distinguishes between bondsmen, whose estates are at their lord's will and pleasure, and freemen, whose property none can invade, change or take away, but by their own consent; a several property in the subject is so sacred as nothing more."[42] Significantly, however, this landmark decision did not create an absolute right to free trade. Instead it insisted that Parliament as the representative of the people, the people who created property through their labor, could regulate trade.

Holt's decision shattered the legal basis for James II's centralized authoritarian empire. Shower made explicit the imperial consequences of his reasoning. Where Jeffreys had insisted under his definition of property that in a regime governed by Jacobite political economy, all acquired territory outside of England would be governed as the king saw fit, Shower outlined a very different imperial regime. Because the acquired property was the result of the labor of English men and women, Shower took "it for a truth, that in all parts of the world where the Englishmen are under the government of any English subjects, their rules must be the laws of this land, and if they punish without jury, they may be punished for it by action of trespass when they return hither, and this we have in practice here everyday in case of the insolency of governors in plantations, as in the East Indies and Barbados." "They cannot proceed there but in the methods allowed here," Shower summarized in contradistinction to the opinion advanced by Jeffreys and the practice followed by the East India Company. "Trial by jury is the right of every English subject all the world over, wheresoever Englishmen have command derived from the Crown of England." The decision rendered by Holt in Nightingale, one modern commentator correctly concludes, "destroyed prerogative control of the economy."[43]

Chief Justice Holt's ruling was in perfect accord with "our present vogue of a free-trade." Roger Coke, for example, argued powerfully that "all nations, as well as the inhabitants, by equal right or the law of nature, may entertain trade or commerce with one another." African traders among a whole host of others railed against the exclusive rights of joint-stock companies, claiming that a free trade would quadruple exports of English manufactures. Petitions poured into the House of Commons from all over the country complaining of the deleterious effects of the overseas trading monopolies. The Royal African Company withstood the legislative charge from its Whig critics, but only by conceding that its monopoly depended on parliamentary statute, not on royal prerogative.[44]

The Whigs' larger target, and one that became even easier to attack after Justice Holt's ruling, was the East India Company. Given Child's success in purging the company of his most powerful Whig rivals, the company's failure to generate profits for its stockholders, and the unpopular ideological orientation of Child's political economic program, one would expect the East India Company to come under fire immediately after the revolution. And it did. "What great and indefatigable industry hath been employed? What arts and devices made use of, to blast the reputation of the present East India Company, is notoriously evident to all, who either give themselves the trouble of listening to those calumnies, daily inculcated in all noted coffee-houses against them, or to the reading of those prints exposed publicly, and delivered gratis in the said coffee-houses to all such as will accept them," complained one of the East India Company's defenders. Whigs advanced a wide range of arguments for the dissolution or at least radical reorganization of the East India Company. The radical Roger Coke suggested that the only defense of an exclusive monopoly, that it was needed to combat the imperial ambitions of the Dutch, was based on a ridiculous overestimation of Dutch power in the Indies. In fact, he pointed out, the "greatest fear the company have" was of the success of the English interlopers—hardly possible if the Dutch had a monopoly of trade. Others elevated this critique to a more theoretical level. "There is nothing that can conduce more to the peopling and enriching a kingdom, or commonwealth, than a free and open trade," argued one of Child's more bitter critics. This antimonopolist was no libertarian defender of small government, however. He hastened to add that because trade "by sea is the principal source of such happiness, it may very well deserve the government's most particular care and application to advance it."[45]

A wide variety of commentators argued that the East India Company's imports had a profoundly negative effect on English manufactures. John Cary pointed out that anyone committed to a political economy that prioritized labor over land, manufactures over husbandry, should be extremely skeptical of the East India trade. East India calicoes and wrought silks, because they competed with domestically made clothing, Cary thought, "do us more prejudice in our manufactures than all the advantage they bring either to private purposes or to the nation in general." The Dutch in this respect provided a poor model, because their circumstances dictated an economy based on "buying and selling [rather] than manufacturing." As a result, Cary concluded that for England no trade was "so detrimental as that to the East-Indies." Indian calicoes, one pamphleteer pointed out, were quickly replacing English manufactured cloths such as says or perpetuanas. Calicoes, muslins, and Indian wrought silks had recently become "the general wear in England," observed the Whig clothier John Blanch. The result was disastrous for the English economy. These cloths, "fully manufactured abroad," Blanch concluded, "do our nation the greatest mischief at present" of any imports. The East India Company "trade to the loss of the nation," agreed John Locke's friend the Whig MP from Taunton Edward Clarke. This was because "by bringing home wrought silks, calicoes, and muslins," the East India Company destroyed the demand for English manufactures both at home and in Europe. The fantastic wealth gained by the leading East India merchants, Clarke concluded, was thus at the expense "of their fellow subjects." During James II's reign manufacturers in Gloucestershire, Suffolk, and Essex had complained bitterly about the dislocations and unemployment caused by the East India Company's imports. In the 1680s these pleas fell on deaf ears. Not so in the 1690s. In 1697 the Board of Trade issued a report concluding that the East India Company's imported goods valued more than ten times what it exported.[46] After the revolution the Whig critics of the East India Company, the supporters of a political economy of manufacturing, had the ideological upper hand.

These Whig critics of the East India Company quickly took political action. By February 1689 John Cholmley, no friend to Child's company, had the confidence to "expect a new company or a regulation so soon as matters of state are settled," predicting as well that "the matters of difference betwixt us and the Dutch in India will be adjusted and settled in a friendly manner." Petition after petition against the company was sent to the Commons committee delegated to investigate the matter. When the committee debated the issue, it did so "with some heat." The following year the company's position remained precarious. "The present East India Company still continues, but they are winding up their bottoms," reported Cholmley. "We do not question the next sessions of Parliament there will be a new company settled." The House of Commons quickly signaled its distaste for the East India Company both by taxing owners of its stock in the Poll Tax and increasing impositions on East India goods. By the autumn of 1691, the East India Company's Whig critics had formalized their meetings "to consider the best way of procuring a regular and lawful establishment of the East India trade upon a new national stock clear of all encumbrances." This self-described new East India Company, undoubtedly merely continuing the name that the interlopers of the 1680s had assumed, promoted a comprehensive strategy that included proposing new East India legislation, petitioning Parliament, publishing and distributing tracts and treatises critical of the East India Company, and lobbying MPs both in Westminster and at Garraways coffeehouse in the City. The East India Company's enemies had good reason to expect success. "The dissolving this present joint-stock, and establishing a new national one, is that which agrees and falls in with the genius of the most considerable part of the nation at this day," contended one of the company's bitterest critics with some apparent justice, "and in public reformations it hath generally seemed expedient to the wisdom of Parliaments to proceed in, and take such methods as are most agreeable to the constitution of the nation, the laws of the land, right of the subject, and consonant to the bent and spirit of the best and most thinking part of the people, which seems absolutely against confirming any illegal, or grafting, clouting, patching, splicing, any weak, doubted, failing drooping nominal stock."[47]

Despite repeated and well-informed predictions of the company's demise, it survived, ultimately receiving statutory legitimization in 1698. Apparently the company owed its continuance to a combination of effective propaganda, more effective bribery, and significant tactical concessions.[48] The East India Company survived temporarily as an exception to a developing antimonopolist rule. Although the company's Whig opponents failed to destroy the monopoly they so detested, they did succeed in demolishing the Tory stranglehold on economic policymaking. Instead of continuing the parliamentary battle against the company, they assaulted land-based political economy on new terrain.

Although the East India Company, its policies, and its political influence generated a good deal of furor in James II's reign, after the revolution the major issue in political economy quickly became that of financing the war. Within a year of James II's flight, the tone of the parliamentary debates over finance had become desperate, not to say hysterical. The difficulty of fighting Europe's greatest power on two fronts while relying on land-based conceptions of property were readily apparent. William III and his government faced two alternatives: scale back the war against Louis XIV as the Tories wished or adopt the full radical implications of the Whig understanding of political economy. The choice became one of accepting the limited European war aims of the Tories or adopting the radical structural reforms long advocated by the Whig opponents of Child's political economy. By 1694 William was prepared to throw in his lot with the Whigs.

The starting point of this reorganization was for the Whigs to establish that finance, not land or virtue, was the sinews of war. By February 1689 the Whiggish lower house already accepted without argument the claim that "money is the sinews of war." "It is certainly impossible, in the present state of things, that this government should subsist, and much less be able to bear its part in the alliance against our common enemies, unless there be great sums of money given," asserted the Whig John Hampden. "These are the sinews of war, and all other business." This truism was so well known that William James mentioned almost in passing that "the safety of the King, Queen, and kingdom stands in the multitude and riches of the people."[49]

This understanding of the relation between wealth and power, so foreign to the writers of classical antiquity and the Italian Renaissance, was the direct result of the changing circumstances of European warfare in the seventeenth century. "As honest Wallop used to say," noted the author of one well-circulated *Rambling Letter to a Friend,* "war is changed from fighting into eating, drinking and campaiging. To carry on which new sort of military art, I am sure money is the one thing necessary." "Princes do not come to the field as in ancient times to void their quarrels," remarked Robert Molesworth, but instead determined their wars by economic attrition. James Whiston offered an almost identical analysis, adding only that "the discovery of the wealth of the Indies" as well as technological innovation in warfare had contributed to making war "rather an expence of money than men." Therefore he thought that nothing was "more conspicuous than the advantages of trade" in making "a prince and people happy at home and formidable abroad."[50]

Those who have insisted on the continuity and hegemony of anticapitalist discourse after the revolution have noted the ubiquity of the notion that money was thought to be the sinews of war without coming to grips with the radical implications of this observation. If wealth was a prerequisite for political survival in the modern world, then concerns about luxury and virtue, the dominant themes in classical and Renaissance anticapitalist discussions, would necessarily be secondary. Indeed, it is remarkable how little the concern about luxury occurs in the fierce political economic debates of the early 1690s. When the term did reemerge in the later 1690s—the period to which the humanists have devoted almost exclusive attention—it did not loom as large or play the decisive role that it had played earlier. Even then, as scholarship has now shown, few advanced classical or Renaissance arguments. Even the Tory polemicist Charles Davenant, one of the humanists' prime examples, thought the dangers from poverty far outweighed the risks from luxury. Even he believed that it was impossible to return to the simpler world of ancient virtue. Both Whigs and Tories recognized that the new economic demands of the state had fundamentally transformed the rules of politics.[51]

It was in this ideological context, then, that the Whig proponents of labor- and manufacturing-based political economy faced the problem of financing the war against France. Their preferred solution was the creation of a national bank. Proposals and blueprints for banks were to be found everywhere in England in the wake of the Glorious Revolution. "Banks have not wanted both pleaders and writers in their behalf," understated one pamphleteer. Hugh Chamberlain and William Paterson were the most prominent and visible proponents of banks, though lesser-known voices were frequently heard praising the merits of "a common bank." For Nicholas Barbon the question was not whether a bank was desirable but why England had not yet created one. "It is much to be wondered at," Barbon marveled, "that since the City of London is the largest, richest, and chiefest city in the world for trade; since there is so much ease, dispatch and safety in a public bank: and since such vast losses has happened for want of it; that the merchant and traders of London have not long before this time addressed themselves to the government for the establishing of a public bank." The answer to Barbon's puzzle was political. "It is true, in a government wholly despotical, whose support is altogether in the military forces; where trade hath no concern in the affairs of state [and] brings in no revenue, there might be a jealousy that such a bank might tempt a Prince to seize it"—and here there can be no doubt he was referring to James II's regime—"but in England, where the government is not despotical, but the people are free and have a great share in the sovereign legislative power, as the subjects of any states have or ever had . . . and where the flourish of trade is as much the interest of the king as of the people, there can be no such cause of fear: for what objections can any man make, that his money in the bank, may not be as well secured by a law, as his property is?"[52]

Toward the end of the tense session of 1694, Parliament passed legislation creating the Bank of England. The main proponents of the bank were ideologically predictable. William Paterson and the radical Whig Michael Godfrey, "a person of great parts and industry, and well known at court and in the House of Commons," were joined by "some of the late solicitors against the East India Company." The first subscribers to the bank include a variety of Child's East India Company critics, including John Cholmley, Sir John Chardin, Sir Robert Clayton, Sir James and Abraham Houblon, John Ward, Thomas Pitt, and John Paige. Although the bank's proponents had a tough fight in Westminster, they had easier going in the City and the nation at large. William Paterson recalled that the initial subscription to the bank "was completed in about ten days," and "the body of the nation" soon proved "willing generously to venture their money."[53] Whigs who could not stomach Child's land-based zero-sum political economy—MPs, merchants, and the nation at large—turned their hopes away from the creation of a new East India Company toward the creation of a national bank.

The proponents of bank schemes and the defenders of the Bank of England clarified the ideological assumptions that undergirded their enthusiasm. One early proponent claimed that a national bank would make it easier for the king to finance his wars as well making it easier for citizens to make ordinary payments. And, "since London is grown to have as equal a share of trade (if not greater) with those cities of Amsterdam, Hamburg, Genoa, and Venice, where public banks are established, they ought to have the same encouragement from [this] government." For all these reasons, this author concluded with nary a whiff of libertarian assumptions, "it is now become the concern and interest of the government, for promoting the welfare and trade of the nation, that such a bank should be established." The Whig Gilbert Burnet recalled that many at the time argued for the

Premier Map of London and Suburbs: The Bank of England in the Poultry, 1724.
The Bank of England, established in 1694, was a Whig project—the product
of a political economy that took labor, rather than land, to be the source of all
value and had as its goal the furtherance of a manufacturing economy.

bank because "the credit it would have must increase trade and the circulation of money."
On the establishment of the bank, one supporter enthused that it would lower interest
rates, "facilitate the circulation of money," and help finance the war. Significantly, the
value of circulation of money was that it would thereby funnel money to where it could
be productive, to manufactures.[54]

The most eloquent proponent of the Bank of England was H. M., the author of
England's Glory. The bank, H. M. pointed out, could provide "ready money" in case of "a
sudden emergency" to "equip Armadas, supply armies, levy soldiers." When "there is leisure
for deliberation, and . . . the Parliament and King judge it requisite, these banks may be
in a capacity to supply the crown with whatever money it needs at a reasonable rate." This
ability to support the government financially will "tend to the overthrowing our enemies by
sea and land." The bank will also promote wealth and power. "Money in a nation in trade,
is like blood in the veins, if it circulates in all parts, the body is health; if it be wanting in
any parts, it languisheth," H. M. noted. Banks guaranteed the circulation of money that
will "beget trade and people, and they will beget riches. . . . Riches are the conveniencies
of a nation: but trade and people are the glory and strength of the kingdom." He was sure
that a bank would initiate the same sort of infinite knock-on effects discussed by Carew

Reynell because with a bank, "people will increase, for trade will bring in people as well as riches to the nation: where trade is, there will be employment; where employment is, there will people resort; where people are, there will be consumption of all commodities." Luxury, thought H. M. in contrast to Renaissance anticapitalist thinkers, was not a serious problem. "When the people's yolk is lined with peace and plenty," he noted, "it will make them cheerful under it, and not desirous to shake it off. If some few should surfeit and grow wanton, the generality of the people (being content in their condition) would certainly keep them in awe." For all these reasons, the optimistic H. M. could report that "all men are satisfied a bank will be very advantageous to a nation, especially to a trading people."[55]

Other Whig advocates of manufacturing and labor-created property were also enthusiastic about the bank. John Cary declared banks "to be so many shops to let out money, for which they receive such security and for such time, as stands most for the conveniency of trade, and therefore the more the better." "The most visible means to preserve these kingdoms in their trade and navigation," advised Sir Francis Brewster, "is the setting up a national bank." So obvious was this point that Brewster presumed "the usefulness of banks in England is not now controverted." John Locke, who along with his printer Awnsham Churchill was one of the initial subscribers to the Bank of England, thought it "of no small consequence" for his subscriber friend Edward Clarke "and to England."[56]

The Whig defenders of the new political economy, the ideological descendants of the 1650s radicals, drew radically different macropolitical conclusions from Josiah Child and those committed to a land-based zero-sum political economy. Where Child had thought that England's great enemies were the Dutch because they were England's main competitor for commercial empire, the defenders of the new political economy saw French land-based and Europe-centered imperialism as England's greatest threat. Whereas proponents of agrarian political economy either became Jacobites or Tory supporters of a blue-water policy, the defenders of manufactures were the most enthusiastic supporters of Continental commitment in the Nine Years' War against France. One opponent of taxes on manufactures, John Hampden, bragged that "no man in England is more thoroughly sensible than I am of the necessity of carrying on this war." The stakes could not have been higher. He was sure "that the liberty of this nation, the preservation of this government, and the security of the Protestant interest throughout Europe" depended "upon the success of it." "There are but two ways, victory or slavery," James Whiston insisted. "There remains no terms of peace for us, but what would fix an everlasting infamy upon the English name. In short, the greatness of England and France is now incompatible. If they rise, we must fall." John Cary claimed that the entire purpose of his treatise on trade was to promote the war effort. On the success of that war, he knew, "depends the security of religion, liberty and property, both to [William III's] subjects, and likewise to all the Protestant interest in Europe." Francis Brewster was just as insistent that the French needed to be defeated. "The danger that hath been impending over us for more than thirty years in this of our trade, is from the French," he noted, "and in truth no nation in the world can so well contest it with England as they can."[57]

The Glorious Revolution, then, produced, and by many was intended to produce, a revolution in political economy. James II had devoted himself to an economic understanding that posited property as a natural endowment. In this understanding the world's wealth was necessarily finite and empires were created by taking land from another state. The East India Company was thus ideally poised to create a vast new English imperial dominion by warring with the Dutch and the Mogul Empire. After the revolution, especially after 1694, the Whigs and their understanding of political economy gained the political upper hand. The Whigs believed that England's future lay in being a manufacturing rather than an agrarian society. The Whigs, many of whom had been supporters of the East India interlopers, thought that wealth was created by human endeavor and thus potentially infinite. While these political economic thinkers, writers and actors initially focused their energies on breaking up mercantile monopolies, in particular that of the East India Company, they quickly shifted their emphasis to creating a national bank. The revolution in political economy was thus a prerequisite to the Financial Revolution. Along with the commitment to a national bank came a commitment to drawing on merchants' knowledge in the creation of national policy and a notion that tax policy should be revised to benefit the most valuable area of the economy, the manufacturing sector. In this view, one's true competitors were not states like the United Provinces, which specialized in the carrying trade, but large countries like France, which could compete with England in manufacturing and were doing so by pernicious political means. The proponents of this new political economy were far more concerned with the creation of wealth than they were about the corrosive effects of luxury. They were not obsessed, as some classical and Renaissance thinkers were, with anchoring political personality in real property. Instead they thought that circulation of wealth in an infinite cycle of production and consumption was vital to the maintenance of England's national integrity and identity.

The new political economy did not achieve ideological hegemony. Not only did the defenders of the old East India Company achieve a partial success in retaining the company as a Tory stronghold, albeit on a different constitutional basis, but they waged a long and powerful campaign against the Bank of England. The ideological content of that campaign, however, was not based on classical or Renaissance assumptions. The Tories did not argue that banks and capitalism were incompatible with commonwealth principles. Instead they melded a commitment to agrarian economics with a bitter attack on the political consequences of banks. Rather than indict banks for the danger they posed to commonwealths, the Tories argued that national banks of credit fostered republics.

"There are three sorts of people, how much soever otherwise their interest and humours differ, have . . . unanimously joined issue against this undertaking [of a bank]," noted one of the new institution's proponents, "the Jacobites, who apprehend it may contribute to lessen their monarch of France, and some few usurers and brokers of money, and the third sort are commonly such as have not wherewith to trade." Though a bitter and exaggerated view, this explanation has merit. Tories and Jacobites immediately criticized the bank. The Earl of Nottingham was but one of the more prominent Tory voices to decry the new bank as "pernicious to the public good." The passionately Whig bishop of Salisbury Gilbert Burnet noted the "vehemence of zeal" with which "all the enemies of the government set themselves" against the bank. The Tories apparently followed Sir Edward Seymour in believing that the English should "never lay burdens on ourselves that our forefathers never knew."[58]

The creation of the Bank of England, which accepted deposits in any form, paid out interest, and sought to encourage manufacturers, forced its opponents into action. Tories, always reluctant to support proposals that would benefit those with liquid capital, now threw their support behind a land bank scheme. The National Land Bank, as opposed to the Bank of England, explicitly sought a clientele of landowners. Significantly, four of the leading figures associated with the Land Bank were none other than Sir Josiah Child, his brother-in-law Sir Thomas Cooke, the Tory East India merchant Sir Joseph Herne, and the Tory financier John Briscoe. The eighteenth-century economic writer Adam Anderson was certain that the Land Bank scheme "was principally encouraged" by the "Tory party." When the representatives of the Land Bank scheme made their case before the Treasury, they chose the Tory Sir Thomas Meres as their spokesman, who "made a very florid oration." One scholar has shown that to its enemies the Bank of England seemed "inherently anti-agrarian, too much allied with commercial interests and with the growing bourgeoisie. It appeared to be the spearhead of a financial revolution which was furthering the change from a landed to a commercial economy and was aimed at lowering land values, increasing interest rates, adding more aristocratic support of the war effort, and effectually placing increased control of both national finance and policy in the hands of the war interest." Not surprisingly, the supporters of the Land Bank were also committed to "a peace policy." No wonder the Whig Charles Montagu was convinced that the supporters of the Land Bank "mean something else than doing the king's business." The Tories, along with all the supporters of the Old East India Company, were able to get statutory approval of the Land Bank in 1696. But the scheme quickly "failed completely" because the merchant community refused to subscribe.[59] Though agrarian political economy still had its supporters in Parliament, it had far fewer out of doors.

Classical and Renaissance critics of capitalism may well have supported the agrarian-based Land Bank as a politically responsible alternative to the Bank of England, as a way of containing the corrosive effects of an increasingly commercial economy. But they would never have followed the second line of attack on the Bank of England. When the proposal for the bank was debated in the House of Lords—we have only the sketchiest of accounts of the debates in the Commons—the Tories Halifax, Nottingham, and Rochester were "among its most vocal" critics. A chief objection was that "it would undermine royal authority for banks were only fit for republics." These were not the odd views of a few powerful but ideologically naive aristocrats. The Tory propaganda campaign made this same argument repeatedly against the Bank of England. Just a "perusal" of the names of "the zealots for upholding the Bank and some of the chief trustees in managing of it," observed one critic, reveals a group of "whom it may be pronounced without doing them injustice, that their bias was never very remarkable toward kingship." Drawing on a traditional Tory trope for Whig-bashing, another opponent of the bank described the bank's supporters as part of a "faction for private advantage." The bank's enemies found this social alignment predictable since banks were ineluctably tied to republican forms of government. It "doth not look too favourably upon the constitution of the government that all national banks have hitherto been peculiar to commonwealths," worried another polemicist, "nor can models convertible with republics have a good effect upon crowned heads, or be found consistent with a monarchical constitution, but either the king will swallow up the bank, or the bank supplant the king." Many of the bank's opponents noted incorrectly, in an accusation fraught with political significance in the wake of the Glorious Revolution, that its model "came from Holland"—the republican homeland of William of Orange. The association of banks with republicanism was no new thing. "The nature and use of banks and public funds have been the discourse and expectation of many years," recalled one proponent of the bank with a good deal of justice, "but all this while our more refined politicians assured us, that we must never think of settling a bank in England without a commonwealth: and this notion became so universal, that it was a matter of derision for anyone to seem to be of a contrary opinion." It was still commonly said that "the very establishing of a bank in England, will of course alter the government for that is to entrust the fund of the nation in the hands of subjects, who naturally are, and will always be sure to be of the popular side, and will insensibly influence the church and state." The bank's defenders made little effort to ease these traditional Tory concerns. One responded bitterly that "such politicians as would not allow of banks here (because 'tis no commonwealth) mistook the English constitution very much, for, till the time of Charles the Second, nobody was ashamed to call it a commonwealth."[60]

Reviewing the polemical responses to the bank reveals an odd juxtaposition of arguments. Far from adopting a coherent classical and Renaissance critique of capitalism, opponents developed a two-pronged approach. First, they argued that a national bank would transform the basis of English society from a reliance on land to a reliance on manufacturing. It is extremely important to note that this line of analysis was prominently advanced in the first instance not by the radical Whigs like Robert Molesworth or John Trenchard, both of whom subscribed to the Bank of England and strongly supported Whig schemes for carrying on a Continental war, but by Josiah Child and his Tory East India Company friends. Second, the enemies of the bank repeatedly insisted that a national bank would turn England into a commonwealth. This line of argument was antithetical to the classical and Renaissance commonwealth tradition. Classical and Renaissance modes of thought were incapable of providing a key to understanding postrevolutionary political economy.

England enjoyed a phenomenal period of economic growth in the later seventeenth century. While most of Continental Europe was suffering through economic recession and deurbanization, the English economy was growing at a respectable rate. It was during this period that England's economy diverged from the European pattern. Stimulated by developments in overseas trade, England's towns became larger and more prosperous, England's economic infrastructure—its roads, its postal services, its transportation networks—developed tremendously, and the English people benefited from a whole new range of consumer amenities. This transformation of English society and the English economy made it possible for English politicians to imagine and implement vast modern projects for state improvement.

Later seventeenth-century England was an age of state-building projects. "The past ages have never come up to the degree of projecting and inventing, as it refers to matters of negoce, and methods of civil polity, which we see this age arriv'd to," observed Daniel Defoe in his *Essay upon Projects*. Defoe made it clear that by projects he meant endeavors "of public advantage, as they tend to improvement of trade, and employment of the poor, and the circulation and increase of the public stock of the kingdom." These were not mere inventions. "The true definition of a project, according to modern acceptation, is," Defoe explained, "a vast undertaking, too big to be managed, and therefore likely enough to come to nothing." Projects were political economic schemes to promote the common good achievable only in the modern age. It was for this reason that Defoe could "trace the original of the projecting humor that now reigns, no farther back than the year 1680, dating its birth as a monster then, though by times it had indeed something of life in the time of the late Civil War."[61]

Defoe understood something fundamental about the nature of political economic debate in later seventeenth-century England. At about the time of the Exclusion Crisis the nature of political argument in England was fundamentally transformed.[62] England did not become a secular society. English men and women did not stop arguing about the succession, about the nature of royal authority, about the proper relation between the state and the salvation of souls. But at or about 1680 party politicians did add the question of the people's secular welfare to the list of central issues. Defoe was right to perceive that trading projects had become political issues already in the 1640s and 1650s. But in those decades and the 1660s and 1670s, debates over political economic issues were extremely fluid. They did not map easily onto other political preferences. However, from the mid-1670s, when future Whigs departed the Royal African Company in droves, through Josiah Child's purge of the Whigs from the East India Company in the early 1680s, political economic preferences began to meld more readily with other party political issues. By the

1680s Whigs and Tories divided over their political economic visions as much as they did over their views of church and state.

Historians, convinced that the Revolution of 1688–89 was fundamentally about the succession, the constitution, or confessional issues, have missed a vibrant and significant discussion of political economy in later seventeenth-century England. These debates taking place in trade company committee rooms, on the floor of the House of Commons and the House of Lords, on the exchange, and in the taverns and coffeehouses scattered across England both preceded and deeply influenced the events of 1688–89. Those historians have failed to note the revolution in political economy that was an intended outcome of many of the revolutionaries of 1688–89.

The controversy in political economy in the 1680s and 1690s was not between libertarian capitalists and neoclassical anticapitalists, nor was it between mercantilists and free traders. Polemicists on both sides of the debate were committed to promoting the common good rather than the profit of private individuals. Polemicists on both sides were sure that the common good or national interest was something conceptually distinct from the summation of the private interests of England's population. Similarly, both the defenders and the opponents of the Bank of England were committed to the notion that the government needed to intervene in the economy. The seventeenth-century advocates of free trade were fierce opponents of exclusive foreign trading concerns created by royal prerogative but were also great supporters of a state-supported national bank and progressive taxation schemes.

The discussion of political economy was not narrowly, as one scholar has asserted, a discipline that "provided the means to describe and explain the relationships among the three kingdoms." Political economy was not primarily a jurisdictional dispute about "the triangular relations between England, Ireland and Scotland."[63] The debate about political economy was about England's economic identity and its relations with Europe and the Indies East and West. Debates about the proper relationship with Ireland and Scotland certainly played a role. Nevertheless, those discussions took place in the broader context of England's relations with France and the United Provinces, with the East Indies and the Americas.

The debate that so deeply influenced the Revolution of 1688–89 and its aftermath was, in fact, between those who understood property as a natural creation and those who knew it to be the result of human endeavor. Sir Josiah Child, James II's court, and a wide range of Tories were committed to an agrarian political economy, one that posited a zero-sum world of commercial exchange. The corollary of that commitment was support of territorial imperialism in India and war against the Dutch. After the revolution, Child and his Tory allies opposed the creation of the bank both because it would transform England into a manufacturing society based on mobile wealth and because that very transformation would turn England into a commonwealth.

Whigs who opposed this agrarian understanding of political economy developed an equally sophisticated description of their social environment. They argued that since property was the result of human labor, it was potentially infinite. Manufacturing rather than land was the key to England's future wealth and power. They were therefore, on the whole, critical of the East India Company's trade to the extent that it imported finished products that competed with English manufactures while failing to export England's finished goods. They also saw little point in military conflict with the Dutch since there was by definition enough potential property for both countries to enjoy unlimited economic success. Most important, they were committed to the creation of a national bank based on mobile wealth, since only such a bank could both finance the ideologically urgent conflict with France and ensure the proper circulation of money. Only the circulation of money, they believed, could guarantee the development of English manufactures. Most Whig supporters of the revolution did not celebrate amoral, profit-seeking individualists. Instead, they celebrated the English nation both for its participatory politics and for its rich communal culture.

Party political allegiances were extremely fluid in the 1690s, yet these two ideological visions correspond closely to the divisions between Tory and Whig. The supporters of the East India Company and the Land Bank were overwhelmingly Tory, the critics of the Old East India Company and subscribers to the bank heavily Whig. Where the supporters of the agrarian notion of political economy were deeply skeptical of the Continental war effort (preferring a blue-water strategy), the advocates of the manufacturing economy were the most enthusiastic supporters of confrontation with Louis XIV in Europe.

The political economic achievements that have come to be known as the Financial Revolution were Whig achievements. Whigs were determined to demolish the Royal African and East India Companies not because they were opposed to government intervention in the economy but because they believed those institutions were harming England's manufacturing sector. Whigs wanted to replace the Hearth Tax with a land tax not because they wanted to limit taxation but because they wanted tax policies appropriate to a manufacturing society. Tories wanted to create a territorial empire and the Land Bank not because they were critics of capitalism but because they believed that territory represented a real limit on economic growth.

Given these deep ideological differences between Whigs and Tories in the 1680s and 1690s, neo-Whig social scientists are wrong to posit a postrevolutionary political consensus that created institutions designed to guarantee absolute property rights. There were no new constitutional guarantees. The Whig Colley Cibber was surely right to suggest that the events of 1688–89 created no new rights, advanced no new constitutional guarantees, but gave those that already existed "a real being." Indeed, there was nothing in the Bill of Rights of 1689 to secure property rights that had not been part of the Instrument of Government creating the Cromwellian Protectorate in December 1653. The instrument, like the Bill of Rights, had followed directly on the violent deposition of a monarch who had in the view of his critics been guilty of irresponsible behavior. What distinguished the 1650s from the 1690s was not the existence or absence of political institutions or credible commitments but the reality that in the 1690s Continental war against France had the full support of the Whig party and its commercial allies while in the 1650s Cromwell had precious little support from any segment of the merchant community for his war against Spain. What distinguished the 1650s from the 1690s was the presence, by the end of the century, of a political party capable of establishing the institutions necessary for funding foreign wars. Party strife not political consensus and rational bargaining gave rise to England's Financial Revolution.[64]

The Revolution of 1688–89 was the result of a vicious multilayered party conflict. The Whigs initiated the economic program of the 1690s, the so-called Financial Revolution, after a full-scale and hard-fought victory over their political opponents. Their economic program was no compromise. They sought to demolish and emasculate the political economic institutions of their enemies—first the Old East India and the Royal African Companies, and then, in 1696, the Land Bank. It was the fact that the Bank of England was created by and supported by the Whigs, that explains why periods of Whig political control in Westminster led "to increased credibility of debt repayment."[65] Had the Tories succeeded in replacing the Bank of England with a Land Bank in 1696, England would in all likelihood have followed a very different economic path.[66] Between 1689 and Sir Robert Walpole's rise to power in the 1720s, most Whigs remained committed to a political economic program that understood property to be created by human labor and favored the development of England's manufacturing sector. It was because Walpole began to abandon Whig political economic principles in the 1720s and 1730s that Opposition Whigs attacked him with such fury. For these men and women the Excise Crisis of 1733 was not merely a political miscalculation. Opposition Whigs believed that Walpole's plan to raise revenue by means of a tax on consumer goods in order to lower the land tax was an abandonment of the political and economic principles established in the revolution.

The revolution in political economy achieved in the aftermath of the events of 1688–89 had been the work of political as well as economic radicals. Their political achievement lay in creating the financial mechanisms that allowed England to carry on Continental wars on a previously unimaginable scale, against an enemy that was more powerful and more ambitious than any previously faced. Their ideological achievement was just as great. They had forced issues of political economy to the fore. Both Tories and Whigs had to embrace the full financial and commercial implications of their ideological commitments. For the Whigs this meant developing financial institutions and embracing tax policies that could support full-scale Continental war. For Tories this meant embracing not only a blue-water foreign policy but also a commitment to overseas territorial empire that would allow England to remain a first-class power. The Revolution of 1688–89 was a turning point in this struggle between two competing modern economic programs. The Whigs triumphed in the political cut and thrust of the 1690s, but they did not achieve hegemony. Defenders of Tory political economy never vanished. In fact, a strong case could be made that they regained the political upper hand in the 1760s and 1770s.

CHAPTER THIRTEEN

Revolution in the Church

harles Leslie, the Irish-born son of the bishop of Clogher who refused to
take the oath of allegiance to William and Mary, and Gilbert Burnet, the
Scottish child of a puritanical lawyer and a devout Presbyterian mother,
agreed on little. Both, however, were certain that William and Mary had
transformed the English episcopate and the ideological tenor of the Church
of England. "We see among the new-made bishops those who were formerly fanatical
preachers; and those who of all our number, are least zealous for the church, and most
latitudinarian, for a comprehension of dissenters, and a dispensation with our liturgy and
discipline," seethed Leslie in 1694. "In two years time the King had named fifteen new
bishops; and they were generally looked on as the most learned, the wisest, and best men,
that were in the church," countered Burnet, the Williamite bishop of Salisbury. Though
these men were "both of moderate principles and of calm tempers," even Burnet could
not deny that the postrevolutionary church was bitterly "broken" apart into "high and
low church" groupings. The new bishops, in Burnet's account, had become the leaders of
the Low Church party.[1]

Contemporary narratives of the radical transformation after 1689 stand in stark
contrast to the scholarly insistence that the revolution did little to change the Church of
England. If the Revolution of 1688–89 was a minor constitutional adjustment, it makes

---

(above) *Toleration Act,* 1689. Parliament passed the Toleration Act, which
granted freedom of worship to Protestant Dissenters, in 1689. This medal
commemorates the act as a key moment in the expansion of English rights,
depicting the figure of Religion holding up the cap of liberty in her left hand.

perfect sense that it would scarcely alter the Church of England. And that is exactly what historians of the late seventeenth century have argued. One school of thinking about the Church in the later seventeenth century accepts that there were profound divisions within Anglicanism but maintains that William and Mary's initial episcopal appointments did not constitute a new departure in the Church's ideological or political orientation. The new monarchs, argues Henry Horwitz, "leaned increasingly on [the Earl of] Nottingham's advice in ecclesiastical affairs." Predictably, the Tory churchman Nottingham chose men with his own sympathies. "In the two years following the Revolution an unprecedented series of vacancies occurred in bishoprics and deaneries," notes the church historian G. V. Bennett; by and large, "the places were filled by moderate Tories, men of real distinction and learning."[2]

Other scholars have denied that there were any meaningful ideological differences within the Church of England. As a result, they have emphasized the continuities between the pre- and postrevolution church. From the perspective of Anglicanism, argues Gerald Straka, "the Revolution was not a departure, but a restoration of true divine right Protestant monarchy and a return to the national unity of Elizabeth's great days." More recently Tony Claydon has described the postrevolutionary program of godly reformation as "a theological middle ground"—a position equally attractive to Whigs and Tories—which was dependent on an "early Protestant worldview."[3]

This second group emphasizes two important areas of continuity in the postrevolutionary church. First, they insist that there was no sharp break in the political outlook of the postrevolutionary Church of England. "The Church of England continued to be associated with the divine right of kings in its most extreme form," asserts J. P. Kenyon. Opposition to political resistance, notes Jonathan Clark, allowed Church of England divines to seize a moderate position between Calvinist and Roman Catholic doctrines. "The Church of England's doctrine of non-resistance"—enunciated both before and after the revolution—"occupied a middle ground between resistance theories advanced by denominations on either side. It was because it was a moderate doctrine that so many Whigs and Tories subscribed to it." Even those scholars like John Marshall and Craig Rose who have identified a unique brand of postrevolutionary churchmanship have insisted that politically the new episcopate was hardly distinctive. "The Anglican hierarchy was uniformly hostile to Exclusion of James and very few clerics of the Church of England were openly supportive of Exclusion," maintains John Marshall. "Almost all clerics of the Church of England were hostile to any form of armed resistance." The Latitudinarians, whom one might suspect to have more radical political opinions, "were energetic preachers of non-resistance." "The new bishops," Craig Rose opines in describing those preferred after 1688, "were not Whigs in any meaningful sense of the term. Many of them were close associates of the earl of Nottingham, champion of moderate Toryism, and may have shared his convictions that the Whigs wanted to dismantle the establishment."[4]

Those who argue for a unified rather than a divided church have also claimed that the postrevolutionary church remained adamantly opposed to religious toleration. The supposed Latitudinarianism of many of the postrevolutionary bishops should not blind us to their basic hatred of dissent, argue these scholars. Their support for comprehension—a broadening of the Church of England to accommodate the most moderate dissenters—was accompanied by an abhorrence of schism and a defense of persecution. "Within the framework of restoration politics, a policy of comprehension advanced by Anglicans functioned as part of an attempt to defeat the policy of toleration, while legitimating the prosecution of religious dissent," avers Richard Ashcraft. In this context, the Latitudinarians were merely "the shock troops of persecution in the war against nonconformity." Noting that John Tillotson and Edward Stillingfleet, Latitudinarians and postrevolution bishops both, were "vocal opponents of toleration," Jon Parkin insists that "comprehension and toleration were mutually exclusive concepts." According to Tony Claydon, Tillotson and Simon Patrick, another prominent postrevolution bishop, "joined a united Anglican defense of a monopolistic national church and were not unduly sympathetic to dissent."[5] In the view of these scholars, then, the postrevolutionary Church of England was united in its commitment to intolerance and persecution.

Against these views—that William and Mary initially embraced moderate Tory churchmanship on one hand or that there was a basic and profound consensus within the Church of England on the other—I maintain that there was a revolution in the ideological and religious commitments of the episcopate in the wake of the events of 1688–89. Far from being united before the revolution, Anglican clerics were deeply divided over a range of issues, divisions that became increasingly pronounced during the reign of James II. These divisions make it impossible to describe prerevolution groupings in terms of simple divisions between Dissenters and Anglicans. These divisions also make clear the insufficiency of accounts of the period in terms of impermeable, and internally cohesive, religious identities. Identity politics are a wholly inadequate guide to the political and religious divisions of the late seventeenth century. The range of William and Mary's episcopal appointments and translations from 1689 to 1692 demonstrate the new monarchs' commitment to supporting one particular ideological grouping. Although Latitudinarian is probably too restrictive a term for the postrevolutionary episcopate—they shared neither a common Cambridge background nor a distinctive theological outlook—the new bishops were decidedly Low Church. The social connections, ideological pronouncements, and political actions of these churchmen reveal a church hierarchy largely committed to Whig politics, comprehension, *and* toleration.[6]

"The poor Church of England is undone again," Joseph Hill lamented to his fellow moderate churchman Sir William Trumbull in early 1689. The reign of James II as well as his eventual downfall had indeed been difficult times for the Church of England. The bishops had unfailingly asserted James's rights when Duke of York in the trying days of the Exclusion Crisis. After that crisis the commitments of the Church and its bishops were clarified. The Commission for Ecclesiastical Promotions set up by Charles II in 1681, led by William Sancroft, archbishop of Canterbury, preferred a series of men to episcopal sees who were "thorough-paced Anglicans, imbued with a sense of *jure divino* monarchy," who were also sympathetic to Sancroft's highly ritualistic and intolerant program of church reform.[7] These were men such as Francis Turner, the newly preferred bishop of Ely, who were deeply committed both to divine right monarchy and to an activist, uniform national church. They insisted on political and religious conformity.

Although Charles II had done everything he could to prepare the Church of England for James II's accession, it soon became clear that the episcopal bench, so long and so bitterly opposed to religious dissent, was not prepared to support James II's Declaration of Indulgence. James therefore soon felt compelled to prefer a new set of churchmen with different ideological commitments. Thomas Cartwright, who became bishop of Chester in 1686, "stood at the centre of a group of divines whose theological view of kingship left little or no room for the role of positive law or human institutions in the political life of the state." The Whiggishly inclined cleric William Denton commented that Cartwright was "famous for his sermon preaching up arbitrary power to that height that he hath thereby purchased a name." Others who enjoyed the king's favor and unflinchingly supported his policies were Thomas Watson, bishop of St. David's, Nathaniel Crewe, bishop of Durham, Samuel Parker, bishop of Oxford, and Parker's successor in Oxford, Timothy Hall.[8] These were men whose commitment to royal absolutism knew no limits but who were willing to stomach their master's limited support for liberty of conscience. Their support of monarchy, like their Gallican fellow-supporters of James II, called for active, not just passive, obedience.

The personal and ideological cleavages between these two groups of divines became apparent almost immediately. When the bishops of Chester, Oxford, St. David's, Durham, and Rochester (Thomas Sprat) decided to address their king in April 1687, thanking him for his Declaration of Indulgence, the Caroline appointees responded with fury. "The inevitable consequence of this address," wrote the archbishop of Canterbury, William Sancroft, "must be a fatal division among the clergy and either beget a new schism, or widen the old ones, which are already too deplorable." Many churchmen fell in behind their metropolitan and his denunciation of schism. "Some sort of churchmen say these bishops that have subscribed the Address are renegados to the Church of England, and Tories, and they have nothing to do with them," recorded the London Presbyterian Roger Morrice. "I do not know that any London divines have subscribed it." For the balance of James II's reign Sancroft and his friends on the episcopal bench expressed their distaste for Cartwright, Crewe, Parker, and Watson in every conceivable manner. When the Seven Bishops, including Sancroft, were brought to trial for opposing James's second Declaration of Indulgence in June 1688, Cartwright, Crewe, and Watson offered their brethren no support. These real and profound differences were over the relative weight the divines were willing to accord their commitment to absolute monarchy and their detestation of schism. Neither Sancroft's followers nor Cartwright's supporters were willing to countenance political resistance. Neither the addressers nor their opponents wanted a broader or more tolerant church.[9]

The deposition of James II brought no relief. Although the bishops were overjoyed that William had halted James II's Catholicizing policies, they could not stomach any move that went beyond passive obedience. Sancroft, who had "opposed King James before in never acknowledging his son or showing him the least civility," now refused to "pay the least sort of respect to the Prince of Orange." Whereas Sancroft merely withdrew from public life, most of the rest of the bishops spent December 1688 and the early months of 1689 caballing and agitating against the new regime. Their "design," thought Roger Morrice, was "to reduce all things to the state they were brought into *anno* 1662 and continued to the beginning of *anno* 1688." The bishops wanted to return to a world in which a monolithic and intolerant church would receive the full support of a monarch who ruled by indefeasible hereditary divine right. This was clearly not to be. As soon as William and Mary were declared king and queen, Edward Harley noted that "many of the Bishops [were] withdrawn from the Lords House, [and] pretend they will not take the oaths" to the new regime. Sure enough, only eight of the twenty-seven English and Welsh bishops swore allegiance to William and Mary.[10] The withdrawal of the bishops from the House of Lords was soon followed by the refusal of four hundred other clerics to take the oaths.

Nevertheless the moral consistency and literary achievement of the nonjurors has led many to overestimate their significance. The vast majority of England's ten thousand clerics did take the oaths, a much larger proportion than conformed in 1662. The impression of most contemporaries was that there was overwhelming subscription on the part of the clergy. "There are very few of the clergy (one or two) that do refuse the oaths," reported the High Churchman Sir William Boothby from Derbyshire. "The refusers are but a small number in comparison to those that have sworn," mourned the nonjuror Charles Trumbull, "a plain instance of our infirmity and frailty, how far the affectation of popularity, opposition to Popery, and carnal interest may prevail over us contrary to the doctrine of our church and the former public professions of so many of our own members in their treatises and sermons." With more distance, and less personal pique, one might say that the failure of the mass of English clerics to follow the lead of their bishops reveals the veracity of one religious historian's claim that in the 1680s, clerical "dissidents were never far beneath the surface of parish and cathedral life."[11]

The eventual deprivation of the nonjurors coupled with the deaths of a number of other bishops gave William and Mary the opportunity to reshape the episcopal bench, perhaps to tap into that simmering dissidence within the prerevolutionary church. From 1689 to 1692 the new monarchs called on eighteen men to fill vacant sees.[12] Were these men moderate Tories, putting into practice the religious policies of the Earl of Nottingham and his moderate High Church associates? Did they instead merely continue the practices and policies of their deprived and deceased brethren? Or did these new bishops adopt a distinctively new style of churchmanship and in so doing transform the Church of England?

The claim advanced by revisionist scholars that the postrevolutionary bishops had a moderate Tory political outlook rests largely on an analysis of their social networks. The association of many of the new regime's appointees with the impeccably Tory and High Church Finch family certainly renders this assertion plausible. On examination, however, the postrevolutionary bishops had a much wider range of personal associations, a range that points toward a very different sort of churchmanship.

There can be no doubting the variety and significance of Finch ecclesiastical patronage. As solicitor general, attorney general, lord keeper, and eventually lord chancellor, Heneage Finch had a number of ecclesiastical appointments at his disposal. Relying, apparently, on the advice of his chaplain John Sharp, Finch offered his patronage to Edward Stillingfleet, John Tillotson, Richard Kidder, John Moore, Thomas Tenison, and Simon Patrick—all men who would become bishops after the revolution. After his death, Finch's son Daniel, Earl of Nottingham, maintained the family connections with these young and increasingly prominent clerics. Nevertheless, too much can be made of the ideological significance of this connection. When Lord Chancellor Finch made Richard Kidder a prebend of Norwich, for example, he had never met the cleric. The lord chancellor's patronage appears to have been determined more by the social circles of his chaplains than by his political predispositions. Gilbert Burnet, who decried the lord chancellor's proclivity for justifying "the court in all debates in the House of Lords," found himself able to praise "the great care" and "worthy men" with which Heneage Finch filled "the church livings that belonged to the seal."[13]

Many of the postrevolutionary bishops who were part of the Finch circle were also active in other networks with very different religious and political tinctures. Edward Stillingfleet's "introduction" to London came as preacher at the Rolls Chapel, an appointment he owed to the Presbyterian former parliamentarian Sir Harbottle Grimstone, who was then master of the rolls. On Stillingfleet's departure, Grimstone briefly appointed Richard Kidder to be preacher at the Rolls. Grimstone then appointed Gilbert Burnet to succeed Kidder, despite the heavy-handed objections raised by the High Churchman Sir Joseph Williamson. "The obligations [Sir Harbottle Grimstone] has laid on me are such," Burnet later gushed, that "the gratitude and service of my whole life, is the only equal return I can make for them."[14]

The Earls of Bedford and Essex and their relatives, families whose names were closely associated with Parliamentarianism and then radical Whiggery, also did much to promote the careers of several of the postrevolutionary bishops. The Earl of Bedford offered the benefice of St. Paul's Covent Garden to Simon Patrick in 1662. In 1664, the Earl of Essex, "who was known to be a true friend to the church," presented Richard Kidder with a living in Essex in 1664. Both John Tillotson and Gilbert Burnet maintained close contacts with the Russell family. Burnet praised William, Lord Russell, for his "zeal for true religion, and the other virtues that have from the beginnings of the Reformation, in a continued entail, adorned that noble family of Bedford, beyond most others of the kingdom." When Lord Russell was condemned to death for his participation in the Rye House Plot, Tillotson and Burnet ministered to him in his last days. Both men maintained close contact with Lord Russell's widow, Rachel Russell. Tillotson offered Lady Russell words of consolation and then consulted with her about ecclesiastical affairs after the revolution. It was in part because of Lady Russell's recommendation that Burnet was introduced to the Prince and Princess of Orange on his arrival in the United Provinces. Not surprisingly, given these close associations with Whig families, Burnet instructed Robert Boyle to deliver the first manuscript copies of his soon-to-be famous *Travels* to the Ladies Essex and Russell.[15]

Several postrevolutionary bishops were intimates of the great natural philosopher Robert Boyle himself. Boyle was a deeply religious man and a lifelong communicant of the Church of England. But he was also well known "for moderation to those who dissented from us." "If he was sharp in any point," noted one of Boyle's contemporaries, "it was against persecution which he thought immoral." Boyle had no close ties with High Churchmen. Instead he confided in and conversed with Burnet, Kidder, Tenison, and Stillingfleet, "for whose depth of learning and solid judgement he had always the greatest value and esteem." It is true, of course, that Boyle's closest clerical acquaintance, the man "whom he called his confessor," was Thomas Barlow, bishop of Lincoln. Barlow, though perhaps theologically old-fashioned, was deeply implicated in Whig politics. He had been "a bitter enemy" of the Duke of York during the Exclusion Crisis and such an enthusiastic supporter of the revolution that it was said that "no Bishop was more ready than he to supply the places of those of the clergy of the diocese that refused the oaths."[16]

John Locke, the Earl of Shaftesbury's former secretary and Whig polemicist, also had close ties to many of the Williamite bishops. Locke was a lifelong communicant of the Church of England. He maintained friendships with Richard Kidder and William Lloyd. Though he was personally more distant from Burnet, he deeply admired the Williamite bishop of Salisbury's commitment to toleration and his pastoral style. Locke was particularly close to Edward Fowler, the Williamite bishop of Gloucester, who visited the philosopher in his last days. Locke exchanged books with, and referred his friends to, the postrevolutionary archbishop of Canterbury, John Tillotson. At Tillotson's death, Locke mourned "that great and candid searcher after truth," a man who had been Locke's "friend of many years, steadfast, candid, and sincere." Now, Locke explained to his confidant Philippus Van Limborch, "I have scarcely anyone whom I can freely consult about theological uncertainties."[17]

If many of the Williamite bishops enjoyed the patronage of the High Church Tory

Finch family, they had at least as many significant associations with notorious Whigs and advocates of religious toleration. Indeed, that the Williamite bishops maintained these Whiggish associations when it was distinctly unfashionable to do so reveals more about their ideological proclivities than their willingness to accept preferment from those in power under Charles and James.

For most of the postrevolutionary bishops their most important social and intellectual ties were with fellow clerics. When Burnet, William's first episcopal creation, arrived in London from his native Scotland in 1662, he "easily went into the notions of the Latitudinarians." While the meaning and utility of the term "Latitudinarian" has been queried by scholars, it is clear that Burnet meant it in the loosest possible way. Where the Presbyterian divine Richard Baxter described this group of Cambridge-educated men as holding a series of theological principles—they were said to be "platonists or cartesians, and many of them Arminians with some additions, having more charitable thoughts than others of the salvation of heathens and infidels, and some of them holding the opinions of Origen about the preexistence of souls"—Burnet defined the group more vaguely and less theologically. For Burnet, the group was defined by a series of attitudes and friendships rather than by a set of doctrines or beliefs. The friendships in the first instance included Simon Patrick, Edward Stillingfleet, and John Tillotson. The attitudes were, above all, "very moderate," a moderation no doubt defined against the intolerant Act of Uniformity then being advocated by Gilbert Sheldon, bishop of London and soon-to-be archbishop of Canterbury. Burnet's friends were men who though they "loved the constitution of the church, and the liturgy . . . did not think it unlawful to live under another form." They were men who "wished that things might have been carried with more moderation" toward Dissenters. And they were men "who continued to keep a good correspondence with those who had differed from them in opinion, and allowed a great freedom both in philosophy and divinity."[18] Although Burnet has no doubt overemphasized his friends' commitment to philosophical and religious pluralism—they all certainly believed passionately that the Church of England was the best of all possible churches—their style and affect certainly differed sharply from the hotter and more rigid High Church supporters of Archbishop Gilbert Sheldon.

The Williamite bishops were not all Cambridge men. Nor were the associations these men began to have in the 1660s limited to former students of the Cambridge Platonists. Another of Burnet's early friends, for example, was William Lloyd, who was translated from the see of St. Asaph to that of Lichfield and then to that of Worcester by William III. Lloyd was an acolyte of John Wilkins, warden of Wadham College and bishop of Chester. Wilkins, though "exactly conformable himself" to the Church of England, was notorious for being "very tender to those that differed from him." He was, Anthony Wood noted, "for a comprehension and a limited indulgence for Dissenters in religion." Wilkins was hated by both Sheldon and John Fell, bishop of Oxford and the great patron of that university's High Churchmen. Unsurprisingly, Wilkins was a lifelong friend of John

Tillotson's, in whose London house he died. Wilkins also did much to promote the career of his student, successor at Wadham, and Williamite bishop Gilbert Ironside. Ironside was himself probably friendly with another enemy of John Fell's and Gilbert Sheldon's, the master of Pembroke and Williamite bishop of Bristol John Hall.[19]

Throughout the Restoration Fell's and Sheldon's enemies strengthened and expanded their networks of friendships. Tillotson was one of the "intimate friends" of John Sharp, Williamite archbishop of York. So close was their friendship, which was "improved perpetually by an intimate conversation for many years," that Sharp asked Tillotson to officiate at his wedding. Tillotson had another admirer in Richard Kidder. In addition to Tillotson, Kidder knew "intimately" Richard Cumberland, Edward Fowler, and Simon Patrick "from their youth up." Patrick, in turn, knew Thomas Tenison sufficiently well to recommend him for the vicarage of St. Martin-in-the-Fields in 1680. During the difficult summer of 1688, Kidder concealed William Lloyd to protect him from the king's fury in the wake of the Seven Bishops' trial. Lloyd then stayed with Gilbert Burnet during William's march on London. John Moore, the Williamite bishop of Norwich, also considered Burnet to be "a particular friend." Burnet thought sufficiently well of Edward Fowler that he recommended him to Stillingfleet for the living of St. Giles Cripplegate.[20] Burnet's ties with Lloyd and Tillotson were so close that he submitted his writings "to their censure in everything."[21]

This group of Low Church friends and associates engaged in several distinctive schemes. First, many of them were involved in projects for comprehension *and* indulgence, for broadening membership of the Church, and for tolerating those outside it. Tillotson and Stillingfleet were members of John Wilkins's "club for a comprehension and limited indulgence for dissenters in religion." After Wilkins's death in 1672, the club continued to meet in the chambers "of that great trimmer and latitudinarian Dr. Hezekiah Burton in Essex House, without Temple Bar, being the habitation of Sir Orlando Bridgeman, to whom Burton was chaplain." Since Richard Cumberland was an "intimate" of Burton as well as a chaplain of Sir Orlando Bridgeman, he was likely another member of this club. Indeed, Cumberland was probably one of those churchmen whose "haughty and yet flattering brow," in Samuel Parker's opinion, persuaded Bridgeman to lend his authority to comprehension schemes. This group worked with a Dissenting delegation to draw up a plan for comprehension in 1674. Though the project came to nothing, Richard Baxter later maintained that Stillingfleet and Tillotson were "the likeliest men to have a hand in an agreement, if such a thing should be attempted." Although the other members of this club for comprehension and indulgence remain speculative, the Oxford High Churchman William Jane's later quip makes it clear that a number of other Williamite bishops were involved.[22]

This group of friends more successfully brought to fruition a second project in the later 1670s and early 1680s, *The History of the Reformation*. The *History* specifically targeted the High Church account of the Reformation produced by Peter Heylin. Burnet claimed that Heylin, in his narrative of a clerically driven Reformation, was either "very ill informed or very much led by his passions." Unsurprisingly, the *History* was never a favorite of the High Churchmen. Archbishop Sancroft tried to block Burnet's access to vital manuscripts, and nonjurors attacked the published results. By contrast, the project received enthusiastic support from the Whigs William Russell, George Savile (before his gradual turn to Toryism), and the republican Anthony Keck. "That great performance, *The History of the Reformation*," which was "universally applauded," was formally the work of Gilbert Burnet, but was in fact the work of a group of Low Churchmen. Thomas Tenison joined Burnet in reading through relevant manuscripts at Corpus Christi College, Oxford. "The famous and eminently learned Doctor Stillingfleet" loaned Burnet some manuscripts of "great value." William Lloyd "did engage me chiefly to this work," according to Burnet, "and furnished me with a curious collection of his own observations." Burnet submitted the finished manuscript of both parts of his *History* to Lloyd, Stillingfleet, and John Tillotson, who all closely commented on the text before awarding it "their hearty approbation."[23]

The defeat of the Whig attempt to exclude James from the throne and the subsequent Tory reaction in the early 1680s did not stop the meetings and discussions of the moderate divines. Samuel Parker reported in 1685 that William Lloyd, bishop of St. Asaph, was "president of a Trimmer cabal of London divines." This "cabal," no doubt a continuation of the earlier club, which met in Hezekiah Burton's chambers, were probably the same "worthy and eminent men" whom Burnet praised for refraining from Tory excesses in the 1680s. The roll call of honor included a wide range of Williamite bishops: Stillingfleet, Tillotson, Lloyd, Thomas Tenison, John Sharp, Simon Patrick, Edward Fowler, and John Moore, among others. These, Titus Oates later wrote, were "the sober and moderate men of the Church of England" whom Tories stigmatized "with the name of Trimmers."[24]

Far more open and publicly acknowledged than Lloyd's Trimming cabal were the lectures, discussions, and publishing projects promoted in London by the Low Church divines. John Sharp "spent his vacant and leisure hours" in "frequent stated meetings and conferences" with other London divines. At these meetings, which Sharp's son recalled included Tillotson, Patrick, and Stillingfleet, among others, the divines discussed "such subjects as pertained to their own profession, or such passages of scripture, as any of them proposed to treat in the pulpit." Sharp and Tillotson were active participants in the Tuesday and Friday lectures at St. Lawrence Jewry in the City. These lectures were attended by "above a hundred divines" who then met "usually at the Divines Coffee-House hard-by, immediately after, and do business with one another." These frequent discussions and debates among the City divines—and it is probably safe to assume that besides those specifically mentioned, Robert Grove, Nicholas Stratford, Thomas Tension, Richard Cumberland, Edward Fowler, and Richard Kidder were frequent participants as well—shaped a common outlook and ideological perspective. This outlook was further shaped by a publishing scheme developed in 1670, when "several divines in London met and dined together, intending to consult how they might most efficaciously promote true religion by their ministry." The result was a plan to publish a series of "plain" and cheap books "on such subjects as were much misunderstood." Although these books appeared anonymously, both Kidder and Patrick later claimed to have been among the sixteen divines who participated.[25] The London divines were thus a tight-knit community devoted to pastoral activism long before the accession of James II.

In the face of the perceived Catholic threat, the London divines merely turned their efforts from practical to controversial divinity. Richard Kidder remembered that "they met often and consulted," producing what Simon Patrick called "several little treatises" distinguishing and defending the Church of England from Roman Catholicism. In this context it is hardly surprising that the London divines achieved such unanimity in the face of James II's Second Declaration of Indulgence. It was because of their successful apologetic project that William Sancroft called on Tillotson, Stillingfleet, Patrick, Tenison, Robert Grove, and William Sherlock—all except Sherlock to become Williamite bishops—to help the bishops frame their response to the king's demand that the declaration be read in their churches.[26]

Clearly, those preferred and translated by William and Mary were united by social and intellectual networks wider and more profound than mere ties to the Finch family. Indeed, the new monarchs consulted a range of people about ecclesiastical affairs. The Earl of Nottingham did not have a monopoly. William often discussed the Church with the Marquis of Halifax, for example. Halifax had been a promoter of the Low Church *History of the Reformation,* a loyal friend of Gilbert Burnet, and in 1688 was well known to be "treating with, and offering bishoprics to some of the moderate clergymen of greatest note in the Church of England." From their accession William and Mary also consulted the Whig Lord John Somers on church matters. More important still, no doubt, was the influence of John Tillotson. William appointed Tillotson clerk of the closet in April 1689, an office that, his biographer Thomas Birch correctly noted, "required his frequent attendance near their Majesties' persons." William placed the greatest confidence in Tillotson, designing him for the archiepiscopal see of Canterbury as early as the spring of 1689. The list of Williamite bishops reads like a list of Tillotson's closest friends—including John Sharp, for whom Tillotson is known to have interceded—so the new clerk of the closet appears to have used his "frequent attendance" to good effect. Another man who had the king's ear in the first few months of his reign was William Lloyd, bishop of St. Asaph. Lloyd, the Earl of Clarendon sneered, would give William "no quiet" until he had appointed Gilbert Burnet bishop of Salisbury. In the late summer it was again Lloyd who proposed that Simon Patrick be preferred to the see of Chichester.[27]

Queen Mary, however, proved to be the most important ecclesiastical patron in the immediate aftermath of the revolution: she placed an indelible mark on the Church of England. "The filling the bishoprics," Mary recorded in her memoirs, was "the only thing of business I concerned myself in" while William was in England. After Archbishop Tillotson's death and shortly before her own, Mary "interested herself so much in the behalf of the Bishop of Lincoln [Thomas Tenison]; that there could be no denial." Tenison was soon translated to Canterbury as Tillotson's successor. Mary had strong Low Church preferences in religious matters. Her experience in the United Provinces and her marriage to the Calvinist William deeply colored her religious outlook. The Princess of Orange "told me herself more than once," James II's ambassador to the United Provinces wrote in November 1688, "that there was little or no difference between the Church of England and the Presbyterians and she goes constantly to both churches." Edward Fowler, then bishop of Gloucester, later recalled Mary's "charity towards sober Dissenters among our selves." The queen herself expressed "mortification" at the inability of the English clerics to settle on a comprehension scheme in 1689 that would broaden the Church of England and the same time grant toleration outside it. Mary's friendships were deeply partisan and firmly Low Church. Mary frequently consulted with and admired the works of Burnet, Tillotson, Tension, and Lloyd. By contrast, Nottingham, Mary thought, was "too violent for his party." She bemoaned her sister Anne's "making a party" with "all our High Church men and the Bishop of London," men who along with Anne "seemed to endeavour . . . to find fault with everything that was done, especially to laugh at afternoon sermons."[28]

The friendships, social ties, and patronage networks of the Williamite bishops, then, were much wider than the moderate Tory label usually assigned to them. Their connections and publishing projects certainly point to a distinctive ideological position, a position that was more sophisticated and partisan than that suggested by what historians have described as an "early protestant worldview" or a consensual Anglicanism. What, then, were the political and ecclesiological commitments of the Williamite bishops? Were they as a group Low Churchmen?

However divided scholars have been about the religious beliefs of the Williamite bishops, they have agreed that the new sees were filled by men who opposed political resistance. The episcopal bench, scholars maintain, remained committed to passive obedience. The bishops understood the revolution to have been exclusively the work of God's providence. The new bishops, like their predecessors, were not in any meaningful sense Whigs.

There can be no question that both the Caroline bishops appointed during the Tory reaction of the 1680s and James's appointments after 1685, whatever their differences over the extent of the prerogative and the wisdom of toleration by indulgence, agreed that there could be no room for political resistance to a monarch ruling by indefeasible hereditary divine right. "I am sure," wrote John Fell, who was responsible for educating, training, and promoting the careers of so many High Churchmen, "the poor Church of England is infinitely concerned to recommend herself by all offices of devotion and duties of religion to that overruling power and goodness she entirely subsists by." In this view, no right-thinking person could conceive of altering monarchy by hereditary succession.

"No man could be an Exclusioner," wrote the rector of East Allington in Devon Edmund Elys, "unless first he violated the bonds" of the Church of England. If any in England felt their religion or property threatened by the rule of James II, advised Thomas Sprat, bishop of Rochester, in his widely circulated denunciation of the Rye House Plot, "let them but remember and consider sadly what was the issue of the very same murmurs, and tumults against his Royal father of blessed memory; whether the first and most eminent instruments of subverting, for a time this renowned and ancient monarchy, were not themselves beguiled by the same methods into the meanest slavery, both spiritual and temporal."[29]

Not surprisingly, most of the bishops reacted to the arrival of the Prince of Orange in 1688 as an opportunity to reaffirm their principles of nonresistance and passive obedience. Francis Turner, bishop of Ely, on hearing that William had indeed put to sea, preached two sermons in Cambridge "for non-resistance and passive obedience." He then held meetings at Ely House attended by several bishops and London divines. The goal of these meetings, he told Sancroft, was "to proceed in the design of drawing up propositions of our doctrine against deposing, electing, or breaking the succession." Most bishops echoed Turner's views. Thomas Ken, who would later refuse to take the oaths to the new regime, promised his old friend the Earl of Dartmouth when William's arrival appeared imminent that "I shall always be ready to serve my sovereign to the utmost of my power, as far as can be consistent with my superior duty to God and to that holy religion I profess." John Lake of Chichester preached in the City against rebellion. Bishop William Thomas of Worcester wrote a stinging pastoral letter warning clergy not to take the oaths to the new regime. Given these ideological commitments, it is no wonder that "the bishops have been for restoring [the government] to its former channel by calling home the king and binding him to the church by laws and so secure the loyalty and bishoprics."[30]

It was not only nonjurors and future Jacobite plotters who retained their commitment to passive obedience and indefeasible hereditary divine right. Many of those who took the oaths to the new regime did so with reservations. They recognized William and Mary as reigning de facto but insisted that James II was still their king de jure. This was certainly the position, for example, of two men who seemed destined for bishoprics before James's accession: William Jane and Robert South. Jane as Regius Professor of Divinity at Oxford had been the chief protagonist in drafting the infamous Oxford decree of 1683 condemning all books that authorized resistance to princes. After the revolution he formed part of the effective Christ Church–based "Tory patronage network," a set of connections devoted to the old principles of passive obedience and nonresistance. South, who had been recommended for a bishopric in the reigns of both Charles II and James II, was also a High Church protégé of John Fell. Throughout his life he "continued a strenuous assertor of the prerogative of the crown against such as were industrious towards its diminution." When asked to join in the invitation to William in the summer of 1688, South refused, insisting that "his religion had taught him to bear all things, and howsoever it should please God that he should suffer, he would by the divine assistance, continue to abide by his allegiance, and use no other weapons but his prayers and tears for the recovery of his sovereign from the wicked and unadvised counsels wherewith he was entangled."[31]

While nonjurors and High Churchmen were adamant in their opposition to resistance and convinced in their Toryism, most of the Williamite Bishops had very different ideological commitments. Several postrevolutionary bishops had a long history of opposition to absolutism; more came to defend resistance and to become involved in Whig politics.

The revelations of the Popish Plot and the subsequent Exclusion Crisis created a context in which a good number of churchmen could make clear that they were less enthusiastically committed to indefeasible divine right monarchy than many had expected. William Lloyd, then vicar of St. Martin-in-the-Fields, was at the center of the Popish Plot. It was he who whipped Londoners into a frenzy with his impassioned funeral sermon for his murdered friend Sir Edmund Berry Godfrey. His belief that the Jesuits were responsible for Godfrey's death was so deep that he repeated the charge to the archbishop of Canterbury long after it had become deeply unfashionable. It was Lloyd who took the decisive evidence of Miles Prance that did so much to corroborate the revelations of Titus Oates. These two actions made Lloyd into a Whig hero. Samuel Parker, always quick to smell out Whiggery, claimed that Lloyd was "the very founder of the plot and of all our troubles, for the plot had never come to anything without Godfrey's murder, nor Godfrey's murder without Prance's evidence, nor Prance's evidence without the Bishop of St. Asaph." No less inflammatory was the *Letter Written upon the Discovery of the Plot,* published to great popular acclaim by William Lloyd's close friend Gilbert Burnet. John Hall, then master of Pembroke College, similarly fanned the flames of Whig resentment in Oxford when he preached "sharply and bitterly against the Papists" at St. Mary's Church on 5 November 1678. Edward Fowler ostentatiously smashed "an idolatrous window" at Gloucester Cathedral at the height of the Popish Plot and was strongly rumored to be among the Earl of Shaftesbury's friends. John Tillotson, then dean of Canterbury, "was so deeply affected with a just apprehension of the danger of the Popish successor to the civil as well as religious liberties of his country, that he could not but wish success to the exclusion bill." Indeed his "zeal" for Exclusion was such that he did all he could "to divert" his friend Viscount Halifax from falling in with the bill's opponents.[32]

Despite what must have been immense pressure from the court and their superiors in the Church, many Low Churchmen continued to express sympathy for the Whig cause even in its darkest hour. John Hall, for example, "several times prayed" with the condemned Protestant joiner Stephen College in the days before College's execution for treason in 1681. Although Thomas Sprat vitriolically denounced the Rye House Plot by radical Whigs to assassinate Charles II and his brother James in 1683, Tillotson and Burnet ministered to the plotter William, Lord Russell, in his last hours, an act that apparently earned Burnet at least the Duke of York's permanent enmity. Richard Kidder, a less bold man, claims to have hinted strongly in his sermons and publications at his political misgivings during the Tory reaction. It was a time, he recalled, in which "we seemed to ruin ourselves." "We were weary of our franchises and liberties," Kidder lamented in distinctly Whiggish tones, "and courted chains and slavery; we made way for arbitrary power, and too many courted the advent of Popery. We were for giving away our charters, though at the time we were bound by oath to defend them. . . . We were mad with what we called loyalty, the law itself could set it no bounds." After the accession of James, Edward Fowler was accused by his parishioners of "Whiggism." In 1685 Samuel Parker accused Simon Patrick of being "the sourest Whig in the nation." John Hall, while desperately attempting to "show himself loyal" by preaching the coronation sermon for James at St. Mary's in Oxford, could manage only a "lukewarm, trimming sermon."[33]

In the decisive final year of James II's reign, many of the postrevolutionary bishops were deeply implicated in the Prince of Orange's preparations. Thomas Tenison was in frequent and secret correspondence with the Prince and Princess of Orange in the winter of 1688. That summer he was in a position to inform Simon Patrick and his brother John with "assurance" that "the Prince of Orange intended to come over with an army to our relief from the danger in which we were." Edward Fowler spent "a great part of his time" that year in Highgate with William Claggett, who was proclaiming to his friends that resistance "in some cases" might be "lawful." Four days before the trial of the Seven Bishops, William Lloyd predicted to Sancroft's chaplain Henry Wharton that the "injustice and tyranny" of James II and his government had "so exasperated the minds of the people in general, that the latter would soon drive them out of England." He concluded by telling Wharton that "a wonderful change of things was approaching." Unsurprisingly, Lloyd's friend Richard Davies recalled that the news of William's landing gave "great satisfaction to the bishop." Richard Kidder, with whom Lloyd stayed after the trial, also appears to have been well informed of William's imminent arrival in the summer of 1688. Gilbert Burnet, of course, was an active revolutionary. On arriving in the United Provinces after his trip through France, the Swiss cantons, and Italy, he spewed out pamphlet after pamphlet attacking James II, Louis XIV, and their policies. He translated William's *Declaration of Reasons* justifying his intervention in English affairs, joined William's fleet, and on the eve of their departure prayed to God to set the Prince of Orange "and the Princess, on thy good time, on the throne."[34]

Drumming up Whig sentiment during the Exclusion Crisis, supporting Whigs, and encouraging William's intervention strongly suggest that the postrevolutionary bishops were not the passive obedience men and moderate Tories of the scholarly literature. But all this does not quite prove that the Williamite bishops actually justified resistance. Indeed, recent scholarship on the debate over the postrevolutionary oath of allegiance has emphasized the conservatism of the new regime's supporters. These statements should not be read at face value, however. The allegiance controversy of 1689–94 was about persuading recalcitrant clerics to swear allegiance to the new regime; it was an attempt to allay the fears of the conservative members of the political nation. "I do not think that now when we are at quiet it is convenient to write much upon the subject of proving the right of the people's defending themselves when the whole constitution is in danger of being overturned," Gilbert Burnet explained to the Earl of Shrewsbury during the allegiance debate, but "whensoever a new occasion is given by the violence of the government to examine it, authors and matter will be found to support it." Many divines of the Church of England, Burnet later wrote, "owned a reserve for resistance in case a total subversion . . . though they did not think it necessary to mention it."[35]

The Williamite bishops, like many of their nonjuring and High Church opponents but unlike many Puritans and adherents of the early Protestant worldview, did abhor the notion that religious beliefs could justify rebellion. Resistance against James II because he was a Catholic was anathema. John Moore, Williamite bishop of Norwich, denounced "those who take upon them to absolve whole nations from their sworn duty to their prince, on the score of religion." In a speech written while imprisoned in the Tower, William Lloyd insisted that our "holy religion teaches us under pain of damnation not to rebel against our king, though he be of another religion; nay though he should be an enemy to our religion." Even in bitter exile Gilbert Burnet "preached a whole sermon at The Hague" in which he spoke "against the lawfulness of subjects rising against the sovereign on account of religion." "I do not know one of all the divines that have sworn to the present government," he summarized aptly in the 1690s, "who are not still of the same opinion that they were formerly of, and that do not still judge resistance on the account of religion to be unlawful."[36]

For the Low Churchmen the only legitimate justification for resistance in 1688 was political. It was never acceptable to resist a legitimate magistrate because he or she was ungodly or a heretic. To make such a claim was to collapse the distinction between church and state. "I am still as much as ever fixed in that persuasion, that the Christian religion gives no warrant to defend it by arms, but on the contrary forbids all resistance," Burnet wrote as he prepared to join with William's fleet in the autumn of 1688. "But"—and this is the qualification that historians have long failed to include in their analyses—"still it is to be understood that if this religion has laws on its side, in a legal government, where the king's prerogative is shut up within such limits, then as the right of professing that religion *comes to be one of the civil liberties,* so the king by breaking through all the limits of law, assumes an authority which he has not, and by consequence he may be withstood." Defense of the religion established by law was justified not qua religion but as a political act in defense of civil society. This was exactly how Edward Fowler, Williamite bishop of Gloucester, understood the Revolution of 1688–89. "Whether our monarchy be absolute or limited; or if limited whether in its exercise of power, or in the right of sovereignty: how far the limitation gives a right of resistance, in case of the breach of it," Fowler averred, "are nice questions, but not to be resolved by the rules of the Church; but by our legal constitution and the general reason of mankind." If, Fowler insisted, James II "could have been satisfied not to subject himself to the Triple Crown, and not to be governed by the counsels of Jesuits, and by the dictates of the greatest enemy we are capable of having [Louis XIV]," all of which violated English law, "and to let his people enjoy their religion and laws; he might have reigned as happily, notwithstanding his being a son of the Church of Rome, as ever did any of his royal Protestant predecessors." The Low Churchmen who were enthusiastic supporters of William and Mary did not retreat from their detestation of religiously justified resistance. They were "still of their former opinion in that which is theological," observed the Williamite bishop of Salisbury, "yet in matters of law and policy" they came to admit some previous "mistakes."[37]

While the Williamite bishops did believe that the Glorious Revolution had been providential, they did not see God's involvement as obviating the need for human action. That all deliverances are from God "does not imply," John Moore insisted, "that God will deliver us, if we do nothing ourselves towards obtaining our safety; he has promised that his grace shall attend and promote our honest endeavours, but gives no ground to the idle and negligent to hope for his help, who will make no use of their natural powers derived from him for their own preservation." "It is not enough to be merely contented with Providence," agreed Edward Stillingfleet, the Williamite bishop of Worcester, "but we ought to be active and useful in our own places to promote the common interest." "I do not go about to found the right of government merely on Providence," Stillingfleet later explained, "for that were to overthrow all legal constitutions, whenever rebellion meets with success; and the acts of providence do not of themselves determine right and wrong in such cases; but leave them to the rules which are proper for them, viz. the general right of nations, and the particular laws of several countries."[38]

It was on the general right of nations and the particular laws of England that the Williamite bishops founded their justification for resistance. Though deeply religious men, their justification of resistance was political, not religious. Their arguments for revolution had much more in common with the ideas of Locke than with Calvin.

The Williamite archbishop of Canterbury John Tillotson is often wrongly thought to have been adamant in his opposition to resistance. This claim is based upon his *Letter Written to My Lord Russel in Newgate, the Twentieth of July, 1683,* which was published without his consent and reprinted several times by the archbishop's High Church enemies. It is true that Tillotson "thought it a sin to resist only upon jealousies and consequences, upon some illegal acts, and remote fears, but did not think it a sin to resist when a total subversion was openly declared, and actually begun." That resistance was justified in case of a total subversion of the government, Tillotson's biographer assures us, was such a deeply held position of the archbishop that "he did not decline to explain himself in that way as often as there was occasion for it." His difference with his friend the Whig Rye House plotter Lord Russell, then, were not theoretical but "with regard to the attempts already made upon the constitution" in 1683. Tillotson doubted that Charles II had subverted the constitution, but he was absolutely convinced that James II had done so. He advised his auditors in 1693 to bask in "the happiness we now enjoy under their present Majesties, by whom, under God, we have been delivered from that terrible and imminent danger which threatened our religion and laws, *and the very constitution it self of our ancient government.*"[39] For Tillotson, who played such a large role in shaping the contours of William and Mary's ecclesiastical regime, the actions of James II had fully justified resistance.

The three bishops most often allowed Whiggish sympathies, Fowler, Hall and Hough, certainly advocated political resistance when an aspiring absolute monarch actively sought to subvert the government. Fowler, bishop of Gloucester, thought that resistance in such cases had until recently been advocated by the divines of the Church of England. From a study of pre–Civil War divines, Fowler concluded, "it is plain, that it was then thought not only lawful but a duty, to prevent the dangerous growth of such a monarchy which designs to suppress religion and civil liberties; and not only to give assistance those who join in the same design, but to pray to God to bless and prosper it." Fowler believed deeply that the good of the people provided the measure of submission to any government. "No oath can bind any longer than the obligation thereof is consistent and reconcilable with the *salus populi,* the welfare (the spiritual and temporal welfare) of the people which is the sole end of all government," he argued in 1689. It was on this base that Fowler was sure that "any unbiased person, that competently understands that nature of government" would agree to "divest King James of his title to the governing these kingdoms," would agree that his actions "dissolve our obligations to him, and transfer the right to those who now reign over us."[40]

John Hall and John Hough, two Oxfords heads of house as well as Williamite bishops, were less public and prolific in their pronouncements but no less adamant in their views. The High Churchman Thomas Hearne was sure that despite all his learning and his talents as a preacher, John Hall had the principles of "a thorough paced Calvinist [and] a defender of the republican doctrines." Hough, the deprived president who became the hero of the Magdalen College case of 1687, was perceived by Thomas Cartwright to be of the "popular" party—a term that described Hough's ideological commitments as much as the extent of his affections. Just as Fowler would do in print after the revolution, Hough justified his resistance to the Commission for Ecclesiastical Causes in 1687 on his political rights as an Englishman rather than on any perceived religious slight. "I am the only instance of any man in England that has been deprived of a freehold wherein he was legally invested and of which he was quietly possessed without either being summoned or heard," Hough exclaimed. Given these sentiments expressed in the most difficult of circumstances, it is hardly surprising that after 1689 he was "found to be a man of Revolution principles," a "man immoderate in his concern for the honour of King William," the darling of "the Whiggish interest."[41]

Simon Patrick, successively bishop of Chichester and of Ely, lived up to his "sour" Whig principles during the revolutionary moment. In December 1688 he was already proclaiming that the arrival of William "has freed us from slavery both in body and soul." In sermon after sermon thereafter Patrick repeated his assessment that James II and his cronies had undermined the entire frame of English government. His constant refrain was that "we saw our laws so boldly violated and trampled under feet, that we could not but fear the loss of all our liberties. . . . In one word, we saw the very foundations of our ancient government about to be razed, and in great measure overturned." Although Patrick never quite enunciated a full-blown theory of resistance, his emphasis on "the universal consent" of the people in 1688–89 made it clear that he believed resistance was in fact justified by James II's actions. Simon Patrick advocated a radical rather than a conservative understanding of the revolution. He was not content merely to restore the constitution to where it had been before James II acceded to the throne. He hoped "to see both our civil and religious rights and liberties secured to us and to our posterity, so as they have not been since we were a nation." The revolution, he proclaimed when bishop of Ely, was "a kind of new birth of this nation."[42]

John Moore, Williamite bishop of Norwich and supposedly one of those closest to the moderate Tory circle of Daniel Finch, made his advocacy of resistance clearest on a sermon delivered on Charles the Martyr day. Moore quickly signaled the tenor of his sermon by denouncing those "who would persuade governors to rule by arbitrary power, and not to have respect to the laws, and the general good in their administration." Having warmed to his theme, Moore chose this unlikely moment to authorize popular resistance. While placing a high standard on those who would commence a revolution, the bishop of Norwich made explicit his view that in some circumstances such action was justified. "Nothing therefore but the assuming a power to set the laws all aside; a general invasion of property, and the endeavouring to destroy the fundamental constitution of a society," he told the House of Lords, "can break the bands of it asunder, and leave the people at liberty to take care of themselves." This, of course, is exactly what Moore believed had happened during James II's reign. "In the time of the late king," Moore averred, "the laws, the rights, and the liberties of the nation, were in a manner subverted." Given these ideological commitments it is hardly surprising that contemporaries emphasized not Moore's associations with the Finch clan but "his intimacy with the low church party."[43]

Humphrey Humphreys, Williamite bishop of Bangor, has received nary a mention in discussions of the Church in the 1690s. Nevertheless, his political views were distinctly Whiggish. Unlike High Churchmen who celebrated the royalist cause of the 1640s, Humphreys denounced Charles I's supporters for "their looseness and irreligion." Like Moore, he used the opportunity of a commemorative service for the death of Charles I to enunciate a Whiggish understanding of government. "The chief end of government," according to the bishop of Bangor, "is to promote the public good, and to prevent any evil that may endanger the common safety." These commitments were clarified when Humphreys placed "his skill in the British antiquities" at the service of the prolific Whig polemicist James Tyrrell. The resulting publication, Tyrrell's multivolume *General History of England,* was, according to one commentator, "a work of propaganda," Whig propaganda.[44]

Another of Tyrrell's literary associates who shared his Whig commitments was the Williamite bishop of Peterborough, Richard Cumberland. Cumberland's great philosophical treatise, *De Legibus Naturae* (1672) has been the subject of much scholarly inquiry because of its serious engagement with Hobbesian ideas. Though Cumberland did not openly advocate revolution in his treatise—that would have been quite remarkable at the time—he did leave an unusual amount of scope for contemplating limits on royal power. Cumberland suggested that whether or not resistance could be justified, the likelihood of such an outcome should teach monarchs not to be tyrants. That Cumberland approved of James Tyrrell's translation and abridgement of his arguments in Tyrrell's *Brief Description of the Law of Nature* (1692) made it clear in what direction his political sentiments had developed. He had, according to his scholarly biographer, "allowed it to appear that he took what may be termed an extreme Whig view of the Revolution." It is hardly surprising, then, that Cumberland suffered from the "party heat" of the High Churchmen, who found Cumberland's "principles" and "the maxims on which he had acted . . . disagreeable."[45]

The most prolific and flamboyant defender of resistance was the Williamite bishop of Salisbury, Gilbert Burnet. Burnet, as he noted privately just before he embarked with William's fleet in 1688, had "copiously" justified his and his comrades' actions in his *Enquiry into the Measures of Submission*. Burnet began his exposition, like all good Whigs, by asserting that "with relation to the law of nature, all men are born free: and this liberty must still be supposed entire, unless so far as it is limited by contracts, provisions and laws." Unlike the High Churchmen, Burnet did not believe that the Church of England did or could place any special political obligations on its members. Although "considerations of religion do indeed bring subjects under strict obligations to pay all due allegiance and submission to their princes," he explained, "they do not at all extend that allegiance further than the law carries it." As a result, in England it was clear that subjects had a delimited right to resist. "There is nothing more evident," the future bishop of Salisbury exclaimed, "than that England is a free nation, that has its liberties and properties reserved to it by many positive and express laws: if then we have a right to our property, we must then likewise be supposed to have a right to preserve it: for those rights are by law secured against the invasions of the prerogative, and by consequence we must have a right to preserve them against those invasions." If a king "goes to subvert the whole foundation of the government, he subverts that by which he himself has his power, and by consequence he annuls his own power; and then he ceases to be king, having endeavoured to destroy that upon which his own authority is founded." Over and over again, in pamphlet after pamphlet, Burnet insisted that "the King's suspending of laws strikes at the root of this whole government and subverts it quite." No wonder, then, that the Earl of Clarendon found Burnet in January 1689 to be "always so bitter in deposing the king."[46]

Contemporaries and scholars have detected inconsistency in this position and Burnet's earlier caution about resistance, his frequent condemnation of religious rebellion, and his last-minute advice to William Russell, yet there was in fact no tension in Burnet's mind. He set a high standard for resistance, the total subversion of government, and that standard was consistently a political rather than a religious one. It was Burnet's "constant principle," his son correctly summarized, "that resistance was not lawful on account of single acts of injustice or oppression, unless the very basis of the constitution was struck at." Burnet himself insisted that the "principle that I had been bred to, and from which I never departed" was "that in the case of total subversion of a constitution the Prince might be resisted." Burnet did not back away from either his principles or those expressed in William's *Declaration of Reasons,* which he had translated, after William and Mary were successfully placed on the throne. In his coronation sermon Burnet reminded the new monarchs that their power was "not an absolute dominion." Instead, the new monarchs should "make the law the measure of their will," for "in all other paths they must be often divided between an irreconcilable variety of interests and passions."[47]

Burnet's close friend and literary collaborator William Lloyd, who was translated to Lichfield from St. Asaph by William and Mary, was a somewhat more circumspect and subtle—not to say quirky—defender of revolution principles. No doubt Lloyd's prominent role in the Exclusion Crisis convinced him that ideological discretion was necessary during the reign of James II. Lloyd told William Sancroft that "in almost every sermon" he preached against "rebellion of the people." He planned to inform the justices at the trial of the Seven Bishops that "holy religion teaches us under pain of damnation not to rebel against the king, though he be of another religion, nay though he should be an enemy to our religion." This emphasis on not rebelling for religious reasons, however, was the key to Lloyd's political ideas. The bishop of St. Asaph, like so many postrevolutionary bishops, denied that religion could ever justify resistance. Political tyranny, however, was another matter. Lloyd was perfectly right, therefore, to insist in *A Discourse of God's Ways of Disposing Kingdoms,* a pamphlet that explicated revolution principles, that "I have delivered no other doctrine than that which has been received and past for current in the Church of England ever since the Reformation."[48]

Lloyd was certain that, while religious preferences of the magistrate could never provide grounds for rebellion, tyrannical acts by the king could loosen the bonds of obedience to the point of tearing them asunder. "For the people's union with their Prince; though it cannot be dissolved but by a sentence from God," Lloyd argued, "yet by the Prince's own act it may be so loosened that it may be next to dissolution. The laws are the bond of union between Prince and people: by these, as the Prince holds his prerogative, so do the people their just rights and liberties." Just as an abused wife may turn to a judge to dissolve a marriage, so Lloyd contended that an oppressed people can turn to a foreign deliverer. If such a deliverer should appear, then the oppressed people "are not only free to defend themselves, but are obliged to join with him against their oppressor." For Lloyd, then, the revolution was unequivocally beneficial for England. The "guides of our King's conscience" before the revolution "did approve of the example [of Louis XIV] and were mad to have him follow it." James II's deployment of the dispensing power, Lloyd was certain, soon "would have reached all our laws." The events of 1688–89, by contrast, will "make our kings more just and more apt to rule by law."[49]

The Williamite bishop of Worcester Edward Stillingfleet, though he grew more politically and religiously conservative in his old age, had no qualms about defending the right to resist and its application in 1688–89. Stillingfleet deployed his massive learning in history and the law to consider the case of allegiance. In England, Stillingfleet was certain, there was a mutual contract between king and people. "For where laws are made by mutual consent" as in England, he contended, "they are of a nature of a common agreement between the prince and people, which both are bound to observe." Similarly, Stillingfleet argued that oaths of allegiance were not absolute in their obligations. "The rule and measure" of an oath of allegiance is to be taken "from the general good," he reasoned, "for there is a common good of humane society which mankind have an obligation to antecedent to that obligation they are under to particular persons." Should a king rule tyrannically, should his actions threaten the fundamental constitution, Stillingfleet contended, the oath no longer bound the subject, who was then free to resist. "If the keeping of the oath be really and truly inconsistent with the welfare of a people, in subverting the fundamental laws which support it," he pointed out in 1689, "I do not see how such an oath continues to oblige." "Although a due regard ought to be showed to the persons of princes," the bishop of Worcester reasoned, "yet when they declare a willful resolution rather to abandon all, than not to pursue their illegal designs; I cannot understand but under such circumstances the nation is at liberty to take care of its own security in a way most agreeable to its ancient constitution." Of course, James II had shown just such a "willful resolution" in his adamant defense of the dispensing power, a power "that no divine of the Church of England can in conscience approve of . . . because it subverts the legal constitution of our government." The alternative to allowing resistance in such cases was fraught with danger. "But if we suppose that Princes do receive their power so immediately from God, as to be incapable of any such restraint from laws, and that they may take away the force of them when they please," Stillingfleet warned, "the consequence will be, that as there can be no security to the people, so there will be very little to themselves: for there will be a perpetual jealousy and mistrust on both sides, which is generally attended with fatal consequences." In a concession to nonjurors, he did accept that William and Mary were de facto rather than de jure monarchs. But he did not allow that James II remained the rightful king. For Stillingfleet, "a king *de facto* is one who comes in by consent of the nation, but not by virtue of an immediate hereditary right."[50] For him, then, de facto kingship was a regular rather than an exceptional occurrence in England's past. Resistance had a venerable English history.

Alongside these explicit defenders of resistance were three bishops whose views fit more closely the moderate Tory label assigned to all the Williamite bishops by revisionist scholars. In each case, however, it is important to note how far they were ideologically from the passive obedience of the late Caroline appointees or the active absolutism of the Jacobite appointments. Thomas Tenison, the Williamite bishop of Lincoln and later Tillotson's successor at Canterbury, was cautious when it came to political pronouncements. But he was clearly no absolutist. His praise for the "wholesome laws, which are the nerves of society," was much more effusive than that uttered by any High Churchman. His legal critique of the Commission for Ecclesiastical Causes placed ideological distance between him and such Tory churchmen as Thomas Sprat and William Jane. As the 1690s wore on, Tenison increasingly gained the reputation, a reputation that he very much earned, as a supporter of "comprehension" and "everything that makes for the Whigs and Presbyterians."[51]

Robert Grove, who was elevated to the see of Chichester in 1691, never enunciated a theory of resistance. In fact, in early 1685 Grove advised voters in that year's parliamentary elections to "be very cautious that you do not favour any whom you can suspect to have the least taint of the Bill of Exclusion." Nevertheless, Grove was adamant and consistent in his opposition to absolutism. "The prince," he declared, "is the loser when the subject is enslaved; and he is in truth far more absolute that has the hearts of the people at his devotion, than he that treads upon their backs." He celebrated Parliaments and Gothic constitutions, praising England for bucking the European trend toward absolutism. "The Parliamentary way of consulting for the public good has been a very ancient usage in all these parts of Europe, and some footsteps of it are still remaining in most of our neighboring nations," Grove observed, "but the freedom and dignity of those assemblies has been no where so entirely preserved as it is in this." Unlike passive obedience men, Grove insisted on the absolute right to dissent and the right to private property. He insisted that "every man may be allowed to speak his own judgement, and to differ from whom he pleases . . . to be menaced and frighted out of this innocent freedom, is of all slaveries the most intolerable." "The best encouragement to everyman's private industry," Grove asserted, was the assurance in England "that whatever he gains is his own property, and that not one farthing shall be demanded of him without the consent of prudent and worthy persons, freely chosen and entrusted by the body of the nation." In early 1685 Grove advised his compatriots to place their faith in James II because he had promised to preserve the government in church and state. He suggested that anyone concerned about "liberty and property" should "consult but his own experience." Grove cataloged a series of questions that each and every Englishman should put to himself: "Has he ever been illegally imprisoned? Has any part of his goods been violently wrested from him? Has his house been rifled? Have his barns been robbed? Have his cattle been driven off his grounds? Has he suffered anything under colour of authority that could not be justified by the known laws?"[52] Although the answers to these questions were undoubtedly negative for most in England in the spring of 1685, Grove hinted strongly that resistance might not be so unreasonable should the answers prove otherwise. In the wake of the misdeeds of James II's standing army, the king's purge of the corporations, and his insistence on the dispensing power, one can only suppose where Grove's sentiments lay. Certainly William and Mary were not being unreasonably hopeful to guess that Grove would prove a loyal and adamant defender of their new regime.

The only Williamite bishop whose Toryism was manifest was John Sharp, archbishop of York. In January 1689 Sharp had offended the House of Commons with his critical comments about "the deposing power." Sharp's son acknowledged that the archbishop "was observed more generally to approve and favour [Tory] principles, and to go more along with them, than those of the other side." Nevertheless, even Sharp placed significant limits on political obedience. In May 1688, when considering James II's Second Declaration of Indulgence, he argued that "even our obedience to the king is to be extended no further than *licita et honesta*." Sharp, according to his biographer, "always laid down the laws of the land as the rule and measure of obedience."[53] The ideological distance between the most Tory of the Williamite bishops and the likes of Thomas Cartwright or Francis Turner was immense indeed.

Not only did the vast majority of Williamite bishops express Whig opinions, but they also took Whig actions. Edward Stillingfleet and John Tillotson, much to Francis Turner's disgust, did everything in their power to "lead the London clergy" to take the oaths to the new regime. Tillotson's enthusiasm for the new regime knew no limits. "I thank God I have lived to have my last desire in this world which was this happy revolution," he gushed to Willem Bentinck in 1689, "and now I care for no more but to see it established." The Earl of Clarendon discovered that William Lloyd "was most strangely busy to persuade the clergy to take the new oaths." Nicholas Stratford bragged about his success in satisfying people "in their scruples." Simon Patrick and his friends took "abundance of trouble" in 1689 "in endeavouring to satisfy men's scruples about our present settlement, both by discourse and writing letters." Dr. Gilbert Ironside, the future bishop of Bristol, "before ever King William had any pretended right to the Crown from the convention administered the oath of allegiance to King William in the congregation house at Oxford." When Henry Dodwell lobbied hard in Oxford coffeehouses against taking the oaths to the new regime, Ironside intended to use his authority as vice chancellor to encourage Dodwell "to absent himself from Oxon."[54]

The voting records of the Williamite bishops in the House of Lords were impeccably Whiggish. Gilbert Burnet, Richard Cumberland, John Hall, John Hough, Simon Patrick, and Thomas Tension were all reliable Whig voters in the Lords. None of the Williamite appointees were regular Tory voters. Nicholas Stratford, bishop of Chester, joined with Gilbert Burnet in 1690 and "the Whig peers" to impose an oath abjuring James II on all officeholders—a move that no one who believed James II remained king de jure could possibly have supported.[55] In almost every meaningful sense, then, the Williamite bishops were overwhelmingly Whiggish in their political outlook.

The Williamite bishops, it turns out, were remarkably different from their predecessors. They were not moderate Tories; they did not take ambiguous positions that could be seen to strike a middle ground. Fifteen of the eighteen Williamite appointments took Whiggish positions. Eleven of the eighteen appointments explicitly defended resistance. Only John Sharp, Nicholas Stratford, and Edward Jones were not clearly Whigs. Sharp, despite indications that he would take Whiggish positions, became the leader of the Tory bishops. Stratford and Jones have proven difficult to categorize.

The Whig political commitments of the Williamite bishops suggest a shift in the views of a culturally significant portion of the clergy. The loud professions of loyalty of the passive obedience men in the 1680s may have been drowning out the views of a younger set of men. Certainly John Gadbury detected in 1685 that "we have some as arrant true Protestant Jesuits in the Church of England, as any in France, Italy, Spain," men whose political views were as dangerous as "the wickedest of the Dissenters." The events of James II's reign convinced many passive obedience men to reconsider their political ideas. "Those English divines who preached and wrote most for passive obedience and nonresistance, mostly perceive that they laboured under a mistake," recorded the Scottish Episcopalian minister Robert Kirk in 1690 after months of discussions with English divines. These men now understood that "though according the confession of faith, no difference of religion in the prince his private judgement and practice can dissolve the subjects' ties to him, yet when he endeavours to subvert the government and fundamental laws of the nation, he is to be no more looked on as a punisher of evil and protector of the laws and subjects, but as a destroyer of all." The Whig party was now much broader than the party of Dissenters and their friends. The revolution made it clear that the political principles of many in the Church of England had been dramatically transformed. "I can but blush and admire that the bishops of the English Church should be so changed since the days of pious Laud. Then it was submit and obey, now it is resist and rebel," lamented one High Churchman in the wake of the revolution. It was now clear "that many were Whigs or Common-wealth men in state, that were Church of England men and not phanaticks in matters ecclesiastic."[56]

Many churchmen were probably convinced that they had misunderstood political obligation under Charles II and James II, but many more certainly retained their long-held views. There was a revolution in political ascendancy more than there was a sea change in political opinion within the Church of England. In astonishing numbers William and Mary preferred Low Churchmen—men whose political commitments made them suspect in the reigns of Charles II and James II. These men believed, according to Gilbert Burnet, who counted himself among them, "that obedience and submission that is settled by our laws, to the persons of our princes, ought to be paid them for conscience sake." "But," Burnet continued, "if a misguided Prince shall take on him to dissolve our constitution, and to subject the laws to his pleasure, [the Low Churchmen] think that if God offers a remedy, it is to be received with all thankfulness." Burnet's fellow Low Churchmen were convinced that "there is a full power in the legislature to settle the Crown, and to secure the nations." Unlike their High Church predecessors, these clergymen "know of no unalterable or indefeasible right, but what is founded on the law." Given that these political opinions were widely held among the Williamite bishops, it is hardly surprising that their preferment and translation "served much to remove the jealousies that some other steps the King had made were beginning to raise in the Whigs, and very much softened the ill humour that was spread among them."[57] William and Mary had created a largely Whig episcopate.

Those who have emphasized the consensual nature of the Church of England before and after the revolution of 1688–89 have not only insisted on the political conservatism of the clergy, but also on the clergy's ecclesiastical rigidity. The Low Churchmen, we are told by these scholars, had little sympathy for dissenters. They wanted a coercive and uniform national church. Comprehension, the accommodation of moderate Dissenters within the Church, was the gentle face of Anglican persecution. In this interpretative context, the Low Churchmen were, according to one of these scholars, the 'shock troops' of coercion.[58]

Attention to the cut and thrust of religious debate both before and after the revolution reveals a more ideologically divided Church. The Low Churchmen who became Williamite bishops overwhelmingly supported both a more inclusive church and toleration outside that church. Whatever their attitudes toward Dissenters in the 1660s, 1670s, and 1680s, most of the new bishops had come to support a gentler attitude by the later 1680s. Their position stood in stark contrast both to the High Churchmanship of the prerevolutionary bishops, an ecclesiastical posture that refused to accept any modification in the Church of England or any latitude toward Dissenters, and to the moderate Toryism of some of the revolutionary clergy, men such as John Sharp and Henry Compton, who could stomach a broader Church of England but were hostile to toleration.

High Churchmen had always despised diversity within the Church and toleration outside it. Although Restoration clergymen had long deployed Erastian arguments, arguments that religious pluralism necessarily weakened the state, in the 1670s they began to develop a theological case against diversity. Many argued that "coercion is a justifiable and effective instrument of education and persuasion." This line of reasoning "gained momentum as Charles's reign wore on." It was the "characteristic" position of "the new high-church movement that reached maturity in the decade after 1675." These High Churchmen who came to dominate the Church and the episcopal sees in the 1680s could not stomach a broader church; they resented any change in the fabric of the liturgy. "To high churchmen," one scholar pithily notes, "comprehension was a cant word for the destruction of the church." Although it is true that William Sancroft initiated discussions about comprehension in 1688, he did so with his feet dragging. It was the "London clergy"—men like Tillotson, Grove, Fowler, Stillingfleet, Stratford, Kidder, and Tenison—"who brought pressure to bear upon the archbishop and won him over to making a serious attempt at a scheme of comprehension." However serious the attempt may have been, at least one commentator has concluded that Sancroft was not "prepared to make significant concessions to dissenters."[59]

The events of 1688–89 quickly and radically altered the situation. In January 1689 Stillingfleet, then dean of St. Paul's, hosted a meeting "to consult about such concessions as might bring in dissenters to our communion." In addition to Stillingfleet, this meeting included Patrick, Tillotson, Lloyd, Tenison, and Kidder's close friend Edmund Prideaux.

All but the last of these men were to enjoy preferment or translation from William and Mary. Their meeting resulted in the drawing up of "ten or eleven heads" of a parliamentary bill for comprehending religious dissenters within the Church of England. Tillotson and Stillingfleet, of course, had a long history of support for comprehension schemes. Patrick could hardly contain his enthusiasm for accommodating Dissenters, proclaiming that "I do not see how we can fail to come to an happy agreement." To Clarendon's disgust, he found Tenison very "fond" of the "designed comprehension." William Lloyd was also "deep in that comprehending project." Richard Kidder, who was close to all those who consulted at Stillingfleet's house in January, averred that "now to make such alterations as are proposed [is] a thing so absolutely necessary as ought not any longer to be deferred." Lord Yester was certainly right to inform his father that "there is great inclinations among all sober men even among the best of the clergy to yield to all that can be rationally proposed for the admitting all Protestant dissenters to the church."[60]

Deep ideological divisions within the Church of England, however, defeated the plan for comprehension. "Some of the high churchmen," Lord Yester quickly perceived, were adamantly opposed to any scheme of comprehension. While the clerics most closely associated with the Finch circle pursued a generous plan for comprehension, the Earl of Nottingham himself drew up a bill that made few of the concessions to Dissenters that he himself had been willing to make "9 or 10 years since." The limited bill proposed convinced the Dissenter Roger Morrice that "Toryism is very rampant." After deeply partisan debates in both houses, Parliament failed to pass a comprehension bill in the spring of 1689. As a result, of the planned twin bills for comprehension and toleration, only the Toleration Act passed into law.[61] So while Nottingham and the Tories sought a restricted plan for comprehension, the future Williamite bishops were advancing proposals with much broader appeal to Dissenters. The Low Churchmen were performing their roles as the shock troops of persecution very badly indeed.

Bitter divisions between High and Low Churchmen continued to bedevil plans to accommodate Dissenters both within and outside the Church. In an attempt to revive plans for comprehension before the meeting of Convocation, in early autumn 1689 William III authorized "several bishops and others to consider such alterations in the liturgy, etc. as might give some satisfaction to the Dissenters." Although a range of clerics was invited to participate in the discussions in the Jerusalem Chamber, profound divisions quickly emerged. The High Churchmen—including William Jane and Henry Aldrich— "did either not appear, or did soon desert their other brethren, upon a high notion, that either no alterations ought to be made, or at least that this was not a seasonable time for making them." Their actions provoked the normally mild-mannered Thomas Tenison to lambast the High Churchmen for their "narrowness." By contrast, those who would come to make up the Williamite episcopal bench were remarkably diligent and productive in their efforts. Patrick, Grove, Burnet, Stillingfleet, Tillotson, Kidder, Stratford, Sharp, Tenison, and Lloyd were all active and eager participants in the doomed plan.[62]

Convocation, the assembled gathering of the Church of England clergy, provided another stage for this ideological conflict. When Convocation assembled on 21 November 1689, the prolocutor of the upper house Henry Compton duly called on the clergy "to take into their consideration the alteration of Common Prayer in favor of the Dissenters, and expressed himself freely enough in that matter." In the lower house, however, the clergy elected the High Churchman William Jane despite the efforts of William III and John Sharp to promote the election of John Tillotson. The results were predictable. "In spite of all the endeavours of Dr. Tenison, Fowler, Kidder &c.," recalled one observer, "such was the pretended zeal for the Church, and the chimerical fear of dangers that would arise from this desirable union" that nothing could make the high fliers "drop their too violent animosities to their Christian brethren." The lifelong courtier Sir Charles Cotterell described the actions of the High Church party in Convocation in similar terms. "Many of our clergymen in [Convocation] are so stiff," Cotterell commented disgustedly to his friend Sir William Trumbull, "that they will not suffer the least alteration to be made, as if the church must presently be down if the least tittle be changed, though the King give all possible assurance of his adhering to the Church of England."[63]

The debate over comprehension in Parliament, the Jerusalem Chamber, and Convocation revealed deep cleavages between the High and Low Church parties. The High Churchmen, including Nottingham, were unwilling to make any substantive changes in the liturgy to accommodate Dissenters. The Low Churchmen, including almost all of those who would enjoy preferment from William and Mary, were eager to explore a variety of forms of compromise with Dissent.

Although many of the Williamite bishops had written in favor of uniformity in the 1670s and 1680s—a good number of them, one suspects, under considerable pressure—after the revolution they proved remarkably supportive of Dissenters in particular and of religious toleration in general. For the Williamite bishops, comprehension was not the acceptable face of repression; it was part of a program simultaneously to broaden the Church of England and to expand the English political nation. These Low Churchmen wanted to diminish doctrinal barriers to church membership while virtually eliminating doctrinal barriers to membership in the political nation.

Many of the Williamite bishops had close ties to Dissenters. Even those bishops whose later reputations were not particularly associated with friendliness to religious diversity, had in fact old and deep ties to the Dissenting community. John Sharp's father "was not a little inclined to Puritanism, according to the temper of those times, and much favoured the parliament party" in the Civil War. When Sharp's Presbyterian prospective mother-in-law asked the great Presbyterian preacher Richard Baxter his opinion of the proposed match, he replied that he held Sharp in such "esteem" that "had he a daughter of his own to dispose of, he would not refuse her to Mr. Sharp." Robert Grove was the nephew of the prominent Hampshire Dissenter Thomas Grove. When he was chaplain to the bishop of London, Grove was "the only man" willing to license Baxter's writings for the press during the reign of Charles II. Grove was therefore both speaking from the heart and reflecting on his own actions when he declared that "I love [Dissenters] all as men, and more especially as Christians." Edward Stillingfleet was among the mourners at the "fanatical burying place near the Artillery Yard"—Bunhill fields—in London when the Dissenting divine John Fairclough was laid to rest in 1682.[64] Such a display in the midst of the Tory reaction must have been intended as a public as well as a personal act of sympathy.

The ties of other Williamite bishops to the Dissenting community were less surprising but no less profound. Edward Fowler's father was the ejected Presbyterian minister of Westerleigh in Gloucestershire. This family association no doubt gave him an introduction to Richard Baxter, with whom he corresponded, and who counted him "a very ingenious sober conformist." When William Lloyd became pastor of St. Martin's-in-the-Fields, Baxter so much approved of his sentiments that he invited Lloyd to preach regularly at Baxter's own chapel in Oxenden Street. On his preferment to St. Asaph, Lloyd widened his associations among Dissenters. He held discussions with the range of Dissenters in his diocese and soon became friendly with a number of Quakers. Indeed, in his memoirs the Quaker Richard Davies thought it "worthy to take notice of the several kindnesses, upon account of our suffering friends, I received from this Bishop Lloyd in his several dioceses." Richard Kidder's mother had "the name of a Puritan fixed upon her." Kidder himself went up to Emmanuel College—famous for its Puritanism—where he was taught by the Congregationalist friend of New England Samuel Craddock. Simon Patrick's father, similarly, had "got the name of a puritan." John Hall, master of Pembroke College, had the reputation in Oxford of being a Presbyterian and after the revolution was known to allow "Thomas Gilbert, a nonconformist independent," to instruct students at Pembroke.[65]

The Williamite archbishop of Canterbury John Tillotson had long and deep ties to Dissent. Tillotson's father was a Puritan clothier who "very early" became an Anabaptist. His "first education and impressions," recalled his close friend Gilbert Burnet, "were among those who were then called puritans." Tillotson's tutor at Clare Hall was the Presbyterian David Clarkson. At Cambridge the future archbishop "took the covenant, and was esteemed a precious young man, and of great hopes of doing good honour for and to the blessed cause." As late as 1661 Tillotson was still considered to be a Presbyterian. He enjoyed the patronage of the Dissenter Sir Samuel Barnardiston and Cromwell's former attorney general Edmund Prideaux. Throughout his career, Tillotson "usually" gave "most of the pieces which he published to Mr. John Howe," the influential Presbyterian minister. No wonder the Oxford High Churchman Thomas Hearne remembered Tillotson as "this fanatical prelate."[66]

Gilbert Burnet had deep familial ties to Presbyterianism. Burnet's mother was "a warm zealot for the Presbyterian discipline." Burnet's father, a Scottish lawyer, though not a Presbyterian was vocal in his distaste for the Scottish bishops and "was generally called a puritan." Gilbert Burnet's first wife, Lady Margaret Kennedy, was a woman whose "sentiments inclined thoroughly towards the Presbyterian." Given these Scottish family ties, it is hardly surprising that when Burnet came to England he not only fell in with Low Churchmen like William Lloyd, Edward Stillingfleet, and John Tillotson but became an intimate of Richard Baxter's.[67]

Not only did the Williamite bishops support plans for comprehension that made real concessions to Dissenters, not only did they have close and enduring ties to the Dissenting community, but most of the Williamite bishops became champions of religious toleration. For them comprehension was not the gentle face of persecution but part of a program simultaneously to attract as many Dissenters into the Church as possible while tolerating those who chose to remain outside it.

Tillotson was outspoken in his opposition to religious persecution. He believed that "every man's conscience is a kind of God to him. . . . And therefore we ought to take great care not to offend against the light and conviction of our own mind." Certainly the conscience could not be altered by any outside force. "No body can force [our conscience] from us, whether we will or no," Tillotson proclaimed. As a result, compulsory religious uniformity was an illusory goal. The consequence of pursuing such an objective—very much the aim of Gilbert Sheldon, William Sancroft, and Tillotson's High Church predecessors—was to create religious factions. Again and again Tillotson denounced the creators of religious parties. These were men who were "so zealous about small things" that "they neglect the weightier things of the law, faith, and mercy, and judgment and the love of God." These were men who "by inflaming our needless differences about lesser things, have so great a hand in pulling down religion." These men, in short, infused the nation with "heats and animosities." Tillotson hoped because religious divisions were so destructive of "the peace and happiness of this church and nation, that these names and distinctions of parties should be laid down and abolished forever." These commitments had made Tillotson a longtime proponent of "a comprehension of such of the Dissenters as could be brought into the church, and a toleration of the rest."[68]

Tillotson, who was advising William and Mary on ecclesiastical appointments from early 1689, set the tone for the rest of the Williamite bench. The Dutch remonstrant Philippus Von Limborch felt the "same assurance" about Gilbert Burnet's commitment to toleration as he did of John Locke's. It was Burnet's experience in the United Provinces in the 1660s that "fixed" him "in that strong principle of universal charity, and of thinking well of those that differed from him." Again and again throughout his varied career Burnet reaffirmed this fixed principle. It was therefore with a sense of triumph that he welcomed the Toleration Act of 1689. "God be thanked for it," he bellowed from the pulpit in November 1689, "that there is an end put to all persecution in matters of conscience; and that the first and chief right of human nature, of following the dictates of conscience in the service of God is secured to all men amongst us." Burnet remained an advocate "for toleration and for treating Dissenters with gentleness," even though he knew how much these commitments infuriated the High Churchmen. The Welshman William Lloyd had a similar history of commitment to toleration. While still a London parish priest, and at a time when justifying religious coercion was fashionable, Lloyd had argued that "it seems very unreasonable to go about to force men to change their judgments in any thing that hurts none but themselves, and especially in so weighty a matter as is that of religion." Lloyd proudly told the House of Lords that "neither our religion, nor our church, is of a persecuting spirit." During the trial of the Seven Bishops he informed Sancroft's chaplain Henry Wharton that he was resolved "to procure the admission of the sober and pious Dissenters into the Church, a thing so much wished for, [and] to relieve even those who were obstinate by abolishing the penal laws." After the passage of the Toleration Act, Lloyd made it known that he was "well satisfied with it."[69]

Simon Patrick, successively bishop of Chichester and Ely, is usually taken to be a prime example of a supporter of comprehension and opponent of toleration. Patrick's early writings are seized on as evidence that even Low Churchmen could not stomach Dissenters. Certainly Patrick's extremely popular *Friendly Debate betwixt Two Neighbours* (1668) provides fuel for such an argument. The experience of the next two decades, however, convinced Patrick "to become afterward more moderate." By 1688 Patrick had become extremely skeptical of religious persecution. In one sermon he asked his auditors, "How come one sort of men by a right to judge, censure, and condemn all the rest? Why may not others take the same authority over them? And then there will be nothing but cursing and damning throughout the Christian world." Patrick thought that "we ought to forbear judging those who are not of our mind, or act not as we do, if otherwise they do well." Consciences should be free since "the secrets of men's hearts do not fall within our cognizance." After the revolution he made his conversion to toleration more explicit. Uniformity, Patrick had come to believe, was an illusory and destructive goal. "Men do not differ more in their countenances than they do in the frame of their understandings," Patrick preached, "and therefore we must not spend our pains in making all men think alike; for it is impossible to be affected." Before the House of Lords Patrick denounced his fellow Church of England communicants for "their extreme severity towards those who differed from them in some things, though in most they perfectly agreed." He had become an advocate of toleration in deed as well as word. In Queen Anne's reign he voted against the Occasional Conformity Bill, which would have punished those Dissenters who took communion in the Church of England while continuing to attend their Dissenting chapels, because it would make "a manifest breach upon the act of indulgence [the Toleration Act] which had made great peace, quiet, and love among us."[70]

The vast majority of the Williamite bishops shared the commitment to toleration expressed by Tillotson, Lloyd, Burnet, and latterly Patrick. Gilbert Ironside, successively bishop of Bristol and Hereford, was a lifelong opponent of the High Churchman and defender of uniformity John Fell. At the height of the Tory reaction, Ironside argued that the inevitability of religious diversity might well make toleration "not only lawful but necessary." "As for ceremonies and circumstances," he asked rhetorically, "who will insist upon them, so as to make a schism"? Given these sentiments, Ironside's turning out John Locke's antitolerationist antagonist Jonas Proast from his chaplaincy at All Soul's was all too predictable. Thomas Tenison was a longtime advocate of liberty of conscience. "No man's mind can be forced," Tenison argued, "for it is beyond the reach of humane power." Richard Kidder, the Williamite bishop of Bath and Wells, was thought "a very moderate man" by Burnet and therefore acceptable to the Whig Earl of Bedford. This was undoubtedly, in part, because of Kidder's opposition to religious persecution. "St. Paul tells us plainly, there must be heresies among you," Kidder explained to his London parishioners; therefore, "it is a vain thing to pretend a remedy against that evil against which God himself hath provided none." In another London sermon Nicholas Stratford garnered the approval of the Dissenting diarist Roger Morrice by advising "the Church as their true interest to come to a good understanding and coalescency with the Nonconformist Dissenters." Stratford's position was that though the Dissenters were "mistaken it was not an obstinate mistake . . . and pressed this good understanding very affectionately." Edward Fowler, another opponent of the Occasional Conformity Bill when bishop of Gloucester, was a longtime proponent of liberty of conscience. "Nor can I well conceive how any ingeniously-minded person can admit so much as an hard thought of any merely upon their account of their not being of his mind in matters that have been controverted," Fowler maintained. "I declare for my part, and I care not who knows it," he therefore announced with his usual brashness, "that I love with my heart a sober and peaceably minded Nonconformist, as much Conformist as I am myself."[71]

Two of the Williamite bishops were less enthusiastic supporters of toleration. John Sharp, despite his friendship with Tillotson and his lifelong association with Dissenters, became an increasingly reliable ally of the High Churchmen in the 1690s. Unlike most Williamite appointments, he "was entirely for bringing in an act for preventing occasional conformity, and espoused it whenever it was proposed." Edward Stillingfleet, who has established his reputation with the publication of *Irenicum*—a learned and moderate call for kindness to Dissenters—also appears to have backed away from his earlier support of comprehension and toleration. Stillingfleet consciously distanced himself from *Irenicum*. Nevertheless, his ideological retreat was not complete. He did write against "an unlimited toleration," but left space for a more limited indulgence. After the revolution he still criticized the strict High Church insistence on uniformity and doctrinal purity. "The spirit of love and a sound mind," he contended when bishop of Worcester, "consists in laying aside private animosities and heats for a public and general good."[72] The two exceptions to the Williamite episcopal rule of support for toleration—if exceptions they both are—tend to confirm the rule. When William and Mary preferred these two divines, they had good reasons to believe that they would support a program of comprehension and toleration. That Sharp and Stillingfleet both proved to be moderate conservatives shows that ideological commitments of individuals are not always predictable, not that William and Mary were committed to a moderate Tory episcopate or that the new monarchs could not find tolerant churchmen.

Scholars have recently highlighted the limits of the new regime's commitment to toleration. The Toleration Act, it is often pointed out, did not extend to Roman Catholics. Indeed, many scholars insist that the revolution itself was based upon rabid antipopery. Nevertheless, there is good reason to believe that for all of their rhetoric against "popery," many of the Williamite bishops had no such animus against Roman Catholics. Gilbert Burnet, normally taken to be the fieriest of English opponents of Catholicism, was in fact explicit in his pleas for moderation and toleration. "Nor am I set on by any sour or ill-governed zeal against Popery," he noted in his private meditations on the eve of William's expedition to England. "I love all men that love God, and that live well," he insisted. "I have very large notions of the goodness of that God I love whose mercies I could never limit to any form or party of religion, and so I am none of those that damn all Papists; for I have known many good and religious men among them." Indeed, Burnet's famous account of his travels in Europe after his exile from England were filled with praise for Catholic governors and for the moderation of the pope and papal policy. He reserved his scorn for the Jesuits, a society that Burnet elsewhere noted were "decried at Rome itself for its violence." In fact, Burnet did all he could during the Exclusion Crisis to prevent the execution of condemned Roman Catholics. In a statement as much prescriptive as descriptive, he insisted in 1687 that "a cessation of all severities" against Roman Catholics would be easily submitted to by the vast majority of the English. This was not a position from which he receded when in power. In the full flush of victory, in December 1688, Burnet preached that "we are Christians, and therefore we must not only love our brethren, but even our enemies and our persecutors and so overcome their evil with good." With specific reference to Roman Catholics, Burnet pleaded that though "we have declared openly against the injustice and cruelty of our enemies, we govern ourselves by the rule of doing as we should be done by."[73]

William Lloyd, who was translated to Lichfield by William and Mary, is another Williamite bishop normally associated with bitter attacks on Roman Catholicism. Yet he, too, made a distinction between "popery" and Roman Catholicism. The problem, Lloyd pointed out, was that "among the ignorant vulgar, there are many false and wild notions of popery." For Lloyd "the very chief thing in popery" was the assertion of the pope's political and spiritual authority in England. Since he believed the pope's right to depose kings had been denied in England long before the Reformation, Lloyd did not share the early Protestant worldview. Lloyd denied that there was any great eschatological struggle between Roman Catholics and Protestants, for in his own observation, many Catholics "are esteemed by their Protestant neighbours honest, well-meaning men, such as they cannot use hardly, without great and evident cause." In the Netherlands, Lloyd pointed out, Roman Catholics have proved loyal to the state even when that state was fighting a Roman Catholic enemy. Unlike the view developed by John Foxe and perpetuated in early Stuart polemic, Lloyd believed that neither the executions of Protestants in England during Mary's reign nor the St. Bartholomew's Day Massacre in France were evidence of

Catholic perfidy. Rather, they were political massacres. "Had they been all of the same religion," Lloyd insisted, "the barbarous violence would not have been less cruel." Lloyd therefore suggested that England treat those who professed Catholic theology differently from those who believed in papal political authority. "Though such men" that wholly deny the pope's supremacy "believe the same erroneous tenets, and use the same superstitious and idolatrous rites that papists do; namely, such as the Pope himself has made the terms of communion, and therefore are properly in communion with him, yet those tenets and rites are not properly popery." Toleration of such Catholics, Lloyd declared, was "consistent with the safety of the kingdom, and with obedience to government, and with justice of contracts, and love of neighbours."[74]

Although the failure of the Toleration Act to include Roman Catholics under its purview was indeed a limitation to the liberty granted at the revolution, the ideological commitments of the Williamite episcopate profoundly changed the nature of the Catholic experience. William Lloyd bragged that Roman Catholics "are more at ease under King William, than under any Protestant king since the Reformation." The Whig historian and bishop White Kennett perhaps not surprisingly concurred, claiming that "not only foreigners, but English-papists, were used with so much clemency, that they too were really gainers by the Revolution." When the Frenchman Henri Misson commented on the English religious scene in the 1690s, he marveled at the "universal toleration" afforded Catholics in England despite the legal limitations. "All the laymen among them have full liberty of conscience, of trade and residence," Misson noted, a situation that was in stark contrast to the condition of Protestants "in France, Spain, Italy, etc." This was not mere party polemic. The General Assembly of the Catholic Clergy in England recorded that after "the unexpected revolution" they found to their surprise the "government favorable enough to Catholics as to the exercise of their religion." "If we reflect on all the circumstances under which" the Toleration Act was passed, concurred the late-eighteenth-century Catholic lawyer and activist Charles Butler, "we must admit that the general cause of civil liberty gained by it considerably."[75]

The notion that the Low Churchmen who became bishops after the revolution were hostile to Dissent does not mesh with the evidence. The overwhelming majority of William and Mary's appointments were supporters of both comprehension and toleration. They established a religious climate in which not only Protestant Dissenters but even Roman Catholics enjoyed religious liberty. It is true, of course, that this religious liberty was tenuous. There were periods in which the cry that the Church was in danger was heard with real urgency. But that was the cry of the High Churchmen, the ecclesiastical party that was nudged away from the highest offices in the Church of England at the revolution.

Deep divisions that had long rent the Church of England were made manifest during the reign of James II. Although the bishops preferred by James II and Charles II differed in their attitudes toward royal authority vis-à-vis the Church, they shared an antipathy for political resistance and for toleration both inside and outside the Church.

They did not, however, enjoy hegemonic control. Many younger divines within the Church developed a strong social network and a corpus of ideas that distinguished them from their colleagues. These Low Churchmen, men who gained substantial prestige for their literary responses to the onslaught of French Catholic apologetic in the reign of James II, by and large defended the legitimacy and necessity of political resistance and called for both a more inclusive church and greater liberty for those outside it. These men helped forge the revolution and were immediately rewarded with episcopal sees by William and Mary in its aftermath.

The revolutionaries who took action in 1688, then, had an ambitious and well-developed agenda. They were not pragmatically responding to an unanticipated crisis. Instead, the revolutionaries seized the moment to implement an alternative modernizing agenda to that which James II had been putting into place since his accession. The revolutionaries transformed English foreign policy, reoriented the economic commitments of the English state, and radically altered the ideological and ecclesiological priorities of the English church. Their program, however, was a party program. Although Whigs had made common cause with Tories in overthrowing James II, the Tories shared none of their revolutionary fervor. As a consequence the Whigs' revolutionary achievement was fragile and contested in the early 1690s. Fortuitously for the Whigs, James II and his ally Louis XIV gave them an opportunity to consolidate their ideological achievement in 1696. The Whigs aggressively seized the moment.

PART V

Conclusion

CHAPTER FOURTEEN

Assassination, Association, and the Consolidation of Revolution

At nine o'clock on the evening of 14 February 1696 a man urgently demanded admission to the Earl of Portland's lodgings at Whitehall. On admission, this man, formerly unknown to William III's favorite, begged him to "persuade the King to stay at home tomorrow, for if he goes abroad to hunt he will be murdered." Portland took the warning seriously. Not only was the informant, Thomas Prendergrass, a man with impeccable Jacobite credentials—he had been pilloried for his 1689 Jacobite tract *A Short History of the Convention*—but his revelations confirmed in detail other news Portland had gathered. Continental informers had hinted at French and Jacobite preparations for a grand design. Domestic intelligence had provided vague reports of a plot against the king. And on the previous day, Francis De La Rue had told Portland that "His Majesty would be attacked at Turnham Green, on his return from hunting."[1] The specificity and similarity of the last two reports allowed Portland to convince his king to alter his plans and save his life.

Although contemporaries and historians have long debated whether the Assassination Plot was ordered by Louis XIV and the exiled James II, all agree that the plotters

---

(above) *William III: National Association, 1696.* After the 1696 plot to assassinate William III was uncovered, the House of Commons, the House of Lords, and cities, counties, and boroughs across the nation signed associations to protect the life of the king. The content and circulation of the Association Rolls, asserting that William was rightful and lawful king, confirmed a radical understanding of the revolution current among Whigs in the mid-1690s and testified to the extent to which the politics of the later seventeenth century had produced a transformed and vastly expanded political nation.

expected much more than the assassination of the king they hated. "The minute the blow is given," the plotters intended to raise King James II's standard, the sign for a general Jacobite rising. Whether James II had had anything to do with the plotters, there can be no doubt that in late December 1695 he had given orders for a general rebellion.[2]

James II had good reason to think the country ripe for rebellion. England was suffering a nationwide shortage of coin precipitated by the cost of the war against France. Clipped coins were circulating widely. Uncertainty about the government's response created a national panic. "In a week or two . . . there will be no silver to be had," Richard Edge reported from London in early February 1696. Royal action only exacerbated the country's fears. When Parliament debated the coinage issue in February, "all the halls, painted chamber, Speaker's chamber, and the lobby and coffee houses" were "full of people" anxiously awaiting the outcome. "The business of our money has so near brought us to our ruin," William Molyneux informed his friend John Locke, "that, till the plot broke out, it was everybody's talk, everybody's uneasiness." John Toland agreed that "all the discourse of late has been almost only of coin." The Yorkshire antiquary Abraham de la Pryme was not exaggerating when he claimed that the coinage crisis "undoubtedly . . . gave breeding unto the late great plot."[3]

The revolutionary regime faced other problems as well. Anglo-Scottish relations were extremely tense in the winter of 1695–96. The Scottish parliament's creation of a new Scottish East India Company had infuriated England's Tories. The new company was wildly popular in Scotland. But in England the House of Commons voted that all subscribers to the company residing in England "shall be impeached of high crimes and misdemeanors." The Scots, in turn, were "incensed." Parliament itself, James II and his advisers were informed, "began to jar with the usurper" and "were highly disgusted." "In general things are ill, the nation sinks, men are puzzled, and no real prospect of a remedy," the Jacobite-leaning Earl of Huntingdon was informed in February 1696.[4]

In this context of domestic discontent, James II sent his illegitimate son the Duke of Berwick to England in January to organize a general rising. Berwick's contacts insisted that James II arrive in England with an army. Yet Berwick assured both his father and Louis XIV "that King James has a great party both in England and Scotland who will take up arms as soon as they hear he is landed."[5]

That a massive French invasion was planned and prepared there can be no doubt. Rumors poured into England that French troops were massing in the west. "We received information from Flanders," recalled the Earl of Portland, "that the enemy had collected a great body of troops at Dunkirk and Calais"—a body estimated at between twenty thousand and one hundred thousand men—"as well as a large number of transport vessels and ships of war, that the troops were either on board or being embarked, and that is was well known there that they were assembled for the invasion of England."[6]

All agreed that in February 1696 the British Isles lay on the brink of a counterrevolution. The French court was abuzz with hopes for a "grand coup." Jacobites "proudly bragged throughout the nation that the late King James would be here within a month." Williamite spies reported that "King James himself really believed that he was to be replaced on his throne, and that nothing was more easy." "We were on the brink of a precipice and ready to fall," the Earl of Portland confided to the Earl of Lexington, "when, by a manifest interposition of providence, we were made aware of the danger which threatened us and all Europe."[7]

Thomas Prendergass's revelations of the plot to assassinate William III transformed the political and ideological landscape. Jacobite hopes quickly turned into fears. Once Portland persuaded William of the seriousness of the plot and of the reality of the invasion threat, the government took swift and decisive action. Jacobites and suspected Jacobites were rounded up all over England, Scotland, and Ireland. County militias and urban trained bands were placed on high alert. Within days both the House of Commons and the House of Lords "voted an association to protect the King's person and to avenge his death, if it should so happen."[8] Localities in all three kingdoms and abroad quickly followed in Parliament's footsteps.

What was remarkable about the revelations of February 1696 was not that there had been a plot to kill the king—such plots, even plots tied to dignitaries of church and state, were commonplace on the early modern British and European scene—but that the accused owned and defended their actions. Initially, it is true, both the French court and some British Jacobites, "pretend to be infidels in matters of plots, and would have it thought that none were intended which are not executed." However, it soon became implausible to deny the reality of the plot, the plans for an insurrection, or the intended French invasion. Hours of painstaking evidence gathering and witness interrogation convinced William and his advisers that there was "undeniable proof" of a serious threat to the regime. The subsequent rapid succession of confessions made Sir William Trumbull conclude that the plot "is thoroughly owned in all parts of it." Newspaper reports, trial transcripts, and the published statements of the conspirators soon made public what the government already knew. By mid-April clerics throughout England preached to their congregations that there were now "irrefragible arguments" that "must satisfy all the world" that there had been plans for an assassination, a rebellion, and an invasion. Even Jacobites and their sympathizers admitted that the threat to the regime had been serious. "Among all the ill characters [the Jacobites] bestow on the witnesses," James Vernon averred, "yet they abate them the name of perjured." William III's reign "was far from being bloody," the Earl of Ailesbury, who was himself arrested for complicity in the plot, "for those that would have assassinated him in February 1695/6 owned their bloody design." Supporters of the regime were similarly convinced. "There was never any plot so clearly made out as this is and will be," Martha Lockhart assured her friend Lady Masham. "No fact of this kind was ever proved and made appear so soon to the universal satisfaction of all sorts of persons," the Whig poet Sir Richard Blackmore explained in his official history of the plot, "for the evidence was free and voluntary, and perfectly delivered from all suspicions of tampering and subornation."[9]

Because of the clarity of the evidence, because the plotters defended their actions

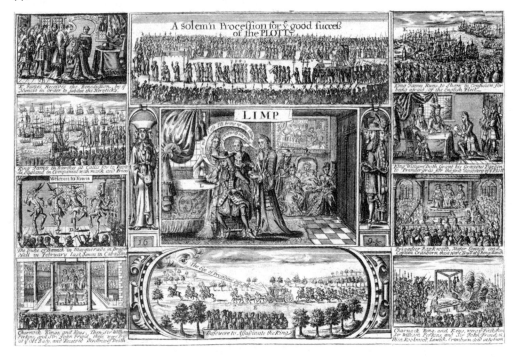

The Triumphs of Providence over Hell, France & Rome, in Defeating & Discovering of the Late Hellish and Barbarous Plott, for Assassinating His Royall Majesty King William the III, 1696. Williamites quickly disseminated narratives of the Jacobite plot to assassinate William III, in newspapers, pamphlets, and prints like this one.

rather than denying them, the revelations in late winter and spring of 1696 generated widespread discussion throughout the three kingdoms and Europe. "The late conspiracy in this kingdom has been for some time the principal object of the curiosity of the public," observed one early commentator. When the news reached Yorkshire, Abraham de la Pryme recalled that it "put the nation into an exceeding great fright." Martha Lockhart reported that the plot was "the subject at present that all sorts of people talk on from morning to night." When three nonjuring divines offered two of the confessed conspirators absolution on the scaffold, John Evelyn noted that it "produced much altercation on both sides."[10]

Because the plotters explained their motivations, the revelations of February 1696 generated ideological debate as well as titillating gossip. Jacobites and Williamites engaged in a wide-ranging and vigorous discussion over the meaning and merits of the Revolution of 1688–89. This debate, quantitatively as extensive and qualitatively as rich as the better-known debate, the Allegiance Controversy conducted between 1689 and 1694 over whether and under what conditions civil and ecclesiastical office holders could take the oath of allegiance to the postrevolutionary regime, has received almost no attention from scholars. The Assassination Plot of 1696 has been studied not as an ideological discussion but as a conspiratorial event.

Scholars have ignored the debates of 1696–97 because the meaning of the revolution has seemed so clear. Almost all commentators on Williamite ideology have followed the establishment Whigs in denying the revolutionary nature of the new regime. Most have agreed that while James II's regime was certainly toppled in 1688–89, there was no ideological caesura. The new regime was defended on traditional, conservative, and moderate grounds. The Revolution of 1688–89 was not so much innovative as it was sensible. Central to the moderation of the revolution, in the view of many scholars, was the compromise formulation that William was in fact the reigning monarch, ruling de facto, while James II remained the rightful if absent king. This theory allowed those English with tender consciences to accept William as their king while denying that James had been overthrown. John Kenyon, in his influential *Revolution Principles,* argues that "the strict *de facto* theory" was "in possession of the field" in the 1690s; "that is, the theory that the Revolution, whatever its precise nature, had resulted in an ineluctable situation in which the king *de jure* [James II], without prejudice to his long-term right, had simply been replaced by a king *de facto* [William III], to whom a qualified and limited allegiance was owing, but who enjoyed no legal rights." In other words defenders of the Revolution of 1688–89 denied that William III and his supporters had legitimately resisted James II. This, according to Kenyon, explains why John Locke's theories, which justified popular political resistance against a tyrannical government, were mentioned only in order "to heap abuse upon them." Mark Goldie has similarly argued that the events of 1688–89 were "hardly a Revolution of 'Revolution principles.'" Like Kenyon, Goldie finds de facto theory dominating the ideological field—a theory that explicitly denies that William was the rightful and lawful king. For Goldie, Williamite ideology was characterized by "ambiguity," moderation, and the seizure of the "doctrinal middleground," and it was this moderate ideological position that "was profoundly to affect the future pattern of party philosophies." The most recent study of Williamite propaganda has reached similar conclusions. Tony Claydon has discovered that Williamite propagandists deployed their rhetoric of "courtly reformation" to "help William occupy the middle ground." In Claydon's view, William and his defenders were able to occupy this moderate position by deploying a profoundly conservative rhetoric, the rhetoric of "the early protestant worldview."[11]

The debate over the Assassination Plot of 1696 and the subsequent association is an excellent vantage point from which to evaluate these claims, to reconsider the meaning of the revolution. Most scholars have used the Allegiance Controversy of the early 1690s to assess the debate over the revolution, but there are good reasons to believe that the debates that followed the Assassination Plot provide a more accurate picture of contemporary understandings of the revolution. First, defenders of the regime during the Allegiance Controversy were trying to persuade the reticent to support the revolution. Immediately after James II's flight, the fragile new regime was constrained to court moderates and conservatives. Arguments deployed during the Allegiance Controversy necessarily emphasized continuity and conservatism, minimizing the profundity of change. One scholar, whose study of the Anglican reaction to the Revolution focused largely on those same early years, observes that Anglican theory "was from the first interested in salving the conscience of the nonjuror, and in this preoccupation other groups were ignored." Jacobites had reason to emphasize breaks with the past; Williamites in this earlier period had reason to highlight continuities. Second, political historians have described the plot of 1696 as a "watershed" and a "dramatic reversal of the tide." Changes in policy direction are often accompanied by changes in political mood and political sentiment. Third, revolutions are not made overnight. Studies of the Glorious Revolution have been remarkable for their narrow chronological focus. By contrast, major works on revolutions outside the British Isles allow themselves much longer time spans to examine the unfolding of the full revolutionary implications of the collapse of one regime and the emergence of a new one.[12]

The debate following the Assassination Plot reveals a very different ideological landscape than that uncovered during the Allegiance Controversy. The veracity and extent of the Jacobite Plot that unfolded in the context of a massive European war squeezed the Tories out of the debate. The Tory view that there had been a minor constitutional adjustment in 1689, that the war was merely a defense of that adjustment in Britain, and that all opponents of the regime were Catholic extremists was thoroughly implausible in 1696. Tories were left to choose between the defenders of two equally unpalatable modernizing strategies, those of the Jacobites and the Whigs. In 1696–97 Jacobites and Whigs agreed that a revolution had taken place; they disagreed profoundly and bitterly about whether that revolution was beneficial. From the wide-ranging debate, three primary areas of contention between Whigs and Jacobites emerged. First, the Jacobites argued that no legitimate resistance could take place against a hereditary monarch and that William was therefore no more than an usurper. Whigs countered that resistance was legitimate in some cases and that James had therefore lost his legal claim to the throne. Second, Jacobites argued that the revolution had destroyed the Church of England, while Whigs argued that the Church had been shed of archaic and misguided doctrines. Third, Jacobites argued that William and Mary had destroyed the English (and British) economy, while the Whig defenders of the regime countered that despite a costly war, the new monarchs had adopted an economic strategy appropriate for a commercial nation.

The adoption in both the House of Commons and House of Lords of associations that insisted on William's right to rule, as opposed to asserting merely his presence on the throne, made it impossible to maintain the kind of ambiguity about his political title adopted by so many polemicists of the Allegiance Controversy. This was a point contemporaries understood well. Those who were "accounted disaffected to the government" had no difficulty taking the oath of allegiance, William Streeter observed from Chester, but "now not one of them will subscribe the address or Association."[13] While the association rolls that circulated first in Parliament and then in the country at large were explicitly modeled on the Elizabethan Association of 1584, the Association of 1696 had little in common with its venerable predecessor. The Association of 1696 was stripped of the confessional and apocalyptic language of that earlier document. The circulation of the 1696 association—both who signed the document and where the document was signed—demonstrates the social gulf separating the Williamite political nation from its Elizabethan predecessor. The Assassination Plot and the subsequent association in defense of the Williamite regime highlight the ideological and social contours of the Glorious Revolution. Both defenders and detractors of the new regime were convinced that a revolution had taken place. The arguments for and against the revolution, and the extent of the political nation that took part in that discussion, demonstrate that this was, in fact, the first modern revolution.

Jacobites, nonjurors, and those disaffected from William's regime did not disappear from the English or British social landscape at the revolution. They constituted a culturally vibrant and socially significant minority on the post-1688 political scene. Although the government attempted to keep a close eye on their activities, they were able to meet, discuss their views, and disseminate their opinions. Criticism of the government in the 1690s was more open and less subject to repression than it had been in the 1680s. As a consequence the Jacobites developed a sophisticated political ideology in the years following James II's deposition. That ideology provided the intellectual basis for the invasion plans and Assassination Plot of 1696.

Jacobites and their sympathizers met actively in a variety of venues in 1695–96, settings that afforded them an opportunity to discuss and refine their views. Jacobites and nonjurors gathered in a number of locales in and around London and Westminster. Will's Coffee House in Covent Garden, where the fashionable supporters of the Duke of York had met during the Exclusion Crisis, continued to be a gathering place for James II's supporters. The government knew that "several clubs are kept on Thursdays of that diabolical crew" near the King's Bench prison. Another group who were "zealous for the rights of St. Germain's" met weekly at the Castle near Doctors' Commons. A "Jacobite Conventicle" was known to hold regular services at a cheesemonger's house on Newgate Street. Jacobites also gathered at the Old King's Head in Leadenhall Street and at Mrs. Mountjoy's in St. James's Street. MPs with Jacobite sympathies, including Sir Edward Seymour and Sir Christopher Musgrave, "had entered into a sort of Association" that "met usually at the late earl of Arlington's at Lindsay House by the Palace yard." The most notorious Jacobite meeting place in 1695 was the Dog Tavern in Drury Lane, where a full-scale Jacobite riot broke out on 10 June during celebrations of the birthday of the Prince of Wales.[14]

Criticism of the regime was not an exclusively metropolitan phenomenon. In Staffordshire and Lancashire "private cabals" met at cock matches and horse races and gamblers placed bets on the date of James II's arrival in London. Oliver Heywood was sure that he could perceive "the spirits of papists and Jacobites" working in Nottinghamshire in late December 1695. Perhaps Heywood knew of the "clubs and meetings of Non-Jurats" being held regularly at the house of the postmaster of Tuxford. The Jacobite "fraternity" resorted to an exempt chapel just outside Norwich where they could hear prayers for "King James." When in town "all the principal Jacobites" of Norwich flocked to the Goat Tavern, where they met "in a private club." The Jacobites in Bristol must have had several gathering places since they enjoyed the support of two prominent former MPs, Sir Richard Hart and Sir John Knight. There was a Jacobite bowling club "held at least three days a week" at Deale Castle in Kent. The two university towns were well-known gathering places for James II's admirers. The Low Church bishop of Oxford John Hough had warned the government "that the spirit of Jacobitism is too prevalent in this university." The longtime spy and Oxford don John Wallis worried that many of "the great concourse" of foreign students were really agents of James sent "to take measure of the inclinations of the king-dom." Abraham de la Pryme had himself attended "once or twice" Jacobite gatherings in Cambridge, where "they were frequently exceeding bold, and would talk openly against the government, which the government connived a little at, for fear of raising any bustle." "It is not doubted," wrote Thomas Percival with good reason, "but the treasonable infec-tion was in some degree or other spread into most parts of these kingdoms, amongst the ringleaders of the Jacobite Clubs and lawless conventicles in town and country."[15]

Jacobites and nonjurors did not, however, restrict their activities to gambling, drinking, and grumbling. They did much more than toast the king who resided over the water, squeeze a rotten orange, celebrate royal birthdays, and mock Williamite fast days. Jacobites and their fellow travelers developed and enunciated an ideological case against the revolution. They distributed pessimistic glosses on current events. Clerics, "both jurors and non-jurors," preached "very impertinently of the horrid murder of King Charles the First, insinuating the abdication of James the Second to be of the same complexion," and at the same time "they took occasion to exclaim against the Rebellion in 1641, and of the Duke of Monmouth's, not sticking to represent the Prince of Orange's glorious expedition parallel thereunto."[16]

Jacobite and nonjuring material circulated widely, both in print and in manuscript. After the revelation of the plot, the government discovered the press of John Redmonds, who was said to have "printed all the libels against the Government since the Revolution." Another "private printing press near Doctors Commons" was discovered along with "1000 virulent libels against the government" hot off the press. In January Richard Kingston had discovered a set of Jacobite woodcuts that "were printed off at a nobleman's house in the country." In March an "abundance of scurrilous pamphlets were scattered about the streets reflecting upon the government." While the Association was making its away around the country, "the enemies of the peace of these realms" were circulating a pamphlet that "prevailed with several to refuse signing the Association." In the aftermath of the plot, Jacobites were able to supplement these covert publications and fly-by-night presses with the official last speeches of the plotters themselves. As a result of these combined efforts, Williamites complained of "scurrilous libels and seditious pamphlets" that "flew up and down the land" and of "traiterous books" that "swarmed in all places."[17]

What was the Jacobite case? What arguments were laid out in these pamphlets, speeches, and sermons? It is in fact very difficult to discuss *the* Jacobite argument. Notorious differences divided the Jacobites, just as deep divisions had bedeviled James II's regime. What is clear is that the positions Jacobites advanced in 1695–96 were not confessional; they did not promote the religious arguments of the ultra-Catholic faction of the Earl of Melfort and Sir Edward Hales.[18]

The Jacobite position advanced publicly in England in 1695–96, whether in pamphlets, poems, or scaffold speeches, was sophisticated, internally consistent, and committed to the notion that the revolution had dramatically altered and deformed English politics, religion, and society. The widest-ranging version of the Jacobite case was advanced by the former radical Whig polemicist Robert Ferguson in his fiery *A Brief Account of the Late Depredations* written just at the time that James II decided to authorize a Jacobite rising. It was this widely distributed pamphlet, as well as his complicity in the wider plot, that landed Ferguson in Newgate in the spring of 1696. This product of "his restless spirit, fluent tongue, subtle brain and hellish malice" led at least one commentator on the plot to describe Ferguson as "the great incendiary, and common agitator of the whole conspiracy."[19] This, of course, was to accord Ferguson too much credit. What can be said safely, however, is that his December 1695 pamphlet gave voice to the range of Jacobite arguments being publicly advanced in 1695–96.

Jacobite polemic, like so much of later seventeenth-century political argument, was framed in European terms. James II and his supporters, who had often been accused of being un-English before 1688, turned the nationalist tables after the revolution. Jacobite poems, squibs, and pamphlets all emphasized the extent to which England had become prey to "the projects of Dutch politicians." Robert Ferguson complained in his influential tract that England was now ruled by "a Dutch King influenced by Dutch councils." James II asserted in 1696 that popular sentiment had turned against his rival because the English now "repented themselves heartily of the loss of peace, plenty, and the ancient laws, [and] longed for nothing more than to see the kingdom free again from Dutch servitude."[20] England, and the British Isles more generally, had—in Jacobite eyes—become the eighth Dutch province. The English, Scots, and Irish had lost their national identity.

William's treatment of the Church of England was very much a Jacobite grievance. Yet James II's supporters in 1695–96 were not fighting a confessional war. They did not see themselves as taking part in the struggle between the forces of the Protestant and Catholic Reformations. Of the nine men executed for their parts in the Assassination Plot, five—Major Robert Lowick, Robert Charnock, Ambrose Rookwood, Thomas Keyes, and Captain Edward King—were Roman Catholics. Another conspirator, Sir George Barclay was known for his "bigotry to the Romish persuasion." But some of the most important government informers were Catholics as well, including Thomas Prendergrass, Francis De La Rue, and Brice Blair. Both Charnock and King insisted that "the body of Roman Catholics" had "no manner of knowledge of this design" to kill the king.[21]

Protestant involvement in the Assassination Plot and the rebellion in general was at least as prominent. Sir William Parkyns, Sir John Friend, Sir John Fenwick, and Charles Cranburn all publicly professed their allegiance to the Church of England on the scaffold. Three prominent nonjuring clerics, William Snatt, Jeremy Collier, and Shadrach Cook, created "a great noise" at the execution of Parkyns and Friend when, "contrary to their duty and allegiance," they gave "absolution" to the two condemned traitors. Protestant involvement in the plot and rebellion was known to spread much wider than those who appeared on the scaffold. The Quaker William Penn, for example, had suspiciously accepted five hundred pounds from the plot's treasurer, Sir John Friend, not long before his death. In Edinburgh the Episcopalian meetinghouses were silent because "all the ministers" were arrested for their parts in the plot. The nonjuring bishop of Gloucester Robert Frampton was publicly examined before the Privy Council for having donated money to the plotters. So certain was James Vernon that the Jacobite opposition was not a confessional one that he complained loudly to the Earl of Lexington of the Protestant "vipers we nourish who seek to betray their country, and to deliver it into the power of a foreigner and its natural enemy." The Jacobite-leaning minister of Richmond Abiel Borfet drew the same conclusion. Jacobite opposition to the government, he informed his congregation, "is not caused by the malignant influence their religion hath upon them" but "by their fancying in [William] a want of legal right and title to rule over us."[22]

That William lacked a legal right to the Crown was one of the central claims advanced by the Jacobites and their fellow travelers. They repeatedly and vociferously denied that any legitimate resistance could ever take place against a monarch ruling by indefeasible hereditary divine right. "Our monarch is and has been always an hereditary monarch and not an elective," proclaimed Robert Ferguson with nary a whiff of his former Whiggery. So, "the Prince of Orange [William III], that hath no hereditary right to the Crown, but hath only obtained it by the illegal and merely pretended choice of the people, which is, in other terms, to have usurped it." Therefore, Ferguson drew the necessary conclusion, "we are bound both in law and in conscience to raise hue and cry after [William III], and to pursue him, and make him accountable for the crimes which have entitled him to the names of robber of his neighbor's crown, and intruder into and usurper of another man's throne."[23]

The notion that political resistance had always been and would always be illegitimate was central to the Jacobite case. "The doctrine of passive obedience is disowned [by the new regime]," the nonjuror Jeremy Collier announced with disgust. "The whole Revolution stands upon the ruins of this principle." "This doctrine," he reminded his readers, "is the distinguishing glory of the Church of England. 'Twas not only preached up by the men, but established by authority and constitution." Anyone who rejected the principle of passive obedience, anyone who no longer supported the claims of James II, Collier argued, could neither be an Englishman or a member of the Christian church. Collier's fellow absolver and fellow nonjuror William Snatt was heard to say "that it was no more sin to kill the Prince and Princess of Orange than to kill a cat or a dog." Less bloodthirsty in tone but identical in implications was the point made by James II's former propagandist Nathaniel Johnston. "If oaths were such binding obligations," he asked rhetorically, "how could we justify our selves in departing from those made to King James." Tendering a new oath, like that called for in the new association, would "infer a change in the constitution." The oath of allegiance was of limited political utility in the face of a Jacobite rebellion according to James II's sympathizers. "I think the people are bound to assist" a King in possession of the throne "in the advancement of trade and commerce, the administration of civil justice, etc.," argued the influential nonjuror George Hickes, "and to aid and assist him against all invasions and rebellions reared against him *saving* such as are made by the rightful sovereign or for his service."[24]

Those associated with the plot repeatedly advanced the claims that all resistance to the hereditary king of England was illegitimate, that William III was a usurper, and that oaths taken to the revolutionary regime were invalid. Sir John Friend, the wealthy London brewer and Jacobite treasurer, insisted that "the laws of the land . . . do require a firm duty and allegiance to our sovereign" and that "no foreign, so neither any domestic, power can alienate our allegiance." For Friend it was "unintelligible" to suppose "that the King's subjects can depose and dethrone him on any account, or constitute any that have not an immediate right in his place." It was therefore "justifiable and our duty" to help James II "in the recovery of his right." Robert Charnock, the sometime Catholic fellow of Magdalen College, was the other conspirator who offered an expansive account of his political views. "So sacred is the settled succession of our crown, and its ancient hereditary rights in the eyes of our law," Charnock asserted in agreement with Friend, that it was "the highest treason" for "any body of men indeed jointly or separately" to "harbour the least thought to alter and dispossess" their rightful king. Therefore William III, whom Charnock compared to Oliver Cromwell and Julius Caesar, could be no more than a usurper. As such, Charnock concluded, "it is the duty of every loyal subject that has the courage and opportunity to do it, to rid the world of a public enemy who has kindled war all over Europe, and sacrificed more lives of men and millions of money in his time to his unsatiable ambition and usurpation, than all your Marius's and Sulla's, Caesar's and Pompey's put together."[25] Friend and Charnock, layman and cleric, Protestant and Catholic, enunciated almost identical defenses of their actions. In their view, a de facto king only deserved obedience when there was no hope of restoring the de jure king. Their denunciation of the revolution was typical of Jacobite and nonjuring sentiment.

Few other executed plotters of 1696 offered such expansive defenses of their positions, but they said enough to indicate their overall concurrence. Charles Cranburn on the scaffold announced that he came to die "for his loyalty to his lawful king." Ambrose Rookwood emphasized he was dying for doing his duty "chiefly to my true and liege sovereign King James." "I believed King James was a coming to assert his own right," Major Robert Lowick recalled, "and I should, if on shore, have done anything in my power to have assisted him." Sir John Fenwick insisted that the government would be "settled upon a right foot" only after the "true and lawful sovereign King James" sat on the throne again. Sir William Parkyns was much influenced by "the principles of *Jure Divino,* Non-resistance, and passive obedience." "Taking the laws and constitution of my country for my guide," Parkyns believed James II to be deprived of his throne "contrary to all right and justice" and therefore "looked upon it [as] my duty, both as a subject and an Englishman, to assist him in the recovery of his throne." A Jacobite medal minted in Paris captured perfectly Jacobite sentiments on political legitimacy. On one side an engraved head was accompanied by the legend, "William Henry of Nassau, Prince of Orange, tyrant of Great Britain"; on the other was engraved a figure hanging from a tree with the legend, "Here is the great Absalom."[26]

The second element of the Jacobite case was that the revolution had destroyed the Church of England. Robert Ferguson, the former Presbyterian, bemoaned "the tottering state of the Church of England." The Church, he thought, necessarily suffered from "contempt" because of the "influence of Belgic advice, and in complacency to the Hogen Mogen constitution abroad." The Dutch king had brought with him the Dutch commitment to religious toleration and had found Dutch-influenced theologians to run the Church of England. George Hickes found abhorrent the broad church inclinations of William's new bishops. "As far as our Presbyterian preachers," he scoffed with the vitriol of one who had turned on his own Presbyterian brother, "they ought to be told that no church in the world would formerly have admitted such nefarious schismatics to the right orders." Jeremy Collier denounced the new churchmen for reducing the church to "many points of morality." For this influential nonjuror, "the New Guides" preferred by William had ruined the Church. "We are not to countenance their prevarications, and join with them in their defection," he insisted. "Are we indeed obliged to wait upon schism to the altar, to help to consecrate the revolt, and to pray against our conscience and inclinations?" he asked his readers. The lay nonjuror the Earl of Clarendon was convinced that the Williamite government was run by either "professed enemies to our church, or at best [those] unconcerned for any church."[27]

For many Jacobites and nonjurors, the postrevolutionary Church's position on resistance was itself sinful. Ferguson excoriated the "episcopal men" for "their apostasy from the doctrine of the Church of England from the doctrine of their church in reference to civil government, and legal governors." The newly approved doctrines of "deposing of kings, and dispensing with oaths, and resolving conscience into public good" convinced Jeremy Collier that the postrevolutionary Church was guilty of "a flaming malignity" in which "the distinctions of right and wrong are unintelligible." On this ground Collier declared "the Revolutioners schismatical" so that "their hierarchy is in effect deposed." Another nonjuror asked in 1695 "whether a man, whose allegiance is owing to his natural and rightful sovereign prince, both by the laws of God and his country, and bound faster upon him by the solemn and sacred obligation of oaths, can depart from, and renounce such allegiance, without offending the God of righteousness and truth?"[28] By implication, this nonjuror suggested, it was sinful for a Church to depart from its oaths and its doctrines; for a churchman to resist his sovereign.

These views were shared by a number of the plotters and their sympathizers. Sir John Fenwick, for example, insisted that it was "my religion that taught me my loyalty," a loyalty to the "crown of England in the true and lineal course of descent, without interruption."[29] Friend and Parkyns made their views known by appearing on the scaffold with the nonjurors Collier, Cook, and Snatt. The large scale of the donations gathered by William Lloyd and others on behalf of nonjuring clerics demonstrate the scale of opposition to the Williamite church.

Finally, Jacobites complained about the political economy of the Williamite regime. Here, too, the revolutionaries were denounced for importing Netherlandish practices. Robert Charnock accused William III of a design "to waste and destroy the English nation in favour of his darling country-men the Dutch." Robert Ferguson complained of "the rapines committed upon our trade, and the many guileful arts that have been practiced to enslave and impoverish us since the beginning of 1689."[30]

Jacobites complained of two forms of economic depravations: the expense of the war and the destruction of Tory joint-stock companies. Complaints about the cost of King William's war were especially salient during the coinage crisis of 1695–96. Robert Charnock bemoaned "the many millions of English money yearly sent into Holland," a tragedy that would end only by restoring James II and "that peace and plenty [England] enjoyed in the time of his reign." Richard Edge heard a Jacobite, "a great rogue I believe," exclaim at the height of the English currency shortage "that what milled money is made, or making, must be all sent to Holland." "Most men saw how unequally the burden was divided betwixt the Dutch and them," James II noted of his subjects. The Dutch achieved the "draining the English coin," in the view of James and his courtiers, because "the Prince of Orange was in effect their factor, and never served them so well when he was their subject as that he was a sovereign, who by making the Kingship truckle to the Stadholder, rendered three kingdoms in effect but provinces to the seven he came from."[31]

Jacobite commentators on political economy also complained that Williamites had destroyed England's great joint-stock companies. Gilbert Burnet knew that it was a common complaint of those who looked on the regime with "spiteful malice" that it "was designed that we should suffer in our trade, that the Dutch might carry it from us." "Asia and Africa can witness how [the Dutch] triumph over us and insult us in those remote parts of the universe; representing us a poor, feeble, and dastardly people," claimed Robert Ferguson in language redolent of the three Anglo-Dutch wars. The East India Company was "so long neglected in all applications they made to the great man at Kensington" because "the Hollanders were to be encouraged and assisted in the supplanting and worming them out of that opulent trade." Ferguson understood the creation of the new Scottish East India Company as yet another pernicious Dutch-inspired attempt to destroy the English East India Company. The Duke of Shrewsbury had heard it "whispered by some here" that plans to suspend the East India Company charter "arises from the suggestions of persons in Holland, who hope by their means, to ruin this company, and would, before any other is set up, destroy the English trade, and possess themselves of it." The editor of the *Flying Post* learned "that the Jacobites did also send advices from England, that the people there were highly discontented because of the decay of their trade, and their great losses, particularly of the East India Company, the African Company, Hudson's Bay Company."[32]

Although England's depredations from the war had been extremely widespread, the Jacobites chose to emphasize areas consonant with their own economic ideology. The costs of the war necessarily hit the landed classes hardest. More telling, however, the companies selected for sympathy were exactly those most committed to the land-based, zero-sum political economy of Josiah Child and his friends. The East India Company, Royal African Company, and Hudson's Bay Company were exactly those companies with the highest proportion of Tory investors and exactly those companies that had evinced the greatest degree of Jacobite sympathy.[33]

The Assassination Plot of 1696, then, was much more than a desperate attempt by a group of men, with or without the sanction of James II, to kill William III. The plot was an expression of Jacobite ideology and an opportunity to promote this ideology. This ideology emphasized that England (as well as Scotland and Ireland) had experienced a revolution, a revolution that all should deplore. The Jacobites and their sympathizers maintained that the English constitution denied subjects the right, under any circumstances, to resist their lawful hereditary king. Certainly the people had no right to elect their king. William III, in this view, was no more than a usurper—a usurper who could be resisted at any opportunity. The Jacobites also insisted that William and his new bishops had desecrated the Church of England. They had done this by advocating a church so broad that it reduced Christianity to mere morality, by supporting a policy of toleration outside the Church, and by jettisoning the Church's doctrine of passive obedience. Finally, the Jacobites argued powerfully during a period of severe economic crisis that Williamite political economy was deleterious to his new kingdoms. William's war had impoverished the country. His commercial policies had destroyed the great trading companies. Jacobites argued, in short, that William III had imposed Netherlandish policies and practices on the British Isles to disastrous effect. Dutch commonwealth politics, Dutch tolerationist religious practices, and Dutch-tinted economic policies had destroyed England.

Supporters of the revolution did not seek the middle ground in 1696. The defenders of the government did not, on the whole, seek to massage the consciences of the recalcitrant as they had done during the Allegiance Controversy. Instead, they chose to meet the Jacobite case head on. Williamites admitted that "our divisions upon the score of the Revolution . . . have been very arduous and of dangerous consequence." Although the Williamites hoped to persuade everyone to support the revolution, they no longer sought to downplay the changes brought about by the revolution so as to achieve the middle ground. They no longer sought consensus by ideological concession. "Who ever knew, or can imagine," asked one Williamite rhetorically and pointedly in 1696, "an exact agreement of a great multitude of men in one opinion"?[34]

Williamites repeatedly and persistently framed the revolution and the Assassination Plot as part of a great European struggle. The editor of the *Post-Man* informed his readers that "the prosperity of Europe in general depend[ed] no less on his Majesty's life than the safety of this kingdom." This was because a Jacobite success was a French victory. "The consequence" of a Jacobite triumph, warned the Anglican cleric James Gardiner, "would have been a French government." Had the plot succeeded, the Low Church bishop of Gloucester Edward Fowler preached, "'twill be crime enough to be an English man." No wonder that the London merchant Richard Lapthorne noted that "the people" reacted to the plot "in most part[s] of England and Scotland" by being "very forward to assert King William's cause against the French." No wonder "the populace" in Shrewsbury celebrated the Thanksgiving day for the plot by carrying "the French King in effigy through the streets" and then "committed him to the flames, with loud acclamations of God Save King William." The Jacobites, Sir Richard Blackmore concluded in his official history, "to revenge themselves on the Deliverer of England, were satisfied to give up the liberties of Europe."[35]

The defenders of the revolution understood the plot as part of Louis XIV's drive for universal dominion. "The power and influence of France" was being deployed for the "setting up an universal monarchy," Samuel Barton informed the House of Commons. "Nothing can satisfy the pride and ambition of that prince less than an universal monarchy," William Talbot explained to his collected auditors in the cathedral at Worcester. Louis XIV's "design is to make himself the sole emperor of the West," agreed Francis Gregory of Hambledon in Buckinghamshire. In Cork, Walter Neale described Louis XIV as "the public enemy of Christendom." "All Europe is sufficiently acquainted," noted another Williamite pamphleteer, that the ends of France are "the enslaving of all the sovereign princes of Europe." "Proud prince, ambitious Louis, cease / To plague mankind, and trouble Europe's peace," begged the young Joseph Addison.[36]

For Williamites, and especially Williamite Whigs, the struggle against France, the fight for European as well as English liberties, had been central to revolution principles. James II, they argued repeatedly, had supported Louis XIV abroad while imitating his governmental style at home. "If the line which succeeded that great Queen [Elizabeth] had religiously pursued the holy politick of her reign," argued William Stephens before the lord mayor of London. "Europe had never heard of the overgrown greatness of France." "Time was when England was in the interests of France, giving her helping hand to the enslaving the nations of Europe," agreed the dean of Worcester.[37]

James II, according to the defenders of the revolution, had become a French king. He had offered the English a stark but easy choice between English and French rule.

James II had "refused to rule us himself," insisted one cleric, "but stooped over to France to fetch fetters thence to enslave us to the boundless tyranny of that monstrous prince." John Strype, usually noted for his social observations, knew that had William III not arrived in November 1688, "the common enemy of the peace of Christendom" would "undoubtedly before now [have] made us a miserable people, like his own." To go back to James II now would be to choose French slavery over English liberty. "It is an unaccountable stupidity in a sort of people among us," exclaimed a Welsh Dissenter, "to prefer the garlic and onions of Egypt before the showers of manna that fall about our tents; to prefer French slavery, which is worse than Turkish, before English liberty." "The questions is come to this short issue," echoed William Talbot in Worcester Cathedral, "whether we live like a free people under our English laws and government" or "exchange these for a French servitude."[38]

The revolutionaries had rejected French policies and a French alignment for an English state and a Dutch alliance and in so doing had aligned England with the cause of European liberties. "Those reigns are past," announced one Williamite commentator. "The cards are all mixed; and the last revolution which advanced King William to the throne, was the most terrible blow that ever was given to France." The Revolution of 1688–89 was decisive "not only for the preservation of the Protestant religion, and the rights and liberties of" England, thundered William Perse in York Minster, "but also for the recovery of the rights and possessions of most of the Princes of Europe which have been invaded and encroached on by the common disturber of the peace, and welfare of Christendom." At long last "this kingdom has broke with France, and joined with the other princes of Christendom, in defending their common liberties and rights, and opposing that torrent that was overwhelming them all."[39]

One might be tempted to read this shift in orientation, this swing from a French to a Dutch alignment, as a confessional shift. France was, of course, the leading Catholic power. Plots against the Crown and government in England had, since the age of Elizabeth, usually been associated with "popery." A few Williamites did describe the revolution and the plot in confessional terms. The Dissenter John Shower insisted that the plot and attendant French invasion would have resulted in "nothing less, than the extirpation of the Protestant religion." Even though emphasis on confessional strife was more common among Dissenters, some Church of England men, such as William Perse, blamed that "religion, if we may call it one, which authorizes, allows, and commands the acting of such barbarous villainies, for promoting the interest of the Roman Catholic faith."[40]

This traditional reaction, this early Protestant worldview, however, was becoming increasingly untenable. One can hear the shift in attitudes in sermons delivered on the plot Thanksgiving day. The Hampshire Dissenter Charles Nicholetts initially announced, "This was a conspiracy of the papists and Popishly affected ones, to root the Protestant religion out of the land." But then, reflecting on the extensive participation of nonjurors, he conceded that "this was a Linsey Woolsey conspiracy; a strange mixture of nations, and parties united together (though otherwise of sentiments differing enough) to oppose the welfare of our Zion." Vincent Alsop, who had once been one of James II's few Dissenting supporters, opened his sermon with a conventional denunciation of the "Antichrist" that seeks the "rooting out the name of Protestants." By the end of his sermon, however, he had brought himself to the "highest transports of indignation" against the Protestant plotters and their nonjuring clergymen. He then found it necessary to sound a conciliatory note toward Roman Catholics. "I rejoice," he told his congregation at parting, "that a Papist can be found that will discover the treason." Similarly, John Moore preached before William III that "where Popery has a full influence upon men, they will break through all ties, natural, civil, or divine, to serve that interest." But he came to admit that even though "it is most unaccountable how any Protestant should have been concerned" in the plot, "yet it cannot be denied, that some there were of that religion and church."[41] For some Dissenters and Anglicans the undeniable evidence of Protestant plotters shattered their beliefs in the ineluctable and exclusive relation between Roman Catholicism on one hand and king killing, intolerance, and tyranny on the other.

Most, even most clerics, in England had already moved away from confessional politics and beyond the early Protestant worldview. They had no trouble asserting the multiconfessional nature of the Assassination Plot and of the struggle against French imperial aspirations. Edward Fowler reminded the House of Lords that the Jacobite rebellion depended on "the combined forces of papists and a strange sort of Protestants among our selves." He later emphasized that these "restless Protestant country-men" have "longed for nothing more than the downfall of this government." James Smallwood knew well that "the Jesuit and the [Protestant] Jacobite are equally well-wishers to the present government." "In this plow lately going, in the carrying on this plot," noted Deuel Pead, "an ox and an ass were yoked together, a Papist and a Protestant." In fact, many commentators argued that the Catholic plotters were less blameworthy than their Protestant counterparts. "I don't question but Popish priests are as malicious as our schismatick clergymen, but they have more prudence and discretion," noted one of the early commentators on gallows absolution, "and therefore will have their men to explain themselves; and to convince people that their church is not so black as we have represented it. They don't go about to justify their action by its principles, as the disciples of Cook, Collier and Snatt have done by the doctrine of theirs."[42]

Understanding the plot, the invasion, and intended rebellion of February 1696 as a traditional "popish plot" simply made no sense. William Stephens with much reason but little historiographical prescience argued that "he who (an age to come) shall read the history of the late embarkation, in order to a French invasion, and know that the Papist was but the two hundredth man in the kingdom . . . will admire from whence the French should have drawn their encouragement to make a conquest of England." Surely the author of one contemporary Williamite pamphlet was right when he stated that it was the political views of the supporters of James II and Louis XIV, not "the religion of Princes that gives an occasion to these fatal conspiracies."[43]

Not only did most Williamites deny that their opponents were motivated primarily by older views of confessional strife, but they insisted that the war against France, so central to the revolutionary agenda, was not part of a Protestant crusade. The interests of "all good catholic Princes," noted one Williamite pamphleteer, "are so closely united to those of the Protestant Princes, since they fight at this day for the same cause, which is to free their dominions from the tyranny of the common enemy." Sir John Fenwick's parting Jacobite salvo prompted another Williamite to remind Britons that "most of the princes and states of Christendom, reformed and un-reformed, are linked in a great and extraordinary confederacy, for a common mutual support of their property." "Have not French invasions already joined different nations of differing religions together in one common league for mutual safety?" asked the Whig cleric William Stephens.[44]

In response to the plot, Williamites did more than turn from an earlier emphasis on confessional politics. They also decisively rejected the moderate constitutional positions they had enunciated during the Allegiance Controversy. Most Williamites reacted to the Assassination Plot by demanding much more than allegiance to a king de facto.

Commentator after commentator, including those with the clear imprimatur of the government, insisted that England was a limited monarchy by law. William Wake, who was at the time one of William III's chaplains, reminded his audience in St. James's Westminster that the English monarchy is "in the very frame and constitution of it a limited monarchy; and established not upon the imperial laws of a few visionary politicians, but upon the fundamental laws of its own making, or allowing." The implication was clear: "I must solemnly profess that either I am incapable of judging what sense and reason is; or, it must follow, that an absolute monarch, a Prince not bounded by law, but governing only by the arbitrary notions of his own will, is no King of our acknowledging: Our constitution knows no such monarch, nor did we ever oblige ourselves to obey such a one." James II, all agreed, had become just such a king. One cleric reminded his auditors that under James II, England was "well nigh enslaved by arbitrary power." Still another pointedly dismissed James as "the late Tarquin." Samuel Barton, the chaplain to the House of Commons, argued that James II had forced on the English "a new constitution of government, according to the pattern of a neighbouring nation." "By seizing the customs, and raising taxes without authority of Parliament, dispensing with the laws of the kingdom, raising and keeping a standing army in the time of peace, and the like enormities," argued the prominent Whig lawyer William Atwood, James II "violated that constitution which would have made or kept him king." As a result, he had "manifestly ceased to be king, before his abdication."[45]

The notions that England was a limited monarchy and that James II had ruled in a French and absolute manner, were not, of course, new. What was remarkable in the wake of the plot, was that more than 80 percent of those who commented on political allegiance rejected passive obedience, notions of de facto kingship, and defended political resistance.[46] Defenders of the postrevolutionary regime, even those most closely associated with it, now eschewed a moderate and ambiguous interpretation of the events of 1688–89.

Defenders of the postrevolutionary regime now baldly denounced the doctrines of passive obedience and indefeasible hereditary divine right. If James II indeed had "a divine and indefeasible right to our passive obedience," William Stephens, admitted in his Thanksgiving day sermon, delivered before the lord mayor of London, then William III had no right to the throne. However, Stephens thundered, while "passive obedience to the law of the land, is the doctrine of Jesus; passive obedience to the will of the prince is the doctrine of Judas; a false and traitorous doctrine, whereby all civil governments and legal rights are betrayed to arbitrary power." Deuel Pead, the Duke of Newcastle's chaplain, listed among those "pestilent doctrines" that "you will do well to avoid" "the doctrine of *Jure Divino*, and the consequent thereof, the Dispensing Power," as well as "the doctrine of passive obedience, and its consequent, non-resistance." William Atwood argued that in fact it was the *jure divino* men who were the ideological innovators, dating their doctrine to the accession of James I.[47]

Far from being in possession of the field, the de facto theory of allegiance was now the target of almost every preacher and pamphleteer. The very ambiguity of the oath of allegiance, "which so many Jacobites have played with," can no longer be allowed to stand, argued Henry Day. It was now "clear as the sun, that the *de facto* doctrine missed but narrowly of taking away not only both [William III's] crown and life. But also our religion, laws and properties." William Stephens hoped that "the knavish distinction of *De Facto*, which was the foundation-stone of the late designed assassination, insurrection and invasion" will cease to be associated with the royal title. Deuel Pead heaped abuse on the "uncouth notion of a King *De Facto*," pointing out that it led some of the plotters to the scaffold. Those who "make one *de facto*, one *de jure* king," rhymed the poet Richard Bovet, "such politicians would a claim reserve, / The French designs to complement, and serve: / To pamper their insatiable avarice, / They'd Europe sell, and England sacrifice."[48]

Williamites in 1696 preferred to advance theories of active resistance rather than passive obedience. They insisted that William was king de jure as well as de facto. Despite providence's obvious support for England and its king, both in 1688 and in 1696, Williamites were not content to wait passively on divine action. The popular preacher and future archbishop of Canterbury William Wake advised his auditors not "to imagine that because we are commanded to trust in God, therefore we must take no farther care of, nor make any suitable provision for the success of our affairs." Providential arguments "alone," Samuel Barton told the House of Commons, "will be found a very dangerous and uncertain way of arguing."[49] Prudent politics required an active rather than a passive political nation.

Contractual arguments and utilitarian polemics based on the public good supplemented historical claims in the Williamite briefs for political resistance. Since it was "absurd to say, that a whole kingdom may have a right to its laws and liberties, and yet have no right to defend them, though they should never so apparently, or in such considerable instances, be broken in upon," reasoned William Wake, "then had this kingdom also reason to stand up in defense of its laws, and its religion, established by those laws." The editor of the *Post-Man* referred his readers to European precedents and James Tyrrell to prove the justice of political resistance. He then argued that as soon as a king "goes about to overthrow the constitution and fundamental laws, and break the chief clauses of his coronation oath, he abdicates *ipso facto,* his royal authority, ceases to be king, and the people have a right to fill the throne, which is thereby become vacant." Henry Day defended political resistance by referring his auditors to John Locke's *Two Treatises,* assuring them that he had "solidly" refuted Robert Filmer's pernicious notions. Another commentator, the most explicitly utilitarian among the contributors to the debate, argued for an ahistorical justification for government. "As every man is presumed most fond of his own interest, so the greater number must be supposed to be equally careful of theirs," asserted this Williamite pamphleteer. This notion that "what is done by the majority is best for the whole," he reasoned, was "a much plainer and firmer foundation for obedience, than all the fine-spun schemes of policy and government; which some pretended rakers into the rubbish of antiquity, have squeezed and strained out of old mysterious unintelligible record; or which by the changeable distinctions of some casuists have been proposed for convenience sake." William Stephens also ridiculed notions of good rule based exclusively on "right by succession." Instead, he argued, "public liberty" should be the proper standard to judge rulers. When a ruler makes "it his business to subvert the religion, laws, and liberties" of his realm, Stephens suggested, then "the people are not only permitted, but obliged by the duty they owe to their country, their posterity, and their own souls effectually, by force of arms to remove the cause of such an insupportable calamity."[50]

In 1696 Williamites were not shy in proclaiming that the people had overthrown James II and made William III their king. Popular support was a legitimate standard of political legitimacy. James Smallwood recalled in St. James's Westminster that William III was "called in by the voice of the people." More significant than the Protestant wind was "the turning about the hearts of the people so universally at that time, and making even those that were pitched upon as the instruments to bring us into slavery, so readily go over to the other side," Samuel Barton told the House of Commons. "The people of England called this great prince to their succor," maintained another commentator, "because the Most Christian King reigned no less in the three kingdoms of Great Britain, than in France."[51]

Not only did the people invite William to England, but they chose to make him their king. Citing John Locke for theoretical justification, Henry Day claimed that "the majority of the people chose their valiant deliverer to be their king." "The States of the realm, and the heads of the tribes of the English Israel, by consent of the whole nation," recalled the Lutheran J. E. Edzard, "have proclaimed [William] their king, and confirmed the crown upon him." William became king by "national assent," which was "the best foundation of allegiance," asserted one of the plotter John Fenwick's interlocutors. The "Country Gentleman" noted that William III "was enacted and declared King by the majority" in Parliament, "which election by the way implies the assent of every voter to all the acts of those persons so chosen." Francis Gregory thought to reaffirm William's right by imaginary plebiscite. "I am persuaded," he told his parishioners, "that of twenty religious and sober protestants, nineteen would vote for King William."[52]

Williamites not only rejected the prerevolutionary definitions of political allegiance advanced by the Jacobites, they also argued that the Protestant Jacobites and their supporters desired an outmoded and inferior Church of England. They asserted that the postrevolutionary religious settlement was radically different and substantially superior. The postrevolutionary Church was better, they claimed, because it promoted tolerance, because it placed limits on political authority, and because it emphasized moral behavior.

Both Dissenters and Anglicans emphasized the disappearance of religious persecution after the revolution. "Great and wide was the breach in the late reigns between the Church of England and those of the Dissenting way," the Hampshire Dissenter Charles Nicholetts recalled bitterly. But now "the breach is competently made up." Nicholetts, who had initially received James II's Declarations of Indulgence with enthusiasm only to cool toward them, as had many Dissenters, distinguished between liberty "granted" as in former reigns and that "secured and made firm by law." Indeed, so significant was this difference that he thought there "would have been no plotting" against William and his regime by High Churchmen had William not signed the Act of Toleration. The controversial Quaker George Keith also remembered sadly the situation "some years since" when "we could not meet and assemble together without great hazard and suffering." He therefore urged his fellow Friends to reject William Penn's example and actively support the Williamite regime in which those "that are sober and godly and of tender consciences may enjoy the happy freedom and liberty to serve and worship God according to their faith and persuasion." "We hear no more of the encouraging of informers," remarked another Dissenter. "None have any cause to complain of grievances for religion's sake."[53]

Church of England men, too, celebrated the new tolerant regime. "Persecution for matters of opinion, is what, I thank God, I have ever abhorred," William III's chaplain William Wake told his auditors at St. James's Westminster. "True religion," that which was promoted by the postrevolutionary church, he implied, "desires the welfare and happiness of those who are at the greatest distance from its own persuasion." In the same pulpit a fortnight earlier, James Smallwood had celebrated the fact that "here are no persecutions now for conscience sake." Force, William Stephens preached to the lord mayor of London, may "compel" a man "through hypocrisy to make a show of any religion." Much better, he suggested, to tolerate a broad swath of beliefs as the Williamite regime did. "Such opinions which are merely speculative, tending to no immoral practice (whether true or false)," he reasoned, "are innocent, and can therefore give no reason of disturbance."[54]

Williamites also rejected the nonjurors' notion that Christianity forbade political resistance. Not only did they enunciate a theory of resistance, but they consistently argued that there was no biblical justification for passive obedience. Henry Day "reproached" clergymen for "running too much out of their province to meddle with affairs that concerned them not, principally state affairs, in the late reigns." Dr. Richard Kingston similarly maintained against Sir John Fenwick that "our laws, and not our religion, does determine our loyalty." In publishing *A Declaration of the Sense of the Archbishops and Bishops* against the scaffold absolution of Parkyns and Friend by Collier, Snatt, and Cook, the Church hierarchy made its abhorrence of passive obedience quite clear. "Those great, eminent, and pious Bishops, who are now at the head of our Church," the *Post-Man* correctly observed, believed that when a king "goes about to overthrow the whole constitution, as King James did, then people are bound in prudence, honor, and conscience to disobey him." Both Dissenters and Anglicans agreed that what passed for orthodoxy during the reigns of James II and Charles II was simply indefensible.[55]

Williamites also celebrated the postrevolution church for a third reason. Whereas Collier and his nonjuring brethren had castigated the new bishops for reducing religion to mere morality, the new establishment continued the Low Church tradition of arguing that the pathological fear of Dissent among High Churchmen had destroyed conscientiousness within the Church. The *Post-Man,* for example, accused the nonjurors of having created a church that "would stick at nothing to promote their interest" but treated "the greatest crimes" as "not so much as Peccadilloes." By contrast, the Church of England establishment now emphasized moral behavior before doctrinal purity. John Tillotson, the recently deceased archbishop of Canterbury, had taken great pride in bringing the duke of Shrewsbury "to our religion," in converting him from his family's long-term devotion to Roman Catholicism, yet he thought it far more important that Shrewsbury "should continue a good and virtuous man than become a Protestant." This was because Tillotson was convinced "that the ignorance and errors of men's understandings will find a much easier forgiveness with God, than the faults of their wills." Almost in passing James Smallwood condemned any "religion" that "comes to supplant moral honesty." "What is religion good for," he asked in a query that had become commonplace among the Low Churchmen who now dominated the Anglican hierarchy, "but to reform the manners and dispositions of men, to restrain human nature from violence and cruelty, from falsehood and treachery, from sedition and treason."[56]

Reorientation of England's European commitments, redefinition of political allegiance, and realignment of the Church of England were, in the eyes of the Williamites, accompanied by a healthy reorganization of the English state's economic commitments. Whereas the Jacobites had pointed to the economic crisis of 1695–96 to prove the manifest failure of Williamite economics, the defenders of the Revolution blamed the downturn on Jacobite-inspired economic mischief. Where the Jacobites complained of the harsh treatment of the East India, Royal African, and Hudson's Bay Companies, the Williamites pointed to foot-dragging of the Tories and their opposition to the Bank of England. Whereas the Jacobites had continued to support an economics committed to land, the Williamites were the champions of manufacturing.

The Williamites responded to Jacobite charges of economic mismanagement by insisting that their antagonists had not grasped the realities of modern political economy. Modern warfare placed huge pressures on the treasuries of states, requiring innovative economic practices. Even though wartime taxation required national sacrifice, the extent of that sacrifice was magnified by Jacobite plotting and economic manipulation. Many pointed out that the war had placed inevitable pressure on the economy. The government, James Smallwood suggested, had done "nothing that is heavy or grievous to the subject, but what the misfortune of a war makes unavoidable." The Welsh Dissenter J. O. urged his auditors to "cheerfully pay our taxes, as heavy as they seem to be" because "they are absolutely necessary for the carrying on a just war in defense of our religion and liberties, which ought to be dearer to us than our estates, than our lives."[57]

Williamites, however, did more than suggest that the country's economic woes were the inevitable result of revolutionary foreign policy. They argued that Jacobite and Tory economic practices had brought on the crisis. Louis XIV and James II, Deuel Pead claimed, "took counsel how they might persuade evil-minded men to clip and debase and adulterate the coin of the nation," hoping that the ensuing economic confusion would be "sufficient to embroil the nation, and give them a fair opportunity for the invasion, assassination and massacre." The story Pead told now appears wildly improbable, yet he was not alone in believing in a Jacobite economic plot. The Whig MP and close friend and associate of John Locke Edward Clarke insisted that Tory recoinage proposals, "ill attempts upon our coin," were certainly "part of the Plot." Sir Richard Blackmore, in his official history of the plot vetted by the Whigs Lord Somers and the Duke of Shrewsbury, told a similar story. "Our coin had for many years past, been gradually lessened or debased, but within these three last years" had been "extremely clipped and counterfeited," Blackmore recalled. Although some of this was undoubtedly due to "the sordid covetousness of particular persons," Blackmore was sure that "there must have concurred the diligent assistance of our enemies, who by this means endeavored to streighten and distress the government."[58]

Why did Williamites blame the coinage crisis on the Jacobites? Why did they not simply explain the country's economic difficulties by pointing to the necessary costs of a just war? The explanation is that differences over political economy were central to the meaning of the revolution. Economic issues in general, and financial concerns in particular, were front and center in the partisan debates of 1695–96. So fierce were the "heats about trade" in the House of Commons in December 1695 that one commentator claimed "there never were such speeches in the House in any Parliament since that of '41." The contentious and socially far-reaching question of the coinage had become a party issue. John Locke, who was deeply involved in this controversy, had weighed in with a series of pamphlets and memoranda in 1695 and 1696. To radical supporters of the revolution, such as John Toland, John Cary, and John Freke, as well as to more mainstream Williamites, such as the Bank of England apologist E. H., Henry Capel, lord lieutenant of Ireland, and John Evelyn, Locke's financial pamphlets "cannot be sufficiently valued." Locke's views, however popular among Whigs, were not universally accepted. His published works were attacked by a flurry of retorts by Tories, including Sir Richard Temple and Nicholas Barbon. Political economy had become central to party differences in the 1690s.[59]

The opponents of the government achieved a modicum of success in modifying Locke's Whig coinage scheme, but their real success came in the establishment of the National Land Bank. Although there had been a number of land bank proposals with a wide variety of ideological implications, the united Land Bank adopted by the House of Commons "was chiefly managed by Foley, Harley and the Tories." The ideological commitments of the National Land Bank could not have been clearer. The National Land Bank echoed the economic arguments enunciated by Tory and Jacobite propagandists throughout the 1690s and the policies adopted at James II's court from 1685 to 1688. It was the parliamentary project of many whom the Earl of Ailesbury recalled "were born and bred whigs" but now shared his "sentiments." The National Land Bank was fully committed to the notion that land, and only land, was the basis of wealth. Land Bank supporters believed that property was necessarily finite and that England's economic survival depended on the government's supporting an agrarian rather than a manufacturing economy. "The National Land Bank," John Briscoe, one of its founders, noted, "is properly so called, the fund being land, the society landed men, who appoint landed men to be trustees, governors, treasurers." This bank, unlike other land bank schemes, Briscoe insisted, would have nothing to do with "monied men." The Tory and notorious East India Company supporter Sir Dalby Thomas insisted in his description of a land bank that "land (and that only)" is the "durable estate of the kingdom, and the *primum mobile* of all things therein." In this context, it was hardly surprising to find that Briscoe, "that set on foot the Land Bank," was involved in Jacobite plans to embarrass the government with John Fenwick's revelations. Nor is it surprising to find two of Fenwick's relatives on an early list of National Land Bank subscriptions.[60]

Given this ideological context, it was easy to understand why William Stephens thought that the discovery of the plot guaranteed "the preservation" of the Bank of England, the target of the National Land Bank men. No wonder John Locke was convinced that "these raisers of our coin and the subscribers of the Land bank" were covert Jacobites and no supporters of the Williamite regime. The Bank of England, the Tory Thomas, pointed out, "will not answer the ends of the landed-men." The great supporters of the Bank of England, John Briscoe reminded his readers in a comment redolent with ideological significance in the context of the Jacobite pamphleteer Ferguson's claims about the new regime's political economic program, included "several of the very same gentlemen, who for some years past have so strenuously opposed the establishment of the East India and African companies." Different economic ideologies explain the opposition between the two bank schemes, the party squabbles in the House of Commons, and the difference between Whig and Tory/Jacobite economic policies. Whereas the National Land Bank men thought that land was the basis of wealth, the Bank of England defenders insisted that "nothing does more advance and promote an inland trade, than a quick vend of our manufactures from the manufacturers; and nothing does this more effectually than a Bank." Locke's friend John Cary thought that the best economic policy was not to support landed men but "our manufactures, which will employ our people; the wealth of England arises chiefly from the labor of its inhabitants." For Williamites, then, the Plot and its aftermath dealt the final deathblow to Jacobite economics. The National Land Bank scheme was the economic counterattack of Sir Josiah Child and those who shared his political economic principles. The bank's failure to achieve the necessary subscriptions may well have been largely because of economic circumstances. But it cannot have helped that it was closely associated with Tory and Jacobite economics and was opposed so powerfully by the now politically triumphant Whig Junto.[61]

Far from minimizing the revolutionary consequences of the events of 1688–89, then, the Williamites in the aftermath of the Assassination Plot of 1696 emphasized ideological discontinuities. They agreed with their Jacobite opponents that much had changed in England after 1688. Unlike the Jacobites, however, they insisted that this change was for the better. They argued that England had freed itself from French thralldom. Not only had the revolutionaries initiated their long-desired Continental war against French absolutism, but they had ensured that the English state was no longer modeled on the Sun King's centralized, bureaucratic, and autocratic regime. The Williamites also defended new notions of allegiance. They now rejected doctrines of passive obedience, indefeasible hereditary divine right, and de facto kingship. Instead they based their allegiance on notions of the public good and contract. Williamites also defended the reorientation of the Church of England toward toleration. Clerics, Williamites argued, should instill good manners before they concerned themselves about doctrinal purity. Finally, Williamites defended a political economy that defined England as a manufacturing nation. They defended the Bank of England against the National Land Bank. They defended domestic manufactures against the importation of finished goods by the East India and Royal African Companies. They defined property as created by human labor rather than as being inherent in the land.

Not only did the Whig supporters of the revolutionary regime seize on the Assassination Plot to sharpen and enunciate their understanding of the meaning of the Revolution, but they also used their now extensive political capital to shape and define their vision of a modern English political nation. England's revolutionaries, like revolutionaries elsewhere, sought to enforce ideological purity on postrevolutionary society. The revolutionaries insisted that the English, first in Parliament, and then throughout the width and breadth of England, Scotland, Ireland, and the colonies, sign an association affirming their commitment to the legality and justice of the transformation they had wrought. They wanted to make manifest in society at large their radical revolution. In so doing they defined a qualitatively and quantitatively different polity from that of the Tudors and early Stuarts.

Contemporaries believed that the revelation of the plot and the wide-ranging debate about the nature of the revolution that those revelations generated had shifted public opinion decisively in a Williamite direction. Commentator after commentator noted that "King William gains new hearts every day." "I observe 'tis very lately that we were full of discontents, fly-blown with jealousies and fears, and these crawled about in murmurings and repinings at many things, at every thing," recalled Vincent Alsop suggestively, but "now it's clear that all these disquiets, these frettings of spirit that made the people uneasy are buried in the grave of the Plot." "The people were never so closely united, nor more zealous against the French King and the late King James than they are now, and the Jacobites never so low and dispirited," observed the editor of the *London News-Letter*.[62]

Many believed the events and debates of 1696–97 would convert Jacobites into Williamites. James Graham of New York thought that even William's "greatest enemies" would now become supporters. John Evelyn, who abhorred the entire Jacobite design, observed that "many did formerly pity King James's condition" but "this design of assassination and bringing over a French army did much alienate many of his friends and was like to produce a more perfect establishment of King William." Others also noted "how many trimming Jacobites are now upon reverse" and crying up the Williamite regime. Even James II appears to have thought that "the people and parliament (who otherwise began to waver)" were now "in the Prince of Orange's interest more than ever."[63]

The official Thanksgiving day in England, 16 April 1696, gave many localities an opportunity to demonstrate their commitment to the revolutionary regime. Taunton, long a hotbed of Whiggery, held an ecumenical celebration. After "excellent sermons" had been delivered "in both our churches and all the separate congregations," the town's notables of "all persuasions" gathered in the town hall, where they "with great affection drank the health of King William their deliverer." "All the gates of the town, fort, and top of the steeple, were decked with colours flying" in Rye. "All persons" in this East Sussex town "demonstrated their zeal for the preservation of His majesty" by drinking the king's health and "wishing him victory over all his enemies, and a long and happy reign." In Norwich the Thanksgiving day was celebrated "with greater marks of loyalty and devotion than I have ever hitherto seen," reported the *Post-Man*'s correspondent there. In Worcester the incorporated companies paraded to the cathedral church in the morning. The evening was marked with bonfires, the ringing of bells, and "all the demonstrations of loyalty and joy imaginable, as also the utmost detestation of the black and devilish designs of the courts of Versailles and St. Germains." The Sheldonian Theatre in Oxford was "extremely thronged" with people who heard several hours of "declamations and speeches" both "in prose and verse" demonstrating "our duty and affections to His Majesty." The inhabitants of both Durham and Great Yarmouth took part in colorful and enthusiastic displays of "devotion and loyalty" to the revolutionary regime. Throughout London and Westminster "there were illuminations, bonfires, and other public rejoicings."[64]

Many other developments leave the impression of a shift in political sentiments toward the Williamite cause. Gilbert Burnet recalled that "the discovery of a conspiracy turned men's thoughts" so that in Parliament "all angry motions were let fall, and the session came to a very happy conclusion." "The country people" in Warwickshire "pulled down" Sir William Parkyns's house "that it might no longer be a receptacle for traitors." The men of Ayrshire in Scotland greeted news of the plot by offering "10,000 men to serve His majesty for ten day *gratis,* and afterwards upon pay during any trouble." Throughout the country "many brave seamen, seeing the nation was in such visible danger, came out of their lurking holes, in which they were hiding themselves from the press, and offered their service."[65]

This impressionistic and anecdotal evidence, though suggestive of a change in mood, may indicate little more than a momentary shift in public demeanor. Political developments quickly forced the vast majority of William's subjects to take a firm and public stance on the nature of the revolution, however. On 24 February, the same day in which William had revealed the existence of the plot in a speech in the House of Lords, the House of Commons drew up an association to defend the king "against the late King James and all his adherents." The association, which was consciously reminiscent of the Elizabethan bond of 1584, created to protect Elizabeth I after the Catholic Throckmorton Plot had threatened her life, was far more forceful on the issue of allegiance than the oath tendered after the revolution. The association agreed to in the House of Commons insisted that William was much more than a king de facto; he was "rightful and lawful king of these realms." The following day members of the House of Commons were called upon to sign the association. On 27 February the clerk recorded the subscriptions county by county. The results were suggestive. Despite the swell of public sentiment for William after the revelations, about 20 percent of the House refused to sign, refused to accept William as king de jure.[66] This was hardly evidence that de facto theory was in possession of the field. In the context of a real and present danger of a French invasion and Jacobite rebellion, this vote did suggest, however, that there was profound disagreement as to whether the revolution had been desirable.

In the House of Lords there was a more bitter and lively debate about the association. In the end, the wording of their association was slightly different. Instead of asserting William to be "rightful and lawful king," the Lords' association claimed that "his present Majesty King William hath right by law to the crown of these realms; and that neither the late King James, nor the pretended Prince of Wales, nor any other person, hath any right whatsoever to the same." Though the language appeared less traditional, the result was the same. No one who signed the association could maintain the distinction between a king de facto and a king de jure. The *Flying Post* was right to claim that the association of the House of Lords was "nothing less zealous for the government than that of the Commons." The result of the subscription in the Lords was statistically similar to that in the Commons. In both cases, no doubt, the ideological implications of not signing were clear. When he heard that the Earl of Nottingham had spoken passionately against the association, the

English Whig diplomat George Stepney commented that Nottingham had become "the most violent man in England against the King's interest." Stepney hoped that Nottingham would be punished alongside the convicted plotters, but he knew that the former secretary of state "knows the laws too well, and goes no further than he can do with safety."[67]

The parliamentary associations soon became a model for county, city, borough, and corporate associations. Every locality, every group, every company in England, Wales, and beyond began drawing up associations and signing association rolls. In early April the House of Commons ordered that its association "and all other Associations of the commons of England, be lodged among the records in the Tower, as a perpetual memorial of their loyalty and affections to his Majesty."[68]

The conscious Elizabethan referents in the Williamite discussion of the association has led some scholars to assert a fundamental ideological, social, and political continuity between the later sixteenth and later seventeenth centuries. Patrick Collinson has posited a conceptual unity "for a long seventeenth century which may be said to have had its roots in the late sixteenth century." The Elizabethan bond of association, he suggests, had a "persistent afterlife in the seventeenth century." That association set the pattern by defining "an essentially protestant political nation"—"a loyalty defined and expressed confessionally."[69]

The evidence from 1696 and 1697 points to both an ideological and a social break. The kingdoms ruled over by William III were very different both socially and politically from those governed by Elizabeth I. The political nation was broader, more diverse, and geographically more far-flung. The ideological commitments of the postrevolutionary regime were radically different from those of its predecessor, to say nothing of the Elizabethan regime. To posit a fundamental unity of the long seventeenth century is to ignore several aspects of revolutionary change.

Neither the association adopted in the House of Lords nor that approved in the House of Commons defined allegiance in confessional terms. Both associations blamed the plot on "Papists and other wicked and traitorous persons." Neither association placed a confessional test on allegiance. Indeed, it would have been surprising had they done so. Both the Lords and the Commons were well aware that many Protestants as well as many Catholics had been rounded up all over England for their roles in the plot. All in Parliament and elsewhere were just as aware that they were engaged in multiconfessional struggle against Louis XIV, a struggle that was defined in terms of European liberties rather than confessional aims.[70]

The extent of social discontinuity between the Elizabethan and Williamite associations is staggering. In the early eighteenth century John Oldmixon claimed that numerical estimates were available for less than 10 percent of the association rolls. This partial tally is remarkable in itself: more than 450,000 are reported to have subscribed an association declaring William to be rightful and lawful king. Comparisons with the Elizabethan rolls are telling. Two Elizabethan subscriptions stood out for their extent. In Yorkshire, for which the roll does not survive, there were reportedly seventy-five hundred subscriptions to the 1584 bond. In 1696 more than twenty-four thousand signed the Williamite association in Yorkshire. In Worcester, which was apparently remarkable for allowing "common citizens to join," more than two hundred signatures were gathered in 1584. Worcester, which appears to have been unusual in its social exclusivity in 1696, had more than a thousand names on its Williamite roll. The Elizabethan Cornish bond lists 115 names. The Cornish Tinners alone gathered five thousand hands in 1696. In 1584 the Earl of Derby gathered sixty-six subscriptions from Lancashire. In 1696 it was "believed that the number of the subscribers will be about 100,000." Generally Elizabethan association rolls contained tens or at most hundreds of names. Williamite subscriptions numbered in the thousands and tens of thousands. In most cases Elizabethan subscriptions were restricted "to officeholders and gentlemen." In 1696 association rolls were subscribed at assizes, at quarter sessions, and at company meetings. In some cases subscriptions were gathered door to door. In Norfolk, the county association, for example, went "through every parish." It is likely that almost every one—or at least almost every male—was offered an opportunity to sign an association. In Warwick "all the male inhabitants of 16 years and upwards" were asked to sign. Similarly, in Barbados "all men in general from the age of 14 to 60" were offered the association.[71] In the 1690s, the political nation was far wider than the county elite.

Merely comparing the numbers of associators in the two eras does not begin to describe the differences in social composition between the Elizabethan and Williamite bonds. While the Elizabethan bond was tendered to "the more senior of the clergy" and the doctors and proctors of the Court of Arches, the Williamite oath was circulated among a wide variety of professional organizations. The remarkable breadth of these organizations, and their perceived stake in the political nation, demonstrates the great social gulf that divides Elizabethan from Williamite England.[72]

Unlike in the Elizabethan era, when only a select few of the clerical establishment signed the bond, clergymen from all levels were tendered the association in 1696. In Norfolk all the clergy in Humphrey Prideaux's archdeaconry were asked to subscribe. Each and every dean and archdeacon throughout England and Wales returned similar associations. Similarly, all the "professors of the ecclesiastical and civil laws, and laws of nations, together with the officers and others belonging to the ecclesiastical and admiralty courts," presented an association.[73] Again, the Williamite bond circulated far more widely among civil lawyers than had its Elizabethan predecessor.

Religious associations extended well beyond the Church of England. Bonds presented by Dissenting groups not only set this campaign apart from its Elizabethan predecessor but also differentiated it from Restoration petitioning campaigns, where Dissenters and Church of England groups were unlikely to appear on the same side of a particular issue. In 1696, freed by the Act of Toleration to appear as good Englishmen, the Dissenters responded enthusiastically with their pens. Dissenters, as a whole, had long since jettisoned their fleeting excitement about James II's Declarations of Indulgence. As in the June 1688 trial of the Seven Bishops, Dissenters stood alongside their Anglican brethren not in support of a confessional state but in support of one defending religious and civil liberty in the British Isles, Continental Europe, and beyond. Early in March the Presbyterian John How, "with a great number of Nonconformist ministers," presented William III with "a very loyal address" on the detection of the plot. A second group of Dissenting ministers addressed William at Althorp House with language echoing the Commons' association, complete with the assertion that William was their "rightful" sovereign. Encouraged by these public performances, performances that were seconded by the spate of Dissenting sermons delivered on 16 April, many Dissenting congregations signed their own association rolls. Dissenting ministers in London, Exeter, and the County of Somerset presented their own rolls. Dissenting ministers along with their congregations systematically collected signatures and presented rolls from the counties of Hampshire, Westmorland, and Cumberland. These county efforts were supplemented by rolls from individual congregations throughout the country. "Several Baptists ministers" saw fit to present their own association. Quakers, who had been more loyal to James II than any Dissenting group and who had religious objections to oaths, nevertheless eventually found means to associate. George Keith drew up a testimony, insisting that William was "rightful and lawful king of these realms," for his London auditors to sign. Quakers in Holderness in the East Riding of Yorkshire were probably one among the many Friends' meetings to take advantage of the parliamentary stipulations that Quakers need sign only a Declaration of Fidelity.[74] Dissenters, naturally, were free to sign the association rolls in their civic corporations and in their counties, and the vast majority did so. The significance of Dissenting associations of 1696, then, is that they could associate as legal entities. Because of the passage of the Williamite Toleration Act, the state now recognized religious life outside the Church of England. Dissenters took advantage of that right to assert their place in the political nation.

The state itself played a large role in the 1696 association effort. There had been no state-based association rolls in 1584, in large part because there was little to the Elizabethan state. The armed forces that had expanded greatly after the outbreak of the Civil War in midcentury, presented a range of association rolls. The general officers of the army in England and Flanders presented separate associations modeled on the Commons' bond. Entire regiments presented separate associations. Garrisons in both England and the Netherlands drew up associations with accompanying addresses.[75] The ordnance office, a recent creation, presented its own roll. The standing army, as the English were to hear very publicly in the next few years, was a post-Elizabethan addition to the state. These associations, which supplemented those drawn up by the more traditional county and local militias, indicated the army's newfound political and social importance.[76]

Elizabethan England did have a navy—though hardly any permanent vessels. Since midcentury the professional navy had played an increasingly significant part in English politics both at home and abroad. It was therefore entirely appropriate that associations were drawn up by the officers of His Majesty's fleet both in England and in the

Mediterranean. These bonds were supplemented by that submitted by "the commissioners for transporting His Majesty's forces" to the battlefields of Europe.[77]

The association rolls of 1696 revealed the extent of the Williamite state. Both the offices of the Treasury and the Exchequer returned rolls. Tax collectors, including excise officers, wine licensers, prize officers, and county tax officers, all presented association lists. The post office, which had become a much more extensive and prominent operation since Elizabeth's day, presented its own association. The pacquet-boat operators, responsible for overseas letters, also presented an association. Mint officers, so much at the center of political discussion in 1696, signed an association. So did the "masters, artisans, and other artificers employed in His Majesty's service of the works."[78] By the 1690s, the English state was more than a local affair.

Many professional and artisanal organizations drew up and signed associations in 1696. No such groups drew up bonds in 1584. The College of Arms and the Royal College of physicians signed associations. At least three of the four Inns of Court presented associations. Officers of the Courts of Westminster and King's Bench presented William III with association rolls.[79]

Commercial and manufacturing associations reflected the increased importance of those sectors in the English polity. All of the London companies drew up associations based on the Commons' model. The Trinity-Houses of Deptford, Kingston-upon-Hull, and York, "being the body corporate of the seamen of England," all signed and presented associations. The clothiers of York, the weavers of Norwich, the tin miners of Cornwall, and the seafaring men of Kent all drew up associations. The Royal Lustring Company and those employed in the rebuilding of St. Paul's also thought it important to associate. A wide variety of merchants living outside England drew up and signed associations. Merchants from Dordrecht and Rotterdam in the United Provinces and Malaga in Spain subscribed to surviving association rolls, suggesting that other merchant groups drew up associations as well.[80]

Whereas the Elizabethan bond was limited to England and Wales, the Williamite association extended beyond the Tweed across the Irish Sea and even across the Atlantic. The political nation had become more geographically extensive as well as more socially diverse. The lord deputy and Irish Privy Council set a model for Ireland when they drew up an association on 23 March. The Irish Parliament soon followed suit. Soon associations poured in from cities, towns, villages, counties, and professional groups throughout Ireland. As in England, these associations were supplemented by those coming from the army, the clergy, and tax officers.[81]

Associations in Scotland may have been somewhat less pervasive than in Ireland. Once again the central government took the lead. The Scottish Privy Council, Lords of the Session, and the Committee for the Plantation of Churches signed an association in early April. This was soon followed by an association from the "taxmen of His Majesty's excise and customs" in Edinburgh and the Duke of Queensberry's troop. In late March, before any official action had been taken, more than seven hundred inhabitants of Edinburgh met in Grey Friars churchyard in order to enlist in the king's service and sign the association. By mid-April the inhabitants of Edinburgh were eagerly signing associations "for the defence of their religion, king, laws, lives, liberties and estates, against the common enemy of all Christendom." These Edinburgh associations were supplemented by one organized by the Scots lord conservator in the United Provinces and signed by "gentlemen, students, ministers and merchants" residing in the Netherlands. The Scots Church in Rotterdam sent its own association, declaring William to be "rightful and lawful" king a few weeks later.[82]

Unlike in the sixteenth century, when the geographical limits of associating were much more narrowly delimited, Williamite associations were eagerly drawn up in North America and the West Indies. In New York City "the model of Association is well received by all hands, and unanimously assented unto by all the inhabitants of the City," wrote James Graham to William Blathwayt. Graham was not exaggerating. More than five hundred people subscribed the association in New York City—a figure more than double the size of any Elizabethan urban bond. Barbados, Virginia, the province of New York, Antigua, Nevis, Montserrat, and St. Christopher's all returned their own association rolls. Captain Shadrach Walton zealously drew up and had signed an association in Fort William and Mary, New Hampshire, long before he had received any instructions to do so from London. That association contained more signatures than the one returned from Elizabethan Lancashire. The most extensive and thorough association was that returned from Bermuda, where "except [for] four Quakers" all the inhabitants signed "with a great deal of readiness and willingness." The Quakers of Bermuda, it turned out, returned their own association.[83]

The Williamite associations were quantitatively and qualitatively on a different scale from their Elizabethan predecessors. The size of the Williamite political nation was well over an order of magnitude larger than the Elizabethan one had been. Where the Elizabethan political nation was limited largely to the aristocracy and gentry, the number of subscriptions in 1696 suggests that most English men and some women assigned themselves a political role.[84] The Williamite rolls registered the increased importance of professional organizations, merchant groups, and artisanal labor in the political process. Whereas the Elizabethan rolls included subscriptions only from the upper clergy of the Church of England, the Williamite associations were tendered to all Church of England clergymen and a range of ministers and congregations outside the church. By 1696 the state had a political and social prominence that it did not have in 1584. This is reflected in the many association rolls presented from army officers and regiments, the navy, the post office, and a wide variety of tax collectors. The Elizabethan rolls came from a few localities in England and Wales. In 1696 association rolls poured in from every county and the tiniest of villages in England and Wales. In 1696, however, this was not the limit of allegiance to the revolutionary regime. Associations were drawn up and subscribed all over Ireland and at least in some parts of Scotland. Englishmen in Europe signed their own associations. So did those living in the North American and West Indian colonies.

A great social and institutional gulf separated the 1690s from the 1580s. The differences between the two sets of Association rolls were truly revolutionary. But was there ideological discontinuity as well as social discontinuity? Was the mental world of the Williamites the same as the Elizabethans? Were they also engaged in a confessional conflict?

Much of the ideological discontinuity was not and could not have been registered in the association rolls. Nothing in any version of the association mentioned the political economic issues or justifications for resistance that loomed large in the printed debates about the meaning of the plot. Nevertheless, evidence from the association campaign itself suggests that, with the possible exception of Ireland, the revolution was not understood in confessional terms. The language adopted in both the House of Lords and House of Commons that set the model for subsequent local, professional, and clerical associations emphasized the multiconfessional nature of the plot against William III. There was no insistence, as in the Elizabethan bond, on an international Catholic conspiracy. Unsurprisingly, therefore, the response to the call to associate was multiconfessional. In Ireland, it is true, many associations proclaimed themselves to be from the "Protestant nobility, gentlemen, freeholders and the rest of the subscribing Protestants." However, this language was nowhere to be found in the associations returned from England, Wales, Scotland, or the various colonies and overseas merchants. Instead, a good deal of evidence suggests that the association was understood outside Ireland in a nonconfessional spirit. There was no evidence for the continuity of the early Protestant worldview. Parliament's decision to associate in defense of their sovereign was followed almost immediately in The Hague not by the Dutch alone but by the entire Congress of confederate princes, both Protestant and Catholic. This confederacy, including the Catholic Holy Roman Emperor and the Catholic king of Spain, pledged "themselves never to sheath their swords, till they have rendered the French King unable to abet conspirators and assassins against neighboring princes or states." There was no hint of confessional strife in this association. Indeed, there was even rumor of a design by some Catholic princes to petition the pope to excommunicate James II for his role in the plot.[85]

Nor, apparently, did English Catholics think the association was anti-Catholic. Few Catholics refused the association. Newspapers reported that in London Roman Catholics were eager to sign association rolls. The imperial envoy Count Auersperg worked with the Bavarian envoy Baron Scarlatti "to persuade the English priests and other papists to sign a declaration of their fidelity to the King and government, and of the abhorrence of the hateful maxim that a Protestant king may be assassinated." Sir Edmund Warcup later learned of "an address from the body of the papists" asserting that "they will take the oaths to the government and will give such other securities as may [make] clear that they are in the interest and will cordially act for the government against all enemies."[86] Since most Catholics felt along with most Protestant Britons that the plot and intended invasion had no confessional basis, they were certain that the 1696 associations were not part of a confessional conflict. Many, if not most, Catholics felt they could be simultaneously good Catholics and good Englishmen in the postrevolutionary era.

The ability of Catholics to sign association rolls in great numbers raises the possibility that the associations reveal little about the ideological contours of postrevolutionary England. Perhaps the association was yet another example of the moderation and consensus-building aspirations of the Williamite regime. No doubt the promoters of the association in the Commons, the Lords, and the country at large hoped that everyone would sign an association roll. But the insertion of the clause "rightful and lawful" in the majority of association rolls, and a close approximation in the rest, suggests anything but moderation. It was impossible for someone to believe that William was merely de facto king and sign the association.

The evidence suggests that a significant minority of the English very much understood the ideological significance of the associational language and refused to sign. Even after subscribing an association became legally compulsory in April, a substantial number refused to do so. While contemporaries spoke of unanimity, only 80 percent of the nation signed the association. Sir Edward Seymour eloquently explained his refusal to the House of Commons. "He was not so far abandoned of his reason as to believe that this was not an hereditary kingdom," Seymour told his colleagues. "There was a great difference between what was done upon an emergency and in state difficulties and what was to be done upon deliberation to violate the constitution of the realm," he lectured. A fifth of Seymour's colleagues in the Commons were joined by the same proportion in the Lords in their refusal. In Norwich, apparently, one out of five citizens attempted to sign an association that omitted the word "rightful" in describing King William. The newspapers were filled with accounts of the occasional refuser. Many more probably evaded. Among the clergy, especially in the lower ranks, many refused to subscribe. Gilbert Burnet estimated that one hundred failed to sign the clerical Associations.[87]

Many in England did not accept the Williamite revolution. As one would expect after a revolutionary transformation, many people did not, could not, or would not embrace the social, economic, religious, institutional, and ideological transformations demanded by the new regime. Large numbers lost their offices and positions for their failure to associate. The Marquis of Normanby and the Earl of Nottingham were dismissed from the Privy Council. Sir William Williams suffered the same fate, while "the credit of some suspected gentlemen sinks very low." The clearest evidence for substantial opposition to the Williamite revolution came after the parliamentary act requiring association. The failure of large numbers of state employees to associate resulted in massive purges in local administration. At least eighty-six justices of the peace and 104 deputy lieutenants lost their positions for failing to sign association rolls. These were people who despite the pressure of public opinion, and the threat of losing their offices, followed their principles. These were men who could not accept that William was rightful and lawful king. Two experts on Williamite politics have noted how "thorough" and "extensive" these purges were. Sir John Lowther of Lowther was undoubtedly right to conclude that, far from creating consensus, the association served to "divide us." The Association of 1696 made explicit the extent of political obligation required by the new regime. The level of commitment to the new regime and its ideology was understood by many as revolutionary.[88]

The extensive association campaign of 1696 was socially and ideologically very different from its Elizabethan model. Tens if not hundreds of thousands more signatures were gathered in the 1690s than in the 1580s. The extent of the participation was evidence of a geographically far-flung and socially deep political nation. William III ruled over a people very different from that governed by Elizabeth I. The Association of 1696 suggests that that people understood their political situation differently, too. Whereas Elizabethans embraced a confessional and perhaps apocalyptic struggle when they drew up and signed their associational bonds, most Williamites thought they were doing nothing of the sort. Only in Ireland did subscribers designate themselves "Protestant" as a mark of distinction. Elsewhere signatories described themselves as loyal supporters of the Williamite regime. Far from insisting on confessional language, the associations noted the nonconfessional nature of the plot against William III. England might still have been a Protestant nation, but it was not a Protestant nation that rejected Catholic participation. It was to this more capacious definition of Englishness that Catholics responded. It was for this reason that so few Catholics failed to sign their local associations. It was for this reason that some Catholic communities sought to draw up their own associations. A revolutionary change had taken place in English political culture.

The revelation of the Assassination Plot of 1696 and the subsequent political developments forced people to take sides, to clarify their positions. The Jacobites developed a sophisticated and widely circulated position against the postrevolutionary regime. In many ways it was a more coherent defense of Jacobite policies than anything circulated before November 1688. The Jacobites argued that William had in effect made the British Isles into Dutch colonies. Dutchmen were governing England. Dutch political ideas were being deployed to justify the new regime. Dutch notions of religious toleration and religious practice had transformed and distorted the Church of England. Dutch economic preferences had convinced William to destroy the English East India and Royal African Companies to enhance Dutch profits.

Williamites, and especially Williamite Whigs, responded with more confidence and less trepidation than they had in the years of the Allegiance Controversy. The time for courting the moderates had passed. Many Williamite Whigs used the plot of 1696 to demonstrate that ambiguity and moderation merely enabled the regime's enemies to appear loyal to their de facto king while covertly working for their de jure king. Instead of minimizing the transformations that had taken place, instead of relying exclusively on criticisms of James II's regime, the Williamite Whigs defended their revolution.

Williamite Whigs insisted that the English faced a choice of subjugation to French rule and governance or support for the new regime. They pointed out that the events of 1688–89 had transformed England from a virtual French viceroyalty into the leader of the European confederation against French tyranny. The English were now defending European liberties against French hegemony. The English, Williamites said, now rejected French-style absolutism for limited monarchy. A limited monarchy, they pointed out, necessitated that the people could enforce those limits. Neither the English constitution nor the Church of England precluded political resistance against tyranny. Williamite Whigs also argued that the true Church was a tolerant church and a broad church. The postrevolution church, they claimed, rightly saw good manners and moral behavior as a higher human good than pure doctrine. The English Church needed to resist the French practice of religious conversion by dragonnade. Finally, Williamite Whigs argued in favor of a political economy that emphasized English manufactures rather than land-based agriculture and imported finished goods. They supported a political economy that celebrated the importance of human labor rather than the importance of land ownership. The Williamite Whigs celebrated a Bank of England that distributed economic resources to productive sectors of the economy, rather than a Land Bank that ensured that economic resources would remain with the landed few.

On the whole the Williamite Whigs made their case. In the wake of the Assassination Plot and the intended French invasion, they were able to convince most in the vastly expanded political nation that William was and had to be their rightful and lawful king. They were able to persuade many that the best way to prevent French hegemony was full and unconditional support for King William. They were able to convince many, in effect, to support the policies of the Whig Junto ministers.

This was not, of course, a permanent victory. The English public did not finally and permanently reject Tory politicians like Robert Harley or the Earl of Nottingham. Revolutions, as we now know, have their radical, moderate, and reactionary moments. But the plot and intended French invasion did have lasting significance. First, that all officeholders and MPs were now required to sign an association proclaiming William's right to the Crown was a decisive and formal rejection of de facto theory. It was a legal recognition that resistance had taken place in 1688, and that English kings did not rule by indefeasible hereditary divine right. De facto theory had permanently lost possession of the field. Second, the aftermath of the plot doomed the Land Bank scheme. It is true, of course, that the Land Bank was launched at an unpropitious moment. However, in the context of the plot investors feared that support for the Land Bank was support for the Jacobite cause. The result was that the government was committed exclusively to a political economy favoring manufactures over raw agricultural produce, labor over land. Third, the plot clarified the distinctive Tory position on Europe. Tories could no longer complain about William's pro-Dutch policies without offering an alternative that could be construed as pro-French. For a brief period in the later 1690s this did not matter, for England was at peace. At the outbreak of the War of the Spanish Succession, however, the Tories revived their distinctive take on foreign policy, demanding that the English pay exclusive attention to the seas. The Tories were committed to keeping the oceans open for commerce but unconcerned with keeping open European markets to English manufactures or preventing the spread of absolutism on the Continent. Tory political resurgence depended on their enunciation of a non-Jacobite alternative to the Whig position on Europe.

The Assassination Plot narrowed the ideological choices available to English men and women. Tories, who had insisted that war against Louis XIV was necessary only to consolidate the slight constitutional adjustment made necessary by James's perfidy, were deeply damaged. They had wanted to end the war to prevent radical social, economic, and religious change. They distinguished themselves from Jacobites by insisting that they were loyal subjects of William and that they would have no truck with Roman Catholics. But the plot had revealed both that William could never be safe as long as Louis XIV remained a powerful force in Europe and that Jacobitism was not a confessional movement. The plot made it possible for the Whigs to consolidate their radical revolution.

CHAPTER FIFTEEN

Conclusion
The First Modern Revolution

Enlightenment commentators from David Hume and Voltaire to John Wilkes and Monsieur Navier of Dijon understood the Revolution of 1688–89 as a fundamentally transformative event in English and European history. This book has recovered the reasons why these men thought, and were right to think, that something radical and radically new happened in later seventeenth-century England. What, then, have been the central claims of this book?

England's Revolution of 1688–89 was the first modern revolution. It was a revolution that took place over a number of years rather than a number of months. It had both long-term causes and long-term intended consequences. Many of the revolutionaries wanted to radically remake English state and society. And they succeeded in doing so. The Revolution of 1688–89 drastically transformed, and was intended to transform, English foreign and imperial policy, English political economy, and the Church of England. The Revolution of 1688–89 resulted in a war against France, the creation of the Bank of England, and the Toleration Act of 1689, which had widespread support among the new English episcopal bench.

The Revolution of 1688–89 was the first modern revolution not only because it transformed English state and society but also because, like all modern revolutions, it was

---

(above) *William and Mary: Coronation,* by R. Arondeaux, 1689. This medal, showing an orange tree growing up where an oak has fallen, celebrates the accession of King William and Queen Mary. The open book that sits beneath the busts of the two monarchs is inscribed "The Laws of England," and it is flanked by cornucopias inscribed "The Safety of Kingdom" and "Public Happiness."

popular, violent, and divisive. The revolutionaries of 1688–89 numbered in the thousands. They were not a tiny political elite. England in 1688–89 was ripped apart by violent acts against property and people. This was not a bloodless revolution. Thousands more lost their lives in the set-piece battles that took place on the Continent, in Ireland, and in Scotland as a direct consequence of the revolutionary transformations in England. James II and his regime may have provoked passionate resentment among a wide range of the English population, but it did not generate unanimous opposition. A substantial minority of the English retained their loyalty to James and his political projects. There were deep divisions even among those who took arms and expended their resources to get rid of their king. Tories, by and large, wanted merely to dismantle the state edifice erected by James. Whigs not only believed that England's political troubles began long before James ascended the throne but fervently hoped that the revolution would allow them to create a radically different and new English polity. The Revolution of 1688–89 was not the aristocratic, bloodless, and consensual affair described in establishment Whig historiography.

The Revolution of 1688–89 was popular, violent, and divisive precisely because James II had not been a defender of traditional society. He had been a radical modernizer. James, to use Max Weber's terminology, promoted a modern bureaucratic rather than a traditional patrimonial state. In contrast to patrimonial regimes, he promoted "binding norms and regulations" for his tax collectors in an effort to create a "well-disciplined bureaucracy." He sought to centralize his authority by replacing the local official, reliant on "his own social prestige within his local district," with technical experts of known ideological reliability. And at least after the defeat of the Duke of Monmouth's rebellion in 1685, James was not overly concerned to legitimate his claims with reference to the "traditional" powers of English rulers.[1] He had followed the French Sun King, Louis XIV, in trying to create a modern Catholic polity. This involved not only trying to Catholicize England along Gallican lines but also creating a modern, centralizing, and extremely bureaucratic state apparatus. The French-style Catholicism James favored and promoted was ideologically suited to creating a modern polity. The emphasis of French Catholic apologists, such as Jacques-Benigne Bossuet, on ideological unity and unfettered sovereignty was perfectly suited to the French model of modern state building. Gallicanism provided the ideological prop necessary to expand significantly the state bureaucracy—from the post office to Hearth Tax collectors—and to devise ideological tests to enforce the loyalty of the local bureaucrats to the central regime. The effectiveness, efficiency, and unity of this civil bureaucracy, coupled with the massive new standing army, made it certain that any attempt to overthrow James II's regime would have to be violent. That James II (and his brother, Charles II) had extended the tendrils of the central state much deeper and farther than they had ever gone before did much to ensure that the revolution against the Catholic modernizing state would be popular. And James's jettisoning the rhetoric of continuity in favor of one of change divided his opponents between those who wanted to maintain the old order and those who disagreed with his vision of modernity.

The Revolution of 1688–89, then, like all modern revolutions, was a struggle ultimately waged between two competing groups of modernizers. The revolution did not pit defenders of traditional society against advocates of modernity. Both Whigs and Jacobites were modernizers. It was the Tories who wished to defend a version of the old order. The Tories were placed in the unpalatable position of having to choose between two very imperfect political outcomes.

Nevertheless, it was not immediately clear that the Tories would fail. By focusing so heavily on the immediate aftermath of James's flight, scholars have overemphasized the extent of Tory political success. Between the middle of 1689 and late 1693 the Tories were winning the majority of political skirmishes; these victories infuriated most Whigs. But from 1694 onward the Whigs began to consolidate their position. They convinced the largely unsympathetic King William that winning the war against France required him to adopt their political and economic vision. They demonstrated that they were the only party fully committed to William's plan for Continental warfare. And, most important, after the failed Assassination Plot of 1696 the Whigs were able to show that only their political ideology and their version of the Church of England could guarantee political stability. The Whigs felt free in 1696 to emphasize the revolutionary transformations they had begun since 1688. While apologists for the oath of allegiance between 1689 and 1694 felt constrained to leave ambiguous the question as to whether James II had been legitimately deposed, the Association of 1696 unequivocally stated that the revolution was a justifiable act of political resistance. The hundreds of thousands of signers of the Association of 1696 formally accepted that the Revolution of 1688–89 had signaled the death knell of the theory of indefeasible hereditary divine right.[2] Revolutions take years rather than months. A narrow focus on the immediate aftermath of the events of 1688–89 has obscured the radical implications of the revolution.

Why have commentators on the Revolution of 1688–89 misunderstood its significance for so long? No doubt much of the answer lies in the political utility of insisting that English history was fundamentally different from that of the rest of world. But two basic misconceptions have also led interpreters astray, misconceptions founded on central assumptions of the establishment Whig account of the revolution. These Whig assumptions have been largely accepted by late-twentieth-century revisionist scholars as well. First, the great achievement of Thomas Babington Macaulay's celebrated third chapter of his *History* was not so much the invention of social history as it was the successful severing of questions of social and economic change from those of religious and political transformation.[3] By insisting that England's great social and economic development happened only after the revolution, Macaulay and his followers were able to ignore any possible socioeconomic causes of the revolution. In this book I have argued, by contrast, that English society and the English economy was changing rapidly in the second half of the seventeenth century. England deviated from the Continental pattern in these years, and these transformations had a number of profound implications for later seventeenth-century politics. The growth of English trade buoyed the intake of royal customs and made the Crown less dependent on extraordinary parliamentary grants and hence on Parliament itself. The development of the post office and the extension of the road system, among other improvements in English infrastructure, facilitated the geographical expansion of James II's modern state apparatus. These developments in English infrastructure, including the rapid spread of coffeehouses across England, radically extended and socially deepened the possibilities for popular political discussion.[4] And England's rapid transformation into a trading nation transformed the very nature of political argument there. In the later seventeenth century English politicians for the first time began to argue openly and explicitly about issues of political economy. By the early 1680s, the Tories and Whigs had clearly adopted differing approaches to England's economic future.

Second, Macaulay and subsequent Whig scholars wrote English foreign policy and English popular concerns about developments overseas out of the history of the Revolution of 1688–89. In the view of most scholars, only on William's arrival were the English forced to look beyond the North and Irish Seas. In fact, as we have seen, the English and their governors were intensely interested in foreign affairs. Neither James II nor his opponents prioritized domestic over foreign policy. This was hardly surprising. Both James II and his opponents agreed that one of the primary duties of an English monarch was to reestablish the kingdom's status as an important player on the European scene. A central function of the state, almost all early modern commentators concurred, was to fight foreign wars. Because so many agreed that foreign affairs were a crucial issue of statecraft, it was in this arena that ideological and political tensions came to the fore. James's decision to ally himself with France against the United Provinces revealed not only his predilections for absolutism as against more popular forms of government, but also his government's belief that the Dutch rather than the French represented the greatest threat to England's economic well-being. Because the scale of early modern warfare had increased dramatically since the late sixteenth century, the decision of later seventeenth-century monarchs to involve themselves on the world scene required them to marshal resources on an unprecedented scale. This need for greater resources, in turn, brought a wider range of people—from metropolitan merchants to provincial consumers—into the political process. All of these people inevitably asked questions about what the government was doing with the money they were collecting in hearth taxes or customs assessments. By writing off English foreign policy, by assuming that James had no international agenda, scholars have missed a central and dynamic area of political contestation.[5]

The English Revolution of 1688–89 was the first modern revolution. It transformed the English church, the English state, and, in the long run, English society. It was an event that involved large swaths of the English nation in political violence and partisan political contestation. In many ways the Revolution of 1688–89 was an inspiration for late-eighteenth-century revolutionaries in France, in North America, and elsewhere. This was not the conservative and restorative revolution described in the establishment Whig historiography.

What of the revisionist scholarship? What of the claim that the Revolution of 1688–89 was fundamentally a confessional struggle in which a Catholic king was overthrown by narrow-minded Protestant English men and women? What of the claim that Tory defenders of the Church of England disposed of James because they detested his tolerationist policies? At the heart of this now dominant interpretation is that James was a political moderate who had modest aims. James was overthrown not because he was an absolutist but because he offended traditional religious sensibilities.

James II was known to be a devout Roman Catholic when he ascended the throne in 1685. James's Catholicism and the knowledge of English antipathy for "popery" prompted the Duke of Monmouth to invade England's West Country in the summer of 1685. Monmouth may have had radical friends, and he may or may not have shared their political ideas, but it is clear that his army was made up of men who were interested in replacing a Catholic James with a Protestant James. They were much less interested in radically transforming the monarchy. In fact, many of the radical revolutionaries of 1688, even those from the West Country, wanted nothing to do with Monmouth. His rebellion failed precisely because few people were willing to engage in rebellious activity for exclusively religious reasons.

That the uprising against James II in 1688, in the West Country and throughout England, was so much more successful owes a great deal to the nature of his regime. James's regime was not merely a Catholic regime; it was a modernizing Catholic regime. Its operating ideological premises were taken from French Catholic arguments directed not against Protestants in the first instance but against pope Innocent XI and his defenders. James's modern Catholic monarchy married notions of absolute sovereignty to a campaign to re-Catholicize England. James's bureaucratic state built on the Gallican model infuriated English Catholics as well as English Protestants.

James was not overthrown in a confessional struggle. But James's policies did heighten and transform religious divisions within England. By offering liberty of conscience while severely restricting the discussions that could take place in religious gatherings and simultaneously increasing royal authority in other areas, James divided the Nonconformist community. Some, like the Quaker William Penn, were grateful that James had ended a brutal period of religious persecution. Most, however, came to believe that religious liberty was of little value without civil liberty. Most religious Dissenters turned against James by 1688, became active revolutionaries, and were the postrevolutionary regime's most active supporters. Anglicans, too, were deeply divided by James II's actions. A few Church of England clerics and laymen exalted in James's firm use of sovereign powers. Many more were deeply disturbed by James's Catholicizing policies but felt paralyzed by their own deep commitment to the Anglican doctrine of passive obedience. Anglican Low Churchmen, with an active group of London clerics playing a prominent role, took the lead in responding to the mass of French Catholic apologetics flooding into England. This group of Anglican clerics developed an increasingly principled commitment to religious toleration and eventually came to believe that political resistance, as distinct from religious resistance, was sometimes necessary.

The study of religion in the Early Modern period has been bedeviled by a set of false binary oppositions. Scholars have argued that later seventeenth-century England was either a secular society or a religious society. This narrow set of interpretative options has made it difficult to narrate, describe, and analyze religious change. The resulting interpretative schema either that "religion ceased to be such an important issue after 1660" or that "domestic religious issues" were of "central significance" are unsatisfactory. The issue in the later seventeenth century was not that religion came to mean less to English men and women but that it came to mean something different.[6] Recent scholarship has demonstrated how complex and dynamic religious disputes were in the later seventeenth century and how much of their syntax depended on earlier debates. But none of that signifies that religion meant the same thing. It did not. Religious discontent was a necessary but insufficient explanation for the Revolution of 1688–89.

The Revolution of 1688–89 was not a struggle between Catholics and Protestants. It was not one of the last battles in the war between the forces of the Protestant and Catholic Reformations. This was in part because the binary confessional divisions that had cut across Europe in the sixteenth and early seventeenth centuries had been superseded. In northern Europe, visions of Protestant political unity had been replaced by the reality of bitter divisions between Calvinist and Lutheran states. The Lutheran king of Sweden, for example, was more concerned about the Calvinist elector of Brandenburg than he was about the Catholic king of France.[7] Louis XIV had succeeded in dividing Catholic Europe into groups that supported France and those that supported the pope. The Holy Roman Emperor saw the French king rather than Europe's Protestant monarchs as his greatest enemy. By failing to place English religious debates in the context of the broader European discussions of which they were a part, scholars have overemphasized continuity in the religious sphere. They have mistaken the extensive and brutal anti-Catholic violence of 1688 and 1689 for a manifestation of traditional anti-Catholic prejudice, when those acts can be better understood as attacks on the instruments and symbols of James II's modern and Gallican state. Similarly, scholars have been too ready to understand the postrevolutionary regime's fanatical commitment to a war against Catholic France as the realization of early-seventeenth-century ideals of the Protestant cause. In fact, the English fought the Nine Years' War in formal alliance with Catholic Spain and the Holy Roman Empire. English men and women were aware of this and understood full well that papal sympathies lay with the empire, Spain, England, and the Protestant United Provinces of the Netherlands rather than with Catholic France. This was explicable to the English because most of them knew that the early Protestant worldview, the view that Protestants and Catholics were locked in a final eschatological struggle for religious hegemony, was no longer tenable.

Revisionist scholars, those who see the revolution as a Protestant struggle against a

Catholic king or an Anglican struggle against a tolerationist king, are also wrong to focus so narrowly on religious issues. Although religious issues were important both to James II and to his opponents, they were not the only issues that energized them. The advocates of a religious interpretation of the revolution have shared with the proponents of the establishment Whig interpretation the view that English men and women of the seventeenth century were too insular to interest themselves in political and economic developments beyond the British Isles and too traditional to engage in political arguments about the economy at home. In fact, matters related to both foreign policy and political economy convinced a wide range of English men and women to risk their lives and fortunes in 1688. The revolutionaries of 1688–89 were motivated to overthrow James II and create a new kind of English government because they were concerned not only about their religion but also about England's foreign policy and England's political economy. The revolutionaries of 1688–89 were motivated by a far broader ideological vision than defenders of the religious interpretation have allowed.

If the Revolution of 1688–89 was the first modern revolution, where does that leave the Revolution of 1640–60, which has so fascinated generations of scholars? It was that earlier revolution which Perez Zagorin calls "the first great manifestation of the modern revolutionary temper." It was that revolution which Christopher Hill describes as "a turning point in human history." It was those events that, according to John Adamson, ended "the 'military age' of the nobility" in England. It was the "revolution of the Saints" that took place between 1640 and 1660 which Michael Walzer claims marks "a crucial phase in the modernization process." In fact, students of the two English revolutions, that of 1640–60 and that of 1688–89, long battled for interpretative supremacy. By the early nineteenth century, however, "the balance of sympathy" had "shifted in favour of the first upheaval." It was this sense of competition and priority that leads Christopher Hill to dismiss the Revolution of 1688–89 as "a restoration to power of the traditional ruling class." Robert Brenner more sympathetically sees the Revolution of 1688–89 as "the consolidation of certain long-term patterns of development that had already marked off socio-political evolution in England from that of most of the continent during the early modern period."[8] From the 1640s, in this view, England decisively diverged from the European pattern of social, political, and cultural development. The events of 1688–89 were at most putting the finishing touches on the great changes that had been set in motion at midcentury and before.

In fact, I suggest, many of the great changes England experienced between 1640 and 1660 proved ephemeral. From the Restoration in 1660, and especially after James II's accession to the throne in 1685, England did not diverge from the European pattern of political development. England was quickly becoming an absolutist regime. Between 1660 and 1688 the later Stuart kings did much to ensure that the monarch would have a monopoly of political power not only in theory but also in practice.[9] More precisely, Charles II increasingly and James II with fanatical energy committed themselves to adapting the French political model to England. The modern absolutist state of the Restoration Stuart kings, one that had the infrastructure to make good its older theoretical claims, was not doomed to failure. At various points in the later seventeenth century both later Stuart kings even enjoyed widespread popular support for their state-building projects. They were not pursuing ill-advised strategies whose failure was preordained, as advocates of the decisive midcentury break have implied. It was not inevitable that James's Catholic modernization strategy would fail. James II was overthrown because of the contingent confluence of two factors. First, he squandered the political capital he enjoyed in the wake of Monmouth's rebellion by moving too quickly to modernize the English state. In so doing he provoked widespread popular political opposition within England. Second, sealing James's demise, his ally Louis XIV fomented a European political crisis that simultaneously gave William broad political support within the United Provinces and across Europe and made it possible for William to risk an invasion. Had James not stimulated so much political opposition, his massive standing army would have been free to crush William's force. Indeed, without widespread political discontent in England, William might have had trouble financing and manning his invading force. Had the Anglo-Dutch invading force not arrived in England in November 1688, it is also likely that James's crack troops would have eventually been able to subdue the widespread popular uprisings. In either case, the English polity would have followed far more closely the French pattern. James almost certainly would have succeeded had it not been for the combined effect of the widespread popular uprisings and the Anglo-Dutch invading force.

To say that the Revolution of 1688–89 was not inevitable, however, is not to say that it lacked long-term causes. The socioeconomic changes that had taken place in England over the seventeenth century did make it inevitable that English state and society would be fundamentally transformed. The question was whether the modernized polity would follow the path desired by James or that desired by his Whig opponents. The midcentury crisis played a central role in shaping the contours of Whig notions of statecraft and political economy. The fundamental Whig notion that labor created property and that property was therefore infinite emerged as an important theme in radical critiques of Oliver Cromwell's protectorate. It was during the 1650s that a number of writers, for the first time, publicly advanced economic arguments against the political regime. It was also during the 1650s that many of the same critics began to highlight the dangers of growing French power and to insist that foreign policy be discussed in terms of national interests rather than religious groupings.[10] Just as important, fissures in church and state, from the Elizabethan period onward, opened up a space for public discussion that widened and intensified during the midcentury crisis. Without these developments, without the midcentury crisis, there would not have been a Revolution in 1688–89.

The English Civil War and its aftermath did have radical and transformative effects. Those events, as Michael Walzer points out, generated "whole sets of clamorous demands . . . for the reorganization of the church, the state, the government of London, the educational system, and the administration of the poor laws." Those years did witness "the formation of groups specifically and deliberately designed to implement those demands." It was in the period between 1640 and 1660 that "political journalism" emerged in England. And many English men and women in that period did enunciate an "awareness of need for and the possibility of reform." But for all that, Walzer's first three revolutionary effects—the transformation of "the very nature of monarchy," the "appearance of a well-disciplined citizens' army," and the effort "to write and re-write the constitution"—were all reversed with the Restoration of the monarchy in 1660.[11] Many English men and women became revolutionaries in the middle of the seventeenth century. But they did not achieve a revolution.

Why was this? Why were the revolutionaries of the midcentury unable to make all of their achievements permanent? There were, of course, a range of social, religious and political reasons for the fall of the Commonwealth and the demise of the Protectorate. However, what fundamentally distinguished the later seventeenth-century Revolution from its midcentury predecessor was the nature of the monarchy itself. Charles I, for all of his political ineptitude, was fundamentally willing and able to defend the traditional society and the traditional polity. The document that did more than anything to define royalist ideology after Charles I's death was the deeply traditionalist *Eikon Basilike,* which essentially reasserted the divine basis of royal power while simultaneously narrating Charles I's saintly life. It was thus possible for royalists both before and after his death to offer the English a political choice between tradition and modernization, and ultimately between stability and revolutionary instability. Each political misstep by the governments in the 1650s made restoration a more palatable option for an ever larger group of people. "People are not so easily got out of their old forms," John Locke perceptively observed. The "slowness and aversion in the people to quit their old constitutions, has in many revolutions, which have been seen in this kingdom, in this and former ages," noted Locke in obvious reference to the events of midcentury, "still kept us to, or, after some interval of fruitless attempts, still brought us back again to our old legislative of king, lords, and commons: and whatever provocations have made the crown to be taken from some of our princes' heads, they never carried the people so far as to place it in another line." Given a choice, Locke argued, most people preferred an old, imperfect government to any innovative alternative. Locke implied that things would be different in the later seventeenth century. Neither the revolutionaries nor the king were defending the "old forms." James II, in contrast to his father, chose to cast himself as a modernizer. He modernized England's infrastructure, England's army, England's navy, English local government, and English political techniques. He and his polemicists asserted a modern, more expansive view of royal power and insisted on new limits on political expression. When forced to defend his grant of religious liberty without civil liberty, James and his polemicists described their effort in terms of a "new great charter for liberty of conscience."[12] By embracing modernity, by adopting a program of political and social modernization, James had eliminated conservatism as a viable political option. There was no possibility of restoring the old regime.

In 1688, unlike in the 1640s and 1650s, English men and women were forced to choose between alternative paths to modernity.

The Revolution of 1688–89 was not a self-contained event lasting only a few months. To understand it in such narrow chronological terms is to miss the radical significance of the revolution. Instead, it is best to understand the revolution as a process set in motion in the wide-ranging crisis of the 1620s, which unleashed an opposition movement deploying modernizing polemical strategies and coming to an end only when the Whig prime minister Sir Robert Walpole chose to consolidate his power by guaranteeing that revolutionary change would go no farther. Walpole's decision in the 1720s and 1730s to appeal to moderate Tories by rolling back the land tax and by refusing to extend civil rights to Dissenters marked the end of the Whig revolution. Revolutionary rumblings had begun with debates over foreign policy, the nature of the English Church, and the role of state finance in the tumultuous decade of the 1620s.[13] By the end of the revolutionary century, English state, society, culture, and religion had been transformed. England had diverged from the Continental pattern on every dimension.

Was this revolutionary transformation a bourgeois revolution? Not in the sense that a self-conscious class, the bourgeoisie, overthrew another class to place itself in power. The middling sort of the late seventeenth and eighteenth centuries, as one historian has noted, were characterized by "conflict, insecurity, and uncertainty" rather than by "unity or group consensus." There was no cohesive middle class to bring about a bourgeois revolution. In fact, the popular uprisings that ultimately overthrew James II involved the spectrum of English society, from humble men and women who volunteered with their pitchforks as their only weapons to wealthy businessmen and aristocratic landowners who provided their considerable prestige and thousands of pounds to the cause. Jacobites came from similarly diverse backgrounds. Unsurprisingly, given the social diversity of the revolutionaries, they did not transform the class basis of English politics. The percentage of merchants in the House of Commons rose only marginally from about 9 percent of the total in the period from 1660 to 1689 to 10.7 percent in the years from 1690 to 1715.[14]

Nevertheless, it is, I claim, justifiable to understand the Revolution of 1688–89 as a bourgeois revolution in a cultural and political sense. England in the later seventeenth century was, a wide variety of commentators agreed, a trading nation. "It is very well known," observed one commentator, "that the strength, riches, and welfare of this kingdom, is supported and maintained by trade and commerce."[15] "Till the Civil Wars in the reign of Charles I," recalled the social commentator Guy Miege, the nobility set the cultural standard in England; but now "the case is altered." In the later seventeenth century, England had become "one of the most trading countries in Europe" where "the greatest body of the commonalty is that of traders, or men that live by buying and selling." In England, according to two French diplomats, merchants played a critical role in shaping public opinion.[16] Both James II and his opponents were well aware that England had become a commercial society. But James II's modernizing program, for all its commitment

End,
Whig Revolution

to trade and empire, was not a bourgeois vision. The exponents of James II's political-economic program were critical of urban populations and placed territorial acquisition at the heart of their imperial program. Merchants were to have no independent political role. Indeed, the social ideal expressed in Sir Josiah Child's economic writings was for the merchant to make a fortune so that his heirs could live as landed gentlemen. James's ideological achievement was to harness commercial society to landed norms. His program was simultaneously modernizing and antibourgeois.

Had the revolutionaries not succeeded in overthrowing James II's Catholic modernizing regime, it is hard to imagine that eighteenth-century English culture and society would have developed the way it did. James had no interest in restoring the cultural world of Charles I, a world in which the English aristocracy and gentry "lived with suitable splendor and magnificence; keeping a plentiful table, and a numerous attendance, with several officers; delighting in noble exercises, and appearing abroad according to their rank and quality." James found this world abhorrent precisely because of the decentralization that it implied. In that world each "Lord's house was then looked upon as a well disciplined court."[17] James wanted discipline to flow exclusively from the court at Whitehall. James also had no truck with the open and unfettered discussion valued by the urban middle classes. While merchants yearned for a world in which economic, political, and social information was freely available, James saw informational transparency as politically dangerous.[18] His cultural vision, not surprisingly, had much more in common with that of Louis XIV and Jean-Baptiste Colbert than it shared with that of James's father.

James's opponents, the revolutionaries of 1688–89, by contrast embraced urban culture, manufacturing, and economic imperialism. The ideological descendants of the new colonial merchants of the middle of the seventeenth century emphasized commercial rather than territorial hegemony.[19] These men and women not only wanted England to be a commercial society, they also wanted it to be a bourgeois society with urban rather than landed values. This was the revolutionaries' cultural program. These were the Whigs' revolution principles. England increasingly became a bourgeois society in the wake of the Revolution of 1688–89 because the political-economic program of the revolutionaries privileged urban and commercial values.

The Whig revolutionary triumph brought with it a new bourgeois culture. The revolution in political economy brought with it a revolution in cultural values. Political economic transformation—new tax structures, new institutions, and a new imperial agenda—encouraged the new cultural dominance of the urban middle classes. Even though the urban middle classes made up no more than 5 percent of England's population in 1700, in the wake of the Revolution of 1688–89 it was able to set the cultural agenda. Whigs, one scholar points out, succeeded in "identifying 'politeness' as the cultural concomitant of post-1688 liberty." The new culture of politeness consolidated by Locke's student the 3rd Earl of Shaftesbury and popularized by the great Whig journalists Joseph Addison and Richard Steele in Whig hands had a "self-conscious modernism." Despite its origins in courtly culture, politeness in the late seventeenth and eighteenth centuries had become a bourgeois ideology. "Politeness represented an alternative to the picture of the English gentleman as a denizen of the country attached with fierce loyalty to his economic independence, his moral autonomy and his virtuous simplicity." "During the seventeenth century," concurs one literary critic while commenting on less elite sources, England had been transformed from "a rural culture to an urban one—or, rather, from a rural past into one that looked toward modernity with eagerness and anticipation." "The middle classes were creating a completely new culture for themselves," concurs one social historian. This culture was "a bourgeois culture that was destined to become the dominant national culture."[20]

The Revolution of 1688–89 did not make England into a commercial society, but it did ensure that the cultural values of the bourgeoisie would become predominant. The bourgeoisie came to matter out of all proportion of their numbers. This was true in politics. Merchant associations were able to influence parliamentary activity disproportionate to their numbers in the general population "particularly after 1689." After the Revolution, noted a recent commentator on English merchant culture, trade became "a party issue" under "the sustained pressure of the commercial classes." After the revolution the "success-rate" for economic legislation in the House of Commons was "dramatically enhanced." Most dramatically, of course, Whig merchants and their political allies were able to create the Bank of England in 1694 and destroy the Land Bank in 1696. No doubt because of these successes, the Revolution of 1688–89 represented the victory of those who supported manufacturing, urban culture, and the possibilities of unlimited economic growth based on the creative potential of human labor. This effect of the revolution meant that traders felt no need to aspire to the culture and estates of the landed elite. In fact, the aristocracy and the gentry began to act more bourgeois in the wake of the Revolution of 1688–89. The Buckinghamshire Verneys were surely not the only gentry family that "gradually absorbed the values of London's urban culture." Margaret Hunt is certainly right to see "a deep ambivalence among trading people toward upper-class mores." The powerful urban middle classes, especially those who shared Whig political and ideological preoccupations, had no desire to become aristocrats.[21]

The Revolution of 1688–89 was the first modern revolution because England was already quickly becoming a modern society before 1688. The crisis of the middle of the seventeenth century had guaranteed not that England would diverge politically from the Continental pattern but that no English government was likely ever again to rest on patrimonial principles. Both the later Stuarts and their political enemies understood this. All understood that for England to be a major player on the European scene, England needed to harness its commercial energies to a bureaucratic state. Revolutionary change became possible when Charles II, and particularly James II, harnessed the new economic and administrative resources at their disposal to the creation of a modern state. The revolutionaries of 1688–89 offered their version of English modernity as a powerful alternative to that created by James II and his supporters. Both groups wanted England to be a first-rate power both in Europe and throughout the world, both groups wanted to modernize English religious practice, and both groups wanted England to be a commercial society.[22] They differed, and differed dramatically, in their proposed means to achieve those ends. Modernization, in this as in all subsequent revolutions, was a cause, not a consequence, of revolution.

The First Modern Revolution radically transformed England and ultimately helped to shape the modern world. I have necessarily told a complex story about the transformation of a society, a state, a church, and an empire. A central point of this narrative has been that the hyperspecialization of history has not only made historical writing accessible to ever narrower audiences but that the breakdown of historical processes into social, religious, intellectual, political, constitutional, military, and diplomatic history has made it impossible to specify broad revolutionary shifts and identify their causes. Early modern men and women experienced their lives whole. It is time that historians return to writing history tout court.

Historical reintegration is essential in a second sense. Because the mid-seventeenth century crisis and the Revolution of 1688–89 were part of the same process, they need to be integrated into a single story. Scholars miss a great deal by defining their periods as beginning or ending with 1640, 1660, or 1688. By writing about a modern period that begins after 1688, scholars also miss the extent to which the radical transformations that were cause and consequence of the Revolution of 1688–89 shaped the contours of modern British and world history.

The Revolution of 1688–89 was a radically transformative event in England's century of revolution. The revolutionaries reversed England's foreign policy, rearranged England's economic priorities, and reconfigured the Church of England. Like all revolutions, the Revolution of 1688–89 arose out of competing visions of social, economic, and political modernity—visions made possible only by the social and economic developments of the second half of the seventeenth century. The Revolution of 1688–89 was the culmination of a long and vitriolic argument about how to transform England into a modern nation. The depth of the argument, the intensity of the ideological differences, and the breadth of the social implications explain why the revolution involved such a broad swath of English society, why it was so violent, and why it was so divisive. It was this protracted argument, rather than a speedy palace coup against an inept king, that transformed England and then Britain into a great European and imperial power.

Abbreviations

Add.	Additional manuscripts
AWA	Archbishop of Westminster's Archives
Axminster	K. W. H. Howard, ed., *The Axminster Ecclesiastica, 1660–1698* (Sheffield: Gospel Tidings, 1976)
Beinecke	Beinecke Rare Book and Manuscript Library, Yale University
Bodleian	Bodleian Library, Oxford University
BL	British Library
Campana	Marquise Emilia Campana di Cavelli, ed., *Les derniers Stuarts à Saint-Germain en Laye,* 2 vols. (Paris: Librairie Academique, 1871)
CKS	Centre for Kentish Studies, Maidstone
CSPD	Calendar of State Papers, Domestic
CSPV	Calendar of State Papers, Venetian
DWL	Doctor Williams Library
EIC	East India Company
Evelyn, *Diary*	E. S. De Beer, ed., *The Diary of John Evelyn,* 6 vols. (Oxford: Clarendon Press, 1955)
Foley	Henry Foley, ed., *Records of the English Province of the Society of Jesus,* vol. 5 (London: Burns and Oates, 1879)
FSL	Folger Shakespeare Library, Washington, DC
Grey	Anchitell Grey, ed., *Debates of the House of Commons,* 10 vols. (London: D. Henry and R. Cave, 1763)
HEH	Henry E. Huntington Library, San Marino, CA
HLRO	House of Lords Record Office, London
HMC	Historical Manuscripts Commission
HRC	Harry Ransom Center, University of Texas

Indiana	Lilly Library, Indiana University, Bloomington
IOL	India Office Library (now in British Library), London
Jeaffreson	John Cordy Jeaffreson, ed., *A Young Squire of the Seventeenth Century: From the Papers (A.D. 1676–1686) of Christopher Jeaffreson of Dullingham House, Cambridgeshire,* vol. 2 (London: Hurst and Blackett, 1878)
JRL	John Rylands Library, Manchester
Life of James II	J. S. Clarke, ed., *The Life of James II* (London: Longman, Hurst, Rees, Orme and Brown, 1816)
Locke Correspondence	*The Correspondence of John Locke,* 8 vols., ed. E. S. De Beer (Oxford: Clarendon Press, 1976–89)
LPL	Lambeth Palace Library
MAE	Ministère des Affaires Étrangères, Paris
MSS	Manuscripts
NA	National Archives, Kew Gardens
NAS	National Archives of Scotland, Edinburgh
NLS	National Library of Scotland, Edinburgh
NMM	National Maritime Museum, London
Penn Papers	*The Papers of William Penn,* ed. Mary Maples Dunn and Richard S. Dunn, vol. 3: *1685–1700,* ed. Marianne S. Wokeck et al. (Philadelphia: University of Pennsylvania Press, 1986)
PRONI	Public Record Office of Northern Ireland, Belfast
RO	Record Office
SCA	Scottish Catholic Archives, Edinburgh
Singer	Samuel Weller Singer, ed., *The Correspondence of Henry Hyde, Earl of Clarendon, and of His Brother Laurence Hyde, Earl of Rochester,* 2 vols. (London: Henry Colburn, 1828)
SOAS	School of Oriental and African Studies, London
Thoresby, *Diary*	Joseph Hunter, ed., *The Diary of Ralph Thoresby,* 2 vols. (London: Henry Colburn and Richard Bentley, 1830)
UL	University Library
WYAS	West Yorkshire Archive Service, Leeds

Notes

Introduction

1. Statistics that highlight the bloodiness of the French Revolution inevitably include the Napoleonic Wars: see, e.g., Jack A. Goldstone, *Revolution and Rebellion in the Early Modern World* (Berkeley: University of California Press, 1991), 477; and Goldstone, "The Outcomes of Revolutions," in *Revolutions: Theoretical, Comparative, and Historical Studies,* ed. Goldstone (New York: Harcourt Brace, 1986), 207–8. By including the Nine Years' War (1689–97) and the wars in Ireland and Scotland—all direct consequences of the Revolution of 1688–89—the percentages of dead and wounded are comparable to the French case.

2. Frederick Cooper, *Colonialism in Question* (Berkeley: University of California Press, 2005), 113–49; John D. Kelly, "Alternative Modernities or an Alternative to 'Modernity,'" in *Critically Modern: Alternatives, Alterities, Anthropologies,* ed. Bruce M. Knauft (Bloomington: Indiana University Press, 2002), 262–77.

3. John Evelyn to Evelyn Jr., 18 December 1688, BL, Evelyn Papers, JEJ 1.

4. The analysis in this paragraph is deeply indebted to Bernard Yack, *The Fetishism of Modernities: Epochal Self-Consciousness in Contemporary Social and Political Thought* (Notre Dame, IN: University of Notre Dame Press, 1997), esp. 35–37; Bjorn Wittrock, "Modernity: One, None, or Many? European Origins and Modernity as a Global Condition," *Daedalus* 129 (2000): 1, 38.

CHAPTER 1. *The Unmaking of a Revolution*

1. Monsieur Navier, Address, 30 November 1789, printed in Richard Price, *A Discourse on the Love of Our Country,* 4 November 1789, 2nd ed. (London: T. Cadell, 1789), "Additions," 14–15. The French revolutionaries did not quickly abandon their admiration for the Glorious Revolution. In 1791 supporters of the revolution in Marseille wrote the English Revolution Society that "we have admired you for a century: for a century we have envied your happiness." Revolution Society, Anniversary Meeting, 4 November 1791, BL, Add. 64814, fol. 48v; *The Correspondence of the Revolution Society with the National Assembly, and with Various Societies of the Friends of Liberty in France and England* (London, 1792). American revolutionaries in 1776 also claimed to be acting on principles established at the Glorious Revolution: James Wilson and John Dickinson, "Address to the Inhabitants of the Colonies," 13 February 1776, in *Journals of the Continental Congress,* vol. 4, ed. W. C. Ford (Washington, DC: GPO, 1906), 145.

2. David Hume, *History of England, from the Invasion of Julius Caesar to the Revolution in 1688,* vol. 6 (London: T. Cadell, 1841), 329; John Millar, *An Historical View of the English Government,* 4th ed., vol. 4 (London: J. Mawman, 1818), 95; Robert Viscount Molesworth, *The Principles of a Real Whig* (1711; London, 1775), 5–6; John Wilkes, "Introduction to Proposed History," in *The Correspondence of the Late John Wilkes,*

vol. 5, ed. John Almon (London: Richard Phillips, 1801), 161; Charles James Fox, *The History of the Early Part of the Reign of James the Second* (London: William Miller, 1808), 58; J. R. Dinwiddy, "Charles James Fox as an Historian," *Historical Journal* 12, no. 1 (1969): 23–34; Henry St. John, Viscount Bolingbroke, "Dissertation upon Parties," 1733–34, in *The Works of Lord Bolingbroke*, vol. 2 (Philadelphia: Carey and Hart, 1841),27. See the similar comments by Andrew Kippis, *A Sermon Preached at the Old Jewry*, 4 November 1788 (London, 1788), 2. The 6th Duke of Devonshire was thinking in this tradition when he had inscribed over the fireplace of the Painted Hall at Chatsworth House that it had been "begun in the year of English liberty 1688." Private communication from Charles Noble, keeper of the Devonshire Collection, Chatsworth House.

3. Molesworth, *Principles*, 13–14; Wilkes, "Introduction," 204; Henry Hunter, "Sermon III," 1788, in *Sermons*, vol. 2 (London, 1795), 102; Kippis, *Sermon*, 32; Price, *Discourse*, 31–32. Later that year the Revolution Society, with Price present, emphasized that British Revolution principles had taken root in America and were now "pervading Europe": Revolution Society, 30 December 1789, BL, Add. 64814, fol. 27r.

4. Abstract of the History and Proceedings of the Revolution Society, 4 February 1789, BL, Add. 64814, fols. 12–13; Kippis, *Sermon*, 2–3. Kathleen Wilson, "A Dissident Legacy: Eighteenth-Century Popular Politics and the Glorious Revolution," in *Liberty Secured? Britain before and after the Glorious Revolution*, ed. J. R. Jones (Stanford, CA: Stanford University Press, 1992), 301–12; Caleb Evans, *British Freedom Realized*, 5 November 1788 (Bristol, 1788), 28; Hunter, "Sermon III," 101.

5. Blair Worden, *Roundhead Reputations: The English Civil Wars and the Passions of Posterity* (London: A. Lane, 2001), 228; Hugh Trevor-Roper, *From Counter-Reformation to Glorious Revolution* (Chicago: University of Chicago Press, 1992), 233; Barry Price (secretary of the William and Mary Tercentenary Trust), "Some Observations on the Tercentenary," 25 June 1989, HLRO, WMT/2; Price, *Anglo-Netherlands Society Newsletter*, March 1988, HLRO, WMT/22/Pt. 2; John Rae, *Times*, 16 July 1987, HLRO, WMT/22/Pt. 2; Viscount Whitelaw, 27 March 1984, Lords Debates, HLRO, WMT/1/Pt. 2; Patricia Morrison, *Daily Telegraph*, 21 September 1988, HLRO, WMT/22/Pt. 2; *Financial Times*, 12 September 1988, HLRO, WMT/22/Pt. 2; *Daily Post* (Liverpool), 4 November 1988, HLRO, WMT/22/Pt. 2.

6. Charles Tilly, *European Revolutions, 1492–1992* (Oxford: Basil Blackwell, 1993), 104; Crane Brinton, *The Anatomy of Revolution*, rev. ed. (New York: Vintage, 1965), 19.

7. Gary S. De Krey, "Political Radicalism in London after the Glorious Revolution," *Journal of Modern History* 55, no. 4 (1983): 586–87. I disagree with J. P. Kenyon, "The Revolution of 1688: Resistance and Contract," in *Historical Perspectives: Studies in English Thought and Society, in Honour of J. H. Plumb*, ed. Neil McKendrick (London: Europa, 1974), 69; and H. T. Dickinson, "The Eighteenth-Century Debate on the 'Glorious Revolution,'" *History* 61 (February 1976): 44.

8. Dickinson, "Eighteenth-Century Debate," 29; Peter N. Miller, *Defining the Common Good: Empire, Religion, and Philosophy in Eighteenth-Century Britain* (Cambridge: Cambridge University Press, 1994), 88.

9. Worden, *Roundhead Reputations*, 162; Mark Goldie, "The Roots of True Whiggism, 1688–1694," *History of Political Thought* 1, no. 2 (1980): 197, 220–25; Goldie and Clare Jackson, "Williamite Tyranny and the Whig Jacobites," in *Redefining William III: The Impact of the King-Stadholder in International Context*, ed. Esther Mijers and David Onnekink (Aldershot: Ashgate, 2007), 178–79, 184–85.

10. Henry Sacheverell, *The Perils of False Brethren, both in Church and State* (London, 1709). I dissent from Goldie's claim that by the later 1690s "the mainstream of whiggism" had "dissociated itself from radicalism." Goldie, "Roots," 195.

11. Nicholas Lechmere, *The Tryal of Dr. Henry Sacheverell* (London: Jacob Tonson, 1710), 7, 88, 94; Gilbert Burnet, *The Bishop of Salisbury's and the Bishop of Oxford's Speeches in the House of Lords* (London, 1710), 2; Benjamin Hoadly, *The Foundation of the Present Government Defended* (London, 1710), 22, 26. In 1714 Walpole was an active member of the Loyal and Friendly Society of the Blue and Orange, a radical group dedicated to the celebration of the revolution. Its members included Walter Moyle, the son of John Locke's

close friend Sir Walter Yonge, and the West Country Whig Sir Francis Henry Drake. BL, Egerton 2346, fol. 6r.

12. Lechmere, *Tryal,* 34. The clarity of Lechmere's position makes it difficult to agree with Dickinson's claim that there was a "general reluctance to rest the Whig case on the principles of John Locke." Dickinson, "Eighteenth-Century Debate," 35.

13. Lechmere, *Tryal,* 36; Molesworth, *Principles,* 15–16, 21–22.

14. J. P. Kenyon, *Revolution Principles: The Politics of Party, 1689–1720* (Cambridge: Cambridge University Press, 1977), 202; Dickinson, "Eighteenth-Century Debate," 36.

15. Paul Langford, *The Excise Crisis: Society and Politics in the Age of Walpole* (Oxford: Clarendon Press, 1975), 32–35; Langford, *A Polite and Commercial People: England, 1727–1783* (Oxford: Clarendon Press, 1989), 9–44; *The True Principles of the Revolution Revived and Asserted* (London, 1741), 14–15; John Hervey, *Ancient and Modern Liberty Stated and Compar'd* (London, 1734), 45. I think the radical interpretation focused on a wider set of issues than the "principles of political accountability and trusteeship" that Wilson emphasizes. Wilson, "Dissident Legacy," 300, 314.

16. William Pulteney, *A Review of the Excise Scheme* (London, 1733), 50; Sir William Blackstone, *Commentaries on the Laws of England,* 4 vols. (Oxford: Clarendon Press, 1765–69), 4:433. Although Blackstone may have been involved in Tory politicking in Oxford, his *Commentaries* were decidedly Opposition Whiggish: *The Livery-Man* (London, 1740), 7–8, 13; Hunter, "Sermon III," 105–6.

17. Pulteney, *Review of Excise Scheme,* 49–50. See also George Coade, *A Letter to a Clergyman,* 2nd ed. (London, 1747), 38; and *Livery-Man,* 6. The willingness of Opposition Whigs to deploy Locke's arguments either explicitly, as here and in discussions of political economy, or implicitly, in references to the original contract, makes me unable to accept John Dunn's claim that Locke's *Two Treatises* "enjoyed no immediate éclat" or that "it was only one work among a large group of other works which expounded the Whig theory of the revolution, and in its prominence within this group is not noticeable until well after the general outlines of the interpretation had been consolidated." John Dunn, "The Politics of Locke in England and America in the Eighteenth Century," in *John Locke: Problems and Perspectives; A Collection of New Essays,* ed. John W. Yolton (Cambridge: Cambridge University Press, 1969), 57, 80. I share Mark Goldie's skepticism about this assessment: Goldie, "Introduction," in *The Reception of Locke's Politics,* 6 vols., ed. Goldie (London: Pickering and Chatto, 1999), 1:xvii–lxxi. Caleb Evans, *British Freedom Realized,* 5 November 1788 (Bristol, 1788), 14–15; Committee of the Revolution Society, 6 October 1788, BL, Add. 64814, fol. 5v.

18. Kippis, *Sermon,* 26–27, 29; Bolingbroke, "Dissertation upon Parties," 71. Bolingbroke's "Dissertation" was written while he was making common cause with the Opposition Whigs in the *Craftsman;* Wilkes, "Introduction," 162, 200–201; Blackstone, *Commentaries,* 4:427; Hunter, "Sermon III," 108; *Examiner,* 6 November 1712 (no. 49), 237. Voltaire made a similar point: *The Age of Lewis XIV,* 2 vols. (London: R. Dodsley, 1752), 1:238.

19. Robert Wallace, *The Doctrine of Passive Obedience and Non-Resistance Considered* (Edinburgh, 1754), 34–35; G. B., *The Advantages of the Revolution* (London: W. Owen, 1753), 5; Wilkes, "Introduction," 189. I see Wilkes's history as an Opposition Whig document, not "the highly conventional" text described by Linda Colley, *Britons: Forging the Nation, 1707–1737* (New Haven and London: Yale University Press, 1992), 111. Kippis, *Sermon,* 28; Committee of the Revolution Society, 16 June 1788, BL, Add. 64814, fol. 2r.

20. Kathleen Wilson, *The Sense of the People: Politics, Culture, and Imperialism in England, 1715–1785* (Cambridge: Cambridge University Press, 1995), 140–65; Langford, *Polite and Commercial People,* 49–57; *The Late Minister Unmask't* (London, 1742), 14–15; Blackstone, *Commentaries,* 1:315; Wilkes, "Introduction," 186–87.

21. Millar, *An Historical View of the English Government,* 3:1–2, 4:78, 102–3; Adam Anderson, *An Historical and Chronological Deduction of the Origins of Commerce,* 2 vols. (London: A. Millar et al., 1764), 1:vii, 2:189.

22. Hume, *History,* 6:336; Anderson, *Origins of Commerce,* 1:viii; Blackstone, *Commentaries,* 1:311, 314, 4:426–27. The point that English society and economy were modernizing before the revolution was also made in the nineteenth century by Tocqueville: Alexis de Tocqueville, *The Old Regime and the French Revolution,* trans. Stuart Gilbert (New York: Anchor, 1983), 18–19.

23. *Some Thoughts on the Land Tax* (London, 1733), 9, 12; Nicholas Amhurst, *The Second Part of an Argument against Excises* (London, 1733), 55; Millar, *Historical View,* 4:106–7; G. B., *Advantages of the Revolution,* 8.

24. Millar, *Historical View,* 4:100; G. B., *Advantages of the Revolution,* 17; Anderson, *Origins of Commerce,* 2:195; Kippis, *Sermon,* 33.

25. Price, *Discourse,* 31–32, 34.

26. Edmund Burke, *Reflections on the Revolution in France* (1790; London: Penguin Books, 1968), 110–11, 117; Don Herzog, *Poisoning the Minds of the Lower Orders* (Princeton, NJ: Princeton University Press, 1998), 13–33.

27. Revolution Society Minutes, 4 November 1789, 4 November 1790, BL, Add. 64814, fols. 22v, 40–41. Horne Tooke toasted that "should Mr. Burke be impeached . . . may his trial last as long as that of Mr. Hastings," referring to the trial of Warren Hastings, governor-general of Bengal, which had begun in 1787 and was not yet concluded. Burke played a leading role in prosecution.

28. Worden, *Roundhead Reputations,* 226; Wilson, "Dissident Legacy," 324; Dickinson, "Eighteenth-Century Debate," 31; *North Briton* no. 30, 25 December 1762, 64; Joseph Towers, *Observations on Public Liberty, Patriotism, Ministerial Despotism, and National Grievances* (London, 1769), 5; Wilkes, "Introduction," 180; Price, *Discourse,* 35; Blackstone, *Commentaries,* 1:325–26.

29. John Cartwright, *The Legislative Rights of the Commonalty Vindicated,* 2nd ed. (London, 1777), 70. Burke gave plausibility to this argument. His great complaint against the new men brought in at the accession of George III was that they sought "to get rid of the great Whig connections," the Whig aristocratic families. He sought to marginalize the importance of William Pitt and his populist patriots: Edmund Burke, *Thoughts on the Cause of the Present Discontents,* 3rd ed. (London: J. Dodley, 1770), 20; Catherine Macaulay, *The History of England,* vol. 8 (London, 1783), 330–34.

30. Thomas Paine, *Rights of Man* (London, 1791), 82; Paine, *Rights of Man; Part the Second,* 2nd ed. (London, 1792), 13–14, 52; John Callow, *King in Exile: James II, Warrior, King and Saint, 1689–1701* (Stroud: Sutton, 2004), 28; Ann Hughes, *Guardian,* 27 June 1988, HLRO, WMT/22, Pt. 2.

31. Thomas Babington Macaulay, *The History of England from the Accession of James II,* 5 vols. (New York: Harper and Brothers, 1849–61), 2:611–17.

32. David Cannadine, *G. M. Trevelyan: A Life in History* (London: Harper Collins, 1992), 85; G. M. Trevelyan, *The English Revolution, 1688–89* (1938; reprint ed., Oxford: Oxford University Press, 1965), 3–5, 129.

33. Recent exceptions to this rule are two scholars who have seen the events of 1688–89 as revolutionary: Melinda S. Zook, *Radical Whigs and Conspiratorial Politics in Late Stuart England* (University Park: Pennsylvania State University Press, 1999), xv; and Tim Harris, *Revolution: The Great Crisis of the British Monarchy, 1685–1720* (London: Allen Lane, 2006), 15. But in both cases the interpretative focus has been on James II's overthrow rather than on the consequences of the revolution. Zook looks at radical writers on the constitution. Harris ends his narrative with 1690–91. Neither focuses on the socioeconomic or foreign political consequences.

34. J. R. Jones, "The Revolution in Context," in *Liberty Secured?* ed. Jones, 12; John Morrill, "The Sensible Revolution," in *The Anglo-Dutch Moment: Essays on the Glorious Revolution and Its World Impact,* ed. Jonathan Israel (Cambridge: Cambridge University Press, 1991), 103; Jonathan Scott, *Algernon Sidney and the Restoration Crisis, 1677–1683* (Cambridge: Cambridge University Press, 1991), 27; Hugh Trevor-Roper, *Counter-Reformation to Glorious Revolution* (Chicago: University of Chicago Press, 1992), 246. See also Eveline Cruickshanks, *The Glorious Revolution* (Basingstoke: Macmillan, 2000), 18–19; and Lionel K. J.

Glassey, "Introduction," in *The Reigns of Charles II and James VII and II,* ed. Glassey (New York: St. Martin's, 1997), 9.

35. Dale Hoak, "The Anglo-Dutch Revolution of 1689," in *The World of William and Mary,* ed. Hoak and Mordechai Feingold (Stanford, CA: Stanford University Press, 1996), 26; David H. Hosford, *Nottingham, Nobles, and the North: Aspects of the Revolution of 1688* (Hamden, CT: Archon, 1976), 120; John Pocock, "The Machiavellian Moment Revisited: A Study in History and Ideology," *Journal of Modern History* 53, no. 1 (1981): 60; Mark Goldie, "The Political Thought of the Anglican Revolution," in *The Revolutions of 1688,* ed. Robert Beddard (Oxford: Clarendon Press, 1991), 104. Others have highlighted the lack of "revolutionary ideology," and the relative unimportance of the ideas of John Locke: J. R. Western, *Monarchy and Revolution: The English State in the 1680s* (London: Blandford, 1972), 283; Cruickshanks, *Glorious Revolution,* 37; J. P. Kenyon, *Revolution Principles: The Politics of Party, 1689–1720* (Cambridge: Cambridge University Press, 1977), 61; Gerald M. Straka, *Anglican Reaction to the Revolution of 1688* (Madison: State Historical Society of Wisconsin, 1962), viii–ix.

36. Western, *Monarchy and Revolution,* 1; Robert Beddard, *Kingdom without a King: The Journal of the Provisional Government in the Revolution of 1688* (Oxford: Phaidon, 1988), 11; W. A. Speck, *Reluctant Revolutionaries: Englishmen and the Revolution of 1688* (Oxford: Oxford University Press, 1988), 242; Jack A. Goldstone, *Revolution and Rebellion in the Early Modern World* (Berkeley: University of California Press, 1991), 318. J. C. D. Clark, who agrees there was no social revolution, insists that the Crown actually gained power after 1688: Clark, *Revolution and Rebellion: State and Society in the Seventeenth and Eighteenth Centuries* (Cambridge: Cambridge University Press, 1986), 89.

37. Howard Nenner, "Introduction," in *Politics and the Political Imagination in Later Stuart Britain,* ed. Nenner (Rochester, NY: University of Rochester Press, 1997), 1; Dickinson, "Eighteenth-Century Debate," 29; Wilson, "Dissident Legacy," 299.

38. Auberon Waugh, *Independent,* 2 April 1988, HLRO, WMT/22/Pt. 2; Tony Benn, 7 July 1988, *Hansards,* 1234, HLRO, WMT/22/Pt. 1; Sir Bernard Braine, 7 July 1988, *Hansards,* 1234, HLRO, WMT/22/Pt. 1. See the also *Times,* 18 July 1988, HLRO, WMT/22/Pt. 1; and John Crosland in the *Times,* 7 November 1988, HLRO, WMT/22/Pt. 2. Sir Geoffrey Howe appears to have expressed similar views, although this may well have been an instrumental assessment so as to procure Dutch financing of the tercentenary celebrations. Sir Geoffrey Howe to Sir Charles Troughton, 17 December 1984, HLRO, WMT/1/Pt. 2.

39. Charles Wilson to Barry Price, 28 March 1988, HLRO, WMT/12/Pt. 2; Noel Annan, "Glorious It Was for British Liberties," *Times,* 22 August 1986, HLRO, WMT/12/Pt. 1; Sir Bernard Braine, 7 July 1988, *Hansards,* 1234, HLRO, WMT/22/Pt. 1; Address by Lord Hailsham, Banqueting House, 29 June 1988, HLRO, WMT/12/Pt. 2; Margaret Thatcher, 7 July 1988, *Hansards,* 1230, HLRO, WMT/22/Pt. 1. The Labour MP for Liverpool Eric Heffer argued that "it was neither glorious nor a revolution. It was not a revolution because the real revolution had already taken place." Heffer, 7 July 1988, *Hansards,* 1242, HLRO, WMT/22/Pt. 1. Henry Roseveare was the lone dissenting voice consulted by the historians' committee. He complained about the "narrow and, probably, unhistorical emphases—with Parliament hogging the whole show." Roseveare to Charles Wilson, 5 January 1987, HLRO, WMT/12/Pt. 1. The commemoration of the revolution in the United States celebrated the high political achievement: Joint Resolution of the 99th Congress of the United States, 2nd Sess., 23 August 1986, HLRO, WMT/25; Speech of Senator John Warner, 25 June 1986, HLRO, WMT/25. Senator Warner was long frustrated by President Ronald Reagan's delays in signing the joint resolution.

40. In this narrow point I dissent from Mark Knights, "The Tory Interpretation of History in the Rage of Parties," in *The Uses of History in Early Modern England,* ed. Paulina Kewes (San Marino, CA: Huntington Library, 2006), 349. Knights is right that "historians across the early modern period" *profess* to "reject both the Whig methodology and the Whig interpretation." But most historians and public intellectuals have in fact propounded "Whiggish conclusions" about the Revolution of 1688–89.

CHAPTER 2. *Rethinking Revolutions*

1. Gilbert Burnet, *The History of the Reformation of the Church of England; First Part,* 2nd ed. (London: T. H. for Richard Chiswell, 1681), sig. (b)r ; Alexis de Tocqueville, *The Old Regime and the French Revolution,* trans. Stuart Gilbert (New York: Anchor, 1983), 5; Theda Skocpol, *States and Social Revolutions: A Comparative Analysis of France, Russia, and China* (New York: Cambridge University Press, 1979), 8.

2. Samuel P. Huntington, *Political Order in Changing Societies* (New Haven: Yale University Press, 1968), 264. Although I share Charles Tilly's concerns about the causal analysis in Huntington's account, I find his assertion that by Huntington's definition "one might reasonably argue that no revolution has ever occurred" peevish: Tilly, "Does Modernization Breed Revolution?" *Comparative Politics* 5, no. 3 (1973): 433. Huntington's definition is not too far removed from that offered by Thomas Paine: see Paine, *Rights of Man; Part the Second,* 2nd ed. (London, 1792), 5; Jeff Goodwin, *No Other Way Out: States and Revolutionary Movements, 1945–1991* (Cambridge: Cambridge University Press, 2001), 4; Isaac Kramnick, "Reflections on Revolution," *History and Theory* 11, no. 1 (1972): 31; Richard Price, *Observations on the Importance of the American Revolution* (London, 1784), 2; Guy Miege, *The New State of England under Their Majesties K. William and Q. Mary,* 2 vols. (London: H. C. for Jonathan Robinson, 1691), sig. A2r; see similar comments by John Evelyn to John Evelyn Jr., 18 December 1688, British Library, Evelyn Papers, JEJ 1; John Aubrey, *The Natural History and Antiquities of the County of Surrey,* 4 vols. ([1673–92]; London: E. Curll, 1719), 3:17; and Thomas Story, *A Journal of the Life of Thomas Story* (Newcastle-upon-Tyne: Isaac Thompson, 1747), 10.

3. Skocpol, *States and Social Revolutions,* 4. The classic social interpretation of the revolution was laid out by Georges Lefebvre, *The Coming of the French Revolution, 1789,* trans. R. R. Palmer (Princeton, NJ: Princeton University Press, 1947); and by Albert Soboul, *The French Revolution, 1787–1799: From the Storming of the Bastille to Napoleon,* trans. Alan Forrest and Colin Jones (New York: Vintage, 1975). For current state of play, see James Livesey, *Making Democracy in the French Revolution* (Cambridge, MA: Harvard University Press, 2001), 3–14; Steven Laurence Kaplan, *Farewell, Revolution: The Historians' Feud, France, 1789/1989* (Ithaca, NY: Cornell University Press, 1995), esp. 99–108; and Rebecca Spang, "Paradigms and Paranoia: How Modern Is the French Revolution?" *American Historical Review* 108, no. 1 (2003): esp. 120–24. One of the opening salvos in the assault on the class struggle interpretation was fired by the British academic Colin Lucas, "Nobles, Bourgeois and the Origins of the French Revolution," *Past and Present* 60 (August 1973): 84–126. A class-based interpretation of the French Revolution is beginning to reemerge; see John Markoff, *The Abolition of Feudalism: Peasants, Lords, and Legislators in the French Revolution* (University Park: Pennsylvania State University Press, 1996); and Henry Heller, *The Bourgeois Revolution in France, 1789–1815* (New York: Berghahn, 2006).

4. Skocpol, *States and Social Revolutions,* 4; John Foran, *Taking Power: The Origins of Third World Revolutions* (Cambridge: Cambridge University Press, 2005), 8; Hannah Arendt, *On Revolution* (London: Penguin Books, 1963), 64. My point is that the analysis is so narrow as to tell us more about the political preferences of the scholar than about the nature of revolutions. Society is invariably reconfigured dramatically in revolutions. But the social can be reconfigured in many ways. The replacing of one dominant class with another is a tiny subset of the possibilities.

5. Huntington, *Political Order in Changing Societies,* 264–74; Tilly, "Does Modernization Breed Revolution?" 435. For an earlier modernization story, see Chalmers Johnson, *Revolutionary Change* (Boston: Little, Brown, 1966), 61–62. For a description of the broader family of modernization stories, see Goodwin, *No Other Way Out,* 17.

6. Skocpol, *States and Social Revolutions,* 13, 19, 23, 47.

7. Skocpol, *States and Social Revolutions,* 24. The point I am making is also emphasized by Goodwin, *No Other Way Out,* 19–20.

8. Huntington, *Political Order in Changing Societies,* 275; Skocpol, *States and Social Revolutions,* 5.

9. Jack A. Goldstone, *Revolution and Rebellion in the Early Modern World* (Berkeley: University of California Press, 1991), xxiv, 27, 37.

10. Goldstone, *Revolution and Rebellion*, xxv, 3.

11. Goldstone, *Revolution and Rebellion*, 318. Skocpol dismisses that revolution as "a political revolution." Skocpol, *States and Social Revolutions*, 141, 144, 294. Karl Marx, "The East India Company," in Karl Marx, *Surveys from Exile: Political Writings*, vol. 2, ed. David Fernbach (London: Penguin, 1973), 308; Sir William Blackstone, *Commentaries on the Laws of England*, 4 vols. (Oxford: Clarendon Press, 1765–69), 1:397–98, 4:435.

12. Jonathan I. Israel, *The Dutch Republic: Its Rise, Greatness and Fall, 1477–1806* (Oxford: Clarendon Press, 1995), 796–806; Pieter Geyl, *Orange and Stuart, 1641–1672*, trans. Arnold Pomerans (New York: Charles Scribner's Sons, 1939), 345–400; Herbert H. Rowen, *John de Witt, Grand Pensionary of Holland, 1625–1672* (Princeton, NJ: Princeton University Press, 1978), 840–84.

13. Knud Jespersen, *History of Denmark*, trans. Ivan Hill (Houndmills: Palgrave, 1994), 40–46. Contemporaries made the same point. See Robert Molesworth, *Account of Denmark* (London: Timothy Goodwin, 1692).

14. A. F. Upton, *Charles XI and Swedish Absolutism, 1660–1697* (Cambridge: Cambridge University Press, 1998), 10, 31–89; Michael Roberts, *Essays in Swedish History* (London: Weidenfeld and Nicolson, 1967), 230, 233, 247–49.

15. John Lynch, *Bourbon Spain, 1700–1808* (Oxford: Basil Blackwell, 1989), 37, 60.

16. In chapter 3 I discuss the socioeconomic modernization that took place in England in the later seventeenth century. That modernization was necessary to underwrite James II's state modernization program, described in chapter 6.

17. Tilly, "Does Modernization Breed Revolution?" 432, 447. It should be noted that Skocpol has claimed a fundamental compatibility between her claims and Tilly's because they share a belief "that the mass, lower-class participants in revolution cannot turn discontent into effective political action without autonomous collective organization and resource to sustain their efforts." Theda Skocpol, *Social Revolutions in the Modern World* (Cambridge: Cambridge University Press, 1994), 241. However, the evidence presented by Tilly in this essay seems to raise more fundamental questions about the relation between class definition and revolution than Skocpol allows.

18. Tocqueville, *Old Regime*, viii–ix, 32, 57–58, 60, 171, 176–79, 188, 193–94, 201. This point is admitted by Heller, the most trenchant contemporary defender of the social interpretation of the French Revolution. The problem, he notes, was that "the attempt at reform from above was too indecisive to stave off ultimate economic crisis and financial bankruptcy." Heller, *Bourgeois Revolution*, 67. Recent scholarship has detailed Louis XVI's commitment to state modernization: see Gail Bossenga, *The Politics of Privilege: Old Regime and Revolution in Lille* (Cambridge: Cambridge University Press, 1991); Michael Kwass, *Privilege and the Politics of Taxation in Eighteenth-Century France* (Cambridge: Cambridge University Press, 2000); and Stephen Miller, *State and Society in Eighteenth-Century France* (Washington, DC: Catholic University of America Press, 2008), 101–40.

19. The evidence for this is presented in the chapters that follow.

20. Friedrich Katz, "Mexico: Restored Republic and Porfiriato, 1867–1910," in *Cambridge History of Latin America*, vol. 5, ed. Leslie Bethell (Cambridge: Cambridge University Press, 1986), 35, 38, 56, 64; Alan Knight, *The Mexican Revolution*, vol. 1 (Cambridge: Cambridge University Press, 1986), 15, 18, 23.

21. Nader Sohrabi, "Historicizing Revolutions," *American Journal of Sociology* 100 (1995): 1392.

22. Sheila Fitzpatrick, *The Russian Revolution* (Oxford: Oxford University Press, 1982), 15–16, 31–36.

23. Hamdan Nezir Akmese, *The Birth of Modern Turkey* (London: I. B. Tauris, 2005), 19–21; Sohrabi, "Historicizing Revolutions," 1391.

24. Jonathan D. Spence, *The Gate of Heavenly Peace: The Chinese and Their Revolution, 1895–1980* (London: Penguin, 1982), 90–91; Michael Gasster, "Reform and Revolution in China's Political Modernization," in *China's Revolution*, ed. Mary Claburgh Wright (New Haven: Yale University Press, 1968), 75, 81. This point has been made by Skocpol as well. Skocpol, *States and Social Revolutions*, 77.

25. Said Amir Arjomand, *The Turban for the Crown: The Islamic Revolution in Iran* (Oxford: Oxford University Press, 1988), 191, 194, 206–7; G. Hassein Razi, "The Nexus of Legitimacy and Performance: The Lessons of the Iranian Revolution," *Comparative Politics* 19, no. 4 (1987): 454–56; Ali Shariati, who has been called "the ideologist of the revolt," blended "Islam with modern ideas." Nikki R. Keddie, *Modern Iran: Roots and Results of Revolution,* rev. ed. (New Haven and London: Yale University Press, 2003), 200, 227. Arjomand has highlighted some modern elements of the Iranian revolution, the establishment of the Majles, the "keen interest in technology," and "the commitment to rural development and improvement of the lot of the peasantry." Theda Skocpol has admitted that the Iranian revolution poses some fundamental problem for her interpretation. Skocpol, "Rentier State and Shi'a Islam in the Iranian Revolution," in Skocpol, *Social Revolutions in the Modern World,* 240–43, 245–47.

26. Jorge I. Domínguez, "The Batista Regime in Cuba," in *Sultanistic Regimes,* ed. H. E. Chehabi and Juan J. Linz (Baltimore: Johns Hopkins University Press, 1998), 125; James O'Connor, *The Origins of Socialism in Cuba* (Ithaca, NY: Cornell University Press, 1970), 29; Foran, *Taking Power,* 60.

27. Carles Boix, *Democracy and Redistribution* (Cambridge: Cambridge University Press, 2003), 28.

28. Huntington, *Political Order in Changing Societies,* 275; Skocpol, *Social Revolutions in the Modern World,* 241; Goodwin, *No Other Way Out,* 26.

29. There has been much dispute over the nature of French absolutism in the seventeenth century, but most commentators agree that Louis XIV vastly increased state power in France. See James B. Collins, *The State in Early Modern France* (Cambridge: Cambridge University Press, 1995), 79–124; and David Parker, *The Making of French Absolutism* (London: Edward Arnold, 1983), 118–36.

30. Thomas M. Huber, *The Revolutionary Origins of Modern Japan* (Stanford, CA: Stanford University Press, 1981), 1; W. G. Beasley, *The Rise of Modern Japan* (London: Weidenfeld and Nicolson, 1990), 54–69; E. H. Norman, *Origins of the Modern Japanese State* (New York: Pantheon, 1975), 114–15. Huber describes the Meiji Restoration as a service revolution. However, as Beasley points out, the Meiji Restoration failed the usual standard of revolution. There was no mass popular movement; there was no new conception of time. The popular debate was not about establishing a new political order. The Meiji Restoration seems to me a classic example of thoroughgoing state modernization.

31. Boix, *Democracy and Redistribution,* 93.

32. Peter Burke, *The Fabrication of Louis XIV* (New Haven and London: Yale University Press, 1992).

33. Barrington Moore Jr., *Social Origins of Dictatorship and Democracy: Lord and Peasant in the Making of the Modern World* (Boston: Beacon, 1966), 3–155, 413, 418, 433.

34. Boix has modified Moore's argument by distinguishing political outcomes in weakly industrialized and strongly industrialized countries. Boix, *Democracy and Distribution,* 40. Although I find Boix's argument more analytically satisfying and I share his enthusiasm for resuscitating the questions posed by modernization theorists, he is asking a fundamentally broader question than I am. He is asking about "democratic transitions"; I am asking more narrowly why some revolutions give rise to more democratic regimes and why others give rise to more authoritarian ones.

35. Arendt, *On Revolution,* 215.

36. Arendt, *On Revolution,* 25, 92.

37. Moore, *Social Origins of Dictatorship and Democracy,* 414; Arendt, *On Revolution,* 23; Steven Pincus, "Whigs, Political Economy, and the Revolution of 1688–89," in *"Cultures of Whiggism:" New Essays on English Literature and Culture in the Long Eighteenth Century,* ed. David Womersley (Newark: University of Delaware Press, 2005); T. H. Breen, *The Marketplace of Revolution: How Consumer Politics Shaped American Independence* (Oxford: Oxford University Press, 2004), xvi–xviii.

38. Tocqueville, *Old Regime,* 12–13. Martin Malia also argues that "a millenarian impulse is necessary to fuel the initial revolutionary breakthrough." Martin Malia, *History's Locomotives: Revolutions and the Making of the Modern World* (New Haven and London: Yale University Press, 2006), 58.

39. The first approach was pioneered by Thomas Paine, *The Decline and Fall of the English System of Finance,* 2nd American ed. (New York, 1796), 33. It has continued through the work of Foran, *Taking Power,* 18. The literature for the second is summarized and critically reviewed by Lawrence Stone, "Theories of Revolution," *World Politics* 18, no. 2 (1966): 164ff.

40. Crane Brinton, *The Anatomy of Revolution,* rev. ed. (New York: Vintage, 1965), 39; Fiztpatrick, *Russian Revolution,* 16.

CHAPTER 3. *Going Dutch*

1. Thomas Machell was one who complained that Camden had based his county descriptions on authority: Thomas Machell, Westmoreland, Cumbria SRO, Carlisle, D&C Machell MSS, 1:47; Edmund Gibson to Dr. Charlett, 31 March 1694, Bodleian, Ballard MSS 5, fol. 23r. Plans were well under way to revise Stow: Gibson to Charlett, 4 June, 4 August 1694, Bodleian, Ballard MSS 5, fols. 44r, 60v; Edmund Gibson, *Camden's Britannia* (London: F. Collins for A. Swalle and A. and J. Churchill, 1695), sig. [A2r].

2. Thomas Babington Macaulay, *The History of England from the Accession of James II,* 5 vols. (New York: Harper and Brothers, 1849–61), 1:260, 262, 265 299–300, 333, 346, 352. Macaulay thought that "the mode in which correspondence was carried on between distant places may excite the scorn of the present generation": *History,* 359.

3. As the following pages make clear, social historians offer a different picture. However, social historians have been guilty of their own vices. Most significantly, an overwhelming majority of social histories either stop in 1640 or begin in 1700, presumably explaining either the outbreak of the English Civil War or the onset of the Industrial Revolution. The problem with those assumptions is underscored below. Others have noted the same problem: David Hey, *The Fiery Blades of Hallamshire: Sheffield and Its Neighbourhood, 1660–1740* (Leicester: Leicester University Press, 1991), 1; D. C. Coleman, *Economy of England, 1450–1750* (Oxford: Oxford University Press, 1977), 158. This group of political historians includes W. A. Speck, J. R. Jones, Eveline Cruickshanks, G. M. Trevelyan, and John Miller.

4. J. C. D. Clark, *English Society, 1660–1832,* 2nd ed. (Cambridge: Cambridge University Press, 2000), 15, 446, 452. This is very similar to Macaulay's view that "in our own land, the national wealth has, during at least six centuries, been almost uninterruptedly increasing." Macaulay, *History,* 1:261. Jonathan Scott, *Algernon Sidney and the Restoration Crisis, 1677–1683* (Cambridge: Cambridge University Press, 1991), 6.

5. Jan de Vries and Ad van der Woude, *The First Modern Economy: Success, Failure, and Perseverance of the Dutch Economy, 1500–1815* (Cambridge: Cambridge University Press, 1997), 693.

6. The examples in printed pamphlet literature are too numerous to mention. The Newcastle merchant Ambrose Barnes commented extensively on all of these topics. W. H. D. Longstaffe, ed., *Memoirs of the Life of Mr. Ambrose Barnes . . . ,* Publications of the Surtees Society, vol. 50 (Durham: Published for the Society, 1867), 46–48, 213 (hereafter cited as *Memoirs of Barnes*). The London Dissenter Roger Morrice kept a collection of pamphlets on comparative political economy: see "A Catalogue of Roger Morrice's Books," DWL, 31 M, 14 May 1697, unfolioed. John Evelyn framed his introduction to his intended history of the Third Anglo-Dutch War in explicitly comparative terms. John Evelyn, *Navigation and Commerce* (London: Benj. Tooke, 1674), esp. 7–8. John Houghton, "A Proposal for Improvement of Husbandry and Trade," BL, Sloane 2903, fol. 164v.

7. "An Essay on the Interest of the Crown in American Plantations and Trade," 1685, BL, Add. 47131, fol. 22. For some not altogether compatible explanations for the decline of Spain, see William Garroway, 15 November 1667, Grey, 1:40; Evelyn, *Navigation and Commerce,* 6–7, 15; P. B., *The Means to Free Europe from the French Usurpation* (London: R. Bently, 1689), 99; *A Discourse of the Necessity of Encouraging Mechanick Industry* (London: Richard Chiswell, 1690), 9–10; John Cary, *An Essay on the State of England in Relation to Its Trade* (London: Sam. Crouch, 1695), sig. [A5v]; *The Irregular and Disorderly State of the Plantation Trade* [London, 1695?], [1]. See also Matthew Wren, *Monarchy Asserted* (Oxford: F. Bowman, 1659), 30; John

Houghton, *England's Great Happiness* (London: J. M. for Edward Croft, 1677), 8; and the instant classic Sir William Temple, *Observations upon the United Provinces of the Netherlands* (London: Sa. Gellibrand, 1673). For the general significance of the Dutch in English economic thought, see Joyce Oldham Appleby, *Economic Thought and Ideology in Seventeenth-Century England* (Princeton, NJ: Princeton University Press, 1978), 73–98.

8. Guy Miege, *The New State of England under Their Majesties K. William and Q. Mary,* 2 vols. (London: H. C. for Jonathan Robinson, 1691), 1:110, 158. Part 1 of this text was based on travels Miege took in the 1680s. Gibson, *Camden's Britannia,* 439; Thomas Baskerville, "London and Dover Journey," HMC *Portland,* 2:280; Robert Lord Wenlock, ed., *Lorenzo Magalotti: Travels of Cosmo the Third* (London: J. Mawman, 1821), 11 April 1665, 147 (hereafter cited as *Magalotti: Travels*); Andrew Yarranton, *England's Improvement by Sea and Land* (London: R. Everingham, 1677), 48–49.

9. C. G. A. Clay, *Economic Expansion and Social Change: England, 1500–1700,* 2 vols. (Cambridge: Cambridge University Press, 1984), 1:60, 165, 2:102; Sir William Coventry, 27 February 1668, Grey, 1:97; Gibson, *Camden's Britannia,* 411–12, 509; Yarranton, *England's Improvement,* 50; Houghton, *England's Great Happiness,* 11–12; Evelyn, *Diary,* 30 August 1654, 1:135; John Edward Jackson, ed., *Wiltshire: The Topographical Collections of John Aubrey* [c. 1670] (Devizes: Wiltshire Archaeological and Natural History Society, 1862), 9–11; Carole Shammas, *The Pre-Industrial Consumer in England and America* (Oxford: Clarendon Press, 1990), 2, 17, 28; de Vries and van der Woude, *First Modern Economy,* 695; I thank Kathy Conzen for providing me with the US statistics, which are based on material gleaned from US Bureau of the Census, *Historical Statistics of the United States* (Washington, DC: GPO, 1960).

10. Clay, *Economic Expansion,* 2:3, 80. For the later seventeenth-century assessments and comparisons, see Jacob M. Price, *Overseas Trade and Traders* (Aldershot: Variorum, 1996), 106; John M. Hatcher, *Before 1700: Towards the Age of Coal* (Oxford: Clarendon Press, 1993), 419; and Coleman, *Economy of England,* 159.

11. Clay, *Economic Expansion,* 1:194, 2:99. I discuss several examples below. For the Peak District, see Andy Wood, *The Politics of Social Conflict* (Cambridge: Cambridge University Press, 1999), 93, 97–98; for Hallamshire, Hey, *Fiery Blades,* 1; for Birmingham, William Hutton, *An History of Birmingham,* 2nd ed. (Birmingham: Pearson and Rollason, 1783), 19. My thinking about regional economies has been influenced by Pat Hudson, "The Regional Perspective," in *Regions and Industries: A Perspective on the Industrial Revolution in Britain,* ed. Pat Hudson (Cambridge: Cambridge University Press, 1989), 5–38.

12. Miege, *New State of England,* 1:18–19, 2:7; Clay, *Economic Expansion,* 2:44; Coleman, *Economy of England,* 160.

13. John Joliffe, 18 November 1670, Grey, 1:292–93; *Reasons Humbly Offered to the Honourable House of Commons Why No Farther Duty or Excise Be Laid upon Wines* [1690s], [1]; *The Trade between England and Italy Truly Stated* [1690s], [1]; Shammas, *Pre-Industrial Consumer,* 96.

14. Clay, *Economic Expansion,* 2:15–16; Petition of the Clothiers of the City of Coventry, 7 May 1686, NA, SP 31/5, fol. 48r; Privy Council Minutes, 7 May 1686, NA, PC 2/71, fol. 137r. This assessment echoed the view of Yarranton, *England's Improvement,* 55, 100; Paul Slack, "Poverty and Politics in Salisbury, 1597–1666," in *Crisis and Order in English Towns, 1500–1700,* ed. Peter Clark and Paul Slack (Toronto: University of Toronto Press, 1972), 170–71; Peter Clark and Paul Slack, *English Towns in Transition, 1500–1700* (Oxford: Oxford University Press, 1976), 102–3; Miege, *New State of England,* 1:206; Gibson, *Camden's Britannia,* 152; Eric Kerridge, *Textile Manufactures in Early Modern England* (Manchester: Manchester University Press, 1985), 241.

15. Narcissus Luttrell, "Travells," 3 July–21 September 1678, Beinecke, OSB Shelves b.314, 63; Miege, *New State of England,* 1:81, 157, 192–93; Clay, *Economic Expansion,* 2:17–18; *Magalotti: Travels,* 6–7 April 1669, 128, 132–33; Luttrell, "Travells," 1677, fol. ev; Maurice Exwood and H. L. Lehmann, eds., *The Journal of William Schellinks' Travels in England, 1661–1663,* Camden 5th Ser., vol. 1 (London: Royal Historical Society, 1993), 18 July 1661, 25 July 1662, 33, 111 (hereafter cited as *Journal of Schellinks*); Henri Misson, *M. Misson's Memoirs and Observations in His Travels over England,* trans. John Ozell (London: D. Browne et al.,

1719), 77; Misson's observations were based on his travels in England in the late 1680s and early 1690s; Luttrell, "Travells," 22 July–22 August 1679, 156; Thomas Baskerville, "Journeys," HMC *Portland*, 2:270; *Reasons Humbly Offered to the Honourable House of Commons, by the Clothiers of Essex* [1690s], [1]; Baskerville, "Journey to Essex," 1662, HMC *Portland*, 2:283. The New Draperies came first to East Anglia and the southeast in the late sixteenth century: Keith Wrightson, *Earthly Necessities: Economic Lives in Early Modern Britain* (New Haven and London: Yale University Press, 2000), 166–67; Clark and Slack, *English Towns*, 86–87; Peter Clark and Paul Slack, "Introduction," in *Crisis and Order*, ed. Clark and Slack, 32; Ralph Thoresby, *Ducatus Leodiensis* (London: Maurice Atkins, 1715), vi. Thoresby began working on his history of Leeds in the 1680s, he remarked on the clothing character of his home region much earlier: Thoresby, *Diary*, 17 October 1680, 1:66; John Smail, *The Origins of Middle-Class Culture* (Ithaca, NY: Cornell University Press, 1994), 22–23.

16. Ralph Thoresby, "Autobiography," WYAS, Thoresby MSS 26, 64; Miege, *New State of England*, 1:48, 127, 237–38; Gibson, *Camden's Britannia*, 798–99. Manchester parish was said to have twenty-seven thousand communicants in 1650: Clark and Slack, "Introduction," 30; John K. Walton, "Proto-Industrialisation and the First Industrial Revolution," in *Regions and Industries*, ed. Hudson, 46, 59; Sir Daniel Fleming, Lancashire, 1674, Cumbria SRO, Carlisle, D/Lons/L12/2/18, fols. 2, 12r; Clay, *Economic Expansion*, 2:38; Thoresby, *Diary*, 19 September 1694, 1:266; The Case concerning the General Sessions in Westmoreland, ca. 1680s, Cumbria SRO, Kendal, WD/RY, Box 35; Machell, Westmoreland, 2:27; Roger North, *Lives*, ed. Augustus Jessopp (London: George Bell and Sons, 1890), 1:183; Fleming, Westmoreland, Cumbria SRO, Kendal, WD/Cr/11/65, 4–5; C. B. Phillips, "Town and Country: Economic Change in Kendal, c. 1550–1700," in *The Transformation of English Provincial Towns, 1600–1800*, ed. Peter Clark (London: Hutchinson, 1984), 115–17.

17. Kerridge, *Textile Manufactures*, 67; Luttrell, "Travells," 22 July–22 August 1679, 189; Baskerville, "London and Dover Journey," 2:281; Miege, *New State of England*, 1:153; *Journal of Schellinks*, 12 October 1662, 160; Bonrepaus (London) to Seignelay, 1/11 February 1686, NA, PRO 31/3/164, fols. 39–40; Misson, *Memoirs*, 182.

18. William Grey, *Chorographia, or a Survey of Newcastle-upon-Tyne* (Newcastle: S. B., 1649), 34, 37; Hatcher, *Before 1700*, 68, 480–90; David Levine and Keith Wrightson, *The Making of an Industrial Society: Whickham, 1560–1765* (Oxford: Clarendon Press, 1991), 4–5; J. U. Nef, *The Rise of the British Coal Industry*, vol. 1 (Hamden, Conn.: Archon Books, 1966), 19–20; Catherine Glover and Philip Riden, eds., *William Woolley's History of Derbyshire* Derbyshire Record Society, 6 (1981), 46 (hereafter cited as *Woolley's History of Derbyshire*); Luttrell, "Travells," 3 July–21 September 1678, 56; Gibson, *Camden's Britannia*, 82–248; Machell, Westmoreland, 1:67; Colonel Birch, 14 March 1670, Grey, 1:232. There appears to have been a tenfold increase in production in Macaulay's barbaric northwest. Miege, *New State of England*, 1:20, 75, 77–78, 164–68; Misson, *Memoirs*, 192–93; John Conyers, Northern Journey, 11 September 1676, Essex SRO, D/DW Z6/2, 18–19; Thoresby, *Diary*, 11 November 1682, 1:141; Evelyn, *Diary*, 10 September 1677, 4:115–16; Richard Colman, 13 April 1671, Grey, 1:443. King's Lynn also benefited from transporting coal: *Journal of Schellinks*, 7 October 1662, 154; Craig Muldrew, *The Economy of Obligation* (New York: St. Martin's Press, 1998), 18–19.

19. John Evelyn, "A Character of England," 1659, in *The Writings of John Evelyn*, ed. Guy de la Bedoyere (Woodbridge: Boydell, 1995), 82; Evelyn, "Fumifugium," 1661, in *Writings of Evelyn*, ed. de la Bedoyere, 137; Evelyn, *Diary*, 28 May 1684, 4:380; Memoire de M. Robert, 27 December/6 January 1685/86, fol. 81r; Misson, *Memoirs*, 37–38, 81; Miege, *New State of England*, 1:33–34.

20. W. H. B. Court, *The Rise of the Midland Industries, 1600–1838* (Oxford: Oxford University Press, 1938), 69; Hatcher, *Before 1700*, 450. This marks a slight modification of Nef's dating. Clay, *Economic Expansion*, 2:48.

21. Clay, *Economic Expansion*, 2:57–58; Wood, *Politics of Social Conflict*, 89, 99; Gibson, *Camden's Britannia*, 78, 782–83; Miege, *New State of England*, 1:20, 47, 54–55, 188; Luttrell, "Travells," 3 July–21 September 1678, 55–56; *Journal of Schellinks*, 22 July 1662, 108; Thoresby, "Autobiography," 46; Thoresby, *Diary*, 20 July

1681, 1:91; Evelyn, *Diary,* 8 July 1685, 4:451–52; *Woolley's History of Derbyshire,* 8, 24, 176–77, 196. Woolley's history is especially valuable because he had made his fortune as a lead merchant in London before retiring to his native Derbyshire to write his history.

22. Clay, *Economic Expansion,* 2:58–59; Luttrell, "Travells," fols. Zv, aar; Miege, *New State of England,* 1:41; *Magalotti: Travels,* 3 April 1669, 119; *Journal of Schellinks,* 14 August 1662, 119–20.

23. Thomas Baskerville, "Journey to the North," HMC *Portland,* 2:309; Conyers, *Northern Journey,* 19 September 1676, 25; Luttrell, "Travells," 18 August–25 September 1680, 273; Baskerville, "Inland Towns," HMC *Portland,* 2:293–94; Thoresby, *Diary,* 20 September 1694, 1:269; Gibson, *Camden's Britannia,* 180, 245, 267, 509; Court, *Rise of Midland Industries,* 78; H. N., *The Compleat Tradesman* (London: John Dunton, 1684), 158; Gregory King, "Of the Naval Trade of England," 1688, in *Two Tracts by Gregory King,* ed. George E. Barnett (Baltimore: Johns Hopkins University Press, 1936), 69. Oxfordshire's post–civil war deforestation may also have been caused by the iron industry: Robert Plot, *The Natural History of Oxfordshire* (Oxford: Theatre, 1677), 51; Yarranton, *England's Improvement,* 56, 58 (this was not Yarranton's position; he had been an iron master in the Forest of Dean); Miege, *New State of England,* 1:20, 85, 149.

24. Clay, *Economic Expansion,* 2:55; Price, *Overseas Trade,* 113; *The Case of the Company of Cutlers in Hallamshire* [ca. 1680], [1]; Hey, *Fiery Blades,* 61, 94, 184; Misson, *Memoirs,* 171; Miege, *New State of England,* 1:235, 262; Gibson, *Camden's Britannia,* 723 (section written by Ralph Thoresby); Thoresby, *Diary,* 19 July 1681, 1:88; Yarranton, *England's Improvement,* 57–58; Court, *Rise of Midland Industries,* 70–71, 77, 147; Marie B. Rowlands, *Masters and Men in the West Midland Metalware Trades before the Industrial Revolution* (Manchester: Manchester University Press, 1975), 13, 149.

25. Clay, *Economic Expansion,* 2:37; Eleanor S. Godfrey, "The Development of English Glassmaking, 1560–1640" (PhD diss., University of Chicago, 1957), 3, 320; *An Answer to the Insinuations and Suggestions of the Commissions for Receiving the Duties on Glass-Wares* [1690s], [1]; Evelyn, *Diary,* 18 September 1676, 4:98–99; Alberti to Inquisitors of State, 6 January 1673, CSPV, 2; Alberti to Doge and Senate, 21 April 1673, CSPV, 38–39; Alberti to Inquisitors of State, 15 September 1673, CSPV, 116; Alberti to Doge and Senate, 15 June, 6 July 1674, CSPV, 265, 272; Court, *Rise of Midland Industries,* 121; Gibson, *Camden's Britannia,* 523, 579; Luttrell, "Travells," 18 August–25 September 1680, 256, 272–73; Baskerville, "Inland Towns," 2:292, 294; Grey, *Chorographia,* 40; Yarranton, *England's Improvement,* 156; Charles Palmer, *The Glass-Makers Case* [1690s], [1]; *The Allegations of the Glass-Makers Examined and Answered* [1690s], [1]; *The Case of the Working Glass-Makers in England* [1690s], [1]; Alberti to Doge and Senate, 23 February 1674, CSPV, 222–223; *The Miserable Case of the Glass-Makers, Considered* [1690s], [1–2]; *The Case of the Poor Work-Men Glass-Makers* [1690s], [1]; Houghton, *England's Great Happiness,* 5–6.

26. Plot, *Natural History of Oxfordshire,* 250–51; *The Case of the Journeymen Potmakers* [1690s], [1]; Robert Plot, *The Natural History of Stafford-Shire* (Oxford, 1686), 122, 128; Hatcher, *Before 1700,* 454; Lorna Weatherill, *The Pottery Trade and North Staffordshire, 1660–1760* (New York: Augustus M. Kelley, 1971), 1–9; *The Deplorable Case of the Journeymen Potmakers* [1690s], [1]; *Reasons Humbly Offered to the Honourable House of Commons for Encouraging of the English Manufactures of Earthen-Wares* [1690s], [1].

27. *An Answer to the Sugar-Bakers or Sugar-Refiners Paper* (London, 1695), 1; *Irregular and Disorderly State,* [2–3]; *A State of the Present Condition of the Island of Barbadoes* (London: Tho. Northcott, [1690s?]), 2; Hatcher, *Before 1700,* 447; *A Reply to a Paper Entitled An Answer to the Sugar-Refiners Paper* [1695], 1; *The Case of the Refiners of England* [1690s], [1]; Richard B. Sheridan, *Sugar and Slavery: An Economic History of the British West Indies, 1623–1775* (Baltimore: Johns Hopkins University Press, 1973), 395; John J. McCusker, *Rum and the American Revolution,* vol. 1 (New York: Garland, 1989), 42.

28. *Magalotti: Travels,* 4 May 1669, 197; Samuel Sorbiere, *A Voyage to England* (London: J. Woodward, 1709), 12 (Sorbiere traveled in 1664); Luttrell, "Travells," 3 July–21 September 1678, 49, 113, 115; Gibson to Charlett, 12 May 1694, Bodleian, Ballard MSS 5, fol. 35r; Gibson, *Camden's Britannia,* 132–33, 219, 229–30, 359; Clay, *Economic Expansion,* 1:197; David Harris Sacks and Michael Lynch, "Ports, 1540–1700," in *The Cambridge Urban History of Britain,* 3 vols., ed. Peter Clark (Cambridge: Cambridge University Press,

2000), 2:385–86; Clark and Slack, *English Towns,* 36–38; Thomas Baskerville, "Abingdon to Southampton," 1679, HMC *Portland,* 2:287; Memoire de M. Robert, 27 December/6 January 1685/86, fol. 94r; Miege, *New State of England,* 1:113–15; Baskerville, "London and Dover Journey," 2:276–78; Luttrell, "Travells," 30 April 1678, 36; *Journal of Schellinks,* 14 July 1661, 46; Luttrell, "Travells," 22 July–22 August 1679, 184–85; Sainte Marie to Denz., 2 May 1685, in Georges Roth, ed., *Un Voyageur Francais a Londres en 1685: M. de Sainte-Marie* (Paris: Didier, 1968), 16.

29. I have refrained from using J. U. Nef's celebrated and controversial phrase "an early industrial revolution." However, it should be clear that the growth in manufacturing in the seventeenth century was nothing short of transformative for England both absolutely and relative to other European countries. See Nef, *Rise of the British Coal Industry,* 165–89; Peter Earle, *The Making of the English Middle Class* (Berkeley: University of California Press, 1989), 18. I dissent from the characterization offered by David Rollison, *The Local Origins of Modern Society: Gloucestershire, 1500–1800* (London: Routledge, 1992), 18.

30. Clay, *Economic Expansion,* 1:165; John Langton, "Urban Growth and Economic Change: From the Late Seventeenth Century to 1841," in *Cambridge Urban History,* ed. Clark, 2:462; William Petty estimated 33 percent: William Petty, "Essay about Analysis of Property," c. 1686, BL, Add. 72866, fol. 54r; de Vries and van der Woude, *First Modern Economy,* 60; US Bureau of the Census, *Historical Statistics of the United States* (Washington, DC: GPO, 1961), 14. These statistics, based on the definition of urban at a population of 2,500, yield a 26 percent urbanization rate. Paul Glennie and Ian Whyte, using a roughly similar basis, argue that England had a 30–33 percent urbanization rate in 1700: Glennie and Whyte, "Towns in an Agrarian Economy, 1540–1700," in *Cambridge Urban History,* ed. Clark, 2:169; Peter Clark, "Introduction," in *Cambridge Urban History,* ed. Clark, 2:3. Even the Netherlands experienced deurbanization after 1675: de Vries and van der Woude, *First Modern Economy,* 60.

31. Jeremy Boulton, "London, 1540–1700," in *Cambridge Urban History,* ed. Clark, 2:316; Clay, *Economic Expansion,* 1:169–70. For contemporary impressions: Sorbiere, *Voyage to England,* 13; Misson, *Memoirs,* 177; Sainte Marie to Denz., 8 May 1685, in Roth, ed., *Voyageur Francais,* 45; *Magalotti: Travels,* 11 May 1669, 395; Evelyn, *Diary,* 12 June 1684, 4:382; Gibson, *Camden's Britannia,* 331.

32. John Evelyn, *The State of France* (London: M. M., G. Bedell and T. Collins, 1652), 111–12; Miege, *New State of England,* 1:283–84, 332; Sainte Marie to Denz., 11 May 1685, in Roth, ed., *Voyageur Francais,* 69; Misson, *Memoirs,* 323; Petty, "Essay about Analysis of Property," fol. 53r. See also Thoresby, *Diary,* 22 February 1678, 1:12.

33. Clay, *Economic Expansion,* 1:169; Clark and Slack, *English Towns,* 38–40; Clark and Slack, "Introduction," 30; Paul Slack, "Great and Good Towns, 1540–1700," in *Cambridge Urban History,* ed. Clark, 2:351–352; Court, *Rise of Midland Industries,* 33, 47; Hutton, *History of Birmingham,* 41; Sacks and Lynch, "Ports, 1540–1700," 2:384; Fleming, Lancashire, 1674, fol. 9r; Thoresby, *Diary,* 8 June 1682, 1:124; Gibson, *Camden's Britannia,* 776, 797–798; Hey, *Fiery Blades,* 64, 304; Miege, *New State of England,* 1:264–65; Smail, *Origins of Middle-Class Culture,* 19–22; Conyers, Northern Journey, 28 August 1676, 6. Thoresby, *Ducatus Leodensis,* provides the most complete account of Leeds's impressive development. For a discussion of the problematic politics resulting in large part from Leeds's rise to eminence as a manufacturing town, see Derek Hirst, "The Fracturing of the Cromwellian Alliance: Leeds and Adam Baynes," *English Historical Review* 108 (1993): 868–94.

34. *Memoirs of Barnes,* 90, 214; Sacks and Lynch, "Ports, 1540–1700," 2:384; Miege, *New State of England,* 1:167; Conyers, Northern Journey, 1 September 1676, 8; Gibson, *Camden's Britannia,* 871; Grey, *Chorographia,* 26; *Journal of Schellinks,* 11 October 1662, 158; Penelope Corfield, "A Provincial Capital in the Late Seventeenth Century: The Case of Norwich," in *Crisis and Order,* ed. Clark and Slack, 263–66; Baskerville, "Journeys," 2:268.

35. Sacks and Lynch, "Ports, 1540–1700," 2:384, 386, 404–5; Paul G. E. Clemens, "The Rise of Liverpool, 1665–1750," *Economic History Review,* n.s., 29, no. 2 (1976): 211–15; Gibson, *Camden's Britannia,* 801; Perry Gauci, *Politics of Trade: The Overseas Merchant in State and Society, 1660–1720* (Oxford: Oxford University

Press, 2001), 55–62; Fleming, *Lancashire, 1674,* fol. 5r; Miege, *New State of England,* 1:50, 127; Gibson, *Camden's Britannia,* 801, 840–41; Sylvia Collier, *Whitehaven, 1660–1800* (London: HMSO, 1991), 2; J. V. Beckett, *Coal and Tobacco: The Lowthers and the Economic Development of West Cumberland* (Cambridge: Cambridge University Press, 1981), 39–40, 103–4, 120, 181; Thoresby, *Diary,* 20 September 1694, 1:269; Sir Daniel Fleming, Cumberland, Cumbria SRO, Kendal, WD/Cr/11/65, 1; Thomas Denton, History of Westmoreland and Cumberland, 1687–88, Cumbria SRO, Carlisle, D/Lons/L/2/4/2/Box 1061, 29; Whitehaven Port Book, Exports, 1678–1685, Cumbria SRO, Carlisle, D/Hud/6/1; Sir John Lowther of Whitehaven, General Notebook, 1685–1694, Cumbria SRO, Carlisle, D/Lons/W1/33, 19.

36. *Magalotti: Travels,* [April] 1669, 121–25; *Journal of Schellinks,* 8 August 1662, 115; Clark and Slack, "Introduction," 31–32; Clark and Slack, *English Towns,* 47, 51–52; Luttrell, "Travells," 1677, 3 July–21 September 1678, fols. l, R–S, 73–74; Miege, *New State of England,* 1:43, 60–61; Memoire de M. Robert, 27 December/6 January 1685/86, fols. 82–84r; *Journal of Schellinks,* 21 August 1662, 125; Jonathan Barry, "South-West," in *Cambridge Urban History,* ed. Clark, 2:83; Slack, "Great and Good Towns," 2:352; Sacks and Lynch, "Ports, 1540–1700," 2:384, 400; Earl of Bath (Plymouth) to Earl of Sunderland, 9 October 1688, NA, SP 31/4, fol. 107v.

37. Sacks and Lynch, "Ports, 1540–1700," 2:384, 400–401; *Journal of Schellinks,* 14 July 1662, 102; Miege, *New State of England,* 1:87; Evelyn, *Diary,* 30 June 1654, 3:102; Luttrell, "Travells," 3 July–21 September 1678, 47; Clark and Slack, *English Towns,* 52; Sir John Knight, 7 November 1670, Grey, 1:277; Memoire de M. Robert, 27 December/6 January 1685/86, fols. 80–81; North, *Lives,* 1:156.

38. Sacks and Lynch, "Ports, 1540–1700," 2:384, 406; John K. Walton, "North," in *Cambridge Urban History,* ed. Clark, 2:114; Clark and Slack, *English Towns,* 12; Luttrell, "Travells," 22 July–22 August 1679, 167; Miege, *New State of England,* 1:154–55.

39. J. D. Marshall, ed., *The Autobiography of William Stout of Lancaster, 1665–1752* (Manchester: Chetham Society, 1967), 77; Carl Bridenbaugh, *Cities in the Wilderness: The First Century of Urban Life in America, 1625–1742* (New York: Alfred A. Knopf, 1964), 143.

40. Angus McInnes, "The Emergence of a Leisure Town: Shrewsbury, 1660–1760," *Past and Present* 120 (August 1988): 84; Sylvia McIntyre, "Bath: The Rise of a Resort Town, 1660–1800," *Country Towns in Pre-Industrial England,* ed. Peter Clark (New York: St. Martin's, 1981), 201; *Journal of Schellinks,* 19 July 1662, 105; *An Historical Account of Mr. Rogers's Three Years Travels over England and Wales* (London: J. Moxon and B. Beardwell, 1694), 25–26; Tweeddale (Bath) to ?, 31 August 1685, NLS, 7026, fol. 7r; Luttrell, "Travells," 3 July–21 September 1678, 43–45; Misson, *Memoirs,* 14; Sir John Floyer, *An Enquiry into the Right Use and Abuses of the Hot, Cold and Temperate Baths in England* (London: R. Clavel, 1697), sig. [A8r].

41. Gibson, *Camden's Britannia,* 216; James Fraser (London) to Sir Robert Southwell, 16 August 1687, FSL, V.b. 287 (29); Luttrell, "Travells," 29 July–11 August 1680, 231–37; John Evelyn (Deptford) to John Evelyn Jr., 14 August, 13 August 1689, BL, Evelyn Papers, JEJ 1, unfolioed (since recataloged); Miege, *New State of England,* 1:115–16; John Evelyn (Deptford) to Susanna, 14 August 1689, BL, Evelyn Papers, JE A2, fol. 63r; Roger Morrice, Entering Book, 13 August 1685, DWL, 31 P, 478.

42. John Aubrey, *The Natural History and Antiquities of the County of Surrey* [1673–1692] (London: E. Curll, 1719), 2:191–92; *An Exclamation from Tunbridge and Epsom against the Newfound Wells at Islington* (London: J. How, 1684), 1; Gibson, *Camden's Britannia,* 165, 306, 477, 732–33, 844; *Journal of Schellinks,* 5 June, 11 June 1662, 87, 91; Luttrell, "Travells," 29 May–7 June 1680, 208–10; Miege, *New State of England,* 1:55, 222; Floyer, *Enquiry,* sig. A3v; Baskerville, "Journey to the North," 2:314; Gibson to Charlett, 4 August 1694, Bodleian, Ballard MSS 5, fol. 60v; London Newsletter, 24 August 1686, FSL, L.c. 1699; Misson, *Memoirs,* 161.

43. *Magalotti: Travels,* 11 May 1669, 219; Miege, *New State of England,* 1:35, 140, 178; Gibson, *Camden's Britannia,* 379; Peter Borsay, *The English Urban Renaissance: Culture and Society in the Provincial Town, 1660–1770* (Oxford: Clarendon Press, 1989), 182, 187–88; McInnes, "Emergence of a Leisure Town," 75.

44. Houghton, *England's Great Happiness,* 19; Jackson, ed., *Wiltshire,* 14; Edward Chamberlayne, *Angliae Notitiae; or, The Present State of England,* 15th ed. (London: John Playford, 1684), 1:19; M. W. Barley, "Rural Building in England," in *The Agrarian History of England and Wales,* vol. 5, 2 vols., ed. Joan Thirsk (Cambridge: Cambridge University Press, 1984), 2:591–98; Hatcher, *Before 1700,* 451–52; Baskerville, "Journeys," 2:272; W. G. Hoskins, "The Rebuilding of Rural England, 1570–1640," *Past and Present* 4 (November 1953): 44–59; R. Machin, "The Great Rebuilding: A Reassessment," *Past and Present* 77 (November 1977): 37; Shammas, *Pre-Industrial Consumer,* 163; Borsay, *English Urban Renaissance,* 42; Miege, *New State of England,* 2:31; Earle, *Making of the English Middle Class,* 292–93.

45. Evelyn, "Character of England," 1659, in *Writings of Evelyn,* 78–82; Sainte-Marie to Denz, 4 May, 8 May, 11 May, 14 May 1685, in Roth, ed., *Voyageur Francais,* 21, 46, 64, 76; Miege, *New State of England,* 1:283–85; Misson, *Memoirs,* 134–35, 148; *Magalotti: Travels,* 11 May 1669, 394–95; "A Particular of New Buildings within the Bills of Mortality," 11 March 1678, NA, SP 29/402, fol. 54.

46. Conyers, Northern Journey, 21 September 1676, 28; Baskerville, "Inland Towns," 2:289; Gibson, *Camden's Britannia,* 441; Thoresby, "Autobiography," 12; Hey, *Fiery Blades,* 85; *Woolley's History of Derbyshire,* 23; *Memoirs of Barnes,* 214; Baskerville, "Journeys," 2:267; Borsay, *English Urban Renaissance,* 55; Luttrell, "Travells," 1677, 22 July–22 August 1679, fols. Mr, 157, 167.

47. Borsay, *English Urban Renaissance,* 69; Evelyn, *Diary,* 31 July 1662, 3:328; Evelyn, *A Parallel of the Antient Architecture with the Modern* (London: Thomas Roycroft, 1664), sig. [b2r]; Miege, *New State of England,* 1:335; Aubrey, *Natural History of Surrey,* 4:149; Fleming, Lancashire, 1674, fol. 17r; Luttrell, "Travells," 3 July–21 September 1678, fol. 67; McInnes, "Emergence of a Leisure Town," 71; Conyers, Northern Journey, 1 September 1676, 8; Thoresby, *Diary,* 15 November 1682, 1:148–49; Luttrell, "Travells," 1677, fol. Iv.

48. Jonathan I. Israel, *Dutch Primacy in World Trade, 1585–1740* (Oxford: Clarendon Press, 1989), 357; Miege, *New State of England,* 1:336; Misson, *Memoirs,* 172; E. S. De Beer, "The Early History of London Street Lighting," *History* 25 (March 1941): 311–24; Malcolm Falkus, "Lighting in the Dark Ages of English Economic History," in *Trade, Government and Economy in Pre-Industrial England,* ed. D. C. Coleman and A. H. John (London: Weidenfeld and Nicolson, 1976), 248–73; *An Act of the Common Council for Lighting of Streets,* 25 October 1695 (London: Samuel Roycroft, 1695); Borsay, *English Urban Renaissance,* 72.

49. Gibson, *Camden's Britannia,* 728, 783; Thoresby, "Autobiography," 61; Luttrell, "Travells," 22 July–22 August 1679, 177; Slack, "Great and Good Towns," 2:367; Conyers, Northern Journey, 23 August 1676, 2; Sainte Marie to Deng, 8 May 1685, in Roth, ed., *Voyageur Francais,* 49–50; Miege, *New State of England,* 1:287; *Journal of Schellinks,* 20 August 1661, 58; Borsay, *English Urban Renaissance,* 162–72; McInnes, "Emergence of a Leisure Town," 67.

50. *Some Considerations about the Most Proper Way of Raising Money in the Present Conjuncture* [1693], 28–29; Gibson, *Camden's Britannia,* 425; Jackson, ed., *Wiltshire,* 8.

51. T. S. Willan, *River Navigation in England, 1600–1750* (Oxford: Oxford University Press, 1936), 133; Clay, *Economic Expansion,* 1:167–68, 181; Gibson, *Camden's Britannia,* 161; Court, *Rise of Midland Industries,* 10–11; Malcolm Wanklyn, "The Impact of Water Transport Facilities on the Economies of English River Ports, c. 1660–1760," *Economic History Review,* n.s., 49, no. 1 (1996): 25; Baskerville, "Inland Towns," 2:291; *Journal of Schellinks,* 11 July, 14 August 1662, 100–101, 120; Luttrell, "Travells," 16 March–18 April 1678, 11, 22; Miege, *New State of England,* 1:180; *Woolley's History of Derbyshire,* 57–58, 177; Conyers, Northern Journey, 1 September 1676, 8; *Memoirs of Barnes,* 92.

52. Sainte Marie to Deng, 2 May, 8 May 1685, in Roth, ed., *Voyageur Francais,* 18–19, 50; Miege, *New State of England,* 1:278; Misson, *Memoirs,* 21.

53. Luttrell, "Travells," 22 July–22 August 1679, 177–78; *Journal of Schellinks,* 20–21 July 1661, 11 October 1662, 20–21, 158; Thomas Baskerville, "Account of Some Remarkable Things in a Journey between London and Dover," HMC *Portland,* 2:276; T. S. Willan, *The English Coasting Trade, 1600–1750* (Manchester: Manchester University Press, 1938), 203–7; Wrightson, *Earthly Necessities,* 246.

54. Sir John Lowther of Whitehaven, Notebook, ca. 1680s, Cumbria SRO, Carlisle, D/Lons/W1/63, 1–2; Thomas Bradyll to Roger Kenyon, 27 October 1690, Lancashire SRO, DD/Ke/9/63/28; William Albert, *The Turnpike Road System in England, 1663–1840* (Cambridge: Cambridge University Press, 1972), 14–29; Dan Bogart, "Turnpike Trusts and the Transportation Revolution in Eighteenth-Century England," *Explorations in Economic History*, 42 (2005): 481–82.

55. J. A. Chartres, "Road Carrying in England in the Seventeenth Century: Myth and Reality," *Economic History Review*, 30, no. 1 (1977): 78–80; George Chalmers, *An Estimate of the Comparative Strength of Britain* (London: C. Ditty and J. Bowen, 1782), 146; Nehemiah Grew, "The Means of a Most Ample Increase of the Wealth and Strength of England," 1707–8, HEH, HM 1264, 13; Miege, *New State of England*, 1:188, 280, 2:46; Luttrell, "Travells," 1677, 16 March–18 April, 3 July–31 September 1678, 22 July–22 August 1679, fol. U, 31, 43, 79, 105, 111, 156, 166, 176; Evelyn, *Diary*, 19 April 1644, 2:135; Sainte Marie to Deng, 2 May, 4 May 1685, in Roth, ed., *Voyageur Francais*, 17, 23–24; Gibson, *Camden's Britannia*, 874; Machell, Westmoreland, 2:43; Sir John Lowther of Whitehaven, General Notebook, 1685–94, Cumbria SRO, Carlisle, D/Lons/W1/33, 5; N. H., *Compleat Tradesman*, 1755ff.; Baskerville, "Inland Towns," 2:291; Baskerville, "Journey to the North," 2:313.

56. *Reasons Humbly Offered to the Consideration of Parliament, for the Suppressing Such of the Stage-Coaches and Caravans* [1680s], 2–3, 11; H. N., *Compleat Tradesman*, 42; Jackson, ed., *Wiltshire*, 9; Miege, *New State of England*, 2:46–47; *City Mercury*, 4 July 1692; Clay, *Economic Expansion*, 1:182; Luttrell, "Travells," 1677, 16 March–18 April, 3 July–21 September 1678, 22 July–22 August 1679, 29 July–11 August, 18 August–25 September 1680, fol. cv, 12, 17, 48, 101, 108, 113, 117, 183, 230–31, 257, 268.

57. *Magalotti: Travels*, 11 May 1669, 401; Sir Richard Temple, Insertion in Hackney Coach Bill, 1667?, HEH, STT Parliamentary Box 3(6); Sainte Marie to Deng, 11 May, 14 May 1685, in Roth, ed., *Voyageur Francais*, 69, 72–73; *The Case of the Hackney-Coachmen* [1690s], 1; Misson, *Memoirs*, 39.

58. Post Office Accounts, 1638–39, NA, E 351/2757; Post Accounts of Stephen Lilly, 1685–1686, NA, E251/2758; Association of Officers Concerned in the Post Office, 1696, NA, C213/379. The gross financial intake of the Post Office remained fairly constant in the immediate aftermath of the Revolution: Receipts of Public Money, 5 November 1688–30 June 1690, 27 June 1690–27 June 1691, NA, T 48/87, fols. 244, 248–49; J. P., *The Merchant's Daily Companion* (London: Tho. Malthus, 1684), 388; Lords of the Treasury's Order for the Increase of Salaries in the Post Office, 5 April 1688, British Postal Museum and Archive, POST 1/1, fol. 51r; Frank Staff, *The Penny Post* (London: Lutterworth, 1964), 22–33; Howard Robinson, *Britain's Post Office* (Oxford: Oxford University Press, 1953), 10–28; Kenneth Ellis, *The Post Office in the Eighteenth Century* (Oxford: Oxford University Press, 1958), 1–7.

59. Roger Whitley (London) to Mr. Bull, 21 December 1672, 1 January 1673, British Postal Museum and Archive, POST 94/12, unfolioed; Whitley (London) to Mr. Cole, 27 May 1673, British Postal Museum and Archive, POST 94/12, unfolioed; Whitley (London) to Mr. Rowlands, 5 June 1674, British Postal Museum and Archive, POST 94/20, unfolioed; Whitley (London) to Mr. Rowes, 5 February 1676, British Postal Museum and Archive, POST 94/16, unfolioed; Whitley (London) to Mr. Lott, 30 March 1676, British Postal Museum and Archive, POST 94/16, unfolioed; Thomas Gardiner, Survey of the Post Office, 1677, British Postal Museum and Archive, Ref 1-10B, fols. 2–4, 9, 18r; Proposals for the Better Management of the Post Office, 1681 or 1682, Staffordshire SRO, D742/5/1/5; H. N., *Compleat Tradesman*, 41; Post Accounts of Stephen Lilly, 1686, NA, E 351/2578; Sir Willoughby Aston, Diary, 19–20 January 1690, Liverpool SRO, 920 MD 173.

60. William Myrcott, "An Account of Mr. Castleton," 1689, BL, Add. 61690, fol. 16r; Maurice Ashley, "John Wildman and the Post Office," in *For Veronica Wedgwood These*, ed. Richard Ollard and Pamela Tudor-Craig (London: Collins, 1986), 204–16.

61. Robert Murray to ?, 2 July 1680, printed in Staff, *Penny Post*, 157–58; William Dockwra, "Humble Memorial," 24 November 1682, Staffordshire SRO, D742/5/1/8; Post Accounts of Stephen Lilly, 1685–1686, NA, E 251/2758; Post Accounts of Stephen Lilly, 1687–1688, NA, E 351/2760; *The Practical Method of Conveyance of*

Letters (1682); William Dockwra, *The Case of William Dockwra, Merchant* [1690s], 2; Miege, *New State of England*, 1:336–37; John Evelyn, *Numismata: A Discourse of Medals, Antient and Modern* (London: Benjamin Tooke, 1697), 164; Misson, *Memoirs*, 22. Dockwra was an active Whig: he smuggled Dissenters out of the country and agitated against the Tory Royal African Company: ? to Sir John Gordon, 4 April 1684, Beinecke, OSB Shelves, Gordonstoun Papers, Box 1/Folder 14; *The Case of Edmund Harrison, William Dockwra, John Thrale and Thomas Jones of London, Merchants* [1690s], 1.

62. *An Advertisement from the Insurance-Office for Houses,* 16 September 1681, 1; *Observations on the Proposals of the City to Insure Houses in Case of Fire* (1681), 1; Journal of the Court of Common Council, 15 November 1681, Corporation of London SRO, Journal 49, fol. 267r (including William Ashurst, Robert Clayton, Patience Ward, John Shorter, and Thomas Player); John Houghton, *An Account of the Bank of Credit in the City of London* (London: John Gain, 1683?), 2; Nicholas Barbon, *A Letter to a Gentleman in the Country* [1684], 2; Miege, *New State of England*, 1:337–38; Reasons Humbly Offered by Mr. Craven Howard and Others, ca. 1695, HEH, EL 9904; John Strype, *A Survey of the Cities of London and Westminster* (London: A. Churchill et al., 1720), 1:239; Robert Evans, "The Early History of Fire Insurance," *Journal of Legal History* 8, no. 1 (1987): 89–90; Andrea Finkelstein, "Nicholas Barbon and the Quality of Infinity," *History of Political Economy* 32, no. 1 (2000): 95; H. A. L. Cockerell and Edwin Green, *The British Insurance Business* (Sheffield: Sheffield Academic Press, 1994), 26–28.

63. William Blundell, in *Crosby Records: A Cavalier's Notebook,* ed. Ellison T. Gibson (London: Longmans, Green, 1880), 127–28; Sir Edward Seymour, 27 October 1670, Grey, 1:271–72; Hoare's Bank Bonds, HB/8/B; Hoare's Bank Releases, HB/8/A; Hoare's Bank Money's Lent, HB/5/H/1; Hoare's Bank Letters to Customers, HB/8/8/T/1; Larry Neal and Stephen Quinn, "Networks of Information, Markets, and Institutions in the Rise of London as a Financial Centre, 1660–1720," *Financial History Review* 8, no. 1 (2001): 9; Coleman, *Economy of England,* 147; Earle, *Making of the English Middle Class,* 49; Stephen Quinn, "The Glorious Revolution's Effect on English Private Finance," *Journal of Economic History* 61, no. 3 (2001): 602; Stephen Quinn, "Goldsmith-Banking: Mutual Acceptance and Interbanking Clearing in Restoration London," *Explorations in Economic History* 34, no. 4 (1997): 411–13; Frank Melton, *Sir Robert Clayton and the Origins of English Deposit Banking, 1658–1685* (Cambridge: Cambridge University Press, 1986), 16–39, 207–27, 233–42. Melton has identified more than ninety goldsmith-bankers operating in London, 1670–1700.

64. Houghton, *England's Great Happiness,* 19; *The Trade of England Revived* (London: Dorman Newman, 1681), 28, 42; Miege, *New State of England,* 1:334; Grew, "Meanes of a Most Ample Increase," 158–59; Nancy Cox, *The Complete Tradesman: A Study of Retailing, 1550–1820* (Burlington: Ashgate, 2000), 17–28, 75; Nancy Cox and Karin Dannehl, *Perceptions of Retailing in Early Modern England* (Burlington: Ashgate, 2007), 13–14, 47; Nancy Cox, "'Beggary of the Nation': Moral, Economic and Political Attitudes to the Retail Sector in the Early Modern Period," in *A Nation of Shopkeepers,* ed. John Benson and Laura Ugloni (New York: I. B. Tauris, 2003), 26–51; Shammas, *Pre-Industrial Consumer,* 235, 258.

65. *Journal of Schellinks,* 19 July, 13 August, 17 August 1661, 11 July, 24 July, 8 September, 17 October 1662, 34, 44, 53–54, 101, 110, 135, 162; *Magalotti: Travels,* 19 May 1669, 296; Baskerville, "Journeys," 2:265; Baskerville, "Journey to the North," 2:308–9; Luttrell, "Travells," 80; Sainte Marie to Deng, 11 May 1685, in Roth, ed., *Voyageur Francais,* 64–65, 69; Robert Kirk, "Sermons, Occurrences . . . ," 1690, Edinburgh UL, La. III.545, fol. 159r; Miege, *New State of England,* 1:38, 299; Clay, *Economic Expansion,* 1:177–78.

66. *Coffee-Houses Vindicated* (London, 1675), 2–3; Evelyn, "Character of England," 82–83.

67. William Sachse, ed., *The Diurnal of Thomas Rugg, 1659–1661,* Camden Society, 3rd Ser., 91 (1961): 10; Robert Latham and William Matthews, eds., *The Diary of Samuel Pepys,* 11 vols. (London: Bell and Hyman, 1970–95) (hereafter cited as Pepys, *Diary*); Henry W. Robinson and Walter Adams, eds., *The Diary of Robert Hooke, 1672–1680* (London: Taylor and Francis, 1935); R. T. Gunther, ed., *Early Science in Oxford,* vol. 10: *The Life and Work of Robert Hooke* (Oxford: Clarendon Press, 1935); William Matthews, ed., *The Diary of Dudley Ryder, 1715–1716* (London: Methuen, 1939); [Antoine Muralt], *Letters Describing the Characters and*

Customs of the English and French Nations (London, 1726), 82; Edward Hatton, *A New View of London . . . ,* 2 vols. (London: R. Chiswell, A. and J. Churchill, T. Horne, J. Nicholson, and R. Knaplock, 1708), 1:30.

68. *Coffee-Houses Vindicated,* 3; Steve Pincus, "'Coffee Politicians Does Create': Coffeehouses and Restoration Political Culture," *Journal of Modern History* 67, no. 4 (1995): 813; M. G. Hobson, ed., *Oxford Council Acts, 1665–1709* (Oxford: Oxford University Press, 1939), 16 July 1677, 98; Thomas Newey (Oxford) to James Harrington, 30 May 1688, BL, Add. 36707, fol. 28v; Peter Millard, ed., *General Preface and Life of Dr. John North* (Toronto: University of Toronto Press, 1984), 115; Baskerville, "Inland Towns," 2:295; Robert Newton, *Eighteenth Century Exeter* (Exeter: University of Exeter, 1984), 24; W. G. Hoskins, *Industry, Trade and People in Exeter, 1688–1800* (Exeter: University of Exeter, 1968), 24; Sir Richard Temple, Ledgerbook, 20 April 1687, HEH, ST 152, fol. 199v; Blake Tyson, ed., *The Estate and Household Accounts of Sir Daniel Fleming* (Kendal: Cumberland and Westmorland Antiquarian and Archaeological Society, 2001), 14 May 1698, 297 (hereafter cited as Fleming, *Accounts*); Hey, *Fiery Blades,* 154; Sir Henry Brabant (Newcastle) to Earl of Sunderland, 14 November 1685, NA, SP 31/1, fol. 141; Luttrell, "Travells," 3 July–21 September 1678, 49; Richard Bower (Yarmouth) to Joseph Williamson, 21 October 1667, NA, SP 29/220, fol. 93; Fleming, *Accounts,* 21 April 1690, 107 (Penrith); Diary of Lawrence Rawstorne, 6, 9, 10, 12, 13, 23 May 1687, Lancashire SRO, Rawstorne Diary, 36ff. (Preston); Aston, Diary, 11 April 1681 (Chester); John Rastrick, Life, HEH, HM 6131, fol. 53v (Stamford); William Le Hardy, ed., *County of Buckingham, Calendar of Session Records,* vol. 1 (Aylesbury: Guy R. Crouch, 1933), 7 October 1680, 61 (Buckingham); J. Cooper (Newark) to Williamson, 27 July 1667, NA, SP 29/211, fol. 28 (Nottingham); Brian Cowan, *The Social Life of Coffee: The Emergence of the British Coffeehouse* (New Haven and London: Yale University Press, 2005), 175 (York); The Declaration of the Gentlemen, Merchants . . . of Boston, 18 April 1689, NA, CO 5/1905, fol. 52v.

69. Guy Miege, *New State of England,* 2:42; James Van Horn Melton, *The Rise of the Public in Enlightenment Europe* (Cambridge: Cambridge University Press, 2001), 240; Brian Cowan, *Social Life of Coffee,* 30, 94, 177.

70. Jean Leclant, "Coffee and Cafés in Paris, 1644–1693," in *Food and Drink in History,* ed. Robert Forster and Orest Ranum (Baltimore: Johns Hopkins University Press, 1979), 89–92; Peter Albrecht, "Coffee-Drinking as a Symbol of Social Change in Continental Europe in the Seventeenth and Eighteenth Centuries," in *Studies in Eighteenth-Century Culture,* ed. John W. Yolton and Leslie Ellen Brown (East Lansing, MI: Colleagues, 1988), 94; [Muralt], *Letters,* 82–83; Ned Ward, *The London Spy: The Vanities and Vices of the Town Exposed to View,* ed. Arthur C. Hayward (New York, n.d.), 10; *Knavery in All Trades* (London, 1664), sig. D3r; Miege, *New State of England,* 2:42; Saint Marie to Deng, 1/11 May 1685, in Roth, ed., *Voyageur Francais,* 70; Dena Goodman, *The Republic of Letters: A Cultural History of the French Enlightenment* (Ithaca, NY: Cornell University Press, 1994), 122.

71. Henry Peacham, *The Worth of a Penny* (London: Samuel Keble, 1687), 15; *Coffee-Houses Vindicated,* 3; Charles W. Dawes, ed., *Samuel Butler, 1612–1680: Characters* (Cleveland, OH: Case Western Reserve University Press, 1970), 256–57; *The Character of a Coffee-House* (London: Jonathan Edwin, 1673), 3; *The Women's Petition* (London, 1674), 4; *A Description of the Academy* (London, 1673), 9; Sainte Marie to Deng, 1/11 May 1685, in Roth, ed., *Voyageur Francais,* 70; [Muralt], *Letters,* 2–4, 10, 82.

72. Ralph S. Hattox, *Coffee and Coffeehouses* (Seattle: University of Washington Press, 1985), esp. 81, 94; John Houghton, "A Discourse of Coffee," *Philosophical Transactions,* 1699, 312; Cowan, *Social Life of Coffee,* 98; Anthony Wood, Diary, 1663, Bodleian, MSS Wood's Diaries, 7, fol. 4r; George Davenport to William Sancroft, 4 December 1666, Bodleian, Tanner 45, 125r; Leclant, "Coffee and Cafés," 89.

73. Sir Benjamin Bathurst to Col. Hender Molesworth, 22 May 1686, BL, Loan 57/83, unfolioed; Moscovy Company Court Minutes, 15 November 1686, Guildhall Library, 11741/2, 77; Houghton, *A Collection for Improvement of Husbandry and Trade,* 6 April 1692; Henri Misson, *Memoires et Observations faites par un voyageur en Angleterre* (The Hague: Henri van Bulderen, 1698), 62; Yarranton, *England's Improvement,* 20; *Corporation Credit* (London: John Gain, 1682), 6; *The Factious Citizen; or, The Melancholy Visioner* (London: Thomas Maddocks, 1685), 10; *The Art of Getting Money* (London, 1691), 1; "An Essay on the Interest of the

Crown in American Plantations," 1685, BL, Add. 47131, fol. 25r; *Coffee-Houses Vindicated*, 3–4; Misson, *Memoirs*, 39–40. I disagree with Brian Cowan's emphasis on the "disproportionate influence of the virtuosi, a small subculture within England's social elite" in defining the nature of England's coffeehouse culture. I dissent from his assertion that the emergence of coffeehouse culture needs to be sharply distinguished from any story "of the making of the modern world." Cowan, *Social Life of Coffee*, 3, 261.

74. *The Character of a Coffee-House* (London, 1673), 2–3; Thomas Sydserf, *Tarugo's Wiles* (London, 1668), 24; *Magalotti: Travels, 1668*, 124; Misson, *Memoirs*, 203–4; [Muralt], *Letters*, 82; Thomas Jordan, *The Triumphs of London* (London: John Playford, 1675), 23; *A Letter to a Friend about the Late Proclamation* (London, 1679), 2.

75. Thomas Sheridan, *A Learned Discourse on Various Subjects* (London: H. Sawbridge, 1685), 10; Sainte Marie to Deng, 1/11 May 1685, in Roth, ed., *Voyageur Francais*, 70; Misson, *Memoirs*, 102; Henry Savile (Whitehall) to Weymouth, 25 November 1686, Longleat House, Thynne MSS 35, fol. 63; James Brydges, Journal, 2 April 1697, HEH, ST 26/1.

76. *The Transproser Rehears'd* (London, 1673), 35–36; Roger North, *Examen* (London, 1740), 140; Notes by Joseph Williamson, 18 February 1676, CSPD, 17, 563; *A Pacquet of Advice and Animadversions* (London, 1676), 6–7, 46; *Mr. Tho. Dangerfields Particular Narrative of the Late Popish Design to Charge Those of the Presbyterian Party with a Pretended Conspiracy against His Majesties Person and Government* (London, 1679), 16–17; Sir William Batten (Harwich) to Samuel Pepys, 14 May 1665, NA, SP 29/112, fol. 49; Tim Harris, *London Crowds in the Age of Charles II: Propaganda and Politics from the Restoration until the Exclusion Crisis* (Cambridge: Cambridge University Press, 1987), 170; Information to Secretary of State Bennet, 9 March 1665, NA, SP 29/114, fol. 90.

77. Pepys, *Diary*, 3 February 1664, 37; F. N. L. Poynter, ed., *The Journal of James Yonge, 1647–1721, Plymouth Surgeon* (1678; Hamden, CT: Archon, 1963), 156–57; Ward, *London Spy*, 172; Thomas Duffet, *The Amorous Old-Woman* (London, 1674), sig. A4r; Thomas Otway, *Alcibiades* (London, 1675), sig. A3r; Henry Oldenburg to Robert Boyle, 6 October 1664, in Henry Oldenburg, *Correspondence*, vol. 2, ed. A. Rupert Hall and Marie Boas Hall (Madison: University of Wisconsin Press, 1965), 249; William Tong, *Some Memoirs of the Life and Death of the Reverend Mr. John Shower* (London: John Clark and Eben. Scadgel, 1716), 16; Aphra Behn, *The Emperor of the Moon* (London, 1687), sig. A3r; Brydges, Journal, 21 August, 24 September 1697; Houghton, "A Description of Coffee," *Philosophical Transactions* (1699): 312.

78. Leclant, "Coffee and Cafés," 91; Larry Neal, *The Rise of Financial Capitalism: International Capital Markets in the Age of Reason* (Cambridge: Cambridge University Press, 1990), 21–22; John J. McCusker and Cora Gravesteijn, *The Beginning of Commercial and Financial Journalism* (Amsterdam: NEHA, 1991), 291. There had been such a price list in Lyons that ceased publication in 1679. Alberti to doge and Senate, 12 January 1674, CSPV, 38, 195; Martin Lister, *A Journey to Paris in the Year 1698*, 2nd ed. (London, 1699), 22, 165; *Tatler*, 22 October 1709, 35–36; *Tatler*, 30 May 1710, 472. Dutch coffeehouse culture was far closer to the English than the French: William Montague, *The Delights of Holland* (London, 1696), 164, 183–84, 192, 200.

79. Coleman, *Economy of England*, 92, 135, 200–201; Douglass C. North and Robert Paul Thomas, *The Rise of the Western World: A New Economic History* (Cambridge: Cambridge University Press, 1973), 109, 113, 118; Jan de Vries, *The Economy of Europe in an Age of Crisis* (Cambridge: Cambridge University Press, 1976), 17, 244–54; E. A. Wrigley, *Poverty, Progress and Population* (Cambridge: Cambridge University Press, 2004), 44–67; Clay, *Economic Expansion*, 1:3. From the 1630s England's population remained steady at around 5 million. François Crouzet, *A History of the European Economy, 1000–2000* (Charlottesville: University Press of Virginia, 2001), 74; Alberti to doge and Senate, 29 March 1675, 23 November 1674, CSPV, 380, 313–14; John Houghton, *A Collection of Letters for the Improvement of Husbandry and Trade*, 27 April 1682, 49; Houghton, *England's Great Happiness*, 20; Abstract of a Representation of the General State of Trade, 23 December 1697, HEH, EL 9874, 1; Report of the Board of Trade, 23 December 1697, BL, Add. 2902, fol. 171v; W. E. Minchinton has claimed that "the Restoration was the economic exit from medievalism and the period

1660–1688 a period of commercial expansion": Minchinton, ed., *The Growth of Overseas Trade in the Seventeenth and Eighteenth Centuries* (London: Methuen, 1969), 11.

80. This insularity is not a uniquely British phenomenon: Paul Burton Cheney, "The History and Science of Commerce in the Century of Enlightenment" (PhD diss., Columbia University, 2002), 18–19; Price, *Overseas Trade,* 267; J. A. Chartres, *Internal Trade in England, 1500–1700* (London: Macmillan, 1977), 10–11, 65; Wrightson, *Earthly Necessities,* 181.

81. Daron Acemoglu, Simon Johnson, and James Robinson, "The Rise of Europe: Atlantic Trade, Institutional Change, and Economic Growth," *American Economic Review* 95, no. 3 (2005): 546–49; de Vries, *Economy of Europe in an Age of Crisis,* 154; Crouzet, *History of European Economy,* 91; de Vries and van der Woude, *First Modern Economy,* 172; Lionel Rothkrug, *Opposition to Louis XIV: The Political and Social Origins of the French Enlightenment* (Princeton, NJ: Princeton University Press, 1965), 264.

82. Coleman, *Economy of England,* 92, 134, 140–41, 146–47; Nuala Zahedieh, "Overseas Expansion and Trade in the Seventeenth Century," in *The Oxford History of the British Empire,* vol. 1, ed. Nicholas Canny (Oxford: Oxford University Press, 1998), 399, 407; Ralph Davis, "English Foreign Trade, 1660–1700," in *Growth of Overseas Trade,* ed. Minchinton, 78, 94; Court, *Rise of Midland Industries,* 76.

83. J. P., *Merchant's Daily Companion,* sig. A4, 363; King, "Naval Trade of England," 63. Commentators then and now feel that King significantly underestimated the amount of foreign trade in the late seventeenth century: H. J., *A Letter from a Gentleman in the Country to His Friend in the City* (London: G. C. for William Miller, 1691), 11; Davis, "English Foreign Trade," 85; *State of Barbados,* 1, 3; William Blathwayt, "Reflections on a Paper," 1685, HEH, BL 416; Richard Blome, *The Present State of His Majesty's Isles and Territories in America* (London: H. Clash, 1687), sig. [A3]; Southwell to Nottingham, 23 March 1689, HEH, BL 418; *Certain Considerations Relating to the Royal African Company* (1680), 1; *Reasons Humbly Offered by the Persons Concerned to the Plantations* [1690s], [1]; *A Rambling Letter to a Friend* [1690], 1; Brethren of Trinity House to James II, 28 July 1688, NMM, SOU/8, fols. 120–21; Report of the Board of Trade, 23 December 1697, BL, Sloane 2402, fols. 173–74.

84. Davis, "English Foreign Trade," 80; Miege, *New State of England,* 2:38; Misson, *Memoirs,* 311; Sir George Downing, 12 November 1670, Grey, 1:286; John Jones, 12 November 1670, Grey, 1:286; *Journal of Schellinks,* 17 August 1662, 121; Luttrell, "Travells," 1677, fol. Xv; Thomas Baskerville, "Morage to Winchcombe," HMC *Portland,* 2:303; Shammas, *Pre-Industrial Consumer,* 78: this was enough for one half of the population to smoke one pipe of tobacco per day.

85. Miege, *New State of England,* 2:37; S. D. Smith, "Accounting for Taste: British Coffee Consumption in Historical Perspective," *Journal of Interdisciplinary History* 27, no. 2 (1996): 190; EIC to General and Council in Bombay, 6 December 1686, IOL, E/3/91, fol. 115v; Robert Balle (Livorno) to Thomas Goodwyn, 10 March 1688, NA, FO 335/7, fol. 3; EIC to general and council of Bombay, 27 August 1688, IOL, E/3/91, fol. 275v. My calculation for coffee consumption is based on numbers gleaned from Smith's article: coffee consumption was about a tenth of a pound per head; one ounce of coffee was mixed with one quart of water. I estimate four cups of coffee per quart.

86. Thomas Tryon, *Tryon's Letters upon Several Occasions* (London: Geo. Conyers, 1700), 219–21; Zahedieh, "Overseas Expansion and Trade," 410; Davis, "English Foreign Trade," 81; Russell R. Menard, *Sweet Negotiations: Sugar, Slavery, and Plantation Agriculture in Early Barbados* (Charlottesville: University of Virginia Press, 2006), 67–68; A Short Account of His Majesty's Plantations in America, 1695, BL, Add. 72572; Shammas, *Pre-Industrial Consumer,* 81–82.

87. Downing, 12 November 1670, Grey, 1:285; Sir Richard Ford, 14 March 1670, Grey, 1:231; Hugh Boscawen, 12 November 1670, Grey, 1:285; Zahedieh, "Overseas Expansion and Trade," 416; Hey, *Fiery Blades,* 172; Luttrell, "Travells," 22 July–22 August 1679, 145; *State of Barbados,* [2]; Davis, "English Foreign Trade," 85; Coleman, *Economy of England,* 138; Clay, *Economic Expansion,* 2:21.

88. Zahedieh, "Overseas Expansion and Trade," 407; Price, *Overseas Trade,* 122; Acemoglu, Johnson, and Robinson, "Rise of the West," 550; Sir John Lowther, Notebook, 1680s and 1690s, Cumbria RO, Carlisle,

D/Lons/W1/63, 9; [Thomas Tomkins], *The Modern Pleas for Comprehension, Toleration . . .* (London: R. Royston, 1675), 197.

89. Fleming, Lancashire, 1674, fol. 3r; Misson, *Memoirs,* 313; Miege, *New State of England,* 2:35; J. A. Chartres, "Marketing of Agricultural Produce," in *Agrarian History of England and Wales,* ed. Thirsk, 2:407; Shammas, *Pre-Industrial Consumer,* 259; Hey, *Fiery Blades,* 156; Hatcher, *Before 1700,* 453; Lorna Weatherill, *Consumer Behavior and Material Culture in Britain, 1660–1760,* 2nd ed. (London: Routledge, 1996), 32.

90. Price, *Overseas Trade,* 123; Zahedieh, "Overseas Expansion and Trade," 418–20.

91. Crouzet, *History of the European Economy,* 86; de Vries, *Economy of Europe in an Age of Crisis,* 122–23; Eli Heckscher, *Mercantilism,* trans. Mendel Shapiro (London: George Allen and Unwin, 1955), 81ff.; Sir Thomas Littleton, 27 February 1668, Grey, 1:95; House of Lords Committee Book, 30 October 1669, HLRO, Main Papers, 2, fol. 287r; Alberti to doge and Senate, 23 February, 23 November 1674, CSPV, 221–22, 314; *Trade of England Revived,* 15; J. P., *Merchant's Daily Companion,* sig. A3v; William Carter, *The Reply of W. C.* (London, 1685), 3–4; Bevil Skelton (Paris) to Sunderland, 25 January/4 February, 18/28 January 1688, NA, SP 78/151, fols. 138v, 134; J. Hill (Paris) to Sir William Trumbull, 19 November 1687, Berkshire SRO, D/ED/C33; James Johnston (London) to ?, 6/16 February 1688, BL, Add. 34515, fol. 47r; Henry Ashurst (London) to Conrad Calkbarner, 25 October 1687, Bodleian, Don.c.169, fol. 60r.

92. Israel, *Dutch Primacy in World Trade,* 358; de Vries and van der Woude, *First Modern Economy,* 341–44, 458–62. De Vries and van der Woude point out that the united VOC did export some Dutch manufactured goods, but the proportion was small. The Dutch failed to establish a robust Atlantic economy to consume Dutch manufactured goods. In the 1680s Sir Richard Temple hinted that this was what proved the value of the colonies: "An Essay upon Government," Bodleian, Eng.Hist.c.201, fol. 12r; Coleman, *Economy of England,* 197–98.

93. P. W. Hasler, ed., *House of Commons, 1558–1603,* vol. 1 (London: History of Parliament Trust, 1981), 8, 40, 56; D. Brunton and D. H. Pennington, eds., *Members of the Long Parliament* (Cambridge, MA: Harvard University Press, 1954), 54; Gauci, *Politics of Trade,* 199. Gauci in fact reveals a small drop in the percentage of trading MPs in the years 1660–90, with a sharp rise after the Glorious Revolution. W. E. Buckley, ed., *Memoirs of Thomas, Earl of Ailesbury,* 2 vols. (Westminster: Nichols and Sons, 1890), 1:98 (hereafter cited as Ailesbury, *Memoirs*); Benjamin Bathurst (London) to Col. Hender Molesworth, 2 November 1685, BL, Loan 57/83 unfolioed; Houghton, *England's Great Happiness,* 11; Pepys, *Diary,* 1 January 1668, 9:1.

94. Houghton, *Collection of Letters,* 8 September 1681, 21; Gibson, *Camden's Britannia,* 335, 813; Alberti to Inquisitors of State, 6 January 1673, CSPV, 2; Lowther of Whitehaven, Notebook, 1680s and 1690s, 11; Memoirs of the Flemings, ca. 1690, Cumbria SRO, Kendal, WD/Ry/Box 25; *Magalotti: Travels,* 22 May 1669, 312; Alberti to doge and Senate, 15 June 1674, CSPV, 264; "A Short Character of King Charles the Second," 1680s, HEH, EL 8773a; Bonrepaus (London) to Seignelay, 28 December/7 January, 31 December/10 January 1685/86, NA, PRO 31/3/163, fols. 27–30, 47r; Ailesbury, *Memoirs,* 1:103; Albert to doge and Senate, 30 November, 23 November, 21 December 1674, CSPV, 317, 313, 324; Newsletter, 17 January 1685, Longleat House, Thynne MSS 12, fol. 51; Owen Wynne (Whitehall) to Edmund Poley, 14 October 1687, Beinecke, OSB MSS 1, Box 2/Folder 68; James Vernon (London) to Albeville, 30 March 1688, Indiana, Albeville MSS.

95. Evelyn, *Diary,* 12 February, 1 September 1672, 3:602–3, 624; Lowther of Whitehaven, Notebook, 1680s and 1690s, 9; Evelyn, *Diary,* 22 June 1664, 3:374; Ralph Thoresby, "Autobiography," 44; Fleming, Lancashire, 1674, fol. 2r; Miege, *New State of England,* 2:230; Sir Francis Brewster, *Essays on Trade and Navigation* (London: Tho. Cockeril, 1695), 76; Cary, *Essay on the State of England,* sig. [A6r]; Alberti to doge and Senate, 2 February 1674, CSPV, 206.

96. *Memoirs of Barnes,* 48–49; Sainte Marie to Deng, 11 May 1685, in Roth, ed., *Voyageur Francais,* 71; Miege, *New State of England,* 2:231; Richard Wolley, *The Present State of France* (London: Gilbert Cownty, 1687), 314; Andrew Yarranton, *England's Improvement by Sea and Land: The Second Part* (London, 1681), 3; Evelyn, *State of France,* 77; *Popery and Tyranny; or, The Present State of France* (London: M. P. for Randall Taylor, 1689), 14.

97. Houghton, *England's Great Happiness,* 19; Miege, *New State of England,* 2:229; Jackson, ed., *Wiltshire,* 9; Dr. Charles Aldworth, Commonplace Book, Essex SRO, D/Dby Z56; Sir Edward Hales, Treatise on Government, 1692, AWA, Old Brotherhood Papers, Book 3/258; Sir Henry Capel, 2 December 1689, Grey, 9:469; *Memoirs of Barnes,* 213; "Essay on the Interest of the Crown," fols. 24–25.

98. J. P., *Merchant's Daily Companion,* sig. A4v; H. N., *Compleat Tradesman,* 2; Carew Reynell, *A Necessary Companion; or, The English Interest Discovered and Promoted* (London: William Budden, 1685), sig. A7r; Sir John Cotton, "Concerning the Adding Sicily to the Address," 1670s, FSL, V.a. 343, fol. 17r; Slingsby Bethel, *An Account of the French Usurpation upon the Trade of England* (London, 1679), 4; Charles Molloy, *De Jure Maritimo et Navali,* 4th ed. (London: John Bellinger and John Walthoe, 1688), sig. [a8v].

99. Miege, *New State of England,* 2:12.

CHAPTER 4. *English Politics at the Accession of James II*

1. Evelyn, *Diary,* 6 February 1685, 4:407; Duke of Newcastle (Wellbeck) to Sir John Reresby, 17 February 1685, WYAS, MX 31/27; Colley Cibber, *An Apology for the Life of Colley Cibber,* ed. Robert Lowe (New York: AMS, 1966), 29–30; John Evelyn (Sayes Court) to Lord Godolphin, 11 February 1685, BL, JE A2, 2:fol. 29r (since recataloged); Henry Hunter (London) to Harry Wrotesley, 9 February 1685, Berkshire SRO, D/EHr/B2; John Curtois, *A Discourse* (London: Jo. Hindmarsh, 1685), 15–16.

2. Earl of Burlington (London) to Henry, Lord Fairfax, 2 February 1685, HRC, Pforzheimer 1m.

3. W. A. Speck, *Reluctant Revolutionaries: Englishmen and the Revolution of 1688* (Oxford: Oxford University Press, 1988), 233, 235; Jonathan Scott, "England's Troubles," in *The Politics of Religion in Restoration England,* ed. Tim Harris, Mark Goldie, and Paul Seaward (Oxford: Basil Blackwell, 1990), 110; J. C. D. Clark, *The Language of Liberty, 1660–1832: Political Discourse and Social Dynamics in the Anglo-American World* (Cambridge: Cambridge University Press, 1994), 238.

4. Melinda S. Zook, *Radical Whigs and Conspiratorial Politics in Late Stuart England* (University Park: Pennsylvania State University Press, 1999), xii–xiii, xvii, xx; Richard L. Greaves, *Secrets of the Kingdom: British Radicals from the Popish Plot to the Revolution of 1688–1689* (Stanford, CA: Stanford University Press, 1992), 1, 332.

5. Zook, *Radical Whigs and Conspiratorial Politics,* xiii–xiv; Greaves, *Secrets of the Kingdom,* 290, 340.

6. Thomas Babington Macaulay, *The History of England from the Accession of James II,* 5 vols. (New York: Harper and Brothers, 1849–61), 1:436.

7. Thomas Cartwright, *A Sermon Preached upon the Anniversary Solemnity of the Happy Inauguration of Our Dread Sovereign Lord King James II,* 6 February 1686, 2nd ed. (London: Walter Davis, 1686), 15; John Towill Rutt, ed., *An Historical Account of My Own Life by Edmund Calamy, 1671–1731,* 2 vols. (London: H. Colburn and R. Bentlley, 1829), 1:116; Burlington (London) to Reresby, 14 February 1685, WYAS, MX 31/30; Sir Robert Southwell (London) to Duke of Ormonde, 21 February 1685, Beinecke, OSB MSS 41/Box 3. See also Clarendon (Whitehall) to Abingdon, 10 February 1685, Bodleian, Clarendon MSS 128, fol. 11v; George Halley, *A Sermon Preached in the Cathedral and Metropolitan Church of St. Peter in York,* 14 February 1689 (London: R. C., 1689), 14; *Dilucidator,* no. 4, February 1689, 87; *Mercurius Reformatus,* 31 July 1689, [1]; and *Quadriennium Jacobi* (London: James Knapton, 1689), 7.

8. Hunter (London) to Wrotesley, 9 February 1685, Berkshire SRO, D/EHr/B2; Phillip Madoxe (Whitehall) to Southwell, Bodleian, Eng.Lett.c.53, fol. 205r; *London Gazette,* 16 February 1685; Sir John Reresby, 10 February 1685, in *Memoirs of Sir John Reresby,* 2nd ed., ed. Andrew Browning (London: Royal Historical Society, 1991), 352 (hereafter cited as Reresby, *Memoirs*); Southwell (Kingsweston) to Ormonde, 9 February 1685, Victoria and Albert Museum, Forster and Dyce Collection, F.47.A.40, 2:fol. 112r; William Aubone (mayor of Newcastle-upon-Tyne) to Sunderland, 13 February 1685, NA, SP 31/1, fol. 11; *London Gazette,* 19 February (Durham, Lyme Regis, Colchester), 2 March 1685; James Howard (sheriff of Northumberland) to Sunderland, 19 February 1685, NA, SP 31/1, fol. 27; *London Gazette,* 16 February 1685 (Winchester, Reading,

Boston, Portsmouth, Plymouth, Stamford); Sir Henry Beaumont (Leicester) to Earl of Huntingdon, 14 February 1685, HEH, HA 656; Benjamin Canfield, *A Sermon,* Leicester, 10 February 1685 (London: Charles Brome, 1685), sig. A3r. See also Strafford to Halifax, 18 February 1685, BL, Althorp C3 (Rotherham); Ezekiel Everest (Harwich) to Lord Middleton, 10 February 1685, BL, Add. 41803, fol. 152r; Earl of Gainsborough (Southampton) to Middleton, 10 February 1685, BL, Add. 41803, fol. 154r; and James Cross (Southampton) to Owen Wynne, 9 February 1685, BL, Add. 41803, fol. 138r.

9. Anthony Wood, 11 February 1685, in *The Life and Times of Anthony Wood,* 3 vols., ed. Andrew Clark (Oxford: Clarendon Press, 1894), 3:129–30; *London Gazette,* 16 February, 19 February 1685; *Supplex Recognitio et Gratulatia Solennis Universitatis Oxoniensis,* 21 February 1685 (Oxford: Sheldonian Theatre, 1685), sigs. A (Bertie), F (Wright), H1 (Wase); *Moestissimae ac Laetissimae Academiae Cantibrigiensis Affectus* (Cambridge: Joan. Hayes, 1685), sigs. T4r (Prior), Gg4 (Stepney), Bb3r–Cc1v (Montague).

10. John Whiting, *Persecution Exposed,* 2nd ed. (London: James Phillips, 1791), 267; Thoresby, *Diary,* February 1685, 1:180; Rutt, ed., *Life of Calamy,* 1:117; William Stout, 1685, in *The Autobiography of William Stout of Lancaster, 1665–1752,* ed. J. D. Marshall (Manchester: Chetham Society, 1967), 82; John Peobbles (London) to Reresby, 19 February 1685, WYAS, MX 30/2; Evelyn, *Diary,* 5 March 1685, 4:419; Sir John Lowther, *Memoirs of the Reign of James II* (London: H. G. Bohn, 1857), 450. See also Thomas Penn (mayor of Bridgewater) to Sunderland, ?10 February 1685, NA, SP 31/1, fol. 49; Thomas Ludlam (mayor of Leicester) to Huntingdon, 18 February 1685, HEH, HA 8410; and Wood, 4 March 1685, in *Life and Times,* ed. Clark, 3:134.

11. Evelyn, *Diary,* 6 February 1685, 4:407–9; *London Gazette,* 9 February 1685.

12. James Fraser (Whitehall) to Southwell, 7 February 1685, BL, Add. 46961, fols. 216–17; Burlington (London) to Reresby, 10 February 1685, WYAS, MX 31/26; Robert Grave, *Seasonable Advice to the Citizens, Burgesses, and Free-Holders of England* (London: Walter Kettilby, 1685), 2. See the similar recollection in James Ellesby (vicar of Chiswick, Middlesex), *The Doctrine of Passive Obedience* (London: William Crooke, 1685), sig. A2v; Christopher Jeaffreson (London) to Capt. James Phipps, 19 February 1685, in Jeaffreson, 170; Isaac Tyrwhitt (London) to Sir Richard Temple, 10 February 1685, HEH, STT 2436.

13. Sir Henry Coker (Warminster) to Sunderland, 11 February 1685, NA, SP 31/1, fol. 9; Sir Andrew Hacket (Moxhul near Colsil) to Sunderland, 3 March 1685, NA, SP 31/1, fol. 53; Henry Watkinson (York) to Sir William Trumbull, 11 February 1685, BL, Trumbull Misc. 23, unfolioed (since recataloged); Reresby (York) to ?, February 1685, WYAS, MX 35/23; Reresby, *Memoirs,* 10 February 1685, 353; John Baber, *A Poem upon the Coronation* (London, 1685), 2–3. For similar poetic sentiments, see *A Loyal New-Years Gift* (London: George Croom, 1685); and *Suspiria, or Sighs on the Death of the Late Most Illustrious Monarch Charles the II King* (London: L. C., 1685).

14. February/March 1685, in P. Braybrooke, ed., *The Autobiography of Sir John Bramston,* Camden Society, 32 (1845): 166 (hereafter cited as Bramston, *Autobiography*); Richard Thompson, *A Sermon Preached in the Cathedral Church of Bristol,* 21 June 1685 (London: Luke Meredith, 1685), 24; *London Gazette,* 2 March 1685. The county of Northampton and the towns of Ipswich and Newark-upon-Trent were the only other addresses I found that could be read as defending absolutism. See *London Gazette,* 16 February (Ipswich), 9 March (Newark), 16 March 1685. The most complete run of addresses is to be found in the official newspaper.

15. *London Gazette,* 16 February, 16 March 1685.

16. *London Gazette,* 16 February (Canterbury), 26 February (Warwick, Chichester), 9 March (Hereford, Westbury), 12 March (Brackley), 16 March (Portsmouth), 30 March 1685 (Nottingham). These examples are but a tiny fraction of the addresses from boroughs and corporations.

17. *London Gazette,* 19 March (Devon, Essex, Hertfordshire), 26 March (Sussex), 6 April 1685 (Berkshire).

18. *London Gazette,* 19 March (Carmarthen), 30 March 1685 (Anglesey, Carnarvon).

19. William Turner (London) to Reresby, 12 February 1685, WYAS, MX 29/14; J. Adderly to high constable, 12 February 1685, BL, Add. 71691, fol. 52v. This is forwarding the instructions sent from Whitehall.

20. Richard Lewis (Edington) to Sunderland, 21 February 1685, NA, SP 31/1, fol. 33; John Evelyn (Sayes Court) to George Evelyn, 23 February 1685, BL, Evelyn Papers, JE A2, fol. 29v (since recataloged).

21. Plymouth (Hull) to Sunderland, 18 February 1685, NA, SP 31/1, fol. 20; Newcastle (Welbeck) to Sunderland, 19 February 1685, NA, SP 31/1, fol. 23; Winchilsea (Eastwell) to Sunderland, 19 February 1685, NA, SP 31/1, fol. 26; Derby to Sunderland, 20 February 1685, NA, SP 31/1, fol. 28; Lewis (Edington) to Sunderland, 21 February 1685, NA, SP 31/1, fol. 33; John Evelyn (Sayes Court) to George Evelyn, 23 February 1685, BL, Evelyn Papers, JE A2, fol. 29v (since recataloged); Winchester (Castle Bolton) to Sunderland, 24 February 1685, NA, SP 31/1, fol. 41; John Lake (bishop of Chichester) to William Sancroft, 30 March 1685, Bodleian, Tanner 31, fol. 4r.

22. ? to Sir Richard Bulstrode, 10 April 1685, HRC, Pforzheimer (since recataloged); George Jeffreys (Bulstrode) to Sunderland, 5 April 1685, NA, SP 31/1, fol. 82; Everest (Harwich) to Sunderland, 26 March 1685, NA, SP 31/1, fol. 73; Robert Tazer (Chichester) to Sunderland, 17 February 1685, NA, SP 31/1, fol. 19; Thomas Penn (Bridgwater) to Sunderland, 10 February 1685, NA, SP 31/1, fol. 49; Penn to Sunderland, 28 February 1685, NA, SP 31/1, fol. 44.

23. Sir Charles Holt to Sunderland, 21 February 1685, NA, SP 31/1, fol. 30; Sir Edward Abney (Wellesley) to Huntingdon, 21 March 1685, HEH, HA 4; Gervase Jacques (Ashby-de la-Zouche) to Huntingdon, 21 March 1685, HEH, HA 7743; Dr. John Guy (Swepston) to Huntingdon, 20 March 1685, HEH, HA 3975; Sir Richard Newdigate (Arbury) to Sunderland, 21 February 1685, NA, SP 31/1, fol. 31.

24. W. E. Buckley, ed., *Memoirs of Thomas, Earl of Ailesbury,* 2 vols. (Westminster: Nichols and Sons, 1890), 1:100 (hereafter cited as Ailesbury, *Memoirs*); Sir William Boothby to George Vernon, 21 February 1685, BL, Add. 71691, fol. 57v; Elizabeth Adams (Baddon) to Sir Ralph Verney, 4 March 1685, Buckinghamshire SRO, Verney MSS; John Mellington (Derby) to Halifax, 16 March, 23 March 1685, BL, Althorp C2. A similar event took place at Newcastle-under-Lime in Staffordshire: Wood, 1 April 1685, in *Life and Times,* ed. Clark, 3:137; Beaumont (Leicester) to Huntingdon, 28 March 1685, HEH, HA 658; Dr. John Guy (Swepston) to Huntingdon, 27 March 1685, HEH, HA 3976; John Grevil Verney (Alexton) to Huntingdon, 27 March 1685, HEH, HA 12967; Bath (Plymouth) to Sunderland, 28 August 1685, NA, SP 31/1, fol. 124; Henry Muddiman's Notebook, 16 May 1685, Longleat House, Muddiman MSS, unfolioed.

25. Rochester to William, 24 March 1685, NA, SP 8/1/Pt. 2, fol. 3v; ? to Bulstrode, 30 March 1685, HRC, Pforzheimer (since recataloged); Edward Dering (London) to Sir John Percival, 31 March 1685, BL, Add. 46961, fol. 255; Sir Benjamin Bathurst to Col. Thomas Dungan, 11 May 1685, BL, Loan 57/83, unfolioed; Ailesbury, *Memoirs,* 1:98.

26. This analysis is based on the volumes produced by the History of Parliament Trust: Basil Duke Henning, ed., *The House of Commons, 1660–1690,* 3 vols. (London: Secker and Warburg, 1983).

27. Here I follow the lines of analysis laid out by Mark Knights, *Politics and Opinion in Crisis, 1678–81* (Cambridge: Cambridge University Press, 1994), 343–46.

28. Reresby, *Memoirs,* 23 April, 22 May, 24 May 1685, 362, 366–67; Evelyn, *Diary,* 7 May 1685, 4:439.

29. Robert Grove, *Seasonable Advice to the Citizens, Burgesses, and Free-Holders of England* (London: Walter Kettilby, 1685), 6–7, 11, 13–14, 18–19, 24. The arguments and language of this pamphlet convinces me that Anthony Wood is surely wrong to claim that George Hickes, the future nonjuror, was the author of this pamphlet. For the claim see Anthony Wood, *Athenae Oxonienses,* 3 vols., 2nd ed. (London: R. Knaplock, D. Midwinter, J. Tonson, 1721), 1004.

30. *The Mischief of Cabals,* 7 May 1685 (London: Randal Taylor, 1685), 23–24, 34; Andrew Allam (London) to Anthony Wood, 5 May 1685, Bodleian, MSS Wood F.39, fol. 43r; Edward Chamberlaine, *England's Wants* (London: Randal Taylor, 1685), 31–32.

31. Reresby, *Memoirs,* 23 April 1685, 362; Roger Morrice, Entering Book, 28 May, 4 June 1685, DWL, 31 P, 462, 465; Evelyn, *Diary,* 22 May 1685, 4:442–44.

32. Reresby, *Memoirs,* 10 February 1685, 352–53; Wood, 12 February 1685, in *Life and Times,* ed. Clark, 3:130; John Fell (Oxford) to Lord Hatton, 12 July 1683, in *Correspondence of the Family of Hatton,* vol. 2,

ed. Edward Maunde Thompson, Camden Society, n.s., 23 (1878): 27–28 (hereafter cited as *Hatton Correspondence*).

33. John Dalrymple, *Memoirs of Great Britain and Ireland,* 2nd ed., 2 vols. (London: W. Strahan and T. Cadell, 1771), 1:115–16; Reresby, *Memoirs,* 11 June 1685, 373; Bramston, *Autobiography,* [June 1685], 184–85; Bathurst (London) to Col. Hender Molesworth, 17 July 1685, BL, Loan 57/83, unfolioed; John Marten (Lavington) to Rev. William Moore, 17 June 1685, BL, Add. 38012, fol. 2r; Southwell (London) to Percival, 23 June 1685, BL, Add. 46962, fol. 62v; Jeaffreson (London) to Colonel Hill, 5 August 1685, Jeaffreson, 220–21; Evelyn, *Diary,* 8 July 1685, 4:451–53; *An Elegy on James Scot, Late Duke of Monmouth* (London: C. W., 1685), [16 July 1685]; "The Late King's Farewell," 1685, NA, C 104/63 (Rev. John Henry Cary Papers); Sir Edward Harley (Hereford) to Robert Harley, 9 July 1685, BL, Add. 70013, fol. 252v; Jacques (Ashby) to Huntingdon, 11 July 1685, HEH, HA 7747; *A Description of the Late Rebellion in the West* (London: P. Brooksby, 1685), MS in Wing copy: 10 September 1685.

34. Ailesbury, *Memoirs,* 1:108.

35. *Axminster,* 11 June 1685, 93; Rochester to William, 16 June 1685, NA, SP 8/1/Pt. 2, fol. 7r; Ailesbury, *Memoirs,* 1:108; Macaulay, *History,* 1:522–23.

36. *The Declaration of James Duke of Monmouth* [1685], 1–2.

37. *Declaration of Monmouth,* 2–6.

38. *Declaration of Monmouth,* 5.

39. Zook, *Radical Whigs and Conspiratorial Politics,* 135; Earl of Perth (Edinburgh) to Earl of Arran, 27 June 1685, NAS, GD 406/1/3328; Bramston, *Autobiography,* [July 1685], 188; Monmouth to James II, 8 July 1685, in "Original Letters of the Duke of Monmouth," ed. Sir George Duckett, *Camden Miscellany, 8,* Camden Society, n.s., 31 (1883): 4; Reresby, *Memoirs,* 9 July 1685, 385; Evelyn, *Diary,* 15 July 1685, 4:455–56; Andrew Paschall, "Account of Monmouth's Rising," LPL, MS 742/34, 10; Ailesbury, *Memoirs,* 1:116; Adam Wheeler, "Iter Bellicosum," 25 June 1685, in Henry Elliott Malden, ed., *Camden Miscellany, 12,* Camden Society, 3rd Ser., 18 (1910): 160; Fell (Oxford) to Hatton, 25 June 1685, *Hatton Correspondence,* 56; Examination of Richard Goodenough, 20 July 1685, Examination of Nathaniel Wade, 28 September 1685, BL, Lansdowne 1152A, fols. 243r, 310r.

40. Aaron Hodges (Rotterdam) to Middleton, 17/27 June 1685, BL, Add. 41817, fol. 179r; Peter Wyche (Hamburg) to Middleton, 9/19 June 1685, BL, Add. 41824, fol. 249v; Lois Schwoerer, "Propaganda in the Revolution of 1688," *American Historical Review* 82 (1977): 843–74; Macaulay, *History,* 1:522n; Reresby, *Memoirs,* 15 June 1685, 374; Henry Booth, Lord Delamere, *The Works* (London: John Lawrence and John Dunton, 1694), 75. Delamere testified that he never received any copies of the *Declaration:* Examination of Henry, Lord Delamere, 26 July 1685, BL, Lansdowne 1152A, fol. 294r; *A Warning to Traytors,* 2 July 1685 (London: E. Mallet, 1685), 2; Andrew Weston, *The True Account of the Behaviour and Confession of William Disney* (London: George Croom, 1685).

41. Ford, Lord Grey, *The Secret History of the Rye-House Plot and of Monmouth's Rebellion* (London: Andrew Millar, 1754); *Life of James II,* 2:29; Edmund Everard (Amsterdam) to Bevil Skelton, 8/18 November 1685, BL, Add. 41812, fol. 235r.

42. Skelton (Hague) to Middleton, 28 April/8May 1685, BL, Add. 41812, fol. 36r; "An Exact Relation," 11 June 1685, BL, Harleian 6845, fol. 254; Dalrymple, *Memoirs,* 1:121; Sir Hugh Cholmondley, 12 November 1685, DWL, 31 T 3, 31–32; Jeaffreson to Mr. Lewis, 18 July 1685, Jeaffreson, 211; Andrew Paschall, "Account of Monmouth's Rising," LPL, MS 942/34, 2; *A Description of the Late Rebellion in the West* (London: P. Brooksby, 1685), MS in Wing copy: 10 September 1685; Notes from Mrs. Langford, 4 January 1686, BL, Add. 36988, fol. 246r.

43. Edward Pelling, *A Sermon Preached at Westminster Abbey,* 26 July 1685 (London: Samuel Keble, 1685), 25–26; Shadrach Cooke, *A Sermon Preached at Islington,* 26 July 1685 (London: R. N., 1685), 11–12; Charles Hutton, *The Rebels Text Opened and Their Solemn Appeal Answered,* 26 July 1685 (London: Walter Kettilby,

1686), 2; S. Rich, *A Sermon Preached at Chard,* 21 June 1685 (London: R. N. for Charles Brome, 1685), 24; *The Countrey's Advice to the Late Duke of Monmouth* (London: T. M., 1685), MSS in Wing: 4 July 1685, [1].

44. William Jenkyn to Mother, 29 September 1685, in *The Bloody Assizes,* ed. J. G. Muddiman (London: William Hodge, 1929), 75–76 (hereafter cited as Muddiman); "The Behaviour and Dying Words of Mr. Roger Satchel," in Muddiman, 121; Examination of John Madden, 20 July 1685, BL, Lansdowne 1152A, fol. 240v; William Orme, ed., *Remarkable Passages in the Life of William Kiffin* (London: Burton and Smith, 1823), 53–54; *Axminster,* 93–94; "The Behaviour and Dying Speech of Mr. Joseph Speed of Culleton," in Muddiman, 82; Major Abraham Holmes, in Muddiman, 84; "An Account of those Executed at Sherborn," in Muddiman, 93; Joseph Tyler's Hymn, September 1685, in Muddiman, 89. John Tutchin produced his martyrology from memory several years after the rebellion. See Robin Clifton, *The Last Popular Rebellion: The Western Rising of 1685* (London: Maurice Temple Smith, 1984), 235. However, Tutchin was himself a rebel, and he did know firsthand many of the formidable information-gathering resources. Finally, in describing the rebels' motivations, Tutchin's account accords with other evidence. Where he seems most unreliable, as Muddiman himself points out, was in his depictions of Jeffereys. It should be noted that Clifton himself sees the rebellion primarily in religious terms: "Religion, in the form of the heir apparent's Catholicism, was of course the central issue in the six years' preparation for the revolt." Clifton, *Last Popular Rebellion,* 284.

45. Deposition of Miles Musgrave and John Sherborn, 23 February 1685, NA, SP 31/1, fol. 38; "Mr. John Hickes' Last Speech," 1685, in Muddiman, 107; Benjamin Keach, *Distressed Sion Relieved* (London: Nath. Crouch, 1689), 34; "Last Speech of Henry Boddy," in Muddiman, 104; Examination of Samson Lark, 16 July 1685, BL, Lansdowne 1152A, fol. 238v; Christopher Heyricke, *The Character of a Rebel,* 26 July 1685, Market Harborough (London: Samuel Heyricke, 1685), 27–28; Life of Sir John Fryer, Guildhall Library, 12017, fol. 14r; Nathaniel Gauden (Chelmsford) to Sir John Bramston, 11 June 1685, Essex SRO, D/Deb 25/24; J. H. E. Bennett and J. C. Dewhurst, eds., *Quarter Session Records with Other Records of the Justices of the Peace for the County Palatine of Chester, 1559–1760,* vol. 1 (Record Society of Lancashire and Cheshire, 1940), 12 July 1685, 186–87.

46. Skelton (Hague) to Middleton, 8/18 May 1685, BL, Add. 41812, fols. 58–59.

47. Skelton (Hague) to Middleton, 10/20 April 1685, BL, Add. 41812, fol. 17r; Grey, *Secret History,* 117; ? (Utrecht) to Skelton, 24 April/4 May, 12/22 May 1685, BL, Add. 41812, fols. 43r, 77v; Skelton (Hague) to Middleton, 8/18 May, 7/17 July 1685, BL, Add. 41812, fols. 58–59, 138r.

48. I disagree with Richard Ashcraft, *Revolutionary Politics and Locke's "Two Treatises of Government"* (Princeton, NJ: Princeton University Press, 1986), 452–66, and share the views of Mark Goldie, "John Locke's Circle and James II," *Historical Journal* 35 (1992): 568. Depositions taken after the rebellion suggest that the Locke who gave money to Argyle and Monmouth was Nicholas Locke, a tobacconist: Nathaniel Wade's Information, 4 October 1685, BL, Harleian 6845, fol. 272r; Burton's Information, August 1685, Goodenough's Information, 25 July 1685, BL, Lansdowne 1152A, fols. 227r, 227v; ? (Utrecht) to Middleton, 17/27 May 1685, BL, Add. 41812, fol. 85v; Jean Le Clerc, *An Account of the Life and Writings of Mr. John Locke,* 2nd ed. (London: John Clarke and E. Curll, 1713), 23.

49. Everard (Amsterdam) to Skelton, 15/25 November 1685, BL, Add. 41812, fol. 248; Everard (Amsterdam) to Skelton, 11/21 December 1685, BL, Add. 41813, fol. 15v; Slingsby Bethel to Skelton, 5/15 May 1686, BL, Add. 41819, fol. 95v; Greaves, *Secrets of the Kingdom,* 296; Information of Robert Cragg, 20 December 1689, HMC 12th Report, appendix pt. 6, 395; Grey, *Secret History,* 110, 122; Examination of John Jones, 16 August 1685, Examination of William Williams, 16 July 1685, BL, Lansdowne 1152A, fols. 303r, 237; Clifton, *Last Popular Rebellion,* 154; Nathaniel Wade's Confession, 29 July 1685, BL, Harleian 6845, fols. 264, 269; Everard (Amsterdam) to Skelton, 11/21 November 1685, BL, Add. 41813, fol. 136; *The Life, Birth, and Character of John L. Haversham* (London, 1710), 3; *Memoirs of the Late Right Honourable John Lord Haversham* (London: J. Baker, 1711), 2–3; Thomas Burnet, "Life of Gilbert," in *Bishop Burnet's History of His Own Time,* ed.

Burnet (London: A. Millar, 1753), xxxii; Examination of Robert Cragg, 15 December 1685, BL, Lansdowne 1152A, fol. 266r.

50. Examination of William Williams, 16 July 1685, Examination of Nathaniel Wade, 28 September 1685, BL, Lansdowne 1152A, fols. 237v, 310; Lady Rachel Russell (Southampton House) to Dr. Fitzwilliam, 21 July 1685, in *Letters of the Lady Rachel Russell; from the Manuscripts in the Library at Woburn Abbey* (London: Edward and Charles Dilly, 1773), 39.

51. Sir Charles Lyttleton (Whitehall) to Viscount Hatton, 6 March 1685, BL, Add. 29578, fol. 50r; Southwell (London) to Percival, 4 March 1685, BL, Add. 46961, fol. 226r; Ailesbury, *Memoirs,* 1:114. Though at the time the Earl of Dartmouth, one of the king's closest confidants, claimed that James was "entirely pleased" with William's support: Dartmouth (London) to Skelton, 9 June 1685, Staffordshire SRO, D(w) 1778/I/i/1114; Skelton (Hague) to Middleton, 23 June/3 July, 15/25 May 1685, BL, Add. 41812, fols. 130v, 76; J. Boscawen to John Evelyn, 29 June 1685, BL, Evelyn Papers, JE A9, unfolioed (since recataloged).

52. Pelling, *Sermon,* 26 July 1685, 14–15; Evelyn, *Diary,* 17 June, 15 July 1685, 4:449, 455–56; Charles Bertie (London) to Moore, 6 July 1685, BL, Add. 38012, fol. 25r; Bramston, *Autobiography,* 6 July 1685, 185–86; Reresby, *Memoirs,* 24 June, 2 July 1685, 381, 383; *The Rampant Alderman; or, News fom the Exchange* (London: Randal Taylor, 1685), 13; Information from Henry Lee, 16 August 1686, BL, Add. 41804, fol. 210r; Sir Richard Temple, "The False Patriot Unmasked," ca. 1690, HEH, STT Lit (9), 9; Southwell (London) to Percival, 23 June 1685, BL, Add. 46962, fol. 62r; Andrew Paschall, "Account of Monmouth's Rising," LPL, MS 742/34, 10. Dalrymple later wrote that Monmouth "was joined by none of the nobility or gentry of condition." Dalrymple, *Memoirs,* 1:119–20. See also William Hamilton (Whitehall) to Earl of Arran, 25 June 1685, NAS, GD 406/1/3474. Here I disagree with Peter Earle: see Earle, *Monmouth's Rebels: The Road to Sedgemoor, 1685* (London: Weidenfeld and Nicolson, 1977), 134.

53. Clifton, *Last Popular Rebellion,* 244–45, 270; J. Boscawen to John Evelyn, 29 June 1685, BL, Evelyn Papers, JE A9, unfolioed (since recataloged). Clarendon thought them "ill armed and ill mounted": Clarendon (Whitehall) to Abingdon, 4 July 1685, Bodleian, Clarendon 128, fol. 53r; William Lloyd (bishop of St. Asaph) to Sir Robert Owen, 13 June 1685, National Library of Wales, Brogynton MSS no. 842; Southwell (London) to Percival, 13 June 1685, BL, Add. 46962, fol. 53v; William Dugdale (London) to Anthony Wood, 23 June 1685, Bodleian, Wood F.41, fol. 180ar; Rochester to William, 16 June 1685, NA, SP 8/1/Pt. 2, fol. 7r; Sunderland (Whitehall) to Arran, 20 June 1685, NAS, GD 406/1/7657; Melfort (Whitehall) to Arran, 20 June 1685, NAS, GD 406/1/3308; Sir William Trumbull, 12 November 1685, Grey, 8:357.

54. Duchess of Beaufort (Chelsea) to Duke of Beaufort, 23 June 1685, HMC 12th Report, appendix 9, 89; Boscawen to John Evelyn, 6 July 1685, BL, Evelyn Papers, JE A9, unfolioed (since recataloged); Marten (Lavington) to Moore, 1 July 1685, BL, Add. 38012, fol. 18r; Bertie (London) to Moore, 6 July 1685, BL, Add. 38012, fol. 25r; Clarendon (Whitehall) to Abingdon, 2 July 1685, Bodleian, MSS Clarendon 128, fol. 47v; John Speke (Amsterdam) to Skelton, 25 April/5 May 1686, BL, Add. 41819, fol. 51r; *Axminster,* 97.

55. "Information of Robert Cragg," 20 December 1689, HMC 12th Report, appendix part 6, 395.

56. Sir John Lowther, Memoirs of the Reign of James II, Cumbria SRO, D/Lons/L2/5; Burlington (London) to Reresby, 24 March 1685, WYAS, MX 31/21; J. Porter (London) to Bulstrode, 16 March 1685, BL, Egerton 3680, fol. 176r; Bathurst to Molesworth, 29 May 1685, BL, Loan 57/83, unfolioed.

57. William Petty (London) to Southwell, 22 August 1685, BL, Add. 72853, fol. 21v; Edmund Warcup (Northmore) to Hugh Jones, 14 September 1685, Bodleian, Rawl. Lett. 48, fol. 11v; *A New Song upon the Coronation* (London: James Dean, 1685), MS in Wing copy: 25 April 1685.

CHAPTER 5. *The Ideology of Catholic Modernity*

1. R. D. (London) to ?, 27 December 1688, BL, Egerton 2717, fol. 418v; John Evelyn (London) to Countess of Sunderland, 12 January 1690, BL, Evelyn Papers, JE A2, fol. 64v (since recataloged).

2. Thomas Babington Macaulay, *The History of England from the Accession of James II,* 5 vols. (New York: Harper and Brothers, 1849–61), 2:5–6, 46, 60, 109, 333–34, 394, 418; G. M. Trevelyan, *The English Revolution, 1688–89* (1938; reprint ed., Oxford: Oxford University Press, 1965), 34.

3. Macaulay, *History,* 2:99, 193 218–36, 242, 393, 396, 402–3. See also Gary S. De Krey, "Reformation and 'Arbitrary Government': London Dissenters and James II's Policy of Toleration, 1687–1688," in *Fear, Exclusion and Revolution,* ed. Jason McEllicott (Aldershot: Ashgate, 2006), 14.

4. Macaulay, *History,* 2:9–10, 58. Jonathan Clark's claim that "it was the men who felt most strongly . . . who were prepared to act . . . in 1688," is wholly consonant with Macaulay's emphasis on the English rallying around their "common Protestantism": J. C. D. Clark, *Revolution and Rebellion: State and Society in England in the Seventeenth and Eighteenth Centuries* (Cambridge: Cambridge University Press, 1986), 65.

5. Robert Beddard, *A Kingdom without a King: The Journal of the Provisional Government in the Revolution of 1688* (Oxford: Phaidon, 1988), 14; John Miller, *James II* (London: Methuen, 1978), 126, 128; Mark Goldie, "James II and the Dissenters' Revenge," *Historical Research* 66 (February 1993): 53; J. R. Western, *Monarchy and Revolution: The English State in the 1680s* (London: Blandford, 1972), 186, 190; Eveline Cruickshanks, *Glorious Revolution* (New York: St. Martin's, 200), 19–21; Tim Harris, *Revolution: The Great Crisis of the British Monarchy, 1685–1720* (London: Allen Lane, 2006), 195; Lionel Glassey to Sir John Riddell, 7 July 1986, HLRO, WMT/12/Pt. I.

6. Sir Richard Temple, "The False Patriot Unmasked," ca. 1690, HEH, STT Lit (9), 9–10; Henry St. John, Viscount Bolingbroke, *A Dissertation upon Parties,* 3rd ed. (London, 1735), 78; Goldie, "James II and the Dissenters' Revenge," 54; Mark Goldie, "The Political Thought of the Anglican Revolution," in *The Revolutions of 1688,* ed. Robert Beddard (Oxford: Clarendon Press, 1991), 111; Mark Goldie, "John Locke's Circle and James II," *Historical Journal* 35, no. 3 (1992): 559, 569, 584; Western, *Monarchy and Revolution,* 226; Cruickshanks, *Glorious Revolution,* 18.

7. Harris, *Revolution,* 183–84, 199, 236; Goldie, "John Locke's Circle," 558, 579; Goldie, "Anglican Revolution," 107–8, 111, 117–18; Western, *Monarchy and Revolution,* 139–40, 266, 274. See also Lionel K. J. Glassey, "Introduction," in *The Reigns of Charles II and James VII and II,* ed. Glassey (New York: St. Martin's, 1997), 9.

8. George Etherege (Ratisbon) to Sunderland, 9/19 January 1688, Harvard Theatre Collection, fMS THR 11, 237; London Newsletter, 17 November, 22 December 1687, FSL, L.c. 1884, 1896; Bevil Skelton (Paris) to Sunderland, 4/14 January 1688, NA, SP 78/151, fol. 131r; Eugène Michaud, *Louis XIV et Innocent XI,* 4 vols. (Paris: G. Charpentier, 1882–83), 2:242–47; Skelton (Paris) to Sunderland, 10/20 December 1687, NA, SP 78/151, fol. 123r; London Newsletter, 3 January, 14 January, 28 January 1688, FSL, L.c. 1903, 1908, 1914; Peter Wyche (Hamburg) to Middleton, 3 February 1688, BL, Add. 41826, fol. 260v; Etherege (Ratisbon) to Albeville, 16/26 April 1688, Indiana, Albeville MSS.

9. Michaud, *Louis XIV et Innocent XI,* 3:168, 195–96; J. R. Jones, *The Revolution of 1688 in England* (New York: W. W. Norton, 1972), 206; Western, *Monarchy and Revolution,* 250; ? to Thomas Felton, 18 August 1688, BL, Add. 39487, fol. 21v; Skelton (Paris) to Sunderland, 15/25 August 1688, NA, SP 78/151, fol. 200v; John Lytcott (Rome) to Sir Richard Bulstrode, 29 September/9 October 1688, BL, Egerton 3683, fol. 160r; J[ames] Fr[aser] (London) to John Ellis, 16 October 1688, BL, Add. 4194, fol. 382v; Pierre Blet, *Les Nonces du pape à la cour de Louis XIV* ([Paris]: Perrin, 2002), 159; *Mercurius Reformatus,* 26 June 1689, [1]; *The Intrigues of the French King at Constantinople* (London: Dorman Newman, 1689), 23–24; Edmund Bohun, *The History of the Desertion* (London: Ric. Chiswell, 1689), 4–5; *The Politicks of the French King Lewis the XIV Discovered* (London: Mat. Wotton, 1689), 2–3; W. E. Buckley, ed., *Memoirs of Thomas, Earl of Ailesbury,* 2 vols. (Westminster: Nichols and Sons, 1890), 1:166 (hereafter cited as Ailesbury, *Memoirs*).

10. William Leslie (Rome) to Louis Innes (?), 15/25 April 1687, SCA, Bl 1/105/8; Gilbert Burnet, "Reasons against the Repealing," 1687, in *A Collection of Eighteen Papers Relating to the Affairs of Church and State during the Reign of King James the Second* (London: John Starkey and Richard Chiswell, 1689), 3; Gilbert Burnet,

History of His Own Time, 2 vols. (London: Thomas Ward, 1724), 1:595, 706; Leslie (Rome) to Melfort, 3 March 1688, SCA, Bl 1/116/5.

11. Raymond J. Maras, *Innocent XI: Pope of Christian Unity* (Notre Dame, IN: Cross Roads Books, 1984), 107–29; Joseph Bergin, *Crown, Church and Episcopate under Louis XIV* (New Haven and London: Yale University Press, 2004), 234–38; *The Present French King Drawn to the Life* (London: R. Baldwin, 1690), 71; *The Spirit of France and the Politick Maxims of Lewis XIV* (London: Awnsham Churchill, 1689), 14–15; M. Roux, ed., *Mémoires de l'abbé Le Gendre* (Paris: Charpentier, 1865), 45; Wyche (Hamburg) to Middleton, 5 April 1687, BL, Add. 41826, fol. 96v; Newsletter from Rome, 12 May 1687, NA, SP 85/12, fol. 187r; London Newsletter, 29 November 1687, FSL, L.c. 1888; William Westby, Memoirs, 26 January 1688, FSL, V.a. 469, fol. 7v.

12. Louis O'Brien, *Innocent XI and the Revocation of the Edict of Nantes* (Berkeley, CA, 1930), 130; *Spirit of France,* 69.

13. Gilbert Burnet, *The History of the Rights of Princes* (London: J. D. for Richard Chiswell, 1682), 3, 34; James Fraser (London) to Sir Robert Southwell, 15 December 1687, FSL, V.b. 287 (39); Alexander Dunbar (Edinburgh) to Innes, 30 October 1688, SCA, Bl 1/111/8; Roger Morrice, Entering Book, 6 November 1686, DWL, 31 P, 650. The bishop of Lincoln, the military man Sir Charles Lyttleton, and the lawyer Whitelocke Bulstrode eagerly followed the Franco-papal disputes: Thomas Barlow (bishop of Lincoln) to Robert Boyle, 1 October, 22 November 1686, in *The Works of the Honourable Robert Boyle,* vol. 6, ed. Thomas Birch (London: W. Johnston et al., 1772), 315, 317; Sir Charles Lyttleton (Richmond) to Hatton, 14 June 1684, in *Correspondence of the Family of Hatton,* vol. 2, ed. Edmund Maunde Thompson, Camden Society, n.s., vol. 23 (1878): 47; Whitelocke Bulstrode, Commonplace Book, January 1686, HRC, Pforzheimer, Misc. MS 817, fols. 56–57. See also *The True Interest of Christian Princes* (1686), 23–24. When Innocent XI died, one Protestant Englishman wrote in his commonplace book that "he was a man of great resolution and bravery, whom Louis XIV, the great hector of Christendom, could not overrule": Whitelocke Bulstrode, Meditations, August 1689, HRC, Pforzheimer 2k. The Whiggish West Country divine John Walker of Hadley bought a copy of Burnet's tract in 1688: John Walker of Hadley, Account Book, 15 April 1688, Somerset SRO, DD/Whb/3185.

14. Father Francis Sanders, *An Abridgement of the Life of James II* (London: R. Wilson, 1704), 13; Foley, 5; Edward Gregg, "New Light on the Authorship of the Life of James II," *English Historical Review* 108 (1993): 959; Letter from a Jesuit of Liege to a Jesuit of Freiburg, 2 February 1688, Beinecke, OSB MSS 2/Box 5/Folder 109. Gilbert Burnet has made a powerful case that this letter was no forgery: Burnet, *History of His Own Time,* 1:712; Charles Dodd, *The History of the English College at Doway* (London: Bernard Lintott, 1713), 32; Geoffrey Scott, "The Court as a Centre of Catholicism," in *A Court in Exile: The Stuarts in France, 1689–1718,* ed. Edward Corp (Cambridge: Cambridge University Press, 2004), 242, 247; Michael A. Mullett, *Catholics in Britain and Ireland, 1558–1829* (New York: St. Martin's, 1998), 81; Skelton (Paris) to Sunderland, 19/29 November 1687, NA, SP 78/151, fol. 117v; Letter from a Jesuit of Liege, 2 February 1688. Edward Coleman, who was appointed secretary to Mary of Modena by James, was in close contact with La Chaise in the 1670s: HMC, *Report XIII,* 89–94, 95–97. See also Andrew Barclay, "The Rise of Edward Colman," *Historical Journal* 42, no. 1 (1999): 126–28; Morrice, Entering Book, 25 September 1686, DWL, 31 P, 628; Gilbert Dolben (London) to Sir William Trumbull, 2 January 1686, BL, Trumbull MSS 54 (since recataloged); and "Over the Lord D[over]'s Door," in *Lampoon* (1687). This was also the view of interested Dutch observers: Barillon (London) to Louis XIV, 23 May/2 June 1687, NA, PRO 31/3/170, fol. 5v. Continentals also remembered James II's court in this way: see W. H. Quarrell and Margaret Mare, eds., *London in 1710 from the Travels of Zacharias Conrad von Uffenbach* (London: Faber and Faber, 1934), 14; and Voltaire, *The Age of Lewis XIV,* 2 vols. (London: R. Dodsley, 1752), 1:239.

15. James (Brussels) to Dartmouth, 8 May, 25 July 1679, Beinecke, OSB Shelves fb.190/II, fols. 40, 52; *Life of James II,* 1:441–42; Bonrepaus (London) to Seignelay, 11/21 March 1686, NA, PRO 31/3/169, fol. 66r; Barillon (London) to Louis XIV, 22 February/4 March 1686, NA, PRO 31/3/165, fol. 2r; Bonrepaus (London) to Seignelay, 24 December/3 January 1686, NA, PRO 31/3/163, fols. 20–21; Barillon (London) to Louis XIV,

26 April/6 May 1688, NA, PRO 31/3/177, fol. 7; John Sheffield, "Memoirs," in *Works,* 2 vols. (London: John Barber, 1723), 2:12. See also Captain Robert Parker, *Memoirs of the Most Remarkable Military Transactions* (Dublin: Geo. and Alex Ewing, 1746), 4.

16. Barillon (London) to Louis XIV, 5 March 1685, NA, PRO 31/3/160, fol. 70r; Bonrepaus (London) to Seignelay, 1/11 February 1686, NA, PRO 31/3/164, fol. 36; Barillon (London) to Louis XIV, 9/19 February 1685, NA, PRO 31/3/160, fols. 39–40; Barillon (Windsor) to Louis XIV, 13/23 September 1686, NA, PRO 31/3/167, fol. 11v; Barillon (London) to Louis XIV, 25 October/4 November, 8/18 November, 11/21 November, 29 November/9 December, 2/12 December 1686, NA, PRO 31/3/167, fols. 40r, 47–48, 50–51, 58v, 60r; Barillon (London) to Louis XIV, 23 December/2 January 1686/87, 13/23 January 1687, NA, PRO 31/3/168, fols. 1r, 15r; Bonrepaus (Windsor) to Seignelay, 11/21 July 1687, NA, PRO, 31/3/171, fol. 67r; Bonrepaus (London) to Seignelay, 29 September/9 October, 14/24 November 1687, NA, PRO 31/3/173, fols. 22r, 124r; Barillon (London) to Louis XIV, 8/18 December 1687, NA, PRO 31/3/174, fols. 41–42; Bonrepaus, Report on the State of England, 1687, NA, PRO 31/3/174, fols. 80–86; Thomas Birch, *The Life of the Reverend Dr. John Tillotson* (London: J. and R. Tonson et al., 1752), 146; Sir Edward Hales, Treatise on Government, 1692, AWA, Old Brotherhood Papers, Book 3/258.

17. Barillon (London) to Louis XIV, 2/12 November, 3/13 December 1685, NA, PRO 31/3/162, fols. 10v, 44–45; Barillon (Windsor) to Louis XIV, 13/23 September 1686, NA, PRO 31/3/167, fol. 12v; Bonrepaus (London) to Seignelay, 7/17 January 1686, NA, PRO 31/3/163, fol. 55r; Morrice, Entering Book, 9 April 1687, DWL, 31 Q, 87. Warner, in particular, never "missed an opportunity to express his zeal and his attachment" to Louis XIV: Barillon (London) to Louis XIV, 28 March/7 April 1687, NA, PRO, 31/3/168, fol. 63r; Placidus Fleming (Ratisbon) to Mr. Whyteford, 13/23 March 1688, SCA, Bl 1/111/9; Charles Dodd, *The Church History of England,* 3 vols. (Brussels, 1742), 3:415–16.

18. William Leslie (Rome) to Innes, 5/15 April 1687, SCA, Bl 1/105/18; Walter Leslie (Rome) to Mr. Whyteford, 23 August/2 September 1687, SCA, Bl 1/103/7; Barillon (London) to Louis XIV, 6/16 January 1687, NA, PRO 31/3/168; Etherege (Ratisbon) to Lord Taaffe, 2/12 1687, Harvard Theatre Collection, fMS THR 11, 69; Morrice, Entering Book, 26 November 1687, DWL, 31 Q, 210; Van Citters (London) to States General, 1/11 May 1688, BL, Add. 34512, fol. 78r; John Miller, *Popery and Politics in England, 1660–1688* (Cambridge: Cambridge University Press, 1973), 236; James Johnston (London) to ?, March 1688, BL, Add. 34515, fol. 58r.

19. Jones, *Revolution of 1688,* 81; Barillon (London) to Louis XIV, 11/21 November 1686, NA, PRO 31/3/167, fols. 50–51; Bonrepaus (London) to Seignelay, 1/11 February 1686, NA, PRO 31/3/164, fol. 36r; James II to the pope, 16 June 1687, Foley, 277–78; Barillon (Windsor) to Louis XIV, 7/17 June 1686, NA, PRO 31/3/166, fol. 22r; Morrice, Entering Book, 8 January, 12 November 1687, DWL, 31 Q, 41, 200; London Newsletter, 12 November 1687, FSL, L.c. 1882; Ailesbury, *Memoirs,* 1:99, 121; Annual Letters of the Province, 1685–1690, Foley, 276; Ethelred Luke Taunton, *The History of the Jesuits in England, 1580–1773* (London: Methuen, 1901), 448; Barillon (London) to Louis XIV, 21 February/3 March, 28 February/10 March 1687, NA, PRO 31/3/168, fols. 37r, 40v; William Blathwayt (Whitehall) to Southwell, 12 November 1687, Nottingham SUL, PwV 53/57; Barillon (London) to Louis XIV, 22 November/2 December 1686, PRO, PRO 31/3/167, fol. 56r.

20. Bonrepaus, Report on the State of England, 1687, NA, PRO 31/3/174, fols. 78–80; Barillon (London) to Louis XIV, 19 February 1685, NA, PRO 31/3/160, fol. 40; Earl of Perth (London) to Hamilton, 10 December 1685, NAS, GD 406/1/9223; Dolben (London) to Trumbull, 22 January 1686, BL, Trumbull MSS 54 (since recataloged); Barillon (London) to Louis XIV, 26 December/5 January 1687/88, NA, PRO 31/3/175, fol. 5v; Bridget Croft to Huntingdon, 9 May 1687, HEH, HA 1791; Henry Thynne (London) to Earl of Weymouth, 30 June 1688, Longleat House, Thynne MSS 14, fol. 234r; Morrice, Entering Book, 30 June 1688, DWL, 31 Q, 277; Van Citters (Windsor) to States General, 27 September/7 October 1687, BL, Add. 54512, fol. 62v; Bonrepaus (Windsor) to Seignelay, 25 May/4 June 1687, NA, PRO 31/3/170, fols. 18–19; Ronquillo (London) to Don Francisco Bernardo de Quixon, 5 April 1686, BL, Add. 35402, fol. 61v; Morrice, Entering

Book, 19 June 1686, DWL, 31 P, 553; Barillon (London) to Louis XIV, 16/26 January 1688, NA, PRO, 31/3/175, fol. 14r.

21. Barillon (London) to Louis XIV, 8/18 December 1687, NA, PRO 31/3/174, fols. 41–42; Morrice, Entering Book, 17 September 1687, DWL, 31 Q, 169; Earl of Clarendon, Diary, 4 January 1688, Singer, 2:153; Blathwayt (Whitehall) to Southwell, 20 October 1687, Nottingham SUL, PwV 53/55; Van Citters (London) to States General, 14/24 October 1687, BL, Add. 34510, fol. 53v; John Oldmixon, *The False Steps of the Ministry after the Revolution,* 3rd ed. (London, 1714), 15; ? (Whitehall) to Sir Richard Bulstrode, 11 April 1687, HRC, Pforzheimer/Box 10; Robert Yard (Whitehall) to Albeville, 12 April 1687, Indiana, Albeville MSS; London Newsletter, 12 April 1687, FSL, L.c. 1796; Roger North, *The Life of Sir Dudley North* (London, 1744), 162; Bonrepaus (London) to Seignelay, 17/27 October 1687, NA, PRO 31/3/173, fols. 59–60; Barillon (London) to Louis XIV, 17/27 October 1687, NA, PRO 31/3/173, fol. 64. Butler played no small role in Rochester's demise: Barillon (Windsor) to Louis XIV, 8/18 July 1687, NA, PRO 31/3/166, fol. 39; Blathwayt (Windsor) to Southwell, 22 June 1686, Nottingham SUL, PwV 53/36. As a result of Butler's professional activities he had a large interest in the City, and presumably within the Dissenting community. This explains his large role in the project to reform England's corporations in 1687 and 1688: Morrice, Entering Book, 5 May 1688, DWL, 31 Q, 254.

22. Barillon (London) to Louis XIV, 24 September/4 October 1685, NA, PRO, 31/3/161, fols. 53–54; Barillon (London) to Louis XIV, 1/11 March 1686, NA, PRO 31/3/165, fol. 4r; Duke of Hamilton (Hamilton) to Earl of Arran, 16 August 1686, NAS, GD 406/1/7190; Miller, *James II,* 210; Bruce Lenman, "The Scottish Nobility and the Revolution 1688–90," in *Revolutions of 1688,* ed. Beddard, 144; Morrice, Entering Book, 8 December 1688, 2 March 1689, DWL, 31 Q, 339–40, 485; William Fuller, Autobiography, Beinecke, OSB Shelves fc.66, 15; Van Citters (London) to States General, 2/12 November 1688, BL, Add. 34510, fol. 163r; Bonrepaus (Windsor) to Seignelay, 11/21 August 1687, NA, PRO 31/3/172, fol. 20r; Bonrepaus, Report on the State of England, 1687, NA, PRO 31/3/174, fol. 82r; Perth to Mme. de Crolly, 1685, in Ch. Urbain and E. Levesque, eds., *Correspondance de Bossuet,* vol. 3 (Paris: Librairies Hachette, 1910), 544; François Gaquère, *Vers L'Unité Chrestienne: James Drummond et Bossuet* (Paris: Beauchesnes, 1963), 22–28, 52–160; Perth (London) to Bossuet, 12 November 1685, in Urbain and Levesque, eds., *Correspondance de Bossuet,* 160; Robert Francis Strachan (Paris) to William Leslie, 16/26 November 1685, SCA, Bl 1/92/12; Innes to Perth, 13 November 1686, SCA, SM 2/12/II; Barillon (London) to Louis XIV, 14/24 January 1686, NA, PRO 31/3/163, fol. 12v; Bonrepaus (London) to Seignelay, 1/11 March 1686, 5/15 April 1686, NA, PRO 31/3/165, fols. 52r, 133r; Morrice, Entering Book, 7 July 1688, DWL, 31 Q, 283; Van Citters (London) to States General, 6/16 November 1688, BL, Add. 34510, fol. 167v. Melfort and Petre came into conflict in June 1688, but that quarrel was over their respective assessments of Sunderland's reliability—both pursued Francophilic policies. Perth to ?, 10 June 1688, SCA, Bl 1/117/13; Morrice, Entering Book, 7 July 1688, DWL, 31 Q, 283.

23. James Fitzjames, Duke of Berwick, *Memoirs of the Marshal Duke of Berwick,* vol. 1 (London: T. Cadell, 1779), 1–2; Dodd, *Church History,* 3:493; Foley, 292. Apparently James originally hoped to have James Francis Edward educated by Jesuits as well: Scott, "Court as a Centre of Catholicism," 257.

24. ? (Whitehall) to William III, 1 June 1686, NA, SP 8/1/Pt. 2, fol. 26; London Newsletter, 18 October 1687, FSL, L.c. 1871; Morrice, Entering Book, 18 February 1688, DWL, 31 Q, 239(3); Barillon (London) to Louis XIV, 11/21 March 1686, PRO, PRO 31/3/165, fol. 11r; Bonrepaus (London) to Seignelay, 8/18 February 1686, NA, PRO 31/3/164, fol. 57; Geoffrey Scott, "A Benedictine Conspirator: Henry Joseph Johnston," *Recusant History* 20, no. 1 (1990): 58–62; Francis Turner (bishop of Ely) to Trumbull, 29 May 1686, BL, Trumbull 46 (since recataloged); William Clagett, *The Present State of the Controversy* (London: Tho. Basset et al., 1687), 13; Burnet, *History of His Own Time,* 1:673.

25. Father Peter Hamerton, An Account of the Beginning and Progress of Oates' Plot, Foley, 23; Barillon (London) to Louis XIV, 21/31 December 1685, NA, PRO 31/3/162, fol. 69r; James Wellwood, *Memoirs,* 3rd ed. (London: Tim. Goodwin, 1700), 181–82; Burnet, *History of His Own Time,* 1:707; Miller, *James II,* 152–53. Castlemaine not only allied himself with the Jesuits when in Rome but also associated himself with the

deeply Francophilic Order of the Knights of Malta: D. F. Allen, "Attempts to Revive the Order of Malta in Stuart England," *Historical Journal* 33, no. 4 (1990): 947; quoted in F. A. J. Mazure, *Histoire de la révolution de 1688 en Angleterre,* vol. 2 (Paris: Charles Gosselin, 1825), 241.

26. E. S. De Beer, "The Marquis of Albeville and His Brothers," *English Historical Review* 45 (1930): 397–408; Barillon (Windsor) to Louis XIV, 13/23 September 1686, NA, PRO 31/3/167, fol. 14r; Bonrepaus (London) to Seignelay, 1/11 February 1686, NA, PRO 31/3/164, fol. 36r; Barillon (Windsor) to Louis XIV, 23 August/2 September, 13/23 September 1686, NA, PRO 31/3/167, fols. 1v, 13–14; Barillon (London) to Louis XIV, 26 August/5 September 1686, NA, PRO 31/3/167, fol. 4r; Yard (Whitehall) to Albeville, 8 April 1687, Indiana, Albeville MSS; Barillon (London) to Louis XIV, 1/11 November 1686, NA, PRO 31/3/167, fol. 43; Barillon (London) to Louis XIV, 28 February/10 March 1687, NA, PRO 31/3/168, fol. 44v; Bonrepaus quoted in Mazure, *Histoire de la révolution,* 331–32; Wyche (Hamburg) to Albeville, 10/20 May 1687, Indiana, Albeville MSS.

27. Barillon (Windsor) to Louis XIV, 26 July/5 August, 5/15 August, 9/19 August 1686, NA, PRO 31/3/166, fols. 48v, 53v, 54v; Fleming (Ratisbon) to Charles Whyteford, 11/21 January 1687, SCA, Bl 1/101/2; Barillon (Windsor) to Louis XIV, 12/22 August 1686, NA, PRO 31/3/166, fol. 57v.

28. Louis XIV to Barillon, 30 September 1688, in John Dalrymple, *Memoirs of Great Britain and Ireland,* 2nd ed. (London: W. Strahan and T. Cadell, 1771), 2:appendix/1:234.

29. For its devotional precepts, see Scott, "Court as a Centre of Catholicism," 238–39. I dissent from Michael Mullet's view that English Catholicism can only be understood to have "a European profile after 1688": Michael A. Mullett, *Catholics in Britain and Ireland, 1558–1829* (New York: St. Martin's, 1998), 82; Scott, "Benedictine Conspirator," 62; Patrick Riley, "Introduction," in *Bossuet: Politics Drawn from Holy Scripture,* ed. Riley (Cambridge: Cambridge University Press, 1990), xli–lvii; Fraser (London) to Southwell, 31 December 1687, FSL, V.b. 287 (43); John Dryden in his translation of Maimbourg's *History of the League* (London: Jacob Tonson, 1684), postscript: 48. Burnet had already drawn attention to the absolutist implications of Maimbourg's work two years earlier: *History of the Rights,* 39–40; Louis Maimbourg, *A Discourse Concerning the Foundation and Prerogative of the Church of Rome,* trans. Archibald Lovell (London: Jos. Hindmarsh, 1688), 345, 347–48, 350–52.

30. James Maurice Corker, *Roman-Catholick Principles* [1687], 4. On Corker's relations with James II, see Scott, "Benedictine Conspirator," 60; Charles Trinder, *The Speech,* 8 January 1688 (London: Randal Taylor, 1688), 4. For Trinder, see Dodd, *Church History,* 3:460; John Wilson, *Jus Regium Coronae* (London: Henry Hills, 1688), 7; Lex Coronae, ca. 1687, Centre for Kentish Studies, U386/Z8/5; *Some Reflections on the Bulls of Paul the Third and Pius the Fifth* (1686), 2; *A Letter in Answer to Two Main Questions* (London: M. T., 1687), 10.

31. *Some Reflections on the Bulls,* 2. The same tract was published under the title *The Bulls of the Popes* (1686); "The Case of Several English Catholics," ca. 1680s, Georgetown SUL, Milton House Archives, Box 3/Folder 10; Edward Scarisbrick, "Catholic Loyalty," 30 January 1688, in *A Select Collection of Catholick Sermons Preach'd before Their Majesties,* vol. 1 (London, 1741), 235. Scarisbrick claimed this "the truly Catholic doctrine of that Society whereof the author hath the honor to be a member" (226). On Scarisbrick, see Foley, 350.

32. Dryden in Maimbourg, *History of the League,* 1684, postscript: 2. Dryden continued to translate French Catholic texts at the king's behest after James's accession: see James Anderson Winn, *John Dryden and His World* (New Haven and London: Yale University Press, 1987), 412, 421–22. Dryden was converted to Catholicism by Corker: Geoffrey Scott, *Gothic Rage Undone: English Monks in the Age of Enlightenment* (Bath: Downside Abbey, 1992), 13; Wilson, *Jus Regium Coronae,* 6–7; Scarisbrick, "Catholic Loyalty," 238.

33. Philip Michael Ellis, Sermon, 5 December 1686, in *Select Collection,* 83. Ellis was himself French educated: Joseph B. Gavin, "An Englishman in Exile," *Recusant History* 15, no. 1 (1979): 11; Scarisbrick, "Catholic Loyalty," 252; *A Pastoral Letter from the Four Catholic Bishops to the Lay-Catholics of England* (London: Henry Hills, 1688), 6.

34. *Pastoral Letter,* 7; Scarisbrick, "Catholic Loyalty," 254; Ellis, Sermon, 77.

35. John Kettlewell, *The Religious Loyalist,* 28 August 1685 (London: Robert Kettlewell, 1685), 15, 27–28; Richard Thompson, *A Sermon Preached in the Cathedral Church of Bristol,* 21 June 1685 (London: Luke Meredith, 1685), 5. See also John Curtois, *A Discourse* (London: Jo. Hindmarsh, 1685), 19, 30–31; James Ellesby, *The Doctrine of Passive Obedience,* 30 January 1685 (London: William Crooke, 1685), 16; Thomas Fysh, *A Sermon Preached . . . in Lyn-Regis in Norfolk,* 29 May 1685 (London: Sam. Smith, 1685), 27–28; John Scott, *A Sermon Preached at the Assizes at Chelmsford,* 31 August 1685 (London: M. Flesher, 1686), 2–3, 8–9; Erasmus Warren, *Religious Loyalty, or Old Allegiance to the New King,* 8 February 1685 (London: Robert Clavell, 1685), 26; John Petter, *A Sermon,* 5 July 1685 (London: Samuel Walsel, 1685), 19–20; Robert Almond, Account of Magdalen College, 19 October 1687, Magdalen College Archives, 908/26, 1; "An Account of the Magdalen College Vistation," 21 October 1687, NA, SP 8/1/Pt. 2, fol. 166r; "An Account of the Visitation of S. M. Magd. College," 21 October 1687, Bodleian, Tanner 29, fol. 93r; Thomas Cartwright, *A Sermon Preached upon the Anniversary Solemnity of the Happy Inauguration of Our Dread Soveraign Lord King James II,* 6 February 1686, 2nd ed. (London: Walter Davis, 1686); Cartwright, *An Answer of a Minister of the Church of England* (London: J. L., 1687), 10; and Burnet, *History of His Own Time,* 1:695–96. For Parker, see Bonrepaus, "Report on the State of England," 1687, NA, PRO 31/3/174, fols. 106–7; and Parker, *A Discourse of Ecclesiastical Politie* (London: J. Martyn, 1670). For the others, see Morrice, Entering Book, 5 February 1687, DWL, 31 Q, 57; *Speech of the Right Honourable Thomas, Earl of Stamford* (London: Richard Baldwin, 1692), 6; and Memorandum on William's Descent, 1688, NA, SP 8/2/Pt. 3, fol. 67r. Significantly, in 1687 Parker was known to be minimizing the theological differences between the Church of England and Roman Catholicism: Nathaniel Johnston to Sir John Reresby, 18 December 1687, WYAS, MX/R50/54.

36. *A Proclamation,* 12 February 1687 (Edinburgh: Andrew Anderson, 1687); Gilbert Burnet, "Some Reflections on His Majesty's Proclamation," 1687, reprinted in *A Collection of Eighteen Papers Relating to the Affairs of Church and State during the Reign of King James the Second* (London: John Starkey and Richard Chiswell, 1689), 10–11. This pamphlet was widely copied during James's reign in both England and Scotland. For one example, see Hertfordshire SRO, D/EP F 26.

37. Barillon (Windsor) to Louis XIV, 13/23 September 1686, NA, PRO 31/3/167, fols. 11–13; Ailesbury, *Memoirs,* 1:174–75; Dodd, *Church History,* 3:416. Hales was a close friend of the Earl of Melfort. Hales, *Treatise on Government.* See Daniel Szechi, "A Blueprint for Tyranny? Sir Edward Hales and the Catholic Response to the Revolution of 1688," *English Historical Review* 116 (2001): 342–67; Hales to Melfort, 27 May 1692, AWA, Old Brotherhood Papers, Book 3/253.

38. James II's speech in Vincent Alsop, *The Humble Address of the Presbyterians* ([London]: J. W., 1687), 7; Robert Barclay, *A Genealogical Account of the Barclays of Urie* (Aberdeen, 1740), 56; James (Hague) to Dartmouth, 25 April 1679, NMM, LBK/49, 5; William Penn (London) to Thomas Lloyd, 16 March, ca. 18 May 1685, *Penn Papers,* 42, 45; J. Tucker to Arran, 19 April 1687, NAS, GD 406/1/3445; London Newsletter, 19 April 1687, FSL, L.c. 1799; James II's answer to William Penn's speech, 24 May 1687, BL, Add. 5540, fol. 43; Ailesbury, *Memoirs,* 1:169.

39. John Marshall, *John Locke, Toleration and Early Enlightenment Culture* (Cambridge: Cambridge University Press, 2006), 396–417; Jacques Benigne Bossuet, *A Pastoral Letter from the Lord Bishop of Meaux* [London: Henry Hills, 1686], 2–3, 36; Maimbourg, *Discourse,* sigs. [A6r], a4v–[a5r]; Evelyn, *Diary,* 3 November 1685, 4:486. Evelyn referred to the "Harangue," delivered by Daniel de Cosnac at Versailles on 14 July 1685: "Harangue," in *Memoires de Daniel de Cosnac,* ed. Comte Jules de Cosnac (Paris: Jules Renouard, 1852), 2:316–22; *The Proceedings of the Clergy of France* (Lille: I. Chrysostome Malte, 1686), [ii]. William Clagett claimed that Bossuet had written a letter, which was quickly suppressed, that did "both own and justify the persecution." Clagett, *Present State of the Controversy,* 24; Dominique Bouhours, *The Life of St. Ignatius* (London: Henry Hills, 1686), 1–2.

40. Joshua Basset, *Reason and Authority* (London: Henry Hills, 1687), 12. Unsurprisingly Basset prevented his college from celebrating the anniversary of the Gunpowder Plot: John Verney (London) to Sir Ralph Verney, 17 November 1687, Buckinghamshire SRO, Verney MSS. I disagree with Mark Goldie's description

of Basset as one who held "principles which modern liberals and secularists hold dear: a university open to a plural society." Mark Goldie, "Joshua Basset, Popery, and Revolution," in *Sidney Sussex College Cambridge: Historical Essays,* ed. D. E. D. Beales and H. B. Nisbet (Woodbridge: Boydell, 1996), 119; William Darrel, *A Vindication of St. Ignatius* (London: Anthony Boudet, 1688), sig. A2r; Dryden, *History of the League,* post-script: 8; Trinder, *Speech,* 8 January 1688, 5–6; John Betham, Sermon, 6 January 1686, in *Select Collection,* 215.

41. Etherege (Ratisbon) to Mr. Maule and Mr. Wynne, 28 February/10 March 1687, Harvard Theatre Collection, fMS THR 11, 83; Perth to Hamilton, 1687, NAS, GD 406/1/9201; Lawrence Dowdall (Champagne) to James II, 22 June/2 July 1688, NA, SP 78/151, fol. 190r; Sir Edward Hales to Melfort, 27 May 1692, AWA, Old Brotherhood Papers, Book 3/253; Hales, Treatise on Government; *A Speech Spoken by Mr. Hayles, Student of University-College of Oxford* (London: A. M., 1687), 1–2; Burnet, *History of His Own Time,* 1:661.

42. Barillon (London) to Louis XIV, 31 January/10 February 1687, NA, PRO 31/3/168, fol. 24v; Barillon (Windsor) to Louis XIV, 10/20 September 1685, NA, PRO 31/3/161, fol. 47r; Barillon (London) to Louis XIV, 11/21 March 1686, NA, PRO 31/3/165, fol. 10v; Barillon (London) to Louis XIV, 2/12 May 1687, NA, PRO, 31/3/169, fol. 26r. James made similar statements to Bonrepaus: Bonrepaus, Report on the State of England, 1687, NA, PRO 31/3/174. fol. 75r; Barillon (Windsor) to Louis XIV, 12/22 July 1686, PRO, PRO 31/3/166, fol. 40v; Barillon (London) to Louis XIV, 7/17 January 1686, NA, PRO 31/3/163, fol. 8v. In his *Treatise Concerning the Correction of the Donatists,* Augustine justified the use of magisterial forces against both schismatics and heretics on the grounds that once they had been exposed to the truth, those who did not follow it were obstinate and needed to be forcibly corrected. The fourth-century Donatists had called into question the sacrament of penance and had argued that the quality of the sacraments depended on the personal character, rather than on the office of the priest. Augustine took the lead in suppressing this movement. As Mark Goldie has pointed out these were exactly the arguments advanced against toleration in the 1670s by English High Churchmen: see Goldie, "Religious Intolerance in Restoration England," in *From Persecution to Toleration,* ed. Ole Peter Grell, Jonathan Israel, and Nicholas Tyacke (Oxford: Clarendon Press, 1991), 335–68. Goldie notes how powerful this argument for intolerance was in the French Catholic polemic of the 1680s (338–39); Letter from Jesuit of Liege, 2 February 1687; Léon Lecestre, ed., *Mémoires de Gourville,* 2 vols. (Paris: Librairie Renouard, 1895), 2:122.

43. Barillon (London) to Louis XIV, 19/29 October 1685, NA, PRO 31/3/161, fol. 66r; Ronquillo (London) to Quixon, 5 April 1686, BL, Add. 34502, fol. 61; Barillon (London) to Louis XIV, 21 September/1 October, 8/18 October 1685, NA, PRO 31/3/161, fols. 51r, 60v; Barillon (London) to Louis XIV, 4/14 January 1686, NA, PRO 31/3/163, fol. 7r. Although James did officially welcome Huguenot refugees to England, they could receive support only if they willingly conformed to the Church of England: Jones, *Revolution of 1688,* 112–13; Sir William Trumbull, Autobiography, All Souls College, MSS 317, [42]; Barillon (London) to Louis XIV, 10/20 May 1686, NA, PRO 31/3/166, fol. 8v; Jean Claude, *An Account of the Persecutions and Oppressions of the Protestants of France* (London, 1686); Barillon (Windsor) to Louis XIV, 1/11 October 1685, NA, PRO 31/3/161, fols. 57–58; Barillon (London) to Louis XIV, 25 March/4 April 1686, NA, PRO 31/3/165, fol. 17v.

44. Bonrepaus (London) to Seignelay, 11/21 January 1686, NA, PRO 31/3/163, fol. 63r; James (Edinburgh) to Dartmouth, 14 December 1679, Beinecke, OSB Shelves fb.190/II, fol. 70r; Hamilton (London) to Duchess of Hamilton, 4 October 1687, NAS, GD 406/1/6236; Barillon (London) to Louis XIV, 19/29 April 1686, NA, PRO 31/3/165, fol. 30v; Innes (Paris) to William Leslie, 20/30 September 1686, SCA, Bl 1/94/10. James established a Jesuit college at the seat of government in Holyroodhouse. For the efforts to Catholicize Scotland and Ireland, see Harris, *Revolution,* 127–29, 166–69, 179–81; Charles Scarburgh (Lisbon) to Sunderland, 11/21 April 1687, NA, SP 89/16, fol. 323; Barillon (Windsor) to Louis XIV, 21 September/1 October 1685, NA, PRO 31/3/161, fol. 51v; William Stanley (Hague) to William Sancroft, 24 January/3 February 1688, Bodleian, Tanner 29, fol. 130v.

45. James II in Father Francis Sanders, *An Abridgement of the Life of James II* (London: R. Wilson, 1704), 174, 176–77.

46. Eustache Le Noble, *The History of Father La Chaise* (London: H. Rhodes, 1693), 342; Ailesbury, *Memoirs,* 1:152, 165–66. See also Edward Gregg, "France, Rome and the Exiled Stuarts, 1689–1713," in *Court in Exile,* ed. Corp, 17.

47. *A Memorial of God's Last Twenty-Nine Years Wonders in England* (London: J. Rawlins, 1689), 116; Wellwood, *Memoirs,* 178, 180; Barillon (Windsor) to Louis XIV, 14/24 June 1686, NA, PRO 31/3/166, fol. 25; London Newsletter, 31 May 1687, FSL, L.c. 1814; John Phillips, *The Secret History of the Reigns of K. Charles II and K. James II* (London, 1690), 195; John Warner, The Origins of Government, ca. 1694, University of Chicago, MSS 416, 2:1325; White Kennett, *A Complete History of England,* vol. 3 (London: Brab. Aylmer et al., 1706), 444; Barillon (Windsor) to Louis XIV, 17/27 June 1686, NA, PRO 31/3/166, fol. 26v; William Leslie (Rome) to Innes, 5/15 August 1687, SCA, Bl 1/105/18; J. Hill (Paris) to Trumbull, 15 February 1688, Berkshire SRO, D/ED/C33; Innes (London) to Whyteford, 17 February 1688, SCA, Bl 1/113/11; Ailesbury, *Memoirs,* 1:166.

48. Barillon (London) to Louis XIV, 15/25 February 1686, NA, PRO 31/3/164, fol. 17v.

49. Barillon (London) to Louis XIV, 26 November/6 December 1685, NA, PRO 31/3/162, fol. 38r; Barillon (London) to Louis XIV, 28 February/10 March 1687, NA, PRO 31/3/168, fol. 40v; Van Citters (London) to States General, 11/21 November 1687, BL, Add. 34510, fol. 61r; ? (London) to Dijkvelt, [January 1688], Warwickshire SRO, CR 2017/C7, fol. 17r; Morrice, Entering Book, 25 September 1686, 6 November 1686, DWL, 31 P, 628, 650; "Father Hay's Memoirs of His Own Time," in *Genealogie of the Hayes of Tweeddale,* ed. Richard Augustin Hay (Edinburgh: Thomas G. Stevenson, 1835), 82; Wellwood, *Memoirs,* 179; Southwell (Kingsweston) to Weymouth, 16 January 1688, Longleat House, Thynne MSS 15, fol. 219v; Ailesbury, *Memoirs,* 1:152, 165. These practices of James's modern Catholic policies are discussed in chapter 6.

50. Bonrepaus (London) to Seignelay, 21/31 January 1686, NA, PRO 31/3/163, fol. 78r; Bonrepaus (London) to Seignelay, 15/25 February 1686, NA, PRO 31/3/164, fol. 85r; Wellwood, *Memoirs,* 152; Barillon (London) to Louis XIV, 30 November/10 December 1685, NA, PRO 31/3/162, fol. 41; Barillon (London) to Louis XIV, 4/14 March 1686, NA, PRO 31/3/165, fol. 6v; "A Copy of a Letter," 1689, Bodleian, Rawlinson MSS, D91, 15–16; Edmund Bohun, *The History of the Desertion* (London: Ric. Chiswell, 1689), 35. The imperial ambassador was taking a similar line in late 1688: *A New Declaration of the Confederate Princes and States* (London: Tim. Goodwin, 1689), 19–20; Dr. Thomas Lane (Vienna) to Sunderland, 7/17 October 1688, BL, Add. 41842, fol. 144r.

51. Michael Questier, *Catholicism and Community in Early Modern England* (Cambridge: Cambridge University Press, 2006), 295, 509; Annual Letters of the English Province, 1678/89, Foley, 9–10; Father Peter Hamerton, "An Account of the Beginning and Progress of Oates's Plot," Foley, 19–23; Morrice, Entering Book, 9 July 1687, DWL, 31 Q, 160; "Father Hay's Memoirs," 57–58; Tyrconnel (Dublin) to Mary of Modena, 2 April 1690, BL, Add. 38145, fol. 16v.

52. Barillon (London) to Louis XIV, 11/21 March 1686, NA, PRO 31/3/165, fol. 11r; Letter from a Jesuit of Liege, 2 February 1687; Van Citters (London) to States General, 24 January/3 February 1688, BL, Add. 34512, fols. 68–69; Cary Gardiner (London) to Sir Ralph Verney, 7 December 1687, Buckinghamshire SRO, Verney MSS; Wellwood, *Memoirs,* sig. [A8r]; Daniel Defoe, *Memoirs of Publick Transactions in the Life and Ministry of His Grace the Duke of Shrewsbury* (London: Tho. Warner, 1718), 12–13; Halifax to Weymouth, 21 February 1688, Longleat House, Thynne MSS 15, fol. 53r; Halifax (London) to Prince of Orange, 12 April 1688, NA, SP 8/1/Pt. 2, fol. 203r; Morrice, Entering Book, 1 September 1688, DWL, 31 Q, 290; Van Citters (London) to States General, 18/28 November 1687, BL, Add. 34510, fol. 64r; Gardiner (London) to Sir Ralph Verney, 30 July 1688, Buckinghamshire SRO, Verney MSS.

53. John Irvine and Innes to Whyteford, Spring 1688, SCA, Bl 1/114/4; Burnet, *History of His Own Time,* 1:662; Thomas Nicholson (Padua) to ?, 22 January/1 February 1687, SCA, Bl 1/96/2; Ailesbury, *Memoirs,* 1:148, 152; Morrice, Entering Book, 15 December 1688, DWL, 31 Q, 351; Privy Council Minutes, 10 July 1685, NA, PC 2/71, fol. 62r; William Fuller, Autobiography, 15–16; *Memoirs of the Secret Service of John Mackey* (London: Nichols and Sons, 1895), 136; Bonrepaus, Report on the State of England, 1687, NA, PRO 31/3/174,

fol. 83r. Middleton did not in fact convert to Catholicism until after the revolution; his wife, however, was a Roman Catholic: Barillon (London) to Louis XIV, 6/16 February 1688, NA, PRO, 31/3/175, fol. 33r; *London Mercury,* December 1688; Questier, *Catholicism,* 324; Dodd, *Church History,* 3:466; Dodd, *The History of the English College at Doway* (London: Bernard Lintott, 1713), 28, 33; Morrice, Entering Book, 25 September 1686, DWL, 31 P, 628; Walter Leslie (Rome) to Whyteford, 17/27 April 1688, SCA, Bl 1/115/6.

54. Barillon (London) to Louis XIV, 3/13 December 1685, PRO, PRO, 31/3/162, fols. 44–45; Barillon (London) to Louis XIV, 16/26 March 1685, NA, PRO 31/3/160, fols. 95–96; Philanax Verax, *A Letter to the King When Duke of York* (London: Richard Janeway, 1688), 5–6; Ailesbury, *Memoirs,* 1:126; Sir Henry Hunloke (Wingermouth) to Huntingdon, 14 July 1688, HEH, HA 6949; Fuller, Autobiography, Beinecke, OSB Shelves fc.66, 16–17; Southwell (Kingweston) to Weymouth, 29 November 1686, Longleat House, Thynne MSS 15, fol. 157v; Morrice, Entering Book, 6 November 1686, DWL, 31 P, 650; Van Citters (Westminster) to States General, 1/11 November 1687, BL, Add. 34512, fol. 65r; James Johnston (?) to ?, 8 December 1687, Nottingham SUL, PwA 2112c; Van Citters (London) to States General, 3/13 January 1688, BL, Add. 34510, fol. 77v; Dodd, *Church History,* 3:420; *Reflexions on Monsieur Fagel's Letter,* 12 January 1688 (1688), 3; David Lindsay (London) to Innes, 28 May 1688, SCA, Bl 1/117/1; Van Citters (London) to States General, 1/11 June 1688, BL, Add. 34510, fol. 123r.

55. P. Conne (London) to Innes, 29 November 1688, SCA, Bl 1/110/6; H. Hughes (Ratisbon) to Earl of Nottingham, 4/14 December 1690, PRO, SP 81/106, fol. 29r; Fleming (Ratisbon) to Innes, 8/18 December 1688, SCA, Bl 1/111/15.

CHAPTER 6. *The Practice of Catholic Modernity*

1. J. P. Kenyon, "The Earl of Sunderland and the Revolution of 1688," *Cambridge Historical Journal* 11, no. 3 (1955): 277.

2. John Callow, *James II: The Triumph and the Tragedy* (Kew: National Archives, 2005), 16–18; James (Edinburgh) to Dartmouth, 5 January 1680, 1 November 1681, Beinecke, OSB Shelves fb.190, 2:fols. 76, 152r.

3. Van Citters (London) to States General, 10/20 July 1685, BL, Add. 34512, fol. 24r; Humphrey Prideaux (Oxford) to John Ellis, 9 July 1685, BL, Add. 28929, fol. 113v; Speeches by the Tory Sir Edward Seymour and the maverick Sir Richard Temple (who was to become a Tory in the 1690s): 12 November 1685, DWL, 31 T 3, 5–7. See also Sir John Lowther, *Memoirs of the Reign of James II* (London: H. G. Bohn, 1857), 456–57; and Guy Miege, *The New State of England under Their Majesties K. William and Q. Mary,* 2 vols. (London: H. C. for Jonathan Robinson, 1691), 1:195.

4. John Childs, *The Army, James II and the Glorious Revolution* (Manchester: Manchester University Press, 1980), 1–4, 204; William A. Shaw, ed., *Calendar of Treasury Books, 1681–1685,* 7:1, 8:1; "An Estimate of the Cost of the Expence for One Year," October 1688, NA, SP 8/2/Pt. 2, fol. 22.

5. List of Winter Quarters, 1687, HEH, HA Military Box 2 (19); Barillon (Windsor) to Louis XIV, 22 September/2 October 1687, NA, PRO 31/3/173, fol. 1r. The expenditures on garrisons can be followed in Shaw, ed., *Calendar of Treasury Books,* 8:1.

6. Thoresby, *Diary,* 1685, 1:181; Diary of Lawrence Rawstorne, 17 October 1688, Lancashire SRO, Rawstorne Diary, 91; C. Hatton (Carlisle) to Huntingdon, 16 May 1687, HEH, HA 6225; John Eames (Aylesbury) to Huntingdon, 23 July 1685, HEH, HA 2404; Sir Ralph Verney (Claydon) to John Verney, 2 August 1685, Buckinghamshire SRO, Verney MSS; Eames (Chester) to Huntingdon, 9 March 1687, HEH, HA 2407; William Blathwayt (Windsor) to Lord Langdale, 15 September 1688, NA, WO 4/1, fol. 50v

7. Barillon (Windsor) to Louis XIV, 27 August/6 September 1685, NA, PRO 31/3/161, fols. 36–37; Samuel Johnson, *Notes upon the Phoenix Edition of the Pastoral Letter* (London, 1694), 82–83; "Abstract of Particular Account of All the Inns, Alehouses in England," 1686, NA, WO 30/48; Charles Morgan (Hull) to Huntingdon, 26 September 1685, HEH, HA 9383; Petition of Marmaduke Ayscough, [1686/87], WYAS, MX 46/21; Roger Morrice, Entering Book, 6 August 1687, DWL, 31 Q, 164; Roger Kenyon, Diary, 27 October 1688,

HMC *Kenyon,* 200; "Letter Sent to Every English Merchant in the United Provinces," 8/18 September 1686, BL, Add. 41820, fol. 3r; Childs, *Army,* 16.

8. Van Citters (London) to States General, 1/11 June 1686, BL, Add. 34512, fols. 36–37; ? (Whitehall) to William III, 1 June 1686, NA, SP 8/1/Pt. 2, fol. 26; Miege, *New State of England,* 2:60; Childs, *Army,* 91–92.

9. Barillon (London) to Louis XIV, 31 October/10 November 1687, NA, PRO 31/3/173, fol. 85r; Blathwayt to Sir William Trumbull, 25 January 1686, BL, Trumbull Misc. 24 (since recataloged). These were presumably the bases on which Blathwayt wrote *His Majesties Orders for Regulation of the Musters* (London: Charles Bill, Henry Hills, et al., 1687). The handbook for soldiers produced in 1686 did not explicitly refer to France as a model but drew heavily on French examples: *The Soldier's Guide* (London: Benjamin Tooke, 1686); John Chichely (London) to Richard Legh, 6 March 1686, John Rylands Library, Legh of Lyme MSS, Box 2/Folder 14; Blathwayt (Whitehall) to Sir John Reresby, 9 September 1686, WYAS, MX 43/16. Others have noted the French influence on James II's army: Robin Clifton, *The Last Popular Rebellion: The Western Rising of 1685* (London: Maurice Temple Smith, 1984), 95; Childs, *Army,* 84. For a recent discussion of Louis XIV's military reforms placed in the context of "the creation of the modern state," see James B. Collins, *The State in Early Modern France* (Cambridge: Cambridge University Press, 1995), 93–95.

10. Journal of Samuel Atkins, 22 August 1685, NMM, JOD/173, fol. 236v; Charles Reresby (London) to Sir John Reresby, 3 July 1686, WYAS, MX 44/18; Barillon (Windsor) to Louis XIV, 1/11 July 1686, NA, PRO 31/3/166, fol. 35v; London Newsletter, 8 July 1686, FSL, L.c. 1679; E. Resresby (Hounslow) to Sir John Reresby, 16 July 1687, WYAS, MX 49/24; Will Hay (London) to Tweeddale, 18 July 1687, NLS, 14407, fol. 116r; James Wellwood, *Memoirs,* 3rd ed. (London: Tim. Goodwin, 1700), 221; Thomas Nicholson (Padua) to William Leslie, 31 August 1685, SCA, Bl 1/91/20; Walter Lorenzo Leslie (Rome) to Leslie, 22 May/1 June 1686, SCA, Bl 1/95/6; Nicholson (Padua) to ?, 23 July/2 August 1686, SCA, Bl 1/96/7; A Litany for the Holy Time of Lent, 1686 or 1687, Hertfordshire SRO, D/EP F27, fol. 10v.

11. Henry Shere (Frome) to Dartmouth, 1 July 1685, Staffordshire SRO, D(w) 1778/I/i/1132; Sir Charles Lyttleton (Taunton) to Hatton, 7 October 1685, BL, Add. 29578, fol. 67r; John Wyndham of Salisbury, 16 November 1685, DWL, 31 T 3, 15 (speech in Parliament); Morrice, Entering Book, 23 January 1686, DWL, 31 P, 517; Information of William Martyn (Exeter), 18 February 1686, NA, SP 31/3, fol. 77r; John Wyndham, Diary, 1687, Somerset SRO, DD/Wy/Box 185; John Whiting, *Persecution Exposed,* 2nd ed. (London: James Phillips, 1791), 300–302; William Nicolson (Carlisle) to Sir Christopher Musgrave, 18 October 1686, Cumbria SRO, Carlisle, CB/ME/Box 32/6; C. Hatton (Carlisle) to Huntingdon 11 April 1687, HEH, HA 6224; John Tichell, *The History of the Town and County of Kingston upon Hull* (Hull: Thomas Lee, 1798), 578–79; Talbot Lascelles (Hull) to Huntingdon, 21 February 1686, HEH, HA 8156; Sunderland (Whitehall) to Legh, 6 October 1685, John Rylands Library, Legh of Lyme Box 3/Folder 22; William Hamilton (Whitehall) to Arran, 5 October 1686, NAS, GD 406/1/3307; Packer (Chester) to Huntingdon, 29 November 1685, HEH, HA 9816; William Lloyd (bishop of Norwich) to William Sancroft, 2 December 1687, Bodleian, Tanner 29, fol. 116r; Morgan (York) to Sir John Reresby, 25 October 1686, WYAS, MX 43/49; Petition of Thomas Woodhouse, Serjeant at Mace City of York, [December 1686], WYAS, MX 45/13; Bryan Fairfax (York) to Sir John Reresby, 2 September 1687, WYAS, MX/R50/33; Edward Baldock (York) to Sir John Reresby, 26 February 1688, WYAS, MX/R50/68; George Prickett (York) to Sir John Reresby, 1 March 1688, WYAS, MX/R53/4; Baldock (York) to Sir John Reresby, 5 March 1688, WYAS, MX/R50/83; Sir John Reresby, *Memoirs,* ed. Mary K. Geiter and W. A. Speck (London: Royal Historical Society, 1991), 10 July 1688, 502; Louis Innes (London) to Whyteford, 25 April 1687, SCA, Bl 1/102/4; Hamilton (Whitehall) to Arran, 26 April 1687, NAS, GD 406/1/3467; Barillon (London) to Louis XIV, 28 April/8 May 1687, NA, PRO 31/3/169, fol. 24v; Journal of Atkins, 10 July 1687, fol. 245v; James Vernon (London) to Albeville, 20 January 1688, Indiana, Albeville MSS; John Verney (London) to Sir Ralph Verney, 20 June 1688, Buckinghamshire SRO, Verney MSS; John Verney (London) to Edmund Verney, 22 August 1688, Buckinghamshire SRO, Verney MSS; John Strype, *A Survey of the Cities of London and Westminster* (London: A. Churchill et al., 1720), 1:77; Lloyd to Sancroft, 5 March 1688, Bodleian, Tanner 29, fol. 141r; John Verney (London) to Edmund Verney, 2 April

1688, Buckinghamshire SRO, Verney MSS; Baldock (York) to Sir John Reresby, 21 January 1688, WYAS, MX/R50/66; Dr. Henry Paman (London) to Sir Ralph Verney, 17 August 1687, Buckinghamshire SRO, Verney MSS; Sir Nicholas Slanning (Salisbury) to Blathwayt, 2 November 1686, Beinecke, OSB MSS 2/Box 8/Folder 172; Blathwayt (London) to Sir Robert Douglas, 16 October 1686, NA, WO 4/1, fol. 18v; Memoire de M. Robert, 27 December/6 January 1685/86, NA, PRO 31/3/163, fol. 82r; George Bulle (York) to Sir John Reresby, 15 January 1686, WYAS, MX 43/29; David Hay (Batrie) to Tweeddale, 22 October 1688, NLS, 14405, fol. 179r; Charles Macarty (Guernsey) to Blathwayt, 12 September 1686, OSB MSS 2/Box 6/Folder 121; Barillon (London) to Louis XIV, 27 May/6 June 1686, NA, PRO 31/3/166, fol. 16v.

12. *Axminster,* 110; George Whitehead, *The Christian Progress of That Ancient Servant and Minister* (London, 1725), 615; Henry Newcome, 15 March 1686, in *The Autobiography of Henry Newcome,* vol. 2, ed. Robert Parkinson, Chetham Society 27 (Manchester: Chetham Society, 1852), 262; Daniel Defoe, *The Advantages of the Present Settlement* (London: Richard Chiswell, 1689), 13–14. See also Thomas Comber, *Three Considerations Proposed to Mr. William Pen* [1687], 3; *A Remonstrance and Protestation of all the Good Protestants . . . with Reflections Thereupon* (London: Randall Taylor, 1689), 13; Edmund Bohun, *The History of the Desertion* (London: Ric. Chiswell, 1689), 1; Gilbert Burnet, "A Letter concerning Some Reflections," 1687, in Burnet, *A Collection of Papers Relating to the Present Juncture of Affairs in England* (1688/89), 26–27; Evelyn, *Diary,* 4 December 1685, 4:490; Sir David Nairne, Journal, April 1686, NLS, 14266, fol. 7v; Barillon (Windsor) to Louis XIV, 1/11 July 1686, NA, PRO 31/3/166, fol. 36r; Sir Ralph Verney (Middle Claydon) to Edmund Verney, 15 August 1686, Buckinghamshire SRO, Verney MSS; Sir Robert Southwell (Kingsweston) to Weymouth, 27 January 1687, Longleat House, Thynne MSS 15, fol. 162r; and Duke of Hamilton (Hamilton) to Arran, 8 May 1688, NAS, GD 406/1/7593.

13. Reresby, *Memoirs,* 30 May 1685, Geiter and Speck, 370; Geoffrey W. Symcox, "The Navy of Louis XIV," in *The Reign of Louis XIV,* ed. Paul Sonnino (Atlantic Highlands, NJ: Humanities Press, 1990), 130–36; Charles Woolsey Cole, *Colbert and a Century of French Mercantilism* (New York: Columbia University Press, 1939), 1:451–64; Bonrepaus (London) to Seignelay, 8/18 February 1686, NA, PRO 31/3/164, fol. 58r; Bonrepaus (London) to Seignelay, 11/21 June 1687, NA, PRO 31/3/170, fols. 120–21; Bonrepaus (London) to Seignelay, 18/28 July 1687, NA, PRO 31/3/171, fol. 87r.

14. Samuel Pepys, Report of the State of the Navy, 31 December 1684, NMM, SOU/8, fol. 113; J. R. Tanner, ed., *Pepys' Memoires of the Royal Navy, 1679–1688* (Oxford: Clarendon Press, 1906), 12–13, 31 (hereafter cited as Pepys, *Memoires*); Bonrepaus (London) to Seignelay, 8/18 February 1686, NA, PRO 31/3/164, fols. 58–59; Barillon (London) to Louis XIV, 29 April/9 May 1686, NA, PRO 31/3/166, fol. 4r; Journal of Atkins, 15 March 1686, fol. 237v; ? (London) to Ellis, 23 March 1686, BL, Add. 4194, fol. 47v; Morrice, Entering Book, 16 October 1686, DWL, 31 P, 636; N. A. M. Rodger, *The Command of the Ocean* (New York: W. W. Norton, 2004), 110–11.

15. J. D. Davies, *Gentlemen and Tarpaulins: The Officers and Men of the Restoration Navy* (Oxford: Clarendon Press, 1991), 198; D.C. Coleman, "Naval Dockyards under the Later Stuarts," *Economic History Review,* n.s., 6, no. 2 (1953): 136, 139–41; King James's Expenses, 1685–1688, HEH, EL 8583; C. Johnston (York) to Sir John Reresby, July 1686, WYAS, MX 43/9; Barillon (Windsor) to Louis XIV, 19/29 August 1686, NA, PRO 31/3/166, fol. 60r; Barillon (London) to Louis XIV, 6/16 September 1686, NA, PRO 31/3/167, fol. 8r; Barillon (Windsor) to Louis XIV, 13/23 September 1686, NA, PRO 31/3/167, fol. 14; London Newsletter, 23 September 1686, FSL, L.c. 1711; Thomas Harley to Sir Edward Harley, 19 October 1686, BL, Add. 70119, unfolioed; Barillon (London) to Louis XIV, 9/19 December 1686, NA, PRO 31/3/167, fol. 62r; Bonrepaus (Windsor) to Seignelay, 8/18 August 1687, NA, PRO 31/3/172, fols. 11–12; J. R. Tanner, "The Administration of the Navy from the Restoration to the Revolution, Part III (1679–1688)," *English Historical Review* 14 (1899): 49, 52; Tanner, "The Administration of the Navy from the Restoration to the Revolution, Part III (1679–1688)," *English Historical Review* 14 (1899): 266–68; Edward B. Powley, *The English Navy in the Revolution of 1688* (Cambridge: Cambridge University Press, 1928), 161–71; Charles Sergison, Abstract of Workmen in the

Naval Yards, August 1686, August 1688, NMM, SER/131, fols. 6r, 10r; Edward Bettine, "The Method of Building," 23 April 1685, BL, Harleian 4716, fols. 67–68.

16. London Newsletter, 6 November 1686, FSL, L.c. 1730; Bonrepaus (London) to Seignelay, 5/15 May 1687, NA, PRO 31/3/169, fol. 29r; Bonrepaus (Windsor) to Seignelay, 18/28 July 1687, NA, PRO 31/3/171, fol. 88r; Pepys, *Memoires,* 130–31.

17. David Parker, *The Making of French Absolutism* (London: Edward Arnold, 1983), 132–36; Peter Burke, *The Fabrication of Louis XIV* (New Haven and London: Yale University Press, 1992), 151–58; Edward Pelling, *A Sermon Preached at Westminster Abbey,* 26 July 1685 (London: Samuel Keble, 1685), 24; *The Speech of Sir George Pudsey, Serjeant at Law, Recorder of the City of Oxford,* 30 September 1685 (London: Timothy Goodwin, 1685), 2; *The Reward of Loyalty* (London: J. Hazzey, 1685); *The Factious Citizen, or, the Melancholy Visioner* (London: Thomas Maddocks, 1685), epilogue. See also Jacob Bury, *Advice to the Commons* (London: Henry Hills, 1685), 49; Edward Fowler, *The Great Wickedness and Mischievous Effects of Slandering,* 15 November 1685 (London: Brabazon Aylmer, 1685), 19; and Sir George MacKenzie, *Jus Regium* (London: Richard Chiswell, 1684), 55.

18. James Walker, "The Secret Service under Charles II and James II," *Transactions of the Royal Historical Society,* 4th Ser., 15 (1932): 214–15; Barillon (Windsor) to Louis XIV, 20/30 September 1686, NA, PRO 31/3/167, fol. 20r; Hudson (London) to Gilbert Burnet, 25 April 1687, BL, Add. 41804, fol. 278r; *The Late Revolution: or, The Happy Change* (London: Richard Baldwin, 1690), 12.

19. Roger Whitley (London) to Mr. Williston, 29 April 1673, British Postal Museum and Archive, POST 94/12, unfolioed; Walker, "Secret Service," 230–32; John Lauder, "Historical Observes," 1683, NLS, Adv. 24.4.6, fol. 165r; Proclamation for Enforcing . . . Post Office, 7 September 1685, NA, PC 2/71, fol. 72; *London Gazette,* 5 March 1685. For use of alternative letter carriers: Francis Atterbury (Christ Church, Oxford) to Jacob Tonson, 15 November 1687, FSL, Cc1(3); Sir William Boothby (Ashbourne) to Anthony Horneck, 2 December 1688, BL, Add. 71692, fol. 56r.

20. William Alchorne to William Atwood, 31 December 1686, NA, C 109/23/1; James Lunn to John Wildman, 24 September 1689, BL, Add. 61689, fol. 90r; Meredith Bromhead and Robert Mason (Westminster) to Wildman, 5 November 1689, BL, Add. 61689, fol. 106r; Sir Daniel Fleming (Rydal) to James Holles Jr., 16 July 1686, CRO Kendal, WD/RY 3019; S G (Oxford) to James Harrington, 6 May 1688, BL, Add. 36707, fol. 28r; John Covel (Grantham) to Sancroft, 1 December 1688, Bodleian, Tanner 28, fol. 270r; Robert Frampton, bishop of Gloucester (Gloucester), to William Wake, 18 December 1687, Christ Church, William Wake Papers, 250, fol. 14r; ? (London) to Ellis, 27 February 1686, BL, Add. 4194, fol. 41; Robert Strachan (Edinburgh) to Louis Innes, 7 January 1687, SCA, Bl 1/107/8; Lady Sunderland (Windsor) to Henry Sidney, 11 September 1688, BL, Add. 32681, fol. 309v; Owen Wynne to Trumbull, 19 November 1685, BL, Trumbull Misc. 23 (since recataloged); Earl Rivers (London) to Sidney, 17 November 1687, Nottingham SUL, PwA 2097a; Katherine Gorye (Coggeshall) to her son, 6 July 1685, BL, Add. 41804, fol. 7r; Hudson (London) to Burnet, 25 April 1687, BL, Add. 41804, fol. 278r; Winchelsea (Richmond) to earl of Weymouth, 19 July 1688, Longleat House, Thynne MSS 17, fol. 194r; Sir James Haye (London) to Tweeddale, 15 July 1686, NLS, 7010, fol. 117r; Mary Thynne to Weymouth, 8 June 1688, Longleat House, Thynne MSS 32, fol. 181r; R. D. (London) to ?, 3 November 1688, BL, Egerton 2717, fol. 411r; Richard Leigh (London) to Sir Richard Newdigate, 1 September 1688, Warwickshire SRO, CR 136/B240A; Christopher Jeaffreson (London) to ?, 29 January 1686, Jeaffreson, 269; Nathaniel Cholmly (Whitby) to ?, 20 January 1686, North Yorkshire SRO, ZCG, unfolioed; Henry Hunter (London) to Alexander Jacobs et al., 26 June 1688, Berkshire SRO, D/EHr/B2; William Squire (London) to James Chetwood, 18 June 1686, NA, FO 355/15, fol. 4; George Hickes (Worcester) to Thomas Turner, 20 June 1687, Bodleian, Rawlinson MSS, Letters 91, fol. 50r; Paman (London) to Lloyd, 28 October 1686, LPL, 3898/4; Thomas Birch, *The Life of the Reverend Dr. John Tillotson* (London: J. and R. Tonson et al., 1752), 94; Jo. Hill to John Swynfen, 11 November 1686, BL, Add. 29910, fol. 206r; Lawrence Clayton (London) to Sir John Percival, 2 July 1685, BL, Add. 46962, fol. 69r; C. Reresby (London) to Sir John Reresby, 23 March 1686, WYAS, MX 46/39; John Stewkeley to Sir Ralph Verney, 6 October 1686,

Buckinghamshire SRO, Verney MSS; Sir Ralph Verney (Claydon) to John Verney, 31 October 1686, Buckinghamshire SRO, Verney MSS; Sir Charles Cotterell to Katherine Trumbull, 18 March 1689, BL, Trumbull MSS 39 (since recataloged); Halifax to Sir William Trumbull, 22 March 1686, BL, Trumbull Misc. 24 (since recataloged); Gilbert Dolben (London) to Sir William Trumbull, 28 January 1686, BL, Trumbull MSS 54 (since recataloged).

21. Bevil Skelton (Paris) to Sunderland, 28 February/10 March 1688, NA, SP 78/151, fol. 154v; Sir Henry Brabant (Newcastle) to Sunderland, 14 November 1685, NA, SP 31/1, fol. 141; Hen. De Puy (Whitehall) to Ellis, 19 January 1686, BL, Add. 4194, fol. 14r; Jeaffreson (London) to Colonel Hill, 20 January 1686, Jeaffreson, 261; Southwell (Kingsweston) to Weymouth, 12 March 1686, Longleat House, Thynne MSS 15, fol. 125v; ? (London) to Louis Innes, 5 November 1688, SCA, Bl 1/119/6; Proclamation of the Mayor, Journal of Common Council, 19 January 1686, Corporation of London SRO, Journal 50, fol. 151v; Morrice, Entering Book, 14 August 1686, DWL, 31 P, 599; London Newsletter, 9 October 1688, BL, Add. 4194, fol. 366r; Whitehall Newsletter, 12 October 1688, Beinecke, OSB MSS 1/Box 2/Folder 90.

22. London Newsletter, 4 September 1686, 19 January, 14 February 1688, FSL, L.c. 1704, 1910, 1919; Instructions for Sir Edmund Andros, 12 September 1686, NA, CO 5/904, fol. 148r; Newsletter from London, 16 June 1686, NA, ADM 77/3/9; Newsletter, 17 June 1686, BL, Trumbull Newsletters (since recataloged); Morrice, Entering Book, 30 October 1686, DWL, 31 P, 646; *The Designs of France against England and Holland Discovered* [1686], 1; Barillon (Windsor) to Louis XIV, 19/29 August 1686, NA, PRO 31/3/166, fol. 60v; Morrice, Entering Book, 19 November 1687, DWL, 31 Q, 207; James Fraser (London) to Southwell, 12 April 1688, FSL, V.b. 287 (59); Lyttleton to Hatton, 29 March 1687, *Correspondence of the Family of Hatton,* vol. 2, ed. Edward Maunde Thompson, Camden Society, n.s., 23 (1878): 67; Henry Fleming (Oxford) to Sir Daniel Fleming, 28 July 1687, CRO Kendal, WD/RY 3122; *A Letter in Answer to Two Main Questions* (London: M. T., 1687), 2; Examination of Richard Lambert, Bookseller of York, 14 September 1687, BL, Add. 41804, fol. 315v; London Newsletter, 24 September 1687, FSL, L.c. 1861; Van Citters (London) to States General, 27 December/6 January 1687/88, BL, Add. 34510, fol. 76v; Fraser (London) to Southwell, 29 December 1687, FSL, V.b. 287 (42); Van Citters (London) to States General, 20/30 January 1688, BL, Add. 34510, fol. 78v; Edward Harley (London) to Sir Edward Harley, 15 February 1688, BL, Add. 70118, unfolioed; Robert Yard (Whitehall) to Albeville, 15 May 1688, Indiana, Albeville MSS; James Johnston (London) to ?, 4 April 1688, BL, Add. 34515, fol. 61.

23. Privy Council Minutes, 6 November 1685, NA, PC 2/71, fol. 79v; Evelyn, *Diary,* 5 November 1685, 4:487; Lauder, "Historical Observes," 5–6 November 1685, fol. 133r; Owen Wynne (London) to Ellis, 13 November 1686, BL, Add. 4194, fol. 107r; Stewkeley (London) to Sir Ralph Verney, 18 November 1686, Buckinghamshire SRO, Verney MSS; Morrice, Entering Book, 10 December 1686, DWL, 31 Q, 33; Van Citters (London) to States General, 28 October/7 November 1687, BL, Add. 34510, fol. 58v; John Verney (London) to Sir Ralph Verney, 6 December 1687, Buckinghamshire SRO, Verney MSS; *A Proclamation Inhibiting all Persons after the Four and Twentieth Day of June Next to Use the Trade of a Pedlar or Petty Chapman, Unless They Be Licensed,* 7 May 1686 (London: Charles Bill, Henry Hills, and Thomas Newcomb, 1686); Proclamation of the Mayor, 2 June 1687, Journal of Common Council, Corporation of London SRO, Journal 50, fol. 318r.

24. Brook Bridges, Notabilia, Beinecke, OSB Shelves b.333; Newsletter from Whitehall, 21 June 1686, BL, Trumbull Newsletters (since recataloged); Wynne to Sir William Trumbull, 21 June 1686, BL, Trumbull 46 (since recataloged); Evelyn Cruickshanks, Stuart Handley and D. W. Hayton, eds., *The House of Commons, 1690–1715* (Cambridge: Cambridge University Press, 2002), 3:661; Katherine Bromfield to Sir Edward Harley, 16 May 1685, BL, Add. 70013, fol. 236r; Edward Harley to Sir Edward Harley, 9 March 1686, BL, Add. 70013, fol. 332r; John Oldmixon, *The History of England during the Reigns of the Royal House of Stuart* (London: John Pemberton et al., 1730), 697; Robert Frances, *The Dying Speech of Robert Frances of Gray's Inn,* 24 July 1685 (London: George Croom, 1685), 3; *A Warning to Traytors,* 2 July 1685 (London: E. Mallet, 1685).

25. This is an impression based on a not very systematic trawl through county record offices; Amy Edith Robinson, ed., *The Life of Richard Kidder, D. D. Bishop of Bath and Wells Written by Himself*, Somerset Record Society, vol. 37 (Frome: Somerset Record Society, 1924), 38–39 (hereafter cited as *Life of Kidder*); Newsletter, 1687, Lancashire SRO, DD/HK/19/3/80; Newsletter (Whitehall), 19 August 1687, Beinecke, OSB MSS 1/Box 2/Folder 64; Gilbert Burnet, *History of His Own Time*, 2 vols. (London: Thomas Ward, 1724), 1:591; Robert Harley to Sir Edward Harley, 9 February 1686, BL, Add. 70013, fol. 322r; London Newsletter, 27 November 1686, FSL, L.c. 1739.

26. "Tunbridge Satyr," 1686, NLS, Adv. 19.1.12, fol. 178v; Edmond Willis (Lisburne) to Sir Arthur Rawdon, 4 March 1686, HEH, HA 14664; *A Letter to the Author of the Dutch Design Anatomized*, 8 November 1688 [1688], 1; John Cotton (Stratton) to Dr. Thomas Smith, 30 June 1687, Bodleian, MS Smith 48, 253; Lauder, "Historical Observes," April 1686, fol. 127r; Richard Bentley to John Evelyn, 4 September 1686, BL, Evelyn In-Letters 2, no. 155 (since recataloged); Skelton (Paris) to Sunderland, 6/16 June 1688, NA, SP 78/151, fol. 178v; Samuel Masters, *The Case of Allegiance in Our Present Circumstances Consider'd* (London: Ric. Chiswell, 1689), 2–3.

27. Collins, *State in Early Modern France*, 116; Parker, *Making of French Absolutism*, 121. The revisionist position on French absolutism of Nicholas Henshall, *The Myth of Absolutism: Change and Continuity in Early Modern European Monarchy* (London: Longman, 1992), 35–60, has been rebutted: Marie-Laure Legay, *Les états provinciaux dans la construction de l'état moderne aux XVIIe et XVIIIe siècles* (Geneva: Droz, 2001); Fanny Cosandey and Robert Descimon, *L'absolutisme en France: Histoire et historiographie* (Paris: Seuil, 2002); John J. Hurt, *Louis XIV and the Parlements: The Assertion of Royal Authority* (Manchester: Manchester University Press, 2002); Edward Foss, *The Judges of England*, 9 vols. (London: Longman, Brown, Green, and Longmans, 1848–64), 7:4, 201. Twelve of twenty-six judges were superseded. Foss intimates that after dismissing all of the prerevolutionary judges, William and Mary never dismissed a judge for political reasons.

28. Yard to Sir William Trumbull, 26 November 1685, BL, Trumbull Newsletters (since recataloged); Wynne to Sir William Trumbull, 21 December 1685, BL, Trumbull Misc. 23, unfolioed (since recataloged); Barillon (London) to Louis XIV, 23 November/3 December 1685, NA, PRO 31/3/162, fol. 36r; Barillon (London) to Louis XIV, 25 January/4 February 1686, NA, PRO 31/3/164, fol. 1v; Bonrepaus (London) to Seignelay, 11/21 February 1686, NA, PRO 31/3/164, fol. 81r; Barillon (London) to Louis XIV, 31 December/10 January 1685/86, NA, PRO 31/3/163, fol. 4v; Barillon (London) to Louis XIV, 15/25 February 1686, NA, PRO 31/3/164, fol. 17r; Barillon (London) to Louis XIV, 19/29 April 1686, NA, PRO 31/3/165, fol. 33r; Barillon (London) to Louis XIV, 22 April/2 May 1686, NA, PRO 31/3/186, fol. 1r; Lionel Glassey, *Politics and the Appointment of Justices of the Peace, 1675–1720* (Oxford: Oxford University Press, 1979), 69; J. Tucker to Arran, 23 April 1687, NAS, GD 406/1/3446; Barillon (London) to Louis XIV, 15/25 April 1686, NA, PRO 31/3/165, fol. 29r; Barillon (London) to Louis XIV, 22 April/2 May 1686, NA, PRO 31/3/166, fol. 1.

29. Yard (London) to Sir Richard Bulstrode, 30 April 1686, HRC, Pforzheimer Collection; ? (Whitehall) to William of Orange, 1 June 1686, NA, SP 8/1/Pt. 2, fol. 73v; Nathaniel Johnston (London) to Sir John Reresby, 29 June 1686, WYAS, MX 44/32; Newsletter from Whitehall, 21 June 1686, BL, Trumbull Newsletters (since recataloged); London Newsletter, 22 June 1686, FSL, L.c. 1674. Sir Isaac Newton was one among many who took careful notes on the case: King's College, Cambridge, Keynes MSS 149; *The Case of Sir Edward Hales* (London: J. Watts, 1689), 9, 11; Barillon (London) to Louis XIV, 30 November/10 December 1685/86, NA, PRO 31/3/162, fol. 40; Barillon (Windsor) to Louis XIV, 24 June/4 July 1686, NA, PRO 31/3/166, fol. 30v; Barillon (Windsor) to Louis XIV, 13/23 September 1686, NA, PRO 31/3/167, fol. 17r. See also Gilbert Burnet, "Reasons against the Repealing," 1687, in *A Collection of Eighteen Papers Relating to the Affairs of Church and State during the Reign of King James the Second* (London: John Starkey and Richard Chiswell, 1689), 4; and Henry Booth, Lord Delamere, "Speech of Corruption of the Judges," in Delamere, *The Works* (London: John Lawrence and John Dunton, 1694), 138.

30. Parker, *Making of French Absolutism*, 120–22; Collins, *State in Early Modern France*, 115–16.

31. Barillon (London) to Louis XIV, 19/29 October 1685, NA, PRO 31/3/161, fol. 66v; Barillon (London) to Louis XIV, 26 October/5 November, 30 November/10 December 1685, NA, PRO 31/3/162, fols. 3, 42r; Privy Council Register, 21 October 1685, NA, PC 2/71, fol. 77v; J. Taylor (London) to Sir Robert Southwell, 22 October 1685, BL, Add. 28569, fol. 56r; Robert Harley (London) to Sir Edward Harley, 24 October 1685, BL, Add. 70013, fol. 280r; Morrice, Entering Book, 24 October 1685, DWL, 31 P, 483; Privy Council Register, 23 December 1685, NA, PC 2/71, fol. 93r; Blathwayt (Whitehall) to Southwell, 24 December 1685, Nottingham SUL, PwV 53/15; Barillon (London) to Louis XIV, 24 December/3 January, 28 December/7 January 1685/86, NA, PRO 31/3/163, fols. 1, 2; Barillon (London) to Louis XIV, 3/13 June 1686, NA, PRO 31/3/166, fol. 19v; Barillon (Windsor) to Louis XIV, 24 June/4 July 1686, NA, PRO 31/3/166, fol. 30v; Barillon (Windsor) to Louis XIV, 13/23 September 1686, NA, PRO 31/3/167, fol. 14v; Barillon (London) to Louis XIV, 7/17 October 1686, NA, PRO 31/3/167, fol. 29v.

32. Yard (Whitehall) to Sir Richard Bulstrode, 9 November 1685, HRC, Bulstrode Newsletters; Barillon (London) to Louis XIV, 3/13 December 1685, NA, PRO 31/3/162, fols. 46–47; Robert Harley to Sir Edward Harley, 15 December 1685, BL, Add. 70013, fol. 304r; Wynne to Sir William Trumbull, 21 December 1685, BL, Trumbull Misc. 23 (since recataloged); Barillon (London) to Louis XIV, 28 December/7 January 1685/86, NA, PRO 31/3/163, fol. 2r; Barillon (London) to Louis XIV, 17/27 January 1687, NA, PRO 31/3/168, fol. 16v; John de la Bere (London) to Kinnard de la Bere, 29 January 1687, NA, FO 335/15, unfolioed; Barillon (London) to Louis XIV, 31 January/10 February 1687, NA, PRO 31/3/168, fol. 24r; Musgrave to Sir Thomas Clarges, 25 February 1687, CRO Kendal, WD/RY 3098; Yard (London) to Bulstrode, 28 February 1687, HRC, Bulstrode Newsletters; C. Johnston to Sir John Reresby, 21 March 1687, WYAS, MX 47/17; Fraser (London) to Ellis, 22 March 1687, BL, Add. 4194, fol. 163r; Nathaniel Johnston (London) to Sir John Reresby, 9 April 1687, WYAS, MX 48/35.

33. Barillon (London) to Louis XIV, 6/16 January 1687, NA, PRO 31/3/168, fol. 11r. This was also the view of the Whigs Gilbert Burnet and Lord Delamere: Burnet, "Reasons against the Repealing," 5; Delamere, "Some Observations on the Prince of Orange's Declaration," in Delamere, *Works,* 365.

34. James II (Whitehall) to Perth, 7 March 1687, NAS, GD 160/369, fols. 86–87; Barillon (London) to Louis XIV, 31 January/10 February, 7/17 February, 17/27 February, 21/31 March, 27 December/6 January 1686/87, NA, PRO 31/3/168, fols. 24r, 28v, 34, 58v, 4r; Lady Sunderland to William III, 7 March 1687, NA, SP 8/1/Pt. 2, fol. 34; Yard (Whitehall) to Albeville, 15 February, 15 March 1687, Indiana, Albeville MSS; Morrice, Entering Book, 12 March 1687, DWL, 31 Q, 81–82; Barillon (London) to Louis XIV, 14/24 1687, NA, PRO 31/3/168, fol. 53r.

35. Barillon (London) to Louis XIV, 21/31 March, 18/28 April 1687, NA, PRO 31/3/168, fols. 57v, 75v.

36. "The King's Instructions," in *Penal Laws and Test Act,* 2 vols., ed. Sir George Duckett (London: n.p., 1883), 1:ix. Interestingly, questionnaires were themselves made use of by Jean-Baptiste Colbert in the 1670s: Collins, *State in Early Modern France,* 112; Ailesbury, *Memoirs,* 1:164–65; Morrice, Entering Book, 9 February 1688, DWL, 31 Q, 236; Southwell (Kingsweston) to Weymouth, 7 November 1686, Longleat House, Thynne MSS 15, fol. 143v. For the regulators, see "Report of the Regulators to James II," 19 April 1688, *Penal Laws and Test Act,* ed. Duckett, 2:218.

37. Van Citters (London) to States General, 3/13 June 1687, BL, Add. 34510, fol. 37; Edmund Verney (East Claydon) to John Verney, 12 June 1687, Buckinghamshire SRO, Verney MSS; Johnston (London) to Sir John Reresby, 12 June, 5 July 1687, WYAS, MX 48/17, 29; Fraser (London) to Ellis, 9 July 1687, BL, Add. 4194, fol. 202r; H. Aubrey (Hereford) to Ellis, 24 August 1687, BL, Add. 4194, fol. 218r; J. Fitzpatrick to William III, 1 September 1687, NA, SP 8/1/Pt. 2, fol. 147r; Samuel de Pay (Windsor) to Edmund Poley, 30 September 1687, Beinecke, OSB MSS 1/Box 2/Folder 67; London Newsletter, 1 November 1687, FSL, L.c. 1877; Roger Kenyon, Note, December 1687, Lancashire SRO, DD/Ke/6/26; Barillon (London) to Louis XIV, 15/25 December 1687, NA, PRO 31/3/174, fol. 45r; T. Fairfax to Reresby, 21 February 1688, WYAS, MX/R51/56; Sir John Lowther of Whitehaven (London) to Sir Daniel Fleming, 4 October 1687, CRO Kendal, WD/RY 3/38; Nathaniel Johnston (London) to Sir John Reresby, 18 December 1687, WYAS, MX/R50/54. For the mixed opin-

ions, see for optimists: Johnston (London) to Reresby, 3 January 1688, WYAS, MX/R51/3; Report of the Regulators to James II, 19 April 1688, *Penal Laws and Test Act,* ed. Duckett, 2:220–21. For pessimists: Bonrepaus (London) to Seignelay 17/27 October 1687, NA, PRO 31/3/173, fol. 57r; Van Citters (London) to States General, 3/13 February 1688, BL, Add. 34510, fol. 83v. For thoroughness: "Memorandum for Those That Go into the Country," 1688, All Souls College, MSS 257.

38. London Newsletter, 23 July 1687, FSL, L.c. 1834; Cotterell (London) to his daughter, 16 October 1687, BL, Trumbull MSS 39 (since recataloged); Newsletter, 8 December 1687, BL, Add. 34515, fol. 38v; James Tyrell (London) to John Locke, 14 December 1687, *Locke Correspondence,* 3:311–12; Robert Harley to Sir Edward Harley, 25 February 1688, BL, Add. 70014, fol. 49r; Morrice, Entering Book, 3 March 1688, DWL, 31 Q, 243–44; Report of the Regulators to James II, September 1688, *Penal Laws and Test Act,* ed. Duckett, 2:235; Paul Halliday, *Dismembering the Body Politic: Partisan Politics in England's Towns, 1650–1730* (Cambridge: Cambridge University Press, 1998), 95, 238, 248; Paman (London) to Lloyd, 18 August 1687, LPL, 3898/6/1; London Newsletter, 18 August 1687, FSL, L.c. 1845; Morrice, Entering Book, 25 February 1688, DWL, 31 Q, 239 (4); Van Citters (Windsor) to States General, 7/17 October 1687, BL, Add. 34510, fol. 51v; Mark Knights, "A City Revolution: The Remodeling of the London Livery Companies in the 1680s," *English Historical Review* 112 (1997): 1158–62; William Nott (London) to Sir Joseph Williamson, 6 October 1687, NA, SP 31/3, fol. 146r; Victor L. Stater, *Noble Government: The Stuart Lord Lieutenancy and the Transformation of English Politics* (Athens: University of Georgia Press, 1994), 166, 169–72; Jo. Cooke (Whitehall) to Poley, 11 November 1687, Beinecke, OSB MSS 1/Box 2/Folder 72; Glassey, *Politics and the Appointment of Justices of the Peace,* 84–91.

39. Barillon (Windsor) to Louis XIV, 29 September/19 October 1687, NA, PRO 31/3/173, fol. 9r; John Phillips, *The Secret History of the Reigns of K. Charles II and K. James II* (London, 1690), 193.

40. Halliday, *Dismembering the Body Politic,* 239; Knights, "City Revolution," 1176. The phrase about modern politics comes from Mark Kishlansky, *Parliamentary Selection: Social and Political Choice in Early Modern England* (Cambridge: Cambridge University Press, 1986), 9; Andreas Schedler, "The Logic of Electoral Authoritarianism," in *Electoral Authoritarianism: The Dynamics of Unfree Competition,* ed. Schedler (Boulder, CO: Lynn Rienner, 2006), 1–3; Bernard Grofman, ed., *Race and Redistricting in the 1990s* (New York: Agathon, 1998).

41. Halliday, *Dismembering the Body Politic,* 248; Barillon (Windsor) to Louis XIV, 29 July/8 August 1686, NA, PRO 31/3/166, fol. 33v (this letter is misdated); Barillon (London) to Louis XIV, 30 August/ 9 September 1686, NA, PRO 31/3/167, fol. 5v; Barillon (Windsor) to Louis XIV, 13/23 September 1686, NA, PRO 31/3/167, fol. 16r; Barillon (London) to Louis XIV, 6/16 January 1687, NA, PRO 31/3/168, fol. 11v; Yard (Whitehall) to Albeville, 18 February, 29 March 1687, Indiana, Albeville MSS; John Verney (London) to Sir Ralph Verney, 6 December 1687, Buckinghamshire SRO, Verney MSS; James Johnston (London) to ?, 16 December 1687, BL, Add. 34515, fol. 42v; London Newsletter, 8 March 1688, FSL, L.c. 1925; Tanner, "Administration of the Navy," 282; Van Citters (London) to States General, 18/28 May 1688, BL, Add. 34512, fols. 79–80; Andrew Newport (Exeter) to Lord Herbert of Cherbury, 19 May 1688, NA, PRO 30/53/8, fol. 60v; Commissioners of the Customs (London) to Noble Waterhouse, 15 March 1688, HEH, STT 882.

42. Patrick K. O'Brien and Philip A. Hunt, "The Rise of a Fiscal State in England, 1485–1815," *Historical Research* 66 (June 1993): 151. This slightly but for our purposes, significantly, revises Michael Mann's claim that the increases came after 1688, and during a period of warfare. Mann, *States, War, and Capitalism: Studies in Political Sociology* (Oxford: Blackwell, 1992), 104–11. Barillon (London) to Louis XIV, 3/13 December 1685, NA, PRO 31/3/162, fol. 43r; C. D. Chandaman, *The English Public Revenue, 1660–1688* (Oxford: Clarendon Press, 1975), 256–61, 332–33. Sir Nicholas Butler and Sir Dudley North also tried to increase efficiency in the customs collection. After the revolution one Peter Coston recalled that Butler and North claimed that their job was "to get what they could for the King." Peter Coston, London Customs House Committee Minutes, 1689, Guildhall Library, 8493A, fol. 21v; Richard Grassby, *The English Gentleman in Trade: The Life and*

Works of Sir Dudley North, 1641–1691 (Oxford: Clarendon Press, 1994), 167–76; Bonrepaus (London) to Seignelay, 29 August/8 September 1687, NA, PRO 31/3/172, fol. 62r.

43. Delamere, "Some Observations on the Prince of Orange's Declaration," in Delamere, *Works*, 355; Barillon (Windsor) to Louis XIV, 10/20 September 1685, NA, PRO 31/3/161, fol. 47v; *An Account of the Pretended Prince of Wales* (1688), 6; *An Account of the Reasons of the Nobility and Gentry's Invitation* (London: Jonathan Robinson, 1688), 7–8; Evelyn, *Diary*, 7 September 1701, 5:475; Bonrepaus (Windsor) to Seignelay, 25 May/4 June 1687, NA, PRO 31/3/170, fol. 8r; Phillips, *Secret History*, 159. See also John Partridge, *Mene Mene, Tekel Upharsin* (London: Richard Baldwin, 1689), 23–24; and Gilbert Burnet, *Reasons against Repealing the Acts of Parliament Concerning the Test* (1687), 4.

44. Evelyn, *Diary*, 18 February 1685, 4:418; John Evelyn (London) to Mary Evelyn, 5 March 1685, BL, Evelyn Papers, ME 2 (since recataloged); Evelyn, *Diary*, 5 March 1685, 29 December 1686, 4:419, 535; Barillon (Windsor) to Louis XIV, 10/20 September 1686, NA, PRO 31/3/161, fol. 147r.

45. Barillon (London) to Louis XIV, 26 February 1685, NA, PRO 31/3/160, fol. 55v; Stewkeley to Sir Ralph Verney, 20 March 1686, Buckinghamshire SRO, Verney MSS; Barillon (London) to Louis XIV, 5/15 April 1686, NA, PRO 31/3/165, fol. 22r; Yard (Whitehall) to Albeville, 28 January 1687, Indiana, Albeville MSS; Thomas Booth (London) to Capt. John Booth, 24 March 1687, FSL, F.c. 28; Robert Francis Strachan (Paris) to William Leslie, 16/26 November 1685, SCA, Bl 1/92/12; Yard (London) to Bulstrode, 19 April 1686, HRC, Bulstrode Newsletters; Thomas Harley to Sir Edward Harley, 16 October 1686, BL, Add. 70119, unfolioed; Barillon (London) to Louis XIV, 21/31 October 1686, NA, PRO 31/3/167, fol. 37r; Henry Thynne (London) to Weymouth, 31 March 1687, Longleat House, Thynne MSS 14, fol. 145r; Yard (Whitehall) to Albeville, 1 April 1687, Indiana, Albeville MSS; London Newsletter, 2 April 1687, BL, Add. 4182, fol. 67r; London Newsletter, 2 April 1687, FSL, L.c. 1792; Stewkeley (London) to Sir Ralph Verney, 7 April 1687, Buckinghamshire SRO, Verney MSS; Morrice, Entering Book, 16 April 1687, DWL, 31 Q, 93; Newsletter from Rome, 17 May 1687, NA, SP 85/12, fol. 187r; Barillon (London) to Louis XIV, 12/22 November 1685, NA, PRO 31/3/162, fol. 20r; Barillon (London) to Louis XIV, 25 January/4 February 1685/86, NA, PRO 31/3/164, fol. 1r; Barillon (London) to Louis XIV, 1/11 April 1686, NA, PRO 31/3/165, fol. 20v; Evelyn, *Diary*, 17 January 1687, 4:535; Van Citters (London) to States General, 1/11 April 1687, BL, Add. 34510, fol. 21r; Lyttleton to Hatton, 5 April 1687, BL, Add. 29578, fol. 99r.

46. Burnet, *History of His Own Time*, 1:683; John Lake, bishop of Chichester (Chichester), to Sancroft, 5 July 1685, Bodleian, Tanner 31, fol. 128r. See also Cotterell to Sir William Trumbull, 26 March 1688, BL, Trumbull MSS 39 (since recataloged); Halifax (London) to William III, 18 June 1687, NA, SP 8/1/Pt. 2, fol. 31; Joseph Hill (London) to Sir William Trumbull, 2 April 1686, 19 November 1687, Berkshire SRO, D/ED/C33.

47. John Leyburn to Vicars Foran, 23 June 1687, AWA, Ser. A, 35:8.

48. William Blundell, Note, in *Crosby Records: A Cavalier's Notebook*, ed. Ellison T. Gibson (London: Longmans, Green, 1880), 205; Journals, 1685, Foley, 90–91; Innes (Paris) to William Leslie, 20/30 September 1686, SCA, Bl 1/94/10; Henry Compton (bishop of London) to William III, 5 September 1687, NA, SP 8/2/Pt. 2, fols. 146–47.

49. General Assembly Book of the Catholic English Clergy, 21 April 1687, AWA, Old Brotherhood Papers, 112; Leyburn to Foran, 27 June 1687, AWA, Ser. A, 35:7–8; Dodd, *History of the English College*, 31; Hickes (Worcester) to Turner, 31 December 1686, 20 June 1687, Bodleian, Rawlinson MSS, Letters 91, fols. 42r, 50; Annual Letters, 1685–1690, Foley, 526; *Life of Kidder*, 38; T. Musgrave (York) to Reresby, 20 June 1687, WYAS, MX/R50/16; A. B. (York) to Sir Daniel Fleming, 22 December 1687, CRO Kendal, WD/RY 3155; Baldock (York) to Reresby, 1 February 1688, WYAS, MX/R50/64; Foley, 394–95; Morrice, Entering Book, 8 May 1686, DWL, 31 P, 532; Supplement of the History of the English Province, 1688, Foley, 151–52; Dodd, *Church History*, 3:418.

50. On the presses: Barillon (London) to Louis XIV, 15/25 March 1686, NA, PRO 31/3/165, fol. 12r; Morrice, Entering Book, 30 January 1686, DWL, 31 P, 520–21; Sunderland (Whitehall) to Sancroft, 16 November

1686, Bodleian, Tanner 30, fol. 143r; Cotterell to his daughter, May–June 1686, BL, Trumbull MSS 39 (since recataloged); Tyrell (London) to Locke, 6 May 1687, *Locke Correspondence,* 3:192. On the content: London Newsletter, 4 March, 11 March, 30 September, 23 October, 14 December 1686, FSL, L.c. 1632, 1635, 1714, 1724, 1747; Sir William Coventry (London) to Weymouth, 27 February 1686, Longleat House, Thynne MSS 16, fol. 420r; Sir Richard Temple, Ledgerbook, 27 February 1686, HEH, ST 152, fol. 185r; James Johnston (London) to ?, 23 May 1688, BL, Add. 34515, fol. 64v; Foley, 265–66; Barillon (Windsor) to Louis XIV, 26 May/5 June 1687, NA, PRO 31/3/170, fol. 32r; London Newsletter, 26 April, 24 May, 24 September, 17 November, 31 December 1687, FSL, L.c. 1802, 1811, 1861, 1884, 1902; Wood, *Athenae,* 2:838–39; The Examination of John Taffe (Capuchin Monk), ca. 1690, BL, Add. 36913, fols. 177–78; Jesuit Annual Letters, 1685–1690, Foley, 319, 450, 526, 621, 662, 727; Rules for Catholic Clergy of Staffordshire, 1686, AWA, Ser. A, 34:1078–79; Wellwood, *Memoirs,* 195.

51. Sir William Petty, "Remedies for the King," 1687, BL, Add. 72866, fol. 59r; "Concerning the King's Wealth," 1685, BL, Add. 72866, fol. 19; "The Use and Application," 1686, BL, Add. 72866, fol. 35; "Intimations to the King," 1686/87, BL, Add. 72866, fol. 53; "Essay about the Analysis of Property," 1686/87, BL, Add. 72866, fol. 57; "Things to Be Done for the Public Good," 1687, BL, Add. 72866, fol. 153. For the Compton Census data, see Anne Whiteman, ed., *The Compton Census* (London: British Academy, 1986), ccxiii–ccxiv; Foley, 334; J. A. Hilton, *Catholic Lancashire* (Chichester: Philimore, 1994), 44; John Paul Jameson (Rome) to Walter Leslie, 30 March 1685, SCA, Bl 1/91/3; Supplement of the History of the English Province, 1688, Foley, 152.

52. *His Majesties Gracious Declaration to All His Loving Subjects for Liberty of Conscience* (London: Charles Bill, Henry Hills, and Thomas Newcomb, 1687), 1–2.

53. Sunderland (Windsor) to Sancroft, 4 September 1685, Bodleian, Tanner 31, fols. 198–99; Burnet, *History of His Own Time,* 1:639; James II to archbishops of Canterbury and York, 5 March 1686, CSPD, Ser. 4A, 2:57; Bonrepaus (London) to Seignelay, 11/21 March 1686, NA, PRO 31/3/165, fol. 79r; Newsletter to Bulstrode, 15 March 1686, HRC, Bulstrode Newsletters; Henry Thynne (London) to Weymouth, 18 March 1686, Longleat House, Thynne MSS 14, fol. 109r; Barillon (London) to Louis XIV, 25 March/4 April 1686, NA, PRO 31/3/165, fol. 18r; Jonathan Trelawney to Sunderland, 21 May 1686, NA, SP 31/3, fols. 70–71.

54. John Gother, *Good Advice to the Pulpits* (London: Henry Hills, 1687), 56–57, 67–68; Thomas Cartwright, *An Answer of a Minister of the Church of England* (London: J. L., 1687), 18, 22–23.

55. Vincent Alsop, *Mr. Alsop's Speech to the King* [1687]; London Newsletter, 21 June 1687, FSL, L.c. 1823; "The Manifestation of Joy," April 1687, in *The Pepys Ballads,* 8 vols., ed. Hyder Edgar Rollins (Cambridge, MA: Harvard University Press, 1929–32), 3:279; *A Poem Occasioned by His Majesties Most Gracious Resolution* (London: George Larkin, 1687); *The Dissenter's Description of True Loyalty* (London: Andrew Sowle, [1687]); Cartwright, *Answer of a Minister,* 22.

56. Gother, *Good Advice,* sig. A2v; Cartwright, *Answer of a Minister,* 24; Wellwood, *Memoirs,* 196. See also Burnet, "Letter Concerning Some Reflections," 1687, 29.

57. Barillon (Windsor) to Louis XIV, 20/30 September 1686, NA, PRO 31/3/167, fol. 20; Jeaffreson (London) to Capt. J. Phipps, 8 September 1686, Jeaffreson, 316; Ailesbury, *Memoirs,* 1:161; *Life of Kidder,* 45; Thomas Newcome, ed., *The Life of John Sharpe,* vol. 1 (London: C. and J. Rivington, 1825), 73; Lloyd to Sancroft, 6 February 1688, Bodleian, Tanner 29, fol. 133r; James Harris to ?, 22 January 1687, Bodleian, Clarendon MSS 89, fol. 12r.

58. Privy Council Minutes, 17 July 1686, NA, PC 2/71, fol. 153v; J. P. Kenyon, "The Commission for Ecclesiastical Causes, 1686–1688," *Historical Journal* 34, no. 3 (1991): 727–36; James II (Whitehall) to Perth, 10 February 1686, NAS, GD 160/569, fol. 82r; Arundel of Wardour to Perth, 11 February 1688, NAS, GD 160/529, fol. 25r. On the Edinburgh Riots, see Tim Harris, *Revolution: The Great Crisis of the British Monarchy, 1685–1720* (London: Allen Lane, 2006), 151–53. For some examples of informal attempts to suppress anti-Catholic preaching, see Dolben to Sir William Trumbull, 8 February 1686, BL, Trumbull MSS 54 (since recataloged); Frampton to Sancroft, 27 March 1686, Bodleian, Tanner 30, fol. 7r; Barillon (London) to

Louis XIV, 3/13 June 1686, NA, PRO 31/3/166, fol. 19v; Barillon (Windsor) to Louis XIV, 24 June/4 July, 1/11 July, 8/18 July, 22 July/1 August 1686, NA, PRO 31/3/166, fols. 30v, 35v, 39r, 46v.

59. Proceedings of the Ecclesiastical Commission, 3 August 1686, HEH, HA Religious Box 2 (5); Evelyn, *Diary,* 24 June 1686, 4:516. The case was a widely publicized cause célèbre. See, e.g., George Clarke's copy among his papers at Worcester College, Oxford: Worcester College, MSS 58; Barillon (London) to Louis XIV, 8 March 1685, NA, PRO 31/3/160, fol. 75v; Barillon (London) to Louis XIV, 29 March/8 April, 1/11 April 1686, NA, PRO 31/3/165, fols. 19r, 20v; Barillon (Windsor) to Louis XIV, 26 July/5 August, 5/15 August 1686, NA, PRO 31/3/166, fols. 48–49, 53r; Burnet, *History of His Own Time,* 1:674.

60. Charles Montagu (Trinity College, Cambridge) to George Stepney, 6 November 1686, NA, SP 105/82, fol. 5v; Yard (Whitehall) to Albeville, 14 January 1687, Indiana, Albeville MSS; London Newsletter, 15 January 1687, FSL, L.c. 1761; Diary of Thomas Cartwright, 31 January 1687, BL, Add. 24357, fol. 60v; Thomas Foley (Witley) to Robert Harley, 5 April 1687, BL, Add. 70226, unfolioed; ? (London) to Arran, 12 May 1687, NAS, GD 406/1/3448; Bonrepaus (London) to Seignelay, 19/29 May 1687, NA, PRO 31/3/169, fol. 90r; Wood, *Athenae,* 2:1178; Captain Robert Parker, *Memoirs of the Most Remarkable Military Transactions* (Dublin: Geo. and Alex Ewing, 1746), 7.

61. Morrice, Entering Book, 23 October 1686, DWL, 31 P, 640; Comber, *Three Considerations,* 3.

62. London Newsletter, 4 March, 28 September, 7 October 1686, FSL, L.c. 1632, 1713, 1717; Henry Compton, *Episcopalia* (London: Timothy Westly, 1686); William Wake, Autobiography, 1687, LPL, 2932, fols. 22–23, 55–57; William Wake, *A Discourse Concerning the Nature of Idolatry* (London: William Rogers, 1688). It was published anonymously.

63. Sir Leoline Jenkins (Whitehall) to Dartmouth, 4 April 1684, Beinecke, OSB Shelves fb.190, 3:fol. 223r; Cotterell to his daughter, 17 June 1686, BL, Trumbull MSS 39 (since recataloged); ? (London) to Ellis, 4 January 1687, BL, Add. 4194, fol. 130v; Dartmouth (London) to Clarendon, 31 January 1687, Glasgow SUL, MS Hunter 73 (T.3.11), fol. 25r; Bonrepaus, Report on the State of England, 1687, NA, PRO 31/3/174, fol. 84r; Barillon (Windsor) to Louis XIV, 2/12 June 1687, NA, PRO 31/3/170, fol. 61r; Barillon (London) to Louis XIV, 23 December/2 January 1686/87, NA, PRO 31/3/168, fol. 1v; Thomas Booth (London) to Capt. John Booth, 8 January 1687, FSL, F.c. 25; Barillon (London) to Louis XIV, 4/14 April 1687, NA, PRO 31/3/168, fol. 66v; Daniel Defoe, *Memoirs of Publick Transactions in the Life and Ministry of His Grace the Duke of Shrewsbury* (London: Tho. Warner, 1718), 13; Petition of Four Gentlemen-Ushers, Quarter Waiters, c. 1689, CKS, U269/O73; For Anne: Barillon (London) to Louis XIV, 26 March 1685, NA, PRO 31/3/160, fol. 92v; Barillon (Windsor) to Louis XIV, 17/27 June 1686, NA, PRO 31/3/166, fol. 27; Barillon (London) to Louis XIV, 3/13 March, 24 March/3 April 1687, NA, PRO, 31/3/168, fols. 48r, 61r; Edward Gregg, *Queen Anne* (New Haven and London: Yale University Press, 2001), 42–45. For Mary: William Stanley (The Hague) to Sancroft, 24 January/3 February 1688, Bodleian, Tanner 29, fol. 130; "Some Account of the Revolution," BL, Add. 9363, fol. 3v.

64. ? (Whitehall) to William III, 1 June 1686, NA, SP 8/1/Pt. 2, fol. 75v; Barillon (London) to Louis XIV, 27 May/6 June 1686, NA, PRO 31/3/166, fol. 16r; Barillon (Windsor) to Louis XIV, 27 June/7 July 1687, NA, PRO 31/3/171, fol. 13r; Barillon (London) to Louis XIV, 14/24 October 1686, NA, PRO 31/3/167, fol. 33r; Childs, *Army,* 22–23, 193; Fraser (London) to Ellis, 9 July 1687, BL, Add. 4194, fol. 202r; Barillon (London) to Louis XIV, 9/19 June 1687, NA, PRO 31/3/170, fol. 115r; James Fitzjames, Duke of Berwick, *Memoirs of the Marshal Duke of Berwick,* vol. 1 (London: T. Cadell, 1779), 19–20; Sir Martin Beekman, "The Reasons Why I Have Been Accounted a Papist," December 1688, ed. N. B. White, *Notes and Queries* 170 (21 March 1936), 200; J. Cunningham (Cambrai) to ?, 5/15 May 1688, NA, SP 8/2/Pt. 2, fol. 17.

65. Childs, *Army,* 20–21; Bonrepaus (London) to Seignelay, 12/22 September 1687, NA, PRO 31/3/172, fols. 90–91; Sir Edward Hales, Treatise on Government, 1692, AWA, Old Brotherhood Papers, Book 3/258.

66. Morrice, Entering Book, 19 February 1687, DWL, 31 Q, 71; J. Hill (Paris) to Sir William Trumbull, 15 February 1688, Berkshire SRO, D/ED/C33; Thomas Bligh (London) to his brother, 13 January 1687, PRONI, T2929/1/7; Stater, *Noble Government,* 166–67; Barillon (London) to Louis XIV, 25 October/4 November

1686, NA, PRO 31/3/167, fol. 40v; Glassey, *Politics and the Appointment of Justices of the Peace,* 70–77; John Miller, *Popery and Politics in England, 1660–1688* (Cambridge: Cambridge University Press, 1973), 219; Morrice, Entering Book, 20 November 1686, DWL, 31 Q, 10.

67. London Newsletter, 28 December 1686, FSL, L.c. 1753; ? (London) to Ellis, 1 January 1687, BL, Add. 4194, fol. 126v; The Petition of His Highness Prince Rupert's Watermen, c. 1689, CKS, U269/O73; David Lemmings, *Gentlemen and Barristers: The Inns of Court and the English Bar, 1680–1730* (Oxford: Clarendon Press, 1990), 65; Goldie, "James II and the Dissenters' Revenge," 61; H.A. (Herefordshire) to Ellis, 2 August 1687, BL, Add. 28876, fol. 23r; London Newsletter, 1 November 1687, FSL, L.c. 1877.

68. G. Reresby (Cambridge) to Reresby, 6 January 1687, WYAS, MX 49/15; T. Bedford (Trinity College, Cambridge) to Stepney, 22 July 1687, NA, SP 105/82, fol. 8r; Paman (London) to Sir Ralph Verney, 27 July 1687, Buckinghamshire SRO, Verney MSS; Fellows of Sidney Sussex College to Sancroft, 14 October 1688, Bodleian, Tanner 28, fol. 197r.

69. Proceedings of the Ecclesiastical Commission, 7 April 1687, HEH, HA Religious Box 2(5); C. Reresby (London) to Sir John Reresby, 28 April 1687, WYAS, MX 49/1; Tyrrell (London) to Locke, 6 May 1687, *Locke Correspondence,* 3:192; Barillon (London) to Louis XIV, 9/19 May 1687, NA, PRO 31/3/169, fol. 62r.

70. Bonrepaus (London) to Seignelay, 8/18 March 1686, NA, PRO 31/3/165, fols. 58–59; Evelyn, *Diary,* 5 May 1686, 4:510; Barillon (London) to Louis XIV, 6/16 September 1686, NA, PRO 31/3/167, fol. 9v; Thomas Barlow (bishop of Lincoln) to Robert Boyle, 4 January 1687, in, *The Works of the Honourable Robert Boyle,* vol. 6, ed. Thomas Birch (London: W. Johnston et al., 1772), 317; Dr. John Guise (Aleppo) to Turner, 3 March 1687, Bodleian, Rawlinson MSS, D60, fol. 94r.

71. Gabriel Hastings (Oxford) to Huntingdon, 18 October 1686, HEH, HA 5267; Burnet, *History of His Own Time,* 1:696; Wood, *Athenae,* 2:934, 1028; R. A. Beddard, "James II and the Catholic Challenge," in *Seventeenth-Century Oxford,* ed. Nicholas Tyacke (Oxford: Clarendon Press, 1997), 921, 939; Foley, 822.

72. Henry Aldrich, *A Reply to Two Discourses Lately Printed at Oxford* (Oxford, 1687), 2; Robert Harley to Sir Edward Harley, 12 March 1686, BL, Add. 70013, fol. 333r; Bonrepaus (Oxford) to Seignelay, 4/14 September 1687, NA, PRO 31/3/172, fol. 78r; London Newsletter, 28 September 1686, FSL, L.c. 1713; Wood, *Athenae,* 2:934.

73. Dr. Thomas Smith's Narrative, 28 March 1687, in *Magdalen College and King James II,* ed. J. R. Bloxam (Oxford: Clarendon Press, 1886), 4; London Newsletter, 9 April 1687, FSL, L.c. 1795; F. Overton to Sir Richard Temple, 2 August 1687, HEH, STT 1541; Diary of Cartwright, 22 June 1687, fol. 90v; Clarges (London) to Weymouth, 23 April 1687, Longleat House, Thynne MSS 12, fol. 216v; Stewkeley (London) to Sir Ralph Verney, 9 June 1687, Buckinghamshire SRO, Verney MSS; Morrice, Entering Book, 11 June 1687, DWL, 31 Q, 152; London Newsletter, 14 June 1687, FSL, L.c. 1820; Thynne (London) to Weymouth, 23 June 1687, Longleat House, Thynne MSS 14, fol. 163r; J. Fr. (London) to Ellis, 25 June 1687, BL, Add. 4194, fol. 200v; Samuel de Pay (Whitehall) to Poley, 29 July 1687, Beinecke, OSB MSS 1/Box 2/Folder 63; Ralph Trumbull (Witney) to Sir William Trumbull, 5 October 1687, BL, Add. 72511, fol. 75v; "An Account of Magdalen College Visitation," 21 October 1687, NA, SP 8/1/Pt. 2, fol. 168v; "The Visitation of Magdalen College," 22 October 1687, Bodleian, Tanner 29, fol. 88r.

74. Wynne to Sir Robert Owen, 20 October 1687, National Library of Wales, Brogynton MSS, 860; Wynne (Whitehall) to Poley, 21 October 1687, Beinecke, OSB MSS 1/Box 2/Folder 69; Magdalen College Plea, 22 June 1687, in the Newdigate Papers, Warwickshire SRO, CR 136/B788; Sir Ralph Verney (Middle Claydon) to John Verney, 26 June 1687, Buckinghamshire SRO, Verney MSS; Thomas Ken (bishop of Bath and Wells) to Wake, 12 August 1687, Christ Church, William Wake Papers, 250, fol. 21r; Stewkeley (London) to Sir Ralph Verney, 27 October 1687, Buckinghamshire SRO, Verney MSS; Wynne (Whitehall) to Poley, 28 October 1687, Beinecke, OSB MSS 1/Box 2/Folder 70; Henry Holden (Oxford) to ?, 31 October 1687, Magdalen College Archives, MSS 421, fol. 1; London Newsletter, 28 January 1688, FSL, L.c. 1914.

75. Bonrepaus and Barillon (Oxford) to Seignelay, 4/14 September 1687, NA, PRO 31/3/172, fol. 77r; James II, Interview with Dr. Hedges, 14 October 1687, Magdalen College Archives, MSS 249, fol. 91v;

"Visitation of Magdalen College," 22 October 1687, fol. 88r; Thomas Cartwright, bishop of Chester, Speech to Magdalen College, [November] 1687, Beinecke, OSB Files 2854; Newsletter from London, 25 October 1687, BL, Add. 4182, fol. 70r; Bishop of Chester's Speech at Magdalen College, 16 November 1687, Warwickshire SRO, CR 136/B735; London Newsletter, 25 October 1687, FSL, L.c. 1874; Henry Holden (Oxford) to ?, 31 October 1687, Magdalen College Archives, MSS 421, fol. 1; Angus Macintyre, "The College, King James II and the Revolution, 1687–1688," in *Magdalen College and the Crown: Essays for the Tercentenary of the Restoration of the College, 1688,* ed. Laurence Brockliss, Gerald Harriss, and Angus Macintyre (Oxford: Printed for the College, 1988), 31–82.

76. Wynne (Whitehall) to Poley, 4 November 1687, Beinecke, OSB MSS 1/Box 2/Folder 71; William Sherwin (Oxford) to Turner, 4 August 1687, Bodleian, Rawlinson MSS, Letters 91, fol. 62v; R. W. to ?, November 1687, Bodleian, Tanner 29, fol. 112r.

77. Macintyre, "College, James II, and Revolution," 66; Thomas Newey (Oxford) to James Harrington, December 1687, BL, Add. 36707, fol. 17r; Edmund Verney (East Claydon) to John Verney, 4 December 1687, Buckinghamshire SRO, Verney MSS; Paul Foley (Oxford) to Sir Edward Harley, 20 February 1688, BL, Add. 70114, unfolioed; Moses Carter (Oxford) to Smith, 5 April 1688, Bodleian, MSS Smith 48, 47; Henry Fleming (Oxford) to Sir Daniel Fleming, 29 July 1688, CRO Kendal, WD/Ry 3230; Beddard, "James II and the Catholic Challenge," 945–47.

78. Dr. John Hough to ?, 9 October 1687, LPL, MSS 933/33; Proceedings of the Ecclesiastical Commission, 3 November 1687, HEH, HA Religious Box 2(5); John Freke to Locke, 3 June, 10 May 1687, *Locke Correspondence,* 3:210, 200–201.

79. Memoire de M. Robert, 27 December/6 January 1685/86, fol. 98r; Bonrepaus (London) to Seignelay, 1/11 March 1686, NA, PRO 31/3/165, fol. 47r; Edward Harley to Robert Harley, 8 March 1687, BL, Add. 70236, unfolioed; London Newsletter, 27 September 1687, 6 March 1688, FSL, L.c. 1862, 1924; Evelyn, *Diary,* 15 April 1688, 4:581; Burnet, *History of His Own Time,* 1:664.

80. I am more sympathetic with the interpretation of Robin Gwynn, "James II in the Light of His Treatment of Huguenot Refugees in England, 1685–1686," *English Historical Review* 92 (1977): 320–33, than I am with John Miller, "The Immediate Impact of the Revocation in England," in *The Huguenots and Ireland: Anatomy of an Emigration,* ed. C. E. J. Caldicott, H. Gough, and J.-P. Pittion (Dublin: Glendale, 1987), 161–74; Barillon (Windsor) to Louis XIV, 3/13 September 1685, NA, PRO 31/3/161, fol. 41v; Barillon (London) to Louis XIV, 28 January/7 February 1686, NA, PRO 31/3/164, fol. 8; Bonrepaus (London) to Seignelay, 28 December/7 January 1685/86, NA, PRO 31/3/163, fol. 31r; Bonrepaus (Calais) to Seignelay, 25 April/5 May 1686, NA, PRO 31/3/166, fol. 66; Robin Gwynn, "The Huguenots in Britain, the 'Protestant International,' and the Defeat of Louis XIV," in *From Strangers to Citizens: The Integration of Immigrant Communities in Britain, Ireland, and Colonial America, 1550–1750,* ed. Randolph Vigne and Charles Littleton (Brighton: Sussex Academic Press, 2001), 412–24; Sir William Trumbull, Diary, 21 September 1685, BL, Add. 52279, fol. 5r; Bonrepaus (London) to Seignelay, 24 December/3 January 1685/86, NA, PRO 31/3/163, fol. 22r; ? (Whitehall) to William III, 1 June 1686, NA, SP 8/1/Pt. 2, fol. 26; Barillon (London) to Louis XIV, 19/29 April 1686, NA, PRO 31/3/165, fol. 32v.

81. Evelyn, *Diary,* 3 November 1685, 4:487; Bonrepaus (London) to Seignelay, 4/14 January 1686, NA, PRO 31/3/163, fol. 52r ; London Newsletter, 13 April 1686, FSL, L.c. 1646; Barillon (London) to Louis XIV, 3/13 May, 6/16 May, 10/20 May 1686, NA, PRO 31/3/166, fols. 5r, 7v, 8r; Jeaffreson (London) to Phipps, 3 May 1686, Jeaffreson, 286. For evidence that private knowledge of Huguenot sufferings was widespread: Barillon (Windsor) to Louis XIV, 21 September/1 October 1685, NA, PRO 31/3/161, fol. 51v; William Penn (London) to James Harrison, 25 October 1685, *Penn Papers,* 65–66; Lady Rachel Russell (Woburn Abbey) to Dr. Fitzwilliam, November 1685, in *Letters of the Lady Rachel Russell; from the Manuscripts in the Library at Woburn Abbey* (London: Edward and Charles Dilly, 1773), 50; Newport (London) to Herbert, 12 December 1685, NA, PRO 30/53/8, fol. 33r; Bonrepaus (London) to Seignelay, 11/21 January 1686, NA, PRO 31/3/163, fols. 63–64; Nathaniel Cholmley (Whitly) to John Evance, 18 January 1686, North Yorkshire SRO, ZCG, unfolioed;

Tweeddale (London) to Lord Yester, 19 January 1686, NLS, 7026, fol. 33r; Henry Compton (bishop of London), Circular Letter, 2 April 1686, Bodleian, Tanner 30, fol. 10r; Will Haward (London) to Smith, 4 December 1686, Bodleian, MSS Smith 50, 57.

82. Van Citters (London) to States General, 1/11 June 1686, BL, Add. 34512, fol. 35v; ? (Whitehall) to William III, 1 June 1686, NA, SP 8/1/Pt. 2, fol. 26; Barillon (London) to Louis XIV, 28 October/7 November 1686, NA, PRO 31/3/167; Barillon (London) to Louis XIV, 9/19 November 1685, NA, PRO 31/3/162, fol. 17; Barillon (London) to Louis XIV, 15/25 February 1686, NA, PRO 31/3/164, fols. 18–19; Newsletter, 8 March 1686, HRC, Bulstrode Newsletters; Francis Thompson (Whitehall) to Sir William Trumbull, 29 April 1686, BL, Trumbull Misc. 24 (since recataloged); Barillon (London) to Louis XIV, 9/19 November 1685, NA, PRO 31/3/162, fol. 17r; Barillon (London) to Louis XIV, 19/29 April 1686, NA, PRO 31/3/165, fol. 32v; John Verney (London) to Sir Ralph Verney, 13 April 1686, Buckinghamshire SRO, Verney MSS; Bonrepaus (London) to Seignelay, 29 March/8 April 1686, NA, PRO 31/3/165, fol. 101r; Bonrepaus (London) to Seignelay, 11/21 November 1687, NA, PRO 31/3/173, fol. 117r.

CHAPTER 7. *Resistance to Catholic Modernity*

1. James II's Speech to His Irish Parliament, 15 May 1689, HEH, EL 9882; Henry St. John, Viscount Bolingbroke, "Dissertation upon Parties," 1733–34, in *The Works,* vol. 2 (Philadelphia: Cary and Hart, 1841), 75; Sir Joseph Williamson, 26 April 1690, Grey, 10:86–87.

2. James was not only interested in creating a well-drilled and well-armed military force; he also actively sought to disarm English civilian society: Sunderland to ?, 6 December 1686, WYAS, MX 33/3; Daniel Fleming to constables in Kendal and Lonsdale Wards, 12 January 1687, Cumbria SRO, Kendal, WD/RY Box 35; Robert Harley to Sir Edward Harley, 10 November 1685, BL, Add. 70013, fol. 290r; Owen Wynne to Sir William Trumbull, 9 November 1685, BL, Trumbull Misc. 23 (since recataloged); Sir Thomas Clarges, 12 November 1685, DWL, 31 T 3, 3; William Bridgeman (Whitehall) to Sir William Trumbull, 12 November 1685, BL, Trumbull Misc. 23 (since recataloged); Francis Cholmondley to Richard Legh, 16 November 1685, JRL, Legh of Lyme MSS, Box 2/Folder 17; Newsletter from Whitehall, 9 November 1685, BL, Trumbull Newsletters (since recataloged); Newsletter from Whitehall, 16 November 1685, BL, Trumbull Newsletters (since recataloged); Barillon (London) to Louis XIV, 23 November/3 December 1685, NA, PRO 31/3/162, fols. 35–36; *Memoirs of the Late Right Honourable John Lord Haversham* (London: J. Baker, 1711), 3; Newsletter from Whitehall, 19 November 1685, BL, Trumbull Newsletters (since recataloged); Barillon (London) to Louis XIV, 19/29 November, 23 November/3 December 1685, NA, PRO 31/3/162, fols. 32v, 34–35; Gilbert Dolben (London) to Sir William Trumbull, 12 November 1685, BL, Trumbull MSS 54 (since recataloged).

3. Barillon (London) to Louis XIV, 3/13 December 1685, NA, PRO 31/3/162, fol. 44; Robert Yard (Whitehall) to Sir Richard Bulstrode, 20 November 1685, HRC, Bulstrode Newsletters; J. Tucker (Whitehall) to Sir William Trumbull, 23 November 1685, BL, Trumbull Misc. (since recataloged).

4. Sir Ralph Verney (Claydon) to John Verney, 2 August 1685, Buckinghamshire SRO, Verney MSS; John Eames (Ailesbury) to Huntingdon, 23 July 1685, HEH, HA 2404; Eames (Ailesbury) to Huntingdon, 25 July 1685, HEH, HA 2405; Thoresby, *Diary,* 1685, 1:181; C. Hatton (Carlisle) to Huntingdon, 16 May 1687, HEH, HA 6225; Charles Morgan (Hull) to Huntingdon, 26 September 1685, HEH, HA 9383; Talbot Lascelles (Hull) to Huntingdon, 21 February 1686, HEH, HA 8156; William Blathwayt (Windsor) to Lord Langdale, 3 March 1688, NA, WO 4/1, fol. 50v; ? (York) to Sir John Reresby, 29 February 1688, WYAS, MX/R53/6; T. Fairfax (York) to Reresby, 3 March 1688, WYAS, MX/R54/1; Charles Macarty (Guernsey) to Blathwayt, 12 September 1686, Beinecke, OSB MSS 2/Box 6/Folder 121; Macarty (Guernsey) to ?, 11 June 1687, Beinecke, OSB MSS 2/Box 6/Folder 121; Memoire de M. Robert, 27 December/6 January 1685/86, NA, PRO 31/3/163, fol. 82r; Eames (Chester) to Huntingdon, 9 March 1687, HEH, HA 2407; Sir Nicholas Slanning (Salisbury) to Blathwayt, 2 November 1686, Beinecke, OSB MSS 2/Box 8/Folder 172; Roger Morrice, Entering Book, 6 August 1687, DWL, 31 Q, 164; Deposition of Robert Vesey, Jasper Green, and William Green, 2

March 1686, Staffordshire SRO, D(w) 1778/I/i/1158 B (reporting on statements by Sir John Moore); Barillon (London) to Louis XIV, 27 May/6 June 1686, NA, PRO 31/3/166, fol. 16v.

5. Blathwayt (London) to Sir Robert Douglas, 16 October 1686, NA, WO 4/1, fol. 18v; William Hamilton (Whitehall) to Earl of Arran, 26 April 1687, NAS, GD 406/1/3467; Dr. Henry Paman (London) to Sir Ralph Verney, 17 August 1687, Buckinghamshire SRO, Verney MSS; George Bulle (York) to Reresby, 15 January 1686, WYAS, MX 43/29; Thomas Comber (York) to William Sancroft, 15 January 1687, Bodleian, Tanner 30, fol. 176r; ? (York) to Reresby, 29 February 1688, WYAS, MX/R53/6.

6. Gilbert Burnet, "A Letter concerning Some Reflections," 1687, in Burnet, *A Collection of Papers Relating to the Present Juncture of Affairs in England* (1688/89), 26–27.

7. Evelyn, *Diary,* 4 December 1685, 9 June 1686, 12 June 1687, 24 August 1688, 4:490, 514, 553, 596–97; Charles Jackson, ed., *The Diary of Abraham De La Pryme,* Publications of the Surtees Society, vol. 54 (Published for the Society, 1869–70), 1686, 8; Barillon (Windsor) to Louis XIV, 29 September/9 October 1687, NA, PRO 31/3/173, fol. 9r. See also Hamilton (Hamilton) to Arran, 8 May 1688, NAS, GD 406/1/7593; Sir David Nairne, Journal, April 1686, NLS, 14266, fol. 7v; "A Letter Sent to Every English Merchant in the United Provinces," 8/18 September 1686, BL, Add. 41820, fol. 3r; Barillon (Windsor) to Louis XIV, 1/11 July 1686, NA, PRO 31/3/166, fol. 36r; Barillon (Windsor) to Louis XIV, 13/23 June 1687, NA, PRO 31/3/170, fol. 138r; Barillon (Bath) to Louis XIV, 6/16 September 1687, NA, PRO 31/3/172, fol. 151r.

8. Barillon (London) to Louis XIV, 23 February/5 March 1685, NA, PRO 31/3/160, fol. 68r; R. L. to mayor of Bridgewater, 24 February 1685, NA, SP 31/1, fol. 40; Burnet, "Letter Concerning Some Reflections," 26; Morrice, Entering Book, 8 January 1687, DWL, 31 Q, 40; Richard Grassby, *The English Gentleman in Trade: The Life and Works of Sir Dudley North, 1641–1691* (Oxford: Clarendon Press, 1994), 162–76.

9. Henry Newcome, 17 January 1686, in *The Autobiography of Henry Newcome,* vol. 2, ed. Robert Parkinson, Chetham Society 27 (Manchester: Chetham Society, 1852), 261 (hereafter cited as Newcome, *Autobiography*); William Haward (Scotland Yard) to Dr. Thomas Smith, 19 January 1686, Bodleian, MSS Smith 50, 45; Newcastle (Wellbeck) to Reresby, 22 January 1686, WYAS, MX 34/7.

10. Barillon (Windsor) to Louis XIV, 28 June/8 July 1686, NA, PRO 31/3/166, fol. 32r; Gilbert Burnet, *Reasons against Repealing the Acts of Parliament Concerning the Test* (1687), 5.

11. Dolben (London) to Sir William Trumbull, 22 January 1686, BL, Trumbull MSS 54 (since recataloged); Henry Howard, Information against People of Buckinghamshire (George Danver), 3 December 1688, HEH, STT Manorial Box 6 (41); Thomas Legh (London) to Richard Legh, 14 May 1685, JRL, Legh of Lyme, Box 2/Folder 15; Letter from a Father in London, 18 May 1685, Foley, 77; Newsletter, 13 August 1687, BL, Add. 4194, fol. 213r; Newsletter (Whitehall), 17 August 1688, Beinecke, OSB MSS 1/Box 2/Folder 88; Edward Scott (Guernsey) to Blathwayt, 2 April 1688, Beinecke, OSB MSS 2/Box 8/Folder 170.

12. Barillon (London) to Louis XIV, 22 October/1 November 1688, MAE, CP/Angleterre 167, fol. 2v; Morrice, Entering Book, 25 February 1688, DWL, 31 Q, 239 (4); Newsletter [James Johnston], 27 February 1688, BL, Add. 34515, fol. 51r; William Westby, Memoirs, 2 March 1688, FSL, V.a. 469, fol. 15r; London Newsletter, 24 September 1687, FSL, L.c. 1861; Henry Rowe (Wigan) to Richard Kenyon, 6 September 1688, HMC Kenyon, 196; London Newsletter, 12 January 1688, FSL, L.c. 1907; Van Citters (London) to States General, 3/13 January 1688, BL, Add. 34510, fol. 77; Paul Halliday, *Dismembering the Body Politic: Partisan Politics in England's Towns, 1650–1730* (Cambridge: Cambridge University Press, 1998), 248–49, 255.

13. Barillon (Windsor) to Louis XIV, 13/23 September 1686, NA, PRO 31/3/167, fol. 16r; Danby (London) to William, 27 March 1688, NA, SP 8/1/Pt. 2, fol. 198r; Halifax (London) to William, 12 April 1688, NA, SP 8/1/Pt. 2, fol. 203; James Johnston to ? 25 November 1687, Nottingham SUL, PwA 2103; James Johnston to ?, 8 December 1687, Nottingham SUL, PwA 2110a. For Tories, see also Bath (Stowe) to ?Sunderland, 28 September 1688, NA, SP 8/2/Pt. 2, fol. 21. For Whigs, see also Sir John Lowther, *Memoirs of the Reign of James II* (London: H. G. Bohn, 1857), 459; Gilbert Burnet, "Reasons against Repealing," 1687, in *A Collection of Eighteen Papers Relating to the Affairs of Church and State during the Reign of King James the Second* (London: John Starkey and Richard Chiswell, 1689), 5; and "To the King," 1694, HEH, EL 9925.

14. Bonrepaus (London) to Seignelay, 12/22 September 1687, NA, PRO 31/3/172, fols. 91–94A; Bonrepaus (London) to Seignelay, 29 September/9 October 1687, NA, PRO 31/3/173, fols. 17–18; Bonrepaus (London) to Seignelay, 24 November/4 December 1687, NA, PRO 31/3/174, fols. 6–7; Barillon (London) to Louis XIV, 21 November/1 December 1687, NA, PRO 31/3/174, fol. 1; Barillon (London) to Louis XIV, 19/29 January, 16/26 February 1688, NA, PRO 31/3/175, fols. 17r, 56r; Barillon (London) to Louis XIV, 3/13 May 1688, NA, PRO 31/3/177, fol. 16r; Philippe Hoffmann (London) to Leopold, 6/16 January 1688, Campana, 1:160–64; Antoine Moreau (The Hague) to king of Poland, 29 November/9 December 1687, 27 December/6 January, 17/27 January, 17/27 April 1688, all in BL, Add. 38494, fols. 3r, 10v, 20r, 59r.

15. Yard (Whitehall) to Albeville, 20 July, 21 July 1688, Indiana, Albeville MSS; George Vernon (Derby) to Huntingdon, 6 August 1688, HEH, HA 12980; Morrice, Entering Book, 8 September 1688, DWL, 31 Q, 291; James Wellwood, *Memoirs,* 3rd ed. (London: Tim. Goodwin, 1700), 213–14; Bonrepaus (London) to Seignelay, 12/22 September 1687, NA, PRO 31/3/172, fol. 93r; Bonrepaus (London) to Seignelay, 10/20 October 1687, NA, PRO 31/3/173, fol. 39r; Barillon (London) to Louis XIV, 5/15 January 1688, NA, PRO 31/3/175, fol. 10r; Van Citters (London) to States General, 2/12 March 1688, BL, Add. 34510, fols. 99–100; Moreau (The Hague) to king of Poland, 20/30 March 1688, BL, Add. 38494, fol. 51. See also George Mackenzie (Edinburgh) to William, 29 June 1687, NA, SP 8/1/Pt. 1, fol. 44; Cary Gardiner (London) to Sir Ralph Verney, 8 August 1688, Buckinghamshire SRO, Verney MSS; Westby, Memoirs, 17 August 1688, fol. 34v; Clarendon (London) to William, 15 December 1687, NA, SP 8/1/Pt. 2, fol. 188; and Halifax (London) to William, 25 July 1688, NA, SP 8/1/Pt. 2, fol. 244r.

16. Information to William, 1688, NA, SP 8/2/Pt. 2, fol. 51; Gardiner (London) to Sir Ralph Verney, 30 July 1688, Buckinghamshire SRO, Verney MSS; Theophilus Brookes (Hormark) to Huntingdon, 8 August 1688, HEH, HA 1041; Col. John Hales (Canterbury) to Blathwayt, 9 September 1688, Beinecke, OSB MSS 2/Box 4/Folder 92; Henry Fleming (Oxford) to Sir Daniel Fleming, 20 September 1688, Cumbria SRO, Kendal, WD/Ry 3258.

17. James Fraser (London) to Sir Robert Southwell, 7 July, 29 July 1688, FSL, V.b. 287 (77, 82); Halifax (London) to William, 25 July 1688, NA, SP 8/1/Pt. 2, fol. 244v; Sir William Boothby (Ashbourne) to Dr. Anthony Horneck, 23 September 1688, BL, Add. 71692, fol. 33v. See also Van Citters (London) to States General, 7/17 September 1688, BL, Add. 34510, fol. 143v.

18. Lord Chancellor Jeffreys, "An Account of the Proceedings . . . against the Lord Bishop of London," 4 August 1686, LPL, Fulham Papers/Compton MSS 2, fol. 68v; Thomas Pennington to Earl of Strafford, 13 August 1686, BL, Add. 31141, fol. 9r; Wynne to Sir William Trumbull, 15 July 1686, NL, Trumbull MSS 46, unfolioed (since cataloged); Evelyn, *Diary,* 14 July 1686, 4:519; Gardiner to Sir Ralph Verney, 4 August 1686, Buckinghamshire SRO, Verney MSS; *The King's Power in Ecclesiastical Matters Truly Stated* [1686?], 8.

19. Christopher Jeaffreson (London) to Major Crispe, 8 September 1686, Jeaffreson, 307; Sir Ralph Verney (Middle Claydon) to Edward Verney, 15 August 1686, Buckinghamshire SRO, Verney MSS; Sir Ralph Verney (Middle Claydon) to Paman, 5 September 1686, Buckinghamshire SRO, Verney MSS; "The Bishop of London's Own Defence," August 1686, Warwickshire SRO, CR 136/B791; Barillon (Windsor) to Louis XIV, 13/23 September 1686, NA, PRO 31/3/167, fol. 14v; Dr. John Guise (Aleppo) to Dr. Thomas Turner, 3 March 1687, Bodleian, Rawlinson MSS, D60, fol. 94r. See also London Newsletter, 14 August 1686, FSL, L.c. 1696; Barillon (Windsor) to Louis XIV, 9/19 September 1686, NA, PRO 31/3/169, fol. 10; and Huntingdon (Kempton Park) to Dr. Grey, 31 August 1686, HEH, HA 6055.

20. Jeffreys, "Account of the Proceedings," 9 August 1686, fol. 71r; Southwell (Kingsweston) to Weymouth, 10 August 1686, Longleat House, Thynne MSS 15, fol. 139; Evelyn, *Diary,* 8 September 1686, 4:524; *A Letter to a Gentleman at Brussels,* 22 December 1688 (London, 1689), 14–15. See also William Stanley (Dieren) to Compton, 16/26 August 1686, Bodleian, Rawlinson MSS, C983, fol. 101r; and Barillon (London) to Louis XIV, 26 August/5 September 1686, NA, PRO 31/3/167, fol. 3r.

21. Barillon (Windsor) to Louis XIV, 19/29 August 1686, NA, PRO 31/3/166, fol. 61r; Morrice, Entering Book, 14 August, 21 August 1686, DWL, 31 P, 602, 611, 613. I disagree with Douglas R. Lacey's claim that

this was a unique moment: Lacey, *Dissent and Parliamentary Politics in England, 1661–1689* (New Brunswick, NJ: Rutgers University Press, 1969), 177; Sir John Lowther, 9 August 1686, in *A Complete Collection of State Trials,* vol. 11, ed. T. B. Howell (London: T. C. Hansard, 1811), 1160.

22. William Sherwin (Oxford) to Thomas Turner, 27 June 1687, Bodleian, Rawlinson MSS, Letters 91, fol. 58v; Henry Care, *A Vindication of the Proceedings of His Majesties Ecclesiastical Commissioners* (London: Tho. Milbourn, 1688), 1–2; Gilbert Burnet, *History of His Own Time,* 2 vols. (London: Thomas Ward, 1724), 1:701; Barillon (Bath) to Louis XIV, 6/16 September 1687, NA, PRO 31/3/172, fol. 151r; Barillon (London) to Louis XIV, 21 November/31 December 1687, NA, PRO 31/3/174, fol. 1r; *A Memorial of God's Last Twenty-Nine Years Wonders in England* (London: J. Rawlins, 1689), 110; *A Letter to a Gentleman at Brussels,* 22 December 1688, 15.

23. Southwell (Kingsweston) to Weymouth, 18 July 1687, Longleat House, Thynne MSS 15, fol. 190; J. R. Bloxam, ed., *Magdalen College and King James II* (Oxford: Clarendon Press, 1886), 219, 222–23; Thomas Ken (bishop of Bath and Wells) to William Wake, 28 December 1687, Christ Church, William Wake Papers, 250, fol. 25r; Barillon (London) to Louis XIV, 21 November/1 December 1687, NA, PRO 31/3/174, fol. 1r; Newsletter, 8 December 1687, BL, Add. 34515, fols. 39–40; Burnet, *History of His Own Time,* 1:701.

24. James Johnston to ?, 21 December 1687, Nottingham SUL, PwA 2120b; James Johnston (London) to ?, BL, Add. 34515, fol. 43r; Charles Caesar, *Numerus Infaustus* (London: Ric. Chiswell, 1689), 114–15; Daniel Defoe, *The Advantages of the Present Settlement* (London: Richard Chiswell, 1689), 11.

25. Samuel Johnson, *A Letter from a Freeholder* (1688), 3; Sir Richard Cocks, "A Charge," Michaelmas 1695, Bodleian, Eng.Hist.b.209, fol. 301; Bloxam, ed., *Magdalen College and James II,* 230, 253. See also Wellwood, *Memoirs,* 206.

26. *Life of James II,* 2:152; William Butterfield (Middle Claydon) to Sir Ralph Verney, 13 May 1688, Buckinghamshire SRO, Verney MSS; Simon Patrick, Autobiography, in *The Works of Symon Patrick,* vol. 9, ed. Alexander Taylor (Oxford: Oxford University Press, 1858), 510–11; Earl of Clarendon, Diary, 12 May 1688, Singer, 2:171. The bishop of London was present but did not sign presumably because he was under sentence of suspension. The bishops subsequently wrote to their fellow bishops who were not present, and all but the bishops of Rochester, Durham, Chester, and St. David's agreed to support the petition: Yard (Whitehall) to Albeville, 22 May 1688, Indiana, Albeville MSS; William Beaw, bishop of Llandaff, to Sancroft, 27 May 1688, Bodleian, Tanner 28, fol. 44r; Thomas Smith, bishop of Carlisle, to Sir Daniel Fleming, 2 June 1688, Cumbria SRO, Kendal, WD/Ry 3203; Smith to Francis Turner, 4 June 1688, Bodleian, Tanner 28, fol. 50r; James Johnston to Dr. John Hutton, 23 May 1688, Nottingham SUL, PwA 2161; Morrice, Entering Book, 19 May 1688, DWL, 31 Q, 255.

27. W. E. Buckley, ed., *Memoirs of Thomas, Earl of Ailesbury,* 2 vols. (Westminster: Nichols and Sons, 1890), 170 (hereafter cited as Ailesbury, *Memoirs*); Bishops' Petition, 18 May 1688, Bodleian, Tanner 28, fol. 35ar; Sir Charles Cotterell to Sir William Trumbull, 28 May 1688, BL, Trumbull MSS 39 (since recataloged).

28. Yard (Whitehall) to Albeville, 25 May 1688, Indiana, Albeville MSS; Barillon (London) to Louis XIV, 21/31 May 1688, NA, PRO 31/3/177, fol. 42; Southwell (Kingsweston) to Weymouth, 21 May 1688, Longleat House, Thynne MSS 15, fol. 235; Smith to Sir Daniel Fleming, 2 June 1688, CRO Kendal, WD/Ry 3203; Patrick, Autobiography, 511–12; William Sancroft, "Some Proceedings," 18 May 1688, Bodleian, Tanner 28, fol. 38v; Jo. Cooke (Whitehall) to Edmund Poley, 25 May 1688, Beinecke, OSB MSS 1/Box 2/Folder 79; *Life of James II,* 2:155.

29. By all accounts, the declaration was read in at most six parish churches in the City and suburbs: A. M. (London) to James Harrington, May 1688, BL, Add. 36707, fol. 27r; Clarendon, Diary, 16 May 1688, 2:172; Van Citters (London) to States General, 18/28 May 1688, BL, Add. 34512, fol. 80v; Edward Harley to Sir Edward Harley, 19 May 1688, BL, Add. 70014, fol. 68r; Clarendon, Diary, 20 May 1688, 2:172–73; Yard (Whitehall) to Albeville, 22 May 1688, Indiana, Albeville MSS; John Horton (London) to Viscount Hatton, 22 May 1688, BL, Add. 29563, fol. 162r; Wynne (Whitehall) to Poley, 25 May 1688, Beinecke, OSB MSS 1/Box 2/Folder 79; Yard (Whitehall) to Albeville, 25 May 1688, Indiana, Albeville MSS; Morrice, Entering

Book, 26 May 1688, DWL, 31 Q, 261; Yard to Albeville, 29 May 1688, Indiana, Albeville MSS; *A Letter from a Clergy-Man in the City to His Friend in the Country,* 22 May 1688, 8; Westby, Memoirs, 20 May 1688, fol. 21v; *An Answer to the City Ministers Letter from His Country Friend* (1688), 1; Westby, Memoirs, 27 May 1688, fols. 22–23; Van Citters (London) to States General, 15/25 June 1688, BL, Add. 34510, fol. 132v; Patrick, Autobiography, 512; Butterfield (Middle Claydon) to Sir Ralph Verney, 20 May 1688, Buckinghamshire SRO, Verney MSS; Thomas Newey (Oxford) to Harrington, 30 May 1688, BL, Add. 36707, fol. 28v; Brookes (Hormark) to Huntingdon, 2 June 1688, HEH, HA 1040; Smith to Francis Turner, 4 June 1688, Bodleian, Tanner 28, fol. 50v; Mary Thynne (Longleat) to Weymouth, 8 June 1688, Longleat House, Thynne MSS 32, fol. 181v; Yard (Whitehall) to Albeville, 8 June 1688, Indiana, Albeville MSS; Willoughby, Lord Aston (Tiscall, Staffordshire) to Sunderland, 9 June 1688, NA, SP 31/4, fol. 42r; Andrew Newport (Exeter) to Lord Herbert of Cherbury, 9 June 1688, NA, PRO 30/53/8, fol. 63r; Sir Ralph Verney (Middle Claydon) to Edmund Verney, 10 June 1688, Buckinghamshire SRO, Verney MSS.

30. There were clearly divisions within the king's inner circle over how to proceed. James, however, never appears to have wavered: Barillon (London) to Louis XIV, 24 May/3 June 1688, NA, PRO 31/3/177, fols. 56–57; Clarendon, Diary, 14 June 1688, 2:177; *Life of James II,* 2:157–58; Minutes for His Grace of Canterbury to Have Been Spoken at the Trial, June 1688, Bodleian, Tanner 28, fol. 98r; Speech of Bishop of St. Asaph Not Spoken, 29 June 1688, BL, Add. 72426, fol. 103r.

31. Charles Dodd, *The Church History of England,* 3 vols. (Brussels, 1742), 3:420; Nathaniel Johnston (London) to Reresby, 9 April 1687, WYAS, MX 48/35; Albeville (The Hague) to Middleton, 29 July/8 August 1687, BL, Add. 41815, fol. 21r; Barillon (London) to Louis XIV, 20/30 October 1687, NA, PRO 31/3/173, fol. 65v; Paman (London) to Sir Ralph Verney, 21 November 1687, Buckinghamshire SRO, Verney MSS; Henry Care, *Draconica* (London: George Larkin, 1687), 2; *An Answer from the Country to a Late Letter to a Dissenter* (London: M. R., 1687), 5–6, 20; Samuel Parker, *Reasons for Abrogating the Test* (London: Henry Bonwicke, 1688); London Newsletter, 17 December 1687, FSL, L.c. 1896; Anthony Wood, *Athenae Oxonienses,* 3 vols., 2nd ed. (London: R. Knaplock, D. Midwinter, J. Tonson, 1721), 2:820; London Newsletter, 3 September, 15 September 1687, FSL, L.c. 1852, 1857; James Fraser (London) to Southwell, 18 September 1687, FSL, V.b. 287 (32); London Newsletter, 20 September 1687, FSL, L.c. 1859; Robert Harley (Witby) to Sir Edward Harley, 26 September 1687, BL, Add. 70014, fol. 41v; Sir Edward Harley (Brampton Bryan) to Robert Harley, 28 September 1687, BL, Add. 70253, unfolioed; Povey (Whitehall) to Southwell, 8 October 1687, Nottingham SUL, PwV 61/29; Barillon (London) to Louis XIV, 20/30 October 1687, NA, PRO 31/3/173, fol. 65v; Morrice, Entering Book, 29 October 1687, DWL, 31 Q, 182; James Johnston to ?, 4 January 1688, Nottingham SUL, PwA 2124g; "Savliana," post-1695, BL, Althorp C8; Henry Care, *Animadversions on a Late Paper* (London: John Harris, 1687), 7–8; Edmund Elys, "The Third Letter to the Truly Religious and Loyal Gentry," 1687, Bodleian, Tanner 29, fol. 15v; Roger L'Estrange, *An Answer to a Letter to a Dissenter* (London: R. Sare, 1687), 47–48; *A Letter in Answer to Two Main Questions* (London: M. T., 1687), 1; Henry Neville Payne, *An Answer to a Scandalous Pamphlet* (London: N. T., 1687), 5; Lady Rachel Russell to Dr. Fitzwilliam, 1 April 1687, in *Letters of the Lady Rachel Russell; from the Manuscripts in the Library at Woburn Abbey* (London: Edward and Charles Dilly, 1773), 77; Yard (Whitehall) to Albeville, 1 April 1687, Indiana, Albeville MSS; Duke of Hamilton (London) to Duchess of Hamilton, 10 November 1687, NAS, GD 406/1/7673; London Newsletter, 8 February 1688, FSL, L.c. 1918; Westby, Memoirs, 9 February 1688, fol. 12r.

32. Fraser (London) to Southwell, 7 January 1688, FSL, V.b. 287 (44); Hoffmann (London) to Leopold, 20/30 January 1688, in *Les derniers Stuarts,* ed. Campana, 1:166; On Monsieur Fagel's Letter, 1688, Georgetown SUL, Milton House Archives, Box 3/Folder 16; London Newsletter, 9 January 1688, HRC, Pforzheimer/Box 10/Folder 5; Letter from England, 12 January 1688, Nottingham SUL, PwA 2126b–c; London Newsletter, 12 January 1688, FSL, L.c. 1907; Louis Innes (London) to Charles Whyteford, 16 January 1688, SCA, Bl 1/113/6; Albeville (The Hague) to Middleton, 24 January/3 February 1688, BL, Add. 41815, fol. 127r; Morrice, Entering Book, 28 January 1688, DWL, 31 Q, 234; George Etherege (Ratisbon) to Albeville, 20 February/1 March 1688, Indiana, Albeville MSS; Robert Banks (Hoston) to Reresby, 7 March 1688, WYAS,

MX/R51/61; Sunderland to Reresby, 28 February 1688, CSPD, 3:153; Sunderland to mayor of Bristol, 15 March 1688, CSPD, 3:166; Newsletter, 4 April 1688, BL, Add. 34515, fol. 61r; Westby, Memoirs, 1688, January 1688, fols. 3r, 7v; London Newsletter, 24 January 1688, FSL, L.c. 1912; Sir John Lowther of Whitehaven (London) to Sir Daniel Fleming, 31 January 1688, Cumbria SRO, Kendal, WD/Ry 3175; Westby, Memoirs, February 1688, fol. 14r; Sir Daniel Fleming (Rydal) to Lowther, 6 April 1688, Cumbria SRO, Carlisle, D/Lons/L1/33.

33. George Savile, Marquis of Halifax, *A Letter to a Dissenter* (London: G. H., 1687), 5–6; Edmund Everard (Amsterdam) to Bevil Skelton, December 1686/January 1687, BL, Add. 41818, fol. 205r; Gilbert Burnet, *The Bishop of Salisbury His Speech in the House of Lords* (London, 1710), 12–13; *Letter from a Clergy-Man in the City*, 6; Letter to Viscount Hatton, 30 June 1688, BL, Add. 29563, fol. 207r; Newsletter from London, 2 July 1688, BL, Add. 34487, fol. 8r; Lowther, *Memoirs*, 467; H. Hall (London) to Justice Dawtrey, 2 July 1688, Essex SRO, D/DFa/F22. See also Yard (Whitehall) to Albeville, 15 March 1687, Indiana, Albeville MSS; Wellwood, *Memoirs*, 210; and Barillon (London) to Louis XIV, 21/31 May 1688, NA, PRO 31/3/177, fols. 43–44.

34. Van Citters (London) to States General, 8/18 June 1688, BL, Add. 34510, fol. 126v; ? (London) to Harrington, 9 June 1688, BL, Add. 36707, fol. 31r; Morrice, Entering Book, 9 June 1688, DWL, 31 Q, 268; Cary Stewkley (London) to Sir Ralph Verney, 12 June 1688, Buckinghamshire SRO, Verney MSS; Van Citters (London) to States General, 12/22 June 1688, BL, Add. 34510, fols. 129–30; Denton (London) to Sir Ralph Verney, 13 June 1688, Buckinghamshire SRO, Verney MSS; Dr. John Nalson to his wife, 14 June 1688, Bodleian, Tanner 28, fol. 64r; John Stewkley (London) to Sir Ralph Verney, 14 June 1688, Buckinghamshire SRO, Verney MSS; Southwell to Weymouth, 15 June 1688, Longleat House, Thynne MSS 15, fol. 244r; Clarendon, Diary, 15 June 1688, 2:177; Letter to Viscount Hatton, 16 June 1688, BL, Add. 29563, fol. 192r; John Verney (London) to Sir Ralph Verney, 20 June 1688, Buckinghamshire SRO, Verney MSS; Diary of Mary Woodforde, 8 June 1688, in *Woodforde Papers and Diaries,* ed. Dorothy Heighes Woodforde (London: P. Davies, 1932), 17; Sir Ralph Verney (Middle Claydon) to Edmund Verney, ca. 29 June 1688, Buckinghamshire SRO, Verney MSS; Boothby (Asbourne) to Horneck, 8 June 1688, BL, Add. 71692, fol. 9v; Westby, Memoirs, June 1688, fol. 23v; Yard (Whitehall) to Albeville, 1 June, 5 June 1688, Indiana, Albeville MSS; Fraser (London) to Southwell, 5 June 1688, FSL, V.b. 287 (68); Sir Ralph Verney (Middle Claydon) to Edmund Verney, 10 June 1688, Buckinghamshire SRO, Verney MSS; Wynne (London) to John Ellis, 16 June 1688, BL, Add. 4194, fol. 232r; Westby, Memoirs, 18 June 1688, fol. 27r; Anna Grigg to Locke, 22 June 1688, *Locke Correspondence,* 3:483–84; Yard (Whitehall) to Albeville, 15 June 1688, Indiana, Albeville MSS; John Le Neve, *The Lives and Characters of the Most Illustrious Persons British and Foreign, Who Died in the Year 1712* (London: S. Holt, 1714), 110; Newsletter from London, June 1688, BL, Add. 34487, fol. 7r; James Johnston (London) to ?, 18 June 1688, BL, Add. 34515, fol. 82v; Boothby (Ashbourne) to Mr. Horton, 19 June 1688, BL, Add. 71692, fol. 11r; Van Citters (London) to States General, 26 June/6 July 1688, BL, Add. 34510, fols. 137–38, 245; Aston to Sunderland, 30 June 1688, NA, SP 31/4, fol. 69r.

35. Lowther, *Memoirs,* 467–68; Abigail Prowse, "Memorandums concerning Bishop Hooper," LPL, 3016, fol. 5v; Clarendon, Diary, 30 June 1688, 2:179; Wynne (London) to John Ellis, 30 June 1688, BL, Add. 4194, fol. 247r; Robert Slater (London) to Edward Parker, [30] June 1688, Lancashire SRO, DD/B/85/9; John Shorter and B. Shower (London) to Sunderland, 1 [July] 1688, NA, SP 31/4, fol. 39r; Wynne (Whitehall) to Poley, 2 July 1688, Beinecke, OSB MSS 1/Box 2/Folder 84; Newsletter from London, 2 July 1688, BL, Add. 34487, fol. 8v; Newsletter, 3 July 1688, BL, Add. 4194, fol. 250r; Van Citters (London) to States General, 3/13 July 1688, BL, Add. 34510, fols. 138–39; Jo. Cooke (Whitehall) to Poley, 3 July 1688, Beinecke, OSB MSS 1/Box 2/Folder 84; Newsletter, 3 July 1688, BL, Add. 4194, fol. 250r; N. Gerrard to Edward Norton, 4 July 1688, BL, Add. 34487, fol. 9r.

36. Sir Ralph Verney (Middle Claydon) to Edmund Verney, 8 July 1688, Buckinghamshire SRO, Verney MSS; Southwell (Kingsweston) to Weymouth, [4] July 1688, Longleat House, Thynne MSS 15, fol. 249v; Patrick, Autobiography, 512–13; Westby, Memoirs, 7 July 1688, fol. 30r; Boothby (Ashbourne) to Horneck, 7 July 1688, BL, Add. 71692, fol. 12v; Gerrard (Hertford) to Norton, 12 July 1688, BL, Add. 34487, fol. 13r;

Moreau to king of Poland, 13/23 July 1688, BL, Add. 38494, fol. 83; Cotterell to Sir William Trumbull, 24 July 1688, BL, Trumbull MSS 39 (since recataloged); Ailesbury, *Memoirs,* 1:171; Wellwood, *Memoirs,* 211.

37. Robert H. Murray, ed., *The Journal of John Stevens* (Oxford: Clarendon Press, 1912), 5; Halifax (London) to William, 25 July 1688, NA, SP 8/1/Pt. 2, fol. 244; Wellwood, *Memoirs,* 207–8. See also Westby, Memoirs, 10 August 1688, fol. 34r; Barillon (London) to Louis XIV, 21/31 May 1688, NA, PRO 31/3/177, fols. 42–43; and Moreau to king of Poland, 4/14 September 1688, BL, Add. 38495, fols. 14–15.

38. Westby, Memoirs, 6 August 1688, fol. 33r; Boothby (Ashbourne) to Mr. Watts, 22 August 1688, BL, Add. 41692, fol. 21r; London Newsletter, 1 September 1688, BL, Add. 4194, fol. 356r; Van Citters (London) to States General, 15/25 June 1688, BL, Add. 34510, fol. 134v; Fraser (London) to Southwell, 16 June 1688, FSL, V.b. 287 (72); List of Bails for the Bishops, June 1688, Bodleian, Tanner 28, fol. 76r; Southwell (Bristol) to Weymouth, 31 May 1688, Longleat House, Thynne MSS 15, fol. 239v; Hall (London) to Dawtrey, 2 July 1688, Essex SRO, D/DFa/F22; Gerrard to Norton, 4 July 1688, BL, Add. 34487, fol. 9r; Newcome, *Autobiography,* 2 July 1688, 267. See also MacKenzie to William Sancroft, [July 1688], Bodleian, Tanner 28, fol. 113r.

39. Sir Roger L'Estrange, *An Answer to a Letter to a Dissenter* (London: R. Sare, 1687), 4, 48–49.

40. Charles Thornton (London) to John Rawlinson, 21 March 1682, Lancashire SRO, DD/Sa/37/4; *Axminster,* 1683, 80; Edmund Calamy, *Memoirs of the Life of the Late Reverend Mr. John Howe* (London: Sam. Chandler, 1724), 113; George Whitehead, *The Christian Progress of That Ancient Servant and Minister* (London, 1725), 573, 608; Christopher Story, *A Briefe Account of the Life, Convincement, Sufferings, Labours and Travels of . . . Christopher Story* (London: J. Sowle, 1726), 48; *Axminster,* 1682, 80; *Presentments at the Grand-Jury for the Town and Borough of Southwark* (London: Benj. Tooke, 1683); William Stout, 1864, in *The Autobiography of William Stout of Lancaster, 1665–1752,* ed. J. D. Marshall (Manchester: Chetham Society, 1967), 81; *Upon the Suppression of Conventicles* (London, 1685), [2]; Whitehead, *Christian Progress,* 570–71. For an account of one of these circles of informers, see Mark Goldie, "The Hilton Gang and the Purge of London in the 1680s," in *Politics and the Political Imagination in Later Stuart Britain,* ed. Howard Nenner (Rochester, NY: University of Rochester Press, 1998), 43–73; *Axminster,* 91–92, 96–97; John Whiting, *Persecution Exposed,* 2nd ed. (London: James Phillips, 1791), 265, 294, 322–23; Burnet, *History of His Own Time,* 1:651. See also Lowther, *Memoirs,* 450; Journal of Thomas Gwin of Falmouth, Friends House Library, MS Vol. 77, unfolioed; J. Fall (Paris) to Robert Wyllie, 31 January 1683, NLS, Wodrow Qu 30, fol. 139v; Thoresby, *Diary,* 10 February 1683, 1:153–54; Newcome, *Autobiography,* 11 August 1684, 256; and John Ashe, *A Short Account of the Life and Character of the Reverend Mr. William Bagshaw* (London: Tho. Parkhurst, 1704), 7.

41. Oliver Heywood, "Solemn Covenants," January 1688, in *The Rev. Oliver Heywood, B. A., 1630–1702: His Autobiography, Diaries, Anecdote and Event Books,* 4 vols., ed. J. Horsfall Turner (Bridghouse: A. B. Bayes, 1882), 3:227; Friends Newsletter, 25 July 1686, Friends House Library, Port 15/48; *A Letter to a Friend in Answer to a Letter to a Dissenter* (London: J. Harris, 1687), 1; Bridgewater (London) to Herbert, 11 April 1687, NA, PRO 30/53/8, fol. 45r; Andrew Paschall to John Aubrey, 23 April 1687, Bodleian, MS Aubrey 13, fol. 81r; Albeville (Hague) to Middleton, 29 April/9 May 1687, BL, Add. 41814, fol. 226; Mr. Scott (London) to Walter Leslie, 3 May 1687, SCA, Bl 1/107/6; Yard (Whitehall) to Albeville, 3 May 1687, Indiana, Albeville MSS; Ralph Trumbull to Sir William Trumbull, 5 October 1687, BL, Add. 72511, fol. 75r; J. Hill (Paris) to Sir William Trumbull, 10 October 1687, Berkshire SRO, D/ED/C33; Thomas Booth (London) to Capt. John Booth, 13 December 1687, FSL, F.c. 29. See also Stephen Lobb, *A Second Letter to a Dissenter* (London: John Harris, 1687), 1–2; Newcome, *Autobiography,* 12 June 1687, 265; and Samuel Rosewell, *An Account of the Life and Death of the Reverend Mr. Thomas Rosewell* (London: John Clark and Richard Ford, 1718), 72.

42. For Penn and Barclay: William Penn (London) to Stephen Crisp, 28 February 1685, *Penn Papers,* 30; Penn (London) to James Harrison, 23 September 1686, *Penn Papers,* 123; London Newsletter, 22 March, 24 March 1687, FSL, L.c. 1787, 1788; Morrice, Entering Book, 26 March 1687, DWL, 31 Q, 86; James Fraser (London) to John Ellis, 5 April 1687, BL, Add. 4194, fol. 177r; Povey (Whitehall) to Southwell, 5 April 1687, Nottingham SUL, PwV 61/4; London Newsletter, 12 April 1687, BL Trumbull Newsletters (since recataloged); Barillon (London) to Louis XIV, 18/28 April 1687, NA, PRO 31/3/168, fol. 75r; Blathwayt (Whitehall)

to Southwell, 28 April 1687, Nottingham SUL, PwV 53/50; Southwell (Kingsweston) to Weymouth, 4 July 1687, Longleat House, Thynne MSS 15, fol. 188v; James Tyrell to Locke, 29 August 1687, *Locke Correspondence,* 3:257; James Hamilton (Edinburgh) to Arran, 15 September 1687, NAS, GD 406/1/3421; Van Citters (Windsor) to States General, 4/14 October 1687, BL, Add. 34512, fol. 63v; J. Hill (Paris) to Sir William Trumbull, 10 October 1687, Berkshire SRO, D/ED/C33; William Penn, *Advice to Freeholders and other Electors of Members to Serve in Parliament* (London: Andrew Sowle, 1687); Penn, *A Letter from a Gentleman in the City to a Gentleman in the Country* (1687); Penn, *Three Letters* (London: Andrew Sowle, 1688); Burnet, *History of His Own Time,* 1:694; Wood, *Athenae,* 2:1051. For Vincent Alsop: London Newsletter, 28 April 1687, FSL, L.c. 1803; Vincent Alsop, *The Humble Address of the Presbyterians* ([London]: J. W., 1687); R. A. Beddard, "Vincent Alsop and the Emacipation of Restoration Dissent," *Journal of Ecclesiastical History* 24 (1973): 178. For Sir James Stewart: James Hamilton (Edinburgh) to Arran, 15 September 1687, NAS, GD 406/1/3421; Duke of Hamilton (Edinburgh) to Duchess of Hamilton, 17 September 1687, NAS, GD 406/1/ 6231; James Stewart, "Reasons Why Protestant Dissenters Ought to Concur," 1687, NA, SP 8/1/Pt. 2, fol. 138r; Stewart, *James Stewart's Answer* (London: Andrew Sowle, 1688). For Stephen Lobb: Lobb, *Second Letter;* John Verney (London) to Sir Ralph Verney, 29 August 1688, Buckinghamshire SRO, Verney MSS.

43. Lacey, *Dissent and Parliamentary Politics,* 181; Care, *Draconica;* Care, *Animadversions on a Late Paper;* Care, *Vindication of the Proceedings;* London Newsletter, 20 September 1687, FSL, L.c. 1859; Lois G. Schwoerer, *The Ingenious Mr.Henry Care* (Baltimore: Johns Hopkins University Press, 2001), 189–93; Phil Madoxe (Whitehall) to Southwell, 28 August 1688, Bodleian, Eng.Lett.c.54, fol. 97r; Morrice, Entering Book, 17 September 1687, DWL, 31 Q, 169; Lowther (London) to Sir Daniel Fleming, 9 October 1687, Cumbria SRO, Kendal, WD/Ry 3138; Wood, *Athenae,* 2:1009–10; Richard Burthogge, *Prudential Reasons for Repealing the Penal Laws* (London: Matthew Turner, 1687); Mark Goldie, "John Locke's Circle and James II," *Historical Journal* 35, no. 3 (1992): 579–84; Skelton (The Hague) to Middleton, 30 April/10 May 1686, BL, Add. 41813, fol. 122r; Yard (Whitehall) to Albeville, 15 March 1687, Indiana, Albeville MSS; London Newsletter, 14 April 1687, FSL, L.c. 1797; Morrice, Entering Book, 16 April 1687, DWL, 31 Q, 96; London Newsletter, 10 May, 10 December 1687, FSL, L.c. 1806, 1893; Thomas Halyburton, *Memoirs of the Life of the Reverend Mr. Thomas Halyburton* (Edinburgh: Andrew Anderson, 1714), 22; List of Those Pardoned by James II, 1686–1688, HEH, HA Misc. Box 1 (24); An Abstract of All Pardons, Temp. James II, HLRO, HL/PO/JO/10/1/414/154(p); Wood, *Athenae,* 2:1092. Williams was rumored to have been reconciled to the Catholic Church: ? (Whitehall) to Sir Richard Bulstrode, 11 April 1687, HRC, Pforzheimer/Box 10; Morrice, Entering Book, 17 September, 29 October 1687, DWL, 31 Q, 169, 182; Denton (London) to Sir Ralph Verney, 9 November 1687, Buckinghamshire SRO, Verney MSS; Yard (Whitehall) to Albeville, 6 July 1688, Indiana, Albeville MSS; Clarendon, Diary, 6 July 1688, 2:180; Morrice, Entering Book, 7 July 1688, DWL, 31 Q, 281; Clarendon (London) to William, 7 July 1688, NA, SP 8/1/Pt. 2, fol. 236; John Verney (London) to Sir Ralph Verney, 11 July 1688, Buckinghamshire SRO, Verney MSS.

44. Barillon (London) to Louis XIV, 28 December/7 January 1686, NA, PRO 31/3/163, fol. 2r; J. Hill (London) to Sir William Trumbull, 6 May 1686, Berkshire SRO, D/ED/C33; Wynne (London) to John Ellis, 5 March 1687, BL, Add. 4194, fol. 151r; Wynne (London) to John Ellis, 19 March 1687, BL, Add. 4194, fol. 158r; Morrice, Entering Book, 26 March 1687, DWL, 31 Q, 85; Yard (Whitehall) to Albeville, 1 April 1687, Indiana, Albeville MSS; Burnet, *History of His Own Time,* 1:672–73; Ronquillo (London) to king of Spain, 7/17 March 1687, BL, Add. 34502, fol. 96; Barillon (London) to Louis XIV, 11/21 April, 18/28 April 1687, NA, PRO 31/3/168, fols. 70r, 75r; Yard (Whitehall) to Albeville, 19 April 1687, Indiana, Albeville MSS; Barillon (London) to Louis XIV, 25 April/5 May, 2/12 May 1687, NA, PRO 31/3/169, fols. 3v, 25r; Bonrepaus (London) to Seignelay, 12/22 September 1687, NA, PRO 31/3/172, fol. 91r.

45. John Lake (bishop of Chichester) to Sancroft, 18 April 1687, Bodleian, Tanner 29, fol. 9r; Reresby (York) to Halifax, May 1687, BL, Althorp C2; H. A. (Hereford) to John Ellis, 27 June 1687, BL, Add. 28876, fol. 13; Jonathan Trelawney (bishop of Bristol) to Sancroft, 1 July 1687, Bodleian, Tanner 29, fol. 42r; Duke

of Hamilton (Holyroodhouse) to Arran, 11 August 1687, NAS, GD 406/1/6206; Samuel Sanders (Normanton) to Huntingdon, 19 December 1687, HEH, HA 10669.

46. John Howe, *The Case of the Protestant Dissenters* (London, 1689), 2; Defoe, *Advantages of the Present Settlement,* 8; Burnet, *History of His Own Time,* 1:702; Whiting, *Persecution Exposed,* 363; James Fraser (London) to John Ellis, 19 April 1687, BL, Add. 4194, fol. 179v; Robert Harley to Sir Edward Harley, 21 May 1687, BL, Add. 70014, fol. 5r; Morrice, Entering Book, 23 April, 11 June 1687, 29 December 1688, DWL, 31 Q, 102, 149, 391–92.

47. Ronquillo (London) to king of Spain, 7/17 March 1687, BL, Add. 34502, fol. 76v; Dr. Samuel Freeman (Clare College, Cambridge) to Lord Hatton, 7 July 1687, *Correspondence of the Family of Hatton,* vol. 2, ed. Edward Maunde Thompson, Camden Society, n.s., 23 (1878): 68; Letter from England, 8 December 1687, Nottingham SUL, PwA 2110; Edward Watson (Lancaster) to Sir Daniel Fleming, 25 November 1687, Cumbria SRO, Kendal, WD/Ry 3144; Sir Daniel Fleming (Rydal) to Lowther, 2 December 1687, Cumbria SRO, Kendal, WD/Ry 3149; Sir George Duckett, ed., *Penal Laws and Test Act,* 2 vols. (London, 1883).

48. Letter from England to Bentinck, 17 November 1687, Nottingham SUL, PwA 2099b; Nathaniel Johnston (London) to Reresby, 24 January 1688, WYAS, MX/R51/53; Defoe, *Advantages of the Present Settlement,* 6–7; William Orme, ed., *Remarkable Passages in the Life of William Kiffin* (London: Burton and Smith, 1823), 84; Gilbert Burnet, *An Apology for the Church of England* [Amsterdam, 1688], 2; Edmund Bohun, *The History of the Desertion* (London: Ric. Chiswell, 1689), 2; Thomas Long, *A Resolution of Certain Queries* (London: R. Baldwin, 1689), sig. A2r.

49. Van Citters (London) to States General, 22 May/1 June 1688, BL, Add. 34512, fols. 82–83; *Letter from a Clergy-Man in the City,* 8; James Johnston (London) to ?, 23 May 1688, BL, Add. 34515, fol. 65; Yard (Whitehall) to Albeville, 25 May 1688, Indiana, Albeville MSS; Wellwood, *Memoirs,* 220.

50. Fraser (London) to Southwell, 18 February 1688, FSL, V.b. 287 (52); Halifax (London) to William, 12 April 1688, NA, SP 8/1/Pt. 2, fols. 203–4; James Johnston (London) to ?, 23 May 1688, BL, Add. 34515, fol. 66.

51. Yard (Whitehall) to Albeville, 29 March 1687, Indiana, Albeville MSS; London Newsletter, 31 March 1687, FSL, L.c. 1791; James Johnston (London) to ?, 23 May 1688, BL, Add. 34515, fol. 66r; Lacey, *Dissent and Parliamentary Politics,* 180. I have not discussed Scottish Presbyterian opposition. The pattern was probably similar; see William Carstares (The Hague) to Willem Bentinck, 1 August, 2 August 1687, NA, SP 8/1/Pt. 2, fols. 134, 141; Morrice, Entering Book, 14 May, 21 May 1689, 31 March 1688, DWL, 31 Q, 129, 132, 249; James Johnston (London) to ?, BL, Add. 34515, fols. 78–79; *Memoirs of the Life of the Late Reverend Mr. John Howe* (London: Sam. Chandler, 1724), 5, 67, 127, 130–32; Burnet, *History of His Own Time,* 1:708; John Rastrick (Kirkton), "A Narrative," HEH, HM 6131, fol. 50r; A. W. Brink, ed., *The Life of the Reverend Mr. George Trosse* (Montreal: McGill-Queen's University Press, 1974), 125, 129–30; John Ashe, *A Short Account of the Life and Character of the Reverend Mr. William Bagshaw* (London: Tho. Parkhurst, 1704), 7; Joshua Sager's Sermon Notes, Frankland's Nonconformist Academy, 1687/88, BL, Add. 54185, fol. 59v. See also Newcome, *Autobiography,* 264; and Thoresby, *Diary,* April 1687, 1:186.

52. Morrice, Entering Book, 9 April, 14 May 1687, Paper of May 1688, 16 June 1688, DWL, 31 Q, 88, 129, 257–58, 269; Rosewell, *Account of Thomas Rosewell,* 73; Calamy, *Memoirs of Howe,* 135.

53. *Axminster,* 128, 133; Wood, *Athenae,* 2:920–21; Thomas Jollie (Pendleton, Lancashire) to ?, 10 December 1687, DWL, 12.78, unfolioed. This letter supplements the biographical detail offered in H. Fishwick, ed., *The Note Book of the Rev. Thomas Jolly,* Chetham Society, n.s., 33 (1894). The evidence regarding John Bunyan is equivocal at best: John Eston (Bedford) to Henry Mordaunt, Earl of Peterborough, 22 November 1687, in *Penal Laws and Test Acts,* ed. Duckett, 1:59; John Bunyan, *Grace Abounding* (London: W. Johnston?, 1750?), 171–73; Christopher Hill, *A Tinker and a Poor Man: John Bunyan and His Church, 1628–1688* (London: W. W. Norton, 1988), 319–20; Richard Greaves, *John Bunyan and English Non-Conformity* (London: Hambledon, 1992), 69.

54. The Presbyterian Roger Morrice was perhaps typical of many who excoriated those groups: Morrice, Entering Book, 14 August 1686, DWL, 31 P, 611; Morrice, Entering Book, 29 October 1687, DWL, 31 Q, 181; Orme, ed., *Life of Kiffin*, 84–85; *Innocency Vindicated* (London: J. Darby, 1689), 1–2; Morrice, Entering Book, 11 September 1688, DWL, 31 P, 623.

55. Letter from England to Bentinck, 17 November 1687, Nottingham SUL, PwA 2099c; Letter from England, 8 December 1687, Nottingham SUL, PwA 2112d–e; James Johnston (London) to ?, 6/16 February 1688, BL, Add. 34515, fol. 47r; Clarendon, Diary, 23 June 1688, 2:178; Bonrepaus (London) to Seignelay, 12/22 September 1688, NA, PRO 31/3/172, fols. 91–92; Letter from England, 8 December 1687, Nottingham SUL, PwA 2112g; Burnet, *History of His Own Time*, 1:703; Thomas Story, *A Journal of the Life of Thomas Story* (Newcastle-upon-Tyne: Isaac Thompson, 1747), 3.

56. On use of the term "Whig": Bonrepaus (London) to Seignelay, 11/21 June 1687, NA, PRO 31/3/170, fol. 124r; Bonrepaus (Windsor) to Seignelay, 23 June/3 July 1687, NA, PRO 31/3/171, fol. 6r. On Dijkvelt: Yard (Whitehall) to Albeville, 13 February 1687, Indiana, Albeville MSS; Barillon (London) to Louis XIV, 10/20 March, 28 March/7 April 1687, NA, PRO 31/3/168, fols. 51r, 63r; Halifax to William, 31 May 1687, NA, SP 8/1/Pt. 2, fol. 133v. On opposition organization: Barillon (Windsor) to Louis XIV, 16/26 June 1687, NA, PRO 31/3/170, fol. 142; Barillon (Windsor) to Louis XIV, 4/14 June 1687, NA, PRO 31/3/171, fol. 45; Barillon (Windsor) to Louis XIV, 26 September/6 October 1687, NA, PRO 31/3/173, fol. 6v; Halifax (London) to William, 31 May 1687, NA, SP 8/1/Pt. 2, fol. 132; Nottingham (London) to William, 2 September 1687, NA, SP 8/1/Pt. 2, fol. 149v; Morrice, Entering Book, 4 June 1687, 15 August 1688, DWL, 31 Q, 190, 288. One recent commentator who dissents from the now-fashionable view: Halliday, *Dismembering the Body Politic*, 261; Fraser (London) to Southwell, 29 December 1687, FSL, V.b. 287 (42); ? (Windsor) to Dijkvelt, 20 September 1687, Warwickshire SRO, CR 2017/C17, fol. 19r; Moreau to king of Poland, 22 November/2 December 1687, BL, Add. 38494, fol. 1r; Barillon (London) to Louis XIV, 15/25 December 1687, NA, PRO 31/3/174, fol. 45v. James Wellwood shared this view: Wellwood, *Memoirs*, 214. My conclusions are similar to those advanced, using different evidence, by John Miller in *Cities Divided: Politics and Religion in English Provincial Towns, 1660–1722* (Oxford: Oxford University Press, 2007), 230–37.

57. Bonrepaus, Report on the Stage of England, 1687, NA, PRO 31/3/174, fol. 116r; Shrewsbury (London) to William, 30 May 1687, NA, SP 8/1/Pt. 2, fol. 130; Halifax (London) to William, 25 August 1687, NA, SP 8/1/Pt. 2, fol. 143r; Daniel Petit (The Hague) to Middleton, 11/21 October 1687, BL, Add. 41815, fol. 60v; "To the King," 1694, HEH, EL 9925; Daniel Defoe, *Memoirs of Publick Transactions in the Life and Ministry of His Grace the Duke of Shrewsbury* (London: Tho. Warner, 1718), 9; Burnet, *History of His Own Time*, 1:712; Barillon (London) to Louis XIV, 25 April/5 May 1687, NA, PRO 31/3/169, fol. 4r; ? (London) to Arran, 12 May 1687, NAS, GD 406/1/3448; Devonshire to William, 31 May 1687, NA, SP 8/2/Pt. 2, fol. 10; Barillon (Windsor) to Louis XIV, 22 September/2 October 1687, NA, PRO 31/3/173, fol. 1; Bonrepaus, Report on the State of England, 1687, NA, PRO 31/3/174, fol. 116r; Skelton (Paris) to Sunderland, 6/16 June 1688, NA, SP 78/151, fol. 178v; Morrice, Entering Book, 18 September 1686, DWL, 31 P, 627; Denton (London) to Sir Ralph Verney, 14 June 1687, Buckinghamshire SRO, Verney MSS; Bonrepaus, Report on the State of England, 1687, NA, PRO 31/3/174, fols. 117r, 116r; Wood, *Athenae*, 2:1057.

58. Thomas Foley (Witley) to Sir Edward Harley, 7 October 1687, BL, Add. 70026, unfolioed; Morrice, Entering Book, 22 October 1687, DWL, 31 Q, 177. James II's regulators thought he would stand as a court candidate. But Foley was no reliable supporter. He seized Worcester for William during the revolution; Thomas Mariet (Warwickshire) to Penn, early 1688, *Penn Papers*, 174; London Newsletter, 10 January 1688, FSL, L.c. 1906; Sir Robert Howard, *A Two-Fold Vindication* (London, 1696), 15, 174; George Evelyn (Wotton) to John Evelyn Jr., 16 September 1688, BL, Evelyn MSS, M2, unfolioed (since recataloged); Isaac Newton, 1687, King's College, Cambridge, Keynes MSS 118, unfolioed; Letter from England, 4 January 1688, Nottingham SUL, PwA 2124c; ? (Amsterdam) to Albeville, 29 January 1688, Indiana, Albeville MSS. On Starkey: ? (Amsterdam) to Albeville, 19/29 January 1688, Indiana, Albeville MSS; Albeville (The Hague) to Middleton, 20/30 January 1688, BL, Add. 41815, fol. 124v.

59. Patrick Curry, *Prophecy and Power: Astrology in Early Modern England* (Cambridge: Polity, 1989), 79–80; John Phillips, *Sam, Ld. Bp. Of Oxon, His Celebrated Reasons for Abrogating the Test* (London, 1688); Wood, *Athenae*, 2:820, 1119; Daniel Defoe, *A Letter to a Dissenter from His Friend at The Hague* (Hague: Hans Verdraeght, 1688), 1–3; Maximillian E. Novak, *Daniel Defoe: Master of Fictions* (Oxford: Oxford University Press, 2003), 89–90.

60. Penn (London) to Duke of Buckingham, 16 February 1687, NAS, GD 406/1/10038; Buckingham to Penn, ca. February 1687, NAS, GD 406/1/10037; James Johnston (London) to ?, 6/16 February 1688, BL, Add. 34515, fols. 47–48; ? to Herbert, 14 July 1688, NA, PRO 30/53/8, fol. 117r; Edward Verney (London) to Sir Ralph Verney, 11 July 1688, Buckinghamshire SRO, Verney MSS.

61. Tyrell (London) to Locke, 6 May 1687, *Locke Correspondence*, 3:191–93; Isabella Duke (Otterton) to Locke, 3 October 1687, *Locke Correspondence*, 3:279; John Freke to Locke, 8/18 February 1687, *Locke Correspondence*, 3:135; Dr. David Thomas (London) to Locke, 29 November 1687, *Locke Correspondence*, 3:307; Philippus van Limborch to Locke, 27 January/6 February 1689, *Locke Correspondence*, De Beer, 3:542; Jean Le Clerc, *An Account of the Life and Writings of Mr. John Locke*, 2nd ed. (London: John Clarke and E. Curll, 1713), 22; Tyrell (London) to Locke, 6 May, 3 November 1687, *Locke Correspondence*, 3:193, 289; Lord Lieutenants' Return for Buckinghamshire, 29 February 1688, *Penal Laws and Test Act*, ed. Duckett, 1:147; Tyrell to Dr. David Thomas, 9 March 1688, *Locke Correspondence*, 3:410; Edward Clarke (London) to John Trenchard, 2 August 1679, Somerset SRO, DD/SF/3082; ? (Utrecht) to Skelton, 8/18 July 1685, BL, Add. 41817, fol. 218v; To all JPs, mayors, constables, August 1685, Somerset SRO, DD/SF/285; Mary Clarke to Edward Clarke, 30 May 1687, Somerset SRO, DD/SF/4515/Pt. 1/3; *Locke Correspondence*, 3:494; Mary Clarke (Chipley) to Edward Clarke, 28 March 1690, Somerset SRO, DD/SF/4515/Pt. 1/6; Tyrell (London) to Locke, 14 December 1687, *Locke Correspondence*, 3:312; Freke to Locke, 19 March 1688, *Locke Correspondence*, 3:418; Report of the Regulators to James II, 19 April 1688, *Penal Laws and Test Act*, ed. Duckett, 2:221; Dr. Charles Goodall to Locke, 27 December 1688, *Locke Correspondence*, 3:530; Mark Goldie, "James II and the Dissenters' Revenge," *Historical Research* 66 (February 1993): 75; J. R. Jones, "James II's Whig Collaborators," *Historical Journal* 3, no. 1 (1960): 66.

62. Yard (Whitehall) to Albeville, 13 May 1687, Indiana, Albeville MSS; J. R., *Life of the Right Honourable Sir John Holt* (London, 1764), 3; Morrice, Entering Book, 3 December 1687, DWL, 31 Q, 213–14; London Newsletter, 24 December, 23 June, 30 June 1687, FSL, L.c. 1899, 1824, 1827; Fraser (London) to Southwell, 16 August 1687, FSL, V.b. 287 (29); Paman (London) to William Lloyd, bishop of Norwich, 18 August 1687, LPL, 3898/6/1; Morrice, Entering Book, 23 August 1687, DWL, 31 Q, 166; Ronquillo (London) to king of Spain, 5/15 September 1687, BL, Add. 34502, fol. 125; Bonrepaus (London) to Seignelay, 1/11 November 1687, NA, PRO 31/3/173, fol. 98r; Morrice, Entering Book, 15 October 1687, DWL, 31 Q, 174; Morrice, Entering Book, 5 November 1687, DWL, 31 Q, 189; London Newsletter, 8 November 1687, FSL, L.c. 1880; Wynne (Whitehall) to Poley, 11 November 1687, Beinecke, OSB MSS 1/Box 2/Folder 72; Van Citters (London) to States General, 11/21 November 1687, BL, Add. 34510, fol. 61v; Morrice, Entering Book, 12 November 1687, DWL, 31 Q, 201; Ailesbury, *Memoirs*, 1:175; Povey (Whitehall) to Southwell, 17 August 1687, Nottingham SUL, PwV 61/23; Paman (London) to Sir Ralph Verney, 17 August 1687, Buckinghamshire SRO, Verney MSS; Paman (London) to Lloyd, 18 August 1687, LPL, 3898/6/1; London Newsletter, 30 August, 3 November, 5 November 1687, FSL, L.c. 1850, 1878, 1879; Povey (Whitehall) to Southwell, 12 November 1687, Nottingham SUL, PwV 61/35; Morrice, Entering Book, 22 September 1688, DWL, 31 Q, 293; Orme, ed., *Life of Kiffin*, Orme, 85–87; Morrice, Entering Book, 11 December 1686, DWL, 31 Q, 29; Van Citters (London) to States General, 21/31 October 1687, BL, Add. 34510, fol. 55r; Mark Knights, "A City Revolution: The Remodeling of the London Livery Companies in the 1680s," *English Historical Review* 112 (1997): 1164–67, 1177.

63. Sir John Dugdale (Coventry) to Dr. Thomas Smyth, 9 July 1687, Bodleian, MSS Smith 49, 183; Dr. Charles Aldworth, Commonplace Book, later 1680s, Essex SRO, D/DBy Z56; Henry Booth, Lord Delamere, Speech at Boden Downs, November 1688, Somerset SRO, DD/SF/3110; Henry Booth, *The Charge*, Chester, 25 April 1693 (London: Richard Baldwin, 1693), 5–6; Calamy, *Memoirs of Howe*, 135; Morrice, Entering Book,

14 May 1687, DWL, 31 Q, 129; Burnet, *History of His Own Time,* 1:691; Burnet, "Some Reflections on His Majesty's [Scottish] Proclamation," 1687, in Burnet, *Collection of Eighteen Papers,* 11.

64. Thomas Brown, *Heraclitus Ridens Redivivus* (Oxford, 1688), 8; Treatise on Magna Carta, 25 October 1687, Beinecke, OSB Shelves b.142, unfolioed; *Three Queries and Answers to Them* (1688), 3; *A Plain Account of the Persecution* (1688), 4; *Reflexions on Monsieur Fagel's Letter,* 12 January 1688 (1688), 1–2.

65. Morrice, Entering Book, 25 September 1686, DWL, 31 P, 628; Sir John Reresby, *Memoirs,* ed. Mary K. Geiter and W. A. Speck (London: Royal Historical Society, 1991), 3 March 1689, 561; R. L. to mayor of Bridgewater, 24 February 1685, NA, SP 31/1, fol. 40; Van Citters (London) to States General, 9/19 April 1686, BL, Add. 34512, fol. 28r; Bonrepaus (London) to Seignelay, 12/22 September 1687, NA, PRO 31/3/172, fol. 94r; James Johnston to ?, 8 December 1687, BL, Add. 34515, fol. 39r; Abel Boyer, *The History of King William the Third,* XX vols. (London: A. Roper and F. Coggan, 1702–3), 1:59–60; Defoe, *Memoirs of Publick Transactions,* 13.

66. Duke of Ormonde (Hampton Court) to Southwell, 6 May 1686, Victoria and Albert Museum, Forster and Dyce Collection, F.47.A.41, fol. 23v; Barillon (London) to Louis XIV, 24 October/3 November 1687, Bonrepaus (London) to Seignelay, 14/24 November 1687, Barillon (London) to Louis XIV, 14/24 November 1687, Barillon (London) to Louis XIV, 17/27 November 1687, all in NA, PRO 31/3/173, fols. 68v, 123–124, 119r, 133; Placidus Fleming (Ratisbon) to Mr. Whyteford, 12/22 July 1688, SCA, Bl 1/101/5; Morrice, Entering Book, 25 September 1686, DWL, 31 P, 628; Thomas Birch, *The Life of the Reverend Dr. John Tillotson* (London: J. and R. Tonson et al., 1752), 33. The Duke of Gordon shared he opposition of Fleming and the Catholic priests to the Drummond brothers: John Drummond, Earl of Perth, to Innes, 10 June 1688, Aberdeen, MS 2403, 13.

67. Barillon (London) to States General, 7/17 April 1687, NA, PRO 31/3/168, fol. 69v; Barillon (London) to Louis XIV, 25 April/5 May 1687, NA, PRO 31/3/169, fol. 3v; Bonrepaus (Windsor) to Seignelay, 11/21 July 1687, NA, PRO 31/3/171, fol. 18r; John Evelyn (Deptford) to Lady Tuke, 14 June 1693, BL, JE A2, fol. 89r (since recataloged); Robert Throckmorton (London) to ?, 17 March 1696, HEH, EL 9423.

68. ? to Countess of Suffolk, 12 July 1688, BL, Add. 34487, fol. 11v; Proceedings of the Ecclesiastical Commission, 12 July 1688, HEH, HA Religious Box 2(5); ? to Herbert, 14 July 1688, NA, PRO 30/53/8, fol. 117v; Newsletter (Whitehall), 20 July 1688, Beinecke, OSB MSS 1/Box 2/Folder 86; Proceedings of the Ecclesiastical Commission, 16 August 1688; Newsletter to Countess of Suffolk, 9 July 1688, BL, Add. 34487, fol. 15v; Matthew Henry (Chester) to Philip Henry, 6 August 1688, Bodleian, Eng.Lett.e.29, fol. 80r; Westby, Memoirs, 20 August 1688, fol. 35r; London Newsletter to Thomas Holton, 21 August 1688, BL, Add. 34487, fol. 23r; John Verney (London) to Sir Ralph Verney, July 1688, Buckinghamshire SRO, Verney MSS; Oliver Le Neve (Norfolk) to Peter Le Neve, 11 July 1688, BL, Add. 71573, fol. 51r; ? (Astrop, Northamptonshire) to Harrington, 28 July 1688, BL, Add. 36707, fol. 38r; Pen Stewkley (London) to Sir Ralph Verney, 8 August 1688, John Verney (London) to Sir Ralph Verney, 8 August 1688, both in Buckinghamshire SRO, Verney MSS; Southwell (Kingsweston) to Weymouth, 10 August 1688, Longleat House, Thynne 15, fols. 263–64; Newsletter from Whitehall, 24 August 1688, Beinecke, OSB MSS 1/Box 2/Folder 88; Bishop of Rochester's Paper, 6 November 1688, Bodleian, Tanner 28, fol. 235r. For an example from the Middlesex Quarter Sessions, see the Recognizances, 31 July 1688: "Middlesex Sessions Rolls: 1688–9," *Middlesex County Records* (1892), 4:321–28, available at: http://www.british-history.ac.uk/report.aspx?compid=66098. William Rogers was an acolyte of Obadiah Walker at University College, Oxford, and donated the statue of James II still preserved there: John Fendley, "William Rogers and His Correspondence," *Recusant History* 23, no. 3 (1997): 291–92.

69. James Johnston to ?, 18 June 1688, Nottingham SUL, PwA 2173/1–2; Devonshire to William, 10 July 1688, NA, SP 8/2/Pt. 2, fol. 43r; Henry Booth, Lord Delamere, "Some Observations on the Prince of Orange's Declaration," in Delamere, *The Works* (London: John Lawrence and John Dunton, 1694), 366; Danby (Leicester) to Chesterfield, [September] 1688, in *Thomas Osborne, Earl of Danby and Duke of Leeds, 1632–1712,* vol. 2, ed. Andrew Browning (Glasgow: Jackson, Son, 1944), 135.

70. Morrice, Entering Book, 1 January 1687, DWL 31 Q, 38; Information to William III, 1688, NA, SP 8/2/Pt. 2, fol. 51; Barillon (Windsor) to Louis XIV, 29 September/9 October 1687, NA, PRO 31/3/173, fol. 8r; Barillon (London) to Louis XIV, 5/15 January 1688, NA, PRO 31/3/175, fol. 10r; John Oldmixon, *The History of England during the Reigns of the Royal House of Stuart* (London: John Pemberton et al., 1730), 730; Morrice, Entering Book, 15 August 1688, DWL, 31 Q, 288–89.

71. Newsletter, 19 September 1688, BL, Add. 34487, fol. 29r; Van Citters (London) to States General, 21 September/1 October 1688, BL, Add. 344512, fol. 101r; William Longueville (London) to Viscount Hatton, 22 September 1688, BL, Add. 29563, fol. 268r; Yard (Whitehall) to Albeville, 25 September 1688, Indiana, Albeville MSS; Bath (Stowe) to Sunderland, 28 September 1688, NA, SP 8/2/Pt. 2, fol. 46r; Morrice, Entering Book, 29 September 1688, DWL, 31 Q, 296–97; J. Boscawen (Whitehall) to John Evelyn, 30 September 1688, BL, Evelyn MSS, JE A9 (since recataloged); Wynne (Whitehall) to Poley, 2 October 1688, BL, Add. 45731, fol. 7r; Clarendon, Diary, 5 October 1688, 2:193; Evelyn, *Diary,* 6 October 1688, 4:600; Newcome, *Autobiography,* 7 October 1688, 267–68.

72. Evelyn, *Diary,* 18 September, 6 October 1688, 4:597, 599–600; Van Citters (London) to States General, 25 September/5 October 1688, BL, Add. 34512, fol. 103r; Van Citters (London) to States General, 9/19 October 1688, BL, Add. 34510, fol. 15; Barillon (London) to Louis XIV, 14/24 December 1688, MAE, CP/Angleterre 167, fol. 227r.

73. Morrice, Entering Book, 26 December 1688, DWL, 31 Q, 401; Steve Pincus, "John Evelyn: Revolutionary," in *John Evelyn and His Milieu,* ed. Frances Harris and Michael Hunter (London: British Library, 2003), 185–219.

74. Delamere, "Essay upon Government," 1687, in Delamere, *Works,* 38, 89–91; Delamere, "Advice to His Children," 20 September 1688, in Delamere, *Works,* 6, 9–10, 12, 15; Delamere, "Some Observations on the Prince of Orange's Declaration," in Delamere, *Works,* 375.

75. John Humfrey, *Advice Before It Be Too Late* [1689], 3–4.

CHAPTER 8. *Popular Revolution*

1. Samuel Pufendorf, *An Introduction to the History of the Principal Kingdoms and States of Europe,* 2nd ed. (London: M. Gilliflower, 1697), 153; Robert Ferguson, *The History of all the Mobs, Tumults, and Insurrections* ([London]: J. Moore, [1715]), 1–2; James Wellwood, *Memoirs,* 3rd ed. (London: Tim. Goodwin, 1700), 1; John T. Gilbert, ed., *A Jacobite Narrative of the War in Ireland, 1688–1691* (New York: Barnes and Noble, 1971), 39, 184; Robert Kirk, "Sermons, Occurrences . . . ," 1690, Edinburgh SUL, La.III.545, fol. 129v.

2. Charles Tilly, *European Revolutions, 1492–1992* (Oxford: Basil Blackwell, 1993), 9; Thomas Doubleday, *A Financial, Monetary and Statistical History of England* (London: Effingham Wilson, 1847), 61; Robin Clifton, *The Last Popular Rebellion: The Western Rising of 1685* (London: Maurice Temple Smith, 1984), 281; J. R. Western, *Monarchy and Revolution: The English State in the 1680s* (London: Blandford, 1972), 264; Jonathan Scott, *England's Troubles: Seventeenth-Century English Political Instability in European Context* (Cambridge: Cambridge University Press, 2000), 206; Stephen Saunders Webb, *Lord Churchill's Coup: The Anglo-American Empire and the Glorious Revolution Reconsidered* (New York: Alfred A. Knopf, 1995), 165. See also Jonathan Israel, "Introduction," in *The Anglo-Dutch Moment: Essays on the Glorious Revolution and Its World Impact,* ed. Jonathan Israel (Cambridge: Cambridge University Press, 1991), 2; and William A. Speck, *Reluctant Revolutionaries: Englishmen and the Revolution of 1688* (Oxford: Oxford University Press, 1988), 73.

3. G. M. Trevelyan, *The English Revolution, 1688–1689* (1938; reprint ed., Oxford: Oxford University Press, 1965), 7; Christopher Hill, *The Century of Revolution, 1603–1714* (Edinburgh: T. Nelson, 1961), 276; David Hosford, *Nottingham, Nobles, and the North: Aspects of the Revolution of 1688* (Hamden, CT: Archon, 1976), 120–21; J. R. Jones, *The Revolution of 1688 in England* (New York: W. W. Norton, 1972), 301. See also Speck, *Reluctant Revolutionaries,* 6.

4. Israel, "Introduction," 2, 5; John Morrill, "The Sensible Revolution, 1688," in *Anglo-Dutch Moment,* ed. Israel, 106; Craig Rose, *England in the 1690s: Revolution, Religion, and War* (Oxford: Blackwell, 1999), 8. See also Scott, *England's Troubles,* 11; and Trevelyan, *English Revolution,* 4.

5. Isaac Kramnick, "Reflections on Revolution," *History and Theory* 11, no. 1 (1972): 28; Nikki R. Keddie, "Introduction," in *Debating Revolutions,* ed. Keddie (New York: New York University Press, 1995), ix; John Dunn, *Modern Revolutions: An Introduction to the Analysis of a Political Phenomenon* (Cambridge: Cambridge University Press, 1972), 2; Chalmers Johnson, *Revolutionary Change,* 2nd ed. (Stanford, CA: Stanford University Press, 1982), 1, 7; Thomas Babington Macaulay, *The History of England from the Accession of James II,* 5 vols. (New York: Harper and Brothers, 1849–61), 2:610–11, 614; Trevelyan, *English Revolution,* 4; Scott, *England's Troubles,* 216; Tim Harris, "London Crowds and the Revolution of 1688," in *By Force or by Default? The Revolution of 1688–89,* ed. Eveline Cruickshanks (Edinburgh: John Donald, 1989), 54.

6. Macaulay, *History,* 2:563; Trevelyan, *English Revolution,* 5, 129; Hosford, *Nottingham, Nobles, and the North,* 124; Western, *Monarchy and Revolution,* 376; Morrill, "Sensible Revolution," 103. The notion of consensus in 1688 has come in for criticism recently: Israel, "Introduction," 4–6. Robert Beddard, "The Unexpected Whig Revolution of 1688," in *The Revolutions of 1688,* ed. Beddard (Oxford: Clarendon Press, 1991), 11–101; Tim Harris, "London Crowds," 57. Eveline Cruickshanks, "The Revolution and the Localities: Examples of Loyalty to James II," in *By Force or By Default?* ed. Cruikshanks, 28–41.

7. Crane Brinton, *The Anatomy of Revolution,* rev. ed. (New York: Vintage, 1965), 3; George Rudé, *The Crowd in the French Revolution* (Oxford: Clarendon Press, 1959), 232. It is worth noting that 156 people were killed at the siege of the Bastille, and fifty were killed at the so-called massacre at the Champ de Mars. Rudé, *Crowd in the French Revolution,* 56, 81.

8. George Etherege (Ratisbon) to Albeville, 22 October/1 November 1688, Indiana, Albeville MSS; Robert Yard (Whitehall) to Albeville, 20 July 1688, Indiana, Albeville MSS; Daniel Petit (Amsterdam) to Middleton, 14/24 August 1688, BL, Add. 41816, fol. 157r; Newsletter to Earl of Suffolk, 16 August 1688, BL, Add. 34487, fol. 19v; Bevil Skelton (Paris) to Sunderland, 18/28 August 1688, NA, SP 98/151, fol. 201; Peter Wyche (Hamburg) to Edmund Poley, 21 August 1688, Beinecke, OSB MSS 1/Box 2/Folder 88; Wyche (Hamburg) to Middleton, 24 August 1688, BL, Add. 41827, fol. 76v; James Fraser (London) to Sir Robert Southwell, 25 August 1688, FSL, V.b. 287 (86); Albeville (Hague) to Middleton, 28 August/7 September 1688, BL, Add. 41816, fol. 170v; Petit (Amsterdam) to Middleton, 28 August/7 September 1688, BL, Add. 41816, fol. 167; Albeville (Hague) to Middleton, 4/14 September 1688, BL, Add. 41816, fol. 177r; J. Stafford (Madrid) to Sunderland, 27 September/7 October 1688, NA, SP 94/72, fol. 248; Sir Richard Bulstrode (Brussels) to Sunderland, 8 October 1688, NA, SP 77/55, fol. 491r; James Fitzjames, Duke of Berwick, *Memoirs of the Marshal Duke of Berwick,* vol. 1 (London: T. Cadell, 1779), 22. James and his court quickly acted on the reports: Roger Morrice, Entering Book, 15 August 1688, DWL, 31 Q, 288; Newsletter, 22 August 1688, BL, Add. 34487, fol. 25r; James II to Sir Roger Strickland, 23 August 1688, NA, ADM 2/1742, 143; William Westby, Memoirs, 24 August 1688, FSL, V.a. 469, fol. 36r; ? (London) to John Ellis, 25 August 1688, BL, Add. 4194, fol. 311r; Sir John Reresby, *Memoirs,* ed. Mary K. Geiter and W. A. Speck (London: Royal Historical Society, 1991), 25 August 1688, 506; Sunderland (Windsor) to Skelton, 27 August 1688, NA, SP 104/19, fol. 95v; William Blathwayt (Windsor) to Captain Shakerley, 28 August 1688, NA, WO 4/1, fol. 47r; John Verney (London) to Edmund Verney, 29 August 1688, Buckinghamshire SRO, Verney MSS; Robert Fairfax (the Downs) to his mother, 30 August 1688, NMM, MS 81/116; Newsletter, 25 September 1688, Bodleian, Don.c.38, fol. 295r. The information that James had about the size of William's invading force was surprisingly accurate: Yard (Whitehall) to Albeville, 24 August 1688, Indiana, Albeville MSS; Newsletter (Whitehall), 7 September 1688, Beinecke, OSB MSS 1/Box 2/Folder 89; Benjamin Bathurst (London) to John Allicock, 25 September 1688, BL, Loan 57/70, fol. 4r; Will Culliford (Customs House, London) to Ellis, 27 September 1688, BL, Add. 4194, fol. 347r; East India Company to General and Council of India, 8 October 1688, IOL, E/3/91, fol. 295v; Robert Balle (Livorno) to Goodwyn and Delabere, 28 October/7 November 1688, NA, FO 335/7, fol. 3; Alexander Dunbar (London) to Louis Innes, 13 September 1688, SCA, Bl 1/111/7; Andrew Cotton to Hatton,

6 September 1688, BL, Add. 29563, fol. 257r; Henry Hunter (London) to George Hales, 25 September 1688, Berkshire SRO, D/EHr/B2; Henry Fleming (Oxford) to Sir Daniel Fleming, 21 October 1688, Cumbria SRO, Kendal, WD/Ry 3290; *Axminster,* October 1688, 135; John Verney (London) to Edmund Verney, 29 August 1688, Buckinghamshire SRO, Verney MSS; Sir John Lowther, Memoirs, Cumbria SRO, Carlisle, D/Lons/L2/5, 94.

9. James II (Whitehall) to Dartmouth, 5 October 1688, Staffordshire SRO, D(w) 1778/v/1403, 116–17; Yard (Whitehall) to Albeville, 11 October 1688, Indiana, Albeville MSS; Reresby, *Memoirs,* 30 October 1688, 524; ? (London) to Innes, 5 November 1688, SCA, Bl 1/119/6; James II (Whitehall) to Dartmouth, 20 October 1688, NMM, LBK/49, 143; John Childs, *The Army, James II and the Glorious Revolution* (Manchester: Manchester University Press, 1980), 4; Webb, *Churchill's Coup,* 141.

10. Yard (Whitehall) to Albeville, 31 August 1688, Indiana, Albeville MSS; Dartmouth (Ouze Edge) to James II, 17 October 1688, NMM, DAR/17; James II (Whitehall) to Dartmouth, 8 October 1688, Staffordshire SRO, D(w) 1778/v/1403, 118.

11. Yard (Whitehall) to Albeville, 25 September 1688, Indiana, Albeville MSS; ? (London) to Albeville, October 1688, Indiana, Albeville MSS; Newsletter from Whitehall, 5 October 1688, BL, Add. 45731, fol. 11; Sunderland (Windsor) to Skelton, 27 August 1688, NA, SP 104/19, fol. 95v.

12. Thomas Bligh (London) to his brother, 27 September 1688, PRONI, T2929/1/20; Nathaniel Molyneux to Roger Kenyon, 18 October 1688, HMC Kenyon, 204; Elizabeth Powis (St. James's) to Lord Montgomery, 30 October 1688, NA, PRO 30/53/8, fol. 129v; Sir Ralph Verney (London) to Lady Bridgeman, 4 October 1688, Buckinghamshire SRO, Verney MSS; Thomas Brathwait (Salisbury) to Sir Daniel Fleming, November 1688, Cumbria SRO, Kendal, WD/Ry, unfolioed.

13. William Lawrence to Col. Henry Norwood, [April 1688], IOL, European MSS, E387/B, fol. 45; Thomas [Smith] (bishop of Carlisle) to Sir Daniel Fleming, 14 May 1688, Cumbria SRO, Kendal, WD/Ry 3198; Robert H. Murray, ed., *The Journal of John Stevens* (Oxford: Clarendon Press, 1912), 4 (hereafter cited as Stevens, *Journal*); Colley Cibber, *An Apology for the Life of Colley Cibber,* ed. Robert Lowe (New York: AMS Press, 1966), 63; Evelyn, *Diary,* 24 August 1688, 4:597; James Johnston (London) to ?, 18 June 1688, BL, Add. 34515, fol. 80v.

14. Stevens, *Journal,* October 1688, 6; Bath (Plymouth) to Sunderland, 9 October 1688, NA, SP 31/4, fol. 107r; Sir Christopher Musgrave (Edenhall) to Sir Daniel Fleming, 4 October 1688, Cumbria SRO, Kendal, WD/Ry 3270; Sir Charles Cotterell to Sir William Trumbull, 25 October 1688, BL, Trumbull MSS 39 (since recataloged); Westby, Memoirs, 15 October 1688, fol. 39v; ? (London) to Innes, 5 November 1688, SCA, Bl 1/119/6; Albeville (Hague) to Middleton, 29 September/9 October 1688, BL, Add. 41816, fol. 226.

15. John Whiting, *Persecution Exposed,* 2nd ed. (London: James Phillips, 1791), 388–89; "Some Account of the Revolution," BL, Add. 9363, fol. 1r; William Sancroft, "The Present State of the English Government," January 1689, Bodleian, Tanner 269, fol. 1r.

16. Count Lillieroot (Paris) to Sir William Trumbull, 8/18 September 1688, BL, Trumbull MSS 8 (since recataloged); Dunbar (Edinburgh) to Innes, 30 October 1688, SCA, Bl 1/111/8; London Newsletter, 13 November 1688, Bodleian, Don.c.38, fol. 341r; Anthony Hewitson, ed., *Diary of Thomas Bellingham, an Officer under William III* (Preston: Geo. Toulmin and Sons, 1908), 13 November 1688, 27 (hereafter cited as Bellingham, *Diary*).

17. Jones, *Revolution of 1688,* 209–49; Western, *Monarchy and Revolution,* 249, 253–55; Stephen Baxter, *William III and the Defense of European Liberty* (New York: Harcourt, Brace and World, 1966), 230–34; Edward B. Powley, *The English Navy in the Revolution of 1688* (Cambridge: Cambridge University Press, 1928), 1–15; Gilbert Burnet, *History of His Own Time* (London: William Smith, 1838), 474, 479; Wellwood, *Memoirs,* 253; Daniel Defoe, *The Advantages of the Present Settlement* (London: Richard Chiswell, 1689), 26; Morrice, Entering Book, 6 October 1688, DWL, 31 Q, 300; Bellingham, *Diary,* 24 September 1688, 16; W. Sandford (mayor of Harwich) to Owen Wynne, BL, Add. 41805, fol. 48r; Daniel Defoe, *Memoirs of Publick Transactions in the Life and Ministry of His Grace the Duke of Shrewsbury* (London: Tho. Warner, 1718), 19.

18. Shrewsbury, Devonshire, Danby, Lumley, Compton, Sidney, and Russell to William, 30 June 1688, PRO, SP 8/1/Part 2, fols. 224–25.

19. Carlingford (Vienna) to Middleton, 9/19 September 1688, BL, Add. 41842, fol. 136; Bulstrode (Brussels) to Sunderland, 12 October 1688, NA, SP 77/55, fol. 493r; Wyche (Hamburg) to Poley, 2 November 1688, BL, Add. 45731, fol. 40r; Wyche (Hamburg) to Albeville, 10/20 April 1688, Indiana, Albeville MSS; Wyche (Hamburg) to Middleton, BL, Add. 41827, fol. 86r; Etherege (Ratisbon) to Albeville, 18/28 June 1688, Indiana, Albeville MSS; Skelton (Paris) to Wynne, 24 August/4 September 1688, BL, Add. 41842, fol. 222v; Albeville (Hague) to Middleton, 18/28 September, 21 September/1 October, 26 September/6 October 1688, BL, Add. 41816, fols. 202, 209v, 217v; Extracts of the Resolutions of the States General, 28 October 1688, PRO, C 110/80/6.

20. Sir Robert Southwell, "A Short Account of the Revolution," FSL, V.b. 150, 1:fol. 2v; Samuel Clarke (London) to Joseph Dolling, 9 October 1688, Churchill College Cambridge, Erle 2/16/17; Westby, Memoirs, 14 October 1688, fol. 39r; Reresby, *Memoirs,* 17 October 1688, 522; Van Citters (London) to States General, 12/22 October 1688, BL, Add. 34512, fol. 112r.

21. Morrice, Entering Book, 18 August 1688, DWL, 31 Q, 286; Dunmore to Derby, 1 October 1688, HMC Kenyon, 198.

22. Van Citters (London) to States General, 12/22 October 1688, BL, Add. 34512, fol. 112r; E. W. (York) to Sir Daniel Fleming, 12 October 1688, Bodleian, MSS Don.c.38, fol. 302r; Lord Fairfax (York) to Sunderland, 5 October 1688, NA, SP 31/4, fol. 91r; Walter Partridge (Scarborough) to Sunderland, 5 October 1688, NA, SP 31/4, fol. 94r; Lowther, Memoirs, 96; W. Lord Aston (Tixall) to Sunderland, 29 September 1688, NA, SP 31/4, fol. 82r; W. Molyneux (Croxteth) to Sunderland, 30 September 1688, NA, SP 31/4, fol. 83r; Caryll Molyneux (Wigan) to Sunderland, 5 October 1688, NA, SP 31/4, fol. 92r; Bellingham, *Diary,* 16 October 1688, 22; Caryll Molyneux to Sunderland, 19 October 1688, NA, SP 31/4, fol. 146r; Theophilus Brookes to Huntingdon, 17 November 1688, HEH, HA 1042; Huntingdon, Autobiography, 17 October 1699, HEH, HA Genealogy Box 1 (32); George Vernon and Henry Hamlocke (Derby) to Lord Preston, 1 November 1688, BL, Add. 63780, fol. 14; Sir Jeffrey Palmer (West Carlton) to Huntingdon, 26 October 1688, HEH, HA 9837; Robert Wilimot (Osmaston) to Huntingdon, 27 October 1688, HEH, HA 13420; Draft of a Petition Giving Particulars of a Dispute between the Earl of Derby and Lord Delamere, October–December 1688, HMC Kenyon, 205; Roger Kenyon, Diary, 3 November 1688, HMC Kenyon, 200; Bristol (Sherborn) to Sunderland, 29 September 1688, NA, SP 31/4, fol. 81r; Matthew Hole, *A Sermon Preached at Taunton,* 6 January 1689 (London: Randolph Taylor, 1689), sig. [A2r]; Morrice, Entering Book, 17 November 1688, DWL, 31 Q, 317; Sir Robert Holmes (Isle of Wight) to Viscount Preston, 6 November 1688, BL, Add. 63780, fol. 41r; Sir Ralph Verney (London) to Edmund Verney Jr., 31 October 1688, Buckinghamshire SRO, Verney MSS; Lord Teynham (Lodge) to Sunderland, 8 October 1688, NA, SP 31/4, fol. 103r.

23. Morrice, Entering Book, 13 October 1688, DWL, 31 Q, 302; Earl of Clarendon, Diary, 24 September 1688, Singer, 2:189–90; Philip Frowde (London) to Dartmouth, 4 October 1688, Beinecke, OSB Shelves fb.190, 3:342–43; London Newsletter, 4 October, 6 October 1688, Bodleian, Don.c.38, fols. 297r, 298r; George Jeffries to Sir William Turner, 5 October 1688, Guildhall Library, 5099, unfolioed; Van Citters (London) to States General, 5 October 1688, BL, Add. 34512, fol. 105r; Lady Gardiner (London) to Sir Ralph Verney, 29 November 1688, Buckinghamshire SRO, Verney MSS; John Verney (London) to Edmund Verney Jr., 1 November 1688, Buckinghamshire SRO, Verney MSS.

24. Bath (Plymouth) to Sunderland, 9 October 1688, PRO, SP 31/4, fol. 107r. The previous week he had reported that this was the situation everywhere in the West Country: Bath to Dartmouth, 3 October 1688, Staffordshire SRO, D(w) 1778/I/i/1319; Paul Halliday, *Dismembering the Body Politic: Partisan Politics in England's Towns, 1650–1730* (Cambridge: Cambridge University Press, 1998), 258–60.

25. John Verney (London) to Sir Ralph Verney, 30 August 1688, Buckinghamshire SRO, Verney MSS; Jack Stewkley (London) to Sir Ralph Verney, 29 August 1688, Buckinghamshire SRO, Verney MSS; Van Citters (London) to States General, 14/24 September, 2/12 October 1688, BL, Add. 34512, fols. 95v, 108r;

Anthony Heyford (Norwich) to Blathwayt, 24 September 1688, Beinecke, OSB MSS 2/Box 5/Folder 98; Childs, *Army*, 3; Kitt Redman's London Letter, 16 October 1688, Bodleian, Don.c.38, fol. 312r.

26. Edward Merrye (London) to James Mellifort, 28 August 1688, HEH, STT 1470; Merrye (London) to Mellifort, 13 September 1688, HEH, STT 1471; Dean Montague (London) to Viscount Hatton, 2 October 1688, BL, Add. 29563, fol. 277r; Levant Company (London) to Trumbull, 13 October 1688, BL, Add. 72526, fol. 184v; Van Citters (London) to States General, 9/19 October 1688, BL, Add. 34510, fol. 153v; London Newsletter, 6 October 1688, Bodleian, Don.c.38, fol. 298r; J. Boscawen (Whitehall) to John Evelyn, 30 September 1688, BL, Evelyn MSS, JE A9, unfolioed (since recataloged); Morrice, Entering Book, 13 October 1688, DWL, 31 Q, 303.

27. Albeville (Hague) to Middleton, 28 August/7 September 1688, BL, Add. 41816, fol. 170v; Petit (Amsterdam) to Middleton, 17/27 August 1688, BL, Add. 41816, fol. 160r; C. D. Chandaman, *The English Public Revenue, 1660–1688* (Oxford: Clarendon Press, 1975), 260; Wyche (Hamburg) to Middleton, 18 September 1688, BL, Add. 41827, fol. 90r; Robert Hall (Rye) to Frowde, 30 September 1688, NA, SP 31/4, fol. 84r.

28. Defoe, *Memoirs of Public Transactions*, 18–19; W. E. Buckley, ed., *Memoirs of Thomas, Earl of Ailesbury*, 2 vols. (Westminster: Nichols and Sons, 1890), 1:129–30; Reresby, *Memoirs*, 15 October 1688, 520–21; Albeville (Hague) to Preston, 6/16 November 1688, BL, Add. 34517, fol. 9r. It is interesting that financial support for William figures prominently in the German Ranke's account of the revolution, but not in Macaulay's. For Ranke, see Leopold Von Ranke, *A History of England Principally in the Seventeenth Century*, vol. 4 (New York: AMS, 1966), 399–400.

29. Hugh Speke to William III, 1689, NA, SP 32/2, fol. 88; Sir John Morgan (Chester Castle) to Shrewsbury, 5 April 1690, NA, SP 32/3, fol. 4; Morrice, Entering Book, 22 December 1688, DWL, 31 Q, 370–71; Earl of Dorset's Dorset Proclamation, 30 November 1688, Churchill College, Cambridge, Erle MSS, 4/4/2; Van Citters (Reading) to States General, 9/19 December 1688, BL, Add. 34510, fol. 194r.

30. A General Account of the Money Received of Lt. Col. Coke, 27 November 1688–20 February 1689, BL, Add. 69953, fol. 36r; Private Account of John Coke, [November–December 1688], BL, Add. 69953, fol. 57r; John Wright's Receipts, 28 November 1688, BL, Add. 69953, fol. 5r; Robert Kirk, "Sermons, Occurrences . . . ," March 1690, Edinburgh SUL, La.III.545, fol. 94v.

31. Newsletter, 12 January 1689, Bodleian, Don.c.39, fol. 87r; London Newsletter, 12 January 1689, FSL, L.c. 1958; Morrice, Entering Book, 12 January 1689, DWL, 31 Q, 419; London Newsletter, 15 January 1689, FSL, L.c. 1959; Robert Dale (London) to ?, 17 January 1689, BL, Egerton 2717, fol. 425r; Edmund Bohun, *The History of the Desertion* (London: Ric. Chiswell, 1689), 122; Corporation of London SRO, Loan Accounts, MS 40/35; London Newsletter, 15 January 1689, FSL, L.c. 1959; *London Intelligence*, 15–19 January 1689.

32. Alexander Stanhope (Madrid) to James Vernon, 7 June 1690, NA, SP 94/73, fol. 9v; Defoe, *Memoirs of Public Transactions*, 20–22; Albeville (Hague) to Middleton, 9/19 March 1688, BL, Add. 41815, fol. 183v; J. Cutts (Loo) to Middleton, 12 April 1688, BL, Add. 41805, fol. 23; Sir John Narborough to Lord Falkland, 4 May 1688, NMM, LBK/1, fol. 19v; Petit (Amsterdam) to Middleton, 15/25 May 1688, BL, Add. 41816, fol. 32v; Albeville (Hague) to Middleton, 31 July/10 August 1688, BL, Add. 41816, fol. 143r; Wyche (Hamburg) to Poley, 19 October 1688, BL, Add. 45731, fol. 22r; Morrice, Entering Book, 17 November 1688, DWL, 31 Q, 317; London Newsletter, 20 November 1688, Bodleian, Don.c.38, fol. 352v; *London Mercury*, 27–31 December 1688; E. S., *A Petition and Demand of Right and Justice by One of the Commons of England*, 19 January 1702 [1702], 2; Burnet, *History*, 483–87; G. Davies, ed., *Autobiography of Thomas Raymond and Memoirs of the Family of Guise of Elmore, Gloucestershire*, Camden Society, 3rd Ser., 28 (1917): 135–36; Winchester (Basingstoke) to William, 23 April 1688, NA, SP 8/1/Pt. 2, fol. 212v; Albeville (Hague) to Middleton, 8/18 June 1688, BL, Add. 41816, fol. 63r; Clarendon, Diary, 27 September 1688, 2:191; Albeville (Hague) to Middleton, 8/18 May 1688, BL, Add. 41816, fol. 25r; Danby (London) to William, 29 March 1688, NA, SP 8/1/Pt. 2, fol. 199r; Antoine Moreau (Hague) to king of Poland, 2/12 October 1688, BL, Add. 38495, fol. 32r; Albeville (Hague) to Middleton, 20/30 March 1688, BL, Add. 41815, fol. 193v; ? (London) to Innes, 5 November 1688, SCA, Bl 1/119/6; Francis Gwynn (Whitehall) to Blathwayt, 18 October 1688, Beinecke, OSB MSS 2/Box 4/Folder 91;

Moreau (Hague) to king of Poland, 13/23 July 1688, BL, Add. 38494, fol. 83v; Westby, Memoirs, 13 July 1688, fol. 31v; Yard (Whitehall) to Albeville, 13 July 1688, Indiana, Albeville MSS; H. Thynne (London) to Weymouth, 14 July 1688, Longleat House, Thynne MSS 14, fol. 241r; Newsletter to Countess of Suffolk, 17 July 1688, BL, Add. 34487, fol. 15r; John Verney (London) to Sir Ralph Verney, 19 July 1688, Buckinghamshire SRO, Verney MSS; Israel and Geoffrey Parker, "Of Providence and Protestant Winds," in *Anglo-Dutch Moment*, ed. Israel, 354–55.

33. Macaulay's exciting narrative emphasizes the role of aristocratic and gentry "adventurers": Macaulay, *History*, 2:421–22; Catalogue of Nobility and Principal Gentry Said to Be in Arms with the Prince of Orange, December 1688, Beinecke, OSB MSS 1/Box 4/Folder 189; Moreau (Hague) to king of Poland, 23 September/5 October 1688, BL, Add. 38495, fol. 26; Albeville (Hague) to Middleton, 27 September/7 October 1688, BL, Add. 41816, fol. 220r. These included such men as the London merchant and foreman of the first *ignoramus* jury John Wilmer: The Case of John Wilmer, HEH, EL 9614; Petit (Amsterdam) to Middleton, 17/27 August 1688, BL, Add. 41816, fol. 159r; Newsletter to Earl of Suffolk, 25 July 1688, BL, Add. 34487, fol. 17r; Israel and Parker, "Of Providence and Protestant Winds," 354; Albeville (Hague) to Middleton, 20/30 April 1688, BL, Add. 41815, fol. 258r; Ian Gentles, *The New Model Army in England, Ireland and Scotland, 1645–1653* (Oxford: Blackwell, 1992), 35–36; Webb, *Churchill's Coup*, 142.

34. Newsletter to Earl of Suffolk, 25 July 1688, BL, Add. 34487, fol. 17v; Theophilus Brookes (Formark) to Huntingdon, 8 August 1688, HEH, HA 1041; Childs, *Army*, 138–64; Shrewsbury, Devonshire, Danby, Lumley, Compton, Sidney, and Russell to William, 30 June 1688, NA, SP 8/1/Pt. 2, fols. 225–26; Morrice, Entering Book, 17 November 1688, DWL, 31 Q, 320–21; Ambrose Norton, "An Account of the Revolution in the Army in 1688," Bodleian, Rawlinson MSS, D148, fol. 3; Lowther, Memoirs, 106; Reresby, *Memoirs*, 10 September 1688, 510; Charles Gatty, ed., "Mr. Francis Gwyn's Journal," *Fortnightly Review*, n.s., 40 (1886): 363.

35. Gilbert Burnet, in H. C. Foxcroft, ed., *A Supplement to Burnet's "History of My Own Time"* (Oxford: Clarendon Press, 1902), 291; Annual Letters, 1688, Foley, 268–69; Van Citters (London) to States General, 20/30 November 1688, BL, Add. 34510, fol. 180r; Webb, *Churchill's Coup*, 130–33; Childs, *Army*, 148–50. Childs has overemphasized the level of cooperation between these Tory and Whig groups: *Memoirs of the Life of the Most Noble Thomas Late Marquess of Wharton*, 2nd ed. (London: J. Roberts, 1715), 19; Norton, "Account of the Revolution in the Army in 1688," fols. 3–4; William Penn to Dartmouth, 23 October 1688, *Penn Papers*, 3:211; Captain Robert Parker, *Memoirs of the Most Remarkable Military Transactions* (Dublin: Geo. and Alex Ewing, 1746), 9–10; Pen Stewkley (Norham, Leicestershire) to John Verney, 5 November 1688, Buckinghamshire SRO, Verney MSS. Subsequently these troops refused to fight against supporters of the Prince: Henry Compton (Nottingham) to Danby, 2 December 1688, LPL, 1834, fol. 17v; Samuel Pepys (London) to Dartmouth, 10 December 1688, Beinecke, OSB Shelves fb.190, 4: fol. 645r; Letter from Exeter, 21 November 1688, BL, Add. 63780, fol. 101r; Henry Booth, Lord Delamere, *The Works* (London: John Lawrence and John Dunton, 1694), 62.

36. Delamere, *Works*, 63; Reresby, *Memoirs*, 28 November 1688, 535.

37. Sir Willoughby Aston, Diary, 18 November 1688, Liverpool SRO, 920 MD 173; Lord Berkeley (Spithead) to Dartmouth, 21 November 1688, Beinecke, OSB Shelves fb.190, 4: fol. 583r; Middleton (Salisbury) to Preston, 24 November 1688, NA, SP 44/97, fol. 23; Sir Henry Shere (Hartly) to Dartmouth, 25 November 1688, Staffordshire SRO, D(w) 1778/III/123; Bellingham, *Diary*, 29 November 1688, 32; John Evelyn Jr. (Oxford) to John Evelyn, [12 December] 1688, BL, Evelyn MSS JE A4 (since recataloged); Norton, "Account of the Revolution in the Army in 1688," fol. 7; James II (Whitehall) to Dartmouth, 10 December 1688, Staffordshire SRO, D(w) 1778/v/1403, 134; James II (Whitehall) to Feversham, 10 December 1688, NAS, GD 406/1/3401; Cotterell to Trumbull, [28 November 1688], BL Trumbull MSS 39 (since recataloged); *Life of James II*, 2:225–26; Delamere, *Works*, 63; Reresby, *Memoirs*, 28 November 1688, 535; Francis Barrington and Benjamin Steele (London) to Goodwyn and Delabere, 11 January 1689, NA, FO 335/8, fol. 3.

38. *A Memorial of God's Last Twenty-Nine Years Wonders in England* (London: J. Rawlins, 1689), 118; ? to Lord Herbert of Cherbury, 21 July 1688, NA, PRO 30/53/8, fol. 119r; J. D. Davies, *Gentlemen and Tarpaulins:*

The Officers and Men of the Restoration Navy (Oxford: Clarendon Press, 1991), 202–3; London Newsletter, 21 July 1688, Longleat House, Thynne MSS 15, fol. 253r; Albeville (Hague) to Middleton, 31 July/10 August 1688, BL, Add. 41816, fol. 143v; Dartmouth (Ouze Edge) to James II, 22 October 1688, Staffordshire SRO, D(w) 1778/v/1403, 159–60; Dartmouth (Ouze Edge) to James II, 22 October 1688, NMM, DAR/17; Shrewsbury, Devonshire, Danby, Lumley, Compton, Sidney, and Russell to William, 30 June 1688, NA, SP 8/1/Pt. 2, fol. 225v.

39. Norton, "Account of the Revolution in the Army in 1688," fol. 10v; Dartmouth (Ouze Edge) to James II, 22 October 1688, NMM, DAR/17; Robert Price to Beaufort, [November 1688], Bodleian, Carte 130, fol. 313r; *Life of James II,* 2:208; John Knox Laughton, ed., *Memoirs Relating to the Lord Torrington,* Camden Society, n.s., 46 (1889): 27–28; Dartmouth (Ouze Edge) to James II, 17 October 1688, NMM, DAR/17; *The Prince of Orange's Letter to the English Fleet,* [1688]; Arthur Herbert, *Admiral Herbert's Letter to All Commanders of Ships and Sea-men,* [1688]; William III to all the commanders of ships in the English navy, 29 September 1688, BL, Egerton 2621, fol. 13. For the personal letters, see Herbert to Andrew Tucker, 6 November 1688, BL, Add. 63780, fol. 45r; Herbert to Colonel Strangways, 6 November 1688, BL, Add. 63780, fol. 47. See also Moreau (Hague) to king of Poland, 4/14 September 1688, BL, Add. 38495, fol. 15v; Albeville (Hague) to Middleton, 4/14 September 1688, BL, Add. 41816, fol. 177v; Albeville (Hague) to ?, 6/16 November 1688, BL, Add. 34517, fol. 8r; Bulstrode (Brussels) to Sunderland, 12 October 1688, NA, SP 77/55, fol. 493r; Van Citters (London) to States General, 13/23 November 1688, BL, Add. 34510, fol. 172v; Wyche (Hamburg) to Poley, 27 November 1688, BL, Add. 45731, fol. 65v; Edward Russell (Exeter) to Herbert, 13 November 1688, BL, Egerton 2621, fol. 47r; Southwell, "A Short Account of the Revolution," 1:fol. 3r; and Memorial for the King about the Fleet, 28 July 1693, NA, CO 388/4, fol. 67r.

40. Dartmouth to Samuel Pepys, 5 November 1688, NMM, DAR/15, 80; Dartmouth to James II, 5 November 1688, NMM, DAR/17; Davies, *Gentlemen and Tarpaulins,* 215–17.

41. Both Simon Patrick and John Evelyn reported that they had heard about the plans from English friends well before the end of August 1688: Simon Patrick, Autobiography, in *The Works of Symon Patrick,* vol. 9, ed. Alexander Taylor (Oxford: Oxford University Press, 1858), 513–14; Evelyn, *Diary,* 10 August 1688, 4:592; Morrice, Entering Book, 24 November 1688, DWL, 31 Q, 321; Information of Captain Humphrey Okeover, 30 August 1688, BL, Add. 41805, fol. 43r.

42. Delamere, *Works,* 57; Dartmouth (Downs) to James II, 8 November 1688, NMM, DAR/17, 22; Southwell, "A Short Account of the Revolution," 1:fol. 18v; John Whittle, *An Exact Diary of the Late Expedition* (London: Richard Baldwin, 1689), 40–41; *A Political Conference* (London: J. L., 1689), 50.

43. Middleton to Newcastle, 30 October 1688, NA, SP 44/97, fol. 9; Reresby, *Memoirs,* 28 November 1688, 530; *Life of James II,* 2:231; Thomas Osborne, Duke of Leeds, *Copies and Extracts of Some Letters* (London, 1710), vi–vii; Reresby, *Memoirs,* 4 October 1688, 514–15.

44. Reresby, *Memoirs,* 28 November, 22 November 1688, 534, 528–31; Jeremy Mahony (York) to Thomas Ratcliffe, 22 November 1688, BL, Egerton 3335, fols. 80–81; Newsletter, 27 November 1688, Bodleian, Don.c.39, fol. 6r; Reresby, *Memoirs,* 531; Newsletter from London, 24 November 1688, Bodleian, Don.c.39, fol. 7r; Reresby, *Memoirs,* 24 November 1688, 532; Bellingham, *Diary,* 27 November 1688, 31; London Newsletter, 29 November 1688, FSL, L.c. 1941; *Life of James II,* 2:231; London Newsletter, 29 November 1688, FSL, L.c. 1941; William Longueville (London) to Viscount Hatton, 24 November 1688, BL, Add. 29563, fol. 336r; ? to Lady Gerard, November 1688, NAS, GD 406/1/8828.

45. Aston, Diary, 18 November 1688; Newsletter, 24 November 1688, Bodleian, Don.c.39, fol. 11r; ? to Charles Jackson, 17 November 1688, BL, Add. 63780, fol. 92r; J. Smithsby (London) to Huntingdon, 20 November 1688, HEH, HA 12450; Delamere, "Advice to His Children," 20 September 1688, in Delamere, *Works,* 1694, 1–2; Delamere to ?, 1689, NA, SP 8/6, fol. 47; Morrice, Entering Book, 24 November 1688, DWL, 31 Q, 324; "The Glory of the Northern Parts of England," January 1689, in *The Pepys Ballads,* 8 vols., ed. Hyder Edgar Rollins (Cambridge, MA: Harvard University Press, 1929–32), 4:58; Bellingham, *Diary,* 21 November 1688, 30; William Fleming (Lancaster) to Sir Daniel Fleming, 30 November, 24 November 1688,

Bodleian, Don.c.39, fols. 23v, 3v; Robert Price (London) to Beaufort, 22 November 1688, Bodleian, Carte 130, fol. 307r; J. Coke to Francis Thacker, 24 November 1688, BL, Add. 69936, fol. 18r; Newsletter to Countess of Suffolk, 27 November 1688, BL, Add. 34487, fol. 38r; London Newsletter, 29 November 1688, Bodleian, Don.c.39, fol. 28r; Morrice, Entering Book, 22 December 1688, DWL, 31 Q, 371; William Fleming (Lancaster) to Sir Daniel Fleming, 30 November 1688, Bodleian, Don.c.39, fol. 31v.

46. D. P. Davies, *A New Historical and Descriptive View of Derbyshire* (Belper: S. Mason, 1811), 184; London Newsletter, 22 November 1688, Bodleian, Don.c.39, fol. 1r; Van Citters (London) to States General, 20/30 November 1688, BL, Add. 34510, fol. 182r; Devonshire (Nottingham) to Danby, 22? November 1688, BL, Egerton 3335, fol. 59r; A. Mildmay to David Barrett, November 1688, Essex SRO, D/DL/C43/2/101; Bligh (London) to ?, 27 November 1688, PRONI, T2929/1/23; Morrice, Entering Book, 22 December 1688, DWL, 31 Q, 371; Mr. Andrews et al. to ? Sir Richard Temple, 10 November 1688, HEH, STT 48; Newsletter from London, 24 November 1688, Bodleian, Don.c.39, fol. 6r; Anne (Cockpit) to William, 18 November 1688, NA, SP 8/2/Pt. 2, fol. 64; ? to Lady Gerard, November 1688, NAS, GD 406/1/8828; Aston, Diary, 30 November 1688; Compton (Nottingham), to Danby, 2 December 1688, LPL, 1834, fol. 17r; Anne (Nottingham) to Bathurst, 3 December 1688, BL, Loan 57/71, fol. 19r; *Life of James II*, 2:227.

47. Cibber, *Apology,* ed. Lowe, 58–62; Commissioners of His Majesty's Revenue to Lords of Treasury, 4 December 1688, NA, CUST 48/3, 226; Petition of Mary Borradale, 13 November 1691, NA, CUST 48/4, 212; Newsletter from London, 27 November 1688, Bodleian, Don.c.39, fol. 21r.

48. Compton (Nottingham) to Danby, 5 December 1688, BL, Egerton 3336, fol. 34r; Compton (London) to William, 2 December 1688, NA, SP 8/2/Pt. 2, fol. 33; London Newsletter, 2 December 1688, HRC, Pforzheimer/Box 10/Folder 5; London Newsletter, 8 December 1688, Bodleian, Don.c.39, fol. 48r; Devonshire (Nottingham) to William, 2 December 1688, NA, SP 8/2/Pt. 2, fol. 32; Chesterfield, "Memoirs," in *Letters of Philip, Second Earl of Chesterfield* (London: E. Lloyd and Son, 1829), 48–49; *English Currant,* 12–14 December 1688; Lord Grey of Ruthen to Christopher Hatton, December 1688, BL, Add. 29563, fol. 395r.

49. R. Fleming to Sir Daniel Fleming, 22 November 1688, Bodleian, Don.c.39, fol. 2r; Draft of Petition, 24 November 1688, HMC Kenyon, 205–6; William Fleming (Lancaster) to Sir Daniel Fleming, 27 November 1688, Bodleian, Don.c.39, fol. 14r; Aston, Diary, 20 November, 28 November, 30 November 1688; Bellingham, *Diary,* 23 November 1688, 31; Roger Kenyon, Remarques upon the Change of Lieutenancy in Lancashire, ca. 1689, Lancashire SRO, DD/Ke/4/9/; London Newsletter, 18 December 1688, Bodleian, Don.c.39, fol. 73r; Stevens, *Journal,* 8–9.

50. Van Citters (London) to States General, 13/23 November 1688, BL, Add. 34510, fol. 174r; London Newsletter, 4 December 1688, BL, Add. 34487, fol. 44r; Newsletter from London, 4 December 1688, Bodleian, Don.c.39, fols. 36–37; Row Tempest to Edmund Poley, 4 December 1688, BL, Add. 45731, fol. 69v; Jonathan Trelawney, bishop of Bristol (Bristol) to William, 5 December 1688, NA, SP 8/2/Pt. 2, fol. 35; Morrice, Entering Book, 8 December 1688, DWL, 31 Q, 343; Memoirs of Edward Harley, 11 December 1688, BL, Add. 34515, fol. 1; Samuel Saunders (Hereford) to Sancroft, 10 December 1688, Bodleian, Tanner 28, fol. 283r; Newsletter from Whitehall, 7 December 1688, HRC, Pforzheimer/Box 10/Folder 5; Morrice, Entering Book, 8 December 1688, 343.

51. Middleton (Whitehall) to Beaufort, 16 November 1688, NA, SP 44/97, fol. 18; Stevens, *Journal,* 6–7; Aston, Diary, 21 November 1688.

52. Reresby, *Memoirs,* 8 August 1688, 505; Norfolk (Norwich) to Sunderland, 15 October 1688, NA, SP 31/4, fol. 135v; Van Citters (London) to States General, 16/26 October 1688, BL, Add. 34512, fol. 115r; Charles Dodd, *The Church History of England,* 3 vols. (Brussels, 1742), 3:447; William Lloyd, bishop of Norwich (Norwich) to Sancroft, 19 November 1688, Bodleian, Tanner 28, fol. 258r; R. D. (London) to ?, 6 December 1688, BL, Egerton 2717, fol. 414r; Duke of Norfolk's Speech at Lynn Regis, 10 December 1688, BL, Add. 22640, fol. 54v; *London Mercury or Moderate Intelligencer,* 15 December 1688.

53. Bohun, *History of the Desertion,* 39; *Quadrennium Jacobi* (London: James Knapton, 1689), 196; Whittle, *Exact Diary,* 45–46; *A True and Exact Relation of the Prince of Orange His Publick Entrance into Exeter* (1688); "Relation du Voyage d'Angleterre," 9/19 November 1688, Warwickshire SRO, CR 2017/C8, fol. 56r.

54. Southwell, "Short Account of the Revolution," 1: fol. 18v; Huntingdon (Honiton) to Countess of Huntingdon, 7 November 1688, HEH, HA 6066; Whittle, *Exact Diary,* 50–51; Morrice, Entering Book, 17 November 1688, DWL, 31 Q, 316; *Quadrennium Jacobi,* 199. Among them was the London innholder George Arnold: Colchester, Manchester, and Sidney to lords of the Treasury, 1 May 1691, NA, CUST 48/4, 132.

55. William (Exeter) to Edward Herbert, 10/20 Novembber 1688, BL, Egerton 2621, fol. 41r; Aikenhead (Edinburgh) to Tweeddale, 13 November 1688, NLS, 7011, fol. 119r; Southwell, "Short Account of the Revolution," 1: fol. 18r; Gilbert Burnet to Edward Herbert, 16 November 1688, BL, Egerton 2621, fol. 51r; ? (Exeter) to John Candy, 21 November 1688, BL, Add. 63780, fol. 103r; Nottingham to Lord Hatton, 15 November 1688, BL, Add. 29594, fol. 131v; James (Whitehall) to Dartmouth, 9 November 1688, Staffordshire SRO, D(w) 1778/v/1403, 123; Dartmouth to Pepys, 11 November 1688, NMM, DAR/15, 95; Narcissus Luttrell, *A Brief Historical Relation of State Affairs,* vol. 1 (Oxford: Oxford University Press, 1857), November 1688, 474.

56. *Memoirs of Wharton,* 21; Southwell, "Short Account of the Revolution," 1:fol. 18r; Letter from Exeter, 17 November 1688, BL, Add. 63780, fol. 93r; Alexander Sampson (Exeter) to Frowde, 19 November 1688, BL, Add. 63780, fol. 99r; London Newsletter, 20 November 1688, FSL, L.c. 1937; London Newsletter, 20 November 1688, Bodleian, Don.c.38, fol. 361r; London Newsletter, 22 November 1688, FSL, L.c. 1938; Newsletter from London, 24 November 1688, Bodleian, Don.c.39, fol. 8r; Morrice, Entering Book, 24 November 1688, DWL, 31 Q, 322; Burnet (Exeter) to Edward Herbert, 16 November 1688, BL, Egerton 2621, fol. 51v; Bligh (London) to ?, 27 November 1688, PRONI, T2929/1/23; Henry Fleming (Oxford) to Sir Daniel Fleming, 17 November 1688, Cumbria SRO, Kendal, WD/Ry 3324; Sir John Chichely to Peter Legh, 1 December 1688, JRL, Legh of Lyme MSS, Box 4/Folder 26; Cotterell to Trumbull, [28 November 1688], BL, Trumbull MSS 39 (since recataloged); EIC to general and council of India at Bombay, 5 December 1688, IOL, E/3/91, fol. 297r.

57. Middleton (Salisbury) to Preston, 23 November 1688, NA, SP 44/97, fol. 22; Nottingham to Lord Hatton, 24 November 1688, BL, Add. 29594, fol. 135r; Morrice, Entering Book, 24 November 1688, DWL, 31 Q, 322; John Cowper (London) to [Thomas Dawtry], 27 November 1688, Essex SRO, D/Dfa/F22.

58. *A Letter to a Gentleman at Brussels,* 22 December 1688 (London, 1689), 5.

59. Albeville (Hague) to Middleton, 17/27 April 1688, BL, Add. 41815, fol. 249v; Morrice, Entering Book, 28 July 1688, DWL, 31 Q, 285; commissioners of His Majesty's revenue to lords of the Treasury, 4 December 1688, NA, CUST 48/3, 226; Morrice, Entering Book, 2 December 1688, 387; [Sir William] Portman (Orchard near Taunton) to Col. Thomas Erle, 19 December 1688, Churchill College, Cambridge, 2/50/2.

60. *Great News from Salisbury,* 6 December 1688 (1688); Whittle, *Exact Diary,* 61.

61. Albeville (Hague) to Middleton, 1/11 October 1688, BL, Add. 41816, fol. 230v; Sandford to Wynne, 26 September 1688, BL, Add. 41805, fol. 46r; London Newsletter, 6 October 1688, Bodleian, Don.c.38, fol. 298r; Southwell, "Short Account of the Revolution," 1:fols. 7–8; Sir Ralph Verney (Middle Claydon) to John Verney, 9 December 1688, Buckinghamshire SRO, Verney MSS; London Newsletter, 8 December 1688, Bodleian, Don.c.39, fol. 48v; John Evelyn Jr. (Radley) to John Evelyn, 15 December 1688, BL, Eveelyn MSS, JE A4, 646 (since recataloged); Henry Fleming (Oxford) to Sir Daniel Fleming, 19 January 1689, Cumbria SRO, Kendal, WD/Ry 3426.

62. Bath to William, 18 November, 27 November 1688, NA, SP 8/21/Pt. 2, fols. 56r, 58r; Huntingdon, Autobiography, 17 October 1699, HEH, HA Genealogy Box 1(32); *English Currant,* 12 December 1688, [1]; Huntingdon (Plymouth) to Countess of Huntingdon, 26 November 1688, HEH, HA 6074.

63. ? to Innes, 11 December 1688, SCA, Bl 1/119/2; London Newsletter, 8 December 1688, Bodleian, Don.c.39, fol. 48r; London Newsletter, 8 December 1688, BL, Add. 34487, fol. 46r; Reresby, *Memoirs,* 3 December 1688, 535–36; Devonshire (Nottingham) to Danby, 8 December 1688, BL, Egerton 3336, fol. 40v; *Life*

of James II, 2:230–31; Childs, *Army,* 192–93; John Tichell, *The History of the Town and County of Kingston upon Hull* (Hull: Thomas Lee, 1798), 583; Newsletter from Whitehall, 7 December 1688, HRC, Pforzheimer/Box 10/Folder 5; *English Currant,* 12 December 1688, [1].

64. Pepys (London) to Dartmouth, 10 December 1688, Beinecke, OSB Shelves fb.190, 4:fol. 644r; ? to Innes, 11 December 1688, SCA, Bl 1/119/2; *English Currant,* 12–14 December 1688; Russell Billingsby (Berwick) to Sir Charles Porter, 16 December 1688, BL, Egerton 3336, fol. 77r; London Newsletter, 15 December 1688, Bodleian, Don.c.39, fol. 65r; *English Currant,* 14–19 December 1688.

65. William Carstares to William, [summer–autumn] 1688, NA, SP 8/2/Pt. 2, fol. 109r; Lord Lindsay, ed., *Memoirs Touching the Revolution in Scotland by Colin Earl of Balcarres* (Edinburgh: Bannatyne Club, 1841), 8–9, 11–12; Ginny Gardner, *The Scottish Exile Community in the Netherlands, 1660–1690* (East Linton: Tuckwell, 2004), 182–85; J. Aglionby to Sir John Lowther, 11 November 1688, Cumbria SRO, Carlisle, D/Lons/L1/1/34/19; John Ker, *Memoirs of John Ker of Kersland* (London, 1726), 10; T. S., *The History of the Affaires of Scotland* (London: Tho. Salusbury, 1690), sig. A3r, 21–22; *Five Letters from a Gentleman in Scotland* (London, 1689), 25 December 1688, 4, 8. Ker and his gang seized the Catholic ritual objects hidden at Traquair House by the 4th earl and burned them at the cross at Peebles: see mss letter, 1688, Traquair House, priest's room; Douglas Duncan, ed., *History of the Union of Scotland and England by Sir John Clerk of Penicuik* (Edinburgh: Scottish History Society, 1993), 81. I differ from Ian B. Cowan, "The Reluctant Revolutionaries: Scotland in 1688," in *By Force or By Default?* ed. Cruickshanks, 65ff. I am in closer agreement with Tim Harris, "Reluctant Revolutionaries? The Scots and the Revolution of 1688–89," in *Politics and the Political Imagination in Later Stuart Britain,* ed. Howard Nenner (Rochester, NY: University of Rochester Press, 1997), 97–117.

66. Patrick Kelly, "Ireland and the Glorious Revolution," in *Revolutions of 1688,* ed. Beddard, 169; The Case of the Governor and Garrison of Londonderry, ca. 1700, Lancashire SRO, D/DK/1745; Gilbert, ed., *Jacobite Narrative,* 40–41; Petition of George Hause, 3 September 1689, NA, SP 32/2, fol. 3; Simon Digby (bishop of Limerick), Diary, 9 October 1688, LPL, 3152, fols. 7–8; Philip O'Regan, *Archbishop William King, 1650–1729, and the Constitution in Church and State* (Dublin: Four Courts Press, 2000), 22; Gilbert, ed., *Jacobite Narrative,* 42.

67. Mr. Riggs's Narrative of the Proceedings at Boston, 18 April 1689, NA, CO 5/905, fol. 47r; lieutenant governor and council of New York to Committee of Trade, 15 May 1689, NA, CO 5/905, fol. 45r; Webb, *Churchill's Coup,* 182–216; Address of the president and Council for Safety (Boston), 20 May 1689, NA, CO 5/905, fol. 60; Morrice, Entering Book, 29 June 1689, DWL, 31 Q, 583; E. R. and S. S., *The Revolution in New England Justified* (Boston: Joseph Brumay, 1691), 2; Edward Randolph, A Short Narrative, 29 May 1689, NA, CO 5/905, fols. 69–70; Stephen Lobb to Preston, 4 December 1688, BL, Add. 63773, fol. 197r; Lieutenant Governor Nicholson (New York) to Committee of Trade, 15 May 1689, NA, CO 5/905, fol. 45v; Petition of the New York House of Representatives, 15 May 1699, HEH, EL 9777; London Newsletter, 27 August 1689, FSL, L.c. 2056; The State of Lord Baltimore's Case, 1712, BL, Add. 70160, unfolioed; *The Declaration of the Reasons and Motives of the Present Appearing in Arms of Their Majesties Protestant Subjects in the Province of Maryland* (St. Mary's, MD: William Nuthead, 1689), 25 July 1689, 3.

68. Georges Lefebvre, *The Great Fear of 1789,* trans. Joan White (Princeton, NJ: Princeton University Press, 1973), 56. In the following paragraphs I have followed and learned much from a paper by Adam Fox: "Rumour and Panic in Late Stuart England: The 'Irish Fright' of December 1688." See his earlier discussion in *Oral and Literate Culture in England, 1500–1700* (Oxford: Clarendon Press, 2000), 380–82; George Hilton Jones, "The Irish Fright of 1688: Real Violence and Imagined Massacre," *Bulletin of the Institute of Historical Research* 55 (November 1982): 148–53.

69. Lowther (London) to Mr. Tichell, 9 October 1688, Cumbria SRO, Carlisle, D/Lons/W2/1/23; Musgrave (Edenhall) to Sir Daniel Fleming, 11 October 1688, Cumbria SRO, Kendal, WD/Ry 3279; William Fletcher (Whitehaven) to Sir Daniel Fleming, 15 October 1688, Cumbria SRO, Kendal, WD/Ry 3284; Lawrence Rawstorne to Kenyon, 16 October 1688, HMC Kenyon, 203; Bellingham, *Diary,* 17 October 1688, 22; Aston, Diary, 20 October 1688; Parker, *Memoirs,* 8; Lieutenant Colonel Norton (Yarmouth) to Blathwayt,

10 September 1688, FSL, X.d. 436 (36); London Newsletter, 9 October, 11 October 1688, Bodleian, Don.c.38, fols. 299r, 299v; Van Citters (London) to States General, 30 October/9 November 1688, BL, Add. 34510, fol. 161r; *The Prince of Orange His Third Declaration,* [28 November 1688], 3; Morrice, Entering Book, 15 December 1688, DWL, 31 Q, 362; Bohun, *History of the Desertion,* 89; Luttrell, *Brief Historical Relation,* 8 December 1688, 485; Hugh Speke, *The Secret History of the Happy Revolution in 1688* (London: S. Keimer, 1715), 32–33; A. Pye (London) to Abigail Harley, 28 October 1688, BL, Add. 70014, fol. 115r; London Newsletter, 29 November 1688, Bodleian, Don.c.39, fol. 27r; London Newsletter, 29 November 1688, FSL, L.c. 1941; Edward Harley (Stoke) to Robert Harley, 9 December 1688, BL, Add. 40621, fol. 1r; ? (Carlisle) to Lowther, 10 December 1688, Cumbria SRO, Carlisle, D/Lons/L1/1/34/21; William Fleming (Lancaster) to Sir Daniel Fleming, 24 November 1688, Bodleian, Don.c.39, fol. 3v; Kenyon to mayor of Wigan, 28 November 1688, HMC Kenyon, 209; Simon Digby, Bishop of Limerick, Diary, 26 October 1688, LPL, 3152, fol. 7v; Cotterell to Trumbull, 25 October 1688, BL, Trumbull MSS 39 (since recataloged); Wellwood, *Memoirs,* 220–21; London Newsletter, 11 December, Bodleian, Don.c.39, fol. 54v; Ferguson, *History of Mobs,* 49.

70. Speke, *Secret History,* 42; Norton, "An Account of the Revolution in the Army," fol. 10v.

71. Morrice, Entering Book, 15 December 1688, DWL, 31 Q, 352; R. D. (London) to ?, 13 December 1688, BL, Egerton 2717, fol. 416r; ? (London) to James Harrington, 13 December 1688, BL, Add. 36707, fol. 51r; John Verney (London) to Sir Ralph Verney, 13 December 1688, Buckinghamshire SRO, Verney MSS; London Newsletter, 13 December 1688, Bodleian, Don.c.39, fol. 62r; Luttrell, *Brief Historical Relation,* 13 December 1688, 487; Parker, *Memoirs,* 12; Martha Harley (Brampton Bryan) to Sir Edward Harley, 14 December 1688, BL, Add. 70118, unfolioed; Francis Holdsworth (Chesterfield) to Danby, 14 December 1688, BL, Egerton 3336, fol. 58r; Sir William Boothby (Ashbourne) to Mr. Wolley, 15 December 1688, BL, Add. 71692, fol. 59r; *London Mercury,* 15–18 December 1688; Roger Whitley, Diary, 15 December 1688, Bodleian, Eng. Hist.c.711, fol. 100r; Aston, Diary, 15 December 1688; *English Currant,* 21–26 December 1688; Thomas Shearson (mayor of Lancaster) to Sir Daniel Fleming, 15 December 1688, Cumbria SRO, Kendal, WD/Ry 3393; Draft of a Petition Giving Particulars of a Dispute between the Earl of Derby and Lord Delamere, 15 December 1688, HMC Kenyon, 206; Bellingham, *Diary,* 15 December 1688, 36; William Fleming (Lancaster) to Sir Daniel Fleming, 15 December 1688, Bodleian, Don.c.39, fol. 67r; Thoresby, *Diary,* 1:191; *English Currant,* 19–21 December 1688; *London Mercury,* 24–27, 27–31 December 1688; *Five Lettters from a Gentleman in Scotland,* 25 December 1688, 4; Speke, *Secret History,* 45–48; Thomas Halyburton, *Memoirs of the Life of the Reverend Mr. Thomas Halyburton* (Edinburgh: Andrew Anderson, 1714), 23; Annual Letters of the Residence, 1685–90, Foley, 729; Theophilus Brookes (Derbyshire) to Huntingdon, 19 December 1688, HEH, HA 1043; Musgrave (Edenhall) to Sir Daniel Fleming, 25 December 1688, Cumbria SRO, Kendal, WD/Ry 3409.

72. William Fleming (Lancaster) to Sir Daniel Fleming, 18 December 1688, Bodleian, Don c. 39, fol. 69r; Lowther (London) to T. Tichell, 25 December 1688, Cumbria SRO, Carlisle, D/Lons/W2/1/23; Morrice, Entering Book, 15 December 1688, DWL, 31 Q, 359; Stevens, *Journal,* 11; Annual Report, 1688, Foley, 731; Speke, *Secret History,* 44.

73. *English Currant,* 19 December 1688, [2]; Whittle, *Exact Diary,* 71; Countess of Huntingdon (London) to Huntingdon, 18 December 1688, HEH, HA 4807; Thomas Carleton (London) to Huntingdon, 18 December 1688, HEH, HA 1227; Wyche (Hamburg) to Poley, 22 January 1689, BL, Add. 45731, fol. 99r; Morrice, Entering Book, 22 December 1688, DWL, 31 Q, 377–78. Orange women were known to have distributed Orange ballads in December 1688. See "Buy My Oranges," 1688, Essex SRO, D/Dby Z5; "A Congratulatory Poem to His Royal Highness the Prince of Orange," "The Prince of Orange Welcome to London," "The Prince of Orange's Triumph," "A Third Touch of the Times," "A New Song of an Orange," and "The Rare Virtue of an Orange," all in *Pepys Ballads,* ed. Rollins, 3:319; Bohun, *History of the Desertion,* 105; John Evelyn to John Evelyn Jr., 18 December 1688, BL, Evelyn MSS, JEJ 1 (since recataloged); London Newsletter, 20 December 1688, FSL, L.c. 1949; Hamon London Newsletter, 20 December 1688, Beinecke, OSB Shelves fb.210; *Quadrennium Jacobi,* 252; R. D. (London) to ?, 18 December 1688, BL, Egerton 2717, fol. 417r.

74. Countess of Huntingdon (London) to Huntingdon, 3 December 1688, HEH, HA 4801; Joseph Hill (Paris) to Trumbull, 8 December 1688, Berkshire SRO, D/ED/C33; Henry Newcome, 30 November 1688, in *The Autobiography of Henry Newcome,* vol. 2, ed. Robert Parkinson, Chetham Society 27 (Manchester: Chetham Society, 1852), 269; Countess of Huntingdon (London) to Huntingdon, 20 November 1688, HEH, HA 4712; Thomas Legh (Norton) to Peter Legh, 22 November 1688, JRL, Legh of Lyme, Box 4/Folder 29; Levant Company to Trumbull, 15 December 1688, NA, SP 105/114, fol. 444; Cibber, *Apology,* ed. Lowe, 70; Stevens, *Journal,* 4; *Life of James II,* 2:230.

75. Delamere, *Works,* 68; *A Dialogue between Dick and Tom* (London: Randal Taylor, 1689), 9.

76. Sir Richard Temple, "Essay on Monarchy," ca. 1690s, HEH, STT Lit (17); Stevens, *Journal,* 98; Cotterell to Trumbull, 31 December 688, BL, Trumbull MSS 39 (since recataloged); Thomas and Robert Ball (Leghorn) to Kinard de la Bere, January 1689, NA, FO 335/15, unfolioed; *A New Declaration of the Confederate Princes and States* (London: Tim. Goodwin, 1689), 24; *Reflections upon Our Late and Present Proceedings in England* (London, 1689), 5; *A Friendly Debate* (London: Jonathan Robinson, 1689), 11; Philip Warre (Whitehall) to Edmund Poley, 4 December 1688, BL, Add. 45731, fol. 71; Huntingdon (Plymouth) to Sir Edward Abney, 7 December 1688, HEH, HA 6078; *Dilucidator,* 5 March 1689, 110; London Newsletter, 28 December 1688, HRC, Pforzheimer/Box 10/Folder 5; Pierre Jurieu, *Monsieur Jurieu's Judgment* (London: John Lawrence, 1689), 23–24.

77. Delamere, *Works,* 67–68; *Life of James II,* 2:233, 241–42; James II (Whitehall) to Feversham, 10 December 1688, NAS, GD 406/1/3401; Reresby, *Memoirs,* 10 December 1688, 536; ? to Sancroft, 30 January 1689, Bodleian, Tanner 28, fol. 336r.

CHAPTER 9. *Violent Revolution*

1. Roger Morrice, Entering Book, 8 December 1688, DWL, 31 Q, 343.

2. Samuel Rudder, *A New History of Gloucestershire* (Cirencester, 1779), 351; J. Keeling to Roger Kenyon, November 1688, HMC Kenyon, 210; Anthony Hewitson, ed., *Diary of Thomas Bellingham, an Officer under William III* (Preston: Geo. Toulmin and Sons, 1908), 18 November 1688, 29–30 (hereafter cited as Bellingham, *Diary*); *Life of James II,* 2:217; John Verney (London) to Sir Ralph Verney, 29 November 1688, Buckinghamshire SRO, Verney MSS; Thomas Babington Macaulay, *The History of England from the Accession of James II,* 5 vols. (New York: Harper and Brothers, 1849–61), 2:473–74; London Newsletter, 11 December 1688, Bodleian, Don.c.39, fol. 54; Samuel Pepys (London) to Dartmouth, 10 December 1688, Beinecke, OSB Shelves fb.190, 4: fols. 644–45; Newsletter from Whitehall, 10 December 1688, HRC, Pforzheimer/Box 10/Folder 5; George Rudé, *The Crowd in the French Revolution* (Oxford: Clarendon Press, 1959), 89.

3. Middleton (Whitehall) to Bristol, 8 November 1688, NA, SP 44/97, fol. 14; John Verney (London) to Sir Ralph Verney, 28 November, 29 November 1688, Buckinghamshire SRO, Verney MSS; London Newsletter, 6 December 1688, FSL, L.c. 1944; Capt. Robert Parker, *Memoirs of the Most Remarkable Military Transactions* (Dublin: Geo. and Alex Ewing, 1746), 12–13.

4. *English Currant,* 12–14 December 1688; London Newsletter, 8 December 1688, FSL, L.c. 1945; Dartmouth (Spithead) to Col. Richard Norton, 18 December 1688, NMM, DAR/17, 53; *English Currant,* 19–21 December 1688.

5. Philip Warre (Whitehall) to Edmund Poley, 4 December 1688, BL, Add. 45731, fol. 71v; Robert H. Murray, ed., *The Journal of John Stevens* (Oxford: Clarendon Press, 1912), 7 (hereafter cited as Stevens, *Journal*); Commissioners of the Revenue to Lords of the Treasury, 26 December 1688, NA, CUST 48/3, 228–29.

6. Charles Dodd, *The Church History of England,* 3 vols. (Brussels, 1742), 3:435; Annual Letters, 1688, Foley, 269; *A Memorial of God's Last Twenty-Nine Years Wonders in England* (London: J. Rawlins, 1689), 138; Sir Richard Bulstrode (Brussels) to Poley, 9 January 1689, BL, Add. 45731, fol. 95v.

7. London Newsletter, 13 October 1688, Bodleian, Don.c.38, fol. 303r; Jesuit Annual Letters, 1688, Foley, 269; Supplement to the History of the Province, 1688, Foley, 271; Morrice, Entering Book, 3 November 1688,

DWL, 31 Q, 310; London Newsletter, 30 October 1688, Bodleian, Don.c.38, fol. 326v; John Verney (London) to Edmund Verney Jr., 1 November 1688, Buckinghamshire SRO, Verney MSS; Letter to Viscount Hatton, 1 November 1688, BL, Add. 29563, fol. 312r.

8. Middleton (Whitehall) to lord mayor of London, 13 November 1688, NA, SP 44/97, fol. 15; Nottingham to Hatton, 15 November 1688, BL, Add. 29594, fol. 131r; ? (London) to James Harrington, 13 November 1688, BL, Add. 36707, fol. 47r; William Longueville (London) to Hatton, 13 November 1688, BL, Add. 29563, fol. 323r; Humphrey Griffith (Whitehall) to Poley, 13 November 1688, BL, Add. 45731, fol. 51r; London Newsletter, 13 November 1688, BL, Add. 34487, fol. 35r; London Newsletter, 13 November 1688, FSL, L.c. 1934; Van Citters (London) to States General, 16/26 November 1688, BL, Add. 34510, fol. 177; London Newsletter, 17 November 1688, Bodleian, Don.c.38, fol. 353v; London Newsletter, 17 November 1688, FSL, L.c. 1936.

9. *English Currant*, 12–14 December 1688; Lady Cary Gardiner (London) to Sir Ralph Verney, 12 December 1688, Buckinghamshire SRO, Verney MSS; Jack Stewkley (London) to Sir Ralph Verney, 11 December 1688, Buckinghamshire SRO, Verney MSS; London Newsletter, 11 December 1688, FSL, L.c. 1946; John Aubrey (London) to Anthony Wood, 22 December 1688, BL, Egerton 2231, fol. 120r; John Verney (London) to Sir Ralph Verney, 13 December 1688, Buckinghamshire SRO, Verney MSS; Sir Charles Cotterell to Sir William Trumbull, 31 December 1688, BL, Trumbull MSS 39 (since recataloged); Morrice, Entering Book, 15 December 1688, DWL, 31 Q, 352; Thomas Carleton (London) to Huntingdon, 13 December 1688, HEH, HA 1226; London Newsletter, 13 December 1688, FSL, L.c. 1947; London Newsletter, 13 December 1688, Bodleian, Don.c.39, fol. 62r.

10. *An Account of the Proceedings at White-Hall, Guildhall, in the City of London and at the Tower*, 11 December 1688 [1688]; Morrice, Entering Book, 15 December 1688, DWL, 31 Q, 348, 361; *English Currant*, 12–14 December 1688; London Newsletter, 13 December 1688, Bodleian, Don.c.39, fol. 62r; Bulstrode (Brussels) to Poley, 9 January 1689, BL, Add. 45731, fol. 95v; *London Mercury*, 15 December 1688; Van Citters (Westminster) to States General, 14/24 December 1688, BL, Add. 34510, fol. 198; London Newsletter, 13 December 1688, Bodleian, Don.c.39, fol. 62r; John Chichely (London) to Peter Legh, 11 December 1688, JRL, Legh of Lyme MSS, Box 4/Folder 26.

11. R. D. (London) to ?, 11 December 1688, BL, Egerton 2717, fol. 415r; Philip Frowde (London) to Dartmouth, 11 December 1688, Beinecke, OSB Shelves fb.190, 4: fol. 649r; Edmund Bohun, *History of the Desertion* (London: Ric. Chiswell, 1689), 98; *Quadrennium Jacobi* (London: James Knapton, 1689), 245–46; "The Downfall of Popery," January 1689, in *The Pepys Ballads,* 8 vols., ed. Hyder Edgar Rollins (Cambridge, MA: Harvard University Press, 1929–32), 4:74.

12. Row Tempest to Poley, 11 December 1688, BL, Add. 45731, fol. 77r; Sir Robert Southwell, "A Short Account of the Revolution in England," 11 December 1688, FSL, V.b. 150, 1: fol. 10v; Supplement to the History of the Province, 1688, Foley, 271; Paul de Rapin de Thoyras, *The History of England,* 5th ed., vol. 12, trans. N. Tindal (London: T. Osborne et al., 1752), 164; *London Mercury,* 15–18, 18–22, 22–24 December 1688; London Newsletter, 22 December 1688, Bodleian, Don.c.39, fol. 75r; Annual Letters, 1688, Foley, 781; Van Citters (London) to States General, 23 October/2 November 1688, BL, Add. 34510, fol. 159v; Norfolk (Norwich) to Sunderland, 15 October 1688, NA, SP 31/4, fol. 135Ar; *English Currant,* 2 January 1689, [2]; London Newsletter, 6 December 1688, FSL, L.c. 1944. On this I disagree with Macaulay, *History,* 2:521.

13. Anthony Wood, *Athenae Oxonienses,* 3 vols., 2nd ed. (London: R. Knaplock, D. Midwinter, J. Tonson, 1721), 2:617; Father Henry Pelham to Father John Clare, 2 May 1690, Foley, 956; London Newsletter, 6 December 1688, FSL, L.c. 1944; Morrice, Entering Book, 29 December 1688, DWL, 31 Q, 410; *London Mercury,* 22–24 December 1688.

14. *English Currant,* 14 December 1688; Dodd, *Church History,* 3:449. For other anti-Catholic activity in Wales, see Foley, 893, 943; Andrews et al. to ?, 10 November 1688, HEH, STT 48; Newsletter from London, 1 December 1688, Bodleian, Don.c.39, fol. 35r; Annual Letters of the College, 1688, Foley, 420, 447; Newsletter from London, 4 December 1688, Bodleian, Don.c.39, fol. 37r; Foley, 488, 621; Annual Letters of the

Residence, 1688, Foley, 683; John Tickell, *History of the Town and County of Kingston upon Hull* (Hull: Thomas Lee, 1798), 582; Annual Letters of the Residence, 1685–90, Foley, 727–30; *London Mercury,* 15–18 December 1688; Annual Letters (Durham), 1688, Foley, 650; Annual Letters, 1688, Foley, 356; Annual Letters, 1685–1690, Foley, 319. Mobs throughout Scotland also attacked Catholic supporters of James II and the edifices they created: Kitt Redman's London Newsletter, 16 October 1688, Bodleian, Don.c.38, fol. 312v; Charles Whyteford (Paris) to Walter Leslie, 7/17 January 1689, SCA, Bl 1/126/3; Tweeddale (Edinburgh) to Yester, 11 December 1688, NLS, 7026, fols. 81–82; John Clerk of Pennicuik, Journal, 10 December 1688, NAS, GD 18/2090; "Diary of Andrew Haye," in *Genealogie of the Hayes of Tweeddale,* 60, 63; *London Mercury,* 18–22 December 1688; *Five Letters from a Gentleman in Scotland* (1689), 1–4; Paul Hopkins, *Glencoe and the End of the Highland War* (Edinburgh: John Donald, 1986), 120; ? (Edinburgh) to Hamilton, 23 December 1688, NAS, GD 406/1/3504; Clerk of Pennicuik, Journal, 25 December 1688; Charles Whyteford (Paris) to ?, 5/15 February 1689, SCA, Bl 1/126/7; *English Currant,* 2 January 1689; Charles Whyteford (Paris) to Walter Leslie, 28 January/7 February 1689, SCA, Bl 1/126/6.

15. Bohun, *History of the Desertion,* 85.

16. Robert Ferguson, *The History of All the Mobs, Tumults and Insurrections in Great Britain* ([London]: J. Moore, [1715]), 48–49; Diary of Mary Woodforde, 5 November 1688, in *Woodforde Papers and Diaries,* ed. Dorothy H. Woodforde (London: P. Davies, 1932), 19; Countess of Huntingdon (London) to Huntingdon, 15 December 1688, HEH, HA 4806; *The True Copy of a Paper Delivered by Lord Delamere,* 21 November 1688; Barillon (London) to Louis XIV, 14/24 December 1688, MAE, CP/Angleterre 167, fols. 227–28.

17. William Westby, Memoirs, 30 November 1688, FSL, V.a. 469, fol. 52r; Samuel Clay (London) to Barbara Newton, 8 December 1688, Staffordshire SRO, D 1344/2/1/20/27; Philip Musgrave (London) to Dartmouth, 11 December 1688, Staffordshire SRO, D(w) 1778/III/124; Philip Musgrave (London) to Dartmouth, 13 December 1688, Staffordshire SRO, D(w) 1778/III/127; *London Mercury,* 15 December 1688; London Newsletter, 11 December 1688, Bodleian, Don.c.39, fol. 54v; Sir Edmund King (London) to Hatton, 13 December 1688, BL, Add. 29585, fol. 140r; Nottingham to Hatton, 13 December 1688, BL, Add. 29594, fol. 137r; Morrice, Entering Book, 15 December 1688, DWL, 31 Q, 351.

18. London Newsletter, 13 December 1688, Bodleian, Don.c.39, fol. 62r; *An Account of the Flight, Discovery and Apprehending of George Lord Geffries* [December 1688]; King (London) to Hatton, 13 December 1688, BL, Add. 29585, fol. 140r; London Newsletter, 13 December 1688, FSL, L.c. 1947; John Verney (London) to Sir Ralph Verney, 13 December 1688, Buckinghamshire SRO, Verney MSS; *English Currant,* 14 December 1688; London Newsletter, 13 December 1688, Bodleian, Don.c.39, fol. 62r; London Newsletter, 18 December 1688, FSL, L.c. 1949; London Newsletter, 18 December 1688, BL, Add. 4182, fol. 71v; *London Courant,* 5–8 January 1689.

19. London Newsletter, 22 November 1688, Bodleian, Don c. 39, fol. 11r; Thomas Morgan (Deane Forest) to Ormond, 23 January 1689, BL, Add. 28876, fol. 176r; Molly McClaim, *Beaufort: The Duke and His Duchess, 1657–1715* (New Haven and London: Yale University Press, 2001), 178–88; Samuel Rudder, *History and Antiquities of Gloucester* (Cirencester, 1781), 149; *English Currant,* 12–14 December 1688; Stevens, *Journal,* 7–8; *English Currant,* 14–19 December 1688; Roger Whitley, Diary, 27 November 1688, Bodleian, Eng.Hist.c.711, fol. 99v; William Fleming (Lancaster) to Sir Daniel Fleming, 18 December 1688, Bodleian, Don.c.39, fol. 69r; *Orange Gazette,* 31 December 1688.

20. John Covel (vice chancellor of Cambridge) to all masters and heads of colleges, 15 December 1688, Trinity College, Cambridge, MS R.4.43, fol. 1r; William Whiston, *Memoirs of the Life and Writings* (London, 1749), 23; *London Mercury,* 24–27 December 1688; *London Mercury,* 31 December 1688–3 January 1689; Hamon London Newsletter, 1 January 1689, Beinecke, OSB Shelves fb.210; Sir John Reresby, *Memoirs,* ed. Mary K. Geiter and W. A. Speck (London: Royal Historical Society, 1991), 22 November 1688, 531. The pattern was similar in Scotland: William Carstares to ? William III, July 1688, NA, SP 8/2/Pt. 2, fol. 52; ? (London) to Lewis Innes, 5 November 1688, SCA, Bl 1/119/6; Livingstone, Dunmore, and Dundee (Watford)

to William, 11 December 1688, NA, SP 8/2/Pt. 2, fol. 37; Robert Dale (London) to ?, 17 January 1689, BL, Egerton 2717, fol. 425r.

21. Daniel Szechi, *The Jacobites: Britain and Europe, 1688–1788* (Manchester: Manchester University Press, 1994), 49, 51–59.

22. Yester (London) to Tweeddale, 19 January 1689, NLS, 14404, fol. 7r; T. Vincent (Yorkshire) to Edward Brereton, 24 July 1689, Bodleian, Carte 79, fol. 239r.

23. William Banks to Kenyon, 21 February 1689, HMC Kenyon, 218; London Newsletter, 29 June 1689, FSL, L.c. 2034; Thomas Tobin (Lancashire) to Mrs. Throckmorton, 10 June 1689, NA, SP 32/1, fol. 71; Lord Massarene (Fishwick) to Sir Richard Newdigate, 8 May 1689, Warwickshire SRO, CR136/B293; Morrice, Entering Book, 11 May 1689, DWL, 31 Q, 551; London Newsletter, 7 May 1689, FSL, L.c. 2012.

24. Deposition of Allan Bateman, Merchant, Deposition of Benjamin Reay, Merchant, Deposition of Thomas Mortimer, Gentleman, Deposition of Robert Maddison, Yeoman, and Deposition of Francis Johnson, Merchant, Newcastle, 23 May 1689, all in NA, SP 32/1, fol. 53; Charles Fitzwilliam (Newcastle) to Col. John Coke, 14 May 1689, BL, Add. 69936, fols. 74–75.

25. Robert Kirk, "Sermons, Occurrences . . . ," 28 November 1689, Edinburgh SUL, La.III.545, fol. 127r; James Fenton (Lancaster) to Sir Thomas Rawlinson, 11 October 1689, Bodleian, Rawlinson Letters D 863, fol. 37r; William Harbord, 15 March 1689, Grey, 9:165; Banks to Kenyon, 21 February 1689, HMC Kenyon, 218.

26. Charles Whyteford (Paris) to Walter Leslie, 25 February/7 March, 4/14 March 1689, SCA, Bl 1/126/11, 13; Halifax's Notes of Conversations with King William, 30 December 1688, BL, Althorp C9, fol. 26r; Hamilton (London) to Duchess of Hamilton, 21 September 1689, NAS, GD 406/1/6344; A Brief Account, 7 March 1689, Bodleian, Rawlinson MSS, D1039, fol. 40r; Rupert Browne (London) to Sir William Trumbull, 17 March 1689, BL, Add. 72527, fol. 25r; Shrewsbury (London) to Hamilton, 13 April 1689, NAS, GD 406/1/3521; Keith Brown, *Kingdom or Province? Scotland and the Regal Union, 1603–1715* (New York: St. Martin's, 1992), 172–73; Hopkins, *Glencoe*, 126–27; Derek J. Patrick, "Unconventional Procedure: Scottish Electoral Politics after the Revolution," in *The History of the Scottish Parliament*, ed. Keith Brown and Alastair J. Mann (Edinburgh: Edinburgh University Press, 2005), 2:208–44. I thank Keith Brown for sending me a PDF file of this volume when I was unable to procure it through conventional means.

27. *An Account from Scotland and London-Derry* (London: George Groom, 1689), 7 June, 1; Sir John Lowther, 27 February 1689, Grey, 9:124; *An Account from Scotland and London-Derry*, 1689, 2.

28. Charles Whyteford (Paris) to Walter Leslie, 27 May/6 June 1689, SCA, Bl 1/127/1; *An Account of Dundee's Rendezvous* (1689), 2; Hamilton (Holyrood House) to Melville, 8 June 1689, NAS, GD 406/1/3581; *An Account from Scotland and London-Derry*, 7 June 1689, 2; Francis Cahane (London) to Major General Matthews, 10 June 1689, NA, SP 32/1, fol. 69I; Hamilton (Holyrood House) to Melville, 2 July 1689, NAS, GD 406/1/3587; Argyll (Inveraray) to Hamilton, 22 July 1689, NAS, 406/1/3564; Hopkins, *Glencoe*, 128–56; Szechi, *Jacobites*, 44.

29. *A Letter from a Friend in the City*, 27 July 1689; John T. Gilbert, ed., *A Jacobite Narrative of the War in Ireland, 1688–91* (New York: Barnes and Noble, 1971), 86; "On Lord Dundee," HEH, EL 8770, 25; Hamilton (Holyrood House) to Melville, 30 July, 1 August 1689, NAS, GD 406/1/3596, 3597; Hopkins, *Glencoe*, 158–61, 178–90; Szechi, *Jacobites*, 44; Bruce Lenman, *The Jacobite Risings in Britain, 1689–1746* (London: Eyre Methuen, 1980), 31. Dundee's forces represented about 0.2 percent of Scotland's population. Assuming Mackay's forces were largely Scots as well, the combined forces in arms at Killiecrankie represented 0.6 percent of the Scottish population. This was exactly equivalent, for example, to the percentage of the U.S. population in arms in 1945. I owe the information on U.S. mobilization to Jim Sparrow.

30. Francis Barrington and Benjamin Steele (London) to Goodwyn and Delabere, 8 September 1689, NA, FO 335/8, fol. 3; Robert Kirk, "Sermons, Conferences . . . ," September 1689, Edinburgh SUL, La.III.545, fol. 9v; James Hay (London) to Tweeddale, 13 August 1689, NLS, 14407, fol. 165r; Thomas Buchan (Dublin) to

Innes, 12 December 1689, SCA, Bl 1/120/6; Phil Babington (London) to Francis Henry Cary, 9 January 1690, NA, C 104/135, unfolioed.

31. John Miller, "The Earl of Tyrconnel and James II's Irish Policy, 1685–1688," *Historical Journal* 20, no. 4 (1977): 813–14, 817–19; J. G. Simms, *Jacobite Ireland, 1685–1691* (Dublin: Four Courts, 2000), 24–25, 32–34, 70; *London Mercury,* 22–24 December 1688; London Newsletter, 8 January 1689, FSL, L.c. 1957; Yester (London) to Tweeddale, 15 January 1689, NLS, 14404, fol. 5r; *London Intelligence,* 15–19 January 1689; Gilbert, ed., *Jacobite Narrative,* 36–38, 51–52; A List of King James's Army Clothed and Armed, 1689, NA, SP 8/2/Pt. 2, fol. 48; Harman Murtagh, "The War in Ireland, 1689–91," in *Kings in Conflict,* ed. W. A. Maguire (Belfast: Blackstaff, 1990), 62.

32. Morrice, Entering Book, 9 February 1689, DWL, 31 Q, 456; Ralph Palmer (London) to John Verney, 30 March 1689, Buckinghamshire SRO, Verney MSS; Martyn and Goodwyn (Adithe) to Goodwyn and Delabere, 12/22 March 1689, NA, FO 335/7, fol. 112; London Newsletter, 19 March 1689, FSL, L.c. 1990; Bellingham, *Diary,* 24 March 1689, 59; Simms, *Jacobite Ireland,* 60–63; Murtagh, "War in Ireland," 62; J. Hogan, ed., *Negotiations de M. le Comte d'Avaux en Irlande, 1689–90* (Dublin, 1934); Sheila Mulloy, ed., *Franco-Irish Correspondence, December 1688–February 1692,* 3 vols. (Dublin: Irish Manuscripts Commission, 1983).

33. Gilbert, ed., *Jacobite Narrative,* 46; William Bankes (London) to Peter Legh, 4 April 1689, JRL, Legh of Lyme MSS, Box 4/Folder 26.

34. There were those who thought it to be well trained and well armed: Gilbert, ed., *Jacobite Narrative,* 47–48; Charles Whyteford (Paris) to Walter Leslie, 27 May/6 June 1689, SCA, Bl 1/127/1; Richard Doherty, *The Williamite War in Ireland, 1688–1691* (Dublin: Four Courts, 1998), 25, 37. Others thought it underprepared and poorly armed: Stevens, *Journal,* 17 May, 5 September 1689, 63–66, 78; Simms, *Jacobite Ireland,* 69–73; Szechi, *Jacobites,* 43; Michael Boyle (Dublin) to William Sancroft, 14 January 1689, Bodleian, Tanner 28, fol. 322ar; Bellingham, *Diary,* 27 March 1689, 60; London Newsletter, 28 March 1689, FSL, L.c. 1995; ? (Dublin) to Perth, 28 March 1689, NAS, GD 406/1/3513; Whyteford (Paris) to Leslie, [10/20 February], 13/23 May 1689, SCA, Bl 1/126/10, 23; Stevens, *Journal,* 17 May 1689, 60–61; Massarene (Fisherworth) to Newdigate, 8 May 1689, Warwickshire SRO, CR 136/B293.

35. *London Mercury,* 22–24 December 1688; Sir William Boothby (Ashbourne, Derbyshire) to Dr. Anthony Horneck, 25 December 1688, BL, Add. 71962, fol. 64r; Cary Gardiner (Bucks) to Sir Ralph Verney, 8 February, 1689, Buckinghamshire SRO, Verney MSS; Hamon London Newsletter, 8 January 1689, Beinecke, OSB Shelves fb.210; Shrewsbury (Whitehall) to Robert Lundy, 8 March 1689, NA, SP 44/97, fol. 38; Robert Balle (Livorno) to Goodwyn and Delabere, 1/11 May 1689, NA, FO 335/8, fol. 2; Whyteford (Paris) to Leslie, 15/25 April 1689, SCA, Bl 1/126/18; Morrice, Entering Book, 29 June 1689, DWL, 31 Q, 582; Doherty, *Williamite War,* 51, 70; Ian McBride, *The Siege of Derry in Ulster Protestant Mythology* (Dublin: Four Courts, 1997), 18; Morrice, Entering Book, 4 May 1689, 548; London Newsletter, 30 April, 4 June 1689, FSL, L.c. 2009, 2024; George Walker and John Mitchelburne (Londonderry) to Maj. Gen. Percy Kirke, 19 July 1689, NAS, GD 406/1/3527.

36. John Hampden Jr., 21 March 1689, Grey, 9:185; Massarene (London) to Newdigate, [March 1689], Warwickshire SRO, CR 136/B297; *Mercurius Reformatus,* 21 August 1689, [1]; Paul Rycaut (Hamburg) to Clarendon, 8 April 1690, Bodleian, Eng.Lett.c.8, fol. 3–4; Alexander Stanhope (Groyne) to James Vernon, 1 May 1690, NA, SP 94/73, fol. 7r; William King, *Europe's Deliverance from France and Slavery* (London: Tim. Goodwin, 1691), 2; Stevens, *Journal,* 17 May 1689, 67; Gilbert, ed., *Jacobite Narrative,* 74, 90.

37. Simms, *Jacobite Ireland,* 109–13; Murtagh, "War in Ireland," 65–69; McBride, *Siege of Derry,* 18–19; Szechi, *Jacobites,* 45–46; Doherty, *Williamite War,* 70; Capt. George Rooke (Cape of Kintyre) to Hamilton, 2 August 1689, NAS, GD 406/1/3536; Bellingham, *Diary,* 7 August 1689, 78; Francis Barrington and Benjamin Steele (London) to Goodwyn and Delabere, 8 September 1689, NA, FO 335/8, fol. 3; Parker, *Memoirs,* 14; King, *Europe's Deliverance,* 16 November 1690, 18.

38. London Newsletter, 20 August 1689, FSL, L.c. 2053; Barrington and Steele (London) to Goodwyn and Delabere, 8 September 1689, NA, FO 335/8, fol. 3; London Newsletter, 3 September 1689, FSL, L.c. 2059; Doherty, *Williamite War,* 89–100; John De La Bere (London) to Kinard De La Bere, 24 August 1689, NA, FO 335/15, unfolioed; Capt. George Rooke to Hamilton, 9 August 1689, NAS, GD 406/1/3539; Cary Gardiner (London) to Sir Ralph Verney, 18 September, 25 September 1689, Buckinghamshire SRO, Verney MSS; Simms, *Jacobite Ireland,* 120–35; Murtagh, "War in Ireland," 70–71.

39. Dr. William Denton (London) to Sir Ralph Verney, 8 October 1689, Buckinghamshire SRO, Verney MSS; Father Ath. Maxwell (Dublin) to ?, 27 November 1689, SCA, Bl 1/124/5; Lord Waldegrave (St. Germain) to Albeville, 15 February 1690, Indiana, Albeville MSS; Stevens, *Journal,* 1690, 101; Simms, *Jacobite Ireland,* 139–40.

40. London Newsletter, 30 January 1690, FSL, L.c. 2069; Lord Dursley (The Hague) to Nottingham, 11/21 March 1690, Berkeley Castle, MSS 36A, fol. 17v; Ralph Trumbull (Witney) to Sir William Trumbull, 16 June 1690, BL, Add. 72511, fol. 95v; Szechi, *Jacobites,* 46; Simms, *Jacobite Ireland,* 141–42; Numbers of Forces to Be Transported to Ireland, 1690, NA, SP 8/8, fol. 35; The Intended Disposition of All Their Majesty's Forces, 1690, NA, SP 8/8, fol. 36; Gilbert, ed., *Jacobite Narrative,* 90, 95.

41. Szechi, *Jacobites,* 47–48; Simms, *Jacobite Ireland,* 147; Carmarthen (London) to William, 28 June 1690, NA, SP 8/7, fol. 68; Queen Mary (Whitehall) to William III, 24 June 1690, NA, SP 8/7, fol. 62; William, Lord Paget (Vienna), to Sir William Dutton Colt, 3/13 July 1690, BL, Add. 34095, fol. 54v.

42. Parker, *Memoirs,* 20; Bellingham, *Diary,* 1 July 1690, 130–31; Gilbert, ed., *Jacobite Narrative,* 103–8; Simms, *Jacobite Ireland,* 148–52, 158–86; Doherty, *Williamite War,* 109–25; Murtagh, "War in Ireland," 73–82; Stevens, *Journal,* 1 July 1690, 123.

43. At Aughrim about seven thousand Jacobites and two thousand Williamites were killed: Murtagh, "War in Ireland," 89; Bellingham, *Diary,* 26 January 1689, 46; Parker, *Memoirs,* 6; Bellingham, *Diary,* 11, 13 December 1688, 35; *London Mercury,* 18–22 December 1688, 6–11 February 1689; Gilbert, ed., *Jacobite Narrative,* 42, 44; Simms, *Jacobite Ireland,* 49, 55, 125, 198–200; D. W. Hayton, *Ruling Ireland, 1685–1742* (Woodbridge: Boydell, 2004), 21–23; Bellingham, *Diary,* 4 March 1689, 55–56; *London Intelligence,* 15–19 January, 22–24 January 1689; Massarene to Newdigate, 8 February 1689, Warwickshire SRO, CR 136/B291; Stevens, *Journal,* 17 May 1689, 61–62; Thomas Aske to Oliver St. George, 30 September 1689, NA, SP 32/2, fol. 32; William King, June 1690, in *A Great Archbishop of Dublin, William King, D.D., 1650–1729,* ed. Sir Charles Simeon King (London: Longmans, Green, 1908), 28.

44. Melville (London) to Hamilton, 13 August 1689, NAS, GD 406/1/3648; William King, March 1691, *A Great Archbishop of Dublin,* King, 32–36; Stevens, *Journal,* 90, 102–4, 109–10; Robert Heslip, "Brass Money," in *Kings in Conflict,* ed. Maguire, 122–35; Henry Mervyn (London) to Huntingdon, 9 August 1690, HEH, HA 9246.

45. Upton and Martyn (Livorno) to Goodwyn and Delabere, 16/26 October 1690, PRO, FO 335/8/7; John Hartstope (London) to Sir Robert Southwell, 8 July 1690, BL, Add. 38015, fol. 353r; ? (Westminster) to Henry Paget, 12 July 1690, SOAS, PP MS 4/Box 17/Bundle 74; Chesterfield (Bretby) to Halifax, 20 July 1690, BL, Althorp C3; *Axminster,* July 1690, 142. See also Sunderland (Althorp) to Dijkvelt, 29 August 1690, Warwickshire SRO, CR 2017/C8/56; Gilbert Burnet, *A Sermon Preached before the King and Queen at Whitehall,* 19 October 1690 (London: Richard Chiswell, 1690), 24–25; and Rycaut (Hamburg) to Colt, 22 October/1 November 1690, BL, Add. 34095, fol. 155v.

46. Colt (Hanover) to Richard Warre, 25 July 1690, NA, SP 81/159, fol. 308; Abraham Kick (Hague) to Nottingham, 18/28 July 1690, NA, SP 84/221, fol. 163; Dursley (Hague) to Nottingham, 18/28 July 1690, Berkeley Castle, MSS 36A, fol. 56r; Simms, *Jacobite Ireland,* 144.

47. Warre (Whitehall) to Colt, 8/18 July 1690, BL, Add. 34095, fol. 39r; Newsletter from London, 11 July 1690, BL, Add. 72528, fol. 81v; F. Overton (London) to Sir Richard Temple, 9 August 1690, HEH, STT 1545; Sir William Fawkener (London) to Sir William Trumbull, 24 October 1690, BL, Add. 72528, fol. 183v; P. Barkman (London) to Huntingdon, 8 August 1690, HEH, HA 398; Melfort (Rome) to Mary of Modena,

30 August/9 September 1690, BL, Lansdowne 1163C, fol. 22r; Melfort to Innes, 8/18 July 1690, BL, Lansdowne 1163B, fol. 79v; Melfort (Rome) to James II, 26 August/5 September 1690, BL, Lansdowne 1163C, fols. 13v–14r; Sir Edward Hales (St. Germain) to Tyrconnel, 20 May 1691, AWA, Old Brotherhood Papers, Book 3/240; Melfort (Rome) to ?, 24 March 1691, AWA, Old Brotherhood Papers, Book 3/239.

48. Gilbert, ed., *Jacobite Narrative*, 121–22; Weymouth (Longleat) to Halifax, 20 July 1690, BL, Althorp C5; Levant Company to Sir William Trumbull, 17 July 1690, NA, SP 105/114, fol. 502; Queen Mary (Whitehall) to William, 3/13 July 1690, NA, SP 8/7, fol. 75; Henry Newcome, 5 July 1690, in *The Autobiography of Henry Newcome,* vol. 2, ed. Robert Parkinson, Chetham Society 27 (Manchester: Chetham Society, 1852), 272; Kick (Hague) to Nottingham, 11/21 July 1690, NA, SP 84/221, fol. 170r; Robert Molesworth (Copenhagen) to Colt, 22 July/1 August 1690, BL, Add. 34095, fol. 78r; Burnet, *Sermon,* 23; Petition of Diverse Mariners, July 1690, HEH, EL 9094; Carmarthen (London) to William, 13 July, 15 July 1690, NA, SP 8/7, fols. 95, 96; Queen Mary to William, 13/23 July 1690, NA, SP 8/7, fol. 94; William Aglionby (Hague) to Warre, 7 July 1690, NA, SP 84/221, fol. 158r; Balle, Henshaw, and Scudamore (Genoa) to Thomas Goodwyn, 1 July 1690, NA, FO 335/8, fol. 7; Craig Rose, *England in the 1690s: Revolution, Religion, and War* (Oxford: Blackwell, 1999), 122.

49. *Axminster,* 1690, 142; A. Pye (London) to Abigail Harley, 12 July 1690, BL, Add. 70014, fol. 333r; Elizabeth Oxenden (Deane) to Lady Trumbull, 31 August 1691, BL, Add. 72529, fol. 95r; Gilbert, ed., *Jacobite Narrative,* 109; G. Bradbury (London) to Tom Wharton, 25 July 1690, Bodleian, Carte 79, fol. 317r; Carmarthen (London) to William, 15 July 1690, NA, SP 8/7, fol. 96; ? (London) to William Dunlop, 2 August 1690, NLS, 9250, fol. 186; Thomas Legh to Peter Legh, 29 June 1690, JRL, Legh of Lyme, Box 4/Folder 29; Melfort (Rome) to James II, 29 August/9 September 1690, Lansdowne 1163C, fol. 19r; The Numbers of the Militia in the Several Counties in England and Wales, 1690, NA, SP 8/8, fol. 51.

50. Carmarthen (London) to William, 12 August 1690, NA, SP 8/7, fol. 139; Edward Ridley to Huntingdon, 26 July 1690, HEH, HA 10491.

51. Memoire from Zurich, 31 May 1690, NA, SP 8/7, fol. 43; John Childs, *The Nine Years' War and the British Army, 1688–1697* (Manchester: Manchester University Press, 1991), 135; Dursley (Hague) to Carmarthen, 13/23 June 1690, Berkeley Castle, MSS 36A, fol. 39v; Carmarthen (London) to William, 23 June 1690, NA, SP 8/7, fol. 61; William, Lord Paget (Vienna), to Colt, 3/13 July 1690, BL, Add. 34095, fol. 54; Gilbert, ed., *Jacobite Narrative,* 122–23.

52. Cotterell (London) to Trumbull, 24 November 1691, BL, Trumbull MSS 39 (since recataloged). "Monsieur" was a reference to Louis XIV; James Brydges to his father, 8 July 1694, HEH, STT 57, 1:20.

CHAPTER 10. *Divisive Revolution*

1. Lady Sunderland (Windsor) to Henry Sidney, 3 September 1688, BL, Add. 32681, fol. 309v; Antoine Moreau (The Hague) to king of Poland, 4/14 September 1688, BL, Add. 38495, fol. 14v; Sir Charles Sedley, "To the King on His Birth-Day," 1690, in Sedley, *The Miscellaneous Works* (London: J. Nutt, 1702), 91; Countess of Huntingdon (London) to Huntingdon, 15 December 1688, HEH, HA 4806; Tregonwell Frampton (Morton) to Thomas Erle, 6 December 1688, Churchill College, Cambridge, 2/25/1; Levant Company (London) to Sir William Trumbull, 14 December 1688, BL, Add. 72526, fol. 192r; John Ollyffe, *England's Call to Thankfulness,* Preached 14 February 1689 (London: Jonathan Richardson, 1689), 15; Colley Cibber, *An Apology for the Life of Colley Cibber,* ed. Robert Lowe (New York: AMS, 1966), 62; *The Late Revolution: or, The Happy Change* (London: Richard Baldwin, 1690), 55.

2. Lois G. Schwoerer, *The Declaration of Rights, 1689* (Baltimore: Johns Hopkins University Press, 1981), 109–16; Daniel Petit (Amsterdam) to Middleton, 5/15 October 1688, BL, Add. 41816, fols. 236–37; Albeville (The Hague) to Middleton, 18/28 October 1688, BL, Add. 41816, fol. 263; London Newsletter, 23 October 1688, Bodleian, Don.c.38, fol. 314v; Earl of Clarendon, Diary, 31 October 1688, Singer, 2:248; ? (London) to James Harrington, 1 November 1688, BL, Add. 36707, fol. 45r; London Newsletter, 1 November 1688, Bod-

leian, Don.c.38, fol. 330r; William Sancroft, "A Journal of What Passed between the King and Some of the Bishops," 2 November 1688, Bodleian, Tanner 28, fol. 219v; Van Citters (London) to States General, 2/12 November 1688, BL, Add. 34510, fol. 164r; Sir John Reresby, *Memoirs*, ed. Mary K. Geiter and W. A. Speck (London: Royal Historical Society, 1991), 3 November 1688, 524; Roger Morrice, Entering Book, 3 November 1688, DWL, 31 Q, 310; London Newsletter, 3 November 1688, BL, Add. 4194, fol. 369r; ? (London) to Lewis Innes, 5 November 1688, SCA, Bl 1/119/6; John Reresby to Lord Preston, 10 November 1688, BL, Add. 63780, fol. 68r; Newsletter (Whitehall) 20 November 1688, Beinecke, OSB MSS 1/Box 2/Folder 91; Bath (Plymouth) to William, 1 December 1688, NA, SP 8/2/Pt. 2, fol. 30; *Quadrennium Jacobi* (London: James Knapton, 1689), 212; John Whittle, *An Exact Diary of the Late Expedition* (London: Richard Baldwin, 1689), 43, 48; Huntingdon (Plymouth) to James II, 29 November 1688, HEH, HA 6075; Huntingdon (Plymouth) to Countess of Huntingdon, 26 November 1688, HEH, HA 6074; Bath (Plymouth) to William, 27 November 1688, NA, SP 8/2/Pt. 2, fol. 27; London Newsletter, 27 November 1688, Bodleian, Don.c.39, fol. 19r; Thoresby, *Diary*, November/December 1688, 1:188; Anthony Hewitson, ed., *Diary of Thomas Bellingham, an Officer under William III* (Preston: Geo. Toulmin and Sons, 1908), 9 December 1688, 34 (hereafter cited as Bellingham, *Diary*); Sir Willoughby Aston, Diary, 14 December 1688, Liverpool SRO, 920 MD 173; *London Mercury*, 15–18 December 1688; *English Currant*, 14–19 December 1688.

3. *Life of James II*, 2:232; Morrice, Entering Book, 12 January 1689, DWL, 31 Q, 421; Lord Del[amere]'s Speech, in *A Collection of Papers Relating to the Present Juncture of Affairs in England* (1688), 23–24. The speech was circulating in manuscript in November 1688: Aston, Diary, 23 November 1688; Roger Kenyon, Diary, 16 November 1688, HMC Kenyon, 201; W. E. Buckley, ed., *Memoirs of Thomas, Earl of Ailesbury*, 2 vols. (Westminster: Nichols and Sons, 1890), 1:133; *The True Copy of a Paper Delivered by the Lord De[lamere] to the Mayor of Derby*, 21 November 1688 (London: John Goodman, 1688); G. S. (South Lambeth) to Harrington, 27 December 1688, BL, Add. 36707, fol. 54r; Halifax's Notes of the Debate of the Assembly of the Lords, 24 December 1688, BL, Althorp C8; Kenyon, Diary, 30 October, 1 November 1688, HMC Kenyon, 200; Delamere to Derby 10 December 1688, HMC Kenyon, 206; *The Declaration of the Nobility, Gentry and Commonalty at the Rendezvous at Nottingham, Nov. 22 1688* [1688]; Edmund Bohun, *History of the Desertion* (London: Ric. Chiswell, 1689), 78; John Miller, "Proto-Jacobitism? The Tories and the Revolution of 1688–89," in *The Jacobite Challenge*, ed. E. Cruickshanks and J. Black (Edinburgh: John Donald, 1988), 13.

4. J. R. Western, *Monarchy and Revolution: The English State in the 1680s* (London: Blandford, 1972), 276; Miller, "Proto-Jacobitism," 12. This was almost certainly because of Danby's connections. His own political manifesto was politically ambiguous: Thomas Osborne, Earl of Danby, *The Thoughts of a Private Person: About the Justice of the Gentlemens Undertaking at York* (1689), 9, 11, 14, 19–21; Newsletter from York, 17 November 1688, Bodleian, Don.c.38, fol. 349v; Reresby, *Memoirs*, 15 October 1688, Geiter and Speck, 521; Danby (York) to Sir John Hanmer, 30 November 1688, BL, Egerton 3335, fol. 92; Sir Richard Temple, "The False Patriot Unmasked," 1690, HEH, STT Lit (9), 10; Sir Richard Bulstrode (Brussels) to Edmund Poley, 9 January 1689, BL, Add. 45731, fol. 96r; Chesterfield to Danby, November 1688, in *Letters of Philip, Second Earl of Chesterfield* (London: E. Lloyd and Son, 1829), 338–39.

5. Sir Daniel Fleming (Rydal) to Sir John Lowther, 20 August 1688, Cumbria SRO, Carlisle, D/Lons/L1/33; Lowther to Fleming, 5 December 1688, Cumbria SRO, Kendal, WD/Ry 3371; Petition of the Gentlemen of Cumberland and Westmoreland, 1 December 1688, Cumbria SRO, Kendal, WD/Ry 3363; John Agliony (Carlisle) to Lowther, 16 December 1688, CRO Carlisle, D/Lons/L1/1/34/unnumbered; Sir John Lowther, Memoirs, October/November 1688, CRO Carlisle, D/Lons/L2/5, 97–98; Clark Stuart Colman, "The Glorious Revolution of 1688 in Cumberland and Westmoreland," *Northern History* 40, no. 2 (2003): 237–58.

6. Sir Thomas Clarges, 14 December 1689, Grey, 9:483. It had become Tory doctrine that the Seven Bishops' Trial of June 1688 made the revolution: Daniel Defoe, *The Englishman's Choice, and True Interest* (London, 1694), 28. For a recent explication of this point of view, see Mark Goldie, "The Political Thought of the Anglican Revolution," in *The Revolutions of 1688*, ed. Robert Beddard (Oxford: Clarendon Press, 1991), 102–

36; Temple, "False Patriot Unmasked," 10; Godfrey Davies, "The Political Career of Sir Richard Temple (1634–97) and Buckinghamshire Politics," *Huntington Library Quarterly* 4, no. 1 (1940): 80–81. Temple himself had been very slow to support William in 1688; Sir John Guise, 14 December 1689, Grey, 9:483; ? (London) to Lowther, 1 December 1688, Beinecke, OSB Files 9245; *A Smith and Cutler's Plain Dialogue about Whig and Tory* (1690), [2].

7. Sir Charles Cotterell to Sir William Trumbull, 14 February 1689, BL, Trumbull MSS 39 (since recataloged); Bohun, *History of the Desertion,* 122; *Mercurius Reformatus,* 24 July 1689, [2]; Schwoerer, *Declaration of Rights,* 138–39; J. H. Plumb, "The Elections to the Convention Parliament of 1689," *Cambridge Historical Journal* 5, no. 3 (1937): 248; Sir Robert Southwell, "A Short Account of the Revolution in England," 31 December 1688, FSL, V.b. 150, 1:fol. 13r; Basil D. Henning, ed., *The House of Commons, 1660–1690* (London: History of Parliament Trust, 1983), 1:106–7, 125–522; Henry Horwitz, "Parliament and the Glorious Revolution," *Bulletin of the Institute of Historical Research* 17 (May 1974): 40–41. Macaulay was wrong to think that "the elections went on rapidly and smoothly. There were scarcely any contests": Thomas Babington Macaulay, *The History of England from the Accession of James II,* 5 vols. (New York: Harper and Brothers, 1849–61), 2:554; "Some Account of the Revolution," Bodleian, Eng.Hist.b.205, fol. 106r.

8. Sir William Boothby to Mr. Adderley, 9 January 1689, BL, Add. 71692, fol. 69r. Ironically, even this account was subject to party differences. The Whig Edward Harley claimed that Sacheverell was defeated for "his not appearing for the Prince": Edward Harley (London) to Robert Harley, 19 January 1689, BL, Add. 40621, fol. 3; Sir William Cowper, *The Case of the Ancient Borough of Hertford,* [January 1689], Hertford Borough Archive, vol. 23, no. 331, 2; Lowther to Sir Daniel Fleming, 5 December 1688, Cumbria SRO, Kendal, WD/Ry 3371; Sir Christopher Musgrave (Edenhall) to Sir Daniel Fleming, 25 December 1688, Cumbria SRO, Kendal, WD/Ry 3409; Philip Musgrave (London) to Dartmouth, 26 December 1688, Staffordshire SRO, D(w) 1778/III/143; Sir Christopher Musgrave (Edenhall) to Sir Daniel Fleming, 11 January 1689, Cumbria SRO, Kendal, WD/Ry 3420; Sir Daniel Fleming (Rydal) to Earl of Thanet, 12 January 1689, Cumbria SRO, Kendal, WD/Ry 3419a; Petition of John Trenchard and Edward Clarke, 1689, Somerset SRO, DD/SF/1084; Roger Morrice, Entering Book, 12 January 1689, DWL, 31 Q, 419; Plumb, "Elections," 240–41, 249–50; Schwoerer, *Declaration of Rights,* 152, 172. The evidence suggests that the fears of Tories and Jacobites that "most members that are chosen are fanatics" was very much overblown. For the fears, see Charles Whyteford (Paris) to Walter Leslie, 14/24 January 1689, SCA, Bl 1/126/4; Boothby (Ashbourne) to Sir Gilbert Clarke, 2 February 1689, BL, Add. 71692, fol. 76v; and Temple, "False Patriot Unmasked," 10–11.

9. London Newsletter, 26 January 1689, FSL, L.c. 1964; John Maynard, 29 January 1689, Grey, 9:32; Dartmouth, "Reasons about the Succession," 1688 or 1689, Staffordshire SRO, D(w) 1778/v/117; *Better Late than Never* [1689], [1]; Boothby (Ashbourne) to Sir Gilbert Clarke, 2 February 1689, BL, Add. 71692, fols. 76–78; Whyteford (Paris) to ?, 5/15 February 1689, SCA, Bl 1/126/7; ? (London) to Harrington, 22 December 1688, BL, Add. 36707, fol. 52r; Halifax's Notes of Conversations with William, 30 December 1688, BL, Althorp C9, fol. 27r; "A Brief Account of Matters of Fact," 30 January 1689, Bodleian, Rawlinson MSS, D1079, fol. 5r; Morrice, Entering Book, 2 February 1689, DWL 31 Q, 449; Cotterell to Sir William Trumbull, 14 February 1689, BL, Trumbull MSS 39 (since recataloged); Sir Robert Southwell (Kingsweston) to Beaufort, 14 December 1688, HMC 12th Report, app. 9, 94; Whyteford (Paris) to Walter Leslie, 7/17 January, 28 January/7 February 1689, SCA, Bl 1/126/3, 6; John Chichely (London) to Peter Legh, 5 February 1689, JRL, Legh of Lyme MSS, Box 4/Folder 26; Schwoerer, *Declaration of Rights,* 144–48, 153–54; J. R. Jones, *The Revolution of 1688 in England* (New York: W. W. Norton, 1972), 313–15; Keith Feiling, *A History of the Tory Party, 1640–1714* (Oxford: Clarendon Press, 1924), 247–50; Locke to Edward Clarke, 29 January 1689, *Locke Correspondence,* 3:545–546; William Stainforth, *A Sermon Preached in the Cathedral and Metropolitan Church of St. Peter in York,* 30 January 1689 (London: Walter Kettilby, 1689), 37.

10. Yester (London) to Tweeddale, 31 January 1689, NLS, 14404, fol. 14r; Morrice, Entering Book, 12 January 1689, DWL, 31 Q, 423–24; Douglas R. Lacey, *Dissent and Parliamentary Politics in England, 1661–1689* (New Brunswick, NJ: Rutgers University Press, 1969), 225–26; Morrice, Entering Book, 16 March, 27 April

1689, DWL, 31 Q, 504–5, 542; Horwitz, "Parliament and the Glorious Revolution," 40; Yester (London) to Tweeddale, 22 January 1689, NLS, 14404, fol. 8r; *Journal of the House of Commons,* 28 January 1689, 10:14; Southwell, "A Short Account of the Revolution in England," 28 January 1689, 1:fol. 13v; London Newsletter, 29 January 1689, FSL, L.c. 1965; Sir Christopher Musgrave (London) to Sir Daniel Fleming, 31 January 1689, Cumbria SRO, Kendal, WD/Ry 3435; Southwell, "A Short Account of the Revolution in England," 6 February 1689, 1:fol. 14v; Robert Kirk, "Sermons, Occurrences. . . . ," 1690, Edinburgh SUL, La.III.545, fol. 101r; *Smith and Cutler's Plain Dialogue,* 1.

11. Yester (London) to Tweeddale, 22 January, 29 January 1689, NLS, 14404, fols. 8, 12v; *Journal of the House of Lords,* 29 January 1689, 14:110; Beddard, "Unexpected Whig Revolution," in *Revolutions of 1688,* ed. Beddard, 80; Horwitz, "Parliament and the Glorious Revolution," 44–45; Morrice, Entering Book, 22 December 1688, DWL, 31 Q, 382; Hamon London Newsletter, 31 January 1689, Beinecke, OSB Shelves fb.210; Edward Harley to Robert Harley, 2 February 1689, BL, Add. 40621, fol. 12r; Earl of Warrington (formerly Lord Delamere), Essay, ca. 1690, Beinecke, OSB File 15756.

12. *London Intelligence,* 2–5 February 1689; *London Mercury,* 6 February 1689; "The Humble Petition," Hertfordshire SRO, D/EP F 26; Morrice, Entering Book, 2 February 1689, DWL, 31 Q, 454; Reresby, *Memoirs,* 2 February 1689, 548–49; William Banks to Roger Kenyon, 2 February 1689, HMC Kenyon, 216; Mark Knights, "London's 'Monster' Petition of 1680," *Historical Journal* 36 (1993): 40; Knights, *Representation and Misrepresentation in Later Stuart Britain* (Oxford: Oxford University Press, 2005), 119; Robert Brenner, *Merchants and Revolution: Commercial Change, Political Conflict, and London's Overseas Traders, 1550–1653* (London: Verso, 2003), 325; David Cressy, *England on Edge: Crisis and Revolution, 1640–1642* (Oxford: Oxford University Press, 2006), 183–84; Anthony Rowe, 2 February 1689, Grey, 9:45; Clarendon, Diary, 2 February 1689, 2:258; Beddard, "Unexpected Whig Revolution," 82–84; Schwoerer, *Declaration of Rights,* 130, 211.

13. "Some Account of the Revolution," BL, Add. 9363, fols. 13–14; Banks to Kenyon, 2 February 1689, HMC Kenyon, 216; Sir Edward Seymour, 2 February 1689, Grey, 9:45; *Journal of the House of Commons,* 2 February 1689, 10:18; *Journal of the House of Lords,* 2 February 1689, 14:114; Clarendon, Diary, 2 February 1689, 2:258; Henry Newcome, 5 February 1689, in *The Autobiography of Henry Newcome,* vol. 2, ed. Robert Parkinson, Chetham Society 27 (Manchester: Chetham Society, 1852), 269 (hereafter cited as Newcome, *Autobiography*).

14. *Journal of the House of Lords,* 6 February 1689, 14:118–19; Beddard, "Unexpected Whig Revolution," 86–91; Schwoerer, *Declaration of Rights,* 219–20; Horwitz, "Parliament and the Glorious Revolution," 45–46; *Revolution Politicks* (London, 1733), 4 February 1689, 8:38; Morrice, Entering Book, 2 February 1689, DWL, 31 Q, 446, 454. I am not persuaded as De Krey seems to be that the "petitions' sponsors discreetly sought to avoid the appearance of any coercion of parliament by the people." Gary Stuart De Krey, *A Fractured Society: The Politics of London in the First Age of Party, 1688–1715* (Oxford: Clarendon Press, 1985), 56. De Krey is following the establishment Whig interpretation: Gilbert Burnet, *Reflections upon a Pamphlet* (London: R. Chiswell, 1696), 123; Macaulay, *History of England,* 2:646.

15. Morrice, Entering Book, 9 February 1689, DWL, 31 Q, 459, 462; "A Brief Account," 6 February 1689, Bodleian, Rawlinson MSS, D1079, fol. 13r; Southwell, "A Short Account of the Revolution in England," 13 February 1689, 1:fol. 16r; London Newsletter, 14 February 1689, FSL, L.c. 1976; Yester (London) to Tweeddale, 14 February 1689, NLS, 14404, fol. 19r; *London Mercury,* 14 February 1689; Cotterell to Sir William Trumbull, 14 February 1689, BL, Trumbull MSS 39 (since recataloged); Thoresby, *Diary,* 14 February 1689, 1:191; *Orange Gazette,* 15 February 1689, [1–2]; Morrice, Entering Book, 16 February 1689, DWL, 31 Q, 467; William Chaplyn (Buckingham) to Sir Richard Temple, 17 February 1689, HEH, STT 413; Aston, Diary, 18 February 1689; Bellingham, *Diary,* 18 February 1689, 52; Isaac Newton (London) to John Covel, 21 February 1689, Trinity College, Cambridge, MS R.4.43, fol. 7r; Ralph Trumbull (Witney) to Sir William Trumbull, 23 February 1689, BL, Add. 72511, fol. 84r; Whyteford (Paris) to Walter Leslie, 25 February/7 March 1689, SCA, Bl 1/126/11; Moses Carter (Oxford) to Dr. Thomas Smith, 5 March 1689, Bodleian, MS Smith 48, 43;

London Mercury, 14 February 1689; "A Brief Account," 21 February 1689, Bodleian, Rawlinson MSS, D1079, fol. 25v.

16. *Journal of the House of Lords,* 6 February 1689, 14:119; London Newsletter, 7 February 1689, FSL, L.c. 1973.

17. Morrice, Entering Book, 26 January 1689, DWL, 31 Q, 432; Whyteford (Paris) to ?, 5/15 February 1689, SCA, Bl 1/126/7; Anthony Cary, Lord Falkland, 1 March 1689, Grey, 9:133–34; Hamilton (London) to Duchess of Hamilton, 3 September 1689, NAS, GD 406/1/6339; London Newsletter, 9 March 1689, FSL, L.c. 1986; Whyteford (Paris) to Walter Lorenzo Leslie, 25 March/4 April 1689, SCA, Bl 1/126/16; Lowther to Shrewsbury, 11 August 1689, NA, SP 32/1, fol. 129; Nottingham (Whitehall) to William, 24 June 1690, NMM, SOU/12; Jeremiah Bubb (Carlisle) to Lowther, 25 March 1689, NA, SP 32/1, fol. 13; William Harbord, 15 March 1689, Grey, 9:164–65; Aston, Diary, 15 March 1689; London Newsletter, 16 March 1689, FSL, L.c. 1989; Morrice, Entering Book, 16 March 1689, DWL, 31 Q, 503; Rupert Browne to Sir William Trumbull, 17 March 1689, BL, Trumbull Misc. 26 (1688–89) (since recataloged); Sir Edward Harley (London) to Robert Harley, 12 March 1689, BL, Add. 70014, fol. 178r; London Newsletter, 12 March 1689, FSL, L.c. 1987.

18. John Howe, 25 February, 26 February 1689, Grey, 9:110, 112; Hugh Boscawen, 1 March 1689, Grey, 9:131; London Newsletter, 5 March 1689, FSL, L.c. 1984; Robert Harley to Sir Edward Harley, 15 March 1689, BL, Add. 70014, fol. 181r; John Wildman, 15 March 1689, Grey, 9:168; Mr. Bowtell (witness to House of Commons), 21 March 1689, Grey, 9:183.

19. Reresby, *Memoirs,* 1 January 1689, 544–45; Tyrconnel (Dublin) to Mary of Modena, 11 March 1690, BL, Add. 38145, fols. 12–13. Beaufort's modern biographer doubts the veracity of the claims: Molly McClain, *Beaufort: The Duke and His Duchess, 1657–1715* (New Haven and London: Yale University Press, 2001), 192–93. The evidence seems to me inconclusive. That Beaufort refused to sign the association in 1696 suggests determined Jacobite views. Matthew Henry (Chester) to Philip Henry, 23 May 1689, Bodleian, Eng.Lett.e.29, fol. 88r; Morrice, Entering Book, 18 May 1689, DWL 31 Q, 556; Examination of Joan Wood, 16 September 1689, NA, SP 32/2, fol. 17; Robert Howson (minister of All Saints, Dorchester) to Shrewsbury, 30 September 1689, NA, SP 32/2, fol. 35; Charles Herbert Mayo, ed., *The Municipal Records of the Borough of Dorchester* (Exeter: William Pollard, 1908), 409; Morrice, Entering Book, 8 June 1689, DWL, 31 Q, 570; Paul Halliday, *Dismembering the Body Politic: Partisan Politics in England's Towns, 1650–1730* (Cambridge: Cambridge University Press, 1998), 259; Commissioners of the Revenue to Lords of the Treasury, 8 November 1689, NA, CUST 48/3, 280–81.

20. Compare: J. H. Overton, *The Nonjurors* (London: Smith, Elder, 1902), 471–96, with John Spurr, *The Restoration Church of England, 1646–1689* (New Haven and London: Yale University Press, 1991), 43.

21. Overton, *Nonjurors,* 179–84; Moses Carter (Oxford) to Dr. Thomas Smith, 23 February 1690, Bodleian, Smith 48, 53. Charles Ellis (Christ's College, Cambridge) to John Ellis, 21 February 1689, BL, Add. 28931, fol. 27r; William Davies to Hilkiah Bedford, 13 May 1689, Bodleian, Rawlinson MSS, Letters 42, fol. 9r; London Newsletter, 22 June 1689, FSL, L.c. 2031; William Whiston, *Memoirs of the Life and Writings* (London, 1749), 30; Dr. Thomas Hyde (Oxford) to Robert Boyle, 23 February 1689, in *The Works of the Honourable Robert Boyle,* 6 vols., ed. Thomas Birch (London: W. Johnston et al., 1772), 577; Sir Richard Newdigate, Diary, 1689, Warwickshire SRO, CR 136/A/23, fol. 47r; Morrice, Entering Book, 29 June 1689, DWL, 31 Q, 582; Bolton to Shrewsbury, 27 September 1689, NA, SP 32/2, fol. 25; ? (Stamford) to Earl of Stamford, 13 April 1689, NA, SP 32/1, fol. 21; Tamworth Newsletter, 22 March 1690, HEH, HM 30659/5; William Amies and John Baker (Churchwardens at Faversham) to James Vernon, 29 April 1690, NA, SP 32/3, fol. 15; *The Character of a Jacobite* (London, 1690), 7, 20; Yester (London) to Tweeddale, 24 April 1689, NLS, 14404, fol. 39v. See also John Berners (Hull) to Thomas Wharton, 13 May 1689, Bodleian, Carte 79, fol. 216r; Robert Harley (Hereford) to Sir Edward Harley, 20 February 1689, BL, Add. 70014, fol. 159r; Morrice, Entering Book, 23 February 1689, DWL, 31 Q, 476; Robert Harley (Brampton) to Sir Edward Harley, 5 March, 29 March 1689, BL, Add. 70014, fol. 170r, 196r.

22. Hamon London Newsletter, 18 December 1688, Beinecke, OSB Shelves fb.210; Cotterell to his daughter, 31 December 1688, BL, Trumbull MSS 39 (since recataloged); Israel Fielding (Pembroke) to Shrewsbury, 1 June 1689, NA, SP 32/1, fol. 57; London Newsletter, 14 September 1689, FSL, L.c. 2063; Cary Gardiner (London) to Sir Ralph Verney, 4 September 1689, Buckinghamshire SRO, Verney MSS.

23. Robert Harley (Brampton) to Sir Edward Harley, 12 March 1689, BL, Add. 70014, fol. 176; Abigail Harley (Brampton) to Sir Edward Harley, 14 December 1689, BL, Add. 70014, fol. 276r; Edward Harley to Sir Edward Harley, 27 January 1690, BL, Add. 70014, fol. 281v; Col. Charles Trelawney (Chester) to Shrewsbury, 2 September 1689, NA, SP 32/2, fol. 1; Sir John Morgan (Chester Castle) to Shrewsbury, 29 March 1690, NA, SP 32/2, fol. 113; Derby to Kenyon, 28 February 1689, HMC Kenyon, 219; Banks to Kenyon, 9 March 1689, HMC Kenyon, 219; Bellingham, *Diary,* 12 March 1689, 57; London Newsletter, 30 March 1689, FSL, L.c. 1996; Col. Edward Matthews (Preston) to Shrewsbury, 15 June 1689, NA, SP 32/1, fol. 80; Brandon (Preston) to Shrewsbury, 15 June 1689, NA, SP 32/1, fol. 81; Morrice, Entering Book, 22 June 1689, DWL, 31 Q, 578; W. Hammond (Parkhead) to Kenyon, 15 February 1690, Lancashire SRO, DD/Ke/9/63/6; Sir John Morgan (Chester Castle) to Shrewsbury, 26 March 1690, NA, SP 32/2, fol. 111; Sir Jonathan Jennings, 15 March 1689, Grey, 9:165; Christopher Tankard (Whitby) to Danby, 29 June 1689, BL, Egerton 3335, fol. 10r; Lumley to Shrewsbury, 17 June 1689, NA, SP 32/1, fol. 86; Col. Rupert Billingsley (Berwick) to Shrewsbury, 12 June 1689, NA, SP 32/1, fol. 73.

24. This has been a subject of much debate, but the most recent scholarship presents damning evidence: Mary K. Geiter, "William Penn and Jacobitism: A Smoking Gun?" *Historical Research* 73 (June 2000): 213–18; Geiter, *William Penn* (London: Longman, 2000), 66–72; William Penn to Halifax, 28 June 1689, BL, Althorp C8; London Newsletter, 29 June 1689, FSL, L.c. 2034; Morrice, Entering Book, 29 June, 6 July 1689, DWL, 31 Q, 584, 585. For other views, see Mary Maples Dunn, *William Penn: Politics and Conscience* (Princeton, NJ: Princeton University Press, 967), 161; Vincent Buranelli, *The King and the Quaker: A Study of William Penn and James II* (Philadelphia: University of Pennsylvania Press, 1962), 172–73; Robert Harley (Worcester) to Sir Edward Harley, 19 April 1689, BL, Add. 70014, fol. 219v; and Melfort (Rome) to Cardinal Howard, 3/13 May 1690, BL, Lansdowne 1163A, fol. 115r.

25. Paul Kleber Monod, *Jacobitism and the English People, 1688–1788* (Cambridge: Cambridge University Press, 1989), 47; "A Brief Account," 2 March 1689, Bodleian, Rawlinson MSS, D1079, fol. 35v; Melfort (Rome) to Mary of Modena, 12/22 March 1690, BL, Lansdowne 1163A, fol. 37r; Edward Harley to Sir Edward Harley, 22 February 1690, BL, Add. 70014, fol. 291r; Wildman, 15 March 1689, Grey, 9:168; John Birch, 6 April 1689, Grey, 9:209; R. Clerke (Calais) to Innes, 6 August 1689, SCA, Bl 1/120/9; *Dilucidator,* 5/15 March 1689, 115; Oxford (London) to Shrewsbury, 7 June 1689, NA, SP 32/1, fol. 65; *Mercurius Reformatus,* 24 July 1689, [1]; John Verney (London) to Sir Ralph Verney, 28 August 1689, Buckinghamshire SRO, Verney MSS; Nottingham (Whitehall) to Southwell, 11 June 1690, NMM, SOU/12; William Chaplyn (Buckingham) to Temple, 17 March 1689, HEH, STT 424; Humphrey Gower (St. John's College, Cambridge) to Covel, 2 May 1689, BL, Add. 22910, fol. 307r; Robert Buckett (Wressle) to Shrewsbury, 29 September 1689, NA, SP 32/2, fol. 30; Belingham, *Diary,* 30 March 1689, 60–61; [James II], *A Declaration of His Most Sacred Majesty James II to All His Loving Subjects in the Kingdom of England,* 8 May 1689 (1689); London Newsletter, 13 June 1689, FSL, L.c. 2028; William Bankes (London) to Legh, 13 June 1689, JRL, Legh of Lyme MSS, Box 4/Folder 26; Col. Henry Trelawney (Plymouth) to Shrewsbury, 14 June 1689, NA, SP 32/1, fol. 79; Morrice, Entering Book, 15 June, 22 June 1689, DWL, 31 Q, 573, 577; Brandon (Ormskirk) to Shrewsbury, 25 June 1689, NA, SP 32/1, fol. 99; Sir John Morgan (Chester Castle) to Shrewsbury, 12 June 1689, NA, SP 32/1, fol. 74.

26. Howe, 25 March 1689, Grey, 9:189; Monod, *Jacobitism and the English People,* 244–47; Robert Harley (Stoke) to Sir Edward Harley, 22 March 1689, BL, Add. 70014, fol. 186r; Information of Thomas Chappell of Chippenham, 31 July 1689, NA, SP 32/1, fol. 106 (ii); Information of Davies Noble of Chippenham, 31 July 1689, NA, SP 32/1, fol. 106 (i); Examination of John Newton, 16 September 1689, NA, SP 32/2, fol. 17; Affidavit of Nathaniel Chamberlaine, Citizen of London, 4 July 1689, NA, SP 32/1, fol. 104; Cotterell (Hadly) to

Sir William Trumbull, 23 December 1689, BL, Trumbull MSS 40 (since recataloged); Morrice, Entering Book, 15 June 1689, DWL, 31 Q, 573; London Newsletter, 9 July 1689, FSL, L.c. 2038; Bridget Croft to Huntingdon, 5 July 1690, HEH, HA 1795.

27. Paul Hopkins, "Sham Plots and Real Plots in the 1690s," in *Ideology and Conspiracy: Aspects of Jacobitism, 1689–1759,* ed. Eveline Cruickshanks (Edinburgh: John Donald, 1982), 89–110; John Hampden, 1 March 1689, Grey, 9:129–30; London Newsletter, 2 March 1689, FSL, L.c. 1983; Anthony Heyford (Newcastle) to Shrewsbury, 20 April 1689, NA, SP 32/1, fol. 33(a); London Newsletter, 11 May 1689, FSL, L.c. 2014; Morrice, Entering Book, 1 June 1689, DWL, 31 Q, 561; London Newsletter, 1 June, 18 June 1689, FSL, L.c. 2023, 2030; Brandon (Preston) to Shrewsbury, 15 June 1689, NA, SP 32/1, fol. 81; ? to Monmouth, 19 July 1689, NA, SP 32/1, fol. 110(i); London Newsletter, 23 July 1689, FSL, L.c. 2044; John Verney (London) to Edward Verney, 24 July 1689, Buckinghamshire SRO, Verney MSS; Abigail Harley (London) to Sir Edward Harley, 7 September 1689, BL, Add. 70014, fol. 258; London Newsletter, 7 September 1689, FSL, L.c. 2060; Massarene (London) to Sir Richard Newdigate, 10 September 1689, Warwickshire SRO, CR 136/B294; Abigail Harley (London) to Sir Edward Harley, 11 September 1689, BL, Add. 70014, fol. 259v; Information of Thomas James, 23 December 1689, NA, SP 32/2, fol. 63; ? (London) to William Dunlop, 1 July 1690, NLS, 9250, fol. 158r; Cotterell to Sir William Trumbull, 22 July 1690, BL, Trumbull MSS 39 (since recataloged); Jo. Knight (London) to Charles Fox, 7 August 1690, BL, Add. 51335, fol. 26v; Daniel Szechi, *The Jacobites: Britain and Europe, 1688–1788* (Manchester: Manchester University Press, 1994), 54–55; Sir Henry Goodrick, 14 May 1690, Grey, 10:140; Delamere to ?, 1689/90, NA, SP 8/6, fol. 97.

28. George Middleton (Kilkenny) to Maj. Robert Middleton, 25 March 1689, NAS, GD 406/1/3510; D. Nairne (Dublin) to Laird of St. Foord Nairne, 29 March 1689, NAS, GD 406/1/3507; James Lincoln (Paris) to Albeville, 5 April 1689, Indiana, Albeville MSS; Whyteford (Paris) to Walter Leslie, 15/25 April, 6/16 May, 13/23 May 1689, SCA, Bl 1/126/18, 21, 23; Robert H. Murray, ed., *The Journal of John Stevens* (Oxford: Clarendon Press, 1912),15 October 1689, 94; Innes (Paris) to William Leslie, 28 October/7 November 1689, SCA, Bl 1/122/14; Tyrconnel (Dublin) to Mary of Modena, 12/22 December 1689, BL, Add. 38145, fol. 5; Rene Grahame (St. Germain) to Huntingdon, 6 January 1690, HEH, HA 4087; Melfort (Rome) to Bevil Skelton, 25 March/4 April 1690, BL, Lansdowne 1163A, fol. 56v; Melfort (Rome) to Innes, 6/16 May 1690, BL, Lansdowne 1163A, fol. 119r; Melfort (Rome) to Mr. Ployden, 27 May/6 June 1690, BL, Lansdowne 1163B, fol. 13v; Melfort (Rome) to Mr. Nelson, 26 July/5 August 1690, BL, Lansdowne 1163B, fol. 112r; Birch, 25 June 1689, Grey, 9:362; Edward Harley (London) to Sir Edward Harley, 26 April 1690, BL, Add. 70014, fol. 322r. See also Massareene (Fisherwick) to Newdigate, 8 May 1689, Warwickshire SRO, CR 136/B293; Jo. Dalrymple (London) to Hamilton, 16 May 1689, NAS, GD 406/1/3545; A. [Pye] (London) to Abigail Harley, 16 May 1689, BL, Add. 70014, fol. 227v; ? to Robert Harley, 5 June 1689, BL, Add. 70014, fol. 231r; and Richard Cromwell to Oliver Cromwell, 4 October 1689, Beinecke, Osborn Files 19385.

29. Robert Kirk, "Sermons, Occurrences . . . ," October 1689, Edinburgh SUL, La.III.545, fol. 26r.

30. Walter Lorenzo Leslie (Rome) to Whyteford, 19 February/1 March 1689, SCA, Bl 1/123/4; Tyrconnel (Dublin) to Mary of Modena, 10/20 May 1690, BL, Add. 38145, fol. 23v; Brandon (Preston) to Shrewsbury, 23 June 1689, NA, SP 32/1, fol. 94; Brandon (Ormskirk) to Shrewsbury, 25 June 1689, NA, SP 32/1, fol. 99; Bohun, *History of the Desertion,* sig. [A4]; J. Hill (London) to Sir William Trumbull, 26 October 1691, Berkshire SRO, D/ED/C33. See also Melfort (Rome) to Mary of Modena, 27 February/9 March 1690, BL, Lansdowne 1163A, fol. 16v; Ralph Trumbull (Witney) to Sir William Trumbull, 8 July 1689, BL, Add. 72511, fol. 86r; Cotterell to Sir William Trumbull, 14 December 1689, BL, Trumbull MSS 39 (since recataloged).

31. This was "the irreducible minimum of support" described by Szechi, *Jacobites,* 60.

32. Browne to Sir William Trumbull, 17 March 1689, BL, Trumbull Misc. 26 (since recataloged); J. Hill (Venice) to Trumbull, 20 August 1689, Berkshire SRO, D/ED/C33. By contrast, when Tories controlled the ministry, some Whigs began to speak in tones that sound, at least to some scholars, Jacobite.

33. Schwoerer, *Declaration of Rights,* esp. 43–101, 283–85; Sir William Williams, 29 January 1689, Grey, 9:30; Robert and Thomas Balle (Livorno) to Goodwyn and Delabere, 12/22 March 1689, NA, FO 335/8, fol. 2; Morrice, Entering Book, 9 February 1689, DWL, 31 Q, 464–65.

34. Yester (London) to Tweeddale, 9 April 1689, NLS, 14414, fol. 37r; Morrice, Entering Book, 23 March 1689, DWL, 31 Q, 507–11; Henry Horwitz, *Revolution Politicks: The Career of Daniel Finch, Second Earl of Nottingham, 1647–1730* (Cambridge: Cambridge University Press, 1968), 86–95; Horwitz, *Parliament, Policy and Politics in the Reign of William III* (Manchester: Manchester University Press, 1977), 23–26; Edward Harley (London) to Robert Harley, 26 March 1689, BL, Add. 70014, fol. 194r; *Axminster,* 1689, 141.

35. George Fleming (Oxford) to Sir Daniel Fleming, 16 August 1689, Cumbria SRO, Kendal, WD/RY 3602; Boothby (Ashbourne) to Mr. Smith, 26 February 1689, BL, Add. 71692, fol. 86r; William Wake, Autobiography, 1689, LPL, 2932, fol. 66v; Mark Goldie, "The Revolution of 1689 and the Structure of Political Argument," *Bulletin of Research in the Humanities* 83 (1980): 473–564.

36. Claire McEachern, *The Poetics of English Nationhood, 1590–1612* (Cambridge: Cambridge University Press, 1996), 9. I am more persuaded by the account of early Stuart ideological contestation provided by J. P. Sommerville than the particularist story of J. G. A. Pocock: J. P. Sommerville, *Politics and Ideology in England, 1603–1640* (London: Longman, 1986), esp. 9–111; J. G. A. Pocock, *The Ancient Constitution and the Feudal Law* (Cambridge: Cambridge University Press, 1987), esp. 30–69; Kirk, "Sermons, Occurrences . . . ," 1690, fol. 115v; *A Brief Vindication of the Parliamentary Proceedings against the Late King James II* (London: Randall Taylor, 1689), 5–6; Samuel Masters, *The Case of Allegiance in Our Present Circumstances Consider'd* (London: Ric. Chiswell, 1689), 8.

37. Richard Claridge, *A Defence of the Present Government* (London: R. Baldwin, 1689), 2; Thomas Long, *A Resolution of Certain Queries* (London: R. Baldwin, 1689), 4; Thomas Long, *A Full Answer to All the Popular Objections* (London: R. Baldwin, 1689), 8–9; Richard Booker, *Satisfaction Tendred to All That Pretend Conscience* (London: Richard Janeway, 1689), 4; Goldie, "Revolution of 1689," 532; Daniel Defoe, *Reflections upon the Late Great Revolution* (London: Richard Chiswell, 1689), 56–57; Defoe, *The Advantages of the Present Settlement* (London: Richard Chiswell, 1689), 4 July 1689, 19–20; Daniel Whitby, *Considerations Humbly Offered for Taking the Oath of Allegiance* (London: Awnsham Churchill, 1689), 35; John Wildman, *Some Remarks upon Government* [London, 1689], January 1689, 12–13. See also *Four Questions Debated* (London, 1689), January/February 1689, 6; William Denton, *Jus Regiminis*: Being a Justification of Defensive Arms in General (London, 1689), 15, 17; Algernon Sidney in *The Dying Speeches of Several Excellent Persons, Who Suffred for Their Zeal against Popery and Arbitrary Government* (London, 1689), 19; *Dilucidator,* no. 4, February 1689, 86; and Elizabeth Lane Furdell, "Dilucidating the *Dilucidator,*" *Quaerendo* 30, no. 1 (2000): 51–63.

38. *The Revolution in New England Justified* (Boston: Joseph Brunning, 1691), 1; Bridgewater, Notes, ca. 1690, HEH, EL 9842; Robert Harley (Hereford) to Sir Edward Harley, 27 July 1689, BL, Add. 70014, fol. 241r; Newcome, *Autobiography,* 19 January 1690, 271; Whitelocke Bulstrode, Meditations, 28 April 1689, HRC, Pforzheimer 2k; Jean Leclerc, *An Account of the Life and Writings of Mr. John Locke,* 2nd ed. (London: John Clarke and E. Curll, 1713), 29–30; Kirk, "Sermons, Occurrences . . . ," October 1689, fol. 25.

39. Yester (London) to Tweeddale, 26 March 1689, NLS, 14404, fol. 32v; A. M. (London) to Harrington, 21 March 1689, BL, Add. 36707, fol. 62r; Sir Edward Harley (London) to Robert Harley, 1 April 1689, BL, Add. 70014, fol. 203; Morrice, Entering Book, 30 March 1689, DWL, 31 Q, 515; John Dalrymple (London) to Duke of Hamilton, 16 May 1689, NAS, GD 406/1/3545; Lionel K. J. Glassey, *Politics and the Appointment of Justices of the Peace, 1675–1720* (Oxford: Oxford University Press, 1979), 100–108; Halliday, *Dismembering the Body Politic,* 265–91; Morrice: Entering Book, 16 March, DWL, 31 Q, 503, 508.

40. Horwitz, *Revolution Politicks,* 99–107; Craig Rose, *England in the 1690s: Revolution, Religion, and War* (Oxford: Blackwell, 1999), 71–76. One measure of the shift in attitude was the treatment of the 1640s and 1650s radical and regicide Edmund Ludlow. In February 1689 a group of Whigs had "begged that he might with safety come home," and William agreed "with all his heart." But when Ludlow did come, the Tories in the House of Commons, with William's acquiescence, forced him back into exile: Morrice, Entering Book,

23 February 1689, DWL, 31 Q, 480; John Verney (London) to Sir Ralph Verney, 7 November 1689, Bucking-hamshire SRO, Verney MSS; Barbara Taft, "Return of a Regicide: Edmund Ludlow and the Glorious Revolution," *History* 76 (June 1991): 219–20.

41. John Evelyn (London) to Countess of Sunderland, 12 January 1690, BL, Evelyn MSS JE A2, fol. 64v; Tamworth Newsletter, 30 January 1690, HEH, HM 30659/4; Nottingham to Hatton, 15 February 1690, BL, Add. 29594, fol. 196; William Hamilton (London) to Arran, 20 February 1690, NAS, GD 406/1/3462; Edward Harley to Sir Edward Harley, 25 February 1690, BL, Add. 70014, fol. 294r; Robert Kirk, "Sermons, Occurrences . . . ," March 1690, Edinburgh SUL, La.III.595, fols. 92–95; Edward Warcup (Northmoor) to Hugh Jones, 3 March 1690, Bodleian, Rawlinson MSS, Letters 48, fol. 26r; Edward Beresford (London) to Legh, 11 March 1690, JRL, Legh of Lyme, Box 4/Folder 32; Edward Harley (London) to Sir Edward Harley, 11 March 1690, BL, Add. 70014, fol. 303r; Cotterell to Katherine Trumbull, 11 March 1690, BL, Trumbull MSS 39 (since recataloged); Melfort (Rome) to Mary of Modena, 25 March/4 April 1690, BL, Lansdowne 1163A, fol. 55r; Charles Montagu to George Stepney, 6/16 October 1690, NA, SP 105/82, fol. 21v; Gilbert Burnet, "History," BL, Add. 63057B, fol. 143v; D. W. Hayton, "Introductory Survey," in *The House of Commons, 1690–1715,* vol. 1, ed. D. W. Hayton (Cambridge: History of Parliament Trust, 2002), 218; Cotterell to Sir William Trumbull, 1 April 1690, BL, Trumbull MSS 39 (since recataloged); Tom Foley (London) to Sir Edward Harley, 5 April 1690, BL, Add. 70014, fol. 316r; Montagu to Stepney, 27 May 1690, NA, SP 105/82, fol. 17r; Gilbert Dolben to Sir William Trumbull, 8 December 1691, BL, Trumbull MSS 54 (since recataloged).

42. Morrice, Entering Book, 2 March 1689, DWL, 31 Q, 487; Edward Harley to Robert Harley, 5 March 1689, BL, Add. 70014, fol. 169r; Morrice, Entering Book, 23 March 1689, DWL, 31 Q, 507; "A Dialogue betwixt the Ghosts of Sidney and Russell," 1689, HEH, EL 8770, 43; Richard Hampden (Westminster) to Tom Wharton, 15 June 1689, Bodleian, Carte 79, fol. 228r; Macclesfield to Shrewsbury, 23 July 1689, NA, SP 32/1, fol. 112.

43. Morrice, Entering Book, 8 June 1689, and Petitition of Gentlemen, Citizens, and Inhabitants of London, 1 June 1689, DWL, 31 Q, 566–68, 566; *A True Account of the Proceedings of the Common Hall,* 24 June 1689 (London: George Larkin, 1689), [2]; De Krey, *Fractured Society,* 56–57.

44. Massareene (London) to Newdigate, 10 October 1689, Warwickshire SRO, CR 136/B296; "A Brief Account," 1690, Bodleian, Rawlinson MSS, D1079, fol. 95v; ? to John Swynfen, 9 May 1690, BL, Add. 29910, fol. 256r; Mary Clarke (Chipley) to Edward Clarke, 28 April 1690, Somerset SRO, DD/SF/4515/Pt. 1/8; James Johnston to Sir William Dutton Colt, 4 June 1690, BL, Add. 34095, fol. 9r; Sir John Thompson, 14 May 1690, Grey, 10:143; John Hampden (Farringdon) to Sir Edward Harley, 9 November 1690, BL, Add. 70014, fol. 353v; Cotterell to Katherine Trumbull, 13 May 1690, BL, Trumbull MSS 39 (since recataloged); Cotterell to Sir William Trumbull, 2 October 1690, BL, Trumbull MSS 40 (since recataloged); Gilbert Burnet, "History," BL, Add. 63057B, fol. 143v; Shrewsbury to William, 22 December 1689, in *Private and Original Correspondence of Charles Talbot, Duke of Shrewsbury,* ed. William Coxe (London: Longman, Hurst, Rees, Orme, and Brown, 1821), 15; Horwitz, *Parliament, Policy, and Politics,* 57.

45. John Pulteney (Whitehall) to Sir William Dutton Colt, 27 March 1691, BL, Add. 34095, fol. 295r; Henry Mordaunt, 21 November 1692, Grey, 10:265; John Lower, "A Familiar Epistle to King William," 1692 or 1693, Worcester College, Clarke MSS, 267/2, fol. 31r; Beinecke, OSB Shelves fb.207; "To the King," 1694, HEH, EL 9925; John Oldmixon, *The False Steps of the Ministry after the Revolution,* 3rd ed. (London, 1714), 6.

46. Melfort (Rome) to Cardinal d'Este, 15/25 March 1690, BL, Lansdowne 1163A, fol. 41v; Kirk, "Sermons, Occurrences . . . ," March 1690, fol. 99r.

47. Warrington, Essay, Beinecke, Osborn File 15756. I am extremely grateful to Professor Mark Knights for calling this valuable document to my attention.

48. Thomas Wharton to William, 25 December 1689, BL, Add. 4107, fols. 78–88. The letter is reprinted in its entirety in Christopher Robbins, *The Earl of Wharton and Whig Party Politics, 1679–1715* (Lewiston, NY: Edwin Mellen, 1991), 297–309; the context is discussed at 69–72.

49. Robert Boyle (London) to Leclerc, 30 May 1689, *Works,* ed. Birch, 3:61; Cotterell to Katharine Trumbull, 18 March 1689, BL, Trumbull MSS 39 (since recataloged); Yester (London) to Tweeddale, 3 April 1689, NLS, 14404, fol. 34r; Williams, 6 April 1689, Grey, 9:207; Elizabeth Adams (London) to Sir Ralph Verney, 14 May 1689, Buckinghamshire SRO, Verney MSS; Charles Trumbull (London) to Sir William Trumbull, 6 May 1689, BL, Add. 72513, fol. 14v; J. Hill (Rome) to Sir William Trumbull, 10 November 1689, Berkshire SRO, D/ED/C33; Ralph Trumbull (Witney) to Sir William Trumbull, 14 December 1689, BL, Add. 72511, fol. 88r; *Advice to English Protestants,* 5 November 1689 (London: J. D. for Awnsham Churchill, 1689), 2; Halifax (London) to Sir William Trumbull, 14 February 1690, BL, Add. 72527, fol. 167r; Cotterell to Sir William Trumbull, 22 January 1690, BL, Trumbull MSS 39 (since recataloged); William Sacheverell, 17 April 1690, Grey, 10:55; Queen Mary (Whitehall) to William, 30 July 1690, NA, SP 8/7, fol. 118.

50. Parker, *Memoirs,* 51; A. Pye to Abigail Harley, 25 February 1690, BL, Add. 70014, fol. 295r; Dursley (The Hague) to Carmarthen, 22 August/2 September 1690, Berkeley Castle, MSS 36A, fol. 68v; Melfort (Rome) to Innes, 11/21 February 1690, BL, Add. 37660, fol. 125v; Evelyn, *Diary,* 16 February 1690, 5:6; Francis Lane (Glendon) to Sir William Trumbull, 26 December 1689, BL, Add. 72527, fol. 143r; J. Hill (Venice) to Sir William Trumbull, 20 August 1689, Berkshire SRO, D/ED/C33; Hill (The Hague) to Sir William Trumbull, 1/11 October 1691, BL, Add. 72529, fol. 140v.

51. J. H. (Rotterdam) to Southwell, 2/12 June 1690, BL, Add. 38015, fol. 347r; John Dutton Colt to Robert Harley, 22 March 1690, BL, Add. 70014, fol. 311r; Paul Foley, 23 November 1692, Grey, 10:275; *The State of Parties and of the Publick* [London, 1692], 1; L'Hermitage (London) to States General, 1/11 September 1693, BL, Add. 17677NN, fol. 226r; Howe, 13 November 1693, Grey, 10:316.

52. Long, *Resolution of Certain Queries,* 8 April 1689, sig. A2v; Guise, 2 May 1690, Grey, 10:109; Carmarthen (London) to William III, 2 August 1690, BL, Add. 78919, fol. 49r; William Ettrick, 14 May 1690, Grey, 10:144; *Smith and Cutler's Plain Dialogue,* 1.

53. Henry St. John, Viscount Bolingbroke, *A Letter to Sir William Windham,* 2nd ed. (Dublin: Richard Watts and James Potts, 1760), 13–14; African Company (London) to Sir Nathaniel Johnston, 26 February 1689, NA, T 70/57, fol. 39v; Henry Booth, Lord Delamere, "Some Observations on the Prince of Orange's Declaration," in Delamere, *The Works* (London: John Lawrence and John Dunton, 1694), 367; Warrington, Essay, ca. 1690s, Beinecke, Osborn File 15756.

CHAPTER II. *Revolution in Foreign Policy*

1. *The Last Years Transactions Vindicated* (London: Richard Baldwin, 1690), 14; P. B., *The Means to Free Europe from the French Usurpation* (London: R. Bently, 1689), 36–37.

2. Craig Rose, *England in the 1690s: Revolution, Religion, and War* (Oxford: Blackwell, 1999), 105; G. C. Gibbs, "The Revolution in Foreign Policy," in *Britain after the Glorious Revolution, 1689–1714* ed. Geoffrey Holmes (Basingstoke: Macmillan, 1969), 59–79; Robert McJimsey, "Shaping the Revolution in Foreign Policy: Parliament and the Press, 1689–1730," *Parliamentary History* 25, no. 1 (2006): 17–31.

3. J. R. Jones, *Britain and the World, 1649–1815* (Glasgow: Fontana, 1980), 12; Ronald Hutton, *The Restoration: A Political and Religious History of England and Wales, 1658–1667* (New York: Oxford University Press, 1985), esp. 157; J. R. Jones, *Charles II: Royal Politician* (London: Allen and Unwin, 1987), 6; Jones, *The Revolution of 1688 in England* (New York: W. W. Norton, 1972), 187; Jonathan Israel, "The Dutch Republic and the 'Glorious Revolution' of 1688/89 in England," in *1688: The Seaborne Alliance and Diplomatic Revolution,* ed. Charles Wilson and David Proctor (London: National Maritime Museum, 1989), 32. Jonathan Scott is a partial exception to this rule. Though he fits squarely in the religious interpretation camp, Scott does suggest that "there is arguably no aspect of the European history of this period more genuinely responsible for ushering in the modern than the reformation, counter-reformation and their consequences": Scott, *England's Troubles: Seventeenth-Century English Political Instability in European Context* (Cambridge: Cambridge University Press, 2000), 353–54.

4. Thomas Babington Macaulay, *The History of England from the Accession of James II,* 5 vols. (New York: Harper and Brothers, 1849–61), 2:1–3; W. A. Speck, *James II* (London: Longman, 2002), 131–32, 134; Jeremy Black, *A System of Ambition? British Foreign Policy, 1660–1793* (London: Longman, 1991), 25–26, 120; J. D. Davies, "International Relations, War and the Armed Forces," in *The Reigns of Charles II and James VII and II,* ed. Lionel K. J. Glassey (New York: St. Martin's Press, 1997), 230–31; Tim Harris, *Revolution: The Great Crisis of the British Monarchy, 1685–1720* (London: Allen Lane, 2006), 185; Wout Troost, *William III, the Stadholder-King,* trans. J. C. Grayson (Aldershot: Ashgate, 2005), 174; John Miller, "William III: The English View," in *The Last of the Great Wars,* ed. Bernadette Whelan (Shannon: University of Limerick Press, 1995), 18; Gibbs, "Revolution in Foreign Policy," 60; Rose, *England in the 1690s,* 105.

5. Black, *System of Ambition,* 29, 119; Macaulay, *History of England,* 3:96; Gibbs, "Revolution in Foreign Policy," 59; Gary De Krey, *Restoration and Revolution in Britain: Political Culture in the Era of Charles II and the Glorious Revolution* (London: Palgrave, 2007), 295; Jonathan Israel, *The Dutch Republic: Its Rise, Greatness and Fall, 1477–1806* (Oxford: Oxford University Press, 1995), 852; Troost, *William III,* 239; Miller, "William III," 17–18; Daniel Szechi, *The Jacobites: Britain and Europe, 1688–1788* (Manchester: Manchester University Press, 1994), 41; Henry Horwitz, *Parliament, Policy, and Politics in the Reign of William III* (Manchester: Manchester University Press, 1977), 20.

6. Tony Claydon, *William III and the Godly Revolution* (Cambridge: Cambridge University Press, 1996), 5, 139, 229; Claydon, *William III* (London: Longman, 2002), 137. In more recent work, Claydon has softened his language: now he suggests that "anti-popery was used alongside other discourses to sell the war." There could be no "simple Protestant crusade," he says. Claydon, *Europe and the Making of England, 1660–1760* (Cambridge: Cambridge University Press, 2007), 155. Nevertheless, he contends, "the nation continued to consider foreign policy in spiritual terms" (160); Jonathan Scott, *Algernon Sidney and the Restoration Crisis* (Cambridge: Cambridge University Press, 1991), esp. 8, 16, 30, 39–41, 106; Scott, "Radicalism and Restoration: The Shape of the Stuart Experience," *Historical Journal* 31 (1988): esp. 458–62; Scott, "England's Troubles: Exhuming the Popish Plot," in *The Politics of Religion in Restoration England,* ed. Tim Harris, Mark Goldie, and Paul Seaward (Oxford: Basil Blackwell, 1990), 110; Davies, "International Relations," 215. Scott has accused me of unfairly summarizing his position: *England's Troubles,* 351–52. I remain uncertain how else to parse the phrase "it was concern about religion, not about politics or economics." My point is that the choices were not narrowly confessional but between a modern Catholic foreign policy and a modern multiconfessional policy. Rose, *England in the 1690s,* 106.

7. For the notion of consensus: Claydon, *William III,* 135. I dissent from Rose's claim that blue-water strategy was "a vein of violent whiggery": Rose, *England in the 1690s,* 118.

8. Sir Daniel Fleming, Lancashire, 1674, Cumbria SRO, Carlisle, D/Lons/L12/2/18, fol. 3r; Robert Lord Wenlock, ed., *Lorenzo Magalotti: Travels of Cosmo the Third* (London: J. Mawman, 1821), 11 May 1669, 397; Thoresby, *Diary,* 1 August 1678, 1:19; *The Case of the Booksellers Trading beyond Sea* [1690s], II.

9. Sir Gyles Isham, ed., *The Diary of Thomas Isham of Lamport* (Farnborough: Gregg International Publishers, 1971), 25 November 1671, 3 February 1672, 67, 81; W. H. D. Longstaffe, ed., *Memoirs of the Life of Mr. Ambrose Barnes . . . ,* Publications of the Surtees Society, vol. 50 (Durham: Published for the Society, 1867), 138; Sir John Lowther's Books, April 1698, Cumbria SRO, Carlisle, D/Lons/L2/6, 42–66; John Verney (London) to Sir Ralph Verney, 24 November 1686, Buckinghamshire SRO, Verney MSS; Lady Damaris Masham to John Locke, 3 October 1687, *Locke Correspondence,* 3:278; Sir Walter Yonge to Locke, 6 September 1687, *Locke Correspondence,* 3:264; Sir John Reresby, *Memoirs,* ed. Mary K. Geiter and W. A. Speck (London: Royal Historical Society, 1991), 21 October 1683, 316; James Brydges, Journal, 7 August 1697, HEH, ST 26/1; Burlington (London) to Sir John Reresby, 10 February 1685, WYAS, MX 31/26; John, Lord Ashburnham (Ashburnham), to James Mackburnye, 22 February 1696, East Sussex SRO, ASH/840, 35; ? to Sir Joseph Williamson, 24 March 1678, NA, SP 29/402, fol. 133.

10. *Remarques on the Humours and Conversations of the Town* (London: Allen Banks, 1673), 126–27; *The Character of a Coffee-House* (1665), 3–4; see, e.g., the 1670 deck of cards in the Huntington at HEH 47507;

and Henry Brome, *Geographical Playing Cards* (London, 1676); Francis Benson to Leoline Jenkins, 11 September 1677, Huntington MSS HM 30314.

11. William King, *Europe's Deliverance from France and Slavery,* Preached 16 November 1690, St. Patrick's, Dublin (London: Tim. Goodwin, 1691), sig. [A4v]; Barillon (London) to Louis XIV, 28 February/10 March 1687, NA, PRO 31/3/168, fol. 42r; George Philips, *The Interest of England in the Preservation of Ireland* (London: Rich. Chiswell, 1689), sig. A2r.

12. *Europae Modernae Speculum* (London: T. Leach, 1665), 4, 103; Edmund Everard, *Discourses on the Present State of the Protestant Princes in Europe* (London: Dorman Newman, 1679), 37; *The French Intrigues Discovered* (London: R. Baldwin, 1681), 8; Charles Davenant, *Essays upon I The Ballance of Power II The Right of Making War, Peace, and Alliances. III Universal Monarchy* (London: James Knapton, 1701), 259.

13. *The Character and Qualifications of an Honest Loyal Merchant* (London: Robert Roberts, 1686), 13; Charles Molloy, *De Jure Maritimo et Navali* (London: John Bellinger, 1676), sigs. A2–A3, A6r; *French Intrigues Discovered,* 23; William Aglionby, *The Present State of the United Provinces of the Low Countries* (London: John Starkey, 1669), 154; "A Letter from a Gentleman in Holland to a Worthy Member of the House of Commons," 13/23 December 1677, BL, Add. 28092, fol. 11r. See also Jacob H. Hollander, ed., *Samuel Fortrey on England's Interest and Improvement, 1663* (Baltimore: Johns Hopkins University Press, 1907), 7; Sir Walter Raleigh, *Judicious and Select Essays and Observations* (London: A. M., 1667), 20. John Evelyn, *Navigation and Commerce, Their Original and Progress* (London: Benjamin Tooke, 1674), 15–17; Roger Boyle, Earl of Orrery, "The Black Prince," in *The Dramatic Works of Roger Boyler Earl of Orrery,* ed. William Smith Clark (Cambridge, MA: Harvard University Press, 1937), 1:372; Edmund Waller, 5 February 1678, Grey, 5:90–91; and Sir William Temple, "A Survey of the Constitutions and Interests," May 1671, in Sir William Temple, *The Works,* vol. 2 (London: F. C. and J. Rivington et al., 1814), 210. I have developed this theme at length in *Protestantism and Patriotism* (Cambridge: Cambridge University Press, 1996).

14. *A True Relation of the Unjust, Cruel, and Barbarous Proceedings against the English at Amboyna,* 3rd ed. (London: Tho. Mabb for William Hope, 1665), sig. A4v; Aglionby, *Present State of the United Provinces,* sig. A4, 163–64, 236. See also *Europae Modernae Speculum,* 66–67; and Henry Coventry, 7 February 1673, Grey, 2:10–11.

15. Charles Molloy, *Holland's Ingratitude: or, A Serious Expostulation with the Dutch* (London: T. J. for Fr. K., 1666), 4; *The Glorious and Living Cinque-Ports of Our Fortunate Islands* (Oxford: H. M., 1666), 1; *Hogan-Moganides: or, The Dutch Hudibras* (London: William Cademan, 1674), 7–8. See also *The Frog, or The Low-Countrey Nightingale, Sweet Singer of Amsterdam* (?1672), 3; and John Ogilby, *The Fables of Aesop* (London: Thomas Roycroft, 1665), 206–11.

16. John Crouch, *The Dutch Imbergo upon Their State Fleet* (London: Edward Crowch, 1665), 7; Robert Wild, *A Panegyricke Humbly Addresst to the King's Most Excellent Majesty* (London: A. P. for Philip Brooksby, 1673), 3; *The Complaisant Companion,* 2 vols. (London: H. B., 1674), 2:32; Sir Philip Warwick, "Of Government," 28 August 1679, Huntington Library, MSS HM 41956, 182.

17. *The Present Interest of England Stated* (London: D.B., 1671), 30–31; Robert MacWard, *The English Balance* (1672), 14–15, 30.

18. *French Intrigues Discovered,* 5–6, 15; Slingsby Bethel, *Observations on the Letter Written to Sir Thomas Osborne* (London: J. B., 1673), 11, 19; *Popery and Tyranny: or, The Present State of France* (London, 1679), 13; Slingsby Bethel, *An Account of the French Usurpation upon the Trade of England* (London, 1679), 6; *Englands Glory by the Benefit of Wool Manufactured Therein, from the Farmer to the Merchant; and the Evil Consequences of Its Exportation Unmanufactured* (London: T. M., 1669), 8; *The Reply of W. C.* (1685), 3–4, 6–7, 9–10; *The Ancient Trades Decayed, Repaired Again* (London: T. N., 1678), 14–15. See also William Sacheverell, 31 October 1673, Grey, 2:202; Joseph Hill, *The Interest of These United Provinces* (Middelburg: T. Berry, 1673), sig. N4v; Francois de Lisola, *The Buckler of State and Justice against the Designs Manifestly Discovered of the Universal Monarchy, under the Vain Pretext of the Queen of France Her Pretension* (London: Richard Royston, 1673), 13; *A Relation of the French King's Late Expedition into the Spanish Netherlands* (London: John Starkey,

1669), sig. A3r; "Marquis de Fresno's Memorial," 20 December 1673, HEH, EL 8457; Roger Coke, *A Discourse of Trade* (London: H. Brome, 1670), sig. B1v; *A Free Conference Touching the Present State of England both at Home and Abroad* (London: Richard Royston, 1678), 48–49; Ludlow, "A Voyce," Bodleian, Eng. Hist.c.487, 1052; and *The Emperour and the Empire Betray'd* (London: B.M., 1681), 68, 71–72. Whig polemic drew heavily on a pan-European literature: Hubert Gillot, *Le regne de Louis XIV et l'opinion publique en Allemagne* (Nancy: A. Crepin-Leblond, 1914); P. J. W. Van Malssen, *Louis XIV d'après les pamphlets répandus en Hollande* (Amsterdam: H. J. Paris, [1937]).

19. *Popery and Tyranny,* 9, 11; *Free Conference,* 38–39, 49–50; *French Intrigues Discovered,* 4–5; Bethel, *French Usurpation,* 4, 6–7; Bethel, *Observations,* 13; *Discoures upon the Modern Affairs of Europe,* 3; *Europae Modernae Speculum,* 91–92.

20. M. Appelbome to chancellor of Spain, 6/16 October 1665, Bodleian, Clarendon MSS 83, fol. 251r; Slingsby Bethel, *The Present Interest of England Stated* (London: D. B., 1671), sigs. A2-A3; Slingsby Bethel, *The Present State of Christendome and the Interest of England* (London: J. B., 1677), 11, 15; Bethel, *French Usurpation,* 1–2; Slingsby Bethel, *Interest of Prince and States of Europe* (London: John Wickins, 1680), sigs. A3–A4, A6; Algernon Sidney, "Court Maxims," 1666, Warwickshire SRO, 152, 155; "Lord Holles's Letter to Van Beuningen at Amsterdam, 1676," in *State Tracts Being a Collection of Several Treatises Relating to the Government Privately Printed in the Reign of K. Charles II* (London, 1693), 458; Andrew Marvell, *An Account of the Growth of Popery and Arbitrary Government in England* (Amsterdam, 1677), 16. See also *The Fortune of France* (London: Jonathan Edwin, 1678), 3–4; *A Letter from the States General of the United Provinces of the Low Countries to the King of Great Britain,* 9/19 December 1673 (The Hague, 1673), 5; *Free Conference,* 8–9; Hill, *Interest of These United Provinces,* sig. C3v; *French Intrigues Discovered,* 11; *Discoures upon the Modern Affairs of Europe,* 1; *The French Politician Found Out* (London: Robert Harford, 1680), 2:11; and *French Intrigues; or, The History of Their Delusory Promises since the Pyrenean Treaty* (London: W. Hensman, 1685), 1.

21. *The Designs of France against England and Holland Discovered* [1686], 7; [Johann Grueber], *China and France* (London: T. N. for Samuel Loundes, 1676), 201–2.

22. Richard Mountagu to Danby, 18 January 1678, in Thomas Osborne, Earl of Danby, *An Explanation of the Lord Treasurer's Letter* (1679), 10; Danby, Memorandum, December 1673, "Memorandum to the King," 4 April 1677, "Memorandums for the King, June 1677, "Memorandums about the Duke of York," September 1679, all in *Thomas Osborne, Earl of Danby and Duke of Leeds, 1632–1712,* vol. 2, ed. Andrew Browning (Glasgow: Jackson, Son, 1944) 63–64, 67–68, 70–71, 89–90; Stephen Temple to Sir Richard Temple, 11/21 October 1672, HEH, STT 2201; Steven Pincus, "From Butterboxes to Wooden Shoes: The Shift in English Popular Sentiment from Anti-Dutch to Anti-French in the 1670s," *Historical Journal* 38 (1995): 333–61.

23. William Garroway, 19 April 1675, Grey, 3:8; Col. John Birch, 10 May 1675, Grey, 3:127; "Letter from a Gentleman in Holland," fol. 15r; Henry Thynne to Francis Parry, 20 December 1677, FSL, V.b. 285; Huntingdon to John Geary, 24 January 1678, HEH, HA 5943; Huntingdon to Geary, 10 January 1678, HEH, MSS HA 5942; Birch, 14 March 1678, Grey, 5:238–39; Danby to Essex, 4 December 1677, *Osborne,* ed. Browning, 62; Francis Benson to Leoline Jenkins, 15 February 1678, Huntington Library, MSS HM 30314; Newsletter from Whitehall, 22 February 1678, Huntington Library, MSS HM 30314; Thomas Thynne to Halifax, 9 December 1677, BL, Althorp MSS C5, unfolioed; *Advice to a Souldier* (London: John Shadd for John Gay, 1680); Marchamont Nedham, *Pacquet-Boat Advice* (London: Jonathan Edwin, 1678), 6; Nedham, *Christianissimus Christianandus* (London: Henry Hills, 1678), 72.

24. Reresby, *Memoirs,* 11 May 1677, Geiter and Speck, 115; "A Short Character of King Charles the Second," ca. 1685–90, HEH, EL 8773a; Charles II's Paper, 27 March 1678, House of Lords Journal, 13:196; Charles II's Speech, 28 January 1678, House of Lords Journal, 13:130; Coventry, 28 January, 4 February 1678, Grey, 5:7–8, 75.

25. George Plaxtone, *The Loyal Speech* (Edinburgh: Heir of Andrew Anderson, 1685), 2; *A Poem on the Coronation of Our Most Illustrious Sovereign K. James II* (London: Nathaniel Thompson, 1685), 5; *A New Song upon the Coronation* (London: James Dean, 1685); *England's Second Happiness* (London: James Dean, 1685),

[February]; *The Reward of Loyalty* (London: J. Hazzey, 1685); "The Happy Return," November 1685, in *The Pepys Ballads,* 8 vols., ed. Hyder Edgar Rollins (Cambridge, MA: Harvard University Press, 1929–32), 3:181; William Basset, *A Panegyrick on the Coronation of King James II* (London: Walter Davis, 1685), 2; Roger Morrice, Entering Book, 12 March 1685, DWL, 31 P, 457; Sir John Lowther, Memoirs of the Reign of James II, Cumbria SRO, Carlisle, D/Lons/L2/5; Gilbert Burnet, *History of His Own Time,* 2 vols. (London: Thomas Ward, 1724), 1:624; *Mercurius Reformatus,* 31 July 1689, [1]; James Fraser to Sir Robert Southwell 7 February 1685, BL, Add. 46961, fol. 217r; John Evelyn (London) to May Evelyn, 8 February 1685, BL, ME 2; Charles Davenant (London) to Sir John Reresby, 12 February 1685, WYAS, MX 29/27; Christopher Phillipson (London) to Sir Daniel Fleming, 14 February 1685, Cumbria SRO, Kendal, WD/Ry 2852; William Petty (London) to Southwell, 22 August 1685, BL, Add. 72853, fol. 21v; Edmund Warcup (Northmoor) to Hugh Jones, 14 September 1685, Bodleian, Rawlinson MSS, Letters 48, fol. 11v; Thomas Chichely to Sir Richard Legh, 17 February 1685, JRL, Legh of Lyme, Box 2/Folder 13; Benjamin Bathurst (London) to Colonel Hender Molesworth, 5 September 1685, BL, Loan 57/83, unfolioed; Charles Reresby (London) to Sir John Reresby 22 September 1685, WYAS, MX 39/49; Gerard Reresby (Cadiz) to Sir John Reresby, 24 December 1685, WYAS, MX 42/35; Thomas Durfey, *An Elegy upon the late Blessed Monarch King Charles II* (London: Jo. Hindmarsh, 1685), 10; Dr. John Nalson, *The Present Interest of England,* 2nd ed. (London: Thomas Dring, 1685), 44; *To the King: A Congratulatory Poem* (London: R. Bentley, 1685), 6; T. R. d. L., *The All-Conquering Genius of the Most Potent and Most Serene Prince James II* (London: John Harefinch, 1685), 5; *A Poem on the Present Assembly of Parliament, November 9th 1685* (London: George Powell, 1686), 4; Morrice, Entering Book, 12 October 1685, DWL, 31 P, 481.

26. "Sur le marriage de Jacques Stuart," MAE, MD/Angleterre 75, fol. 4r.

27. *Life of James II,* 1:659; Barillon (London) to Louis XIV, 16/26 November 1688, MAE, CP/Angleterre 167, fol. 103; Newsletter, 25 September 1688, Bodleian, Don.c.38, fol. 295r; Sir William Trumbull, Autobiography, All Souls College, MSS 317, [21]; Morrice, Entering Book, 26 January 1689, DWL, 31 Q, 437. Contemporaries and Barillon's own extensive correspondence suggest that Voltaire was unfair when he derided Barillon as "a man of pleasure . . . better versed in the intrigues of James's mistresses than the affairs of Europe": Voltaire, *The Age of Lewis XIV,* 2 vols. (London: R. Dodsley, 1752), 1:236–37.

28. ? (Chantilly) to Albeville, 9 March 1685, Indiana, Albeville MSS; Barillon (London) to Louis XIV, 1/11 December 1688, MAE, CP/Angleterre, 167, fol. 173r; Barillon (London) to Louis XIV, 12/22 February, 16/26 March, 16/26 February, 23 February/5 March 1685, NA, PRO 31/3/160, fols. 48, 92r, 53r, 68v; Barillon (London) to Louis XIV, 9/19 April 1685, NA, PRO 31/3/161, fol. 16v; Barillon (Windsor) to Louis XIV, 31 August/10 September 1685, NA, PRO 31/3/161, fol. 39v; Barillon (London) to Louis XIV, 11/21 March 1686, NA, PRO 31/3/165, fol. 10v; Bonrepaus (London) to Seignelay, 3/13 December 1687, NA, PRO 31/3/174, fol. 29r; Bonrepaus (London) to Seignelay, 27 January/6 February 1686, NA, PRO 31/3/164, fols. 24–25; Barillon (Windsor) to Louis XIV, 3/13 October 1687, NA, PRO 31/3/173, fol. 24r; Barillon (London) to Louis XIV, 1/11 April 1686, NA, PRO 31/3/165, fol. 21; Nathaniel Molyneux to Roger Kenyon, 18 October 1688, HMC Kenyon, 204.

29. Barillon (London) to Louis XIV, 16/26 March 1685, NA, PRO 31/3/160, fol. 88v; Barillon (London) to Louis XIV, 28 November/8 December 1687, NA, PRO 31/3/174, fol. 15; Bonrepaus, Report on the State of England, 1687, NA, PRO 31/3/174, fols. 75–76; Barillon (London) to Louis XIV, 8/18 February 1686, NA, PRO 31/3/164, fols. 13–14; Barillon (Windsor) to Louis XIV, 10/20 September 1685, NA, PRO 31/3/161, fol. 47v; Barillon (London) to Louis XIV, 26 April/6 May 1688, NA, PRO 31/3/177, fol. 7r; Barillon (London) to Louis XIV, 16/26 March 1685, NA, PRO 31/3/160, fol. 94r; Barillon (London) to Louis XIV, 28 February/10 March 1687, NA, PRO 31/3/168, fol. 42r; Bevil Skelton (Paris) to Sunderland, 16/26 November 1686, NA, SP 78/151, fol. 116r; Sir William Trumbull to William of Orange, 4/14 January 1686, BL, Trumbull Misc. 24, unfolioed (since recataloged).

30. Petty (London) to Southwell, 30 September 1686, BL, Add. 72853, fol. 112r; Petty, "Matters in Transaction and Discourses," 1687, BL, Add. 72866, fol. 114r; Petty, "Of a Mare Clausum," 1687, BL, Add. 72866,

fol. 122r; Petty, "Considerations upon Shipping and Seamen, Naval Force, Foreign Commerce," 1686, BL, Add. 72867, fol. 37r; Morrice, Entering Book, 11 September 1686, DWL, 31 P, 622; Evelyn, *Diary*, 12 September 1686, 4:524–25; Petty, "For an Alliance with the French," ca. 1686, BL, Add. 72867, fol. 32r; Petty, "About Alliance with the French," ca. 1686, BL, Add. 78267, fol. 35; Petty, "Essay about Analysis of Property," ca. 1686, BL, Add. 72866, fol. 53v.

31. Trumbull, Autobiography, [8–9]; Barillon (London) to Louis XIV, 19/29 January 1685, NA, PRO 31/3/160, fol. 19r; Barillon (London) to Louis XIV, 29 October/8 November 1685, NA, PRO 31/3/162, fol. 7r.

32. Barillon (London) to Louis XIV, 16/26 March 1685, NA, PRO 31/3/160, fol. 91v; Barillon (London) to Louis XIV, 16/26 November, 3/13 December 1685, NA, PRO 31/3/162, fol. 26v, 46r; Barillon (London) to Louis XIV, 21 November/1 December 1687, NA, PRO 31/3/174, fol. 2r; Bonrepaus, Report on the State of England, 1687, NA, PRO 31/3/174, fol. 80r.

33. Barillon (London) to Louis XIV, 9/19 February, 16/26 February 1685, NA, PRO 31/3/160, fols. 40, 52v, 54r.

34. Privy Council Minutes, 15 June 1685, NA, PC 2/71, fol. 56v; Adam Anderson, *An Historical and Chronological Deduction of the Origins of Commerce,* 2 vols. (London: A. Millar et al., 1764), 2:182; Gabriel de Sylvius (Copenhagen) to Sir William Trumbull, 29 December 1685, BL, Trumbull Misc. 23, unfolioed (since recataloged); Hill (The Hague) to Sir William Trumbull, 1 April 1686, BL, Trumbull Misc. 24, unfolioed (since recataloged).

35. Edward Randolph (Whitehall) to Francis North, 3 December 1685, HEH, BL 232; Sunderland to Sir William Trumbull, 1 November 1685, BL, Trumbull Misc. 7, unfolioed (since recataloged); Bonrepaus (London) to Seignelay, 7/17 January 1686, NA, PRO 31/3/163, fols. 53–54; Bonrepaus (London) to Seignelay, 8/18 February 1686, NA, PRO 31/3/164, fol. 56r; Bonrepaus (London) to Seignelay, 22 February/4 March 1686, NA, PRO 31/3/165, fol. 36r; ? (London) to John Ellis, 27 February 1686, BL, Add. 4194, fol. 40r; Van Citters (London) to States General, 5/15 March 1686, BL, Add. 34512, fol. 26r; London Newsletter, 11 March 1686, FSL, L.c. 1635; Henry Savile (Whitehall) to Halifax, 13 April 1686, BL, Althorp C17, fol. 10v; Hill (The Hague) to Sir William Trumbull, 1 April 1686, BL, Trumbull Misc. 24, unfolioed (since recataloged); London Newsletter, 7 December 1686, FSL, L.c. 1744; Barillon (London) to Louis XIV, 29 November/ 9 December 1686, NA, PRO 31/3/167, fol. 58r; Bonrepaus (London) to Seignelay, 29 March/8 April 1686, NA, PRO 31/3/165, fol. 109r; Petition of the Hudson's Bay Company, 25 April 1689, NA, CO 135/1, fol. 69v; The Case of the Hudson's Bay Company, ca. 1697, HEH, EL 9824; Anderson, *Origins of Commerce,* 2:186; Barillon (London) to Louis XIV, 8/18 November 1686, NA, PRO 31/3/167, fol. 47r.

36. London Newsletter, 27 November 1686, FSL, L.c. 1739; Bonrepaus and Barillon (Windsor) to Louis XIV, 11/21 July 1687, NA, PRO 31/3/171, fol. 73r; Bonrepaus (Windsor) to Seignelay, 4/14 August 1687, NA, PRO 31/3/172, fol. 6r; Barillon and Bonrepaus (Bath) to Seignelay, 21/31 August 1687, NA, PRO 31/3/172, fol. 30r; Petition of the Hudson's Bay Company, 25 April 1689, NA, CO 135/1, fol. 69r; Barillon and Bonrepaus (Windsor) to Louis XIV, 2/12 June 1687, NA, PRO 31/3/170, fol. 49r; Bonrepaus (London) to Seignelay, 10/20 October 1687, NA, PRO 31/3/173, fol. 37r; Bonrepaus (London) to Seignelay, 24 November/4 December 1687, NA, PRO 31/3/174, fol. 5r.

37. Barillon (Windsor) to Louis XIV, 6/16 October, 7/17 November 1687, NA, PRO 31/3/173, fols. 26r, 106r; Barillon (London) to Louis XIV, 24 November/4 December, 28 November/8 December 1687, NA, PRO 31/3/174, fols. 13r, 15r; Barillon (London) to Louis XIV, 26 December/5 January 1687/88, NA, PRO 31/3/175, fol. 3v; Barillon (London) to Louis XIV, 31 October/10 November 1687, NA, PRO 31/3/173, fols. 85–86; Barillon (London) to Louis XIV, 1/11 November 1688, MAE, CP/Angleterre 167, fol. 49v; Barillon (Salisbury) to Louis XIV, 22 November/1 December 1688, MAE, CP/Angleterre 167, fol. 130v; Barillon (Andover) to Louis XIV, 25 November/4 December 1688, MAE, CP/Angleterre, 167, fols. 145–46.

38. John Paul Jameson (Rome) to Walter Leslie, 30 March 1685, SCA, Bl 1/91/3; Trumbull, Autobiography, [42]; Count Lillieroot (Paris) to Trumbull, 26 January/5 February 1686, BL, Trumbull MSS 8 (Lillieroot Correspondence), since recataloged; George Etherege (Ratisbon) to Lord Godolphin, 30 December/9 Janu-

ary 1686, Harvard Theatre Collection, fMS THR 11, 57; *Mercurius Reformatus,* 7 August 1689, [1]; Newsletter from the Hague, 7/17 December 1686, BL, Add. 41820, fol. 69r; Bevil Skelton (The Hague) to Middleton, 14/24 May 1686, BL, Add. 41813, fol. 136v; Mr Hughes, "Account of What I Heard in Amsterdam," 14/24 October 1685, BL, Add. 41818, fol. 97r. See also Speech of Daniel de Cosnac, 4/14 July 1685, Bodleian, Tanner 31, fol. 126v; and Gabriel-Jules Comte de Cosnac and Edouard Pontal, eds., *Mémoires du Marquis de Sourches,* vol. 2 (Paris: Hachette, 1883), 23 January/2 February 1688, 132.

39. Barillon (London) to Louis XIV, 21/31 January 1686, NA, PRO 31/3/163, fol. 16; Barillon (London) to Louis XIV, 29 March/8 April 1686, NA, PRO 31/3/165, fol. 19v; Don Pedro de Ronquillo (London) to king of Spain, 2/12 August 1686, BL, Add. 34502, fols. 77–78; Philippe Hoffmann (London) to Holy Roman Emperor, 3/13 February 1688, Campana, 2:175; Francesco Terriesi (London) to Grand Duke of Tuscany, 31 May/10 June 1686, Campana, 2:108; Terriesi (London) to Secretary of State of the Grand Duke of Tuscany, 9/19 July 1686, Campana, 2:113; John Towill Rutt, ed., *An Historical Account of My Own Life by Edmund Calamy, 1671–1731,* 2 vols. (London: H. Colburn and R. Bentley, 1829), 1:70; Trumbull, Autobiography, [45], [53]. For Terriesi, see Stefano Villani, "Note su Francesco Terriesi (1635–1715)," *Nuevo Archivio Veneto,* n.s., 10 (2003). Bevil Skelton, James's envoy-extraordinary in France, helped frame d'Avaux's memorial proclaiming the existence of the alliance for which he was immediately recalled from Paris and imprisoned in the Tower. He was just as quickly released and placed at the head of a regiment and then lieutenant of the Tower. *An Account of . . . the Private League* (London: Richard Baldwin, 1689), 12.

40. *Life of James II,* 2:443; James (Edinburgh) to Dartmouth, 4 May, 5 July 1681, Beinecke, OSB Shelves 190/2, fols. 123r, 136r; Sir Richard Bulstrode, *Memoirs and Reflections* (London: N. Mist, 1721), 377; Lord Godolphin (Whitehall) to William, 18 April 1684, NA, SP 8/1/Pt. 1, fol. 96; Barillon (London) to Louis XIV, 5/15 January, 2/12 February 1685, 29 December/8 January 1684/85, NA, PRO 31/3/160, fols. 9r, 28, 5.

41. Barillon (Windsor) to Louis XIV, 7/17 September 1685, NA, PRO 31/3/161, fol. 46r; Barillon (London) to Louis XIV, 9/19 April 1688, NA, PRO 31/3/176, fol. 114v; Barillon (London) to Louis XIV, 3/13 November 1687, NA, PRO 31/3/173, fols. 99–100.

42. Barillon (Windsor) to Louis XIV, 12/22 July 1686, NA, PRO 31/3/166, fols. 40–41; Barillon (Windsor) to Louis XIV, 13/23 September 1686, NA, PRO 31/3/167, fol. 15v; Barillon (London) to Louis XIV, 18/28 October 1686, NA, PRO 31/3/167, fol. 34r; Barillon (Bath) to Louis XIV, 13/23 September 1687, NA, PRO 31/3/172, fol. 155r; Van Citters (London) to States General, 9/19 June 1685, BL, Add. 34512, fol. 27r; Skelton (The Hague) to Sunderland, 11/21 June 1686, NA, SP 84/220, fols. 18–19; Skelton (The Hague) to Sir William Trumbull, 12/22 June 1686, BL, Trumbull MSS 46, unfolioed (since recataloged); Skelton (The Hague) to Sir William Trumbull, 15/25 June 1686, BL, Trumbull 46, unfolioed (since recataloged); J. Hill (The Hague) to Sir William Trumbull, 22 March/1 April 1686, BL, Trumbull Misc. 24, unfolioed (since recataloged); Edmund Everard (The Hague) to [Daniel Petit], 29 July/18 August 1686, BL, Add. 41819, fol. 224v; Albeville, "Reasons to Recall Troops," 15/25 December 1687, NA, PRO 31/3/174, fol. 47r. See also Everard (Amsterdam) to Skelton, 23 January/2 February 1686, BL, Add. 41818, fol. 229v; Henry Ball (Amsterdam) to Skelton, 28 May/7 June 1685, BL, Add. 41817, fol. 107r; and Owen Wynne to Sir William Trumbull, 6 May 1686, BL, Trumbull Misc. 24, unfolioed (since recataloged).

43. ? (Utrecht) to Skelton, 31 July/10 August 1685, BL, Add. 41817, fol. 265v; Skelton (The Hague) to Middleton, 12/22 June 1685, BL, Add. 41812, fol. 119r; Skelton (The Hague) to Middleton, 14/24 August 1685, BL, Add. 41812, fol. 174v; Petit (Amsterdam) to Skelton, 29 August/8 September 1685, BL, Add. 41812, fol. 199r; Skelton (The Hague) to Middleton, 31 August/10 September 1685, BL, Add. 41812, fol. 195r; Dr. Michael Carney (Amsterdam) to Petit, 31 August/10 September 1685, BL, Add. 41818, fol. 50r; Everard (Amsterdam) to Skelton, 22 September/2 October 1685, BL, Add. 41818, fol. 79; Hughes, "Account of What I Heard in Amsterdam," fol. 98v; Everard (Amsterdam) to Skelton, 25 November/5 December 1685, BL, Add. 41818, fol. 156v; ? (Utrecht) to Skelton, 19/29 December 1685, BL, Add. 41818, fol. 185v; Everard (Amsterdam) to Petit, 16/26 March 1686, BL, Add. 41818, fol. 281r; ? (Utrecht) to Skelton, 17/27 May 1686, BL, Add. 41819, fol. 104; Skelton (Amsterdam) to Middleton, 10/20 September 1686, BL, Add. 41814, fol. 8v; Skelton (Rotterdam) to

Middleton, 30 June/10 July 1685, BL, Add. 41812, fol. 135r; Skelton (The Hague) to Middleton, 18/28 August 1685, BL, Add. 41812, fol. 177r; James Kennedy (Rotterdam) to Skelton, 13/23 October 1686, BL, Add. 41820, fol. 30v; William Hamilton (Whitehall) to Arran, 18 October 1686, NAS, GD 406/1/3306; Kennedy (Rotterdam) to Skelton, 19/29 October 1686, BL, Add. 4180, fols. 45–46; Petit (The Hague) to Middleton, 22 October/1 November 1686, BL, Add. 41814, fol. 64r; Skelton (The Hague) to Middleton, 18/28 May 1686, BL, Add. 41813, fol. 138v; Halifax (London) to William, 18 January 1687, NA, SP 8/1/Pt. 2, fol. 92r; Albeville (The Hague) to Middleton, 17/27 May 1687, BL, Add. 41814, fol. 239; Gilbert Burnet, *The Citation,* 27 June 1687 [1687], 5; Skelton (The Hague) to Middleton, 7/17 July, 21 April/1 May, 24 April/4 May, 8/18 May 1685, BL, Add. 41812, fols. 138r, 33r, 34v, 58–59; ? (Utrecht) to Skelton, 13/23 August 1685, BL, Add. 41818, fol. 17; Skelton (The Hague) to Middleton, 1/11 September 1685, BL, Add. 41812, fol. 20; Skelton (Utrecht) to Middleton, 20/30 October 1685, BL, Add. 41812, fol. 208r; ? (Utrecht) to Skelton, 8/18 March, 18/28 March 1686, BL, Add. 41818, fols. 273, 283; Skelton (The Hague) to Middleton, 30 March/9 April 1686, BL, Add. 41813, fol. 94v; ? (Utrecht) to Skelton, 25 June/5 July 1686, BL, Add. 41819, fols. 177–78; ? (Utrecht) to Skelton, 5/15 July 1686, BL, Add. 41813, fol. 179r; Skelton (The Hague) to Middleton, 6/16 July 1686, BL, Add. 41813, fol. 176r; Skelton (Nijmegen) to Middleton, 6/16 August 1686. BL, Add. 41813, fol. 228v; Skelton (The Hague) to Middleton, 13/23 August 1686, BL, Add. 41813, fol. 229; Albeville (The Hague) to Middleton, 5/15 April 1687, BL, Add. 41814, fol. 208r. For Leeuwarden: Everard (Amsterdam) to Skelton, 31 January/10 February 1686, BL, Add. 41818, fols. 234–35; Petit (The Hague) to Middleton, 5/15 February 1686, BL, Add. 41813, fol. 69r; ? (Utrecht) to Skelton, 8/18 March 1686, BL, Add. 41818, fol. 274; Solomon Slater (Amsterdam) to Skelton, 19/29 April 1686, BL, Add. 41813, fol. 114r; Skelton (The Hague) to Sunderland, 20/30 April 1686, NA, SP 84/220, fol. 14; Benjamin Alsop (Leeuwarden) to Joseph Tiley, 21/31 May 1686, BL, Add. 41819, fol. 108r; Tiley (Amsterdam) to Skelton, 28 May/7 June 1686, BL, Add. 41819, fol. 122; Tiley (Amsterdam) to Slater, 18/28 July 1686, BL, Add. 41813, fol. 201v. For Groningen: Everard (Amsterdam) to Skelton, 6/16 March 1686, BL, Add. 41818, fol. 269v; Albeville (The Hague) to Middleton, 6/16 May 1687, BL, Add. 41814, fols. 229–30. For Luneburg: Peter Wyche (Hamburg) to Middleton, 16/26 June 1685, BL, Add. 41824, fol. 253v; Wyche (Hamburg) to Middleton, 4/14 August 1685, BL, Add. 41825, fol. 7v; Skelton (The Hague) to Middleton, 2/12 April 1686, BL, Add. 41813, fol. 96v; Albeville (The Hague) to Middleton, 15/25 May 1688, BL, Add. 41816, fol. 34v; Henry Ball (Amsterdam) to Middleton, 8/18 January 1685, BL, Add. 41810, fol. 234v; G. Neale [Joseph Tiley] (Rotterdam) to ? Harrison, 12/22 April 1685, BL, Add. 41812, fol. 40r; ? (Utrecht) to Skelton, 12/22 May 1685, BL, Add. 41812, fol. 77r; Skelton (Rotterdam) to Middleton, 30 June/10 July 1685, BL, Add. 41812, fol. 134v; Hughes, "Account of What I Heard at Amsterdam," fol. 99r; ? (Utrecht) to Skelton, 23 March/2 April 1686, BL, Add. 41818, fol. 285r; Richard L. Greaves, *Secrets of the Kingdom: British Radicals from the Popish Plot to the Revolution of 1688–1689* (Stanford, CA: Stanford University Press, 1992), 295–312.

44. Everard (Amsterdam) to Skelton, 8/18 November 1685, BL, Add. 41812, fol. 235r; ? (Utrecht) to Skelton, 25 November/5 December 1685, BL, Add. 41812, fols. 260–61; Petit (The Hague) to Middleton, 24 February/5 March 1686, BL, Add. 41813, fol. 80v; Sir Richard Bulstrode (Brussels) to Sunderland, 7/17 September 1686, NA, SP 77/55, fol. 91r; Barillon (Windsor) to Louis XIV, 18/28 July 1687, NA, PRO 31/3/171, fol. 78r; Van Citters (London) to States General, 19/29 July 1687, BL, Add. 34510, fol. 44r; London Newsletter, 16 August 1687, FSL, L.c. 1844; Dr. William Denton (London) to Sir Ralph Verney, 24 August 1687, Buckinghamshire SRO, Verney MSS; Barillon (London) to Louis XIV, 19/29 December 1687, NA, PRO 31/3/174, fol. 49v; Morrice, Entering Book, 6 August 1687, DWL, 31 Q, 162; Newsletter (Whitehall), 26 August 1687, Beinecke, OSB MSS 1/Box 2/Folder 64; J. Hill (Paris) to Sir William Trumbull, 10 October 1687, Berkshire SRO, D/ED/C33; Petit (The Hague) to Middleton, 21/31 October 1687, BL, Add. 41815, fol. 66v; Newsletter to Earl of Suffolk, 16 August 1688, BL, Add. 34487, fol. 19v; William Westby, Memoirs, 10 August 1688, FSL, V.a. 469, fol. 34r; Barillon (London) to Louis XIV, 9/19 April 1688, NA, PRO 31/3/176, fol. 114v; Barillon (London) to Louis XIV, 21/31 May 1688, NA, PRO 31/3/177, fol. 44r.

45. Barillon (Windsor) to Louis XIV, 31 May/10 June 1686, NA, PRO 31/3/166, fol. 18r; Barillon (London) to Louis XIV, 25 November/5 December 1686, NA, PRO 31/3/167, fol. 57r; Barillon (London) to Louis XIV, 24 May/3 June 1688, NA, PRO 31/3/177, fol. 58v; Barillon (London) to Louis XIV, 16/26 April 1685, NA, PRO 31/3/161, fol. 25v; Barillon (London) to Louis XIV, 18/28 October 1686, NA, PRO 31/3/167, fol. 34r; Barillon (Windsor) to Louis XIV, 23 September/3 October 1686, NA, PRO 31/3/167, fol. 22r; Court Memorandum, 9 November 1686, Beinecke, OSB MSS 2/Ser. 2/Box 4/Folder 76; Barillon (London) to Louis XIV, 7/17 February 1687, NA, PRO 31/3/168, fol. 28v; Barillon (Windsor) to Louis XIV, 11/21 August 1687, NA, PRO 31/3/172, fol. 135v; Barillon (Bath) to Louis XIV, 13/23 September 1687, NA, PRO 31/3/172, fol. 155r; Barillon (London) to Louis XIV, 2/12 January 1688, NA, PRO 31/3/174, fol. 9r; "An Essay on the Interest of the Crown in the American Plantations," 1685, BL, Add. 47131, fol. 26; Barillon (Windsor) to Louis XIV, 30 May/9 June 1687, NA, PRO 31/3/170, fol. 33; Barillon and Bonrepaus (Windsor) to Seignelay, 20/30 June 1687, NA, PRO 31/3/170, fols. 151–52; Barillon (Bath) to Louis XIV, 10/20 September 1687, NA, PRO 31/3/172, fol. 153r. James also believed that Orange in particular had caused mischief in the Scottish parliament: Barillon (Windsor) to Louis XIV, 21 June/1 July, 12/22 July 1686, NA, PRO 31/3/166, fols. 29r, 40r; Barillon (Windsor) to Louis XIV, 30 May/9 June 1687, NA, PRO 31/3/170, fol. 33r; Barillon (London) to Louis XIV, 24 October/3 November, 27 October/6 November 1687, NA, PRO 31/3/173, fols. 69r, 76v; William Blathwayt (Whitehall) to Southwell, 20 February 1686, Nottingham SUL, PwV 53/23; Barillon (London) to Louis XIV, 7/17 May 1688, NA, PRO 31/3/177, fol. 22.

46. James (Edinburgh) to Dartmouth, 12 November 1681, Beinecke, OSB Shelves fb.190, 2:fol. 159r; Bonrepaus (London) to Seignelay, 19/29 May 1687, NA, PRO 31/3/169, fol. 90r; Bonrepaus (London) to Seignelay, 11/21 June 1687, NA, PRO 31/3/170, fols. 127–28; Bonrepaus (London) to Seignelay, 28 December/7 January 1685/86, NA, PRO 31/3/163, fol. 28r; "Essay on the Interest of the Crown," fols. 22–23; Barillon (Windsor) to Louis XIV, 2/12 June 1687, NA, PRO 31/3/170, fol. 64r. These views were no doubt encouraged by stories circulated from the East India Company: Captain Goldsbrough (Gombroon) to East India Company, 10 June 1687, NA, CO 77/14, fol. 156r; Sir Josiah Child to Middleton, 31 August 1686, BL, Add. 41822, fol. 91r; William Petty, "The Weight and Force of the Crown of England," 1687, BL, Add. 72866, fol. 135r; Petty, "Of Ingrossing Trade," 1687, BL, Add. 72866, fol. 124.

47. Barillon (London) to Louis XIV, 6/16 April 1685, NA, PRO 31/3/161, fol. 12v; Barillon (London) to Louis XIV, 31 May/10 June 1686, NA, PRO 31/3/166, fol. 18r; Barillon (London) to Louis XIV, 15/25 November 1686, NA, PRO 31/3/167, fol. 52v; Barillon (London) to Louis XIV, 7/17 April 1687, NA, PRO 31/3/168, fol. 68r; Bonrepaus (Windsor) to Seignelay, 25 July/4 August 1687, NA, PRO 31/3/172, fol. 103r; Barillon (London) to Louis XIV, 5/15 March 1688, NA, PRO 31/3/176, fol. 33v; Barillon (London) to Louis XIV, 10/20 December 1685, NA, PRO 31/3/162, fol. 54r; Barillon (London) to Louis XIV, 25 April/5 May 1687, NA, PRO 31/3/169, fol. 3r; Barillon (Windsor) to Louis XIV, 20/30 June 1687, NA, PRO 31/3/170, fol. 157.

48. *Life of James II*, 1:450.

49. Barillon (Windsor) to Louis XIV, 21 September/1 October 1685, NA, PRO 31/3/161, fol. 51r; Barillon (Windsor) to Louis XIV, 5/15 August 1686, NA, PRO 31/3/166, fols. 52–53; Morrice, Entering Book, 23 October 1686, DWL, 31 P, 641; Barillon (London) to Louis XIV, 4/14 November 1686, NA, PRO 31/3/167, fol. 46r; Van Citters (London) to States General, 19/29 November 1686, BL, Add. 41820, fol. 61r; Barillon (London) to Louis XIV, 29 November/6 December 1686, NA, PRO 31/3/167, fol. 58r; Barillon (London) to Louis XIV, 7/17 February 1687, NA, PRO 31/3/168, fol. 28v; Barillon (Windsor) to Louis XIV, 21/31 July 1687, NA, PRO 31/3/171, fol. 100v. See also Barillon (London) to Louis XIV, 2/12 November 1685, NA, PRO 31/3/162, fol. 11r; Barillon (London) to Louis XIV, 8/18 March 1686, NA, PRO 31/3/165, fol. 8r; Barillon (London) to Louis XIV, 4/14 November 1686, NA, PRO 31/3/167, fol. 45r; Bonrepaus (London) to Seignelay, 31 December/10 January 1685/86, NA, PRO 31/3/163, fol. 47r; Bonrepaus (London) to Seignelay, 8/18 February 1686, NA, PRO 31/3/164, fol. 60r; Morrice, Entering Book, 23 October 1686, 641; and Barillon (Windsor) to Louis XIV, 12/22 August 1686, NA, PRO 31/3/166, fol. 57r.

50. There is some countervailing evidence: Hoffmann to Holy Roman Emperor, 23 January/2 February, 9/19 March 1688, Campana, 2:168, 179. Sunderland also told Barillon that James was in no capacity to attack the Netherlands in February, but he was once again angling to get the French to finance the war: Barillon (London) to Louis XIV, 12/22 March 1688, NA, PRO 31/3/176, fol. 47v.

51. Van Citters (London) to States General, 23 July/3 August 1686, BL, Add. 34512, fol. 41v; Ronquillo (London) to king of Spain, 2/12 August 1686, BL, Add. 34502, d. 77r; Van Citters (London) to States General, 17/27 August 1686, BL, Add. 34512, fol. 49r; Van Citters (London) to States General, 23 July/3 August, 30 July/9 August 1686, BL, Add. 35412, fols. 41–43, 46v; Court Memorandum, 2/12 August 1686, BL, Add. 34502, fol. 79; "Remonstrances Faites au Roy d'Angleterre par Son Conseil Privé," 1686, BL, Add. 41820, fol. 93; Barillon (London) to Louis XIV, 26 August/5 September 1686, NA, PRO 31/3/167, fol. 3r; John Oldmixon, *The History of England during the Reigns of the Royal House of Stuart* (London: John Pemberton et al., 1730), 713.

52. ? (Whitehall) to William III, 1 June 1686, NA, SP 8/1/Pt. 2, fol. 26; London Newsletter, 15 April, 1 June, 8 June 1686, FSL, L.c. 1647, 1665, 1668; J. Fr. (London) to John Ellis, 21 July 1686, BL, Add. 4194, fol. 81v; Anderson, *Origins of Commerce,* 2:186; London Newsletter, 15 April, 28 September 1686, FSL, L.c. 1647, 1713.

53. Robert Harley to Sir Edward Harley, 2 January 1686, BL, Add. 70013, fol. 311v; Lady Rachel Russell (London) to Dr. Fitzwilliam, 23 March 1686, in *Letters of the Lady Rachel Russell; from the Manuscripts in the Library at Woburn Abbey* (London: Edward and Charles Dilly, 1773), 57; J. Fr. (London) to John Ellis, 30 March 1686, BL, Add. 4194, fol. 175v; Morrice, Entering Book, 22 May 1686, DWL, 31 P, 540; Will Haward (Scotland Yard) to Dr. Thomas Smith, 26 June 1686, Bodleian, MSS Smith 50, 51; Barillon (Windsor) to Louis XIV, 5/15 August 1686, NA, PRO 31/3/166, fol. 52v; Skelton (The Hague) to Middleton, 1/11 January 1686, BL, Add. 41813, fols. 53–54; London Newsletter, 18 February 1686, FSL, L.c. 1627; Everard (Amsterdam) to Skelton, 10/20 February 1686, BL, Add. 41818, fol. 248v; Bulstrode to Sunderland, 28 May 1686, NA, SP 77/55, fol. 37r; Barillon (Windsor) to Louis XIV, 2/12 August 1686, NA, PRO 31/3/166, fol. 50.

54. Morrice, Entering Book, 31 July 1686, DWL, 31 P, 587.

55. Barillon (London) to Louis XIV, 26 January/5 February, 13/23 February, 30 January/9 February 1688, NA, PRO 31/3/175, fols. 20v, 46r, 24v; Barillon (London) to Louis XIV, 3/13 November 1687, NA, PRO 31/3/173, fol. 99r; Barillon (London) to Louis XIV, 26 December/5 January 1687/88, NA, PRO 31/3/175, fols. 2–3, 18v.

56. Barillon (London) to Louis XIV, 8/18 November 1686, NA, PRO 31/3/167, fol. 47v; ? (London) to John Swynfen, 13 November 1686, BL, Add. 29910, fol. 203r; ? (London) to William Sherman, 18 November 1686, NA, SP 110/16, fol. 21r; Petit (Amsterdam) to Middleton, 23 November/3 December 1686, BL, Add. 41814, fol. 88v; Kennedy (Delft) to Middleton, 2/12 November 1686, BL, Add. 41820, fol. 52r. See also London Newsletter, 21 October 1686, FSL, L.c. 1723; Petit (Amsterdam) to Middleton, 16/26 November 1686, BL, Add. 41814, fol. 83v; London Newsletter, 25 November 1686, FSL, L.c. 1738; Dr. William Denton to Sir Ralph Verney, [November] 1686, Buckinghamshire SRO, Verney MSS; Barillon (London) to Louis XIV, 4/14 November 1686, NA, PRO 31/3/167, fols. 45–46; London Newsletter, 11 November 1686, FSL, L.c. 1732; and Southwell (Kingsweston) to Viscount Weymouth, 15 November 1686, Longleat House, Thynne MSS 15, fol. 145v.

57. Jonathan Israel, *Dutch Primacy in World Trade, 1585–1740* (Oxford: Oxford University Press, 1989), 334; Barillon (London) to Louis XIV, 16/26 March 1685, NA, PRO 31/3/160, fol. 94v; Morrice, Entering Book, 9 January 1686, DWL, 31 P, 509; Robert Harley to Sir Edward Harley, 9 January 1686, BL, Add. 70013, fol. 314r; Wynne to Sir William Trumbull, 4 March 1686, BL, Trumbull Misc. 24, unfolioed (since recataloged); London Newsletter, 27 March, 24 April, 27 April, 14 October, 16 October, 9 November 1686, FSL, L.c. 1640, 1651, 1652, 1720, 1721, 1731; Christopher Jeaffreson (London) to Colonel Hill, 8 September 1686, Jeaffreson, 314–15; Barillon (London) to Louis XIV, 11/21 November, 4/14 November 1686, NA, PRO 31/3/167, fols. 49v, 46r; Bonrepaus (Windsor) to Seignelay, 23 May/2 June 1687, NA, PRO 31/3/170, fol. 1r;

Barillon (London) to Louis XIV, 23 May/2 June 1687, NA, PRO 31/3/170, fols. 5–6; Bonrepaus (London) to Seignelay, 11/21 June 1687, NA, PRO 31/3/170, fol. 128; Barillon (Windsor) to Louis XIV, 7/17 July 1687, NA, PRO 31/3/171, fol. 48v.

58. Barillon (London) to Louis XIV, 16/26 January, 19/29 January 1688, NA, PRO 31/3/175, fols. 14v, 16–17. James's arguments followed closely the Marquis d'Albeville's "Reasons to Recall the Troops," 15/25 December 1687, NA, PRO 31/3/74, fol. 47. James told Hoffmann that the Dutch "talk, write, print, and agitate more than the English themselves against the abolition of the Test": Hoffmann (London) to Holy Roman Emperor, 23 January/2 February, 3/13 February, 9/19 March, 23 March/2 April 1688, Campana, 2:168–69, 171, 179, 181; Benjamin Furley (Rotterdam) to Locke, 12/22 February 1688, *Locke Correspondence,* 3:363; Antoine Moreau (The Hague) to king of Poland, 2/12 October 1688, BL, Add. 38495, fol. 29r.

59. Marmaduke Williams to Lovelace, 24 January 1688, BL, Add. 63465, fol. 15r; Van Citters (London) to States General, 23 July/3 August 1686, BL, Add. 34512, fols. 39–40; Barillon (London) to Louis XIV, 29 November/9 December 1686, NA, PRO 31/3/167, fol. 58v; Bonrepaus (Windsor) to Seignelay, 6/16 June 1687, NA, PRO 31/3/170, fol. 89r; Bonrepaus and Barillon (Windsor) to Louis XIV, 20/30 June 1687, NA, PRO 31/3/170, fol. 162r; Bonrepaus (Windsor) to Seignelay, 23 June/3 July 1687, NA, PRO 31/3/171, fol. 5r; Barillon (Bath) to Louis XIV, 23 August/2 September 1687, NA, PRO 31/3/172, fol. 141r; Barillon (London) to Louis XIV, 30 January/9 February 1688, NA, PRO 31/3/175, fol. 24r.

60. Barillon (London) to Louis XIV, 16/26 February 1688, NA, PRO 31/3/175, fol. 54v; Sir John Lowther of Whitehaven (London) to Sir Daniel Fleming, 13 March 1688, Cumbria SRO, Kendal, WD/RY 2482; Barillon (London) to Louis XIV, 12/22 March 1688, NA, PRO 31/3/176, fol. 50r. James formed three new regiments from the recalled soldiers, giving each a new Roman Catholic commander: Barillon (London) to Louis XIV, 15/25 March, 19/29 April 1688, NA, PRO 31/3/176, fols. 64r, 136–37. The percentage of officers returning was probably smaller: one estimate had thirty-three of the 180 officers returning, all but five of whom were Catholics: Lothar Hobelt, "Imperial Diplomacy and the 'Glorious Revolution,'" *Parliaments, Estates and Representation* 11 (1991): 63; Barillon (London) to Louis XIV, 27 February/8 March 1688, NA, PRO 31/3/176, fol. 18r. James later blamed the recalcitrance of the Seven Bishops on support from "the party of the Prince of Orange." Barillon (London) to Louis XIV, 21/31 May 1688, NA, PRO 31/3/177, fol. 43v; Albeville (The Hague) to Middleton, 29 March/8 April 1688, BL, Add. 41815, fol. 211r; Barillon (London) to Louis XIV, 9/19 April 1688, NA, PRO 31/3/176, fol. 114r.

61. Morrice, Entering Book, 4 February 1688, DWL, 31 Q, 235; Letter from a Jesuit of Liege to a Jesuit of Freiburg, 2 February 1688, Beinecke, OSB MSS 2/Box 5/Folder 109; Skelton (Paris) to Sunderland, 4/14 February 1688, NA, SP 78/151, fol. 146; Barillon (London) to Louis XIV, 23 February/4 March, 12/22 March, 20 February/1 March, 1/11 March 1688, NA, PRO 31/3/176, fols. 11–12r, 49v, 1r, 24r; Barillon (London) to Louis XIV, 14/24 May 1688, NA, PRO 31/3/177, fol. 32r; Cosnac and Pontal, eds., *Mémoires du Marquis de Sourches,* 23 January/2 February 1688,132; Barillon (London) to Louis XIV, 13/23 February 1688, NA, PRO 31/3/175, fol. 45v; Barillon (London) to Louis XIV, 23 April/3 May, 3/13 May, 17/27 May 1688, NA, PRO 31/3/177, fols. 2, 16r, 38r; Morrice, Entering Book, 4 February 1688, DWL, 31 Q, 235; ? (Whitehall) to Bulstrode, 6 April [1688], HRC, Pforzheimer/Box 10; R[obert] Y[ard] (London) to Bulstrode, 13 April 1688, HRC, Pforzheimer/Box 10; Barillon (London) to Louis XIV, 16/26 April 1688, NA, PRO 31/3/176, fols. 127–28.

62. Moreau (The Hague) to king of Poland, 2/12 October 1688, BL, Add. 38495, fol. 29v.

63. I have outlined this problem with a more thorough discussion of the theoretical issues at stake in "'To Protect English Liberties': The English Nationalist Revolution of 1688–1689," in *Protestantism and National Identity: Britain and Ireland, c.1650–c.1850,* ed. Tony Claydon and Ian McBride (Cambridge: Cambridge University Press, 1998), 75–104.

64. Mr. Leyenberg (London) to Sir W. Trumbull, 17 May 1686, BL, Trumbull Misc. 24 (March–May 1686), unfolioed (since recataloged); Henry Newcome, *Autobiography,* 19 December 1686, in *The Autobiography of Henry Newcome,* vol. 2, ed. Robert Parkinson, Chetham Society 27 (Manchester: Chetham

Society, 1852), 264; Longford (Dublin) to Dartmouth, 27 June 1685, Beinecke, OSB Shelves fb.190, 3:fol. 263r; *A Short Discourse upon the Designs, Practices and Counsels of France* (London: Randal Taylor, 1688), 8; *The Mischief of Cabals,* 7 May 1685 (London: Randal Taylor, 1685), 5–6; *Designs of France against England and Holland Discovered,* 2; Thomas Sheridan, *A Learned Discourse on Various Subjects* (London: H. Sawbridge, 1685), 115–16; Edmund Verney (East Claydon) to John Verney, 1 May 1686, Buckinghamshire SRO, Verney MSS; *Modern History, or, The Monthly Account* 2, no. 1 (October 1688): 17; Barillon (London) to Louis XIV, 16/26 November, 3/13 December 1685, NA, PRO 31/3/162, fols. 23–24, 45–48; Barillon (London) to Louis XIV, 29 November/9 December 1686, NA, PRO 31/3/167, fol. 58r; Jeaffreson (London) to Colonel Hill, 19 February 1685, Jeaffreson,167–68; Barillon (London) to Louis XIV, 13/23 April 1686, NA, PRO 31/3/161, fol. 20v. See also Captain Robert Parker, *Memoirs of the Most Remarkable Military Transactions* (Dublin: Geo. and Alex Ewing, 1746), 1; *The True Interest of Christian Princes* (1686), 23; *French Intrigues,* 149–50; and *Reflexions on Monsieur Fagel's Letter,* 12 January 1688 (1688), 2.

65. *The Case of the People of England in Their Present Circumstances Considered* (London: Randall Taylor, 1689), 2–3; *True Interest of Christian Princes,* 12; Gabriel de Sylvius (Copenhagen) to Sir William Trumbull, 27 February 1686, BL, Trumbull Misc. 24, unfolioed (since recataloged); *French Intrigues,* 150–51; Morrice, Entering Book, 9 October 1686, DWL 31 P, 630; Barillon (London) to Louis XIV, NA, PRO 31/3/167, fol. 36v; Morrice, Entering Book, 6 November 1686, 649; Winchelsea (Richmond) to Weymouth, 18 November 1686, Longleat House, Thynne MSS 17, fols. 144–45; Evelyn, *Diary,* 24 August 1688, 4:596; T. Yarborough (London) to Sir JohnReresby, 12 March 1685, WYAS, MX 29/2; *True Interest of Christian Princes,* sig. A2r; *The Bounds Set to France* (London: Richard Baldwin, 1694), 56; William Lawrence to William Paulett, 27 October 1693, IOL, European MSS, E3871B, fol. 46r. See also Richard Booker, *Satisfaction Tendered to All that Pretend Conscience* (London: Richard Janeway, 1689), 5; Sir William Coventry (London) to Weymouth, 9 February 1686, Longleat House, Thynne MSS 16, fol. 412r; London Newsletter, 13 May, 10 June 1686, FSL, L.c. 1659, 1669; and Morrice, Entering Book, 9 October 1686, 630.

66. *A Discourse to the King* [Amsterdam, 1688], May/June 1688, 1; William Crofts, *Deliverance: A Poem to the Prince of Orange* (London: R. Baldwin, 1689), 3; Whitelocke Bulstrode, Meditations, 30 June 1688, HRC, Pforzheimer 2k; Maj. John Wildman, 2 November 1689, Grey, 9:391–92; Samuel Barton (chaplain of St. Saviors), *A Sermon Preached before . . . the Lord Mayor and Aldermen of the City of London* (London: Thomas Cockerill, 1689), 23; "The Reason of the Suddenness of the Change in England," in *The Twelfth and Last Collection of Papers,* vol. 1 (London: Richard Janeway, 1689), 7; *A Justification of the Whole Proceedings* (London: Randall Taylor, 1689), 2; James Wellwood, *An Answer to the Late King James's Declaration* (London: Dorman Newman, 1693), 8. See also "A Satyr," late 1680s, Bodleian, Eng.Poet.d.53, fol. 23; *A Congratulatory Poem to His Highness,* 19 December 1688, broadside; and *An Essay upon the Original and Design of Magistracie* (1689), January/February, 13.

67. "The Impartial Trimmer," ca. 1682, NLS, Adv. 19.1.12, fol. 15r; "England's Congratulation," 1690, FSL, M.b. 12, fol. 153v; *Monthly Account* 2, no. 3 (December 1688): 98; Daniel Defoe, *The Advantages of the Present Settlement* (London: Richard Chiswell, 1689), 4 July 1689, 16. See also "England's Present State," 1685, in *Pepys Ballads,* ed. Rollins, 3:163; "Satyr on the Affairs of the Camp," 1686, NLS, Adv. 19.1.12, fol. 159r; and Richard Wolley, *Present State of France* (London: Gilbert Cownly, 1687), 17.

68. *A Friendly Debate* (London: Jonathan Robinson, 1689), 37; *An Account of the Pretended Prince of Wales* (1688), 6; *A Brief Account of the Nullity of King James's Title* (London: Richard Chiswell, 1689), 7.

69. "Reasons against Repealing the Acts of Parliament Concerning the Test," 1687, BL, Add. 69955, fols. 1–2; *An Account of the Reasons,* 1688, 7–8; Sir George Treby, 28 January 1689, Grey, 9:14; John Phillips, *The Secret History of the Reigns of K. Charles II and K. James II* (London, 1690), 193. See also *History of the Late Revolution in England* (London: Thomas Salusbury, 1689), 2.

70. Jacob Bury, *Advice to the Commons* (London: Henry Hills, 1685), 44–45; Gilbert Burnet, *A Sermon Preached before the House of Peers,* 5 November 1689 (London: Richard Chiswell, 1689), 29.

71. The Information of John Tilly of Huntspell, 13 August 1687, Somerset SRO, Q/SR/169/2; *English Currant,* 12 December 1688, [1–2]; London Newsletter, 22 December 1688, FSL, L.c. 1951; Captain Thomas Plunket, *The Character of a Good Commander* (London: William Marshal, 1689), 6; William Westby, Memoirs, 26 November 1688, FSL, V.a. 469, fol. 49v.

72. Dr. William Denton (London) to Sir Ralph Verney, 29 August 1688, Buckinghamshire SRO, Verney MSS; John Verney (London) to Edmund Verney, 8 August 1688, Buckinghamshire SRO, Verney MSS; Morrice, Entering Book, 15 August 1688, DWL, 31 Q, 288; Wynne (London) to Edmund Poley, 19 October 1688, BL Add. 45731, fol. 24v; John Verney (London) to Sir Ralph Verney, ca. 4 September 1688, Buckinghamshire SRO, Verney MSS; Westby, Memoirs, 24 September, 22 November 1688, fols. [36ar], 48r.

73. Sir Richard Cocks, "Charge Spoke at Midsummer Sessions 1694," Bodleian, Eng.Hist.b.209, fol. 28v; James Wellwood, *Memoirs,* 3rd ed. (London: Tim. Goodwin, 1700), 242; Robert Kirk, "Sermons, Occurrences . . . ," March 1690, Edinburgh SUL, La.III.545, fol. 98v; J. R. Jones, "Revolution in Context," in *Liberty Secured? Before and after 1688,* ed. Jones (Stanford, CA: Stanford University Press, 1992), 36; Arthur Herbert to Andrew Tucker, 6 November 1688, BL Add. 63780, fol. 45r.

74. Moreau (The Hague) to king of Poland, 9/19 April 1689, BL, Add. 34895, fol. 97r.

75. Southwell (Kingsweston) to Ormonde, 14 December 1688, Victoria and Albert Museum, Forster and Dyce Collection, F.47.A.41, no. 28 (folios illegible); Levant Company to Sir William Trumbull, 14 December 1688, BL, Trumbull MSS Misc. 26, unfolioed (since recataloged); Van Citters (London) to States General, 30 November/10 December 1688, BL, Add. 34510, fol. 192v; Sir Edmund Warcup (Oxford) to Hugh Jones, 22 December 1688, Bodleian, Rawlinson MSS, Letters 48, fol. 19r; EIC to general and council at Bombay, 5 December 1688, IOL, E/3/91, fol. 297r. See also London Newsletter, 28 December 1688, HRC, Pforzheimer/Box 10/Folder 5.

76. Locke to Edward Clarke, 29 January 1689, *Locke Correspondence,* 3:546; Locke (Whitehall) to Charles Mordaunt, 21 February 1689, De Beer, *Locke Correspondence,* 3:575–76; Henry Powle in *An Account of the Proceedings of the Lords and Commons* (London: W. D., 1688), [22 January 1689]; Thomas and Robert Balle (Leghorn) to Kinard de la Bere, January 1689, NA, FO 335/15, unfolioed; J. Hill (Geneva) to Sir William Trumbull, 18/28 February 1689, Berkshire SRO, D/ED/C33; R. B. Walker, "The Newspaper Press in the Reign of William III," *Historical Journal* 17 (1974): 695; *A Dialogue between Dick and Tom* (London: Randal Taylor, 1689), 18; "A Brief Account," 4 March 1689, Bodleian, Rawlinson MSS, D1079, fol. 36v.

77. *A Congratulatory Poem to His Highness,* 19 December 1688 [1688], broadside; *To the Most Illustrious and Serene Prince* (London: Thomas Salusbury, 1688), broadside; "The Prince of Orange's Triumph," December 1688, in *Pepys Ballads,* ed. Rollins, 3:328; *An Appendix to the Translation of Tully's Panegyrick on Julius Caesar* (London: Walter Kettilby, 1689), January/February 1689, 11; Richard Rigby, "A New Song," January 1689, in *Pepys Ballads,* ed. Rollins, 4:84; *The Civil Orange; or, The United Hearts of England* (London: J. Black, 1689); Sir William Cowper, "A Poem," 1689, Hertfordshire SRO, D/EP F49, fol. 9r; Henry Pollexfen, 14 March 1689, Grey, 9:163–64.

78. Daniel Riches, "The Culture of Diplomacy in Brandenburg-Swedish Relations, 1575–1697" (PhD diss., University of Chicago, 2007).

79. Moreau (The Hague) to king of Poland, 2/12 October 1688, BL, Add. 38495, fol. 31v; Albeville (The Hague) to Middleton, 18/28 September 1688, BL, Add. 41816, fol. 202v; Moreau (The Hague) to king of Poland, 25 December/4 January 1688/89, 8/18 January 1689, BL, Add. 38495, fols. 71r, 74r.

80. *An Address Agreed upon at the Committee for the French War,* 14 April 1689 (London: Richard Janeway, 1689), 1–6; "Humble Address," HRC, Pforzheimer/Box 10/ Folder 5; Claydon, *William III and the Godly Revolution,* 142.

81. *Their Majesties Declaration against the French King,* 7 May 1689 (London: Charles Bill and Thomas Newcomb, 1689); compare Claydon, *William III and the Godly Revolution,* 143; Isaac Newton (Westminster) to John Covel, 28 February 1689, Trinity College, Cambridge, MS R.4.43, fol. 8r; Francis Barrington and Benjamin Steele (London) to Goodwyn and Delabere, 11 March 1689, NA, FO 335/8, fol. 3; Sir Edward

Harley (London) to Robert Harley, 16 April 1689, BL, Add. 70014, fol. 215r; Martyn and Goodwyn (Livorno) to Goodwyn and Delabere, 11/21 June 1689, NA, FO 335/7, fol. 13.

82. Instructions for Thomas, Earl of Pembroke, 30 May 1689, BL, Add. 34340, fol. 49v; Further Instructions for Robert Molesworth, 12 July 1689, BL, Lansdowne 1152B, fol. 155r; Additional Instructions to Viscount Dursley, 4 September 1689, BL, Add. 34340, fol. 54r; Instructions to William, Lord Paget, 4 September 1689, BL, Lansdowne 1152B, fol. 199r; Dursley (The Hague) to Carmarthen, 16/26 September 1690, Berkeley Castle, MSS 36A, fol. 75v; Paul Rycaut (Hamburg) to Sir William Dutton Colt, 11 June 1690, BL, Add. 34095, fol. 16v; Colt (Cell) to Paget, 23 October 1690, SOAS, PP MS 4/Box 8/Bundle 39.

83. Thomas Tenison, *A Sermon against Self-Love* (London: Richard Chiswell, 1689), 22, 25; compare Claydon, *William III and the Godly Revolution,* 144; William Wake, *A Sermon Preached before the House of Commons* (London: Richard Chiswell, 1689), 31–32.

84. King, *Europe's Deliverance from France and Slavery,* 9, 13–14; John Tillotson, *A Sermon Preached before the King and Queen at Whitehall,* 27 October 1692 (London: Brabazon Aylmer, 1692), 25, 32; compare Rose, *England in the 1690s,* 107; John Petter, *A Sermon Preached before Their Majesties, K. William and Q. Mary's Forces at Gant in Flanders* (London: J. H., 1694), 30, 33–34.

85. Morrice, Entering Book, DWL, 31 Q, 400, 410; Barillon (London) to Louis XIV, 22 October/1 November 1688, MAE, CP/Angleterre, 167, fol. 13v; *Reflexions upon the Conditions of Peace Offer'd by France* (London: Matt. Wotton, 1694), 7; Barillon (London) to Louis XIV, 5/15 November 1688, MAE, CP/Angleterre, 167, fols. 68–69; *London Intelligence,* 29 January–2 February, 15–19 January 1689.

86. *The Detestable Designs of France Expos'd; or, The True Sentiments of the Spanish Netherlanders* (London: Robert Clavel, 1689), 16; *The Spirit of France and the Politick Maxims of Lewis XIV* (London: Awnsham Churchill 1689), 2, 68, [73]; *A Letter Written by the Emperor to the Late King James* (London: Ric. Chiswell, 1689), 5–6; Hobelt, "Imperial Diplomacy," 66; *A View of the True Interest of the Several States of Europe* (London: Thomas Newbourg and John Bullord, 1689), 54; *The Happy Union of England and Holland* (London: Richard Baldwin, 1689), 46; P. B., *Means to Free Europe,* 153, 160–61.

87. *Monthly Account* 2, no. 3 (December 1688): 91; Robert Southwell, "A Short Account of the Revolution in England," FSL, V.b. 150, 1:fol. 1v; Voltaire, *The Age of Lewis XIV,* 2 vols. (London: R. Dodsley, 1752), 1:233, 2:184; *The Intrigues of the French King at Constantinople* (London: Dorman Newman, 1689), sig. B1, 23–24; Jo. Lytcott (Rome) to Bulstrode, 11/21 May 1689, BL, Egerton 3683, fol. 173r; London Newsletter, 25 April 1689, FSL, L.c. 2007; Bohun, *History of the Desertion,* 10 April 1689, 4–5; Morrice, Entering Book, 8 June 1689, DWL, 31 Q, 569. Papal attitudes changed little with the death of Innocent XI in August 1689 and his replacement by Alexander VIII: Lytcott (Rome) to Bulstrode, 19 November 1689, Beinecke, Osborn Files 9358; Melfort (Rome) to Father Maxwell, 13/23 April 1690, BL, Lansdowne 1163A, fol. 84v; *Bounds Set to France,* 33; Perth (St. Germain) to William Leslie, 14 July 1697, Aberdeen, MS 2403, 37.

88. *A Letter from a Roman Catholick* (London: R. Baldwin, 1689), 2; *Appendix to the Translation of Tully's Panegyrick on Julius Caesar,* 16–17; *Detestable Designs of France Expos'd,* 15; Sir John Lowther, *Memoirs of the Reign of James II* (London: H. G. Bohn, 1857), 470–71; *Dilucidator,* no. 2, [19/29 January] 1689, 48–49; Dr. Thomas Lane (Vienna) to Sunderland, 7/17 October 1688, BL, Add. 41842, fols. 144–45; Bohun, *History of the Desertion,* 10 April 1689, 5. See also Melfort (Rome) to Mary of Modena, 11/21 February 1690, BL, Add. 37660, fol. 124v; *Dilucidator,* no. 1, 5/15 January 1689, 9; *Dilucidator,* no. 4, 4 February 1689, 91.

89. *Happy Union of England and Holland,* 4; *View of the True Interest,* 45; *Popish Treaties Not to Be Rely'd On: In a Letter from a Gentleman at York* [London, 1688], 4. See also *Spirit of France,* 4; "A Speech Made by a Member of the Convention of the States in Scotland," in *An Eleventh Collection of Papers* (London: Richard Janeway, 1689), 31–32; P. B., *Means to Free Europe,* 11–12, 50; and *The Detestable Designs of France Expos'd,* 18.

90. *Means to Free Europe,* 154; *Monthly Account* 2, no. 4 (January 1689): 124; Sir Richard Cox, "A Charge," Michaelmas 1695, Bodleian, Eng.Hist.b.209, fol. 30r. See also Bohun, *History of the Desertion,* 10 April 1689, 4; and Wellwood, *Memoirs,* 240.

91. *A Short Discourse upon the Designs, Practices and Counsels of France,* 29 December 1688, 4–5.

92. Bonrepaus (London) to Seignelay, 1/11 March 1686, NA, PRO 31/3/165, fol. 57r; *Detestable Designs of France Expos'd*, 18; *Dilucidator*, no. 1, 5/15 January 1689, 9; *Dilucidator*, no. 2, [19/29 January] 1689, 44.

93. *The True Interests of the Princes of Europe in the Present State of Affairs* (London: Richard Baldwin, 1689), 35–36; *Dilucidator*, no. 1, 5/15 January 1689, 22–23; Morrice, Entering Book, 29 December 1688, DWL, 31 Q, 398; Bohun, *History of the Desertion*, 10 April 1689, 4.

94. Gilbert Burnet, *An Exhortation to Peace and Union*, Sermon Preached at St. Lawrence-Jury, 26 November 1689 (London: Richard Chiswell, 1689), 5–9; Carew Reynell, *A Necessary Companion; or, The English Interest Discovered and Promoted* (London: William Budden, 1685), 60–61.

95. Sir Richard Cox, "Charge Delivered Easter Sessions 1694," Bodleian, Eng.Hist.b.209, fol. 27v; George Savile, Marquis of Halifax, "Character of a Trimmer," in *The Works of George Savile, Marquis of Halifax,* ed. M. B. Brown (Oxford: Clarendon Press, 1989), 237. For the pamphlet's wild popularity, see J. F. (London) to ?, 17 January 1685, BL, Add. 32095, fol. 214v; Letter to Dr. Hutton, 30 December 1687, Nottingham SUL, PwA 2122c; and Sir William Boothby (Ashbourne, Derbyshire) to Mr. Horton, 14 August 1688, BL, Add. 71692, fol. 18v. The pamphlet went through at least three editions in 1689 alone.

96. Daniel A. Baugh: see Baugh, "Great Britain's 'Blue-Water' Policy, 1689–1815," *International History Review* 10 (1988): 40; Baugh, "Maritime Strength and Atlantic Commerce," in *An Imperial State at War,* ed. Lawrence Stone (London: Routledge, 1994), 188–203; and Baugh, "British Strategy in the First World War in the Context of Four Centuries," in *Naval History: The Sixth Symposium of the U.S. Naval Academy,* ed. Daniel M. Masteron (Wilmington, DE: Scholarly Resources, 1987), 86–90; compare: Henry Horwitz, *Revolution Politicks: The Career of Daniel Finch, Second Earl of Nottingham, 1647–1730* (Cambridge: Cambridge University Press, 1968), 129; and Horwitz, *Parliament, Policy and Politics in the Reign of William III* (Manchester: Manchester University Press, 1977), 317.

97. Col. John Granville, 29 April 1690, Grey, 10:96; Sir Thomas Clarges, 1 May 1690, Grey, 10:107; Morrice, Entering Book, 27 April, 8 June 1689, DWL 31 Q, 546–47, 568; Daniel Defoe, *The Englishman's Choice, and True Interest* (London, 1694), 3. See also *A Smith and Cutler's Plain Dialogue about Whig and Tory* (1690), 1.

98. John Brewer, *The Sinews of Power: War, Money and the English State, 1688–1783* (London: Routledge, 1989), 29–40, 89; Sir John Trevor, 2 November 1689, Grey, 9:393; Garroway, 2 November 1689, Grey, 9:392; Sir Edward Seymour, 2 November 1689, Grey, 9:390.

99. Mary Clarke (Chipley) to Sir Edward Clarke, 17 December 1690, Somerset SRO, DD/SF/45/5/20; Warcup (Northmoor) to Jones, 23 June 1690, Bodleian, Rawlinson MSS, Letters 48, fol. 29r; Sir Christopher Musgrave, 9 November 1691, in *The Parliamentary Diary of Narcissus Luttrell,* ed. Henry Horwitz (Oxford: Clarendon Press, 1972), 10 (hereafter cited as *Luttrell's Parliamentary Diary*); Sir Thomas Clarges, 9 November 1691, *Luttrell's Parliamentary Diary,* 9; Paul Foley, 9 November 1691, Grey, 10:168; Foley, 19 November 1691, *Luttrell's Parliamentary Diary,* 30; Sir John Thompson, 27 November, 19 November 1691, Grey, 10:187, 176. See also Cary Gardiner (London) to Sir Ralph Verney, 6 November 1689, Buckinghamshire SRO, Verney MSS; "Tarquin and Tullia," 1689, HEH, EL 8770, 60; Edward Harley to Sir Edward Harley, 14 December 1689, BL, Add. 70014, fol. 276r; Sir Charles Lyttleton (London) to Sir William Bruce, 9 January 1692, NAS, GD 29/1927/30; and Charles Davenant, "Observations upon the State of the Value and Strength . . . ," 15 July 1696, Beinecke, OSB Shelves b.153, 36.

100. Seymour, 13 November 1689, Grey, 9:413; Clarges, 24 November 1689, Grey, 9:449–50; Barrington and Steele (London) to Goodwyn and Delabere, 15 December 1690, NA, FO 335/8, fol. 9; John Bridges (London) to Sir William Trumbull, 31 March 1690, BL, Add. 72490, fol. 10v; Levant Company to Sir William Trumbull, 14 August 1689, NA, SP 105/114, fol. 459; John Verney (London) to Edward Verney, 4 December 1689, Buckinghamshire SRO, Verney MSS; [Thomas] Sheridan to ?, 30 November 1689, NA, SP 32/2, fol. 56; Kirk, "Sermons, Occurrences . . . ," fol. 106v; Sherman (Aleppo) to William Sherman, 28 December 1689, NA, SP 110/16, fol. 59; Julian Hoppit, *A Land of Liberty? England, 1689–1727* (Oxford: Oxford University Press, 2000), 100; D. W. Jones, *War and Economy in the Age of William III and Marlborough*

(Oxford: Basil Blackwell, 1988), 131, 158–59; Rose, *England in the 1690s*, 126; G. N. Clark, *The Dutch Alliance and the War against French Trade* (Manchester: Manchester University Press, 1923), 126–29.

101. Dursley (The Hague) to Carmarthen, 12/22 August, 1690, Berkeley Castle, MSS 36A, fol. 63v; Dursley (The Hague) to Carmarthen, 11/21 November 1690, Berkeley Castle, MSS 36B, fol. 5v; Edward Harley (London) to Sir Edward Harley, 3 December 1690, BL, Add. 70014, fol. 373r; Clarges, 19 November 1691, *Luttrell's Parliamentary Diary*, 31; Theodore Bathurst, 18 November 1691, *Luttrell's Parliamentary Diary*, 26; Foley, 23 November 1692, Grey, 10:274; Nottingham (London) to James Johnston, 12 August 1690, BL, Add. 21551, fol. 1v; Nottingham (The Hague) to Sir William Trumbull, 3/13 February 1691, BL, Add. 72529, fol. 4r; Horwitz, *Revolution Politicks*, 128–42.

102. *Fair-Warning to All English-Men* [1688 or 1689]; *England's Crisis; or, The World Well Mended* [September 1689]; *To the Brave Apprentices, Journey-Men, and Honest Porters, Labourers and Others* [September, 1689]; "Second Thoughts or A Caution to My Countrymen," 1689, BL, Egerton 2651, fol. 200r; Sir John Reresby, *Memoirs*, ed. Mary K. Geiter and W. A. Speck (London: Royal Historical Society, 1991), 1 February 1689, 547; Kirk, "Sermons, Occurrences . . . ," fol. 101r; "The Dutchess of York's Ghost," 1690, HEH, EL 8770, 79; Defoe, *Englishman's Choice, and True Interest*, 27.

103. Clarges, 16 November 1685, Grey, 8:366; DWL, 31 T 3, 17; Clarges, 19 November 1691, 21 November 1692, Grey, 10:177, 264; Seymour, 21 November 1692, Grey, 10:271; [Robert] Harley, 21 November 1692, Grey, 10:268; Sir Richard Temple, "An Essay upon Government," Bodleian, Eng.Hist.c.201, fols. 6–7, 13; *A Letter Written to One of the Members of Parliament* (London, 1692), 2. The author is summarizing the position to criticize it; Charles Leslie, *Delenda Carthago* (London, 1695), 1.

104. Thomas Papillon, 14 March 1689, 22 March 1690, Grey, 9:160, 10:7; John Maynard, 29 April, 5 May 1690, Grey, 10:96–115; White Kennett, *A Complete History of England*, vol. 3 (London: Brab. Aylmer et al., 1706), 526; *Journal of the House of Commons*, 19 April 1689, 10:93–95; London Newsletter, 16 April 1689, FSL, L.c. 2003; Robert Molesworth (Copenhagen) to Colt, 17/27 November, 29 July/8 August 1690, 18/28 April 1691, BL, Add. 34095, fols. 177, 78r, 339; Sir John Lowther, 22 March 1690, Grey, 10:4; Lowther, 19 November 1691, *Luttrell's Parliamentary Diary*, 29; "The Address of the JPs of Westmoreland," January 1695, extolled the war for defending "the common liberty of Europe": Cumbria SRO, Kendal, WD/RY 4767; Colt (Zell) to Paget, 5 June, 13 July 1690, SOAS, PP MS 4/Box 8/Bundle 39; Cocks, "Charge Spoke Midsummer Sessions 1694," fol. 28v; Lawrence to Sir Michael Hickes, 29 March 1693, IOL, European MSS, E387/B, fols. 34–35; Lawrence to Paulett, 27 October 1693, IOL, European MSS, E387/B, fol. 46r; Sir Charles Sedley, "The Soldier's Catch," 1690, in Sedley, *The Miscellaneous Works* (London: J. Nutt, 1702), 68; *Athenian Mercury*, 25 August 1691, [1].

105. Lowther, 31 March 1690, Grey, 10:23; Sacheverell, 22 March 1690, Grey, 10:6; Sir John Guise, 19 November 1691, Grey, 10:176; Anne Pye to Abigail Harley, 14 June 1689, BL, Add. 70014, fol. 232r; Edward Littleton, *A Project of a Descent upon France* (London: Richard Baldwin, 1691), 24. Littleton produced two other Whiggish pamphlets on the war: *Descent upon France Considered* (London: Richard Baldwin, 1693) and *Management of the Present War against France Consider'd* (London: R. Clavel et al., 1690). Abigail Swingen has highlighted the Whiggish aspects of his famous *Groans of the Plantations*: Swingen, "The Politics of Labor and the Origins of the British Empire, 1650–1720," vol. 2 (PhD diss., University of Chicago, 2007), 271. See also *A Remonstrance and Protestation of All the Good Protestants . . . with Reflections Thereupon* (London: Randall Taylor, 1689), 15; *Advice to English Protestants* (London: J. D. for Awnsham Churchill, 1689), 22; and *The Fate of France* (London: Richard Baldwin, 1690), sig. A2v.

106. *True Interest of Christian Princes*, 1689, 14; P. B., *Means to Free Europe*, 1689, 117–18; *The Politicks of the French King Lewis the XIV Discovered* (London: Mat. Wotton, 1689), 3; Defoe, *Advantages of the Present Settlement*, 30; Thomas Manley, *Present State of Europe* (London: Richard Baldwin, 1689), 2; *Case of the People of England*, 2–3; George Phillips, *The Interest of England in the Preservation of Ireland* (London: Rich. Chiswell, 1689), 26; *Spirit of France*, 3, 18, 35; *Nero Gallicanus* (London: R. Taylor, 1690), 2; *King Lewis of France, the Hector of Europe* (London: Richard Baldwin, 1690), 2; John Tutchin, *Reflections upon the French*

King's Declaration (London: Langley Curtis, 1690), [1]; *A New Discovery of the Private Methods of France* (London: J. Weld, 1691), 4; *A Brief Display of the French Counsels* (London: Randall Taylor, 1694), 44; Kirk, "Sermons, Occurrences . . . ," fol. 95r; Lawrence to Hickes, 7 October 1692, IOL, European MSS, E387/B, fol. 22; *A Letter Written to One of the Members of Parliament* (London, 1692), 4–5, 9–10; Defoe, *Englishman's Choice, and True Interest*, 11, 26–27; Treby, 19 November 1691, Grey, 10:179.

107. Wildman, 2 November 1689, Grey, 9:391; Lowther, 19 November 1691, *Luttrell's Parliamentary Diary*, 29; Sedley, "Soldier's Catch," 67; *Letter Written to One of the Members of Parliament*, 3; *Reflexions upon the Conditions of Peace*, 29.

108. Francis Barrington and Benjamin Steele (London) to Goodwyn and Delabere, 20 May 1689, NA, FO 335/8, fol. 3; Wyche (Hamburg) to Poley, 19 March 1689, BL, Add. 45731, fol. 126v; M. Lane, "The Diplomatic Service under William III," *Transactions of the Royal Historical Society*, 4th Ser., 10 (1927): 92. The political positions of Albeville, Skelton, and Castlemaine have been discussed earlier in this chapter. For Sir Richard Bulstrode, envoy in Brussels, see Bulstrode, Misc. Notes, Beinecke, OSB Shelves fb.124; Bulstrode, *Memoirs and Reflections* (London: N. Mist, 1721), 395–96. For George Etherege: see Etherege (Ratisbon) to Albeville, 23 February/4 March, 15/15 July 1688, Indiana, Albeville MSS. For John Locke, see Locke to Mordaunt, 21 February 1689, *Locke Correspondence*, 3:573; Jean Leclerc, *An Account of the Life and Writings of Mr. John Locke*, 2nd ed. (London: John Clarke and E. Curll, 1713), 27–28. For Hampden, see Henry Ashurst (London) to Richard Hampden, 9 March 1689, Bodleian, Don.c.169, fol. 71r; Greaves, *Secrets of the Kingdom*, 352; Instructions to Thomas, Earl of Pembroke, 30 May 1689, BL, Lansdowne 1152B, fol. 185v; Leclerc, *Life of Locke*, 30; Locke to Philippus Von Limborch, 7 June 1689, *Locke Correspondence*, 3:634–35; Pembroke (London) to William, 2 March 1684, NA, SP 8/1/Pt. 1, fol. 101; Instructions to Envoy Extraordinary Dursley, 31 August 1689, BL, Add. 34340, fol. 52r; Locke to Van Limborch, 10 September 1689, *Locke Correspondence*, 3:691; William Aglionby (The Hague) to James Vernon, 27 May/6 June 1690, NA, SP 84/221, fol. 137r; John, Lord Hervey, *Some Materials towards Memoirs of the Reign of King George II*, vol. 1, ed. Romney Sedgwick (London: KPE, 1931),37; Kennett, *Complete History*, 546; Thomas Coxe (Gravesend) to Shrewsbury, 14 August, 24 September/4 October 1689, NA, SP 96/7, unfolioed; Coxe (The Hague) to Vernon, 24 September/ 4 October 1689, NA, SP 96/7, unfolioed; Coxe (Zurich) to Shrewsbury, 6/16 November 1689, NA, SP 96/7, unfolioed; Instructions to James Johnston, 27 February 1690, BL, Lansdowne 1152B, fol. 218v; Johnston to Henry Sidney, 17 November 1687, Nottingham SUL, PwA 2097/1–3; James Johnston, *An Account of the Ceremony of Investing His Electoral Highness of Brandenburgh with the Order of the Garter* (London: Ric. Chiswell, 1690), 16; Instructions to Sir William Trumbull, 5 August 1689, NA, SP 105/145, 155–56; Barillon (London) to Louis XIV, 15/25 February 1686, NA, PRO 31/3/164, fol. 18r.

109. John Freke to Edward Clarke, 26 February 1690, Somerset SRO, DD/SF/3110; Gilbert Burnet (Salisbury) to Colt, 14/24 October 1690, BL, Add. 34095, fol. 160r. Carmarthen threw his support behind bluewater policy in this period: compare Carmarthen (London) to William, 18 July 1691, 22 March 1692, BL, Add. 78919, fols. 73, 83r; Horwitz, *Revolution Politicks*, 86–146; Hoppit, *Land of Liberty?* 145–51; Molesworth (Copenhagen) to Colt, 23 December/2 January 1691/92, BL, Add. 36662, fol. 263v; James Cressett (Zell) to Sir John Trenchard, 8 December 1693, Beinecke, OSB Shelves fb.239, 1:9; Cressett (Hanover) to Trenchard, 29 December 1693, Beinecke, OSB Shelves fb.239, 1:15; Coxe (Bern) to Paget, 20 January 1692, SOAS, PP MS 4/Box 9/Bundle 45 (ii); *Mercurius Reformatus*, 15 May 1689, [2]; William Duncombe (Stockholm) to Colt, 3/13 July 1690, BL, Add. 34095, fol. 57r; Duncombe (Stockholm) to Paget, [July 1690], SOAS, PP MS 4/Box 9/Bundle 40; Dursley (The Hague) to Nottingham, 27 May/6 June, 26 September/6 October 1690, Berkeley Castle, MSS 36A, fols. 37v, 77r; Cressett (Hanover) to Trenchard, 7 November 1693, Beinecke, OSB Shelves fb.239, 1:1; Cressett (Zell) to Shrewsbury, 4 May 1694, Beinecke, OSB Shelves fb.239, 1:48; Colt (Zell) to Paget, 10 April, 122 May 1690, SOAS, PP MS 4/Box 8/Bundle 39; Sir William Trumbull (Constantinople) to Paget, 5/15 May 1690, BL, Add. 8880, fol. 199v; Duncombe (Stockholm) to Paget, 10 January 1691, SOAS, PP MS 4/Box 9/Bundle 40; Portland (Gemblous) to Paget, 4 July 1691, SOAS, PP MS 4/Box 4/Bundle 26; Paget (Vienna) to ?, 5 December 1691, SOAS, PP MS 4/Box 1/Bundle 4; Aglionby

(The Hague) to Richard Warre, 15/25 April 1690, NA, SP 84/221, fol. 101v; Dursley (The Hague) to ?, 6/16 August 1690, Berkeley Castle, MSS 36B, fol. 1r; Dursley (The Hague) to Nottingham, 12/22 August 1690, Berkeley Castle, MSS 36A, fol. 63r; Nathaniel Loddington (Tripoli) to Shrewsbury, 18 July 1690, NA, SP 71/22/Pt. 1, fol. 84r.

110. Dursley (The Hague) to Carmarthen, 3/13 October 1690, Berkeley Castle, MSS 36A, fol. 81v; Molesworth (Copenhagen) to Colt, 3/13 March 1691, 22 July/1 August 1690, BL, Add. 34095, fols. 268r, 73r; Robert Molesworth, Memoirs, c. 1712, BL, Add. 61639, fol. 3v; Molesworth (Copenhagen) to Dutton Colt, 17/27 March, 118/28 March, 11/21 April 1691, BL, Add. 34095, fols. 285r, 299v, 333r; Troost, *William III,* 245. See also Duncombe (Stockholm) to Paget, 12 April 1690, SOAS, PP MS 4/Box 9/Bundle 40; Paget (Vienna) to Colt, 12/22 June 1690, BL, Add. 34095, fol. 31v; and Colt (Zell) to Paget, 23 October 1690, SOAS, PP MS 4/Box 8/Bundle 39.

111. Timothy Goodwin's preface to John Robinson, *An Account of Sueden* (London: Tim. Goodwin, 1694), sig. A3r; Paul Ries, "Robert Molesworth's 'Account of Denmark': A Study in the Art of Political Publishing and Bookselling in England and the Continent before 1700," *Scandinavica* 7 (1968): 108–22; Anthony Wood, *Life and Times,* 13 January 1694, in *The Life and Times of Anthony Wood,* 3 vols., ed. Andrew Clark (Oxford: Clarendon Press, 1894), 3:441; Mogens Skeel (envoy extraordinary of Denmark), Premier Memoire, 18/28 December 1693, BL, Sloane 3828, fol. 172r; Nicholas Luttrell, *A Brief Historical Relation of State Affairs,* vol. 3 (Oxford: Oxford University Press, 1857), 23 December 1693, 4 January, 13 January 1694, 244, 250, 253; Rene Saunière de l'Hérmitage (London) to States General, 22 December/1 January 1693/94, BL, Add. 17677, fol. 15v; Paul Rycaut (Hamburg) to George Stepney, 3/13 January 1694, BL, Add. 37407, fol. 13r.

112. Caroline Robbins, *The Eighteenth-Century Commonwealthman* (Cambridge, MA: Harvard University Press, 1961), 99; J. A. I. Champion, *The Pillars of Priestcraft Shaken: The Church of England and Its Enemies, 1660–1730* (Cambridge: Cambridge University Press, 1992), 178; Mark Goldie, "The Roots of True Whiggism, 1688–94," *History of Political Thought* 1, no. 2 (1980): 220, 235–36. For one account that emphasizes Molesworth's "internationalism," see Blair Worden, "Republicanism and the Restoration, 1660–1683," in *Republicanism, Liberty, and Commercial Society, 1649–1776,* ed. David Wootton (Stanford, CA: Stanford University Press, 1994), 176, 187; D. B. Horn, *The British Diplomatic Service, 1689–1789* (Oxford: Clarendon Press, 1961), 286; Knud J. V. Jespersen, "Surviving in a World of Great Powers," in *The Last of the Great Wars,* ed. Bernadette Whelan (Shannon: University of Limerick Press, 1995), 57.

113. Robert Molesworth, Memoir, fol. 4r. Although Molesworth admitted that he did not side with his "brother Whigs" during the standing army controversy, perhaps because he saw that as a moment in which real European disarmament was possible, he claimed "this in a Whig is no insensible crime." He was, he said, committed to the core Whig program: he was "for the Association [1696], for the attainder of Sir John Fenwick, for all bills of naturalization, liberty of conscience, for all supplies [for the wars against France]" (fol. 4r). Molesworth developed in the *Account of Denmark* a defense of political economic principles central to the Whig agenda and the foundation of the Bank of England. This program has been elucidated at length in Hugh Mayo, "Robert Molesworth's *Account of Denmark:* Its Roots and Its Impact" (PhD diss., University of Odense, 2000). I thank Hugh Mayo for allowing me to read his extremely useful dissertation.

114. Robert Molesworth, *An Account of Denmark as It Was in the Year 1692,* 3rd ed. (London: Timothy Goodwin, 1694), sigs. br, a[7]r.

115. Molesworth, *Account of Denmark,* 38–43, 74–75, 86, 166–67, 146.

116. Molesworth, *Account of Denmark,* 205; Molesworth, Memoir, fol. 3v; Molesworth (Copenhagen) to Colt, 5/15 September 1691, 23 April/3 May 1692, BL, Add. 36662, fol. 153v, 380r.

117. Molesworth, *Account of Denmark,* 43, 118–19.

118. Molesworth, *Account of Denmark,* sigs. b2–b3, 235–36; William Phillips (Preston) to Edward Clarke, 22 January 1696, Somerset SRO, DD/SF/3833.

119. Samuel Johnson, *Notes upon the Phoenix Edition of the Pastoral Letter* (London, 1694), 5–6; A Speech Intended to be Given by Mr. John Smith, 1694, HEH, EL 9920; Sir Robert Atkyns, *The Lord Chief Baron Atkyns's Speech to Sir William Ashurst* (London: Richard Baldwin, 1693), 2.

120. J. F. Chance, ed., "William Duncombe's 'Summary Report' of His Mission to Sweden, 1689–92," *English Historical Review* 39 (1924): 576–77, 584–85. There is another copy of the "Summary Report" in BL, Lansdowne 1152B, fols. 171–75. Duncombe's report is consistent with his diplomatic dispatches, which can be read in NA, SP 95/13; Robinson, *Account of Sueden*, 96–97, 111–12; John Robinson (Stockholm) to Shrewsbury, 8 December 1694, BL, Add. 72531, fol. 145r. Robinson's subsequent career was as a moderate Tory. In the 1690s, however, he was a firm advocate of Continental commitment. In any event, Goodwin clearly published the tract without Robinson's consent for his own Whiggish purposes.

121. *Nero Gallicanus*, 3–4; *Bounds Set to France*, 73; William Lloyd, *The Pretences of the French Invasion Examined* (London: R. Clavel, 1692), 7–8; *Reflexions upon the Conditions*, 10–11; Evelyn, *Diary*, 5 February 1693, 5:130; King, *Europe's Deliverance from France and Slavery*, 11; Atkyns, *Speech*.

122. *Descent upon France Considered*, 7; Sir John Darrell, 5 December 1693, Grey, 10:340–41; Sir Thomas Littleton, 5 December 1693, Grey, 10:342; Sir Charles Sedley, 5 December 1693, Grey, 10:341; Lord Colchester, 5 December 1693, Grey, 10:343.

123. Horwitz, *Revolution Politicks*, 149; Sir Thomas Clarges, 28 November 1693, Grey 10:332; Sir Christopher Musgrave, 5 December 1693, Grey, 10:340; Dr. Nicholas Barbon, 5 December 1693, Grey, 10:340; Col. Henry Cornewall, 11 December 1693, Grey, 10:358; Mayo, "Robert Molesworth's *Account of Denmark*," 12–13; Morrice, Entering Book, DWL, 31 Q, 597; Jodocus Crull, *Denmark Vindicated* (London: T. Newborough, 1694), sig. [A7r]; Thomas Rogers, *The Common-wealths Man Unmasqu'd* (London: Randal Taylor, 1694), 2–3; William King, *Animadversions on a Pretended Account of Denmark* (London: Tho. Bennet, 1694), sig. [A6v]. This author is not to be confused with his namesake, the Whiggish dean of St. Patrick's Dublin.

124. P. B., *Means to Free Europe*, 142–43; William Sherlock, *A Letter to a Member of the Convention* [January 1689], 4; *True Interest of Christian Princes*, 1689, 37–38; *A Brief Vindication of the Parliamentary Proceedings against the Late King James II* (London: Randall Taylor, 1689), sigs. A3–A4; Newsletter, 15 January 1689, Bodleian, Don.c.39, fol. 89r; Wellwood, *Memoirs*, 257; Trumbull, Autobiography, 46–46bis; *A Letter Written by the Emperor to the Late King James* (London: Ric. Chiswell, 1689), 3–5; Bonrepaus (London) to Seignelay, 15/25 February 1686, NA, PRO 31/3/164, fol. 83r; Barillon (London) to Louis XIV, 22 October/1 November 1688, MAE, CP/Angleterre, 167, fol. 13v. See also William Nicolson to ?, May 1689, BL, Add. 34265, fol. 5r.

125. For the interpretation that the succession was "the central issue at stake in 1688–89," see Edward Vallance, *The Glorious Revolution: 1688—Britain's Fight for Liberty* (London: Little, Brown, 2006), 17.

CHAPTER 12. *Revolution in Political Economy*

1. John Toland, *The Oceana of James Harrington and His Other Works* (London, 1700), iii; compare J. G. A. Pocock, *Virtue, Commerce, and History: Essays on Political Thought and History, Chiefly in the Eighteenth Century* (Cambridge: Cambridge University Press, 1985), 233.

2. Pocock, *Virtue, Commerce, and History*, 108, 230; J. G. A. Pocock, *The Machiavellian Moment: Florentine Political Thought and the Atlantic Republican Tradition* (Princeton, NJ: Princeton University Press, 1975), 423–26; J. G. A. Pocock, "Early Modern Capitalism: The Augustan Perception," in *Feudalism, Capitalism and Beyond*, ed. Eugene Kamenke and R. S. Neale (London: E. Arnold, 1975), 68–71.

3. P. G. M. Dickson, *The Financial Revolution in England* (London: Macmillan, 1967), 17; John Brewer, *The Sinews of Power: War, Money and the English State, 1688–1783* (London: Routledge, 1989), 138, 153, 157. See also Quentin Skinner, *Liberty before Liberalism* (Cambridge: Cambridge University Press, 1998), 96; and David Armitage, *The Ideological Origins of the British Empire* (Cambridge: Cambridge University Press, 2000), 156–68.

4. Douglass C. North and Barry R. Weingast, "Constitutions and Commitment: The Evolution of Institutions Governing Public Choice in Seventeenth-Century England," *Journal of Economic History* 49 (1989): 815–16, 819, 831; Barry R. Weingast, "The Political Foundations of Democracy and the Rule of Law," *American Political Science Review* 91(1997): 252–53; Weingast, "The Political Foundations of Limited Government: Parliament and Sovereign Debt in Seventeenth- and Eighteenth-Century England," in *The Frontiers of New Institutional Economics,* ed. John N. Drobak and John V. C. Nye (New York: Academic, 1997), 23. This story fits nicely with C. B. Macpherson, *The Political Theory of Possessive Individualism: Hobbes to Locke* (Oxford: Oxford University Press, 1962), 1, 3, 258, 270.

5. Compare: Pocock, "Early Modern Capitalism," 72; Armitage, *Ideological Origins of the British Empire,* 3.

6. Steve Pincus, "Neither Machiavellian Moment nor Possessive Individualism: Commercial Society and the Defenders of the English Commonwealth," *American Historical Review* 103 (1998): 720–21.

7. Carew Reynell, *A Necessary Companion; or, The English Interest Discovered and Promoted* (London: William Budden, 1685), sig. A7r, 17–18, 71–72. John Locke was impressed by Reynell's work: Bodleian, MSS Locke, c.30, fols. 18–19.

8. Reynell, *Necessary Companion,* sigs. A5v–A7r (a1)v–(a2)r, 5, 17–18, 48.

9. Reynell, *Necessary Companion,* sig. A4, 1–2, 6, 16.

10. Reynell, *Necessary Companion,* 13–14.

11. I disagree with historians and economists who insist that no notion of sustained economic growth was available in the seventeenth century: D. C. Coleman, "Labour in the English Economy of the Seventeenth Century," *Economic History Review,* n.s., 8, no. 3 (1956): 287–88; Antony Brewer, "The Concept of Growth in Eighteenth Century Economics," *History of Political Economy* 28, no. 4 (1995): esp. 609–10. I also disagree with the vast number of writers who have posited a mercantilist consensus. Kenneth Morgan, "Mercantilism and the British Empire," in *The Political Economy of British Historical Experience, 1688–1914,* ed. Donald Winch and Patrick K. O'Brien (Oxford: Oxford University Press, 2002), 165, 168. For one exceptional view: Richard C. Wiles, "The Theory of Wages in Later English Mercantilism," *Economic History Review,* n.s., 21 (1968): 113–26; Richard Blome, *The Present State of His Majesty's Isles and Territories in America* (London: H. Clash, 1687), 127; William Carter, *The Reply of W. C.* (London, 1685), 49; John Locke, "Second Treatise of Government," in *Political Writings of John Locke,* ed. David Wootton (New York: Mentor, 1993), 281–82; Locke to Edward Clarke, 30 June 1694, and Locke to Clarke, 6 August 1694, in *The Correspondence of John Locke and Edward Clarke,* ed. Benjamin Rand (Cambridge, MA: Harvard University Press, 1927), 395, 397.

12. Andrew Yarranton, *England's Improvement by Sea and Land* (London: R. Everingham, 1677), 20, 22–23; Mark Lewis, *Proposals to the King and Parliament* (London: Henry Million, 1678), sig. A2r; Adam Anderson, *An Historical and Chronological Deduction of the Origins of Commerce,* 2 vols. (London: A. Millar et al., 1764), 1:vii, 2:189, 2:564; Sir John Lowther, Notes on Trade, ca. 1680, Cumbria Record Office, D/Lons/W1/63, 1–2. See also *The Mischief of Cabals,* 7 May 1685 (London: Randal Taylor, 1685), 35–36.

13. *Some Remarks upon the Present State of the East-India Company's Affairs* (London, 1690), 3, 6; Nathaniel Cholmley (Whitby) to Cholmely Stephens, 30 December 1684, North Yorkshire SRO, ZCG, unfolioed; Cholmley to John Heatfield, [January 1686], North Yorkshire SRO, ZCG, unfolioed; John Williams to Arthur Charlett, 20 March 1683, in Robert Beddard, ed., "A Whig View of Tory Oxford in 1683: Lord Herbert of Cherbury's Criticism of the University," *Bodleian Library Record* 15 (1995): 179; Sir William Coventry to Viscount Weymouth, [1685], Longleat House, Thynne MSS 16, fol. 442v. It is possible that Jean Chardin's "great disgust" with the company and his decision to sell off three-fourths of his shares was related to this purge: Bonrepaus (London) to Seignelay, 8/18 March 1686, NA, PRO 31/3/165, fol. 59r; Cholmley (Whitby) to Mr. Mohun, 30 December 1684, North Yorkshire SRO, ZCG, unfolioed; *Reasons Humbly Offered against Grafting and Splicing and for Dissolving This Present East-India Company* [London, 3 January 1690], 6; EIC to agent and council in Bengal, 9 June 1686, IOL, E/3/91, fol. 73v; EIC to general and council at Bombay,

3 August 1687, IOL, E/3/91, fol. 163r; Dr. John St. John, His Information Regarding India, 1685–1688, CKS, U269/O82; Roger Morrice, Entering Book, 23 March 1689, DWL, 31 Q, 509; William Letwin, *Sir Josiah Child: Merchant Economist* (Cambridge, MA: Harvard University Press, 1959), 22.

14. Bruce G. Carruthers, *The City of Capital: Politics and Markets in the English Financial Revolution* (Princeton, NJ: Princeton University Press, 1996), 146; Gary De Krey, *A Fractured Society: The Politics of London in the First Age of Party, 1688–1715* (Oxford: Clarendon Press, 1985), 24; Henry Horwitz, "The East India Trade, the Politicians, and the Constitution, 1689–1702," *Journal of British Studies* 17 (1978): 1; Sir William Wilson Hunter, *A History of British India,* vol. 2 (London: Longmans, Green, 1900), 247; K. N. Chaudhuri, *The Trading World of Asia and the English East India Company, 1660–1760* (Cambridge: Cambridge University Press, 1978), 116, 429; Letwin, *Josiah Child,* 23; W. J. Ashley, "The Tory Origin of Free Trade Policy," *Quarterly Journal of Economics* 11, no. 4 (1897): 353; James Mill, *The History of British India,* vol. 2 (1817; New Delhi: Associated Publishing House, 1972), 82; Morrice, Entering Book, 1 June 1689, DWL, 31 Q, 560–61; K. G. Davies, *The Royal African Company* (London: Longmans, Green, 1957), 103; Bonrepaus (London) to Seignelay, 14/24 January 1686, NA, PRO 31/3/163, fol. 67r; Cholmley (Whitby) to Richard Eliot, 30 December 1684, North Yorkshire SRO, ZCG, unfolioed; Cholmley to Heatfield, 1 January 1685, North Yorkshire SRO, ZCG, unfolioed; *Some Remarks,* 1690, 3–4; *Reasons Humbly Offered against Grafting,* 4–6; Christopher Phillipson (London) to Sir Daniel Fleming, 14 February 1685, Cumbria SRO, Kendal, WD/Ry 2852; Brook Bridges, Notabilia, 7–8 April 1685, Beinecke, OSB Shelves b.233; London Newsletter, 30 May 1689, FSL, L.c. 2022.

15. Shafaat Ahmad Khan, *The East India Trade in the Seventeenth Century* (Oxford: Oxford University Press, 1923), 193.

16. Sir Josiah Child, *A Discourse Concerning Trade and That in Particular of the East Indies; Published with A Supplement* (London: Andrew Sowle, 1689), 25 June 1689, 1. Debates over political economy were fluid in the later Stuart period. At the very least, Child changed his ideological emphasis as he grew older. So, after the revolution his enemies published his earlier writings to discredit him, just as Child and the defenders of the old East India Company appear to have been behind republication of Thomas Papillon's early writings.

17. Sir Josiah Child, *A Discourse of the Nature, Use and Advantages of Trade* (London: Randal Taylor, 1694), 2, 7–8, 10–11; *The Argument of the Lord Chief Justice of the Court of King's Bench Concerning the Great Case of Monopolies* (London: Randal Taylor, 1689), 7; Child, *Discourse Concerning Trade,* 3. In 1669 Child told the lords' committee on trade that "all trade [is] a kind of warfare": quoted in Letwin, *Josiah Child,* 28. Compare: Thomas Leng, "Commercial Conflict and Regulation in the Discourse of Trade in Seventeenth-Century England," *Historical Journal* 48 (2005): 954; Armitage, *Ideological Origins of the British Empire,* 166.

18. Child, *A New Discourse of Trade* (London: Sam. Crouch et al., 1694), sig. [A4v]; Child, *Discourse of the Nature,* 17, 27–28; EIC Memorandum, 1670s, NA, PRO 30/24/44/75, fol. 52r.

19. Child to Middleton, 1 September 1683, BL, Add. 41822, fol. 25r; Child, *Supplement,* 2; president and council of Surat to EIC, 21 April 1685, IOL, E/3/45/5365.

20. James held three thousand pounds' worth of stock in the company that he transferred to Sir James Grahame at Rochester only on the eve of his final departure from England: "An Answer of the Royal African Company," 1690, PRO, T 70/169, fol. 76; William A. Pettigrew, "Free to Enslave: Politics and the Escalation of Britain's Transatlantic Slave Trade, 1688–1714," *William and Mary Quarterly,* 3rd ser., 64 (2007): 8; Davies, *Royal African Company,* 60, 65, 103–4, 156; Morrice, Entering Book, 6 August 1687, DWL 31 Q, 164.

21. *Certain Considerations Relating to the Royal African Company of England* (1680), 1, 6–8; "Reasons of the African Company," August 1683, NA, CO 268/1, fol. 59r. This was the standard company line. After the revolution, Sir Robert Harley, the new Tory leader in the House of Commons, presented a petition by the Royal African Company using almost identical language: Petition of the Royal African Company, 24 January 1694, NA, T 70/169, fol. 106v.

22. Sir Benjamin Bathurst to Col. Hender Molesworth, 5 February 1685, BL, Loan 57/83, unfolioed; Barillon (London) to Louis XIV, 2/12 February 1685, NA, PRO 31/3/160, fol. 28r; Sir John Holt's Argu-

ments, EIC v. Sandys, Bodleian, Rawlinson MSS, C130, fols. 34–35, 38; Daniel Finch's Arguments, 19 April 1684, EIC v. Sandys, fol. 84.

23. Sir Henry Pollexfen's Arguments, 21 April 1684, EIC v. Sandys, fol. 128v; Sir George Treby's Arguments, EIC v. Sandys, fols. 50v, 59v, 74v.

24. Justice Walcott's Opinion, 31 January 1685, EIC v. Sandys, fol. 220v; Justice Holloway's Opinion, 31 January 1685, EIC v. Sandys, Bodleian, fol. 223v; Chief Justice Jefferies's Opinion, 31 January 1685, EIC v. Sandys, in *A Complete Collection of State Trials,* vol. 10, ed. T. B. Howell (London: T. C. Hansard, 1811), 523, 526, 534; Roger North, *Lives,* vol. 1, ed. Augustus Jessopp (London: George Bell and Sons, 1890), 283; Justice Witkins's Opinion, 31 January 1685, EIC v. Sandys, fol. 229v.

25. Jefferies' Opinion, 31 January 1685, EIC v. Sandys, fol. 238v. See also Witkins' Opinion, 31 January 1685, EIC v. Sandys, fol. 227r.

26. Jefferies's Opinion, 31 January 1685, EIC v. Sandys, in *Complete Collection,* ed. Howell, 522, 534, 550–51.

27. Richard R. Johnson, *Adjustment to Empire: The New England Colonies, 1675–1715* (New Brunswick, NJ: Rutgers University Press, 1981), 50–70; Stephen Saunders Webb, *Lord Churchill's Coup: The Anglo-American Empire and the Glorious Revolution Reconsidered* (New York: Alfred A. Knopf, 1995), 61–62; Viola Florence Barnes, *The Dominion of New England: A Study in British Colonial Policy* (New Haven: Yale University Press, 1923), esp. 5–46; Bathurst to Molesworth, 5 February 1685, BL, Loan 57/83, unfolioed; Committee of Trade and Plantations, Minutes, 3 March 1685, NA, CO 391/5, fol. 52r; London Newsletter, 30 March 1685, HRC, Pforzheimer/Box 10/Folder 6; John Freke to Locke, 28 June 1687, *Locke Correspondence,* 3:217–18; Philip S. Haffenden, "The Crown and the Colonial Charters, 1675–1688: Part II," *William and Mary Quarterly,* 3rd Ser., 15 (1958): 463–65.

28. EIC to general of India and president and council of Fort St. George, 25 January 1688, IOL, E/3/91, fol. 245r. After the revolution Child continued to insist that for the East India Company "to hold up against the Dutch and other foreign nations in India," it needed to have "no less than absolute sovereign power in India": Josiah Child (Wansted) to Sir Thomas Papillon, 22 October 1698, CKS, U1015/O17/2; EIC to president and council of Fort St. George, 24 February, 9 June 1686, IOL, E/3/91, fols. 54r, 70v; EIC's Commission for Establishing President and Council, [3 November 1686], IOL, E/3/91, fol. 113v; EIC to president and council of Surat, 23 March 1687, IOL, E/3/91, fol. 135v; EIC to general and council at Bombay, 28 September 1687, IOL, E/3/91, fol. 196r; EIC to president and council at Fort St. George, 28 September 1687, IOL, E/3/91, fol. 214v; EIC to general and council at Bombay, 27 August 1688, IOL, E/3/91, fols. 275–76.

29. London Newsletter, 14 January 1688, FSL, L.c. 1908; Child, *Supplement,* 7–8; Om Prakash, *European Commercial Enterprise in Pre-Colonial India* (Cambridge: Cambridge University Press, 1998), 148.

30. Child, *New Discourse of Trade,* 1; sig. [B3r], C6r; Child to Middleton, 1 September, 6 September 1683, BL, Add. 41822, fols. 25r, 28r; Child, *Supplement,* 1; Child, *A Discourse Concerning Trade,* 6–7; Child to Middleton, 6 September 1683, BL, Add. 41822, fol. 28v; Barillon (London) to Louis XIV, 14/24 December 1685, NA, PRO 31/3/162, fol. 66r; Bonrepaus (London) to Seignelay, 31 December/10 January 1685/86, NA, PRO 31/3/163, fol. 36r; Barillon (London) to Louis XIV, 8/18 April 1686, NA, PRO 31/3/165, fol. 23v; Barillon (London) to Louis XIV, 4/14 November 1686, NA, PRO 31/3/167, fol. 46r; Barillon and Bonrepaus to Louis XIV, 2/12 June 1687, NA, PRO 31/3/170, fols. 43–44; EIC to president and council of Fort St. George, 14 January, 22 October 1686, IOL, E/3/91, fols. 30v, 104; EIC to general and council at Bombay, 3 August 1687, IOL, E/3/91, fol. 160v; EIC to governor and council at York Fort at Bencoolen, 4 April 1688, IOL, E/3/91, fol. 258v; *An Impartial Vindication of the English East-India Company* (London: Samuel Tidmarsh, 1688), 90–96; EIC to president and council at Fort St. George, 22 October 1686, IOL, E/3/91, fols. 106–7; EIC to governor and council of India at Bombay, 3 August 1687, IOL, E/3/91, fol. 160r.

31. Child to Middleton, 6 September 1683, BL, Add. 41822, fol. 28v; Representation of the Deputies of Amsterdam, 1686, BL, Add. 41814, fol. 119v; EIC to general of India and council at Bombay, 27 August 1688, IOL, E/3/91, fol. 273r; Bonrepaus (London) to Seignelay, 11/21 March 1686, NA, PRO 31/3/165, fol. 74r;

London Newsletter, 9 July, 16 July 1687, FSL, L.c. 1821, 1831; Sir John Jacob to Huntingdon, 12 July 1687, HEH, HA 7148.

32. Mill, *History of British India,* 85–87; Secret Instructions to Capt. John Cribb, 9 July 1686, IOL, E/3/91, fol. 78r; Instructions for agent and council at Bengal, 14 January 1686, IOL, E/3/91, fols. 34–40; Bonrepaus (London) to Seignelay, 25 August/4 September 1687, NA, PRO 31/3/172, fols. 51–52; Dr. John St. John, His Information Regarding India, 1685–1688, CKS, U269/O82; Chaudhuri, *Trading World of Asia,* 117; Prakash, *European Commercial Enterprise,* 150; London Newsletter, 4 August 1688, Add. 4194, fol. 291v; Child, *Supplement,* 9; Newsletter addressed to Earl of Suffolk, 25 July 1688, BL, Add. 34487, fol. 17v; John Verney (London) to Sir Ralph Verney, ca. 24 July 1688, Buckinghamshire SRO, Verney MSS; *Some Remarks,* 4, 6–7; Tamworth Newsletter (London), 29 May 1690, HEH, HM 30659/10.

33. Cholmley (London) to John Aelst, 25 November 1684, North Yorkshire SRO, ZCG, unfolioed; Cholmley and Ambrose Isted to Aelst, November 1684, North Yorkshire SRO, ZCG, unfolioed; Newsletter from London, 14 August 1688, BL, Add. 4194, fol. 299. It is true that James's Declarations of Indulgence mentioned the association of labor and wealth creation. However, contemporaries knew that this was a late addition to the declaration meant solely to counter opposition arguments: Barillon (London) to Louis XIV, 3/13 May 1688, NA, PRO 31/3/177, fol. 16v.

34. Haffenden, "Crown and Colonial Charters," 452.

35. Armitage, *Ideological Origins of the British Empire,* 166; Terence Hutchinson, *Before Adam Smith: The Emergence of Political Economy, 1662–1776* (Oxford: Basil Blackwell, 1988), 56; T. R. Malthus, *Principles of Political Economy* (London: John Murray, 1820), 2.

36. Nicholas Barbon, *A Discourse of Trade* (London: Tho. Melbourn, 1690), sigs. A2–A3.

37. Barbon, *Discourse of Trade,* sig. A3; *Considerations Requiring Greater Care for Trade in England* (London: S. Crouch, 1695), 1–2, 11–12; *The Character and Qualifications of an Honest Loyal Merchant* (London: Robert Roberts, 1686), 11. See also Sir Francis Brewster, *Essays on Trade and Navigation* (London: Tho. Cockeril, 1695), 76.

38. William James, *Englands Interest* (London, 1689), 2; Daniel Defoe, *Taxes no Charge* (London: R. Chiswell, 1690), 12; James Whiston, *A Discourse of the Decay of Trade* (London: Samuel Crouch, 1693), 3; H. M., *England's Glory; or, The Great Improvement of Trade in General by a Royal Bank* (London: Tho. Bever, 1694), 20–21; sigs. A2v-A3r; Brewster, *Essays on Trade,* 1; Roger Coke, *A Detection of the Court and State of England,* 2 vols. (London, 1694), 2:15; Simon Patrick, "Sermon Preached before the King and Queen," 16 April 1690, in *The Works of Symon Patrick,* vol. 8, ed. Alexander Taylor (Oxford: Oxford University Press, 1858), 431; John Cary, *An Essay on the State of England in Relation to Its Trade* (London: Sam. Crouch, 1695), sig. [A7], 2, 6, 12, 23; Locke to John Cary, 2 May 1696, in *Correspondence of Locke and Clarke,* ed. Rand, 472; Customs Officers to Lords of the Treasury, 5 January 1694, BL, Add. 72564, fol. 43r. See also *A Discourse of the Necessity of Encouraging Mechanick Industry* (London: Richard Chiswell, 1690), 15, 21; Sir Richard Cocks, "A Charge," Michaelmas 1695, Bodleian, Eng.Hist.b.209, fol. 29v; and Bridgewater, "State Propositions," 1690s, HEH, EL 8443.

39. C. D. Chandaman, *The English Public Revenue, 1660–1688* (Oxford: Clarendon Press, 1975), 77–81, 87–88, 93; Michael J. Braddick, *The Nerves of State: Taxation and the Financing of the English State, 1558–1714* (Manchester: Manchester University Press, 1996), 102, 158–59, 172–74; For resentment, see William Williamson to Secretary Nicholas, 3 July 1662, CSPD, 428; Information by A. Bradley, 1662, CSPD, 614; ? to Charles II, 2 June 1664, CSPD, 604–5; Lord Treasurer Southampton and Lord Ashley to JPs for Lancashire, 8 November 1664, CSPD, 58; Proposal by Eady, 1664, CSPD, 148; Edward Bodham (King's Lynn) to Joseph Williamson, 5 December 1666, CSPD, 321; Case of the Borough of Southwark, 1665, CSPD, 179; Petition of William Harwood (Yorkshire), 11 April 1666, CSPD, 346; Wives of the Shipwrights and Ropers of Woolwich to Arlington, 1670, CSPD, 633. For evasion: Charles II to lord mayor and aldermen of London, 13 August 1662, CSPD, 459; Jonathan Trelawney to Joseph Williamson, 11 December 1663, CSPD, 371; Daniel Fleming (Penrith) to Joseph Williamson, 7 January 1664, CSPD, 433; Thomas Dade (Tannington, Suffolk) to

Charles II, 4 April 1664, CSPD, 544; Abraham Nelson (Garsdale, Yorkshire) to Charles II, 18 November 1664, CSPD, 78; George Williamson to Joseph Williamson, 4 March 1665, CSPD, 238. On riots: Testimony of Capt. Robert Atkinson, 26 November 1663, CSPD, 352; Testimony of Dobson, 1 February 1664, CSPD, 464; Warrant to the Warden of the Fleet, 17 August 1666, CSPD, 48; Muddiman's Newsletter, 24 November 1666, CSPD, 285; Advice Received from Norwich, 30 January 1668, CSPD, 204; Henry Coventry to Sir Robert Holt, 17 September 1672, CSPD, 626–27; John Lamplugh to Joseph Williamson, October 1675, CSPD, 369; David Hey, *The Fiery Blades of Hallamshire: Sheffield and Its Neighbourhood, 1660–1740* (Leicester: Leicester University Press, 1991), 136–39; Deposition of Robert Johnson, 30 May 1687, NA, CUST 48/3, 1117 (Staffordshire); Samuel Hardwicke to commissioners of excise and hearth tax, November 1687, NA, CUST 48/3, 161 (Cornwall); Commissioners of His Majesty's revenue to lords of the Treasury, 4 December 1688, NA, CUST 48/3, 226; London Newsletter, 28 February, 1689, HRC, Pforzheimer/Box 10/Folder 5; *Journal of the House of Commons,* 5 March 1689, 10:42; Col. John Birch, 1 March 1689, Grey, 9:130; Isaac Newton (Westminster) to John Covel, 2 March 1689, Trinity College, Cambridge, MS R.4.43, fol. 9r; "Speech against the Hearth Money," ca. 1689, BL, Stowe 304, fol. 70v; Halifax's Notes of Conversations with King William, 28 July 1689, BL, Althorp C9, fol. 37r.

40. Henry Horwitz, *Parliament, Policy and Politics in the Reign of William III* (Manchester: Manchester University Press, 1977), 40; Braddick, *Nerves of State,* 98–99; Colin Brooks, "Public Finance and Political Stability: The Administration of the Land Tax, 1688–1720," *Historical Journal* 17 (1974): 281–300; John Swynfen, 2 April 1690, Grey, 10:37; John Hampden, *Some Considerations about the Most Proper Way of Raising Money in the Present Conjuncture* [1691], 34; *A Proposal for an Equal Land-Tax* (London: Randall Taylor, 1691), 3, 13; Sir Richard Temple, Ledgerbook, 23 December 1677, 4 December 1684, 13 May 1687, HEH, ST 152, fols. 172v, 201r; Sir Richard Temple, *An Essay upon Taxes* (London: Tim. Goodwin, 1693), 5, 8, 22; William Bankes (London) to Roger Kenyon, 28 February 1689, Lancashire SRO, DD/KE/92, fol. 19r; Simon Harcourt, 2 April 1690, Grey, 10:37–38; Sir Christopher Musgrave, 1 April 1690, Grey, 10:37; Sir Edward Seymour, 11 January 1692, Grey, 10:227; David Stasavage, *Public Debt and the Birth of the Democratic State: France and Great Britain, 1688–1789* (Cambridge: Cambridge University Press, 2003), 108, 120.

41. H. J., *A Letter from a Gentleman in the Country to His Friend in the City* (London: G. C. for William Miller, 1691), 8–9; Charles Whyteford (Paris) to Walter Leslie, 29 April/9 May 1689, SCA, Bl 1/126/20; Aston, Diary, 13 March 1690; James Finton (Lancaster) to Sir Thomas Rawlinson, 23 September 1689, Bodleian, Rawlinson MSS, D863, fol. 35r.

42. "The Case of the Royal African Company," September/October 1689, NA, T 70/169, fol. 69v; Anderson, *Historical and Chronological Deduction,* 2:566; Shower was later retained as a lawyer by the opponents of the East India Company: New East India Company Minutes, 24 November 1692, Bodleian, Rawlinson MSS, C449, unfolioed; Sir Bartholomew Shower's Arguments, Nightingale and others v. Bridges, in *The English Reports,* vol. 89, ed. Max A. Robertson and Geoffrey Ellis (London: Stevens and Sons, 1908), 498–500.

43. Sir Batholomew Shower's Arguments, 500; W. Darrell Stump, "An Economic Consequence of 1688," *Albion* 6 (1974): 28; Horwitz, "East India Trade," 3; Pettigrew, "Free to Enslave," 11.

44. *The Interest of England Considered* (London: Walter Kettilby, 1694), sig. [A5r]; Roger Coke, *A Reply to an Answer from a Friend to the Apology for the English Nation* (London, 1692), 3; William Wilkinson, *Systema Africanum* (London, 1690), 5–6; Davies, *Royal African Company,* 46, 104, 129–30; Tim Keirn, "Monopoly, Economic Thought, and the Royal African Company," in *Early Modern Conceptions of Property,* ed. John Brewer and Susan Staves (London: Routledge, 1995), 427–66; Petition of the Royal African Company, 16 August 1689, PRO, T 70/169, fol. 63v.

45. N. T., *A Modest and Just Apology for; or, Defence of the Present East India Company* (London, 1690), 1; Letwin, *Josiah Child,* 23; Coke, *Reply to an Answer,* 4; *Reasons for Settling Admiralty Jurisdiction* (1690), 1.

46. Cary, *Essay on the State of England,* 47, 49, 52; Chaudhuri, *Trading World of Asia,* 96; Prakash, *European Commercial Enterprise,* 105, 119, 240; Bonrepaus, Report on the State of England, 1687, NA, PRO

31/3/174, fols. 113–14; *The Ancient Trades Decayed, Repaired Again* (London: T. N., 1678); John Blanch, *The Naked Truth* (London, 1696), 4–5, 13. John Blanch was a friend of the Whig Edward Clarke: Blanch (London) to Edward Clarke, 15 June 1696, Somerset SRO, DD/SF/3839; Blanch, *The Interest of England Considered* (London: Walter Kettilby, 1694); Edward Clarke, Notes on the EIC, 1690s, Somerset SRO, DD/SF/2604a; Entries Relating to Trade, 26 March, 7 May 1686, NA, CO 389/12, fols. 17–18, 21v. These complaints were renewed after the revolution: L'Hermitage (London) to States General, 1/11 September 1693, BL, Add. 17677NN, fol. 227r; The Case of the Japanners, ca. 1690s, Lancashire SRO, DD/K/1745; Proofs before the Committee for a Free Exportation of the Woolen Manufactures, 1693, Somerset SRO, DD/SF/4515/4; Report of Board of Trade, 23 December 1697, BL, Sloane 2902, fol. 173v; Khan, *East India Trade,* 246, 257–73.

47. Cholmley (London) to Robert Freeman, 12 February 1689, North Yorkshire SRO, ZCG, unfolioed; Cholmley to John Heatfield, 16 February 1689, North Yorkshire SRO, ZCG, unfolioed; Cholmley to John Chardin and Salvador Rodriguez, [March 1689], North Yorkshire SRO, ZCG, unfolioed; London Newsletter, 23 April 1689, FSL, L.c. 2006; Letter from London, 10/20 June 1689, MAE, CP/Angleterre 170, fol. 112r; John Verney (London) to Sir Ralph Verney, 2 May 1689, Buckinghamshire SRO, Verney MSS; Cholmley to Richard Browne, 1690, North Yorkshire SRO, ZCG, unfolioed; *Journal of the House of Commons,* 4 April 1689, 10:79; "A State of All the Duties," 14 September 1694, BL, Add. 72564, fol. 51; New East India Company Minutes, 12 October, 22 October, 24 October 1691, 6 October, 9 November, 15 November 1692, Bodleian, Rawlinson MSS, C449, unfolioed; John Pulteney (Whitehall) to Sir William Dutton Colt, 30 October 1691, BL, Add. 36662, fol. 198r; L'Hermitage (London) to States General, 1/11 September 1693, BL, Add. 17677NN, fol. 226v; *Reasons Humbly Offered against Grafting,* 7; Child (Wansted) to Papillon, 22 October 1698, CKS, U1015/O17/2.

48. Cholmley to ?, 14 January 1691, North Yorkshire SRO, ZCG, unfolioed; J. Hill (London) to Sir William Trumbull, 26 October 1691, Berkshire SRO, D/ED/C33; Horwitz, "East India Trade," 1–18; Chaudhuri, *Trading World of Asia,* 120. For the propaganda and lobbying: *A Letter to a Friend Concerning the Credit of the Nation* (London: E. Whitlock, 1697), 14. For the bribery: Cholmley to ?, 14 January 1691, North Yorkshire SRO, ZCG, unfolioed; Edward Clarke, Notes, 1690s, Somerset SRO, DD/SF/2604a; Joint Committee Report, 23 April 1695, HLRO, HL/PO/JT/1/1; Evelyn, *Diary,* 25 April 1695, 5:209; Sir Richard Temple, "The False Patriot Unmasked," ca. 1690, HEH, STT Lit (9), 15. Josiah Child recommended to the company that it buy the Duke of Bolton's lead to secure his support in Parliament: Child (Wansted) to Sir Thomas Cooke, 5 December 1693, IOL, H/40, fol. 154r. For the concession that Parliament not the king had the right to grant commissions to govern by martial law: EIC to Capt. Leonard Browne, 15 June 1689, IOL, E/3/92, fol. 30r.

49. *Orange Gazette,* 1 March 1689, [2]; Hampden, *Some Considerations,* 11; James, *Englands Interest,* 3. See also Thomas, *Historical Account,* 1.

50. *A Rambling Letter to a Friend* [1690], 1–2; Robert Molesworth (Copenhagen) to George Stepney, 11 October 1690, BL, Add. 37407, fol. 6r; Barbon, *Discourse of Trade,* sig. A2; Whiston, *Discourse of the Decay,* 2–3; Whiston, *To the King's Most Excellent Majesty* [1693], [1].

51. Istvan Hont, "Free Trade and the Economic Limits to Modern Politics: Neo-Machiavellian Political Economy Reconsidered," in *The Economic Limits to Modern Politics,* ed. John Dunn (Cambridge: Cambridge University Press, 1990), 64–65. Charles Davenant was on the East India Company's payroll for much of the 1690s: Davenant, Receipts of Payment from the East India Company, Bodleian, Rawlinson MSS, D747, fols. 194–201. Davenant had served as commissioner of the excise under James II: *Memoirs of the Secret Services of John Mackey* (London: Nichols and Sons, 1895), 91; Commissioners for the Excise to ?, 11 March 1691, NA, CUST 48/4, 111.

52. *Some Useful Reflections upon a Pamphlet Called a Brief Account of the Intended Bank of England* [1694], 3; Jerry Squirt, *Some Account of the Transactions of Mr. William Paterson* (London, 1695), 1–2; *Proposals Humbly Offer'd to the Consideration of This Present Parliament* (London: W. Pardoe, 1689), [1]; William Paterson, "An Inquiry into the State of the Union," 1717, in *The Writings of William Paterson,* 2nd ed., ed. Saxe Bannis-

ter (London: Judd and Glass, 1859), 2:63–64; John Dalrymple (The Hague) to Hamilton, 14/24 October 1691, NAS, GD 406/1/3557; Barbon, *Discourse of Trade,* 29–31.

53. Squirt, *Some Account,* 4–5; Horwitz, "East India Trade," 6–7; *A List of the Names of All the Subscribers to the Bank of England* [1694]; D. W. Jones, *War and Economy in the Age of William III and Marlborough* (Oxford: Basil Blackwell, 1988), 12–13, 296–301. The group may have first come together in agitating against the French trade in the 1670s: see "A Scheme of the Trade between England and France," 28 November 1674, BL, Add. 72890; Paterson, "Inquiry into the State of the Union," 64, 67.

54. *A Proposal to Raise a Million of Money by Credit on a Public Bank* [1692]; Gilbert Burnet, *History of His Own Time* (London: William Smith, 1838), 599; *A Brief Account of the Intended Bank of England* (London: Randal Taylor, 1694), 1–4.

55. H. M., *England's Glory; or, The Great Improvement of Trade in General by a Royal Bank* (London: Tho. Bever, 1694), sigs. A3r-A4r, 11–12, 18–19, 21–24, 31.

56. Cary, *Essay on the State of England,* 32; Brewster, *Essays on Trade,* 6, 109; Locke to Clarke, 6 August 1694, in *Correspondence of Locke and Clarke,* ed. Rand, 397; *A List of the Names,* 1694; Edward Clarke, Notes on the Bank, 1695/96, Somerset SRO, DD/SF/2764; Edward Clarke's Money Assets at the Time of His Death, 1710, Somerset SRO, DD/SF/1789; compare Craig Rose, *England in the 1690s: Revolution, Religion, and War* (Oxford: Blackwell, 1999), 135.

57. Hampden, *Some Considerations,* 31; Whiston, *Discourse of the Decay,* 9; Cary, *Essay on the State of England,* sig. A3r; Brewster, *Essays on Trade,* 1.

58. *Brief Account of the Intended Bank,* 16–17; Carruthers, *City of Capital,* 141–42; Extrait d'un Lettre de Londres, 9 February 1695, MAE, CP/Angleterre 173, fol. 35v; Burnet, *History of His Own Time,* 599; Sir Edward Seymour, 30 November 1689, Grey, 9:466; Paterson, "Inquiry into the State of the Union," 64.

59. Rubini, "Battle for the Banks," 697, 702, 712; Brewer, *Sinews of Power,* 153; Charles Montague to William Blathwayt, 3 July 1696, BL, Add. 34355, fol. 10v; Land Bank Minute Book, University of London, Senate House Library, MS 61; Anderson, *Origins of Commerce,* 2:211; Montague to Blathwayt, 29 May 1696, BL, Add. 34255, fol. 1v; Peter Le Neve (London) to Oliver Le Neve, 23 January 1696, Beinecke, Osborn Files 8983/8; John Lord Ashburnham (Ashburnham) to Richard Hoare, 15 April 1696, East Sussex SRO, ASH/840, 48; Montague to Blathwayt, 17/27 July 1696, BL, Add. 34355, fol. 14v; Carruthers, *City of Capital,* 142.

60. Henry Horwitz, *Parliament, Policy and Politics,* 131; *Some Considerations Offered against the Continuance of the Bank of England* [1694], 2; *Observations upon the Constitution of the Bank of England* [1694], 1; John Briscoe, *A Discourse of the Late Funds of the Million-Act, Lottery-Act, and Bank of England,* 2nd ed. (London: R. Baldwin, 1694), 4; Paterson, "Inquiry into the State of the Union," 64; *A Brief Account of the Intended Bank,* 2, 8; Burnet, *History of His Own Time,* 599; *Some Useful Reflections upon a Pamphlet,* 3. Defenders of the East India Company at this time accused their opponents, many of whom were involved in creating the bank, "of levelling," comparing their aspirations unfavorably to "our Levellers of England and anciently the tribunes of Rome": "The Humble Answer of the East India Company," May 1692, IOL, H/40, fol. 176r.

61. [Daniel Defoe], *An Essay upon Projects* (London, 1697), 1–2, 10–11, 19–20, 24; Defoe clearly distinguishes his discussion from the kind of projects delineated by Joan Thirsk in her *Economic Policy and Projects: The Development of a Consumer Society in Early Modern England* (Oxford: Clarendon Press, 1978), 1, 9.

62. Sir John Lowther similarly perceived a transformation in political discourse at about this moment: Lowther, Trade in General, 1680s, Cumbria SRO, Carlisle, D/Lons/W1/63, 11; Paul Slack, "The Politics of Consumption and England's Happiness in the Later Seventeenth Century," *English Historical Review* 122 (2007): 609–25.

63. Armitage, *Ideological Origins of the British Empire,* 148.

64. Colley Cibber, *An Apology* (London: John Watts, 1740), 40; Steve Pincus, "England and the World in the 1650s," in *Revolution and Restoration: England in the 1650s,* ed. John Morrill (London: Collins and Brown, 1992), 143–46; David Smith, "The Struggle for New Constitutional and Institutional Forms," in *Revolution*

and Restoration, ed. Morrill, 21–23; Allan I. Macinnes, *The British Revolution, 1629–1660* (New York: Palgrave, 2005), 209–10; Robert Brenner, *Merchants and Revolution: Commercial Change, Political Conflict, and London's Overseas Traders, 1550–1653* (London: Verso, 2003), 648.

65. David Stasavage, "Partisan Politics and Public Debt: The Importance of the 'Whig Supremacy' for Briatin's Financial Revolution," *European Review of Economic History* 11 (2007): 124.

66. For a powerful argument that state policies shaped the direction of the English economy after 1689, see David Ormrod, *The Rise of Commercial Empires: England and the Netherlands in the Age of Mercantilism, 1650–1770* (Cambridge: Cambridge University Press, 2003), 342–46.

CHAPTER 13. *Revolution in the Church*

1. Charles Leslie, "Querela Temporum," 1694, in *A Collection of Scarce and Valuable Tracts,* 2nd ed., vol. 9, ed. Walter Scott (London: T. Cadell and W. Davies et al., 1813), 518; Melfort (Rome) to John Caryl, 12/22 March 1690, BL, Lansdowne 1163A, fol. 39r; Gilbert Burnet, *History of His Own Time* (London: William Smith, 1838), 569; Burnet, *The New Preface and Additional Chapter* (London: D. Midwinter and B. Cowse, 1713), 9.

2. Henry Horwitz, *Revolution Politicks: The Career of Daniel Finch, Second Earl of Nottingham, 1647–1730* (Cambridge: Cambridge University Press, 1968), 99; G. V. Bennett, "Conflict in the Church," in *Britain after the Glorious Revolution, 1689–1714,* ed. Geoffrey Holmes (Basingstoke: Macmillan, 1969), 161, 165; Bennett, "King William III and the Episcopate," in *Essays in Modern Church History,* ed. G. V. Bennett and J. D. Walsh (New York: Oxford University Press, 1966), 105, 122, 124–31; Gordon Rupp, *Religion in England, 1688–1791* (Oxford: Clarendon Press, 1986), 74; John Spurr, *The Restoration Church of England, 1646–1689* (New Haven and London: Yale University Press, 1991), 379.

3. Gerald M. Straka, *Anglican Reaction to the Revolution of 1688* (Madison: State Historical Society of Wisconsin, 1962), ix; Tony Claydon, *William III and the Godly Revolution* (Cambridge: Cambridge University Press, 1996), 44, 159–60, 229. At one point John Spurr denied that there was a distinctively Latitudinarian outlook: Spurr, "'Latitudinarianism' and the Restoration Church," *Historical Journal* 31 (1988): 77, 82. Spurr appears since to have modified his position in Mark Goldie and Spurr, "Politics and the Restoration Parish: Edward Fowler and the Struggle for St. Giles Cripplegate," *English Historical Review* 109 (1994): 572–96. Marshall says they became less distinctive after 1689. John Marshall, *John Locke, Toleration and Early Enlightenment Culture* (Cambridge: Cambridge University Press, 1994), 39.

4. J. P. Kenyon, *Revolution Principles: The Politics of Party, 1689–1720* (Cambridge: Cambridge University Press, 1977), 77; Straka, *Anglican Reaction,* viii; J. C. D. Clark, *English Society, 1660–1832,* 2nd ed. (Cambridge: Cambridge University Press, 2000), 84; Claydon, *William III and the Godly Revolution,* 58–59; Marshall, *Locke,* 284; Marshall, "John Locke and Latitudinarianism," in *Philosophy, Science, and Religion in England, 1640–1700,* ed. Richard Kroll, Richard Ashcraft, and Perez Zagorin (Cambridge: Cambridge University Press, 1992), 282; Craig Rose, *England in the 1690s: Revolution, Religion, and War* (Oxford: Blackwell, 1999), 182.

5. Richard Ashcraft, "Latitudinarianism and Toleration: Historical Myth versus Political History," in *Philosophy, Science, and Religion in England, 1640–1700,* ed. Kroll, Ashcraft, and Zagorin, 154, 160; Jon Parkin, *Science, Religion and Politics in Restoration England: Richard Cumberland's "De Legibus Naturae"* (Woodbridge: Boydell, 1999), 29, 33; Claydon, *William III and the Godly Revolution,* 163. See also Kenyon, *Revolution Principles,* 84.

6. Others have made gestures in this interpretative direction: Mark Goldie, "John Locke, Jonas Proast and Religious Toleration, 1688–1692," in *The Church of England, c. 1689–c. 1833,* ed. John Walsh, Colin Haydon, and Stephen Taylor (Cambridge: Cambridge University Press, 1993), 143–71; Goldie and Spurr, "Politics and the Restoration Parish," 572–73; G. M. Trevelyan, *The English Revolution, 1688–89* (Oxford: Oxford University Press, 1938), 87.

7. Joseph Hill (Geneva) to Sir William Trumbull, 18/28 February 1689, Berkshire SRO, D/ED/C33; Andrew Swatland, *The House of Lords in the Reign of Charles II* (Cambridge: Cambridge University Press, 1996), 255; Bennett, "Conflict in the Church," 156; Robert Beddard, "The Commission for Ecclesiastical Promotions, 1681–1684: An Instrument of Tory Reaction," *Historical Journal* 10 (1967): 15, 39.

8. Beddard, "Bishop Cartwright's Death-Bed," *Bodleian Library Record* 11 (1984): 220–21; Dr. William Denton to Sir Ralph Verney, 25 August 1686, Buckinghamshire SRO, Verney MSS; Anthony Wood, *Athenae Oxonienses,* 3 vols., 2nd ed. (London: R. Knaplock, D. Midwinter, J. Tonson, 1721), 2:1170, 1173 1721; Thomas Birch, *The Life of the Reverend Dr. John Tillotson* (London: J. and R. Tonson et al., 1752), 149; Newcastle (Newcastle) to Sunderland, 4 October 1688, NA, SP 31/4, fol. 89r; ? (Yorkshire) to James Harrington, March 1688, BL, Add. 36707, fol. 20v; Sir Charles Cotterell to Sir William Trumbull, 26 March 1688, BL, Trumbull MSS 39, unfolioed; William Westby, Memoirs, 21 March 1688, FSL, V.a. 469, fol. 16v; White Kennett, *A Complete History of England,* vol. 3 (London: Brab. Aylmer et al., 1706), 491; "A Brief Account Concerning Matters of Fact Touching the Prince of Orange," Bodleian, Rawlinson MSS, D1079, fol. 1r.

9. William Sancroft, "Reason against Subscription," 1687, Bodleian, Tanner 29, fol. 13r; Morrice, Entering Book, 30 April 1687, 31 Q, 114, 107; Worcester (Oxford) to Thomas Turner, 31 May 1687, Bodleian, Rawlinson MSS, Letters 91, fol. 66r; Dr. Paman (London) to Sir Ralph Verney, 4 May 1687, Buckinghamshire SRO, Verney MSS; Jonathan Trelawney, bishop of Bristol (Bristol) to Sancroft, 1 July 1687, Bodleian, Tanner 29, fol. 42v; Morrice, Entering Book, 10 November 1688, 312; Earl of Clarendon, Diary, 20 February, 12 May, 3 November 1688, Singer, 2:163–64, 171, 200; Francis Turner, bishop of Ely (Ely), to Sancroft, 6 June 1687, Bodleian, Tanner 29, fol. 34r; William Lloyd, bishop of St. Asaph, to Sancroft, 21 June 1687, Bodleian, Tanner 29, fol. 39v. The possible exception is Herbert Croft, bishop of Hereford. Even though Lloyd detested Cartwright, Parker, Crew, and Watson, he should not be grouped as a follower of Sancroft. He had a long history of sympathy for Dissent and was willing to countenance resistance. Not surprisingly, he was the lone prerevolutionary bishop to enjoy translation after 1688.

10. "Some Account of the Revolution," Bodleian, Eng.Hist.b.205, fol. 98v; London Newsletter, 26 March 1689, FSL, L.c. 1994; Morrice, Entering Book, 26 January 1689, 29 December 1688, 5 January, 12 January, 16 March 1689, DWL, 31 Q, 433, 406–7, 415, 422, 503; Edward Harley to Robert Harley, 23 February 1689, BL, Add. 40621, fol. 26r; Birch, *Life of Tillotson,* 155; Kennett, *Complete History,* 517.

11. Rose, *England in the 1690s,* 154; Straka, *Anglican Reaction,* 29; Spurr, *Restoration Church of England,* 34–36, 83. In 1689 about 4 percent lost their places for failure to accept the new regime; in 1662 around 20 percent lost their places; Sir William Boothby (Ashbourne, Derbyshire) to Dr. Anthony Horneck, 9 July 1689, BL, Add. 71692, fol. 105; Robert Harley (Brampton) to Sir Edward Harley, 11 April 1689, BL, Add. 70014, fol. 211r; Charles Trumbull (Hadleigh) to Sir William Trumbull, 25 October 1689, BL, Add. 72513, fol. 17r; Isaac Newton (Westminster) to John Covel, 2 March 1689, Trinity College, Cambridge, MS R.4.43, fol. 9r.

12. These men were John Tillotson (Canterbury, 1691); Richard Kidder (Bath and Wells, 1691); Gilbert Ironside (Bristol, 1689; Hereford, 1691); John Hall (Bristol, 1691); Simon Patrick (Chichester, 1689; Ely, 1691); Robert Grove (Chichester, 1691); Edward Fowler (Gloucester, 1691); William Lloyd (Lichfield, 1692); Thomas Tenison (Lincoln, 1692); John Moore (Norwich, 1691); John Hough (Oxford, 1690); Richard Cumberland (Peterborough, 1691); Gilbert Burnet (Salisbury, 1689); Edward Stillingfleet (Worcester, 1689); Humphrey Humphries (Bangor, 1689); Edward Jones (St. Asaph, 1692); John Sharp (York, 1691); and Nicholas Stratford (Chester, 1689). Although this chapter is based on analysis of the writings of all these bishops, it has proved impossible to discover much about Edward Jones.

13. Horwitz, *Revolution Politicks,* 262; Thomas Newcome, ed., *The Life of John Sharpe,* vol. 1 (London: C. and J. Rivington, 1825), 15 (hereafter cited as *Life of Sharpe*); Timothy Goodwyn, *The Life and Character of That Eminent and Learned Prelate, the Late Dr. Edward Stillingfleet* (London: J. Heptinstall, 1710), 59; John Sharp to Nottingham, 1689, in *Life of Sharpe,* 104–5; Amy Edith Robinson, ed., *The Life of Richard Kidder,*

D. D. Bishop of Bath and Wells Written by Himself, Somerset Record Society, vol. 37 (Frome: Somerset Record Society, 1924), 24–25 (hereafter cited as *Life of Kidder*); Burnet, *History of His Own Time,* 241–42.

14. Goodwyn, *Life of Stillingfleet,* 19; David Underdown, *Pride's Purge: Politics in the Puritan Revolution* (London: George Allen and Unwin, 1971), 104–5; Richard Cust, "Politics and the Electorate in the 1620s," in *Conflict in Early Stuart England,* ed. Cust and Ann Hughes (London: Longman, 1989), 157; *Life of Kidder,* 21; Thomas Burnet, "Life of Gilbert Burnet," in *Bishop Burnet's History of His Own Time,* ed. T. Burnet (London: A. Millar, 1753), xxi–xxii; Gilbert Burnet, *The History of the Reformation of the Church of England; First Part,* 2nd ed. (London: T. H. for Richard Chiswell, 1681), sig. [(b)2r].

15. Simon Patrick, Autobiography, in *The Works of Symon Patrick,* vol. 9, ed. Alexander Taylor (Oxford: Oxford University Press, 1858), 438. Patrick later maintained a friendship with Lady Rachel Russell: Lois G. Schwoerer, *Lady Rachel Russell: "One of the Best of Women"* (Baltimore: Johns Hopkins University Press, 1988), 150, 194–95; *Life of Kidder,* 11–12; Gilbert Burnet, *History of the Reformation of the Church of England; Second Part,* 2nd ed. (London: T. H. for Richard Chiswell, 1683), sig. [a2r]; Birch, *Life of Tillotson,* 131; Burnet, "Life of Gilbert Burnet," xxxv; Gilbert Burnet (Hague) to Robert Boyle, 4 June 1686, in *The Works of the Honourable Robert Boyle,* ed. Thomas Birch (London: W. Johnston et al., 1772), 6:626 (hereafter cited as Boyle, *Works*).

16. Thomas Dent to William Wotton, 20 May 1699, and Gilbert Burnet, "Memorandum," both in *Robert Boyle by Himself and His Friends,* ed. Michael Hunter (London: William Pickering, 1994), 105–6, 28; *Life of Kidder,* 17; Robert Boyle to Burnet, [June 1686], Boyle, *Works,* 6:626–27; Burnet to Boyle, 4 June 1686, in Boyle, *Works,* 6:625–26; Burnet, *History of the Reformation; First Part,* sig. [(b)2r]; Wood, *Athenae,* 2:877. Barlow, unlike Boyle, had come to despise religious toleration. See Robert Beddard, "Tory Oxford," in *Seventeenth-Century Oxford,* ed. Nicholas Tyacke (Oxford: Clarendon Press, 1997), 884; Tyacke, "Religious Controversy," in *Seventeenth-Century Oxford,* ed. Tyacke, 605–6.

17. N. Toinard to Locke, 11/21 March 1689, in *Locke Correspondence,* 3:581; Marshall, *Locke,* 78, 80; Marshall, "John Locke and Latitudinarianism," 253; Locke (London) to Edward Clarke, 13 April 1689, *Locke Correspondence,* 3:603; Locke (London) to Philippus Von Limborch, 11 December 1694, *Locke Correspondence,* 5:237–38, 3:603; Mark Goldie, "John Locke, Jonas Proast and Religious Toleration," in *The Church of England, c. 1689–c. 1833,* ed. John Walsh, Stephen Taylor, and Colin Haydon (Cambridge: Cambridge University Press, 1993), 144, 152, 157, 165.

18. Matthew Sylvester, ed., *Reliquiae Baxterianae,* 3 vols. (London: T. Parkhurst et al., 1696), 2:386; Burnet, "Autobiography," in *A Supplement to Burnet's History of My Own Time,* ed. H. C. Foxcroft (Oxford: Clarendon Press, 1902), 463; Spurr, *Restoration Church of England,* 47–49; Birch, *Life of Tillotson,* 60; Burnet, *History of His Own Time,* 128–29.

19. Burnet, *History of His Own Time,* 130; William Lloyd, *A Sermon Preached at the Funeral of the Right Reverend Father in God John Late Lord Bishop of Chester* (London: A. C. for Henry Brome, 1672), 34; Wood, *Athenae,* 2:506–7, 1184; Barbara Shapiro, *John Wilkins, 1614–1672: An Intellectual Biography* (Berkeley: University of California Press, 1969), 4, 151–52, 251–53; Birch, *Life of Tillotson,* 6; Beddard, "Restoration Oxford," in *Seventeenth-Century Oxford,* ed. Tyacke, 834.

20. Burnet, "Life of Gilbert Burnet," xxi.

21. *Life of Sharpe,* 28–29; *Life of Kidder,* 46, 48–49, 62; Patrick, Autobiography, 472; Clarendon, Diary, 14 December 1688, 2:225; William Whiston, *Memoirs of the Life and Writings* (London, 1749), 41; Burnet, "Autobiography," 487.

22. Philip Bliss, ed., *Athenae Oxenienses* (London: Lackington et al., 1820), 4:512–13; "Archdeacon Payne's Life of Cumberland," in *Richard Cumberland: A Philosophical Enquiry into the Laws of Nature,* ed. John Towers (Dublin: Samuel Powell, 1750), app., 71; Thomas Newlin, trans., *Bishop Parker's History of His Own Time* (London: Charles Purington, 1727), 323–24; Sylvester, *Reliquiae Baxterianae,* 3:157; Kennett, *Complete History,* 302; William Jane, *A Letter to a Friend Concerning Some Quaeries* [1689], 2.

23. Burnet, *History of the Reformation; First Part,* sig. (b)v, [(b)2]; Dr. Thomas Barlow to R. S., in *The Genuine Remains of That Learned Prelate Dr. Thomas Barlow* (London: John Dunton, 1693), 181; Burnet, *History of the Reformation; Second Part,* sigs. av-[a2r]; Burnet, "Life of Gilbert Burnet," xxii–xxiii. James II hated the *History:* Daniel Defoe, *The Advantages of the Present Settlement* (London: Richard Chiswell, 1689), 13; Gilbert Burnet, *Reflections upon a Pamphlet* (London: R. Chiswell, 1696), 80; William Lloyd, *A Sermon Preached before the House of Lords* (London: M. C. for Henry Brome, 1680), 26; Birch, *Life of Tillotson,* 60–61; J. A. I. Champion, *The Pillars of Priestcraft Shaken: The Church of England and Its Enemies, 1660–1730* (Cambridge: Cambridge University Press, 1992), 64, 78–79; Sir Robert Howard, *A Two-Fold Vindication* (London, 1696), 95.

24. Samuel Parker to ?, 1685, Bodleian, Tanner 31, fol. 173v; Burnet, *History of His Own Time,* 307; Titus Oates, *A Display of Tyranny, First Part* (London, 1689), sig. [A5]r.

25. *Life of Sharpe,* 30–31, 48–49; Robert Kirk, "Sermons, Occurrences . . . ," 1690, Edinburgh SUL, La.III.545, fol. 137r; Patrick, Autobiography, 454; *Life of Kidder,* 37.

26. *Life of Kidder,* 37; Patrick, Autobiography, 490, 509–10; Goodwyn, *Life of Stillingfleet,* 58–59; William Sancroft, "Some Proceedings," May 1688, Bodleian, Tanner 28, fol. 38r; John Tillotson (London) to Sancroft, [May 1688], Bodleian, Tanner 28, fol. 37r; James Johnston to ?, 23, 27 May 1688, BL, Add. 34515, fols. 65v, 67v.

27. Morrice, Entering Book, 5 May 1688, DWL, 31 Q, 254; Burnet, "Life of Gilbert Burnet," xxx, xxxii; Burnet, *History of the Reformation; Second Part,* sig. [a2]; Halifax, "Spencer House Journals," in *The Life and Letters of Sir George Savile, Bart. First Marquis of Halifax,* vol. 2, ed. H. C. Foxcroft (London: Longmans, Green, 1898), 216, 226; Thomas Warton, *The Life and Literary Remains of Ralph Bathurst* (London: R. and J. Dodsley, C. Bathurst, J. Fletcher, 1761), 63; Birch, *Life of Tillotson,* 151; Kennett, *Complete History,* 642; *Life of Sharpe,* 109–10. Sharpe's later Toryism came as a great surprise to many who knew him well: Burnet, "Original Memoirs," in *Supplement,* ed. Foxcroft, 359; Burnet, "Autobiography," 504; Clarendon, Diary, 11 March 1689, 2:269; Patrick, Autobiography, 520.

28. Richard Doebner, ed., *Memoirs of Mary Queen of England, 1689–1693* (London: David Nutt, 1886), 14, 18, 21, 24, 37, 39, 43; *Memoirs of the Life and Times of the Most Reverend Father in God, Dr. Thomas Tennison,* 3rd ed. (London: J. Roberts, 1716?), 19, 23; Goldie, "John Locke, Jonas Proast and Religious Toleration," 163; Albeville (Hague) to Lord Preston, 9/19 November 1688, BL, Add. 34517, fol. 11v; Edward Fowler, *Memoirs of the Life and Death of Our Late Most Gracious Queen Mary,* 2nd ed. (London: B. Aylmer and J. Wyat, 1712), 12; Burnet, *New Preface,* 18.

29. John Fell (bishop of Oxford) to Lord Hatton, 12 July 1685, in *Correspondence of the Family of Hatton,* vol. 2, ed. Edward Maunde Thompson, Camden Society, n.s., 23 (1878): 58–59; Edmund Elys, "The Third Letter of the Truly Religious and Loyal Gentry," 1687, Bodleian, Tanner 29, fol. 16v; Thomas Sprat (bishop of Rochester), *A True Account and Declaration of the Horrid Conspiracy against the Late King* (London: Thomas Newcombe, 1685), 159; Thomas Sprat to Sancroft, 11 April 1685, Bodleian, Tanner 31, fol. 22r.

30. Morrice, Entering Book, 22 December 1688, DWL, 31 Q, 379, 381–82; Edward Harley to Robert Harley, 22 January 1689, BL, Add. 40621, fol. 5r; Francis Turner to Sancroft, [11 January 1689], Bodleian, Tanner 28, fols. 318–21; Lloyd to Bentinck, 17 December 1688, NA, SP 8/2/Pt. 2, fol. 91r; Thomas Ken (bishop of Bath and Wells) to Dartmouth, 23 September 1688, Staffordshire SRO, D(w) 1778/I/i/1280; Morrice, Entering Book, 2 February 1689, DWL, 31 Q, 450; Wood, *Athenae,* 2:988.

31. Beddard, "Tory Oxford," 893–97; G. V. Bennett, "Against the Tide: Oxford under William III," in *The Eighteenth Century,* ed. L. S. Sutherland and L. G. Mitchell (Oxford: Clarendon Press, 1986), 42; William Pittis, *Memoirs of the Life of the Late Reverend Dr. South* (London: E. Curll, 1721), 108, 114; Sancroft to James II, 29 July 1686, Bodleian, Tanner 30, fol. 93r; Beddard, "Restoration Oxford," 839.

32. William Lloyd, *A Sermon at the Funeral of Sir Edmund-Bury Godfrey* (London: M. Clark for Henry Brome, 1678); Lloyd to Sancroft, 20 April 1686, Bodleian, Tanner 30, fol. 24r; A. Tindal Hart, *William Lloyd, 1627–1717* (London: SPCK, 1952), 30–34; Samuel Parker to ?, 1685, Bodleian, Tanner 31, fol. 173r;

Gilbert Burnet, *A Letter Written upon the Discovery of the Plot* (London: H. Brome and R. Chiswell, 1678); Wood, 5 November, 23 December 1678, in *Life and Times,* ed. Clark, 2:422, 428; Goldie and Spurr, "Politics and the Restoration Parish," 584; Birch, *Life of Tillotson,* 81–82.

33. Wood, [August 1681], 29 November 1684, in *Life and Times,* ed. Clark, 2:553, 3:118; Wood, *Athenae,* 2:994, 1029; *Life of Kidder,* 36; Goldie and Spurr, "Politics and the Restoration Parish," 572–96; Parker to ?, 1685, Bodleian, Tanner 31, fol. 172r; Patrick, Autobiography, 451, 541; Wood, 9 April, 23 April 1685, in *Life and Times,* ed. Clark, 3:137, 141; J. T. (Oxford) to Philip Henry, 6 May 1685, Bodleian, Eng.Lett.e.29, fol. 8r.

34. William Stanley (Hague) to Sancroft, 24 January/3 February 1688, Bodleian, Tanner 29, fol. 132r; Patrick, Autobiography, 513; William Wake, Autobiography, LPL, 2932, fols. 55, 61–62; Birch, *Life of Tillotson,* 167–68; Richard Davies, *An Account of the Convincement, Exercises, Services and Travels of that Ancient Servant of the Lord Richard Davies* (London: J. Sowle, 1710), 243; *Life of Kidder,* 46; Van Citters (London) to States General, 24 February/5 March 1688, BL, Add. 34510, fol. 98; James Fraser (London) to Sir Robert Southwell, 7 April 1688, FSL, V.b. 287 (57); Southwell (Kingsweston) to Weymouth, 4 April 1687, Longleat House, Thynne MSS 15, fol. 169v; Gilbert Burnet, "Meditations on the Impending Expedition," 1688, in *Supplement,* ed. Foxcroft, 522, 527.

35. Burnet to Shrewsbury, 7 September 1689, NA, SP 32/2, fol. 6; Burnet, *Reflections,* 38–39.

36. John Moore, *Sermons on Several Subjects* (London: W. Taylor, J. Hooke, and T. Caldecott, 1715), "Sermon 2: 27 January 1684," 69–70; William Lloyd, "Speech Prepared . . . to Have Been Spoken at the Trial," June 1688, Bodleian, Tanner 28, fol. 101r; Gilbert Burnet, *The Citation,* 27 June 1687 [1687], 6; Burnet, *An Answer to a Paper Printed with Allowance* [1687], 6; Burnet, *An Enquiry into the Measures of Submission* [London, 1688], 5–6; Burnet, *Reflections,* 43.

37. Burnet, "Meditations on the Impending Expedition," 524; Edward Fowler (bishop of Gloucester), *An Answer to the Paper Delivered by Mr. Ashton at His Execution* (London: Robert Clavell, 1690), 21; Fowler, *Memoirs of the Life and Death of Our Late Most Gracious Queen Mary,* 2nd ed. (London: B. Aylmer and J. Wyat, 1712), 25; Burnet, *Reflections,* 45.

38. John Moore (bishop of Norwich), *A Sermon Preach'd before the King* (London: Will. Rogers, 1696), 7; Edward Stillingfleet (bishop of Worcester), *Christian Magnanimity* (London: Henry Mortlocke, 1690), 36; Edward Stillingfleet, "Sermon not Preached," 1694, in *Miscellaneous Discourses on Several Occasions* (London: S. Buckley, 1735), 399–400.

39. Burnet, *Reflections,* 40, 42, 90–91; Birch, *Life of Tillotson,* 123; John Tillotson, "Sermon Preached 29 May 1693," in *The Works of the Most Reverend Dr. John Tillotson,* 10th ed., vol. 1, ed. Ralph Berker (London: J. J. and P. Knapton, 1735), 1:214.

40. Fowler, *Answer to the Paper,* 18, 23; Fowler, *A Vindication of the Divines of the Church of England* (London: Brabazon Aylmer, 1689), 13–14. Late in Charles II's reign Fowler had been under immense pressure to clear himself from the aspersions of Whiggery. He then preached a sermon very much circumscribing the right to resist. But even then, he had left a clear opening for resistance in extreme cases: Fowler, *A Sermon Preached at the General Meeting of Gloucestershire-Men* (London: T. B. for Brabazon Aylmer, 1685), 10.

41. Thomas Hearne, 6 February 1710, in *Remarks and Collections of Thomas Hearne,* 2 vols., ed. C. E. Doble (Oxford: Oxford Historical Society, 1885–86), 2:343; "An Account of the Visitation of S. M. Magd. College," 22 October 1687, Bodleian, Tanner 29, fol. 97v; "An Account of the Visitation," 21 October 1687, Bodleian, MSS Tanner 29, fol. 94v; Hearne, 17 February 1706, in *Remarks and Collections,* ed. Doble, 1:187; William Nicolson, 16 December 1702, in *The London Diaries of William Nicolson, Bishop of Carlisle, 1702–1718,* ed. Clyve Jones and Geoffrey Holmes (Oxford: Clarendon Press, 1985), 146; Hearne, 16 September 1706, in *Remarks and Collections,* ed. Doble, 1:288.

42. Morrice, Entering Book, 29 December 1688, DWL, 31 Q, 394; Simon Patrick, "A Sermon Preached before the Lords," 26 November 1691, in *Works,* vol. 8, ed. Taylor, 448–49, 460; Patrick, *A Sermon Preached at St. Paul's Covent Garden,* 31 January 1689 (London: Richard Bentley, 1689), 22, 24; Patrick, "A Sermon against Murmering," 17 March 1689, in *Works,* vol. 8, ed. Taylor, 414–16.

43. John Moore, *A Sermon Preach'd before the House of Lords,* 31 January 1698 (London: R. R. for W. Rogers, 169[8]), 7, 24; Moore, *Sermon Preach'd before the King,* 17; Hearne, 7 March 1706, in *Remarks and Collections,* ed. Doble, 1:200.

44. Humphrey Humphreys (bishop of Bangor), *A Sermon Preach'd before the House of Lords,* 30 January 1696 (London: John Everingham, 1696), 20, 27; Hearne, 14 April 1706, in *Remarks and Collections,* ed. Doble, 1:224–25; J. W. Gough, "James Tyrrell, Whig Historian and Friend of John Locke," *Historical Journal* 19, no. 3 (1976): 605.

45. Linda Kirk, *Robert Cumberland and Natural Law* (Cambridge: James Clarke, 1987), 18–19, 76; "Archdeacon Payne's Life of Cumberland," app. 74.

46. Burnet, "Meditations on the Impending Expedition," 522; Gilbert Burnet, *An Enquiry into the Measures of Submission* [London, 1688], [1], 2, 7, 9–10; Gilbert Burnet, "A Letter concerning Some Reflections," 1687, in Burnet, *A Collection of Papers Relating to the Present Juncture of Affairs in England* (1688/89), 4; Burnet, *Reflections,* 36–37; Burnet, *Reasons against Repealing the Acts of Parliament Concerning the Test* (1687), 6; Clarendon, Diary, 11 January 1689, 2:244.

47. Burnet, "Life of Gilbert Burnet," xxxii; Burnet, *Reflections,* 31–32; Gilbert Burnet, *A Sermon Preached at the Coronation,* 11 April 1689 (London: J. Starkey and Richard Chiswell, 1689), 5,13. See also Burnet, *An Exhortation to Peace and Union,* Sermon Preached at St. Lawrence-Jury, 26 November 1689 (London: Richard Chiswell, 1689), 9.

48. Lloyd to Sancroft, 1685?, Bodleian, Tanner 33, fol. 4r; Lloyd, Speech not Spoken, 29 June 1688, BL, Add. 74246, fol. 105; Lloyd, *A Discourse of God's Ways of Disposing Kingdoms* (London: H. Hills for Thomas Jones, 1691), sig. A2r.

49. Lloyd, *Discourse of God's Ways,* 64–66; Lloyd, *A Sermon Preached before Their Majesties at Whitehall,* 5 November 1689 (London: Robert Clavell, 1689), 27–29; Lloyd, *The Pretences of the French Invasion Examined* (London: R. Clavel, 1692), 12.

50. Stillingfleet, "Sermon not Preached," 403–4, 439; Stillingfleet, *A Discourse Concerning the Unreasonableness of a New Separation* (London: Richard Chiswell, 1689), 5, 30; Stillingfleet, "Case of Reading King James' Declaration 1688," in *Miscellaneous Discourses,* 369–70.

51. Thomas Tenison, *A Sermon Concerning Doing Good to Posterity* (London: Richard Chiswell, 1690), 21; Tension, *A Discourse Concerning the Ecclesiastical Commission Open'd in the Jerusalem Chamber* (London: Richard Chiswell, 1689), 1; Clarendon, Diary, 7 January 1690, 2:300; Hearne, 23 June 1708, in *Remarks and Collections,* ed. Doble, 2:115.

52. Robert Grove, *Seasonable Advice to the Citizens, Burgesses, and Free-Holders of England* (London: Walter Kettilby, 1685), 6–7, 11, 13, 18–19, 32; Grove, *A Short Defence of the Church and Clergy of England* (London: J. Macock for Walter Kettilby, 1681), 78.

53. London Newsletter, 31 January 1689, FSL, L.c. 1966; Hamon London Newsletter, 31 January 1689, Beinecke, OSB Shelves fb.210; *Life of Sharpe,* 65, 95, 256.

54. Dr. Francis Turner (bishop of Ely) to ?, 17 February 1689, in Robert Beddard, ed., "The Loyalist Opposition in the Interregnum: A Letter of Dr. Francis Turner, Bishop of Ely, on the Revolution of 1688," *Bulletin of the Institute of Historical Research* 40 (1967): 109; Burnet, *Reflections,* 49–50; Tillotson to Bentinck, 1689, in Birch, *Life of Tillotson,* 153; Clarendon, Diary, 23 May 1689, 2:277; Nicholas Stratford to James Harrington, 9 March 1689, BL, Add. 36707, fol. 61r; Patrick, Autobiography, 519; Hearne, 25 November 1705, in *Remarks and Collections,* ed. Doble, 1:97; Wood, 31 August 1689, in *Life and Times,* ed. Clark, 3:309.

55. Horwitz, *Parliament, Policy and Politics,* 56, 337.

56. John Gadbury (London) to Sir Robert Owen, 16 May 1685, National Library of Wales, Brogynton MSS [841]; John Walker (counselor in Norwich) to W. Sancroft, Bodleian, Tanner 28, fol. 323r; Kirk, "Sermons, Occurrences . . . ," 1690, fols. 142–43.

57. Burnet, *New Preface,* 12–13; Burnet, *History of His Own Time,* 569–70.

58. The phrase is Richard Ashcraft's.

59. Mark Goldie, "The Theory of Religious Intolerance in Restoration England," in *From Persecution to Toleration,* ed. Ole Peter Grell, Jonathan I. Israel, and Nicholas Tyacke (Oxford: Clarendon Press, 1991), 334; Bennett, "William III and the Episcopate," 111; Rose, *England in the 1690s,* 184, 298.

60. Patrick, Autobiography, 516–17; Tillotson, "Sermon at the Yorkshire Feast," 3 December 1678, *Sermons on Several Subjects and Occasions,* 3 vols. London: R. Ware, et al., 1742), 25; Patrick, *Sermon Preached at St. Paul's,* 36; Clarendon, Diary, 25 April, 11 March 1689, 2:275, 269; Richard Kidder, *A Letter to a Friend Relating to the Present Convocation at Westminster* (London: Brabazon Aylmer, 1690), 2; Yester (London) to Tweeddale, 15 January 1689, NLS, 14404, fols. 5–6.

61. Yester (London) to Tweeddale, 15 January 1689, NLS, 14404, fol. 6r; Boothby (Ashbourne) to Horneck, 3 September 1689, BL, Add. 71692, fol. 112r; Morrice, Entering Book, 16 March, 9 March 1689, DWL, 31 Q, 498, 493; Horwitz, *Parliament, Policy and Politics,* 23–25; Morrice, Entering Book, 13 April 1689, DWL, 31 Q, 527.

62. *Life of Kidder,* 49; Patrick, Autobiography, 522–25; Morrice, Entering Book, 21 September 1689, DWL, 31 Q, 601; *Memoirs of Tenison,* 13; Kennett, *Complete History,* 551; Thomas Tenison, *A Discourse Concerning the Ecclesiastical Commission Open'd in the Jerusalem Chamber* (London: Richard Chiswell, 1689), 10; Birch, *Life of Tillotson,* 190–91; *Life of Sharpe,* 106.

63. Wood, *Athenae,* 2:968–69; *Memoirs of Tenison,* 16–18; *Life of Sharpe,* 106; Cotterell to Sir William Trumbull, 14 December 1689, BL, Trumbull MSS 39 (since recataloged), unfolioed.

64. *Life of Sharpe,* 5, 28; Sylvester, *Reliquiae Baxterianae,* 3:86; Grove, *Short Defence of the Church,* 5; Wood, 10 July 1682, in *Life and Times,* ed. Clark, 3:23–24.

65. Wood, *Athenae,* 2:1029; Sylvester, *Reliquiae Baxterianae,* 3:85, 179; Davies, *Account of the Convincement,* 207, 244; *Life of Kidder,* 1, 3; Patrick, Autobiography, 410; Wood, 31 December 1664, 24 May 1676, 6 January 1692, in *Life and Times,* ed. Clark, 2:26, 346, 3:379.

66. Birch, *Life of Tillotson,* 2–3, 15, 18, 65; Gilbert Burnet, *A Sermon Preached at the Funeral of the Most Reverend Father in God, John Tillotson* (London: Jacob Milner, 1694), 8; Anthony Wood, *Athenae Oxenienses,* ed. Philip Bliss (London: Lackington et al., 1820), 4:511–12; Hearne, 17 November 1705, in *Remarks and Collections,* ed. Doble, 1:85.

67. Burnet, "Life of Gilbert Burnet," iv–v, xvii; Burnet, "Autobiography," 463.

68. Tillotson, "A Conscience Void of Offence towards God and Men," 27 February 1691, *Sermons,* 3:86–87, 103; Tillotson, "The Care of Our Souls," 14 April 1689, *Sermons,* 2:432; Tillotson, "How to Keep a Truly Religious Fast," *Sermons,* 3:122–23; Tillotson, "The Way to Prevent the Ruin of a Sinful People," *Sermons,* 3:77–78; Birch, *Life of Tillotson,* 42; Burnet, *History of His Own Time,* 129.

69. Von Limborch (Amsterdam) to Locke, 2/12 April 1689, *Locke Correspondence,* 3:589; Burnet, "Life of Gilbert Burnet," xi; Burnet, *History of the Reformation; Second Part,* sig. [c2r]; J. Fall (Paris) to Robert Wyllie, 4 March 1683, NLS, Wodrow, Qu 30, fol. 144r; Thomas Burnet, *A Character of the Right Reverend Father in God, Gilbert Lord Bishop of Sarum* (London: J. Roberts, 1715), 7; Burnet, *Exhortation to Peace and Union,* 27; Burnet, *A Sermon Preached before the House of Commons* (London: John Starkey and Richard Chiswell, 1689), 22; Burnet, "Autobiography," 499; Burnet, *New Preface,* 9–10; William Lloyd, *Considerations Touching the True Way to Suppress Popery* (London: Henry Brome, 1677), 38; Lloyd, *A Sermon Preached before the House of Lords* (London: M. C. for Henry Brome, 1680), 20; Birch, *Life of Tillotson,* 168; Davies, *Account of the Convincement,* 243.

70. Patrick, "A Friendly Debate betwixt Two Neighbours," 1668, in *Works,* vol. 5, ed. Taylor, 253–691; Burnet, *History of His Own Time,* 130; Birch, *Life of Tillotson,* 214; Patrick, "Sermon against Censuring," 1688, in *Works,* vol. 8, ed. Taylor, 271–72, 282; Simon Patrick, *A Sermon Preached at St. Paul's Covent-Garden* (London: Richard Chiswell, 1689), 34–35; Patrick, "Sermon Preached before the Lords," 452; Patrick, Autobiography, 450, 554–55.

71. Wood, *Athenae,* 2:1184; Wood, 16 August 1687, in *Life and Times,* ed. Clark, 3:224; Gilbert Ironside, *A Sermon Peached before the King* (Oxford: Leonard Lichfield, 1685), 17–18; Hearne, 25 November 1705, in

Remarks and Collections, ed. Doble, 2:97–98; Thomas Tenison, *An Argument for Union* (London: Tho. Basset, Benj. Tooke, F. Gardiner, 1683), 40; Gilbert Burnet to ?Shrewsbury, 7 September 1689, NA, SP 32/2, fol. 6; Richard Kidder, *The Judgment of Private Discretion in Matters of Religion* (London: Brabazon Aylmer, 1687), 21; Morrice, Entering Book, 2 April 1687, DWL, 31 Q, 86; Edward Fowler, *The Principles and Practices of Certain Moderate Divines of the Church of England* (London: Lodowick Lloyd, 1670), 28.

72. *Life of Sharpe,* 304; Burnet, *History of His Own Time,* 129; Hearne, 17 April 1710, in *Remarks and Collections,* ed. Doble, 2:173; Spurr, *Restoration Church of England,* 144; Robert Grove, *An Answer to Mr. Lowth's Letter to Dr. Stillingfleet* (London: Randal Taylor, 1687), 5; Stillingfleet, "Case of Reading King James' Declaration, 1688," 371; Edward Stillingfleet, *Christian Magnamity* (London: Henry Mortlocke, 1690), 29.

73. Burnet, "Meditations on the Impending Expedition," 523–24; Gilbert Burnet, *Dr. Burnet's Travels* (Amsterdam: Peter Savouret and W. Fenner, 1687), 22, 34–35; Burnet, *Some Letters* (London: J. Robinson and Awnsham Churchill, 1689), 201–2; Burnet, "Reasons against the Repealing," 1687, in *A Collection of Eighteen Papers Relating to the Affairs of Church and State during the Reign of King James the Second* (London: John Starkey and Richard Chiswell, 1689), 3, 6; Burnet, "Life of Gilbert Burnet," xxix; Burnet, *A Sermon Preached in the Chapel of St. James's,* 23 December 1688, 2nd ed. (London: Richard Chiswell, 1689), 28–29.

74. William Lloyd, *Considerations Touching the True Way to Suppress Popery* (London: Henry Brome, 1677), 1, 4, 18, 25–26, 30; Lloyd, *A Conference between Two Protestants and a Papist* (1673), 15, 29.

75. Lloyd, *Pretences of the French Invasion,* 13; Kennett, *Complete History,* 532; Henri Misson, *M. Misson's Memoirs and Observations in His Travels over England,* trans. John Ozell (London: D. Browne et al., 1719), 204–6; General Assembly Book of the English Catholic Clergy, July 1694, AWA, Old Brotherhood Papers, Book 3/116; Charles Butler, *Historical Memoirs of the English, Irish, and Scottish Catholics,* 3rd ed. (London: John Murray, 1822), 3:132.

CHAPTER 14. *Assassination, Association, and the Consolidation of Revolution*

1. Richard Kingston, *A True History of the Several Designs and Conspiracies* (London: Abel Roper, 1698), 186; Portland to Lexington, 3/13 March 1696, in *The Lexington Papers,* ed. H. Manners Sutton (London: John Murray, 1851), 178–79 (hereafter cited as *Lexington Papers*); Jane Garrett, *The Triumphs of Providence* (Cambridge: Cambridge University Press, 1980); Mark Goldie, "The Revolution of 1689 and the Structure of Political Argument," *Bulletin of Research in the Humanities* 83, no. 4 (1980): 499; John Gellibrand to Sir William Trumbull, 21 February 196, HMC Downshire, 1:Pt. 2:625; Galway to Lexington, 3/13 February 1696, *Lexington Papers,* 163; Gilbert Burnet, *History of His Own Time* (London: William Smith, 1838), 622.

2. For examples of those insisting on James II's role in the assassination plot: *London Gazette,* 5 March 1696; M. De Chenailles to Trumbull, 27 February/8 March 1696, HMC Downshire, 1:Pt. 2:628; Blancart to George Stepney, 27 March/ 6 April 1696, *Lexington Papers,* 200. For the opposite case, which was maintained by the plotters: W. E. Buckley, ed., *Memoirs of Thomas, Earl of Ailesbury,* 2 vols. (Westminster: Nichols and Sons, 1890), 2:366 (hereafter cited as Ailesbury, *Memoirs*); Ambrose Rookwood, "Paper," in *True Copies of the Papers Which Brigadier Rookwood and Major Lowick Delivered to the Sheriffs,* 29 April 1696 (London: John Lawrence and William Rogers, 1696); Robert Charnock, *Mr. Charnock's Letter, Writ to a Friend after His Condemnation* [1696], 2; "Mr. Charnock's Paper," in *A True Copy of the Papers Delivered* (London: William Rogers, 1696), [1]; Henry Crymes to Trumbull, 17 February 1696, HMC Trumbull, 1:Pt. 2:623; *Life of James II,* 2:547. The commission was dated 17/27 December 1695.

3. Richard Edge (London) to Roger Kenyon, 10 February 1696, HMC Kenyon, 402; John Lloyd (London) to Earl of Huntingdon, 9 January 1696, HEH, HA 8356; J. H. to Robert Harley, 8 October 1695, BL, Add. 70018, fol. 64r; Charles Jackson, ed., *The Diary of Abraham De La Pryme,* Publications of the Surtees Society, vol. 54 (Durham: Published for the Society, 1869–70), 2 January 1696, 77–78 (hereafter cited as De La Pryme, *Diary*); Edge (London) to Kenyon, 13 February 1696, HMC Kenyon, 403; William Molyneux to John Locke, 5 April 1696, *Locke Correspondence,* 5:594; John Toland, *A Discourse upon Coins* (London:

Awnsham and John Churchill, 1696), iii (Toland dated his introduction 1 March 1696); De la Pryme, *Diary*, March 1696, 84; *Life of James II*, 2:531.

4. *Flying Post*, 7 March 1696; *Post Boy*, 19 March 1696; Edge to Kenyon, 21 January 1696, HMC Kenyon, 396; Locke to John Freke and Edward Clarke, 27 January 1696, *Locke Correspondence*, 5:525; *Life of James II*, 2:530; Ailesbury, *Memoirs*, 1:358; Jean Gailhard to Huntingdon, 20 February 1696, HEH, HA 3345; *Simeon and Levi: Or, Jacobite Villany and French-Treachery, Hand in Hand* (London, 1696), 17; *Flying Post*, 3 March 1696; Galway to Lexington, 20 February 1696, *Lexington Papers*, 167; John Evelyn, *Diary*, 26 February– 1 March 1696, 5:232–33; Sir Richard Blackmore, *A True and Impartial History of the Conspiracy* (London: James Knapton, 1723), 29–30; *Post-Man*, 7 March 1696.

5. James Fitzjames, Duke of Berwick, *Memoirs of the Marshal Duke of Berwick*, vol. 1 (London: T. Cadell, 1779), 129–35; *Life of James II*, 2:540–42; *Post-Man*, 2 March 1696; ? (Paris) to Lexington, 20 Febru- ary/2 March 1696, and Lexington to William Blathwayt, 23 February/5 March 1696, both in *Lexington Papers*, 170–72, 173–74; *An Account of a Most Horrid Conspiracy* (London: John Chaplin, 1696); *Post Boy*, 5 March 1696.

6. Portland to Lexington, 3/13 March 1696, *Lexington Papers*, 179; J. Hill (Antwerp) to Trumbull, 20/ 30 January 1696, BL, Add. 72570, fol. 126r; Villiers (The Hague) to Trumbull, 24 February 1696, BL, Add. 72570, fol. 186; Edge to Kenyon, 27 February 1696, HMC Kenyon, 405; *Post-Man*, 18 April, 25 February 1696; Galway to Lexington, 10/20 February 1696, *Lexington Papers*, 166–67; *Post Boy*, 25 February, 3 March 1696; *The Flying Post*, 10 March 1696; Shrewsbury to Galway, 28 February/10 March 1696, in *Private and Original Correspondence of Charles Talbot, Duke of Shrewsbury*, ed. William Coxe (London: Longman, Hurst, Rees, Orme, and Brown, 1821), 283; Evelyn, *Diary*, 1 March 1696, 5:234.

7. De Chenailles to Trumbull, 3/13 March 1696 HMC Downshire, 1:Pt. 2:636; Thomas Percival, *The Rye-House Travestie* (London: A. Bell, 1696), 7; *Flying Post*, 7 March 1696; ? (Paris) to Lexington, 9/19 March 1696, and Portland to Lexington, 3/13 March 1696, both in *Lexington Papers*, 184, 177–78.

8. George Fleming to Sir Daniel Fleming, 5 March 1696, in *The Flemings in Oxford*, vol. 3, ed. John Richard Magrath (Oxford: Oxford Historical Society, 1924), 271–73; William Gilpin (Whitehaven) to Sir John Lowther, 2 March 1696, in *The Correspondence of Sir John Lowther of Whitehaven, 1693–1698*, ed. D. R. Hainsworth (London: British Academy, 1983), 266; Richard Lapthorne (London) to Richard Coffin, 7 March 1696, in *The Portledge Papers*, ed. Richard J. Kerr and Ida Coffin Duncan (London: Jonathan Cape, 1928), 222; Daniel Bret (London) to Huntingdon, 27 February 1696, HEH, HA 955; Evelyn, *Diary*, 10 April 1696, 5:235; *Post Boy*, 25 February, 14 March, 17 March, 19 March, 21 April 1696; De la Pryme, *Diary*, 29 March 1696, 86; *Flying Post*, 25 February, 27 February 1696; *Life of James II*, 2:554; Lapthorne to Coffin, 28 February 1696, *Portledge Papers*, ed. Kerr and Coffin Duncan, 221; *London Gazette*, 12 March 1696; *Post Boy*, 3 March 1696.

9. James Vernon to Lexington, 13 March 1696, and ? (Paris) to Lexington, 16/26 March 1696, both in *Lexington Papers*, 186–87, 191; *Flying Post*, 3, 7 March 1696; de Chenailles to Trumbull, 12/23 March 1696, HMC Downshire, 1:Pt. 2:641; *Post-Man*, 24, 26 March 1696; Vernon to Lexington, 3 March 1696, and Trumbull to Lexington, 3 April 1696, both in *Lexington Papers*, 181, 196; *London Gazette*, 27 February 1696; *Post-Man*, 25 February 1696; *Flying Post*, 10, 21 March, 4 April 1696; *Post Boy*, 7 March 1696; *London Gazette*, 20, 23 April 1696; *Flying Post*, 19 March 1696; J. Horsfall Turner, ed., *The Rev. Oliver Heywood, B. A., 1630– 1702: His Autobiography, Diaries, Anecdote and Event Books*, 4 vols. (Bridghouse: A. B. Bayes, 1882), 28 Febru- ary 1689, 4:154; John Ellis (Whitehall) to Matthew Prior, 20 March 1696, Longleat House, Prior MSS 2, fol. 68r; Lapthorne to Coffin, 22 March 1696, *Portledge Papers*, ed. Kerr and Coffin Duncan, 224; Kingston, *True History*, 198; James Gardiner (rector of St. Michaels Crooked-Lane), *A Thanksgiving Sermon Preached at St. Michaels Crooked-Lane*, 16 April 1696 (London: B. Aylmer, 1696), 1–2; Edward Fowler (bishop of Gloucester), *A Sermon Preached before the House of Lords*, 16 April 1696 (London: B. Aylmer, 1696), 24; J. E. Edzard (minister of the German Lutheran Congregation in Trinity-Lane), *The Finger of God over His An- nointed*, 16 April 1696 (London: F. Collins, 1696), sig. [A3r]; Evelyn, *Diary*, 12 April 1696, 5:235–36; Ailes-

bury, *Memoirs*, 1:279, 2:366; Martha Lockhart to Lady Masham, 21 March 1696, *Locke Correspondence*, 5:574; Blackmore, *True and Impartial History*, 27.

10. *The History of the Late Conspiracy against the King and the Nation* (London: Daniel Brown and Tho. Bennet, 1696), 1; De La Pryme, *Diary*, February 1696, 82; Lockhart to Masham, 21 March 1696, *Locke Correspondence*, 5:574; Evelyn, *Diary*, 19 April 1696, 5:236. There was debate in Europe too: *Post-Man*, 18 April 1696.

11. J. P. Kenyon, *Revolution Principles: The Politics of Party, 1689–1720* (Cambridge: Cambridge University Press, 1977). I quote from the paperback edition of 1990, 1, 32; Kenyon notes in the 1990 edition that his argument is "merely paraphrasing" an interpretation "which went back as far as Macaulay" (x); Goldie, "Revolution of 1689," 489–90, 513, 516–17, 519; Tony Claydon, *William III and the Godly Revolution* (Cambridge: Cambridge University Press, 1996), 157, 229.

12. Gerald M. Straka, *Anglican Reaction to the Revolution of 1688* (Madison: State Historical Society of Wisconisn, 1962), 122; Dennis Rubini, *Court and Country, 1688–1702* (London: Rupert Hart-Davis, 1967), 67; Henry Horwitz, *Parliament, Policy and Politics in the Reign of William III* (Manchester: Manchester University Press, 1977), 175; Thomas Babington Macaulay, *The History of England from the Accession of James II*, 5 vols. (New York: Harper and Brothers, 1849–61), 4:585; Craig Rose, *England in the 1690s: Revolution, Religion, and War* (Oxford: Blackwell, 1999), 92; Garrett, *Triumphs of Providence*, 262.

13. William Streeter (Chester) to Sir Willoughby Aston, 16 March 1696, BL, Add. 36913, fol. 246r.

14. Ailesbury, *Memoirs*, 1:353, 359; Tim Harris, *London Crowds in the Reign of Charles II: Propaganda and Politics from the Restoration until the Exclusion Crisis* (Cambridge: Cambridge University Press, 1987), 170; Robert Young to William, 23 April 1696, BL, Add. 72535, unfolioed; William Fuller to Trumbull, 15 April 1696, BL, Add. 72535, unfolioed; [Richard Kingston] to Trumbull, 21 June 1695, BL, Add. 72570, fol. 8r; *Flying Post*, 7 April 1696; *Post-Man*, 17 April, 24 March 1696; Percival, *Rye-House Travestie*, 27; Paul Kleber Monod, *Jacobitism and the English People, 1688–1788* (Cambridge: Cambridge University Press, 1989), 167; De Krey, *Fractured Society*, 193.

15. *Flying Post*, 14 March 1696; Oliver Heywood, *Diaries*, 27 December 1695, in Turner, ed., *Rev. Oliver Heywood*, 4:153–54; Henry Baker to Trumbull, 23 February 1696, BL, Add. 75270, fol. 185r; *Flying Post*, 10, 12 March 1696; Humphrey Prideaux (Norwich) to John Ellis, *Letters of Humphrey Prideaux*, ed. Edward Maunde Thompson, Camden Society, n.s., 15 (1875): 177; Monod, *Jacobitism*, 169–70; Richard Kingston, "A Journey into Kent," 9–27 July 1695, BL, Add. 72570, fol. 50v; Dr. Robert Gorge (Oxford) to Trumbull, 16 July 1695, HMC Downshire, 1: Pt. 2:509; William Hayley to Trumbull, 10 October 1695, HMC Downshire, 1:Pt. 2:561; De La Pryme, *Diary*, 3 October 1695, 70; Percival, *Rye-House Travestie*, 13; Blackmore, *True and Impartial History*, 17.

16. *Post Boy*, 23 April 1696; De La Pryme, *Diary*, 70–71; Peter Newcome (vicar of Aldenham, Hertfordshire), *A Sermon Preached in the Parish Church of Aldenham*, 16 April 1696 (London: John Wyat, 1696), 15; Percival, *Rye-House Travestie*, 7–8.

17. Capt. W. Courtenay to Sir Stephen Fox, 17/27 September 1696, HMC Downshire, 1:Pt. 2:690; *Post-Man*, 29 February 1696; Kingston to Trumbull, 4 January 1696, BL, Add. 72570, fol. 100r; *Post Boy*, 12 March 1696; William Atwood, *Reflections upon a Treasonable Opinion, Industriously Promoted, against Signing the National Association* (London: E. Whitlock, 1696), 1; Deuel Pead, *The Protestant King Protected* (London: T. Parkhurst, 1696), 19; Percival, *Rye-House Travestie*, 3.

18. Daniel Szechi, "A Blueprint for Tyranny? Sir Edward Hales and the Catholic Response to the Revolution of 1688," *English Historical Review* 116 (2001): 346.

19. James Ferguson, *Robert Ferguson, the Plotter* (Edinburgh: David Douglas, 1887), 267; Monod, *Jacobitism*, 23–24; Daniel Szechi, *The Jacobites: Britain and Europe, 1688–1788* (Manchester: Manchester University Press, 1994), 22; Kingston to Trumbull, 19 February 1696, HMC Downshire, 1: Part 2:623–24; *Flying Post*, 12, 14 March 1696; Edge to Kenyon, 12 March 1696, HMC Kenyon, 407; Lapthorne to Coffin, 22 March 1696, *Portledge Papers*, ed. Kerr and Coffin Duncan, 224; De La Pryme, *Diary*, 8 June 1696, 96; Garrett,

Triumphs of Providence, 75–76; Percival, *Rye-House Travestie,* 16–17. The arguments that Ferguson advanced in 1695 were inconsistent with Whig ideology of the 1690s.

20. "On the Promoted Bishops," 1691, in *Poems on Affairs of State: Satirical Verse, 1660–1714,* vol. 5, ed. William J. Cameron (New Haven and London: Yale University Press, 1971), 5:314; Robert Ferguson, *A Brief Account of Some of the Late Incroachments and Depredations,* 20 December [1695], 5; *Life of James II,* 2:531.

21. "Major Robert Lowick's Paper," *True Copies,* 29 April 1696 (broadside); *A True Account,* 29 April 1696 (broadside); Lapthorne to Coffin, 2 May 1696, *Portledge Papers,* ed. Kerr and Coffin Duncan, 229; Garrett, *Triumphs of Providence,* 28–32, 108–9, 118, 202; Kingston, *True History,* 171; *Post Boy,* 24 March 1696; "Mr. King's Paper," *True Copy,* William Rogers, 1696), [2]; "Mr. Charnock's Paper," [1].

22. "Sir William Parkyns's Paper" and "Sir John's Paper," both in *A True Copy of the Papers Delivered by Sir John Friend, and Sir William Parkyns,* 3 April 1696 (London: William Rogers, 1696), [2], [1]; *A True Account of the Dying Behaviour of Ambrose Rookwood, Charles Cranburne, and Major Lowick,* 29 April 1696 (London: R. Green, 1696); Sir John Fenwick, *A True Copy of the Paper,* 28 January 1697 (London: R. Bentley, [1697]), [1]; *An Answer to Mr. Collier's Defence* (London: R. Baldwin, 1696), 1; *Post-Man,* 2, 4, 9 April 1696; *Flying Post,* 4 April 1696; *Post Boy,* 4 April 1696; *London Gazette,* 9 April 1696; Lapthorne to Coffin, 4 April 1696, *Portledge Papers,* ed. Kerr and Coffin Duncan, 226; Burnet, *History of His Own Time,* 627; Whitehall Treasury Minute, 30 July 1696, Historical Society of Pennsylvania, Penn Papers, Acc. No. 2641; *Flying Post,* 9, 14 April 1696; Vernon to Lexington, 17 March 1696, *Lexington Papers,* 192; Abiel Borfet, *The Minister of Richmond's Sermon* (London, 1696), 2.

23. Ferguson, *Brief Account,* 23, 65–67.

24. Jeremy Collier, *A Perswasive to Consideration, Tender'd to the Royalists* (London, 1695), 5–6, 23; *Flying Post,* 25 April 1696; Nathaniel Johnston to Huntingdon, 4 February 1696, HEH, HA 7836; "Life of John Kettlewell," in John Kettlewell, *A Compleat Collection of the Works,* vol. 1 (London: D. Browne, et al., 1719), 21; George Hickes (Worcester) to Dr. Charlett, 8 July 1689, Bodleian, Ballard MSS 12, fol. 29r. In 1696 Johnston was living with the Jacobite Earl of Peterborough: Johnston to Huntingdon, 18 February 1696, HEH, HA 7837.

25. *Post Boy,* 14 March 1696; *History of the Late Conspiracy,* 100; "Sir John Friend's Paper," [1]; *Post Boy,* 4 April, 7 April 1696; *Post-Man,* 9 April 1696; Finch to Trumbull, 2/12 February 1696, HMC Downshire, 1:Pt. 2:625; Vernon to Lexington, 13 March 1696, *Lexington Papers,* 187; Ailesbury, *Memoirs,* 1:352; Charnock, *Mr. Charnock's Letter,* 3–6; *Life of James II,* 2:555–56.

26. "Charles Cranburn's Speech," in *True Account; Post-Man,* 30 April 1696; Rookwood, "Paper"; "Major Robert Lowick's Paper"; Fenwick, *True Copy of the Paper,* [2]; *Flying Post,* 28 March 1696; "Sir William Parkyns's Paper," [2]; ? (Paris) to Lexington, 9/19 March 1696, *Lexington Papers,* 184.

27. Ferguson, *Brief Account,* 2–3; Hickes to Charlett, 6 September 1690, Bodleian, Ballard MSS 12, fol. 38r; Collier, *Perswasive,* 14–15; Clarendon (London) to Abingdon, 16 February 1690, Newberry Library, CASE MS E5.5434.

28. Ferguson, *Brief Account,* 3; Collier, *Perswasive,* 15, 21; *A Letter from a Minister of the Church of England to a Gentleman in the Country* (London, 1695), 5.

29. Fenwick, *True Copy of the Paper,* [1].

30. Charnock, *Mr. Charnock's Letter,* 3; Ferguson, *Brief Account,* 2.

31. Charnock, *Mr. Charnock's Letter,* 6–7; Edge to Kenyon, 28 January 1696, HMC Kenyon, 398; *Life of James II,* 2:530–31.

32. Burnet, *History of His Own Time,* 621; Ferguson, *Brief Account,* 12, 16–17, 57; Shrewsbury to William, 24 August/3 September 1694, *Private Correspondence of Shrewsbury,* ed. Coxe, 71–72; *Flying Post,* 7 March 1696.

33. D. W. Jones, *War and Economy in the Age of William III and Marlborough* (Oxford: Basil Blackwell, 1988), 12–13, 274–75, 294–302; Gary Stuart De Krey, *A Fractured Society: The Politics of London in the First Age of Party, 1688–1715* (Oxford: Clarendon Press, 1985), 24–25; Bruce G. Carruthers, *City of Capital: Politics*

and Markets in the English Financial Revolution (Princeton, NJ: Princeton University Press, 1996), 148–49, 154–55.

34. Deuel Pead, *Sheba's Conspiracy,* 29 March 1696 (London: T. Parkhurst, 1696), 26; *The Country Gentleman's Notion Concerning Governments,* 29 May 1696 (London: Eliz. Whitlock, [1696]), 3.

35. *Post-Man,* 27 February 1696; *London News-Letter,* 6 May 1696; Gardiner, *Thanksgiving Sermon,* 6; Fowler, *Sermon,* 31; Lapthorne to Coffin, 7 March 1696, *Portledge Papers,* ed. Kerr and Coffin Duncan, 223; Locke to Clarke, 25 March 1696, *Locke Correspondence,* 5:579; *Flying Post,* 23 April 1696; Blackmore, *True and Impartial History,* 10–11. See also Walter Neale, *A Sermon Preached in Christ-Church, Cork,* 23 April 1696 (London: Abel Swall and Tim. Child, 1696), 14; John Moore, *A Sermon Preach'd before the King,* 16 April 1696 (London: Will. Rogers, 1696), 11.

36. Samuel Barton (chaplain to the House of Commons), *A Sermon Preach'd before the House of Commons,* 16 April 1696 (London: Tho. Cockerill, 1696), 17; W. Talbot (dean of Worcester), *A Sermon Preach'd at the Cathedral Church of Worcester,* 16 April 1696 (London: T. Bennet, 1696), 14; Francis Gregory, *A Thanksgiving Sermon,* 16 April 1696 (London: R. Sare, 1696), 14; Neale, *Sermon,* 15; *The Art of Assassinating Kings* (London: E. Whitlock, 1696), 6–7; Joseph Addison, *A Poem to His Majesty* (London: Joseph Tonson, 169[6]), 6. See also James Smallwood (chaplain to the Earl of Romney); *A Sermon Preach'd at St. James's Church Westminster,* 2 April 1696 (London: E. Whitlock, 1696), 27; and *Flying Post,* 7 May 1696.

37. William Stephens (rector of Sutton, Surrey), *A Thanksgiving Sermon Preach'd before the Right Honourable the Lord Mayor,* 16 April 1696 (London: B. Aylmer, 1696), 15–16; Talbot, *Sermon,* 15. See also *Art of Assassinating Kings,* 19–20.

38. T. B., *David and Saul* (London, 1696), 26; John Strype (vicar of Low-Leyton, Essex). *David and Saul,* 16 April 1696 (London: B. Aylmer, 1696), 15; J. O., *Salvation Improved,* 16 April 1696, Preached at Oswestry (London: J. Salusbury, 1696), 16; Talbot, *Sermon,* sig. A2r. See also Charles Nicholetts (minister at Havenet, Southampton), *The Cabinet of Hell Unlocked,* 16 April 1696 (London: William Marshall and John Marshall, 1696), 19–20.

39. *Art of Assassinating Kings,* 20; William Perse (rector of West Heslerton, chaplain to Earl of Feversham), *A Sermon Preach'd in the Cathedral of St. Peters in York,* 5 November 1689 (York: John Bulkley, 1689), 28–29; Talbot, *Sermon,* 15.

40. John Shower, *A Thanksgiving Sermon,* 16 April 1696 (London: B. Aylmer, 1696), 11; Perse, *Sermon,* 25. See also Andrew Burnett, *A Sermon Preach'd at Barbican,* 16 April 1696 (London: Rich. Baldwin, 1696), 14; and Newcome, *Sermon,* 11.

41. Nicholetts, *Cabinet of Hell Unlocked,* 11–12; Vincent Alsop, *A Sermon upon the Wonderful Deliverance* (London: J. Barnes, 1696), 7, 32–33; Moore, *Sermon,* 13, 17.

42. Fowler, *Sermon,* 21–22, 28; Smallwood, *Sermon,* 19–20; Pead, *Protestant King,* 14; *True Copy,* 29 April 1696, [1]. See also Talbot, *Sermon,* 12; Neale, *Sermon,* 17; Henry Day, *A Thanksgiving Sermon Preach'd at Sutton in Surrey,* 16 April 1696 (London: Richard Baldwin, 1696), 7–8; and Blackmore, *True and Impartial History,* 6.

43. Stephens, *Thanksgiving Sermon,* sig. [A3v]; *Art of Assassinating Kings,* 72.

44. *Art of Assassinating Kings,* 72–73; *Reflections on the Paper Deliver'd to the Sheriffs of London and Middlesex by Sir John Fenwick* (London: Richard Baldwin, 1697), 5; Stephens, *Thanksgiving Sermon,* 16, 21.

45. William Wake, *A Sermon Preached in the Parish Church of St. James Westminster,* 16 April 1696 (London: Richard Sare, 1696), 10; A. S., *God Glorified and the Wicked Snared* (London: R. Baldwin, 1696), 24; *Simeon and Levi,* 10–11; Barton, *Sermon,* 17; Atwood, *Reflections,* 59. See also Newcome, *Sermon,* 9; and J. O., *Salvation Improved,* 14–15.

46. The only exceptions I have found are Abiel Dorfet, *The Minister of Richmond's Reasons* (London: John Harris, 1696), 4; and Theophilus Dorrington, *The Honour Due to the Civil Magistrate Stated and Urg'd* (London: John Wyat, 1696).

47. Stephens, *Thanksgiving Sermon,* 23–24; Pead, *Sheba's Conspiracy,* 25; Atwood, *Reflections,* 57. See also Fowler, *Sermon,* 31–32; Gregory, *Thanksgiving Sermon,* 9.

48. Day, *Thanksgiving Sermon,* 12, 18; Stephens, *Thanksgiving Sermon,* sig. [A3v]; Pead, *Sheba's Conspiracy,* sig. A2; Richard Bovet, *Poem* (London: Richard Baldwin, 1696), 9. See also Atwood, *Reflections,* 62; and Percival, *Rye House Travestie,* 8.

49. Wake, *Sermon,* 16; Barton, *Sermon,* 13.

50. Wake, *Sermon,* 9–10; *Post-Man,* 7 April 1696; Day, *Thanksgiving-Sermon,* 10, 21; *Country Gentleman's Notion,* 3, 7; Stephens, *Thanksgiving Sermon,* 19, 22. See also *Reflections on a Paper,* 1697, 14; *A Full Answer Paragraph by Paragraph to Sir John Fenwick's Paper* (London: Richard Baldwin, 1697), 9; *Post-Man,* 5 May 1696; Kingston, *True History,* 202; and Pead, *Sheba's Conspiracy,* 11.

51. Smallwood, *Sermon,* 21; Barton, *Sermon,* 18–19; *Art of Assassinating Kings,* 28.

52. Day, *Thanksgiving-Sermon,* 11; Edzard, *Finger of God,* 19; *Full Answer,* 25; *Country Gentleman's Notion,* 6; Gregory, *Thanksgiving Sermon,* 10–11. See also Burnett, *Sermon,* 16; *Reflections on a Paper,* 5; and Pead, *Sheba's Conspiracy,* 15.

53. Nicholetts, *Cabinet of Hell Unlocked,* 13; George Keith, *A Sermon Preached at the Meeting of Protestant Dissenters, Called Quakers, in Turners-Hall, London,* 16 April 1696 (London: B. Aylmer, 1696), 15; T. B., *David and Saul,* 18.

54. Wake, *Sermon,* 25–26; Smallwood, *Sermon,* 28; Stephens, *Thanksgiving Sermon,* 10–12.

55. Day, *Thanksgiving-Sermon,* 8–9; Kingston, *True History,* 201–2; *A Declaration of the Sense of the Archbishops and Bishops,* 10 April 1696 (London: John Everingham, 1696); *Flying Post,* 14 April 1696; *Post-Man,* 5 May 1696; Pead, *Sheba's Conspiracy,* 13; T. B., *David and Saul,* 8, 13.

56. Mark Knights, "'Meer Religion' and the 'Church-State' of Restoration England," in *A Nation Transformed: England after the Restoration,* ed. Alan Houston and Steve Pincus (Cambridge: Cambridge University Press, 2001), 64; *Post-Man,* 5 May 1696; John Tillotson to Shrewsbury, 23 October 1692, Bodleian, Ballard MSS 9, fol. 11r; Smallwood, *Sermon,* 17–18.

57. Smallwood, *Sermon,* 28; J. O., *Salvation Improved,* 25.

58. Pead, *Protestant King,* 20; Clarke to Locke, 31 March 1696, *Locke Correspondence,* 5:587; Blackmore, *True and Impartial History,* sig. A2v, 30.

59. J. Harvey to Mercier, 13 December 1695, HMC Downshire, 1:Pt. 2:597–98; E. H., *Decus and Tutamen* (London, 1696), 1; Freke to Locke, 5 December 1695, *Locke Correspondence,* 5:475; John Toland, *A Discourse upon Coins* (London: Awnsham and John Churchill, 1696), ii–iv; Edmund Bohun to John Cary, 31 July 1696, in *The Diary and Autobiography of Edmund Bohun,* ed. Wilton S. Rix (Beccles, 1853), 140; Steve Pincus, "John Evelyn: Revolutionary," in *John Evelyn and His Milieu,* ed. Frances Harris and Michael Hunter (London: British Library, 2003), 185–219; Molyneux (Dublin) to Locke, 24 December 1695, HRC, Pforzheimer 21; Patrick Hyde Kelly, "General Introduction," in *Locke on Money,* vol. 1, ed. Kelly (Oxford: Clarendon Press, 1991), 35.

60. Burnet, *History of His Own Time,* 625; Horwitz, *Parliament, Policy and Politics,* 163, 166–67, 327; *Post-Man,* 6 February 1696; Ailesbury, *Memoirs,* 1:359; John Briscoe, *Mr Briscoe's Reply* [1695 or 1696], 2; Dalby Thomas, *Propositions for General Land-Banks.* [1695], [1]; Vernon to Shrewsbury, 1 October 1696, Boughton House, Shrewsbury MSS, Vernon Letters, 4/3 (read on microfilm); *A List of the Names of the Subscribers to the Land-Bank,* 22 November 1695 (London: Thomas Cockerill, 1695). Contemporaries noted the strong relationship between Tory coinage proposals and the national land bank scheme: E. H., *Decus and Tutamen,* 2–3.

61. Stephens, *Thanksgiving-Sermon,* sig. [A4v]; Locke to Freke and Clarke, 28 March 1696, and Locke to Clarke, 4 August 1696, both in *Locke Correspondence,* 5:581, 674; Thomas, *Propositions,* [1]; John Briscoe, *Reasons Humbly Offered for the Establishment of the National Land-Bank,* 3 February [1696], [1]; *A Letter to a Friend* (London, 1696), 5–6; Cary to Locke, 11 January 1696, *Locke Correspondence,* 5:515; Obadiah Sedgwick to ?, 11 June 1696, Bodleian, Tanner 24, fol. 126r; Shrewsbury to William, 5/15 June 1696, *Private*

Correspondence of Shrewsbury, ed. Coxe, 122; *Flying Post,* 1 August 1696; Shrewsbury to William, 29 May/ 8 June 1696, *Private Correspondence of Shrewsbury,* ed. Coxe, 120; *Flying Post,* 18 August 1696.

62. *Simeon and Levi,* 23; Shower, *Thanksgiving Sermon,* 15–16; Gregory, *Thanksgiving Sermon,* 11; Perse, *Sermon,* 27; Shrewsbury to Galway, 21 April/ 1 May 1696, *Private Correspondence of Shrewsbury,* ed. Coxe, 286; ? to Lexington, 6/16 March 1696, *Lexington Papers,* 183; Alsop, *Sermon,* 33–34; *London News-Letter,* 6 May 1696. See also Pawling to Locke, 14 March 1696, *Locke Correspondence,* 5:568.

63. James Graham (Fontabell, New York) to Blathwayt, 31 May 1696, Colonial Williamsburg Foundation, William Blathwayt Papers, 10/Folder 7; Evelyn, *Diary,* 26 February–1 March 1696, 5:233; Nicholetts, *Cabinet of Hell Unlocked,* 16 April 1696, 21; *Life of James II,* 2:537. See also Perse, *Sermon,* 16 April 1696, 28; and *Simeon and Levi,* 23.

64. *Post Boy,* 23, 21 April 1696; Prideaux to Ellis, 17 April 1696, Thompson, 171; *Post-Man,* 23 April 1696; *London Gazette,* 23 April 1696; *London Gazette,* 27, 20 April 1696.

65. Burnet, *History of His Own Time,* 621, 623; *Post-Man,* 5 March 1696; *Post Boy,* 17 March 1696.

66. *Flying Post,* 27 February 1696; *Post Boy,* 31 March 1696; *Journal of the House of Commons,* 24, 25, 27 February 1696, 11:466–67, 468, 470–74; Freke and Clarke to Locke, 27 February 1696, *Locke Correspondence,* 5:549; Edge to Kenyon, 27 February 1696, HMC Kenyon, 405; *Flying Post,* 4 April 1696; Gailhard (London) to Huntingdon, 27 February 1696, HEH, HA 3346.

67. *Journal of the House of Lords,* 26 February 1696, 15:683; *Flying Post,* 29 February 1696; Freke and Clarke to Locke, 27 February 1696, *Locke Correspondence,* 5:549–50; Stepney to Lexington, 11 April 1696, *Lexington Papers,* 198–99; Horwitz, *Revolution Politicks: The Career of Daniel Finch, Second Earl of Nottingham, 1647–1730* (Cambridge: Cambridge University Press, 1968), 156–57; Daniel Bret (London) to Huntingdon, 27 February 1696, HEH, HA 955.

68. *Journal of the House of Commons,* 3 April 1696, 11:544; *London Gazette,* 6 April 1696; *Flying Post,* 7 May 1696.

69. Patrick Collinson, "The Elizabethan Exclusion Crisis and the Elizabethan Polity," *Proceedings of the British Academy* 84 (1994): 53, 64–65, 68–69. Others have noted social discontinuity while accepting ideological continuity: David Cressy, "Binding the Nation: The Bonds of Association, 1584 and 1696," in *Tudor Rule and Revolution,* ed. Delloyd J. Guth and John W. McKenna (Cambridge: Cambridge University Press, 1982), 227, 234; Edward Vallance, "Loyal or Rebellious? Protestant Associations in England, 1584–1696," *Seventeenth Century* 17, no. 1 (2002): 2, 16.

70. *Journal of the House of Lords,* 26 February 1696, 15:683; *Journal of the House of Commons,* 24 February 1696, 11:466–67; *Post-Man,* 5 March, 7 April 1696; *London Gazette,* 9 April 1696; *Post-Man,* 18 April 1696; *Flying Post,* 7 April 1696.

71. John Oldmixon, *The History of Addresses* (London, 1709), 198; Cressy, "Binding the Nation," 222–24, 232–33; *London Gazette,* 4 May 1696; *Flying Post,* 25 April 1696; Patrick Collinson, "The Monarchical Republic of Queen Elizabeth," *Bulletin of John Rylands Library* 69 (1986–87): 414; *London Gazette,* 21 May 1696; *Flying Post,* 29 February 1696; *Post-Man,* 25 April 1696; *London Gazette,* 14 May 1696; *Flying Post,* 14 May 1696; Prideaux to Ellis, 8 April 1696, Thompson, 166–67; *London Gazette,* 30 March 1696; Francis Russell (Barbados) to Blathwayt, 22 July 1696, Colonial Williamsburg Foundation, William Blathwayt Papers, 31/ Folder 5.

72. Collinson, "Elizabethan Exclusion Crisis," 64; Leah S. Marcus, Janel Mueller, and Mary Beth Rose, eds., *Elizabeth I: Collected Works* (Chicago: University of Chicago Press, 2000), 183.

73. Prideaux to Ellis, 16 May 1696, Thompson, 174; *London Gazette,* 23 March 1696. These associations were thoroughly reported on in the *London Gazette.* See the following issues: 9 April, 30 April, 4 May, 14 May, 21 May, 25 May, 28 May, 4 June, 11 June, 15 June, 29 June, 2 July, 16 July, 30 July, and 20 August.

74. *Post-Man,* 5 March, 28 March 1696; *Flying Post,* 2 April 1696; *London Gazette,* 4 May, 18 June, 13 April, 30 April, 25 June, 4 May, 7 May, 25 May 1696; *Flying Post,* 25 April 1696; "A Testimony of Our Faithful Obedience and Subjection," in Keith, *Sermon,* 29; *Flying Post,* 9 April 1696; *London Gazette,* 21 May 1696;

Mary Geiter, "Affirmation, Assassination and Association: The Quakers, Parliament and the Court in 1696," *Parliamentary History* 16 (1997): 277–88.

75. *London Gazette,* 26 March 1696; *Flying Post,* 14 April 1696.

76. Steve Hindle, *The State and Social Change in Early Modern England, c. 1550–1640* (Basingstoke: Macmillan, 2000), 17; Thomas Cogswell, *Home Divisions: Aristocracy, the State and Provincial Conflict* (Manchester: Manchester University Press, 1998), 3; John Brewer, *The Sinews of Power: War, Money and the English State, 1688–1783* (London: Routledge, 1989), 7–9, 250; *London Gazette,* 23 April, 4 May 1696; *Post Boy,* 7 March 1696; *London Gazette,* 23 March, 26 March, 30 March 1696; *Flying Post,* 14 March 1696; *London Gazette,* 23 March, 6 April, 30 April, 17 May 1696.

77. Brewer, *Sinews of Power,* 10–11; *London Gazette,* 19 March, 30 April, 27 April 1696.

78. *London Gazette,* 30 April, 26 March, 2 April, 7 May, 11 May, 14 May, 27 April, 30 March 1696.

79. *London Gazette,* 23 April, 27 April, 6 July, 23 July, 7 May 1696.

80. *Post-Man,* 28 March 1696; *London News-Letter,* 1 May 1696; *London Gazette,* 13 August, 16 April, 20 April, 23 April, 7 May, 11 May, 18 May 1696; Prideaux to Ellis, 8 April 1696, Thompson, 167; Wallace Gandy, ed., *The Association Rolls of the British Plantations* (San Bernardino, CA: Borgo, 1993), 70–73.

81. *London Gazette,* 30 March, 6 April 1696; *Post-Man,* 9 April, 11 April 1696; *London Gazette,* 13 April, 27 April, 7 May, 18 May, 4 June, 11 June, 15 June, 18 June, 25 June, 2 July, 24 August, 27 August.

82. *Flying Post,* 18 April 1696; *London Gazette,* 23 April 1696; Tamworth Newsletter, 16 April 1696, HEH, HM 30659/66; *Post Boy,* 21 April 1696; *London Gazette,* 4 May 1696; *Flying Post,* 28 May 1696; *Post-Man,* 9 April, 18 April 1696; *Flying Post,* 21 May, 4 June 1696.

83. Graham (Fontabell, New York) to Blathwayt, 31 May 1696, Colonial Williamsburg Foundation, William Blathwayt Papers, 10/Folder 7; Gandy, ed., *Association Oath Rolls of the British Plantations,* 34–60; *London Gazette,* 27 August 1696; John Usher (Newcastle, New Hampshire) to Blathwayt, 6 October 1696, Blathwayt Papers, 12/Folder 3; J. Goddard (Bermuda) to Blathwayt, 9 November 1696, Blathwayt Papers, 36/Folder 4; Bridgewater's Notes, Board of Trade, 21 April 1697, HEH, EL 9691.

84. *London Gazette,* 2 April, 4 May 1696; *Flying Post,* 16 May, 21 May, 26 May 1696.

85. For Ireland: *London Gazette,* 6 April, 13 April, 14 May, 28 May, 13 August; *Flying Post,* 14 March 1696; *Post-Man,* 11 April 1696; *Flying Post,* 5 May, 28 March 1696.

86. Vallance, "Loyal or Rebellious?" 22; *Post Boy,* 21 March 1696; *Flying Post,* 7 April 1696; Blancart to Stepney, 27 March/6 April 1696, *Lexington Papers,* 200–201; Edmund Warcupp (London) to Dr. Charlett, 16 May 1696, Bodleian, Ballard MSS 11, fol. 74r.

87. *Flying Post,* 9 April 1696; Evelyn, *Diary,* 24–28 May 1696, 5:242–43; Burnet, *History of His Own Time,* 624–25; Horwitz, *Parliament, Policy and Politics,* 176; *Flying Post,* 26 March 1696; *Post Boy,* 4 April 1696; *Flying Post,* 27 June 1696; Prideaux to Ellis, 24 April 1696, Thompson, 172; De La Pryme, *Diary,* 17 June 1696, 99; *Post-Man,* 7 May 1696; Edzard, *Finger of God,* 19–20; Bovet, *Poem,* 10; Barton, *Sermon,* 16 April 1696, 21–22; John Gery to Huntingdon, 13 April 1696, HEH, HA 4005; Macaulay, *History,* 4:616; Daniel Bret (London) to Huntingdon, 27 February 1696, HEH, HA 955; Rev. George Fleming to Sir Daniel Fleming, 5 March 1696, Magrath, 3:269–71; Percival, *Rye House Travestie,* 51; *Post-Man,* 9 April 1696; Prideaux to Ellis, 29 April 1696, Thompson, 173; Prideaux to Ellis, 8 April 1696, Thompson, 168.

88. *Post Boy,* 10 March 1696; Vernon to Lexington, 17 March 1696, *Lexington Papers,* 192; *Flying Post,* 30 July 1696; De La Pryme, *Diary,* 30 July 1696, 109; Kenyon to G. Wentworth, 13 September 1696, HMC Kenyon, 411; Rubini, *Court and Country,* 67; Horwitz, *Parliament, Policy and Politics,* 179; Bret (London) to Huntingdon, 27 February 1696, HEH, HA 955.

CHAPTER 15. *Conclusion*

1. Guenter Roth and Claus Wittich, eds., *Max Weber: Economy and Society* (Berkeley: University of California Press, 1978), 1:231–232, 2:1020, 1030, 1039–40; Julia Adams, *The Familial State: Ruling Families*

and Merchant Capitalism in Early Modern Europe (Ithaca, NY: Cornell University Press, 2005), 16–19, 175–87. I disagree with Adams about the long-term implications of the revolution.

2. Many of course continued to defend monarchy on that basis. The Association of 1696 simply demonstrated unequivocally that this was a minority position.

3. Keith Wrightson, *Earthly Necessities: Economic Lives in Early Modern Britain* (New Haven and London: Yale University Press, 2000), 9–10.

4. Peter Lake and Steve Pincus, "Rethinking the Public Sphere in Early Modern England," *Journal of British Studies* 45, no. 2 (2006): 270–92.

5. Robert Brenner, *Merchants and Revolution: Commercial Change, Political Conflict, and London's Overseas Traders, 1550–1653* (London: Verso, 2003), 648.

6. Tim Harris, "Revising the Restoration," in *The Politics of Religion in Restoration England,* ed. Tim Harris, Paul Seaward, and Mark Goldie (Oxford: Basil Blackwell, 1990), 2, 11; Blair Worden, "The Question of Secularization," in *A Nation Transformed: England after the Restoration,* ed. Alan Houston and Steve Pincus (Cambridge: Cambridge University Press, 2001), 30–40; Keith Thomas, *Religion and the Decline of Magic: Studies in Popular Beliefs in Sixteenth and Seventeenth Century* (Harmondsworth: Penguin, 1985), 205–6.

7. Daniel Riches, "The Rise of Confessional Tensions in Brandenburg's Relations with Sweden in the Late Seventeenth-Century," *Central European History* 37 (2004): 568–92.

8. Perez Zagorin, *The English Revolution: Politics, Events, Ideas* (Aldershot: Ashgate, 1998), 25; Christopher Hill, "A Bourgeois Revolution?" in *Three British Revolutions,* ed. J. G. A. Pocock (Princeton, NJ: Princeton University Press, 1980), 136; J. S. A. Adamson, "The Baronial Context of the English Civil War," in *The English Civil War,* ed. Richard Cust and Ann Hughes (London: Arnold, 1997), 98; John Adamson, *The Noble Revolt: The Overthrow of Charles I* (London: Weidenfeld and Nicolson, 2007); Michael Walzer, *The Revolution of the Saints: A Study in the Origins of Radical Politics* (New York: Atheneum, 1976), 19; Blair Worden, *Roundhead Reputations: The English Civil Wars and the Passions of Posterity* (London: A. Lane, 2001), 228; Christopher Hill, *The Century of Revolution, 1603–1714* (New York: W. W. Norton, 1980), 235; Brenner, *Merchants and Revolution,* 713.

9. Angus MacInnes, "When Was the English Revolution?" *History* 67 (October 1982): 384–87; Wrightson, *Earthly Necessities,* 228.

10. Steve Pincus, "Neither Machiavellian Moments nor Possessive Individualism," *American Historical Review* 103 (1988): 705–36; Pincus, "England and the World in the 1650s," in *Revolution and Restoration,* ed. John Morrill (London: Collins and Brown, 1992), 144–46; Pincus, "From Holy Cause to Economic Interest," in *Nation Transformed,* ed. Houston and Pincus, 272–98.

11. Peter Lake, "Wentworth's Political World in Revisionist and Post-Revisionist Perspective," in *The Political World of Thomas Wentworth, Earl of Strafford, 1621–1641,* ed. J. F. Merritt (Cambridge: Cambridge University Press, 1996), 266–69; Walzer, *Revolution of the Saints,* 10.

12. Lois Potter, *Secret Rites and Secret Writing: Royalist Literature, 1641–1660* (Cambridge: Cambridge University Press, 1989), 170–76; John Locke, *Two Treatises of Government,* ed. Ian Shapiro (New Haven and London: Yale University Press, 2003), 198–99; William Penn, *Three Letters* (London: Andrew Sowle, 1688), 10; Henry Neville Payne, *An Answer to a Scandalous Pamphlet* (London: N. T., 1687), 5; Stephen Lobb, *A Second Letter to a Dissenter* (London: John Harris, 1687), 11; *An Answer by an Anabaptist* (London: Andrew Sowle, 1688), 4.

13. Lawrence Stone, "The Results of the English Revolutions of the Seventeenth Century," in *Three British Revolutions,* ed. Pocock, 23; Thomas Cogswell, "'Published by Authoritie': Newsbooks and the Duke of Buckingham's Expedition to the Ile de Re," *Huntington Library Quarterly* 67 (2004): 1–25; Thomas Cogswell, "John Felton, Popular Political Culture and the Assassination of the Duke of Buckingham," *Historical Journal* 49 (2006): 357–85; Mark Knights, *Representation and Misrepresentation in Later Stuart Britain* (Oxford: Oxford University Press, 2005), 3.

14. Margaret R. Hunt, *The Middling Sort: Commerce, Gender, and the Family in England 1680–1780* (Berkeley: University of California Press, 1996), 14; Daniel Szechi, *The Jacobites: Britain and Europe, 1688–1788* (Manchester: Manchester University Press, 1994), 12–26; Basil D. Henning, "Introductory Survey," in *The Commons, 1660–1690,* vol. 1, ed. Henning (London: History of Parliament Trust, 1983), 10; David W. Hayton, "Introductory Survey," in *The Commons, 1690–1715,* ed. Hayton (Cambridge: History of Parliament Trust, 2002), 1:302; Perry Gauci, *The Politics of Trade: The Overseas Merchant in State and Society, 1660–1720* (Oxford: Oxford University Press, 2001), 198.

15. *Proposals Humbly Offered to the Honourable House of Commons* [1690s], [1].

16. Guy Miege, *The New State of England under Their Majesties K. William and Q. Mary,* 2 vols. (London: H. C. for Jonathan Robinson, 1691), 2:218–19, 229; Barillon and Bonrepaus (Windsor) to Louis XIV, 2/12 June 1687, NA, PRO, 31/3/170, fol. 49r.

17. Miege, *New State of England,* 2:218–19.

18. Miege, *New State of England,* 2:218–19; Steve Pincus, "The State and Civil Society in Early Modern England: Capitalism, Causation and Habermas' Bourgeois Public Sphere," in *The Politics of the Public Sphere in Early Modern England,* ed. Peter Lake and Pincus (Manchester: Manchester University Press, 2007).

19. Compare Brenner, *Merchants and Revolution,* 713.

20. Peter Earle, *The Making of the English Middle Class* (Berkeley: University of California Press, 1989), 10, 335; L. E. Klein, "The Political Significance of 'Politeness' in Early Eighteenth-Century Britain," in *Politics, Politeness, and Patriotism,* ed. Gordon J. Schochet (Washington, DC: Folger Shakespeare Library, 1993), 84–87; Lawrence Klein, "Liberty, Manners and Politeness in Early Eighteenth-Century England," *Historical Journal* 32 (1989): 588; J. Paul Hunter, *Before Novels: The Cultural Contexts of Eighteenth-Century English Fiction* (New York: W. W. Norton, 1990), 97; Ian Watt, *The Rise of the Novel* (Berkeley: University of California Press, 1957) .

21. Gauci, *Politics of Trade,* 94, 109–10, 209, 272; Julian Hoppit and Joanna Innes, "Introduction," in *Failed Legislation, 1660–1800,* ed. Julian Hoppit (London, 1997), 8–10; Susan Whyman, *Sociability and Power in Late-Stuart England* (Oxford: Oxford University Press, 1999), 80; Hunt, *Middling Sort,* 3.

22. Compare Linda Colley, *Britons: Forging the Nation, 1707–1737* (New Haven and London: Yale University Press, 1992), 135.

Manuscripts Consulted

University of Aberdeen, Special Libraries and Archives, Aberdeen

MS 2126 Diary of James Gordon of Foveran
MS 2403 Letters of James Drummond
MS 2740 Ogilvie-Forbes Papers
  Box 3/Bundle 12 Pittrichie Papers
MS 2957 King Family of Tertowie

All Souls College, Oxford, Codrington Library

221–222, 257 Owen Wynne Papers
317 Sir William Trumbull, Autobiography

Bank of England Archives, London

AC 27 Stock Ledgers
AC 28 Stock Book Transfers
ADM 7 General Ledger
G4 Minutes of the Court of Directors
G7 Minutes of the General Court of
  Proprietors
M1 Museum Book and Document Collections
M5 Secretary's Department
M6 Museum Documents
M7 Miscellaneous Books

Beinecke Library, Yale University, New Haven

OSB Files
OSB MSS 1 Edmund Poley Papers
OSB MSS 2 William Blathwayt Papers
OSB MSS 11 Birchall Papers
OSB MSS 41 Southwell Papers
OSB MSS 44 Temple Family Letters
OSB MSS 60 Newsletters, 1691–1694
OSB Shelves b.33 Brook Bridges, Notabilia
OSB Shelves b.100 Sir William Dutton Colt
  Letters
OSB Shelves b.142 Treatise on Magna Carta,
  1687
OSB Shelves b.153 Trade Tracts Late
  Seventeenth Century
OSB Shelves b.314 Narcissus Luttrell, "Travells"
OSB Shelves b.316 Henry Sidney Letters to
  Blathwayt
OSB Shelves b.317 Shrewsbury to Blathwayt
  Letters
OSB Shelves fb.27 Late Seventeenth Century
  Tracts
OSB Shelves fb.53 Parliamentary Collections
OSB Shelves fb.70 Political Poetry, 1680–1700
OSB Shelves fb.85 Lorenzo Magalotti
  Collection
OSB Shelves fb.124 Sir Richard Bulstrode
  Papers
OSB Shelves fb.190 Letters to Dartmouth
OSB Shelves fb.207 Poetical Commonplace
  Book

OSB Shelves fb.210 Newsletters to Lady
  Clopton, 1688–1689
OSB Shelves fb.239 James Cressett
  Correspondence
OSB Shelves fc.66 William Fuller,
  Autobiography
OSB Shelves Gordonstoun Papers
Gen MSS 216 Chardin Papers

BERKELEY CASTLE MUNIMENT ROOM

MSS 36A-B Diplomatic Correspondence of
  Earl Berkeley, 1689–1693

BERKSHIRE RECORD OFFICE, READING

D/EHr Henry Hunter Papers
D/ED Downshire Manuscripts

BODLEIAN LIBRARY, OXFORD

Aubrey MSS
Ballard MSS
Carte MSS
Clarendon MSS
Don.b.16 Letters of Edward Tucker, 1662–1707
Don.c.38–c.39 Fleming Newsletters
Don.c.169 Henry Ashurst Letterbook
Eng.Hist.b.193 Letters to Edward Fisher, 1688
Eng.Hist.b.205 Papers of John Warner
Eng.Hist.b.209 Sir Richard Cocks Papers
Eng.Hist.c.201 Sir Richard Temple Papers
Eng.Hist.c.476 Herrick Family Papers
Eng.Hist.c.487 Edmund Ludlow "A Voyce
  from the Watchtower"
Eng.Hist.c.711 Roger Whitley Diary
Eng.Lett.c.8 Paul Rycaut-Clarendon
  Correspondence
Eng.Lett.c.28–29 Letters to Henry Dodwell
Eng.Lett.c.53–54 Philip Madoxe–Robert
  Southwell Correspondence
Eng.Lett.c.200 Letters to Benjamin Furley
Eng.Lett.e.29 Henry Family Correspondence
Eng.Poet.d.53 Misc. Poetry
Locke MSS

Rawlinson MSS

A266 Sunderland letters to Ambassadors
A326 Papers on Foreign Affairs, 1686–1702
A336 Misc. Papers
B497 Letters of Dr. Robert Huntington,
  1684–1688
C130 Proceedings and Judgment in East India
  Company v. Sandys
C417 Sylvius Despatches, 1685–1686
C449 Minute Book of New East India
  Company
C746 Royal Africa Company Letters, 1681–1699
C983 Misc. Letters
D60 Miscellaneous Letters
D91 "A Copy of a Letter," 1689
D148 Colonel Norton's "Account of the
  Revolution in the Army 1688"
D747 East India Company Papers
D749 Sir Gabriel Sylvius Papers, 1685–1689
D863 Rawlinson Family Papers
D1079 Account of Revolution, 1688–1689
Lett. 42 Misc. Letters
Lett. 47–48 Edmund Warcup–Hugh Jones
  Correspondence
Lett. 91 Letters to Dr. Thomas Turner
Smith MSS
Tanner MSS
Wood F.39–F.45 Anthony Wood Papers

BRITISH LIBRARY, LONDON (BL)

Additional MSS (Add.)

2902 Collection of Papers: Trade
3828 Miscellaneous Legal and Historical Papers
4107 Birch Papers
4182 Newsletters, 1684–1695
4194 Letters to John Ellis
4236 Birch Collection: Tillotson Papers
4292 Birch Collection
4295 Toland Papers
5540 John Cary Papers
7080 Letters to R. Newport, 1689–1692
8880 Paget Letters
9363 Political Tracts
9735 Blathwayt Papers
9807 Letters of Sir W. D. Colt
11513 Sir George Etherege Letterbook
11689 Scudamore Papers

15857–15858 Sir Richard Browne and John Evelyn Correspondence

15949 Evelyn Correspondence

17677 Netherlands Transcripts (multiple volumes)

18979 Fairfax Papers

19254 James Drummond Letters

21483 Letters to James II

21494 Letters to Sir Robert Southwell, 1686–1705

21551 Letters to George Stepney, 1690–1706

22185–22186 Sir Henry Johnson Papers

22640 John Greene's Verse Collection

23722 Political Poetry Collection

24357 Thomas Cartwright Diary

27395–27397 Gawdy Family Correspondence

27440 Charles Allestree Memoirs

27447–27448 Paston Correspondence

28079 Godolphin-Osborne Papers: Danby's Tracts Relating to Trade

28087 Edward Osborne Letters

28089 Papers Relating to Colonies in America

28226 John Caryll Letters and Papers

28227 Caryll Family Correspondence

28569 Savile and Finch Correspondence

28875–28876 Ellis Papers

28929 Humphry Prideaux–John Ellis Correspondence

28930–28931 Ellis Family Correspondence

28955 Ellis Collection of Political and Satyrical Pieces

29563 Hatton Family Correspondence

29578 Sir Charles Lytlleton–Christopher Hatton Correspondence

29582–29583 John Fell–Christopher Hatton Correspondence

29585 Sir Edmund King–Christopher Hatton Correspondence

29594 Nottingham-Hatton Correspondence

29910 Swynfen Papers

29911 Jervis Correspondence

30277 Hugo Papers

31141 Lord Strafford Correspondence

31152 Political Verse

32095 Malet Collection

32681 Correspondence of Henry Sidney, 1681–1691

34095–34096 Letters to Sir William Dutton Colt, 1690–1693

34152 Kent Letters

34340 Negotiations between England and the Netherlands

34487 Mackintosh Collection—Newsletters

34502 Mackintosh Collection—Ronquillo Letters

34507–34512 Mackintosh Collection—Political Correspondence from Dutch Archives

34515 Mackintosh Collection—Correspondence from Portland Collection

34519 Charles Talbot-Shrewsbury Correspondence

34730 West Papers

36540 Paston Family Correspondence

36662 Letters to R. D. Colt

36707 Letters to James Harrington

36988 Paston Correspondence

37660 Letterbook of Earl of Melfort, 1689–1690

38012 Letters to Rev. William Moore

38013 Correspondence of Thomas Coxe, 1689–1692

38052 Sir Robert Southwell Correspondence

38329 Liverpool Papers

38493–38495 Letterbook of Antony Moreau (Polish Ambassador at The Hague)

33847 Hodgkin Papers

38855 Hodgkin Papers

38695 War Office Correspondence, 1688–91

40060 Political Poems

40160 William Lloyd's Commonplace Book

40621 Harley Papers

40629 Cassiobury Papers

40771 Vernon Papers

40794 Vernon Papers—Memoirs of James Vernon

40800 Letterbook of Hugh Greg, 1694–1695

41804–41805 Middleton Papers

41809–41821 Middleton Papers—Letters to Secretaries from Foreign Envoys

41823 Middleton Papers—Middleton's Outgoing Letters

41824–41827 Middleton Papers—Hamburg Correspondence

41842 Middleton Papers—Miscellaneous Correspondence

42586 Brockman Family Correspondence

45731 Poley Papers

46961–46962 Egmont Papers—Correspondence of Sir John Percival

47022 Egmont Papers—Correspondence Re: Public Affairs

47131 Egmont Papers—The Interest of the Crown in American Plantations, 1685

47840 Radclyffe Papers

49605 Wilson Papers

51319 Holland House Papers—Correspondence of Sir Stephen Fox

51335 Holland House Papers—Papers of Charles Fox

52279 Diary of Sir William Trumbull

52475A BRA Papers—Letters to Sir Richard Temple

54185 Joshua Sager Sermon Notes from Nonconformist Academy nr. Sheffield

56245 Blathwayt Correspondence

61689–61690 Blenheim Papers: Wildman Correspondence

61903 Peter Le Neve Diary

62081 Pythouse Papers—Bennett Family Correspondence

62453 Sir Robert Clayton's Monmouth Rebellion Papers

63465 Wentworth Papers

63629 Albemarle Papers

63765 Preston Papers—Letters from England

63770 Preston Papers—Letters from Informants

63773 Preston Papers—Elections and North America

63776 Preston Papers—Newsletters and Political Verse

64814 Revolution Society Minutes

69936 John Coke Correspondence

69943 John Coke Correspondence

69953 Coke Papers—Devonshire Horse Regiment

69955 Coke Papers—Test and Corporation materials

70013–70014 Harley Papers

70235 Sir Edward Harley–Robert Harley Letters

70095 Harley Verses

70112–70125 Sir Edward Harley Correspondence

70140 Sir Edward Harley–Edward Harley Correspondence

70158–70159 Harley Excise and Customs papers

70225–70226 Foley-Harley Correspondence

70289 Musgrave-Harley Correspondence

70236 Edward Harley-Robert Harley Correspondence

70358 Letters to Matthew Prior

70500 Cavendish Papers

70504 Earl of Clare Papers

71573 Oliver Le Neve Letters

71691–71692 Sir William Boothby Letterbooks

72481–72620 Trumbull MSS (some read before given Add mss numbers)

72853 Petty/Southwell Correspondence

72866 Petty Economic Papers temp. James II

72867 Petty Projects

72889 Petty Papers on Liberty of Conscience

72890 Petty Statistical Papers

78299 John Evelyn Letterbook, 1679–1698 (read before number assigned)

78919 Osborne Papers, 1690–1699

Althorp MSS

C2 Letters to Halifax regarding Yorkshire Elections

C3 Letters to Halifax from Strafford and Chesterfield

C5 Letters to Halifax from Weymouth and Sunderland

C8 Halifax Correspondence

C17 Miscellaneous Halifax Letters

Egerton MSS

1169 Autograph Letters

1533 Autograph Letters

1717 Bentinck Papers

2231 John Aubrey Correspondence

2346 Papers of the Blue and Orange Society, 1714

2395 Papers Relating to English Settlements in America

2618 Historical Letters and Papers

2651 Barrington Papers

2717 Gawdy Family Papers

3335–3336 Danby Correspondence

3680 Bulstrode Papers—Letters to Sir Richard Bulstrode
3681 Bulstrode Papers—Letters from Skelton, Wyche
3683 Bulstrode Papers—Letters from Sir John Lytcott

Evelyn Papers

EL 3 John Evelyn's Library Catalogue, 1687
JE A2 Letterbook, 1679–1698
JE A4 Letters from Family, 1652–1705
JE A6 Letters from Family, 1636–1699
JE A9 Godolphin Correspondence
JE A11 Letters from Tuke Family and Lady Sunderland
JE A15 Letters from Ralph Bohun, Samuel Pepys, and Benjamin Tooke
JE A19 General Correspondence, 1680–1689
JE D7 Notes on Trades
JE F5 Sermon Notes
JE G1 Public Affairs
JEJ 1 John Evelyn Jr. Letters
ME 2 Mary Evelyn's Letters from John Evelyn
UP 1–2 Autograph Letters of Nobility
UP 6–8 Autograph Letters of Writers and Antiquaries

Harleian MSS

1283 Edward Battine, "The Method of Building," 1685
4716 Thomas Baskerville Collections
6845 Historical Papers

Lansdowne MSS

1152 A–B Bridgman's Collections
1163 A–C Earl of Melfort Letterbooks

Loan MSS

57/1 Bathurst Papers
57/20 Bathurst Papers
57/70 Bathurst-Allicock Correspondence
57/71 Bathurst-Anne Correspondence
57/83 Bathurst Papers—Outletters as Sub-Governor of Royal Africa Company
57/84 Bathurst Outletters, 1692–1709

Sloane MSS

2903 Philosophical Papers

Stowe MSS

292 State of England, 1695

304 Sir Richard Temple Papers
746–747 Dering Correspondence

BRITISH POSTAL MUSEUM AND ARCHIVE, LONDON

POST 1/1 Early Letter Book
POST 23/1 Early Documents
POST 94/12 Whitley Letter Book
POST 94/16 Whitley Letter Book
Ref 1-10B Thomas Gardiner, Survey of the Post Office, 1677

BUCKINGHAMSHIRE RECORD OFFICE

Claydon House Papers (Verney MSS) (read on microfilm)

CENTRE FOR KENTISH STUDIES, MAIDSTONE

U23 Wykeham Martin MSS
U120 Filmer Papers
U133 Dering MSS
U145 Faunce-Delaune MSS
U269 Sackville Papers
U386 Darrell MSS
U951 Knatchbull Papers
   F15 Diary of Philip Skippon
   F46 Diary of Sir John Knatchbull
U1015 Papillon MSS
U1475 De L'Isle MSS
U1500 Sidney MSS
U1590 Stanhope of Chevening Papers

CHRIST CHURCH, OXFORD

William Wake Papers

CHURCHILL COLLEGE, CAMBRIDGE

Thomas Erle Papers

COLONIAL WILLIAMSBURG FOUNDATION, WILLIAMSBURG, VIRGINIA

William Blathwayt Papers

Cumbria Record Office, Carlisle

CB/ME Purchased Musgrave Records
D/Hud Huddleston family papers
D/Lons Lonsdale Papers
D/Mus Musgrave papers
D&C Machell MSS Topographical notes of
  Thomas Machell
D&C Nicolson MSS Antiquarian materials
  of William Nicolson

Cumbria Record Office, Kendal

WD/CAT Curwen Archives Trust—Musgrave
  MSS
WD/Cr Crewdson Family Papers
WD/Ry Rydal Hall MSS (Fleming)
WSMB/A Borough of Appleby Records
WDX/1229 Tryon-Wilson Family Papers
WDY/165 Fleming Photocopies

Doctor Williams' Library, London

DWL 12.78 Thomas Jollie Papers
DWL 31 Roger Morrice Papers
  J Chronological Account of Eminent Persons
  M Miscellaneous MSS
  P, Q Entering Books
  T Debates in Parliament 1685
DWL 90.4 Sarah Savage's Letterbook
DWL 201.38 Stillingfleet Letterbook

Duke University, Special Collections Library, Durham, North Carolina

6th 16:A (sm. Brit. Coll., Box 4) Le Neve
  Letters

East Sussex Record Office, Lewes

ASH Asburnham Papers (Diaries and
  Letterbooks)

Edinburgh University Library

La.II.60 Gray Correspondence
La.III.545 Diary of Robert Kirk, Minister of
  Aberfoyle

Essex Record Office, Chelmsford

D/DP Petre Family Papers
D/DU Blyth Family Papers
D/DL Dacre Family Papers
D/Dfa Dawley and Cutler Family Papers
D/Deb Bramston Family Papers
D/Dby Braybrooke Papers
D/DW Z6/2 John Conyers' Northern Journey

Folger Shakespeare Library, Washington, DC (FSL)

F.c. 17–34 Thomas Booth Letters
L.c. Newdigate Newsletters
M.b. 12 Political Satires, 1672–1704
V.a. 343 Sir John Cotton Papers and Speeches
V.a. 399 Poetry Commonplace Book, 1675–1725
V.a. 469 William Westby Memoirs
V.b. 25 Sir T. Gresly–Sir John Moore Letters
V.b. 150 Sir Robert Southwell Papers
V.b. 287 James Fraser Letters
V.b. 294 Edward Southwell Papers
V.b. 305 Norfolk County Collections
X.d. 439 Blathwayt Papers
X.d. 451 Rich Papers

Friends House Library, London

MS Box C3 John Field Account of Life and
  Sufferings
MS Box E Swarthmore MSS
MS Box G1/6 Diary of Jonathan Burnyeat
Port 8/163
Port 15/139
MS Vol. 77 Journal of Thomas Gwin
MS Vol. 268 A History of Joseph Pike of Cork
  by Himself

Georgetown University Library, Washington, DC

Jesuit Commonplace Book
Milton House Archives

Guildhall Library, London

507 Sir John Moore Papers
3504 Sir John Moore Personal Papers

5099 London Charter Papers, 1688

7927 A New England Company Letterbook, 1688–1761

7932 New England Company Evidences, 1662–1780

7936 New England Company Original Correspondence, 1657–1714

7952 New England Company Loose Court Minutes, 1655–1816

7955 New England Company Correspondence from Boston, 1677–1761

7956 New England Company General Correspondence, 1664–1780

8493A Robert Clayton's Papers

10116 East India Company Chaplain Licensing Papers, 1685–1689

10823 George Boddington Commonplace Book

11741/2 Russia Company Court Minutes, 1683–1699

12017 Sir John Fryar Autobiography

17626 Sir John Shorter Papers

HAMPSHIRE RECORD OFFICE, WINCHESTER

63M84/235 Samuel Heathcote of Hackney Notebook

HARRY RANSOM CENTER, UNIVERSITY OF TEXAS, AUSTIN (HRC)

HRC 119 Oliver Freeman Diary
Pforzheimer Collection

HARVARD UNIVERSITY, THEATRE COLLECTION, CAMBRIDGE, MASSACHUSETTS

FMS THR 11 George Etherege Letterbook

HERTFORDSHIRE ARCHIVES AND LOCAL STUDIES

Cowper MSS

HOARE'S BANK, LONDON

HB/5/H/1 Money's Lent, 1696–1701
HB/8/A Releases
HB/8/B Bonds

HOUSE OF LORDS RECORD OFFICE (PARLIAMENTARY ARCHIVES), LONDON (HLRO)

HC House of Commons Papers
HL House of Lords Papers (including Main Papers)
WIL Willcocks Collection
WMT William and Mary Tercentenary Trust Papers

HUNTINGTON LIBRARY, SAN MARINO, CALIFORNIA (HEH)

Blathwayt Papers (BL)
Edmund Gibson Collection
Ellesmere Papers (EL)
Hastings Papers (HA)
HM 929 John Tillotson "Dialogue"
HM 1264 Nehemiah Grew "The Means of a Most Ample Increase of the Wealth and Strength of England"
HM 6131 Life of John Rastrick
HM 30659 Tamworth Newsletters
Parker Family Letters (uncataloged)
Shovell-Rooke Papers
Stowe-Grenville Papers (STG)
Stowe-Nugent Papers (STN)
Stow-Temple Papers (STT)
Stowe General Volumes (ST)
   9 Royal African Company Papers
   13 James Brydges' Notes, 1697
   26 James Brydges's Journal, 1697–1702 (2 vols.)
   31 Excise Papers, 1662–1718
   57 Chandos Out-Letterbooks (vol. 2)
   152 Sir Richard Temple's Ledgerbook, 1677–1688
   153 Sir Richard Temple's London House Book, 1688–1691

INDIA OFFICE LIBRARY, LONDON (IOL)

E/3 Correspondence with the East
/44 26 March 1684–24 March 1685
/45 29 March 1685–24 March 1686
/46 9 April 1686–March 1687
/47 11 April 1687–March 1689
/90 Despatch Book, 1682–1685
/91 Despatch Book 21 October 1685–
   10 December 1688

H/36 Home Out-Letters, 1688–1699
H/40 Josiah Child Letters, 1691–1694

European MSS
D1076 Thomas Bowrey Papers
E210 Sir Streynsham Master Papers
E387/B Lawrence Letterbook

KING'S COLLEGE, CAMBRIDGE

Keynes MSS 118, 119, 149 Newton MSS

LAMBETH PALACE LIBRARY (LPL)

Fulham Papers/Compton MSS
Fulham Papers/American Colonial Section
Gibson Papers
742/34 Andrew Paschall, "Account of
   Monmouth's Rising"
746 Accounts of Taxes, 1688–1698
933 Misc. Letters
1029 Tenison Letters
1834 Misc. Mss.
2932 William Wake Autobiography
3016 Abigail Prowse, "Life of Bishop George
   Hooper"
3152 Journal of Simon Digby, Oct. 1688–
   Feb. 1689
3894 Sancroft-Lloyd Correspondence,
   1680–1692
3895 Frampton-Lloyd Correspondence,
   1680–1703
3898 Lloyd Papers, 1687–88

LANCASHIRE RECORD OFFICE, PRESTON

DD/B Parker of Brownsholme Papers
DD/Ba Bankes of Winstanley Papers

DD/Bb Blundell of Halsall papers
DD/Bl Blundell of Little Crosby Papers
DD/HK Hawkshead-Talbot of Chorley Papers
DD/In Blundell of Ince Blundell
DD/K Derby Papers
DD/Ke Kenyon of Peel Papers
DD/M Molyneux, Earl of Sefton Papers
DD/Sa Sandys of Esthwaite and
Graysthwaite Papers
   (Rawlinson Family Correspondence)
MSS of The Rawstorne Diary, 1687–1689
   (edited by Richard D. Harrison)

LICHFIELD RECORD OFFICE, LICHFIELD

B/A/19 Letterbook and Papers of John
   Husband

LILLY LIBRARY, INDIANA UNIVERSITY,
BLOOMINGTON (INDIANA)

Albeville MSS
Augustan MSS

LIVERPOOL RECORD OFFICE, LIVERPOOL

920 MD 172–174 Diary of Sir Willoughby
   Aston (1640–1702)
   Diary Covers, 1680–1701

LONGLEAT HOUSE, WILTSHIRE

Muddiman MSS
Prior MSS
Thynne MSS

MAGDALEN COLLEGE ARCHIVES, OXFORD

MINISTÈRE DES AFFAIRES ÉTRANGÈRES,
PARIS (MAE)

Correspondance Politique (CP)
Angleterre
Hollande

Mémoires et Documents (MD)
Angleterre

NATIONAL ARCHIVES OF SCOTLAND, EDINBURGH (NAS)

GD 18 Clerk of Pennicuik Papers
GD 29 Kinross House Papers
GD 112 Breadalbane Muniments
GD 124 Earls of Mar and Kellie
GD 158 Hume of Marchmont Papers
GD 160 Drummond Castle Papers
GD 406 Hamilton Muniments
SP 3 Letterbooks of James Johnston, 1692–1694
SP 4 Warrant Books of the Secretary for Scotland

NATIONAL LIBRARY OF SCOTLAND, EDINBURGH (NLS)

Adv. 24.4.6 John Lauder, "Historical Observes"
974 Angus Papers
2781 Commonplace Book of Rev. John Hunter of Ayr, 1685–1711
2785 Late Seventeenth Century Commonplace Book
3807 Satirical Poems
5071 Erskine-Murray Correspondence
6141 Liston-Fowlis Correspondence
6409 Pitfirrance Papers
7010–14, 7026–27, 7035, 7104, 14403–4, 14407, 14414, 14417 Yester/Tweeddale Papers
9250 Dunlop Papers
17498 Fletcher of Saltoun Papers
Wodrow Manuscripts

NATIONAL MARITIME MUSEUM, LONDON (NMM)

DAR/ Dartmouth Papers
JOD/6 Diary of Rev. Henry Teonge
JOD/173 Journal of Samuel Atkins
LBK/1 Sir John Narborough's Letterbook
LBK/3 Sir Anthony Deane's Letterbook
LBK/49 James II–Dartmouth Correspondence
MS 81/116 Papers of Rear Admiral Robert Fairfax
GOS/9 Edward Randolph's Discourse on Pirates
PLA/ Phillips Collection
SER/ Sergison Papers
SOC/21 Royal Navy Club Minutes

SGN/A/2 Fighting Instructions, 1687
SOU/ Southwell Papers

NORTH YORKSHIRE RECORD OFFICE, NORTHALLERTON

ZCG Nathaniel Cholmley Letterbook, 1682–1691
John Cholmley Letterbook, 1664–1695

NOTTINGHAM UNIVERSITY LIBRARY, NOTTINGHAM

PwA Willem Bentinck Papers/Portland Papers
PwV Portland Papers
  53 Blathwayt-Southwell Correspondence
  60–61 Povery-Southwell Correspondence

PEPYS LIBRARY, MAGDALENE COLLEGE, CAMBRIDGE

2869–2880 Miscellany of Matters Historical, Political and Naval

PROVINCIAL ARCHIVES OF MANITOBA, WINNIPEG

Hudson's Bay Company Archives
  HBCA A.1/8–10 Court and Committee Minutes

NATIONAL ARCHIVES, KEW GARDENS (NA)

ADM 2 Admiralty Out-Letters
ADM 77 Newsletters
C 104 Chancery Master Exhibits
  /63 Rev. John Henry Cary papers
C 110 Chancery Masters Exhibits
  /81–82 Thomas Pitt Correspondence
C 213 1696 Association Rolls
C 214 1696 Association Rolls
CO 1 Colonial Office General Series
CO 5 Board of Trade
  /904 Reports, 1679–88
CO 77 East Indies
  /14 1678–86
  /16 1689–1725

CO 134 Hudson's Bay
/1 1675–1689
CO 135 Hudson's Bay Company
/1 1670–1689
/2 Anglo-French Negotiations re Hudson's
Bay, 1687–1688
CO 268 Ivory Coast
/1 Africa Company Letters and Petitions,
1670–1691
CO 388 Board of Trade
/2 Petitions, 1662–1693
CO 391 Board of Trade Entry Books
/5 1684–1686
/6 1686–1690
CUST 37 Revenue Statistics
/1 Gross and Net Produce of the Customs
CUST 48 Excise Board Correspondence
/3–4 1685–1692
E 351/1324 Excise General Accounts 1685
E 351/2757–2760 Declared Accounts:
Post Office
FO 95/ 573–574 D'Avaux Papers
FO 335 Foreign Office Tunis Records
PC 2 Privy Council Minutes
PRO 30/24 Shaftesbury Papers
PRO 31/3 Baschet Transcripts
SP 8/ King William's Chest
SP 9/ Joseph Williamson's Papers
SP 29/ State Papers, Domestic, Charles II
SP 31/ State Papers, Domestic, James II
SP 44/ State Papers, Entry Books
SP 77/ State Papers, Foreign, Flanders
SP 78/ State Papers, Foreign, France
SP 79/ State Papers, Foreign, Genoa
SP 80/ State Papers, Foreign, Germany Empire
SP 81/ State Papers, Foreign, Germany States
SP 84/ State Papers, Foreign, Holland
SP 85/ State Papers, Foreign, Rome
SP 89/ State Papers, Foreign, Portugal
SP 92/ State Papers, Foreign, Savoy
SP 94/ State Papers, Foreign, Spain
SP 95/ State Papers, Foreign, Sweden
SP 96/ State Papers, Foreign, Switzerland
SP 98/ State Papers, Foreign, Tuscany
SP 99/State Papers, Foreign, Venice
SP 101 Newsletters
/79 Rome. 1673–1705

SP 103 Treaty Papers
/104 Grand Alliance. 1689–1702
SP 104 Foreign Entry Books
/19 France. 1680–1689
SP 105 British Legations
/82 Correspondence to George Stepney.
1686–1695
/83 Memorandum Book of George Stepney.
1689–1695
/145 Register Book of the Levant Company.
1668–1710
/155 Minute Book of the Levant Company.
1685–1699
/343 Correspondence and Papers of Factory
at Aleppo. 1687–1842
SP 110 Aleppo Letterbooks
/16 Letterbooks of Factors at Aleppo,
1683–1690
T 48 William Lowndes Papers
/35 Papers regarding Hearth Tax Collection,
1680–1689
/87 Miscellany
/88 Miscellany
T 64 Miscellaneous Records
/88 Journal of William Blathwayt,
1680–1697
/302 Papers of Gregory King
T 70 Africa Company Papers
/11 Abstracts from Africa, 1683–98
/12 Abstracts from the Indies, 1683–1698
/57 Plantations Letterbook, 1687–1701
/81 Court of Assistants Minute Book,
1684–1687
/82 Court of Assistants Minute Book,
1687–1690
/163 Advice Books, 1685–1694
/164 Advice Books, 1694–1696
/169 Petitions
/1433 Reports/Complaints, 1685–1702
WO 4
/1 General Letters, 1684–1690
WO 30
/48 "Abstract of Particular Account of All
the Inns, Alehouses in England," 1686
WO 89 Courts Martial
/1 1666–1697

PUBLIC RECORD OFFICE OF NORTHERN
IRELAND, BELFAST (PRONI)

T2929 Rossmore Papers

SCHOOL OF ORIENTAL AND AFRICAN
STUDIES, LONDON (SOAS)

PP MS 4 Paget Papers

SCOTTISH CATHOLIC ARCHIVES,
EDINBURGH (SCA)

Bl Blairs MSS
SM Scots Mission MSS

SION COLLEGE LIBRARY, LONDON

L 40.2/E 41 Thomas Bennet Notebook,
1686–1719

SOMERSET RECORD OFFICE, TAUNTON

DD/L Luttrell Papers
DD/PH Phelips Papers
DD/SF Sanford Papers (Edward Clarke)
DD/SPK Speke Papers
DD/Whb Button-Walker-Heneage Muniments
DD/Whh Helyar of Coker Hall Papers
DD/WO Trevelyan Papers
DD/WY Wyndham Papers
Q/SR Quarter Session Records

STAFFORDSHIRE RECORD OFFICE,
STAFFORD

D(w) 1734 Paget Papers
D(w) 1778 Dartmouth Papers
D742 Further Dartmouth Papers
D 1366/2 Newton Papers

TRINITY COLLEGE, CAMBRIDGE

MS R.4.43 Newton-Covel Letters

UNIVERSITY COLLEGE, OXFORD

P2 Anthony Wood Correspondence

VICTORIA AND ALBERT MUSEUM, LONDON

Forster and Dyce Collection
F.47.A.40 Ormonde Papers

WARWICKSHIRE RECORD OFFICE,
WARWICK

CR 136 Newdegate of Arbury Papers
CR 1998 Throckmorton Papers
CR 2017 Fielding of Newnham Paddox Papers
Algernon Sidney "Court Maxims"

WESTMINSTER DIOCESAN ARCHIVES,
LONDON

Old Brotherhood Archives
Archbishops of Westminster Archives
"A" Series

WEST YORKSHIRE ARCHIVE SERVICE,
LEEDS (WYAS)

MX Mexborough MSS
Thoresby MSS

Index